of evidence is transliterations of Greek words into Latin, e.g. *cithara* (for κιθάρα), and, in particular, transliterations of Latin names into Greek, in the Greek authors who wrote on Roman history — e.g. Κικέρων (*Cicerō*), Βροῦτος (*Brūtus*), Ἰούλιος (*Iūlius*), Γερμανικός (*Germānicus*), Οὐαλέριος (*Valerius*).

Single vowels in any given Latin word are either long by nature (e.g. *fās, nūbēs*) or short by nature (e.g. *lăpĭdĕ, pĭŭs* — though the quantity of short vowels is not usually marked). The difference between the sounds of long and short vowels is partly a matter of actual length — i.e. the time taken in pronouncing them — and partly a matter of quality or timbre. The following is a list of the Latin long and short vowels, together with some English, French, and German words containing approximately similar vowel-sounds:

Latin	English	French	German
ā	f*a*ther	p*a*ge	V*a*ter
ă	*a*ha	p*a*tte	M*a*nn
	footp*a*th		
ē		*é*glise	W*e*h
ĕ	f*e*d	av*e*c	B*e*tt
ī	mach*i*ne	l*i*vre	*i*hn
ĭ	p*i*t		m*i*t
ō		d*o*s	S*o*hn
ŏ	n*o*t	b*o*tte	G*o*tt
ū	br*u*te	r*ou*ge	d*u*
ŭ	f*u*ll		*u*nd
ȳ		d*u*r	*ü*ber
y̆			H*ü*tte

When two vowels come together in a Latin word, they are often pronounced quite separately, as in *ăēnĕŭs, ăĭt, rĕmĕăt, crĕĕt, dĕīs, ĕōs, rĕŭs, pĭās, dĭēī, dŭbĭōs, gĕnĭŭs, clŏācă, rĕbŏĕt, sŭās, stătŭĕt, mŏnŭĭt, strēnŭōs, tŭŭs*[1]. Sometimes, however, two vowels form a diphthong. Each keeps its proper sound as nearly as possible, but they are run together by means of a "glide" so as to make a monosyllable. The following are the Latin diphthongs, with

[1] The first of the two vowels which come together is nearly always short. Moreover, in compound words, a naturally long vowel, or the diphthong *ae*, is shortened in this position: e. g. *deamat* (*dē* + *amat*), *dehīscēns, prohibet* (*prō* + *habet*), *praeacūtus* (*prae* + *acūtus*), *praeeunte, praeustus*. The rule, however, does not apply to Greek words adopted into Latin, e. g. *Aenēās, āēr, hērōus*. Exceptions in genuine Latin words are *diēī, rēī* (and some other nouns of the fifth declension); *fīō*; *Gāī*; *nullīus* (and other genitives in *-ius*, though in most cases the *i* can also be scanned short).

English and German words containing similar sounds (French has no diphthongs):

Latin	English	German
ae	f*i*nd	St*ei*n
au	h*ou*se	H*au*s
ei	gr*ey*	
eu		
oe	t*oi*l	h*eu*te
ui		pf*ui*

Notes: (1) Latin *ae* should probably be pronounced more broadly than the diphthong in *find* — more like the *ai* commonly heard in *Isaiah.*

(2) In certain words, *au* tended to be pronounced in colloquial Latin as *ō*, and it was often so written: e.g. *Clōdius* for *Claudius, cōpa* as a feminine corresponding to the masculine *caupō.*

(3) The diphthong *ei* is very rare. It occurs in the interjection *ei,* and in *Pompei,* vocative of *Pompēịus.*

(4) The sound of the Latin *eu* was perhaps similar to that of the *eu* in Italian *neutro* — though this is not a true diphthong, the two vowels being pronounced more or less separately. This Latin diphthong is rare. It occurs in *ceu, heu, neu, seu,* and *neuter.*

(5) The diphthong *ui* is rare. It occurs in the interjection *hui,* and in *huic* and *cui.* (In *quis, quī, quid,* &c., the *u* is consonantal.)

The Latin consonants, except as noticed below, were pronounced more or less as they generally are in English.

Notes: **bs** (e.g. *urbs*) was pronounced as *ps*; **bt** (*obtineō*) as *pt.*

c (*cīvis*) was always 'hard', as *k* (never as *s*); **ch** (*pulcher*) as *kh* (as in English *deck-hand*).

g (*gemma*) was always 'hard', as in English *go* (never as in English *gem*).

Consonantal **i** (*iaciō* — sometimes written *jaciō*) was pronounced as the *y* in English *young.*

m at the end of a word (*bellum*) was not sounded, but the preceding vowel was slightly nasalized, somewhat as in the French *un.* Compare the forms *circuit, circuitiō* for *circumit, circumitiō.*

ng (*angulus*) was pronounced as in English *angle.*

q was used only before consonantal *u* (*quaerō*); the combination *qu* was pronounced *kw,* as in English.

s (*rosa*) was always 'hissed', as in the English *sit* (never as in English *rose*).

t (*ratiō*) always had its proper sound; *ra-ti-ō* was pronounced as it is written (not with the sound of *sh* as in English *rational*, nor with the sound of *ts*, although in many Italian words *t* has been replaced by a *z* which is pronounced as *ts* — e.g. *giustizia* from Latin *iūstitia*).

Consonantal **u** (*uīuō* — often written *vīvō*) was pronounced as the *w* in English *wet*; **gu** (*anguis*) as in English *anguish*.

x was pronounced *ks*, as in English *extra* (not *gz* as in *examine*, nor *kz* as in *exonerate*).

ph and **th** were used in words borrowed from Greek (e.g. *philosophia*, *theātrum*) to represent the Greek letters φ and θ. Properly speaking, each of these Latin consonants should have its normal sound — *ph* as in the English *loophole*, *th* as in *hothouse*. But *ph* is generally pronounced as *f* (a sound which it acquired only about the fifth century A.D.), and even *th* is often pronounced as in the English *thin*.

IV. **Accent.** A syllable is said to be accented either because it is pronounced at a higher musical pitch than the neighbouring syllables (pitch-accent or musical accent), or because, in pronouncing it, the breath is expelled with more force (stress-accent or 'exspiratory' accent). In practice, both kinds of accent are often used together, and it is not easy to demonstrate that any accent is purely a matter of pitch or purely a matter of dynamic stress. However, accentuation in various languages is easily recognizable as being mainly pitch-accent or mainly stress-accent. In Greek and some other Indo-European languages, and — it can be confidently assumed — in the parent Indo-European itself, it was mainly pitch-accent. In English and in German it is mainly stress-accent.

The nature of Latin accent is debatable. The ancient grammarians are unanimous in describing it as a pitch-accent. But there is reason to think that they can not have been altogether right. In some period preceding that of the earliest extant Latin literature, it is clear that the main accent of most Latin words, however many syllables they contained, was on the first syllable. And some of the changes which took place in the following — i.e. the unaccented — syllables suggest strongly that there was at any

rate a considerable element of dynamic stress in this first-syllable accent. These changes are mainly of two kinds:

(1) *Weakening of vowels.* Unaccented short vowels in middle syllables were frequently weakened. Under certain conditions, *a*, *e*, *o*, *u* could all become *i*; *a* and *o* could also become *u*; and *a* could become *e*. Long vowels resisted weakening, but the diphthong *ae* became *ī*, and *au* became *ū*. These changes are especially common in verbs compounded with prepositions. Thus, *a'bigō* from *ab* + *agō*; *ob'sideō* from *ob* + *sedeō*; *ī'licō* for *in locō*; *ob'stipuī* for *obstupuī*; *sur'rupuī*, later *surripuī*, from *sub* + *rapuī*; *e'pistula* for *epistola* (from the Greek ἐπιστολή); *re'periō* from *re* + *pariō*; *oc'cīdō* from *ob* + *caedō*; *in'clūdō* from *in* + *claudō*.

(2) *Syncope.* In words of three or more syllables, a short vowel in the second syllable, immediately following the accented first syllable, was often 'syncopated' — i.e. the second syllable disappeared as a separate syllable, although it might leave traces behind. Thus *auceps*, 'bird-catcher', stands for **a'vi-cap-s* (formed from *avis* and *capiō*); *vīndēmia*, 'vintage', is for **vī'ni-dēmia* (from *vīnum* and *dēmō*); *quīndecim* is formed from *quīnque* and *decem*; *repperī* is for **re'-peperī*, *rettulī* for **re'-tetulī*, the double consonants preserving a trace of the unsyncopated forms. This process continued to some extent in the historical period. Plautus wrote *balineum* ('bath', from the Greek βαλανεῖον), while a little later the word appears as *balneum*; similarly, Plautus' *columen*, 'summit', became *culmen*. It is difficult to imagine that syncope on such a large scale could take place except under the influence of an accent having a considerable stress-element.

As to the nature of the Latin accent in the literary period, there is no agreement. Some think it was, as the grammarians say it was[1], a pitch-accent (in which case, the stress-element which appears to have been present in a pre-literary period must have been merely a temporary phenomenon); some think it was a stress-accent; and some think that it may ave contained both elements, the stress-element being the more prominent in the popular speech, and the pitch-element in the consciously refined speech of the educated class, most of whom knew some Greek.

* The asterisk indicates that these forms are not found in manuscripts or inscriptions, but are assumed to have preceded the extant forms.

[1] Cicero himself (*Orator* 58) calls the Latin accent *acuta vox*, which would most naturally describe a pitch-accent.

However that may be, there is general agreement that, if the accent was a stress-accent, it was a much less vigorous stress than is used in English or German, and that, in speaking Latin, quantity is more important than accent. Every effort should be made to observe the proper length of each syllable, and unaccented syllables, whether long or short, must never be slurred over as they often are in English.

About the *position* of the accent in historical times there is no doubt at all. Its position was bound up with the quantity of the penultimate syllable in any given word. The rules are very simple:

(a) Words of two syllables are accented on the first syllable: *dū'-rī, bi'-bit, Rō'ma, fe'-rās.*

(b) Words of more than two syllables are accented

(i) on the penultimate syllable, if it is long: *lē-gā'-tus, hor-tā-ban'-tur, sol-li-ci-tā'-re*;

(ii) on the antepenultimate syllable, if the penultimate is short: *cōn'-fe-rō, ha-bu'-e-ris, mi-se-ri-cor'-di-a.*

These rules apply to words lengthened by the addition of an enclitic — *-que, -ve, -ne, -ce*: thus, *vi-rum'-que, de-us'-ve, po-test'-ne, hū-ius'-ce.* The following are only apparent exceptions: *tan-tōn'* (= *tan-tō'-ne*), *dī-xīn'* (= *dī-xī'-ne*), *il-līc'* (= *il-lī'-ce*).

V. **Division of syllables. 1.** A single consonant goes with the following vowel: *de-li-be-ra-bo.* (Notice that *qu, ch, ph, th* count as single consonants: *a-qua, e-chi-nus, e-le-phas, Ce-the-gus.*) This rule holds good for compounds such as *a-bi-go, i-ne-o,* although, in dictionaries and grammars, such words are often written *ab-igo, in-eo,* in order to show their etymology. Syllables ending with vowels are known as open syllables.

2 (*a*). Two consonants coming together are generally divided between syllables: *col-lum, ma-gis-ter, om-nes, in-gen-ti-a.* The first of the two syllables in question, ending with one of the two consonants, is called a closed syllable.

(*b*). This rule is subject to an important exception. Consonant-groups consisting of a mute (*p, b, t, d, c, g*) or *f*, followed by *l* or *r*, are generally (always, in prose and in the earliest poetry) left undivided: thus, *a-pri-cus, a-gros, re-flu-o.* This does not apply, however, to compound words in which the first of the two consonants belongs to a preposition; in this case, the two consonants are *always* divided: e.g. *ab-rupi, ad-latus* (= *al-latus*), *sub-ripuit* (= *sur-ripuit*).

3. When three consonants come together, they are divided either 2 + 1 or 1 + 2: e.g. *sanc-tus, cons-tat, sump-se-ro, im-bris, e-ques-tris*. Four consonants are divided 2+2: *mons-trum.*

VI. **Length of syllables.** The length of syllables, which is important both for correct pronunciation and for the scanning of verse, is not the same thing as the length of the vowels contained in the syllables. In a given word a vowel is either short or long, and its length can not be altered by the presence of consonants. What consonants *can* do is to make *syllables* long. The following are the main rules for determining the length of syllables:

(1) *Open* syllables containing a short vowel are short: *dĕ-ōs, ă-mās, flō-rĕ,* and generally *pă-trēs.*

(2) *All* syllables containing a long vowel or a diphthong[1] are long: *gra-dū, pēs, lēx, rē-gis, ā-ēr, bo-nae, lau-dī.*

(3) *All* closed syllables — i.e. those which, according to the principles explained above, end with a consonant — are long, irrespective of the quantity of their vowels. In practice, this means that, when a vowel is followed by two or more consonants (excluding the particular consonant-groups mentioned above under Section V, **2** (*b*)), the syllable containing that vowel is long: e.g. *pan-dō, trac-tus, mis-sus.* The two consonants need not be both in the same word; the same principle applies when a word ending with a consonant is followed by a word beginning with a consonant: e.g. *dī-vi-di-mus mū-rōs.*

(4) When the consonant-groups mentioned under Section V, **2** (*b*) occur inside a word, the classical poets often treat them just like other consonant-groups — i.e. they divide them between syllables. Thus, the words ordinarily pronounced *vo'-lu-crēs, te'-ne-brae* can, if it suits a poet's convenience, be pronounced *vo-luc'-rēs, te-neb'-rae.* In this case the syllables *-luc-, -neb-* are closed, and are therefore long syllables. As explained above, in compounds such as *ab-ri-pi-ō, sub-le-vā-re* the consonants are *always* divided.

In scanning verse, it is usual to place a 'long' mark over all vowels in closed syllables (*pāndō, trāctus, mīssus*). Although this is a convenient way of indicating the length of the syllables, it is, strictly speaking, incorrect, because it involves marking as long many vowels which are in fact short. A better method would be to indicate the length of the syllables by placing a stroke over both the vowel and the consonant following it.

[1] The *ae* of *prae* is short when it is compounded with a word beginning with a vowel or *h*. (See above, Section III.).

Observe that the letter *h* does not count as a consonant, and has no effect on syllable length. On the other hand, syllables in which a vowel is followed by *x* or *z* are always long, these being regarded as double consonants (*x* stands for *cs*, *z* probably for *ds* or *dz*).

In compounds of *iaciō* the *a* is weakened into *i*, and the consonantal *i̯* is omitted in writing: thus, *abiciō*, *adiciō*, *coniciō*, *iniciō*, *subiciō*. The first syllable however is generally scanned as a closed, and therefore long, syllable, just as though the *i̯* were present; and the words were probably pronounced *ab-i̯iciō*, etc.

VII. **'Hidden' quantities.** Since a closed syllable is necessarily scanned long, we often have no means of knowing the quantity of the vowel which it contains. Sometimes other forms of the word make it clear. Since the *e* of *necem* is short, it is a safe deduction that the *e* of *nex* is also short, although the syllable, being closed because of the *x*, is scanned long; conversely, since *ultrīcem* has *ī*, the *i* of *ultrīx* must also be long; similarly, *iūs* shows the quantity of the *u* in *iūstus*. Ancient authors give us some information on the subject. Cicero (*Orator* 159), for example, tells us that the vowels of *in* and *con* were always long before *s* or *f* (*īnsānus*, *īnfēlix*, *cōnsuēvit*, *cōnfēcit*), and this probably applies to all vowels before *ns* and *nf*. Some evidence is supplied by inscriptions, on which long vowels may be found indicated in various ways: e.g. PAASTORES (i.e. *pāstōrēs*); QVEINCTIVS (*Quīnctius*); QVA'RTO (*quārtō*). The evidence obtained from these sources can often be confirmed (though sometimes, unfortunately, it is contradicted) by an examination of the forms assumed by Latin words when they passed into Romance languages. In this dictionary, vowels in closed positions are marked long when it is fairly certain that they are long; but in many cases the quantity is uncertain or unknown.

Notes on this Dictionary

I. **Vocabulary.** This dictionary presents a substantially complete vocabulary of the most widely read authors of classical Latin, down to A.D. 140. The following are the chief authors:

T. Maccius **Plautus*** (c. 251 — 184 B.C.); P. **Terentius** Afer (Terence: ? 195 — 159); M. Tullius **Cicerō** (106 — 43); C. Iūlius **Caesar** (? 102 — 44); Cornēlius **Nepōs** (c. 99 — c. 24); T. **Lucrētius** Cārus (? 94 — ? c. 51); C. **Sallustius** Crispus (Sallust: 86 — c. 34); C. Valerius **Catullus** (c. 84 — c. 54); P. **Vergilius** Maro (Virgil: 70 — 19); Q. **Horātius** Flaccus (Horace: 65 — 8); T. **Līvius** (Livy: 59 B.C. — A.D. 17); Albius **Tibullus** (? c. 50 to 19 B.C.); Sex. **Propertius** (? c. 50 — after 16 B.C.); P. **Ovidius** Nāso (Ovid: 43 B.C. — A.D. ? 17); Phaedrus (c. 15 B.C. to A.D. c. 50); L. Annaeus **Seneca** (Seneca the Younger: c. 5 B.C. — A.D. 65); Ti. **Sīlius Italicus** (A.D. c. 26 — c. 101); A. **Persius** Flaccus (34 — 62); M. Annaeus **Lūcānus** (Lucan: 39 — 65); M. Valerius **Martiālis** (Martial: c. 40 — c. 104); P. Papinius **Stātius** (c. 45 — 96); D. Iūnius **Iuvenālis** (Juvenal: between 45 and 65 — after 127); Cornēlius **Tacitus** (c. 55 — after 115); C. **Valerius Flaccus** (? c. 60 — 92 or 93); C. **Plīnius** Caecilius Secundus (Pliny the Younger: 61 or 62 — before 114); C. **Suētōnius** Tranquillus (c. 69 — c. 140).

The following are not included: (1) some words which occur only in surviving fragments of lost works; (2) most of the words found only in inscriptions, in technical writers (e.g. Cato, Varro, Seneca the Elder, Columella, Pliny the Elder, Quintilian), or in Petronius; (3) a few rare technical terms occurring only in certain authors of the first and second centuries of the Christian era.

II. **Spelling.** The consonantal *i̯* is printed as *i*, and is treated as forming one letter with the vowel *i*. In deference, however, to the usage of most printed texts, consonantal *u̯* is printed as *v*, and is listed separately from the vowel *u* — although to the Romans they were one and the same letter.

* This dictionary contains a more complete list of Plautine words than is to be found in other Latin-English dictionaries. Practically all the words whose authenticity is reasonably certain have been included — generally with the spelling given by W. M. Lindsay in his *Oxford Classical Text* of Plautus.

The standardization of spelling in most languages is comparatively recent, having resulted chiefly from the invention of printing and the compilation of full and accurate dictionaries. Since the entire life of the Latin language falls within a period when these things did not exist, it is not surprising that many words are variously spelt. It must be remembered, too, that classical Latin literature covers a period of some centuries, and that all the manuscripts we possess were written centuries later than the literature which they preserve.

Many of the variations in spelling are indicated in the dictionary by means of cross-references. The following are some of the most important:

(1) Compounds formed with prepositions: e.g. *ac-curro* or *ad-curro* (and similarly in words beginning with *f, g, l, n, p, r, s, t*); *a-scribo* or *ad-scribo*; *a-spicio* or *ad-spicio*; *a-sto* or *ad-sto*; *col-laudo* or *con-laudo*; *il-lido* or *in-lido* (and similarly in words beginning with *m* or *r*); *im-buo* or *in-buo*; *im-pello* or *in-pello*; *op-secro* or *ob-secro*; *op-tineo* or *ob-tineo*; *sum-mitto* or *sub-mitto* (and similarly in words beginning with *c, f, g, p, r*); *trans-duco* or *tra-duco* (and similarly in words beginning with *i, l, m, n, v*).

(2) Some words were spelt with or without an initial *h* — e.g. *(h)arena, (h)erus, (h)olus, (h)umerus, (h)umidus.*

(3) Many spellings varied in different periods:

(a) The early Latin forms *servos, volnus, voltus* were later replaced by *servus, vulnus, vultus.*

(b) Early spellings such as *equos, equom, antiquos, antiquom, aquola* were afterwards replaced by *ecus, ecum, anticus, anticum, acula,* and later still by *equus, equum, antiquus, antiquum, aquula* (most of these words are listed in the dictionary in the latest forms, because they are the forms most commonly found in printed texts).

(c) The verbs *verro* and *verto* (and their compounds) were in early Latin spelt *vorro, vorto*; the same variation of spelling occurs in words derived from these verbs — e.g. *devorticulum, revorsio.*

(d) Many words show a variation between *i* and *u*, the spellings with *u* being the older — e.g. *optimus, optumus*; *monimentum, monumentum*; *recipero, recupero*; *manifestus, manufestus*; *sacrifico, sacrufico*; *carnifex, carnufex.*

III. Many Latin participles are used as adjectives. Some of the more important are separately listed; some others will be found at the end of the articles on the verbs to which they belong.

To save space, regularly formed adverbs are not listed, unless they have meanings different from those of the corresponding adjectives.

In the alphabetical word-list (but not always in the course of the articles), long vowels are marked thus: **ā**. Short vowels (**ă**) are marked only when it is desired to call particular attention to their quantity.

The figures 1, 2, 3, 4, placed after verbs, indicate the conjugation to which they belong. The figures 2, 3 placed after adjectives, participles, or pronouns, indicate the number of different terminations which they have in the nominative singular.

Abbreviations

abbr.	abbreviation
abl.	ablative
acc.	accusative
acc.c.inf.	accusative with infinitive
adj.	adjective
adv.	adverb
alci	*alicui*
alcis	*alicuius*
alqa	*aliqua*
alqd	*aliquid*
alqm	*aliquem*
alqo	*aliquo*
alqos	*aliquos*
c.	*circa*
cj.	conjunction
coll.	collective
comp.	comparative
dat.	dative
depon.	deponent
dim(in).	diminutive
esp.	especially
exclam.	exclamatory
f	feminine
fig.	figuratively
fut.	future
gen.	genitive, generally
genit.	genitive
gram.	grammatical
hort.	horticultural term
imperat.	imperative
impers.	impersonal(ly)
indecl.	indeclinable
indef.	indefinite
indic.	indicative
int.	interjection
intens.	intensive
interr(og).	interrogative
intr(ans).	intransitive
jur.	juridical term
lit.	literally
liter.	literary term
loc.	locative
m	masculine
med.	medical term
metaph.	metaphorical
mil.	military term
mus.	musical term
n(eut).	neuter
nom(in).	nominative
opp.	opposed to
P.	passive
part.	participle
pers.	personal
pf., perf.	perfect
pl.	plural

poet.	poetical	*subst.*	substantive (noun *or* pronoun)
pol.	political term	*sup.*	supine
pos.	positive	*superl.*	superlative
poss.	possessive	*thea.*	theatrical term
prep.	preposition	*trans.*	transitive
pron.	pronoun	*usu.*	usually
reflex.	reflexive	*vb.*	verb
rel(at).	relative	*v/i.*	verb intransitive
rhet.	rhetorical term	*v/t.*	verb transitive
sc.	*scilicet* (that is to say)	*vulg.*	vulgar
sg.	singular	*w.*	with
subj.	subjunctive		

⚔ military term ⚓ nautical term ⚘ botanical term

Latin-English Dictionary

A

A *abbr.* **1.** = **Aulus; 2.** = **antiquo** (*legem*) *or* **absolvo; 3. a. d.** = **ante diem; 4. a.u.c.** = **anno urbis conditae.**
ā, āh *int.* alas!, ah!
ā, ab (**abs te** = **a te**) *prep. with abl.* **1.** (*of space*) from, away from, out of, down from; distant from a point; at, on, in (*a tergo, a latere, a dextra parte*); **2.** (*of time*) after, from, since, since the time of; **3.** (*of relation*) by, from, of, on the part of, in respect of, on account of, in consequence of, from, against (*defendere*).
abacus, ī, *m* table; counting *or* play board.
ā-baetō 3 = **abito.**
ab-aliēnātiō, ōnis *f* alienation (*of property*).
ab-aliēnō 1 to alienate; **a**) to sell, withdraw (*rem*); to deprive (*alqm re*); **b**) to estrange (*ab alqo*).
ab-avus, ī, *m* great-great-grandfather; ancestor.
ab-dicātiō, ōnis *f* abdication, resignation.
ab-dicō[1] 1 to renounce; **a**) to disown, reject (*alqm*); **b**) to resign, abdicate (*se magistratu*).
ab-dīcō[2] 3 to forbid; to disapprove of.
ab-ditus 3 hidden, concealed, secret.
ab-dō, didī, ditum 3 **a**) to remove, put aside, withdraw; **b**) to hide, conceal, bury (*alqd in locum, in loco*): **c**) **se abdere** to hide oneself, withdraw, retire, escape; to plunge oneself (*in rem, in re, re*).
ab-dōmen, inis *n* belly, paunch.
ab-dūcō 3 to lead *or* conduct away from, take away, carry off, rob (*alqd ab, de, ex re, alqm ab alqo*); **a**) to separate, seduce, alienate, remove, draw away (*a re, ab alqo, ad alqm*): **b**) to reduce, degrade.
ab-eō, iī, itum, īre to go away *or* off (*ab alqo, de, ex, a re, in* or *ad alqd*); **a**) to resign, retire from (*an office, magistratu*); **b**) to come off, turn out, end; **c**) to pass away, disappear; **d**) to turn aside, deviate from (*ab re ad* or *in alqd*); **e**) to be transformed, changed into (*in alqd*): **f**) **abi** begone! be off!
ab-equitō 1 to ride away.
ab-errātiō, ōnis *f* escape, relief.
ab-errō 1 to wander, go astray, lose one's way (*ab* or *ex re*): to deviate, wander in thought, forget for a time (*a re ad alqd*).
ab-hibeō 2 to keep off.
ab-hinc *adv.* (*with acc., seldom abl.*) from this time, ago.
ab-horrēns, tis incongruous, inappropriate.
ab-horreō, uī, — 2 to shrink back from, abhor (*a re*); **a**) to be averse *or* disinclined to (*a re*); **b**) to vary *or* differ from, be inconsistent with, be opposed to (*a re*).
āb-iciō (*and* **ăb-**), **iēcī, iectum** 3 **1.** to throw *or* cast away *or* down; a) to squander; b) to fling away, give up, abandon; **2.** to strike to the ground; **se ābicere** to prostrate oneself (*ad pedes alcis*); to degrade, humble.
ab-iectiō, ōnis *f* dejection.
ab-iectus 3 cast away *or* down; **a**) dispirited, low; **b**) common, mean, contemptible; **c**) cowardly, despondent.
abiegnus 3 of fir-wood.
abiēs, etis *f* fir(-tree); **a**) ship; **b**) spear; **c**) writing-tablet.
ab-igō, ēgī, āctum 3 to drive away *or* off; **a**) to procure abortion; **b**) to banish, expel; **c**) to repel.
ab-itiō, ōnis *f* a going away.
ā-bītō 3 to go away.
ab-itus, ūs *m* a going away, departure; egress, outlet.
ab-iūdicō 1 to deprive of by judicial decree (*alqd ab alqo, alci alqd*).
ab-iungō, iūnxī, iūnctum 3 to unyoke, detach.
ab-iūrō 1 to abjure, deny by *or* on oath.
ab-lēgātiō, ōnis *f* a sending away.
ab-lēgō 1 to send away *or* off; **a**) to remove, banish; **b**) to dismiss, dislodge (⚔).

ab-ligūr(r)iō 4 to squander.
ab-locō 1 to lease, farm out.
ab-lūdō 3 to differ from.
ab-luō, luī, lūtum 3 to wash (away), cleanse.
ab-natō 1 to swim away.
ab-negō 1 **a**) to deny, refuse; **b**) to disown, abnegate.
ab-nepōs, pōtis *m*, **ab-neptis, is** *f* great-great-grandson *or* -daughter.
ab-noctō 1 to sleep out.
ab-normis, e irregular.
ab-nuō, nuī, nuitūrus 3 to deny, refuse, decline (by a sign) (*alci alqd* or *de re*); **a**) to reject; **b**) to deny, disclaim (*alqd*; *acc. c. inf.*).
ab-nūtō 1 = **abnuo.**
ab-oleō, ēvī, itum 2 **a**) to destroy, annihilate, to do away with, abolish (*alqd*); **b**) to take away, remove.
ab-olēscō, lēvī, — 3 to disappear, vanish.
ab-olitiō, ōnis *f* abolition; amnesty.
abolla, ae *f* thick cloak.
ab-ōminor 1 **a**) to deprecate as an evil omen; **b**) to detest, execrate, abominate.
ab-orior 4, **ab-orīscor** 3 to fail, perish.
ab-ortiō, ōnis *f*, **ab-ortus, ūs** *m* miscarriage.
ab-ortīvus 3 prematurely born.
ab-rādō, rāsī, rāsum 3 to scrape *or* shave off (*alqd ab alqo*).
ab-ripiō, ripuī, reptum 3 to snatch away, tear off, drag off; **se abr.** to hurry away.
ab-rogātiō, ōnis *f* repeal (*of a law*).
ab-rogō 1 **a**) to repeal, annul, abrogate (*alqd*); **b**) to take away (*alci alqd*).
abrotonum, ī, *n* southernwood (*a plant*).
ab-rumpō, rūpī, ruptum 3 **1.** to break off *or* away; **2.** to tear, rend, burst; **a**) to sever, end; **b**) to violate.
ab-ruptiō, ōnis *f* a breaking off; divorce.
ab-ruptus 3 torn *or* broken off; precipitous, steep; **abruptum, ī** *n* precipice.
abs-cēdō, cessī, cessum 3 to go away, withdraw, retire (*ab alqo*, *ab*, *ex*, *de re*); **a**) to desist from, abandon, give up (*re*); **b**) to disappear, to be lost.
abs-cessiō, ōnis *f* a going away, diminution.
abs-cessus, ūs *m* a going away, departure, absence.
abs-cīdō, cīdī, cīsum 3 to cut off, hew off (*alci alqd*); **a**) to separate; **b**) to take away.
ab-scindō 3 to take *or* break off (*alqd a* or *de re*); **a**) to rip open (*venas*); **b**) to divide, separate; **c**) to hinder.
abs-cīsus 3 cut off; **a**) precipitous, steep; **b**) short.
abs-conditus 3 concealed, hidden; **a**) secret; **b**) abstruse.
abs-condō, con(di)dī, conditum 3 to conceal, hide (*alqd in loco*); to make a secret of.
ab-sēns, tis absent, remote.
ab-sentia, ae *f* absence; want.
ab-siliō 4 to leap away.
ab-similis, e unlike.
absinthium, iī *n* wormwood.
absis, īdis *f* arch, vault.
ab-sistō, stitī, — 3 to go away, withdraw (*a re, re*); **a**) to desist from; **b**) leave off (*with inf.*).
ab-solūtiō, ōnis *f* **a**) acquittal; **b**) perfection.
ab-solūtōrius 3 belonging to acquittal.
ab-solūtus 3 **a**) complete, perfect; **b**) unconditional.
ab-solvō 3 to loosen; **a**) to set free, release (*alqd alqa re, ab alqo*); **b**) to acquit, absolve; **c**) to complete, finish, bring to an end; **d**) to relate.
ab-sonus 3 inharmonious, discordant (*a re* or *w. dat.*); incompatible.
ab-sorbeō, uī, — 2 to swallow down, devour.
absque *prep. with abl.* apart from, without.
abs-tēmius 3 abstemious, temperate.
abs-tergeō 2 **a**) to wipe off, dry by wiping; ⚓ to break off; **b**) to remove.
abs-terreō 2 to frighten away, drive away (*alqm a re*); to deter.
abs-tinēns, tis abstinent, continent; chaste.
abs-tinentia, ae *f* abstinence; integrity; self-denial, contentedness.
abs-tineō, tinuī, (**tentum**) 2 **a**) to keep off *or* back (*alqm* or *alqd a re* or *re*); **b**) to abstain, refrain (*re*, *a re*); **c**) to spare.
ab-stō 1 to stand at a distance.

abs-trahō 3 to draw *or* drag away *or* off (*alqm* or *alqd ab, de, ex re, ad* or *in alqd*); **a**) to pull away, remove, detach (*alqd a re*); **b**) to carry on (*ad alqd*); **c**) to estrange.
abs-trūdō 3 to thrust away, conceal (*alqd in rem* or *in re*).
abs-trūsus 3 **a**) concealed, hidden, secret; **b**) abstruse.
ab-sum, ā-fuī (ā-futūrus) ab-esse **1.** to be away from, be absent (*a re*); **a**) (*alci* or *ab alqo, a re*) to stand off, take no part, to be missing *or* wanting, to abandon, not to help; **b**) to be inconvenient, inconsistent with, different (*a re*); **c**) to be free from (*a re*); **2. haud multum (longe) abest, quin** it is not far from being the case that; **tantum abest, ut ... ut** so far is it from ... that.
absūmēdō, inis *f* a consuming.
ab-sūmō 3 **a**) to take away, diminish, consume; **b**) to waste; **c**) to destroy; **d**) to spend (*time*). **P.** to perish, be killed.
ab-surdus 3 unmelodious, out of tune, harsh; **a**) foolish, silly, unreasonable; **b**) incongruous, inconsistent.
ab-undāns, tis overflowing; **a**) abundant, rich, abounding (*w. abl.* or *gen.*); **b**) living in abundance, plentiful; **c**) overloaded.
ab-undantia, ae *f* abundance, plenty, fulness; an overcharging.
ab-unde *adv.* plentifully, more than enough, copiously.
ab-undō 1 to overflow, stream over; **a**) to abound (*re*), be rich in; **b**) to enjoy.
ab-ūsiō, ōnis *f* incorrect use of a figure of speech.
ab-usque (*w. abl.*) = **usque ab.**
ab-ūsus, ūs *m* a using up.
ab-ūtor 3 **a**) to use up, consume, to use fully (*with abl.*); **b**) to abuse, use wrongly, misapply, waste.
ac, *see* **atque.**
acalanthis, idis *f* goldfinch, thistle-finch.
acanthus, ī *m* (and *f*) **1.** bear's--breech (*a plant*); **2.** gum arabic.
a-capnus 3 smokeless.
ac-cantō 1 to sing beside.
ac-cēdō 3 **1.** to go *or* come to, to approach, come near (*ad alqm, ad alqd,* with *acc.,* with *dat.*); a) to approach as an enemy (*ad alqd,* with *dat.*); b) to enter upon some work, to undertake (*ad alqd*); c) to assent, agree (*ad alqm, ad alqd*); d) to come near, be like (*ad alqd*); **2.** to be added (*ad alqd,* with *dat.*); **accēdit ut** *or* **quod** = moreover.
ac-celerō 1 **a**) to accelerate; **b**) *intr.* to hasten.
ac-cendō, cendī, cēnsum 3 to kindle, set on fire, light; **a**) to lighten up; **b**) to inflame, excite, arouse, stir, provoke; **c**) to increase.
ac-cēnseō 2 to reckon to.
ac-cēnsus, ī *m* **1.** apparitor, attendant of a magistrate; **2.** light-armed soldier.
ac-centus, ūs *m* accent.
ac-ceptiō, ōnis *f* a receiving, accepting.
ac-ceptō 1 to receive (*repeatedly*).
ac-ceptor, ōris *m*, **ac-ceptrīx, īcis** *f* receiver, approver.
ac-ceptus 3 welcome, pleasing, agreeable (*alci*).
ac-cersō 3 = **arcesso.**
ac-cessiō, ōnis *f* **1.** a coming to, approach; audience, admission; **2.** increase, addition, appendage; progress.
ac-cessus, ūs *m* **1.** = **accessio; 2.** a) entrance; b) inclination (*ad alqd*).
ac-cidō¹, cidī, — 3 [*cado*] **1.** to fall down, to fall to; a) to fall at the feet of; b) to reach, strike (*the senses*); **2.** to come to pass, happen, take place; **accidit ut** it happens that; a) to occur; b) to fall out, turn out.
ac-cīdō², cīdī, cīsum 3 [*caedo*] to cut *or* hew at; **a**) to consume; **b**) to weaken, ruin.
ac-cingō 3 **1.** to gird to *or* on; **2.** to equip with (*abl.*), arm, furnish, provide; **se acc.** *or* **P.** to gird oneself, make oneself ready, to be ready (*ad,* seldom *in rem, dat., acc., inf.*).
ac-ciō 4 to call to, summon, send for; **accītus** outlandish.
ac-cipiō, cēpī, ceptum 3 **1.** to take, receive, get, accept (*alqd ab alqo*); **acceptum, ī** *n* what is received (*money*); a) *alci alqd acceptum referre* to enter to the credit, to give credit for; b) to suffer, bear; c) to admit, approve of; **2.** to receive as a guest; a) to entertain; b) to treat, deal with; **3.** to hear, perceive; a) to learn, understand; b) to feel; c) to take,

interpret, explain (*in bonam partem, in omen, falsa pro veris*); **4.** a) to obtain; b) to suffer (*detrimentum, cladem*).
accipiter, tris *m* a hawk, bird of prey.
accipitrīna, ae *f* hawk's talon.
ac-cītus, ūs *m* summons, call.
ac-clāmātiō, ōnis *f* cry, shout.
ac-clāmō 1 **a**) to call, cry, shout at; **b**) to name by acclamation.
ac-clārō 1 to make clear, reveal.
ac-clīnis, e leaning on, inclined to (*dat.*).
ac-clīnō 1 to lean on, incline to (*se in alqm* or *ad alqd*).
ac-clīvis, e *and* **-vus** 3 inclined upwards, ascending, sloping.
ac-clīvitās, ātis *f* acclivity, ascent.
ac-cognōscō 3 to recognize.
ac-cola, ae *m* one who dwells near, neighbour.
ac-colō 3 to dwell near (*alqd*).
ac-commodātiō, ōnis *f* **a**) an adjusting, accommodation; **b**) complaisance.
ac-commodātus 3 adapted, fitted, fit, suitable (*alci, ad alqd*).
ac-commodō 1 to put on, apply, fit; **a**) to adjust, adapt (*alci alqd, ad alqd*); **b**) to attribute, ascribe; **c**) to make use of.
ac-commodus 3 fit for (*with dat.*), suitable.
ac-crēdō 3 to give credence.
ac-crēscō 3 **a**) to grow, increase; **b**) to come as an addition.
ac-crētiō, ōnis *f* increase.
ac-cubitiō, ōnis *f*, **ac-cubitus, -us** *m* a lying at table.
ac-cubō 1 to lie at, recline at table.
ac-cubuō *adv.* lying near.
ac-cūdō 3 to coin.
ac-cumbō, cubuī, cubitum 3 to lie down, to lie beside; to lie at table.
ac-cumulātor, ōris *m* one who heaps up.
ac-cumulō 1 **a**) to heap up, amass, to give in abundance, to heap upon; **b**) to overwhelm (*alqm re*).
ac-cūrātiō, ōnis *f* accuracy, exactness, carefulness.
ac-cūrātus 3 exact, careful; nice, precise.
ac-cūrō 1 to do carefully.
ac-currō, (cu)currī, cursum 3 to run to *or* up, to hasten to (*ad alqm, ad* or *in alqd*).
ac-cursus, ūs *m* a running to.
accūsābilis, e worthy of blame.
accūsātiō, ōnis *f* **a**) accusation, complaint; prosecution, indictment; **b**) bill of indictment.
accūsātor, ōris *m* accuser, prosecutor.
accūsātōrius 3 like an accuser.
accūsātrīx, īcis *f* female accuser.
ac-cūsitō 1 to accuse.
ac-cūsō 1 **a**) to accuse, prosecute (*alqm rei* or *de re*); **b**) to complain of, blame, reproach (*alqd, alqm de re, in re*; with *quod*).
acer[1], **eris** *n* maple(-tree).
ācer[2], **ācris, ācre** sharp, cutting, piercing; **a**) penetrating, pungent, biting, shrill; **b**) acute, sagacious, subtle; **c**) violent, energetic, active, ardent, spirited, brave; **d**) passionate, hot, fierce; **e**) severe, cruel.
acerbitās, ātis *f* bitterness, sourness; **a**) severity, harshness; **b**) bitterness, painfulness; **c**) misery, affliction, distress.
acerbō 1 to make bitter *or* worse.
acerbus 3 bitter, sour; **a**) raw, unripe; **b**) harsh, severe, rough, angry, morose; **c**) grievous, distressing.
acernus 3 of maple (wood).
acerra, ae *f* casket for incense.
acersecomēs, ae *m* long-haired youth.
acervālis, e like a heap.
acervātim *adv.* by heaps, in heaps; to sum up, briefly.
acervō 1 to heap up.
acervus, ī *m* heap, pile; **a**) mass, multitude; **b**) (*in logic*) argument by accumulation.
acēscō, — 3 to become sour.
acētābulum, ī *n* (vinegar-)bowl, cup.
acētum, ī *n* sour wine, vinegar; wit.
acidus 3 sour, sharp; disagreeable.
aciēs, ēī *f* **1.** sharp edge, point; a) keenness, piercing look, sight; b) eye, pupil; c) insight, acuteness; **2.** a) line of battle, battle-array; army; b) battle; c) battle in words, disputation.
acina, ae *f* = **acinus.**
acīnacēs, is *m* Persian sabre.
acinus, ī *m and* **-um, ī** *n* berry (*of the grape*).
acipēnser, eris *m* a sea-fish, sturgeon.
aclys, ydis *f* small javelin.

acoenonoētus 3 curmudgeonly (*or* stupid ?).
aconītum (*and* **-on**), **ī** *n* a poisonous plant, aconite; poison.
acosmos unadorned.
ac-quiēscō 3 **1.** to come to rest, to repose (*a re*); a) to die; b) to have peace; **2.** a) to be content with (*re*); b) to find comfort in.
ac-quīrō, quīsīvī, quīsītum 3 **a**) to acquire in addition; **b**) to obtain, gain, win.
acrāto-phorum, ī *n* vessel for unmixed wine.
acrēdula, ae *f* a bird.
ācriculus 3 irritable; hothead.
ācrimōnia, ae *f* sharpness; energy.
ācriter *adv. of* **ācer.**
acroāma, atis *n* **a**) anything heard with pleasure; **b**) musician, singer, reader, actor.
acroāsis, is *f* lecture.
acta[1], **ae** *f* sea-shore, beach.
ācta[2], **ōrum** *n/pl.* actions, deeds; **a**) public *or* legal acts, proceedings, ordinances; **b**) register, minutes, records; **c**) journal, gazette (*diurna*).
āctiō, ōnis *f* a doing, performing, action; **1.** enterprise, business; a) public action; b) office; **2.** a) a performing, rendering (*of an orator* or *actor*); b) action in a court of justice, suit at law, process; c) permission *or* right to bring an action.
āctitō 1 to do *or* perform often.
āctīvus 3 active, practical.
āctor, ōris *m* **1.** driver, shepherd; **2.** agent, performer; a) manager, executor; b) accuser, plaintiff; c) actor, player.
āctuāriola, ae *f* a small boat.
āctuārius[1] 3 easily driven, swift; **āctuāria, ae** *f* swift-sailing vessel.
āctuārius[2], **i** *m* shorthand writer; registrar of documents.
āctum, ī *n, see* **acta**[2], **orum.**
āctuōsus 3 active, full of life, effective; passionate.
āctus, ūs *m* **1.** a driving, motion, impulse; a) driving of cattle; b) right of way for driving cattle; **2.** a) movement of the body, gesture; b) recital, presentation of a play; c) division of a play, act.
actūtum *adv.* immediately, directly.
acula, ae *f* = **aquula.**
aculeātus 3 provided with prickles *or* stings, stinging; cunning.
aculeus, ī *m* sting, point; **a**) sagacity, cunning; **b**) sarcasm; **c**) spur, goad.
acūmen, inis *n* point, sharpness; spear-point; **a**) cunning, trickery; **b**) acuteness.
acuō, uī, ūtum 3 to point, sharpen, whet; **a**) to exercise, practise; **b**) to spur, stimulate; **c**) to tease, grieve; **d**) to raise, enhance.
acus, ūs *f* needle; *acu pingere* to embroider.
acūtulus 3 somewhat sharp, rather subtle.
acūtus 3 pointed, sharpened, sharp; **a**) cutting, pungent, piercing, hot; **b**) acute, cunning, penetrating, sagacious; **c**) crafty, subtle.
ad *prep.* with *acc.* **1.** (*of space*) a) to, towards, in the direction of, to the vicinity of, against, before; b) up to (*ad unum omnes* all, to a man); c) at, near, close by; **2.** (*of time*) a) about, toward; till, to, even to, up to, *ad tempus* for some time, in due time, temporarily, for a certain time; b) at, on; **3.** (*of relation*) a) (*with numbers*) about, near to, almost; b) for the purpose of; c) with respect to; d) according to, in consequence of; e) compared with; f) besides, in addition to (*ad hoc, ad haec*).
ad-āctiō, ōnis *f* enforcing.
ad-āctus, ūs *m* a driving in.
ad-aequē *adv.* in like manner.
ad-aequō 1 to make equal (*alqd alci rei*); **a**) to compare to, to put on a par (*alqd cum re*, or with *dat.*); **b**) to come near to (*with acc.*).
ad-aestuō 1 to surge.
adamantēus 3, **-tinus** 3 of steel; hard as steel.
adamās, antis *m* steel; adamant; hardness, inflexibility.
ad-ambulō 1 to walk near.
ad-amō 1 to fall in love with.
ad-aperiō 4 to throw open, open fully.
ad-apertilis, e capable of being opened.
ad-aptō 1 to adjust to.
ad-aquō 1 to water.
ad-auctus, ūs *m* growth.
ad-augeō 2 to increase.
ad-augēscō 3 to begin to grow.
ad-bibō, bibī, — 3 to drink (in); *fig.* to listen eagerly to.
ad-bītō, —, — 3 to go near.

adc..., *see* **acc...**
ad-decet 2 it befits.
ad-dēnseō 2 to make compact.
ad-dīcō 3 **1.** to assent, to be propitious; **2.** a) to award, adjudge (*in servitutem; alci alqd*); **addictus, ī** *m* 3 debtor, bondsman; b) to knock down to (*in auctions, alci alqd*); c) to sell, make over; d) to dedicate, devote, consecrate (*alci alqd*); *se add.* to give oneself up to.
ad-dictiō, ōnis *f* an adjudging, award.
ad-discō 3 to learn in addition (*alqd*).
additāmentum, ī *n* addition, accession.
ad-dō, didī, ditum 3 to give *or* put to; **1.** a) to bring to, add to, increase; b) to impart, bestow; **2.** to add (*in reckoning*); to say *or* write in addition; *adde* moreover (*alci alqd, in rem*).
ad-doceō 2 to teach in addition.
ad-dormīscō 3 to fall asleep.
ad-dubitō 1 to incline to doubt, to hesitate (*de re, in re*); *trans.* to doubt.
ad-dūcō 3 **1.** to draw (tight) to oneself, to stretch, draw together; **2.** to lead to, bring to *or* along (*alqd ad* or *in alqd*), *in iudicium* or *in ius* to bring to justice; a) to bring to a certain condition *or* state of mind; b) to induce, prevail upon (*alqm in* or *ad alqd*, with *ut*); **P.** to be influenced, persuaded.
ad-ductus 3 drawn together, wrinkled; severe, stern.
ad-edō, ēdī, ēsum 3 to gnaw at; to consume.
ad-ēmptiō, ōnis *f* a taking away.
ad-eō[1], iī, itum, īre to go *or* come to *or* up, to approach (*ad, in alqd,* with *acc.*); to draw near; **a)** to accost, address, apply to; **b)** to travel to, to visit; **c)** to approach as an enemy, to attack; **d)** to undertake, enter on (*alqd* or *ad alqd*), take in hand; to undergo, incur (*alqd*).
ad-eō[2] *adv.* to that point, thus far, so far; **a)** so long; **b)** so much, to that degree; **c)** even, indeed, truly, just, precisely; *atque adeō* and what is more.
adeps, ipis *m and f* soft fat of animals.
adeptiō, ōnis *f* an obtaining.
ad-equitō 1 to ride up to (*with dat.* or *ad alqm, in alqd*).
ad-errō to wander *or* travel to (*with dat.*).
ad-ēsuriō 4 to hunger after.
adf..., *see* **aff...**
adg..., *see* **agg...**
ad-haereō 2 to cleave, stick *or* hang to, to adhere (*with dat.*); **a)** to border on, be near; **b)** to be attached, to cling to.
ad-haerēscō, haesī, haesum 3 to stick to, adhere; **a)** to cling to, remain (*ad alqd* or *in re,* with *dat.*); **b)** to stick fast, stop.
ad-haesiō, ōnis *f* a clinging to.
ad-hibeō, uī, itum 2 to bring to, hold to, lay on (*alqd ad alqd* or with *dat.*); **a)** to apply to, use, show, employ; **b)** to summon, call, invite (*in convivium*); to consult; **c)** to treat, handle.
ad-hinniō 4 to neigh to (*alci*); to crave, long for (*ad alqd*).
ad-hōc *adv.* = **adhuc.**
ad-hortātiō, ōnis *f* exhortation, encouragement.
ad-hortātor, ōris *m* one who exhorts.
ad-hortor 1 to exhort, encourage, rouse (*alqm ad alqd* or with *ut, ne*).
ad-hūc *adv.* **1.** thus far, hitherto; **2.** a) till now, up to the present time; b) as yet, still, even now; **3.** still more, besides, in addition.
ad-iaceō 2 to lie at, by the side of; to adjoin (*ad alqd,* with *dat.* or *acc.*).
ād-iciō (*and* **ăd-**), **iēcī, iectum** 3 **1.** to throw to, cast to, to direct to (*alqd in, ad alqd,* with *dat.*); **2.** to apply to, to add.
ad-iectiō, ōnis *f*, **ad-iectus, ūs** *m* addition.
ad-igō, ēgī, āctum 3 to drive to; **a)** to drive home; **b)** to thrust *or* push to (*alqd in* or *ad alqd, in re,* with *dat.*); **c)** to compel, urge (*alqm ad alqd*; with *ut*), *alqm ad ius iurandum* to bind by oath.
ad-imō, ēmī, ēmptum 3 to take away, to take from (*alci alqd*).
adipātus 3 **a)** fatty, greasy; **-ta, ōrum** *n/pl.* food made with *or* cooked in fat; **b)** turgid, bombastic.
ad-ipīscor, adeptus sum 3 to reach, come up to, overtake (*alqm*); to obtain, get, attain (*alqd ab alqo*).
ad-itiālis, e connected with an entry into office, inaugural.

ad-itiō, ōnis *f* a going to, approach.
ad-itus, ūs *m* a going to, approach (*ad rem, ad alqm*); **a**) entrance, entry, access (*in rem, ad alqm*); **b**) audience; admittance; **c**) beginning, commencement; **d**) possibility of entrance; opportunity, chance.
ad-iūdicō 1 to award, adjudge, adjudicate (*alci alqd*); to assign, ascribe.
ad-iūmentum, ī *n* help, assistance, support.
ad-iūnctiō, ōnis *f* a joining to, union (*rei ad alqd*); **a**) addition, connexion; **b**) restriction.
ad-iūnctor, ōris *m* one who adds.
ad-iūnctus 3 closely joined, connected, united; belonging to (*with dat.*); **adiūnctum, ī** *n* **a**) characteristic *or* essential attribute; **b**) accessory circumstance.
ad-iungō 3 to yoke, harness, *or* bind to (*alqd alci rei*); **a**) to join, connect, attach (*alqd ad alqd* or with *dat.*); **adiūnctum esse** to border on; **b**) to add, annex, associate (*alqd ad alqd* or with *dat.*); **c**) to win as a friend *or* ally; **d**) to unite; **e**) to give, attribute, confer; **f**) to direct to.
ad-iūrō 1 **a**) to swear in addition; **b**) to swear to; **c**) to confirm *or* promise by oath.
adiūtābilis, e helping.
ad-iūtō 1 to help, assist (*alqm*).
adiūtor, ōris *m* helper, assistant; **a**) aid, adjutant; **b**) deputy, secretary; **c**) secondary player (*in the theatre*).
adiūtōrium, ī *n* help.
adiūtrīx, īcis *f* female helper *or* assistant.
ad-iuvō, iūvī, iūtum 1 to help, assist, aid (*alqm in re, ad alqd*); **a**) to encourage, support, further (*alqd*); **b**) to be of good service, to avail, be useful.
adl..., *see* **all...**
ad-mātūrō 1 to hasten still more.
ad-mētior 4 to measure out to.
ad-migrō 1 to be added to.
adminiculō 1 to support by props.
adminic(u)lum, ī *n* prop, support, stake; **a**) aid, help; **b**) instrument.
ad-minister, trī *m* assistant, helper, servant, attendant; *fig.* tool.
ad-ministra, ae *f* female helper *or* assistant.
ad-ministrātiō, ōnis *f* help, aid; **a**) management, direction; **b**) administration, government.
ad-ministrātor, ōris *m* manager, administrator.
ad-ministrō 1 to direct, administer, manage, execute (*alqd*).
ad-mīrābilis, e **a**) admirable, wonderful; **b**) strange, astonishing.
ad-mīrābilitās, ātis *f* admirableness.
ad-mīrandus 3 = **admirabilis.**
ad-mīrātiō, ōnis *f* **a**) admiration; **b**) wonder, astonishment.
ad-mīrātor, ōris *m* admirer.
ad-mīror 1 **a**) to admire; **b**) to wonder at, be astonished at (*alqd, in alqo, alqm in* or *de re*, with *acc. c. inf.* or *quod*).
ad-misceō 2 **1.** to mix with, admix; a) to add to by mixing (*alqd alci rei*); **b**) to join, mingle (*alqd alqa re*); **2.** to implicate (*alqm ad alqd*).
ad-missārius, ī *m* stallion.
ad-missiō, ōnis *f* audience.
ad-missum, ī *n* trespass, crime.
ad-missūra, ae *f* breeding, breeding-stud.
ad-mittō 3 **1.** to let go, let loose, set in motion (*alqd in alqm*), to put to a gallop (*equum*); **2.** a) to admit (*alqm in* or *ad alqd*), to give audience; b) to give a share in; c) to allow, permit; d) to commit (*a crime*); **3.** to grant, to be propitious.
ad-mixtiō, ōnis *f* admixture.
ad-moderātē suitably.
ad-moderor 1 to moderate.
ad-modum *adv.* **a**) (*with numbers*) to full measure, at least; **b**) (*of degree*) wholly, entirely; completely, quite, altogether; *non* ~ not at all, ~ *nihil* nothing at all; **c**) (*in answers*) certainly.
ad-moeniō 4 to blockade.
ad-mōlior 4 to move *or* bring to.
ad-moneō 2 **1.** to remind, to call to mind (*alqm alcis rei* or *de re*; with *acc. c. inf.*); to put in mind of a debt; **2.** to admonish, warn (*alqm*); a) to advise, suggest; b) to urge, incite (*alqm, ut* or *ne*).
ad-monitiō, ōnis *f* **a**) a reminding; **b**) admonition, suggestion, exhortation.
ad-monitor, ōris *m* admonisher.
ad-monitrīx, īcis *f* female admonisher.
ad-monitum, ī *n* = **admonitio.**

ad-monitus, ūs *m* = **admonitio.**
ad-mordeō, momordī, morsum 2 to gnaw at, bite at.
ad-mōtiō, ōnis *f digitorum* application (*to a stringed instrument*).
ad-moveō 2 to move *or* bring to *or* near (*alqm* or *alqd ad alqd* or *dat.*); **a**) to bring up, lead on, conduct; *se ad alqd* to draw near; **b**) *calcaria* or *stimulos* to give the spur, to goad; **c**) to bring up (*war-machines*); **d**) *fig.* to apply, direct to.
ad-mūgiō 4 to low *or* bellow to (*dat.*).
ad-murmurātiō, ōnis *f* a murmuring.
ad-murmurō 1 to murmur.
ad-mutilō 1 to fleece.
adn..., *see* **ann...**
ad-oleō[1] 2 to smell.
ad-oleō[2], **uī,** — 2 to pile up on *or* with; to burn.
ad-olēscēns, tis growing up, young; *subst.*, *see* **adulescens.**
ad-olēscentia, ae *f* = **adulescentia.**
ad-olēscō, olēvī, (**ultum**) 3 to grow up, grow; to be piled high.
ad-operiō 4 **a**) to cover, veil; **b**) to close, shut.
ad-opīnor 1 to conjecture.
ad-optātīcius 3 adopted.
ad-optātiō, ōnis *f* = **adoptio.**
ad-optiō, ōnis *f* adoption.
ad-optīvus 3 belonging to adoption; adopted; *hort.* grafted.
ad-optō 1 **a**) to choose in addition, to select; **b**) to adopt; **c**) *hort.* to graft.
ador, ōris (*and* **ŏris**) *n* spelt.
adōrea (*or* **-ia**), **ae** *f* praise, glory, reward of valour.
adōreus 3 of spelt.
ad-orior 4 to rise against; **a**) to attack, assail, assault (*alqm, alqd*); **b**) to address (*with entreaties*); **c**) to undertake, attempt (*alqd*; *inf.*).
ad-ōrnō 1 **a**) to fit out, equip, prepare, provide; **b**) to adorn, embellish.
ad-ōrō 1 to speak to; **a**) to implore, entreat; **b**) to reverence, worship; **c**) to ask for.
adp..., *see* **app...; adqu...,** *see* **acqu...; adr...,** *see* **arr...**
ad-rādō 3 to scrape at; to cut.
ads..., adsc...; adsp..., adstt..., ad-..., *see* **ass..., asc..., asp..., ast..., att...**
ad-sum, *see* **as-sum.**
adūlātiō, ōnis *f* a fawning; flattery.
adūlātor, ōris *m* flatterer; servile person.
adūlātōrius 3 flattering, cringing.
adulēscēns, entis *m* young man, youth; *f* young woman, maiden.
adulēscentia, ae *f* youth; young people.
adulēscentulus, ī *m*, **ula, ae** *f* a young man, woman.
adūlō 1 to fawn; to wipe off.
ad-ūlor 1 to fawn on (*alqm*); to flatter, cringe, to revere in a servile manner (*alqm, alci*).
adulter, erī *m* **a**) adulterous; adulterer; **b**) gallant, paramour.
adultera, ae *f* adulteress.
adulterīnus 3 forged, counterfeit, false, not genuine.
adulterium, ī *n* adultery.
adulterō 1 **a**) to commit adultery; **b**) to falsify, corrupt; **c**) to seduce to adultery.
adultus 3 grown up, adult, mature.
adumbrātim in outline.
adumbrātiō, ōnis *f* sketch, outline.
ad-umbrō 1 to sketch, to shade; **a**) to represent vaguely; **b**) to imitate; **ad-umbrātus** 3 sketched, shadowed; a) vague, dim, imperfect; **b**) unreal, feigned, vain, fictitious.
ad-uncitās, ātis *f* hooked shape.
ad-uncus 3 bent inwards, hooked.
ad-ūnō 1 to unite.
ad-urgeō 2 to press to; to pursue eagerly.
ad-ūrō, ussī, ustum 3 to set on fire, kindle; **a**) to scorch, singe; **b**) to nip, freeze.
ad-usque *prep.* with *acc.* = **usque ad;** *adv.* all the way.
advectīcius 3 imported, foreign.
ad-vectō 1 to convey continually.
ad-vectus, ūs *m* a conveying.
ad-vehō, vexī, vectum 3 to carry *or* bring to a place; **P.** to be brought, conveyed, borne to; to arrive, land.
ad-vēlō 1 to veil; to crown.
ad-vena, ae *m* stranger, foreigner, immigrant; novice.
ad-veneror 1 to honour.
ad-veniō 4 to come to, to arrive at (*in locum, ad alqd*); **a**) to approach, appear; **b**) to happen (*ad alqm*).

adventīcius 3 coming in addition; foreign, strange.
adventō 1 to approach, advance, draw near.
ad-ventor, ōris *m* visitor, guest.
adventus, ūs *m* approach, arrival.
ad-verberō 1 to strike.
adversārius 1. *adj.* 3 opposed, contrary, hostile, noxious (*with dat.*); **2.** a) ~ ī *m* opponent, adversary, enemy, antagonist; **b) adversāria, ōrum** *n/pl.* arguments of an opponent; memoranda; notebook.
ad-versātrīx, īcis *f* female adversary.
ad-versiō, ōnis *f* direction.
ad-versitor, ōris *m* slave who goes to meet his master.
ad-versō 1 *animum* to watch.
ad-versor 1 to resist, oppose, withstand (*with dat.* or *quominus*).
ad-versus[1] 3 turned towards, fronting, opposite, in front; **dentes** front teeth; (*vulnus*) on the breast; **in adversum os** full in the face; **flumine adverso** up stream; **ex adverso** over against; **in adversum** against; **a)** opposed, hostile; **adverso senatu** against the will of the senate; **b)** odious; unfavourable, unpropitious (*with dat.*) — *subst.* **adversa, ōrum** *n/pl.* **a)** misfortune, calamity, disaster; **b)** the contrary, contrast.
ad-versus[2] *or* **-sum 1.** *adv.* in the opposite direction, to meet; **2.** *prep.* with *acc.* a) opposite, over against, towards; b) in respect of; contrary to; compared with.
ad-vertō 3 to turn to *or* towards (*alqd in alqd*); **a)** to steer, land; **b) animum advertere** to direct one's attention to, to heed, notice (*ad alqd*, with *acc.* or *dat.*); to perceive (*alqd*; *acc. c. inf.*); to punish (*in alqm*); **c)** to draw *or* direct to oneself (*omnium oculos, odia*).
ad-vesperāscit, āvit, — 3 evening approaches.
ad-vigilō 1 to watch, guard.
ad-vocātiō, ōnis *f* **1.** a summoning to advise; a) legal advice; b) the bar, body of advocates; **2.** delay for consultation.
ad-vocātus, ī *m* **a)** one who is called to aid in a trial; **b)** advocate, witness.
ad-vocō 1 to call, summon (*alqm in, ad alqd*); **a)** to call as an adviser *or* witness; **b)** to call to aid, ask for help (*with acc.*).
ad-volātus, ūs *m* a flying to.
ad-volō 1 to fly to *or* towards; to hasten towards (*ad, in alqd*).
ad-volvō 3 to roll to *or* towards; **P.** to throw oneself at the feet of, to fall prostrate before.
ad-vors-, -vort- = **ad-vers-, -vert-.**
adytum, ī *n* the holiest part of a temple, inmost recess (*generally in pl.*).
aedēs (*or* **aedis**), **is** *f* **1.** a) room, chamber, apartment; b) temple, chapel, sanctuary; **2.** *pl.* a dwelling, house, habitation.
aedicula, ae *f* small building, temple, *or* room.
aedificātiō, ōnis *f* **a)** act of building; **b)** building, edifice.
aedificātiuncula, ae *f* a small building.
aedificātor, ōris *m* builder, architect; one who is fond of building.
aedificium, ī *n* building, structure, edifice.
aedi-ficō 1 to build, erect, construct, establish; to build houses.
aedīlicius 3 of an aedile; *subst.* ex-aedile.
aedīlis, is *m* aedile, superintendent of public works.
aedīlitās, ātis *f* office of an aedile.
aedis, *see* **aedes.**
aedituus, ī, aedituēns, entis *m* guardian of a temple.
aēdōn, onis *f* nightingale.
aeger, gra, grum sick, ill, suffering; **a)** feeble, weak, frail; **b)** troubled, dejected, dissatisfied; **c)** painful, sad.
aegis, idis *f* shield of Jupiter, [aegis.]
aegi-sonus 3 sounding with the aegis.
aegocerōs, ōtis (and **-os, ī**) *m* the wild goat (*sign of the zodiac*).
aegrē *adv.* **1.** painfully, distressingly, annoyingly; **aegre facere alci** to mortify, grieve; **aegre ferre** to be grieved, distressed (*alqd*); **2.** a) with difficulty, hardly, scarcely; b) reluctantly, unwillingly.
aegreō, —, — 2 to be sick.
aegrēscō, —, — 3 to fall sick; **a)** to become worse; **b)** to be grieved, mortified.

aegrimōnia, ae *f* sorrow, distress, grief.
aegritūdō, inis *f* **a**) sickness; **b**) grief, uneasiness.
aegror, ōris *m* illness.
aegrōtātiō, ōnis *f* sickness.
aegrōtō 1 to be sick *or* ill; to suffer.
aegrōtus 3 sick, ill, suffering.
aelinos, ī *m* dirge.
aelūrus, ī *m* cat.
aemulātiō, ōnis *f* **a**) emulation, rivalry; **b**) envy, jealousy.
aemulātor, ōris *m* rival; imitator.
aemulātus, ūs *m* = **aemulatio.**
aemulor 1 **a**) to strive after, emulate, vie with, rival (*with acc.*); **b**) to envy (*alci*).
aemulus 3 **a**) striving after, vying with (*alci*); imitator (*alcis*); **b**) envious, jealous.
aēneus 3 of copper, bronze(-coloured); hard as metal.
aenigma, atis *n* riddle, mystery, allegory, enigma.
aēni-pēs, edis bronze-footed.
aēnus 3 = **aēneus; aēnum, ī** *n* bronze vessel.
aequābilis, e uniform, similar, equal; equable; impartial, just.
aequābilitās, ātis *f* equality, uniformity; impartiality.
aequaevus 3 of equal age.
aequālis, e like, equal; **1.** even, level; **2.** a) uniform, steady; b) equal in size, growth, *or* height; c) equal in age, coeval, contemporary (*alcis*).
aequālitās, ātis *f* **a**) equality (*of age, of rights*); **b**) evenness.
aequanimitās, ātis *f* fairness, impartiality; calmness, kindness.
aequātiō, ōnis *f* a making equal; equal distribution.
aequē *adv.* equally, in like manner; **a**) fairly, justly; **b**) **aeque ... ac** as ... as, just as, equally with.
aequi-lībritās, ātis *f* equipoise.
aequi-noctiālis, e relating to the equinox, equinoctial.
aequi-noctium, ī *n* equinox.
aequiperābilis, e comparable.
aequi-perō 1 **a**) to compare (*alqd alci*); **b**) to equal, rival (*with acc.*).
aequitās, ātis *f* uniformity, evenness; **a**) equanimity, patience, calmness; **b**) impartiality, fairness, justice; **c**) equality of rights.
aequō 1 **1.** to make even, level, smooth; to make straight; **2.** to make equal (*alqd alci rei*); **solo aequare** to level with the ground; a) to distribute equally; b) to compare (*alqd cum re* or *dat.*); **se aequare** *or* **P.** to become equal, come up to, reach (*with acc.*).
aequor, oris *n* even surface, level; **a**) flat field, plain; **b**) surface of the sea, sea, ocean.
aequoreus 3 belonging to the sea.
aequus 3 equal; **1.** even, level; *subst.* **aequum, ī** *n* level ground, plain; a) favourable, advantageous; b) friendly, propitious; **aequi** friends; **2.** equal in size *or* height; indecisive; a) even-tempered, calm; b) impartial, fair; **aequum est** it is just; **aequi boni**(**que**) **facere** to be content with; *subst.* **aequum, ī** *n* equity, equal degree *or* right; fairness, what is right; **ex aequo** equitably (*also* = *aeque*); **in aequo** in the same condition.
āēr, āeris *m* **a**) air, atmosphere; **b**) mist, cloud.
aerārius 3 **1.** of copper *or* bronze; a) relating to mining; b) belonging to money, pecuniary; **tribunus aerārius** paymaster; **2.** *subst.* a) **aerārius, ī** *m* citizen of the lowest class; b) **aerāria, ae** *f* copper-mine; c) **aerārium, ī** *n* public treasury, public funds, finances.
aerātus 3 covered *or* fitted with brass; supplied with money, rich.
aereus 3 = **aēneus;** = **aeratus.**
aeri-fer 3 bearing bronze cymbals.
aeri-pēs, pedis brazen-footed.
aeri-sonus 3 sounding with bronze.
āerius 3 belonging to the air, aerial; lofty, high.
aerūgō, inis *f* rust of copper, verdigris; **a**) envy; **b**) avarice.
aerumna, ae *f* toil, hardship, suffering.
aerumnōsus 3, **aerumnābilis, e** full of hardship, troubled, miserable.
aes, aeris *n* **1.** copper, bronze, brass; **2.** anything made of copper *or* bronze; a) copper vessel, image, statue, tablet; b) money, coin, the as; c) means, fortune; **aes alienum** another's money, debt; d) pay, fee, salary.
aesculētum, ī *n* oak-wood *or* -forest.
aesculeus 3 of the oak.
aesculus, ī *f* the winter oak.

aestās, ātis *f* summer; summer heat *or* weather; year.
aesti-fer 3 heat-bringing.
aestimābilis, e valuable.
aestimātiō, ōnis *f* **1.** an appraising, valuation, estimation; assessment of damages, fine; **2.** true value, esteem.
aestimātor, ōris *m* appraiser; one who values a thing according to its worth.
aestimō 1 **1.** to appraise, estimate (*alqd, with gen.* or *abl.* of *value*), to assess a penalty; **2.** to value, esteem, judge (*alqd, re, ex re*).
aestīvō 1 to pass the summer.
aestīvus 3 relating to summer, of summer, summer-like; **aestīva, ōrum** *n/pl.* **a**) summer camp; **b**) campaign; **c**) summer pastures, cattle in summer pastures; **d**) summer-time.
aestuārium, ī *n* **a**) lagoon, shallow water; **b**) inlet of the sea, creek, bay.
aestumō = **aestimo.**
aestuō 1 **1.** to blaze; to burn, glow, be hot, boil, seethe; **2.** to swell, heave; a) to be agitated, excited; b) to hesitate, be in doubt.
aestuōsus 3 **a**) glowing, hot; **b**) surging, agitated.
aestus, ūs *m* **1.** fire, heat, glow, sultriness; summer heat, fever; **2.** a raging, seething; a) tide, surge, swell; b) passion, rage, fervour; c) unrest, anxiety, hesitation.
aetās, ātis *f* **1.** age, life of man, life--time; a) **aetas prima** childhood, youth; b) **aetas constans, media, confirmata** manhood, middle age; c) **aetas extrema, exacta** old age; d) men of a certain age; **2.** time of life, generation; time at which a person lives; **3.** age of the world.
aetātula, ae *f* youthful age.
aeternitās, ātis *f* eternity, endless duration, immortality.
aeternō 1 to immortalize.
aeternus 3 eternal; **a**) immortal, imperishable; **b**) everlasting, permanent.
aethēr, eris *m* the upper air, sky, heaven; heavenly things, upper world.
aetherius 3 relating to the upper air; **a**) etherial, celestial, heavenly; **b**) airy; **c**) of the upper world.
aethra, ae *f* the clear sky.
aevitās, ātis *f* = **aetas.**
aevum, ī *n* (**aevus, ī** *m*) **1.** eternity; **2.** = **aetas.**
af-fābilis, e affable, approachable.
af-fābilitās, ātis *f* affability.
af-fabrē *adv.* cunningly, in a workmanlike manner.
af-fatim *adv.* sufficiently, enough, abundantly (*with gen.*).
af-fātus, ūs *m* a speaking to, address.
affectātiō, ōnis *f* a striving, eager desire.
affectātor, ōris *m* one who strives after a thing.
affectiō, ōnis *f*; **a**) disposition, condition, state of mind; **b**) inclination, partiality, predilection; **c**) influence.
affectō 1 to grasp (*alqd*); to pursue, aim at, strive after, to enter on; **a**) = **afficere; b**) to try to get, to win over; to influence; **c**) to affect, feign, simulate.
affectus[1], **ūs** *m* condition, state, disposition; **a**) passion, feeling, emotion; **b**) affection.
affectus[2] 3 **1.** furnished, provided, gifted, endowed (*with abl.*); disposed, inclined, affected; **2.** indisposed, impaired, weakened, disordered; ending.
af-ferō, attulī, allātum, afferre to carry, bring, convey to (*alci alqd*); **manus** to lay hands on, to do violence (*with dat.*); **manus sibi** to commit suicide; **a**) to bring, carry; **b**) to report, announce, relate (*alqd ad alqm* or *alci, de re,* with *acc. c. inf.*); **c**) to produce; allege; to cause (*alci alqd*); **d**) to contribute, help, assist, be of use (*alqd ad alqd*); **e**) to bring as an addition.
af-ficiō, fēcī, fectum 3 to treat in a certain way (*alqm* or *alqd alqa re*), **vulnere** to wound, **poena** to punish, **iniuria** to outrage, **honore** to honour, **timore** to frighten, **laude** to praise, **muneribus** to present with, **praemio** to reward, **supplicio** to behead, **dolore** to give pain; **P. vulnere affici** to be wounded; **morbo** to fall sick; **a**) to influence, affect, dispose; **b**) to weaken, impair, afflict, attack, oppress.
af-fīgō 3 to fasten to, attach, affix (*alqd ad alqd* or with *dat.*); to pin fast; to imprint (*memoriae*).

af-fingō 3 to form in addition (*alci alqd*); to feign *or* invent in, addition to add falsely.
af-fīnis, e adjoining, bordering on, neighbouring (*alci*); **a**) connected with, privy to, accessory to; **b**) related by marriage (brother-, sister-, father-in-law).
af-fīnitās, ātis *f* **a**) relationship by marriage; **b**) neighbourhood.
af-firmātē *adv.* with positive assurance.
af-firmātiō, ōnis *f* affirmation, solemn assurance.
af-firmō 1 to strengthen; **a**) to confirm, assert; **b**) to assure.
af-flātus, ūs *m* a blowing *or* breathing on; **a**) blast, breath; **b**) inspiration.
af-fleō 2 to weep at.
af-flīctātiō, ōnis *f* pain, torture.
af-flīctō 1 to beat *or* strike repeatedly; **a**) to damage, trouble, harass, torment; **b**) to afflict, grieve.
af-flīctor, ōris *m* a damager, destroyer.
af-flīctus 3 **1.** beaten, shattered, damaged; a) cast down, miserable, wretched, distressed; b) discouraged, spiritless; c) vile, contemptible.
af-flīgō, xī, ctum 3 to strike *or* dash against; **a**) to strike to the ground, throw down; **b**) to damage, shatter, injure, ruin, distress; **c**) to weaken, discourage, humiliate; **d**) to dash to pieces.
af-flō 1 **1.** a) to blow *or* breathe on; to scorch; b) to impart by breathing (*alci alqd*); **2.** *intr. and* **P.** to blow (*propitiously*).
af-fluēns, tis a) affluent, abounding, abundant, plentiful; **b**) provided copiously, rich, full of.
af-fluentia, ae *f* abundance, plenty.
af-fluō 3 to flow to *or* towards; **a**) to come imperceptibly, to glide on; **b**) to flow with, abound (*with abl.*).
af-for 1 to accost, address, implore (*alqm*).
af-fore, af-forem, *see* **assum.**
af-formīdō 1 to be in fear.
af-frangō 3 to dash *or* press against.
af-fremō 3 to roar *or* murmur at.
af-fricō 1 to rub on.
af-fulgeō 2 to shine against *or* upon (*alci*); to beam, glitter, appear bright.
af-fundō 3 **a**) to pour into (*alqd alci rei*); **P.** to be washed by, to be spread out; **b**) to add; **affūsus** prostrate.
af-futūrus 3, *see* **assum.**
afluō = **affluō.**
ā-fore, ā-forem, *see* **absum.**
agāsō, ōnis *m* groom, hostler; churl.
agellus, ī *m* little field *or* estate.
agēma, atis *n* Macedonian horse-guards.
ager, grī *m* field, arable land, estate; open *or* flat country; **a**) territory, district; **b**) **in agrum** in depth (*opp. in breadth*).
ā-gerō (?) 3 to take *or* carry away.
ag-gemō 3 to groan *or* sigh at.
agger, eris *m* **1.** heap, mound, pile, rubbish, soil; **2.** a) rampart, dike, dam, mole; b) fortification, wall; c) rampart marking a boundary; d) causeway constructed with logs; e) elevation, bank of a river; f) funeral pile.
aggerō[1] 1 to form a mound, to heap up; to pile up, amass, increase.
ag-gerō[2] 3 **a**) to carry, bring, *or* convey to; **b**) to bring forward, utter.
ag-gerō[3] = **agero.**
ag-gestus, ūs *m* a bringing to, accumulation.
ag-glomerō 1 to attach.
ag-glūtinō 1 to glue to, stick on.
ag-gravēscō, —, — 3 to become worse.
ag-gravō 1 **a**) to make heavier *or* worse; **b**) to molest, oppress.
ag-gredior, gressus sum 3 to step *or* go to, to approach (*ad alqm* or *alqm*); **a**) to apply to, address (*with acc.*); **b**) to attack, assail, fall upon (*alqm*); **c**) to begin, undertake, attempt, try (*ad alqd, alqd,* with *inf.*).
ag-gregō 1 to add to, join to (*alqm alci, in* or *ad alqd*); **se a.** to attach oneself to.
ag-gressiō, ōnis *f* attack (*on a subject*), introduction.
agilis, e easily moved; **a**) quick, nimble; **b**) active, busy, lively.
agilitās, ātis *f* quickness, agility.
agitābilis, e easily moved.
agitātiō, ōnis *f* motion, movement; **a**) agitation; pursuit, management; **b**) activity.
agitātor, ōris *m* driver; charioteer.
agitō 1 to set in violent *or* constant motion, to drive about *or* onward,

to drive, chase, hunt, shake, toss up and down; **1.** a) to incite, spur, pursue; b) to trouble, vex; to ridicule; c) to stir, rouse, disturb; **2.** to practise, exercise, prosecute, occupy oneself with; a) to celebrate, keep (*a festival*); b) to pass (*time*), to live; c) to discuss, debate (*alqd, de re*); d) to consider, think, deliberate (*alqd, alqd animo, in* or *cum animo, secum*).

agmen, inis *n* **1.** a driving, movement, stream; **2.** what is driven *or* moved; a) band, throng, crowd, troop, multitude; b) army on the march, column, phalanx, army in line of battle; **~ primum** vanguard, **~ medium** the centre, **~ extremum** *or* **novissimum** rear; c) war, battle.

agna, ae *f* ewe-lamb.

agnālia, ium *n/pl.* feast of the ewes.

a-gnāscor, agnātus sum 3 to be born in addition.

a-gnātiō, ōnis *f* blood-relationship on the father's side.

a-gnātus 3 born after; related on the father's side.

agnellus, ī *m* little lamb.

agnīnus 3 of a lamb; **agnīna** (*caro*) lamb's flesh.

agnitiō, ōnis *f* recognition.

a-gnōscō, agnōvī, agnitum 3 a) to perceive, observe (*alqd* or *acc. c. inf.*); **b**) to recognize, acknowledge, identify, approve (with *acc.*, with *acc. c. inf.*).

agnus, ī *m* lamb.

agō, ēgī, āctum 3 **1.** to drive, lead, conduct, chase, hunt, urge; to set in motion (**P.** to go, march); a) to drive away, rob, **ferre atque agere** to rob and plunder; b) to accuse, arraign, impeach, *alqm reum* to bring an action against; c) to impel, excite, prompt (*alqm ad alqd*); **se agere** to behave, bear oneself; **2.** to put in motion (*things*); a) to drive, lead, direct, draw, steer, push, pull, advance; to strike (*root*); b) to construct, build (*roads*); **animam agere** to expire; c) to pass, spend, live; **3.** to pursue, practise, undertake, act, perform, execute, transact, manage; **aliquid agere** to be active *or* busy, **nihil agere** to be inactive, idle, **quid agis?** how are you?, **id agere ut (ne)** to aim at, take care, to have as one's purpose; **bene mecum agitur** I am well; **actum est de me** I am done for; **res agitur** is at stake, is concerned; **4.** a) to keep (*a festival*), observe, celebrate; b) to act (*a play or part*), to deliver, declaim; c) **gratias agere** to thank, give thanks; d) to treat, consider, discuss, speak, transact (*alqd cum alqo*); (*causam*) **agere** to plead, conduct a lawsuit; e) to live, dwell, pass time, do service; *adj.* **agēns** effective, powerful; **age, agite** well then! come!

agōn, ōnis *m* contest, combat in the public games.

agorā-nomus, ī *m* inspector of the market.

agrārius 3 relating to land *or* fields *or* country; **lex** law for the division of land; **triumvir** officer for the division of land; *subst.* **agrāriī, ōrum** *m/pl.* the agrarian party.

agrestis, e living in the fields *or* country; **a**) wild, savage; **b**) rustic, uncultivated, boorish, clownish, brutish; **c**) agricultural; *m* countryman, peasant.

agri-cola, ae *m* tiller of the field, husbandman, farmer.

agri-cultiō, -cultor, -cultūra, *see* **ager** *and* **cultiō** *etc.*

agri-peta, ae *m* colonist, settler.

āh, ā *int.* ah! alas!

ahēneus, ahēnus = **aēneus, aēnus.**

ai *int.* alas!

ain' = **aisne,** *see* **aio.**

āiō 1. to say yes, affirm, assent; **āiēns, tis** affirmative; **2.** to assert, say, state, aver; **ain'** = **aisne** indeed? really? is it possible?, **quid ais** what is your opinion?

āla, ae *f* **a**) wing (*of a bird* or *army*); **b**) armpit, shoulder; **c**) squadron, troop (*of cavalry*).

alabaster, trī *m,* **-trum, ī** *n* unguent-flask.

alacer, cris, cre lively, quick, brisk, eager, excited, active, cheerful.

alacritās, ātis *f* liveliness, quickness, eagerness, cheerfulness, ardour.

alapa, ae *f* box on the ear, slap on the cheek.

ālārius 3, **ālāris, e** belonging to the wing of an army; *pl.* **ālāriī, ōrum** *m/pl.* auxiliary troops.

ālātus 3 winged.

alauda, ae *f* lark.
alāzōn, onis *m* braggart, boaster.
albātus 3 clothed in white.
albeō, uī, — 2 to be white *or* pale.
albēscō, buī, — 3 to become white; to dawn.
albi-capillus 3 white-haired.
albicō 1 to be white.
albidus 3, **albulus** 3 white.
albitūdō, inis *f* whiteness.
albus 3 white (*without lustre*); **a)** clothed in white; **b)** pale, grey; **c)** bright, fortunate, propitious; *subst.* **album, ī** *n* white colour; white tablet (*for advertisements*); register, list.
alcēdō, inis *f* kingfisher.
alcēdōnea, ōrum *n/pl.* winter calm.
alcēs, is *f* elk.
alcyōn, onis *f* kingfisher.
ālea, ae *f* **a)** game with dice, die; **b)** hazard, risk, chance.
āleārius 3 relating to gambling.
āleātor, ōris *m* dicer, gambler.
āleātōrius 3 of a dicer *or* gambler.
ālēc, ēcis *n* = **allec.**
āleō, ōnis *m* = **aleator.**
āles, itis 1. winged; swift, quick; **2.** *subst.* bird; prophetic bird; a) omen, augury; b) poet.
alēscō 3 to grow.
alga, ae *f* sea-weed.
algeō, alsī, — 2 to be *or* feel cold.
algēscō, alsī, — 3 to catch cold.
algidus 3 cold, icy.
algor, ōris (*and* **algus, ūs**) *m* cold.
aliā *adv.* (*sc.* **viā**) by another way.
aliās *adv.* **1.** at another time; **aliās ... aliās** at one time ... at another time; **2.** elsewhere; in another way.
āliātus = **alliātus.**
alibī *adv.* elsewhere, at another place; **alibī ... alibī** here ... there; **alius alibī** one here ... another there; with some other person; in other respects.
alica, ae *f* spelt grits, drink made of spelt.
alicāria, ae *f* wench, prostitute.
alicubī *adv.* anywhere, somewhere.
alicula, ae *f* cape.
alicunde *adv.* from somewhere, from any place.
alid = **aliud.**
aliēnātiō, ōnis *f* **1.** alienation (*of property*), transfer; **2.** separation, desertion, breach, enmity.
aliēni-gena, ae *m* alien, foreign; foreigner.
aliēnō 1 **1.** to make a thing another's, to make over, transfer; a) to cast off, disown; b) to sell; c) to make subject to another; d) to cause one to lose his reason (*mentem*), to drive mad; **2.** to estrange, set at variance, alienate (*alqm* or *alqd ab alqo*); **P.** to have an aversion, to shrink from.
aliēnus 3 belonging *or* relating to another; **aes aliēnum** another's money, debt; **nomina a.** debtors; **aliēnissimus** not related at all; *subst.* **aliēnus, ī** *m* stranger, foreigner; **aliēnum, ī** *n* another man's property, affair of a stranger; **a)** not acquainted with, not related to, strange to (*ab alqo* or *dat.*); **b)** averse, unfavourable, hostile (*ab alqo, a re,* also with *dat.* or *gen.*); strange, unsuitable, unseasonable, disadvantageous.
āliger, gera, gerum bearing wings.
alimentārius 3 belonging to nourishment.
alimentum, ī *n* **1.** food, nourishment, provisions; **2.** return due to parents for the bringing up of children.
alimōnium, ī *n* nourishment.
aliō *adv.* to another place; **alius aliō** one in this direction, another in that; to another person *or* thing.
aliō-quī(n) *adv.* **1.** in other respects, otherwise, for the rest; **2.** besides, moreover, in general, in any case.
aliō(vo)rsum *adv.* in another direction; in a different sense.
āli-pēs, pedis wing-footed, swift-footed.
ālipilus, ī *m* slave who removes superfluous hair.
aliptēs, ae *m* anointer, wrestling master.
aliquā *adv.* (*sc.* **viā**) by any way; somehow.
aliquam-diū *adv.* for a pretty long time.
aliquam multī a good many.
aliquandō *adv.* **1.** at any time, at some time, once, ever; **2.** finally, at length, sometimes.
aliquantillum a little bit.
aliquantisper for a while.
aliquantulus 3 very little *or* small.
aliquantus 3 some, considerable; *subst.* **aliquantum, ī** *n* a good deal, a considerable amount, not a little (*with gen.*).

aliquātenus to some extent.
ali-quī, a, od some, any.
ali-quis, a, id some one, something, anyone, anything; **aliquid** (*adv.*) in some degree.
ali-quō *adv.* to some place, somewhere.
ali-quot some, a few, several.
ali-quotiē(n)s *adv.* several times.
aliquō-vorsum *adv.* to some place.
alis = alius.
aliter *adv.* **1.** otherwise, in another way (*with ac, atque, et, quam*); **non aliter, haud aliter** not otherwise, just as (**ac si, quam si** exactly as if); **alius aliter** one in this way, another in that; **2.** in the contrary manner, in other respects.
aliubi = alibi.
ālium, ī *n* = **allium.**
ali-unde *adv.* from another direction, from elsewhere.
alius, a, ud (*gen.* **alīus** *and* **alterius,** *dat.* **aliī**) **a**) another, other; **aliī — aliī** some — others; **alius aliud fecit** one did this, another that; **alius aliō more vivit** people live in different ways; **alius ex aliō** one after the other; **alius ac, atque, et** other than, different from; **nihil aliud nisi** *or* **quam** nothing else but, only; **b**) different, of another kind.
al-lābor 3 to glide *or* flow to *or* towards (with *dat.* or *acc.*).
al-labōrō 1 to add to by toil.
al-lacrimō 1 to weep at.
al-lāpsus, ūs *m* a gliding up to.
al-lātrō 1 to bark at; to rail at.
al-laudābilis, e praiseworthy.
al-laudō 1 to praise.
allēc, ēcis *n* fish-sauce.
allectō 1 to allure, entice.
al-lectus 3, *see* **allego**[2] *and* **allicio.**
al-lēgātiō, ōnis *f* a sending of negotiators.
allēgātus, ūs *m* instigation.
al-lēgō[1] 1 **a**) to send on business, as a negotiator, *or* deputy (*alqm alci* or *ad alqm*); **b**) to adduce, allege.
al-legō[2] 3 to choose in addition, select.
al-levāmentum, ī *n* means of alleviation.
al-levātiō, ōnis *f* alleviation.
al-levō 1 to lift up, raise, erect; to lighten, alleviate; **P.** to recover.
allex[1]**, icis** *m* little man.
allēx[2]**, ēcis** *f* = **allec.**

alliātus 3 provided with garlic.
al-licefaciō 3 to entice.
al-liciō, lexī, lectum 3 to allure, entice, draw to oneself (*alqm* or *alqd ad alqd, ad se*).
al-līdō, sī, sum 3 to dash *or* strike against; **P.** to suffer damage, to be ruined.
al-ligō 1 **1.** to bind *or* tie to (*alqd ad alqd*); a) to make fast, hold fast; b) to fetter, shackle; c) to bind, oblige by kindness; d) to bind, make responsible; **se all. scelere** to become an accomplice in a crime (**in scelere alligātus** involved in a crime); **2.** (**vulnus, oculum**) to bind up, dress.
al-linō, lēvī, litum 3 to smear on, bedaub.
allium, ī *n* garlic.
al-locūtiō, ōnis *f* = **alloquium.**
al-loquium, ī *n* **a**) a speaking to, address; **b**) exhortation, encouragement, consolation.
al-loquor 3 **a**) to speak to, address; **b**) to exhort, comfort (*alqm*).
al-lubēscit 3 it begins to please.
al-lūceō 2 to shine at *or* upon.
al-lūdiō 1 to play *or* sport with.
al-lūdō 3 to play *or* sport with; **a**) to approach in play *or* by stealth; **b**) to wash (*the shore*); **c**) to add in sport.
al-luō, luī, — 3 to wash (*against*).
al-luviēs, ēī *f* inundation.
al-luviō, ōnis *f* alluvial soil.
almus 3 **a**) nourishing, giving food; **b**) kind, gracious, bountiful, sweet.
alnus, ī *f* alder; ship, boat.
alō, aluī, altum *or* **alitum** 3 to nourish, feed, bring up, rear; **a**) to support, maintain; **b**) to promote, strengthen, increase.
aloē, ēs *f* aloe; bitterness.
alogia, ae *f* folly.
alpha the first letter of the Greek alphabet, A.
als(i)us 3 cold, cool.
altāria, ium *n/pl.* (high) altar.
alter, era, erum a) one of two, the one, the other; the other, the opposite; **b**) the second, **alter Marius** a second M.; **alter ego** one's second self; **c**) neighbour, fellow-man; **unus et alter** the one and the other, one or two, a few; **alterum tantum** as much again.
alterās at any other time.

altercātiō, ōnis *f* dispute, debate, quarrel.
altercor (*and* **cō**) 1 to dispute, quarrel (*cum alqo*).
alternō 1 to do by turns *or* alternately; to change; to hesitate.
alternus 3 one after the other, alternate, reciprocal; **alternīs** (*adv.*) by turns; (*in poetry*) elegiac, in couplets.
alter-uter, utra, utrum one of two, one or the other.
alti-cinctus 3 high-girt.
altilis, e fat; *subst.* fattened fowl.
alti-sonus 3 sounding from on high.
alti-tonāns, tis high-thundering.
altitūdō, inis *f* height; **a**) sublimity, grandeur; **b**) depth; **c**) reserve, secrecy.
altiusculus 3 a little too high.
alti-volāns, tis high-flying.
altor, ōris *m* nourisher, sustainer.
altrin-secus *adv.* at *or* on the other side.
altrīx, īcis *f* foster-mother, nurse.
altrō-vorsum *adv.* on the other side.
altus 3 **1.** a) high; *subst.* **altum, ī** *n* height; heaven; depth, deep sea; b) lofty, elevated, great; **2.** deep; **altum, ī** *n* depth, far distance; **ex altō repetere** to fetch from afar; a) secret, profound, unfathomable; b) ancient, remote.
alucinātiō, ōnis *f* wandering of the mind.
alucinor 1 to wander in mind, to ramble in speech.
alumna, ae *f* foster-daughter, pupil.
alumnus, ī *m* foster-son, nursling; pupil; a young one.
alūta, ae *f* soft leather; shoe; purse; face-patch.
alv(e)ārium, ī *n* beehive.
alveolus, ī *m* small trough; gaming board, play at dice; bed of a small river.
alveus, ī *m* hollow, cavity; **a**) trough, basin, bathing-tub; b) boat, ship; c) bed of a river; d) beehive; e) dice--board.
alvus, ī *f* belly, abdomen; **a**) womb; **b**) stomach; **c**) hold of a ship; **d**) beehive.
ama, ae *f* = **hama.**
amābilis, e lovely, lovable.
amābilitās, tātis *f* lovableness.
ā-mandātiō, ōnis *f* a sending away.
ā-mandō 1 to send away, remove (*alqm in locum*).
amāns, tis loving (*with gen.*), fond, affectionate; friendly, kind; lover.
ā-manuēnsis, is *m* secretary.
amāracinum, ī *n* marjoram ointment.
amāracus, ī *m* marjoram.
amarantus, ī *m* amaranth, unfading flower.
amāritiēs, ēī *f* = **amaritudo.**
amāritūdō, inis *f*, **amāror, ōris** *m* bitterness; exasperation.
amārus 3 bitter, pungent; morose.
amāsius, ī *m* lover.
amātiō, ōnis *f* love-affair.
amātor, ōris *m*, **amātrīx, īcis** *f* lover.
amātorculus, ī *m* little lover.
amātōrius 3 loving, amorous, amatory.
ambactus, ī *m* vassal.
amb-adedō 3 to eat round, consume.
amb-āgēs, um *f/pl.* (*abl. sing.* **āge**) roundabout way; **a**) digression, diffuseness; **b**) evasion, subterfuges; **c**) riddle, ambiguity.
amb-edō 3 to eat round, consume.
amb-ēstrīx, īcis *f* gluttonous woman.
amb-igō, —, — 3 **a**) to doubt, waver, hesitate; **b**) to dispute, contend, argue, debate.
ambiguitās, ātis *f* ambiguity.
ambiguus 3 inclined to both sides; of uncertain nature, hybrid; **a**) wavering, hesitating, uncertain, doubtful; **b**) obscure, ambiguous; **c**) untrustworthy; **d**) irresolute, timid; *subst.* **ambiguum, ī** *n* = **ambiguitas.**
ambiō, īvī *and* **iī, ītum** 4 to go round; **a**) to avoid, shun; **b**) to surround (*alqd re*); **c**) to go round canvassing for votes, for help; to entreat, solicit (*alqm*).
amb-itiō, ōnis *f* a going about; **a**) display, pomp; **b**) canvassing for an office; **c**) a striving after honours *or* for favour, courting, flattery; **d**) desire for popularity, ambition; **e**) striving after something.
ambitiōsus 3 **1.** encompassing, twining around; **2.** a) eager for favour, striving after honours; b) competing for an office; c) vain, ostentatious, pretentious.
amb-itus, ūs *m* **1.** a going round; a) circuit, revolution, circular course,

circle, edge, orbit; b) circumlocution; c) period (*in grammar*); **2.** a) illegal canvassing for an office; b) = **ambitio.**
ambō, ae, ō both, the two.
ambrosius 3 divine; *subst.* **ambrosia, ae** *f* ambrosia, food of the gods.
ambūbāia, ae *f* Syrian flute-player.
ambulācrum, ī *n* walk.
ambulātiō, ōnis *f* a walking about; promenade.
ambulātiuncula, ae *f* a little walk; little promenade.
ambulātor, ōris *m* pedlar.
ambulātōrius 3 movable.
ambulō 1 to walk about, take a walk; **a**) to strut, stalk; **b**) to march, travel; **c**) to traverse, travel over (*alqd*).
amb-ūrō 3 **a**) to burn round, scorch, burn up; consume; **b**) to nip, benumb; **P.** to be injured, damaged.
ambustulātus 3 burnt round.
amellus, ī *m* purple Italian starwort.
ā-mēns, tis senseless, mad; foolish, stupid.
āmentātus 3 furnished with a strap.
ā-mentia, ae *f* senselessness, madness, folly.
āmentō 1 to hurl, whirl.
āmentum, ī *n* strap, thong.
ames, itis *m* fork for a fowler's net.
amethystinātus 3 clad in clothing of amethyst-purple.
amethystinus 3 **a**) of amethyst-purple (*n/pl.* purple garments); **b**) set with amethysts.
amethystus, ī *f* amethyst.
amīca, ae *f* female friend; mistress.
amiciō —, ictum 4 to clothe, wrap round, to cover, envelop.
amīciter, in a friendly way.
amīcitia, ae (*and* **tiēs, ēī**) *f* friendship; **a**) alliance; **b**) friends.
amīcō 1 to make friendly.
amictus, ūs *m* garment, covering.
amīcula, ae *f* sweetheart.
amiculum, ī *n* cloak, mantle.
amīculus, ī *m* (dear) friend.
amīcus 3 **a**) friendly, loving, kindly, well-wishing; **b**) favourable, propitious, pleasing; *subst.* **amīcus, ī** *m* **a**) friend; **b**) ally, minister.
ā-migrō 1 to wander away.
ā-missiō, ōnis *f*, **ā-missus, ūs** *m* loss.
amita, ae *f* aunt (*father's sister*).
ā-mittō 3 **1.** to send away, dismiss, let go; to let slip, to loose; to break one's word (**fidem a**); **2.** to lose, to suffer the loss of.
amni-cola, ae *m and f* dwelling near a river.
amniculus, ī *m* streamlet.
amnis, is *m* river, stream; **a**) torrent; **b**) current, flood; **c**) water.
amō 1 to love, **se am.** to love oneself; **a**) to be in love, to love passionately; to have an amour; **b**) (*with inf.*) to be wont, to be fond of; **c**) **ita** *or* **sic me di ament** *or* **amabunt** so help me the gods!; **amabo (te)** be so good, I entreat you; **d**) (*alqm de,* or *in re*) to be obliged for, to owe gratitude.
amoenitās, ātis *f* pleasantness, delightfulness, loveliness, charm.
amoenus 3 pleasant, delightful, lovely, charming; luxurious.
ā-mōlior 4 to move (away) with effort, to remove; **a**) to put away, avert, get rid of; **b**) to refute, repel.
amōmum, ī *n* an aromatic shrub.
amor, ōris *m* love, affection (*alcis* or *in, erga alqm*); **a**) amour, love-affair, amorous intrigue; **b**) object of love, darling; **c**) desire, passion, longing (*alcis rei*); **d**) the god of love, Cupid.
ā-mōtiō, ōnis *f* a removing.
ā-moveō 2 to move away, remove (*alqd ab, ex re*), **se a.** to retire, withdraw, depart; **a**) to steal; **b**) to banish; **c**) to lay aside, to sway (away) from, get rid of (*alqd a re*).
amphi-bolia, ae *f* ambiguity.
amphi-theātrālis e of the amphitheatre.
amphi-theātrum, ī *n* amphitheatre.
amphora, ae *f* **a**) two-handled vessel (*for wine*), jar, pitcher; **b**) a measure for liquids, *or* of the tonnage of a ship.
ampla, ae *f* handle; opportunity.
am-plector, plexus sum 3 to encircle, surround, encompass, embrace; **a**) to embrace lovingly, to love, esteem, value, welcome, receive; **b**) to embrace with the mind, to consider, understand; **c**) to discuss, comprehend, comprise.
amplexor (*and* **ō**) 1 = **amplector.**
amplexus, ūs *m* a surrounding, encircling; embrace.

ampli-ficātiō, ōnis *f* an enlarging, increasing; amplification.
ampli-ficātor, ōris *m* one who enlarges, amplifier.
ampli-ficē *adv.* splendidly.
ampli-ficō 1 **a)** to enlarge, increase, extend, make wide; **b)** to magnify, amplify, glorify.
ampliō 1 **a)** = **amplifico; b)** to adjourn, delay a judgment.
ampliter *adv.* amply, fully; splendidly.
amplitūdō, inis *f* wide extent, width, size; **a)** greatness, grandeur; **b)** dignity, high rank.
amplius *adv.* **1.** (*of time*) more, longer, further; **2.** in a higher degree; **3.** (*with numbers*) more than; besides, further, more, in addition; **nihil amplius** nothing further; **hoc amplius** besides this.
ampliusculē *adv.* a little too much.
amplus 3 of large extent, ample, large, spacious, roomy; **a)** great, full, copious, abundant, numerous; *subst.* **amplius** *n* a greater amount, larger sum; **b)** strong, violent; **c)** splendid, magnificent, glorious, honourable; **d)** esteemed, distinguished, honoured, illustrious, excellent, noble.
ampulla, ae *f* **a)** a flask for unguents; **b)** bombast, inflated speech.
ampullārius, ī *m* flask-maker.
ampullor 1 to write *or* talk bombastically.
amputātiō, ōnis *f* a cutting off.
amputō 1 **a)** to cut around, to cut off (*alqd, alci alqd*); **b)** to lop, prune; **c)** to curtail.
amurca, ae *f* scum *or* dregs of oil.
amygdala, ae *f* almond-tree.
amygdalum, ī *n* almond (kernel).
amystis, idis *f* the emptying of a cup at one draught.
an *cj.* **1.** *in disjunctive* (*direct* or *indirect double*) *questions:* or; **utrum — an** whether — or; **annon** (*direct*, **necne** *indirect*) or not; **2.** *in indirect simple questions* = **num** whether; **haud scio, nescio, dubito, dubium** *or* **incertum est an** (= whether not) I almost think, I might almost say, perhaps, probably; **3.** *in simple direct questions:* or then, or rather.
anabathrum, ī *n* raised seat.
anadēma, atis *n* headband.
anaglypta, ōrum *n/pl.* work in relief.
ana-gnōstēs, ae *m* a reader.
ana-lecta, ae *m* slave who removes food left over at table and gathers up waste fragments.
analectis, idis *f* shoulder-pad.
anancaeum, ī *n* large drinking cup.
ana-paestus 3 anapæstic; *subst.* **~, ī,** anapæst; **-um, ī** *n* poem in anapæsts.
anas, atis (and **itis**) *f* duck.
anaticula, ae *f* little duck.
anatīnus 3 of a duck.
anatocismus, ī *m* compound interest.
an-ceps, cipitis two-headed; **a)** two-sided, twofold; amphibious; from *or* on both sides; **b)** doubtful, undecided, **ancipiti Marte** with uncertain success; **c)** wavering; **d)** ambiguous; **e)** dangerous.
ancīle, is *n* the shield said to have fallen from heaven in the time of Numa; shield.
ancilla, ae *f* maidservant.
ancillāriolus, ī *m* maidservant's lover.
ancillāris, e of a maidservant.
ancillula, ae *f* a young maidservant.
ancipes = **anceps.**
an-cīsus 3 cut round.
ancora, ae *f* anchor.
ancorāle, is *n* (anchor-)cable.
ancorārius 3 belonging to an anchor.
andabata, ae *m* gladiator who fought blindfold; a blind man.
andro-gynus, ī *m* man-woman, hermaphrodite.
andrōn, ōnis *m* passage between two walls.
ānellus, ī *m* a little ring.
aneō 2 to be an old woman.
anet-, *see* **anat-.**
anēthum, ī *n* dill.
ān-frāctus, ūs *m* a turning, bending round; **a)** circuit, revolution; **b)** circuitous way; diffuseness, prolixity; **c)** intricacies.
angellus, ī *m* small corner.
angina, ae *f* quinsy.
angi-portus, ūs *m or* **-um, ī** *n* narrow lane; by-street.
angō, (anxī), — 3 **1.** to press tight, squeeze, compress; **2.** to choke, strangle; to vex, trouble, torment; **P.** to feel pain, be grieved.

angor, ōris, *m* **a**) strangling, suffocation; **b**) anguish, torment, trouble.
angui-comus 3 with snaky hair.
anguiculus, ī *m* a small snake.
angui-fer 3 serpent-bearing.
angui-gena, ae snake-born.
anguilla, ae *f* eel.
angui-manus 3 snake-armed.
anguineus 3, **anguīnus** 3 of serpents, snaky.
angui-pēs, pedis serpent-footed.
anguis, is *m and f* serpent, snake; the Dragon (*constellation*).
Angui-tenēns, tis *m* the Serpent-holder (*constellation*).
angulātus 3 with corners, angular.
angulus, ī *m* corner; **a**) angle; **b**) secret place, corner, nook, recess, lurking-place.
angustiae, ārum *f/pl.* narrowness, straitness; narrow place; **a**) defile, narrow passage; **b**) shortness (*of breath, of time*); **c**) difficulty, scarcity, poverty, want; distress, perplexity, trouble; **d**) narrow-mindedness, meanness; **e**) captiousness.
angusti-clāvius 3 wearing a narrow stripe of purple.
angustō 1 to make narrow.
angustus 3 narrow, strait, contracted; **a**) short, brief; **b**) confined, slight, faint, limited, needy, scant; **c**) critical, difficult; **d**) base, low, mean; **e**) narrow-minded.
an-hēlitus, ūs *m* a panting, short breath, asthma; **a**) breath, breathing; **b**) exhalation, vapour.
an-hēlō 1 **a**) to pant, gasp, breathe with difficulty; **b**) to roar, crash; **c**) to breathe out *or* forth; **d**) to pant for (*alqd*).
an-hēlus 3 **a**) panting, gasping; **b**) causing to pant.
anicula, ae *f* little old woman.
anīlis, e of an old woman.
anīlitās, ātis *f* old age (*of a woman*).
anima, ae *f* **1.** current of air, wind; a) air; b) breath, breeze; **2.** soul, vital principle, life; **animam efflare, edere** to expire, give up the ghost; **animam agere** to breathe one's last; a) departed spirit, shade (in the nether world); b) living being, person; c) life-blood; d) dear heart, good soul; e) mind.
anim-adversiō, ōnis *f* **1.** perception, observation, investigation, inquiry; **2.** a) censure; b) punishment.
anim-adversor, ōris *m* observer.
anim-advertō 3 **1.** to attend to, pay attention, consider, notice, observe, perceive, discern, apprehend; **2.** a) to blame, censure; b) to punish, chastise (*alqd, in alqm*).
animal, ālis *n* living being, creature; beast, monster.
animālis, e 1. of air; **2.** a) animate, living; b) enlivening.
animāns, tis animate, living; *subst. m and f* = **animal.**
animātiō, ōnis *f* an animating.
animātus 3 **a**) animate, living; **b**) disposed, minded; **c**) courageous.
animō 1 to animate, quicken, give life; **a**) *in alqd* transform into; **b**) to dispose, inspirit, to endow with a certain disposition; to encourage.
animōsus 3 **a**) breathing, living; **b**) courageous, bold, spirited; **c**) audacious, passionate, furious.
animula, ae *f* a little soul, life.
animulus, ī *m* little life, little heart.
animus, ī *m* (*locat.* **animi** in the heart) **1.** *poet.* = **anima**; **2.** soul, mind; a) intellect, mental powers, reason; b) thought, memory, consciousness, self-possession; c) judgment, opinion, belief; d) feeling, sentiment, affection, inclination, heart; e) disposition, character, nature; f) courage, heart, spirit; g) haughtiness, arrogance, pride; h) passion, vehemence, wrath; i) desire, will, wish; k) purpose, design, intention, resolve; l) inclination, pleasure.
annālis, e a) relating to a year, annual, **lex ~** law fixing the age required for an office; **b**) *subst.* **annālēs, ium** *m/pl.* yearly records, chronicles, annals.
an-narrō 1 to relate.
annatō 1 to swim to.
an-ne = **an.**
an-nectō 3 to tie, bind *or* fasten to (*alqd ad alqd*, or with *dat.*); to connect, unite, add (*with dat.*).
an-nexus, ūs *m* connexion.
anniculus 3 a year old.

an-nītor 3 to lean upon *or* against (*ad alqd*); to exert oneself, take pains (*de re, pro alqo*, with *ut*, with *inf.*).
anni-versārius 3 returning every year, yearly.
an-nō 1 to swim up to (*ad alqm, dat., acc.*).
annōna, ae *f* **a**) yearly produce, crop, corn-supply; **b**) corn, grain; **c**) price of grain and other provisions; market-price; high price of corn, dearness.
annōsus 3 full of years, aged.
an-notātiō, ōnis *f* a noting down, remark.
annōtinus 3 of last year, a year old.
an-notō 1 **a**) to note down, mark; **b**) to remark, observe, take notice of.
an-nūbilō 1 to bring up clouds.
an-numerō 1 **a**) to count among, reckon, consider (*alqm alci* or *in re*); **b**) to count out, pay (*alci alqd*).
an-nūntiō 1 **a**) to announce; **b**) to relate in addition.
an-nuō, nuī, — 3 to nod to, make a sign; **a**) to nod assent *or* approval, to agree, assent, grant, promise; **b**) to point out by a nod.
annus, ī *m* a year; **anno** in *or* for a year, a year ago; **annum** during a whole year; **ad annum** for the coming year, **in annum** for a year; **a**) (*pl.*) time of life, age; **b**) season (= **tempus anni**); **c**) produce of the year, harvest.
an-nūtō 1 to nod to.
annuus 3 **a**) of a year, lasting a year; **b**) returning every year, yearly.
an-quīrō, sīvī, sītum 3 to seek *or* search carefully (*alqd*); **a**) to inquire into, examine (*alqd, de re*); **b**) to conduct judicial inquiry *or* examination; to accuse, impeach (*de re, gen.* or *abl.*).
ānsa, ae *f* **a**) handle, haft; **b**) opportunity, occasion (with *gen.* or *ad alqd*).
ānsātus 3 with handles *or* ears.
ānser, eris *m* (*and f*) goose.
ante 1. *adv.* in front, before, forwards; previously, before; **2.** *prep.* with *acc.*; a) (*of space*) before, in front of; b) (*of time*) before; c) (*of relation*) before, more than, above, beyond; **esse ante aliquem** to be superior to; **ante omnes, ante alios** above all others; **ante omnia** before all other things = especially.
anteā *adv.* before, formerly, earlier, previously.
ante-ambulō, ōnis *m* footman (*running before his master*).
ante-capiō 3 to take beforehand, preoccupy; **a**) to receive, obtain previously; **b**) to be beforehand, anticipate.
ante-cēdēns, tis foregoing, preceding.
ante-cēdō 3 to go before, precede (with *acc.* or *dat.*); **a**) to be in the van; **b**) to overtake (*acc.*); **c**) to excel, surpass, to have the precedence *or* advantage of (with *acc.* or *dat.*).
ante-cellō, —, — 3 **a**) to be prominent; **b**) to surpass, excel, distinguish oneself (*alci rei* or *in re, alqa re*).
ante-cessiō, ōnis *f* **a**) a preceding, going forward; **b**) antecedent cause.
ante-cessor, ōris *m* skirmisher.
ante-cursor, ōris *m* forerunner; advanced guard, skirmisher.
ante-eō to go before, precede (with *dat.*, with *acc.*); **a**) to anticipate, be beforehand; **b**) to surpass, excel (*acc.*); **c**) to prevent.
ante-ferō 3 **a**) to bear *or* carry before, in front; **b**) to place before, prefer (*alqm* or *alqd alci rei*).
ante-fīxus 3 fastened before, in front; **antefīxum, ī** *n* ornament affixed to the frieze of a house *or* temple.
ante-gredior, gressus sum 3 = **antecedo.**
ante-habeō 2 to prefer.
ante-hāc *adv.* before this time, before now, hitherto.
ante-logium, ī *n* prologue.
ante-lūcānus 3 before daybreak.
ante-merīdiānus 3 before midday.
ante-mittō 3 to send before.
antenna (-mna), ae *f* (sail-)yard.
ante-occupātiō, ōnis *f* anticipation of an opponent's point.
ante-pertus 3 previously acquired.
ante-pēs, pedis *m* forefoot.
ante-pīlānus, ī *m* soldier who fought before the triarii.
ante-pōnō 3 **a**) to place before; **b**) to prefer (*alqd alci*).

ante-potēns, tis very rich.
ante-quam *cj.* before; **non ante quam** not until.
antēs, ium *m/pl.* rows *of vines.*
ante-signānus, ī *m* a) soldier who fought before the standards; b) leader.
ante-stō, *see* **antisto.**
an-testor 1 to call as a witness.
ante-veniō 4 to come *or* arrive before; a) to anticipate; b) to exceed, surpass; c) to prevent.
ante-vertō 3 to precede; to get the start of; a) to anticipate; b) to prevent, frustrate (*alqd*); c) to prefer to (*dat., ut*).
ante-volō 1 to fly before (*acc.*).
anticipātiō, ōnis *f* preconception, innate notion.
anticipō 1 to take *or* receive before; to anticipate; **viam** to take a shorter way.
antīcus 3 1. in front; 2. = **antiquus.**
antid-eā *adv.* = **antea.**
antid-eō = **anteeo.**
antid-hāc *adv.* = **antehac.**
anti-dotum, ī *n* antidote.
antīquārius 3 antiquarian; *subst.* ~, **ī** *m* antiquary.
antīquitās, ātis *f* ancient time, antiquity; a) men of ancient times, the ancients; b) events of ancient times, the history of ancient times; c) the good old times, primitive virtue.
antīquitus *adv.* a) from antiquity; b) in former times.
antīquō 1 to make obsolete, to reject (*a law*).
antīquus 3 (**antīcus**) 1. what is in front, *comp. and superl.* preferable, of more value *or* importance, more *or* most celebrated; 2. old, ancient, former; a) of old times, venerable, long-established, oldfashioned; **antīquī, ōrum** *m* the ancients, ancient writers; **antīqua, ōrum** *n/pl.* old customs, obsolete things; b) of the good old times, of primitive virtue.
anti-stes, itis *m and f* overseer of a temple, chief priest(ess).
anti-stita, ae *f* = **antistes** *f.*
anti-stō, stetī, — 1 a) to stand before; b) to be superior, to excel, be prominent.
anti-theton, ī *n* antithesis.
antlia, ae *f* machine for pumping water.
antrum, ī *n* cave, cavern, grotto.
ānulārius 3 belonging to a seal-ring; *subst.* ~, **ī** *m* ringmaker.
ānulātus 3 wearing a ring.
ānulus, ī *m* finger-ring, seal-ring.
anus[1], **ūs** *f* old woman; old hag.
ānus[2], **ī** *m* ring.
ānus[3], **ī** *m* fundament.
anxietās, ātis *f* anxiety, solicitude, trouble, grief.
anxi-fer 3 bringing anxiety.
anxitūdō, inis *f* = **anxietas.**
anxius 3 a) anxious, troubled, uneasy, solicitous (*re, de re, pro alqo*); b) tormenting, troublesome.
ap-age away with you, begone, be off!
apēliōtēs, ae *m* east-wind.
aper, prī *m* wild boar.
aperiō, ruī, rtum 4. 1. to uncover, lay bare, to open, unclose, to make accessible; 2. to discover, unveil, display, unfold, make known; to reveal, explain, disclose (*alci alqd,* with *acc.c.inf.*).
apertō 1 to lay bare.
apertus 3 1. uncovered, bare; without deck exposed; 2. not shut, open; a) accessible, free, unobstructed; **apertum, ī** *n* open space, open field; b) clear, manifest, plain, evident; not obscure, intelligible; c) practicable; d) frank, open, candid, straightforward.
apex, icis *m* point, extremity, top, summit; a) top of the helmet; b) conical hat, cap; cap of a priest; crown, tiara; c) highest ornament.
a-phractus, ī *f* (*and* **-um, ī** *n*) ship without deck.
apicātus 3 adorned with a priest's cap.
apicula, ae *f* bee.
apis, is *f* bee.
apīscor, aptus sum 3 to reach, obtain, get.
apium, ī *n* celery.
aplustre, is *n* stern.
apo-clētī, ōrum *m/pl.* committee of the Aetolian league.
apo-dytērium, ī *n* undressing room in a bath.
apo-lactizō 1 to kick away, spurn.
apo-logō 1 to reject.
apo-logus, ī *m* narrative; fable.
apo-phorēta, ōrum *n/pl.* presents given at the Saturnalia

apo-proēgmena, ōrum *n/pl.* what is rejected.
apo-sphrāgisma, atis *n* image of a seal-ring.
apo-thēca, ae *f* store-room, magazine, warehouse.
ap-parātiō, ōnis *f* **a**) preparation; **b**) a preparing.
ap-parātus[1], ūs *m* **a**) a preparing; **b**) tool, implement, instrument, engine; **c**) magnificence, splendour, pomp.
ap-parātus[2] 3 **a**) well prepared, ready; **b**) splendid, sumptuous.
ap-pāreō 2 to appear, become visible, make one's appearance; **a**) to be clear, manifest, evident, perceptible (**appāret** *with acc.c.inf.* it is clear, plain); **b**) to appear as a servant, to attend, serve.
ap-pariō 3 to gain.
ap-pāritiō, ōnis *f* **a**) a waiting upon, service, attendance; **b**) servants.
ap-pāritor, ōris *m* public servant, lictor.
ap-parō 1 to prepare, make ready, equip, provide.
appellātiō, ōnis *f* **a**) an addressing, speaking to; appeal; **b**) a naming, name, title; **c**) pronunciation.
appellātor, ōris *m* appellant.
appellitō 1 to name habitually.
ap-pellō[1] **1.** to address, accost, speak to, greet; **a**) to apply to, entreat, request (*alqm de re*); **b**) to appeal to (*alqm*); **c**) to press (*for money*); **d**) to summon (*alqm*); **e**) to call by name, to name, entitle; to mention; **2.** to pronounce.
ap-pellō[2], pulī, pulsum 3 to drive, move, bring to *or* towards (*alqd ad alqd*), *navem, classem* to bring to land (*ad* or *in locum*); **P.** (*and intrans. active*) to reach land.
appendicula, ae *f* a small appendage.
ap-pendix, icis *f* appendage, supplement, addition.
ap-pendō, ndī, nsum 3 to weigh out.
ap-petēns, tis **a**) striving after, eager for; **b**) grasping, avaricious.
appetentia, ae *f* = **appetitio.**
ap-petītiō, ōnis *f* **a**) a grasping at; **b**) desire, longing for.
ap-petītus, ūs *m* = appetitio.
ap-petō 3 to strive after, long for; **a**) to desire, seek; **b**) to seek to go to, to approach, arrive (*with acc.*); **c**) to draw near (*of time*); **d**) to attack, assail (*alqd alqa re*).
ap-pingō 3 to paint in (*alqd alci rei*); to add in writing.
ap-plaudō 3 **a**) to strike one thing upon another (*with dat.*); to strike with (*abl.*); **b**) to applaud.
ap-plicātiō, ōnis *f* attachment, inclination.
ap-plicō, cāvī, cātum (*or* **cuī, citum**) 1 to apply, attach, add, join to, to place near (*alqd ad alqd* or *alci rei*); **a**) (*navem*) to steer to, bring to land, **P.** to land; **b**) to turn to, direct towards, **se applicāre** *ad alqd* to devote oneself to; *ad alqm* to associate with; **applicātus** *ad alqd* inclined to; **c**) to add (*alqd ad rem*).
ap-plōrō 1 to weep at, bewail.
ap-pōnō 3 to put *or* place at, by, beside, near (*alqd ad rem* or with *dat.*); **a**) to serve, set before, put on the table; **b**) to add to, put to; **c**) to procure.
ap-porrēctus 3 stretched out near.
ap-portō 1 **a**) to carry, convey, bring to; **c**) to cause.
ap-poscō 3 to demand in addition.
ap-positus 3 **a**) placed *or* situated near, contiguous; **b**) appropriate, proper.
ap-pōtus 3 drunk, intoxicated.
ap-precor 1 to pray to, worship.
ap-prehendō 3 to seize, take hold of.
ap-prīmē *adv.* chiefly, exceedingly.
ap-primō, pressī, pressum 3 to press to (*alqd alci rei*).
ap-probātiō, ōnis *f* **a**) approval, assent; **b**) proof.
ap-probātor, ōris *m* one who approves, assents.
ap-probē *adv.* fully, very well.
ap-probō 1 **a**) to approve, assent to, favour; **b**) to bless; **c**) to make acceptable; **d**) to prove.
ap-prōmittō 3 to promise besides.
ap-properō 1 **a**) to hasten, accelerate; **b**) to make haste.
ap-propinquātiō, ōnis *f* approach.
ap-propinquō 1 to approach, draw near (*ad alqd* or with *dat.*) (*of place and time*).
ap-pugnō 1 to fight against, attack, assault.
ap-pulsus, ūs *m* **a**) a driving towards, approach, landing; **b**) influence.

aprīcātiō, ōnis *f* a basking in the sun.
aprīcitās, ātis *f* sunniness, warmth of the sun.
aprīcor 1 to bask in the sun.
aprīcus 3 open to the sun, sunny; fond of sunshine; *subst.* **-um, ī** *n* sunlight.
Aprīlis, e belonging to April; *subst. m* April.
aprūgnus 3 belonging to a wild boar.
aps..., *see* **abs...**
aptō 1 **a**) to fit *or* adapt to, to adjust, accommodate; **b**) to prepare, make ready.
aptus 3 **a**) fastened, connected, joined, allied; **b**) depending upon; **c**) adhering together; **d**) prepared, equipped, fitted out; **e**) suitable, appropriate, fit, proper.
apud *prep.* with *acc.* **1.** at, near, by, with (*of places and persons*); before, in the presence of, among; at the house of; **2.** in the opinion of; in the writings of.
aqua, ae *f* water; **aquā et igni interdicere alci** to exclude from society, to banish; **a**) sea, lake, river, rain, tears; **b**) *pl.* baths, bathing-place; **c**) water-conduit; **d**) water-clock.
aquae-ductus, ūs *m* **a**) aqueduct, conduit; **b**) the right of conducting water (*to a place*).
aquāliculus, ī *m* stomach.
aquālis, e of water; *subst. m* water-jug.
aquārius 3 belonging to water; *subst.* **~, ī** *m* **a**) inspector of conduits; **b**) the Aquarius *or* Water--carrier (*constellation*).
aquāticus 3 *and* **aquātilis, e** growing *or* living in the water; watery.
aquātiō, ōnis *f* a fetching of water.
aquātor, ōris *m* one who fetches water.
aquila, ae *f* eagle; the eagle as the standard of a Roman legion.
aqui-lex, legis *m* water-finder.
aquili-fer, ferī *m* eagle-bearer.
aquilīnus 3 relating to an eagle.
aquilō, ōnis *m* the north-wind; a) storm; **b**) north.
aquilōnius 3 northerly.
aquilus 3 dark-coloured, blackish.
aquola, ae *f* = **aquula.**
aquor 1 to fetch water.
aquōsus 3 full of water, watery, rainy, moist.
aquula, ae *f* a little water, small stream.
ar = **ad.**
āra, ae *f* altar, hearth; refuge, shelter.
arānea, ae *f* **a**) spider; **b**) spider's web.
arāneola, ae *f* (*and* **us, ī** *m*) little spider.
arāneōsus 3 full of cobwebs.
arāneum, ī *n* a spider's web.
arāneus, ī *m* = **aranea.**
arātiō, ōnis *f* **1.** a ploughing; agriculture; **2.** arable land.
arātiuncula, ae *f* small farm.
arātor, ōris *m* **a**) ploughman, husbandman; farmer; **b**) cultivator of public lands.
arātrum, ī *n* plough.
arbiter, trī *m* **1.** spectator, beholder, eyewitness; **2.** arbiter, umpire; a) judge; b) lord, master, ruler, governor.
arbitra, ae *f* female witness.
arbitrārius 3 matter of opinion.
arbitrātus, ūs *m* free-will, choice, pleasure; a) full discretion; **b**) direction; maxim.
arbitrium, ī *n* **1.** decision of an arbiter, judgment; = **arbitratus;** **2.** a) **~ funeris** funeral expenses; b) dominion, mastery, authority.
arbitror 1 (*and* **arbitrō** 1) **a**) to decide as an arbiter, to give judgment; **b**) to consider, think, believe.
arbor (*and* **ōs**), **oris** *f* tree (*coll.* trees); mast, oar, ship.
arboreus 3 of a tree; tree-like.
arbustus 3 full of trees; **-um, ī** *n* plantation, orchard, vineyard; trees, shrubs.
arbuteus 3 of the strawberry-tree.
arbutum, ī *n* fruit of the strawberry-tree.
arbutus, ī *f* strawberry-tree.
arca, ae *f* chest, box; **a**) box for money, coffer; **b**) coffin; **c**) cell.
arcānus 3 secret, private, hidden; silent, trusty; *subst.* **arcānum, ī** *n* a secret.
arceō, uī, — 2 to shut in *or* up, enclose, confine; **a**) to restrain, hinder, prevent, keep at a distance; **b**) to protect from.
arcessītor, ōris *m* one who fetches.

arcessītus, ūs *m* a calling for, summons.
arcessō, īvī, ītum 3 to call, summon, fetch, send for; **a**) to summon before a court of justice (*alqm capitis, crimine, alcis rei*), accuse; **b**) to bring, procure; **c**) to derive, fetch, seek from.
arche-typus 3 original.
archi-magīrus, ī *m* chief cook.
archi-mīmus, ī *m* chief mime--actor.
archi-pīrāta, ae *m* pirate chief.
archi-tectōn, onis = **architectus.**
archi-tector 1 to build; to devise, invent.
architectūra, ae *f* art of building, architecture.
architectus, ī *m* master-builder, architect; **a**) inventor, deviser, maker; **b**) plotter, schemer.
archōn, ontis *m* archon (*of Athens*).
arci-potēns, tis skilful in archery.
arci-tenēns, tis holding a bow; *subst.* **A~** *m* the Archer (*constellation*).
Arcto-phylax, acis *m* (*a constellation*) Boötes.
Arctos, ī *f* the Great Bear; the two Bears; the north; night.
arctōus 3 northern.
Arctūrus, ī *m* the brightest star of Boötes; the rising of Boötes.
arcuātus 3 bent like a bow.
arcula, ae *f* small box, casket.
arculārius, ī *m* casket-maker.
arcus, ūs *m* a bow; **a**) rainbow, triumphal arch, vault; **b**) circle, curve.
ardaliō, ōnis *m* a busybody.
ardea, ae *f* heron.
ārdēns, tis burning, glowing, hot; **a**) glittering, sparkling; **b**) fiery, impassioned.
ārdeō, ārsī, ārsum 2 to burn, be on fire; **a**) to sparkle, flash; **b**) to be inflamed, excited, to burn with passion, with love, to desire ardently (*alqm, in alqo, ad* or *in alqd*).
ārdēscō, ārsī, — 3 to take fire, become inflamed; **a**) to flash, glitter; **b**) to become furious.
ārdor, ōris *m* flame, fire, heat; **a**) brightness, gleam; **b**) eagerness, zeal, desire; **c**) love; a beloved one.
arduus 3 **a**) steep, elevated, lofty; *subst.* **arduum, ī** *n* a steep place, height; **b**) difficult, troublesome, hard.
ārea, ae *f* open space; **a**) building ground, site for a house; **b**) threshing-floor; **c**) playground, racecourse; **d**) bald spot.
āre-faciō 3 to dry.
arēna, ae *f* sand; **a**) sandy place; **b**) sandy desert; **c**) sea-shore, strand, beach; **d**) arena in an amphitheatre.
arēnāria, ae *f* sand-pit.
arēni-vagus 3 wandering in sandy deserts.
arēnōsus 3 sandy.
ārēns, tis dry, arid; thirsty.
āreō, uī, — 2 to be dry *or* arid.
āreola, ae *f* small open space.
ārēscō, āruī, — 3 to become dry, dry up.
aretā-logus, ī *m* babbler about virtue.
argentārius 3 **a**) of silver; **b**) of money; (*taberna*) **argentāria, ae,** *f* banker's shop; *subst.* **argentārius, ī** *m* money-changer, banker.
argentātus 3 ornamented with silver.
argenteolus 3 of silver.
argenteus 3 made of silver; *subst.* **~, ī** *m* silver coin; **a**) ornamented *or* covered with silver; **b**) of a silver colour, silvery; **c**) of the Silver Age.
argentum, ī *n* silver; silver plate; silver money, money.
argīlla, ae *f* white clay, potter's clay.
argītis, idis *f* vine with white grapes.
argūmentātiō, ōnis *f* a proving, argumentation, reasoning.
argūmentor 1 **a**) to adduce proof; **b**) to adduce in proof.
argūmentum, ī *n* **1.** subject, story, representation, statement; theme, matter, contents; plot, drama, tale; reality; **2.** proof, conclusion; mark, token.
arguō, uī, ūtum 3 to make clear *or* known, to manifest, show, prove; **a**) to betray; **b**) to confute, disprove; **c**) to accuse, charge, censure, blame (*alqm alcis rei* or *de re,* with *acc. c. inf.*).
argūtātiō, ōnis *f* creaking.
argūtiae, ārum *f/pl.* **1.** significance; quick movement; **2.** cleverness, sagacity, acuteness, wit; subtlety, cunning.
argūtor (*and* **ō**) 1 to talk much.
argūtulus 3 somewhat subtle.

argūtus 3 **1.** significant, expressive; piercing, noisy, melodious; **2.** a) clear, explicit; b) sagacious, acute, witty; c) sly, cunning, subtle, artful.
argyr-aspides, um *m/pl.* soldiers armed with a silver shield.
āridulus 3 somewhat dry.
āridus 3 dry, arid, parched; *subst.* **āridum, ī** *n* dry land; **a**) thirsty; **b**) poor, meagre, scanty, unadorned.
ariēs, etis *m* ram; battering-ram.
arietātiō, ōnis *f* butting.
arietō 1 to butt like a ram, to strike violently.
arista, ae *f* **a**) beard of an ear of corn; **b**) ear of corn; cereals.
aristolochia, ae *f* (*a plant useful in childbirth*).
arithmētica, ōrum *n/pl.* (and **-ca, ae** *f*) arithmetic.
āritūdō, inis *f* dryness.
arma, ōrum *n/pl.* **1.** tools, implements, tackle, outfit; **2.** weapons, arms, armour; a) shield; b) war, battle; c) warriors, armed men; d) defence.
armamaxa, ae *f* Persian travelling-coach.
armāmenta, ōrum *n/pl.* tackling, equipment of a ship.
armāmentārium, ī *n* arsenal, armoury.
armāriolum, ī *n* little chest.
armārium, ī *n* chest, cupboard.
armātūra, ae *f* armour; **a**) branch of the service; **b**) armed soldiers.
armātus[1], **ūs** *m* = **armatura.**
armātus[2] 3 armed, equipped; *subst.* **armātī, ōrum** *m/pl.* armed men, soldiers.
armentālis, e grazing in herds *or* flocks; belonging to a herd.
armentārius, ī *m* herdsman.
armentum, ī *n* herd, cattle (for ploughing).
armi-fer 3 bearing arms, warlike.
armi-ger 3 **a**) bearing arms; **b**) shield-bearer; man of the body-guard; attendant.
armilla, ae *f* bracelet, arm-ring.
armillātus 3 adorned with a bracelet.
armi-potēns, tis mighty in arms.
armi-sonus 3 resounding with arms.
armō 1 **1.** to furnish with implements, to equip, fit out (*a ship*); **2.** to make ready for battle, to arm (*alqm alqa re, in* or *contra alqm, ad* or *in alqd*); to strengthen, help.
armus, ī *m* shoulder, shoulderblade, upper arm; flank.
arō 1 to plough, till; **a**) to furrow; **b**) to farm, cultivate; **c**) to gain by agriculture.
arquātus 3 jaundiced.
ar-rēctus 3 upright; steep, precipitous.
ar-rēpō 3 to creep to, steal to, to approach gently (*ad alqd* or with *dat.*).
arr(h)abō, ōnis *m* deposit, security.
ar-rīdeō 2 **a**) to laugh *or* smile at, to laugh with; **b**) to be favourable, to please (*alci*).
ar-rigō, rēxī, rēctum 3 **a**) to erect, lift up; **b**) to excite, animate, rouse.
ar-ripiō, ripuī, reptum 3 to snatch, catch; **a**) to seize, lay hold of; **b**) to drag into a court, to accuse; **c**) to seize with violence.
ar-rīsor, ōris *m* fawner.
ar-rōdō 3 to gnaw at.
arrogāns, tis assuming, arrogant, presumptuous, haughty.
arrogantia, ae *f* assumption, arrogance, pride, haughtiness.
ar-rogātiō, ōnis *f* adoption of an adult.
ar-rogō 1 **1.** to associate with (*alqm alci*); **2.** a) to appropriate, claim; b) to confer upon (*alci alqd.*).
ar-rōsor, ōris *m* one who gnaws *or* nibbles.
ars, artis *f* **1.** skill; **2.** a) profession, business, trade; b) fine *or* liberal art, letters; c) science, knowledge; theory, principles of art; manual *or* text-book of any art *or* science; conduct, practice, method, work of art; **3.** character, habit; artificial means, artifice, cunning, trick, fraud, intrigue.
artē *adv. of* **artus**[2].
artēria, ae *f* **a**) artery; **b**) windpipe.
arthrīticus 3 gouty.
articulātim *adv.* **a**) limb by limb, piecemeal; **b**) distinctly.
articulō 1 to speak distinctly.
articulus, ī *m* **1.** a joint; a) limb; finger; b) knot (*of plants*); **2.** a) part, division; b) point, moment, crisis.
arti-fex, icis *m and f* **1.** *adj.* clever, skilled, ingenious (*alcis rei*); **2.** artist, master of an art; a) author, maker, contriver; b) cunning deceiver.

artificiōsus 3 **a**) skilful, full of art; **b**) artistic, skilfully wrought; artificial.
artificium, ī *n* **1.** skill, knowledge, ingenuity, art; a) work of art; b) trick, cunning, craft; c) theory, system; **2.** trade, profession, handicraft.
artō 1 to straiten, press *or* draw together; to contract, limit.
artolaganus, ī *m* cake.
artopta, ae *f* baking-pan.
artua *n/pl.* limbs.
artus[1], **ūs** *m* joint, limb (*mostly pl.*).
artus[2] 3 **a**) tight, narrow, close; *subst.* **artum, ī** *n* narrow space; **b**) dense, firm; **c**) straitened, scanty, small, needy; *subst.* **artum, ī** *n* scantiness, difficulty, precarious position.
artūtus 3 strong-limbed.
ārula, ae *f* small altar.
arundō, *see* **harundo.**
aruspex, *see* **haruspex.**
arvīna, ae *f* grease, fat, lard.
arviō = **rāviō.**
arvum, ī *n* ploughed land, arable field; **a**) crop; **b**) country, field, plain; **c**) pasture-ground.
arvus 3 arable, ploughed.
arx, arcis *f* **1.** castle, citadel, fortress, stronghold; height, eminence; **2.** protection, bulwark, refuge.
as, assis *m* **1.** the whole *or* unity (*divided into twelve parts*), **heres ex asse** sole heir; **2.** a copper coin, the as.
asarōtum, ī *n* mosaic floor.
ascaulēs *m* bagpiper.
a-scendō, ndī, ēnsum 3 a) to mount, ascend, go up (*in* or *ad alqd*); **b**) to rise, reach.
ascēnsiō, ōnis *f* = **ascensus.**
a-scēnsus, ūs *m* a going *or* climbing up, ascent; **a**) a rising; **b**) place of ascending, approach, step, degree.
ascia, ae *f* carpenter's axe.
a-sciō 4 to take to oneself, to adopt.
a-scīscō 3 to take to oneself, receive, adopt (*alqm* or *alqd in* or *ad alqd, inter alqos, sibi socium*); **a**) to appropriate *or* associate with oneself; **b**) to assume, arrogate; **c**) to approve of.
ascop(ēr)a, ae *f* leather wallet.
ā-scrībō 3 to add in writing, to write in addition (*alqd alci rei, in alqd, in alqa re*); **a**) to enter in a list; **b**) to appoint, assign (*alqm tutorem liberis*); **c**) to reckon *or* number among (*alqm in* or *ad alqd*); **d**) to attribute, ascribe (*alci alqd*).
āscrīpticius 3 enrolled in the list of citizens.
ā-scrīptiō, ōnis *f* addition in writing.
āscrīptīvus, ī *m* supernumerary soldier.
ā-scrīptor, ōris *m* one who adds his name, supporter.
asella, ae *f* little she-ass.
asellus, ī *m* little ass.
asīlus, ī *m* gadfly.
asina, ae *f* she-ass.
asinārius, ī *m* donkey-driver.
asinus, ī *m* ass; blockhead.
asōtus, ī *m* libertine.
asparagus, ī *m* asparagus.
a-spectābilis, e visible.
a-spectō 1 to look at attentively *or* with respect; **1.** to lie towards (*alqd*); **2.** to observe (*alqd*).
a-spectus, ūs *m* **1.** a looking at, glance, look; a) limit of vision; b) faculty of seeing; **2.** appearance.
as-pellō, pulī, pulsum 3 to drive away.
asper, era, erum rough, uneven, stormy; **a**) cold, harsh, hard, sharp, coarse; **b**) bitter, abusive; **c**) cruel, severe, unkind, violent; **d**) troublesome, difficult, adverse, dangerous.
a-spergō[1], **rsī, rsum** 3 **1.** to sprinkle, scatter on (*alqd alci*); **2.** to besprinkle, taint (*alqa re*).
a-spergō[2], **inis** *f* a sprinkling; drops, spray.
asperitās, ātis *f* roughness, unevenness; **a**) sharpness, sourness, harshness; **b**) rudeness; **c**) fierceness, severity, austerity; **d**) calamity, difficulty, adversity, violence.
aspernātiō, ōnis *f* disdain, contempt.
a-spernor 1 to despise, reject.
asperō 1 **a**) to make rough *or* uneven; **b**) to sharpen; **c**) to excite, exasperate.
aspersiō, ōnis *f* a sprinkling, a laying on of colours.
a-spiciō, spexī, spectum 3 to look at *or* upon; **1.** to behold, see, observe; **2.** to face; a) to lie towards; b) to inspect, examine, survey; c) to consider, weigh, ponder, respect.

a-spīrāmen, inis *n* something breathed on; favour, gift.
a-spīrātiō, ōnis *f* a breathing upon; exhalation.
a-spīrō 1 **1.** to breathe at *or* upon; to exhale; a) to be favourable (*with dat.*), to assist; b) to strive for, seek to reach, aspire to (*in, ad alqm* or *alqd*); **2.** *trans.* to breathe *or* blow something upon a person; to infuse, instil.
aspis, idis *f* viper, adder.
as-portātiō, ōnis *f* a carrying away.
as-portō 1 to carry *or* bring away.
asprētum, ī *n* rough, uneven, stony place.
assecla, ae *m* = **assectator.**
as-sectātiō, ōnis *f* attendance.
as-sectātor, ōris *m* attendant, follower; disciple.
as-sector 1 to follow, accompany.
assecula, ae *m* = **assectator.**
as-sēnsiō, ōnis *f* **a**) an assenting, assent, applause; **b**) belief in the reality of sensible appearances.
as-sēnsor, ōris *m* one who assents.
as-sēnsus, ūs *m* = **assensio;** echo.
assentātiō, ōnis *f* **a**) an assenting; **b**) flattering assent, flattery, adulation.
assentātiuncula, ae *f* base flattery.
assentātor, ōris *m* flatterer.
assentātōriē *adv.* in a flattering manner.
as-sentātrīx, īcis *f* female flatterer.
as-sentior, sēnsus sum (*and* **assentiō**) 4 to assent, agree (*alci de re, in re*).
as-sentor 1 to assent; to flatter (*alci*).
as-sequor 3 to overtake, reach (*with acc.*); **a**) to become like, to equal; **b**) to obtain, gain; **c**) to comprehend, understand.
asser, eris *m* stake, pole, post.
as-serō[1], seruī, sertum 3 to join to; **a**) to lay hold of, claim; to assume; **b**) to set free, liberate; **c**) (*in servitutem*) to claim as a slave.
as-serō[2], sēvī, situm 3 to sow *or* plant near.
assertiō, ōnis *f* declaration of a person's free status.
assertor, ōris *m* one who asserts a person's free or servile status; defender, champion.
as-serviō 4 to help, assist (*with dat.*).
as-servō 1 to keep carefully, to preserve; to watch.
as-sessiō, ōnis *f*, **as-sessus, ūs** *m* a sitting near.
as-sessor, ōris *m* **a**) assistant; **b**) assessor (of a judge).
as-sevēranter *adv.* earnestly.
as-sevērātiō, ōnis *f* **a**) earnestness, perseverance; **b**) earnest assertion *or* affirmation.
as-sevērō 1 **1.** to do with earnestness; **2.** a) to affirm *or* assert earnestly; b) to show, prove.
as-sideō, sēdī, sessum 2 to sit near, by the side of; **a**) to attend, watch, wait upon; **b**) to encamp before, to besiege, blockade.
as-sīdō, sēdī, sessum 3 to sit down.
assiduitās, ātis *f* a sitting at; **a**) constant attendance, presence, attention; **b**) continual intercourse; **c**) constant repetition; **d**) perseverance, persistence, constancy.
assiduus 3 sitting near; **a**) established, well-off, (man) of substance; **b**) untiring, incessant, unremitting; **c**) perpetual, continuous.
assignātiō, ōnis *f* an assigning, allotment.
as-signō 1 to assign, allot, to commit, intrust; to ascribe, attribute (*alci alqd*).
as-siliō, siluī, (sultum) 4 to leap *or* spring at *or* upon; to assail.
as-similis, e like, similar.
as-simulātiō, ōnis *f* comparison.
as-simulō 1 to make like, copy (*alqd alci rei*); **a**) to compare; **b**) to imitate, counterfeit, feign, pretend (*alqd*, with *acc.c.inf.*, with *quasi*).
as-sistō, stitī, — 3 **a**) to stand at, by, near; **b**) to help, defend.
as-soleō, —, — 2 to be wont, accustomed; **ut assolet** as is usual.
as-sonō, —, — 1 to resound, answer.
as-sūdāscō 3 to get into a perspiration.
as-suēfaciō 3 to accustom to (*alqm alqa re* or *ad alqd*, with *dat.* or with *inf.*).
as-suēscō 3 **1.** to become accustomed (*alqa re, ad alqd*); **2.** to make familiar; **3.** to accustom; **assuētus** 3 a) accustomed; b) usual, customary, familiar.
assuētūdō, inis *f* custom, habit, intercourse.
as-sūgō 3 to suck in.
assula, ae *f* splinter of wood; board, plank.

assulātim *adv.* in splinters *or* fragments.
as-sultō 1 to leap at, assault, attack [(*alqd* or with *dat.*).
assultus, ūs *m* assault, attack.
as-sum, affuī, adesse (afforem = adessem, affore = affutūrum esse); to be at, by, near; to be at hand, be present; **a**) to appear, arrive; **b**) to appear before a tribunal (*in iudicio, ad iudicium*); **c**) to share, participate, assist (*alci rei*); **d**) to be present to witness *or* to support, defend (*alci in re*); **e**) to give attention (*animo*).
as-sūmō 3 to take to oneself, receive; **a**) to take in addition to (*alqd ad alqd* or with *dat.*); **b**) to take for one's assistance; **c**) to appropriate to oneself, to claim, assume, arrogate.
as-sūmptiō, ōnis *f* a taking to one; **a**) approval; **b**) minor proposition of a syllogism.
as-sūmptīvus 3 resting on external evidence.
as-suō 3 to sew on.
as-surgō 3 to rise up, stand up; to mount.
assus 3 roasted; (*nutrix*) dry-nurse; *subst.* **assum, ī** *n* **a**) roast meat; **b**) dry heat bath.
ast = **at.**
a-sternō 3 to strew on, scatter upon.
asticus 3 of a city, city-.
a-stipulātor, ōris *m* **a**) one who joins in accepting a verbal contract; **b**) supporter.
a-stipulor 1 to agree with (*alci*).
a-stituō 3 to add, place to.
a-stō, stitī, — 1 **a**) to stand at, by, near; **b**) to stand upright *or* erect; **c**) to assist, aid.
a-strepō, puī, pitum 3 to make a noise at; **a**) to shout; **b**) to applaud, assent loudly (*alci*).
a-strictus 3 drawn together, tight; **a**) sparing, parsimonious; **b**) concise, brief.
a-strīdō 3 to hiss (at).
astri-fer 3 and **astri-ger** 3 starry.
a-stringō 3 to draw together, contract, bind together (*alqd ad alqd*); **a**) to cause to freeze *or* congeal; **b**) to bind, fetter, oblige (*alqm alqa re*); **c**) to circumscribe, condense.
astro-logia, ae *f* astronomy.
astro-logus, ī *m* **a**) astronomer; **b**) astrologer.
astro-nomia, ae *f* astronomy.
astrum, ī *n* star, constellation; (*pl.*) heaven, immortality, glory.
a-struō 3 to build to, in addition; to add.
astu *n* (*indecl.*) city (Athens).
a-stupeō, —, — 2 to be astonished *or* amazed at (*alci rei*).
astus, ūs *m* cunning, craft; stratagem.
astūtia, ae *f* **a**) skill, adroitness; **b**) cunning, craft, astuteness.
astūtus 3 **a**) shrewd, sagacious; **b**) crafty, cunning.
asȳlum, ī *n* place of refuge, sanctuary, asylum.
asymbolus 3 contributing nothing (to an entertainment).
at *cj.* but, yet, but on the other hand, moreover, but meanwhile; **at contra** but on the contrary, **at vero** *or* **at certe** but certainly, **at tamen** and yet; *si non — at* (*certe, tamen*) if not — but yet *or* nevertheless; but at least.
atābulus, ī *m* south-east wind, sirocco.
atat *int., see* **attat.**
at-avus, ī *m* great-great-great-grandfather; ancestor.
āter, ātra, ātrum black, dead black, dark; **a**) clothed in black; **b**) gloomy, sad, unfortunate, dismal, unlucky; **c**) malicious, virulent, deadly.
āthlēta, ae *m* wrestler, athlete.
āthlēticē like an athlete.
a-tomus, ī *f* indivisible body, atom.
atque *cj.* (*before consonants* **ac**) **a**) and, and also, and moreover, and even, and especially; **b**) *after words of comparison* (*aequus, similis, talis, alius, contra, dissimilis etc.*): as, than; **c**) and so, and thus, and consequently; **atque adeo** and in fact.
at-quī *cj.* yet, however, nevertheless, notwithstanding, rather; (*in syllogisms to introduce the minor proposition*): but, now.
ātrāmentum, ī *n* black liquid, blacking, ink.
ātrātus 3 clothed in black.
ātri-color black.
ātriēnsis, is *m* house-steward.
ātriolum, ī *n* small hall *or* forecourt.
ātritās, ātis *f* blackness.
ātrium, ī *n* forecourt, hall; **a**) principal room of a house; **b**) house, palace.

atrōcitās, ātis *f* **a**) fierceness, harshness, atrociousness; **b**) severity, barbarity.
atrōx, ōcis a) repulsive, horrid, terrible; **b**) savage, fierce, cruel, harsh, severe; **c**) violent, perilous; **d**) morose, gloomy.
at-tāctus, ūs *m* a touching, touch.
attagēn, ēnis *m* (*and* **attagēna, ae** *f*) woodcock.
at-tamen *cj.* but yet, but nevertheless.
attat, attatae *exclamation of surprise, pain, warning etc.:* oh! alas!
attegia, ae *f* hut, tent.
at-temperātē *adv.* appropriately, seasonably.
at-temperō 1 to fit on; to direct, point at.
at-temptō 1 to make a trial of; **a**) to try to corrupt; **b**) to attack, assail.
at-tendō, dī, tum 3 to stretch to, direct to, (*animum*) to give attention to (*ad alqd*), give heed, to mind (*alqd, alci rei* or with *acc.c.inf.*).
at-tentiō, ōnis *f* attentiveness, attention.
at-tentō = **attempto.**
at-tentus 3 **a**) attentive, engaged; **b**) intent on, striving after; **c**) economical
at-tenuō 1 to make thin; **a**) to lessen, diminish; **b**) to weaken, reduce, impair; **attenuātus** 3 concise, meagre, dry, affected.
at-terō 3 **a**) to rub against; **b**) to rub away, wear away; **c**) to destroy, waste, injure.
at-testor 1 to bear witness *or* testimony, to attest.
at-texō 3 to weave *or* plait to; to join closely (*alqd ad alqd* or with *dat.*).
atticissō 1 to be in the Attic manner.
at-tineō, tinuī, (tentum) 2 **1.** to hold fast, detain; a) to delay, keep (*re*); b) to hold, have possession of; **2.** *intr.* to reach, pertain to, a) to concern; **quod attinet ad me** for my part, as far as I am concerned; b) **non** *or* **nihil attinet** it is of no use, does not matter.
at-tingō, tigī, tāctum 3 to touch against, come in contact with (*alqd*); **a**) to arrive at, reach; **b**) to border on; **c**) to touch, strike, lay hands on, seize, attack; **d**) to come in contact with, belong to, be related to; **e**) to engage in, undertake, manage, be occupied in; **f**) to touch, mention, refer to.
at-tollō, —, — 3 **a**) to raise up, lift up; to erect; to raise (*alqd ad* or *in alqd*), elevate, exalt, distinguish, aggrandize; **b**) **P.** to rise up.
at-tondeō, ndī, nsum 2 **a**) to shear, shave, cut; **b**) to lessen, depreciate.
at-tonitus 3 thunder - struck; **a**) stunned, terrified, senseless; **b**) inspired, frantic.
at-tonō 1 to thunder at, strike with thunder; **a**) to stun, terrify; **b**) to inspire.
at-torqueō, —, — 2 to hurl *or* [whirl upwards.]
at-trahō 3 to draw to, attract; **a**) to pull tight; **b**) to drag; **c**) to allure, take with one.
at-trectātus, ūs *m* touching, feeling.
at-trectō 1 to touch, handle; **a**) to lay hands on; **b**) to appropriate; **c**) to busy oneself with.
at-tremō 3 to tremble at (*dat.*).
at-trepidō 1 to go to tremblingly.
at-tribuō 3 to allot, assign to, make over; **a**) to commit, confer, bestow; **b**) to pay out; **c**) to attribute, ascribe, impute; **d**) to add, annex; **e**) to attribute words to.
at-tribūtiō, ōnis *f* **a**) an assigning, assignment; **b**) predicate, attribute (*also* **attribūtum**).
at-trītus 3 worn; shameless.
au *int.* oh! ah! now!
au-ceps, cupis *m* bird-catcher, fowler; **syllabarum** quibbler, wordcatcher.
auctārium, ī *n* addition.
aucti-ficus 3 promoting increase.
auctiō, ōnis *f* **a**) public sale, auction; **b**) goods sold at an auction.
auctiōnārius 3 pertaining to an auction.
auctiōnor 1 to hold an auction.
auctitō 1 to increase greatly.
auctō 1 to increase, augment.
auctor, ōris *m* (and *f*) **1.** guarantor, attesting witness (*alcis rei*); **a**) example, model, teacher, authority; **b**) narrator, historian, writer, author; **c**) voucher, security, **d**) guardian (*of a woman*); **e**) witness; **f**) promoter, producer; **2.** adviser, counsellor; originator, doer, beginner, causer; founder, maker, inventor; progenitor.

auctōrāmentum, ī *n* contract; wages, pay, earnest-money.
auctōritās, ātis *f* **1.** warrant, security, attestation; a) credibility; b) legal ownership, right of possession, property; c) full power, authorisation; d) legal document *or* deed; **2.** a) model, pattern, example, precedent; b) weight, dignity, influence, importance, power, worth, consequence, estimation; c) influential person; **3.** a) counsel, advice, encouragement; b) will, pleasure, decision, bidding, command; c) decree *or* will (*of the Senate*).
auctōrō 1 to bind, oblige, pledge; to hire.
auctumnus, ī *m*, *see* **autumnus.**
auctus[1], **ūs** *m* **a**) an increasing, augmenting; **b**) increase, growth, thriving.
auctus[2] 3 increased, enlarged.
aucupium, ī *n* **a**) bird-catching, fowling; **b**) the hunting after a thing; **verborum** a quibbling.
aucupor (*and* **aucupō**) 1 to strive for, hunt after, lie in wait for (*alqd*).
audācia, ae *f* **a**) courage, daring, boldness, bravery; **b**) temerity, presumption, insolence; **c**) bold action.
audāx, ācis (*adv.* **audācter**) a) courageous, daring, bold, intrepid; **b**) foolhardy, audacious, rash, insolent.
audēns, tis daring, bold, courageous.
audentia, ae *f* boldness, courage.
audeō, ausus sum 2 **a**) to have a mind, to be willing; **b**) to dare, venture, risk.
audiēns, tis *m* hearer, listener.
audientia, ae *f* a hearing, listening; attention; **-am facere alci** to procure a hearing for.
audiō 4 **1.** to hear, to have the faculty of hearing; **2.** to perceive, understand, learn; *subst.* **audītum, ī** *n* hearsay, report; **audītō** on hearing; a) to listen to; b) to hear a case, to examine; c) to lend an ear to a prayer, to grant; d) to approve of, give credence to; e) to obey, follow, **dicto audiēns esse** to obey; **3.** to be called, named, reported, pass for, **bene** (**male**) **audire** to be well (ill) spoken of, to be in good (bad) repute (*ab alqo*).
auditiō, ōnis *f* **a**) a hearing, listening; **b**) hearsay, report.
audītō 1 to hear often.
audītor, ōris *m* hearer, listener; pupil, scholar.
audītōrium, ī *n* lecture-room, (place of) audience.
audītus, ūs *m* a) sense of hearing; **b**) = **auditio.**
au-ferō, abstulī, ablātum 3 **1.** to carry away, bring away (*alqd ab, ex, de re*); **se auferre** to remove oneself, withdraw; **P.** to hurry *or* run away, to disappear; **2.** to take away, carry off, snatch away (*alqd de* or *ab re, alci alqd*); to rob, steal; to destroy, kill; **3.** to gain, obtain, get (*alqd ab alqo*, with *ut*).
au-fugiō 3 to flee away, to flee from (*alqd*).
augeō, xī, ctum 2 to cause to grow; **1.** to increase, augment, enlarge, extend; a) to exaggerate; b) to magnify, extol; **2.** to furnish abundantly, to enrich, load (*alqm re*); to advance, honour; **P.** to grow, become greater.
augēscō, —, — 3 to begin to grow, to become greater.
augmen, minis *n* increase, bulk.
augur, uris *m* augur, diviner.
augurālis, e pertaining to an augur; *subst.* **augurāle, is** *n* the general's tent in a camp.
augurātiō, ōnis *f* a divining.
augurātus, ūs *m* office of an augur.
augurium, ī *n* **a**) interpretation of omens, divination, augury; prophecy; **b**) presentiment, foreboding; **c**) omen, sign.
augurius 3 = **auguralis.**
augurō 1 *and* **auguror** 1 **1.** to act as an augur, to interpret omens; **augurātō** after taking the auguries; **2.** a) to consecrate, dedicate; b) to predict, foretell, prophesy; c) to conjecture, forebode.
augustus 3 **a**) consecrated, sacred, reverend, venerable, majestic, elevated; **b**) **Augustus** 3 relating to the month of August; (*mensis*) *m* August.
aula[1], **ae** *f* **1.** yard, forecourt; **2.** a) royal court, palace; b) royal dignity; c) courtiers.
aula[2], **ae** *f* = **olla.**
aulaeum, ī *n* hangings, canopy, curtain (*esp. in a theatre*).

aulicus 3 belonging to a princely court.
auloedus, ī *m* one who sings to the flute.
aura, ae *f* breath of air, breeze, gentle breeze; **a**) air (*pl.* the upper air, heaven, the upper world); **b**) breath, wind; odour, exhalation; **c**) breath of favour (**aura popularis**); **d**) scent, slight indication.
aurārius 3 relating to gold; *subst.* **aurāria, ae** *f* gold-mine.
aurātus 3 gilded, ornamented with gold; golden.
aureolus 3 = **aureus.**
aureus 3 of gold, golden; (*nummus*) gold coin (*worth 25 denarii*); **a**) gilt, ornamented with gold; **b**) of the colour of gold, glittering like gold; **c**) beautiful, magnificent, excellent; lovely.
auri-chalcum, ī *n* **a**) imaginary precious metal; **b**) = **orichalcum.**
auricilla, ae *f* lobe of the ear.
auri-comus 3 with golden hair, with golden foliage.
auricula, ae *f* lobe of the ear; ear.
auri-fer 3 carrying gold.
auri-fex, ficis *m* goldsmith.
auriga, ae *m* charioteer, driver (*also* **A~** *a constellation*); pilot, helmsman.
aurigārius, ī *m* driver in a chariot--race.
aurigātiō, ōnis *f* a driving in a chariot-race.
auri-gena, ae sprung from gold.
auri-ger 3 bearing gold.
aurigō 1 to drive a racing-chariot.
auris, is *f* the ear; **aures alci praebere** *or* **dare** to give attention to; **a**) (*pl.*) sense of hearing, critical judgment; **b**) earth-board of a plough.
auri-scalpium, ī *n* ear-pick.
auritulus, ī *m* long-eared animal, ass.
auritus 3 long-eared; listening.
aurōra, ae *f* dawn, daybreak; the east.
aurufex = **aurifex.**
aurum, ī *n* gold, **a**) vessel *or* ornament of gold; **b**) coined gold, money; **c**) golden lustre, brightness; **d**) the Golden Age
ausculor 1 = **osculor.**
auscultātiō, ōnis *f* an obeying
auscultātor, ōris *m* listener
auscultō 1 to hear with attention, listen to (*alqd*); to obey (*alci*).
ausim *subjunctive of* **audeō.**
au-spex, icis *m* bird-seer; interpreter of omens; **a**) director, leader, protector; **b**) witness at a marriage.
auspicātus 3, *see* **auspico.**
auspicium, ī *n* **1.** a) divination by means of birds, auspices; b) the right to take auspices; c) command, guidance, power, authority, inclination, will; the beginning; **2.** sign, omen.
(**auspicō** 1 *and*) **auspicor** 1 **1.** to take the auspices, **auspicātō** after taking the auspices; **2.** to begin *or* undertake under good auspices; to begin (*alqd*); **auspicātus** 3 inaugurated, consecrated; favourable, fortunate, lucky, auspicious.
auster, strī *m* the south wind; the south.
austēritās, ātis *f* severity.
austērus 3 sour, harsh; **a**) severe, strict; **b**) morose, gloomy, sad, hard.
austrālis, e southern.
austrīnus 3 due to the south wind.
ausum, ī *n* (*and* **ausus, ūs** *m*) venture, bold undertaking.
aut *cj.* or, or else; **aut ... aut** either — or; **neque aut ... aut** and neither — nor.
autem *cj.* (*never at the beginning of a clause*) **1.** but, however, on the other hand, moreover; **2.** and now, besides, further.
authepsa, ae *f* cooking-apparatus.
auto-graphus 3 written with one's own hand.
auto-maton, ī *n* self-moving machine.
autumnālis, e autumnal.
autumnus 3 autumnal; *subst.* **autumnus, ī** *m* autumn.
autumō 1 to assert, affirm.
auxiliāris, e, -ārius 3 **a**) aiding, helping, assisting; **b**) auxiliary; **auxiliārēs, ium** *m/pl.* auxiliary troops.
auxiliātor, ōris *m* helper, assistant.
auxiliātus, ūs *m* aid
auxilior 1 to help, succour, assist (*alci*).
auxilium, ī *n* help, assistance, aid, **alci auxiliō esse** *or* **auxilium ferre** to come to one's assistance, to help; **auxiliō alcis** with the aid of; *pl.* **a**) expedients, resources; **b**) auxiliary troops, military power.

avāritia, ae (*and* **tiēs, ēī**) *f* avarice, covetousness, greediness.
avārus 3 greedy, covetous, avaricious; eagerly desirous; *adv.* **avārē, avāriter.**
ā-vehō 3 to carry *or* convey off *or* away (*alqd ab alqo, ex re in alqd*). **P.** to ride, sail, drive away.
ā-vellō, vellī *or* **vulsī, vulsum** 3 **a)** to tear, rend, pluck, pull off, snatch away (*alci alqd*); **b)** to separate by force (*alqd ab* or *de re*).
avēna, ae *f* **1.** oats, wild oats; **2.** straw; oaten *or* pastoral pipe.
aveō[1], —, — 2 to long for, desire earnestly, crave (*alqd*).
aveō[2] 2 to fare well; **avē, avēte** hail! farewell!
ā-verrō, verrī, — 3 to sweep away.
ā-verruncō 1 to avert (evil).
ā-versābilis, e abominable.
ā-versātiō, ōnis *f* dislike, aversion.
ā-versiō, ōnis *f* a turning away; **ex āversiōne** from behind.
ā-versor[1] 1 to turn oneself from, to shrink from; to repulse.
ā-versor[2] **ōris** *m* embezzler.
ā-versus 3 turned away *or* backward; back; *subst.* **āversa, ōrum** *n/pl.* the back part; — disinclined, unfavourable, hostile, averse (*with dat.*).
ā-vertō 3 to turn away *or* off, to avert, divert (*alqm* or *alqd ab, ex re ad* or *in alqd*); **P.** to turn oneself away from (*with acc.*); *intr.* to turn away; **a)** to put to flight; **b)** to carry off, purloin, steal, embezzle; **c)** to estrange, alienate; **d)** to keep off, ward off.
avia, ae *f* grandmother.
aviārium, ī *m* haunt of birds, aviary.
aviditās, ātis *f* eagerness, vehement desire, longing; covetousness, greediness.
avidus 3 eager, desirous, longing (*alcis rei, in* or *ad rem*); **a)** greedy, voracious, gluttonous; **b)** avaricious, covetous; **c)** ardent, fiery.
avis, is *f* bird; omen, portent.
avītus 3 of a grandfather, ancestral, hereditary; very old.
āvius 3 **a)** out of the way, remote, unfrequented; *subst.* **āvia, ōrum** *n/pl.* solitude; **b)** wandering.
āvocāmentum, ī *n* distraction, recreation.
ā-vocātiō, ōnis *f* a calling away, diversion.
ā-vocō 1 to call away; **a)** to withdraw, remove (*a re, in rem*); **b)** to divert, distract.
ā-volō 1 to fly away; to flee away, vanish.
ā-vors-, -vort- = **ā-vers-, -vert-.**
avunculus, ī *m* maternal uncle; great-uncle.
avus, ī *m* grandfather; ancestor.
axicia, ae *f* pair of scissors.
axis[1], **is** *m* **1.** axle-tree; wagon, car, chariot; **2.** the North Pole; **3.** the heaven; region, clime.
axis[2], **is** *m* board, plank.
axula, ae *f* = **assula.**

B

babae *int.* wonderful! strange!
bāca (bacca), ae *f* **1.** berry; round fruit, olive; **2.** pearl.
bācātus 3 adorned with pearls.
baccar, aris *n* cyclamen.
bacchābundus 3 raving like the Bacchantes.
Bacchānal, ālis *n* place devoted to Bacchus; feast of Bacchus.
Bacchānālia, ium *n/pl.* feast of Bacchus.
bacchātiō, ōnis *f* bacchanalian orgies.
bacchor 1 to celebrate the festival of Bacchus; **a**) to revel, rave, rage; **b**) to run about wildly.
bāci-fer 3 bearing berries *or* olives.
bacillum, ī *n* a little staff; the lictor's wand.
baculum, ī *n* (*and* **baculus, ī** *m*) stick, staff.
badizō 1 to walk, march.
bāi(i)olō, -olus = **bāiulō, -ulus.**
bāiulō 1 to carry a burden.
bāiulus, ī *m* porter, carrier.
balanātus 3 perfumed with balsam.
balanus, ī *f* **1.** balsam-nut; **2.** a shell-fish.
balatrō, ōnis *m* jester, buffoon.
bālātus, ūs *m* a bleating.
balbus 3 stammering.
balbūtiō 4 to stammer, stutter; to stammer out.
balineum, ī *n* = **balneum.**
bālitō 1 to bleat.
ballaena, ae *f* whale.
ballista, ae *f* military engine for hurling stones.
ballistārium, ī *n* = **ballista.**
balneārius 3 belonging to a bath; *subst.* **balneāria, ōrum** *n/pl.* bathing-rooms.
balneātor, ōris *m* bath-keeper.
balneolum, ī *n* small bathroom.
balneum, ī *n* bathroom, bath; **balnea, ōrum** *n/pl. or* **balneae, ārum** *f/pl.* public baths.
bālō 1 to bleat; *subst.* **bālantēs, ium, um** *f/pl.* sheep.
balsamum, ī *n* balsam(-tree).
balteus, ī *m* (*and* **-um, ī** *n*) sword-belt, baldric.
balūx, ūcis *f* gold-dust.
baptistērium, ī *n* bath.
barathrum, ī *n* abyss, chasm, belly.
barba, ae *f* beard.
barbaria, ae (*and* **barbariēs, ēī**) *f* **1.** foreign country (of the barbarians); **2.** rudeness, roughness, savageness, want of culture.
barbaricus 3 barbarian, foreign.
barbarus 3 **1.** foreign, strange; *subst.* **barbarus, ī** *m* foreigner, barbarian; **2.** rude, savage, uncivilized, cruel.
barbātulus 3 with a small beard.
barbātus 3 bearded; *subst.* **~, ī** *m* an old Roman.
barbi-ger 3 bearded.
barbitos, ī *m* lyre, lute.
barbula, ae *f* small beard.
bardītus, ūs *m* = **barritus.**
bardocucullus, ī *m* (Gallic) hooded cloak.
bardus 3 stupid, dull.
bāris, idos *f* Egyptian rowing-barge.
bārō, ōnis *m* simpleton.
barrītus, ūs *m* war-song of the Germans; war-cry.
barrus, ī *m* elephant.
bascauda, ae *f* bowl (*or* basket?).
bāsiātiō, ōnis *f* a kissing, kiss.
bāsiātor, ōris *m* one who kisses.
basilicus 3 royal, princely; *subst. m* a 'royal' (highest) throw at dice; *f* basilica, public building (*law-court, exchange*).
bāsiō 1 to kiss.
basis, is *f* base; **a**) pedestal; **b**) foundation; **c**) base of a triangle.
bāsium, ī *n* kiss.
batillum, ī *n* = **vatillum.**
batioca, ae *f* cup.
battuō, —, — 3 to beat, strike.
baubor 1 to bark.
baxea, ae *f* a kind of sandal.
bdellium, ī *n* a fragrant gum.
beātitās, ātis *and* **beātitūdō, inis** *f* happiness, felicity.
beātus 3 happy; **1.** prosperous, rich, wealthy, **beātī** the rich; fertile, abundant, excellent; **2.** blessed, fortunate; making happy (*dimin.* **beātulus**).

bellāria, ōrum *n/pl.* dessert, fruit.
bellātor, ōris *m* warrior; warlike.
bellātōrius 3 pertaining to war.
bellātrīx, īcis *f* warlike.
bellāx, ācis *f* warlike.
bellē *adv. of* **bellus.**
belliāt(ul)us = **bellus.**
bellicōsus 3 warlike, martial; fond of fighting *or* war.
bellicus 3 **1.** belonging to war, of war; *subst.* **bellicum, ī** *n* war-signal; **bellicum canere** to blow the war-trumpet; **2.** = **bellicosus.**
belli-ger 3 warlike.
belli-gerō 1 to wage war, to fight.
belli-potēns, tis mighty in war.
bellō 1 (*and* **bellor** 1) to wage war, fight (*cum alqo, adversus alqm, pro alqo*).
bellum, ī *n* war; **in bello** *or* **belli** in war, during war; **domi bellique** in peace and in war; combat, fight, contest.
bellus 3 pretty, charming (*dimin.* **bellulus**).
bēlua, ae *f* wild beast, monster, brute.
bēluātus 3 ornamented with figures of animals.
bēluōsus 3 abounding in monsters.
bene *adv.* (**melius, optimē**) **1.** well (better, best), properly, rightly, exactly, prosperously; **bene agere** to do *or* act well, (*cum alqo* to treat kindly); **bene dicere** to speak well of (*alci*), to commend, praise; **bene facere** to do *or* make well *or* rightly (*alci* to do good, to benefit); **bene factum** good deed, favour; **bene est** it is well, I am glad *or* satisfied; **bene te** (*or* **tibi**) good health to you!; **2.** thoroughly, fully, very much (*bene impudens, bene sanus, bene notus, bene mane*).
benedicē *adv.* with friendly speech.
bene-ficentia, ae *f* kindness, liberality.
bene-ficiārius, ī *m* privileged soldier (*exempt from menial work*).
bene-ficium, ī *n* **a)** kindness, favour, benefit, service; **beneficiō** *alcis rei* by means of; **b)** distinction, honour, promotion, grant; **c)** privilege.
bene-ficus 3 kind, generous, liberal.
bene-volēns, tis = **benevolus.**
bene-volentia, ae *f* **a)** good-will, benevolence (*erga* or *in alqm*); **b)** favour.
bene-volus 3 well wishing, benevolent, kind (*alci*).
benignitās, ātis *f* **a)** kindness, friendliness, mildness, courtesy; **b)** liberality, bounty (*in alqm*).
benignus 3 kind; **a)** goodnatured, friendly, pleasing, benignant; **b)** beneficent, liberal, obliging; fruitful, copious, rich (**benignē facere** *alci* = **bene facere**); **benignē** you are very kind, much obliged to you!
beō 1 to make happy, bless, gladden.
bēryllus, ī *m* a precious stone, beryl.
bēs, bessis *m* two thirds.
bēsālis, e weighing eight ounces.
bēstia, ae *f* beast, animal; beast of prey.
bēstiārius 3 of wild beasts; *subst. m* one who fights with wild beasts.
bēstiola, ae *f* small animal.
bēta[1]**, ae** *f* (*a vegetable*) beet.
bēta[2] the second letter of the Greek alphabet, B.
bētāceus, ī *m* beetroot.
biblio-pōla, ae *m* book-seller.
biblio-thēca, ae *f* library.
biblus, ī *f* papyrus.
bibō, bibī, — 3 to drink; to imbibe, absorb, drink in.
bibulus 3 fond of drinking; absorbent.
bi-ceps, cipitis two-headed; with two peaks.
bi-clīnium, ī *n* dining sofa for two persons.
bi-color, ōris two-coloured.
bi-corniger 3 *and* **bi-cornis, e** two-horned; two-pronged.
bi-corpor, oris with two bodies.
bi-dēns, tis with two teeth *or* prongs; *subst. m* hoe, fork; *f* sheep.
bidental, ālis *n* place struck by lightning.
bīduum, ī *n* space of two days; **bīduō** in two days.
bi-ennium, ī *n* space of two years.
bi-fāriam *adv.* in two ways *or* parts.
bi-fer 3 bearing (fruit) twice.
bi-fidus 3 split into two parts.
bi-foris, e having two doors *or* openings.
bi-fōrmātus 3 double-formed.
bi-fōrmis, e two-formed; two-shaped.
bi-frōns, tis with two foreheads.
bi-furcus 3 two-pronged.
bīgae, ārum *f/pl.* (*also* **bīga, ae**) pair of horses; two-horsed chariot.

bīgātus 3 bearing the figure of a pair of horses; **~, ī** *m* silver coin so stamped.
bi-iugis, e *and* **bi-iugus** 3 yoked two together; *subst.* **biiugī, ōrum** *m/pl.* = **bigae.**
bi-lībra, ae *f* two pounds.
bi-lībris, e weighing *or* holding two pounds.
bi-linguis, e having two tongues; **a**) speaking two languages; **b**) double-tongued, false.
bīlis, is *f* bile, bilious effusion; **a**) anger, wrath; **b**) melancholy, sadness.
bi-līx, īcis with a double thread.
bi-lūstris, e lasting ten years.
bi-maris, e lying on two seas.
bi-marītus 3 husband of two wives.
bi-māter, tris having two mothers.
bi-membris, e with double members; *subst.* **~, is** *m* centaur.
bi-mē(n)stris, e of two months.
bīmulus 3 only two years old.
bīmus 3 two years old.
bīnī, ae, a a) two by two, two for each; **b**) a pair, two.
bi-noctium, ī *n* space of two nights.
bi-nōminis, e having two names.
bi-palmis, e two palms long.
bi-partītus, bi-pertītus 3 (*adv.* **-ō**), in two parts, in two ways.
bi-patēns, tis with two doors open, wide open.
bi-pedālis, e two feet long.
bipenni-fer 3 bearing a two-edged axe.
bi-pennis, e double-edged; *subst.* **~, is** *f* double-edged axe.
bi-pertītus 3 = **bipartitus.**
bi-pēs, edis two-footed, biped.
bi-rēmis, e two-oared; *subst.* **bi-rēmis, is** *f* ship with two sets of oars.
bis *adv.* twice; in two ways.
bi-sulcus 3 (*or* **cis, ce**) forked, split.
bītō 3 to go.
bitūmen, inis *n* mineral pitch, asphalt, bitumen.
bitūmineus 3 bituminous.
bi-vertex, icis with two peaks.
bi-vius 3 having two ways; *subst.* **bivium, ī** *n* place where two roads meet.
blaesus 3 lisping, stammering.
blandi-dicus 3, **blandi-loquus** 3, **blandi-loquentulus** 3 smooth-tongued.
blandi-loquentia, ae *f* flattery.
blandīmentum, ī *n* = **blanditia.**
blandior 4 **a**) to flatter, caress, coax; **b**) to please, gratify, to be favourable (*with dat.*).
blanditia, ae *f* **a**) flattery, caress; **b**) blandishments, allurements; **c**) delight, enticement, charm; **d**) dainty.
blandus 3 **a**) flattering, fondling, caressing; **b**) charming, agreeable, enticing, alluring; — *adv.* **blandē, -diter, -dītim.**
blaterō 1 *and* **blatiō** 4 to babble, prate.
blatta, ae *f* moth, cockroach.
blennus 3 stupid.
bliteus 3 insipid, silly.
blit(e)um, ī *n* a tasteless kitchen-vegetable.
boārius 3 relating to cattle.
boia, ae *f* collar.
bōlētātiō, ōnis *f* mushroom-eating.
bōlētus, ī *m* mushroom.
bolus, ī *m* throw of dice; gain, profit, advantage.
bombax *int.* strange! indeed!
bombus, ī *m* a humming.
bombȳcinus 3 of silk.
bombȳx, ȳcis *m* silk-worm; silk.
bonitās, ātis *f* a) goodness; **b**) virtue, integrity, kindness.
bonum, ī *n* **a**) a good, the good; **b**) excellence; **c**) profit, advantage; **bonō esse** *alci* to be of advantage; **bonum publicum** the common weal; **d**) *pl.* **bona** goods, property.
bonus 3 (*comp.* **melior, us,** *superl.* **optimus** 3, *adv.* **bene**) good; **1.** a) excellent, perfect; b) fit, proper, suitable, able, clever; c) brave, courageous; d) noble, distinguished, genteel, aristocratic, **optimī** *m/pl.* = **optimates;** e) rich, wealthy; f) considerable, large; g) fair, nice, delicate; h) favourable, propitious, kind; **bonae res** good fortune; **2.** a) honest, righteous, virtuous, faithful, chaste; **bonus vir** man of honour; **bonae artes** good qualities, fine arts, liberal sciences; b) kind, auspicious, favourable; c) patriotic, loyal, aristocratic.
boō 1 to roar, to echo.
boreās, ae *m* the north-wind; the north.
borēus 3 northern.
bōs, bovis *m* and *f* ox, bull, cow.

botryō, ōnis *m* bunch of grapes.
botulārius, ī *m* sausage-maker.
botulus (*and* **botellus**), **ī** *m* sausage.
bovārius 3 = **boarius.**
bovīle, is *n* = **bubile.**
bovillus 3 = **bubulus.**
brācae, ārum *pl.* (*and* **brāca,** ae) *f* breeches, trousers.
brācātus 3 **a**) wearing breeches; **b**) foreign; Transalpine.
bracchiālis, e of the arm.
bracchiolum, ī *n, dim. of* **bracchium.**
bracchium, ī *n* the whole arm; **a**) lower arm, fore-arm; **b**) branch of the sea, of trees; yard of a sail.
brassica, ae *f* cabbage.
brattea *and* **bratteola, ae** *f* gold-leaf.
bratteātus 3 gilded; fair-seeming, deceptive.
breviārium, ī *n* summary.
breviculus 3 shortish.
brevi-loquēns, tis short in speaking.
brevis, e short; **1.** a) small, narrow, shallow, *subst.* **breve, is** *n* shallow place, shoal; b) little, indifferent, brief, concise; **brevī** *adv.* in short, shortly; **2.** short in time, **brevī** (*tempore*) in a short time.
brevitās, ātis *f* shortness; brevity, conciseness.
breviter *adv. of* **brevis.**
brūma, ae *f* the shortest day in the year, the winter solstice; winter time, wintry cold.
brūmālis, e belonging to the winter solstice; wintry.
brūtus 3 heavy, inert; stupid.
būbīle, is *n* ox-stall.
būbō, ōnis *m* (*f*) owl.
bubulcitor 1 to be a cowherd.
bubulcus, ī *m* ox-driver, one who ploughs with oxen
būbulus 3 of cattle, of oxen; *subst.* **būbula, ae** *f* beef
bū-caeda, ae *m* one who is whipped with thongs of ox-hide.
bucca, ae *f* cheek, mouth.
buccella, ae *f* small mouthful.
buccō, ōnis *m* babbler, fool.
buccula, ae *f* cheek; cheek-piece.
bucculentus 3 puffy-cheeked.
bū-cer(i)us 3 ox-horned.
būcētum, ī *n* cattle-pasture.
būcina, ae *f* horn, crooked trumpet; **a**) shepherd's horn; **b**) trumpet-call; **c**) Triton's-horn.
būcinātor, ōris *m* trumpeter.
būcolicus 3 belonging to shepherds, bucolic.
būcula, ae *f* young cow, heifer.
būfō, ōnis *m* toad.
bulbus, ī *m* onion, garlic.
būlē, ēs *f* Greek council.
būleuta, ae *m* councillor.
būleutērium, ī *n* senate-house.
bulla, ae *f* **a**) bubble; **b**) boss, stud; **c**) amulet.
bullātus 3 wearing a *bulla* (*i.e.* a boy).
bū-mastus, ī *f* large grape.
būris, is *m* crooked beam holding the ploughshare.
busti-rapus, ī *m* robber of tombs.
bustuārius 3 belonging to a place for burning the dead.
bustum, ī *n* place for burning the dead; pyre, tomb.
bū-thysia, ae *f* sacrifice of oxen.
buxētum, ī *n* plantation of box-trees.
buxeus 3 yellowish.
buxi-fer 3 bearing box-trees.
buxus, ī *f and* **buxum, ī** *n* box(tree); **a**) boxwood; **b**) box flute, pipe, comb, spinning-top.

C

C. *abbr.* **a**) = **Gaius; b**) = **condemno; c**) = **centum; d**) **Cn.** = **Gnaeus; e**) **CIↃ** = 1000.
caballus, ī *m* pack-horse, nag.
cacāturiō 4 to want to evacuate the bowels.
cachinnātiō, ōnis *f* = **cachinnus.**
cachinnō[1] 1 to laugh aloud.
cachinnō[2], **ōnis** *m* scoffer.
cachinnus, ī *m* loud laugh.
cacō 1 to evacuate the bowels; to defile.
caco-ēthes, is *n* disease.
caco-zēlus, ī *m* bad imitator.
cacula, ae *m* servant of a soldier.
cacūmen, inis *n* point, extremity, top, height.
cacūminō 1 to make pointed.
cadāver, eris *n* dead body, corpse; **a**) carcass; **b**) ruins.
cadāverōsus 3 like a corpse.
cadō, cecidī, cāsum 3 to fall; **1.** to fall down, sink down (*de* or *ex re in alqd*), to descend; a) to flow down; b) to slip, drop; c) to be thrown; **2.** to go down, set, to fall down prostrate; a) to be killed, be slain; b) to be conquered, captured, destroyed; c) to lose strength, be overthrown, decline, vanish, decay, cease; **animō cadere** to lose courage, **causā** *or* **in iūdiciō cadere** to lose a law-suit; d) to fall flat, fail (*of theatrical representations*); **3.** to fall into (*in alqd*); a) to get into, to incur, fall under, be subject *or* exposed to; b) to belong, agree, refer, be suitable, fit; c) to happen; d) to terminate, end (*words*); **4.** to occur, come to pass, turn out.
cādūceātor, ōris *m* herald, officer bearing the flag of truce.
cādūceus, ī *m* a herald's staff.
cādūci-fer, ferī *m* bearer of the herald's staff.
cadūcus 3 **1.** falling, fallen; hurled (*flash of lightning*); **2.** inclined to fall; a) frail, perishable, transitory; b) *in law:* rendered void, having no heir *or* owner.
cadus, ī *m* wine-jar.
caeci-genus 3 born blind.
caecitās, ātis *f* blindness.
caecō 1 **a**) to make blind, to blind; **b**) to make obscure.
caecus 3 blind, not seeing; **a**) mentally *or* morally blind; **b**) dark, obscure; **c**) invisible, hidden; **d**) unintelligible, unknown; **e**) vague, uncertain, doubtful, aimless.
caedēs, is *f* **1.** a cutting off *or* down; **2.** a killing, slaughter; a) murder; b) massacre, bloodshed; c) persons slain.
caedō, cecīdī, caesum 3 to cut, hew; **1.** to strike, beat, cudgel; **2.** a) to fell, cut down *or* off, cut to pieces; b) to slay, kill, murder.
caelāmen, inis *n* bas-relief, chased work.
caelātor, ōris *m* chaser, engraver, carver.
caelātūra, ae *f* (art of) engraving.
caelebs, libis unmarried, single.
caeles, itis heavenly; *m/pl.* the gods.
caelestis, e a) belonging to heaven, heavenly, celestial; *subst.* god, deity; **caelestia, ium** *n/pl.* heavenly things *or* bodies; **b**) divine, superhuman, glorious.
caelibātus, ūs *m* celibacy.
caeli-cola, ae *m* dweller in heaven, god.
caelicus 3 heavenly; magnificent.
caeli-fer 3 bearing the heavens.
caeli-potēns, tis mighty in heaven.
caelō 1 to engrave in relief, to chase, carve; to adorn.
caelum[1], **ī** *n* the sky, the heaven; **de caelo tangi** to be struck by lightning; **de caelo servare** to observe the signs of heaven; **a**) the home of the gods, the upper world; **b**) clime, zone, region; **c**) air, atmosphere, weather; **d**) height, highest joy, immortality.
caelum[2], **ī** *n* engraver's chisel.
caementum, ī *n* unhewn stone.
caenōsus 3 muddy.
caenum, ī *n* dirt, mud; lowest strata of society.
caepa, ae *f and* **caepe, is** *n* onion.

caerimōnia, caeremōnia, ae *f* **a**) holy dread, reverence, veneration; **b**) sanctity, sacredness; **c**) religious action *or* usage, ceremony.
caeruleus *and* **caerulus** 3 dark-blue, blue-black; black; (blue-)green, dark; *subst.* **caerula, ōrum** *n/pl.* the blue sea.
caesariātus 3 long-haired.
caesariēs, ēī *f* the hair of the head, bushy hair.
caesīcius 3 cut, tailored (?).
caesim *adv.* by cutting; in short sentences.
caesius 3 (with) bright blue (eyes).
caespes, itis *m* turf, grass; altar of turf.
caestus, ūs *m* boxing-glove made of thongs.
caetra, ae *f* short Spanish shield.
caetrātus 3 armed with a short shield.
calamārius 3 pertaining to a writing-reed.
calamister, trī *m* = **calamistrum.**
calamistrātus 3 curled with the curling-iron.
calamistrum, ī *n* curling-iron for the hair; artificial ornament in speech.
calamitās, ātis *f* **a**) loss, damage, injury, disaster, calamity, ruin; **b**) defeat, misfortune in war.
calamitōsus 3 ruinous, disastrous, destructive; suffering damage, exposed to injury, unhappy.
calamus, ī *m* **a**) reed, cane; **b**) reed-pen, reed-pipe, arrow, fishing-rod, lime-twig.
calathiscus, ī *m*, *dim. of* **calathus.**
calathus, ī *m* **a**) wicker-basket; **b**) bowl, cup.
calātor, ōris *m* attendant (*of priests*).
calcar, āris *n* spur; incitement.
calceāmentum, ī *n* shoe.
calceārium, ī *n* shoe-money.
calceātus, ūs *m* shoes, sandals.
calceō 1 to furnish with shoes.
calceolārius, ī *m* shoemaker.
calceolus, ī *m* little shoe.
calceus, ī *m* shoe, half-boot.
calcitrō[1] 1 to kick; to be stubborn, refractory.
calcitrō[2], **ōnis** *m* a kicker.
calcō 1 to tread, to tread on; **a**) to tread down, trample upon; **b**) to despise, abuse.
calculātor, ōris *m* teacher of arithmetic.
calculus, ī *m* small stone, pebble; **1.** stone used a) in reckoning; b) in playing draughts; c) for voting; **2.** a computing, calculating; **3.** stone (*in the bladder*).
caldārius 3 belonging to warmth; supplied with warm water; *subst.* **-um, ī** *n* room for taking warm baths.
caldus 3 = **calidus.**
cale-facio 3 to make warm *or* hot; to heat, to excite.
cale-factō 1 to make warm.
cale-fīō, P. *of* **calefacio.**
Calendae, ārum *f/pl.* the calends, first day of each month.
calendārium, ī *n* debt-book, account-book.
caleō, uī, calitūrus 2 to be warm *or* hot; **a**) to glow, be inflamed, enamoured; **b**) to be urged on zealously; **c**) to be yet fresh *or* new.
calēscō, luī, — 3 to grow warm *or* hot, to glow.
cal-faciō = **calefacio.**
calidus 3 **a**) warm, hot; **b**) fiery, rash, eager; *subst.* **calida, ae** *f* warm water.
caliendrum, ī *n* wig for women.
caliga, ae *f* half-boot of soldiers.
caligātus 3 wearing soldier's shoes.
cālīginōsus 3 dark, obscure, gloomy.
cālīgō[1], **inis** *f* darkness, obscurity, night; **a**) mist, vapour, fog; **b**) mental darkness; **c**) calamity, affliction.
cālīgō[2] 1 **a**) to cover with darkness, to obscure; **b**) to be dark, gloomy, blind.
calix, icis *m* **a**) cup, goblet, drinking-vessel; **b**) pot.
callainus 3 emerald-green.
calleō, uī, — 2 **a**) to be thick-skinned, callous; **b**) to be clever, experienced, versed, skilful; **c**) to know by experience *or* practice.
calliditās, ātis *f* **a**) shrewdness, skill; **b**) cunning, craft, slyness, artfulness.
callidus 3 dexterous, skilful; **a**) practised, versed, shrewd; **b**) well-wrought, ingenious; **c**) crafty, cunning, artful.
callis, is *f* (*and m*) **a**) stony foot-way, foot-path, mountain-path; **b**) alpine meadow.
callōsus 3 thick-skinned.

callum, ī *n* thick skin; insensibility.
calō[1] 1 to call together.
cālō[2], **ōnis** *m* horse-boy, groom, soldier's servant.
calor, ōris *m* **a**) warmth, heat, glow, summer heat; **b**) heat of passion, fire of love, zeal.
caltha, ae *f* marigold.
calthula, ae *f* yellow robe.
calumnia, ae *f* **a**) artifice, chicanery, deceitful pretence, malicious prosecution; **b**) penalty for false accusation; **c**) false statement, sophistry.
calumniātor, ōris *m* contriver of tricks, intriguer, malicious prosecutor, false accuser.
calumnior 1 **a**) to contrive tricks, to intrigue; **b**) to prosecute maliciously, to censure, depreciate, calumniate.
calva, ae *f* bald head, scalp.
calvitium, ī *n* baldness.
calvor, —, — 3 to deceive.
calvus 3 bald, without hair.
calx[1], **cis** *f* (*m*) **a**) limestone, lime; **b**) goal in a race-course; **c**) counter in a game.
calx[2], **cis** *f* (*m*) heel, hoof.
camella, ae *f* goblet, cup.
camēlus, ī *m* (*f*) camel.
camera, ae *f* **a**) vault, arch; **b**) flat boat with a covering.
camīnus, ī *m* **a**) fire-place; **b**) furnace, forge, smithy.
cammarus, ī *m* lobster.
campester, stris, stre a) pertaining to a field *or* plain, flat, level; **b**) of the Campus Martius, used in sport; *subst.* **campestre, is** *n* leathern apron used in wrestling.
campus, ī *m* **a**) field, plain, level place, open country, level of the sea; **b**) the Campus Martius, place of assemblage for the people in Rome, athletic grounds.
camur, a, um crooked.
canālis, is *m* (*f*) water-pipe, conduit, channel, canal.
cancellī, ōrum *m/pl.* lattice, enclosure, balustrade, grating, railings; boundaries.
cancer, crī *m* **a**) crab (*also* **C~** *sign of the zodiac*); **b**) cancer; **c**) south, summer heat.
candē-faciō 3 to make shining white.
candēla, ae *f* **a**) wax-light, candle; **b**) cord covered with wax.
candēlābrum, ī *n* candlestick, lamp-stand.
candeō, uī, — 2 to be shining white, to glitter, glow.
candēscō, duī, — 3 to become glittering white; to glow.
candidātōrius 3 pertaining to a candidate.
candidātus 3 clothed in white; *subst.* **~, ī** *m* candidate.
candidulus 3 shining white.
candidus 3 shining white, glittering, white; **a**) clothed in white; **b**) bright, clear, fair, beautiful, lucid; **c**) artless, honest, upright; **d**) happy, fortunate, lucky, joyful.
candor, ōris *m* dazzling whiteness, lustre, brightness; **a**) dazzling beauty; **b**) clearness; **c**) integrity, sincerity, frankness.
cāneō, uī, — 2 to be grey, white, hoary.
canē-phoros, ī *f* basket-bearer.
cānēscō, —, — 3 to become grey, white, hoary, old.
canīcula, ae *f* little dog; **C~** the Dog-star, Sirius.
canīnus 3 relating to a dog, of a dog.
canis, is *m and f* dog; **a**) malicious, insolent, shameless person; **b**) parasite; **c**) sea-dog; **d**) the Dog-star; **e**) the worst throw (*in dice*).
canistra, ōrum *n/pl.* plaited basket.
cānitiēs, ēī *f* **a**) grey colour; **b**) grey hair.
canna, ae *f* reed, cane, reed-pipe.
cannabis, is *f* hemp.
canō, cecinī, (cantum) 3 to sound **1.** a) to sing; b) to crow, croak, hoot; c) to play on a musical instrument (*abl.*); **2.** *trans.* to utter; a) to sing, compose (*poems*); b) to celebrate, praise; c) to prophesy, announce; d) **bellicum, classicum, signum canere** to give the signal for battle; **receptui canere** to sound the signal for retreat.
canor, ōris *m* song, sound.
canōrus 3 melodious, harmonious; *subst.* **canōrum, ī** *n* melodious sound.
cantāmen, inis *n* incantation, charm.
cantātor, ōris *m* singer.
cantērīnus 3 of a horse.
cantērius, ī *m* gelding (*horse*).
cantharis, idis *f* Spanish fly.

cantharus, ī *m* **a**) tankard; **b**) a sea fish.
canthērius, ī *m* = **canterius.**
canthus, ī *m* tire; wheel.
canticum, ī *n* musical monologue; song; singsong.
cantilēna, ae *f* old song, silly prattle, gossip.
cantiō, ōnis *f* **a**) song; **b**) incantation.
cantitō 1 to sing often *or* usually.
cantiuncula, ae *f* an alluring song.
cantō 1 **a**) = **cano; b**) to recite incantations, to enchant.
cantor, ōris *m* singer; poet; **a**) reciter, player; **b**) eulogist.
cantrīx, īcis *f* female singer.
cantus, ūs *m* **a**) song, a crowing, croaking; **b**) music, sound; **c**) incantation; **d**) prophecy.
cānus 3 **a**) whitish-grey, white; *subst.* **cānī, ōrum** *m/pl.* grey hair; **b**) old, venerable.
capācitās, ātis *f* room for holding, capacity.
capāx, ācis a) wide, large, spacious, roomy, capacious; **b**) able to grasp, capable, apt, fit for.
capēdō, inis *f* sacrificial bowl.
capēduncula, ae *f* small bowl used in sacrifices.
capella, ae *f* (little) she-goat.
caper, prī *m* he-goat; smell in the arm-pits.
caperrō 1 to be wrinkled.
capessō, sīvī, sītum 3 to seize eagerly, to lay hold of, snatch at; **a**) to take in hand, busy oneself with, enter upon, engage in, **rem publicam** to enter public life; **b**) to strive to reach, to repair to, resort to (*alqd*).
capillāmentum, ī *n* wig; plant-hair.
capillāre, is *n* hair-oil.
capillātus 3 hairy, having hair.
capillus, ī *m* hair of the head *or* of the beard.
capiō, cēpī, captum 3 **1.** to take, seize, grasp; **arma** to take up arms; a) to capture, take, occupy, hold; b) to arrive at, reach (*alqd, portum*); c) to take possession of, catch, make prisoner, take by force of arms; d) to win, gain (*gloriam virtutibus*); e) to undertake, enter upon, engage in, **fugam capere** to flee, **consilium c.** to resolve, plan, propose; f) to win, fascinate, enchain, charm, allure, deceive, mislead, betray, delude; g) to harm, lame, injure, attack, weaken (**mente captus** distracted, mad, lunatic); **2.** to choose, select (*locum, sibi tabernaculum, alqm socium*); **3.** to receive, get, obtain, acquire (*alqd ab alqo, ex re*) **pecuniam** *ab alqo* to accept a bribe; to enjoy, reap (*fructum*), to suffer, be subjected to; **4.** to contain, hold, suffice for; to allow of, comprehend; to comprehend mentally.
capis, idis *f* sacrificial bowl with one handle.
capistrō 1 to harness, halter.
capistrum, ī *n* halter, muzzle.
capital, ālis *n* capital crime.
capitālis, e relating to the head, to life; **a**) capital, deadly, endangering life, **hostis** ~ a deadly enemy; **b**) chief, pre-eminent, distinguished.
capitō, ōnis *m* one who has a large head.
capitulātim *adv.* summarily, briefly.
capitulum, ī *n* small head.
cāpō, ōnis *m* capon.
capparis, is *f* ⚘ caper.
capra, ae *f* she-goat (*also a star*); smell under the armpits.
caprea, ae *f* wild goat, roe.
capreāginus 3 goatish.
capreolus, ī *m* **1.** roebuck; **2.** support, prop.
Capri-cornus, ī Capricorn (*sign of the zodiac*).
capri-fīcus, ī *f* wild fig-tree.
capri-genus 3 born of goats.
capri-mulgus, ī *m* goat-milker, countryman, herdsman.
caprīnus 3 of goats.
capri-pēs, pedis goat-footed.
capsa, ae *f* chest, box, case.
capsārius, ī *m* slave who carried the books of schoolboys.
capsula, ae *f* smal lbox (*for personal property*).
captātiō, ōnis *f* a catching at, eager seizing; **verborum** a quibbling.
captātor, ōris *m* one who seizes eagerly; legacy-hunter.
captiō, ōnis *f* **a**) deceit, fraud, cheat; **b**) fallacy, sophism; **c**) injury, loss.
captiōsus 3 **a**) deceitful; **b**) sophistical, captious; *subst.* **captiōsum, ī** *n* sophism.
captiuncula, ae *f* fallacy, sophism.
captīvitās, ātis *f* **a**) captivity; **b**) conquest, capture.

captīvus 3 taken in war, *subst.* **captīvus, ī** *m* prisoner, captive; **a**) pertaining to a prisoner; **b**) captured, conquered.
captō 1 to strive to seize (*alqd*); **a**) to catch *or* snatch at; **b**) to try to obtain, desire, seek, hunt for (*alqd aure* to listen eagerly).
captūra, ae *f* prey, booty; day's wages.
captus, ūs *m* **a**) a taking, seizing, catching; **b**) power of comprehension, understanding, capacity.
capūdō, inis *f* = **capedo.**
capulāris, e ready for a coffin.
capulus, ī *m* **a**) handle; hilt of a sword; **b**) coffin.
caput, itis *n* the head; **a**) man, person, individual, animal; **b**) top, summit, point, end, extremity; origin, source, mouth (*of a river*); **c**) life; **capitis accusare** to prosecute on a capital charge; **causa** *or* **iudicium capitis** trial of a capital crime; **d**) civil rights, political life, citizenship; **e**) the chief point; chief, leader, author, contriver; chief thing, leading principle, most important part; principal place, capital; principal sum, stock; division, chapter.
carbaseus 3 of linen.
carbasus, ī *f*, **carbasa, ōrum** *n/pl.* linen garment, sail, awning.
carbō, ōnis *m* coal, charcoal.
carbōnārius, ī *m* charcoal-burner.
carbunculus, ī *m* small coal; grief, sorrow.
carcer, eris *m* barrier, starting-place; prison, jail.
carcerārius 3 of a prison.
carchēsium, ī *n* drinking-cup; top of a mast.
carcinōma, atis *n* cancerous ulcer.
cardaces, um *m/pl.* class of Persian soldiers.
cardiacus 3 suffering from a disease of the stomach.
cardō, inis *m* door-hinges, pivot and socket of doors; **a**) pole, turning point; **b**) chief circumstance, crisis.
carduus, ī *m* thistle.
cārectum, ī *n* place full of reeds.
careō, uī, — 2 to be without, be free from, be destitute of (*alqa re*), **a**) to abstain from, deny oneself, make no use of; **b**) to be deprived of, to want, miss.
cārex, icis *f* reed-grass, sedge.
cariēs, ēī *f* decay, rottenness.
carīna, ae *f* **a**) keel of a ship; **b**) vessel, ship.
carinārius, ī *m* dyer with nut-brown.
carinum, ī *n* nut-brown garment.
cariōsus 3 rotten, decayed.
cāris, idis *f* crab.
cāritās, ātis *f* dearness, high price; **a**) scarcity; **b**) high esteem, regard, respect, love, affection.
carmen, inis *n* **a**) song, tune; **b**) poem, poetry, lyric poetry; poetic inscription; **c**) formula (*religious* or *legal*); incantation, prediction, oracle.
carnārium, ī *n* frame of meat-hooks; larder, pantry.
carnārius, ī *m* a lover of flesh.
carni-fex, icis *m* executioner, hangman; **a**) tormentor, murderer; **b**) villain.
carnificīna, ae *f* **a**) the hangman's office; **b**) rack, torture, torment.
carnificius 3 of an executioner.
carnificō 1 to cut to pieces, behead.
carnu-, *see* **carni-.**
carō, carnis *f* flesh.
carpatinus 3 of raw hide.
carpentum, ī *n* two-wheeled carriage, coach.
carpō, psī, ptum 3 to pluck; **a**) to pluck off; **b**) to graze on, eat; **c**) to crop, gather; to enjoy, make use of; **d**) to divide into parts, to take one's way, to pass over, sail along *or* through; **e**) to select, choose out; **f**) to gnaw at (*alqd*); to lacerate; to tear *or* pull to pieces; to weaken, enfeeble; to blame, censure, slander, revile; to harass, alarm.
carptim *adv.* by pieces; **a**) repeatedly; **b**) singly; **c**) by degrees.
carptor, ōris *m* carver.
car(r)ō 3 to card (wool).
carrūca, ae *f* four-wheeled carriage.
carrus, ī *m* cart, wagon.
caruncula, ae *f* a piece of flesh.
cārus 3 dear, valued, loved.
caryōta, ae (*and* **caryōtis, idis**) *f* a kind of date.
casa, ae *f* hut, cottage, cabin.
cascus 3 very old.
cāse(ol)us, ī *m* cheese.
casia, ae *f* **a**) cinnamon; **b**) spurge-laurel.
cassida, ae *f* helmet of metal.
cassis[1], **idis** *f* helmet of metal.

cassis[2], **is** *m* (*mostly* **cassēs, ium** *m/pl.*) hunting-net; a) snare; **b**) spider's web.
cassō 1 to tumble.
cassus 3 empty, hollow; **a**) *with gen.* or *abl.* devoid of, deprived of, without; **b**) vain, futile, useless, fruitless (*adv.* **in cassum** *or* **incassum**).
castanea, ae *f* chestnut (tree).
castellānus 3 pertaining to a castle *or* fortress; *subst.* **~, ī** *m* occupant of a castle.
castellātim *adv.* in single fortresses.
castellum, ī *n* castle, fort, stronghold; refuge.
castēria, ae *f* sleeping room for rowers.
castīgābilis, e deserving punishment.
castīgātiō, ōnis *f* **a**) a correcting, censure, reproof; **b**) punishment.
castīgātor, ōris *m* corrector, reprover.
castīgātōrius 3 reproving.
castīgō 1 **a**) to correct, reprove; **b**) to punish; **c**) to amend; **d**) to restrain, hold in.
castimōnia, ae *f* purity, chastity; abstinence.
castitās, ātis *f* chastity, purity of morals.
castor, oris *m* beaver.
castoreum, ī *n* secretion of the beaver, castoreum.
castrēnsis, e of a camp.
castrō 1 to emasculate, castrate; enervate.
castrum, ī *n* **1.** = **castellum; 2.** *pl.* military camp, encampment; a) military service; b) a day's march; c) political party, philosophic school.
castus 3 pure, innocent; **a**) chaste; **b**) pious, religious; **c**) continent, disinterested.
casula, ae *f* cottage.
cāsus, ūs *m* a falling; **1.** fall; a) false step; destruction; b) end; **2.** a) accident, event, occurrence, chance; b) disaster, misfortune, calamity, death; **3.** (*in grammar*) case.
cata-dromus, ī *m* tight-rope.
cata-gelasimus 3 exposed to ridicule.
cata-graphus 3 painted, coloured.
catamītus, ī *m* catamite.
cata-phractēs, ae *m* a coat of mail with iron scales.
cata-phractus 3 mailed.
cataplēxis *f* a wonder.
cataplūs, ī *m* ship(s) coming to land.
cata-pulta, ae *f* engine of war for throwing arrows.
catapultārius 3 of a catapulta.
cata-racta, ae *f* *and* **-tēs, ae** *m* **a**) waterfall; sluice; **b**) portcullis.
cataractria, ae *f* a kind of spice.
cata-scopus, ī *m* spy-ship.
cata-sta, ae *f* stage for the sale of slaves.
catēia, ae *f* a wooden spear.
catēlla, ae *f* (*and* **catēllus, ī** *m*) a little chain.
catellus, ī *m* (*and* **catella, ae** *f*) little dog.
catēna, ae *f* chain, fetter; **a**) barrier, restraint, check; **b**) bond.
catēnārius 3 kept on a chain.
catēnātus 3 chained, fettered.
caterva, ae *f* crowd, troop, band, throng; company of actors.
catervārius 3 belonging to a troop.
catervātim *adv.* in companies, in troops.
cathedra, ae *f* arm-chair, sedan-chair.
cathedrārius 3 professorial, academic.
catillō 1 to lick plates.
catillus, ī *m* small bowl, dish.
catīnus, ī *m* bowl, dish.
catōmum back (?).
catulus, ī *m* young animal, whelp; young dog.
catus 3 intelligent, sagacious, wise.
cauda, ae *f* tail, **caudam trahere** to be mocked; appendage.
caudeus 3 of rushes.
caudex, icis *m* **a**) trunk of a tree, log; **b**) wooden tablet for writing, book, notebook, account-book.
caudicālis, e relating to wood.
caulae, ārum *f/pl.* **1.** spaces, pores; **2.** sheep-fold.
caulis, is *m* stalk, stem of a plant; cabbage.
caupō, ōnis *m* innkeeper.
caupōna, ae *f* inn, tavern.
caupōnius 3 of a tavern.
caupōnor 1 to traffic *or* trade in.
caupōnula, ae *f* wretched tavern.
caurus, ī *m* the north-west wind.
causa, ae *f* **1.** cause, reason, motive, inducement, occasion (*with gen.* or *quod*, *cur*, *ut*, *inf.*); a) **causā** *with gen.* on account of, for the sake of,

with respect to, **meā causā** for my sake, on my behalf; b) good reason, **cum causā** with good reason; c) well founded excuse; d) pretext, feigned cause, pretence, **per causam** under a pretext; **2.** cause, affair, business; a) lawsuit, judicial process; **causam agere, defendere** to carry on *or* conduct a law-suit, to defend a case; **causam perdere** = **causā cadere** to lose a lawsuit; question, matter for discussion; b) party, side, faction; c) condition, circumstances, situation; d) relation of friendship (*cum alqo*).

causārius 3 sickly, invalid.

causia, ae *f* broad-brimmed hat.

causi-dicus, ī *m* advocate.

causi-ficor 1 to plead an excuse.

causor 1 to give as a reason, to pretend (*alqd*, with *acc. c. inf.*, with *quod*).

caussa, ae *f* = **causa.**

causula, ae *f* petty lawsuit *or* cause.

cautēla, ae *f* caution.

cautēs, is *f* sharp rock, crag.

cautim *adv.* = **caute (cautus).**

cautiō, ōnis *f* **a**) precaution, circumspection; precautionary measure; **b**) security, bond, bail, obligation, warranty.

cautor, ōris *m* **a**) one who is on his guard; **b**) surety.

cautus 3 **a**) circumspect, wary, careful; **b**) secured, safe.

cav-aedium, ī *n* inner yard of a house.

cavea, ae *f* hollow place, cavity; **a**) den, cave, stall, birdcage, beehive; **b**) auditorium in a theatre, theatre, the spectators.

caveō, cāvī, cautum 2 **1.** to be on one's guard, take care, take heed (*alqm*, *ab alqo*, *alqd*, *a re*, *ne*, *ut*); **cavē** (*with following subj.*) take care lest, see that... not; **2.** to provide for, have a care for (*alci a re*); a) to lend aid to; b) to give security *or* bail for (*alci alqa re*, *de re*); c) to make oneself secure, to procure bail for oneself (*ab alqo*); d) to stipulate, order, decree.

caverna, ae *f* hollow, cave, cavern; **a**) hold of a ship; **b**) tank.

cavilla, ae *f* jesting, raillery.

cavillātiō, ōnis *f* a jeering, jesting, railing, scoffing, sneering.

cavillātor, ōris *m* jester, jeerer, humourist.

cavillor 1 **a**) to jest, jeer, rail, scoff, mock (*alqd* or *cum alqo*); **b**) to shuffle.

cavō 1 to make hollow, to hollow out; to pierce through.

cavus 3 hollow, excavated, concave; enveloping; *subst.* (*and* **cavum, ī** *n*) a hollow, hole.

cedo[1] (*pl.* **cette**) **a**) here with it! give here! (*with acc.*); **b**) out with it! let us hear!; **c**) only look!

cēdō[2], **cessī, cessum** 3 **1.** to go, move, go along (= **incedo**); a) *in alqd* to take the place of, to change to, to become; b) *alci* or *in alqm* to fall to the lot of, to accrue; c) *alci* to turn out, result; d) *pro re* to pass for; **2.** to give place, go away, withdraw (with *abl.* or *ex*, *de re*); a) to give up (*property*), to yield, cede; b) to pass away, vanish; c) to retreat before, submit to; **3.** to comply with, yield to, obey.

cedrus, ī *f* cedar, juniper; cedar-wood, cedar-oil.

cēlātor, ōris *m* concealer.

celeber, bris, bre (*also* **celebris, bre**) much visited, frequented, populous; **a**) renowned, distinguished, celebrated; **b**) solemn, festive; **c**) well-known, common, usual; **d**) numerous, frequent.

celebrātiō, ōnis *f* **a**) numerous assembly; **b**) festival.

celebrātor, ōris *m* one who celebrates.

celebrātus 3 = **celeber.**

celebritās, ātis *f* **a**) numerous concourse *or* attendance at; **b**) festivity, celebration; **c**) multitude, large assembly; **d**) frequency, repetition; **e**) fame, renown.

celebrō 1 **1.** to visit frequently *or* in great numbers, to frequent; a) to accompany in great numbers, to crowd round; b) to celebrate, keep a festival; **2.** to do frequently, to practise, engage in, repeat; a) to make known, publish, proclaim; b) to praise, honour, make famous; c) to fill with (*alqd alqa re*).

celer, eris, ere swift, quick, speedy; *subst.* **Celerēs, um** *m/pl.* Roman knights; **a**) quick in mind, lively; **b**) hasty; *adv.* **celeriter** (*and* **celere**).

celeri-pēs, pedis swift-footed.

celeritās, ātis *f* swiftness, quickness; adroitness.
celerō 1 a) to quicken, hasten, accelerate; b) to make haste.
celeuma, atis *n* coxswain's command (*giving the time to a crew*).
cella, ae *f* cell; a) chamber, room, closet; b) granary, cellar, store-room; c) cell of a beehive; d) sanctuary.
cellārius 3 of a store-room; *subst.* storekeeper.
cellula, ae *f dimin.* of **cella.**
cēlō 1 to conceal, hide from (*alqd, alqm*), to keep secret; **P. cēlor de re** to be kept ignorant of.
celōc(u)la, ae *f dimin.* of **celox.**
celōx, ōcis *f* swift-sailing ship, yacht.
celsus 3 a) raised high, lifted, towering; b) high, lofty, elevated; c) noble, high-spirited; d) haughty.
cēna, ae *f* principal meal, dinner; **inter cēnam** at dinner-time.
cēnāculum, ī *n* a) dining-room; b) tenement, flat; attic.
cēnāticus 3 pertaining to a dinner.
cēnātiō, ōnis *f*, **cēnātiuncula, ae** *f* (little) dining-room.
cēnātōria, ōrum *n/pl.* dinner dress.
cēnāturiō 4 to want one's dinner.
cēnitō 1 to be accustomed to dine often *or* repeatedly.
cēnō 1 **1.** to dine, eat; **cēnātus** 3 having dined, after dinner; **2.** *trans.* to eat up, dine upon.
cēnseō, suī, sum 2 **1.** a) to tax, value, estimate, assess, to take an account of the names and property of Roman citizens; to take the census; **capite cēnsī** the lowest class of Roman citizens, whose persons only were counted; b) to make a return to the censor, **P.** to be assessed; **2.** to value, appreciate, weigh; a) to be of opinion, think, hold, judge; b) to vote, propose, recommend by vote; to decree, resolve, order (*alqd*, with *ut, ne, acc. c. inf.*); c) to adjudge to.
cēnsiō, ōnis *f* taxation; opinion.
cēnsor, ōris *m* a Roman magistrate, censor, commissioner of assessment, censurer, critic.
cēnsōrius 3 relating to a censor; censorial; rigid, severe; one who has been a censor.
cēnsūra, ae *f* censorship.
cēnsus, ūs *m* a) a registering of citizens and property, census; b) register of the census, censor's list; c) amount of property.
centaurium *and* **-rēum, ī** *n* a plant, centaury.
Centaurus, ī *m* centaur (*half man, half horse*).
centēnī 3 one hundred each.
centēsimus 3 the hundredth; *subst.* **centēsima, ae** *f* the hundredth part, one per cent.
centi-ceps, cipitis hundred-headed.
centiē(n)s *adv.* a hundred times.
centi-manus 3 having a hundred hands.
centō, ōnis *m* a covering of rags, patch-work.
centum a hundred; many.
centum-geminus 3 a hundred-fold.
centum-plex, icis a hundred-fold.
centum-pondium, ī *n* weight of a hundred pounds.
centum-virālis, e pertaining to centumviri.
centum-virī, ōrum *m/pl.* the centumviri (*a college of judges*).
centunculus, ī *m* patchwork.
centuria, ae *f* a division of one hundred; company of soldiers.
centuriātim *adv.* by centuries.
centuriātus[1], **ūs** *m* office of a centurion; division into centuries.
centuriātus[2] 3 divided into centuries.
centuriō[1], **ōnis** *m* centurion, commander of one hundred soldiers.
centuriō[2] 1 to divide into centuries.
centuriōnātus, ūs *m* election of centurions.
centussis, is *m* a hundred asses.
cēnula, ae *f* a little *or* frugal meal.
cēpa, ae *f* = **caepa.**
cēra, ae *f* wax; a) writing-tablet covered with wax; b) seal of wax; c) image of wax, ancestral portrait; d) waxen paint for the face.
cērārium, ī *n* fee for sealing.
cerastēs, ae *m* horned snake.
cerasus, ī *f* cherry(-tree).
cērātus 3 covered with wax.
cerco-pithēcus, ī *m* long-tailed monkey.
cercūrus, ī *m* swift-sailing vessel, cutter.
cerdō, ōnis *m* workman.
Cereālis, e belonging to Ceres.
cerebellum, ī *n* brain.
cerebrōsus 3 hot-brained, hotheaded.

cerebrum, ī *n* **a**) brain; **b**) understanding; **c**) hot temper.
cēreus 3 of wax, waxen; **a**) wax-coloured; **b**) pliant, soft; *subst.* **cēreus, ī** *m* wax-light.
ceriāria, ae *f* caterer (?).
cērintha, ae *f* honeywort.
cērinum, ī *n* wax-coloured garment.
cernō, crēvī, crētum 3 to separate, sift; **1.** a) to distinguish, discern, see distinctly, perceive (*alqd*); b) to understand, comprehend; **P. cerni** *re, in re* to be shown, show oneself; c) to have regard for; **2.** to decide; a) to resolve, determine (*alqd*); b) to contend, fight (*de, pro re, rem*); c) **hereditatem** to accept *or* enter upon an inheritance.
cernulō 1 to knock down.
cernuus 3 head-foremost.
cērōma, atis *n* wrestler's ointment; wrestling; **cērōmaticus** 3 smeared with *ceroma*.
cerrītus 3 frantic, mad.
certāmen, inis *n* contest, contention, struggle (*de re* or *gen.*); **a**) rivalry, competition; **b**) prize; **c**) fight, battle, combat, war.
certātim *adv.* in rivalry, emulously.
certātiō, ōnis *f* (and **-tus, ūs** *m*) **a**) a contending, contest, competition; **b**) public discussion.
certē *adv.* surely, certainly; **a**) really, undoubtedly; **b**) yet surely; **c**) at least.
certō[1] *adv.* with certainty, surely, really.
certō[2] 1 to fight, struggle, contend, contest (*cum alqo, de* or *pro re*); **a**) to emulate, vie with (*cum alqo, de re,* with *inf.*); **b**) to contend at law.
certus 3 decided **1.** a) determined, resolved, **mihi certum est** (*with inf.*) I have made up my mind; b) resolved upon; **2.** a) settled, established, fixed; b) sure, true, to be depended on; c) informed, assured, *alqm* **certiorem facere** to inform *or* apprise one (*alcis rei, de re*); d) definite, positive, undoubted.
cerūchus, ī *m* halyard.
cērula, ae *f* a little piece of wax; **miniata** red pencil.
cērussa, ae *f* white-lead; (white) paint for the face: **cērussātus** 3 painted with *cerussa*.
cerva, ae *f* hind, deer.
cervīcal, ālis *n* pillow, cushion for the head.
cervīcula, ae *f* a little neck.
cervīnus 3 of a stag *or* deer.
cervīx, īcis *f* (*mostly pl.*) **a**) the nape, neck; **esse in cervīcibus alcis** to be in dangerous proximity; **b**) courage, boldness.
cervus, ī *m* **a**) stag; **b**) forked stakes (*in a fortification*).
cēryx. ӯcis *m* herald.
cessātiō, ōnis *f* a delaying; inactivity.
cessātor, ōris *m* loiterer, idler.
cessiō, ōnis *f* a giving up, cession.
cessō 1 to delay, loiter (*with inf.*); **a**) to be remiss, to be inactive (*in, a re*), idle; **b**) to cease, stop, rest; **c**) to be unemployed, out of action.
cestro-sphendonē, ēs *f* war-engine for hurling stones.
cestus, ī *m* girdle of Venus.
cētārium, ī *n* fishpond.
cētārius, ī *m* fishmonger.
cētē *n* (*pl. of* **cētus**).
cēterō-quī(n) in other respects, otherwise.
cēterus 3 the other, the rest, remainder; **(et) cētera** and so on; *adv.* **a**) **cēterum** *and* **cētera** for the rest, in other respects; **b**) **cēterum** however, but.
cētra, cētrātus, *see* **caetra, caetratus.**
cētus, ī *m* (*pl.* **cētē** *n*) sea-monster, whale, dolphin, shark.
ceu *adv* **a**) as, like as, just as; **b**) (*with subj.*) as if.
cēveō 2 to move the haunches; to fawn.
chalc-aspides, um *m/pl.* soldiers with brazen shields.
chalybēïus 3 of steel.
chalybs, ybis *m* steel.
chaos *n* (*abl.* **chaō**) **a**) boundless, empty space; the nether world; **b**) the shapeless mass out of which the universe was made.
chara, ae *f* plant with edible root.
charistia, ōrum *n/pl.* festival of family reconcilement.
charitōn mia (χαρίτων μία) one of the Graces.
charta, ae *f* **a**) Egyptian papyrus, paper; **b**) writing, book, letter, poem.
chartula, ae *f* paper, letter.
Chēlae, ārum *f/pl.* the arms of Scorpio, *the constellation* Libra.
chelydrus, ī *m* a water-snake.
chelys *f* tortoise-shell lyre.

cheragra = **chiragra.**
chersos, ī *f* land-turtle, tortoise.
chīli-archus, ī *m*, **-ēs, ae** *m* commander of 1000 soldiers; *in Persia*: the grand vizier.
chimaeri-fer 3 producing the chimera.
chīragra, ae *f* gout in the hand.
chīro-graphum, ī *n* **a)** handwriting, autograph; **b)** bond.
chīro-nomōn, ūntis *m* gesticulator.
chīrūrgia, ae *f* surgery.
chīrūrgus, ī *m* surgeon.
chlamydātus 3 dressed in a cloak.
chlamys, ydis *f* (*military*) cloak.
chor-āgium, ī *n* preparation of a chorus.
chor-āgus, ī *m* supplier of a chorus.
chor-aulēs, ae *m* flute-player in a chorus.
chorda, ae *f* **a)** string; **b)** cord.
chorēa (*and* **chorĕa**), **ae** *f* dance in a ring.
chorēus (*and* **-īus**), **ī** *m* trochee.
choro-citharistēs, ae *m* cithara-player in a chorus.
chors, chortis *f* = **cohors.**
chorus, ī *m* dance in a ring, choral dance; dancing troop, chorus; band, crowd.
chrīa, ae *f* sentence used as a theme for logical development, as a rhetorical exercise.
chrȳs-anthus, ī *m* a golden flower.
chrȳs-endetus 3 inlaid with gold.
chrȳso-colla, ae *f* substance used for soldering gold.
chrȳso-lithus, ī *m* chrysolite.
chrȳsos, ī *m* gold.
cibārius 3 **1.** pertaining to food; *subst.* **cibāria, ōrum** *n/pl.* victuals, food, provisions; a) fodder; b) allowance (*of corn*); **2.** common, ordinary.
cibātus, ūs *m* food.
cibō 1 to feed.
cibōrium, ī *n* drinking-cup.
cibus, ī *m* food, victuals, nutriment, fodder; **a)** nourishment, sustenance; **b)** bait.
cicāda, ae *f* cicada, tree-cricket.
cicātrīcōsus 3 full of scars.
cicātrīx, īcis *f* scar, cicatrice.
ciccum, ī *n* pomegranate core, trifle.
cicer, eris *n* the chick-pea.
cichorēum ī *n* chicory.
cicōnia, ae *f* stork.
cicur, uris tame, domesticated.
cicūta, ae *f* **a)** hemlock; **b)** flute of hemlock-stalks.
cieō, cīvī, citum 2 to move, stir, set in motion; **a)** to call to aid, summon; **b)** to call by name, mention by name; **c)** to produce, cause, excite.
cīmex, icis *m* bug.
cinaedicus 3 lewd, unchaste.
cinaedus, ī *m* sodomite, unchaste person.
cincinnātus 3 with curled hair.
cincinnus, ī *m* **a)** (*artificial*) curl of hair; **b)** artificial ornament (*in rhetoric*).
cincticulus, ī *m* little girdle.
cinctus, ūs *m* (*and* **cinctūra, ae** *f*) **a)** a girding; **b)** girdle, apron.
cinctūtus 3 girded.
cine-factus 3 reduced to ashes.
cinerārius, i *m* hairdresser (*with hot irons*).
cingō, cinxī, cinctum 3 to gird (*with acc.*), gird on; **a)** to gird up, to make ready; **P.** to be girded, encircled, to gird oneself; **b)** to surround, enclose (*alqd alqa re*), invest; **c)** to accompany, escort; **d)** to protect, to cut off on all sides.
cingulus, ī *m* zone (of the earth).
cingulum, ī *n and* **cingula, ae** *f* girdle, belt; zone.
cini-flō, ōnis *m* hair-curler.
cinis, eris *m* (*f*) ashes; **a)** ashes of a burnt corpse; ruins of a city; **b)** destruction.
cinnamum (and **-on**), **ī** *n* cinnamon.
ciō, cīvī, citum 4 = **cieo.**
cippus, ī *m* **a)** post; **b)** tomb-stone; **c)** sharpened stake.
circā 1. *adv.* around, round about, all around; in the neighbourhood; **2.** *prep.* with *acc.* a) (*of space*) about, round, on the side of, near to, near by; among; b) (*of time*) about) **c)** (*of number*) about; d) in respect to.
circā-moerium, ī *n* space about a wall.
circēnsis, e belonging to the circus; (*ludi*) **circēnsēs** *m/pl.* the circus--games
circinō 1 to fly through in a circle.
circinus, ī *m* a pair of compasses.
circiter 1. *adv.* about, near; **2.** *prep.* with *acc.* = **circa.**
circitō 1 to perambulate, wander through.
circius, ī *m* north-west wind.

circu-eō = **circumeo.**
circu-itiō, ōnis *f* a going round; **a**) a patrolling; **b**) circumlocution, indirect manner.
circu-itus, ūs *m* a going round in a circle; **a**) revolution; **b**) circuit, compass; **c**) digression, circumlocution; **d**) period.
circulātim *adv.* in a circle.
circulātor, ōris *m* one who runs about; itinerant vendor.
circulātrīx, īcis (*f*) of a mountebank *or* cheap-jack.
circulor 1 **a**) to form a circle of persons; **b**) to converse, to gossip.
circ(u)lus, ī *m* circular figure, circle; **a**) circular course, orbit; **b**) ring, chain; **c**) company, social gathering.
circum *adv.* and *prep.* = **circa** (1 *and* 2a).
circum-āctus, ūs *m* revolution.
circum-agō 3 **1.** to drive, lead, turn round, in a circle; **2.** to turn round, change, turn about, drive about, mislead; **P.** to turn oneself round, to be driven *or* led about; to pass away, be spent.
circum-arō 1 to plough around.
circum-caesūra, ae *f* circumference.
circum-cīdō, cīdī, cīsum 3 to cut around, to cut, clip; to diminish, abridge, cut off.
circum-circā *adv.* round about.
circum-cīsus 3 cut off around; **a**) steep, precipitous, inaccessible; **b**) abridged, short.
circum-clūdō, sī, sum 3 to shut in, enclose, surround.
circum-colō 3 to dwell round about (*alqd*).
circum-cursō 1 to run round.
circum-dō, dedī, datum 1 **a**) to put *or* place around (*alqd alci rei*); **b**) to surround with, encompass, enclose (*alqd re*), to invest, besiege; **P.** to place oneself around.
circum-dūcō 3 to lead, move, draw around; to lengthen, prolong.
circum-ductiō, ōnis *f* **a**) cheating; **b**) rhetorical period
circum-eō to go round, travel, march, drive around (*alqd*); **a**) to surround, encircle, to outflank; **b**) to visit, inspect (*alqd*).
circum-equitō 1 to ride round.
circum-ferō 3 to bear *or* carry round; **a**) to pass around, hand round; **b**) to publish, proclaim, spread around; **P.** to go round, revolve, to move about.
circum-flectō 3 to bend round, turn about.
circum-flō 1 to blow round about.
circum-fluō 3 **a**) to flow round (*alqd*); to surround, encompass; **b**) to overflow; to abound in, be rich (*alqa re*).
circum-fluus 3 **a**) flowing around; **b**) flowed around.
circum-fodiō 3 to dig round.
circum-forāneus 3 **a**) round the forum; **b**) frequenting markets.
circum-fremō 3 to make a noise round.
circum-fundō 3 **a**) to pour around (*alqd alci rei*), **P.** to flow round (*alci rei*); **b**) to cover, enclose, overwhelm with (*alqa re*); to surround, encompass, **P.** to be crowded, surrounded by.
circum-gemō 3 to roar around.
circum-gestō 1 to carry round.
circum-gredior, gressus sum 3 to go round, surround (*in a hostile manner*).
circum-iaceō, —, — 2 to lie *or* dwell round about.
circum-iciō, iēcī, iectum 3 to throw *or* cast round, to put round (*alqd alci rei*), to enclose with; *adj.* **circumiectus** 3 **a**) surrounding; **b**) surrounded.
circum-iectus, ūs *m* encompassing.
circum-itiō, -itus = **circuitio, -itus.**
circum-lātrō 1 to bark *or* roar round about.
circum-ligō 1 **a**) to bind round *or* to (*alqd alci rei*); **b**) to bind with, encompass (*alqd alqa re*).
circum-linō, —, — 3 **a**) to smear around, **b**) to spread all over, cover
circum-litiō, ōnis *f* a coat (e.g. of varnish) spread over something
circum-luō, —, — 3 to wash round, flow around
circum-luviō, ōnis *f* island formed by a river flowing in a new channel.
circum-mittō 3 to send round.
circum-mūniō (*or* **moeniō**) 4 to fortify, to enclose by a wall.
circum-mūnītiō, ōnis *f* an investing, circumvallation.

circum-padānus 3 about the river Po.
circum-pendeō 2 to hang around.
circum-plaudō 3 to applaud on all sides.
circum-plector (*and* **-ō**), **plexus sum** 3 to embrace, enclose.
circum-plicō 1 to wind around.
circum-pōnō 3 to place round.
circum-pōtātiō, ōnis *f* a drinking round in turn.
circum-rētiō 4 to enclose in a net, ensnare.
circum-rōdō 3 **a**) to gnaw round; **b**) to slander.
circum-saepiō 4 to hedge *or* fence around.
circum-scindō 3 to tear off around.
circum-scrībō 3 **1.** to describe a circle round (*alqd*); to enclose in a circle; **2.** a) to define, fix the boundaries of (*alci alqd*), limit; b) to restrain, confine; c) to circumvent, deceive, cheat, defraud; d) to cancel, annul, set aside.
circum-scrīptē *adv.* **a**) by precise definition; **b**) in periods.
circum-scrīptiō, ōnis *f* an encircling; **a**) circumference; **b**) boundary, limit, compass; **c**) period; **d**) a deceiving, cheating, overreaching.
circum-scrīptor, ōris *m* deceiver, cheat.
circum-scrīptus 3 bounded; concise; in periods.
circum-secō 1 to cut around.
circum-sedeō 2 **a**) to sit around; **b**) to besiege, blockade, invest.
circum-sessiō, ōnis *f* a beleaguering, besieging.
circum-sīdō, sēdī, — 3 to besiege.
circum-siliō 4 to leap around.
circum-sistō, stetī, — 3 to stand round, surround.
circum-sonō 1 **a**) *intr.* to resound on all sides; **b**) *trans.* to make echo, surround with noise.
circum-sonus 3 sounding around.
circum-spectātrīx, īcis *f* she who looks round.
circum-spectiō, ōnis *f* caution, circumspection.
circum-spectō 1 (*intens.*) = **circumspicio.**
circum-spectus[1], **ūs** *m* consideration; prospect, view.
circum-spectus[2] 3 cautious, circumspect, considerate.
circum-spiciō, spexī, spectum 3 to look round; **1.** to look about (*cautiously* or *attentively*); **2.** a) to see, observe; b) to view on all sides, to survey; c) to look for, seek for, wait for; d) to consider, weigh, survey.
circum-stō, stetī, — 1 **a**) *intr.* to stand round; **b**) *trans.* to surround, encircle (*alqd*); to threaten, beset.
circum-strepō 3 **a**) to surround with noise; **b**) to shout (*alqd*) round about.
circum-struō 3 to build round.
circum-tentus 3 encased.
circum-terō 3 to crowd round.
circum-textus 3 woven all around.
circum-tonō 1 to thunder round.
circum-tōnsus 3 shorn all around.
circum-vādō, sī, — 3 to attack, assail on every side.
circum-vagus 3 flowing around.
circum-vallō 1 to surround with a wall, to blockade.
circum-vectiō, ōnis *f* **a**) a carrying around; **b**) circuit, revolution.
circum-vectō 1 to carry round.
circum-vector 1 to ride *or* sail round (*alqd*); to go through, describe.
circum-vehor 3 *trans.* to ride *or* sail round (*alqd*).
circum-vēlō 1 to veil around, envelop.
circum-veniō 4 to come around, surround, flow round; **a**) to encircle, enclose; **b**) to invest, to beset, to oppress, distress, overthrow; **c**) to ensnare, cheat, deceive.
circum-vertō 3 to turn *or* twist round; **P.** to turn oneself round.
circum-vestiō 4 to clothe round.
circum-vinciō 4 to bind all round.
circum-vīsō 3 (*intens.*) to look all round.
circum-volitō 1 to fly round (*alqd*).
circum-volō 1 to fly round (*with acc.*).
circum-volvor 3 to roll round; to revolve through (*annum*).
circus, ī *m* **a**) circular line, circle; **b**) race-course, circus.
cīris, is *f* an unknown sea-bird.
cirrātus 3 curly-haired.
cirrus, ī *m* curl; fringe.
cis *prep.* with *acc.* **a**) on this side of; **b**) within.

cis-alpīnus 3 lying on the Roman side of the Alps, Cisalpine.
cisium, ī *n* two-wheeled carriage.
cis-rhēnānus 3 on the left side of the Rhine.
cista, ae *f* chest, box.
cistell(ul)a, ae *f* little box.
cistellātrīx, īcis *f* female slave in charge of the money-box.
cisterna, ae *f* cistern, reservoir.
cisto-phorus, ī *m* Asiatic coin stamped with a cista.
citātim *adv.* quickly, hastily.
citātus 3 speedy, swift, rapid.
citerior, ius a) on this (*the Roman*) side; **b**) nearer, closer.
cithara, ae *f* cithara, lyre.
citharista, ae *m and* **citharistria, ae** *f* player on the cithara.
citharizō 1 to play on the cithara.
citharoedicus 3 of a *citharoedus.*
cithar-oedus, ī *m* one who sings to the cithara.
citimus 3 nearest.
citō *adv. of* **citus.**
citō[2] 1 to put in quick motion, to excite, rouse; **a**) to call, summon, cite; **b**) to call a defendant, a witness; to accuse (*capitis*); **c**) to name, appeal to, quote, recite.
citrā 1. *adv.* nearer, on this side; **2.** *prep.* with *acc.*; a) on this side of, within; b) short of, without, except, setting aside.
citreus 3 of citrus-wood.
citrō *adv.* to this side; **ultrō et citrō** hither and thither, to and fro, reciprocally
citrum, ī *n* (article made of) citrus-wood.
citrus, ī *f* citrus-tree.
citus 3 swift, quick, rapid; *adv.* **citō; non cito** not easily; **citius** sooner, rather.
civicus 3 = **civilis** 1.
cīvīlis, e 1. pertaining to citizens, of citizens; a) **ius cīvīle** civil law, private rights; b) civil, civic, patriotic, political, public; **2.** affable, courteous, polite
cīvīlitās, ātis *f* politeness, courteousness.
cīvis, is *m and f* citizen, a) fellow-citizen, countryman; b) subject.
cīvitās, ātis *f* citizenship; **a**) condition *or* rights of a citizen; **b**) the citizens; city, state, commonwealth.
cīvitātula, ae *f* citizenship of a small town.
clādēs, is *f* damage, injury, disaster, destruction, defeat, slaughter, massacre.
clam 1. *adv.* secretly, privately, in secret; **2.** *prep.* with *abl.* (and *acc.*) without the knowledge of, unknown to.
clāmātor, ōris *m* shouter.
clāmitātiō, ōnis *f* loud crying.
clāmitō 1 *intens. of* **clamo.**
clāmō 1 to cry aloud, shout (*trans.* and *intr.*); **a**) to proclaim, to call aloud to (*alci*); **b**) to call upon, invoke; **c**) to call by name; **d**) to declare.
clāmor, ōris *m* loud shout, call, cry; **a**) acclamation, applause, rejoicing; **b**) outcry, complaint, cry of sorrow, war-cry; **c**) noise, sound, din, echo.
clāmōsus 3 noisy.
clanculārius 3 concealed, anonymous.
clanculum = **clam.**
clandestīnus 3 secret, concealed, hidden.
clangō 3 to resound, peal.
clangor, ōris *m* sound, clang, noise.
clāreō, —, — 2 to be bright *or* clear; to shine.
clārēscō, ruī, — 3 to become bright *or* clear; **a**) to become audible; **b**) to become brilliant, illustrious.
clārigātiō, ōnis *f* demand of satisfaction; fine for transgressing limits.
clāri-sonus 3 clear-sounding.
clāritās, ātis *f* clearness, brightness; **a**) distinctness; **b**) renown, fame, celebrity.
clāritūdō, inis *f* = **claritas.**
clārō 1 to make clear; to make famous.
clārus 3 bright, clear, shining; **a**) distinct, loud, audible; **b**) plain, clear, evident; **c**) illustrious, renowned, notorious
classiārius 3 belonging to the navy; *subst.* **~, ī** *m* soldier on a ship, marine; sailor
classicula, ae *f* little fleet.
classicum ī *n* trumpet-call for battle; war-trumpet
classicus 3 belonging *or* pertaining to the fleet *or* navy; *subst.* **~, ī** *m* = **classiarius.**
classis, is *f* **1.** class *or* division of citizens; **2.** a) army; b) fleet, navy; naval service.

clātrātus 3 latticed.
clātrī, ōrum *m/pl.* bar, lattice.
claudeō 2 *and* **claudō** 3 = **claudico.**
claudicātiō, ōnis *f* a limping.
claudicō 1 **a**) to limp, be lame; **b**) to waver, halt.
claudō, sī, sum 3 **1.** to shut, close, shut up; *subst.* **clausum, ī** *n* enclosure, confinement; a) to close, end, conclude, **agmen claudere** to bring up the rear; **b**) to round (*a period*); **2.** to shut in, imprison, confine (*alqd in rem, in re, re*); a) to make inaccessible, to intercept, dam up, stop; b) to surround.
claudus 3 **a**) limping, halting, lame; **b**) wavering; **c**) crippled, defective.
claustra, ōrum *n/pl.* (*sg. rare*) **a**) lock, bolt, bar, barrier; **b**) gate, dam, dike, barricade; **c**) confinement, den, cage; **d**) key (*of a position*), bulwark, entrenchment.
clausula, ae *f* close, conclusion.
clāva, ae *f* cudgel, club; staff.
clāvārium, ī *n* (*mil.*) money for shoe-nails.
clāvātor, ōris *m* cudgel-bearer.
clāvīcula, ae *f* **a**) small key; **b**) vine tendril.
clāvi-ger 3 **a**) [*clava*] club-bearer; **b**) [*clavis*] key-bearer.
clāvis, is *f* **a**) key; **b**) lock.
clāvus, ī *m* **1.** nail; **2.** a) rudder, helm; b) purple stripe on the tunic.
clēmēns, tis mild, placid, calm, gentle, kind, merciful.
clēmentia, ae *f* mildness, benignity, kindness, forbearance, moderation.
clepō, psī, (ptum) 3 to steal.
cleps-ydra, ae *f* water-clock.
clepta, ae *m* thief.
cliēns, tis *m* dependant, client; adherent, retainer, follower, vassal.
clienta, ae *f* female client.
clientēla, ae *f* **a**) clientship, patronage; **b**) clients, dependants, vassals.
clientulus, ī *m* a poor client.
clīmactēricus 3 critical, climacteric.
clīnāmen, inis *n* inclination (of atoms).
clīnātus 3 inclined, bent.
clīnicus, ī *m* **a**) physician; **b**) undertaker, bearer of a bier.
clipeātus 3 bearing a shield.
clipeus, ī *m* (*and* **clipeum, ī** *n*) round brazen shield; **a**) disk of the sun; **b**) oval medallion.
clītellae, ārum *f/pl.* pack-saddle.
clītellārius 3 bearing a pack-saddle.
clīvōsus 3 hilly, steep.
clīvus, ī *m* gentle ascent, slope, declivity; eminence, hill.
cloāca, ae *f* sewer, drain.
clōstra, *see* **claustra.**
clūdo, cluēns, *see* **claudo, cliens.**
clueō (*and* **clueor**) 2 to hear, be spoken of, to be reputed, famed.
clūnis, is *f* or *m* buttock.
clupeus = **clipeus.**
clūrīnus 3 of apes.
clystēr, ēris *m* enema; syringe.
Cn. (*abbr.*) = **Gnaeus.**
co-acervātiō, ōnis *f* a heaping up.
co-acervō 1 to heap together, heap up, accumulate.
co-acēscō, acuī, — 3 to become sour.
co-āctiō, ōnis *f* a collecting.
co-āctō 1 to constrain, force.
co-āctor, ōris *m* collector of money; rear man (in a column).
co-āctum, ī *n* felt.
co-āctus, ūs *m* compulsion.
co-aedificō 1 to build on.
co-aequō 1 **a**) to make equal, even, level; **b**) to place on the same footing.
co-āgmentātiō, ōnis *f* a joining, connection.
co-āgmentō 1 to join, connect, cement together.
co-āgmentum, ī *n* a joining together, joint.
co-āgulum, ī *n* rennet.
co-alēscō, aluī, alitum 3 to grow together, to become united by growth; **a**) to join together, to unite; **b**) to grow, to take root, become strong.
co-angustō 1 to compress, confine, narrow.
co-arguō 3 to prove fully, to demonstrate, show, establish; **a**) to convict, prove guilty; **b**) to prove to be wrong, to refute.
co-artātiō, ōnis *f* a pressing together.
co-artō 1 **a**) to pack, confine; **b**) to abridge, shorten.
coaxō 1 to croak.
coccinātus 3 clad in scarlet.
coccin(e)us 3 scarlet-coloured.
coccum, ī *n* scarlet dye *or* cloth.
cochlea, coclea, ae *f* snail, snail-shell.

coc(h)lear(e), is *n* spoon.
cocles, itis one-eyed.
coctilis, e baked, burned; of burned bricks.
cocus, ī *m* = **coquus.**
cōda, ae *f vulg.* = **cauda.**
cōdex, icis *m* = **caudex.**
cōdicārius 3 made of tree trunks.
cōdicillus, ī *m* **1.** small wooden block; **2.** (*pl.*) writting tablet; a) note, billet; b) petition; c) imperial rescript; d) addition to a will, codicil.
co-emō 3 to buy up.
co-ēmptiō, ōnis *f* **a**) marriage by fictitious sale; **b**) fictitious marriage.
co-ēmptiōnālis, e bought up with others (as being valueless).
co-eō, iī, (itum), īre 1. to go *or* come together, to meet, assemble; a) to meet in battle, to encounter; b) to be united, to combine; to copulate; to unite in marriage; c) to heal up, close; d) to congeal, curdle; e) to agree; **2.** *trans.* **societatem** to form an alliance (*cum alqo*).
(coepiō), coepī, coeptum 3 to begin.
coeptō 1 (*intens.*) = **incipio.**
coeptum, ī *n* an undertaking, work begun.
coeptus, ūs *m* a beginning, undertaking.
co-epulōnus, ī *m* companion at [a dinner.
co-erceō, cuī, citum 2 to enclose on all sides, to hold together; **a**) to enclose, encompass; **b**) to restrain, confine, control, keep in order, to check, curb, correct, tame.
co-ercitiō, ōnis *f* **a**) a restraining; **b**) (right of) punishing
coetus, ūs *m* **a**) a coming together, meeting; **b**) assembly, company
cōgitābilis, e conceivable.
cōgitātiō, ōnis *f* a thinking; **1.** a) a considering, deliberating, meditation, b) power of thinking, reflection, imagination; **2.** thought; a) idea, notion; b) purpose, plan, design.
cōgitō 1 **1.** a) to think, reflect upon, ponder, weigh (*de re*); to be disposed; b) to think of, have in mind, intend, purpose (*de re* or with *inf.*); **2.** to design, plan (*alqd* or with *inf.*); *adj.* **cōgitātus** 3 well-considered, deliberate, intended; *subst.* **cōgitātum, ī** *n* thought, idea; purpose.
cognātiō, ōnis *f* blood-relationship; **a**) kindred, relations; **b**) resemblance, affinity, agreement.
co-gnātus 3 **a**) related by blood (*with dat.*); **b**) connected, related, similar; *subst.* ~, **ī** *m* kinsman, blood-relation.
cognitiō, ōnis *f* a becoming acquainted with; **a**) a knowing, knowledge, acquaintance (*with gen.*); **b**) notion, idea; **c**) legal inquiry *or* examination, trial.
cognitor, ōris *m* **a**) advocate, procurator, attorney, protector; **b**) witness to identity.
cognitūra, ae *f* public prosecutor's office.
cognitus 3, *see* **cognosco.**
cognōmen, inis *n* surname; **a**) family name; **b**) name.
cognōmentum, ī *n* = **cognomen.**
cognōminis, e of the same name.
cognōminō 1 to surname; **cognōminātus** synonymous.
co-gnōscō, gnōvī, gnitum 3 to become acquainted with, learn, perceive, understand; see; *pf.* to know; **a**) to read, peruse; **b**) to inquire into, investigate, examine, study; **c**) to examine judicially; **d**) to recognize, identify; **e**) to reconnoitre, act as a scout; *adj.* **cognitus** 3 known, tried, proved.
cōgō, coēgī, coāctum 3 **1.** to drive together, bring together (*alqm* or *alqd ab, ex re in, ad alqd*); a) to contract, condense; b) to gather together, assemble, collect, summon; to collect (*money*); (*agmen*) to bring up the rear; **2.** to urge, force, compel (*ut*, or with *inf.*); a) to constrain; b) to drive, press; c) to conclude; **coāctus** 3 constrained, compelled, forced.
co-haerentia, ae *f* coherence, connection
co-haereō, haesī, — 2 to hang together (*cum re, inter se*); **a**) to be united, cohere, adhere; **b**) to hold together, subsist, consist of (*abl.*).
co-haerēscō, haesī 3 to stick together.
co-hērēs, ēdis *m* and *f* co-heir.
co-hibeō, buī, bitum 2 to hold together; **a**) to hold, contain, comprise; **b**) to restrain, confine; **c**) to hinder, hold back; **d**) to control, repress.

co-honestō 1 to honour, celebrate.
co-horrēscō, horruī, — 3 to shudder, shiver.
co-hors, tis *f* **1.** enclosure, cattle-yard; **2.** a) division of soldiers, cohort, **praetoria** body-guard of a general; b) retinue *or* suite of a governor; c) troop, crowd, multitude.
co-hortātiō, ōnis *f* exhortation, encouragement.
cohorticula, ae *f* a small cohort.
co-hortor 1 to exhort, encourage, incite.
cō-iciō = **conicio.**
co-inquinō 1 to defile, pollute.
co-itiō, ōnis *f* a coming together; **a)** conspiracy, plot; **b)** agreement.
co-itus, ūs *m* meeting; sexual union.
colaphus, ī *m* box on the ear.
cōleus, ī *m* sack; scrotum.
cōliculus, ī *m* young stalk, young greens.
col-labāscō 3 to totter.
col-labefactō 1 to cause to totter.
col-labefīō, factus sum, fierī to be made to totter, to fall to pieces, collapse, be ruined.
col-lābor 3 = **collabefio.**
col-lacerātus 3 torn to pieces.
col-lacrimātiō, ōnis *f* a weeping.
col-lacrimō 1 to bewail.
col-lactea, ae *f* foster-sister.
collāre, is *n* collar.
col-lāticius 3 contributed, lent.
col-lātiō, ōnis *f* a bringing together, **signorum** hostile encounter, collision; **a)** contribution of money, collection; **b)** comparison, similitude.
col-lātīvus 3 into which much is collected, i. e. fat, distended.
col-lātor, ōris *m* contributor.
col-lātrō 1 to bark at, abuse.
col-lātus, ūs *m* = **collatio;** *esp.* engagement, attack.
col-laudātiō, ōnis *f* warm praise.
col-laudō 1 to praise very much.
col-laxō 1 to make loose.
col-lēcta, ae *f* contribution.
col-lēctāneus 3 collected.
col-lēcticius 3 gathered in haste.
col-lēctiō, ōnis *f* **a)** a gathering; **b)** a summing up; **c)** inference.
col-lēctus, ūs *m* collection.
collēga, ae *m* partner in office, colleague.
collēgium, ī *n* **1.** colleagueship; **2.** association, guild, corporation, college, company, fraternity.
col-lēvō 1 to make smooth.
col-lībertus, ī *m* fellow-freedman.
col-libet 2 it pleases, is agreeable.
col-līdō, sī, sum 3 **a)** to strike *or* dash together; **P.** to meet in a hostile manner; **b)** to dash to pieces.
col-ligātiō, ōnis *f* a binding together, connection.
col-ligō[1] 1 to bind together; tie, connect, bind (*alqd cum re, inter se*); **a)** to combine, unite; **b)** to fasten, fetter; **c)** to restrain, hinder.
col-ligō[2]**, lēgī, lēctum** 3 **1.** a) to bring together, collect, gather, **vasa** to pack up for a march; b) to put together, to enumerate, reckon; c) to assemble, bring together, concentrate; **2.** a) **se** *or* **animum** to collect one's mind, recover one's senses *or* courage; **b)** to gain, obtain, acquire; c) to consider, reckon; to infer, conclude.
col-līneō 1 to direct in a straight line; to hit the mark.
col-linō, lēvī, litum 3 to besmear; to defile (*alqd alqa re*).
col-liquefactus 3 made liquid, dissolved.
collis, is *m* hill, elevation.
col-locātiō, ōnis *f* **a)** a putting, placing; **b)** a giving in marriage.
col-locō 1 to place, lay, set (*alqm* or *alqd in re*); **a)** to station, quarter, settle; **b)** to lay out, invest, advance (*money*); **c)** to settle (*a woman*) in marriage (*alci in matrimonio*); **d)** to employ, occupy, manage (*alqd in re*).
col-locuplētō 1 to enrich greatly.
col-locūtiō, ōnis *f* conversation.
colloquium, ī *n* conversation, talk.
col-loquor 3 to speak, talk, converse with (*cum alqo de re*), to treat *or* negotiate with; to accost.
col-lubet = **collibet.**
col-lūceō, —, — 2 to shine on all sides, to shine, to be illuminated, to be clear *or* bright.
col-luctor 1 to wrestle with.
col-lūdō 3 to play *or* sport with (*dat.*); to have a secret understanding with (*cum alqo*).
collum, ī *n* (*and* **collus, i** *m*) the neck.
col-luō 3 to wash thoroughly, to rinse.
col-lūsiō, ōnis *f* secret understanding (*cum alqo*).
col-lūsor, ōris *m* playmate, playfellow.

col-lūstrō 1 **a**) to light up on all sides, illuminate; **b**) to survey, review.
col-lutulentō 1 to defile.
col-luviēs, ēī *f* = **colluvio.**
col-luviō, ōnis *f* conflux, collection of filth, washings, dregs, offscourings; medley, rabble.
collybus, ī *m* moneychanging.
collȳra, ae *f* a kind of bread.
collȳricus 3 made with *collyra.*
collȳrium, ī *n* eye-salve.
colō, coluī, cultum 3 to care for; **a**) to till, cultivate, farm; **b**) to tend, adorn; *adj.* **cultus** 3 cultivated, tilled (**culta, ōrum** *n/pl.* tilled land, gardens, plantations), adorned, elegant, polite, accomplished; **b**) to abide, dwell in a place; **c**) to bestow care upon, to guard, protect, honour, revere, worship, cherish, love.
colocāsium, ī *n* waterlily.
cōloephia, ōrum *n/pl.* = **colyphia.**
colōna, ae *f* country-woman.
colōnia, ae *f* **1.** farm, estate; **2.** colony, settlement; colonists.
colōnicus 3 colonial; levied in the colonies.
colōnus, ī *m* **1.** peasant, farmer; **2.** colonist; inhabitant.
color (*and* **colōs**), **ōris** *m* colour, hue, tint; **a**) complexion; **b**) outward show, external appearance *or* condition; **c**) colouring, style, character.
colōrō 1 to colour, dye, tan.
colossēus 3 gigantic.
colossus, ī *m* gigantic statue.
coluber, brī *m* serpent, snake.
colubra, ae *f* female serpent.
colubri-fer 3 serpent-bearing.
colubrīnus 3 snake-like.
cōlum, ī *n* sieve, strainer.
columba, ae *f* pigeon, dove.
columbar, āris *n* collar like a pigeon- hole.
columbīnus 3 of a pigeon *or* dove.
columbus, ī *m* male pigeon *or* dove.
columella, ae *f* small column.
columen, inis *n* column, pillar; **a**) highest part, top; **b**) prop, support
columis, is = **incolumis** (?).
columna, ae *f* column, pillar; prop.
columnāriī, ōrum *m/pl.* rascals, thieves.
columnārium, ī *n* tax on pillars.
columnātus 3 supported by pillars.
colurnus 3 made of hazel-wood.
colus, ūs *and* **ī** *f* (*m*) distaff.
colustrum, ī *n* beestings.
colūtea, ōrum *n/pl.* pod-like fruit.
cōlȳphia, ōrum *n/pl.* meat for athletes.
coma, ae *f* the hair of the head; foliage, leaves.
comāns, tis hairy, covered with hair; having leaves.
cōm-archus, ī *m* ruler of a village.
comātus 3 long-haired; having leaves.
combardus 3 stupid.
com-bibō[1]**, ōnis** *m* drinking-companion.
com-bibō[2]**, bibī,** — 3 to drink up, imbibe, to swallow.
comb-ūrō 3 to burn up, consume, destroy.
com-edō 3 to eat up, consume; to waste, squander, dissipate.
comes, itis *m* and *f* companion, associate, comrade; **a**) guardian, tutor, teacher; **b**) attendant, client; **c**) *pl* retinue.
comētēs, ae *m* comet.
cōmicus 3 of comedy, comic; *subst.* ~**, ī** *m* comic poet *or* actor.
cōmis, e affable, courteous, kind, amiable, obliging.
cōmissābundus 3 revelling, carousing.
cōmissātiō, ōnis *f* a revelling, riotous banquet.
cōmissātor, ōris *m* drinking-companion, reveller, rioter.
cōmissor 1 to revel, riot, carouse.
cōmitās, ātis *f* affability, kindness, friendliness, gaiety.
comitātus, ūs *m* **a**) attendance; **b**) train, escort, retinue; **c**) travelling company; **d**) imperial court *or* suite.
comitiālis, e pertaining to the *comitia*, of an election; **morbus** epilepsy.
comitiātus, ūs *m* assembly of the people in the *comitia.*
com-itium, ī *n* place of assembly; *n/pl.* **-ia, iōrum** assembly of the people for electing magistrates, etc.: election.
com-itor (**com-itō**) 1 to accompany, attend, follow (*alqm, alqd*); **comitātus** *alqo* attended by.
com-maculō 1 to spot, stain, pollute.

com-manipulāris, is *m* one belonging to the same maniple, comrade.
com-marītus, ī *m* fellow-husband.
com-meātus, ūs *m* a going to and fro, free passage; **a**) leave of absence; **b**) transport, convoy, supply-train, caravan; **c**) provisions, supply, food, forage.
com-meditor 1 to imitate.
com-meminī, isse to remember, recollect.
com-memorābilis, e memorable.
com-memorātiō, ōnis *f* **a**) a mentioning, reminding; **b**) remembrance.
com-memorō 1 **1.** to keep in mind, remember; **2.** a) to remind of (*alqd*); b) to mention, recount, relate (*alqd* or *de re*).
commendābilis, e worthy of praise, commendable.
commendātīcius 3 of recommendation.
commendātiō, ōnis *f* **a**) recommendation; **b**) that which recommends, excellence.
commendātor, ōris *m*, *and* **-trīx, īcis** *f* one who recommends.
com-mendō 1 to commit to the care of, to intrust to; to recommend (*alci alqd*, *se alci*); to make agreeable.
commentāriolum, ī *n* short treatise, sketch.
commentārium, ī *n* = **commentarius.**
commentārius, ī *m* notebook, diary, memorandum, notes, sketch, paper, commentary; *pl.* memoirs, records.
commentātiō, ōnis *f* **a**) careful consideration, deep reflection, meditation, study, preparation; **b**) treatise, dissertation.
commentīcius 3 invented, fictitious; **a**) ideal; **b**) feigned, false.
commentor[1] 1 to consider thoroughly, to meditate, think over (*alqd*, *de re*); **a**) to discuss; **b**) to study, prepare (*mentally*), to practise, exercise in speaking *or* writing; **c**) to compose, sketch, write down.
commentor[2], **ōris** *m* inventor, deviser.
commentum, ī *n* **a**) invention, thought, device; **b**) fiction, falsehood.
com-meō 1 **a**) to come and go, go to and fro, go about; **b**) to visit frequently, to resort to.
com-mercium, ī *n* **a**) commercial intercourse, trade, traffic; **b**) the right of trade; **c**) communication, correspondence, communion.
com-mercor 1 to traffic together, to buy up, purchase.
com-mereō (*and* **eor**) 2 **a**) to deserve fully; **b**) to be guilty of.
com-mētior 4 to measure; to measure with, compare.
com-mētō[1] 1 to measure.
com-mētō[2] 1 to go frequently.
com-migrātiō, ōnis *f* wandering.
com-migrō 1 to migrate; to remove to.
com-mīlitēs, um *m/pl.* fellow-soldiers.
commīlitium, ī *n* a serving together as soldiers, comradeship.
com-mīlitō, ōnis *m* fellowsoldier, comrade.
com-minātiō, ōnis *f* a threatening, threat.
com-mingō 3 to make water on; to defile, pollute.
com-minīscor, mentus sum 3 to devise, invent; to feign.
com-minor 1 to threaten (*alci alqd*).
com-minuō 3 to break into small pieces, to crush; **a**) to lessen, diminish; **b**) to weaken, enervate, reduce.
com-minus *adv.* hand to hand; at close quarters; close by, near; face to face.
com-misceō 2 **a**) to mix *or* mingle together (*alqd cum re* or with *abl.*); **b**) to unite, join.
com-miserātiō, ōnis *f* appeal to compassion; pathetic speech.
com-miserēscō 3 to pity.
com-miseror 1 to lament, bewail, excite pity.
com-missiō, ōnis *f* contest, struggle; prize composition.
com-missum, ī *n* **1.** an undertaking; transgression, offence, crime, fault; **2.** secret, trust.
com-missūra, ae *f* connection, joint, knot, juncture.
com-mītigō 1 to make soft.
com-mittō 3 **1.** to bring together, join, combine, connect, unite (*alqd alci rei*); to set *or* bring together in a fight; **2.** to engage in, begin, carry on; a) **proelium** to commence *or* fight a battle; b) to commit, be guilty of (*alqd in*, *erga*, *adversus*

alqm); c) to give cause, allow it to happen (*ut, ne, cur, quare*); d) to forfeit; **3.** to give, intrust, commit to; to resign to, expose, abandon.

commoditās, ātis *f* **a**) just proportion, symmetry, fitness, convenience, comfort, advantage; **b**) courtesy, kindness, indulgence.

commodō 1 **a**) to adapt oneself to suit another person (*alci*); to accommodate; **b**) to furnish, lend, give (*alci alqd*).

commodulē (*and* **lum**) *adv.* conveniently, nicely.

commodum[1] *adv.* opportunely; just, just now.

commodum[2], **ī** *n* **a**) convenience, opportunity; **b**) use, advantage, profit; **c**) favour, privilege, prerogative; **d**) reward, pay; **e**) loan.

com-modus 3 **1.** proper, fit, convenient, suitable, appropriate; a) good, agreeable; b) easy, useful, serviceable, pleasant; **2.** obliging, friendly, polite.

com-mōlior 4 to set in motion.

com-monefaciō 3 = **commoneo.**

com-moneō 2 **a**) to remind, bring to one's recollection (*alqm alcis rei, de re*); **b**) to warn, to exhort (*with ut, ne*).

com-mōnstrō 1 to show *or* point out distinctly.

com-morātiō, ōnis *f* a tarrying, abiding, dwelling on.

com-mordeō 2 to bite; to abuse, slander.

com-morior 3 to die together.

com-moror 1 to tarry, linger, abide, sojourn.

com-mōtiō, ōnis *f* excitement, agitation, commotion.

commōtiuncula, ae *f* slight indisposition.

com-moveō 2 to put in violent motion (*alqm, alqd*); **a**) to remove, drive away, carry away, displace, **castra** to decamp; **b**) to shake, excite, stir, agitate, disturb; **c**) to rouse, make an impression upon, produce (*alci dolorem*); **d**) to disquiet; **commōtus** 3 moved, excited, agitated, disordered.

commūnicātiō, ōnis *f* imparting, communication.

commūnicō (*and* **-or**) 1 **1.** to make common, to unite (*alqd*); a) to share with, have in common with (*alqd cum alqo*); b) to communicate, impart, give a share in, grant; **2.** to inform, take counsel with, confer with (*cum alqo, de re*).

com-mūniō[1] 4 to fortify on all sides, to strengthen, secure.

commūniō[2], **ōnis** *f* communion, mutual participation.

com-mūnis, e a) common, ordinary, general, usual, universal, public; **b**) affable, courteous, condescending; *subst.* **commūne, is** *n* **a**) common property; **b**) commonwealth, state, community, **in commūne** for common use, for all, in general, generally.

commūnitās, ātis *f* **1.** community; **2.** a) public spirit; b) condescension.

com-mūnītiō, ōnis *f* a paving a way.

com-murmuror (*and* **ō**) 1 to murmur, mutter.

com-mūtābilis, e (ex)changeable.

com-mūtātiō, ōnis *f* (*and* **-tus, -ūs** *m*) a changing, change, alteration.

com-mūtō 1 **a**) to change, alter; **b**) to exchange, change for.

cōmō, cōmpsī, cōmptum 3 **1.** to unite; **2.** to adorn, arrange; dress; **cōmptus** 3 adorned, embellished, neat, pretty.

cōmoedia, ae *f* comedy.

cōmoedicē as in a comedy.

cōmoedus, ī *m* comic actor.

comōsus 3 hairy.

com-pacīscor, pactus sum 3 to make an agreement, form a compact; **compactō** *adv.* according to agreement.

com-pāctiō, ōnis *f* a joining together.

com-pāctus 3 sturdy, compact.

compāgēs, is *f* **a**) a joining together; **b**) connection, joint; **c**) structure.

compāgō, inis *f* = **compages.**

com-pār, aris like, similar, equal; *subst. m* companion, comrade, compeer.

comparābilis, e comparable.

comparātiō, ōnis *f* **1.** a) a preparing, preparation; b) a procuring, acquiring; **2.** a comparing, comparison; a) relation; b) agreement, contract.

comparātīvus 3 comparative.

com-parcō 3 to save, lay up; to abstain from (*inf.*).

com-pāreō, ruī, — 2 to appear, be visible, exist.
com-parō[1] 1 [*par*] to bring together as equals, to pair, match; **a**) to bring together for a combat, to oppose; **b**) to compare, make a comparison, to consider by comparing.
com-parō[2] 1 [*parare*] to prepare, make ready, arrange; **a**) to get ready, equip (*soldiers*); **b**) to make arrangements *or* preparations; **c**) to appoint, ordain, establish, settle, institute, **ita comparātus** of such a constitution; **d**) to procure, provide, furnish, obtain, acquire (*alci alqd*).
com-pāscō 3 to feed together.
com-pāscuus 3 for common pasturage.
com-pectus sum, com-pectō = **compactus sum, compacto;** *see* **compaciscor.**
com-pediō 4 to fetter.
compellātiō, ōnis *f* **a**) an accosting, addressing; **b**) a rebuking, reprimand.
com-pellō[1] 1 to accost, address; **a**) to rebuke, reproach, abuse, chide; **b**) to arraign, accuse.
com-pellō[2] **pulī, pulsum** 3 to drive together, to one place (*alqd in* or *ad alqd*); **a**) to force together; **b**) to drive; **c**) to impel, incite, urge, compel (*alqm in* or *ad alqd*).
compendiārius 3 saving time, shortened; **compendiāria via** (*also f and n as subst.*) short cut.
compendium, ī *n* a shortening, abridging; **a**) short way; **b**) a sparing, saving, profit.
compēnsātiō, ōnis *f* equivalent, compensation.
com-pēnsō 1 **a**) to balance, weigh together, counterbalance (*alqd cum re*); **b**) to compensate, make good (*alqd re*).
com-percō = **comparco.**
comperendinātus, ūs *m and* **-tiō, ōnis** *f* an adjourning a trial to the third day.
com-perendinō 1 to adjourn a trial to the third day, to summon a defendant for the third day.
com-periō (*and* **-ior**), **perī, pertum** 4 to find out, learn, discover, get information; **compertus** 3 **a**) known, heard; **b**) ascertained, certain; **c**) convicted.
com-pēs, edis *f* fetter *or* shackle (*for the feet*).
compescō, uī, — 3 to restrain, check, repress, suppress.
com-petītor, ōris *m* rival, competitor.
com-petītrīx, īcis *f* female competitor.
com-petō 3 **a**) to coincide (*cum re*); **b**) to be adequate, capable, suitable, fit; to correspond.
com-pīlātiō, ōnis *f* a pillaging, plundering; compilation.
com-pīlō 1 to plunder, pillage, rob.
com-pingō[1], **pēgī, pāctum** 3 **a**) to join together, frame, construct; **b**) to drive *or* thrust into; to fasten up.
com-pingō[2], **pinxī,** — 3 to paint over, bedaub.
compitālicius 3 belonging to the *Compitalia.*
compitālis, e belonging to a *compitum*; *subst.* **Compitālia, iōrum** *n/pl.* festival in honour of the *Lares compitales*, celebrated on the cross-roads.
compitum, ī *n* cross-roads.
com-placeō 2 to please well.
com-plānō 1 to make level *or* even; to raze to the ground.
com-plector, plexus sum 3 to clasp, embrace; **a**) to surround, encircle, enclose; **b**) to comprehend, comprise; **c**) to understand, grasp mentally; **d**) to esteem, value, honour, care for; **e**) to take into possession, lay hold of.
complēmentum, ī *n* complement.
com-pleō, ēvī, ētum 2 to fill up, fill full, make full (*alqd* with *gen.* or *abl.*); **a**) to complete, fill with men; **b**) to accomplish, fulfil, finish; **c**) to live through, pass.
complexiō, ōnis *f* connection, combination; short summary; sentence, period; syllogism; dilemma.
complexus, ūs *m* embrace, affection; close grip (of an enemy).
com-plicō, uī, ātum 1 to fold together *or* up; **complicātus** 3 confused, intricate.
com-plōdō 3 to strike together, clap (*the hands*).
com-plōrātiō, ōnis *f* (*and* **-us, ūs** *m*) loud complaint, wailing, lamentation.
com-plōrō 1 to bewail, lament loudly.
com-plūrēs, a, ium several, very many.

com-plūriēs *adv.* several times.
com-plūsculī 3 a good many.
com-pluvium, ī *n* open space in the middle of a Roman house.
com-pōnō 3 **1.** to bring, place, put together (*alqd in loco*); a) to collect, unite, concentrate; b) to inter, bury; c) to take in (*sails*); d) to oppose, confront; e) to compare, contrast (*alqd cum re* or with *dat.*); **2.** to compose, compound, make up, construct, form, fashion, make by joining together (*alqd ex re*); a) to compose, write; b) to agree upon together, to appoint, fix, settle; c) to invent, devise, contrive; **3.** to arrange, dispose, regulate, set in order, adjust; to allay, settle, appease, quiet.
com-portō 1 to carry *or* bring together.
com-pos, otis a) partaking of, possessing, participating in, sharing in (with *gen.*, seldom *abl.*); **b**) having the mastery of.
com-positiō, ōnis *f* a putting together, adjusting; matching; composition, arrangement; settlement, reconciliation.
com-positor, ōris *m* arranger, maker.
com-positūra, ae *f* putting together; fabric, texture.
com-positus 3 put together; **a**) well arranged, carefully adjusted *or* assumed; **b**) suitable, prepared; **c**) quiet, calm; **(ex) compositō** by agreement.
com-pōtātiō, ōnis *f* drinking party.
com-potiō 4 to put in possession of (*alqm alqo*).
com-pōtor, ōris *m*, **-trīx, trīcis** *f* drinking-companion.
com-prānsor, ōris *m* dinner-companion.
com-precātiō, ōnis *f* an imploring.
com-precor 1 to implore, supplicate, pray to.
com-prehendō 3 **1.** a) to comprise, express, describe; b) to embrace with kindness; **2.** to take hold of, seize, grasp, catch; a) to arrest, apprehend, capture; b) to detect, discover; c) to perceive, comprehend.
com-prehēnsibilis, e perceptible; conceivable, intelligible.
com-prehēnsiō, ōnis *f* **a**) a seizing, laying hold of; **b**) comprehension, perception; **c**) arrest, hostile seizing; **d**) period, sentence, style.
com-prēndō = **comprehendo.**
com-pressiō, ōnis *f and* **-ssus**[1], **ūs** *m* **a**) a pressing together, pressure, compression; **b**) embrace; **c**) conciseness.
com-pressus[2] 3 pressed together; concise.
com-primō, pressī, pressum 3 **1.** to press *or* squeeze together; a) to compress, to close; b) to embrace, ravish; **2.** to hold back; a) to restrain, check, repress, hinder, subdue; b) to keep to oneself, conceal.
com-probātiō, ōnis *f* approval.
com-probātor, ōris *m* approver.
com-probō 1 **a**) to approve of, assent to, acknowledge; **b**) to prove, confirm.
com-prōmissum, ī *n* mutual agreement to accept an award.
com-prōmittō 3 to agree to abide by the decision of an arbiter.
comptiōnālis = **coemptionalis.**
cōmptulus 3 elegant, foppish.
cōmptus, ūs *m* **a**) union; **b**) neatness.
com-pungō, (nxī), nctum 3 to prick *or* sting.
com-putātiō, ōnis *f* **a**) reckoning; **b**) stinginess.
com-putātor, ōris *m* reckoner.
com-putō 1 to sum up, reckon, compute.
com-putrēscō 3 to rot.
cōnāmen, inis *n* **a**) effort, attempt; **b**) support.
cōnātum, ī *n* attempt, undertaking, venture; effort, exertion; impulse.
cōnātus, ūs *m* = **conatum.**
con-cacō 1 to defile with filth.
con-caedēs, ium *f/pl.* barricade of trees, abattis.
con-calefaciō 3 to warm thoroughly.
con-caleō 2 to be warm.
con-calēscō, luī, — 3 to become warm, to glow.
con-callēscō, luī, — 3 **a**) to become callous, insensible; **b**) to become shrewd.
con-camerātus 3 vaulted over.
con-castīgō 1 to chastise severely.
con-cavō 1 to curve.
con-cavus 3 hollow, concave, curved.

con-cēdō 3 **1.** (*intr.*) to go away, give way; a) to depart, retire; withdraw, remove (*abl.*, *ab*, *ex*); to resort to, to pass (*in alqd*), **in sententiam** *alcis* to assent to; b) to yield (*alci*), to submit, be inferior, give precedence (*with dat.*); **2.** (*trans.*) to concede; to pardon; grant, allow; to hand over, resign.
con-celebrō 1 to visit a place often; to celebrate a festival; **a**) to pursue eagerly; **b**) to publish, proclaim; **c**) to praise, honour, extol.
con-cēnātiō, ōnis *f* a dining together.
con-centiō, ōnis *f* = **concentus.**
con-centuriō 1 to assemble in centuries.
con-centus, ūs *m* a singing together; **a**) harmony, music, concert; **b**) unanimity, concord.
con-ceptiō, ōnis *f*, **a**) = **conceptus; b**) drawing up of a legal formula.
con-ceptus, ūs *m* a) a becoming pregnant, conception; **b**) catching; **c**) collection.
con-cerpō, psī, ptum 3 to tear in pieces, rend; to criticize.
con-certātiō, ōnis *f* contest, dispute, controversy.
con-certātor, ōris *m* rival.
con-certātōrius 3 controversial.
con-certō 1 to contend eagerly, to dispute (*cum alqo de re*).
con-cessiō, ōnis *f* a yielding, concession; admission.
con-cessō 1 to leave off.
con-cessus, ūs *m* only in *abl.* **-u** *alcis* = by permission of.
concha, ae *f* mussel; **a**) mussel shell, Triton's trumpet; **b**) purple-fish; **c**) pearl; **d**) vessel *or* box for unguents; **e**) the vulva.
concheus 3 belonging to a shell-fish.
conchis, is *f* bean.
conchīta, ae *m* gatherer of mussels.
conchȳliātus 3 dyed with *or* dressed in purple.
conchȳlium, ī *n* shell-fish; **a**) oyster; **b**) purple-fish; purple dye, purple clothing.
con-cidō[1]**, cidī,**—3 to fall *or* tumble down; **a**) to sink down, drop; **b**) to fall, be slain, overthrown, defeated, to perish; **c**) to get discouraged.
con-cīdō[2]**, cīdī, cīsum** 3 to cut up, cut to pieces; **a**) to cut down, destroy, kill; **b**) to beat severely; **c**) to prostrate, strike down; *see also* **concīsus.**
con-cieō, cīvī, citum 2 = **concio.**
conciliābulum, ī *n* place of assembly, market-place, court.
conciliātiō, ōnis *f* union, connection; **a**) a making friendly, winning over; **b**) inclination; **c**) recommendation; **d**) an acquiring.
conciliātor, ōris *m* author, promoter, mediator.
conciliātrīcula, ae *f* = **conciliatrix.**
conciliātrīx, īcis *f* a female promoter, match-maker.
conciliātū *m* by union.
conciliātūra, ae *f* match-making.
conciliō 1 to bring together, unite; **a**) to reconcile, make friendly, win over; **b**) to recommend; **c**) to cause, mediate, bring about; **d**) to procure, acquire, gain (*alci alqd*); to play the match-maker. — **conciliātus** 3 **a**) beloved by (*alci*); **b**) inclined to (*ad alqd*).
concilium, ī *n* **a**) union; **b**) assembly, meeting; assembly of the people; council.
concinnitās, ātis *f* symmetry of style; elegance.
concinnitūdō, inis *f* = **concinnitas.**
concinnō 1 to arrange carefully; to cause, produce, make.
con-cinnus 3 **a**) harmonious, elegant, pretty, tasteful, polished; **b**) courteous, obliging.
con-cinō, cinuī, (centum) 3 **a**) to sing *or* sound together; **b**) to sing in harmony, in a chorus; **c**) to celebrate, praise; **d**) to agree together.
con-ciō, cīvī, cītum 4 **1.** to bring together, assemble, summon; **2.** to stir up, move violently; a) to rouse, excite; b) to produce, cause, promote.
concipilō 1 to cut to pieces.
con-cipiō, cēpī, ceptum 3 **1.** to take *or* hold together; to express in words, in a certain form; **2.** to take in, draw in, suck (*fluids*); to catch *or* take (*fire*); a) to conceive, become pregnant; *subst.* **conceptum, ī** *n* fœtus; b) to perceive, comprehend, understand; to imagine, think, fancy; entertain (*odium in alqm*); c) to receive, incur, commit.

con-cīsiō, ōnis *f* a separating *or* cutting up.
con-cīsūra, ae *f* a dividing, distribution.
concīsus 3 concise, brief, short, abrupt.
con-citāmentum, ī *n* incentive.
con-citātiō, ōnis *f* quick movement; **a**) sedition, tumult; **b**) violent passion.
con-citātor, ōris *m* exciter, agitator.
con-citō 1 to move quickly; **a**) to stir up, excite, rouse up, instigate; **b**) to summon; **c**) to cause, produce, occasion; **concitātus** 3 rapid, swift, violent.
concitor, ōris *m* = **concitator.**
con-clāmātiō, ōnis *f* loud shouting together.
con-clāmō (*and* **-mitō**) 1 **1.** to shout together *or* loudly; **vasa** to give the signal for packing; **2.** to call together; to bewail.
conclāve, is *n* room, chamber, apartment.
con-clūdō, sī, sum 3 **1.** to shut up, close, confine; to compress, condense, comprise; **2.** to bring to an end; to conclude, argue, infer; **conclūsum, ī** *n* conclusion (*in a syllogism*).
con-clūsē in rounded phrases.
con-clūsiō, ōnis *f* **1.** a shutting up, blockade; **2.** a) close, end; b) conclusion (*in a syllogism*).
conclūsiuncula, ae *f* paltry conclusion.
con-color, ōris of the same colour.
con-comitātus 3 escorted.
con-coquō 3 to boil thoroughly; a) to digest; **b**) to bear, endure, brook; **c**) to consider maturely, revolve in mind.
concordia, ae *f* concord, unity, harmony; intimate friend.
concordō 1 to be of one mind, be in union, to agree.
con-cors, dis of one mind, concordant, agreeing.
con-crēbrēscō, bruī 3 to grow strong.
con-crēdō 3 to intrust, commit, consign (*alci alqd*).
con-cremō 1 to burn up.
con-crepō, uī, — 1 **a**) to sound violently; to resound, rattle, clash, grate, creak; **b**) to cause to sound.
con-crēscō 3 to grow together; **a**) to condense, harden, stiffen, congeal curdle; **b**) to grow, be formed; **concrētus** 3 **a**) condensed, hardened, thick, hard; **b**) composed of.
con-crētiō, ōnis *f* a condensing, congealing, materiality.
con-crīminor 1 to make an accusation.
con-cruciō 1 to torture.
con-cubīna, ae *f* concubine.
con-cubīnātus, ūs *m* concubinage.
con-cubīnus, ī *m* bedfellow, one living in concubinage.
con-cubitus, ūs *m* a lying together; copulation; coition.
con-cubius 3: **-ā nocte** in the silence of night, at midnight; **-um** *subst. n* the dead of night.
con-culcō 1 to trample upon, to maltreat, despise.
con-cumbō, cubuī, cubitum 3 to lie down; to lie with.
con-cupiēns, tis desirous.
con-cupīscō, pīvī *and* **piī, pītum** 3 to long for, covet (*alqd*).
con-cūrō 1 to take great care of.
con-currō, (cu)currī, cursum 3 **a**) to run together, flock together (*ex re in* or *ad alqd*); **b**) to meet in conflict, rush together, engage in combat; **c**) to meet together (*cum alqo*); **d**) to happen at the same time.
con-cursātiō, ōnis *f* a running together, concourse; a running about, skirmishing.
concursātor, ōris *m* skirmisher.
con-cursiō, ōnis *f* a) a running together, concurrence; **b**) emphatic repetition of words.
con-cursō 1 **a**) *intr.* to run to and fro, to go about; to skirmish; **b**) *trans.* to visit.
con-cursus, ūs *m* **a**) a running together, concourse, throng, tumult; **b**) a meeting together; an encountering, attack, assault; **c**) combination.
con-cussiō, ōnis *f* a shaking, concussion.
con-cussū *m* by a shaking.
con-custōdiō 4 to watch *or* guard closely.
con-cutiō, cussī, cussum 3 **1.** to strike together; **2.** to shake violently, agitate; a) **se concutere** to examine oneself carefully; b) to disturb, alarm, trouble; c) to impair, weaken.

condalium, ī *n* little ring.
con-decet 2 it is proper *or* decent.
con-decorō 1 to adorn carefully.
condemnātor, ōris *m* prosecutor, accuser.
con-demnō 1 **a**) to sentence, condemn, find guilty (*alqm alcis rei, de re*); to accuse of, charge with, blame, disapprove; **b**) to effect the condemnation of a person.
con-dēnsō 1 to press close together.
con-dēnsus 3 very dense, close, thick.
con-diciō, ōnis *f* **1.** agreement; stipulation; a) proposition, condition, terms; b) marriage-contract, marriage; **2.** state, position, situation; place, circumstances, rank, relation, nature, manner.
con-dīcō 3 to agree upon, to appoint (*alci alqd*).
con-dīgnus 3 very worthy.
condīmentum, ī *n* spice, seasoning.
condiō 4 **a**) to make savoury, to prepare (*food*) carefully; to soften, temper: **b**) to pickle, preserve; to embalm; **condītus** 3 savoury, seasoned.
condiscipulātus, ūs *m* companionship in school.
con-discipulus, ī *m* (*and* **-la, ae** *f*) schoolfellow.
con-discō 3 to learn thoroughly.
condītiō, ōnis *f* a seasoning, pickling, preserving.
conditīvum, ī *n* tomb.
conditor, ōris *m* founder, maker, author, contriver, composer.
conditōrium, ī *n* tomb, coffin, urn.
conditūra, ae *f* **a**) preserving; **b**) seasoning.
con-dō, didī, ditum 3 **1.** to put together; a) to found, establish, build; b) to compose, write, describe; **2.** to put in, preserve; a) to store up, hide (*alqd in rem, in re*); b) to bury, inter; c) to pass (*time*); d) to hide, conceal, plunge (*a sword*).
con-docefaciō 3 (*and* **con-doceō** 2) to teach, instruct, train.
con-dolēscō, luī, — 3 to feel pain, suffer.
con-dōnātiō, ōnis *f* a giving away.
con-dōnō 1 to give away, present (*alci alqd*); **a**) to remit; **b**) to give up to, surrender, deliver up; **c**) to forgive, pardon.
con-dormiō 4 to fall asleep.
con-dormīscō, mīvī 3 to fall asleep.
con-dūcibilis, e profitable, advantageous.
con-dūcō 3 **1.** to lead *or* draw together, to assemble, gather (*alqd in locum*), to unite, combine; **2.** to hire, rent, employ, to hire for use, contract for, farm; *subst.* **conductī, ōrum** *m/pl.* hired soldiers, mercenaries; **conductum, ī** *n* hired apartment *or* house; **3. condūcit** it is useful, profitable (*alci, ad alqd*).
con-ductīcius 3 hired.
con-ductiō, ōnis *f* **a**) a bringing together; **b**) a hiring, farming.
con-ductor, ōris *m* **a**) hirer, farmer, tenant; **b**) contractor.
con-duplicātiō, ōnis *f* a doubling; embrace.
con-duplicō 1 to double.
con-dūrō 1 to harden.
condus, ī *m* store-keeper.
cō-nectō, nexuī, nexum 3 to bind together; **a**) to connect, join, link (*alqd cum re* or with *dat.*); **b**) to subjoin a logical conclusion.
cō-nexiō, ōnis *f* logical conclusion.
cō-nexus, ūs *m* a joining.
cōn-fābulor 1 to talk.
cōn-farreō 1 to marry by the ceremony of *confarreatio* (*an offering of bread*).
cōn-fātālis, e determined by the same fate.
cōn-fectiō, ōnis *f* **1.** a composing, finishing, completing; **2.** consumption, a chewing; **3.** exaction of money.
cōn-fector, ōris *m* **1.** finisher, executor; **2.** destroyer.
cōn-ferciō, rsī, rtum 4 to cram together; **cōnfertus** 3 closely compressed, dense, thick, crowded, in close array; filled full.
cōn-ferō, tulī, collātum, cōnferre **1.** to carry *or* bring together (*alqd ex re, in alqd, in* or *ad alqm*); a) to unite, join, connect (**P.** to be concentrated); b) to place together *or* near; to exchange (*words*), to discuss; to bring into hostile contact, set together (*arma, manus, signa*); **signis collātīs** in a pitched battle; **collātō pede** foot to foot; c) to pay in, contribute, to be profitable, of use; d) to compare, contrast (*alqd cum re,* or with *dat.*); **2.** to bring to a place, remove, transfer (*alqd ex re*

in rem); a) **se cōnferre** to betake oneself to, to devote oneself to, join oneself to; b) to put off, defer, postpone; c) to change, transform; d) to bestow on (*alci alqd*); to ascribe, attribute, impute; to transfer, assign (*alqd ad alqm*); e) to direct, apply to, to use.

cōnfertim *adv. of* **confertus.**

cōn-fervēfaciō 3 to melt.

cōn-fervēscō, buī, — 3 to begin to boil *or* to glow.

cōn-fessiō, ōnis *f* confession, acknowledgment.

cōn-festim *adv.* without delay, immediately.

cōn-ficiēns, tis effecting, efficient (*with gen.*).

cōn-ficiō 3 **1.** to make, make ready, prepare, bring about, accomplish, execute, fulfil; a) to compose, write; to settle, finish, bring to an end; to pass over, complete (*of time or space*); b) to produce, cause, procure, provide; c) to get, collect, contribute; d) to infer, show (*in a logical conclusion*); **2.** to grind, chew, digest, waste, consume, weaken, lessen, diminish, kill, destroy, subdue.

cōn-fictiō, ōnis *f* an inventing.

cōn-fīdēns, tis self-reliant, confident, bold, daring; audacious, impudent.

cōn-fīdentia, ae *f* a confiding, confidence; boldness, arrogance, impudence.

cōnfīdenti-loquus 3 speaking boldly.

cōn-fīdō, fīsus sum 3 to trust, confide, rely on (with *dat.* or *abl.*); to be assured, believe firmly, to hope (*with acc. c. inf.*).

cōn-fīgō 3 **a**) to fasten *or* nail together; **b**) to pierce through.

cōn-findō 3 to cleave asunder.

cōn-fingō 3 to invent, devise, fabricate.

cōn-fīnis, e bordering, adjoining (*with dat.*); neighbouring, nearly related, similar.

cōn-fīnium, ī *n* **a**) common boundary; **b**) confine, border, bordering-line; **c**) nearness, intermediate state.

cōn-fīō, —, fierī to be brought together, to be accomplished, brought about.

cōn-firmātiō, ōnis *f* a making firm; a) encouragement, consolation; **b**) a confirming, affirmation.

cōn-firmātor, ōris *m* one who confirms, a surety (*alcis rei*).

cōn-firmitās, ātis *f* obstinacy.

cōn-firmō 1 to make firm, establish, **a**) to strengthen, make lasting; to support, confirm, prove; **b**) to encourage, console, cheer, make bold; **c**) to assert, corroborate, affirm, protest.

cōn-fiscō 1 to lay up in a chest; to confiscate.

cōn-fīsiō, ōnis *f* confidence.

cōn-fiteor, fessus sum 2 **a**) to confess, avow, own, acknowledge (*alqd, de re*; with *acc. c. inf.*); **b**) to reveal, make known; **cōnfessus** 3 **a**) who pleads guilty; **b**) confessed, acknowledged.

cōn-flagrātiō, ōnis *f* a burning.

cōn-flagrō 1 to be in flames.

cōn-flictiō, ōnis *f* collision, conflict.

cōn-flictō 1 to strike together; **a**) to ruin; **b**) *intr. and* **P.** to struggle, contend, fight; to be tormented, afflicted, harassed (*alqa re, ab alqo*).

cōn-flīctus, ūs *m* a striking together.

cōn-flīgō, xī, ctum 3 **a**) to strike together; **b**) *intr.* to be in conflict, to struggle, fight.

cōn-flō 1 **a**) to blow together, blow up, kindle; **b**) to melt (*metals*); to bring together, make up, bring about; **c**) to forge, invent; to cause, produce, occasion.

cōn-fluō, fluxī, — 3 to flow *or* pour together; *subst.* **cōnfluēns, tis** (*also pl.*) confluence.

cōn-fodiō 3 to pierce through, transfix, stab.

cōn-fore (*and* **cōn-futūrum**) to be about to happen.

cōn-fōrmātiō, ōnis *f* a forming, shaping, form, shape; **a**) notion, conception; **b**) figure of speech.

cōn-fōrmō 1 to form, shape; to arrange, fashion, educate.

cōn-frag(ōs)us 3 uneven, rough.

cōn-fremō, uī, — 3 to murmur loudly, to roar.

cōn-fricō 1 to rub.

cōn-fringō, frēgi, frāctum 3 to break in pieces, shiver, shatter; to destroy, undo.

cōn-fugiō 3 to flee, take refuge.

cōn-fugium, ī *n* place of refuge.

cōn-fulgeō 2 to shine, glitter.
cōn-fultus 3 driven together.
cōn-fundō 3 to pour together; **a**) to mix, mingle, join, unite (*alqd in alqd*); **b**) to confound, confuse, throw into disorder, disturb, obscure; **c**) to disconcert, perplex; **cōnfūsus** 3 confused, disorderly; disturbed, disconcerted, blushing, disfigured.
cōn-fūsīcius 3 mixed together.
cōn-fūsiō, ōnis *f* **a**) a mingling, mixing, union; **b**) confusion, disorder.
cōn-fūtō 1 **a**) to silence; **b**) to check, repress; **c**) to confute, refute.
con-gelō 1 **a**) *trans.* to freeze, harden; **b**) *intr.* to freeze, congeal.
con-geminātiō, ōnis *f* a doubling, embrace.
con-geminō 1 to (re)double.
con-gemō 3 to sigh *or* groan loudly.
conger, grī *m* sea-eel, conger-eel.
congeriēs, ēī *f* heap, pile, mass.
con-gerō 3 to carry *or* bring together, to collect; **a**) to heap up, pile up; to build, construct; **b**) to heap upon, load; **c**) to build a nest.
con-gerrō, ōnis *m* companion in amusement.
congestīcius 3 heaped up.
con-gestus, ūs *m* **a**) a bringing together, heaping up; **b**) heap.
congiālis, e holding a *congius*.
congiārium, ī *n* donation, distribution, largess (*in wine, oil, money etc.*).
congius, ī *m* a measure for liquids (6 pints).
con-glaciō 1 to freeze, congeal.
con-gliscō 3 to blaze up anew.
con-globātiō, ōnis *f* a pressing *or* crowding together.
con-globō 1 to gather into a ball, to make round; to press together in a mass *or* crowd.
con-glomerō 1 to roll into a mass.
con-glūtinātiō, ōnis *f* a gluing *or* cementing together.
con-glūtinō 1 to glue *or* cement together, to unite, join, bind closely,
con-graecō 1 to squander in Greek manner.
con-grātulor 1 to wish joy, congratulate one another.
con-gredior, gressus sum 3 **a**) to come together, meet; **b**) to meet in combat, to fight.
congregābilis, e social, sociable.
congregātiō, ōnis *f* union, society.
con-gregō 1 to collect into a flock, to collect, gather together, associate, unite.
con-gressiō, ōnis *f* = **congressus.**
con-gressus, ūs *m* a meeting; **a**) intercourse, conversation, conference; **b**) onset, encounter, fight.
congruēns, tis agreeing, fit, appropriate; accordant, consistent, harmonious (*cum re*, or with *dat.*).
con-gruentia, ae *f* consistency, symmetry.
con-gruō, uī, — 3 to come together, meet; **a**) to coincide; **b**) to agree, harmonize, suit, correspond (*cum re*, or with *dat.*); to be of one mind (*de re, in rem*).
con-gruus 3 in agreement.
cōn-iciō (*and* **cŏn-**), **iēcī, iectum** 3 **1.** to throw together, bring together; to conjecture, guess, infer (*ex, de re*); **2.** to throw, cast, thrust, drive; to direct, turn, urge, force (*in* or *intra alqd*), **se cōnicere** to rush, run, hasten away.
con-iectiō, ōnis *f* **a**) a hurling, throwing; **b**) conjecture, interpretation.
con-iectō 1 to conjecture, guess, infer.
coniector, ōris *m* (*and* **-trīx, īcis** *f*) interpreter of dreams, soothsayer.
coniectūra, ae *f* **a**) conjecture, guess, inference; **b**) interpretation of omens, soothsaying.
con-iectūrālis, e conjectural.
con-iectus, ūs *m* **a**) a throwing together; **b**) a throwing, casting, hurling; **c**) a turning, directing; **teli** reach of a shot.
cōni-fer 3, **cōni-ger** 3 cone-bearing.
cō-nitor 3 **a**) to lean *or* push against; **b**) to strive, struggle, exert oneself, ascend; **c**) to bring forth, give birth.
con-iugātiō, ōnis *f* relationship of words.
con-iugātor, ōris *m* uniter.
coniug(i)ālis, e conjugal.
con-iugium, ī *n* **a**) marriage, wedlock; **b**) husband, wife.
con-iugō 1 = **coniungo.**
con-iūnctim *adv.* jointly.
con-iūnctiō, ōnis *f* union, connection; **a**) friendship, intimacy; **b**) marriage, relationship; **c**) connecting particle.

con-iūnctus 3 connected, joined, united (*cum re*, or with *dat.*); **a**) adjoining, bordering on; **b**) near, associated, intimate, allied, kindred; agreeing with.
con-iungō 3 **a**) to connect, join, unite (*alqd cum re*, or *dat.*); **b**) to add (*alqd alci rei*); **c**) to contract (*a union*).
con-iūnx, iugis *f* wife, spouse consort (*more rarely m* husband); **a**) female; **b**) bride, mate.
con-iūrātiō, ōnis *f* **a**) a swearing together; union confirmed by oath; **b**) conspiracy, plot; conspirators.
con-iūrō 1 to swear together; **a**) to take the military oath; **b**) to combine under oath; **c**) to conspire, plot; **coniūrātus** 3 united by an oath; *subst.* conspirator.
coniux, *see* **coniunx.**
cō-nīveō, (nīvī *or* **nīxī),** — 2 to wink, shut the eyes (*of the eyes*: to be shut); **a**) to be languid, drowsy; **b**) to overlook, leave unnoticed, connive.
conl..., *see* **coll...**
con-nectō, *see* **conecto.**
con-nītor, *see* **conitor.**
con-nīveō, *see* **coniveo.**
cōnōpēum (*and* **cōnōpium**), **ī** *n* mosquito-net.
cōnor 1 to attempt, try, undertake, venture, endeavour (*alqd;* with *inf.*).
con-quassātiō, ōnis *f* a violent shaking, shattering.
con-quassō 1 to shake violently, to shatter, disturb.
con-queror 3 to bewail, lament; to complain (*alqd, de re,* with *acc. c. inf.*).
con-questiō, ōnis *f* a bewailing, complaint.
con-questus, ūs *m* complaint.
con-quiēscō 3 to rest, repose (*ab, ex re*); **a**) to find rest; **b**) to be still, quiet.
con-quinīscō 3 to squat down.
con-quīrō, sīvī, sītum 3 to seek for, bring together; to search out, to collect; **conquīsītus** 3 sought out, choice.
con-quīsītiō, ōnis *f* a seeking out, search for; a collecting; a levying, conscription.
con-quīsītor, ōris *m* recruiting officer.
conr..., *see* **corr...**

cōn-saepiō 4 to fence in, hedge in.
cōn-saeptum, ī *n* enclosure.
cōn-salūtātiō, ōnis *f* a greeting.
cōn-salūtō 1 to greet, salute.
cōn-sānēscō, nuī, — 3 to become healed, to recover.
cōn-sanguineus 3 related by blood, of a brother *or* sister; brother *m*, sister *f*.
cōn-sanguinitās, ātis *f* blood-relationship.
cōn-sauciō 1 to wound severely.
cōn-scelerātus 3 wicked, villainous.
cōn-scelerō 1 to defile with a crime.
cōn-scendō, dī, sum 3 to ascend, mount, climb (*alqd*), to go on board (*navem*).
cōn-scēnsiō, ōnis *f* an ascending, embarking.
cōn-scientia, ae *f* **1.** joint knowledge, a being privy to (*with gen.*); **2.** consciousness, a) feeling; sense; b) good *or* bad conscience, remorse.
cōn-scindō 3 to tear *or* rend to pieces.
cōn-sciō 4 (*sibi*) to be conscious.
cōn-scīscō 3 **a**) to resolve jointly *or* publicly; **b**) **sibi** *alqd.* to bring *or* inflict upon oneself, **mortem** to commit suicide.
cōn-scius 3 **a**) knowing with another (*alci rei* or *alcis rei; alci alcis rei*), conscious; **b**) self-conscious; conscious of guilt (*gen.*); *subst.* **~, ī** *m* partaker, accomplice.
cōn-screor 1 to clear the throat.
cōn-scrībillō 1 to scribble on.
cōn-scrībō 3 to write together; **1.** to enrol; **2.** a) to levy, enlist; b) to enrol in a particular class (**cōnscrīptus** newly chosen senator); c) to write, compose; d) to write all over.
cōn-scrīptiō, ōnis *f* a drawing up in writing, composition, treatise.
cōn-secō 1 to cut to pieces.
cōn-secrātiō, ōnis *f* consecration, dedication; **a**) execration; **b**) apotheosis.
cōn-secrō 1 to dedicate, consecrate (*alqd alci*); **a**) to execrate; **b**) to deify, to make immortal.
cōnsectārius 3 following logically, consequent.
cōn-sectātiō, ōnis *f* a striving after.
cōn-sectātrīx, īcis *f* she who pursues eagerly, friend, adherent.
cōn-sectiō, ōnis *f* a cutting to pieces.

cōn-sector 1 to follow, attend (*with acc.*); **a**) to pursue (*alqm*); **b**) to overtake, catch; **c**) to strive after, emulate.

cōn-secūtiō, ōnis *f* effect, consequence; **a**) sequence; **b**) conclusion.

cōn-senēscō, senuī, — 3 to become old *or* grey; to become weak *or* infirm, to decay, fade, degenerate, grow obsolete.

cōn-sēnsiō, ōnis *f* = **consensus.**

cōn-sēnsus, ūs *m* agreement, unanimity, harmony; **a**) common accord; **b**) conspiracy, plot.

cōnsentāneus 3 agreeing, fit, suitable (*cum re;* with *dat.*); reasonable, consistent.

cōn-sentiō 4 to agree, be of one mind, accord, harmonize (*cum alqo, de re*); **a**) to resolve unanimously (with *inf.* or *ut*); **b**) to conspire, plot (*contra alqm, ad alqd*); (*of things*) to harmonize, suit, fit; **cōnsentiēns, tis** agreeing, accordant, harmonious.

cōn-sequē *adv.* consecutively.

cōn-sequēns, tis according to reason, reasonable, appropriate, consequent; *subst.* **cōnsequēns, tis** *n* consequence.

cōn-sequentia, ae *f* consequence, succession.

cōn-sequor 3 **1.** to follow up, to follow, go after (*alqm* or *alqd*); a) to pursue; b) to imitate, copy, obey; c) to follow as an effect, to result; **2.** to overtake, reach, attain to (*alqm, alqd*); a) to become like *or* equal; to express adequately; b) to understand, perceive, learn.

cōn-serō¹, sēvī, situm 3 **a**) to sow, plant; **b**) to plant in *or* with.

cōn-serō², seruī, sertum 3 to connect, twine together; **a**) to join, fit, bind, tie; **b**) to bring together in a hostile manner (*manus cum alqo* to come to close quarters), to engage (*in battle*); **c**) *in law*: **manum** to lay hands on a thing in dispute.

cōnsertē *adv.* connectedly.

cōn-serva, ae *f* (*female*) fellow-slave.

cōn-servātiō, ōnis *f* preservation, a keeping.

cōn-servātor, ōris *m* preserver, keeper, defender.

cōn-servātrix, īcis *f* preserver.

cōn-servitium, ī *n* joint servitude.

cōn-servō 1 to keep, preserve; **a**) to maintain, observe; **b**) to save, keep safe, keep intact, spare.

cōn-servus, ī *m* fellow-slave.

cōn-sessor, ōris *m* one who sits near *or* by; neighbour, assessor.

cōn-sessus, ūs *m* a sitting together, assembly, spectators, audience.

cōnsīderātiō, ōnis *f* consideration, reflection.

cōnsīderātus 3 **a**) well considered, maturely reflected upon; **b**) thoughtful, prudent, cautious.

cōn-sīderō 1 to look at, regard, contemplate; to consider, weigh, reflect upon.

cōn-sidium, ī committee.

cōn-sīdō 3 **1.** to sit down together, to settle (*in loco*); **2.** to sit down, be seated, take a seat; a) to hold sessions, be in session; b) to take up a position, to encamp, station oneself; c) to settle, stay; d) to land; e) to sink down, give way, subside, abate, cease.

cōn-signō 1 **1.** to seal, sign, subscribe; to attest, certify, vouch for; **2.** to write down, note, register.

cōn-silēscō 3 to become silent.

cōnsiliārius 3 counselling; *subst.* ~, **ī** *m* counsellor, adviser.

cōnsiliātor, ōris *m* adviser, counsellor.

cōnsilior 1 to take *or* give counsel, hold a consultation.

cōnsilium, ī *n* **1.** a taking counsel; a) deliberation, consultation; b) assembly *or* body of counsellors, council, senate, council of war, body of judges; **2.** consideration, understanding, foresight, prudence, judgment; wisdom; a) resolution, plan, determination, measure, design, intention (**cōnsiliō** on purpose); stratagem, device; b) advice, suggestion.

cōn-similis, e similar, like.

cōn-sipiō 3 to be of sound mind.

cōn-sistō, stitī, — 3 **1.** to take one's stand *or* place oneself in company with others, be together (*in loco*); a) to exist, occur, take place; b) to be based upon (*in re*), depend on, consist of; **2.** to place oneself; a) to stand still, stop, halt, stay, to anchor; b) to establish oneself, to settle; to stand firmly; to keep one's ground *or* footing, to continue, endure; c) to stop, dwell, abide, tarry; d) to falter; e) to come to a stand, to rest, cease; f) to contain *or* collect oneself.

cōnsitiō, ōnis *f* a sowing, planting.
cōnsitor, ōris *m* sower, planter.
cōnsitūra, ae *f* = **consitio.**
cōn-sobrīnus, ī *m and* **-a, ae** *f* cousin.
cōn-socer, erī *m* joint father-in-law.
cōn-sociātiō, ōnis *f* union, association.
cōn-sociō 1 to unite, associate, to make common, share with (*alqd cum alqo*); **cōnsociātus** 3 united, harmonious.
cōn-sōlābilis, e consolable.
cōn-sōlātiō, ōnis *f* a consoling, consolation, comfort; consolatory treatise.
cōn-sōlātor, ōris *m* comforter.
cōn-sōlātōrius 3 of consolation.
cōn-sōlor 1 to console, comfort, encourage (*alqm de* or *in re*); to mitigate, alleviate, relieve.
cōn-somniō (?) 1 to dream.
cōn-sonō 1 to sound together, to resound, echo; to agree.
cōn-sonus 3 sounding together, harmonious; agreeing.
cōn-sōpiō 4 to lull to sleep.
cōn-sors, tis having an equal share (*with gen.*); **a**) partaking of; **b**) brotherly, sisterly; **c**) common; *subst.* partner, sharer, associate, comrade.
cōnsortiō, ōnis *f* companionship, community.
cōn-sortium, ī *n* = **consortio.**
cōn-spectus[1] 3, *see* **conspicio.**
cōn-spectus[2], **ūs** *m* **1.** a seeing; **a**) look, sight, view; **b**) an appearing, becoming visible, **in cōnspectū** within sight, **in cōnspectum venire** to come in sight; **2.** mental view, survey, consideration.
cōn-spergō, sī, sum 3 to sprinkle, moisten, besprinkle; to cover.
cōn-spicillum, ī *n* look-out.
cōn-spiciō, spexī, spectum 3 **1.** a) to look at, behold, view; b) to descry, perceive, observe, **P.** to attract notice, be conspicuous, distinguished, admired; **2.** to perceive mentally; — **cōnspectus** 3 visible, distinguished, remarkable; **cōnspiciendus** 3 worth seeing.
cōn-spicor 1 to see, behold.
cōn-spicuus 3 visible; striking, remarkable, conspicuous, eminent.
cōn-spīrātiō, ōnis *f* **a**) union, harmony; **b**) conspiracy.
cōn-spīrō 1 **1.** to breathe together, to sound together; **2.** a) to agree, harmonize (*cum alqo*); b) to conspire, plot; **cōnspīrātus** 3 of one mind; *subst.* conspirator.
cōn-spōnsor, ōris *m* a joint surety.
cōn-spuō 3 to spit upon.
cōn-spurcō 1 to defile.
cōn-spūtō 1 to spit upon.
cōn-stabiliō 4 to establish.
cōn-stāns, tis standing firm; **a**) firm, steady, immovable, constant, unchanging, regular, consistent, harmonious; **b**) resolute, constant, steadfast, faithful.
cōnstantia, ae *f* **a**) firmness, steadiness, constancy, perseverance; agreement, harmony, consistency; **b**) steadfastness, self-possession.
cōnsternātiō, ōnis *f* **a**) dismay, alarm, fright, consternation; **b**) mutiny, tumult.
cōn-sternō[1] 1 **a**) to cause confusion, to confound, perplex; **b**) to terrify, alarm, frighten; **c**) to excite, cause a revolt.
cōn-sternō[2] 3 **a**) to strew over, cover, to thatch, pave; **b**) to throw down, prostrate.
cōn-stīpō 1 to press *or* crowd together.
cōn-stituō, uī, ūtum 3 **1.** a) to place *or* put together; b) to cause to stand, to place, put; **2.** a) to station, post, moor; b) to appoint, settle, fix by agreement; c) to erect, set up; d) to draw up in line, arrange; e) to settle, establish, to found, build, construct; f) to set in order, organize, manage; g) to undertake, make, effect, constitute; h) to designate, assign; i) to determine at law, decide; k) to resolve, take a resolution (*with inf., acc. c. inf.*); — **cōnstitūtus** 3 constituted, arranged, disposed.
cōnstitūtiō, ōnis *f* constitution, condition; **a**) regulation, arrangement; **b**) disposition, nature.
cōnstitūtum, ī *n* **a**) regulation, order; **b**) agreement, appointment; fixed time *or* place for meeting.
cōnstitūtus 3, *see* **constituo.**
cōn-stō, stitī, stātūrus 1 to stand firm, to exist; **a**) to stand still *or* firm, to remain, to remain the same, to be unaltered (*in re*); **b**) to agree, be consistent, correspond (*alci rei, cum* or *in re*); **sibi cōnstāre** to be consistent; **ratio cōnstat** the

reckoning is right; **c**) to be certain, ascertained, known, **inter omnes cōnstat** everybody knows; **d**) to exist, be extant; **e**) to consist of, be composed of, be derived from (*ex* or *in re*; *abl.*); to cost (with *abl.* or *gen.*).
cōn-strātum, ī *n* a covering, floor.
cōn-stringō 3 to bind together; **a**) to fetter, confine; **b**) to strengthen, fortify; **c**) to bind, restrain, limit, compress.
cōnstructiō, ōnis *f* a putting together, construction, building.
cōn-struō 3 to heap up together, to pile up; **a**) to construct, build up, to erect; **b**) to arrange.
cōn-stuprātor, ōris *m* debaucher, ravisher.
cōn-stuprō 1 to ravish, violate.
cōn-suādeō 2 to advise emphatically.
cōn-suāsor, ōris *m* adviser.
cōn-sūcidus 3 juicy.
cōn-sūdō 1 to sweat profusely.
cōn-suēfaciō 3 to accustom, habituate (*alqm* with *inf.*).
cōn-suēscō 3 to accustom oneself to (*inf.*), *pf.* to be accustomed, be wont; **a**) *cum alqo* **cōnsuēvisse** to be intimate with; **b**) **cōnsuētus** 3 accustomed, usual.
cōn-suētiō, ōnis *f* love-affair.
cōnsuētūdō, inis *f* custom, habit, usage, way, usual practice; **a**) form of speech; **b**) social intercourse, intimacy; correspondence (*epistularum*); **c**) love-affair.
cōnsul, ulis *m* consul.
cōnsulāris, e relating to a consul, consular; *subst.* **~, is** *m* **a**) one who has been a consul, ex-consul; **b**) governor of consular rank; *adv.* **cōnsulāriter** in a manner worthy of a consul.
cōnsulātus, ūs *m* the office of consul, consulship.
cōnsulō, luī, ltum 3 **1.** to deliberate, consider, consult (*de re*); **a**) to take care for (*dat.*), have regard, be mindful; **sibi cōnsulere** to look to one's interest; b) to take a resolution, resolve, take measures (*against*) (*de re, in alqm*); **2.** a) to ask the advice of, to consult (*alqm de re*); b) to consult an oracle; *alqd boni* to take in good part; *see also* **cōnsultus.**
cōnsultātiō, ōnis *f* **a**) deliberation; **b**) a consulting, asking for advice, inquiry; **c**) subject of consultation.
cōnsultō 1 **a**) to consider maturely, to weigh, **in medium** for the common good; to provide for (*with dat.*), have a care; **b**) to consult (*alqm*).
cōnsultor, ōris *m* **a**) adviser; **b**) one who asks advice.
cōnsultrīx, īcis *f* she who cares for.
cōnsultum, ī *n* deliberation; resolution, decree, measure; answer of an oracle.
cōnsultus 3 **a**) well considered, weighed, deliberated upon; **b**) knowing, experienced, learned; **iuris** *or* **iure cōnsultus** learned in the law, lawyer, counsellor; *adv.* **cōnsultō** (*and* **-tē**) deliberately, purposely.
cōn-summābilis, e capable of completion *or* perfection.
cōn-summātiō, ōnis *f* completion.
cōn-summō 1 **a**) to sum up; **b**) to finish, accomplish, complete, perfect; **cōnsummātus** 3 complete.
cōn-sūmō 3 **1.** to use up, consume; **a**) to eat up; **b**) to spend, employ, waste, destroy, annihilate, exhaust; **2.** to use, spend upon (*alqd in re*).
cōn-sūmptiō, ōnis *f* a consuming.
cōn-sūmptor, ōris *m* consumer, destroyer.
cōn-suō 3 to stitch together; to plan.
cōn-surgō 3 **a**) to rise, stand up (*together*); **b**) to rise for an action; to strive upwards, aspire.
cōn-surrēctiō, ōnis *f* a rising in a body.
cōn-susurrō 1 to whisper together.
con-tābēfaciō 3 to consume.
con-tābēscō, buī, — 3 to waste away.
con-tabulātiō, ōnis *f* a covering with planks; wooden floor *or* story.
con-tabulō 1 to cover with boards; **a**) to build towers in stories; **b**) to bridge over.
con-tāctus, ūs *m* = **contagio.**
con-tāgēs, is *f* contact.
con-tāgiō, ōnis *f* (*also* **-gium, ī** *n*) **a**) a touching, contact; **b**) contagion, infection; contamination, bad example.
con-tāminō 1 to pollute, contaminate; to blend together.
con-technor 1 to devise.
con-tegō 3 to cover; **a**) to protect; **b**) to conceal, to bury.
con-temerō 1 to violate, defile.

con-temnō, psī, ptum 3 to despise, contemn, to slight, esteem lightly.
contemplātiō, ōnis *f* a viewing, surveying, contemplation.
contemplātīvus 3 speculative, theoretical.
contemplātor, ōris *m* observer.
contemplātus, ūs *m* = **contemplatio.**
contemplor (*and* **-ō**) 1 to look at, view, survey, consider.
contemptim *adv.* contemptuously, scornfully.
contemptiō, ōnis *f* contempt, disregard, disdain.
contemptor, ōris *m* despiser.
contemptrīx, īcis *f* she who despises.
contemptus[1] 3 despised, despicable.
contemptus[2], **ūs** *m* = **contemptio.**
con-tendō, tendī, tentum 3 **1.** to stretch together; a) to put together, to compare, contrast; b) to strive with some one else, to contend, dispute; **2.** to stretch forcibly, to draw tight, strain; a) to hurl, b) to exert oneself, to strive, to pursue earnestly (*in, ad alqd*), to hasten on a journey, try to reach; c) to strive to obtain, to demand (*alqd ab alqo*; with *ut, ne*), ask; d) to assert, affirm, maintain (*alqd*; *acc. c. inf.*).
con-tentē[1] energetically.
con-tentē[2] sparingly.
contentiō, ōnis *f* **1.** a) comparison, contrast; b) contest, combat, contention; dispute, controversy.; **2.** a) exertion, zealous pursuit; b) vehemence, passion.
contentiōsus 3 contentious.
contentus[1] 3 [*contendo*] **a**) stretched, strained, tense; **b**) eager, zealous.
contentus[2] 3 [*contineo*] contented, satisfied (*alqa re*).
con-terminus 3 bordering on, neighbouring.
con-terō 3 to grind, bruise; **a**) to rub away, wear away, waste, consume, spend, destroy; **b**) to esteem lightly; **conteri** *or* **se conterere** (*in re*) to be wearied, to drudge; **contrītus** 3 trite, common.
con-terreō 2 to terrify, frighten.
con-testor 1 **a**) to call to witness; **b**) **litem** to introduce a lawsuit; **contestātus** 3 tried, proved.
con-texō 3 to weave *or* twine together; **a**) to connect, unite (*alqd cum re*); **b**) to continue; **c**) to devise, build, compose.
con-textus[1] 3 woven together, closely connected, continuous.
con-textus[2], **ūs** *m* connection, coherence; sequel.
con-ticēscō, ticuī, — 3 to become silent, still *or* dumb.
con-ticinium (*or* **-cinnum**), **ī** *n* sleeping time, night.
con-tignātiō, ōnis *f* a joining together of beams; floor, story.
con-tignō 1 to construct of beams.
contiguus 3 **a**) contiguous, near; **b**) within reach.
con-tinēns, tis **1.** holding together; moderate, temperate; **2.** a) bordering, neighbouring (*with dat.*); b) following, continuous, in unbroken succession; — *subst.* **continēns, tis** *f* mainland, continent; *n* main point (of a case).
continentia, ae *f* temperance, abstinence, self-restraint.
con-tineō, tinuī, (**tentum**) 2 **1.** to hold *or* keep together; a) to bind together, connect, join; b) to keep, maintain, retain, preserve; **2.** to surround; a) to shut in, enclose, limit; b) to contain, comprise, comprehend, involve, **P.** to depend upon, consist of; **3.** to keep in a place *or* situation, to hold back, stay, stop; a) to check, repress, restrain, curb; b) to keep some one from something.
con-tingō, tigī, tāctum 3 **1.** to touch; a) to reach, take hold of, seize; b) to arrive at, come to; c) to border on, touch, be near, be related to; d) to concern, affect; *part.* **contāctus** 3 defiled, polluted, tainted; **2.** *intr.* to happen, turn out, come to pass.
continuātiō, ōnis *f* unbroken succession; **a**) continuance, prolongation, series; **b**) period.
continuō[1] *adv.* immediately, at once, directly; continuously.
continuō[2] 1 to join in unbroken succession; **a**) to connect, unite, make continuous (*alqd alci rei*), **P.** to be adjacent, border on; **b**) to extend (*alqd alqa re*); **c**) to carry on, draw out, continue, do uninterruptedly, **P.** to follow close upon; **d**) to prolong.

continuus 3 hanging together; **a**) uninterrupted, continuous, successive, following on; **b**) connected with, near; **c**) incessant, unremitting.

contiō, ōnis *f* meeting, assembly, convocation; **a**) public meeting (*of the people* or *of the soldiers*); **b**) speech made to an assembly, public address, harangue. [public.

contiōnābundus 3 speaking in

contiōnālis, e *and* **-nārius** 3 relating to a public assembly; vulgar.

contiōnātor, ōris *m* demagogue, popular orator.

contiōnor 1 **a**) to speak in public; **b**) to form an assembly.

contiuncula, ae *f* **a**) small assembly; **b**) petty speech.

con-tollō 3 = **confero.** [ly.

con-tonat 1 it thunders violent-

contor 1 to inquire.

con-torqueō 2 to twist, whirl, contort; **a**) to turn, direct, influence (*alqm ad alqd*); **b**) to hurl, brandish; **contortus** 3 intricate, confused, complicated; vigorous, vehement.

con-tortiō, ōnis *f* complicated expression. [tricate.

contorti-plicātus 3 entangled, in-

con-tortor, ōris *m* perverter.

contortulus 3 somewhat intricate.

contrā 1. *adv.* opposite, over against; a) on the other side; b) on the contrary (*contrā ac* otherwise than), in return; against; **2.** *prep.* with *acc.* opposite to, over against; against, contrary to.

con-tractiō, ōnis *f* a drawing together; **a**) abbreviation, shortness; **b**) dejection.

contractiuncula, ae *f* dejection, sadness. [against (*alci*).

contrā-dīcō 3 to gainsay, speak

contrā-dictiō, ōnis *f* a speaking in opposition.

con-trahō 3 to draw together; **1.** to draw in, shorten (*orationem*), to make narrow; a) to reduce, confine; b) to check, restrain; **2.** to collect, unite, assemble, concentrate; a) to bring about, accomplish, execute, cause, produce; b) to transact, contract, bargain, complete a business-arrangement; — **contractus** 3 drawn in, contracted, narrow, limited, short; living in retirement; **res contracta** contract.

contrārius 3 lying over against, opposite (*alci rei*); **a**) opposed; **b**) hostile, contrary to, inimical, conflicting; injurious; — *subst.* **contrārium, ī** *n* the opposite, reverse, opposite direction.

con-trectābiliter so as to be felt.

contrectātiō, ōnis *f* a touching, handling.

con-trectō 1 to touch, handle, feel; **a**) to violate, dishonour; **b**) to consider, survey.

con-tremīscō *and* **-ēscō, muī,** — 3 to tremble violently, shake, shudder at (*alqd*); to waver.

con-tremō 3 to quake.

con-tribuō 3 **a**) to unite, incorporate, add, annex.

con-trīstō 1 to make sad *or* sorrowful, to make gloomy.

con-trītus 3 worn out, trite.

contrōversia, ae *f* **a**) quarrel, dispute, debate, question, controversy; **b**) lawsuit; **c**) contradiction.

contrō(-versiōsus,)-versus 3 controverted, disputed.

con-trucīdō 1 to cut down *or* to pieces.

con-trūdō 3 to thrust into, crowd into (*alqm in alqd*).

con-truncō 1 to cut to pieces.

contubernālis, is *m* (*and f*) tent-companion, comrade; **a**) personal follower, attendant of a general; **b**) companion, mate, husband (*f wife*).

con-tubernium, ī *n* **1.** common tent, common dwelling; a) abode of a male and female slave; b) marriage of slaves, concubinage; **2.** tent--companionship, comradeship; intercourse, attendance.

con-tueor, (**tuitus sum**) 2 (*and* **con-tuor** 3) to look on *or* at attentively, to regard, behold, survey.

contuitus *or* **-tūtus, ūs** *m* a beholding, sight.

contumācia, ae *f* **a**) obstinacy, stubbornness; **b**) constancy, firmness.

con-tumāx, ācis a) stubborn, obstinate; **b**) unyielding.

con-tumēlia, ae *f* **a**) injury, violence, damage; **b**) insult, affront, contumely.

contumēliōsus 3 **a**) insulting, abusive; **b**) reproachful.

con-tumulō 1 to cover with a mound, to bury.

con-tundō, tudī, tū(n)sum 3 a) to crush, bruise, break to pieces; **b**) to put down, subdue, destroy.
con-turbātiō, ōnis *f* confusion, consternation.
con-turbātor, ōris *m* ruinously expensive.
con-turbō 1 to throw into disorder, disturb, confound; **a**) to fail (*in business*), be bankrupt; **b**) to disquiet, cause anxiety.
contus, ī *m* pole; spear, pike.
cō-nūbiālis (*and* **-nŭb-**), **e** conjugal.
cō-nūbium (*and* **-nŭb-**), **ī** *n* marriage, wedlock; **a**) nuptials; **b**) right of intermarriage.
cōnus, ī *m* cone; apex of a helmet.
con-vador 1 to bind over to appear in court.
con-valēscō, luī, — 3 **a**) to become strong *or* valid; **b**) to recover, regain health.
con-vallis, is *f* a valley shut in on all sides.
con-vāsō 1 to pack up.
con-vectō 1 *intens. of* **conveho.**
con-vector, ōris *m* fellow-passenger.
con-vehō 3 to carry together to one place; to convey; **P.** to be conveyed *or* carried.
con-vellō 3 **a**) to pull *or* tear away, to pluck up, **signa** to decamp; **b**) to shake, overthrow, destroy.
con-vena, ae meeting together; *subst.* **-nae, ārum** *m/pl.* assembled multitude, strangers, vagabonds.
con-veniēns, tis a) agreeing, unanimous, harmonious; **b**) convenient, corresponding, fit, becoming, appropriate.
con-venientia, ae *f* agreement, harmony, symmetry.
con-veniō 4 **1.** to come together, assemble, meet (*in locum, ad alqm*); a) to come into the power of a man, to marry; b) to visit, meet, address, accost (*alqm*); **2.** to come about, to a decision, be agreed upon; **convenit** it is agreed *or* decided upon; **3.** to be fit, suitable, appropriate (*ad alqd*); to consist, apply, be adapted to; **convenit** it is suitable, proper, becoming.
conventīcium, ī *n* money paid for attendance in an assembly.
con-ventīcius 3 casually met.
conventiculum, ī *n* a coming together, assembly.
con-ventiō, ōnis *f and* **con-ventum, ī** *n* agreement, convention, contract.
con-ventus, ūs *m* a coming together, assembly; **a**) congress, council, judicial session, court of justice; **b**) assembly of the inhabitants of a province, provincial corporation; **c**) union, agreement.
con-verberō 1 to beat severely.
con-verrō 3 to sweep together, to scrape together; to beat.
con-versātiō, ōnis *f* intercourse, conversation.
con-versiō, ōnis *f* a turning round; **a**) periodical return; **b**) revolution, change.
con-versō 1 to turn round; **-sor** to keep company (with).
con-vertō 3 **1.** a) to turn round, back, to the other side, to reverse, **signa** to wheel round, change the direction; **se, terga convertere** to flee; b) to turn in a circle; c) to throw back, to cause to yield; d) to change, alter, transform; e) to convert, pervert; f) to exchange; g) to translate; **2.** to direct, turn (*alqd in* or *ad alqd*); to apply to; **P.** to turn round; *intr.* to turn, return, change.
con-vestiō 4 to clothe, cover.
convexus 3 **a**) vaulted, arched; **b**) sloping, steep; *subst.* **convexum, ī** *n* vault, arch.
convīciātor, ōris *m* slanderer, reviler.
convīcior 1 to revile, rail at, reproach.
convīcium, ī *n* loud cry, noise, clamour; **a**) altercation, contention; **b**) loud disapprobation *or* contradiction; **c**) a reviling, reproach, abuse, censure, reproof.
con-vīctiō, ōnis *f* = **convictus.**
convīctor, ōris *m* table-companion, familiar friend.
con-vīctus, ūs *m* **a**) a living together, social intercourse; **b**) familiar friends; **c**) = **convivium.**
con-vincō 3 **a**) to convict, refute, prove guilty (*alqm alcis rei*) *or* wrong; **b**) to prove *or* demonstrate clearly.
con-vīsō 3 to survey, examine; to shine upon.
convīva, ae *m* table-companion, guest.
convīvālis, e belonging to a banquet.

convivātor, ōris *m* host, entertainer.
convivium, ī *n* feast, banquet, entertainment; company at table, guests.
con-vivō 3 to live with; to eat with.
con-vivor 1 to feast *or* banquet together.
con-vocātiō, ōnis *f* a calling together.
con-vocō 1 to call together, assemble.
con-volō 1 to fly *or* run together.
con-volūtor 1 to go round, go about.
con-volvō 3 **a**) to roll together, roll up *or* round; **b**) to wrap.
con-vomō 3 to vomit upon.
con-vorr-, -vors-, -vort- = **con--verr-, -vers-, -vert-.**
con-vulnerō 1 to wound severely.
co-operiō, ruī, rtum 4 to cover over, to overwhelm.
co-optātiō, ōnis *f* election by way of supplement, co-optation, election.
co-optō 1 to choose, elect (*to an office*).
co-orior 4 to arise, break out *or* forth, to appear.
co-ortus, ūs *m* rising.
cōpa, ae *f* hostess of a tavern.
cophinus, ī *m* basket.
cōpia, ae *f* plenty, abundance (*alcis rei*); **a**) wealth, riches, resources; **b**) provisions, supplies, victuals; **c**) multitude, throng, number; **d**) body of men, troop, band, *pl.* troops, forces; **e**) fulness, copiousness; **f**) ability, power, opportunity, means.
cōpiolae, ārum *f/pl.* small forces.
cōpiōsus 3 well supplied *or* provided, wealthy; **a**) abounding, plentiful, copious (with *abl.* or *a re*); **b**) eloquent.
cōpis, e = **copiosus.**
coprea, ae *m* dirty joker.
copta, ae *f* a very hard cake.
cōpula, ae *f* band; **a**) rope, thong, tie; **b**) grapnel; **c**) connection.
cōpulātiō, ōnis *f* a coupling, union.
cōpulō (*and* **-or**) 1 to bind *or* join together, to couple, connect, unite, fasten.
coquinō 1 = **coquo.**
coquinus 3 of cooks.
coquō, xī, ctum 3 to cook, bake, boil, roast; **a**) to burn, parch, dry up; **b**) to ripen, make mature; **c**) to digest; **d**) to disturb, torment; **e**) to meditate.
coquus, ī *m*, **coqua, ae** *f* cook.
cor, cordis *n* **1.** the heart; a) soul, feeling, *alci* **cordi** *esse* to be dear to, be agreeable, please; b) courage; c) judgment, mind; d) person; **2.** stomach.
corallium, ī *n* red coral.
cōram 1. *adv.* a) openly, publicly, before the eyes of all, face to face; b) personally, in one's own person; **2.** *prep.* with *abl.* in the presence of.
corbis, is *f* (*m*) basket.
corbīta, ae *f* ship of burden.
corbula, ae *f* small basket.
corcodīlus, ī *m* = **crocodilus.**
corcōtārius = **crocotarius.**
corculum, ī *n* a little heart.
cordātus 3 prudent, wise.
cordāx, ācis *m* a lascivious dance.
cor-dolium, ī *n* heartache, grief.
coriandrum, ī *n* coriander.
corium, ī *n* (*and* **corius, ī** *m*) hide, skin; leather.
corneolus 3 horny.
corneus 3 **a**) horny, of horn; **b**) of cornel-wood.
corni-cen, inis *m* horn-blower.
cornīcor 1 to caw like a crow.
cornīcula, ae *f* crow.
corniculārius, ī *m* promoted soldier.
corniculum, ī *n* a little horn; ornament on the helmet.
corni-ger 3 horned.
corni-pēs, pedis horn-footed.
cornīx, īcis *f* crow.
cornu, ūs *n* **1.** horn, antler; a) excrescence on the head; b) horn of the moon; c) branch of a river; d) tongue of land; e) ends of the sail-yards; f) top of a helmet; g) end of a staff round which writings were rolled; h) wing of an army; i) horn of plenty; **2.** horn as a material; a) bugle-horn, trumpet; b) bow; c) funnel; d) horn holding the strings of a lyre.
cornum, ī *n* **a**) = **cornu; b**) cornel-berry; javelin of cornel wood.
cornus[1], **ī** *f* cornel(-tree); javelin.
cornus[2], **ūs** *m* = **cornu.**
cornūtus 3 horned.
corōlla, ae *f* small wreath.
corōllārium, ī *n* garland, chaplet; gift, present.

corōna, ae *f* wreath, garland, chaplet; **a**) crown, diadem; **b**) circle, assembly, audience; **c**) surrounding army, besiegers.
corōnārius 3 of a wreath *or* crown; **aurum corōnārium** present of gold for a victorious general.
corōnis, idis *f* final flourish; end.
corōnō 1 to wreathe, crown with a garland, to surround.
corporātus 3 material.
corporeus 3 *and* **corporālis** e bodily, corporeal, composed of flesh.
corpulentus 3 stout, corpulent.
corpus, oris *n* body; **a**) flesh; **b**) corpse, shade, soul of a dead one; **c**) trunk; **d**) person, individual, being; **e**) substance, essential matter; **f**) mass, frame, system, structure, corporation; collection of writings.
corpusculum, ī *n* little body.
cor-rādō 3 to scrape together.
corrēctiō, ōnis *f* improvement, amendment; correction.
cor-rēctor, ōris *m* improver, amender; corrector, censor.
cor-rēpō 3 to creep, slink.
correptus 3 pronounced short.
cor-rīdeō 2 to laugh aloud.
corrigia, ae *f* shoe-string, -tie.
cor-rigō, rēxī, rēctum 3 to make straight; **a**) to set right; **b**) to correct, improve, amend, reform.
cor-ripiō, ripuī, reptum 3 to snatch up, seize, grasp, take up; **a**) to snatch away violently; **b**) to arrest; **c**) to carry away, catch, attack, seize; **d**) to blame, rebuke, reproach, chide, accuse; **e**) to hasten, quicken, shorten.
cor-rīvō 1 to conduct (*streams*) together.
cor-rōborō 1 to strengthen, invigorate; **P.** to gain strength.
cor-rōdō, sī, sum 3 to gnaw to pieces.
cor-rogō 1 to collect by begging.
cor-rūgō 1 to wrinkle.
cor-rumpō 3 to break completely; to destroy, annihilate, ruin, spoil, waste; **P.** to perish; **a**) to make worse, deteriorate, injure, mar, corrupt; **b**) to falsify, adulterate; **c**) to pervert, degrade; to seduce, entice, mislead; **d**) to gain by gifts, to bribe. — **corruptus** 3 spoiled, bad, marred, corrupted; perverted, perverse.
cor-ruō 3 to fall together, fall down; to be ruined; to cause to fall in a heap.
cor-ruptēla, ae *f* a corrupting, seducing, bribing.
cor-ruptiō, ōnis *f* a corrupting; **a**) corruption; **b**) bribery, seduction.
cor-ruptor, ōris *m* corrupter, seducer, briber.
corruptrīx, īcis *f* she who seduces.
cors, tis *f* = **cohors.**
cortex, icis *m* (and *f*) bark, shell; bark of the cork-tree.
cortīna, ae *f* kettle, caldron; **a**) the Delphic tripod; **b**) oracle.
corulus, ī *f* hazel(-tree).
cōrus, ī *m* = **caurus.**
coruscō 1 **1.** *trans.* to move quickly, vibrate; **2.** *intr.* to be in quick motion, to flash, glitter.
coruscus 3 **a**) shaking, trembling, waving, vibrating; **b**) flashing, glittering.
corvus, ī *m* raven; grappling-iron.
cōrycus, ī *m* sand-bag for athletes.
corylētum, ī *n* hazel-thicket.
corylus, ī *f* = **corulus.**
corymbi-fer 3 bearing clusters of ivy-berries.
corymbus, ī *m* cluster (*of ivy-berries*).
coryphaeus, ī *m* leader, chief, head.
cōrȳtus, ī *m* quiver; quiverful of arrows.
cōs, cōtis *f* **a**) flint-stone; **b**) whetstone, grindstone.
cosmētēs, ae *m* wardrobe-keeper.
cosmicos, ī *m* citizen of the world; **-ca, ōrum** *n/pl.* worldly things.
costa, ae *f* rib; side.
costum, ī *n* (*and* **costos, ī** *f*) balsam-shrub; unguent.
cōtēs, is *f* = **cautes.**
cothurnātus 3 with the cothurnus; lofty, tragic.
cothurnus, ī *m* high shoe of tragic actors, cothurnus; **a**) hunting-boot; **b**) tragic style, tragedy.
cottabus, ī *m* clap, stroke.
cottana(-ona), ōrum *n/pl.* figs.
cot(t)īdiānus 3 daily
cot(t)īdiē *adv.* daily, every day.
cotula, ae *f* small cup (holding one hemina).
cōturnix (*and* **cŏ-**), **īcis** *f* quail.
coturnus, ī *m* = **cothurnus.**
covinnārius, ī *m* one who fights from a chariot (**covinnus, ī** *m*).

coxa, ae *f* the hip.
coxendīx, īcis *f* hip, hip-bone.
crābrō, ōnis *m* hornet.
crambē, ēs *f* cabbage.
crāpula, ae *f* intoxication.
crāpulārius 3 for intoxication.
crās *adv.* to-morrow; in the future.
crassitūdō, inis *f* thickness; density.
crassus 3 thick, dense, solid; **a**) fat, stout; **b**) rude.
crāstinus 3 of to-morrow; *subst.* **-um, ī** *n* the morrow.
crātēr, ēris *m and* **crātēra, ae** *f* mixing-vessel, wine-bowl; **a**) basin; **b**) crater of a volcano; **c**) the Cup (*a constellation*).
crāticula, ae *f* gridiron.
crātis, is *f* (*mostly pl.*) wicker-work, hurdle; **a**) fascines; **b**) joint; rib; honeycomb.
creātiō, ōnis *f* election.
creātor, ōris *m* creator, begetter, founder.
creātrīx, īcis *f* mother.
crēber, bra, brum thick, crowded together, close, frequent, numerous; **a**) abundant, abounding (*re*); **b**) repeated; *adv.* **crēbrō** frequently, repeatedly.
crēb(r)ēscō, b(r)uī, — 3 to become frequent, to increase; to spread abroad.
crēbritās, ātis *f* frequency.
crēdibilis, e worthy of belief, credible.
crēditor, ōris *m* creditor.
crēdō, didī, ditum 3 **1.** to commit, consign, intrust; to lend, give as a loan; **2.** to trust, confide in (*alci*); a) to believe, give credence to (*alci alqd*); b) to think, be of opinion, suppose, imagine; **crēdō** (*parenthetic*) I suppose, believe, think.
crēdulitās, ātis *f* easy belief, credulity.
crēdulus 3 easy of belief, confiding, unsuspecting.
cremō 1 to burn.
cremor, ōris *m* thick juice.
creō 1 to produce, make, create; a) to beget, bring forth; b) to cause, effect (*alci alqd*); c) to choose, elect.
creper, era, erum dark; uncertain.
crepida, ae *f* sole, sandal.
crepidātus 3 wearing sandals.
crepīdō, inis *f* a) pedestal; b) mound, pier, mole, dam.
crepidula, ae *f* little sandal.
crepitācillum, ī *n* rattle.
crepitō 1 (*intens. of* **crepo**) to rattle, clatter, creak, rustle.
crepitus, ūs *m* a rattling, clattering, creaking, rustling.
crepō, uī, itum 1 **1.** *intr.* to rattle, clatter, creak, rustle, crack; **2.** *trans.* to cause to sound, to talk much of, to make ado about.
crepundia, ōrum *n/pl.* a child's rattle; toys.
crepusculum, ī *n* (evening-) twilight.
crēscō, crēvī, (crētum) 3 to grow, grow up; **a**) to spring up, to rise; **b**) to increase, thrive, swell, prosper, become great, increase in power and fame; **crētus** 3 born, sprung from.
crēta, ae *f* chalk; white earth, clay, paint for the face.
crētātus 3 chalked.
crēterra, ae *f* = **crater(a)**.
crēteus 3 of clay.
crētiō, ōnis *f* declaration about accepting an inheritance.
crētōsus 3 abounding in chalk *or* clay.
crētula, ae *f* clay for sealing.
crētus 3, *part. pf.* P. *of* **cerno** *and* **cresco.**
crībrum, ī *n* sieve.
crīmen, inis *n* accusation, reproach, charge; **a**) object of reproach, guilty person *or* thing; **b**) fault, offence, crime, guilt.
crīminātiō, ōnis *f* accusation, calumny.
crīminātor, ōris *m* accuser, slanderer.
crīminor (*and* **-ō**) 1 **a**) to accuse, charge with a crime, to calumniate; **b**) to complain of, denounce.
crīminōsus 3 slanderous, reproachful, backbiting.
crīnālis, e relating to the hair, of the hair; *subst.* **crīnāle, is** *n* hair-band, diadem.
crīni-ger 3 = **crinitus.**
crīniō 4 to cover with hair (i. e. leaves).
crīnis, is *m* (*and f*) the hair; tail (*of a comet*).
crīnītus 3 having hair, hairy.
crisis (*acc.* **-im**) *f* crisis.
crīsō 1 to move the thighs.
crispi-sulcāns, tis winding, serpentine.

crispō 1 **a**) to swing, brandish; **b**) to curl.
crisp(ul)us 3 curly, curly-headed; quivering.
crista, ae *f* **a**) crest, comb (*of a bird*); **b**) plume of a helmet.
cristātus 3 **a**) crested; **b**) having a plume.
criticus, ī *m* judge, critic.
croceus 3 of saffron; yellow, orange.
crocinus 3 saffron-coloured; **-num, ī** *n* saffron-oil.
crōc(c)iō 4 to croak.
crocodīlus, ī *m* crocodile.
crocōt(ul)a, ae *f* saffron-coloured robe.
crocōtārius 3 of saffron robes.
crocum, ī *n and* **crocus, ī** *m* **a**) saffron; **b**) saffron-colour.
crotalistria, ae *f* castanet-dancer.
crotalum, ī *n* rattle, castanet.
cruciābilitās, ātis *f* torture.
cruciābiliter with torture.
cruciāmentum, ī *n* = **cruciatus.**
cruciātus, ūs *m* torture, torment; **a**) execution; **b**) instrument of torture.
cruciō 1 **a**) to torment, put to the rack; **b**) to afflict, grieve.
cruci-salus, ī *m* cross-dancer.
crūdēlis, e cruel; unfeeling, hard, severe, fierce.
crūdēlitās, ātis *f* cruelty, hardness, severity.
crūdēscō, —,— 3 to become violent, grow worse.
crūditās, ātis *f* indigestion.
crūdus 3 raw, bloody, uncooked, unbaked; unripe; **a**) fresh, vigorous; **b**) with full stomach; undigested; **c**) unprepared, undressed; **d**) unfeeling, cruel.
cruentō 1 to make bloody, stain with blood; to wound.
cruentus 3 bloody; **a**) blood-red; **b**) blood-thirsty.
crumēna (and **-mīna**), **ae** *f* purse; money.
crumilla, ae *f* small purse.
cruor, ōris *m* blood from a wound, gore; **a**) drop of blood; **b**) bloodshed, murder.
cruppellārius, ī *m* mail-clad Gallic soldier.
crūri-crepida, ae *m* slave with legs chained.
crūri-fragius, ī *m* slave with legs broken.
crūs, ūris *n* leg, shin.
crūsma, atis *n* music played on a stringed instrument.
crusta, ae *f* crust, rind, bark, shell; inlaid *or* embossed work.
crustō 1 to encrust.
crustulārius, ī *m* confectioner.
crust(ul)um, ī *n* cake, confectionery.
crux, crucis *f* cross, gallows; **a**) crucifixion; **b**) torture, trouble, misery; **c**) gallowsbird, good-for--nothing.
crypta, ae *f* vault, crypt.
crypto-porticus, ūs *f* walled passage.
crystallinus 3 of crystal.
crystallum, ī *n and* **-us, ī** *f* ice; crystal.
cubiculāris, e belonging to a sleeping-room.
cubiculārius, ī *m* valet.
cubiculāta, ae *f* (*sc. navis*) ship furnished with cabins.
cubiculum, ī *n* **a**) sleeping-room, bedroom; **b**) apartment.
cubīle, is *n* resting-place, den, bed, seat.
cubital, ālis *n* elbow-cushion.
cubitālis, e a cubit long.
cubitō 1 to be accustomed to lie.
cubitum, ī *n and* **-tus, ī** *m* **a**) elbow, **b**) cubit (1½ *feet*).
cubitūra, ae *f* lying.
cubitus, ūs *m* = **concubitus.**
cubō, buī, bitum 1 to lie down, rest, repose; **a**) to lie asleep; **b**) to recline at table; **c**) to lie sick; **d**) to slope, slant.
cucullus, ī *m* hood.
cucūl(l)us, ī *m* cuckoo.
cucumis, (er)is *m* cucumber.
cucurbita, ae *f* gourd; cupping--glass.
cūdō[1], (**dī, sum**) 3 to beat, strike, knock, hammer, stamp, coin.
cūdō[2], **ōnis** *m* helmet of raw hide.
cūiās, ātis of what country?, whence?
cuicui-modī of whatever kind.
cūius 3 (*interrog.*) of whom?, whose?; (*rel.*) of whom, whose.
cūius-modī of what kind?
cūiusque-modī of every kind.
culcit(ul)a, ae *f* mattress, pillow.
culex, icis *m* gnat, midge.
culillus, ī *m* = **culullus.**
culīna, ae *f* kitchen; food, fare.

culleus, ī *m* (leather-) bag, sack.
culmen, inis *n* top, summit; culmination; roof, height.
culmus, ī *m* stalk, straw.
culpa, ae *f* guilt, error, fault, defect; **in culpā esse** to be to blame; **a)** mischievous thing, cause of fault; **b)** unchastity.
culpitō 1 to blame, reproach.
culpō 1 **a)** to reproach, accuse, find fault with; **b)** to blame, disapprove.
cultellus, ī *m* little knife.
culter, trī *m* knife; razor.
cultiō, ōnis *f* cultivation.
cultor, ōris *m* cultivator; **a)** planter, husbandman, farmer; **b)** inhabitant; **c)** friend, worshipper, lover.
cultrārius, ī *m* sacrificer.
cultrīx, īcis, *fem. of* **cultor.**
cultūra, ae *f* = **cultus²**.
cultus¹ 3, *see* **colo.**
cultus², ūs *m* cultivation, labour, tilling; **a)** cultivated land; **b)** care, training, education; **c)** culture, civilization, refinement; **d)** veneration, adoration, worship; **e)** way of life; luxury, wantonness; dress, attire, splendour, adornment.
cullullus, ī *m* drinking-vessel.
cūlus, ī *m* the fundament.
cum¹ *prep.* with *abl.* with, together with, in the company of, in connection with, on the side of, at the same time with.
cum² *cj.* **1.** when (*gen. with subj. of past time, with indic. of present or future time*); at the time when (*with indic.*); whenever (*with indic.*; *later, with subj.*); **2.** as, since (*with subj.*); **3.** although, whereas (*with subj.*); — **cum primum** as soon as; **cum praesertim** especially when *or* as; **cum maxime** precisely when; at this *or* that very moment; **cum ... tum** both ... and; while ..., especially.
cūmatile, is *n* sea-green garment.
cumb(ul)a, ae *f* small boat.
cumera, ae *f* box, corn-chest.
cumīnum, ī *n* cumin.
cum-que *adv.* **1.** at any time, always; **2.** = **et cum.**
cumulātus 3 heaped up, increased, augmented, perfect, complete, full.
cumulō 1 to heap up, accumulate, pile; **a)** to fill, load, cover (*alqd alqa re*); **b)** to augment, increase; **c)** to crown, complete, bring to perfection.
cumulus, ī *m* heap, pile, mass; **a)** addition, increase, surplus, summit, point, crown; **b)** immense number.
cūnābula, ōrum *n/pl.* cradle; resting-place, dwelling.
cūnae, ārum *f/pl.* cradle; nest.
cūnctābundus 3 lingering much.
cūnctāns, tis lingering, delaying, slow; tenacious.
cūnctātiō, ōnis *f* a lingering, delaying, tarrying.
cūnctātor, ōris *m* delayer, lingerer, loiterer.
cūnctor (*and* **-ō**) 1 to linger, loiter, delay; to hesitate, doubt.
cūnctus 3 (*mostly pl.*) all collectively, all in a body, all together, the whole; *subst.* **cūncta, ōrum** *n/pl.* all things, everything at once.
cuneātim *adv.* in the form of a wedge.
cuneātus 3 pointed like a wedge.
cuneō 1 to wedge.
cuneolus, ī *m* little wedge.
cuneus, ī *m* wedge; **a)** troops drawn up in form of a wedge; **b)** wedge-formed division of seats in a theatre, the spectators.
cunīculōsus 3 full of rabbits.
cunīculus, ī *m* **a)** rabbit, cony; **b)** underground passage, mine, canal.
cunīla, ae *f* a sort of plant.
cunnus, ī *m* the vulva; unchaste woman.
cunque = **cumque.**
cūpa, ae *f* tub, cask, tun.
cupiditās, ātis *f* a longing, desire, passion; lust; **a)** covetousness, avarice; **b)** desire for love; **c)** ambition; **d)** party-spirit.
cupīdō, inis *f* (*m*) = **cupiditas.**
Cupīdō, inis *m* Cupid, (God of) Love.
cupidus 3 longing, desiring, desirous, wishful, eager, passionate; **a)** covetous (*with gen.*); **b)** lustful, amorous; **c)** ambitious; **d)** eager, fond; **e)** partial, factious.
cupiēns, tis longing, desiring.
cupiō, īvī *and* **iī, ītum** 3 to long for, desire, wish (*alqd*; with *inf.*); to be favourable, wish well, be devoted (*alci*).
cupītor, ōris *m* one who desires.
cuppēdia¹, ōrum *n/pl.* dainties.

cuppēdia[2], **ae** *f* daintiness.
cuppēdinārius, ī *m* confectioner.
cuppēdō, inis *f* desire.
cuppēs *m* one fond of delicate food.
cupressētum, ī *n* cypress-grove.
cupresseus 3 of cypress-wood.
cupressi-fer 3 cypress-bearing.
cupressus, ī (*and* **ūs**) *f* the cypress; box of cypress wood.
cūr *adv.* why?
cūra, ae *f* **1.** care; carefulness, attention, diligence, pains (*alcis rei*); a) an attending, caring, minding, healing, cure; b) administration, management, oversight, command, office, business; c) written work, writing, book; d) guardian, overseer; protégé(e); **2.** care, anxiety, trouble, disquiet, grief; a) disquiet of love; b) object of love, mistress.
cūrābilis, e needing medical treatment (?).
cūralium, ī *n* = **corallium.**
cūrātiō, ōnis (*and* **cūrātūra, ae**) *f* a taking care (of), care, management; treatment.
cūrātor, ōris *m* manager, superintendent; overseer, keeper.
cūrātus 3 anxious, earnest; cared for.
curculiō, ōnis (*dimin.* **curculiunculus, ī**) *m* corn-weevil.
cūria, ae *f* curia **1.** senate-house; senate; **2.** the tenth part of a tribus *or* division of the Roman people; meeting-place of the curiæ.
cūriālis, is *m* member of the same curia.
cūriātim *adv.* by curiæ.
cūriātus 3 relating to the curiæ; **comitia cūriāta** assembly of the people in curiæ; **lex cūriāta** law passed in the comitia curiata.
cūriō[1], **ōnis** *m* priest *or* head of a curia.
cūriō[2] (**ōnis**) wasted by care.
cūriōsitās, ātis *f* desire for knowledge; curiosity.
cūriōsus 3 **a**) careful, attentive, diligent; **b**) inquisitive, curious, prying; **c**) careworn.
curis, is *f* lance, spear.
cūrō 1 to care for, pay attention to, look *or* attend to (*alqd*; with *ut* or *inf.*); **a**) to be solicitous for, think of (*with acc.; de re; inf.*); **b**) to administer, manage, govern, command; **c**) to tend, cure, heal; to refresh; **d**) to procure, provide.
curriculum, ī *n* a running, course; **a**) race, race-course; **b**) orbit; **c**) race-chariot; **d**) career, course, race-ground.
currō, cucurrī, cursum 3 **a**) to run, hasten; to sail, fly, move quickly, flow; to spread; **b**) to traverse, pass over (*with acc.*).
currus, ūs *m* chariot, car; the horses, team; **a**) war-chariot; **b**) triumphal car; **c**) plough; **d**) ship.
cursim *adv.* hastily, quickly.
cursitō *and* **cursō** 1 to run constantly, to run to and fro.
cursor, ōris *m* runner; **a**) racer, charioteer; **b**) courier.
cursūra, ae *f* a running.
cursus, ūs *m* a running; **a**) rapid motion, course, march, voyage, passage, journey; **b**) direction, way; **c**) flow, progress, speed; **d**) flow of words; **e**) race-course; career.
curtō 1 to shorten, abridge.
curtus 3 shortened, mutilated; circumcised; castrated.
curūlis, e belonging to a chariot; curule; (**sella**) ~ *f* curule chair.
curvāmen, inis *n and* **curvātūra, ae** *f* a bending, bend, arching.
curvō 1 to bend, curve, crook, round.
curvus 3 bent, bowed, crooked, curved, arched.
cuspis, idis *f* point, sting; head of a spear; lance, javelin.
custōdēla, ae *f* = **custodia.**
custōdia, ae *f* a watching, guarding, watch, guard, protection, care; **a**) guard, watch, sentinel; watch-station; **b**) custody, confinement, imprisonment, prison; **c**) captive, prisoner.
custōdiō 4 to watch, guard, keep; **a**) to preserve, heed; **b**) to observe, take care of, **se custōdīre** to be on the watch; **c**) to hold in custody.
custōs, ōdis *m and f* watchman, keeper; **a** preserver, protector, defender; **b**) body-guard; watch, spy; **c**) jailer.
cutīcula, ae *f* skin.
cutis, is *f* skin; coating, outside.
cyathissō 1 to fill the cups.
cyathus, ī *m* **a**) ladle for filling drinking-cups; **b**) a measure for liquids (= $^1/_{12}$ *sextarius*).

cybaea, ae *f* transport-vessel (*navis*).
cybiosactēs, ae *m* dealer in salt-fish.
cybium, ī *n* (dish made of) tunny-fish.
cycladātus 3 wearing a cyclas.
cyclas, adis *f* circular robe.
cyclicus 3 belonging to a cycle, cyclic.
Cyclōps, ōpis *m* Cyclops (*one-eyed giant*).
cycnēus (*and* **cyg-**) 3 of a swan.
cycnus (*and* **cyg-**) **ī** *m* swan.
cydōnium, ī *n* quince.
cylindrus, ī *m* cylinder, roller.
cymba, ae *f* = **cumba.**
cymbalum, ī *n* cymbal.
cymbium, ī *n* drinking-vessel.
cynicus 3 doglike, Cynic.
cyno-cephalus, ī *m* ape with a dog's head.
cyparissus = **cupressus.**
cytisus, ī *f* a kind of clover, snail-clover.

D

D *abbr.* **a**) = **Decimus; b**) **Divus;** **c**) 500 (= half of **CIↃ**).
dactylicus 3 dactylic.
dactyliothēca, ae *f* casket for rings.
dactylus, ī *m* a dactyl.
daedalus 3 skilful, artfully constructed.
dāmiūrgus, ī *m* = **demiurgus.**
damma, ae *f* deer; venison.
damnātiō, ōnis *f* condemnation.
damnātōrius 3 condemnatory.
damni-ficus 3, **damni-gerulus** 3 causing damage, injurious.
damnō 1 to condemn, declare guilty (*alqm alcis rei*), **voti damnare** to grant one's wish and exact fulfilment of a vow; **a**) to sentence, doom; **b**) to disapprove, reject, blame (*alqd*); **c**) to consecrate, condemn as a sacrifice; **d**) to bind *or* oblige.
damnōsus 3 **a**) causing damage, injurious, destructive (*alci*); **b**) prodigal.
damnum, ī *n* loss, damage, injury; **a**) fault; **b**) something lost; **c**) fine, penalty.
danīsta, ae *m* money-lender.
danīsticus 3 money-lending.
danunt = **dant** (*see* **do**).
daphnōn, ōnis *m* grove of bay-trees.
dapinō 1 to serve up.
daps, dapis *f* (*mostly pl.*) sacrificial feast; **a**) banquet; **b**) food, victuals.
dapsilis, e sumptuous, costly.
datārius 3 belonging to gifts.
datātim *adv.* by giving, by tossing from one to the other.
datiō, ōnis *f* a giving; the right to give away.
datō 1 to give away.
dator, ōris *m* giver.
datū (*abl.*) by gift.
dē *prep.* with *abl.* **1.** (*of space*) from, down from, away from, out of; **2.** (*of time*) from, immediately after, during, in the course of; **3.** (*of relation*) from, out of a number *or* class (*unus de multis*); on account of; according to, in accordance with; with relation to; concerning; **dē integro** anew, **dē improviso** unexpectedly, **dē industria** purposely.
dea, ae *f* goddess.
de-albō 1 to whitewash.
de-ambulātiō, ōnis *f* a walking, promenading.
de-ambulō 1 to take a walk.
de-amō 1 to love very much.
de-armō 1 to disarm.
de-artuō 1 to tear limb from limb, to ruin.
de-asciō 1 to cheat.
dē-bacchor 1 to revel wildly, to rave.
dē-bellātor, ōris *m* conqueror.
dē-bellō 1 **a**) to finish a war, fight out (*cum alqo*); **b**) to subdue, vanquish.
dēbeō, uī, itum 2 to owe, be indebted; **a**) to be in debt; **b**) to remain indebted; **c**) to be under obligation; **d**) to be bound *or* pledged, one ought, must, should; **e**) to be destined, fated; **f**) to have to thank for; — **dēbitus** 3 due, owing, becoming; destined, doomed; **dēbitum, ī** *n* debt.
dēbilis, e lame, infirm, frail, weak, feeble, helpless.
dēbilitās, ātis *f* lameness, debility, weakness.
dēbilitātiō, ōnis *f* a disabling.
dēbilitō 1 to lame; to weaken, debilitate, unnerve, disable.
dēbitiō, ōnis *f* indebtedness.
dēbitor, ōris *m* debtor; indebted for.
dēbitum, ī *n and* **dēbitus** 3, *see* **debeo.**
dē-blaterō 1 (*alci alqd*) to blab out.
dē-cantō 1 to sing; **a**) to repeat in singing, repeat often, harp on; **b**) to leave off singing.
dē-cēdō 3 to go away, depart (*ab, ex, de re*; with *abl.*); **a**) to march off, to evacuate, to leave a province, surrender (*office*), retire; **b**) **de vita** to depart from life, to die; **c**) to make way, give place (*alci*), yield (*de via*); to yield, be inferior, rank below; to depart, deviate; **d**) to cease, abandon; to disappear, abate, subside.
decem ten.

december, bris, bre belonging to December; *subst. m* December.
decem-iugis, is *m* chariot with ten horses.
decem-peda, ae *f* measuring-rod ten feet in length.
decempedātor, ōris *m* land-surveyor.
decem-plex, plicis tenfold.
decem-scalmus 3 having ten tholes *or* oars.
decem-vir, ī *m* one of a commission of ten men.
decem-virālis, e relating to the decemvirs.
decemvirātus, ūs *m* decemvirate, office of a decemvir.
decēns, tis becoming, seemly, decent; handsome, beautiful.
decentia, ae *f* comeliness, decency.
deceō, uī, — 2 to be comely, seemly, decent, to become, be suitable *or* proper (*alqm*).
dē-ceptor, ōris *m* deceiver.
dec-ēris, is *f* with oars worked by ten rowers.
dē-cernō, crēvī, crētum 3 **1.** to decide, determine, decree (*alqd; acc. c. inf.; ut*); **b**) to judge, vote for, resolve, fix, settle; **c**) to adjudge, award (*alci alqd*); **d**) to proclaim; **e**) to form a purpose *or* resolution; **2. pugnam, proelium** to fight out (*cum alqo*), decide by combat.
dē-cerpō, psī, ptum 3 to pluck off; **a**) to take away; **b**) to enjoy.
dē-certātiō, ōnis *f* contest, decisive battle.
dē-certō 1 to fight to a decision, to fight out.
dē-cessiō, ōnis *f* a going away, departure; decrease.
dēcessor, ōris *m* predecessor.
dēcessus, ūs *m* a going away, departure; **a**) retirement of a magistrate; **b**) death.
dē-cidō[1]**, cidī,** — 3 to fall down (*ab, ex, de re*), fall off; **a**) to sink down, die; **b**) to fail (*a spe*); **c**) to sink, perish.
dē-cīdō[2]**, cīdī, cīsum** 3 to cut *or* hew off; **a**) to decide, terminate, settle; to cut short; **b**) to agree, compromise (*cum alqo de re*).
deciē(n)s *adv.* ten times.
decimānus 3 **1.** belonging to tithes, **ager** ~ land paying a tenth, **frumentum** a tithe of corn; *subst.* **~, ī** *m* tithe-farmer (**-na, ae** *f* tithe-farmer's wife); **2.** belonging to the tenth cohort *or* legion; **porta** main gate of a Roman camp.
decimō 1 to take every tenth man for punishment.
decimus 3 the tenth; *subst.* **a**) **decimum, ī** *n* tenfold yield; **b**) **decima, ae** *f* a tenth part, tithe; largess.
dē-cipiō, cēpī, ceptum 3 to cheat, deceive (*alqm alqa r*·); **a**) to escape notice; **b**) to elude, beguile (*alqd*).
dēcīsiō, ōnis *f* agreement, settlement.
dē-clāmātiō, ōnis *f* practice in public speaking; loud talking.
dē-clāmātor, ōris *m* rhetorician, elocutionist.
dē-clāmātōrius 3 declamatory, rhetorical.
dē-clāmitō 1, *intens. of* **declamo.**
dē-clāmō 1 1. *intr.* to practise public speaking, to speak loudly *or* violently; **2.** *trans.* to declaim.
dē-clārātiō, ōnis *f* exposition, declaration.
dē-clārātor, ōris *m* announcer.
dē-clārō 1 to make clear *or* distinct; to declare, pronounce, explain, proclaim (*alci alqd; acc. c. inf.*).
dēclīnātiō, ōnis *f* a bending aside, turning away, inflection; **a**) an avoiding; **b**) rejection.
dēclīnis, e turning aside, retreating.
dē-clīnō 1 **1.** *trans.* to bend aside, turn away (*alqd ab, de re in alqd*); to avoid, shun; **2.** *intr.* to deviate, digress (*de, ab re*); to incline to (*in alqd*).
dē-clīvis, e sloping, inclined downwards; *subst.* **dēclīve, is** *n* declivity, slope.
dēclīvitās, ātis *f* declivity.
dē-coctor, ōris *m* spendthrift, bankrupt.
dē-collō 1 to behead.
dē-cōlō 1 to trickle away.
dē-color, ōris deprived of colour, discoloured; **a**) dark, tanned; **b**) degenerate.
dēcolōrātiō, ōnis *f* a discolouring.
dē-colōrō 1 to discolour; to stain.
dē-condō 3 to hide away.
dē-coquō 3 to boil; **a**) to boil down; *subst.* **dēcocta, ae** *f* a cold drink; **b**) to become bankrupt.
decor, ōris *m* **a**) comeliness, elegance; **b**) charm, beauty, grace.

decorāmen, inis *n* ornament.
decorō 1 **a**) to adorn, embellish; **b**) to honour, distinguish.
decōrus 3 **a**) fitting, seemly, becoming; **b**) beautiful, graceful, handsome; embellished, adorned.
dē-crepitus 3 very old, decrepit.
dē-crēscō 3 to become less *or* fewer, to decrease, lessen, disappear, vanish.
dēcrētōrius 3 decisive, final.
dēcrētum, ī *n* **a**) decree, decision, resolution; **b**) principle, doctrine.
dē-culcō 1 to kick *or* knock down.
decuma, decumānus = **decima, decimanus.**
decumātēs agrī *m/pl.* tributary *or* tithe-land.
dē-cumbō, cubuī, cubitum 3 to lie down; to fall down.
decuria, ae *f* a body *or* division of ten; division, class.
decuriātiō, ōnis *f and* **-tus, ūs** *m* a dividing into *decuriae.*
decuriō[1] 1 to divide (into *decuriae*).
decuriō[2], **ōnis** *m* **a**) commander of ten horse-soldiers; **b**) member of a municipal senate.
decuriōnātus, ūs *m* office of *decurio.*
dē-currō, (cu)currī, cursum 3 **1.** a) to run *or* hasten down, to fly, flow, sail, march down (*ab, ex, de re in* or *ad alqd*); b) to come away, hasten, travel; to march, manœuvre; c) to have recourse to, take refuge in; **2.** a) to run over, pass through; b) to discuss, treat.
dē-cursiō, ōnis *f and* **-sus, ūs** *m* **1.** a) a running down; b) military evolution, manœuvre; charge, attack; c) course, career; **2.** end of a course, completion.
dē-curtō 1 to curtail, mutilate.
decus, oris *n* **a**) ornament, beauty, splendour, glory, honour, dignity, worth, virtue; **b**) deed of honour, exploit.
decussis, is *m* coin worth ten *asses.*
decussō 1 to divide crosswise.
dē-cutiō, cussī, cussum 3 to shake off, strike down, throw down.
dē-deceō 2 to be unbecoming, unfitting, unseemly (*alqm*).
dē-decor, oris unseemly, shameful.
dē-decorō 1 to disgrace, dishonour, bring to shame.
dē-decōrus 3 disgraceful, shameful, dishonourable.

dē-decus, oris *n* disgrace, dishonour, infamy, shame; **a**) blot, blemish; **b**) crime, evil, vice.
dē-dicātiō, ōnis *f* consecration, dedication.
dē-dicō 1 **1.** to declare, specify; **2.** to dedicate, consecrate, inscribe, devote (*alci alqd*).
dē-dīgnātiō, ōnis *f* a scorning, refusal.
dē-dīgnor 1 to disdain, reject, scorn.
dē-discō 3 to unlearn, forget.
dēditīcius 3 one who has surrendered *or* capitulated unconditionally; prisoner, subject.
dēditiō, ōnis *f* a giving up, surrender, capitulation.
dēditus 3 given up, surrendered; given to, devoted, addicted, engaged in (*with dat.*).
dē-dō, didī, ditum 3 **a**) to give up, surrender, deliver, consign, yield (*alci alqd*); **b**) **se dēdere** to surrender oneself, to capitulate; to apply, devote *or* dedicate oneself (*dat.*).
dē-doceō 2 to cause to unlearn.
dē-doleō 2 to cease grieving.
dē-dolō 1 to hew smooth.
dē-dūcō 3 **1.** to lead *or* bring down; to lead, fetch, draw down *or* away (*ab, ex, de re in* or *ad alqd*); **2.** a) to remove; b) to lead, conduct, escort, accompany; c) to lead forth, found a colony; d) to lead *or* turn away from, to dispossess; e) to seduce, mislead; f) to take away, subtract; g) to spin out (*a thread*), to compose; **3.** a) to conduct a bride to her husband; b) to conduct a young man to a public teacher; c) to divert, derive, deduce, reduce.
dē-ductiō, ōnis *f* a leading down *or* away (*alcis in alqd*); **a**) a leading forth, establishing, colonizing; b) ejection, expulsion; c) diminution, subtraction; d) inference.
dē-ductor, ōris *m* attendant, client.
dē-ductus 3 humble, weak, poor.
de-errō 1 to lose one's way, go astray.
dē-faecō 1 to cleanse, make clear.
dē-faenerō 1 to involve in debt.
dē-fatīgātiō, ōnis *f* weariness, fatigue, exhaustion.
dē-fatīgō 1 to weary out, fatigue, tire.
dēfectiō, ōnis *f* **1.** desertion, defection, rebellion, revolt; **2.** disappearance, eclipse; exhaustion, weakness.

dēfector, ōris *m* rebel, deserter.
dēfectus[1], **ūs** *m* = **defectio.**
dēfectus[2] 3, *see* **deficio.**
dē-fendō, dī, sum 3 **1.** to ward off, drive away, keep off, avert (*alci alqd*); **2.** to defend, protect (*alqm ab alqo, in, adversus*); a) to maintain, sustain, support; b) to assert, allege in defence.
dē-fēnerō = **defaenero.**
dēfēnsiō, ōnis *f* a warding off; defence.
dēfēnsitō 1 *and* **dēfēnsō** 1 to (be wont to) defend; **causas** to be a lawyer.
dēfēnsor, ōris *m* **a**) one who wards off; **b**) defender, protector.
dē-ferō 3 **1.** to bring, bear, carry down, to throw down; **2.** to remove, divert, drive off; **3.** to carry *or* bring to a place (*pecuniam in aerarium*); to confer, transfer, deliver; a) to offer, grant, hand over; b) to bring *or* give an account of, to report, announce, tell; c) to inform against, indict, accuse; d) to register.
dē-fervēscō, fervī (ferbuī), — 3 to cease boiling *or* raging.
dēfetīgō 1 = **defatigo.**
dē-fetīscor, fessus sum 3 to become tired, grow weary *or* exhausted.
dē-ficiō 3 **1.** a) to rebel, revolt, desert, fall off (*ab alqo ad alqm*); b) to be wanting, fail, cease, become less, run out; c) to sink, faint, become weak, expire; d) (*animo*) to lose courage; to become eclipsed; **2.** *trans.* a) to abandon, leave, desert; b) to fail; — **dēfectus** 3 abandoned; enfeebled, weak.
dē-fīcō = **defaeco.**
dē-fīgō 3 to fix *or* fasten into (*alqd in re*); **a**) to drive *or* fix down; **b**) to turn intently, direct (*oculos, lumina*); **c**) to render immovable, make fast, to fix in amazement, stupefy, astonish; to enchant; **d**) to imprint firmly; **P.** to fix oneself, to be deeply engaged in.
dē-fingō 3 **a**) to disfigure; **b**) to form, mould.
dē-fīniō 4 to bound, limit, terminate (*alqd re*); **a**) to define, determine, explain; **b**) to confine, restrict; **c**) to give a definition.
dē-fīnītiō, ōnis *f* a defining, limiting; **a**) a prescribing; **b**) definition.
dē-fīnītīvus 3 definitive, explanatory.
dē-fīnītus 3 **a**) defined, distinct; **b**) plain, perspicuous.
dē-fīō, dēfierī to fail, be wanting (*alci*).
dē-flagrātiō, ōnis *f* a consuming [by fire.
dē-flagrō 1 **a**) to burn down, be consumed by fire; **b**) to consume by fire; **c**) to cease burning, be allayed.
dē-flectō, flexī, flexum 3 **1.** to bend down *or* aside, to turn aside (*alqd de re in alqd, ad alqm*); **2.** to turn away, lead astray; a) to alter; b) to turn oneself aside (*a, de re*).
dē-fleō 2 **a**) to weep for, bewail; to tell with tears; **b**) to weep violently.
dē-floccō 1 to depilate; **dēfloccātus** bald.
dē-flōrēscō ruī, — 3 to fade, wither.
dē-fluō 3 **1.** to flow down; a) to glide *or* fall down; b) to swim *or* sail down; c) to change to (*ad alqd*); **2.** to flow away, cease flowing; to vanish.
dē-fluus 3 flowing down, descending, falling.
dē-fodiō 3 **1.** to dig up; **2.** to dig in, cover with earth (*alqd in re, in rem*); to bury, hide.
dē-fōrmātiō, ōnis *f* a deforming, disfiguring; degradation.
dē-fōrmis, e 1. formless, without shape; **2.** deformed, disfigured; a) hideous, ugly; b) disgraceful, shameful.
dē-fōrmitās, ātis *f* deformity, ugliness.
dē-fōrmō 1 **1.** to form, shape, delineate, depict; **2.** to deform, disfigure; to disgrace, dishonour.
dē-fraudō 1 to deceive, cheat (*alqm alqa re*).
dē-frēnātus 3 unbridled.
dē-fricō 1 to rub down, rub hard; to lash, satirize.
dē-fringō, frēgī, frāctum 3 to break off.
dē-frūdō 1 = **defraudo.**
dē-frūstror 1 to cheat.
dē-frutum, ī *n* must boiled down.
dē-fugiō 3 to flee away; to flee from, avoid, shun (*with acc.*).
dē-fundō 3 to pour down *or* out, to empty.

dē-fungor 3 (*with abl.*) to have done with, to finish, complete, perform, discharge; to be discharged from office; to die.

dē-futūtus 3 worn out by debauchery.

dē-gener, eris degenerate, not genuine, unworthy of one's ancestors (*with gen.*); unworthy, ignoble, base.

dē-generō 1 **1.** *intr.* to become degenerate (*ab alqa re, in alqd*); to become unlike; **2.** *trans.* to cause to degenerate, to dishonour, disgrace.

dē-gerō 3 to carry away.

dē-glūbō 3 to flay, skin.

dēgō, —, — 3 to pass (*time*), to live.

dē-grandinat 1 it hails violently.

dē-grassor 1 to assail.

dē-gravō 1 to press down, weigh down; to burden, distress.

dē-gredior, gressus sum 3 **a**) to go, march *or* walk down; to dismount; **b**) to go away.

dē-grunniō 4 to grunt out.

dē-gustō 1 to taste (*alqd*); to lick; **a**) to graze; **b**) to try, make a trial of, test.

de-hibeō 2 = **debeo.**

dehinc *adv.* from here; **a**) from this time, henceforth; **b**) thereupon, for the future; next.

de-hīscō, —, — 3 to gape, split open.

de-honestāmentum, ī *n* deformity, disgrace, dishonour.

de-honestō 1 to dishonour.

de-hortor 1 to advise to the contrary, to dissuade (*alqm ab re*, with *ne* or *inf.*); to alienate.

dē-iciō, iēcī, iectum 3 to throw, cast, hurl down; **P.** to rush down; **a**) to fell, prostrate, precipitate, tear down; **b**) to destroy, kill; to cast down (*oculos a re*), avert, turn away; **c**) to overthrow; **d**) to drive out, expel, drive from a position, drive off (*loco, re, ex* or *de re, in alqd*); to turn out of possession, dispossess; **e**) to prevent from obtaining, deprive (*abl.*); **f**) to remove, carry off.

dē-iectiō, ōnis *f* ejection, dispossession.

dē-iectus[1] 3 low-lying, sunken; dejected, dispirited.

dē-iectus[2]**, ūs** *m* a throwing down, hurling down; **a**) fall; **b**) declivity, depression.

dē-ierō 1 to swear solemnly.

dein *adv.* = **deinde.**

deinceps *adv.* successively, in order, in succession, following; immediately.

deinde *adv.* from there, then, next; thereafter, afterwards.

dē-iungō 3 to unyoke; to separate.

dē-iuvō 1 to deny help.

dē-lābor 3 **a**) to glide *or* fall down, sink; **b**) to glide away (*ab, de, ex re*); **c**) to be derived from (*ab alqo*); **c**) to fall into, to digress (*in, ad alqd*).

dē-lacerō 1 to tear to pieces.

dē-lambō 3 to lick.

dē-lāmentor 1 to bewail, lament.

dē-lassō 1 to weary, tire out.

dē-lātiō, ōnis *f* information against one, denunciation, accusation.

dē-lātor, ōris *m* informer, denouncer.

dēlēbilis, e destructible.

dēlectābilis, e delightful, pleasant.

dēlectāmentum, ī *n* delight, amusement.

dēlectātiō, ōnis *f* delight, pleasure, amusement.

dēlectō 1 to delight, amuse, please, charm.

dē-lēctus, ūs *m* **a**) selection, choice; **b**) = **dilectus.**

dē-lēgātiō, ōnis *f* a delegating; assignment of a debt.

dē-lēgō 1 to send away, dispatch (*alqm in* or *ad alqd*); **a**) to transfer, give in charge, entrust; to assign, attribute; **b**) to refer to; **c**) to assign, make over a debt.

dē-lēnificus 3 soothing, winning.

dē-lēnīmentum, ī *n* **a**) anything that soothes *or* charms; **b**) blandishment, charm, caress.

dē-lēniō 4 to soothe, charm, caress.

dē-lēnītor, ōris *m* soother, cajoler.

dēleō, ēvī, ētum 2 to blot out, obliterate; to destroy, annihilate, abolish, finish (*bellum*).

dēlētrīx, īcis *f* she who destroys.

dēlīberābundus 3 reflecting, deliberating maturely.

dēlīberātiō, ōnis *f* deliberation, reflection, consideration.

dēlīberātīvus 3 deliberative; requiring deliberation.

dēlīberātor, ōris *m* one who deliberates.

dē-līberō 1 **a**) to weigh carefully, consider, consult (*de re, alqd*); **b**) to resolve, decide; **c**) to consult an oracle.

dē-lībō 1 to take away a little, to take from; **a**) to enjoy; **b**) to detract, diminish (*alqd de re*).
dē-librō 1 to bark, peel.
dē-libūtus 3 besmeared, anointed.
dēlicātus 3 **1.** delightful, charming, pleasing; luxurious, voluptuous, tender, soft; **2.** nice, dainty, effeminate, spoiled.
dēliciae, ārum *f/pl.* (*also* **-ia, ae** *f and* **-ium, ī** *n*) delight, pleasure, luxury, voluptuousness; **a**) favourite, darling, sweetheart; **b**) ornament.
dēliciolae, ārum *f/pl.* (*and* **dēliciolum, ī** *n*) darling.
dē-licō 1 to explain.
dēlictum, ī *n* fault, offence, crime, trespass.
dēlicuus (*or* **-uos**) 3 lacking.
dē-ligō[1], **lēgī, lēctum** 3 to pick, pluck; **a**) to choose, pick out, select; **b**) to separate, remove; **dēlēctī, ōrum** *m/pl.* picked men.
dē-ligō[2] 1 to bind *or* tie together, to fasten (*alqd ad alqd*).
dē-lingō 3 to lick.
dē-linquō, līquī, lictum 3 to fail, commit a crime, transgress.
dē-liquēscō, licuī, — 3 to melt, dissolve.
dē-liquiō, ōnis *f* lack, loss.
dēlīrāmentum, ī *n* folly, nonsense.
dēlīrātiō, ōnis *f* silliness, folly, madness.
dē-līrō 1 to be silly, mad, insane.
dēlīrus 3 silly, mad, insane, crazy.
dē-litēscō, lituī, — 3 to conceal oneself, lie hid.
dē-lītigō 1 to scold *or* rail.
(**delphīn, īnis** *and*) **delphīnus, ī** *m* dolphin.
dēlūbrum, ī *n* sanctuary, shrine, temple.
dē-luctor (*and* **-ō**) 1 to wrestle.
dē-lūdificō (*and* **-or**) 1 to mock, jeer, hoax.
dē-lūdō, sī, sum 3 to mock, delude, deceive.
dē-lumbis, e feeble.
dē-lumbō 1 to make lame, weaken.
dē-madēscō, duī, — 3 to become quite wet.
dē-mandō 1 to give in charge, intrust (*alci alqd*).
dē-mānō 1 to flow down.
dēm-archus, ī *m* ruler of a district, tribune of the people.
dē-mēns, tis out of one's senses, mad, insane, foolish.
dēmentia, ae *f* folly, madness, insanity.
dē-mentiō 4 to be mad.
dē-mereor (*and* **-reō**) 2 to earn; to deserve well of.
dē-mergō, rsī, rsum 3 **a**) to submerge, dip, plunge, immerse; **b**) to cast down, sink, overwhelm.
dē-mētātus 3 measured out, marked.
dē-mētior, mēnsus sum 4 to measure off *or* out.
dē-metō, (messuī,) messum 3 to mow, cut off, reap.
dē-migrātiō, ōnis *f* emigration.
dē-migrō 1 to migrate, emigrate, remove; to depart from.
dē-minuō 3 to make less *or* smaller, to diminish; to take away (*alqd de* or *ex re*).
dē-minūtiō, ōnis *f* a lessening, diminution; **a**) decrease, loss; **b**) loss of dignity, of civil rights.
dē-mīror 1 to wonder at, be amazed.
dē-missīcius 3 hanging down.
dē-missiō, ōnis *f* a letting down, lowering.
dē-mītigō 1 to make mild.
dē-mittō 3 to send *or* let down, to lower, drop, to cast, thrust *or* put down; **a**) to sink down; to fix, drive *or* plunge into; to lead to a lower position; **b**) **se dēmittere** (*or* **P.**) to go, flow, let oneself down, to condescend, stoop, engage in; — **dēmissus** 3 lowered, hanging down, low; **a**) feeble, weak; **b**) modest, humble, unassuming; **c**) downcast, dispirited; **d**) poor, needy.
dēmiūrgus, ī *m* chief magistrate in some Greek states.
dēmō, dēmpsī, dēmptum 3 to take away (*alqd de re; alci alqd*), to withdraw, subtract, remove.
dē-mōlior 4 **a**) to pull *or* throw down, to destroy, demolish; **b**) to remove.
dē-mōlītiō, ōnis *f* a tearing down, demolition.
dē-mōnstrātiō, ōnis *f* a showing, pointing out; **a**) description, representation, explanation, proof; **b**) laudatory speech.
dēmōnstrātīvus 3 **a**) demonstrative; **b**) laudatory.
dē-mōnstrātor, ōris *m* one who points out, indicator.

dē-mōnstrō 1 to show, point out, indicate; **a**) to describe, explain, mention; **b**) to prove, demonstrate.
dē-mordeō 2 to bite (off).
dē-morior 3 to die; to be dying of love for (*alqm*).
dē-moror 1 **1.** to delay, linger; **2.** *trans.* to stop, hinder, delay.
dē-moveō 2 to move *or* put away, remove, drive out; to turn away, divert.
dē-mūgītus 3 filled with the noise of bellowing.
dē-mulceō 2 to stroke caressingly.
dēmum *adv.* **1.** at length, at last; a) now at last, then indeed, not till then; b) only; **2.** precisely, certainly.
dē-murmurō 1 to mutter over.
dē-mūtō 1 to change, alter.
dēnārius 3 containing ten (*asses*); *subst.* **dēnārius, ī** *m* a Roman silver coin.
dē-nārrō 1 to tell, relate exactly.
dē-nāsō 1 to deprive of the nose.
dē-natō 1 to swim down.
dē-negō 1 **a**) to deny; **b**) to refuse, reject a request.
dēnī, ae, a ten each, ten at a time, by tens,
dē-nicālis, e relating to the dead, funeral.
dēnique *adv.* at last, at length, finally; **a**) in short, in a word, in fine; **b**) then indeed; **c**) even, certainly, at least; just, precisely; only.
dē-nōminō 1 to name, call.
dē-normō 1 to make irregular.
dē-notō 1 to mark out, indicate, denote, point out; to stigmatize.
dēns, tis *m* tooth; **a**) the tooth of envy, of slander, of hatred, of time; **b**) spike, prong.
dēnseō, —, — 2 *and* **dēnsō** 1 to make thick, to thicken, press together, condense; to crowd together.
dēnsus 3 thick, close, dense; **a**) crowded together, pressed together; **b**) frequent, following closely, uninterrupted.
dentālia, ium *n/pl.* share-beam of a plough, ploughshare.
dentātus 3 provided with teeth.
denti-frangibulus 3 breaking teeth.
denti-frangibulum, ī *n* instrument for breaking teeth, fist.
denti-legus 3 collecting teeth.
dentiō 4 to cut one's teeth; (of teeth) to grow (through lack of use).
denti-scalpium, ī *n* toothpick.
dē-nūbō 3 to marry (*of a woman*).
dē-nūdō 1 to lay bare, make naked; **a**) to uncover; **b**) to rob, plunder.
dē-numerō 1 to pay (down).
dē-nūntiātiō, ōnis *f* announcement, declaration, proclamation; threat, menace, warning, order.
dē-nūntiō 1 to announce, declare, proclaim; **a**) to menace, threaten; **b**) to foretell, prophesy; **c**) to direct, order, command; **d**) to give notice of.
dēnuō *adv.* anew, again.
dēnus tenth.
de-onerō 1 to unload, disburden.
de-orsum (*and* **-us**) *adv.* downwards, down.
de-ōsculor 1 to kiss affectionately.
dē-pacīscor 3 = **depeciscor.**
dē-pāctūs firmly fixed.
dē-parcus 3 niggardly.
dē-pāscō (*and* **-scor**) 3 to feed on, to consume.
dē-pecīscor, pectus sum 3 **a**) to make an agreement (*cum alqo, ut*); **b**) to bargain for (*sibi alqd*).
dē-pectō —, pexum 3 to comb.
dē-pecūlātor, ōris *m* plunderer, embezzler.
dē-pecūlātus, ūs *m* swindling.
dē-pecūlor 1 to plunder, rob (*alqm alqa re*).
dē-pellō, pulī, pulsum 3 **a**) to drive down; **b**) to drive away, expel, remove (*alqm alqa re, ab, de, ex re*); **c**) to wean; **d**) to keep off; **e**) to displace, avert, to drive out of one's course.
dē-pendeō, —, — 2 to hang down, hang from, to depend upon (*a re*).
dē-pendō, ndī, nsum 3 to pay.
dē-perdō, didī, ditum 3 to ruin, destroy; to lose.
dē-pereō, to perish, be lost, be ruined utterly; (*trans.*) to be desperately in love with.
dē-pilō 1 to depilate.
dē-pingō 3 to depict, paint, portray; to describe.
dē-plangō 3 to bewail, lament.
dē-pleō 2 to empty, exhaust.
dē-plexus 3 winding oneself round, gripping.
dē-plōrābundus 3 lamenting.
dē-plōrātiō, ōnis *f* lamentation.
dē-plōrō 1 **1.** to weep violently (*de re*); **2.** *trans.* to bewail, deplore; to give up as lost.

dē-pluō 3 to rain down.
dē-poliō 4 to smooth, polish.
dē-pōnō 3 to put, place, lay down (*alqd in re, in rem*), **arma** to lay down arms; **a**) to deposit, commit to the charge of (*alqd apud alqm, in re*), to intrust; **b**) to give up, lay aside, resign, get rid of, renounce; **dēpositus** 3 despaired of, given up, dead, **dēpositum, ī** *n* deposit, trust.
dē-populātiō, ōnis *f* a laying waste, pillaging.
dē-populātor, ōris *m* spoiler, pillager.
dē-populor (*and* **-lō**) 1 to lay waste, pillage.
dē-portō 1 **a**) to carry down *or* away (*alqd ex re in* or *ad alqd*), take away; **b**) to bring home; **c**) to banish, exile.
dē-poscō, poposcī, — 3 to demand *or* request earnestly (*alqd, sibi alqd, alqm alqd*); **a**) to demand for punishment; **b**) to challenge.
dēpositum, ī *n, see* **depono.**
dē-postulō 1 to demand.
dē-prāvātē wrongly.
dē-prāvātiō, ōnis *f* **a**) distorting; **b**) perversion, corruption.
dē-prāvō 1 to distort, pervert; **a**) to disfigure; **b**) to spoil, corrupt.
dēprecābundus 3 earnestly entreating.
dē-precātiō, ōnis *f* **1.** an averting by entreaty; a) apology; b) deprecation; **2.** appeal, intercession.
dē-precātor, ōris *m* intercessor, averter.
dē-precor 1 **1.** to avert by entreaty, deprecate, beg to escape (*alqd ab alqo*); to pray for forgiveness; **2.** to pray for, intercede in behalf of (*alqm* or *alqd ab alqo; ut, ne*).
dē-prehendō 3 to seize, lay hold of; **a**) to catch, snatch; **b**) to surprise, detect, overtake, apprehend, discover; **c**) to confine, bring into a difficulty; **d**) to perceive, understand, discover, find.
dē-prehēnsiō, ōnis *f* a catching, detection.
dē-prēndō, ndī, nsum 3 = **deprehendo.**
dē-primō, pressī, pressum 3 to press *or* weigh down; **a**) to sink (*a ship*); to place deep in the ground; **b**) to depress, oppress; **c**) to depreciate; **dēpressus** 3 sunken, low.
dē-proelior 1 to fight furiously.
dē-prōmō 3 to draw *or* bring forth, to bring out, to fetch (*alqd ex, de, ab re*); to derive, obtain.
dē-properō 1 to hasten.
depsō, suī, stum 3 to knead.
dē-pudet, uit — 2 to cease to be ashamed (*alqm* with *inf.*).
dē-pūgis, e with thin buttocks.
dē-pugnō 1 to fight out, to the end, decisively (*cum alqo*).
dēpulsiō, ōnis *f* a driving away *or* off; defence.
dē-pulsō 1 to drive away.
dēpulsor, ōris *m* one who drives away.
dē-pungō 3 to prick, mark.
dē-purgō 1 to clean out.
dē-putō 1 **1.** to cut off; **2.** to reckon, estimate.
dē-pȳgis, e = **depugis.**
dēque = et de; *see* **susque.**
dē-questus 3 (*pf. part. of dequeror*) complaining of (*with acc.*).
dē-rādō to scrape off.
dērēctus 3 = **directus.**
dē-relictiō, ōnis *f* a forsaking.
dē-relinquō 3 to forsake wholly, to abandon, desert.
dē-repente *adv.* suddenly.
dē-rēpō 3 to creep down.
dē-rīdeō 2 to laugh at, mock.
dē-rīdiculus 3 very ridiculous; *subst.* **-culum, ī** *n* object of ridicule, mockery.
dē-rigēscō, riguī, — 3 to become quite stiff.
dē-rigō = **dirigo.**
dē-ripiō, ripuī, reptum 3 to tear down *or* off (*alqd de re*); **a**) to snatch away (*alci alqd*), to pull down; **b**) to curtail, detract from.
dē-rīsor, ōris *m* derider, mocker.
dē-rīsus, ūs *m* mockery.
dērīvātiō, ōnis *f* diversion.
dē-rīvō 1 to lead off, turn away, divert (*alqd ex re in alqd*); to derive.
dē-rogātiō, ōnis *f* partial repeal.
dē-rogō 1 **a**) to take away; detract (*alqd de, ex re; alci alqd*); **b**) to repeal in part.
dē-rōsus 3 gnawed away.
dē-runcinō 1 to plane off; to cheat.
dē-ruō 3 to cast down, overturn.
dē-ruptus 3 precipitous, steep.
dē-sacrō 1 to dedicate.
dē-saeviō 4 to rage furiously.
dē-saltō 1 to dance.

dē-scendō, ndī, nsum 3 to go, come, climb down, to descend (*a, de, ex re in* or *ad alqd*); **a**) to sink down, penetrate; **b**) to descend, stoop, yield, agree to, lower oneself (*ad* or *in alqd*).
dēscēnsiō, ōnis *f and* **dēscēnsus, ūs** *m* a descending; descent, way down.
dē-scīscō, scīvī *and* **sciī, scītum** 3 to revolt from, desert (*ab alqo ad alqm; a re*), to go over; to withdraw, depart, deviate.
dē-scrībō 3 **1.** to copy, transcribe; **2.** to sketch, draw, depict, describe, delineate; a) to define, explain, assign, allot, appoint, fix, prescribe; b) = **discribo.**
dē-scrīptiō, ōnis *f* delineation; a) transcript, copy; b) definition, disposition, division, arrangement; c) description, representation.
dē-scrīptus 3 well arranged, precisely ordered.
dē-secō, cuī, ctum 1 to cut off.
dē-serō, seruī, sertum 3 to forsake, abandon; **a**) to desert, leave; **b**) to give up, neglect; **dēsertus** 3 deserted, forsaken (*a re*), solitary, lonely, waste; *subst.* **dēserta, ōrum** *n/pl.* deserts, wastes, wilderness.
dē-serpō 3 to creep down.
dēsertor, ōris *m* **a**) deserter, runaway, fugitive; **b**) abandoning, neglecting (*gen.*).
dēsertus 3 *and* **-ta** *n/pl., see* **desero.**
dē-serviō 4 to serve diligently (*alci*).
dēses, idis inactive, idle, indolent.
dē-siccō 1 to dry up.
dē-sideō, sēdī, sessum 2 to sit idle.
dēsīderābilis, e desirable, to be longed for.
dēsīderātiō, ōnis *f* = **desiderium.**
dēsīderium, ī *n* a longing, desire, yearning; wish, request.
dē-sīderō 1 to long for, desire, wish for, require, ask (*alqd ab alqo*; with *inf.* or *acc. c. inf.*); to miss, lack, lose; **P.** to be lost.
dēsidia, ae *f* inactivity, idleness.
dēsidiābulum, ī *n* lounging-place.
dēsidiōsus 3 idle, lazy, indolent; causing idleness.
dē-sīdō, sēdī *and* **sīdī,** — 3 to sink down, fall, settle.
dē-signātiō, ōnis *f* designing, describing, appointment.
dē-signātor, ōris *m* = **dissignator.**
dē-signō 1 to mark out, point out by signs; **a**) to allude to; **b**) to designate, represent, copy; **c**) to appoint to a magistracy.
dē-siliō, siluī, (sultum) 4 to leap down.
dē-sinō, siī, situm 3 to leave off, desist, cease (*alcis rei;* with *inf.*); **a**) to end, close (*in alqd*); **b**) to abandon.
dē-sipientia, ae *f* folly.
dē-sipiō, —, — 3 **a**) to be foolish *or* silly; **b**) to act foolishly.
dē-sistō, stitī, — 3 to desist, leave off, cease (*re, de* or *a re,* with *inf.*).
dē-sōlō 1 to make solitary, to forsake, leave alone.
dē-spectō 1 **a**) = **despicio; b**) to tower above.
dēspectus[1] 3 = **despicatus.**
dēspectus[2]**, ūs** *m* **1.** view, prospect; **2.** contempt.
dēspēranter *adv.* despairingly.
dē-spērātiō, ōnis *f* hopelessness, despair.
dē-spērō 1 to be hopeless, to despair (*de re, alqd;* with *acc. c. inf.*); **dēspērātus** 3 **a**) hopeless, desperate; **b**) given up, despaired of.
dēspicātiō, ōnis *f and* **-tus**[1]**, ūs** *m* contempt.
dēspicātus[2] 3 despised, contemptible.
dēspicientia, ae *f* contempt.
dē-spiciō, spexī, spectum 3 **1.** to look down upon; a) to overtop, command; b) to despise, disdain; **2.** to look away.
dē-spoliātor, ōris *m* robber, plunderer.
dē-spoliō 1 to plunder, despoil.
dē-spondeō, spondī, spōnsum 2 **1.** to promise formally, pledge; to betroth, promise in marriage (*alci alqm*); **2. animum** to lose courage, to despond.
dē-sponsō 1 to betroth.
dē-spūmō 1 **a**) to skim; **b**) to dissipate the fumes of (*wine*); **c**) to shed scum; **d**) to cease foaming, abate.
dē-spuō — — 3 to spit out.
dē-squāmō 1 to scale (*fish*).
dē-stertō, tuī, — 3 to cease snoring *or* dreaming.
dē-stillō 1 to drop down, drip.
dē-stimulō 1 = **distimulo.**

dēstinātiō, ōnis *f* determination, resolution; appointment.

dēstinō 1 to make fast *or* firm (*alqd alqa re, ad alqd*); **a**) to fix, determine, settle, resolve; **b**) to aim at, to intend, choose; **c**) to betroth, designate as a wife for; **dēstinātus** 3 determined, fixed, intended; *subst.* **dēstinātum, ī** *n* plan, purpose.

dē-stituō, tuī, tūtum 3 **1.** to set down, place; **2.** to leave, forsake, abandon; to deceive, betray (*alqm in re*), **spe** *and* **a spe** to deprive of hope; **dēstitūtus** 3 forsaken, deceived, deprived, needy, helpless.

dēstitūtiō, ōnis *f* a forsaking; disappointment.

dē-stringō 3 to strip off; **a**) to draw, bare (*the sword*), brandish; **b**) to touch lightly, graze; **c**) to criticize, satirize; **dēstrictus** 3 sharp, severe, rigid.

dē-structiō, ōnis *f* a pulling down; refutation.

dē-struō 3 to pull down, tear down, demolish.

dē-subitō *adv.* suddenly.

dē-sūdāscō 3 to sweat profusely.

dē-sūdō 1 to sweat greatly; to exert *or* fatigue oneself.

dē-suēfiō, fierī to become unaccustomed, estranged (*a re*).

dē-suēscō 3 = **desuefio.**

dēsuētūdō, inis *f* disuse, want of practice.

dē-suētus 3 unused, out of use; unaccustomed (*with inf.*).

dēsultor, ōris *m* leaper, circus--rider.

dēsultōrius 3 (*equus*) circus-rider's horse.

dē-sultūra, ae *f* a leaping down.

dē-sum, fuī, esse to be absent *or* away, to be wanting (*alci rei, ad alqd*); **a**) to fail, abandon, desert, neglect; **b**) to lose the opportunity; **sibi deesse** to betray oneself, to be wanting in one's duty.

dē-sūmō 3 to choose, select.

dē-super *adv.* from above.

dē-surgō 3 to rise.

dē-tegō 3 to uncover, lay bare, unroof; to reveal, disclose.

dē-tendō, —, tēnsum 3 to unstretch, take down.

dē-tergeō 2 to wipe off; **a**) to break off, sweep away; **b**) to cleanse.

dēterior, ius *comp.* worse, inferior, lower, poorer, meaner; *superl.* **dēterrimus** 3 worst, lowest, last.

dē-terminātiō, ōnis *f* boundary, end.

dē-terminō 1 to bound, limit.

dē-terō 3 to rub off *or* away, to file away; **a**) to wear away; **b**) to lessen, weaken, impair.

dē-terreō 2 to frighten off, deter (*alqm a, de re*; with *abl.*; with *ne* or *inf.*); **a**) to prevent, hinder, discourage (*alqm a re*); **b**) to keep off, ward off (*alqd ab alqo*).

dētestābilis, e detestable, execrable, abominable.

dē-testātiō, ōnis *f* a cursing, execration; an averting (*by sacrifice*).

dē-testor 1 to curse, execrate; **a**) to avert, ward off, deprecate (*alqd ab alqo*); **b**) to call down upon (*alqd in alqm*).

dē-texō 3 to weave, plait; to finish.

dē-tineō, tinuī, tentum 2 **a**) to keep back, detain, to check, hold away (*alqm a re*); **b**) to keep, occupy, engage; **c**) to withhold (*money*); **d**) **se dētinēre** to support existence.

dē-tondeō, tondī, tōnsum 2 to shear off, clip; to strip.

dē-tonō, uī, — 1 **a**) to thunder down; **b**) to cease to thunder *or* to rage.

dē-torqueō 2 **a**) to turn away *or* off, bend aside, to avert (*alqd a re ad* or *in alqd*); **b**) to twist, distort.

dē-tractātiō, ōnis *f* = **detrectatio.**

dē-tractiō, ōnis *f* a drawing *or* taking away; removal.

dē-tractō = **detrecto.**

dē-tractor, ōris *m* disparager, detractor.

dē-trahō 3 **1.** to draw *or* take down, pull down (*alqd de, a re, re*); to humiliate; **2.** to take away, remove, withdraw (*de, ex re, alci alqd*), drag; a) to disparage, detract, calumniate, slander; b) to drag away, take from; c) to drag *or* bring to (*alqd ad* or *in alqd*).

dētrectātiō, ōnis *f* a declining, refusal.

dē-trectātor, ōris *m* = **detractor.**

dē-trectō 1 **a**) to decline, refuse; **b**) to detract from, disparage.

dētrīmentōsus 3 hurtful, detrimental.

dētrīmentum, ī *n* damage, loss, injury; defeat.

dē-trūdō 3 **1.** to thrust down *or* away; a) to drive away, dislodge; b) to force away (*de, ex re*); **2.** a) to force, compel (*ad, in alqd*); b) to postpone, put off.
dē-truncō 1 to lop *or* cut off; to mutilate, behead.
dē-tumēscō, muī, — 3 to cease being swollen, to subside.
dē-turbō 1 to thrust down, cast down, drive away (*de, ex, a re*); to eject, dispossess.
dē-turpō 1 to disfigure.
de-unx, cis *m* eleven twelfths.
de-ūrō 3 to burn, destroy; to nip.
deus, ī *m* a god, deity, divine being; **a)** tutelary god; **b)** person in power.
de-ūtor 3 to misuse, maltreat.
dē-vāstō 1 to lay waste, devastate.
dē-vehō 3 to convey, carry *or* bear down *or* away (*alqd ex re in* or *ad alqd*); **P.** to sail.
dē-vellō 3 to pull, pluck *or* tear away.
dē-vēlō 1 to unveil, uncover.
dē-veneror 1 to venerate, worship.
dē-veniō 4 to come to, arrive.
dē-verbeōr 1 to cudgel well.
dē-versor[1] 1 to lodge as a guest, put up.
dē-versor[2], **ōris** *m* guest (*in an inn*).
dēversōriolum, ī *n* little inn.
dēversōrium, ī *n* inn, lodging; tavern; place of retreat.
dēversōrius 3 (fit) for lodging in.
dēverticulum, ī *n* **1.** by-road; digression; refuge; **2.** = **deversorium.**
dē-vertō 3 to turn away *or* aside (*trans.* and *intr.*); to go to lodge (*in alqd, ad* or *apud alqm*), to put up; to digress.
dē-vēscor 3 to devour.
dēvexitās, ātis *f* declivity.
dēvexus 3 inclining, sloping; sinking, steep.
dē-vinciō 4 to bind, tie fast; **a)** to fasten, connect (*alqd cum alqo*); **b)** to pledge, oblige, lay under obligation (*re*); **c)** to devote *or* attach to (*re*); **dēvinctus** 3 devoted to, strongly attached.
dē-vincō 3 to conquer completely, to overcome, subdue; to carry through, enforce (*ut*).
dē-vītātiō, ōnis *f* an avoiding.
dē-vītō 1 to avoid.
dē-vius 3 out of the way, off the road; **a)** retired, sequestered, secluded; **b)** solitary, wandering; c) inconstant, foolish; **dēvium** (*iter*) by-way.
dē-vocō 1 **a)** to call down; **b)** to call away *or* off, to recall (*alqm ab, ex, de re ad* or *in alqd*); **c)** to invite; **d)** to allure, seduce.
dē-volō 1 **a)** to fly down; to hasten down; **b)** to fly away.
dē-volvō 3 to roll down *or* downwards; **P.** to roll oneself down, to fall headlong.
dē-vorō 1 to swallow down, devour; **a)** to consume, waste; **b)** to bear patiently, endure; **c)** to devour eagerly, absorb; **d)** to enjoy.
dēvortium, ī *n* by-way.
dē-vors-, -vort- = **dē-vers-, -vert-.**
dē-vōtiō, ōnis *f* a devoting, consecrating; **a)** vow, curse, execration; **b)** incantation, spell.
dē-vōtō 1 to lay a spell on.
dē-voveō 2 to vow, devote, offer, consecrate; to devote to death (*alci alqd, se pro alqo*); **a)** to curse; to bewitch; **b)** to give up, destine, appoint; — **dēvōtus** 3 devoted (*alci*); accursed.
dextāns, tis *m* five sixths.
dextella, ae *f* a little right hand.
dexter, t(e)ra, t(e)rum right, on the right hand; **a)** propitious; **b)** suitable, fitting; **c)** skilful, handy, dexterous; — *subst.* **dext(e)ra, ae** *f* right hand, right side; fidelity, pledge of friendship, bravery; **dext(e)rā** *adv.* (and *prep.* with *acc.*) on the right (of); *comp.* **dexterior, ius,** *superl.* **dextumus** *and* **dextimus.**
dext(e)rē adroitly.
dexteritās, ātis *f* skilfulness, dexterity.
dextrōrsum (*or* **-sus**) *adv.* towards the right hand, to the right.
dextrō-vorsum = **dextrōrsum.**
dextumus 3, *see* **dexter.**
diabathrārius, ī *m* maker of low Greek shoes.
dia-dēma, atis *n* royal headdress, diadem.
diaeta, ae *f* **a)** mode of living (*prescribed by a physician*); **b)** room.
dia-lecticus 3 dialectical; *subst.* **a)** ~, **ī** *m* dialectician, logician; **b) -a, ae** *f* dialectics, art of discussion.
dialectus, ī *f* dialect.
diālis, e of Juppiter.

dia-logus, ī *m* dialogue, conversation.
dia-nomē, ēs *f* distribution.
dia-pasma, atis *n* powder for sprinkling.
diārium, ī *n* daily ration *or* allowance.
dia-trēta, ōrum *n/pl.* cups decorated with filigree.
di-baphus, ī *f* purple-striped state-robe.
dica, ae *f* lawsuit, action; jury.
dicācitās, ātis *f* pungent wit, raillery.
dicāculus 3 witty, satirical.
dicātiō, ōnis *f* a settling as a citizen in another state.
dicāx, ācis satirical, witty.
dichorēus, ī *m* double-trochee.
diciō, ōnis *f* jurisdiction; authority, power, control.
dicis causā for form's sake, for the sake of appearance.
dicō[1] 1 to dedicate, consecrate, devote to a god (*alci alqd*); to devote, give up to; **se civitati** *or* **in civitatem** to become a citizen of another state.
dīcō[2], **dīxī, dictum** 3 **1.** a) to fix, appoint, settle; b) to name, appoint, proclaim (*alqm dictatorem*); **2.** to say, speak, utter, tell, relate, mention, declare, affirm; a) to plead (*causam*), to pronounce judgment (*ius*); b) to deliver an oration, **ars dīcendī** art of eloquence; c) to name, call (*alqm nomine, alci nomen*); d) to sing, celebrate in verse; e) to describe, narrate.
di-crotum, ī *n* (*and* **-ta, ae** *f*) vessel with two banks of oars.
dictamnus, ī *f and* **-num, ī** *n* dittany (*a plant*).
dictāta, ōrum *n/pl., see* **dicto.**
dictātor, ōris *m* chief magistrate with absolute power, dictator.
dictātōrius 3 of a dictator.
dictātrīx, īcis *f* mistress.
dictātūra, ae *f* dictatorship.
dictērium, ī *n* witty remark.
dictiō, ōnis *f* a saying, speaking, uttering; **causae** defence; **a)** answer of an oracle; **b)** conversation; c) declamation, speech; diction, style.
dictitō 1 to say often, maintain, assert repeatedly.
dictō 1 **1.** to say often, reiterate (*alci alqd*); **2.** a) to dictate; b) to compose, draw up; *subst.* **dictāta, ōrum** *n/pl.* dictation, lesson, precepts.
dictum, ī *n* a saying; **a)** word, remark; **b)** maxim, proverb, sentence; **c)** order, command; **d)** promise; **e)** witty saying.
dī-dō, dīdidī, dīditum 3 to distribute, spread, disseminate.
dī-dūcō 3 to draw apart; **a)** to separate, sever, divide; **b)** to expand, disjoin; **c)** to disperse, scatter, separate forcibly.
diēcula, ae *f* a little while.
dīērēctus 3 (? = crucified) ruined, 'done for'; **(ab)i dīērēctus** *or* **dīērēctē** (*adv.*), go and be hanged!
diēs, ēī *m* (*and f*) **1.** day; daylight, daytime; a day's march *or* journey; **2.** fixed day *or* time, appointed time, term; birthday, day of death; **3.** space of time, period, time.
dif-fāmō 1 to divulge, to spread abroad an evil report, to defame.
differēns, entis different.
differentia, ae (*and* **-feritās, ātis**) *f* difference, diversity.
dif-ferō, distulī, dīlātum 3 **1.** to carry different ways; a) to spread abroad, disperse; to publish, report, circulate; to defame; b) to put off, delay, postpone, protract; c) to separate, scatter; to distract; **2.** *intr.* to differ, be different, vary (*ab alqo, inter se*).
dif-fertus 3 stuffed full (*abl.*).
dif-fībulō 1 to unclasp.
dif-ficilis, e difficult, hard, troublesome; **a)** dangerous, critical; **b)** morose, surly, captious, obstinate; *adv.* **difficulter, difficiliter, difficile.**
difficultās, ātis *f* difficulty, trouble; **a)** need, poverty, distress; **b)** moroseness, obstinacy.
diffīdēns, tis distrustful, uneasy.
dif-fīdentia, ae *f* distrust.
dif-fīdō, fīsus sum 3 to distrust.
dif-findō 3 to cleave asunder, split; to break off; to open; to interrupt.
dif-fingō 3 to transform, form anew.
dif-fiteor, —, — 2 to deny, disavow.
dif-flāgitō 1 to harass with demands.
dif-flō 1 to disperse by blowing.
dif-fluō 3 to flow in different directions, to flow away; to be dissolved, to melt away, disappear.
dif-fringō, —, frāctum 3 to break to pieces.

dif-fugiō, 3 to flee in different directions; to disperse, be scattered.
diffugium, ī *n* dispersion.
dif-fulminō 1 to scatter like a thunderbolt.
dif-funditō 1 to dissipate.
dif-fundō 3 to spread by pouring, to pour forth in all directions; **a**) to spread, scatter, diffuse; **b**) to extend, expand; **c**) to gladden, cheer up; — **diffūsus** 3 extended, extensive, spread out; prolix.
dif-fūsilis, e expansive.
dif-fūsiō, ōnis *f* expansion; *animi* cheerfulness.
dif-futūtus 3 exhausted by debauchery.
di-gamma *n* the digamma; investment- *or* interest-book.
dī-gerō 3 **a**) to separate, divide; **b**) to distribute (*alqd in alqd*); **c**) to put in order, arrange.
dī-gestiō, ōnis *f* (*and* **-tus, ūs** *m*) distribution, enumeration.
digitulus, ī *m* a little finger.
digitus, ī *m* **1.** finger; **extremus digitus** tip of the finger; a finger's breadth, inch; **2.** toe.
dī-gladior 1 to fight for life and death, to contend fiercely.
dīgnātiō, ōnis *f* reputation, honour, rank.
dīgnitās, ātis *f* worthiness, merit; **a**) dignity, grandeur, splendour, dignified exterior, majesty, distinction, eminence; **b**) personal dignity, honour, esteem, authority; **c**) rank, high office.
dīgnō 1 to deem worthy (*alqm alqa re*).
dīgnor 1 **a**) to be deemed worthy; **b**) to deem worthy *or* deserving; to deign, to condescend.
dī-gnōscō, —, — 3 to distinguish, discern.
dīgnus 3 worthy, deserving (*abl.*; with *qui* and *subj.*); fitting, suitable, becoming, proper.
dī-gredior, gressus sum 3 to go apart *or* asunder, to depart; to deviate, digress (*ab alqo, de, ex, a re*).
dī-gressiō, ōnis *f and* **-sus, ūs** *m* a separating, parting, departure; digression.
dī-iūdicātiō, ōnis *f* a deciding.
dī-iūdicō 1 to decide, determine; to distinguish (*alqd a re*).
dī-iungō, dī-iūnctiō, *see* **disiungo, disiunctio.**
dī-lābor 3 **a**) to glide apart; to fall asunder, fall to pieces; to dissolve, disappear, melt away; **b**) to flee, escape, disperse; to slip away.
dī-lacerō 1 to tear to pieces, rend asunder; to ruin.
dī-lāminō to split in two.
dī-laniō 1 to tear to pieces.
dī-lapidō 1 to squander, waste.
dī-largior 4 to lavish, give liberally.
dī-lātiō, ōnis *f* a delaying.
dī-lātō 1 to spread out, extend; to enlarge.
dī-lātor, ōris *m* loiterer.
dī-laudō 1 to praise highly.
dī-lēctus[1] 3, *see* **diligo.**
dī-lēctus[2]**, ūs** *m* a picking out; levy, recruiting; levied soldiers.
dī-līdō 3 to break to pieces.
dīligēns, tis a) careful, attentive, assiduous, accurate, diligent, scrupulous; **b**) careful in house-keeping, thrifty.
dīligentia, ae *f* **a**) carefulness, attentiveness, accuracy, diligence; **b**) frugality.
dī-ligō, lēxī, lēctum 3 to esteem highly, to prize, value, love; **dīlēctus** 3 beloved, dear.
dī-lōrīcō 1 to tear open.
dī-lūceō,—,—2 to be clear, evident.
dī-lūcēscō, lūxī, — 3 to grow light, become day.
dī-lūcidus 3 clear, evident.
dīlūculum, ī *n* daybreak, dawn.
dī-lūdium, ī *n* interval (between plays *or* games).
dī-luō 3 to wash away; **a**) to dissolve; **b**) to weaken, lessen, impair; **c**) to refute; **d**) to remove.
dīluviēs, ēī *f and* **-vium, ī** *n* inundation, flood, deluge.
dīluviō 1 to flood.
dī-madēscō, duī, — 3 to melt away.
dī-mānō 1 to flow different ways, to spread abroad.
dī-mēnsiō, ōnis *f* a measuring.
dī-mētior, mēnsus sum 4 to measure out, lay out.
dī-mētō *and* **-tor** 1 to measure out, to bound by measuring.
dīmicātiō, ōnis *f* fight, struggle, combat.
dī-micō 1 to fight, contend, struggle (*cum alqo, pro, de re*); to strive; to be in conflict.
dīmidiātus 3 halved, half.
dīmidius 3 half; **dīmidium, ī** *n* a half.

dī-missiō, ōnis *f* a sending away *or* out; a dismissing, discharge.
dī-mittō 3 to send in different directions, to send about, send forth; **a**) to dismiss, disband, dissolve, adjourn a meeting; **b**) to discharge; to let loose, let go, release; to repudiate; **c**) to renounce, give up, abandon, forgo.
dim-minuō 3 to break to pieces.
dī-moveō 2 to move asunder, part, separate; **a**) to remove, take away (*alqd a, de re, abl.*); **b**) to estrange.
dī-nōscō 3 = **dignosco.**
dī-notō 1 to distinguish.
dī-numerātiō, ōnis *f* enumeration.
dī-numerō 1 to count up, reckon, enumerate.
di-ōbolāris, e worth two obols.
di-oecēsis, is *f* district of jurisdiction.
di-oecētēs, ae *m* overseer of finances, treasurer.
diōta, ae *f* two-handled winejar.
diplōma, atis *n* document, letter of recommendation.
dipsas, adis *f* a serpent whose bite causes thirst.
di-pyrus 3 twice burnt.
dīrae *f*/*pl*., *see* **dirus.**
dī-rēctus 3 straight, direct; **a**) level; upright, steep; **b**) straightforward, plain, simple.
dirēmptus, ūs *m* separation.
dīreptiō, ōnis *f* a plundering, sack.
dīreptor, ōris *m* plunderer.
dir-ibeō 2 to separate, to sort (*voting-tablets*).
diribitiō, ōnis *f* a sorting of voting--tablets.
diribitor, ōris *m* a sorter of voting--tablets.
diribitōrium, ī *n* house for the sorting of voting-tablets.
dī-rigō, rēxī, rēctum 3 to set straight, arrange in a straight line; **a**) to direct to, send, aim, steer; **b**) to dispose, order.
dir-imō, ēmī, ēmptum 3 to take apart, to separate, divide; **a**) to interrupt, end, disturb, frustrate; **b**) to break up.
dī-ripiō, ripuī, reptum 3 to tear asunder, to tear to pieces; **a**) to plunder, pillage, rob; **b**) to snatch away.
dīritās, ātis *f* misfortune; cruelty.
dī(r)rumpō 3 **a**) to break in pieces, shatter; **P.** to burst; **b**) to break up (*amicitiam*).
dī-ruō 3 to pull down, destroy, demolish.
dīrus 3 ill-omened, ominous, portentous; awful, dreadful, horrible; *subst.* **dīrae, ārum** *f*/*pl*. **a**) bad omens; **b**) curses, execrations; **c**) the Furies.
dis-, *see also* **des-.**
dīs, dītis (*neut.* **dīte**) = **dives.**
dis-calceātus 3 unshod.
dis-cēdō 3 **1.** to go asunder, part, separate (*in alcis sententiam* to take sides with); to disperse; **2.** to go away; a) to march away, depart (*ab, ex, de re*); b) to desert, forsake; c) to get away, come off (*superior, victor, victus*); d) to depart, leave, abandon; e) to pass away, vanish.
disceptātiō, ōnis *f* discussion, debate; **a**) controversy, dispute; **b**) decision.
disceptātor, ōris *m* (*f* **-trīx, īcis**) arbitrator, judge, umpire.
dis-ceptō 1 to discuss, debate, dispute (*de re*); to decide, determine, arbitrate (*in re*).
dis-cernō, crēvī, crētum 3 to separate, divide, set apart; **a**) to distinguish, discern (*alqd a re*); **b**) to decide, settle.
dis-cerpō, psī, ptum 3 to pluck to pieces, to tear asunder; to scatter.
dis-cessiō, ōnis *f and* **-sus, ūs** *m* **a**) separation; **b**) a going away, marching away, departure; division in voting.
discidium, ī *n* separation; **a**) divorce; **b**) absence; **c**) disaffection, alienation.
dis-cīdō 3 to cut in pieces.
dis-cinctus 3, *see* **discingo.**
di-scindō 3 to tear *or* cleave asunder, to rend asunder.
dis-cingō 3 to ungird; **discinctus** 3 ungirt, without a girdle; reckless, dissolute, extravagant.
disciplīna, ae *f* **1.** instruction, teaching; a) learning, knowledge, science; b) method of teaching, system, school; **2.** discipline, training, education; custom, habit, order, way of living.
discipulus, ī *m* (**discipula, ae** *f*) pupil, scholar, disciple.
dis-clūdō, sī, sum 3 to shut up apart, keep apart, separate.

discō, didicī, — 3 to learn (*alqd ab alqo*, with *inf.* or *acc. c. inf.*), become acquainted with, find out; to study; *pf.* to know.
dis-color, ōris of a different colour; party-coloured; different.
dis-condūcō 3 to be inconvenient *or* disadvantageous.
dis-conveniō, —, — 4 to disagree, be inconvenient.
dis-cordābilis, e discordant.
dis-cordia, ae *f* disagreement, dissension, discord.
dis-cordiōsus 3 quarrelsome.
dis-cordō 1 to disagree, quarrel.
dis-cors, dis disagreeing, discordant; **a)** different, at variance, inharmonious; **b)** mutinous.
dis-crepantia, ae *f* (*and* **discrepātiō, ōnis** *f*) disagreement, disunion, difference.
dis-crepitō 1 to differ.
dis-crepō, uī (**āvī**), — 1 to differ in sound; to disagree, be different (*cum* or *a re, inter se*); *impers.* **discrepat** there is a disagreement.
di-scrībō 3 **a)** to divide (*alqd in alqd*); **b)** to distribute, classify, assign (*alci alqd*); **discrīptus** 3 well-arranged; **c)** = **describo.**
dis-crīmen, inis *n* that which divides; dividing line; **a)** interval, distance; **b)** intervening space; **c)** difference, distinction; (power of) discernment; **d)** turning-point, critical moment, crisis, peril, danger, hazard; turn, issue; trial.
dis-crīminō 1 to separate, divide; to mark out.
di-scrīptiō, ōnis *f* distribution, assignment.
dis-cruciō 1 to torture, torment.
dis-cumbō, cubuī, cubitum 3 to recline at table; to go to bed.
dis-cupiō 3 to desire greatly.
dis-currō, (cu)currī, cursum 3 to run different ways, run about.
dis-cursus, ūs *m* (*and* **-sātiō, ōnis** *f*) a running about, to and fro.
discus, ī *m* quoit.
dis-cutiō, cussī, cussum 3 to strike asunder, dash to pieces, to shatter; **a)** to disperse; scatter; **b)** to remove, destroy.
disertē (*and* **-im**) distinctly, lucidly.
disertus 3 well arranged; **a)** eloquent; **b)** well expressed, clear, clever, fluent.
dīs-iciō, iēcī, iectum 3 to throw asunder, drive asunder, disperse; **a)** to tear asunder, ruin, destroy, frustrate; **b)** to squander; **disiectus** 3 scattered, dishevelled; extended.
dis-iectō 1 to toss about.
dis-iectus, ūs *m* scattering.
dis-iūnctiō (*or* **dī-iūnctiō**), **ōnis** *f* separation; logical dilemma.
dis-iungō (*or* **dī-iungō**) 3 to unyoke, unharness; **a)** to separate, sever, disunite, remove (*alqd a re*); **b)** to estrange; **disiūnctus** 3 **a)** separated, distant, remote; **b)** different; **c)** logically opposed.
dis-marītus, ī *m* twice married man.
dis-pālēscō 3 to be divulged.
dis-pālor 1 to wander about, straggle.
dis-pandō (*and* **-pennō**), **pandī, pānsum, pēnsum** *or* **pessum** 3 to stretch out, spread out.
dis-pār, aris unlike, different.
dis-parilis, e unlike, dissimilar.
dis-parō 1 to separate, divide; **disparātum, ī** *n* antithesis.
dispectus, ūs *m* examination, consideration.
dis-pellō, pulī, pulsum 3 to drive asunder, disperse.
dis-pendium, ī *n* expense; loss.
dis-pēnsātiō, ōnis *f* economical management; **a)** administration, direction; **b)** office of a steward.
dispēnsātor, ōris *m* steward, treasurer, paymaster.
dis-pēnsō 1 to distribute, disburse, pay out; to manage, arrange, regulate.
dis-percutiō 3 to knock to pieces.
dis-perdō 3 to ruin *or* destroy fully.
dis-pereō to perish *or* to be lost, undone, ruined.
dī-spergō, sī, sum 3 to disperse, scatter, spread abroad, spread out.
dis-pertiō (*and* **-ior**) 4 to divide, distribute.
dis-pertītiō, ōnis *f* dividing.
di-spiciō, spexī, spectum 3 to open the eyes; to discern, perceive, descry, discover.
dis-plicentia, ae *f* dissatisfaction.
dis-pliceō, uī, (itum) 2 to displease; **sibi displicēre** to be dissatisfied with oneself, to be fretful.
dis-plōdō 3 to burst, cause to explode.

dis-pōnō 3 to set in different places; to arrange, dispose, draw up, assign, adjust; — **dispositus** 3 well-arranged, methodical.
dis-positiō, ōnis *f*, **-tūra, ae** *f*, **-tus, ūs** *m* regular arrangement.
dis-positor, ōris *m* disposer, arranger.
dis-pudet 2 it causes much shame.
dis-pungō 3 to check up, audit.
disputābilis, e arguable.
disputātiō, ōnis *f* a reasoning; discussion; *dimin.* **-tiuncula, ae** *f*.
disputātor, ōris *m* debater, disputer.
dis-putō 1 **a**) to clear up by reckoning; **b**) to discuss, argue, examine, dispute.
dis-quīrō, —, — 3 to investigate.
dis-quīsītiō, ōnis *f* inquiry, investigation.
dis-rumpō 3 = **dirumpo.**
dis-saepiō 4 to separate, divide.
dis-saeptum, ī *n* partition.
dis-sāvior 1 = **dissuavior.**
dis-secō 1 to cut asunder.
dis-sēminō 1 to sow; to scatter, spread.
dis-sēnsiō, ōnis *f* (*and* **-sus, ūs** *m*) disagreement, dissension; **a**) discord; **b**) opposition.
dis-sentāneus 3 contrary.
dis-sentiō 4 to differ in opinion, to dissent, disagree (*ab* or *cum alqo*); to be different (*ab re*), opposed.
dis-serēnāscit, nāvit, — 3 it clears up.
dis-serō¹, sēvī, situm 3 to scatter seed, to plant here and there.
dis-serō², ruī, rtum 3 to set asunder; to discuss, to argue (*alqd* or *de re; cum alqo*).
dis-serpō to steal abroad, spread.
dis-sertiō, ōnis *f* severance.
dis-sertō 1 to discuss, treat of.
dissiciō = **disicio.**
dis-sideō, sēdī, sessum 2 **1.** a) to sit apart; b) to be remote; **2.** to disagree, be at variance, contrary.
dis-signātiō, ōnis *f* arrangement.
dis-signātor, ōris *m* **a**) usher in a theatre; **b**) funeral undertaker.
dis-signō 1 to arrange, regulate, dispose.
dis-siliō, luī, — 4 to leap *or* burst asunder.
dis-similis, e dissimilar, unlike (with *gen.* or *dat.*).
dis-similitūdō, inis *f* unlikeness, difference.
dis-simulanter (*and* **-lābiliter**) *adv.* secretly.
dis-simulantia, ae *and* **-lātiō, ōnis** *f* a dissembling, concealing.
dis-simulātor, ōris *m* dissembler, concealer.
dis-simulō 1 **a**) to dissemble, disguise; **b**) to conceal, hide, keep secret (*alqd; de re; acc. c. inf.*); **c**) to disregard.
dissipābilis, e that may be scattered.
dissipātiō, ōnis *f* a scattering, dispersion.
dis-sipō 1 to scatter, disperse; **a**) to spread abroad, to disseminate; **b**) to rout, put to flight; to overthrow, destroy; **c**) to squander.
dis-sociābilis, e dividing; incompatible.
dis-sociātiō, ōnis *f* separation.
dis-sociō 1 to disunite, separate; to estrange, set at variance.
dis-solūbilis, e that may be dissolved.
dis-solūtiō, ōnis *f* a dissolving, dissolution; **a**) an abolishing, destruction; **b**) refutation; **c**) dissoluteness.
dis-solūtus 3 disjointed, unconnected; **a**) loose, lax, remiss; **b**) negligent, careless; **c**) dissolute, licentious.
dis-solvō 3 to disunite, separate, dissolve; **a**) to abolish, abrogate, annul; **b**) to refute, reply to; **c**) to release, disengage; **d**) to pay (*alci alqd*).
dis-sonus 3 discordant, inharmonious, confused; disagreeing, different.
dis-sors, tis not in common, of a different lot *or* fate.
dis-suādeō 2 to advise against, resist, speak against (*alqd; de re,* with *acc. c. inf.*).
dis-suāsiō, ōnis *f* an advising to the contrary.
dis-suāsor, ōris *m* one who advises to the contrary, opponent.
dis-s(u)āvior 1 to kiss affectionately *or* to one's heart's content.
dis-sultō 1 to leap *or* burst asunder.
dis-suō 3 to unstitch, rip open; **a**) to open wide; **b**) to dissolve by degrees.
dis-taedet 2 it tires.

di-stantia, ae *f* distance, remoteness; diversity.
dis-tendō, tendī, tentum 3 to stretch asunder, extend; **a**) to fill full, distend; **b**) to divide; to disperse.
dis-tentus 3 [*distineo*] busy, occupied.
dis-terminō 1 to limit, separate by a boundary.
dis-terminus 3 separated.
di-stichon, ī *n* couplet.
di-stimulō 1 to squander.
distinctiō, ōnis *f and* **-tus, ūs** *m* a distinguishing; **a**) distinction; **b**) difference.
distinctus 3 separated; marked off, distinguished; **a**) decorated; **b**) adorned, embellished; **c**) distinct.
dis-tineō, tinuī, tentum 2 to keep asunder, separate, keep from uniting; **a**) to occupy, engage; **b**) to hinder, prevent, detain.
di-stinguō, inxī, inctum 3 to separate, divide, part; **a**) to decorate, adorn; **b**) to distinguish, discriminate (*alqd ab alqo*).
di-stō, —, — 1 to stand apart; **a**) to be distant *or* remote; **b**) to differ, to be different; **distat** there is a difference.
dis-torqueō 2 to twist, distort; to torture; **distortus** 3 distorted, misshapen, deformed; perverse.
dis-tortiō, ōnis *f* a distorting.
dis-tractiō, ōnis *f* a pulling asunder, separating; dissension, discord.
dis-trahō 3 to pull *or* draw asunder, to tear to pieces, divide; **a**) to sell in parcels; **b**) to end, adjust; **c**) to prevent, frustrate; **d**) to draw in different directions, to distract, perplex; **e**) to estrange, alienate.
dis-tribuō 3 to divide, distribute (*alci alqd, alqd in alqm*); **a**) to dislocate; **b**) to divide logically; **distribūtus** 3 well arranged.
dis-tribūtiō, ōnis *f* division, distribution.
di-stringō 3 to draw asunder, stretch out; **a**) to keep from uniting; **b**) to torture; **c**) to occupy, engage.
dis-truncō 1 to cut to pieces.
dis-turbātiō, ōnis *f* destruction.
dis-turbō 1 to drive asunder; to demolish, destroy; to disturb, confuse, frustrate.
dīte *neut. of* **dis**, *see* **dives.**
dītēscō, —, — 3 to grow rich.
dīthyrambicus 3 dithyrambic.
dīthyrambus, ī *m* dithyramb, song in honour of Bacchus.
dītiae, ārum *f* riches.
dītō 1 to enrich.
diū *adv.* (*comp.* **diūtius, diŭtius,** *superl.* **diutissimē**) **a**) by day; **b**) a long time, long while; **c**) long since, long ago.
diurnus 3 belonging to the day, of the day; **a**) by day; **b**) daily, of one day, for one day; *subst.* **diurna, ōrum** *n/pl.* official gazette.
dius *adv.* by day.
dīus 3 = **divus.**
diūtinus (and **diŭtinus**) 3 lasting, long, of long duration.
diuturnitās, ātis *f* long duration, length of time.
diuturnus 3 lasting, long, of long duration.
dī-vāricō 1 to spread asunder, stretch apart.
dī-vellō, vellī (vulsī), vulsum 3 to tear apart, rend asunder, tear in pieces, divide forcibly; to remove, separate, tear away (*alqd a re*).
dī-vendō 3 to sell in separate lots.
dī-verberō 1 to strike asunder, cut, divide.
dī-verbium, ī *n* dialogue (*on the* stage).
dīversitās, ātis *f* diversity, contrariety, contradiction.
dī-versus 3 **1.** turned away from, opposite, contrary; a) apart, separate, remote; b) different, various; c) opposed; — **2.** turned *or* going in different directions; a) isolated; b) opposed in character, discordant.
dī-vertō to differ.
dīves, itis rich (with *abl.* and *gen.*), wealthy; fertile, copious; precious, costly.
dī-vexō 1 to tear asunder, to vex, trouble; to destroy.
dīvidia, ae *f* sorrow, grief.
dī-vidō, vīsī, vīsum 3 **1.** to part asunder, separate, divide; to remove from (*alqd ab alqa re*); **2.** a) to divide into parts; b) to distribute, allot.
dīviduus 3 **a**) divisible; **b**) divided, separated.
dīvīnātiō, ōnis *f* **1.** gift of prophecy; divination, prophecy; **2.** selection of a prosecutor.

dīvīnitās, ātis *f* divine nature, godhead, divinity.
dīvīnitus *adv.* by divine influence; excellently, admirably.
dīvīnō 1 to foretell, prophesy, divine, forebode.
dīvīnus 3 of a god *or* deity, divine; **res dīvīna** sacrifice; **res dīvīnae** religion, service of the gods; natural laws, physics; **a**) inspired, prophetic; *subst.* **dīvīnus, ī** *m* diviner, prophet; **b**) divine, excellent, admirable, godlike.
dīvīsiō, ōnis *f* division; distribution.
dīvīsor, ōris *m* divider, distributor of bribes.
dīvīsus, ūs *m* = **divisio.**
dīvitiae, ārum *f/pl.* riches, wealth, treasures; copiousness.
dī-vors-, -vort- = **dī-vers-, -vert-.**
dī-vortium, ī *n* separation; **a**) boundary line, water-shed; **b**) divorce.
dī-vulgō 1 to make public, to publish, spread abroad, divulge.
dīvus 3 divine, godlike; deified; *subst.* **dīvus, ī** *m* god; **dīva, ae** *f* goddess; **dīvum, ī** *n* the sky, the open air.
dō, dedī, dătum, dăre to give, offer, present (*alci alqd*); **datum, ī** *n* gift; **a**) to offer, dedicate (*to the gods*); to furnish, pay; **poenam** to suffer punishment; to give up, deliver, hand over, render, surrender; to confer, grant, yield, leave, abandon; to be ready to give; **b**) to devote, **operam dare** to bestow care *or* pains; **c**) to concede, resign, permit, allow (*alci alqd*); to forgive, let loose, release; to tell, communicate, relate, utter, announce; to attribute, impute, assign, ascribe, reckon (*alci laudi* or *crimini*); **d**) to bring, put, throw, **se dare in** to betake oneself to; **e**) to cause, produce, excite, make, display; to arrange.
doceō, cuī, ctum 2 to teach, instruct (*alqm alqd* or *alqa re*), inform, tell; **a**) to show, prove, explain; **b**) to teach, rehearse (*a play*); **c**) to be a teacher, give instruction.
dochmius, ī *m* the dochmiac foot.
docilis, e easily taught, docile, tractable.
docilitās, ātis *f* docility.
doctor, ōris *m* teacher, instructor.
doctrīna, ae *f* instruction, teaching; **a**) learning, knowledge, erudition; **b**) science.
doctus 3 learned (with *abl.* or *inf.*), trained; **a**) skilled, experienced; **b**) versed in Greek letters; *subst.* **doctus, ī** *m* a learned man, literary man.
documentum, ī (*and* **-men, inis**) *n* lesson; **a**) example, instance, pattern, proof; **b**) a warning.
dōdrāns, tis three fourths.
dōdrantārius 3 of three fourths.
dogma, atis *n* philosophic principle, tenet, doctrine.
dolābra, ae *f* pickaxe.
dolēns, tis causing pain, painful.
dolenter *adv.* painfully.
doleō, luī, litūrus 2 **a**) to suffer pain, feel pain, to grieve, be sorry *or* afflicted (*alqd, de re, quod, acc. c. inf.*); **b**) to cause pain, be painful to (*alci*).
dōliāris, e like a barrel.
dōliolum, ī *n* little cask.
dōlium, ī *n* cask; wine-jar.
dolō[1] 1 to chip with an axe, to hew; to cudgel.
dolō[2]**, ōnis** *m* **1.** iron-pointed staff, sword-stick; sting; **2.** fore-topsail.
dolor, ōris *m* pain, smart, ache; **a**) sorrow, grief, affliction, distress, trouble, mortification; **b**) indignation, resentment.
dolōsus 3 deceitful, cunning, crafty.
dolus, ī *m* fraud, deceit, guile, deception, trickery, malice; fault.
domābilis, e tamable.
domesticātim *adv.* in private houses.
domesticus 3 belonging to a house *or* family; **a**) domestic; **b**) private, native; *subst. m* member of a household.
domicēnium, ī *n* meal eaten at home.
domicilium, ī *n* dwelling, abode, residence; home.
domina, ae *f* mistress of a household, lady, mistress.
dominātiō, ōnis *f* rule, dominion; despotism, tyranny; rulers.
dominātor, ōris *m* ruler, lord.
dominātrīx, īcis *f* mistress.
dominātus, ūs *m* = **dominatio.**
dominicus 3 pertaining to a lord *or* ruler.
dominium, ī *n* property; feast, banquet.

dominor 1 to be lord *or* master, to rule; to domineer; to be ruled; **-āns, antis** (of words) having their ordinary sense.
dominus, ī *m* master, lord, head; owner, proprietor; ruler, lord, despot; entertainer, host.
domi-porta, ae *f* house-carrier, snail.
domitō 1, *intens. of* **domo.**
domitor, ōris *m* tamer, subduer.
domitrīx, īcis *f* tamer, subduer.
domitus, ūs *m* a taming, subduing.
domō, uī, itum 1 to tame, break, subdue, conquer.
domus, ūs *f* house, dwelling; home, native town *or* country; household, family; philosophical school *or* sect; **domum** home, homewards; **domō** from home; **domī** at home, in the house; **domī bellique** (*or* **militiaeque**) in war and peace.
dōnābilis, e deserving of (*alqa re*).
dōnārium, ī *n* altar, temple; votive offering.
dōnātiō, ōnis *f* a giving; gift, present.
dōnātīvum, ī *n* largess, distribution of money.
dōnātor, ōris *m* giver.
dōnec *cj.* as long as, while; until.
dōnicum, dōnique = **donec.**
dōnō 1 **a**) to give as a present (*alci alqd*), bestow, grant, confer; **b**) to sacrifice, give up; **c**) to pardon, forgive, remit; **d**) to present with, endow (*alqm re*).
dōnum, ī *n* present, gift; offering, sacrifice.
dorcas, adis *f* gazelle.
dormiō 4 to sleep; to be inactive, idle.
dormī(tā)tor, ōris *m* sleeper, dreamer.
dormītō 1 to be drowsy, to fall asleep.
dormītōrius 3 belonging to sleep.
dorsum, ī *n* (*and* **-us, ī** *m*) the back; ridge of a mountain.
dory-phoros, ī *m* lance-bearer.
dōs, dōtis *f* dowry, marriage-portion; gift, quality, talent.
dōtālis, e belonging to a dowry.
dōtō 1 to endow, to portion; **dōtātus** 3 endowed, richly provided.
drach(u)ma, ae *f* drachma (*a Greek coin* = **denarius**).
drach(u)missō 1 to hire oneself out for a drachma.

dracō, ōnis *m* serpent, dragon.
dracōni-gena, ae *m and f* dragon-born.
drāpeta, ae *m* runaway slave.
draucus, ī *m* sodomite.
dromas, adis *m* dromedary.
dromos, ī *m* the Spartan race--course.
drōpax, acis *m* depilatory plaster.
Druidae, ārum, *and* **-dēs, um** *m/pl.* druids.
dubitābilis, e doubtful, to be doubted.
dubitanter *adv.* doubtingly; hesitatingly.
dubitātiō, ōnis *f* **a**) doubt, uncertainty; **b**) hesitation, wavering, irresolution.
dubitō 1 **a**) to doubt, be in doubt (*de re; quin*); to deliberate; **b**) to hesitate, waver, be irresolute, delay.
dubius 3 **a**) doubting, uncertain, wavering, irresolute; **b**) doubtful, doubted, undecided, uncertain, dubious; dangerous, precarious, critical; **sine dubiō** without doubt; **in dubiō esse** to be questioned, to be in danger; **in dubium vocare** to make doubtful, call in question.
ducātus, ūs *m* leadership.
ducēnārius 3 relating to two hundred.
ducēnī 3 two hundred each.
ducentēsima, ae *f* tax of one half per cent (½%).
du-centī 3 two hundred.
ducentiē(n)s *adv.* two hundred times.
dūcō, dūxī, ductum 3 **1.** to draw; a) to drag behind, to move by drawing; b) to draw out (*ferrum de vagina*); c) to draw in (*aëra, spiritum*); to quaff, drink in; d) to stretch, draw in, pull at (*frena, arcum*); e) to take, receive, admit (*colorem, cicatricem, formam, notam*); f) to incite, seduce, allure; g) to distort, make wry faces (*os*); h) to form by drawing, to spin; to form, fashion, shape, compose (*carmina, versus*); to hammer out; to construct, build, draw (*fossam, muros*); i) to extend, prolong, protract (*bellum, tempus, rem in noctem*); to keep off *or* in suspense; **2.** to lead, guide, conduct, direct; a) to lead to, conduct, derive (*hostes* or *aquam ex montibus in urbem, alqm secum in castra, ad mortem, originem ab alqo*);

to lead home as a wife, to marry; b) to cause, produce (*soporem, somnum*); c) to take, lead away, carry off; d) to lead, command, march (*copias*); to lead in front, in advance, take the lead, form the van; e) to incite, move (*ad credendum*); **P.** to be moved, incited; **3.** to calculate, reckon, compute; to consider, think, hold, account, esteem, regard (*alqd in malis sive bonis, pro nihilo, alqm victorem, alqd turpe* or *nefas, omnia pericula levia;* with *dat. alqd honori* or *laudi*).

ductilis, e (capable of being) led, conducted.

ductim *adv.* in deep draughts.

ductitō 1 to lead away; to marry (*alqm*); to cheat.

ductō 1, *intens. of* **duco.**

ductor, ōris *m* leader, commander.

ductus, ūs *m* a leading, conducting; **a**) **ōris** lineaments of the face; **b**) command, leadership.

dūdum *adv.* **a**) a short time ago, a little while ago, not long since; **b**) formerly, of old; **iam dūdum** now for a long time.

duellum, duellātor, duellicus = **bellum, bellator, bellicus.**

duim = **dem** (*see* **do**).

dulcēdō, inis *f* sweetness, pleasantness, charm, delightfulness.

dulcēscō, —, — 3 to become sweet.

dulciārius 3 of confectionery.

dulciculus 3 sweetish.

dulci-fer 3 sweet.

dulcis, e sweet; pleasant, delightful, charming, dear.

dulcitūdō, inis *f* = **dulcedo.**

dūlicē *adv.* like a slave.

dum 1. *cj.* a) while, as long as; until; b) provided that; **2.** *adv.* (*joined to other words*) now (*agedum, cedodum*).

dūmētum, ī *n* thicket, thorn-hedge.

dum-modo *cj.* = **dum** provided that, if only.

dūmōsus 3 covered with thorn-bushes, bushy.

dum-taxat *adv.* exactly, strictly speaking, precisely; **a**) only, merely; **b**) at least, in so far; **c**) of course.

dūmus, ī *m* thorn-bush; thicket.

duo, ae, o two; the two, both.

duo-deciē(n)s *adv.* twelve times.

duo-decim twelve.

duo-decimus 3 the twelfth.

duo-dēnī 3 twelve each.

duo-et-vīcēsimānus, ī *m* soldier of the twenty-second legion.

duo-virī = **duumviri.**

du-plex, icis a) twofold, double; **b**) double-tongued, false.

duplicārius, ī *m* a soldier who receives double pay.

duplicō 1 to double; **a**) to fold in two, double up; to bend; **b**) to enlarge, augment.

duplus 3 double, twice as large, twice as much; *subst.* **duplum, ī** *n* double.

du-pondius, ī *m* coin of two asses.

dūrābilis, e lasting, durable.

dūracinus 3 with a hard skin.

dūrāmen, inis *n* frozen state.

dūrāmentum, ī *n* durability, firmness.

dūrateus 3 wooden.

dūrēscō, ruī, — 3 to grow hard.

dureta, ae *f* wooden bathing-tub.

dūritās, ātis *f* = **duritia.**

dūriter *adv.* = **dure** (*see* **durus**).

dūritia, ae (*and* **-tiēs, ēī**) *f* hardness; **a**) austerity; **b**) absence of feeling, insensibility; **c**) harshness, severity, oppression.

dūriusculus 3 somewhat hard *or* harsh.

dūrō 1 **1.** *trans.* to make hard; a) to dry; b) to make hardy, insensible; c) to bear, endure; **2.** *intr.* a) to become hard *or* dry; b) to continue, last, remain.

dūrus 3 hard; **a**) harsh, rough, ugly, awkward; **b**) shameless; **c**) strong, enduring; **d**) insensible, unfeeling, rude, stern, severe, cruel; **e**) hard, difficult, painful, toilsome, oppressive, distressing, adverse.

duum-virātus, ūs *m* office of a duumvir.

duum-virī, ōrum *m/pl.* a commission of two men.

dux, ducis *m* (*and f*) leader; **a**) guide; **b**) commander, general; **c**) prince, ruler.

dynamis, is *f* plenty.

dynastēs, ae *m* ruler, prince.

E

ē, ex *prep.* with *abl.* **1.** (*of space*) out of, from, from within (*ex castris venire, ex patria fugere, ē loco superiore impetum facere, Rhenus oritur ex Alpibus; pugnare ex equo* on horseback; *pendere ex arbore; ex alqo audire* or *cognoscere*); **2.** (*of time*) since, from, immediately upon (*ex Kalendis Martiis, ex eo tempore, ex praetura urbem relinquere; ex quo* from which time, since; *diem ex die* day after day); **3.** (*of relation*) from, of; a) *to denote origin* (*liberos habere ex femina, ex serva natus, soror ex matre*); from among, from, out of (*unus ex multis, ex ephoris quidam*); b) *to denote the material:* out of (*statua ex aere facta*); c) *to denote the cause:* from, on account of, by reason of, in consequence of, through (*Demetrius ex doctrina nobilis est, avem ex pennis cognoscere, ex pedibus laborare, ex vulnere aeger* or *mori, ex eadem causa*); d) *to denote a change:* (*ex beato miser, ex aratore orator factus est*); e) according to (*ex senatus consulto, ex edicto praetoris, ex consuetudine, ex sententia* satisfactorily); f) **ex contrario** on the contrary; **ē regione** opposite to; **ex composito** by agreement; **ex improviso** unexpectedly; **ex usu esse** to be advantageous; **ē re publica esse** to be for the public benefit; **magna ex parte** mostly; **ex itinere** straight from a march.

eā (*sc. via*) *adv.* there, that way.

eādem *adv.* by the same way.

eā-propter = **propterea.**

eā-tenus *adv.* so far, to such a degree.

ebenus, ī *f* ebony-tree; **-num, ī** *n* ebony.

ē-bibō 3 to drink up; to squander.

ē-bītō 3 to go out.

ē-blandior 4 to obtain by flattery.

ēbrietās, ātis *f* drunkenness, intoxication.

ēbriolus 3 tipsy.

ēbriōsitās, ātis *f* love of drink.

ēbriōsus 3 given to drink; drunkard.

ēbrius 3 drunk, intoxicated.

ē-bulliō 4 to bubble up; to boast of.

ebulum, ī *n* dwarf elder.

ebur, oris *n* ivory; work of ivory.

eburātus 3 adorned with ivory.

eburneolus 3 of ivory.

eburneus (**-nus**) 3 (made of) ivory.

ē-castor *int.* by Castor!

ec-ce *adv.* lo! behold!

ecce-re *int.* there! indeed!

ec-clēsia, ae *f* assembly of the Athenian people.

ec-dicus, ī *m* public attorney, prosecutor.

ecf..., *see* **eff...**

eche-nēis, idis *f* ('ship-holder') sucking-fish, remora.

echidna, ae *f* adder, viper.

echīnus, ī *m* **a**) sea-urchin; **b**) rinsing-vessel.

ēchō, ūs *f* echo.

ec-loga, ae *f* selection; eclogue.

ec-quandō *adv.* ever? whether ever.

ecquis, quī, ecqua(e), ecquid, quod (is there) any(one)? whether any(one); *also* **ecquisnam:** *adv.* **ecquid** *interrog. particle* (whether) at all?; **ecquō** anywhere?

eculeus, ī *m* **a**) young horse, colt; **b**) wooden rack (instrument of torture).

ecus = **equus.**

edācitās, ātis *f* voraciousness.

edāx, ācis greedy, gluttonous; consuming.

ē-dentō 1 to knock out the teeth from.

ēdentulus 3 toothless, old.

ede-pol *int.* by Pollux!

edera, ae *f* = **hedera.**

ē-dīcō 3 **a**) to make known, publish, proclaim, declare (*alci alqd*); **b**) to decree, ordain, order, appoint (*alqd; ut, ne*).

ē-dictiō, ōnis *f* edict.

ē-dictō 1 to proclaim, publish.

ē-dictum, ī *n* decree, proclamation, edict.

ē-discō, didicī, — 3 to learn by heart, learn thoroughly.

ē-disserō, ruī, rtum 3 to relate fully, explain.

ē-dissertō 1, *intens. of* **edissero.**
ēditīcius 3 announced, proposed.
ēditiō, ōnis *f* a publishing; statement, proposal.
ēditor, ōris *m* producing.
ēditus 3 elevated, high, lofty; *subst.* **-um, ī** *n* height.
edō[1], **ēdī, ēsum** 3 to eat, consume.
ē-dō[2], **didī, ditum** 3 to give out, put forth; **a**) to breathe, to utter; **b**) to bring forth, give birth; **c**) to publish, make known, spread abroad; to proclaim, ordain, designate, name; **d**) to display, produce, perform, cause, furnish.
ē-doceō 2 to teach *or* instruct thoroughly (*alqm alqd*); to inform, relate.
ē-dolō 1 to hew out, to complete.
ē-domō 1 to tame thoroughly, to subdue.
ē-dormiō 4 to sleep out *or* off (*alqd*).
ēdormīscō 3 = **edormio.**
ēducātiō, ōnis *f* a bringing up, education.
ēducātor, ōris *m* foster-father, tutor.
ēducātrīx, īcis *f* foster-mother.
ē-ducō[1] 1 **a**) to bring up, rear; **b**) to educate.
ē-dūcō[2] 3 **1.** to draw out (*sortem*); **2.** to lead out; a) to march out (*alqm* or *alqd ex re in alqd*); to take out of port; to bring before a court; b) to take away; c) to raise up; to erect, build; d) to bring up, rear, educate.
edūlis, e eatable.
ē-dūrō 1 to last, continue.
ē-dūrus 3 very hard.
ef-farciō, —, fertum 4 to stuff full, fill out.
ef-fātum, ī *n* utterance; **a**) prophecy; **b**) axiom.
effectiō, ōnis *f* **a**) a practising; **b**) efficient cause.
effector, ōris *m* producer, author.
effectrīx, īcis *f* she who effects, produces.
effectus, ūs *m* an effecting; **a**) execution, performance; operation; **b**) result, consequence.
ef-fēminō 1 **a**) to make a woman of; **b**) to make effeminate.
efferciō 4 = **effarcio.**
ef-feritās, ātis *f* savageness.
ef-ferō[1] 1 [*ferus*] to make wild; to enrage.
ef-ferō[2], **extulī, ēlātum** 3 **1.** to bear, carry, bring, take out (*alqd ex, de re, ad* or *in alqd*); a) to carry to the grave, bury; b) to bring forth, produce, bear; c) to utter, express, spread abroad, make known; d) to carry away, transport; **P.** to be carried away (*studio, gaudio*); **2.** a) to raise, lift up, elevate; b) to make haughty; c) to extol, praise.
ef-fertus 3, *see* **effarcio.**
ef-ferus 3 very wild, savage.
ef-fervēscō, ferbuī (*or* **fervī**), — 3 to boil up *or* over; to burst forth.
ef-fervō, —, — 3 = **effervesco.**
ef-fētus 3 exhausted, worn out, weakened.
efficācitās, ātis *f* efficiency.
efficāx, ācis efficient, effective.
efficiēns, tis efficient, effective.
efficientia, ae *f* efficiency.
ef-ficiō, fēcī, fectum 3 to bring about, produce, effect, make; **a**) to bear (*fruit*); to make up (*of number*); **b**) to execute, finish, complete, accomplish; **c**) to cause, carry through (*alqd; ut, ne*); **d**) to prove, show.
effigiēs, ēī (*and* **-ia, ae**) *f* image, copy; **a**) likeness, portrait; **b**) ideal; **c**) phantom; **d**) form, shape.
ef-fingō 3 **1.** to wipe out *or* off; **2.** to form, fashion, copy, imitate; to represent, express.
ef-flāgitātiō, ōnis *f* (*and* **-tātus, ūs** *m*) pressing request, solicitation, demand.
ef-flāgitō 1 to demand *or* ask urgently, to entreat (*alqd ab alqo; ut, ne*).
ef-flīctim *adv.* desperately (*amare*).
ef-flīctō 1 to strike dead.
ef-flīgō, xī, ctum 3 to kill, slay.
ef-flō 1 to breathe *or* blow out.
ef-flōrēscō, ruī, — 3 to blossom, bloom, flourish.
ef-fluō, uxī, — 3 to flow out *or* forth; **a**) to run over; **b**) to slip from, escape (*ex re*); to disappear, vanish, be forgotten.
effluvium, ī *n* outlet.
ef-fodiō 3 **a**) to dig out *or* up; to tear out; **b**) to rummage, ransack.
ef-for, fātus sum 1 to speak out, say, utter; **a**) to define *or* consecrate a place; **b**) to state a proposition.
ef-frāctārius, ī *m* housebreaker, burglar.
ef-frēnātiō, ōnis *f* unbridled impetuosity.

ef-frēnātus 3 unbridled, unrestrained, unruly.
ef-frēnō 1 to let loose.
effrēnus 3 = **effrenatus.**
ef-fricō 1 to rub off.
ef-fringō, frēgī, frāctum 3 to break open *or* away.
ef-fugiō, fūgī, (fugitum) 3 **1.** *intr.* to flee away (*ex re*); **2.** *trans.* to escape from, avoid, shun; to escape observation.
effugium, ī *n* a fleeing away, flight; **a)** escape; **b)** means of escape, way of flight.
ef-fulgeō, lsī, — 2 to shine forth.
ef-fultus 3 supported by, resting upon.
ef-fundō 3 to pour out *or* forth, to shed; **a)** to waste, squander, exhaust; **b)** to send forth; to pour out, utter; **c)** to bring forth *or* produce abundantly; **d)** to loose, let go; **P.** (*also* **se effundere**) to pour out in a crowd; to let oneself go, give way to (*in alqd*).
ef-fūsiō, ōnis *f* a pouring out, shedding; **a)** a pouring forth; **b)** extravagance, profusion; **c)** excess of hilarity.
ef-fūsus 3 poured forth; **a)** widespread, extensive; **b)** let loose, disorderly; extravagant; **c)** unrestrained, immoderate.
ef-fūtiō 4 to chatter, babble forth.
ef-futuō 3 to waste in debauchery.
ē-gelidus 3 mild; cool.
egēns, tis needy (*with gen.*), poor.
egēnus 3 needy (*gen.* or *abl.*), in want, poor.
egeō, uī, — 2 **a)** to be in need, in want (*gen.* or *abl.*), to be needy, poor, to be without; **b)** to desire, wish for, want (*gen.*).
ēgerō (?), **ōnis** *m* one who carries off.
ē-gerō 3 to take *or* bring out; **a)** to discharge, vomit; **b)** to expel.
egestās, ātis *f* **a)** need, poverty; **b)** want.
ē-gestiō, ōnis *f* (*and* **-tus, ūs** *m*) carrying away; squandering.
ē-gignō 3 to produce.
egŏ (*and* **egō**) *pers. pron.* I.
ē-gredior, gressus sum 3 to go out, come forth (*ex re, re, in, ad alqd*); **a)** to march out; to land, to put to sea; to digress (*a re*); **b)** to go up, ascend; **c)** to go beyond (*acc.*), to overstep, pass.
ē-gregius 3 distinguished, select, extraordinary, excellent, admirable, honourable; *subst.* **ē-gregium, ī** *n* honour, glory.
ē-gressus, ūs *m* a going out, egress; **a)** departure; a landing; **b)** outlet, mouth.
ē-gurgitō 1 to pour out, squander.
ehem *int.* = **hem.**
ēheu (*and* **ĕheu**) *int.* ah! alas! woe!
eho *int.* ho! indeed!
ei *int.* = **hei.**
ēia *int.* ha! well then! quick!
ē-iaculor 1 to shoot out.
ē-iciō, iēcī, iectum 3 to throw, cast, *or* drive out, to expel, banish, drive into exile; **se ēicere** to rush out *or* forth; **a)** to cast forth, utter; **b)** to bring to shore; to run aground; **ēiectus** 3 shipwrecked; **c)** to hoot, hiss (*off the stage*), to reject, disapprove.
ēiectāmentum, ī *n* refuse.
ēiectiō, ōnis *f* banishment, exile.
ēiectō 1 (*intens. of* **eicio**) to throw out; to vomit forth.
ē-iectus, ūs *m* emission.
ē-ierō 1 = **eiuro.**
ēiulātiō, ōnis *f and* **ēiulātus, ūs** *m* a wailing, lamenting.
ēiulō 1 to wail, lament.
ē-iūrātiō, ōnis *f* a laying down, resigning.
ē-iūrō 1 to deny *or* refuse on oath; **a)** to resign solemnly, to abdicate; **b)** to abjure, disown, abandon, (*alqd*).
ēius-modī of that sort, of such a kind.
ē-lābor 3 to glide out of, slip away (*ex re in alqd*); to be dislocated (*artus*); **a)** to escape, be lost, fall out; **b)** to fall, glide.
ē-labōrō 1 **a)** to work out, elaborate, produce; **b)** to work hard, endeavour, strive.
ē-lāmentābilis, e lamentable.
ē-languēscō, guī, — 3 to become languid.
ē-lātiō, ōnis *f* elevation, transport, exaltation.
ē-lātrō 1 to bark out, cry out.
ē-lātus 3 **a)** elevated, exalted; **b)** haughty, proud.
ē-lāvī (*perf.*), *see* **ēluō.**
ē-lecebra, ae *f* seductress.
ē-lēctilis, e selected, choice.

ē-lēctiō, ōnis *f* (*and* **-tus, ūs** *m*) choice, selection.
ē-lectō 1 to wheedle out.
ēlectrum, ī *n* **a**) amber; **b**) alloy of gold and silver.
ē-lēctus 3 picked, select.
ēlegāns, tis choice, fine, tasteful, correct, elegant, refined.
ēlegantia, ae *f* taste, refinement, grace, elegance; correctness.
elegēa (*also* **-īa, -īā, -ēïa**), **ae** *f* elegy.
elegēon, ī *n* elegy.
elegī, ōrum *m/pl.* elegiac verses.
elegīdion, ī *n* little elegy.
elementārius 3 learning the elements.
elementum, ī *n* simple substance, first principle, element; *pl.* rudiments, beginnings.
elenchus, ī *m* a kind of pearl.
elephantus, ī (*and* **elephās, antis**) *m* elephant; ivory; (**elephas**) elephantiasis.
eleutheria, ae *f* liberty.
ē-levō 1 to raise, lift up; **a**) to alleviate; **b**) to lessen, impair.
ē-liciō, cuī, citum 3 to entice out, lure forth; **a**) to elicit, bring out; **b**) to search out, find out; **c**) to invite, induce; **d**) to call down, conjure up; **e**) to produce, cause.
ē-līdō, sī, sum 3 **a**) to strike, thrust *or* drive out; **b**) to dash to pieces, shatter, crush.
ē-ligō, lēgī, lēctum 3 to pick out, choose, select.
ē-līminō 1 to carry out of doors.
ē-līmō 1 to file off, polish.
ē-linguis, e speechless; without eloquence.
ē-linguō 1 to 'de-tongue'.
ē-liquō 1 to filter out, to let trickle out.
ē-līsiō, ōnis *f* a squeezing out.
ē-lix, icis *m* furrow for draining.
ē-lixus 3 boiled, soaked.
elleborum *and* **-us** = **hell...**
ē-locō 1 to farm out, let on hire.
ē-locūtiō, ōnis *f* oratorical delivery.
ēlogium, ī *n* inscription; **a**) epitaph; **b**) clause in a will; **c**) judicial record.
ē-loquēns, tis eloquent.
ēloquentia, ae *f* **a**) eloquence; **b**) a pronouncing.
ēloquium, ī *n* **a**) = **elocutio; b**) = **eloquentia.**
ē-loquor 3 to speak out, speak plainly; to utter, pronounce.
ē-lōtus 3 = **ēlūtus** (*ēluō*).
ē-lūceō, xī, — 2 to shine forth, gleam, glitter; to be conspicuous *or* manifest.
ē-luctābilis, e such as one can struggle out of.
ē-luctor 1 **a**) to struggle out, burst forth; **b**) to overcome with difficulty (*alqd*).
ē-lūcubrō, -or 1 to work out by lamplight, to compose at night.
ē-lūdificor 1 to fool completely.
ē-lūdō 3 **1.** to win at play; **2.** to parry, elude; a) to avoid; b) to mock, jeer, ridicule (*alqm*); c) to frustrate (*alqd*).
ē-lūgeō, xī, — 2 to mourn; to have finished mourning.
ē-lumbis, e weak in the loins.
ē-luō, uī, lūtum 3 to wash out, to cleanse; to wash away, efface; *intrans.* (with *pf.* **ēlāvī**) to be cleaned out, ruined.
ē-lūtus 3 washed out; insipid.
ēluviēs, ēī *and* **-viō, ōnis** *f* a flowing off; inundation, flood, pond.
em *int.* there! see!
ēmacerātus 3 emaciated.
emācitās, ātis love of buying.
ē-mancipātiō, ōnis *f* emancipation of a son; transfer of property, surrender.
ē-mancipō 1 to release from the paternal authority; to transfer, make over (property).
ē-maneō 2 to remain outside.
ē-mānō 1 to flow out; **a**) to arise, spring, emanate; **b**) to spread abroad, become known.
ē-marcēscō, rcuī, — 3 to wither away.
ē-mātūrēscō, ruī, — 3 to become ripe; to grow mild.
emāx, ācis fond of buying.
em-blēma, atis *n* embossed *or* inlaid work, relief.
em-bolium, ī *n* interlude.
ēmendābilis, e that may be amended.
ēmendātiō, ōnis *f* amendment, correction.
ēmendātor, ōris *m* corrector.
ēmendātrīx, īcis *f* she who amends.
ē-mendīcō 1 to obtain by begging.
ē-mendō 1 to free from faults, to correct, amend; **ēmendātus** 3 correct, faultless, perfect.
ē-mentior 4 to lie, feign, pretend.
ē-mercor 1 to buy up, bribe.

ē-mereō *and* **-eor** 2 **1.** to deserve, obtain by service; to deserve well of (*alqm*); **2.** to serve out; **ēmeritus** 3 veteran.
ē-mergō 3 **1.** to cause to rise up; **se ēmergere** *or* **P.** to raise oneself up, rise (*ex re*); **2.** *intr.* to come forth *or* up, to emerge, to extricate oneself.
ē-mētior, mēnsus sum 4 to measure out; **a**) to pass over, traverse (*alqd*); to live through, survive; **b**) to impart, bestow.
ē-metō 3 to mow down, reap.
ē-micō, uī, ātum 1 to spring forth, dart forth, to break out; to rush up; to project; to shine forth.
ē-migrō 1 to wander forth, emigrate.
ē-minātiō, ōnis *f* threatening.
ēminēns, tis projecting; **a**) lofty, eminent; **b**) prominent, illustrious, excellent.
ēminentia, ae *f* prominence; the lights of a painting.
ē-mineō, uī, — 2 to project; **a**) to be conspicuous; **b**) to be eminent, distinguish oneself.
ē-minor 1 to threaten.
ē-minus *adv.* at a distance, from afar.
ē-mīror 1 to wonder at, be astonished at (*alqd*).
ēmissārium, ī *n* outlet, drain.
ēmissārius, ī *m* emissary, spy.
ē-missīcius 3 prying.
ē-missiō, ōnis *f* (*and* **ēmissus, ūs** *m*) a sending forth, hurling.
ē-mittō 3 to send out; **a**) to send forth, hurl; to utter; **b**) to let loose, let go, set free; **c**) to send forth from oneself.
emō, ēmī, ēmptum 3 to buy, purchase; to pay, bribe.
ē-moderor 1 to moderate.
ē-modulor 1 to sing, praise, celebrate.
ē-mōlior 4 **a**) to heave up, agitate; **b**) to accomplish.
ē-molliō 4 to soften; to make mild; to make effeminate.
ē-molō 3 to use up by grinding.
ēmolumentum, ī *n* advantage, profit.
ē-moneō 2 to admonish.
ē-morior 3 to die off, to perish, pass away.
ē-mortuālis, e belonging to death.
ē-moveō 2 to move out *or* away, to remove, expel.
empīricus, ī *m* physician guided only by experience.
emporium, ī *n* place of trade.
emporus, ī *m* merchant.
ēmptiō, ōnis *f* a buying, purchase.
ēmptitō 1 to buy up, purchase.
ēmptor, ōris *m* buyer, purchaser.
ē-mūgiō 4 to bellow out.
ē-mulgeō, —, **lsum** 2 to empty, drain.
ē-mungō, mūnxī, mūnctum 3 **a**) to blow the nose; **ēmūnctus** 3 refined; **b**) to cheat.
ē-mūniō 4 to wall off, fortify; to make passable.
ēmussitātus 3 (made true with a workman's ruler) perfect.
ēn *int.* lo! behold! see! there! come!
ē-nārrābilis, e that may be related *or* told.
ē-nārrātio, ōnis *f* **a**) exposition; **b**) scanning (of verse).
ē-nārrō 1 to explain fully.
ē-nāscor 3 to grow out of, to arise.
ē-natō 1 to swim from, to escape (by swimming).
ē-nāvigō 1 **a**) to sail away; **b**) to sail through (*acc.*).
encaustus 3 burnt in, encaustic.
endromis, idis *f* athlete's wrap.
ē-necō, cuī, ctum 1 to kill, destroy; to exhaust.
ē-nervis, e nerveless, weak.
ē-nervō 1 to enervate, weaken, make effeminate.
ē-nicō 1 = **eneco.**
enim *cj.* for; for instance, namely; truly, certainly, in fact.
enim-vērō *adv.* truly, certainly, to be sure; but indeed.
ē-niteō, tuī, — 2 to shine forth.
ē-nitēscō, tuī, — 3 to begin to shine forth.
ē-nītor, nīxus *or* **nīsus sum** 3 **1.** to struggle up, force one's way out, to ascend; to strive; **2.** to bring forth, bear.
ē-nīxus 3 earnest, zealous.
enlychnium, ī *n* lamp-wick.
ē-nō 1 = **enato.**
ē-nōdātē plainly.
ē-nōdātiō, ōnis *f* explanation.
ē-nōdis, e without knots, smooth; clear.
ē-nōdō 1 to free from knots; to explain.
ē-normis, e a) irregular; **b**) exceedingly big.

ē-nōtēscō, tuī, — 3 to become known.
ē-notō 1 to make notes on.
ēnsiculus, ī *m* little sword.
ēnsi-fer *and* **-ger** 3 sword-bearing.
ēnsis, is *m* sword.
enterocēlē, ēs *f* rupture, hernia; **-cēlicus** 3 suffering from hernia.
entheātus 3 divinely inspired.
entheus 3 **a)** divinely inspired; **b)** inspiring.
enthȳmēma, atis, *n* reflection; a type of logical argument.
ē-nūbō 3 to marry out of her station *or* town (of a woman).
ē-nucleō 1 to take out the kernel; to explain in detail; **ēnucleātus** 3 clean, clear.
ē-numerātiō, ōnis *f* a counting up, enumeration.
ē-numerō 1 to reckon, count up.
ēn-umquam (*in questions*) ever?
ē-nūntiātiō, ōnis *f and* **-tum, ī** *n* enunciation, proposition.
ē-nūntiātīvus 3 declaratory.
ē-nūntiō 1 to speak out, tell, to declare, announce, state; to disclose, betray.
ē-nuptiō, ōnis *f* a marrying out of the family.
ē-nūtriō 4 to nourish, bring up.
eō[1] *adv.* **1.** thither, to that place (*rarely* in that place); **2.** so far, so much; **3.** on that account; therefore; *with comp.*: the ...
eō[2], **iī** (*and* **īvī**), **itum, īre** to go; **a**) to walk, march, to ride, sail, &c.; **in sententiam** to vote for, support; **b**) to proceed; **c**) to happen, turn out; **d**) to pass away.
eōdem *adv.* to the same place; in the same place.
Eōs (ē-) *f* (only *nom.*) dawn; the East.
Eōus (ē *and* ĕ) 3 of the morning, of the East; *subst.* ~, **ī** *m* **a**) the morning-star; **b**) man of the East.
epaphaeresis (*acc.* **-in**) *f* repeated removal.
ē-pāstus 3 eaten up.
ephēbus, ī *m* a youth.
ephēmeris, idis *f* day-book, diary.
ephippiātus 3 riding with a saddle.
ephippium, ī *n* horse-cloth, saddle.
ephorus, ī *m* ephor.
epi-bata, ae *m* marine.
epi-chysis, is *f* vessel for pouring out.
epi-cōpus 3 provided with oars.
epi-crocus 3 thin, transparent.
epicus 3 epic.
epi-dīcticus 3 for display.
epi-dīpnis, idis *f* dessert.
epi-gramma, atis *n* inscription; epigram.
epi-logus ī *m* peroration, epilogue.
epi-mēnia, ōrum *n/pl.* month's rations.
epi-nīcia, ōrum *n/pl.* triumphal songs.
epi-rēdium, ī *n* strap attaching a horse to a carriage.
epi-stolium, ī *n* small letter.
epi-stula, ae *f* letter, epistle.
epi-taphius, ī *m* funeral oration.
epi-thēca, ae *f* addition.
epi-toma, ae *and* **-ē, ēs** *f* abridgment, epitome.
epitonion, ī *n* water-tap.
epi-tȳrum, ī *n* olive salad.
epops, opis *m* hoopoe.
epos *n* epic poem.
ē-pōtō 1 to drink up, absorb; *pf. part. P.* **ēpōtus** 3 drunk up, absorbed.
epulae, ārum *f/pl.* **a**) viands, food, dishes; **b**) feast, banquet; entertainment.
epulāris, e belonging to a feast *or* banquet.
epulātiō, ōnis *f* feasting.
epulō, ōnis *m* arranger of a feast; feaster.
epulor 1 to feast, dine.
epulum, ī *n* feast, banquet.
equa, ae *f* mare.
eques, itis *m* and *f* **1.** horseman, rider; a) horse-soldier, cavalry; b) rider and horse; **2.** knight; equestrian order.
equester, tris, tre 1. of a horseman, of cavalry, equestrian; **2.** of knights.
e-quidem *adv.* **a**) truly, indeed; of course; **b**) for my part.
equīle, is *n* stable for horses.
equīnus 3 of horses.
equīria, ōrum *n/pl.* horse-races.
equitābilis, e fit for riding.
equitātus, ūs *m* **1.** a) a riding; b) cavalry; **2.** knights, the equestrian order.
equitō 1 to ride on horseback, to be a cavalry-man.
equola, ae *f* young mare.
equuleus, ī *m* = **eculeus.**
equus, ī *m* horse, steed; stallion; chariot, horse-race; cavalry.
era, ae *f* mistress of a house; mistress.

ē-rādīcō 1 to uproot.
ē-rādō 3 to scrape off, scratch out; to erase, eradicate.
eranus, ī *m* a friendly society.
ē-rēctus 3 upright, erect; **a**) elevated, lofty, noble; **b**) haughty; **c**) attentive, eager, intent; **d**) lively, resolute.
ē-rēmigō 1 to row through.
ē-rēpō 3 **a**) to creep through *or* over; **b**) *trans.* to climb.
ēreptiō, ōnis *f* robbery.
ēreptor, ōris *m* robber.
ergā *prep.* with *acc.* towards, in relation to.
ergastulum, ī *n* house of correction, prison.
ergō (*and* **-ŏ**) **1.** *prep.* with *gen.* on account of, because of; **2.** *adv.* a) consequently, therefore, accordingly, then; **b**) well then, as I was saying.
ēricius, ī *m* hedgehog; cheval de frise.
eri-fuga, ae *m* one who runs away from his master.
ē-rigō, rēxī, rēctum 3 to raise up, set up, place upright; **a**) to erect, build; **b**) to lead to a height; **c**) to arouse, stir, excite; **d**) to encourage, cheer.
erīlis, e of a master *or* mistress.
Erīnȳs, yos *f* goddess of revenge, Fury.
ē-ripiō, ripuī, reptum 3 **a**) to tear out, snatch away, tear *or* pluck out (*alqd ex, a, de re*); **b**) to take away, rob (*alci alqd*); **c**) to rescue, deliver, free; to remove from.
ē-rogātiō, ōnis *f* payment, expenditure.
ē-rogitō 1 to inquire.
ē-rogō 1 to pay out, expend; to bequeath.
erōmenion *n* (ἐρωμένιον) darling.
errābundus 3 wandering about.
errāticus 3 wandering.
errātiō, ōnis *f* a wandering.
errātor, ōris *m* wanderer.
errātum, ī *n* error, mistake, fault.
errātus, ūs *m* a wandering.
errō[1] 1 to wander, stray, rove; to go astray; to err, be in error, be mistaken (*in re*).
errō[2]**, ōnis** *m* vagabond.
errōneus 3 wandering.
error, ōris *m* **1.** a wandering, roving, straying; a) uncertainty, doubt; b) a going astray; **2.** error, infatuation; a) deception; b) mistake, fault.
ē-rubēscō, buī, — 3 to grow red, to blush, to be ashamed of; to respect.
ērūca, ae *f* a plant.
ē-rūctō 1 to belch forth, vomit; to cast out.
ē-rudiō 4 to instruct, teach, educate (*alqm re, de re*); *adj.* **ērudītus** 3 instructed, learned.
ē-rudītiō, ōnis *f* instruction, learning, knowledge.
ē-rudītulus 3 somewhat skilled.
ē-rumpō 3 **1.** *trans.* to cause to break forth, to emit, **se ērumpere** to burst forth, break out; **2.** *intr.* to break out *or* forth; a) to rush *or* sally forth; b) to come to light, become public; c) to turn out, result.
ē-ruō 3 to dig out; **a**) to dig up, to throw out; **b**) to pluck out; **c**) to bring out, search *or* rummage out; **d**) to root out, to destroy utterly.
ē-ruptiō, ōnis *f* a breaking out, bursting forth; sally.
erus, ī *m* master of a house, master; owner, proprietor.
ervum, ī *n* vetch.
ēsca, ae *f* food, victuals; bait.
ēscārius 3 of food; — **ia, ōrum** *n/pl.* dishes.
ē-scendō, ndī, ēnsum 3 to climb up, mount, ascend.
ē-scēnsiō, ōnis *f* a landing; climbing.
ē-scēnsus, ūs *m* a going up, climbing; ascent.
ēsculentus 3 eatable; *subst.* **-a, ōrum** *n/pl.* food.
essedārius, ī *m* fighter in a war-chariot.
essedum, ī *n* (*and* **-da, ae** *f*) war-chariot; travelling-chariot.
essentia, ae *f* essential being, essence.
ēssitō 1 to eat (habitually).
ēssuriālis, e belonging to hunger.
ēs(s)uriō[1] 4 to desire to eat, to be hungry.
ēssuriō[2]**, ōnis** *m* starving person.
ēsurītiō, ōnis *f* a hungering, hunger.
ēsurītor, ōris *m* hungry man.
et *cj.* **1.** and; a) and so, and then; b) and indeed, and in fact; c) and moreover, and besides; **2.** and also, also (= **etiam**); **3. et ... et** as well ... as, both ... and, not only ... but also.

et-enim *cj.* for, and indeed.
etēsiae, ārum *m/pl.* Etesian (summer) winds.
etēsius 3 Etesian.
ētho-logia, ae *f* portrayal of character.
ētho-logus, ī *m* imitator of manners.
etiam *cj.* **1.** as yet, even yet, still; a) again, **etiam atque etiam** again and again, repeatedly; even now, even at this time; b) at once; **2.** also; a) even, nay even, furthermore, besides, then too; **b**) still, even; c) certainly.
etiam-num, -nunc *adv.* yet, still, till now, even to this time.
etiam-sī *cj.* even if, although.
etiam-tum *and* **-tunc** *adv.* even then, till then.
et-sī *cj.* **a**) although, albeit; **b**) and yet, notwithstanding.
etymologia, ae *f* etymology.
eu *int.* well! well done!
euān, euhān *int. the Bacchic cry eu(h)an.*
euāns, tis crying *euan.*
euax *int.* hurrah! bravo!
euge (*and* **eugē**), **eugepae** *int.* well done! bravo!
euhān, *see* **euan, euhoe,** *see* **euoe.**
eunūchus, ī *m* eunuch.
euoe, euhoe *int. the shout of the Bacchantes.*
eurīpus, ī *m* strait, channel.
eurōus 3 eastern, south-eastern.
eurus, ī *m* south-east wind; the east.
eu-schēmē *adv.* becomingly.
ē-vādō 3 **1.** *intr.* to go *or* come out, go forth; a) to climb, ascend (*ex re, in alqd*); b) to escape, get away; c) to turn out, become, result, prove to be; **2.** *trans.* a) to pass, travel over; b) to climb; c) to escape (*alqd*).
ē-vagātiō, ōnis *f* aberration, extension.
ē-vagor 1 **a**) *intr.* to wander, make evolutions; to spread, extend; **b**) *trans.* to transgress.
ē-valēscō, luī, — 3 to grow strong; to prevail; to be able (*with inf.*).
ē-vānēscō, nuī, — 3 to disappear, vanish.
ēvānidus 3 vanishing, passing away.
ē-vāstō 1 to devastate.
ē-vehō 3 to carry *or* convey out (*alqd ex re in* or *ad alqd*); **a**) to lead up, lift up, raise; **b**) **P.** to proceed, advance, sail out, ride away; to be carried away *or* forth; to raise oneself up, to mount.
ē-vellō 3 to tear out, pluck out (*alqd ex re; alci alqd*); to root out, erase, remove.
ē-veniō 4 to come out, come forth; **a**) to come to pass, happen, occur (*ut*); **b**) to fall to the lot of (*alci; ut*); **c**) to proceed, turn out, result, issue (*prospere, bene, male; ut*).
ēventum, ī *n* (*mostly plur.*) = **eventus.**
ēventus, ūs *m* consequence, issue, result; **a**) end; **b**) occurrence, accident, event; **c**) success, fortune.
ē-verberō 1 to strike violently, to beat.
ē-vergō (?) 3 to pour *or* shoot out.
ēverriculum, ī *n* drag-net; that which sweeps up *or* together.
ē-verrō, —, rsum 3 to sweep out; to clean out, plunder completely.
ē-versiō, ōnis *f* an overthrowing; destruction, ruin.
ēversor, ōris *m* destroyer.
ē-vertō 3 to overturn, throw down; **a**) to turn upside down; **b**) to demolish, destroy, ruin; **c**) to turn *or* drive out, expel.
ē-vestīgātus 3 traced out.
ē-vidēns, tis manifest, clear, plain, evident.
ēvidentia, ae *f* clearness, distinctness.
ē-vigilō 1 to watch through; **a**) *trans.* to elaborate carefully; **b**) *intr.* to be wakeful, vigilant.
ē-vīlēscō, luī, — 3 to become vile, worthless.
ē-vinciō 4 to bind *or* wind round.
ē-vincō 3 to conquer completely, to subdue utterly; **a**) to prevail over *or* upon (*ut*); **b**) to prove (*acc. c. inf.*)
ē-virō 1 to emasculate, unman.
ē-viscerō 1 to take out the bowels; to mangle.
ē-vītābilis, e avoidable.
ē-vītō[1] 1 to avoid, shun.
ē-vītō[2] 1 to deprive of life.
ē-vocātiō, ōnis *f* the summoning of a debtor.
ē-vocātor, ōris *m* one who calls to arms.
ē-vocō 1 to call out *or* forth (*alqm ex re, ad se*); **a**) to challenge; **b**) to summon (*for military service*); **ē-vocātī, ōrum** *m/pl.* re-enlisted veterans; **c**) to summon to a place of honour, to raise; **d**) to call forth, produce, stir, elicit; **e**) to seduce.

ēvoe *int.* = **euoe.**
ē-volō 1 to fly out *or* away (*ex re*); **a**) to rush forth; **b**) to hasten away, escape; **c**) to fly up.
ē-volūtiō, ōnis *f* an unrolling, reading.
ē-volvō 3 **1.** to roll out *or* forth; to spin out; **2.** to unroll, unfold; to strip; a) to read; b) to disclose, make clear, narrate.
ē-vomō 3 to vomit forth, cast out.
ē-vors-, -vort- = **ē-vers-, -vert-.**
ē-vulgō 1 to make known, publish.
ēvulsiō, ōnis *f* a pulling out.
ex *prep., see* **e.**
ex-acerbō 1 to exasperate.
ex-āctiō, ōnis *f* **1.** a driving out; **2.** an exacting; a) a collecting of debts, tax, tribute; b) management.
ex-āctor, ōris *m* **1.** driver-out, expeller; **2.** a) collector, exactor; b) executioner.
ex-āctus 3 accurate, precise, exact; perfect.
ex-acuō 3 to sharpen, make sharp *or* pointed; to excite, stimulate, stir up.
ex-adversum (*or* **-advorsum**) *and* **-sus** *adv.* and *prep.* with *acc.* over against, opposite.
ex-aedificātiō, ōnis *f* a building up, finishing.
ex-aedificō 1 to finish building, to build up.
ex-aequātiō, ōnis *f* a making equal.
ex-aequō 1 to make equal, place on a level (*alqd alci rei* or *cum re*); to equal.
ex-aeresimus 3 that may be taken out.
ex-aestuō 1 to boil up, foam up; to effervesce, glow.
ex-aggerātiō, ōnis *f* elevation.
ex-aggerō 1 to heap *or* pile up, dam up; **a**) to accumulate; **b**) to amplify, magnify, heighten.
ex-agitātor, ōris *m* censurer.
ex-agitō 1 to rouse, hunt, chase; **a**) to disquiet, disturb, harass; **b**) to censure, blame, reproach; **c**) to excite, stir up.
ex-agōga, ae *f* exportation (*of goods*).
ex-albēscō 3 to turn white.
ex-ambulō 1 to walk out.
ex-āmen, inis *n* **1.** swarm (*of bees*), multitude; **2.** tongue of a balance; examination, consideration.
exāminō 1 to weigh, consider, examine.
ex-amussim *adv.* (by a workman's ruler) accurately, perfectly.
ex-anclō 1 to drain; to endure.
exanguis, e, *see* **exsanguis.**
ex-animālis, e 1. lifeless; **2.** killing.
ex-animātiō, ōnis *f* breathless terror.
ex-animis, e *and* **-mus** 3 lifeless; senseless, frightened.
ex-animō 1 to deprive of breath; **a**) to deprive of life, to kill; **b**) to exhaust, weaken, discourage, dismay.
ex-antlō 1 = **exanclo.**
ex-ārdēscō, ārsī, — 3 to take fire; **a**) to be kindled, inflamed, to glow (*alqa re*; *ad* or *in alqd*); **b**) to break out.
ex-ārēscō, āruī, — 3 to become quite dry; to be dried up, be gone.
ex-armō 1 to disarm; to dismantle.
ex-arō 1 **a**) to plough out *or* up, to furrow; to obtain by ploughing; **b**) to write, note, set down.
ex-asciātus 3 hewn out, well prepared.
ex-asperō 1 to make quite rough; **a**) to stir up (*waves*); **b**) to make savage, to exasperate.
ex-auctōrō 1 to dismiss from service, discharge; to cashier.
ex-audiō 4 to hear; to catch the sound of; to overhear; to listen, give heed to.
ex-augeō 2 to increase exceedingly.
ex-augurātiō, ōnis *f* deconsecration.
ex-augurō 1 to deconsecrate.
ex-auspicō 1 to take a good auspice.
ex-ballistō 1 to take by storm.
ex-bibō = **ebibo.**
ex-caecō 1 to make blind; to block.
ex-calceō 1 to remove the shoes from; **-ceātus** 3 **a**) barefoot; **b**) not wearing buskins, i.e. acting in comedy or mime.
ex-candēscentia, ae *f* heat, wrath.
ex-candēscō 3 to become hot, to burn with anger.
ex-cantō 1 to charm out, bring forth by incantations.
ex-carnificō 1 to torture to death.
ex-cavātiō, ōnis *f* hollowing out.
ex-cavō 1 to hollow out.
ex-cēdō 3 **1.** to go out, forth, away, to go from; to depart, withdraw, emigrate (*ex, de, a re, re, in* or *ad alqd*); a) to disappear; b) to go beyond, advance, proceed; **c**) to result in; d) to die; **2.** *trans.* a) to transgress; b) to rise above, overtop; c) to exceed, surpass, pass beyond; d) to go out of, leave (*urbem*).

ex-cellēns, tis high, lofty; excellent, distinguished, surpassing, superior.

excellentia, ae *f* superiority, excellence, merit.

ex-cellō 3 to rise, be distinguished, eminent, excellent.

ex-celsitās, ātis *f* loftiness.

ex-celsus 3 elevated, lofty, high; *subst.* **-um, ī** *n* height, high rank, high station.

ex-ceptiō, ōnis *f* **a**) exception; **b**) restriction, limitation; **c**) protest, objection.

ex-ceptiuncula, ae *f* a limitation.

ex-ceptō 1 to take out *or* up; to catch, receive.

ex-cernō 3 to sift, sort.

ex-cerpō, psī, ptum 3 to take *or* pick out; **a**) to select; **b**) to separate, leave out, except.

ex-cessus, ūs *m* a going out *or* away; **a**) death; **b**) digression.

excetra, ae *f* viper.

excidium, ī *n* (*and* **-diō, ōnis** *f*) destruction, demolition, annihilation.

ex-cidō[1], cidī, — 3 to fall out *or* down, to fall from (*e, de re in alqd*); **a**) to slip out, escape; **b**) to fall away, perish, be lost; **c**) to be deprived of (*abl.*).

ex-cīdō[2], cīdī, cīsum 3 to cut out *or* off, to cut *or* hew down; **a**) to hollow out; **b**) to demolish, destroy, extirpate, banish.

ex-cieō, cīvī, citum 2 *and* **exciō** 4 to set in motion; **a**) to rouse, awake, excite, stir up, shake; **b**) to frighten; **c**) to summon, call forth, call to help; **d**) to provoke; **e**) to cause, produce.

ex-cipiō, cēpi, ceptum 3 **1.** to take out (*alqd ex re*), catch up; a) to withdraw, rescue, release; b) to except, make an exception; c) to make a condition, state expressly; **2.** to catch, snatch; a) to capture, take prisoner; b) to catch with the ear, to listen to; c) to await, meet, be exposed to, sustain, obtain; **3.** to receive; a) to welcome, entertain; b) to engage, claim; c) to interpret, take for; **4.** to follow, succeed, take up, continue, prolong.

excīsiō, ōnis *f* a destroying.

ex-citō 1 **1.** to arouse, stir up; a) to awaken, excite; b) to call out *or* forth; c) to cause, produce; **2.** to raise, summon up, call up; a) to erect, construct; b) to kindle; c) to enliven, revive, encourage, comfort; d) to stimulate, excite; **excitātus** 3 excited, lively, vehement.

ex-clāmātiō, ōnis *f* exclamation.

ex-clāmō 1 to cry aloud; to call out *or* aloud; to call upon.

ex-clūdō, sī, sum 3 to shut out, exclude; **a**) to thrust out, remove; **b**) to separate; **c**) to prevent, hinder; **d**) to hatch.

ex-clūsiō, ōnis *f* a shutting out.

ex-cōgitātiō, ōnis *f* a devising, contriving.

ex-cōgitō 1 to devise, contrive, invent.

ex-colō 3 to cultivate, tend, work carefully; **a**) to improve, ennoble, perfect; **b**) to honour, worship.

ex-concinnō 1 to arrange, to furnish (a house).

ex-coquō 3 to boil *or* melt **out;** to dry up.

ex-cors, dis silly, stupid.

excrēmentum[1], ī *n* excrement, spittle, mucus.

excrēmentum[2], ī *n* growth.

ex-crēscō 3 to grow out *or* up, increase.

ex-cruciābilis, e deserving of torture.

ex-cruciō 1 to torture, torment, plague, afflict, trouble.

ex-cubiae, ārum *f/pl.* a lying out on guard; watch, sentries.

excubitor, ōris *m* watchman, guard, sentinel.

excubitus, ūs *m* guard-duty.

ex-cubō 1 to lie *or* sleep out; to keep watch.

ex-cūdō, dī, sum 3 to strike out, hammer out; **a**) to forge, mould; **b**) to hatch out; **c**) to prepare, compose.

ex-culcō 1 to tread down *or* out; to stamp firm.

ex-cūrātus 3 carefully attended to.

ex-currō, (cu)currī, cursum 3 to run out *or* forth, to hasten forward; **a**) to sally forth, make an incursion; **b**) to make an excursion; **c**) to issue forth; **d**) to spread; **e**) to project.

ex-cursō 1 to sally forth repeatedly.

ex-cursiō, ōnis *f* a running out *or* forth; a stepping forward; **a**) excursion; **b**) sally, attack, invasion; **c**) digression.

ex-cursor, ōris *m* skirmisher, scout.

ex-cursus, ūs *m* = **excursio.**

excūsābilis, e excusable.

excūsātiō, ōnis *f* a declining, excusing, excuse, plea.

ex-cūsō 1 **a**) to decline, refuse (*alqd*); **b**) to plead as an excuse, to apologize for, excuse, absolve from, dispense with; **c**) to pretend.
ex-cutiō, cussī, cussum 3 to shake out *or* off; **a**) to cast *or* drive out (*alci alqd*); **b**) to throw down, hurl, send forth; **c**) to drive out *or* away, expel, reject; **d**) to shake out, search, investigate, examine; **e**) to wrest, extort; **f**) to shake about; **g**) to extend; to discharge; **excussō lacertō,** *or* **excussē** (*adv.*), with extended arm.
ex-dorsuō 1 to bone (*fish*).
exec..., *see* **exsec...**
ex-edō, ēdi, ēsum 3 to eat up, consume; **a**) to corrode, hollow out; **b**) to destroy.
ex-edra, ae *f* hall furnished with seats.
ex-edrium, ī *n* sitting-room.
exemplar (*and* **-āre**) **āris** *n* **a**) copy; **b**) image, likeness; **c**) model, pattern, example.
exemplāris, is *m* copy.
exemplum, ī *n* **a**) copy; **b**) tenor, purport, contents; **c**) imitation, image; **d**) pattern, model, specimen, instance, ideal; **e**) way, manner; **f**) example, warning, punishment; **g**) precedent.
ex-enterō 1 to disembowel; to torture.
ex-eō 1. to go out, forth, *or* away; a) to march out; to disembark, land; b) to turn out, result; c) to leave, withdraw; d) to pass away, run out, expire; e) to mount upwards, ascend, rise; f) to spread abroad, become known; **2.** *trans.* a) to exceed; b) to avoid, evade (*alqd*).
exequiae *and* **exequor,** *see* **exs-.**
ex-erceō, uī, itum 2 **1.** to keep in motion; a) to keep busy, at work; to occupy, employ; b) to trouble, disturb, harass; **2.** to exercise, practise, train, discipline (*alqm re, in re, ad alqd*); a) to follow, pursue, employ oneself about; b) to till, work (at), administer; **exercitus** 3 harassed; disciplined, trained; hard, distressing.
exercitātiō, ōnis *f* exercise, training.
exercitium, ī *n* exercise.
exercitō 1 to exercise often; **exercitātus** 3 **a**) practised, versed, trained (*in re*); **b**) troubled, vexed, harassed, worried (*re*).
exercitor, ōris *m* trainer.
exercitus, ūs *m* **1.** exercise; **2.** army, trained body of men, forces; a) land-army, infantry; b) multitude, host, swarm.
ex-errō 1 to wander away.
ex-ēsor, ōris *m* an erosive agent.
exfāfillātus 3 bared.
ex-hālātiō, ōnis *f* exhalation, vapour.
ex-hālō 1 to breathe out, exhale.
ex-hauriō 4 **1.** to draw out, empty; a) to take out, empty out (*alqd ex re*); b) to take away, remove (*alci alqd*); **2.** to drink up, empty; a) to exhaust, bring to an end; b) to undergo, endure.
ex-hērēdō 1 to disinherit.
ex-hērēs, ēdis disinherited.
ex-hibeō, uī, itum 2 to hold forth, tender, present; to deliver, produce, show; **a**) to furnish; **b**) to display, exhibit (*alci alqd*); **c**) to maintain, support; **d**) to procure, occasion, cause.
ex-hilarō 1 to gladden.
ex-horrēscō, ruī, — 3 to tremble, shudder, be terrified (at).
ex-hortātiō, ōnis *f* exhortation.
ex-hortor 1 to exhort, encourage.
ex-igō, ēgī, āctum 3 **1.** to drive out, thrust out, expel (*alqm ex re*); a) to drive, plunge, thrust (*a weapon*); b) to sell, export; **2.** to demand, require, enforce, exact (*money*); a) to inquire after, to ask (*alqd ab* or *de alqo*); b) to measure, estimate, weigh; c) to examine, consider, deliberate; **3.** to complete, finish; a) to pass, live through; b) to establish, settle.
exiguitās, ātis *f* scantiness, littleness, shortness.
exiguus 3 **a**) scanty, small, little, petty, short; **b**) mean, poor, trifling.
ex-īlis, e a) thin, slender, meagre; **b**) poor, feeble, wretched; cheerless; destitute.
exīlitās, ātis *f* leanness, poorness.
exiliō, exilium *see* **exs-.**
exim *adv.*, = **exinde.**
eximius 3 **1.** excepted; **2.** distinguished, extraordinary, excellent.
ex-imō, ēmī, ēmptum 3 to take out *or* away (*alqd de* or *ex re; alci alqd*); **a**) to separate, remove; **b**) to free, release, deliver; **c**) to consume, spend (*time*); **d**) to remove, banish; **e**) to except, make an exception.
exin *adv.* = **exinde.**

ex-ināniō 4 to empty, make empty; to plunder.
ex-inde *adv.* from there; then, after that, next; since then.
exīstimātiō, ōnis *f* **a**) judgment, opinion; **b**) good name, reputation, honour; credit.
exīstimātor, ōris *m* judge, critic.
ex-īstimō 1 **a**) to judge, consider, suppose, think, reckon; **b**) to value, estimate; **c**) to pass judgment on (*de re*); *subst.* **exīstimantēs, ium** *m/pl.* critics.
existō, *see* **exsisto.**
exitiā(bi)lis, e destructive, fatal.
ex-itiō, ōnis *f* a going out.
exitiōsus 3 destructive, pernicious, deadly.
ex-itium, ī *n* destruction, ruin, hurt.
ex-itus, ūs *m* **a**) a going out, egress, departure; outlet, passage; **b**) end, close, conclusion; end of life, death; issue, result, event.
ex-lecebra, ae *f* = **elecebra.**
ex-lēx, lēgis bound by no law, lawless.
ex-obsecrō 1 to beg earnestly.
ex-oculō 1 to knock out the eyes of.
exodium, ī *n* after-play, interlude.
ex-olēscō, lēvī, (lētum) to grow out of use, become obsolete, pass away; *adj.* **exolētus** 3 **a**) grown up (*for prostitution*); **b**) obsolete, forgotten.
ex-onerō 1 to unload, disburden; **a**) to remove, send off; **b**) to discharge, release.
ex-optābilis, e very desirable.
ex-optō 1 to desire *or* wish greatly, to long for (with *inf.* or *ut*); **ex-optātus** 3 longed for, desired.
ex-ōrābilis, e easily entreated.
ex-ōrābula, ōrum *n/pl.* means of entreaty.
ex-ōrātor, ōris *m* one who obtains by entreaty.
ex-ōrdior 4 to lay the warp, begin to weave; to begin, commence (*alqd; inf.*); *subst.* **exōrsum, ī** *n* = **exordium.**
exōrdium, ī *n* a beginning, commencement; introduction.
ex-orior 4 to come out, spring up, rise; **a**) to come forth, appear; **b**) to arise, originate, begin, proceed.
ex-ōrnātiō, ōnis *f* an adorning.
ex-ōrnātor, ōris *m* embellisher.
ex-ōrnātulus 3 rather smart.
ex-ōrnō 1 to fit out, equip, furnish, supply with (*alqd alqa re*); **a**) to arrange, instruct; **b**) to adorn, embellish, extol.
ex-ōrō 1 **a**) to prevail upon, persuade by entreaty; **b**) to obtain by entreaty; to soften, appease (*alqd; ut*).
ex-ōrsum, ī *n* = **exordium.**
ex-ōrsus, ūs *m* = **exordium.**
ex-ortus, ūs *m* a rising.
ex-os, ossis boneless.
ex-ōsculor 1 to kiss.
ex-ossō 1 to bone.
ex-ōstra, ae *f* movable stage in a theatre; open stage.
ex-ōsus 3 hating, detesting (*with acc.*).
exōticus 3 outlandish, foreign.
ex-pallēscō 3 to turn pale; to shrink from (*alqd*).
ex-palliātus 3 deprived of a cloak.
ex-pallidus 3 very pale.
ex-palpō 1 to coax out.
ex-pandō 3 to unfold.
ex-patrō 1 to squander in debauchery.
ex-pavēscō, pāvī 3 to be terrified, frightened (of).
expectō 1, *see* **exspecto.**
ex-pectorō 1 to banish from the mind.
ex-pecūliātus 3 deprived of property.
ex-pediō 4 **1.** *trans.* to disengage, extricate (*alqd ex re*); a) to let loose, set free; **se expedīre** to escape; b) to free from evil *or* obstacle, to bring through critical circumstances, to put in order, arrange, set right; c) to dispatch, hurl; d) to relate, narrate; e) to make ready, prepare, procure; **2.** *intr.* to be serviceable, profitable, advantageous (*expedit alci*).
expedītiō, ōnis *f* enterprise, expedition, special mission; a getting rid of, despatch.
expedītus 3 disengaged; **a**) unimpeded, free, easy; **b**) ready, at hand, ready for action.
ex-pellō, pulī, pulsum 3 to drive out *or* away, to thrust out (*alqd ex re, re, in alqd*); **a**) to expel, banish, eject; **b**) to repudiate, reject; **c**) to rob of (*alqm re*); **d**) to shoot.
ex-pendō, ndī, ēnsum 3 to weigh out, weigh; **a**) to ponder, consider, estimate; **b**) to pay out, pay,

expend, lend out; **c**) to pay, suffer, undergo; *subst.* **expēnsum, ī** *n* payment; *alci alqd* **expēnsum ferre** to enter a sum as paid to someone.
ex-pergēfaciō 3 to awaken, rouse.
expergīscor, perrēctus sum 3 to be awakened, to wake.
expergō, gī, gitum 3 to awaken, rouse.
experiēns, tis enterprising, active; patient of (*alcis rei*).
experientia, ae *f* **a**) trial, proof; **b**) experience, practice.
experīmentum, ī *n* **a**) trial, proof, test; **b**) experience.
experior, pertus sum 4 to try, prove, test; **a**) to undertake, attempt, risk, undergo, experience; **b**) to contend with (*cum alqo*); **c**) to learn *or* know by experience (*alqd in re*).
ex-pers, tis having no part in, not sharing in, devoid of, free from (*with gen.*).
expertus 3 **a**) experienced in (*gen.*); **b**) tried, proved.
expetendus 3 desirable.
expetēns, entis desirous.
ex-petessō 3 to desire, wish for.
expetibilis, e desirable.
ex-petō 3 **a**) to long for, seek after, strive for, aspire to, desire, wish (*alqd ab alqo*); **b**) to befall (*in alqm*).
expiātiō, ōnis *f* atonement.
ex-pīlātiō, ōnis *f* a pillaging.
expīlātor, ōris *m* plunderer.
ex-pīlō 1 to pillage, plunder.
ex-pingō 3 to paint, depict, describe to the life.
ex-piō 1 to atone for, make amends, purify (*alqd a re*); **a**) to expiate, avenge; **b**) to make good; **c**) to appease.
ex-piscor 1 to fish out; to search out (*alqd ab alqo*).
explānābilis, e intelligible.
ex-plānātiō, ōnis *f* explanation, interpretation.
ex-plānātor, ōris *m* interpreter.
explānātus 3 plain; distinct.
ex-plānō 1 **a**) to make plain *or* flat, to spread out; **b**) to explain; interpret.
ex-plēmentum, ī *n* filling, food.
ex-pleō, plēvī, plētum 2 to fill up *or* full (*alqd re*); **a**) to fill, make up, complete (*a number*); to supply, make good; **b**) to finish, accomplish; **c**) to fill, satisfy; **d**) to discharge, execute, perform; **e**) to pass over, live through; **explētus** 3 complete, perfect.
ex-plētiō, ōnis *f* a satisfying.
explicātiō, ōnis *f* an unfolding, uncoiling; exposition, explanation.
explicātor, ōris *m* explainer, expounder.
explicātrīx, īcis *f* she that explains.
explicātus, ūs *m* an unfolding; exposition.
ex-plicō, cāvī *or* **cuī, cātum** *or* **citum** 1 to unfold, unroll, uncoil; **a**) to spread out, loosen, undo; **b**) to spread *or* stretch out, extend, display; **c**) to disentangle, arrange, regulate, settle, adjust, perform; **d**) to set free, release; **e**) to explain, exhibit, express, interpret; **explicātus** 3 well-ordered, regular; plain, clear; **explicitus** 3 easy, plain.
ex-plōdō, sī, sum 3 to drive out, hiss off (*the stage*), explode; to disapprove.
explōrātiō, ōnis *f* investigation, examination.
explōrātor, ōris *m* scout, spy.
explōrātōrius 3 of a scout.
ex-plōrō 1 to search out, examine, explore (*alqd*; *de re*); to spy out, reconnoitre; **explōrātus** 3 ascertained, established, certain, sure.
explōsiō, ōnis *f* a driving off the stage.
ex-poliō 4 to smooth off, polish up; to finish, adorn, embellish.
ex-polītiō, ōnis *f* a polishing, finishing, embellishing.
ex-pōnō 3 to put *or* set out *or* forth; **a**) to expose (*children*); **b**) to set on shore, disembark; **c**) to offer (*cash*); **d**) to leave unprotected, to abandon (*alci alqd*); **e**) to publish; **f**) to exhibit, propose, relate, explain, expound; **expositus** 3 open, accessible; exposed, abandoned; common, vulgar.
ex-porrigō (and **-porgō**) 3 to stretch out.
ex-portātiō, ōnis *f* exportation.
ex-portō 1 to carry out, bring out (*alqd ex re*); **a**) to convey away, export; **b**) to send away, banish.
ex-poscō, poposcī, — 3 to ask *or* beg earnestly (*alqd ab alqo, alqd alqm*); **a**) to request, entreat, implore; **b**) to demand the delivery of a person.

ex-positīcius 3 exposed.
ex-positiō, ōnis *f* **a**) an exposing; **b**) exposition, narration, explanation.
ex-postulātiō, ōnis *f* **a**) demand, request; **b**) expostulation, complaint.
ex-postulō 1 **a**) to demand urgently (*alqd ab alqo*; *ut*), to insist on; **b**) to expostulate (*cum alqo alqd* or *de re; acc.c.inf.*), complain of.
ex-pōtus = **ēpōtus.**
ex-primō, pressī, pressum 3 to press *or* squeeze out; **a**) to force out; **b**) to carry up, raise; **c**) to pronounce, articulate; **d**) to extort, elicit; **e**) to form, represent, portray, express, imitate, copy; **f**) to translate, render; **g**) to describe; **expressus** 3 clearly exhibited, distinct, visible, manifest, clear, plain; translated.
ex-probrātiō, ōnis *f* a reproaching, charge.
ex-probrātor, ōris *m*, **-trīx, īcis** *f* upbraider.
ex-probrō 1 to reproach with, blame for, to charge against (*alci alqd; de re*).
ex-prōmō 3 to bring forth *or* out; **a**) to show forth, exhibit, display; **b**) to utter, declare.
expugnābilis, e assailable.
expugnātiō, ōnis *f* a taking, storming.
expugnātor, ōris *m* stormer, conqueror.
expugnāx, ācis victorious, effectual.
ex-pugnō 1 to take by assault, to storm, capture; **a**) to subdue, overcome, conquer; **b**) to gain by force, to force (*alqd; ut*).
expulsiō, ōnis *f* a driving out, expulsion.
ex-pulsō 1 to knock away.
expulsor, ōris *m* expeller.
expultrīx, īcis *f* she that expels.
ex-pungō, nxī, nctum 3 to strike out, blot out.
ex-pūr(i)gātiō, ōnis *f* excuse.
ex-pūr(i)gō 1 to purge, cleanse, purify; to exculpate, excuse.
ex-pūtēscō 3 to rot.
ex-putō 1 to consider, think.
ex-quaerō = **exquiro.**
ex-quīrō, sīvī, sītum 3 to search out, seek diligently; **a**) to examine; **b**) to inquire out, make inquiry; investigate; **c**) to ask (*alqd ab* or *ex alqo*); to demand; **exquīsītus** 3 carefully studied, choice, refined.
ex-rādīcitus from the roots.
ex-sacrificō 1 to sacrifice.
ex-saeviō 4 to cease raging.
ex-sanguis, e a) bloodless; lifeless; **b**) pale, wan; **c**) weak, feeble.
ex-saniō 1 to drain (*a body*) of watery *or* bloody matter.
ex-sarciō 4 to patch, mend, make good.
ex-satiō = **exsaturo.**
ex-saturābilis, e that may be satiated.
ex-saturō 1 to satiate, satisfy.
exscendō *and* **exscēnsiō, ōnis** *f*, *see* **escendo** *and* **escensio.**
ex-scindō 3 to tear out; to extirpate, destroy.
ex-screō 1 to cough up, to clear the throat.
ex-scrībō 3 to write out *or* off; **a**) to copy; **b**) to write down.
ex-sculpō 3 **a**) to cut *or* chisel out, to carve; **b**) to scratch out, erase.
ex-secō 1 to cut out; **a**) to extort; **b**) to castrate.
exsecrābilis, e a) accursed, execrable; **b**) execrating.
exsecrātiō, ōnis *f* **a**) execration, curse; **b**) solemn oath.
ex-secrātus 3 cursed, execrable.
ex-secror 1 **a**) to curse, execrate; **b**) to take a solemn oath.
ex-sectiō, ōnis *f* a cutting out.
ex-secūtiō, ōnis *f* performance, execution; administration.
ex-secūtor, ōris *m* avenger.
exsequiae, ārum *f*/*pl.* funeral procession, funeral rites.
exsequiālis, e of a funeral.
ex-sequor 3 **1.** to follow to the grave; **2.** to follow, pursue; a) to strive after; b) to investigate, examine; c) to assert, maintain; d) to prosecute, carry out, execute, perform, accomplish; e) to punish, avenge; f) to go through, describe, relate; g) to bear, suffer.
ex-serciō 4, *see* **exsarcio.**
ex-serō, ruī, rtum 3 **a**) to stretch out *or* forth, thrust out, put forth; **b**) to bare, uncover; **se exserere** to come forth.
ex-sertō 1 to stretch forth; to bare.

ex-sībilō 1 to hiss out, to hiss from the stage.
ex-siccō 1 to dry up, make quite dry.
ex-sicō 1 = **exseco.**
ex-signō 1 to write out, note down.
ex-siliō, luī (*and* **līvī**), — 4 **a**) to leap out; **b**) to spring forth, start up.
exsilium, ī *n* **a**) exile; **b**) place of exile, retreat.
ex-sistō, stitī, — 3 to step out, come forth (*ab, ex re*); **a**) to emerge, appear, come to light; **b**) to spring, proceed, arise; **c**) to be visible, to exist, to be.
ex-solvō 3 to loose, unbind, untie; **a**) to deliver, release, set free (*alqm alqa re*); **b**) to discharge, pay (*debts*); **c**) to throw off, lay aside; **d**) to fulfil, keep; **e**) to repay; **f**) to solve, explain.
ex-somnis, e sleepless.
ex-sorbeō, uī, — 2 to suck out, suck up, drain, drink, swallow.
ex-sors, tis free from; deprived of (*with gen.*); chosen, choice.
ex-spatior 1 to wander from the course *or* out of the way; to spread, overflow.
ex-spectātiō, ōnis *f* an awaiting, expectation.
ex-spectō 1 to look out for, await, expect, wait for, wait (*with dum, si, ut; alqd ab* or *ex re;* with *acc.c.inf.*); to hope, long for, desire; to fear, apprehend, anticipate; **exspectātus** 3 expected, longed for, desired, welcome.
ex-spergō 3 to disperse.
ex-spēs (*indecl.*) hopeless (*with gen.*).
ex-spīrātiō, ōnis *f* a breathing out, exhalation.
ex-spīrō 1 to breathe out; to expire, die, cease.
ex-splendēscō, duī, — 3 to shine forth, glitter.
ex-spoliō 1 to spoil, pillage, plunder, rob (*alqm alqa re*).
ex-spuō 3 to spit out; to cast out, expel.
ex-sternō 1 to terrify, dismay.
ex-stillēscō, —, —3 to begin to drip.
ex-stillō 1 to drop *or* trickle out (*re*).
ex-stimulātor, ōris *m* inciter.
ex-stimulō 1 to prick, goad; to excite.
ex-(s)tinctiō, ōnis *f* extinction.
ex-(s)tinctor, ōris *m* extinguisher; destroyer.
ex-(s)tinguō, inxī, inctum 3 to put out, quench, extinguish; **a**) to dry up; **b**) to destroy, kill, ruin; **c**) to abolish, annihilate, annul; **P.** to go out (*fire*); to die, perish, to be forgotten.
ex-stirpō 1 to root out, to eradicate.
ex-stō, —, — 1 to stand out *or* forth, to project (*ex* or *de re*); **a**) to be visible, appear; **b**) to be extant, to exist.
ex-structiō, ōnis *f* an erecting, building up.
ex-struō 3 to pile up; to erect, raise, build up, fill with buildings.
ex-sūdō 1 to sweat out; to sweat at (*acc.*), perform with sweating.
ex-sūgō 3 to suck out.
ex-sul, ulis *m and f* banished person, exile.
ex-sulō 1 to be banished, live in exile.
exsultātiō, ōnis *f* exultation.
ex-sultim *adv.* leaping about, frisking.
ex-sultō 1 to spring, jump, leap up; **a**) to move freely, gambol about; **b**) to exult, rejoice; **c**) to revel, to boast.
ex-superābilis, e superable, surmountable.
ex-superantia, ae *f* superiority, pre-eminence.
ex-superō 1 to mount up, appear above (*alqd*); to surpass, surmount, excel, overcome.
ex-surdō 1 to deafen; to dull.
ex-surgō 3 to rise up, get up, stand up (*contra* or *adversus alqd*); to recover strength.
ex-suscitō 1 to awaken, rouse; to stir up.
exta, ōrum *n/pl.* the internal organs.
ex-tābēscō, buī, — 3 to waste away; to vanish, disappear.
extāris, e for cooking *exta*.
ex-temp(u)lō *adv.* immediately, straightway.
ex-temporālis, e extemporary, without preparation.
ex-temporālitās, ātis *f* faculty of extemporary speech.
ex-tendō, tendī, tentum *or* **tēnsum** 3 to extend, stretch out; **a**) to spread out (*alqd in* or *ad alqd*); **b**) to increase, enlarge, prolong, continue, lengthen; **c**) to spend, pass.

extēnsus, extentus 3 extensive.
ex-tentō 1 to stretch, exert.
ex-tentus, ūs *m* extent, width.
ex-tenuātiō, ōnis *f* diminution.
ex-tenuō 1 to make thin; **a**) to lengthen; **b**) to make small, reduce, diminish, lessen, weaken, extenuate; **extenuātus** 3 faint, weak, reduced.
exter, a, um on the outside, outward, foreign; *comp.* **exterior, ius** outward, outer, exterior, on the outer side; *superl.* (**extimus** *and*) **extrēmus** 3 outermost, utmost, extreme, furthest; **a**) remotest, last; **b**) highest, greatest, lowest, least, meanest, worst.
ex-terebrō 1 to bore out.
ex-tergeō 2 to wipe; to strip clean, plunder.
ex-terminō 1 to drive out *or* away; **a**) to expel, banish; **b**) to remove, put away.
externus 3 outward, external; foreign, strange; **externa, ōrum** *n/pl.* external things, foreign examples; *subst.* **externus, ī** *m* foreigner.
ex-terō 3 to rub out *or* away; to crush.
ex-terreō 2 to frighten, terrify, alarm; to rouse up.
ex-tersus, ūs *m* a wiping.
exterus 3 = **exter.**
ex-texō 3 to unweave; to plunder.
ex-timēscō, muī, — 3 to be greatly afraid (of).
extimus 3, *superl. of* **exter.**
ex-tinguō 3, *see* **ex(s)tinguō.**
exti-spex, icis *m* observer of entrails, diviner.
exti-spicium, ī *n* divination by inspection of entrails.
extō, —, — 1, *see* **exsto.**
ex-tollō, —, — 3 to lift out *or* up, to raise up; **a**) to raise, extol, elevate, praise; **b**) to excite, encourage; **c**) to adorn, beautify.
ex-torqueō 2 to twist *or* wrench out, wrest away (*alqd ex* or *de re*); **a**) to put out of joint, torture; **b**) to extort, obtain by force, tear away.
ex-torris, e exiled, banished.
ex-tortor, ōris *m* snatcher.
extrā *adv.* and *prep.* with *acc.* on the outside, without, externally; outside, without, beyond; except, besides.
ex-trahō 3 to draw *or* drag out (*alqd a, de, ex re in* or *ad alqd*); **a**) to draw forward; **b**) to release, extricate; **c**) to protract, prolong, draw out.
extrāneus 3 external, stranger.
extra-ōrdinārius 3 extraordinary, uncommon, unnatural.
extrārius 3 = **extraneus.**
extrēmitās, ātis *f* extremity, end; circumference.
extrēmus 3, *superl. of* **exter.**
ex-trīcō (*and* **-or**) 1 to disentangle, extricate, clear; to procure with difficulty, hunt up.
extrīn-secus *adv.* **a**) from without; **b**) outside.
ex-trūdō 3 to thrust out *or* forth, drive out *or* away (*alqd ex* or *a re in alqd*); to get rid of.
extruō 3, *see* **exstruo.**
ex-tumefactus 3 swollen up.
ex-tumeō 2 to swell up.
extumus 3 = **extimus.**
ex-tundō, tudī, (**tūsum**) 3 to beat out, strike out; **a**) to hammer *or* forge out; **b**) to form, devise, fashion; **c**) to drive out *or* away; **d**) to dash to pieces.
ex-turbō 1 to drive out *or* away; thrust away; to repudiate, divorce.
ex-ūberō 1 **a**) to grow luxuriantly; **b**) to abound, come forth in abundance (*abl.*).
exul, ulis = **exsul.**
exulcerātiō, ōnis *f* a making sore, inflammation.
ex-ulcerō 1 to make worse; to exasperate, embitter.
ex-ululō 1 to howl, cry out.
ex-undō 1 to flow out, overflow.
ex-unguō 3 to rub away by anointing; to squander on unguents.
ex-uō, uī, ūtum 3 to draw out, take off, pull off; **a**) to lay aside, shake off, put away, divest oneself of (*alqd*); **b**) to unclothe, bare (*alqm re*); **c**) to strip, despoil, deprive.
ex-urgeō 2 to squeeze out.
ex-ūrō 3 **a**) to burn out *or* up, consume by fire; **b**) to dry up; **c**) to inflame; **d**) to destroy.
ex-ustiō, ōnis *f* a burning, combustion.
exuviae, ārum *f/pl.* **a**) what is stripped off, skin of an animal; **b**) clothing, equipment, arms; **c**) spoils, booty.

F

F *abbr.* = **filius.**
faba, ae *f* bean.
fabālis, e of beans.
fābella, ae *f* **a**) short story, fable, tale; **b**) short play.
faber[1], **brī** *m* workman, smith, artificer, carpenter; engineer, sapper.
faber[2], **bra, brum** skilful; workmanlike.
fabrē-faciō 3 to make artistically *or* skilfully.
fabrica, ae *f* **1.** work-shop; **2.** a) trade, profession, art; architecture; b) skilful production, fabric, structure; **c**) crafty device, trick.
fabricātiō, ōnis *f* a framing, construction.
fabricātor, ōris *m* artificer, framer, contriver.
fabricor (*and* **-cō**) 1 **a**) to frame, forge, construct, build; **b**) to form, fashion.
fabrīlis, e of a workman *or* artificer; **-lia, ium** *n/pl.* tools.
fābula, ae *f* **1.** narration, account, tale, story; a) fable, fiction; b) dramatic poem, play; epic poem; c) affair, concern, matter; **2.** common talk, conversation.
fābulāris, e fabulous, legendary.
fābulātor, ōris *m* narrator.
fābulor 1 to talk, chat, speak.
fābulōsus 3 fabulous.
fabulus, ī *m* bean.
facessō, īvī *and* **iī, ītum** 3 **1.** to perform, execute, accomplish; to bring on, cause; **2.** to go away, depart.
facētia, ae *f* drollery; *pl.* **-iae, ārum** *f* wit, pleasantry, humour.
facētus 3 fine, elegant; **a**) courteous, polite; **b**) merry, witty, humorous.
faciēs, ēī *f* external form, outward appearance, shape, figure; aspect; **a**) pretence, pretext; **b**) look, face, countenance; beauty.
facilis, e 1. easy to do, easy, without difficulty; favourable, prosperous; **2.** a) ready, quick; b) good-natured, compliant, willing, yielding, courteous, affable; **3.** *adv.* **facile** easily, without trouble *or* difficulty; certainly, without contradiction, beyond dispute; readily, willingly; agreeably, well; **non** (**haud**) **facile** hardly.
facilitās, ātis *f* **1.** easiness, ease, facility in doing; fluency of expression; **2.** a) inclination (*with gen.*); b) willingness, courteousness, affability.
facinorōsus 3 criminal.
facinus, oris *n* (conspicuous) deed, action; **a**) bad deed, crime, misdeed; **b**) instrument of villainy; **c**) *pl.* criminals.
faciō, fēcī, factum 3 **1.** (*trans.*) to make, produce, effect, create, perform, carry out; a) to build, erect (*castra*); b) to compose, write; to coin, make, earn (*money*); c) to commit, execute, practise; exercise; to celebrate, offer; to suffer (*damnum, naufragium*); d) to cause, occasion; to give, procure (*alci magnas opes, nomen, potestatem*); to deal with (*quid facias hoc homine?* what is to be done with ...?); e) to take care, provide for (*with ut*); **2.** (*trans.*) a) to make into, render, appoint (*with double acc.*); b) to represent, introduce (*with acc. part.*), feign, assert; c) to estimate, value, consider (*with gen.*); to suppose; d) to put under, in the power of (*gen.*); **3.** (*intr.*) a) to do, deal, act in any manner; b) to side, take part (*cum alqo*); c) to be good, of use, of service.
facteon = **faciendum.**
factiō, ōnis *f* a making, doing, preparing; **a**) class, order, sect, party; **b**) faction, partisans, party-spirit, party-organization.
factiōsus 3 factious, seditious; partisan.
factitō 1 to do *or* make frequently, to practise.
factius nihilō (*factus*) not any nearer being done.
factor, ōris *m* **a**) oil-presser; **b**) one who catches a ball (?).

factus 3 done, made, accomplished, created; *subst.* **factum, ī** *n* deed, action, exploit; event.
facul *adv.* = **facile** (*see* **facilis** 3).
facula, ae *f* little torch.
facultās, ātis *f* capability, possibility, opportunity; **a**) permission, power, means; **b**) skill, ability; **c**) plenty, abundance, supply, stock, property.
fācundia, ae *f* eloquence, command of language.
fācunditās, ātis *f* talkativeness.
fācundus 3 eloquent.
faeceus 3 of dregs; filthy.
faecula, ae *f* wine-tartar.
faenebris, e of interest, of usury.
faenerātiō, ōnis *f* usury.
faenerātō with interest (*i.e* 'you (he) shall pay for it').
faenerātor, ōris *m* capitalist, usurer.
faeneror (*and* **-rō**) 1 to lend on interest; to invest.
faenīlia, ium *n/pl.* hay-loft.
faeni-seca, ae *m* hay-cutter, rustic.
faenum, ī *n* hay.
faenus, oris *n* produce; gain, profit; **a**) interest, usury; **b**) burden of debt, lent capital.
faenusculum, i *n* a bit of interest.
faex, cis *f* sediment, lees, dregs; **a**) salt of tartar; **b**) refuse, rabble.
fāgineus *and* **fāginus** 3 of beech, beechen.
fāgus, ī *f* beech-tree; beechwood.
fala, ae *f* a scaffold used in besieging cities; wooden pillar.
falārica, ae *f* fire-dart.
falcārius, ī *m* sickle-maker.
falcātus 3 **a**) furnished with scythes; **b**) sickle-shaped.
falci-fer 3 sickle-bearing.
fallācia, ae *f* deceit, trick, artifice; intrigue (*pl.*).
fallāci-loquus 3 speaking deceitfully.
fallāx, ācis deceitful, deceptive, fallacious.
fallō, fefellī, falsum 3 to deceive, cheat, trick; **P.** to deceive oneself, be mistaken; **a**) to violate, break (*fidem*); **b**) to imitate, counterfeit; **c**) to cause to pass imperceptibly, to beguile, cheat, silence; **d**) to escape the notice of, be concealed, remain undiscovered; **mē fallit** I fail to observe.
falsārius, ī *m* forger.
falsi-dicus 3 speaking falsely.
falsi-ficus 3 acting falsely.
falsi-iūrius 3 swearing falsely.
falsi-loquos (*and* **-locus**) speaking falsely.
falsimōnia, ae *f* deceit.
falsi-parēns, tis having a pretended father.
falsus 3 false **1.** feigned, counterfeit, pretended; a) spurious, supposed; b) untrue, erroneous; **2.** deceitful, hypocritical; *subst.* **falsum, ī** *n* falsehood, deceit, fraud, error; *adv.* **falsō.**
falx, cis *f* **a**) sickle, scythe; **b**) wall--hook.
fāma, ae *f* **a**) report, rumour, fame, tradition; **b**) public opinion, popular voice; **c**) reputation, character, renown, infamy, scandal.
famēlicus 3 famished, starved.
famēs, is *f* hunger; **a**) famine; **b**) poverty; **c**) greed.
fāmigerātiō, ōnis *f* report.
fāmigerātor, ōris *m* talebearer.
familia, ae *f* household; slaves, servants; family property, estate; house, family; company, sect.
familiāris, e belonging to a household *or* family, *m* slave; **res ~** estate, property; **a**) familiar, intimate, friendly, *m* friend, companion; **b**) native, belonging to one's own people.
familiāritās, ātis *f* intimacy, familiar intercourse, friendship.
fāmōsus 3 **a**) famous, renowned; **b**) notorious, infamous.
famul = **famulus.**
famula, ae *f* female slave.
famulāris, e of slaves.
famulātus, ūs *m* servitude.
famulor 1 to serve, be a slave.
famulus, ī *m* servant, slave; *as adj.* serving, servile.
fānāticus 3 inspired, enthusiastic; frantic, furious.
fandus, *see* **for.**
fānum, ī *n* temple, sanctuary.
fār, farris *n* spelt, corn, grain; **a**) grits; **b**) bread.
farciō, sī, tum 4 to stuff, cram.
farferum, ī *n* colt's-foot.
farīna, ae *f* meal, flour; quality of material, character.
farrāgō, inis *f* mixed fodder; medley.

farrātus 3 filled with meal; *subst.* **-tum** *n* porridge.
fartim (*acc.*) stuffing, contents; **-tem** mincemeat.
fartor, ōris *m* sausage-maker; fattener of fowls.
fās *n* (*indecl.*) divine law; the dictates of religion; **a**) what is right, proper, allowable, lawful, permitted; **b**) divine will.
fascia, ae *f* band, bandage, head--band; sock; swaddling-band; brassière; bed-girth; wisp of cloud.
fasciculus, ī *m* small bundle *or* bunch.
fascinō 1 to enchant, bewitch.
fascinum, ī *n* (*and* **-us, ī** *m*) penis.
fasciō 1 to bandage.
fasciola, ae *f* small bandage.
fascis, is *m* bundle, parcel; **a**) burden, load; **b**) **fascēs** *pl.* bundle of rods with an axe; high office, consulship.
fasēlus, *see* **phaselus.**
fāstī, ōrum *m/pl.*, *see* **fastus²**.
fastīdiō 4 to feel disgust *or* loathing; to dislike, disdain, despise.
fastīdiōsus 3 **a**) full of disgust, disdainful; fastidious, nice; **b**) cloying, disgusting.
fāstīdium, ī *n* a loathing, aversion; haughtiness; fastidiousness, nicety.
fastīgātus 3 sloping; descending; pointed.
fastīgium, ī *n* **a**) slope, declivity, descent, depth; **b**) top *or* gable-end of a building; **c**) height, summit, top; highest point *or* degree, high rank *or* dignity; **d**) chief point.
fastōsus 3 proud, lordly.
fastus¹, ūs *m* pride, haughtiness, disdain, contempt.
fāstus² 3 **a**) **dies** ~ judicial day; **b**) *subst.* **fāstī, ōrum** (*and* **-ūs, uum**) *m/pl.* register of judicial days; calendar, almanac, annals.
fātālis, e a) ordained by fate *or* destiny, decreed, fated; **b**) fatal, dangerous, deadly.
fateor, fassus sum 2 **a**) to confess, own, acknowledge; **b**) to indicate, manifest.
fāti-canus, fāti-cinus 3 prophesying, prophetic.
fāti-dicus 3 prophesying; prophetic; *m* prophet.
fāti-fer 3 deadly.
fatīgātiō, ōnis *f* weariness.
fatīgō 1 **a**) to weary, tire, fatigue; **b**) to vex, harass, torment, plague; to importune; **c**) to pass without rest.
fāti-legus 3 death-gathering.
fāti-loqua, ae *f* prophetess.
fatīscō *and* **-or,** —, — 3 **a**) to open in chinks, to gape *or* crack open; **b**) to grow weak, become exhausted, faint.
fatuitās, ātis *f* silliness, folly.
fātum, ī *n* utterance; **a**) prophetic declaration; **b**) determination of the gods, divine will; destiny, fate, law of nature; ill fate, mishap; destruction, ruin, death.
fatuor 1 to talk foolishly.
fatuus 3 silly, foolish; *subst. m and f* fool, jester.
faucēs, ium *f/pl.* throat, gullet; **a**) defile, pass; **b**) gulf, abyss; **c**) narrow inlet, strait.
Faunus, ī *m* Faun.
faustitās, ātis *f* fertility, prosperity.
faustus 3 fortunate, favourable, auspicious.
fautor (favitor), ōris *m* favourer, furtherer, promoter, protector; applauder.
fautrīx, īcis *f* patroness, protectress.
faux, cis *f*, *see* **fauces.**
favea, ae *f* favourite maidservant.
faveō, fāvī, fautum 2 to favour, to be favourable, promote, befriend (*alci*); **a**) to applaud; **b**) (*linguā*) to favour with the tongue, be silent.
favilla, ae *f* (glowing) ashes; spark (*metaph.*).
favōnius, ī *m* the west-wind.
favor, ōris *m* favour, good-will; applause.
favōrābilis, e winning favour, pleasing, agreeable.
favus, ī *m* honeycomb.
fax, facis *f* torch, firebrand; **a**) nuptial-torch, wedding; **b**) funeral-torch; **c**) fiery meteor, shooting-star; **d**) light, fire, flame; **e**) incitement, cause of ruin.
faxim = **fecerim, faciam** (*subj.*); **faxō** = **fecero, faciam** (*fut.*).
febrīcitō 1 to have a fever.
febricula (ī ?), **ae** *f* (slight) fever.
febrīculōsus 3 sick of a fever.
febris, is *f* fever.
Februārius 3 belonging to February; *m* February.
fēcunditās, ātis *f* fertility.

fēcundō 1 to make fruitful.
fēcundus 3 a) fruitful, fertile; rich, abundant; **b**) fertilizing.
fel, fellis *n* gall, bile; choler; anger, bitterness.
fēlēs *or* **fēlis, is** *f* (wild) cat, marten.
felicātus 3 = **filicatus.**
fēlīcitās, ātis *f* a) fruitfulness, fertility; **b**) happiness, good fortune, luck.
fēlīx, īcis a) fruitful, fertile; **b**) happy, fortunate; **c**) favourable, propitious.
fēl(l)ātor, ōris *m* sucker.
fēl(l)ō 1 to suck.
fēmella, ae *f* woman.
fēmina, ae *f* woman, female.
feminālia, ium *n/pl.* thigh-wrappings.
fēmineus 3 womanly, feminine; womanish.
fēminīnus 3 feminine (*only gram.*).
femur, oris *or* **inis** *n* thigh.
fēnebris, e, *see* **faenebris.**
fēnerātiō, fēneror, *see* **faen...**
fenestella, ae *f* small window *or* gate.
fenestra, ae *f* opening; **a**) window; **b**) loophole, entrance.
fēniculum, ī *n* fennel.
fēnīlia, fēnum, fēnus, *see* **faen...**
fera, ae *f, see* **ferus.**
fērālis, e belonging to the dead, to a funeral; deadly, fatal; *subst.* **fērālia** (and **fĕr-**), **ium** *n/pl.* festival of the dead.
ferāx, ācis fruitful, fertile.
ferculum, ī *n* barrow, litter, bier; dish, course.
ferē *adv.* **a**) nearly, almost, about; **non ferē** scarcely, hardly; **b**) for the most part, in general, quite, entirely.
ferentārius, ī *m* light-armed spear-man; energetic helper.
feretrum, ī *n* litter, bier.
fēriae, ārum *f/pl.* festival days, holidays.
fēriātus 3 keeping holiday, unoccupied, idle, at leisure.
fericulum = **ferculum.**
ferīnus 3 of wild beasts; (*caro*) **-a, ae** *f* game, venison.
feriō, —, — 4 to strike, beat, thrust, hit; **a**) to strike dead, kill, slay; **b**) **foedus** to make a compact *or* treaty; **c**) to cheat.
fērior 1 to idle, to keep holiday.
feritās, ātis *f* wildness, savageness.
fermē *adv.* = **fere.**
fermentum, ī *n* **a**) leaven, ferment; **b**) beer; **c**) anger.
ferō, tulī, lātum 3 **1.** to bear, carry, bring; a) **ventrem** to be pregnant; b) **prae se ferre** to manifest, show, display, profess; c) to carry about oneself; d) to bear, suffer, endure; **aegre, moleste, graviter** to be angry *or* vexed at; e) to report, make known, relate, say, tell; **ferunt** people say; **fertur** it is said; f) to celebrate, praise; g) to carry away, take off, snatch, plunder, spoil; h) to get, receive, obtain, earn, win; **2.** to bring, carry (*alci alqd*); a) to take, lead, conduct; b) to offer; c) to propose, move (*a law*); d) to require, allow; e) to bring forth, produce, yield; to cause, create; f) to enter *or* note down (*in an account-book*); **3.** to set in motion, move, drive, carry off, take away; **P.** *or* **se ferre** to rush, run, hasten, speed, flow, rise, mount up.
ferōcia, ae *f* high, defiant, *or* headstrong spirit; overbearing behaviour.
ferōcitās, ātis *f* = **ferocia.**
ferōculus 3 = **ferox.**
ferōx, ōcis a) bold, courageous; **b**) spirited, defiant, headstrong, overbearing.
ferrāmenta, ōrum *n/pl.* iron tools.
ferrāria, ae *f* iron-mine.
ferrārius (faber), ī *m* blacksmith.
ferrātilis, e fettered.
ferrātus 3 covered with iron, iron-clad; *m* soldier in armour.
ferreus 3 of iron; **a**) hard, unfeeling, hard-hearted, cruel; **b**) firm, rigid, unyielding.
ferri-crepīnus 3 clanking chains.
ferri-terium, ī *n* place of fettered slaves.
ferri-terus, ī *m,* **ferri-trībāx, ācis** *m* fettered slave.
ferrūgin(e)us 3 rust-coloured; rusty black, dusky; blue-green (*like verdigris*).
ferrūgō, inis *f* iron-rust; dark colour; verdigris.
ferrum, ī *n* iron; **a**) iron-tool, *e.g.* axe, ploughshare, knife, scissors, chain, pen, curling-iron; **b**) weapon, sword, arrowhead; **ferrō ignique** with fire and sword.

fertilis, e a) fruitful, fertile, productive; **b**) fertilizing.
fertilitās, ātis *f* fertility.
fertum, ī *n* sacrificial cake.
ferula, ae *f* an umbelliferous plant; rod; goad.
ferus 3 **a**) wild, untamed, uncultivated; **b**) rude, savage, cruel; *subst.* (**ferus, ī** *m*), **fera, ae** *f* wild animal.
fervē-faciō 3 to make hot.
fervēns, tis = **fervidus.**
ferveō, ferbuī, — 2 (*and* **fervō,** —, — 3) to boil; **a**) to boil up, foam, rage; **b**) to swarm forth; to be busy, go on busily; **c**) to glow, burn.
fervēscō 3 to become hot, begin to glow.
fervidus 3 **a**) boiling; **b**) burning, glowing, raging; fiery, hot,. vehement, impetuous.
fervō, —, — 3, *see* **ferveo**.
fervor, ōris *m* **a**) a boiling, violent heat; **b**) a raging; ardour, passion.
fessus 3 tired, wearied, exhausted.
festīnanter *adv.* hastily.
festīnātiō, ōnis *f* haste, hurry.
festīnātō *adv.* = **festinanter.**
festīnō 1 **a**) *intr.* to make haste, hasten, be quick; **b**) *trans.* to hasten, make haste with.
festīnus 3 hasty, quick.
festīvitās, ātis *f* **a**) gaiety; **b**) humour, pleasantry.
fēstīvus 3 festive, gay; **a**) pretty, agreeable, pleasant; **b**) humorous, witty; **c**) kind.
festūca, ae *f* rod used by a praetor in freeing slaves.
festūcula, ae *f* pile-driver.
fēstus 3 solemn, festive, festal; *subst.* **fēstum, ī** *n* festival, holiday, feast.
fēteō 2 to stink.
fētiālis, e belonging to the college of the **fētiālēs** (**ium** *m*), diplomatic negotiators.
fētidus 3 stinking, fetid.
fētor, ōris *m* stench.
fētūra, ae *f* **a**) a bringing forth, breeding; **b**) offspring.
fētus[1] 3 pregnant, breeding; **a**) productive, fertile, full of (*abl.*); **b**) *f* **-a** that has brought forth, newly delivered.
fētus[2], **ūs** *m* a bringing forth, bearing; **a**) growth; **b**) production, offspring, progeny; **c**) fruit, produce.
fiber, brī *m* beaver.
fibra, ae *f* **a**) fibre, filament; lobe of lungs *or* liver; **b**) *pl.* entrails.
fībula, ae *f* clasp, buckle, brooch, brace.
fīcēdula (*and* **fīcĕ-**), **ae** *f* a small bird.
fīcētum, ī *n* **a**) fig-orchard; **b**) a crop of piles.
fīcōsus 3 suffering from piles.
fictilis, e made of clay, earthen; *subst.* **-e, is** *n* earthen vessel *or* ware.
fictiō, ōnis *f* invention; formation.
fictor, ōris *m*, **fictrīx, īcis** *f* moulder; **a**) sculptor; **b**) baker of sacrificial cakes.
fictūra, ae *f* a forming, fashioning.
fictus 3 formed, fashioned; **a**) feigned, fictitious; **b**) false, dissembling; **c**) = **fīxus**; *subst.* **fictum, ī** *n* deception, fiction, lie.
fīculnus 3 of a fig-tree.
fīculus, ī *f* little fig.
fīcus, ī *and* **ūs** *f* **a**) fig-tree; **b**) fig; **c**) ~, **ī** *m* piles, haemorrhoids.
fidēlia, ae *f* earthen vessel, pot.
fidēlis, e a) faithful, trusty, sincere; **b**) sure, safe, strong.
fidēlitās, ātis *f* faithfulness, trustiness.
fīdēns, tis confident, bold.
fīdentia, ae *f* confidence.
fidēs[1], **ēī** (*and* **-ĕī**) *f* **1.** a) trust, faith, confidence, belief; **fidem habere** to place confidence in, **fidem facere** *alci* to produce confidence; (*in business*) credit; b) good faith, sincerity, trustworthiness, credibility, faithfulness, conscientiousness, **ex bona fidē** in good faith; c) fulfilment, assurance, confirmation, proof; **2.** a) promise, engagement, word of honour, pledge; b) protection, safe-conduct, guardian care, **in alcis fidem venire** to surrender at discretion.
fidēs[2], **is** *f* **1.** lyre-string; **2.** (*mostly* **fidēs, ium** *f/pl.*) stringed instrument.
fidi-cen, inis *m* lute-player, harpist; lyric poet.
fidi-cina, ae *f* female lute-player.
fidi-cinius 3 of lute-playing.
fidicula, ae *f* small lute; instrument of torture.
fidius, ī *m* the god of faith, **mēdius fidius!** by the god of truth!

fīdō, fīsus sum 3 to confide, trust (*alci; alqa re*); to venture (*inf.*).
fīdūcia, ae *f* **1.** trust, confidence, reliance, assurance; self-reliance; **2.** a) trustiness; b) deposit, pledge, mortgage.
fīdūciārius 3 intrusted.
fīdus 3 = **fidelis.**
fīgō, xī, xum 3 **1.** to fix, fasten, drive in (*alqd in re, in* or *ad rem*), attach, affix; a) to post up, bill; b) to hang up; **2.** a) to transfix, pierce through.
figulāris, e of a potter.
figulus, ī *m* potter; bricklayer.
figūra, ae *f* form, shape, figure; **a**) beauty; **b**) image, appearance; **c**) kind, nature, quality; **d**) figure of speech.
figūrō 1 to form, fashion.
fīlātim thread by thread.
fīlia, ae *f* daughter.
filicātus 3 adorned with fern.
fīliola, ae *f* little daughter.
fīliolus, ī *m* little son.
fīlius, ī *m* son, child.
filix, icis *f* fern, bracken.
fīlum[1]**, ī** *n* thread, yarn; **a**) fillet of wool; **b**) string, cord, fibre, wick; **c**) texture.
fīlum[2]**, ī** *n* figure, shape, outline; manner.
fimbriae, ārum *f/pl.* fringe, curl.
fimbriātus 3 fringed.
fimum, ī *n and* **fimus, ī** *m* dung, manure; dirt.
findō, fidī, fissum 3 to cleave, split, separate, divide.
fingō, finxī, fictum 3 to form, fashion, shape, frame; **a**) to make, mould, represent, **ars fingendī** sculpture, art of statuary; **b**) to arrange, set to rights, **se fingere** *ad alqd* to regulate oneself; **c**) to instruct, teach, train; **d**) to make into something; **e**) to imagine, conceive, think; **f**) to devise, invent, feign, pretend.
fīniēns, tis *m* (*sc.* orbis) horizon.
fīniō 4 to limit, bound, enclose; **a**) to restrain, check; **b**) to determine, prescribe, appoint; **c**) to put an end to, finish, terminate; **d**) to cease speaking; **e**) to cease, end, die; **P.** to come to an end; **fīnītus** 3 limited, restricted; rhythmical.
fīnis, is *m* (*and f*) boundary, limit, border; **fīne** (*with gen.*) up to, as far as; **a**) *pl.* borders, territory, land, country; **b**) *fig.* limit, end, termination, limitation; **c**) end purpose, aim, object; **d**) extremity, highest point *or* degree, **bonōrum** chief good; **e**) end, close, stop; **fīnem facere** to make an end; death.
fīnitimus (**-umus**) 3 bordering upon, adjoining, neighbouring (*alci*); connected with, nearly related; *m* neighbour.
fīnītor, ōris *m* surveyor.
fīō, factus sum, fierī 1. to grow, spring up; a) to be born *or* created; b) to happen, come to pass; **fieri potest, ut** it is possible that; **fieri non potest quin** it is indispensable, inevitable that; **2. P.** *of* **facere:** a) to be made; b) to be turned into, appointed; c) to be estimated.
firmāmen, inis *n* support.
firmāmentum, ī *n* support, prop, stay; main point.
firmātor, ōris *m* one who makes firm.
firmitās, ātis *and* **-tūdō, inis** *f* firmness, strength; steadfastness, constancy, endurance.
firmiter *adv. of* **firmus.**
firmō 1 to make firm *or* strong; **a**) to strengthen, fortify (*alqa re*); **b**) to encourage, animate; **c**) to confirm, assert, affirm, prove.
firmus 3 firm, fast, strong, powerful (*ad alqd*); steadfast, constant, trusty, lasting, faithful; *adv.* **firmē** (*and* **firmiter**).
fiscālis, e belonging to the state-treasury.
fiscella, ae *f* small basket.
fiscina, ae *f* basket.
fiscus, ī *m* money-basket, money-bag; a) treasury, public chest; **b**) imperial treasury.
fissilis, e (that may be) cleft.
fissiō, ōnis *f* a cleaving.
fissum, ī *n* cleft, fissure.
fistūca, ae *f* pile-driver.
fistula, ae *f* pipe; **a**) waterpipe; **b**) shepherd's pipe; **c**) ulcer, fistula; **d**) writing-reed.
fistulātor, ōris *m* piper.
fistulātus 3 fitted with tubes *or* pipes.
fīsus 3, *see* **fido.**

fitilla, ae *f* pap, soft food used at a sacrifice.
fixus 3 fixed, immovable.
flābelli-fera, ae *f* fan-bearer.
flābellulum, ī *n* little fan.
flābellum, ī *n* fan, fly-flap.
flābilis, e airy, breath-like.
flābra, ōrum *n/pl.* breezes, winds.
flacceō, —, — 2 to be languid, flag.
flaccēscō, —, — 3 to flag.
flaccidus 3 feeble.
flaccus 3 flabby; flap-eared.
flagellō 1 to whip, scourge, lash.
flagellum, ī *n* whip, scourge; **a**) thong of a javelin; **b**) vineshoot; **c**) arm of a polypus.
flāgitātiō, ōnis *f* pressing demand, request, importunity.
flāgitātor, ōris *m* demander, dun.
flāgitiōsus 3 shameful, disgraceful, infamous, profligate.
flāgitium, ī *n* **a**) shameful act, outrage; **b**) shame, disgrace; **c**) rascal, scoundrel.
flāgitō 1 to ask *or* demand urgently, entreat (*alqd ab alqo* or *alqm alqd; ut, ne*); **a**) to require; **b**) to demand to know; **c**) to summon, accuse.
flagrāns, tis burning, flaming, blazing; **a**) glowing; **b**) hot, vehement, passionate, eager.
flagrantia, ae *f* glow, heat.
flagri-triba, ae *m* whipped slave.
flagrō 1 to burn, flame, blaze; **a**) to glitter, shine; **b**) to glow, be inflamed with passion, be excited (*alqa re*).
flagrum, ī *n* whip, scourge.
flāmen[1], **inis** *n* a blowing, blast, breath, breeze, wind.
flāmen[2], **inis** *m* priest of a particular deity, *flamen.*
flāminica, ae *f* wife of a *flamen.*
flāminium, ī *n* office of a *flamen.*
flamma, ae *f* flame, blaze; **a**) torch, lightning, star; **b**) fire, glow, heat, glare; **c**) flame of passion, fire of love; **d**) destructive fire, ruin.
flammārius, ī *m* maker of bride's veils.
flammeolum, ī *n* bridal veil.
flammēscō 3 to become fiery.
flammeum, ī *n* bride's veil.
flammeus 3 flaming, fiery(-red).
flammi-fer *and* **-ger** 3 = **flammeus.**
flammō 1 **a**) *intr.* to burn, flame; **b**) *trans.* to burn, consume; to heat, inflame.
flammula, ae *f* little flame.
flāmōnium, ī *n* office of a *flamen.*
flātus, ūs *m* a blowing, breathing; **a**) breeze, wind; **b**) breath, snorting; **c**) haughtiness.
flāvēns, tis = **flavus.**
flāvēscō 3 to become yellow.
flāvus 3 (golden-)yellow, brownish *or* reddish yellow.
flēbilis, e a) lamentable, deplorable, pitiable; **b**) weeping, tearful.
flectō, xī, xum 3 **1.** to bend, turn round, curve; a) to bend, move, persuade, prevail upon, influence; b) to double, pass round; to apply to; **2.** to wind, contort; a) to turn, direct, change (*alqd in alqd*); b) *intr.* to turn, go, march, direct one's course; **flexus** 3 bent, curved, winding.
flēmina, um *n/pl.* swellings in the ankles.
fleō, ēvī, ētum 2 **a**) to weep, cry; **b**) to bewail, lament (*acc.*).
flētus, ūs *m* **a**) a weeping, wailing, lamenting; **b**) tears.
flex-animus 3 **a**) affecting, touching; **b**) touched, affected.
flexibilis, e flexible, pliant; **a**) tractable; **b**) inconstant, fickle.
flexilis, e pliant, pliable.
flexi-loquus 3 ambiguous.
flexiō, ōnis *f* a bending; **a**) shift, excuse; **b**) modulation of the voice.
flexi-pēs, edis with crooked feet.
flexuōsus 3 winding, tortuous.
flexūra, ae *f* a bending, winding.
flexus, ūs *m* a bending, turn; **a**) a winding, curve; **b**) crooked way; **c**) transition, change.
flīctus, ūs *m* a striking, collision.
flō 1 **a**) *intr.* to blow; to sound; **b**) *trans.* to blow at, out, up *or* away; to melt, cast, coin.
floccus, ī *m* flock of wool; trifle.
flōrēns, tis blooming, flowering, flourishing; **a**) shining, bright; **b**) in the prime, in repute, excellent; **c**) flowery.
flōreō, uī, — 2 to bloom, blossom; **a**) to shine, glitter; to froth (*wine*); **b**) to flourish, be prosperous, in the prime, in repute, distinguished.
flōrēscō 3 to begin to blossom.
flōreus 3 of flowers, flowery.
flōridulus 3 blooming.
flōridus 3 **a**) blooming; **b**) flowery.
flōri-fer 3 flower-bearing.

flōri-legus 3 culling flowers.
flōrus 3 blond.
flōs, ōris *m* flower, blossom; **a**) flower-juice; honey; **b**) flourishing condition, prime, best part, top, crown, freshness, splendour, glory, ornament, innocence; downy beard.
flōsculus, ī *m* little flower, floweret; pride, ornament.
flucti-fragus 3 wave-breaking.
flucti-sonus 3 resounding with waves.
flucti-vagus 3 wandering *or* moving in waves.
fluctuātiō, ōnis *f* a wavering, agitation.
fluctuō 1 (*and* **-uor**) to wave, undulate; to waver, hesitate.
fluctuōsus 3 full of waves.
fluctus, ūs *m* a flowing; flood, billow, surge; commotion; disturbance.
fluēns, tis a) flowing, fluent; **b**) lax, enervated, effeminate; **c**) unrestrained.
fluenti-sonus 3 resounding with waves.
fluentum, ī *n* flow, stream.
fluidus 3 flowing, fluid; **a**) lax, languid; **b**) dissolving.
fluitō 1 to flow; **a**) to float, swim; **b**) to wave, undulate; **c**) to waver.
flūmen, inis *n* **a**) stream, flood, flowing water; **b**) river; **c**) flow of words.
flūmineus 3 of a river.
fluō, uxī, (uxum) 3 to flow, stream; **a**) to drip, run down (*alqa re*); **b**) to stream forth *or* along, to spread; **c**) to pass, pass away, proceed; to flow away, vanish, dissolve, perish; **d**) to fall down, flow down, sink.
flūtō 1 = **fluitō.**
fluviā(ti)lis, e of a river.
flūvidus (*and* **flŭvidus**) 3 = **fluidus.**
fluvius, ī *m* river.
fluxus 3 flowing; **a**) loose, slack; **b**) frail, weak, transient, perishable; **c**) impaired.
fōcāle, is *n* neck-cloth.
fōcil(l)ō 1 to warm, restore to life.
fōculum, ī *n* warming-pan.
foculus, ī *m* fire-pan; fire.
focus, ī *m* **a**) fire-place, hearth; **b**) fire-pan, altar; **c**) funeral pile; **d**) home, family.
fodicō 1 to dig, prick, wound.
fodiō, fōdī, fossum 3 **a**) to dig, dig up; **b**) to prick, pierce.
foederātus 3 allied.
foedi-fragus 3 league-breaking.
foeditās, ātis *f* foulness, hideousness, ugliness
foedō 1 to make foul; **a**) to defile, pollute; **b**) to disgrace, disfigure, mar.
foedus[1] 3 foul, filthy, ugly, repulsive, detestable, horrible.
foedus[2], **eris** *n* compact, treaty, league, alliance; **a**) agreement, stipulation; **b**) promise.
foetidus 3 *and* **foetor, ōris** *m*, *see* **fet...**
foliātum, ī *n* unguent made from leaves of spikenard.
folium, ī *n* leaf; foliage.
folliculus, ī *m* little bag, sack; **a**) inflated ball; **b**) pod, shell; egg-shell.
follis, is *m* **a**) purse; **b**) bellows; **c**) punch-ball; **d**) puffed-out cheeks.
follītus 3 in a sack.
fōmentum, ī *n* poultice, bandage; alleviation, mitigation.
fōmes, itis *m* touchwood, tinder.
fōns, tis *m* **a**) spring, fountain, well, source; **b**) origin, cause.
fontānus 3 of a spring *or* fountain.
fonticulus, ī *m* little spring.
for, fātus sum 1 **a**) to say, speak; **fandō audīre** to know by hearsay; **b**) to foretell, prophesy; *subst.* **fandum, ī** *n* right.
forābilis, e that can be bored through, vulnerable.
forāmen, inis *n* hole, opening, aperture.
forās *adv.* out of doors, forth, out.
for-ceps, ipis *f* (*and m*) pair of tongs, pincers.
forda, ae *f* cow in calf.
fore = **futurum esse; forem** = **essem.**
forēnsis, e belonging to the forum *or* market-place; public, forensic.
forfex, icis *f* scissors.
forica, ae *f* public latrine.
foris[1], **is** *f* (leaf of a) door, gate, *pl.* folding-doors, entrance.
forīs[2] *adv.* **a**) out of doors, without, abroad; in public; **b**) from without, from abroad.

fōrma, ae *f* form, shape, figure, appearance; **a**) fine form, beauty; **b**) quality, condition, sort, species; **c**) image, representation, outline, sketch; **d**) model, pattern, shoemaker's last; **e**) stamp, coin.
fōrmālis, e formal, official.
fōrmāmenta, ōrum *n/pl.* shapes.
fōrmātiō, ōnis *f* formation.
fōrmātor, ōris *m* former, fashioner.
fōrmātūra, ae *f* fashioning.
formīca, ae *f* ant.
formīcīnus 3 ant-like.
formīdābilis, e terrible, formidable.
formīdō[1] 1 to fear (*alqd*), be afraid of *or* terrified; **formīdātus** 3 feared.
formīdō[2], **inis** *f* **a**) fear, terror, dread; **b**) that which produces fear, fright.
formīdolōsus 3 **a**) fearful, dreadful; **b**) afraid, timid.
fōrmō 1 to form, shape, fashion; **a**) to make, produce; **b**) to regulate, direct, prepare.
fōrmōnsus = **formosus.**
fōrmōsitās, ātis *f* beauty.
fōrmōsus 3 finely formed, beautiful.
fōrmula, ae *f* fine form, beauty; **a**) rule, prescription; **b**) form of contract, agreement, regulation; **c**) formula, lawsuit, judicial proceedings; **d**) principle.
fornācālis, e belonging to an oven.
fornācula, ae *f* furnace.
fornāx, ācis *f* furnace, oven, kiln.
fornicātus 3 arched, vaulted.
fornix, icis *m* arch, vault; **a**) vaulted opening; **b**) triumphal arch; **c**) brothel.
forō 1 to bore, pierce.
forpex, icis *f* tongs.
fors *f* (*only nom.* and *abl. sg.* **forte**) chance, hap, luck, hazard, accident; **fors** (as *adv.*) perhaps; **forte** by chance, as it happens (happened).
(**fors-an, forsit,**) **forsitan** *adv.* perhaps.
fortasse (**fortassis**) *adv.* perhaps, probably, possibly.
forticulus 3 somewhat brave.
fortis, e strong, vigorous; **a**) enduring, firm; **b**) brave, bold, courageous, manly.
fortitūdō, inis *f* **a**) strength, force; **b**) manliness, firmness, fortitude, bravery, courage, boldness.
fortuītus 3 (*adv.* **-ō**) casual, accidental.
fortūna, ae *f* fate, fortune, luck; **a**) good *or* bad fortune; **b**) **F** ~ the Goddess of Fate; **c**) prosperity; misfortune, adversity; **d**) state, condition, circumstances, fate, lot, position, rank; **e**) (*mostly pl.*) property, possessions.
fortūnō 1 to make prosperous *or* happy; **fortūnātus** 3 prosperous, lucky, happy, fortunate; wealthy, rich.
foruli, ōrum *m/pl.* book-case.
forum, ī *n* **a**) open space; **b**) market-place, market, market-town; **c**) the forum; public affairs; **d**) the courts, jurisdiction; **e**) commerce.
forus, ī *m* (*mostly pl.*) **a**) gangway in a ship; **b**) row of seats in a theatre; **c**) row of bee-cells; **d**) dice-board.
fossa, ae *f* ditch, trench, canal; **a**) pit; **b**) furrow; **c**) watercourse, river-bed.
fossiō, ōnis *f* a digging.
fossor, ōris *m* digger, navvy.
fossūra, ae *f* a digging.
fovea, ae *f* pitfall, pit.
foveō, fōvī, fōtum 2 **a**) to keep warm, to warm; **b**) to cherish, foster, fondle, caress, love.
frāctus 3 broken; weakened, feeble, faint.
fragilis, e a) easily broken, brittle; weak, frail, perishable; **b**) crackling.
fragilitās, ātis *f* weakness, frailty.
fragmen, inis *n* = **fragmentum.**
fragmentum, ī *n* broken piece, fragment, remnant; *pl.* ruins, wreck; faggots.
fragor, ōris *m* **a**) crashing, crash, noise; **b**) breaking.
fragōsus 3 broken; **a**) rough, uneven; **b**) roaring; **c**) brittle.
fragrō 1 to smell (sweet).
frāgum, ī *n* wild strawberry.
framea, ae *f* spear, javelin.
frango, frēgī, frāctum 3 to break *or* dash to pieces, shiver, shatter; **a**) to grind, bruise, crush; **b**) to break (*a promise*); **c**) to break down, subdue; **d**) to weaken, diminish, violate; **e**) to soften, move, touch.
frāter, tris *m* brother (*pl.* brother and sister); **a**) cousin, brother-in-law; **b**) fellow, companion.
frāterculus, ī *m* little brother.
frāternitās, ātis *f* brotherhood.

frāternus 3 of a brother, brotherly, fraternal; **a**) belonging to a relation *or* kinsman; **b**) friendly, allied.
frātri-cīda, ae *m* fratricide.
fraudātiō, ōnis *f* a cheating, deceit.
fraudātor, ōris *m* cheat, deceiver.
fraudō 1 **a**) to deceive, cheat, defraud (*alqm re*); **b**) to embezzle, purloin.
fraudulentia, ae *f* deceitfulness.
fraudulentus 3 deceitful.
fraus, dis *f* a cheating, deceit, imposition, fraud; **a**) self-deception, error, mistake; **b**) injury, damage; **c**) offence, crime.
frausus sit (*depon.*) = **fraudāverit.**
fraxineus (*and* **fraxinus**[1]) 3 of ashwood.
fraxinus[2], **ī** *f* ash-tree; spear, javelin.
fremebundus 3 roaring, snorting, murmuring.
fremidus 3 noisy.
fremitus, ūs *m* a roaring, rushing, noise, murmuring.
fremō, uī, (itum) 3 to growl, resound, roar, murmur, rage, howl, snort, mutter, neigh, grumble.
fremor, ōris *m* a roaring, murmuring.
frēnātor, ōris *m* bridler; hurler.
frendō, —, frēsum 3 (**frendeō, —, —** 2) to gnash the teeth.
frēniger 3 bearing bridles.
frēnō 1 to furnish with a bridle; to bridle, curb, restrain, check.
frēnum, ī *n* (*pl. usually* **-ī, ōrum** *m*) bridle, curb, bit.
frequēns, tis numerous, full, crowded; **a**) populous, much frequented, filled; **b**) frequent, repeated, common, usual.
frequentātiō, ōnis *f* piling up.
frequentia, ae *f* crowding together, concourse, throng.
frequentō 1 **a**) to visit often *or* in crowds; to frequent, attend; **b**) to assemble in numbers, bring together; to fill with a multitude, to crowd, people; **c**) to do often, to repeat.
fretēnsis, e belonging to the Straits of Sicily.
fretum, ī *n* strait, sound, channel; sea; (*metaph.*) seething flood.
fretus[1], **ūs** *m* = **fretum.**
frētus[2] 3 leaning on, supported; relying on, trusting.
fricō, cuī, c(ā)tum 1 to rub.
frīctus 3, *see* **frigo.**
frīge-factō 1 to make cold *or* cool.
frīgeō, (xī), — 2 to be cold *or* chill; **a**) to be inactive, languid, lifeless; **b**) to be coldy received, disregarded.
frīgerō 1 to cool, refresh.
frīgēscō, —, — 3 to grow cold.
frīgidārius 3 for cooling.
frīgidulus 3 somewhat cold *or* languid.
frīgidus 3 cold, cool, chill; *subst. f* cold water; **a**) chilling; **b**) remiss, inactive, indolent, feeble; **c**) dull, insipid, trivial.
frīgō, xī, ctum 3 to roast.
frīgus, oris *n* cold; **a**) frost; **b**) cold shudder; **c**) inactivity, slowness; **d**) cold reception; loss of favour.
friguttiō 4 to chatter, babble.
fringillus, ī *m* finch *or* sparrow.
friō 1 to crumble.
frit (*indecl.*) the tip of an ear of corn.
fritillus, ī *m* dice-box.
frīvolus 3 empty, trifling, worthless; *subst. n/pl.* paltry possessions.
frondātor, ōris *m* pruner.
frondeō, —, — 2 to be in leaf, become green.
frondēscō, —, — 3 to put forth leaves.
frondeus 3 covered with leaves.
frondi-fer 3 leafy.
frondōsus 3 full of leaves.
frōns[1], **dis** *f* leaves, foliage; leafy bough, garland of leaves.
frōns[2], **tis** *f* (*and m*) forehead, brow, front, countenance; **b**) forepart, face; **c**) outside, exterior; appearance.
frontālia, ium *n/pl.* frontlet.
frontō, ōnis *m* with a large forehead.
frūctuārius 3 liable to payment out of the produce.
frūctuōsus 3 fruitful, productive; profitable, gainful.
frūctus, ūs *m* **a**) enjoyment, satisfaction; **b**) fruit, produce; profit, gain, income, return.
frūgālis, e (*only comp.* **-lior** *and superl.* **-lissimus,** *adv.* **-liter**) = **frugi.**
frūgālitās, ātis *f* thrift(iness), orderliness; temperance.
frūgēs, um *pl. of* **frux.**
frūgī (*dat. of* **frux,** *used as adj.*) thrifty, frugal; temperate, honest, worthy, virtuous (*see* **frugalis**).

frūgi-fer 3 fruit-bearing.
frūgi-ferēns, tis fruitful.
frūgi-legus 3 grain-gathering.
frūgi-parus 3 corn-producing.
frūmentārius 3 of *or* producing corn, of provisions; *subst.* ~, **ī** *m* corndealer.
frūmentātiō, ōnis *f* a providing of corn, foraging, distribution of corn.
frūmentātor, ōris *m* purchaser of corn; forager.
frūmentor 1 to fetch corn, to forage.
frūmentum, ī *n* corn, grain, wheat.
frūnīscor 3 to enjoy.
fruor, (frūctus *and* **fruitus sum)** 3, *fut. part.* **fruitūrus,** to make use of, enjoy, delight in (*abl.*); to have the use of.
frustillātim *adv.* in pieces.
frūstrā *adv.* **a**) in error; **b**) in vain, for nothing; **c**) without reason, groundlessly.
frūstrāmen, inis *n* deception.
frūstrātiō, ōnis *f* deception, disappointment; a delaying.
frūstrātus, ūs *m* deceiving.
(**frūstrō** *and*) **frūstror** 1 to deceive, disappoint, elude, frustrate.
frustulentus 3 full of morsels.
frustum, ī *n* piece, bit.
frutex, icis *m* **a**) shrub, bush; **b**) blockhead.
fruticētum, ī *n* thicket.
(**fruticō** *and*) **fruticor** 1 to put forth shoots.
fruticōsus 3 full of shrubs, bushy.
frūx, ūgis *f* (*usually pl.* **frūgēs, um**) fruit, produce; **a**) fruits of the earth *or* of trees; **b**) result, success, value.
fuam, fuās, fuat = **sim, sis, sit.**
fūcō 1 to dye (red), paint; to falsify.
fūcōsus 3 counterfeit, spurious.
fūcus[1], **ī** *m* rock-lichen; **a**) red colour; **b**) propolis, bee-glue; **c**) disguise, deceit, dissimulation.
fūcus[2], **ī** *m* drone.
fuga, ae *f* a fleeing, flight, running away; **a**) banishment, exile; **b**) desire to escape; **c**) an avoiding, shunning, aversion; **d**) swift motion, speed.
fugāx, ācis fleeing, swift, fleet; **a**) timid, shy; **b**) shunning, avoiding; **c**) transitory.
fugiō, fūgī, fugitum 3 **1.** to flee, fly, take flight, run away, escape, be off; a) to become an exile *or* fugitive, to leave the country; b) to vanish, disappear, pass away, perish; **2.** to flee from (*alqm*); a) to avoid, shun, desire to escape; b) to escape, flee away from, elude, forsake, omit, forbear; c) to escape the notice of, be unobserved by, unknown to; **me fūgit** I failed to notice.
fugitīvus 3 fleeing away, fugitive; *m* runaway slave.
fugitō 1 to flee in haste; to avoid, shun.
fugitor, ōris *m* runaway, deserter.
fugō 1 to put to flight, drive away.
fulcīmen, inis *n* prop, support, pillar.
fulciō, lsī, ltum 4 to prop up, stay, support; to secure, sustain, uphold.
fulcrum, ī *n* bedpost, foot of a couch; couch.
fulgeō, lsī, — 2 (*and* **fulgō** 3) to flash, lighten; **a**) to shine, glitter, gleam, glare; **b**) to be conspicuous.
fulgidus 3 flashing.
fulgor, ōris *m* **a**) lightning, flash of lightning; **b**) brightness, splendour; glory.
fulgur, uris *n* **a**) lightning, flash of lightning; **b**) brightness.
fulgurālis, e pertaining to lightning.
fulgurātor, ōris *m* interpreter of lightning.
fulgurītus 3 struck by lightning.
fulgurō 1 to lighten.
fulica, ae *f* coot (*or* cormorant?).
fūlīgō, inis *f* soot; black paint.
fulix, icis *f* = **fulica.**
fullō, ōnis *m* fuller.
fullōnia, ae *f* trade of a fuller.
fullōnius 3 pertaining to a fuller.
fulmen, inis *n* **a**) flash *or* stroke of lightning; thunderbolt; **b**) fiery flashing; **c**) destructive power, crushing blow.
fulmenta, ae *f* heel of a shoe.
fulmineus 3 belonging to lightning; **a**) sparkling, brilliant; **b**) destructive.
fulminō 1 to lighten.
fultūra, ae *f* prop, support.
fulvus 3 reddish yellow, tawny.
fūmeus 3, **fūmidus** 3, **fūmi-fer** 3 smoking, smoky.
fūmi-ficō 1 to burn incense.
fūmi-ficus 3 steaming, smoking.
fūmō 1 to smoke, steam.
fūmōsus 3 full of smoke, smoky, smoked.

fūmus, ī *m* smoke, steam, vapour.
fūnāle, is *n* **a**) thong of a sling; **b**) wax-torch; **c**) candelabrum.
fūnālis, e tied by a rope.
fūn-ambulus, ī *m* rope-walker.
fūnctiō, ōnis *f* performance, execution.
funda, ae *f* sling; sling-stone; casting-net.
(**fundāmen, inis** *n and*) **fundāmentum, ī** *n* foundation, base.
fundātor, ōris *m* founder.
funditō 1 to shoot with a sling, to hurl, pour out (words).
funditor, ōris *m* slinger.
funditus *adv.* from the bottom, completely, entirely.
fundō[1] 1 **a**) to make a foundation for; **b**) to found, secure, establish, confirm; **fundātus** 3 established, firm.
fundō[2], **fūdī, fūsum** 3 to pour out, shed; to melt, cast, found; **a**) to pour forth, scatter, hurl, spread; **b**) to utter; **c**) to bring forth, produce, bear, yield; **d**) to overthrow, overcome, rout, beat; **e**) to throw down, prostrate.
fundus, ī *m* bottom, ground; **a**) piece of land, farm; **b**) foundation; **c**) authority, one who sanctions.
fūnebris, e a) belonging to a funeral, funeral; **b**) deadly, mortal, fatal.
fūnereus 3 = **funebris.**
fūnerō 1 to bury; to kill.
fūnestō 1 to pollute (by death).
fūnestus 3 **a**) polluted by death; in mourning; **b**) deadly; destructive, fatal.
fungīnus 3 of mushrooms.
fungor, fūnctus sum 3 to busy oneself with, be engaged (*abl.*); **a**) to perform, execute, administer, discharge; **b**) to complete, finish; **c**) to suffer.
fungus, ī *m* mushroom; candle-snuff.
fūniculus, ī *m* cord, string.
fūnis, is *m* (*and f*) rope, cord, line.
fūnus, eris *n* funeral, burial, funeral procession; **a**) bier; **b**) corpse, dead body; **c**) death, murder; destruction, ruin.
fur, fūris *m and f* thief; rogue.
fūrāx, ācis thievish.
furca, ae *f* fork; forked prop.
furci-fer, erī *m* rascal.
furcilla, ae *f* hay-fork.
furcillō 1 to pitchfork.
furcula, ae *f* **a**) forked prop; **b**) narrow pass.
furenter *adv.* furiously.
furfur, uris *m* **a**) chaff; **b**) bran.
furia, ae *f* rage, fury, madness; **a**) violent passion, desire; **b**) Goddess of Revenge, Fury.
furiālis, e of the Furies; **a**) furious, raging; **b**) infuriating.
furibundus 3 furious, raging; inspired.
fūrīnus 3 of thieves.
furiō 1 to madden, infuriate.
furiōsus 3 mad, furious.
furnāria, ae *f* baker's trade.
furnus, ī *m* (baker's) oven, fireplace.
furō, —, — 3 to rage, revel, be mad *or* furious.
furor[1], **ōris** *m* rage, madness, fury, passion; **a**) passionate love; **b**) frenzy, inspiration.
fūror[2] 1 to steal (*alqd alci, ab alqo, ex re*), purloin, pilfer; to withdraw secretly.
fūrti-ficus 3 thievish.
fūrtim *adv.* by stealth, secretly.
fūrtīvus 3 **a**) stolen; **b**) secret, furtive.
fūrtum, ī *n* theft; **a**) a stolen thing; **b**) secret action, deceit, trick, artifice; **c**) stratagem; love intrigue.
fūrunculus, ī *m* petty thief.
furvus 3 black, dark, gloomy.
fuscina, ae *f* trident.
fuscō 1 to blacken.
fuscus 3 **a**) dark brown; black; dark; **b**) husky, indistinct.
fūsilis, e molten, fluid.
fūsiō, ōnis *f* an outpouring.
fūstis, is *m* cudgel, club.
fūstitudīnus 3 cudgelling.
fūstuārium, ī *n* a cudgelling to death.
fūsus[1], **ī** *m* spindle.
fūsus[2] 3 poured out; **a**) stretched out, prostrate, extended; **b**) flowing, diffuse, free; **c**) copious, full, plump; broad.
fūt(t)ilis, e that cannot hold *or* contain; brittle; vain, worthless, futile.
fūt(t)ilitās, ātis *f* emptiness, silly talk.
futuō 3 to lie with (*acc.*); *hence* **futūtiō, ōnis** *f*; **futūtor, ōris** *m*; **futūtrīx, īcis** *f*.

G

gabata, ae *f* bowl, dish.
gaesum, ī *n* long javelin.
galbaneus 3 of galbanum.
galbanum, ī *n* resinous sap of a Syrian plant, galbanum.
galbinus 3 greenish-yellow; effeminate.
galbinātus 3 dressed in yellow.
galea, ae *f* helmet.
galeō 1 to arm with a helmet.
galēriculum, ī *n* = **galerum.**
galērītus 3 wearing a cap.
galērum, ī *n and* **galērus, ī** *m* skin cap; wig.
galla, ae *f* gall-nut.
gall-iambus, ī *m* song of the *galli* (priests of Cybele).
gallica, ae *f* Gaulish shoe.
gallīna, ae *f* hen.
gallīnāceus 3 of hens, of fowls.
gallīnārius, ī *m* poultry-keeper.
gallus[1], **ī** *m* cock.
gallus[2], **ī** *m* castrated priest of Cybele.
gamēliōn, ōnis *m an Attic month* (*January to February*).
gānea, ae *f and* **-eum, ī** *n* cookshop; public house; brothel.
gāneō, ōnis *m* glutton, debauchee.
ganniō 4 to growl, snarl.
gannītus, ūs *m* growling, snarling.
garriō 4 to chat, prate, talk, chatter.
garrulitās, ātis *f* a chattering, babbling.
garrulus 3 chattering, talkative.
garum, ī *n* fish-sauce.
gaudeō, gāvīsus sum 2 to rejoice, be glad (*alqa re; quod; acc.c.inf.*); to delight in.
gaudium, ī *n* joy, gladness, delight, enjoyment; darling.
gaulus, ī *m* round dish.
gausape, is *and* **-pum, ī** *n* thick woollen cloth; shaggy beard; *hence* **gausapātus** 3 clothed in woollen cloth; **gausapinus** 3 of woollen cloth, **-na, ae** *f* woollen garment.
gaza, ae *f* treasure, wealth.
gelasīnus, ī *m* dimple.
gelidus 3 icy cold; stiff, cold.
gelō 1 to freeze.
gelū, ūs *n* (also **gelum, ī** *n* and **gelus** *m*) frost, cold, ice.
gemebundus 3 groaning, sighing.
gemelli-para, ae *f* twin-bearing.
gemellus 3 = **geminus.**
geminātiō, ōnis *f* a doubling.
geminō 1 to double; **a**) to repeat; **b**) to pair, couple, unite.
geminus 3 double; **a**) twin; **b**) paired, twofold, both, two; **c**) of double nature; **d**) resembling, similar.
gemitus, ūs *m* a groaning, sighing; **a**) a roaring, roar; **b**) sorrow, pain.
gemma, ae *f* **a**) bud, eye; **b**) precious stone, jewel; goblet (*of precious stones*): seal-ring.
gemmātus 3 set with jewels.
gemmeus 3 set with jewels; sparkling, brilliant.
gemmi-fer 3 producing gems.
gemmō 1 **a**) to put forth buds; **b**) to be adorned (as) with precious stones.
gemō, uī, (itum) 3 **a**) to groan, sigh; to moan, creak; **b**) to lament, bewail (*alqd*).
gena, ae *f* **a**) cheek; **b**) socket of the eye, eye.
geneā-logus, ī *m* genealogist.
gener, erī *m* **a**) son-in-law; **b**) brother-in-law.
generālis, e belonging to a kind *or* species, general, of all.
generāscō 3 to be generated.
generātim *adv.* by kinds, by species, by classes; generally, in general.
generātor, ōris *m* breeder, begetter.
generō 1 to beget, procreate, engender, produce.
generōsus 3 **a**) of noble birth, eminent; **b**) superior, excellent, generous, magnanimous.
genesis, is *f* constellation that presides over one's birth.
genesta, ae *f* = **genista.**
genetīvus 3 pertaining to generation *or* birth; original, native.
genetrīx, īcis *f* she who brings forth, mother.
geniālis, e **a**) nuptial, bridal; **b**) pleasant, delightful, joyous, genial.

geniculātus 3 knotty, knotted.
genista, ae *f* broom(-plant).
genitābilis, e generative.
genitālis, e pertaining to generation; fruitful, generative.
genitīvus 3 = **genetivus.**
genitor, ōris *m* begetter, father.
genitrīx, īcis *f* = **genetrix.**
genitūra, ae *f* = **genesis.**
genius, ī *m* **a**) tutelar deity, guardian spirit; one's essential self; **b**) natural inclination, taste; **c**) talent, genius.
genō 3 = **gigno.**
gēns, tis *f* race, family, clan; **a**) descendant, offspring; **b**) kind, species; **c**) tribe, people; community; **d**) region, country; *pl.* **gentēs, ium** foreign nations, barbarians.
genticus 3 national.
gentīlicius 3 belonging to a clan *or* family.
gentīlis, e a) of the same clan *or* family; **b**) national.
gentīlitās, ātis *f* (relationship between) the members of a *gens.*
genū (*and* **genus**), **ūs** *n* knee.
genuāle, is *n* garter.
genuīnus[1] 3 innate, natural.
genuīnus[2] 3 of the cheek *or* jaw; *subst. m* back tooth.
genus, eris *n* **1.** birth, descent, origin, family; a) high descent, noble birth; b) people, nation, tribe; c) race, line; d) posterity, descendants; **2.** gender; **3.** kind, class, sort, species; a) order, division; b) kind, description, character, (*dicendi*) fashion, manner, way, style; c) respect, relation.
geō-graphia, ae *f* geography.
geō-metrēs, ae *m* geometer.
geō-metria, ae *f* geometry.
geōmetricus 3 geometrical.
geōrgicus 3 agricultural.
germānitās, ātis *f* brotherhood, relationship.
germānus 3 full *or* own (*brother or sister*); **a**) brotherly, sisterly; **b**) genuine, real, true.
germen, inis *n* **a**) shoot, bud, graft; **b**) germ, seed; **c**) embryo.
germinō 1 to sprout, bud.
gerō, gessī, gestum 3 **1.** to bear, wear, carry, have, bring; a) **prae se** to exhibit, display; **persōnam alcis** to represent, act the part of; b) to keep, entertain, cherish; c) to bring forth, produce; d) **se gerere** (*with adv.*) to act, behave, deport oneself, conduct oneself; **2.** to carry out, administer, manage, rule, govern, regulate, transact, accomplish, perform; **rem bene gerere** to be successful, manage business well; **bellum gerere** to wage war; **res gestae** exploits; **alci morem gerere** to gratify, humour; **P.** to happen, take place, be done.
gerrae, ārum *f/pl.* trifles, nonsense.
gerrēs, is *m* a cheap kind of sea-fish.
gerrinum(?) = **cerinum.**
gerrō, ōnis *m* trifler, buffoon.
geruli-figulus, ī *m* accomplice.
gerulus, ī *m* carrier, porter.
gestāmen, inis *n* **a**) thing carried *or* worn; **b**) conveyance, carriage.
gestātiō, ōnis *f* a riding *or* driving for pleasure; carriage drive, promenade.
gestātor, ōris *m* (*and* **-trīx, īcis** *f*) bearer; rider in a carriage.
gestātōrius 3 belonging to a *gestator*; **sella -a** sedan-chair.
gesticulātiō, ōnis *f* pantomimic motion, gesticulation.
gesticulor 1 to gesticulate.
gestiō[1], **ōnis** *f* a managing, performing.
gestiō[2] 4 to exult, be joyful, transported; to desire eagerly, long for passionately (*inf.*).
gestitō 1 to be wont to carry.
gestō 1 to carry, bear, wear; **P.** to ride, drive, sail; (*in sinu, pectore*) to cherish, love.
gestor, ōris *m* carrier.
gestus, ūs *m* bearing, carriage; gesture, action.
gibba, ae *f* (*and* **-us, ī** *m*) hunch, hump.
gibber 3 hunched, humped.
gignō, genuī, genitum 3 to beget, produce; to occasion, cause; **gignentia, ium** *n/pl.* growing things, vegetation.
gilvus 3 pale yellow.
gingīva, ae *f* gum (in the mouth).
glaber, bra, brum hairless, smooth; *subst. m* young slave, page.
glabrāria, ae *f* **a**) a lover of smooth-skinned boys; **b)** shorn bare, robbed.
glaciālis, e icy, frozen.
glaciēs, ēī *f* ice, frost.

glaciō 1 to turn into ice.
gladiātor, ōris *m* swordsman, gladiator; robber, bandit; *pl.* combat of gladiators.
gladiātōrius 3 of gladiators; *subst.* **-ium, ī** *n* pay of gladiators.
gladiātūra, ae *f* the fighting of gladiators.
gladius, ī *m* sword; **a**) weapon; **b**) murder.
glaeba, ae *f* clod; earth; lump.
glaebula, ae *f dimin.* of **glaeba.**
glaesum, ī *n* = **glesum.**
glandi-fer 3 acorn-bearing.
glandiōnida, ae *and* **glandula, ae** *f,* **glandium, ī** *n* gland (in meat, as a delicacy).
glāns, dis *f* acorn, nut; acorn--shaped ball.
glārea, ae *f* gravel.
glāreōsus 3 full of gravel.
glaucina, ōrum *n/pl.* a cheap ointment.
glaucōma, atis *n,* **glaucūma, ae** *f* cataract, blindness.
glaucus 3 grey-green; with light--coloured eyes.
glēba, ae *f* = **glaeba.**
glēsum, ī *n* amber.
glīs, īris *m* dormouse.
glīscō, —, — 3 to blaze up, swell up; to grow, increase.
globōsus 3 globular, spherical.
globus, ī *m* ball, globe, sphere; **a**) round heap; **b**) crowd, mass; **c**) union, clique.
glomerāmen, inis *n* round body, ball.
glomerō 1 to form into a ball; to collect, crowd, assemble.
glomus, (*and* **glō-**), **eris** *n* ball of thread.
glōria, ae *f* glory; **a**) fame, renown; **b**) ornament, pride; **c**) glorious deed; **d**) thirst for glory, ambition, boasting.
glōriātiō, ōnis *f* vainglory.
glōriola, ae *f* little glory.
glōrior 1 **a**) to boast, vaunt (*de re, re*); **b**) to pride oneself (*in re*).
glōriōsus 3 **a**) glorious, famous; **b**) boasting.
glūbō (**psī, ptum**) 3 to bark, peel, rob.
glūten, inis *n* glue.
glūtinātor, ōris *m* bookbinder.
gluttiō 4 to swallow.
gluttus, ūs *m* gulp.
gnārus 3 (*and* **gnāruris, e**) **a**) knowing, skilled, practised; **b**) known.
gnātus, gnāvus etc., *see* **natus, navus.**
gōbius, ī (*and* **-iō, ōnis**) *m* groundling, gudgeon.
gomphus, ī *m* peg, pin.
gōrȳtus, *see* **corytus.**
grabātus, ī *m* couch, camp-bed.
gracilis, e (*and* **-us** 3) thin, slender, meagre, lean; **a**) scanty, poor; **b**) plain, simple, unadorned.
gracilitās, ātis *f* slenderness, thinness.
grāculus, ī *m* (jack)daw.
gradārius 3 slow, deliberate.
gradātim *adv.* step by step.
gradātiō, ōnis *f* climax.
gradātus 3 cut in steps.
gradior, gressus sum 3 to step, walk, go.
gradus, ūs *m* step, pace, **gradum conferre** to come to close combat; **a**) a stepping forward, approach, advance; **b**) station, position, stand; **c**) step, stage, degree; *pl.* stairs, ladder; **d**) dignity, rank.
graecissō 1 to copy the Greek style.
graecor 1 to imitate Greek manners.
grallātor, ōris *m* person that walks on stilts.
grāmae, ārum *f* discharge from the eye.
grāmen, inis *n* grass, blade of grass; plant, herb.
grāmineus 3 grassy; of bamboo.
grammaticus 3 of grammar; *subst. m* grammarian, philologist; **grammatica, ae** *f* (*and* **-ca, ōrum** *n/pl.*) grammar.
grānārium, ī *n* granary.
grand-aevus 3 old, aged.
grandēscō, —, — 3 to become great, to grow.
grandiculus 3 fairly big.
grandi-fer 3 productive.
grandi-loquus 3 boastful.
grandinat it hails.
grandiō 4 to make great, increase.
grandis, e a) full-grown, aged, old; **b**) great, tall, full, abundant, strong, weighty; **c**) lofty, dignified.
grandi-scāpius 3 with a large trunk.
granditās, ātis *f* greatness, grandeur.
grandō, inis *f* hail.

grāni-fer 3 grain-bearing.
grānum, ī *n* grain, seed, corn.
graphiārius 3 relating to a writing--style.
graphicus 3 masterly, exquisite.
graphium, ī *n* writing-style.
grassātor, ōris *m* rioter, footpad.
grassātūra, ae *f* a waylaying.
grassor 1 to move about; **a**) to prowl about for mischief, behave riotously; **b**) to act, proceed; **c**) to attack, use violence.
grātēs *f/pl.* thanks, thanksgiving.
grātia, ae *f* **1. a**) charm, loveliness, grace; **b**) favour, credit, influence, regard; **grātiam inīre** *ab alqo* find favour; c) friendship, love; **in grātiam redīre** *cum alqo* to be reconciled; **2.** favour, kindness, courtesy, service; **grātiam facere** to excuse (*alci alcis rei*); a) **in grātiam** *alcis* to please; b) thanks, thankfulness, gratitude, requital, recompense; **grātiās** *agere* to return thanks; **grātiam** *habēre* to be thankful; **grātiam** *referre* to requite, recompense; c) *abl.* **grātiā** (*with gen.*) for the sake of, on account of, in favour of; d) **grāt(i)īs** out of kindness, for nothing, gratuitously.
grātificātiō, ōnis *f* obligingness, complaisance.
grātificor 1 to do a favour to, to oblige (*alci*); to make a present of, to sacrifice.
grātiōsus 3 obliging; **a**) given out of favour; **b**) in favour, popular, beloved; influential.
grāt(i)īs, *see* **gratia.**
grātor 1 = **gratulor.**
grātuītus 3 without pay *or* reward; free, spontaneous, gratuitous; *adv.* **grātuītō.**
grātulābundus 3 congratulating.
grātulātiō, ōnis *f* **a**) a wishing joy, congratulation; **b**) thanksgiving; joyful festival.
grātulātor, ōris *m* congratulator.
grātulor 1 **a**) to congratulate (*alci alqd, de* or *in re; acc. c. inf.; quod*); **b**) to rejoice; **c**) to render thanks (*alci*).
grātus 3 pleasing, agreeable; **a**) lovely, charming; **b**) acceptable, dear; **gratum** *alci facere* to do a favour; **c**) thankful, grateful.
gravanter *adv.* = **gravate.**
grāvāstellus (?) greyish-headed.
gravātē *and* **-tim** reluctantly, unwillingly.
gravēdinōsus 3 subject to colds *or* catarrhs.
gravēdō, inis *f* cold, catarrh.
gravēscō, —, — 3 to become burdened; to grow worse.
graviditās, ātis *f* pregnancy.
gravidō 1 to impregnate.
gravidus 3 pregnant, with child, with young; loaded, full.
gravis, e heavy, weighty; **a**) burdensome, burdening, oppressive, troublesome; **b**) hard, severe, unpleasant, harsh; **c**) strong (*of smell*), offensive; deep, low (*of sound*); **d**) unwholesome, noxious; **e**) important, weighty, grave, mighty; venerable, having authority; responsible; serious; **f**) loaded, burdened, heavy--armed; **g**) pregnant; **h**) grieved.
gravitās, ātis *f* heaviness, weight; **a**) importance, greatness; **b**) vigour, intensity; **c**) dignity, gravity, seriousness; **d**) oppressiveness, offensiveness; severity, harshness, violence, vehemence; **e**) dulness, slowness.
gravō 1 to make heavy, to load, burden, weigh down; **a**) to oppress; **b**) to make worse *or* more grievous.
gravor 1 **a**) to feel incommoded, annoyed, vexed (*abl.*); **b**) to do unwillingly, to shrink from doing (*alqd*), to refuse, decline.
gregālis, e belonging to a herd; **a**) of a common soldier; **b**) *subst. m/pl.* companions.
gregārius 3 belonging to a herd; (of soldiers) in the ranks, common, private.
gregātim *adv.* in flocks, in crowds.
gregor 1 to assemble (*intr.*).
gremium, ī *n* lap, bosom; the heart, centre.
gressus, ūs *m* a stepping; step, course.
grex, gregis *m* flock, herd; **a**) band, troop, crowd; **b**) company, society, clique.
gruis, is *f* = **grus.**
grūmus, ī *m* hillock.
grundiō *and* **grunniō** 4 to grunt.
grunditus *and* **grunnītus, ūs** *m* a grunting.
grūs, uis *f* (*m*) crane.
gryps, pis *f* griffin.

gubernāc(u)lum, ī *n* **a)** helm, rudder; **b)** guidance, direction.
gubernātiō, ōnis *f* **a)** a steering; **b)** direction, government.
gubernātor, ōris *m* **a)** steersman, pilot; **b)** ruler, governor.
gubernātrīx, īcis *f* directress.
gubernō 1 **a)** to steer, pilot; **b)** to direct, conduct, govern.
gubernum, ī *n* helm, rudder.
gula, ae *f* **a)** gullet, throat; **b)** appetite, gluttony, gormandizing.
gulōsus 3 gluttonous, greedy.
gumia, ae *m* glutton.
gurges, itis *m* whirlpool; **a)** raging abyss, gulf; **b)** waters, stream, sea; **c)** spendthrift.
gurguliō, ōnis *m* **1.** gullet; windpipe; **2.** = **curculiō; 3.** penis.
gurgustium, ī *n* hovel, hut.
gustātōrium, ī *n* (dish containing) hors d'œuvres.
gustātus, ūs *m* (sense of) taste.
gustō 1 to taste, take a little; to enjoy.
gustus, ūs *m* (preliminary) taste; sample; hors d' œuvres.
guttātus 3 speckled.
gutt(ul)a, ae *f* drop; spot.
guttātim drop by drop.
guttur, uris *n* (*and* *m*) gullet, throat.
gūtus, ī *m* narrow-necked jug.
gymnas, adis *f* wrestling.
gymnasi-archus, ī *m* master of a gymnasium.
gymnasium, ī *n* physical training school; practice-ground; lecture--room.
gymnasticus 3 gymnastic.
gymnicus 3 gymnastic.
gynaecēum *and* **-īum, ī** *n*, **gynaecōnītis, idis** *f* the women's apartments.
gypsō 1 to plaster, cover with gypsum.
gypsum, ī *n* gypsum; plaster figure.
gȳrus, ī *m* circle, ring; **a)** circular course, circuit; **b)** place where horses are trained.

H

habēna, ae *f* thong, strap; **a**) whip; **b**) rein, bridle; management, government.
habeō, uī, itum 2 to have **1.** to hold; a) to keep, retain, detain; b) to contain; c) to pronounce, deliver (*orationem*); d) to hold, conduct; e) to treat, use, handle; f) to believe, think, regard (*pro amico*); **sē habēre** (*or intrans.*) to be (in a certain condition); **2.** a) to own, possess, occupy, be master of; be rich; b) to know; c) to keep *or* breed (*animals*); d) to occupy, engage; **3.** to show, exhibit, be characterized by; to cause, produce; — **habitus** 3 **a**) in good condition, fit; **b**) in a certain humour.
habilis, e manageable, handy; **a**) suitable, fit, proper, apt (*ad alqd, alci rei*); **b**) nimble, swift; skilful.
habilitās, ātis *f* aptitude, ability.
habitābilis, e habitable.
habitātiō, ōnis *f* dwelling, habitation; house-rent.
habitātor, ōris *m* dweller, inhabitant, tenant.
habitō 1 **a**) to inhabit (*alqd*); **b**) to dwell, reside, abide; to be habitually, to stay, remain.
habitūdō, inis *f* form, appearance; condition.
habituriō 4 to desire to have.
habitus, ūs *m* **a**) appearance; **b**) dress, attire; **c**) condition, state, quality, nature, character; **d**) disposition, state of feeling.
habrotonum = abrotonum.
hāc *adv.* on this side, by this way.
hāc-tenus *adv.* **a**) to this place, thus far; **b**) up to this time, hitherto; **c**) to this extent, so far.
haedilia, ae *f* (**haedillus** *and* **haedulus, ī** *m*) little kid.
haedīnus 3 of a kid.
haedus, ī *m* young goat, kid.
haereō, haesī, sum 2 to hang to, stick to, cling to, adhere (*in re, ad rem, dat.*); **a**) to remain in a place; **b**) to remain attached, keep close to, keep firm, not to leave; **c**) to stand still, cease; **d**) to be embarrassed, perplexed, at a loss.
haerēscō, —, — 3 to stick, adhere.
haeresis, is *f* philosophical sect; craft, trade.
haesitābundus 3 stammering, perplexed.
haesitantia, ae *f* a hesitating, stammering.
haesitātiō, ōnis *f* a hesitating, stammering; irresolution.
haesitātor, ōris *m* one who is undecided.
haesitō 1 to stick fast, remain fixed; **a**) to stammer; **b**) to hesitate, be at a loss *or* irresolute.
ha(**ha**)**hae** *int.* ha ha!
halagora (?) salt-market.
halcēdō, halcyōn, *see* **alc...**
hāl(l)ēc, ēcis *n*, *see* **allec.**
hali-aeetos, ī *m* sea-eagle.
hālitus, ūs *m* breath, steam, vapour.
hālō 1 to breathe, be fragrant, exhale; to spread (*perfume*).
halo-phanta, ae *m* rogue, scoundrel.
haltēr, ēris *m* leaden weight, dumb-bell.
halucinātiō, -nor, *see* **al-.**
hama, ae *f* water-bucket, pail.
hama-dryas, adis *f* wood-nymph.
hāmātilis, e with hooks.
hāmātus 3 furnished with a hook; crooked.
hāmiōta, ae *m* angler.
hāmulus, ī *m* little hook.
hāmus, ī *m* **a**) hook; **b**) fishhook; **c**) talon; **d**) thorn.
haphē, ēs *f* fine sand (used by wrestlers for dusting the body): dust.
hapsis = absis.
hara, ae *f* pig-sty.
harēna, ae *f*, *see* **arena.**
harēnōsus 3, *see* **arenosus.**
hariolātiō, ōnis *f* soothsaying.
hariolor 1 to foretell, prophesy; to talk foolishly.
hariolus, ī *m* soothsayer.
harmonia, ae *f* consonance, concord.
harpagō[1], ōnis *m* hook, grappling-iron.

harpagō² 1 to rob.
harpastum, ī *n* ball for use in a game.
harpē, ēs *f* sickle-shaped sword.
harundi-fer 3 reed-bearing.
harundinētum, ī *n* reed-plot.
harundineus 3 reedy; made of reed; **carmen -um** a shepherd's song.
harundinōsus 3 full of reed.
harundō, inis *f* reed, cane; **a**) pen; **b**) shepherd's pipe; **c**) fishing-rod; **d**) arrow-shaft; **e**) hobby-horse; **f**) weaver's comb; **g**) splint.
haru-spex, icis *m* inspector of entrails, diviner.
haruspica, ae *f* a female haruspex.
haruspicīnus 3 relating to the inspection of entrails.
haru-spicium, ī *n* inspection of victims.
hasta, ae *f* staff, rod, pole; **a**) spear, lance, pike, javelin; **b**) auction; **sub hastā vendere** to sell by auction.
hastātus 3 armed with a spear; *subst.* soldier of the first line.
hastīle, is *n* spear-shaft, spear, shaft, stick.
hau = **haud.**
haud *adv.* not, not at all.
haud-dum *adv.* not yet.
haud-quāquam *adv.* not at all.
hauriō, hausī, haustum 4 **1.** to draw, draw up *or* out (*alqd ex, de, a re*); a) to spill, shed; b) to derive, borrow; c) to gather, collect; **2.** to drink in, to drain; a) to swallow, devour, exhaust, consume; b) to traverse, pierce; c) to seize eagerly, enjoy, know thoroughly; d) to accomplish.
haustor, ōris *m* drinker.
haustrum, ī *n* bucket.
haustus, ūs *m* a drawing; **a**) the right of drawing; **b**) drawn water, a handful, draught; **c**) drinking, drink.
haut = **haud.**
haveō, —, — 2 = **aveo².**
hebdomas, adis *f* the seventh day.
hebenus, -num = **ebenus, -num.**
hebeō, —, — 2 to be blunt, dull.
hebes, etis blunt, dull; **a**) dim; **b**) sluggish, weak, stupid.
hebēscō, —, — 3 to become blunt, dull, weak, faint.
hebetātiō, ōnis *f* dulness.
hebetō 1 to make blunt, dull, weak.
hecatombē, ēs *f* hecatomb, large-scale sacrifice.
hedera, ae *f* ivy.
hederi-ger 3 ivy-bearing.
hederōsus 3 full of ivy.
hēdy-chrum, ī *n* cosmetic balsam.
hei *int.* ah! woe!
hēia *int.* = **eia.**
hēiulō 1 = **eiulo.**
helciārius, ī *m* boat-hauler.
helica, ae *f* a spiral.
Helicē, ēs *f constellation of the* Great Bear.
hēlio-camīnus, ī *m* apartment exposed to the sun.
helix, icis *f* spiral.
helleborōsus 3 full of hellebore.
helleborus, ī *m and* **-rum, ī** *n* hellebore.
helluātiō, ōnis *f* gluttonous revelry.
helluō, ōnis *m* gormandizer, glutton, squanderer.
helluor 1 to gormandize, devour (*with abl.*).
helops, opis *m* a much-prized fish.
hēlu-, *see* **hellu-.**
helvella, ae *f* a small pot-herb.
hem *int.* oh! well! only see! indeed!
hēmero-dromus, ī *m* courier, fast runner.
hēmi-cyclium, ī *n* semicircle.
hēmīna, ae *f* = ½ *sextarius.*
hēmi-tritaeos, ī *m* semi-tertian fever: *adj.* suffering from such a fever.
hendeca-syllabī, ōrum *m/pl.* hendecasyllabic verses.
hēpatiārius 3 pertaining to the liver.
heptēris, is *f* galley with oars worked by seven rowers (?).
hera, ae *f* = **era.**
herba, ae *f* **a**) grass, blade, herb, herbage, plant, turf; **b**) weeds.
herbēscō, —, — 3 to sprout.
herbeus 3 grass-green.
herbidus 3 grassy.
herbi-fer 3 producing grass.
herbi-gradus 3 going in the grass.
herbōsus 3 grassy; made of herbs.
herbula, ae *f* little herb.
hercīscō, —, herctum 3 *and* **herctum ciēre** to divide an inheritance.
hercle *int.* by Hercules!
here *adv.* = **heri.**
hērēditārius 3 **a**) of an inheritance; **b**) hereditary, inherited.
hērēditās, ātis *f* inheritance.
hērēdium, ī *n* hereditary estate.

hērēs, ēdis *m and f* heir, heiress; successor; owner.
herī *adv.* yesterday.
herīlis, e, *see* **erilis.**
herm-aphrodītus, ī *m* hermaphrodite.
hērōicus 3 heroic, epic.
hērōinē, ae *and* **hērōis, idis** *f* demigoddess.
hērōs, ōis *m* demigod, hero; distinguished man.
hērōus 3 = **heroicus.**
herus, ī *m* = **erus.**
hesternus 3 of yesterday.
hetaeria, ae *f* fraternity, club.
hetaericē, ēs *f* the Macedonian horse-guards.
heu *int.* oh! ah! alas!
heus *int.* ho! there! hark!
hexa-clīnon, ī *n*, couch for six persons.
hexa-meter, trī *m* of six feet; *subst.* hexameter.
hexa-phoron, ī *n* litter borne by six men.
hexēris, is *f* vessel with oars worked by six rowers (?).
hiātus, ūs *m* **a**) an opening, aperture, cleft; open mouth; **b**) pompous language; **c**) eager desire; **d**) hiatus.
hībernāculum, ī *n* tent for winter-quarters; winter-residence.
hībernō 1 to pass the winter.
hībernus 3 wintry, winter-...; *subst.* **hīberna, ōrum** *n/pl.* **a**) winter-quarters; **b**) winter.
hibiscum, ī *n* the marsh-mallow.
hibrida, ae *m* and *f* halfbreed, mongrel, hybrid.
hīc[1], (*and* **hĭc**), **haec, hōc a**) this, this here; **b**) present, actual, **hic ... ille** the latter ... the former; **c**) the following; **d**) such.
hīc[2] *adv.* in this place, here; in this affair, on this occasion, herein, at this point.
hīce, haece, hōce = **hic.**
hīcine, haecine, hōcine *interrog.* = **hic + ne.**
hiemālis, e wintry, of winter; stormy.
hiemō 1 **a**) to pass the winter, to winter; **b**) to be stormy.
hiem(p)s, emis *f* winter, cold; storm.
hiero-nīcae, ārum *m/pl.* victors in the sacred games.
hietō 1 to gape, yawn.
hilariculus 3 = **hilarus.**
hilaris, e = **hilarus.**
hilaritās, ātis (*and* **hilaritūdō, inis**) *f* cheerfulness, gaiety.
hilarō 1 to cheer, gladden.
hilarulus 3 merry.
hilarus 3 cheerful, glad, joyful.
hīlla, ae *f* sausage.
Hīlōta, ae *m* Helot, serf of the Spartans.
hīlum, ī *n* a little thing, trifle.
hinc *adv.* **a**) from this place, hence; **b**) on this side, here; **c**) from this time, hereupon; **d**) from this cause, on this account.
hinniō 4 to neigh.
hinnītus, ūs *m* a neighing.
hīn(n)uleus, ī *m* young deer.
hiō 1 to stand open, gape, yawn; **a**) to be amazed, gape with wonder; **b**) to long for: **c**) to be badly connected.
hipp-agōgus, ī *f* a vessel for cavalry-transport.
hippo-centaurus, ī *m* hippocentaur (*half horse half man*).
hippo-dromus, ī *m* race-course.
hippo-manes, is *n* **a**) slimy discharge of a mare; **b**) membrane on the head of a newborn foal.
hippo-pērae, ārum *f/pl.* saddle-bags.
hippo-toxota, ae *m* mounted archer.
hīra, ae *f* empty gut, jejunum.
hircīnus 3 of a goat.
hircōsus 3 smelling like a goat.
hircus, ī *m* he-goat; smell of a goat; dirty fellow.
hirnea[1], **ae** *f* wine-jar.
hirnea[2], **ae** *f* rupture, hernia.
hirsūtus 3 **a**) shaggy, bristly, rough; **b**) rude, unpolished.
hirtus 3 = **hirsutus.**
hirūdō, inis *f* leech; bloodsucker.
hirundinīnus 3 of swallows.
hirundō, inis *f* swallow.
hīscō, —, — 3 to open, gape, yawn; to utter, speak.
hispidus 3 shaggy, rough.
historia, ae *f* **a**) inquiry, history, historical work; **b**) narrative, account, tale, story; **c**) theme of discourse.
historicus 3 historical; *subst.* **~, ī** *m* historian.
histricus 3 = **histrionalis.**
histriō, ōnis *m* actor, player.
histriōnālis, e of actors, like an actor.
histriōnia, ae *f* dramatic art.

hiulcō 1 to cause to gape.
hiulcus 3 gaping; greedy; with a hiatus.
hōc *adv.* = **huc.**
ho-diē *adv.* to-day, at this time, now; **hodiēque** even to this day, even now.
hodiernus 3 of this day, today's.
holus(culum), holitor, holitōrius, see **ol-.**
homi-cīda, ae *m* and *f* manslayer.
homicīdium, ī *n* manslaughter, homicide.
homō, inis *m* a man; **a)** human being, person; **b)** servant, slave; — *pl.* **a)** man, mankind, the human race; **b)** society, fellows; **c)** foot--soldiers.
homoeo-merīa (*acc.* **an**) *f* the homogeneousness of constituent particles.
homullus, ī *m* little man.
homunciō, ōnis *and* **homunculus, ī** *m* = **homullus.**
honestāmentum, ī *n* ornament.
honestās, ātis *f* **a)** honour, reputation, character; **b)** honesty, probity, integrity, virtue; beauty, grace; — *pl.* honourable men, notabilities.
honestō 1 to honour, dignify, adorn.
honestus 3 **a)** honoured, distinguished, noble; **b)** respectable, honest, worthy, virtuous, decent, proper; fine, beautiful.
honor *and* **-ōs, ōris** *m* **a)** honour, distinction, respect; **honōris causā** out of respect; **b)** esteem, praise; **c)** public honour, official dignity, office, preferment; **d)** honorary gift, reward, recompense, fee; **e)** glory, ornament, decoration, grace, charm, beauty.
honōrābilis, e honourable.
honōrārius 3 for the sake of honour, honorary; *subst.* **-ium, ī** *n* honourable gift.
honōri-ficus 3 honourable.
honōrō 1 to honour, respect; **honōrātus** 3 **a)** honoured, respected; **b)** high magistrate, dignitary; **c)** respectable, conferring honour.
honōrus 3 honourable, conferring honour.
honōs, ōris *m* = **honor.**
hoplo-machus, ī *m* heavy-armed fighter, gladiator.
hōra, ae *f* hour; **a)** time, season; **b)** *pl.* = **horologium.**
hōraeum (?) a pickle of young fish.
hordēia, ae *f* (?) a shell-fish (perhaps also *f adj.* = of barley).
hordeum, ī *n* barley.
hōria *and* **hōriola, ae** *f* fishing-boat.
hōrnōtinus *and* **hōrnus** 3 of this year.
hōro-logium, ī *n* sun-dial, water-clock.
hōro-scopus, ī *m* horoscope.
horrendus 3 = **horribilis.**
horreō, uī, — 2 to stand on end, bristle; **horrēns** bristly, shaggy, rough; **a)** to shake, tremble, shudder (at), be afraid; **b)** to be astonished, amazed at (*alqd*).
horrēscō, ruī, — 3 to rise on end, bristle up; to begin to shudder, to be terrified (at).
horreum, ī *n* storehouse, barn, granary.
horribilis, e a) terrible, dreadful, horrible; **b)** astonishing, wonderful.
horridulus 3 *dimin.* of **horridus.**
horridus 3 **a)** standing on end, rough, shaggy, bristly; **b)** unadorned, rude, wild, savage; **c)** unpolished, uncouth; stern, blunt; **d)** shuddering; **e)** terrible, frightful.
horri-fer 3 chilling, dreadful, horrible.
horri-ficō 1 to ruffle; to terrify; to make dreadful.
horri-ficus 3 dreadful, frightful.
horri-sonus 3 sounding dreadfully.
horror, ōris *m* **a)** a bristling, trembling, shuddering, dread; **b)** awe; thrill.
hōrsum *adv.* hither, this way.
hortāmen, inis *and* **hortāmentum, ī** *n* incitement, encouragement.
hortātiō, ōnis *f* encouragement, exhortation.
hortātor, ōris *m*, **-trīx. īcis** *f* encourager, exhorter.
hortātus, ūs *m* encouragement, exhortation.
hortor 1 to incite, instigate, encourage, cheer, exhort (*alqm ad alqd; ut, ne*); to harangue.
hortulus, ī *m* little garden.
hortus, ī *m* garden; *pl.* park.
hospes, itis *m* **a)** visitor, guest; **b)** entertainer, host; **c)** stranger, foreigner; **d)** one unacquainted with (*in re* or with *gen.*).
hospita, ae *f* hostess; visitor, guest, friend.

hospitālis, e hospitable, of a guest, of a host.
hospitālitās, ātis *f* hospitality.
hospitium, ī *n* hospitality; **a**) hospitable reception, entertainment; **b**) lodging, quarters, guest-chamber.
hospitor 1 to lodge.
hospitus 3 **a**) hospitable; **b**) strange, foreign.
hostia, ae *f* victim, sacrifice.
hostiātus 3 provided with victims.
hosticus 3 hostile; strange, foreign.
hosti-ficus 3 hostile, malicious.
hostīlis, e hostile, inimical.
hostīmentum, ī *n* compensation, requital.
hostiō 4 to recompense.
hostis, is *m* (*and f*) **a**) stranger, foreigner; **b**) enemy, foe.
HS. *abbr.* (*for* **IIS**) = **sestertius.**
hūc *adv.* to this place hither; to this point, so far; **hūcine** hitherto? to this? so far?
hui *int.* ha! ho! oh!
hūiusce-modī, hūius-modī *adv.* of this sort, such.
hūmānitās, ātis *f* human nature, humanity, human race, mankind; **a**) philanthropy, kindness, gentleness, sympathy; **b**) good breeding, education, civilization, elegance, refinement, good manners.
hūmānitus *adv.* **1.** according to the common lot of humanity; **2.** kindly.
hūmānus 3 human, belonging to man; **res hūmānae** human affairs, things happening to man, events of life; **a**) humane, kind, gentle, obliging, polite; **b**) well educated, refined, civilized, learned; — *adv.* **hūmānē** *and* **hūmāniter.**
humātiō, ōnis *f* burial.
humātor, ōris *m* one who buries.
hūmectō, hūmeō, *see* **um...**
humerus, ī *m, see* **um...**
hūmēscō, hūmidus, *see* **um...**
humilis, e low, lowly; **a**) small, slight, petty; **b**) shallow; **c**) mean, humble, poor, obscure; **d**) insignificant; **e**) base, abject, servile, low-spirited.
humilitās, ātis *f* lowness; meanness, insignificance; **a**) low birth; **b**) weakness; **c**) baseness, abjectness.
humō 1 to bury, inter.
hūmor, ōris *m, see* **umor.**
humus, ī *f* **a**) earth, soil, ground; **b**) country, region; *loc.* **humī** on the ground, to the ground.
hyacinthinus 3 of the *hyacinthus*; crimson, purple.
hyacinthus, ī *m* kinds of red *or* purple flower (lilies, corn-flags [?]).
Hyades, um *f/pl.* the Hyades, *a group of seven stars.*
hyaena, ae *f* hyena.
hyalus, ī *m* glass.
hybrida, ae *m and f, see* **hibrida.**
hydra, ae *f* water-serpent.
hydr-aulēs, ae *m* player on the water-organ.
hydr-aulicus 3 belonging to the water-organ.
hydr-aulus, ī *m* water-organ.
hydria, ae *f* jug, ewer, urn.
hydrōpicus 3 dropsical.
hydrōps, ōpis *m* dropsy.
hydrus, ī *m* water-serpent.
Hymēn, (*and* **Hȳmēn**), **enis** *m* the god of marriage; marriage-song.
hymenaeus, ī *m* marriage-song, nuptial hymn; a wedding, nuptials; the god of marriage.
hyper-bolē, ēs *f* exaggeration.
hypo-caustum, ī *n* underground vault for heating a house.
hypo-critēs, ae *m* mime who accompanied the delivery of an actor by his gestures.
hypo-didascalus, ī *m* under-teacher.
hypo-mnēma, atis *n* memorandum, note.
hystericus 3 hysterical.

I

iaceō, uī, (iacitūrus) 2 to lie, lie down; **a**) to lie sick, lie at rest, recline at table; **b**) to lie dead, have fallen; **iacentēs, ium** *m/pl.* the fallen, slain; **c**) to lie prostrate, in ruins; **d**) to be inactive, to linger, tarry, stop; **e**) to hang loose; **f**) to lie low, be flat; **g**) to lie idle, neglected, unemployed; **h**) to be low, despised, discouraged.

iaciō, iēcī, iactum 3 **1.** to throw, cast, fling, hurl (*alqd in alqd*), hit, push; to send forth, emit; **2.** to throw up, to set, to establish, build, construct; **fundamenta** to lay foundations.

iactāns, tis boastful.

iactantia, ae *f* a boasting, vainglory.

iactātiō, ōnis *f* **a**) a throwing to and fro, tossing, shaking, agitation, violent motion, emotion; **b**) ostentation, display, vanity.

iactātor, ōris *m* boaster.

iactātus, ūs *m* = **iactatio.**

iactitō 1 to utter frequently, bandy.

iactō 1 **1.** to throw, cast, hurl often; a) to throw out, emit, spread; b) to pronounce, utter, speak; c) to mention frequently, speak often about; d) to assert in a boastful way, to boast (*re, in re*); **se iactāre** to make a display, to brag; **2.** to throw *or* toss about, drive about, shake; **se iactāre** to be active in (*in re*), devote oneself to.

iactūra, ae *f* a throwing away, throwing overboard; **a**) loss, damage, detriment, sacrifice; **iactūram facere** to suffer a loss, to lose, omit (*gen.*); **b**) expense, cost.

lactus, ūs *m* a throwing, casting, hurling, throw, cast; **intra iactum** within range.

laculābilis, e that can be thrown *or* hurled.

iaculātor, ōris *m* thrower, javelin-thrower.

iaculātrīx, īcis *f* huntress.

iaculor 1 to throw, cast, hurl, throw the javelin; to throw at, strike at, hit (*alqm*); to aim at, strive after (*alqd*).

iaculum, ī *n* dart, javelin; fishing-net.

iaculus 3 that is thrown: *subst. m* a darting serpent; *n* a casting-net.

iāientāculum, ī *n* = **ientaculum.**

iam 1. *adv.* a) already; b) now, **iam ... iam** now ... now; c) forthwith, immediately, presently; **iam iam (-que)** every moment; **non iam** *or* **iam non** not from this time, not now, no longer; **2.** a) now, further, moreover; b) now at last.

iambēus 3 iambic.

iambus, ī *m* iambus; iambic poem.

iānitor, ōris *m*, **iānitrīx, īcis** *f* door-keeper.

ianthinus 3 violet-coloured.

iānua, ae *f* door, house-door; entrance.

Iānuārius 3 of January; *subst. m* [January.]

iānus, ī *m* arched passage.

iaspis, idis *f* jasper.

iātr-alīptēs, ae *m* physician who heals by unguents.

ibī (*and* **ibĭ**) *adv.* in that place, there; **a**) then, thereupon; **b**) in that matter, on that occasion.

ibī-dem (*and* **ibĭ-**) *adv.* **a**) in the same place, in that very place, just there; **b**) at that very moment.

ībis, is *and* **idis** *f* the ibis.

iccircō = **idcirco.**

ichneumōn, onis *m* ichneumon (*Egyptian rat*).

īcō, īcī, ictum 3 to strike, hit, smite, stab; **foedus** to make a covenant *or* league; **ictus** 3 struck, smitten, tormented.

īconicus 3 copied from life

īconismus, ī *m* portrayal.

ictericus 3 jaundiced.

ictus, ūs *m* blow, stroke, stab, cut, thrust; **a**) beat, impulse; **b**) attack; shock.

īcuncula, ae *f* little portrait.

id-circō *adv.* on that account, therefore.

idea, ae *f* Platonic idea, archetype.

ī-dem, eadem, idem the same; **īdem ac** the same as; at the same time, likewise, also.

identidem *adv.* repeatedly, several times.
id-eō *adv.* on that account, therefore.
idiōta *and* **-tēs, ae** *m* ignorant person, outsider.
īdōlum *and* **on, ī** *n* image; apparition.
idōneus 3 fit, proper, suitable, apt, capable, sufficient (with *dat.*, *ad alqd;* with *qui* and *subj.*); responsible, worthy.
īdos *n* form, appearance.
īdūs, uum *f/pl.* the ides, middle of the month.
iecur, oris (*and* **iocineris**) *n* the liver.
iecusculum, ī *n* a little liver.
iēientāculum, ī *n* = **ientaculum.**
iēiūnitās, ātis *f* **a**) a fasting; **b**) dryness, poverty, meagreness.
iēiūnium, ī *n* a fasting; **a**) hunger; **b**) leanness, poorness.
iēiūnus (rarely **iēiūniōsus**) 3 fasting, hungry; **a**) dry, barren; **b**) scanty, poor, insignificant; **c**) feeble, spiritless.
ientāculum, ī *n* breakfast.
ientō 1 to breakfast.
igitur *cj.* then, therefore, accordingly, consequently.
ī-gnārus 3 **a**) ignorant, not knowing, inexperienced, unacquainted with (*gen.*), unaware; **b**) not known, unknown, strange.
īgnāvia, ae *f* **a**) inactivity, laziness; **b**) cowardice.
ī-gnāvus 3 **a**) inactive, lazy, slothful, idle; **b**) cowardly; *adv.* **īgnāvē** (*and* **īgnāviter**).
ignēscō, —, — 3 to take fire, kindle.
igneus 3 fiery, burning hot, glowing.
igniculus, ī *m* little flame, spark.
igni-fer 3 fire-bearing.
igni-gena, ae *m* fire-born.
igni-pēs, edis fiery-footed.
igni-potēns, tis mighty in fire.
ignis, is *m* fire; **a**) conflagration; **b**) firebrand, signal-fire, watch-fire, torch, lightning, thunderbolt, star; **c**) brightness, splendour, brilliancy, lustre, redness; **d**) glow, rage, fury; **e**) flame of love, beloved object, flame; **f**) destruction.
ī-gnōbilis, e unknown, unrenowned, obscure; of low birth, base-born, ignoble.
īgnōbilitās, ātis *f* want of fame, obscurity; low birth.
ī-gnōminia, ae *f* disgrace, dishonour, ignominy.
īgnōminiōsus 3 disgraceful, degraded.
īgnōrābilis, e unknown.
īgnōrantia, ae *f* ignorance, want of knowledge.
īgnōrātiō, ōnis *f* = **ignorantia.**
ī-gnōrō 1 not to know (*alqd*), to be ignorant, unacquainted with;
īgnōrātus 3 unknown.
ī-gnōscō, gnōvī, gnōtum 3 to pardon, forgive, excuse, overlook, indulge (*alci alqd*).
ī-gnōtus 3 **a**) unknown, strange; low-born, base, ignoble; **b**) ignorant of, unacquainted with.
īle *n, see* **ilia.**
īlex, icis *f* holm-oak, ilex.
īlia, ium *n/pl.* groin, flanks; entrails.
ī-licet *adv.* **a**) one may go, let us go! **b**) all is over! all is lost!; **d**) immediately, at once.
īlicētum, ī *n* grove of holm-oaks.
īliceus 3 of holm-oak.
ī-licō *adv.* on the spot, instantly, directly.
īlignus 3 of the holm-oak, oaken.
illā *adv., see* **ille.**
il-labefactus 3 unshaken, unbroken.
il-lābor 3 to fall, slip, glide *or* flow into (*ad alqd*); to fall to ruins.
il-labōrātus 3 not worked out.
il-labōrō 1 to work at *or* upon.
illāc *adv.* that way, on that side, there.
il-lacerābilis, e that cannot be torn *or* rent.
il-lacessītus 3 unprovoked.
il-lacrimābilis, e a) unwept, unlamented; **b**) inexorable.
il-lacrimō *and* **-mor** 1 **a**) to weep at *or* over (*dat.*), to lament; **b**) to drip, drop, distil.
il-laesus 3 unhurt, uninjured.
il-laetābilis, e cheerless, sad.
il-lāpsus, ūs *m* a gliding *or* passing onto something.
il-laqueō 1 to ensnare, entrap.
il-laudābilis, e not worthy of praise.
il-laudātus 3 **a**) unpraised; **b**) detestable.
il-lautus 3, *see* **illotus.**
ille, a, ud that; **hic ... ille** this ... that, the one ... the other; **ille et ille** such and such, one and another;

a) he, she, it; **b**) the well-known, the ancient, the famous, the former; — *adv.* **illā** on that side, there; **illō** to that place, thither.

illecebra, ae *f* enticement, inducement, bait.

illecebrōsus 3 enticing.

il-lēctus[1] 3 unread.

il-lectus[2] 3 allured.

il-lectus[3], **ūs** *m* allurement.

il-lepidus 3 impolite, unmannerly, rude.

il-lēx[1], **ēgis** lawless.

illex[2], **icis** alluring, seducing.

illī *adv.* = **illic.**

il-lībātus 3 undiminished, unimpaired.

il-līberālis, e ignoble, ungenerous; sordid, mean.

il-līberālitās, ātis *f* meanness, stinginess.

illic[1], **aec, uc** that, yonder; he, she, it.

illī(c)[2] *adv.* in that place, there; in that matter.

il-liciō, lexī, lectum 3 to allure, entice; to seduce, mislead.

il-licitātor, ōris *m* sham-bidder, mock-purchaser.

il-licitus 3 forbidden, unlawful.

il-licō *adv.* = **ilico.**

il-līdō, sī, sum 3 **a**) to strike *or* dash against; **b**) to dash to pieces, to crush.

il-ligō 1 to tie, bind *or* fasten on, attach; **a**) to fetter, bind, oblige, encumber; **b**) to entangle, impede.

illim *adv.* = **illinc.**

il-līmis, e without mud.

illinc *adv.* from that place, thence; there.

il-linō 3 **a**) to smear over, to spread *or* lay on (*alqd alci rei*); **b**) to bedaub, anoint (*alqd re*).

il-liquefactus 3 melted, liquefied.

il-līsus, ūs *m* a dashing against.

il-litterātus 3 unlearned, unlettered.

illō(c) = **illuc.**

il-locābilis, e that cannot be disposed of in marriage.

il-lōtus 3 unwashed, unclean, dirty.

illūc *adv.* to that place *or* point.

il-lūceō 2 to blaze upon.

il-lūcēscō, lūxī, — 3 to grow light; to dawn, break.

il-luctāns, tis struggling on *or* against.

il-lūdō 3 to play at *or* with (*dat.*), to sport with; **a**) to make sport with writing (*chartis*), to mock at, laugh at, jeer at, ridicule; **b**) to violate, abuse, disgrace, ruin.

illūminātē *adv.* distinctly.

il-lūminō 1 **a**) to light up, light, illuminate; **b**) to set off, adorn.

il-lūnis, e moonless.

il-lūsiō, ōnis *f* mockery.

il-lūstris, e full of light, lighted, bright, brilliant; **a**) clear, plain, distinct, evident; **b**) distinguished, remarkable; **c**) celebrated, renowned, famous, illustrious; noble.

il-lūstrō 1 to light up, make light; **a**) to bring to light; **b**) to make clear, explain, illustrate; **c**) to adorn, make famous *or* illustrious.

il-lūtilis, e not to be washed out.

il-lūtus 3 = **illotus.**

il-luviēs, ēī *f* **a**) inundation; **b**) dirt, filth.

imāginārius 3 fancied, seeming.

imāginātiō, ōnis *f* imagination, fancy.

imāginor 1 to imagine, fancy.

imāginōsus 3 pertaining to an image; **aes -um** mirror.

imāgō, inis *f* image, representation; **a**) portrait, figure, bust; **b**) waxen figure, portrait of an ancestor; **c**) likeness, counterfeit; **d**) shade, ghost of a dead man, dream, phantom, apparition, vision; **e**) echo; **f**) pretence, appearance; **g**) simile, similitude, comparison; **h**) idea, conception.

imāguncula, ae *f* little image.

imbēcillitās, ātis *f* **a**) weakness, feebleness; **b**) imbecility.

im-bēcillus 3 (*and* **-is, e**) **a**) weak, feeble; **b**) weak in mind.

im-bellis, e unwarlike; **a**) cowardly; **b**) peaceful.

imber, bris *m* shower of rain, violent rain; **a**) storm, raincloud; **b**) water, waves; **c**) shower, fall.

im-berbis, e *and* **-bus** 3 beardless.

im-bibō, bibī, — 3 to drink in, imbibe; **a**) to conceive; **b**) to determine, resolve (*alqd*).

im-bītō 3 to go in.

imbrex, icis *f* hollow tile, gutter-tile.

imbricus 3 bringing rain.

imbri-fer 3 rain-bringing.

im-buō, uī, ūtum 3 to wet, moisten; steep (*alqd re*); **a**) to stain, taint, infect; **b**) to fill; **c**) to train, educate, instruct.

imitābilis, e imitable.
imitāmen, inis *and* **imitāmentum, ī** *n* imitation.
imitātiō, ōnis *f* a copying, imitation.
imitātor, ōris *m* imitator.
imitātrīx, īcis *f* she that imitates.
imitor 1 **a**) to imitate, copy (*acc.*); **b**) to resemble, be like.
im-maculātus 3 unstained.
im-madēscō, duī, — 3 to become moist *or* wet.
im-mānis, e enormous, immense, monstrous; frightful, savage, horrible.
immānitās, ātis *f* hugeness; savageness, barbarity, frightfulness; barbarians.
im-mānsuētus 3 untamed, savage.
im-mātūritās, ātis *f* untimely haste.
im-mātūrus 3 unripe; premature, untimely.
im-medicābilis, e incurable.
im-memor, oris unmindful (*gen.*), forgetful, heedless.
im-memorābilis, e a) unworthy to be repeated; indescribable; **b**) silent.
im-memorātus 3 unmentioned, new.
immēnsitās, ātis *f* immensity.
im-mēnsus 3 immeasurable, immense, boundless.
im-merēns, tis not deserving, innocent.
im-mergō 3 to dip *or* plunge into (*alqd in rem*); **se immergere** to plunge into.
im-meritus 3 **a**) not deserving, innocent; **b**) undeserved, unmerited; *adv.* **immeritō.**
im-mersābilis, e not to be sunk *or* overwhelmed.
im-mētātus 3 unmeasured.
im-migrō 1 to migrate, remove into (*in alqd*).
im-mineō, —, — 2 to project over, bend, incline over, overhang (*dat.*); **a**) to be imminent, threaten; to be near to, be at hand; **c**) to strive eagerly after, be intent upon.
im-minuō 3 to diminish, lessen; to abate (*alqd de re*); to curtail; to weaken, injure, destroy; to slight.
im-minūtiō, ōnis *f* a diminishing, lessening; mutilation.
im-misceō 2 to mix in, mingle with (*alqd alci rei*), entwine; to join, associate.
im-miserābilis, e unpitied.
im-misericors, dis pitiless.
im-missiō, ōnis *f* a letting grow.
im-mītis, e a) harsh, unripe, sour; **b**) rough, cruel, pitiless, stern, inexorable.
im-mittō 3 **1.** to send in, let in; **a**) to dispatch, let go, let loose against (*in* or *ad alqd*); **P.** *and* **se immittere** to throw oneself into, to advance, attack; **b**) to discharge, shoot, cast among; **c**) to put into possession, to install; **d**) to let into, insert, sink into; **e**) to instigate, suborn; **f**) to cause (*alci alqd*); **2.** to let grow; **immissus** 3 long, flowing (*hair*).
immō *adv.* **a**) no indeed, nay rather, on the contrary, by no means; **b**) indeed, assuredly.
im-mōbilis, e immovable, unmoved.
im-moderātiō, ōnis *f* want of moderation, excess.
im-moderātus 3 **a**) without measure, immeasurable; **b**) immoderate, unrestrained, intemperate.
im-modestia, ae *f* intemperate conduct; insubordination.
im-modestus 3 intemperate, excessive, unrestrained.
im-modicus 3 **a**) immoderate, excessive; **b**) unrestrained.
im-modulātus 3 inharmonious.
immolātiō, ōnis *f* a sacrificing.
immolātor, ōris *m* sacrificer.
im-mōlītus 3 built.
im-molō 1 to sacrifice (*alci alqd*).
im-morior 3 to die in *or* upon.
im-moror 1 to stay, linger at a place.
im-morsus 3 bitten; stimulated.
im-mortālis, e a) undying, immortal; *m/pl.* the gods; **b**) imperishable, eternal.
im-mortālitās, ātis *f* immortality, everlasting renown, imperishableness.
im-mōtus 3 unmoved, motionless, immovable, unshaken, steadfast.
im-moveō 2 to move in.
im-mūgiō 4 to roar, resound inwardly.
im-mulgeō 2 to milk into.
im-munditia, ae *f* uncleanness.
im-mundus 3 unclean, impure.
im-mūniō 4 to fortify.
im-mūnis, e not bound, free from obligation; **a**) exempt from taxes

(*with abl.* or *gen.*), from military service, from work; **b**) without gifts; **c**) inactive, doing nothing; **d**) not sharing *or* partaking in, devoid of (*alcis rei*).

immūnitās, ātis *f* exemption from public burdens, immunity, privilege.

im-mūnītus 3 unfortified; unpaved.

im-murmurō 1 to murmur in, at *or* against (*dat.*).

im-mūtābilis[1], **e** unchangeable, unalterable.

im-mūtābilis[2], **e** changed.

im-mūtābilitās, ātis *f* immutability.

im-mūtātiō, ōnis *f* change, alteration; metonymy.

im-mūtātus 3 unchanged.

im-mūtēscō, tuī, — 3 to become silent.

im-mūtō 1 to change, alter, transform.

im-pācātus 3 disinclined to peace, warlike.

im-pallēscō, palluī 3 to grow pale at *or* over.

im-pār, aris unequal; **a**) uneven, odd, awry; **b**) unequal in strength, inferior (*alci*); **c**) inferior in birth.

im-parātus 3 unprepared, unprovided with.

im-pāstus 3 unfed, hungry.

im-patiēns, tis unable to bear *or* to endure (*gen.*); **a**) impatient; **b**) without feeling.

im-patientia, ae *f* inability to endure.

im-pavidus 3 fearless, intrepid.

impedīmentum, ī *n* hindrance, impediment; *pl.* heavy baggage, travelling equipage.

im-pediō 4 to entangle, involve, hold fast, wrap round (*alqd re*); **a**) to make impassable; **b**) to embarrass; to hinder, impede, prevent, obstruct, detain, check (*alqm re, a re, in re; ne, quominus, quin*).

impedītiō, ōnis *f* a hindering, hindrance.

impeditō 1 to impede.

impedītus 3 hindered, impeded; **a**) impassable, inaccessible; **b**) embarrassed, encumbered, burdened, not ready for battle; **c**) difficult, intricate.

im-pellō, pulī, pulsum 3 to strike, strike upon; **a**) to push forward, set in motion, drive on; to impel, propel, wield; **b**) to put to rout, to complete one's ruin, to throw to the ground; **c**) to incite, urge, instigate, persuade, move (*alqm ad* or *in alqd; ut, ne, inf.*).

im-pendeō, —, — 2 to hang over, overhang (*dat.*); to impend, threaten, be near, at hand (*alci, in alqm*).

impendiōsus 3 extravagant.

impendium, ī *n* expense, outlay, cost; loss; interest, usury; *adv.* **impendiō** much, very much.

im-pendō, ndī, ēnsum 3 to expend, lay out (*in alqd*); to devote, employ, apply; **impēnsus** 3 **a**) dear, at a high price, expensive; **b**) earnest, great, vehement.

im-penetrābilis, e impenetrable, inaccessible, unconquerable.

impēnsa, ae *f* expense, outlay, cost; contribution, waste.

imperātor, ōris *m* ruler, lord; **a**) commander; **b**) emperor.

imperātōrius 3 **a**) relating to a general; **b**) imperial.

imperātrīx, īcis *f* female ruler *or* commander.

imperātum, ī *n, see* **impero.**

im-perceptus 3 unperceived.

im-percō 3 to spare.

im-percussus 3 noiseless.

im-perditus 3 not killed.

im-perfectus 3 unfinished, incomplete; undigested.

im-perfossus 3 unpierced.

imperiōsus 3 far-ruling, powerful; imperious, arbitrary.

im-perītia, ae *f* inexperience.

imperitō 1 to govern, rule, command.

imperītus 3 inexperienced, ignorant (*gen.*).

imperium, ī *n* **1.** command, order, direction; **2.** might, power; a) rule; b) command, control, authority; c) supreme power, sway, command-in-chief, highest office; d) magistrate, commander; e) dominion, empire, realm.

im-periūrātus 3 that is not sworn falsely by.

im-permissus 3 unlawful, forbidden.

imperō 1 **a**) to command, order, enjoin (*alci alqd; ut, ne*); **imperātum, ī** *n* command, order; **b**) to give orders for, make requisition

for, levy, demand (*alci naves, obsides*); **c**) to rule, control, govern, be supreme master (*alci*).
im-perpetuus 3 not permanent.
im-perspicuus 3 not perspicuous, obscure.
im-perterritus 3 undaunted.
im-pertiō *and* **-ior** 4 to share with, communicate, bestow, present with (*alci alqd; alqm re*).
im-perturbātus 3 undisturbed, calm.
im-pervius 3 impassable.
impete *archaic abl. of* **impetus.**
impetibilis, e unbearable.
impetis *archaic genit. of* **impetus.**
im-petō 3 to attack (*alqm*).
impetrābilis, e 1. attainable; **2.** able to obtain.
impetrātiō, ōnis *f* an obtaining by request.
impetriō 4 to seek to obtain by good omens.
im-petrō 1 to accomplish, effect, bring to pass; to obtain, procure, get (*by request*) (*alqd ab alqo; ut*).
impetus, ūs *m* violent impulse *or* motion, vehemence, rush, vigour; **a**) attack, assault, onset; **b**) impetuosity, ardour, passion, pressure, instinct; **c**) inclination, desire.
im-pexus 3 uncombed; unpolished, uncouth.
im-pietās, ātis *f* irreverence, undutifulness; treason.
im-piger 3 diligent, active, quick.
impigritās, ātis *f* activity, indefatigableness.
im-pingō, pēgī, pāctum 3 to drive, strike at *or* into, to fasten upon (*alqd alci rei, in alqd*); to thrust, strike, dash against; to force upon.
im-piō 1 to defile with sin.
im-pius 3 ungodly, wicked, impious, unpatriotic, undutiful.
im-plācābilis, e implacable, irreconcilable.
im-plācātus 3 unappeased, unastisfied.
im-placidus 3 ungentle, savage, fierce.
im-plexus 3 entwined, involved.
im-pleō, ēvī, ētum 2 to fill up *or* full, to make full, to fill (*alqd with abl.* or *gen.*); **a**) to satisfy, satiate; **b**) to make pregnant; **c**) to make full (*a certain measure* or *number*), complete; **d**) to finish, end, accomplish; **e**) to fulfil, discharge; **f**) to infect.
implicātiō, ōnis *f* an entwining, entanglement, embarrassment.
im-plicīscor 3 to get confused.
im-plicō, uī (*and* **āvī**), **ātum** *and* **itum** 1 **a**) to enfold, involve, entangle, enwrap, envelop; **b**) to attach, unite, join; **c**) to engage in, to confound, perplex, embarrass; **d**) to twine *or* weave around (*alqa re*); **implicātus, implicitus** 3 entangled, involved, confused.
im-plōrābilis, e that may be invoked to aid. [(*for help*).]
im-plōrātiō, ōnis *f* an imploring
im-plōrō 1 to implore, beseech, entreat (*alqm, alqd ab alqo; ut, ne*).
im-plūmis, e unfledged; bald.
im-pluō, uī, — 3 to rain into *or* upon. [*impluvium*, square.]
impluviātus 3 in the shape of an
im-pluvium, ī *n* small court open to the sky in the middle of a Roman house, with a cistern.
im-polītus 3 **a**) unpolished, unrefined, rude; **b**) unfinished.
im-pollūtus 3 unstained.
im-pōnō 3 to place, set, put into, upon *or* in a place (*alqd in re, in rem, dat.*); **a**) to put on board, embark; **b**) to set over, constitute; **c**) to impose, lay upon, put upon, inflict (*alci alqd*); **d**) to impose upon, deceive, cheat; **e**) to assign, assess, exact; to apply, give, add; **f**) to cause (*alci alqd*).
im-portāticius 3 imported.
im-portō 1 to bring, carry *or* convey into; **a**) to import; **b**) to occasion, cause (*alci alqd*).
importūnitās, ātis *f* importunity, rudeness, ruthlessness.
im-portūnus 3 unsuitable; **a**) troublesome, distressing; **b**) rude, cruel, savage.
im-portuōsus 3 without a harbour.
impos, otis not master of (*gen.*).
im-potēns, tis a) powerless, weak, feeble; **b**) not master of, unable to control (*gen.*); **c**) without self--control, unbridled, headstrong, violent, insolent, excessive, despotic.
im-potentia, ae *f* **a**) inability, poverty; **b**) want of moderation, ungovernableness, passionateness, fury.

im-praesentiārum (= *in praesentia rerum*) for the present, in present circumstances.
im-prānsus 3 without breakfast, fasting.
im-precātiō, ōnis *f* curse.
im-precor 1 to call down upon, imprecate.
im-pressiō, ōnis *f* a) beat, emphasis, impression; **b**) onset, attack, assault.
im-prīmīs *adv.* chiefly, especially.
im-primō, pressī, pressum 3 **a**) to press into *or* upon (*alqd in re, dat.*); **b**) to imprint, mark, stamp (*alqa re*); **P.** to take impressions.
im-probābilis, e not to be approved.
im-probātiō, ōnis *f* disapproval.
im-probitās, ātis *f* wickedness, dishonesty.
im-probō 1 to disapprove, reject.
im-probus 3 **a**) bad, dishonest, disloyal, wicked; **b**) relentless, merciless, shameless, naughty; *dimin.* **improbulus.**
im-prōcērus 3 of small stature.
im-prōdictus 3 not postponed.
im-professus 3 not professing adherence.
im-prōmptus 3 not ready, not quick; hesitating.
im-proper(āt)us 3 not hasty.
im-prosperus 3 unfortunate.
im-prōvidus 3 **a**) not foreseeing, not anticipating; **b**) heedless, improvident.
im-prōvīsus 3 unforeseen, unexpected; (**de, ex**) **imprōvīsō** unexpectedly.
im-prūdēns, tis not foreseeing *or* expecting; **a**) without knowing, unaware, ignorant (*gen.*); **b**) unwise, rash, inconsiderate.
im-prūdentia, ae *f* **a**) want of foresight; **b**) imprudence, ignorance; **c**) inconsiderateness.
im-pūbēs, eris (*and* **impūbis, e**) **a**) under age, youthful, beardless; **b**) unmarried, chaste.
im-pudēns, tis shameless, impudent.
im-pudentia, ae *f* shamelessness, impudence.
im-pudīcitia, ae *f* unchastity, lewdness.
im-pudīcus 3 unchaste. lewd.
impugnātiō, ōnis *f* assault, attack.
im-pugnō 1 to fight against, attack, assail, to oppose.
im-pulsiō, ōnis *f* = **impulsus.**
impulsor, ōris *m* inciter, instigator.
im-pulsus, ūs *m* push, pressure, shock; incitement; impulse, instigation.
impūne *adv.* **a**) with impunity, unpunished; **b**) safely, without danger.
impūnitās, ātis *f* **a**) impunity, safety; **b**) licence, licentiousness.
im-pūnītus 3 **a**) unpunished; **b**) unrestrained.
impūrātus 3 dirty, vile, infamous, abominable.
impūritās, ātis *f* impurity, pollution.
im-pūritia, ae *f* = **impuritas.**
im-pūrus 3 unclean, filthy, foul; defiled, infamous, shameful, impure.
imputātor, ōris *m* one who makes up an account.
im-putātus 3 unpruned.
im-putō 1 to reckon, attribute, ascribe, charge (*alci alqd*).
īmulus 3 lowest.
īmus 3, *see* **inferus.**
in *prep.* **1.** *with abl.* in; a) *of space:* in, on, upon, over, among, before, under; b) *of time:* in, during, within, in the course of, at, on the point of; c) *of other relations:* in the condition of, in the case of, in relation to, subject to, affected by, engaged *or* involved in; **2.** *with acc.* into; a) *of space:* into, up to, down to, towards; b) *of time:* to, till, for; c) *of other relations:* in relation to, about, respecting, towards, against, with a view to, according to.
in-abruptus 3 unbroken.
in-accēnsus 3 unkindled.
in-accessus 3 inaccessible.
in-acēscō, acuī, — 3 to turn sour; to become bitter.
in-adsuētus 3, *see* **inassuetus.**
in-adustus 3 unsinged.
in-aedificō 1 **a**) to build in *or* upon (*in re, in rem*); **b**) to build up, wall *or* block up, barricade.
in-aequābilis, e unequal, uneven.
in-aequālis, e a) unequal, uneven, unlike; **b**) varying, changeable; **c**) making unequal.
in-aequālitās, ātis *f* unevenness.
in-aequātus 3 unequal.

in-aequō 1 to make even, level.
in-aestimābilis, e priceless, inestimable; **a**) valueless, worthless; **b**) unaccountable.
in-aestuō 1 to boil *or* rage within.
in-affectātus 3 unaffected.
in-agitābilis, e immovable.
in-agitātus 3 unmoved.
in-alpinus 3 living on the Alps.
in-amābilis, e repulsive, odious.
in-amārēscō, ruī, — 3 to become bitter.
in-amātus 3 unloved.
in-ambitiōsus 3 unambitious, unassuming.
in-ambulātiō, ōnis *f* a walking up and down.
in-ambulō 1 to walk up and down.
in-amoenus 3 unpleasant.
ināniae, ārum *f/pl.* emptiness.
inānilogista, ae *m* idle talker.
(**in-animālis, e** *and*) **in-animus** 3 lifeless, inanimate.
inānimentum, ī *n* emptiness.
ināniō 4 to make empty.
in-ānis, e empty, void, vacant; **a**) stripped, deserted, abandoned, unoccupied; **b**) empty-handed; **c**) useless, worthless, vain, groundless; **d**) conceited, puffed up; *subst.* **ināne, is** *n* empty space, vanity.
inānitās, ātis *f* emptiness, empty space; vanity, worthlessness.
in-apertus 3 not exposed.
in-arātus 3 unploughed.
in-ārdēscō, ārsī, — 3 to kindle, take fire, burn, glow.
in-ārēscō, ruī, — 3 to become dry.
in-ascēnsus 3 not ascended.
in-aspectus 3 unseen.
in-assuētus 3 unaccustomed.
in-attenuātus 3 undiminished, unimpaired.
in-audāx, ācis timid, fearful.
in-audiō 4 to hear tell, be told of (esp. a secret).
in-audītus 3 **a**) unheard of, unusual; **b**) unheard, without a hearing.
in-augurō 1 **a**) to practise augury; **b**) to inaugurate, consecrate.
in-aurēs, ium *f/pl.* ear-rings.
in-aurō 1 to overlay with gold.
in-auspicātus 3 done without auspices; *adv.* **-ō.**
in-ausus 3 not ventured, not attempted.
inb..., *see* **imb...**
in-caeduus 3 uncut, unfelled.
in-calēscō, luī, — 3 to grow warm *or* hot, to glow.
in-calfaciō 3 to warm, heat.
in-callidus 3 unskilful, unintelligent.
in-candēscō, udī, — 3 to grow hot, to glow.
in-cānēscō, nuī, — 3 to become white *or* grey.
in-cantō 1 to consecrate with charms.
in-cānus 3 quite white.
in-cassum, *see* **cassus.**
in-castīgātus 3 unpunished.
in-cautus 3 **a**) incautious, inconsiderate, heedless; **b**) unforeseen, unexpected; **c**) unguarded, unsafe.
in-cēdō, ssī, ssum 3 to go, step, march along; **a**) to advance, proceed, march (*in, ad alqd*); **b**) to come to, happen, befall, attack, approach, appear; **c**) to go *or* come into (*alqd*).
in-celebrātus 3, **in-celeber, bris, bre** not made known, not famed.
in-cēnātus 3 dinnerless.
incendiārius, ī *m* incendiary.
incendium, ī *n* fire, conflagration; **a**) fire, flame, heat, glow; **b**) vehemence, passion; **c**) destruction.
in-cendō, ndī, ēnsum 3 to kindle, set fire to, set on fire; **a**) to light up, brighten, illumine; **b**) to inflame, fire, rouse, excite, enrage; **c**) to enhance, increase; **d**) to ruin.
in-cēnō 1 to dine in *or* at.
in-cēnsiō, ōnis *f* a setting on fire.
in-cēnsus[1] 3, *part. of* **incendo.**
in-cēnsus[2] 3 not assessed, unregistered.
inceptiō, ōnis *f* = **inceptum.**
in-ceptō 1 to begin, undertake.
inceptor, ōris *m* beginner.
inceptum, ī *n and* **-tus, ūs** *m* a beginning, undertaking, attempt, enterprise, design.
in-cernō 3 to sift.
in-cērō 1 to smear with wax.
incertō 1 to make uncertain.
in-certus 3 **a**) uncertain, unreliable, unsettled, vague, obscure; **b**) doubtful, dubious, doubting, hesitating (*gen.*); *subst.* **incertum, ī** *n* uncertainty.
in-cessō, (īv)ī, — 3 to assault, assail, attack (*acc.*).

in-cessus, ūs *m* **a)** a walking, pace, gait; **b)** attack, invasion; **c)** entrance.
incesti-ficus 3 acting uncleanly.
incestō 1 to pollute, defile.
in-cestus[1] 3 polluted, impure, defiled, sinful, unchaste, lewd; **incestum, ī** *n* unchastity, incest.
in-cestus[2] **ūs** *m* = **incestum,** *see* **incestus**[1].
in-choō, *see* **incoho.**
in-cidō[1], **cidī, cāsum** 3 to fall into *or* upon (*in alqd, dat.*); **a)** to rush at, flow into; **b)** to attack, assault (*in alqm*); **c)** to incur, become involved, fall in with, come upon (*in alqd, dat.*); **d)** to fall out, happen, occur; to come upon, befall (*alci*).
in-cīdō[2], **cīdī, cīsum** 3 **a)** to cut into, cut through; **b)** to cut upon, engrave (*in rem, re*); **c)** to break off, interrupt, stop; **d)** to cut off, remove (*spem*).
incīle, is *n* canal for carrying off [water.]
incīlō 1 to rebuke.
in-cingō 3 to gird, gird about, surround.
in-cinō 3 to begin to sing.
in-cipiō, *pf.* **coepī, coeptum** *and* **inceptum** 3 **a)** to take in hand, begin, commence, undertake (*alqd, a re*; with *inf.*); to have a beginning, [arise.]
in-cipissō 3 to begin.
incīsē, -sim *adv.* in short phrases.
in-cīsiō, ōnis *f*, **in-cīsum, ī** *n* section, division, clause.
incitāmentum, ī *n* incitement, inducement, incentive.
incitātiō, ōnis *f* an inciting, rousing; **a)** violent motion; **b)** ardour, energy.
in-citō 1 to set in rapid motion; **a)** to incite, urge, rouse, spur on; **b)** to excite, stir up, stimulate; **c)** to enhance, increase; **incitātus** 3 hurried, rapid, swift.
in-citus[1] 3 rapid, swift.
in-citus[2] 3 immovable (of pieces in a game); **ad incitās** (*sc. calcēs*) **redigere** to bring to a standstill, checkmate.
in-cīvīlis, e uncivil, hard, cruel.
in-clāmitō 1 to cry against, scold.
in-clāmō 1 to cry out to, call upon; to scold.
in-clārēscō, ruī, — 3 to become known *or* famous.
in-clēmēns, tis unmerciful, harsh.
in-clēmentia, ae *f* harshness, unkindness, rigour.
in-clīnābilis, e inclined, prone to (*ad alqd*).
in-clīnātiō, ōnis *f* a leaning, bending, inclining; **a)** inclination, favour; **b)** alteration, change, inflexion.
in-clīnātus 3 inclined; **a)** bent down, sunken, fallen; **b)** disposed, prone, favourable (*ad alqd, ad* [*alqm*).]
in-clīnis, e bending.
in-clīnō 1 **1.** *trans.* to lean, bend, incline, direct, turn; a) to drive back; b) to sink; c) to change, alter, change for the worse, bring down, cause to decline; d) to give a decisive turn to; **2.** *intr.* (*and* **P.**); a) to turn, incline, sink; b) to yield, give way; c) to change.
inclitus 3 = **inclutus.**
in-clūdō, sī, sum 3 **a)** to shut up *or* in, to confine, enclose, keep in (*alqm in rem, in re*); **b)** to insert, embrace, comprehend; **c)** to obstruct, hinder.
in-clūsiō, ōnis *f* confinement.
in-clutus 3 famous, renowned.
in-coāctus 3 not compulsory.
in-coctus 3 uncooked, raw.
in-cōgitābilis, e, in-cōgitāns, tis inconsiderate.
in-cōgitantia, ae *f* thoughtlessness.
in-cōgitātus 3 unstudied; unthinkable; thoughtless.
in-cōgitō 1 to contrive, design against.
in-cognitus 3 **a)** unknown; **b)** unexamined, untried; **c)** unclaimed.
in-cohō 1 to begin, commence; *part.* **in-cohātus** 3 only begun, unfinished. [resident.]
incola, ae *m* (*and f*) inhabitant.
in-colō 3 (*trans.* and *intr.*) to dwell, abide in, inhabit (*alqd*).
in-columis, e uninjured, safe and sound, unharmed.
incolumitās, ātis *f* safety, soundness, good condition.
in-comitātus 3 unaccompanied.
in-comitiō 1 to insult publicly.
in-commendātus 3 given up, abandoned.
in-commodesticus 3 = **incommodus.** [venience.]
in-commoditās, ātis *f* incon-
in-commodō 1 to be troublesome, to annoy (*dat.*).

in-commodum, ī *n* **a)** inconvenience, trouble; **b)** disadvantage, detriment, injury; **c)** damage, misfortune.

in-commodus 3 inconvenient, unsuitable, unfit; unreasonable; troublesome, disagreeable.

in-commūtābilis, e unchangeable.

in-compertus 3 unascertained, unknown.

in-compositus 3 not arranged, disordered, irregular, artless, rough.

in-comprehēnsibilis, e not to be seized; incomprehensible; unattainable.

in-cōmptus 3 untended, unkempt, unadorned; artless, rude.

in-concessus 3 not allowed, forbidden.

in-conciliō 1 to ensnare; to get by trickery.

in-concinnus 3 awkward, inelegant, absurd.

in-concussus 3 unshaken.

in-conditus 3 confused, unorganized, disorderly; artless, rough.

in-cōnfūsus 3 not disconcerted.

in-congruēns, tis not agreeing, inconsistent.

in-cōnsīderantia, ae *f* thoughtlessness.

in-cōnsīderātus 3 thoughtless, inconsiderate.

in-cōnsōlābilis, e inconsolable.

in-cōnstāns, tis changeable, inconstant, fickle, capricious.

in-cōnstantia, ae *f* inconsistency, fickleness.

incōnsultū *meo* without consulting me.

in-cōnsultus 3 **a)** not consulted; **b)** without advice; **c)** inconsiderate, indiscreet.

in-cōnsūmptus 3 unconsumed; imperishable.

in-contāminātus 3 undefiled.

in-contentus e unstretched.

in-continēns, tis incontinent, intemperate.

in-continentia, ae *f* incontinence, intemperance.

in-conveniēns, tis not agreeing with, dissimilar.

in-coquō 3 to boil in *or* with; to dye, imbue.

in-corporālis, e unsubstantial.

in-corrēctus 3 unamended, uncorrected.

in-corruptus 3 not corrupted, unspoiled, uninjured; **a)** unadulterated, genuine; **b)** pure, upright; **c)** unbribed.

in-crēbrāvit (?) has visited frequently.

in-crēb(r)ēscō, b(r)uī, — 3 to become prevalent *or* strong; to grow, increase.

in-crēdibilis, e incredible, extraordinary.

in-crēdulus 3 unbelieving, incredulous.

in-crēmentum, ī *n* growth, increase; seed, progeny.

in-crepitō 1 **a)** to call loudly to; **b)** to reproach, rebuke.

in-crepō, uī, itum 1 **1.** *intr.* to make a noise; a) to rustle, rattle, roar; b) to be noised abroad; **2.** *trans.* a) to utter aloud, call upon; b) to cause to sound; c) to thunder at, to upbraid, chide, rebuke, reproach.

in-crēscō, crēvī, — 3 to grow in *or* upon; to grow, increase.

in-crētus 3, *part. of* **incerno.**

in-cruentātus 3 not stained with blood.

in-cruentus 3 without bloodshed, unwounded.

in-crustō 1 to cover, incrust.

in-cubitō 1 to defile.

in-cubō, uī, itum 1 to lie in *or* upon; **a)** to pass the night in a temple; **b)** to hatch, brood over; **c)** to watch earnestly over.

in-cūdō, dī, sum 3 to forge, shape.

in-culcō 1 to trample in; to mix in; **a)** to impress, inculcate; **b)** to force upon (*alci alqd*).

in-culpātus 3 unblamed, blameless.

in-cultus[1] 3 uncultivated, untilled; **a)** unarranged, disordered; **b)** unpolished, unrefined; **c)** rude, without education; **d)** waste, desert; rough.

in-cultus[2], **ūs** *m* neglect.

in-cumbō, cubuī, cubitum 3 to lie upon, recline *or* lean upon (*in alqd; dat.*); **a)** to rush towards, throw oneself upon; **b)** to burst upon; **c)** to apply, devote oneself to, exert oneself with; **d)** to incline towards; **e)** to fall upon forcibly.

in-cūnābula, ōrum *n/pl.* cradle clothes; **a)** birth-place, cradle; **b)** origin, beginning.

in-cūrātus 3 unhealed, incurable.
in-cūria, ae *f* want of care, carelessness, negligence, indifference.
in-cūriōsus 3 **a)** careless, negligent; **b)** neglected.
in-currō, (cu)currī, cursum 3 to run to *or* against, run into (*in alqd; dat.*); **a)** to rush at *or* upon, assail, to make an inroad; **b)** to extend to, border on; **c)** to meet, stumble on; to fall into (*an evil*), to incur; **d)** to fall on, coincide with.
in-cursiō, ōnis *f* **a)** a running against; **b)** onset, assault, attack; **c)** inroad, incursion.
in-cursitō 1 to run against, attack.
in-cursō 1 to run *or* strike against (*dat.*); **a)** to attack, to make an incursion into (*in alqd*); **b)** to meet, fall upon.
in-cursus, ūs *m* = **incursio.**
in-curvēscō *and* **-īscō** 3 —, — to bend, curve.
in-curvō 1 to bend (*inwards*), curve.
in-curvus 3 bent, curved, crooked.
in-cūs, ūdis *f* anvil.
in-cūsātiō, ōnis *f* accusation, blame, reproach.
in-cūsō 1 to accuse, find fault with.
in-cussus, ūs *m* a dashing against, shock.
in-cūstōdītus 3 **a)** unwatched, unguarded; **b)** unconcealed.
in-cutiō, cussī, cussum 3 to strike, dash *or* beat against (*alqd in alqd*); **a)** to throw, hurl; **b)** to strike into, inspire with, inflict, (*alci alqd*).
indāgātiō, ōnis *f* inquiry, investigation.
indāgātor, ōris *m* investigator, explorer.
indāgātrīx, īcis *f* she who searches *or* explores.
ind-āgō[1] 1 to trace out; to search, explore.
indāgō[2], **inis** *f* an encircling, enclosing (*esp.* in hunting).
ind-audiō = **in-audiō.**
in-de *adv.* from there, thence, **a)** on that side; **b)** from that time forth, after that, thereupon; **c)** from that cause.
in-dēbitus 3 not owed, not due.
in-decēns, tis unbecoming, improper, indecent.
in-deceō 2 to be unbecoming.
in-dēclīnābilis, e inflexible.
in-dēclīnātus 3 unchanged; firm.
in-decoris, e without honour, shameful.
in-decorō 1 to disfigure, disgrace, dishonour.
in-decōrus 3 unbecoming, unseemly, ugly, disgraceful.
in-dēfatīgābilis, e, in-dēfatīgātus 3 untiring.
in-dēfēnsus 3 unprotected.
in-dēfessus 3 unwearied; indefatigable.
in-dēflētus 3 unwept.
in-dēiectus 3 not thrown down.
in-dēlēbilis, e imperishable.
in-dēlībātus 3 untouched.
in-demnātus 3 uncondemned.
in-demnis, e uninjured.
in-dēplōrātus 3 unwept, unlamented.
in-dēprāvātus 3 uncorrupted.
in-dēprēnsus 3 undetected.
in-dēsertus 3 not forsaken; imperishable.
in-dēspectus 3 unfathomable.
in-dēstrictus 3 unhurt.
in-dētōnsus 3 unshorn.
in-dēvītātus 3 unavoided; unavoidable.
in-dex, icis *m* (and *f*) informer; **a)** betrayer, indicator; **b)** the forefinger; **c)** title, inscription; **d)** touch-stone; **e)** index.
indicātiō, ōnis *f* a valuing, setting a price upon a thing.
indīcente mē without my saying.
indicium, ī *n* discovery, disclosure, evidence; **a)** permission to *or* reward for giving evidence; **b)** mark, proof.
in-dicō[1] 1 to disclose, point out, show, declare; **a)** to make known, tell; **b)** to put a price on, to value.
in-dīcō[2] 3 **a)** to announce, proclaim, declare, to make publicly known; **b)** to impose, enjoin (*alci alqd*).
in-dictiō, ōnis *f* (proclamation of) a tax.
in-dictus 3 unsaid; **indictā causā** without a hearing.
ind-idem *adv.* from the same place.
in-differēns, tis indifferent.
ind-igem (*acc.*) needy.
indi-gena, ae *m* and *f* native, indigenous.
indigentia, ae *f* need, want, insatiableness.
ind-igeō, uī, — 2 to need, want, be in need of (*abl.* or *gen.*); to long for; **indigēns, tis** needy.

indiges, etis, indigenous; native god, deified hero.
in-dīgestus 3 unarranged.
in-dīgnābundus 3 full of indignation, indignant.
in-dīgnāns, tis impatient, indignant.
in-dīgnātiō, ōnis *f* indignation, displeasure, disdain.
indīgnātiuncula, ae *f* little indignation.
in-dīgnitās, ātis *f* **a**) unworthiness, shamefulness, degrading treatment; **b**) indignation.
in-dīgnor 1 to consider as unworthy *or* improper, to be offended *or* indignant at (*alqd*).
in-dīgnus 3 unworthy, not deserving (with *abl.;* with *qui* and *subj.*); undeservedly suffering; **a**) innocent; **b**) unbecoming, shameful; undeserved; **indīgnē ferre** to take ill.
indigus 3 needy, in want of.
in-dīligēns, tis careless.
in-dīligentia, ae *f* carelessness, negligence.
ind-ipīscor (*and* **-ō**), **deptus sum** 3 to attain, obtain.
in-dīreptus 3 unplundered.
in-discrētus 3 **a**) undivided; **b**) without distinction, indistinguishable.
in-disertus 3 not eloquent.
in-dispēnsātus 3 unregulated.
in-dispositus 3 unarranged.
in-dissolūbilis, e indissoluble.
in-distinctus 3 confused.
in-dīviduus 3 indivisible; *subst.* **in-dīviduum, ī** *n* an atom.
in-dīvīsus 3 held in common.
in-dō, didī, ditum 3 to put into, set *or* place in *or* on, insert (*alqd in rem* or *alci rei*); **a**) to give, apply, impose; **b**) to introduce; **c**) to cause, occasion.
in-docilis, e a) unteachable; ignorant; **b**) hard to learn.
in-doctus 3 untaught; unskilful.
in-dolentia, ae *f* freedom from pain, insensibility.
ind-olēs, is *f* natural constitution, inborn quality, nature; disposition, talents.
in-dolēscō, luī, — 3 to feel pain, be grieved.
in-domābilis, e untamable.
in-domitus 3 **a**) untamed, unrestrained, wild; **b**) untamable, invincible.
in-dormiō 4 to sleep in *or* upon; to be asleep; to sleep over.
in-dōtātus 3 without a dowry, without gifts.
in-dubitātus 3 undoubted.
in-dubitō 1 to distrust (*dat.*).
in-dubius 3 not doubtful.
in-dūcō 3 to draw over, overlay (*alqd re*), to draw on; **a**) to strike out; **b**) to repeal, cancel, make invalid; **c**) to bring in, introduce; **d**) to lead in, lead up, bring forward; **e**) to bring upon the stage, produce, represent in speaking *or* writing; **f**) to set down in an account; **g**) to move, excite, persuade, induce, seduce (*alqm ad* or *in alqd; ut*); **(in) animum indūcere** to bring one's mind to, to resolve; to be convinced.
in-ductiō, ōnis *f* **a**) a bringing in, leading to; **b**) introduction; **c**) intention, inclination; **d**) induction, reasoning from instances.
inductor, ōris *m* chastiser.
in-ductus[1]**, ūs** *m* inducement, incitement.
in-ductus[2] 3 imported; foreign.
indūcula, ae *f* a woman's under-garment.
indu-gredior = **ingredior.**
indulgēns, tis kind, tender, indulgent.
indulgentia, ae *f* kindness, indulgence, forbearance; tenderness, affection.
in-dulgeō, lsī, (ltum) 2 to be complaisant, forbearing, to yield, incline, allow, gratify (*dat.*); **a**) to give oneself up to; **b**) to care for; to concede, permit, grant.
ind-ūmentum, ī *n* covering, skin.
ind-uō, uī, ūtum 3 to put on, dress in (*alci alqd*); **a**) to cover, wrap, clothe, array; **b**) to entangle, involve (*alqm re*); to engage in; to assume.
indu-perātor, ōris *m* = **imperator.**
in-dūrēscō, ruī, — 3 to become hard; to be hardened.
in-dūrō 1 to make hard, harden.
indusiārius, ī *m* maker of upper tunics (?).
indusiātus 3 wearing an upper tunic (?).
industria, ae *f* diligence, activity, assiduity, industry; **(de) industriā** purposely, intentionally.

industrius 3 diligent, active, zealous, assiduous.
indūtiae, ārum *f/pl.* truce, armistice.
indūtus, ūs *m* a putting on; attire.
induviae, ārum *f/pl.* clothes.
in-ēbriō 1 to intoxicate; to deafen with talk.
in-edia, ae *f* abstinence from food, fasting.
in-ēditus 3 not published.
in-efficāx, ācis ineffective.
in-ēlabōrātus 3 unstudied.
in-ēlegāns, tis inelegant, tasteless, not fine.
in-ēluctābilis, e inevitable.
in-ēmendābilis, e irremediable.
in-ēmorior 3 to die in *or* at (*dat.*).
in-ēmptus 3 unbought.
in-ēnārrābilis, e indescribable.
in-ēnōdābilis, e inexplicable.
in-eō, iī, itum, īre 1. *intr.* to go in, enter (*in alqd*); to begin, commence; **iniēns aetas** youth; **2.** *trans.* a) to enter; b) to commence a period of time, to begin (*office, business*), to undertake; **ratiōnem reī inīre** to make an estimate, to calculate, consider; **gratiam ab alqo** to obtain the favour of.
ineptia, ae *f* (*mostly pl.*) silliness, absurdity.
ineptiō 4 to play the fool.
in-eptus 3 **a**) unsuitable, unfit, improper; **b**) silly, awkward, absurd.
in-ermis, e *and* **-mus** 3 unarmed, defenceless; harmless.
in-errāns, tis not wandering, fixed.
in-errō 1 to wander in, haunt.
in-ers, tis without skill; **a**) inactive, lazy, idle, cowardly, indolent; **b**) numbing; dull, insipid.
inertia, ae *f* unskilfulness; inactivity, laziness.
in-ērudītus 3 unlearned, illiterate.
in-ēscō 1 to allure with a bait.
in-euschēmē *adv.* unbecomingly.
inēvectus mounted high.
in-ēvītābilis, e inevitable.
in-ēvolūtus 3 not unrolled, unopened,
in-excitābilis, e from which one cannot be roused.
in-excītus 3 unmoved, quiet.
in-excūsābilis, e inexcusable, without excuse.
in-exercitātus 3 untrained.
in-exhaustus 3 unexhausted, inexhaustible.
in-exōrābilis, e a) inexorable; **b**) unobtainable by entreaty.
in-expedītus 3 entangled.
in-experrēctus 3 not awakened.
in-expertus 3 **a**) inexperienced, unpractised, unacquainted with; **b**) untried, untested.
in-expiābilis, e inexpiable; implacable.
in-explēbilis, e insatiable.
in-explētus 3 insatiable.
in-explicābilis, e inextricable, intricate; **a**) impracticable, impassable (*via*); **b**) with no result, endless.
in-explicitus 3 obscure.
in-explōrātus 3 unexplored; *adv.* **-ō** without reconnoitring.
in-expugnābilis, e impregnable, unconquerable.
in-exspectātus 3 unlooked for.
in-exstinctus 3 unextinguished; insatiable.
in-exsuperābilis, e insurmountable, insuperable.
in-extrīcābilis, e inextricable.
īn-fabrē *adv.* unskilfully.
īn-fabricātus 3 unwrought, unfashioned.
īn-facētiae, ārum *f/pl.* coarse jests, absurdities.
īn-facētus 3 without wit, dull, stupid, coarse.
īn-fācundus 3 not eloquent.
īnfāmia, ae *f* ill fame, ill report, shame, disgrace, reproach.
īn-fāmis, e disreputable, infamous; disgraceful.
īn-fāmō 1 to bring into ill repute; to accuse, charge.
īn-fandus 3 unspeakable, unutterable; shocking, abominable.
īn-fāns tis a) speechless; **b**) poor of speech, not eloquent; **c**) young, little, infant; childish, foolish, silly; *subst.* **īnfāns, tis** *m* and *f* (little) child.
īnfantārius 3 fond of children.
īnfantia, ae *f* lack of eloquence; infancy.
īn-fatīgābilis, e tireless.
īn-fatuō 1 to befool, infatuate.
īn-faustus 3 unlucky, unpropitious.
īn-fector, ōris *m* dyer.
īn-fectus[1] 3 dyed.
īn-fectus[2] 3 not done, not made, unfinished, unaccomplished; **īn-**

fectā rē without effecting one's purpose; **a**) impracticable, impossible; **b**) uncoined.
īn-fēcunditās, ātis *f* barrenness.
īn-fēcundus 3 barren, unfruitful.
īn-fēlīcitās, ātis *f* ill-luck, unhappiness.
īn-fēlīcō 1 to bring bad luck to.
īn-fēlīx, īcis a) unfruitful; **b**) unhappy, unlucky, miserable; ill-boding.
īn-fēnsō 1 to treat as an enemy.
īn-fēnsus 3 hostile, ready to attack.
īn-ferciō, rsī, rsum 4 to stuff in, cram in.
īnferiae, ārum *f/pl.* sacrifices in honour of the dead.
īnferior, ius, *see* **inferus.**
īnfernus 3 lower, of the underworld.
īn-ferō, intulī, illātum 3 to bring, bear, carry in *or* to (*alqd in alqd*, or with *dat.*); **a**) to put *or* place on; **b**) to offer, sacrifice, render; to bring forward, introduce, produce; **c**) **bellum alci** to make war on, make an attack; **signa** to advance to the attack; **d**) to produce, cause, occasion, inspire; **P.** *or* **se īnferre** to fall into, to rush, hasten.
īnferus 3 below, beneath; *subst.* **īnferī, ōrum** *m/pl.* the dead, the lower world; — *comp.* **īnferior, ius** lower, further down; subsequent, later, latter; inferior, weaker, meaner; — *superl.* **īnfimus** 3 *and* **īmus** 3 lowest, last, worst, meanest; **īmum, ī** *n* lowest part, bottom.
īn-fervēscō, ferbuī, — 3 to begin to boil.
īn-festō 1 to annoy, attack.
īn-festus 3 **a**) unsafe, insecure, molested; **b**) hostile, inimical, dangerous, troublesome, ready for battle.
īn-ficētus 3 *and* **īnficētiae,** *see* **infacetus, infacetiae.**
īn-ficiō, fēcī, fectum 3 **a**) to dye, colour; to steep; **b**) to poison, stain, taint, infect, corrupt.
īn-fidēlis, e unfaithful, faithless.
īn-fidēlitās, ātis *f* faithlessness.
īn-fīdus 3 faithless, treacherous, false.
īn-fīgō 3 to fasten in *or* to, drive in, affix (*alqd in rem; dat.*); to imprint, impress, fix in (*alqd in re, dat.*).
īnfimātis, is *m* person of the lowest rank.
īnfimus 3, *see* **inferus.**
īn-findō 3 to cut into.
īn-fīnitās, ātis *f* endlessness.
īn-fīnītiō, ōnis *f* infinity.
īn-fīnītus 3 boundless; **a**) endless, unceasing, countless; **b**) indefinite, general.
īn-firmātiō, ōnis *f* invalidation.
īn-firmitās, ātis *f* weakness, infirmity; **a**) want of courage *or* spirit; **b**) unsteadiness, instability.
īn-firmō 1 to weaken; **a**) to shake; **b**) to refute; to annul.
īn-firmus 3 weak, feeble; **a**) invalid, ill; **b**) timorous, superstitious, inconstant; **c**) trivial, inconclusive.
īn-fit he (she) begins.
īnfitiae, ārum *f/pl.* a denying; **īnfitiās īre** to deny.
īnfitiālis, e negative, containing a denial.
īnfitiātiō, ōnis *f* a denying.
īnfitiātor, ōris *m* denier.
īnfitior 1 to deny, disown (*alqd*).
īn-flammātiō, ōnis *f* a kindling; conflagration; an inflaming.
īn-flammō 1 **a**) to kindle, set on fire; **b**) to inflame, excite, stir up, rouse.
īn-flātiō, ōnis *f* a blowing up, flatulence.
īn-flātus[1] 3 blown into; **a**) swollen; **b**) puffed up, pompous, haughty; **c**) scornful.
īn-flātus[2], **ūs** *m* a blowing into, blast; inspiration.
īn-flectō 3 to bend, curve; **a**) to modulate (*the voice*); **b**) to change, alter; **c**) to move, affect.
īn-flētus 3 unwept.
īn-flexibilis, e inflexible.
īn-flexiō, ōnis *f* a bending.
īn-flexus, ūs *m* bending; change.
īn-flīgō, xī, ctum 3 to strike against, dash into (*alci rei alqd*); to inflict, impose (*alci alqd*).
īn-flō 1 to blow into; **a**) to puff out, swell; **b**) to produce by blowing; **c**) to puff up, make proud; **d**) to inspire, encourage.
īn-fluō, uxī, — 3 to flow *or* stream in; to steal into.
īn-fodiō 3 to dig in, bury.
īn-fōrmātiō, ōnis *f* representation, idea, conception.
īn-formīdātus 3 not feared.
īn-fōrmis, e shapeless; deformed, hideous.

īn-fōrmō 1 to form, shape, fashion; **a**) to form an idea, to conceive; **b**) to represent, describe; **c**) to instruct, educate.
īn-forō 1 **a**) to summon to court; **b**) to penetrate.
īn-fortūnātus 3 unfortunate, unhappy.
īnfortūnium, ī *n* misfortune, calamity.
īnfrā 1. *adv*. below, beneath; **2.** *prep.* with *acc.* a) below, beneath; b) later than; c) inferior to.
īn-frāctiō, ōnis *f* a breaking.
īn-frāctus 3 **a**) exhausted, dejected; **b**) disconnected.
īn-fragilis, e unwearied, strong.
īn-fremō 3 to growl, bellow.
īn-frēnātus[1] 3 without a bridle.
īn-frēnātus[2] 3, *part. pf.* P. *of* **infreno.**
īn-frendō 3 to gnash (*the teeth*).
īn-frēnis, e (*and* **-us** 3) unbridled.
īn-frēnō 1 to bridle, harness; to restrain.
īn-frequēns, tis infrequent, in small numbers, seldom doing; **a**) thinly attended, not forming a quorum; **b**) scantily populated, not filled with, not well provided with.
īn-frequentia, ae *f* **a**) small number, scantiness; **b**) solitude, loneliness.
īn-fringō, frēgī, frāctum 3 to break off, break in pieces; to weaken, impair, subdue.
īn-frōns, dis without foliage, treeless.
īn-frūctuōsus 3 fruitless, useless.
īn-frūnītus 3 unsatisfactory; uninteresting, silly.
īn-fūcātus 3 highly coloured.
īnfula, ae *f* bandage; (*sacred*) fillet; ornament.
īnfulātus 3 wearing an *infula*.
īn-fulciō 4 to stuff *or* cram in.
īnfumus, īnfumātis = **infi...**
īn-fundō 3 to pour in *or* on (*alqd in alqd*); **a**) to administer, pour out; **b**) to cause to enter, let stream in *or* on; to spread over; **īnfūsus** 3 spread, lying on (*dat.*).
īn-fuscō 1 to make dark *or* black; to stain, tarnish, disfigure, corrupt, spoil.
in-gemēscō 3 = **ingemisco.**
in-geminō 1 to (re)double, repeat, reiterate; *intr.* to be redoubled.
in-gemīscō, muī, — 3 to groan over, sigh at; lament (*alqd, alqm*).
in-gemō 3 = **ingemisco.**
in-generō 1 to implant; to produce.
ingeniātus 3 disposed by nature.
in-geniōsus 3 naturally gifted, talented; requiring talent; naturally suited.
in-genium, ī *n* innate *or* natural quality; **a**) disposition, temper, character; natural bent; **b**) natural capacity, mental power, talents, abilities, parts, genius, fancy; **c**) man of genius; **d**) clever thought.
in-gēns, tis vast, huge, immense, enormous.
in-genuī (*pf. indic.*) to implant; **ingenitus** inborn.
ingenuitās, ātis *f* **a**) condition of one freeborn; **b**) uprightness, frankness, noble-mindedness.
in-genuus 3 native; **a**) freeborn; **b**) like a freeman, noble, honourable; upright, frank; **c**) weak, delicate.
in-gerō 3 to carry, put, throw *or* heap into *or* on; **a**) to inflict; **b**) to obtrude, force upon (*alci alqd*).
in-glomerō 1 to pile up.
in-glōri(ōs)us 3 inglorious.
in-gluviēs, ēī *f* gullet, crop of birds, maw; gluttony.
in-grātē unwillingly; ungratefully.
ingrāti-ficus 3 unthankful.
in-grāt(i)īs *adv.* unwillingly.
in-grātus 3 **a**) unpleasant; **b**) ungrateful; thankless, unprofitable.
in-gravēscō, —, — 3 to become heavier; to grow worse *or* more oppressive.
in-gravō 1 to make heavy, oppress, molest, make worse.
in-gredior, gressus sum 3 **a**) to go into, enter (*intra* or *in alqd*); **b**) to go along, walk, proceed; **c**) to enter upon, engage in (*alqd*); **d**) to attack; to begin, to undertake; to commence speaking.
in-gressiō, ōnis *f* = **ingressus.**
in-gressus, ūs *m* **a**) an entering, marching in, entrance; **b**) inroad; **c**) a walking, gait, pace; **d**) a beginning.
in-gruō, uī, — 3 to break in, fall upon violently, assail (*in alqd*).
inguen, inis *n* (*mostly pl.* **inguina, um**) the groin; **a**) the privy parts; **b**) tumour.

in-gurgitō 1 to pour in, swill; **se ingurgitāre** to plunge in; to gormandize.
in-gustātus 3 not tasted before.
in-habilis, e unmanageable, unwieldy; unfit, ill adapted to.
in-habitābilis, e uninhabitable.
in-habitō 1 to inhabit, dwell in.
in-haereō, sī, (sum) 2 **a**) to stick in *or* fast, to cling, adhere, remain fast to; **b**) to be inherent, connected (*ad alqd, in re, dat.*). **[inhaereo.]**
in-haerēscō, haesī, haesum 3 = }
in-hālō 1 to breathe at *or* upon.
in-hibeō, uī, itum 2 to hold back *or* in; **a**) to row backwards, to cease rowing; **b**) to check, restrain, hinder; **c**) to practise, use, employ (*alqd alci* or *in alqm*).
in-hibitiō, ōnis *f* a restraining; backward movement.
in-hiō 1 to gape, to open the mouth wide; **a**) to gape at *or* for; **b**) to regard longingly.
in-honestō 1 to dishonour.
in-honestus 3 **a**) dishonourable, shameful, disgraceful; **b**) unseemly, ugly.
in-honōrātus 3 **a**) not honoured, disregarded; **b**) unrewarded.
in-honōri-ficus 3 dishonourable.
in-honōrus 3 unsightly.
in-horreō, —, — 2 to stand erect, bristle.
in-horrēscō, ruī, — 3 a) to rise erect, bristle up; **b**) to shake, shudder, tremble.
in-hospitālis, e inhospitable.
in-hospitālitās, ātis *f* inhospitality.
inhospitus 3 inhospitable.
in-hūmānitās, ātis *f* inhumanity, cruelty; **a**) barbarity, rudeness; **b**) incivility, brutality, unkindness; **c**) niggardliness.
in-hūmāniter uncivilly.
in-hūmānus 3 rude, savage, cruel, barbarous, inhuman; **a**) uncultivated; **b**) uncivil, uncourteous.
in-humātus 3 unburied.
in-ibi *adv.* in that place, there; near (*of time*); therein.
īn-icio, iēcī, iectum 3 **a**) to throw, cast *or* put in *or* into (*alqd in alqd* or *dat.*); **se īnicere** to throw oneself into; **b**) to inspire (*alci alqd*), infuse, occasion, to cause; **c**) to mention, let drop; **d**) to throw on *or* over; to lay on (*alci manum*), to seize.
in-iectiō, ōnis *f* a laying on.
in-iectō 1 to lay on.
in-iectus, ūs *m* a throwing on *or* over.
in-igō, ēgī, āctum 3 to drive, incite.
inimīcitiae, ārum *f/pl.* (*rarely sing.*) enmity, hostility.
inimīcō 1 to make hostile.
in-imīcus 3 hostile, inimical; *subst.* ~, **ī** *m*, **-ca, ae** *f* enemy, foe; hurtful, injurious.
inīquitās, ātis *f* unevenness; **a**) unfavourableness, difficulty, adverseness; **b**) unfairness, injustice, unreasonableness.
in-īquus 3 uneven, unequal, steep; **a**) unfavourable, disadvantageous; **b**) excessive, not of the right measure; **c**) unfair, unjust; **d**) inimical, hostile, adverse; **e**) unwilling, impatient.
initiātiō, ōnis *f* (*and* **initiāmenta, ōrum** *n/pl.*) initiation, consecration.
in-itiō 1 to initiate, admit.
initium, ī *n* a going in; beginning, commencement; **a**) *pl.* constituent parts, elements; **b**) first principles, elements of science; **c**) secret mysteries.
in-itus, ūs *m* arrival; beginning.
in-iūcunditās, ātis *f* unpleasantness.
in-iūcundus 3 unpleasant, harsh.
in-iūdicātus 3 undecided.
in-iungō 3 **a**) to join *or* fasten into (*alqd in alqd*); **b**) to join with, attach to (*alci alqd*); to inflict, bring upon; to impose upon, enjoin.
in-iūrātus 3 unsworn.
iniūria, ae *f* injury, injustice, wrong; **a**) outrage, insult, damage, harm; **b**) unjust acquisition; **c**) revenge for an affront.
in-iūrior 1 to do an injury.
iniūriōsus 3 unjust, wrongful, hurtful (*in alqm*).
in-iūr(i)us 3 wrongful, unjust.
in-iussū without orders *or* command.
in-iussus 3 uncommanded, unbidden.
in-iūstitia, ae *f* injustice.
in-iūstus 3 unjust, wrongful; **harsh**, severe, oppressive.
inl..., inm..., *see* **ill..., imm...**
in-nābilis, e that cannot be swum in.
in-nāscor 3 to be born, grow in *or* upon; **innātus** 3 inborn.

in-natō 1 a) to swim into; **b**) to swim *or* float in *or* upon.
in-nāvigābilis, e not navigable.
in-nectō 3 to tie, join, fasten about, together *or* to.
in-nītor 3 to lean, depend upon.
in-nō 1 **a**) to swim into; **b**) to swim upon, sail upon (*alqd*).
in-nocēns, tis a) guiltless, innocent, blameless; **c**) harmless, inoffensive, upright.
innocentia, ae *f* innocence; **a**) inoffensiveness; **b**) uprightness, disinterestedness.
in-nocuus = **innoxius.**
in-nōtēscō, tuī, — 3 to become known.
in-novō 1 to renew; **se** to return to (*ad*).
in-noxius 3 harmless; innocent; unhurt, free from injury.
in-nūbilus 3 (*and* **in-nūbis, e**) cloudless.
in-nūbō 3 to marry into (*with dat.*).
in-nubus 3 = **innuptus.**
in-numerābilis, e innumerable.
in-numerābilitās, ātis *f* countless number.
in-numerus 3 (*and* **-rālis, e**) numberless.
in-nuō, uī, — 3 to nod to *or* at.
in-nuptus 3 unmarried, virgin; (*nuptiae*) unhappy (*marriage*).
in-nūtriō 4 to bring up in.
in-oblītus 3 mindful.
in-obrutus 3 not overwhelmed.
in-obsequēns, tis disobedient.
in-observābilis, e untraceable.
in-observantia, ae *f* carelessness, disorder.
in-observātus 3 unobserved.
in-occiduus 3 never setting *or* closing.
in-odōrus 3 unscented.
in-offēnsus 3 untouched, unobstructed, undisturbed.
in-officiōsus 3 careless of obligations.
in-olēns, entis without smell.
in-olēscō, lēvī, litum 3 to grow upon *or* into (*dat.*).
in-ōminātus 3 ill-omened.
in-opertus 3 naked.
inopia, ae *f* want, lack; need, poverty, scarcity, helplessness.
in-opinans, tis not expecting, unaware.
in-opīnātus (*and* **in-opīnus**) 3 1. (*seldom*) = **inopinans; 2.** unexpected, unsuspected.
in-opiōsus 3 in need of (*alcis*).
in-ops, opis a) helpless, poor, needy, lacking (*alcis rei* or *alqa re*); **b**) powerless, weak; **c**) poor in words *or* thoughts, mean, pitiful.
in-ōrātā rē without pleading.
in-ōrdinātus 3 not arranged.
in-ōrnātus 3 unadorned, uncelebrated.
inp..., *see* **imp...**
inquam (*defective vb.*) to say.
in-quiēs, ētis restless, unquiet.
in-quiētō 1 to disquiet, disturb.
in-quiētus 3 restless, unquiet.
inquilīnus, ī *m* tenant, lodger.
in-quinō 1 to stain, pollute, defile; **inquinātus** 3 polluted, defiled, foul.
in-quīrō, sīvī, sītum 3 to seek after, search for; **a**) to inquire into, examine; **b**) to seek grounds of accusation (*in alqm*).
in-quīsītiō, ōnis *f* a searching after; investigation, inquiry.
in-quīsītor, ōris *m* inquirer, spy; investigator.
in-quīsītus unexamined.
inr..., *see* **irr...**
īn-saepiō 4 to fence round.
īn-salūbris, bre unhealthy.
īn-salūtātus 3 ungreeted.
īn-sānābilis, e incurable.
īnsānia, ae *f* insanity, madness; frenzy; **a**) rapture, inspiration; **b**) senseless extravagance, excess.
īn-sāniō 4 to be mad, insane; to rage, rave.
īn-sānitās, ātis *f* unsoundness.
īn-sānus 3 insane, mad, raging, raving; **a**) enthusiastic, enraptured, inspired; **b**) monstrous, excessive.
īn-satiābilis, e a) insatiable; **b**) not surfeiting.
īn-satiātus 3 insatiate.
īn-satietās, ātis *f* insatiableness.
īn-saturābilis, e insatiable.
īn-scendō, ndī, ēnsum 3 to climb up, mount (*alqd*).
īn-scēnsiō, ōnis *f* embarkation.
īn-sciēns, tis not knowing, unaware; ignorant, silly, stupid.
īn-scientia, ae *f* ignorance, want of knowledge; inexperience.
īnscītia, ae *f* **a**) awkwardness, unskilfulness; **b**) ignorance; = **inscientia.**

īn-scītus 3 unskilful, blundering.
īn-scius 3 not knowing, ignorant.
īn-scrībō 3 **a**) to write in *or* upon (*in re; dat.*), to inscribe; **b**) to ascribe, assign (*alci alqd*); **c**) to furnish with an inscription *or* title (*alci alqd*); **d**) to mark, characterize.
īn-scrīptiō, ōnis *f* **a**) a writing upon; **b**) inscription, title.
īn-sculpō 3 to engrave, cut *or* carve in *or* upon, to impress (*alqd in re*).
īn-secābilis, e indivisible.
īn-secō[1]**, uī, ctum** 1 to cut into, cut to pieces.
īn-secō[2]**, (sexī)** to tell of, relate the story of (*acc.*).
īn-sectātiō, ōnis *f* pursuit; a railing at.
īn-sectātor, ōris *m* persecutor; censurer.
īn-sector (*and* **-ō**) 1 to pursue, attack; to reproach, rail at.
īn-sēdābiliter unceasingly.
īn-segestus not sown.
īn-senēscō, nuī, — 3 to grow old in *or* at (*dat.*).
īn-sēnsilis, e imperceptible.
īn-sēparābilis, e inseparable.
īn-sepultus 3 unburied.
īn-sequor 3 to follow after (*acc.*), come next; **a**) to pursue; **b**) to censure, reproach, attack; **c**) to strive after; **d**) to overtake.
īn-serēnus 3 overcast.
īn-serō[1]**, sēvī, situm** 3 to sow *or* plant in (*in alqd; dat.*); **a**) to ingraft; **b**) to implant; **insitus** 3 innate, natural.
īn-serō[2]**, ruī, rtum** 3 to put, place *or* set in, insert (*alqd in alqd; dat.*); **a**) to introduce, intermingle with; **se inserere** to meddle with; **b**) to incorporate with, place among.
īn-serpō 3 to steal upon.
īn-sertō 1 to put into.
īn-serviō 4 to serve; **a**) to be a slave *or* serviceable; **b**) to be devoted *or* attached to; to take care of, attend to (*dat.*).
īn-servō 1 to observe.
īn-sībilō 1 to hiss *or* whistle in.
īn-siccātus 3 not dried.
īn-sideō, sēdī, sessum 2 **a**) to sit in *or* upon (*in re*), to be settled, seated, fixed, stamped in; **b**) to keep possession of, occupy; to inhabit (*acc.*).
īnsidiae, ārum *f/pl.* ambush, ambuscade; plot, artifice, snare, trap, deceit, treachery.
īnsidiātor, ōris *m* soldier in ambush, waylayer, lurker.
īnsidior 1 to lie in ambush, in wait for; to wait for; to plot against (*dat.*).
īnsidiōsus 3 deceitful, artful, cunning, treacherous; dangerous.
īn-sīdō, sēdī, sessum 3 **a**) to sit down upon (*in re; dat.*); to settle, become fixed, rooted in; **b**) to occupy, beset.
īnsigne, is *n* token, mark, signal; official badge, decoration, distinction; flag, standard.
īn-signiō 4 to make conspicuous, distinguish.
īn-signis, e distinguished by a mark, noted; **a**) remarkable, distinguished; **b**) extraordinary, excellent, notorious.
īnsignītus 3 marked; **a**) noticeable, plain; **b**) notable, distinguished, conspicuous; *adv.* **īnsignītē.**
īnsilia *n/pl.* treadles (of a loom).
īn-siliō, luī, — 4 to leap, spring, jump in *or* on (*in alqd; dat.* or *acc.*).
īnsimul = simul.
īn-simulātiō, ōnis *f* accusation, charge.
īn-simulō 1 to charge, accuse, blame (*alqm* with *gen.*).
īn-sincērus 3 impure, tainted.
īn-sinuātiō, ōnis *f* a winning favour.
īn-sinuō 1 to push forward into a gap; **P.** *or* **se īnsinuāre** to penetrate (*inter* or *in alqd*), work one's way in; to insinuate oneself (*alci*).
īn-sipiēns, tis unwise, foolish.
īnsipientia, ae *f* folly, stupidity.
īn-sistō, stitī, — 3 **1.** to stand *or* tread upon, set foot on (*in re; dat.*); a) to step on; b) to enter, enter on (*alqd*); c) to pursue, press on (*alci*); d) to persist, insist, apply oneself, be busy about (*alqd*); **2.** to stand still, pause, stop, be fixed *or* obstinate in (*inf.*).
īnsitīcius 3 ingrafted, foreign.
īnsitiō, ōnis *f* a grafting; time of grafting.
īnsitīvus 3 grafted, ingrafted; pretended, foreign, spurious, bastard.
īnsitor, ōris *m* grafter.
īn-situs 3, *part. pf.* P *of* **inserō**[1].
īn-sociābilis, e with whom no alliance is possible.
īn-sōlābiliter inconsolably.

īn-solēns, tis a) unaccustomed (*alcis rei, in re*); **b)** unusual, extravagant, excessive, immoderate; **c)** proud, haughty, arrogant, insolent.
īn-solentia, ae *f* **a)** strangeness, novelty; **b)** extravagance, excess; **c)** pride, arrogance.
īn-solēscō, —, — 3 to become haughty *or* insolent.
īn-solidus 3 weak, tender.
īn-solitus 3 **a)** unaccustomed; **b)** unusual.
īn-solūbilis, e that cannot be paid.
īn-somnia, ae *f* sleeplessness.
īn-somnis, e sleepless.
īn-somnium, ī *n* **1.** dream; **2.** = **insomnia.**
īn-sonō, uī, — 1 to sound (*also alqd*), resound, make a noise, roar, rustle, crack.
īn-sōns, tis innocent, guiltless.
īn-sōpītus 3 sleepless.
īn-sopor, -ōris sleepless.
īn-spectiō, ōnis *f* investigation.
īn-spectō 1 to look at, view.
īn-spector, ōris *m* observer.
īn-spectus, ūs *m* contemplation.
īn-spērāns, tis not hoping, not expecting.
īn-spērātus 3 unhoped for, unexpected.
īn-spergō, rsī, rsum 3 to sprinkle on *or* over, strew on.
īn-spiciō, spexī, spectum 3 to look into *or* upon (*in alqd; rem*); **a)** to read; **b)** to examine, to inspect, view, observe; **c)** to investigate.
īn-spicō 1 to make pointed, sharpen.
īn-spīrō 1 **a)** to breathe into (*dat.*), blow upon; **b)** to inspire, rouse, inflame; to instil, implant (*alci alqd*).
īn-spoliātus 3 not plundered.
īn-spuō 3, **īn-spūtō** 1 to spit on.
īn-spurcō 1 to defile.
īn-stabilis, e unstable, unsteady, not firm, inconstant.
īn-stāns, tis a) present, immediate; **b)** pressing, threatening.
īnstantia, ae *f* **a)** presence; **b)** perseverance.
īnstar *n* (*indecl.*) image, likeness, resemblance; **a)** equal size, number, value; **b)** *with gen.* in the form of, like, as large as, equivalent to.
īnstaurātiō, ōnis *f* renewal.
īnstaurātīvus 3 renewed.
īn-staurō 1 **a)** to establish, set about, prepare; **b)** to renew, repeat; to repair, restore.
īn-sternō 3 to cover over, spread upon; to lay upon.
īnstīgātor, ōris *m* (*f* **-trīx, īcis**) stimulator, instigator.
īn-stīgō 1 to incite, stimulate.
īn-stillō 1 to drop in, instil.
īn-stimulātor, ōris *m* instigator.
īn-stimulō 1 to stimulate, arouse, incite.
īn-stinctor, ōris *m* inciter.
īn-stinctus, ūs *m* incitement.
īn-stinguō, inxī, inctum 3 to incite, impel.
īn-stipulor 1 to stipulate.
īnstita, ae *f* border of a lady's robe.
īn-stitiō, ōnis *f* a standing still.
īnstitor, ōris *m* hawker, pedlar.
īnstitōrium, ī *n* trade of a hawker.
īn-stituō, uī, ūtum 3 **1.** to put *or* place into; a) to plant, fix, set; b) to build, construct, erect, found, establish; c) to draw up in order (*troops*); d) to designate, appoint; **2.** to undertake, begin, commence; a) to purpose, determine, resolve upon; **b)** to introduce, institute; c) to ordain, regulate; **3.** to teach, instruct, educate (*alqm alqa re, ad alqd*).
īnstitūtiō, ōnis *f* = **institutum.**
īnstitūtum, ī *n* arrangement, disposition; **a)** old-established custom, usage; **b)** undertaking, purpose; **c)** instruction; *pl.* principles, method.
īnstō, stitī, (stātūrus) 1 **1.** to stand in *or* on, to enter (*viam*); **2.** to press upon (*dat.*); a) to urge, insist, pursue; b) to be at hand, approach, impend; c) to be intent upon, work hard at, strive after (with *dat.* or *acc.*, *ut*, *ne*, *acc. c. inf.*).
īn-strātus[1] 3 uncovered.
īn-strātus[2] 3, *part. pf.* P. *of* **insterno.**
īn-strēnuus 3 inactive, lazy, idle.
īn-strepō 3 to rattle, creak.
īn-strīdō 3 to hiss in *or* on.
īn-stringō 3 to bind round.
īn-structiō, ōnis *f* a drawing up in order, array; construction.
īnstructor, ōris *m* preparer.
īnstructus[1] 3 **a)** ordered, drawn up; **b)** provided with, furnished; **c)** taught, instructed (*in re, re*).

īn-structus², **ūs** *m* equipment.
īnstrūmentum, ī *n* tool, implement, instrument, apparatus, material; **a**) dress, apparel; **b**) ornament, embellishment; **c**) document; **d**) means.
īn-struō 3 **1.** to build in *or* into; a) to build, erect; b) to draw up in order, set in order; c) to prepare, make ready; **2.** to provide, procure, furnish, equip (*alqa re*), to teach, instruct.
īnsuāsum (?), **ī** *n* = **suasum**
īn-suāvis, e unpleasant, disagreeable.
īn-sūdō 1 to sweat on.
īnsuē-factus 3 accustomed to.
īn-suēscō 3 **a**) to accustom oneself to (*ad alqd; inf.*); **b**) to accustom (*alqm*).
īn-suētus 3 **1.** *part. pf.* P. *of* **insuesco; 2.** a) unaccustomed (*gen., dat., ad alqd, inf.*); b) unusual.
īnsula, ae *f* **a**) island; **b**) tenement house, block of flats.
īnsulānus, ī *m* islander.
īnsulsitās, ātis *f* absurdity, bad taste.
īn-sulsus 3 **a**) unsalted, without taste; **b**) insipid, absurd.
īn-sultō 1 **a**) to leap upon, bound, jump; **b**) to scoff at, taunt, insult (*dat.; in alqd*).
īn-sultūra, ae *f* a leaping on.
īn-sum, īnfuī, inesse to be in *or* on, be contained in, belong to (*in re; dat.*).
īn-sūmō 3 to take for, apply, expend (*alqd in re* or *alci rei*).
īn-suō 3 to sew in *or* into.
īn-super *adv.* above, on the top; from above; over and above, moreover.
īn-superābilis, e insurmountable; unconquerable.
īn-surgō 3 to rise (up), lift oneself; to rise against.
īn-susurrō 1 to whisper in *or* to.
in-tābēscō, buī, — 3 to melt; to pine away.
in-tāctilis, e intangible.
in-tāctus 3 untouched, uninjured; a) untried, unattempted; **b**) undefiled, chaste.
in-tāminātus 3 unsullied.
in-tēctus 3 **1.** *part. pf.* P. *of* **intego; 2.** uncovered, unarmed; frank.
in-tegellus 3 undefiled; uninjured.
in-teger, gra, grum untouched; **a**) unhurt, uninjured; **b**) unimpaired; fresh, sound, vigorous; entire, whole, complete; **c**) undecided, undetermined, open; **d**) inexperienced, ignorant; **e**) healthy, sane, unbiassed; **f**) spotless, blameless, pure, honest, virtuous, impartial, unbribed; — **ab, de, ex integro** afresh.
in-tegō 3 to cover, to protect.
integrāscō 3 to start afresh.
integrātiō, ōnis *f* a renewing, restoring.
integritās, ātis *f* unimpaired condition; **a**) completeness, soundness; **b**) purity, chastity; **c**) honesty, innocence, integrity.
integrō 1 to make whole, restore, repair; to renew, repeat, begin again.
in-tegumentum, ī *n* covering, disguise.
intellēctus, ūs *m* **a**) perception, discernment, understanding; **b**) sense, meaning.
intellegēns, tis intelligent, discerning, well acquainted with (*gen.*); *subst.* connoisseur.
intellegentia, ae *f* intelligence, discernment; **a**) understanding; knowledge, skill, taste; **b**) perception.
intellegibilis, e understandable.
intel-legō, ēxī, ēctum 3 to perceive; **a**) to understand, comprehend (*alqd; acc. c. inf.*), have skill in, be master of; **b**) to judge, think, be of opinion; **c**) to be a connoisseur.
in-temerandus 3 inviolable.
in-temerātus 3 inviolate, pure.
in-temperāns, tis intemperate, immoderate, unrestrained, profligate.
in-temperantia, ae *f* want of moderation, intemperance; insolence, insubordination.
in-temperātus 3 immoderate, extravagant.
in-temperiae, ārum *f/pl.* distemper (of mind).
in-temperiēs, ēi *f* excess, intemperateness; **a**) inclement weather; **b**) intemperate behaviour.
in-tempestīvus 3 untimely, unseasonable.
in-tempestus 3 **a**) timeless; **nox -a** the dead of night; **b**) unhealthy; **c**) stormy.

in-temptātus 3 untried.
in-tendō, ndī, ntum 3 **1.** to stretch, strain; to stretch forth, exert; **2.** to extend; a) to lay *or* put upon (*alci alqd*); to direct, bend, turn, aim (*alqd in* or *ad alqd*); to assail with; b) to direct one's course to, to intend, purpose, endeavour; c) to direct with hostile intention (*alqd alci* or *in alqm*); d) to increase, magnify.
intentātiō, ōnis *f* a stretching out towards.
in-tentātus 3 1. *part. pf.* P. *of* **intento; 2.** = **intemptatus.**
in-tentiō, ōnis *f* a stretching, straining; **a**) exertion, effort; **b**) attention, application; **c**) attack, accusation.
in-tentō 1 to stretch *or* hold out threateningly (*alqd in alqm* or *alci*).
intentus[1], **ūs** *m* a stretching out.
in-tentus[2] 3 stretched, strained; **a**) intent, attentive (*alci rei, in* or *ad alqd*), anxious, eager; vigorous; active.
in-tepeō, —, — 2 to be warm.
in-tepēscō, puī, — 3 to become warm.
inter *prep.* with *acc.* **a**) *of space:* between, among, amid; **b**) *of time:* between, during, in the course of; **c**) *denoting relation:* between, among.
inter-aestuō 1 to be inflamed at intervals (*or* in places).
interāmenta, ōrum *n/pl.* interior woodwork *of a ship.*
inter-aptus 3 joined together.
inter-ārēscō, —, — 3 to become [dry.]
interātim = **interim.**
inter-bibō 3 to drink up.
inter-bītō 3 to perish.
inter-calāris, e *and* **-ius** 3 inserted, intercalary.
inter-calō 1 to insert, intercalate; to put off, defer.
inter-capēdō, inis *f* interruption, interval.
inter-cēdō 3 to go between, come between; **a**) to stand *or* lie between; **b**) to intervene, pass, happen between; **c**) to protest against, interfere, interpose a veto (with *dat.; quominus*); **d**) to occur, happen.
interceptiō, ōnis *f* a taking away.
interceptor, ōris *m* interceptor, embezzler.
inter-cessiō, ōnis *f* intervention.
inter-cessor, ōris *m* **a**) vetoer, preventer; **b**) mediator, surety.
inter-cīdō[1], **cīdī, cīsum** 3 to cut through *or* asunder, cut down.
inter-cidō[2], **cidī, —** 3 **a**) to fall between; to happen; **b**) to perish, decay; **c**) to drop out, be forgotten.
inter-cinō, —, — 3 to sing between.
inter-cipiō, cēpī, ceptum 3 to take by the way, intercept; **a**) to embezzle, steal; **b**) to interrupt, hinder; **c**) to snatch away, carry off prematurely.
intercīsē *adv.* disconnectedly.
inter-clūdō, sī, sum 3 **a**) to shut out *or* off, block up, hinder (*alci alqd*); to cut off, separate.
inter-clūsiō, ōnis *f* a stopping, hindering.
inter-columnium, ī *n* space between two columns.
inter-currō, (cu)currī, cursum 3 to run between; **a**) to step between, intercede; **b**) to run to in the meanwhile.
inter-cursō 1 = **intercurro.**
inter-cursus, ūs *m* intervention.
inter-cus, cutis under the skin.
inter-dīcō 3 **a**) to forbid, prohibit, interdict; **alci aquā et ignī** to banish; **b**) to make a provisional decree; — *subst.* **interdictum, ī** *n* **a**) prohibition; **b**) a prætor's decree, interdict.
inter-dictiō, ōnis *f* a prohibiting.
inter-diū(s) *adv.* by day.
inter-dō 1 to interpose; to diffuse; **non interduim** (*subj.*) I would not give anything, I do not care.
inter-ductus, ūs *m* punctuation.
inter-dum *adv.* sometimes.
inter-eā *adv.* **a**) in the meantime, meanwhile; **b**) nevertheless, however.
inter-ēmptor, ōris *m* murderer.
inter-eō, iī, itum, īre to be lost, perish, go to ruin.
inter-equitō 1 to ride between.
inter-fātiō, ōnis *f* interruption in speaking.
inter-fectiō, ōnis *f* a slaying.
inter-fector, ōris *m* murderer.
inter-fectrīx, īcis *f* murderess.
inter-ficiō, fēcī, fectum 3 to destroy, kill, slay.
inter-fīō to pass away; to be destroyed.

inter-fluō 3 to flow between.
inter-fodiō 3 to pierce.
inter-for 1 to interrupt (*alqm*).
inter-fugiō 3 to flee among.
inter-fulgeō 2 to gleam among.
inter-furō 3 to rage between *or* through.
inter-fūsus 3 flowing between; interposed; stained.
inter-iaceō, —, — 2 to lie between.
inter-ibi *adv.* in the meantime.
inter-iciō, iēcī, iectum 3 to throw, cast, put, place between *or* among; **P.** to intervene; — **interiectus** 3 interposed.
inter-iectus, ūs *m* a putting between, intervention; interval.
interim *adv.* meanwhile, sometimes, however.
inter-imō, ēmī, ēmptum 3 to take from the midst, take away; to destroy, kill, slay.
interior, ius inner, interior; **a**) inland; **b**) more confidential, intimate, secret.
inter-itiō, ōnis *f* destruction, ruin.
inter-itus, ūs *m* destruction, ruin, fall, annihilation.
inter-iungō 3 **a**) to join together, unite; **b**) to unyoke, rest.
inter-lābor 3 to glide *or* fall between.
inter-legō 3 to pluck off here and there.
inter-ligō 1 to bind together.
inter-linō 3 to smear *or* daub between; to falsify by erasure.
inter-loquor 3 to interrupt in speaking.
inter-lūceō, xī, — 2 to shine forth (from its surroundings); to show gaps.
inter-lūnium, ī *n* time of new moon.
inter-luō, —, — 3 to flow between.
inter-maneō 2 to remain among.
inter-mēnstruus 3 between two months; *subst.* **-um, ī** *n* time of the new moon, change of moon.
inter-micō 1 to gleam (amid).
in-terminātus[1] 3 unbounded.
inter-minātus[2] 3, *part. pf.* P. *of* **interminor.**
inter-minor 1 to threaten, forbid with threats.
inter-misceō 2 to mix among, mingle.
inter-missiō, ōnis *f* a leaving off, interval.
inter-mittō 3 to place between; **P.** to lie between; **a**) to leave a space between, separate, isolate; **b**) to leave off, discontinue, interrupt, neglect; **P.** to be discontinued for an interval; **c**) to let pass, suffer to elapse.
inter-morior 3 to die off, perish; to faint away, to wither away; **intermortuus** 3 half-dead, almost perished.
inter-mundia, ōrum *n/pl.* spaces between the worlds.
inter-mūrālis, e between two walls.
inter-nātus 3 grown between.
inter-necīnus 3 annihilating.
inter-neciō, ōnis *f* massacre, utter destruction.
internecīvus 3 murderous, destructive.
inter-necō 1 to destroy utterly.
inter-nectō 3 to bind together.
inter-nigrāns, ntis black in places (on a white ground).
inter-niteō, uī, — 2 to shine forth.
inter-nōdium, ī *n* space between two joints.
inter-nōscō, nōvī, — 3 to distinguish between.
inter-nūntiō 1 to negotiate.
inter-nūntius, ī *m and* **-tia, ae** *f* negotiator, go-between.
internus 3 inward, internal.
in-terō 3 to pound *or* mash together.
interpellātiō, ōnis *f* interruption, disturbance.
interpellātor, ōris *m* disturber.
inter-pellō 1 to interrupt a speaker; **a**) to urge as an objection; **b**) to molest by remarks; **c**) to prevent, hinder, disturb, obstruct.
inter-plicō 1 to weave in, insert; to enfold.
interpolis, e furbished, repaired.
interpolō 1 to furbish, repair; to interpolate, falsify.
inter-pōnō 3 to put, place, lay *or* set between; **a**) to insert, interpose, intermix, falsify; **b**) to let pass, permit to elapse; **P.** to pass between, **spatiō interpositō** some time after; **c**) to introduce, bring forward, admit, **se interpōnere** to engage in, have to do with, meddle, interfere; **d**) to allege as a reason *or* pretext; **fidem interpōnere** to pledge one's word.

inter-positiō, ōnis *f* an introducing, insertion.
inter-positus, ūs *m* interposition.
inter-pres, etis *m and f* negotiator, mediator; **a**) explainer, expounder, interpreter, soothsayer; **b**) translator.
interpretātiō, ōnis *f* explanation, interpretation; translation.
interpretor 1 **a**) to assist, aid (*alci*); **b**) to explain, expound, interpret; **c**) to translate; **d**) to understand, comprehend; **e**) to decide, determine.
inter-primō, pressī, pressum 3 to squeeze, crush.
inter-punctiō, ōnis *f* division by points.
inter-pungō, (nxī), nctum 3 to divide by points; **interpunctus** 3 well divided; *subst.* **-tum, ī** *n* mark of punctuation.
inter-quiēscō, ēvī, — 3 to pause, rest a while.
inter-rēgnum, ī *n* interval between two reigns.
inter-rēx, rēgis *m* regent, interrex.
in-territus 3 undaunted.
inter-rogātiō, ōnis *f* question; **a**) interrogation; **b**) examination (*of witnesses*); **c**) argument, syllogism.
interrogātiuncula, ae *f* short argument.
inter-rogō 1 to ask, question (*alqm; alqm alqd* or *de re*); **a**) to examine judicially; **b**) to accuse, bring an action against.
inter-rumpō 3 to interrupt; **a**) to break asunder *or* to pieces; **b**) to separate; **c**) to disturb.
interruptē *adv.* interruptedly.
inter-saepiō 4 to hedge *or* fence in, shut off; **a**) to block up; **b**) to cut off, separate (*alqd a re; alci alqd*).
inter-scindō 3 to tear asunder, separate.
inter-scrībō 3 to write between.
inter-serō[1]**, sēvī, situm** 3 to sow *or* plant between.
inter-serō[2]**, (seruī, sertum)** 3 to put *or* place between.
inter-sistō, stitī, — 3 to pause, stop in the middle.
inter-sonō 1 to sound among.
inter-spīrātiō, ōnis *f* a breathing between.
inter-stinctus 3 checkered, spotted.
inter-stinguō 3 to extinguish.
inter-stringō 3 to strangle.
inter-struō 3 to connect.
inter-sum, fuī, esse to be between (*inter alqd*); to intervene; **a**) to be different, distinguished from; **b**) to be present at, take part in (*in re* or with *dat.*); **interest** it concerns, it is of importance, of interest (*alcis,* with *inf., acc.c.inf., indirect question; ad alqd*).
inter-texō 3 to intertwine, interweave.
inter-trahō 3 to take away, draw out.
inter-trīmentum, ī *n* loss by attrition, waste, damage.
inter-turbātiō, ōnis *f* disturbance.
inter-turbō 1 to interrupt.
inter-vallum, ī *n* space between; **a**) distance, interval; **b**) interval of time, pause; **c**) difference.
inter-vellō 3 to pull out here and there.
inter-veniō 4 to come between, intervene (*with dat.*); **a**) to break in upon, interrupt (*dat.*); **b**) to interfere, put a stop to.
interventor, ōris *m* visitor, intruder.
interventus, ūs *m* intervention.
inter-vertō 3 to embezzle; **a**) to intercept; **b**) to defraud.
inter-viās on the way.
inter-vireō 2 to show green among.
inter-vīsō, sī, sum 3 to take a look; to visit from time to time.
inter-vol(it)ō 1 to fly among *or* through.
inter-vomō 3 to throw up among.
inter-vortō 3 = **interverto.**
in-testābilis, e a) incapable of bearing witness, infamous; **b**) = **intestatus**[2].
in-testātus[1] 3 **a**) intestate; **b**) not convicted by evidence.
in-testātus[2] 3 castrated.
intestīnus 3 inward, internal; *subst.* **-a, ōrum** *n/pl.* (*rarely sing.*) intestines, entrails.
in-texō 3 **a**) to weave *or* plait in, interweave; **b**) to wind *or* weave around; **c**) to surround.
intibum, ī *n* endive.
intimus 3 inmost; **a**) deepest, most profound, most secret; **b**) most familiar, intimate; *subst.* **~, ī** *m* intimate friend.

in-tingō 3 to dip in.
in-tolerābilis, e a) unable to bear; **b**) unbearable.
in-tolerandus 3 unbearable.
in-tolerāns, tis a) unable to bear, impatient of (*gen.*), intolerant; immoderate; **b**) intolerable.
in-tolerantia, ae *f* insolence.
in-tonō, uī, — 1 to thunder; to resound, make a noise.
in-tōnsus 3 unshorn, with long hair and beard; uncouth.
in-torqueō 2 **a**) to twist *or* turn round, to wind; **b**) to hurl, launch, cast; **c**) to distort.
intrā 1. *adv.* within; **2.** *prep.* with *acc.* within, into; **a**) within, in the space of, during, before the lapse of; **b**) less than, fewer than.
intrābilis, e accessible.
in-tractābilis, e unmanageable, intractable, rude, fierce.
in-tractātus 3 not handled; unattempted.
in-tremō *and* **-mīscō, -uī,** — 3 to tremble.
in-trepidus 3 undaunted, undisturbed.
in-tribuō 3 to contribute.
in-trīcō 1 to entangle, perplex.
intrīn-secus *adv.* inside, inwardly.
in-trītus 3 unexhausted.
intrō[1] *adv.* inside, within.
intrō[2] 1 to go into, enter (*in, ad alqd; alqd*); to penetrate into.
intrō-dūcō 3 to lead *or* conduct into (*alqd in alqd*); **a**) to bring into, introduce; **b**) to bring forward, maintain (*alqd; acc.c.inf.*).
intrō-ductiō, ōnis *f* introduction.
intro-eō, iī, itum, īre to go into, enter.
intrō-ferō, —, lātum 3 to carry in.
intrō-gredior, gressus sum 3 to enter.
intro-itus, ūs *m* an entering, entrance; **a**) beginning; **b**) introduction; passage.
intrō-mittō 3 to send in, let in.
intrōrsum *and* **-sus** *adv.* **a**) towards the inside; **b**) inside, within; internally.
intrō-rumpō 3 to break into; enter by force.
intrō-spectō 1 to look into.
intrō-spiciō, spexī, spectum 3 to look into *or* upon; to observe; to inspect, examine (*alqd* or *in alqd*).
intubum, ī *n* = **intibum.**
in-tueor 2 (*and* **in-tuor** 3) to look at attentively (*in alqd*), gaze at (*alqd*); to consider, contemplate, observe, regard.
in-tumēscō, muī, — 3 to swell up; to swell with, be puffed up.
in-tumulātus 3 unburied.
intumus 3 = **intimus.**
in-tuor 3, *see* **intueor.**
in-turbidus 3 undisturbed, quiet.
intus *adv.* **a**) within, inside, in the heart; **b**) to the inside.
in-tūtus 3 unguarded, unsafe.
inula, ae *f* (*a plant*) elecampane.
īnuleus, ī *m* = **hinnuleus.**
in-ultus 3 unavenged, unpunished.
in-umbrō 1 to overshadow, darken.
in-undātiō, ōnis *f* inundation, flood.
in-undō 1 **a**) to overflow, inundate; **b**) to flow over (*re*), spread.
in-ung(u)ō 3 to anoint; to besmear.
in-urbānus 3 rustic, unmannerly, rude, unpolished; unrefined, inelegant, not witty.
in-urgeō 2 to thrust at.
in-ūrō 3 to burn in; to brand, imprint indelibly; **b**) to inflict.
in-ūsitātus 3 unusual.
in-ustus 3 unburnt (?).
in-ūtilis, e useless, unserviceable; hurtful, injurious.
in-ūtilitās, ātis *f* uselessness; injuriousness.
in-vādō 3 **1.** to go *or* come into (*in rem, rem*); a) to set foot upon; b) to undertake, begin; **2.** to rush upon; a) to attack, invade; b) to fall upon, seize, befall.
in-valēscō, luī, — 3 to become strong *or* stronger; to increase; to prevail.
in-validus 3 weak, feeble, infirm; inefficient.
invectīcius 3 imported; insincere.
in-vectiō, ōnis *f* importation; a sailing in.
in-vehō 3 **1.** to carry *or* bear in *or* into (*alqd in alqd* or *alci rei*); to occasion, bring upon; **2.** *with reflex. pron.*, or **P.** to burst into, attack; to attack with words, inveigh against; to ride, drive, sail in *or* into.
in-vendibilis, e unsalable.
in-veniō 4 to come *or* light upon (*alqd*), meet with; **a**) to find out,

discover, learn, become acquainted with; **b**) to acquire, earn; **c**) to devise, contrive.
inventiō, ōnis *f* (faculty of) invention.
inventor, ōris *m and* **-trīx, īcis** *f* inventor, contriver, discoverer.
inventum, ī *n* invention, discovery, contrivance.
inventus, ūs *m* discovery.
in-venustus 3 without charm, ungraceful.
in-vērē (?) untruthfully.
in-verēcundus 3 shameless, immodest.
in-vergō, —, — 3 to pour upon.
in-versiō, ōnis *f* inversion; irony; allegory.
in-vertō 3 to turn upside down, turn about; **a**) to turn *or* plough up; **b**) to pervert; **c**) to change, alter, reverse.
in-vesperāscit, —,— 3 it becomes evening.
investīgātiō, ōnis *f* an inquiring into, investigation.
investīgātor, ōris *m* inquirer, investigator.
in-vestīgō 1 to trace out, search into, investigate, find out.
in-vestiō 4 to clothe *or* surround with.
in-veterāscō, āvī, — 3 to grow old: to become fixed, established, rooted, *or* obsolete.
in-veterātiō, ōnis *f* an inveterate fault.
in-veterō 1 to establish; **inveterātus** 3 long-established, inveterate.
in-vetitus 3 unrestrained.
in-vicem *adv.* **a**) by turns; **b**) mutually, on both sides; **c**) on the other hand.
in-victus 3 unconquered; unconquerable.
invidentia, ae *f* envy.
in-videō 2 to look askance at (*alqd*); to envy, grudge (*alci, alci rei alcis*); **invidendus** 3 enviable.
invidia, ae *f* envy, grudge, jealousy, ill-will; **a**) cause of envy; **b**) odium, unpopularity.
invidiōsus 3 **a**) envious; **b**) exciting ill-feeling; enviable, envied; **c**) hateful, hated.
invidus 3 envious, jealous.
in-vigilō 1 to be awake, watch at, over *or* on account of; to be watchful over.
in-violābilis, e inviolable, invulnerable.
in-violātus 3 unhurt; inviolable.
in-vīsitātus 3 unseen; new, strange.
in-vīsō, sī, (sum) 3 to go to see, to visit; to get a sight of.
in-vīsus[1] 3 unseen.
in-vīsus[2] 3 **a**) hated, hateful; **b**) malicious.
invītāmentum, ī *n* allurement, incitement.
invītātiō, ōnis *f* invitation; challenge.
invītātus, ūs *m* (*only abl. sg.*) = **invitatio.**
in-vītō 1 to invite (*alqm in* or *ad alqd;* with *abl.*); **a**) to entertain; **se invitāre** to take one's fill; **b**) to summon, challenge; **c**) to allure, entice, attract.
in-vītus 3 unwilling, reluctant.
in-vius 3 impassable.
in-vocātiō, ōnis *f* invocation.
in-vocātus 3 uncalled, uninvited.
in-vocō 1 to call upon.
in-volātus, ūs *m* a flying, flight.
in-volitō 1 to float *or* wave over.
in-volō 1 **a**) to fly into; **b**) to fly at, rush upon; to attack, invade.
involūcrum, ī *n* veil, covering.
in-volūtus 3 involved, intricate.
in-volvō 3 **a**) to roll to, into *or* upon; **b**) to wrap up, envelop; to cover, overwhelm (*alqd re*).
in-volvolus, ī *m* leaf-curling caterpillar.
in-vors-, -vort = **in-vers-, -vert.**
in-vulnerābilis, e invulnerable.
in-vulnerātus 3 unwounded.
iō *int.* ho! hurrah!
iocātiō, ōnis *f* a joking.
iocor 1 to jest, joke.
iocōsus 3 jocose, humorous, facetious.
ioculāris, e = **iocōsus; ioculāria, ium** *n/pl.* jests, jokes.
ioculārius 3 ludicrous.
ioculātor, ōris *m* jester, joker.
ioculor 1 = **iocor.**
ioculus, ī *m* little jest.
iocus, ī *m* jest, joke; **a**) pastime; **b**) trifle; **c**) child's play.
iōta *n* the Greek letter I.
ipse, a, um self; himself, herself, itself; the master, mistress, teacher, the chief person; **per se ipse** of

himself, by himself; **a**) just, very, exactly, identical; **b**) of one's own accord, spontaneously; *comic superl.* **ipsissumus.**
īra, ae *f* anger, wrath, rage.
īrācundia, ae *f* irascibility, wrath, anger.
īrācundus 3 irascible, angry.
īrāscor, — 3 to grow angry.
īrātus 3 angry, enraged (*dat.*).
īrim (*acc.*) *m* hedgehog.
īrōnīa, ae *f* irony.
ir-radiō 1 to irradiate.
ir-rāsus 3 unshorn; unsmoothed.
ir-ratiōnālis, e irrational, unscientific.
ir-raucēscō, rausī, — 3 to become hoarse.
ir-redux, ucis that does not bring one back.
ir-religātus 3 unbound.
ir-religiōsus 3 impious.
ir-remeābilis, e from which there is no return.
ir-remediābilis, e irreconcilable.
ir-reparābilis, e irrecoverable.
ir-repertus 3 undiscovered.
ir-rēpō 3 to creep into.
ir-reprehēnsus 3 blameless.
ir-rēptō 1 to creep upon, steal over.
ir-requiētus 3 restless.
ir-resectus 3 uncut, unpared.
ir-resolūtus 3 not loosed.
ir-restinctus 3 unquenched.
ir-rētiō 4 to catch in a net; to entangle (*alqm re*).
ir-retortus 3 not turned back.
ir-reverēns, tis irreverent, disrespectful.
ir-reverentia, ae *f* disrespect.
ir-revocābilis, e irrevocable; implacable.
ir-revocātus 3 not called again.
ir-rīdeō 2 to laugh at.
ir-rīdiculē *adv.* without wit.
ir-rīdiculum, ī *n* laughing-stock.
ir-rigātiō, ōnis *f* a watering.
ir-rigō 1 **a**) to conduct water to; **b**) to water, irrigate, to inundate; to bathe, flood.
irriguus 3 **a**) supplying water; **b**) well-watered, soaked.
ir-rīsiō, ōnis *f* = **irrisus.**
ir-rīsor, ōris *m* derider, mocker.
ir-rīsus, ūs *m* a scoffing, mockery, derision.
ir-rītābilis, e irritable, excitable.
(**irrītāmen, inis** *n and*) **irrītāmentum, ī** *n* incitement, incentive.
irrītātiō, ōnis *f* incitement, irritation.
irrītātor, ōris *m* inciter.
irrītō 1 to excite, incite, stimulate, to provoke, exasperate.
ir-ritus 3 **a**) invalid, void; **b**) vain, useless, ineffectual.
ir-rogātiō, ōnis *f* an imposing.
ir-rogō 1 **a**) to propose against one; **b**) to impose, inflict, ordain (*alci alqd*).
ir-rōrō 1 to bedew, moisten, trickle down upon.
ir-rubēscō, buī, — 3 to grow red.
ir-ructō 1 to belch at.
ir-rūgō 1 to wrinkle, fold.
ir-rumō 1 to treat obscenely *or* foully; to defile; *hence* **irrumātiō, ōnis** *f*; **irrumātor, ōris** *m.*
ir-rumpō 3 to break *or* rush in *or* into; to intrude, invade.
ir-ruō, uī, — 3 to rush in, invade; to fling in.
irruptiō, ōnis *f* invasion, incursion.
ir-ruptus 3 unbroken.
is, ea, id he, she, it; **a**) **is qui** he who; **b**) this *or* that (*man, woman, thing*); **c**) such, of such a sort *or* kind; **d**) the one mentioned; **isque, et is, atque is** and that too, and indeed.
ischnon (*ἰσχνόν*) slender.
īs-elasticus 3 *adj.* applied to competitions which entitled winners to a triumphal entry into their town; **-um, ī** *n* present given to the winners.
issula *f* (*from ipse*) little mistress.
istāc *adv.* there, by that way.
istāc-tenus thus far.
iste, a, ud that (of yours) (*referring to the person spoken to, or to something mentioned by him*); your client (*in a lawsuit*).
istī *adv.* = **istic**[2].
istic[1], **aec, oc** *or* **uc** = **iste.**
istīc[2] *adv.* there, in that place, here; in this affair.
istim *adv.* = **istinc.**
istinc *adv.* from there, thence.
istīus-modī of that kind, such.
istō(c) *adv.* thither, that way.
istōrsum *adv.* thitherwards, in that direction.
istuc[1] *neutr. of* **istic**[1].

istūc[2] *adv.* thither.
ita *adv.* thus, so, in such manner; **ut ... ita** as ..., so; although ..., yet; **itane?** is it so? really? **quid ita?** why so? how is that?; **a**) and so, consequently, and then; **b**) yes, just so; **c**) accordingly, under these circumstances; **d**) **ita ... ut** so ... that, on the condition that, in so far, only in so far as; **non ita** *or* **haud ita** not very, not especially.
ita-que **1.** = **et ita**; **2.** *cj.* and so, therefore, for that reason.
item *adv.* likewise, besides, also; a second time.
iter, itineris *n* **1.** a going, walk, way; **2.** journey, march, passage; **in itinere** on the march; a) a day's journey; b) legal right of way; c) passage, road, path; d) course, method, custom, means.
iterātiō, ōnis *f* repetition.
iterō 1 to do a second time; **a**) to repeat; **b**) to plough again.
iterum *adv.* a second time, again.
itidem *adv.* in like manner.
itiner, eris *n* = **iter.**
itiō, ōnis *f* = **itus.**
itō 1 to go.
itus, ūs *m* a walking, going (away), departure.
iuba, ae *f* mane; crest (*of a helmet* or *serpent*).
iubar, aris *n* beaming light, radiance; morning star, light of the sun.
iubātus 3 with a mane *or* crest.
iubeō, iussī, iussum 2 to order, command, bid, tell (*alqm, de re, acc.c.inf.*); **a**) to decree, ratify; **b**) to designate, appoint.
iubilum, ī *n* glad cry, shout.
iūcunditās, ātis *f* pleasantness; **a**) delight; cheerfulness; **b**) good office, favour.
iūcundus 3 pleasant, agreeable, delightful.
iūdex, icis *m* (*f*) judge; juryman; critic.
iūdicātiō, ōnis *f* judgment.
iūdicātus, ūs *m* office of judge.
iūdiciālis, e *and* **iūdiciārius** 3 judicial, judiciary, juridical.
iūdicium, ī *n* **1.** judicial investigation (*de re, alcis rei*), trial; a) court of justice; b) body of judges; **c**) jurisdiction; **2.** sentence, decision; a) opinion, judgment; b) power of judging, discernment; c) consideration, discretion.
iūdicō 1 to be a judge, to judge, decide, pass judgment; **a**) to pass sentence against **b**) to resolve, determine, settle; **c**) to consider, hold, think; **d**) to suppose, conclude; **e**) to declare openly.
iugālis, e yoked together; matrimonial, nuptial.
iugātiō, ōnis *f* a binding to rails.
iūgerum, ī *n* a land measure (about $^2/_3$ of an acre).
iūgis, e perpetual, never failing.
iūges, *only:* **iūges auspicium** joined auspice.
iūglāns, dis *f* walnut (-tree).
iugō 1 to bind, connect; to marry.
iugōsus 3 mountainous.
iugulae, ārum *f* Orion's belt.
iugulātiō, ōnis *f* a murdering.
iugulō 1 to cut the throat; **a**) to slay, murder; **b**) to ruin, destroy.
iugulum, ī *n* (*and* **-us** *m*) throat.
iugum, ī *n* yoke; **a**) yoke, span, pair, team; **b**) yoke of slavery, of matrimony; **c**) arch of spears; **d**) the constellation Libra; **e**) beam of a weaver's loom; rowers' bench; **f**) ridge, mountain heights.
Iūlius 3 belonging to July; *m* (*mensis*) July.
iūmentum, ī *n* yoked animal, beast for drawing *or* carrying.
iunceus 3 made of rushes; as thin as a rush.
iuncōsus 3 full of rushes.
iūnctim *adv.* successively.
iūnctiō, ōnis *f* a joining, uniting.
iūnctūra, ae *f* a joining; **a**) joint, juncture, connection; **b**) relationship.
iuncus, ī *m* (bul)rush.
iungō, iūnxī, iūnctum 3 to yoke, harness (*ad alqd*); **a**) to attach, fasten; **b**) to join, unite, connect); **fluvium ponte** to throw a bridge over a river; **c**) to make by joining, bring together, associate; **iūnctus** 3 joined together, connected, united, intimate; **iūnctissimī** *m/pl.* nearest relations.
iūnior, ōris comparatively young.
iūniperus, ī *f* juniper-tree.
Iunius 3 belonging to June; *m* (*mensis*) June.
iūnīx, īcis *f* heifer.
iūrātor, ōris *m* sworn assistant of a censor.

iūrgium, ī *n* quarrel, altercation.
iūrgō 1 to quarrel, brawl, scold.
iūri-diciālis, e relating to right *or* justice.
iūris-dictiō, ōnis *f* administration of justice; jurisdiction.
iūrō 1 to swear, take an oath (*per alqm, in alqd*); **a**) to affirm on oath, swear to; **b**) to deny on oath; **iūrātus** 3 on oath.
iūs[1], **iūris** *n* broth, soup.
iūs[2], **iūris** *n* **a**) right, statutes, law, justice; **b**) privilege, permission, liberty, conceded right; **iūre** rightfully, justly; **c**) legal power, authority; **d**) court of justice.
iūs iūrandum, iūris iūrandī *n* oath.
iussū by order.
iussum, ī *n* order, command, ordinance; prescription.
iūsti-ficus 3 acting justly.
iūstitia, ae *f* justice, equity.
iūstitium, ī *n* judicial vacation; suspension, holiday.
iūstus 3 just, equitable; **a**) fair, upright, righteous; **b**) regular, lawful, rightful, proper; *subst.* **iūstum, ī** *n* justice; **iūsta, ōrum** *n/pl.* rights; due forms and observances; **c**) justified.
iuvenālis, e youthful.
iuvenca, ae *f* heifer; young woman.
iuvencus, ī *m* young bullock; young man; *adj.* young.
iuvenēscō, —, — 3 **a**) to grow up to youth; **b**) to grow young again.
iuvenīlis, e youthful, juvenile.
iuvenis, is young; *subst. m* young man, youth; *f* maiden.
iuvenīx, īcis *f* young cow.
iuvenor 1 to act indiscreetly, to wanton.
iuventa, ae (*and* **iuventās, ātis**) *f* age of youth; **a**) youthful vigour; **b**) the young, young people; **c**) downy beard.
iuventūs, ūtis *f* **a**) time of youth; **b**) young people; young men in the army.
iuvō, iūvī, iūtum 1 to delight, gratify, please; to help, aid.
iuxtā 1. *adv.* near, close, hard by; in like manner, equally; **2.** *prep.* with *acc.* near to, close to, hard by; a) immediately after; b) along with; c) approaching, bordering on.
iuxtim *adv.* close beside; alike.

K

K *abbr.* = **Kaeso.**
Kal. = **Kalendae** (*see* **Calendae**).

L

L *abbr.* **1.** = **Lūcius; 2.** *as a numeral* = 50.
labāscō, —, — 3 to waver, yield.
labea, ae *f* lip.
lābēcula, ae *f* little stain, slight disgrace.
labe-faciō 3 = **labefacto.**
labe-factō 1 to cause to totter, to shake, to weaken, impair, ruin, destroy.
labellum¹, ī *n* little lip.
lābellum², ī *n* small basin.
labeōsus 3 with large lips.
lābēs, is *f* **a**) a falling; downfall; ruin, destruction; **b**) spot, stain; disgrace, ignominy.
labium, ī *n* lip.
labō 1 to totter, waver, be unsteady; to be undecided.
lābor¹, lāpsus sum 3 to glide, slide, slip; **a**) to fall down, sink; **b**) to glide *or* float down; **c**) to glide along *or* off; **d**) to slip, stumble; **e**) to escape, vanish, pass away, elapse; **f**) to fall into (*ad* or *in alqd*); **g**) to be mistaken, err, commit a fault.
labor², ōris *m* work, labour, toil, exertion; **a**) drudgery, hardship; **b**) laboriousness, effort; **c**) trouble, distress, need, difficulty, pain.
labōrātus 3 toilsome.
labōri-fer 3 toil-enduring.
labōriōsus 3 **a**) full of toil *or* hardship; **b**) industrious.
labōrō 1 **1.** a) to work, toil, exert oneself, strive (*in* or *de re; ut, ne, inf.*); b) to suffer, be troubled, vexed; to be in distress, difficulty *or* danger (*ex, ab, in re, re*); **2.** to work out, elaborate, produce with effort (*alqd*).
labōs, ōris *m* = **labor².**
labrum¹, ī *n* lip, edge.
lābrum², ī *n* bathing-tub, basin.
labrusca, ae *f* wild vine.
labruscum, ī *n* wild grape.
labyrinthēus 3 labyrinthine.
labyrinthus, ī *m* labyrinth.
lac, lactis *n* milk; milky juice.
lacer, era, erum a) mangled, lacerated, torn; mutilated; **b**) lacerating
lacerātiō, ōnis *f* a mangling, lacerating.
lacerna, ae *f* cloak.
lacernātus 3 cloaked.
lacerō 1 to mangle, tear to pieces; **a**) to censure, wound; **b**) to waste, squander, ruin.
lacerta, ae *f* lizard.
lacertōsus 3 muscular.
lacertus¹, ī *m* lizard.
lacertus², ī *m* **a**) muscle; **b**) upper arm; **c**) strength, vigour.
lacessō, īvī *and* **iī, ītum** 3 to excite, provoke (*alqm ad alqd, re*), irritate, exasperate; to move, arouse, produce.
lachanizō 1 to be weak.
lacinia, ae *f* flap, corner.
Lacōnicus 3 Spartan; *subst.* **-um, ī** *n* sweating-room (in baths).
lacrima, ae *f* tear; drop.
lacrimābilis, e lamentable.
lacrimābundus 3 weeping.
lacrimō 1 to weep; to drop, distil.
lacrimōsus 3 full of tears; lamentable; plaintive.
lacrimula, ae *f* little tear.
lacruma, -mō = **lacrima, mō.**
lactēns, tis a) sucking (milk), young; **b**) sappy, juicy; **c**) milk-white.
lacteolus 3 milk-white.
lactēs, ium *f/pl.* small guts.
lactēscō, —, — 3 to turn to milk.
lacteus 3 milky; **a**) full of milk; **b**) milk-white.
lactō¹ 1 **a**) to contain milk; **b**) to suck milk.
lactō² 1 to allure, deceive with flattery.
lactūca, ae *f* (**lactūcula, ae** *f*) garden-lettuce.
lacūna, ae *f* hole, pit; **a**) pool, pond; **b**) gap, void, defect.
lacūnar, āris *n* panelled ceiling.
lacūnō 1 to panel.
lacūnōsus 3 full of hollows.
lacus, ūs *m* **a**) basin, tank, (wine-) vat, cistern; **b**) lake; pool.
laedō, sī, sum 3 **a**) to strike at, hurt, wound, injure, afflict; **b**) to insult, offend, annoy.

laena, ae *f* cloak, mantle.
laesiō, ōnis *f* hurt, provocation.
laetābilis, e joyful, glad.
laetātiō, ōnis *f* a rejoicing.
laeti-ficō 1 to cheer, gladden; to fertilize; to be glad.
laeti-ficus 3 pleasing.
laetitiā, ae *f* joy, gladness, delight; beauty, grace.
laetō 1 to delight, gladden.
laetor 1 to be glad, rejoice (*re, de* or *in re; quod; acc. c. inf.*).
laetus 3 glad, joyful, cheerful, joyous; **a**) pleasing, prosperous; **b**) fertile, rich, copious.
laevus 3 left, on the left side; *subst.* **laeva, ae** *f* left hand; **a**) awkward, foolish; **b**) lucky, propitious; **c**) unfavourable, unfortunate.
laganum, ī *n* cake of flour and oil.
lagēna, ae *f* = **lagoena.**
lagēos, ī *f* species of vine.
lagoena, ae *f* flagon.
lagōis, idis *f* grouse.
lagōna, ae *f*, *see* **lagoena.**
laguncula, ae *f* flask.
lalīsiō, ōnis *m* foal of a wild ass.
lallō 1 to sing a lullaby.
lāma, ae *f* bog, fen.
lamberō 1 to lick.
lambō 3 to lick, lap, wash.
lāmella, ae *f* metal plate, coin.
lāmenta, ōrum *n/pl.* lamentation.
lāmentābilis, e lamentable; **a**) mournful; **b**) deplorable.
lāmentārius 3 causing lament.
lāmentātiō, ōnis *f* a lamenting.
lāmentor 1 to wail, moan, weep; lament; (*alqd.*) to bewail.
lamia, ae *f* witch; vampire.
lām(i)**na** *and* **lammina, ae** *f* thin plate, leaf, layer; **a**) plate of iron used for torture; **b**) blade; **c**) money, coin; **d**) peel.
lampas, adis *f* torch, light, lamp; daylight, day.
lāna, ae *f* wool, woollen thread; **a**) working in wool; **b**) down, cotton, fleecy cloud.
lānārius, ī *m* worker in wool.
lānātus 3 woolly; *subst.* **-a, ae** *f* sheep.
lancea, ae *f* lance, spear.
lancinō 1 to rend to pieces, to squander.
lāneus 3 woollen; soft.
langue-faciō 3 to make languid *or* faint.
langueō, guī, — 2 to be faint, weak, languid, weary.
languēscō, guī, — 3 to become faint, weak, languid.
languid(ul)**us** 3 faint, weak, languid, dull; sluggish, inactive.
languor, ōris *m* weariness, feebleness; inactivity, dullness.
laniātus, ūs *m* (*and* **laniātiō, ōnis** *f*) a mangling; anguish.
laniēna, ae *f* a butcher's stall.
lāni-ficium, i *n* wool-work.
lāni-ficus 3 working in wool.
lāni-ger 3 wool-bearing; *subst. m and f* ram, sheep, lamb.
laniō 1 to tear to pieces, mangle.
laniōnius 3 of a butcher.
lanista, ae *m* trainer of gladiators; inciter, instigator.
lānitium, ī *n* wool.
lanius, ī *m* butcher; executioner.
lanterna, ae *f* lantern, lamp.
lanternārius, ī *m* lantern-bearer.
lānūgō, inis *f* down of plants *or* of the beard.
lanx, cis *f* **a**) plate, platter, dish; **b**) scale of a balance.
lapathus, ī *m* sorrel.
lapi-cīda, ae *m* stone-cutter.
lapicīdīnae, arum *f/pl.* quarries.
lapidārius 3 relating to stone.
lapidātiō, ōnis *f* a throwing of stones, stoning.
lapidātor, ōris *m* thrower of stones.
lapideus 3 of stone.
lapidō 1 to throw stones at; **lapidat** it rains stones.
lapidōsus 3 full of stones, stony.
lapillus, i *m* little stone, pebble; precious stone.
lapis, idis *m* stone; **a**) marble; **b**) milestone; **c**) boundary-stone; **d**) tombstone; **e**) precious stone; jewel; **f**) auctioneer's block; **g**) blockhead.
lappa, ae *f* goose-grass.
lāpsiō, ōnis *f* a gliding; tendency.
lāpsō 1 to stumble *or* totter.
lāpsus, ūs *m* a gliding, sliding, flowing; **a**) flight; **b**) a falling, fall; **c**) fault, error.
laqueāre, āris *n* = **lacunar.**
laqueātus 3 panelled.
laqueus, ī *m* noose, snare, trap.
Lār, Laris *m* tutelary god of a house *or* city; home, hearth.
lārdum, ī *n* = **laridum.**
largi-ficus 3 copious.

largi-fluus 3 flowing copiously.
largi-loquos 3 talkative.
largior 4 to give abundantly, bestow, impart (*alci alqd*); to bribe; to grant; to forgive.
largitās, ātis *f* liberality, bounty.
largītiō, ōnis *f* a giving freely, bestowing, lavishing, liberality; **a**) bribery; **b**) a granting.
largītor, ōris *m* bestower, granter; briber; squanderer.
largus 3 **a**) liberal in giving, bountiful; **b**) abundant, plentiful; *adv.* **largē** *and* **largiter.**
lāridum, ī *n* bacon.
larix, icis *f* larch.
(**lārua** *and*) **lārva, ae** *f* spectre, mask.
lāruātus 3 bewitched.
lārvālis, e ghostly.
lasanum, ī *n* cooking-pot; commode.
lāsarpīci-fer = **lāserpīci-fer.**
lascīvia, ae *f* **a**) playfulness, jollity, wantonness; **b**) licentiousness, insolence.
lascīvībundus 3 frolicsome.
lascīviō 4 **a**) to be wanton, insolent, licentious; **b**) to sport.
lascīvus 3 **a**) playful, jolly, wanton; **b**) licentious, unrestrained, insolent.
lāserpīci-fer 3 producing laserpicium.
lāserpīcium, ī *n* the juice of a North African plant (*silphium* or *sirpe*).
lassitūdō, inis *f* weariness.
lassō 1 to make weary, tire.
lassulus 3 somewhat tired.
lassus 3 wearied, tired, faint.
latebra, ae *f* hiding-place, retreat; **a**) concealment; refuge; **b**) subterfuge, pretext.
latebricola, ae frequenting low haunts.
latebrōsus 3 full of hiding-places; full of holes.
latēns, tis hidden, secret.
lateō, uī, — 2 to lie hid *or* concealed; **a**) to be retired, sheltered; **b**) to remain unknown.
later, eris *m* brick, tile.
laterāmen, inis *n* earthenware.
laterculus, ī *m* small brick; cake, biscuit.
laterīcius 3 made of bricks; *subst.* **-ium, ī** *n* brickwork.
latericulus, ī *m* small brick.
latēscō 3 to hide oneself.
latex, icis *m* a liquid, fluid; water, wine, oil.
latibulum, ī *n* = **latebra.**
lāti-clāvius 3 having a broad purple stripe.
lāti-fundium, ī *n* large estate.
latīnitās, ātis *f* **a**) pure Latinity; **b**) Latin rights (limited citizenrights).
lātiō, ōnis *f* a bringing; **auxilii** a rendering assistance; **legis** a proposing; **suffragii** a voting.
latitō 1 to be hidden, concealed.
lātitūdō, inis *f* breadth, width; extent; broad pronunciation; richness of expression.
lātomiae *f/pl.* = **lautumiae.**
lātor, ōris *m* mover, proposer.
lātrātor, ōris *m* barker; dog.
lātrātus, ūs *m* a barking.
lātrīna, ae *f* privy.
lātrō[1] to bark, bark at; to growl, grumble, roar, rage.
latrō[2]**, ōnis** *m* **a**) hired servant, mercenary soldier; **b**) freebooter, highwayman, robber; **c**) hunter; **d**) piece in a game.
latrōcinium, ī *n* **a**) robbery, piracy; **b**) villany, roguery, fraud; **c**) band of robbers.
latrōcinor 1 to practise robbery *or* piracy; to serve as a mercenary.
latrunculārius 3 for playing a game resembling draughts.
latrunculus, ī *m* **a**) robber; **b**) piece in a game.
lātumiae, ārum *f/pl.* = **lautumiae.**
lātūra, ae *f* a carrying of burdens.
lātus[1] 3 **a**) broad, wide, spacious, extended; **b**) diffuse, copious.
latus[2]**, eris** *n* side, flank; **latus dare alci** to expose oneself to; the lungs; the body; flank of an army.
latusculum, ī *n* (little) side.
laudābilis, e praiseworthy.
laudātiō, ōnis *f* praise, eulogy, panegyric; funeral oration.
laudātor, ōris *m*, **laudātrīx, īcis** *f* praiser, eulogizer; funeral orator; witness to character.
laudicēnī, ōrum *m/pl.* persons who applaud an orator in order to get a dinner.
laudō 1 to praise, laud, commend; to deliver a funeral oration; to cite, quote; **laudātus** 3 praiseworthy, excellent.

laurea, ae *f* = **laurus.**
laureātus 3 crowned with bay.
laureola, ae *f* laurel (bay) wreath.
laureus 3 of bay.
lauri-comus 3 covered with bay--trees.
lauri-fer *and* **-ger** 3 crowned *or* decked with bay.
laurus, ī (*and* **-ūs**) *f* bay-tree; a) laurel (bay) wreath; b) triumph.
laus, dis *f* praise, glory; a) commendation, eulogy; b) praiseworthy action, merit.
lautia, ōrum *n/pl.* public entertainment of ambassadors.
lautitia, ae *f* splendour, elegance, magnificence.
lautumiae, ārum *f/pl.* stone-quarry; prison, dungeon.
lautus 3 washed; neat; a) elegant, splendid, sumptuous; b) distinguished, refined.
lavābrum, ī *n* bath.
lavātiō, ōnis *f* a washing, bathing; bath; bathing-apparatus.
lavō, lāvī, lautum, lōtum *or* **lavātum** 1 (*and* 3) a) to wash, bathe; b) to wet; c) to wash away.
laxāmentum, ī *n* mitigation, alleviation, respite.
laxitās, ātis *f* wideness, spaciousness.
laxō 1 to unloose, slacken; a) to extend, expand, stretch out; b) to relax, release, relieve, ease, refresh.
laxus 3 a) loose, lax, relaxed; b) wide, open, extended.
lea *and* **leaena, ae** *f* lioness.
lebēs, ētis *m* basin, kettle, cauldron.
lectīca, ae *f* a) litter; b) bier.
lectīcāriola, ae *f* litter-bearer's lover.
lectīcārius, ī *m* litter-bearer.
lectīcula, ae *f* litter, bier, couch.
lēctiō, ōnis *f* a) a selecting; b) a reading, perusal; a reading aloud.
lecti-sterniātor, ōris *m* slave who prepares couches for a *lectisternium*.
lecti-sternium, ī *n* feast offered to the gods.
lēctitō 1 to read often.
lēctiuncula, ae *f* a reading.
lēctor, ōris *m* reader.
lectulus, ī *m, dim. of* **lectus**[1].
lectus[1]**, ī** *m* a) bed, couch; b) sofa; dining-couch; c) bier.
lēctus[2] 3 chosen, picked, selected; choice.

lēgātārius, ī *m* legatee.
lēgātiō, ōnis *f* a) embassy, public commission; message of an ambassador; b) office of a lieutenant; deputy command; command of a legion.
lēgātor, ōris *m* testator.
lēgātōrius 3 of a deputy.
lēgātum, ī *n* legacy, bequest.
lēgātus, ī *m* a) ambassador; b) deputy, lieutenant, lieutenant-general.
lēge-rupiō, ōnis *f* law-breaking.
lēgi-fer 3 law-giving.
legiō, ōnis *f* a Roman legion; army.
legiōnārius 3 belonging to a legion; *subst.* ~**, ī** *m* legionary.
lēgi-rupa, ae *m* breaker of the law.
lēgitimus (*or* **-umus**) 3 lawful, legal, legitimate; right, just, proper, fit, appropriate.
legiuncula, ae *f* a small legion.
lēgō[1] 1 a) to depute, despatch, send as an ambassador; b) to commission (*alci alqd*); c) to choose as one's lieutenant; d) to bequeath.
legō[2]**, lēgī, lēctum** 3 a) to collect, gather, pick; b) to wind up, spin; c) to receive, pick up; d) to trace out, catch up; e) to coast, pass along *or* over; f) to choose, select, pick out; g) to read, peruse; to read aloud, recite.
lēgulēius 3 pettifogger.
legūmen, inis *n* pulse, bean.
lembunculus, ī *m* small boat.
lembus, ī *m* cutter. boat.
lēmma, atis *n* a) theme, subject; b) (title of) a short poem.
lēmniscātus 3 adorned with ribbons.
lēmniscus, ī *m* ribbon (*attached to a victor's crown*).
lemurēs, um *m/pl.* spirits of the dead, ghosts, spectres; **lemūria, ōrum** *n/pl.* festival for appeasing the spirits of the dead.
lēna, ae *f* procuress, bawd; she that entices.
lēnīmen, inis *and* **-mentum, ī** *n* alleviation, mitigation, solace.
lēniō 4 to alleviate, mitigate, soften, soothe.
lēnis, e soft, smooth, mild, gentle; a) moderate, gradual; b) calm, kind.
lēnitās, ātis *f* mildness, softness, gentleness, smoothness.

lēnitūdō, inis *f* = **lenitas.**
lēnō, ōnis *m* pander, procurer.
lēnōcinium, ī *n* a pandering; enticement, allurement; finery; flattery.
lēnōcinor, 1 to flatter (*alci*); to stimulate, aid.
lēnōnius 3 belonging to a procurer.
lēns, tis *f* lentil.
lentēscō 3 to become sticky *or* pliant; to slacken.
lentīsci-fer 3 bearing mastictrees.
lentīscus, ī *f* (*and* **-um, ī** *n*) mastic tree *or* wood.
lentitūdō, inis *f* slowness; dullness, apathy.
lentō 1 to make flexible, to bend.
lentulus 3 rather slow.
lentus 3 tenacious, sticky; **a**) tough, pliant, flexible; **b**) slow, sluggish, lingering, lazy, drawling; **c**) indifferent, phlegmatic.
lēnullus (*and* **lēnunculus**), **ī** *m* = **leno.**
lēnunculus, ī *m* = **lembunculus.**
leō, ōnis *m* lion.
leōnīnus 3 of a lion, leonine.
lepas, adis *f* limpet.
lepidus 3 pleasant, charming, elegant; witty.
(**lepor, ōris** *and*) **lepōs, ōris** *m* pleasantness, charm; wit.
lepus, oris *m* hare.
lepusculus, ī *m* little hare.
lessus *m* funeral lamentation.
lētālis, e deadly, fatal.
lēthargicus 3 drowsy, lethargic.
lēthargus, ī *m* drowsiness.
lēti-fer 3 = **letalis.**
lētō 1 to kill.
lētum, ī *n* death; ruin.
leuc-aspis, idis bearing white shields.
leucophaeātus 3 clothed in grey.
Leuc-ophryna, ae *f* with white eyebrows (*Diana*).
levāmen, inis *and* **-mentum, ī** *n* alleviation.
levātiō, ōnis *f* alleviation; a diminishing.
leviculus 3 somewhat vain.
levidēnsis, e thin, slight, poor.
levi-fidus 3 worthy of little belief.
levi-pēs, pedis light-footed.
lēvis[1], **e** smooth, smoothed; beardless, slippery, youthful, delicate; flowing (*speech*).
levis[2], **e** light, not heavy; **a**) gentle, soft, mild; **b**) quick, rapid, swift; **c**) trifling, unimportant, insignificant, small; **d**) light-minded, unsteady, capricious, fickle, inconstant.
levi-somnus 3 sleeping lightly.
lēvitās[1], **ātis** *f* smoothness.
levitās[2], **ātis** *f* lightness; **a**) mobility; **b**) groundlessness; **c**) levity, inconstancy.
lēvō[1] 1 to smooth, polish.
levō[2] 1 **1.** to make light, lighten, diminish (*alci alqd*); a) to relieve (*alqm re*); b) to lessen; **2.** to raise, lift up; a) to support; b) to console.
lēvor, ōris *m* smoothness.
lēx, lēgis *f* **1.** formula; a) compact, agreement, covenant; b) stipulation, terms; **2.** proposal of a law, bill; a) law, legal enactment; *pl.* constitution; b) precept, regulation, rule.
(**lībāmen, inis** *and*) **lībāmentum, ī** *n* libation, offering; first-fruits.
lībārius, ī *m* pastry-cook.
lībātiō, ōnis *f* drink-offering.
lībella, ae *f* a) small coin ($^1/_{10}$ *dēnārius*); **hērēs ex lībellā** heir to one tenth of an estate; **b**) builder's level.
libellus, ī *m* little book, pamphlet; **a**) (answer to) a petition; **b**) memorandum-book; journal; **c**) letter; **d**) libel, satire; **e**) programme; **f**) announcement, placard.
libēns, tis willing, with goodwill, with pleasure; *adv.* **libenter.**
liber[1], **brī** *m* **1.** bark of a tree; **2.** book, writing; a) letter; b) list, catalogue.
līber[2], **era, erum** free; **a**) unrestricted, unlimited; **b**) free from care, debt *or* tax; **aedes** uninhabited; **c**) frank, open; **d**) free socially and politically, independent (*re, a re*).
līberālis, e a) belonging to freedom; **b**) worthy of a free man, gentlemanly, decorous, noble, noble-minded; kind, generous, liberal, plentiful, bountiful.
līberālitās, ātis *f* **a**) noble *or* kind disposition *or* character; **b**) liberality, generosity; **c**) gift, present.
līberātiō, ōnis *f* a releasing, delivering, acquittal, discharge.
līberātor, ōris *m* deliverer, liberator.

līberī, ōrum *or* **um** *m/pl.* children.
līberō 1 to set free, liberate (*alqm re, ab* or *ex re*); **a**) to manumit; **b**) to free, deliver, release; **c**) to cancel, render void; **d**) to free from taxes; **e**) **fidem** to keep one's word; **nomina** to settle debts; **f**) to absolve, acquit.
līberta, ae *f* freedwoman.
lībertās, ātis *f* freedom, liberty; **a**) civil *or* political freedom, independence; **b**) frankness.
lībertīnus 3 of the class of freedmen; *subst. m, f* freedman, -woman.
lībertus, ī *m* freedman.
libet, libuit *and* **libitum est** 2 it pleases, is agreeable; *subst.* **libita, ōrum** *n/pl.* pleasure, liking.
libīdinor 1 to indulge lust.
libīdinōsus 3 **a**) luxurious, licentious, lustful; **b**) wilful, wanton.
libīdō, inis *f* desire, pleasure, longing; **a**) wilfulness, caprice; **b**) lust, sensual desire, lewdness.
libita, ōrum *n/pl., see* **libet.**
libitīnārius, ī *m* undertaker.
lībō 1 to take a little away from (*alqd ab* or *ex re*); **a**) to touch, taste; **b**) to diminish; **c**) to sacrifice, offer, consecrate, make a libation (*alci alqd*).
lībra, ae *f* **1.** balance, pair of scales; **lībra et aes** due legal form; builder's level; **2.** the Roman pound.
lībrāmentum, ī *n* **a**) weight, gravity; **b**) level surface, horizontal plane.
lībrāria, ae *f* weigher of wool.
librāriolus, ī *m* = **librarius.**
librārium, ī *n* book-case.
librārius, ī *m* belonging to books; *subst. m* copyist, scribe; bookseller.
lībrātor, ōris *m* **a**) leveller, surveyor; engineer; **b**) = **libritor.**
lībrātus 3 hurled, poised.
lībrīlis, e of a pound weight.
lībritor, ōris *m* hurler, thrower.
lībrō 1 to poise, balance; to swing, hurl.
lībum, ī *n* cake (*for offering*).
liburn(ic)a, ae *f* light warship.
licēns, tis unrestrained, bold, licentious.
licentia, ae *f* freedom, licence; licentiousness, lawlessness, uncontrolled power.
liceō, uī, — 2 to be valued, fetch a price.
liceor, itus sum 2 to bid, offer a price for.
licet, licuit *and* **licitum est** 2 it is allowed, permitted (*alci* with *inf.; acc.* with *inf.*), one may, one is at liberty; *cj.* with *subj.* even if, although.
līchēn, ēnis *m* ringworm.
licitātiō, ōnis *f* a bidding (*at a sale*).
licitātor, ōris *m* bidder.
licitor 1 = **liceor.**
licitus 3 permitted, allowed.
līcium, ī *n* (*usu. plur.*) loops for raising any desired number of warp-threads, in order to pass the woof in front of *or* behind them; thread; woven material.
līctor, ōris *m* lictor, official attendant of a magistrate.
liēn, ēnis *m* spleen.
liēnōsus 3 suffering from a disorder of the spleen.
ligāmen, inis *and* **-mentum, ī** *n* band, tie, bandage.
lignārius, ī *m* carpenter, joiner.
lignātiō, ōnis *f* a procuring of wood.
lignātor, ōris *m* wood-cutter.
ligneolus *and* **ligneus** 3 wooden.
lignor 1 to procure wood.
lignum, ī *n* **a**) wood, firewood; **b**) tree; **c**) spearshaft; **d**) puppet; **e**) writing-table.
ligō[1], **ōnis** *m* mattock, hoe.
ligō[2] 1 to tie, to bind.
ligula, ae *f* = **lingula.**
ligūr(r)iō 4 **a**) to lick, lick up; to pick at; to feed daintily; to prey on; to lust after.
ligūr(r)ītiō, ōnis *f* daintiness.
ligustrum, ī *n* privet.
līlium, ī *n* lily.
līma, ae *f* file; a polishing.
līmāt(ul)us 3 filed, polished.
līmāx, ācis *f* (*and m*) slug.
limbulārius, ī *m* maker of fringes.
limbus, ī *m* hem, edge, border.
līmen, inis *n* threshold; **a**) door, entrance; **b**) starting-point, beginning; **c**) dwelling.
līmes, itis *m* cross-path (*between fields*); **a**) boundary-line, boundary-wall; **b**) path, way, passage, road.
līmō[1] 1 to file, polish; **a**) to rub; **b**) to examine accurately; **c**) to file off, diminish.
līmō[2] 1 to cover with mud.
līmōsus 3 miry, muddy.

limpidus 3 clear, limpid.
līmulus 3 slightly aslant.
līmus[1], ī *m* mud, mire, dirt.
līmus[2] 3 aslant, sideways.
līmus[3], ī *m* priest's apron.
līnea, ae *f* linen thread; **a)** plumb-line; **b)** line, stroke; **c)** bound, limit; **d)** fishing-line.
līneāmentum, ī *n* line, stroke; *pl.* outline, sketch; features.
līneō 1 to make straight.
līneus 3 flaxen, linen.
lingō, līnxī, līnctum 3 to lick.
lingua, ae *f* the tongue; **a)** speech, language; eloquence; **b)** a language *or* tongue, dialect; **c)** tongue of land.
linguārium, ī *n* fine for thoughtless speaking.
lingula, ae *f* **a)** tongue of land; **b)** shoe-strap; **c)** ladle.
linguläca, ae *f* chatterbox.
līniāmentum, ī *n* = **lineamentum.**
līni-ger 3 linen-wearing.
linō, lēvī *or* **līvī, litum** 3 to besmear, anoint; to erase; to bedaub, cover.
linquō, līquī, — 3 to leave, quit; to forsake; abandon, omit (*alqd*).
linteātus 3 clothed in linen.
linteō, ōnis *m* linen-weaver.
linteolum, ī *n* small linen cloth.
linter, tris *f* (*m*) boat, skiff; trough, tub.
linteus 3 of linen; *subst.* **linteum, ī** *n* linen cloth, sail.
lintriculus, ī *m* small boat.
līnum, ī *n* flax, linen; **a)** thread, cord, fishing-line; **b)** linen cloth *or* garment; **c)** rope; **d)** hunter's *or* fisher's net.
lippiō 4 to have sore eyes; to burn.
lippitūdō, inis *f* inflammation of the eyes.
lippus 3 with sore eyes; blind; running with juice.
lique-faciō (*and* **liquē-**) 3 to melt, dissolve; to weaken.
liquēns (*and* **lī-**), **tis** liquid.
liqueō, liquī *or* **licuī,** — 2 to be clear, evident.
liquēscō, —, — 3 to become clear *or* fluid, to melt (away); **a)** to become effeminate; **b)** to putrefy.
liquidiusculus 3 milder, softer.
liquidus (*and* **lī-**) 3 flowing, fluid, liquid; *subst.* **liquidum, ī** *n* a liquid; **a)** clear, bright, limpid; **b)** pure; **c)** clear, evident, certain; *subst.* **liquidum, ī** *n* certainty; *adv.* **liquidō** clearly, certainly.
liquō 1 to melt, liquefy; to strain, purify.
liquor[1] (*and* **lī-**), **ōris** *m* **a)** fluidity, liquidity; **b)** a fluid; **c)** the sea.
līquor[2], —, — 3 to flow; to melt away.
līs, lītis *f* contention, quarrel; **a)** controversy, dispute; **b)** lawsuit.
litāmen, inis *n* sacrifice.
litātiō, ōnis *f* auspicious sacrifice.
litera, ae *f*, *see* **littera.**
liti-cen, inis *m* clarion-blower.
lītigātor, ōris *m* party in a lawsuit.
lītigiōsus 3 **a)** quarrelsome, full of dispute, contentious; **b)** disputed, contested.
lītigium, ī *n* = **lis.**
lītigō 1 to dispute, quarrel.
litō 1 **a)** to sacrifice under favourable auspices, to obtain favourable omens; **b)** to propitiate.
lītorālis, e relating to the shore.
lītoreus 3 belonging to the shore.
littera, ae *f* **1.** letter of the alphabet, *pl.* the alphabet; a handwriting; **2.** *pl.* a writing; a) letter, epistle; b) document, record, deed; **c)** literature; **d)** learning, culture, liberal education.
litterārius 3 relating to reading and writing.
litterātor, ōris *m* elementary teacher.
litterātūra, ae *f* writing; alphabet; grammar.
litterātus 3 inscribed with letters; **a)** literal; **b)** learned, lettered, liberally educated.
litterula, ae *f* **a)** small letter (*of the alphabet*); **b)** *pl.* short letter, note; (knowledge of) literature.
litūra, ae *f* erasure; blot.
lītus, oris *n* sea-shore, coast, beach; bank.
lituus, ī *m* **a)** curved staff of an augur; **b)** clarion, trumpet.
līveō, —, — 2 to be bluish, dark, livid; to envy (*with dat.*).
līvēscō 3 to turn blue.
līvidulus 3 envious.
līvidus 3 bluish, blue-grey; blue--black, black; livid; envious.
līvor, ōris *m* bluish colour, livid spot; envy, malice.

lixa, ae *m* sutler, camp-follower.
locārius, ī *m* seller of theatre seats.
locātiō, ōnis *f* **a**) a placing; **b**) a letting out, leasing; contract.
locātor, ōris *m* landlord.
locitō 1 to hire out.
locō 1 to place, put, lay, set (*alqd in re*); **a**) to give in marriage (*women*); **b**) to let, lease, hire, farm out; to lend money at interest; **c**) to give out on contract.
loculāmentum, ī *n* case, pigeon-hole.
loculus, ī *m* **a**) small place; **b**) receptacle, coffer, satchel.
locuplēs, ētis rich, wealthy, opulent, richly supplied; trustworthy, reliable, credible.
locuplētātor, ōris *m* one who enriches.
locuplētō 1 to enrich; to adorn (*alqm re*).
locus, ī *m* place, spot, locality (*pl.* **loca, ōrum** *n*) **1.** a) the right *or* proper place, (**in**) **loco** in the right place; b) special, appointed place, station, post, position; c) dwelling, residence; d) locality, district, region; e) place in the order of succession (**primo loco** firstly); f) passage in a book (*pl.* **locī**); topic, matter, subject, point, head, division; **loci communes** passages of a general import; g) position, rank, degree, birth (**nobili** *or* **summo loco natus**), **loco** *with gen.* in the condition of (**filii loco esse** *or* **amare** as a son, in the place of, instead of); **2.** time, right time; a) opportunity, occasion; b) condition, situation.
lōcusta, ae *f* locust; crayfish.
locūtiō, ōnis *f* a speaking, pronunciation, speech.
lōdīcula, ae *f* blanket.
lōdīx, īcis *f* blanket.
logī, ōrum *m/pl.* words; empty talk; jest.
logica, ōrum *n/pl.* logic.
lolium, ī *n* darnel.
lolligō, inis (*and* **lollīguncula, ae**) *f* cuttle-fish.
lōmentum, ī *n* cleansing-cream.
long-aevus 3 aged, old.
longē *adv.* **1.** (*of space*) a long way off, far off, at a distance; a) far, from afar; b) by far, very much; c) at length, diffusely; **2.** (*of time*) long, for a long time (*longe ante*).
longinquitās, ātis *f* length, extent, long duration.
longinquus 3 long; **a**) distant, far, remote, foreign, strange; **b**) long in duration, tedious, long deferred, distant.
longiter far.
longitūdō, inis *f* length; long duration.
longiusculus 3 rather long.
longulus 3 somewhat long.
longurius, ī *m* long pole.
longus 3 **1.** (*of space*) long; **navis longa** man-of-war; a) tall, vast, spacious; b) far off, remote, distant; prolix; **2.** of long duration, tedious.
lopas, adis *f* limpet.
loquācitās, ātis *f* talkativeness.
loquāx, ācis *and* **loquāculus** 3 talkative, garrulous.
loquēla (*and* **-ella**), **ae** *f* speech, discourse, language.
loquentia, ae *f* readiness of speech.
loquitor 1 to speak.
loquor, cūtus sum 3 **1.** to speak (*cum, pro alqo, de re*); **2.** to indicate clearly; a) to say (*alqd*); b) to mention.
lōrārius, ī *m* flogger of slaves.
lōrātus 3 bound with thongs.
lōreus 3 made of thongs.
lōrīca, ae *f* **a**) leather cuirass; **b**) breast-work.
lōrīcātus 3 armed with a cuirass.
lōrīcula, ae *f* small breastwork.
lōri-pēs, edis with deformed feet.
lōrum, ī *n* thong; **a**) rein; **b**) whip; **c**) leather amulet.
lōtium, ī *n* urine.
lōtos *and* **-us, ī** *f* (*and m*) lotus; flute (*of lotus-wood*).
lōtus 3 = **lautus** (*lavo*).
lubēns, lubet, lubīdō, *see* **libens, libet, libido.**
lubentia, ae *f* pleasure.
lūbricō 1 to make slippery.
lūbricus 3 slippery; **a**) quickly moving, fleeting; **b**) uncertain, critical, hazardous; **c**) deceitful, tricky.
lūca bōs *f* (Lucanian cow) elephant.
lūcānica, ae *f* smoked sausage.
lūcar, āris *n* salary (*of actors*).
lucellum, ī *n* small gain, little profit.
lūceō, xī, — 2 **a**) to be bright, shine; **b**) to be conspicuous, clear; **lūcet** it is day.

lucerna, ae *f* lamp, oil-lamp.
lūcēscō, lūxī, — 3 to grow light, become day.
lūcidus 3 clear, bright, shining; perspicuous.
lūci-fer 3 light-bringing; *m* the morning-star; day.
lūci-fuga, ae *m* one who shuns daylight.
lūci-fugus 3 light-shunning.
lūcīscō 3 = **lucesco.**
lucrātīvus 3 lucrative, profitable.
lucri-ficābilis, e, lucri-fer 3 profitable.
lucri-fuga, ae *m and f* gain-shunning.
lucri-peta, ae *m and f* greedy of gain.
lucror 1 to gain, win, acquire.
lucrōsus 3 profitable, lucrative.
lucrum, ī *n* gain, profit, advantage; (in) **lucro esse** to be profitable; **lucri facere** *alqd* to gain, to reap the benefit of; **a**) love of gain, avarice; **b**) riches.
luctāmen, inis *n* effort, exertion.
luctātiō, ōnis *f* a wrestling, struggling, contest, fight.
luctātor, ōris *m* wrestler.
lūcti-ficus 3, **lūcti-fer** 3, **lūcti-ficābilis, e** mournful, doleful.
lūcti-sonus 3 sad-sounding.
luctor (*and* **luctō**) 1 to wrestle, struggle, strive.
lūctuōsus 3 mournful, sorrowful, lamentable.
lūctus, ūs *m* sorrow, mourning; mourning apparel.
lūcubrātiō, ōnis *f* a working by lamp-light.
lūcubrātōrius 3 serving for studies at night.
lūcubrō 1 to work by night.
lūculentus 3 **a**) full of light, bright; **b**) distinguished, splendid; *adv.* **lūculentē** *and* **lūculenter.**
lucunzulus, ī *m* a kind of pastry.
lūcus, ī *m* grove, wood.
lūcusta, ae *f* = **locusta.**
lūdia, ae *f* **a**) stage-dancer; **b**) gladiator's wife.
lūdibrium, ī *n* derision, mockery; laughing-stock, plaything.
lūdibundus 3 **a**) playful, sportive, wanton; **b**) without effort *or* danger.
(**lūdicer**), **cra, crum a**) sportive, playful; **b**) belonging to public games *or* stage-plays; *subst.* **lūdicrum, ī** *n* **a**) plaything, toy; **b**) public games, scenic show.
lūdi-faciō 3 to make sport of.
lūdi-ficābilis, e used in mockery.
lūdificātiō, ōnis *f* a deriding, rallying, mockery.
lūdi-ficātor, ōris *m* mocker.
lūdi-ficātus, ūs *m* mockery.
(**lūdi-ficō** *and*) **lūdi-ficor** 1 **a**) to deride, make game of, turn into ridicule, mock; **b**) to thwart, frustrate.
lūdiō, ōnis *and* **lūdius, ī** *m* stage-player.
lūdō, sī, sum 3 to play, sport (*alqd; alqa re*); **a**) to frolic; **b**) to practise as a pastime, play with; **c**) to baffle, ridicule, deceive.
lūdus, ī *m* play, game, pastime; **a**) (*pl.*) public games, spectacles, shows, exhibitions; **b**) stage-play; **c**) child's play, mere sport; trifle; jest, joke; **d**) gladiatorial school; **e**) elementary school.
luella, ae *f* expiation.
luēs, is *f* plague, pestilence; ruin, destruction.
lūgeō, xī, — 2 to mourn, lament.
lūgubris, e belonging to mourning; **a**) mournful, doleful, plaintive; **b**) disastrous; *subst.* **lūgubria, ium** *n/pl.* mourning attire.
lumbi-fragium, ī *n* rupture of the loins.
lumbrīcus, ī *m* earthworm.
lumbus, ī *m* the loin.
lūmen, inis *n* light; **a**) lamp, candle, torch; **b**) daylight, day; **c**) the light of life; **d**) eye, the light of the eye; **e**) window; **f**) splendour, glory, ornament; **g**) salvation, help.
lūmināria, ium *n/pl.* window-shutters.
lūminōsus 3 full of light; conspicuous.
lūna, ae *f* the moon; moonshine; **a**) crescent; **b**) month.
lūnāris, e lunar; moonlike.
lūnō 1 to bend into a crescent.
lūnula, ae *f* crescent-shaped ornament.
luō[1] 3 to wash, cleanse.
luō[2], **luī,** — 3 to expiate, atone for (*alqd*); **a**) to avert by expiation *or* punishment; **b**) to pay, to suffer punishment.
lupa, ae *f* she-wolf; harlot.
lupānar, āris *n* brothel.

lupātus 3 with wolf's teeth; **lupāta, ōrum** *n/pl. and* **-tī, ōrum** *m/pl.* curb armed with sharp teeth.
Lupercālia, i(or)um *n/pl.* festival of Lupercus.
lupīllus, ī *m* lupin.
lupīnus 3 of a wolf, wolf's; *subst.* **lupīnus, ī** *m and* **lupīnum, ī** *n* **a)** lupin; **b)** counter in a game.
lupus, ī *m* **a)** wolf; **b)** voracious fish, pike; **c)** hook; **d)** a horse's bit armed with sharp teeth.
lurcō, ōnis *m* glutton.
lūreō 2 to be ghastly pale.
lūridus 3 (making) sickly yellow, ghastly, lurid.
lūror, ōris *m* paleness.
luscinia, ae *f (and* **-ius, ī** *m,* **-iola, ae** *f)* nightingale.
luscitiōsus 3 dim-eyed.
luscus 3 one-eyed.
lūsiō, ōnis *f* playing, game.
lūsitō 1 to play, sport.
lūsor, ōris *m* player; playful writer; humourist.
lūsōrius 3 used for play *or* pleasure.
lūstrālis, e **a)** relating to expiation; **b)** quinquennial.
lūstrātiō, ōnis *f* **a)** purification by sacrifice; **b)** a wandering, traversing, going about.
lūstricus 3 = **lustralis.**
lūstrō[1] 1 to light up, illuminate.
lūstrō[2] 1 **a)** to purify by expiation; **b)** to review, survey, examine; to go over *or* about, to traverse.
lustror 1 to frequent brothels.
lustrum[1], **ī** *n* **a)** bog, morass; **b)** den *or* lair of wild beasts; **c)** brothel; **d)** debauchery.
lūstrum[2], **ī** *n* **a)** expiatory sacrifice; **b)** period of (five) years; quinquennial festival.
lūsus, ūs *m* play, game, sport, amusement, dalliance.
lūteolus 3 yellow.
luteus[1] 3 of mud *or* clay; worthless; dirty.
lūteus[2] 3 orange, yellow.
lut(it)ō 1 to make dirty.
lutulentus 3 muddy, dirty.
lutum[1], **ī** *n* mud, mire, dirt; loam, clay.
lūtum[2], **ī** *n* dyer's weed, yellow colour.
lūx, lūcis *f (m)* light; **a)** splendour, brightness; **b)** daylight, day; **prīmā lūce** at dawn; **lūce** *or* **lūcī** in the daytime; **c)** light of life; **d)** light of the eye; **e)** clearness, elucidation; **f)** publicity, the sight of men; **g)** help, succour, encouragement, ornament.
luxō 1 to dislocate.
luxor 1 to revel, feast.
luxuria, ae *f and* **-iēs, ēī** *f* rankness, luxuriant growth; riotous living, extravagance.
luxuriō *and* **-or** 1 to be rank, luxuriant, abundant in growth; **a)** to be playful, sportive; **b)** to abound in, swell, increase; **c)** to revel, run riot.
luxuriōsus 3 rank, luxuriant, exuberant; **a)** dissolute, luxurious, voluptuous; **b)** excessive.
luxus, ūs *m* rankness; **a)** luxury, debauchery, sensual excess, extravagance; **b)** splendour.
lychno-bius, ī *m* one who lives by lamp-light.
lychnūchus, ī *m* lamp-stand, candlestick.
lychnus, ī *m* light, lamp.
lygdos, ī *f* white marble.
lympha, ae *f* clear water.
lymphāticus *and* **lymphātus** 3 insane, mad, frantic.
lymphō 1 to make mad.
lynx, cis *m* and *f* lynx.
lyra, ae *f* lyre, lute; lyric poetry, song.
lyricus 3 lyric; *m* lyric poet.
lyristēs, ae *m* lyre-player.

M

M *abbr.* **1.** = **Marcus; 2.** *as a numeral* = 1000; **M'** = **Mānius.**
macellārius, ī *m* victualler.
macellum, ī *n* (*and* **-us, ī** *m*) food-market.
maceō 2 to be lean.
macer, cra, crum lean, meagre.
māceria, ae *f* wall.
mācerō 1 to soak, make soft; to weaken, emaciate, enervate; to tease, torment.
macēscō 3 to become lean.
machaera, ae *f* sword.
machaerophorus, ī *m* swordbearer; halberdier, satellite.
māchina, ae *f* machine, engine (windlass, crane, catapult); device, artifice.
māchināmentum, ī *n* machine, instrument.
māchinātiō, ōnis *f* **a)** mechanism, machinery; **b)** = **machina.**
māchinātor, ōris *m* (*and* **-trīx, īcis** *f*) maker of machines, engineer; contriver, inventor.
māchinor 1 to contrive, devise, invent; to scheme, plot.
māchinōsus 3 ingeniously contrived.
maciēs, ēī *f* leanness, thinness.
macilentus 3 thin, lean.
macrēscō, —, — 3 to grow lean *or* thin.
macritūdō, inis *f* leanness.
macro-cōl(l)um, ī *n* large-sized paper, royal paper.
mactābilis, e deadly.
mactātor, ōris *m* killer.
mactātus, ūs *m* sacrifice.
macte (*voc. of* **mactus**), *pl.* **mactī** magnified, glorified; **macte virtute** hail to thee!, good-luck!, be honoured!, well done!
mactō 1 **1.** to magnify, glorify; honour; **2.** to afflict, punish; to sacrifice, kill.
mactus 3 wounded.
macula, ae *f* **a)** spot, mark; blot, stain, blemish, fault; **b)** mesh (*of a net*).
maculō 1 to stain, pollute, disgrace.
maculōsus 3 **a)** spotted; **b)** stained, polluted; disgraced; abominable.
made-faciō 3 (*and* **-factō** 1) to wet, moisten.
madeō 2 to be wet; **a)** to be made soft by boiling; **b)** to be soaked in (*re*).
madēscō, duī, — 3 to become wet *or* moist.
madidus 3 wet, moist, steeped.
mador, ōris *m* moisture.
madulsa, ae *m* drunkard.
maelēs, is *f* marten, badger.
maena, ae *f* small sea-fish.
maenas, adis *f* bacchante.
maeniānum, ī *n* balcony.
maereō, —, — 2 **a)** to mourn, grieve, lament; **b)** to bemoan, bewail (*acc.*).
maeror, ōris *m* mourning, sadness, grief.
maestiter *adv. of* **maestus.**
maestitia, ae *f* sadness, sorrowfulness, grief, dejection.
maestitūdō, inis *f* = **maestitia.**
maestus 3 **a)** sad, sorrowful, dejected; **b)** causing sorrow, gloomy.
māgālia, ium *n/pl.* huts, cottages.
mage = **magis.**
magicus 3 magical, magic.
magis *adv.* **a)** more, in a higher degree; **non magis quam** not so much ... as, not so ... but rather; **b)** rather, with better reason, more truly.
magister, trī *m* master, chief, ruler, director; **a)** superintendent; **b)** teacher, leader, adviser.
magisterium, ī *n* direction, superintendency, tutorship, guardianship.
magistra, ae *f* mistress, directress, leader, instructress.
magistrātus, ūs *m* dignity *or* office of a magistrate, civil office, magistracy; a magistrate, high civil officer, public functionary.
magmentārius 3 for additional offerings.
magn-animitās, ātis *f* magnanimity.
magn-animus 3 high-minded, high-spirited.

magnēs, ētis *m* (*lapis*) loadstone, magnet.
magni-dicus 3 boastful.
magnificentia, ae *f* grandeur, splendour, magnificence; **a**) loftiness, greatness; **b**) a boasting, pompousness.
magni-ficō 1 to esteem highly.
magni-ficus 3 splendid, fine, costly, sumptuous; **a**) fond of display; **b**) boasting, pompous; **c**) noble, distinguished.
magni-loquentia, ae *f* elevated language, lofty style; boasting.
magni-loquus 3 boastful; sublime.
magnitūdō, inis *f* greatness, size; **a**) number, quantity; **b**) importance, vastness, extent.
magn-opere (*and* **magnō opere,** *superl.* **maximō opere**) *adv.* very much, greatly, exceedingly, particularly; earnestly, urgently.
magnus 3 (*comp.* **māior, ius;** *superl.* **maximus**) **1.** a) (*of size*) large, great, big, high, tall, long, broad, extensive, spacious; b) (*of number or quantity*) considerable, abundant, much, numerous; c) (*of value*) high; **magnī aestimāre, magnō vendere; māior pars** majority; **2.** (*of time*) a) great, long, extended; b) aged, old, advanced; **māior** (*natu*) elder, **maximus** eldest; **māiōrēs** *pl.* fathers, ancestors; **3.** (*of force*) a) strong, powerful, vehement, loud (*vox*); b) considerable, great, mighty, important, weighty; c) high, eminent, noble, powerful; d) haughty, proud, boastful; e) high-minded; f) excessive, intense.
magus, ī *m* magician; *adj.* 3 magic.
magȳdaris *f* seed (*or* stalk?) of the plant *sirpe* or *silphium.*
māiālis, is *m* hog.
māiestās, ātis *f* majesty, grandeur, greatness, elevation, dignity; high-treason.
māior, māius, *see* **magnus.**
Māius 3 of the month of May; (*mensis*) *m* May.
māiusculus 3 somewhat greater *or* older.
māla, ae *f* cheek-bone, jaw; cheek.
malacia, ae *f* calm at sea.
malacissō 1 to render soft.
malacus 3 soft; luxurious; nimble.
malaxō 1 to soften, to make flexible.
male *adv.* (*comp.* **pēius,** *superl.* **pessimē**) **a**) badly, ill, wrong, wickedly; **b**) unfortunately, unsuccessfully; **c**) unseasonably; **d**) excessively, very much, greatly; imperfectly, scarcely, not at all.
male-dicāx, ācis abusive.
male-dīcō 3 to speak ill of, abuse, revile (*alci*).
male-dictiō, ōnis *f* a reviling, abuse.
male-dictum, ī *n* abusive language, curse.
male-dicus 3 abusive, slanderous.
male-faciō 3 to do evil; **male-factum, ī** *n* evil deed, injury.
male-factor, ōris *m* evil-doer.
maleficium, ī *n* evil deed, offence; wickedness, injury.
male-ficus 3 evil-doing; vicious, wicked; mischievous.
male-suādus 3 ill-advising.
male-volēns, tis = **malevolus.**
malevolentia, ae *f* ill-will, malevolence.
male-volus 3 ill-disposed, envious, malevolent.
māli-fer 3 apple-bearing.
malignitās, ātis *f* ill-will, malice, envy; niggardliness.
malignus 3 ill-disposed, wicked, malicious; **a**) barren, unfruitful; **b**) niggardly, scanty.
malitia, ae *f* malice, roguery.
malitiōsus 3 ill-disposed, wicked, knavish, malicious.
malivolentia, malivolus, *see* **male-.**
malleātor, ōris *m* one who hammers, beater.
malleolus, ī *m* fire-dart.
malleus, ī *m* hammer, mallet.
mālō, māluī, mālle to choose rather, prefer; to be more favourable (*alci*).
mālobathron, ī *n* a costly (cinnamon-) oil *or* ointment.
mālum[1]**, ī** *n* apple, quince, citron, pomegranate.
malum[2]**, ī** *n* evil; **a**) fault; **b**) misfortune, calamity, mischief; **c**) punishment, hurt, harm, injury; **d**) wrong-doing, vice; *int.* plague!, wretch.
malus[1] 3 (*comp.* **pēior, us,** *superl.* **pessimus** 3) bad; **a**) evil, wicked, mischievous, wrong, criminal, depraved, malicious; (*subst.*) **malī, ōrum** *m/pl.* unpatriotic citizens;

b) ugly, hideous; c) unlucky, unfortunate, miserable; d) injurious, pernicious, destructive.
mālus², **ī** 1. *m* upright pole, mast, prop; 2. *f* apple-tree; citron.
malva, ae *f* mallow.
mamilla, ae *f* breast; darling.
mamillāre, is *n* brassière.
mamma, ae *f* breast, pap; teat.
mammeātus (*and* **mammōsus**) 3 full-breasted.
mammia *n/pl.* little mothers.
mammicula, ae *f* = **mamilla.**
mānābilis, e penetrating.
manceps, cipis *m* purchaser, renter, contractor; surety.
mancipātiō, ōnis *f* transfer of property, purchase.
mancipium, ī *n* a) a taking possession of; legal purchase; **lex mancipii** contract of sale; right of possession; b) slave obtained by legal transfer.
mancipō 1 to transfer by formal sale, to sell, give up to.
mancup- *see* **mancip-** *and* **manceps.**
mancus 3 maimed, defective.
mandātor, ōris *m* suborner.
mandātū *abl.* by order.
mandātum, ī *n* charge, order, commission, injunction.
mandō¹ 1 to commit to the charge of (*alci alqd; de re*), to order, commission (*alci*).
mandō², **ndī, ānsum** 3 to chew, masticate; to eat, consume.
mandra, ae *f* a) drove of cattle; b) squares on a game-board.
mandūcō 1 to chew, to eat.
mandūcus, ī *m* mask representing a glutton.
māne 1. *n* (*abl.* **-ī**) the early morning; 2. *adv.* early in the morning.
maneō, mānsī, mānsum 2 1. to stay, remain, abide; a) to pass the night; b) to last, endure, continue; to persist, adhere to (*in re*); 2. to await, expect (*acc.*).
mānēs, ium *m/pl.* ghosts *or* shades of the departed; a) corpse; b) the lower world, infernal regions.
mangō, ōnis *m* slave-dealer.
mangōnicus 3 of a slave-dealer.
manicae, ārum *f/pl.* a) long sleeves; b) handcuffs; grapple.
manicātus 3 with long sleeves.
manicula, ae *f* little hand.
manifestārius 3 clear; caught in the act, red-handed.
manifestō 1 to show clearly, manifest, reveal.
mani-festus 3 palpable; a) convicted of, manifestly betraying (*gen.*); b) clear, plain.
maniplāris, -plus, *see* **manipul-.**
manipulāris, e (*and* **-ius** 3) manipular, of a company; *subst.* common soldier.
manipulātim *adv.* in maniples.
manipulus, ī *m* a handful, bundle; maniple *or* company of foot-soldiers.
mann(ul)us, ī *m* small Gallic horse.
mānō 1 to flow, run, drop, trickle (*re*); a) to flow; b) to proceed (*ab, ex, de re*); c) to spread; to pass away.
mānsiō, ōnis *f* a remaining, stay, sojourn.
mānsitō 1 to stay, abide, remain.
mānstrūca, ae *f* = **mastrūca.**
mānsuē-faciō 3 to make tame.
mānsuēs, ētis = **mansuetus.**
mānsuēscō, suēvī, suētum 3 a) to become tame *or* gentle; b) to tame.
mānsuētūdō, inis *f* tameness, mildness, gentleness, clemency.
mānsuētus 3 tame; gentle, soft, mild, quiet, tranquil.
mānsūrus 3, *part. fut. of* **maneo.**
mantēle, is *n* towel, napkin.
mantellum, ī *n* cloak, cover.
mantica, ae *f* wallet.
mantis-cinor 1 *meaning doubtful: either* to help oneself liberally *or* to prophesy.
mantō 1 to wait (for).
manuālis, e thrown by the hand.
manubiae, ārum *f/pl.* money obtained by the sale of booty, prize-money; spoils, plunder.
manubiālis, e, manubiārius 3 coming from *or* producing booty.
manubrium, ī *n* handle, hilt, haft.
manuf- *see* **manif-; manufestārius** 3 plain.
manuleārius, ī *m* maker of long sleeves.
manuleātus 3 provided with long sleeves.
manū-missiō, ōnis *f* a setting free.
manū-mittō 3 to set free.
manu-pretium, ī *n* pay, wages, hire; reward.
manus, ūs *f* the hand; **in manibus habēre** to be engaged on; a) armed

hand, fist; **b**) personal valour; **c**) hand to hand fight, close combat; **manum conferre** *or* **conserere** to come to close quarters; **d**) force, violence, power; jurisdiction (*of a father, of a husband*); **in manū alcis esse** to be in one's power; **e**) work, work of the artist *or* craftsman, workmanship; handwriting; **f**) a handful, band, body of men, corps, armed force; **g**) trunk of an elephant; grappling-iron.

mapālia, ium *n/pl.* huts, cottages, movable dwellings.

mappa, ae *f* napkin; signal-flag.

marceō, —, — 2 to wither, droop; to be faint, feeble, languid.

marcēscō, —, — 3 to begin to droop; to become languid, weak, feeble.

marcidus 3 withered, faded; weak, feeble, languid.

marcor, ōris *m* withering, languor.

marculus, ī *m* small hammer.

mare, is *n* the sea, ocean; **terrā marīque** by sea and land; sea-water.

margarīta, ae *f* (*and* **-tum, ī** *n*) pearl.

marginō 1 to enclose with a margin.

margō, inis *m* (*and f*) border, edge, boundary.

marīnus 3 = **maritimus.**

marisca, ae *f* **a**) fig; **b**) haemorrhoid.

marīta, ae *f*, *see* **maritus.**

marītālis, e matrimonial, nuptial.

maritimus (-umus) 3 relating to the sea, marine, maritime, on the sea, on the sea-coast; *subst.* **maritima, ōrum** *n/pl.* coast.

marītō 1 to wed, marry.

marītus 3 matrimonial, nuptial, wedded; *subst.* **~, ī** *m* husband, **-a, ae** *f* wife.

marmor, oris *n* marble; **a**) marble block, marble work, statue; **b**) surface of the sea.

marmorārius (faber) worker in marble.

marmorātus 3 covered with marble.

marmoreus 3 made of marble; marble-like, smooth, shining.

marra, ae *f* hoe.

Mārs, tis *m* Mars, the God of War; **a**) war, battle, contest, engagement; **b**) manner of fighting, issue of battle, fortune of war; **aequo** (*or* **ancipiti**) **Marte** without decision.

marsuppium (*and* **-sūpium**), **ī** *n* money-bag, purse.

Mārtiālis, e relating to Mars.

Mārtius 3 belonging to Mars; (*mensis*) *m* March.

mās, maris a) *m* man, male being; **b**) *adj.* male, masculine; manly, brave.

masculīnus 3 male, masculine.

masculus 3 male; manly, vigorous.

massa, ae *f* dough; lump, mass.

mastīgia, ae *m* gallows-bird, scoundrel, good-for-nothing.

mastrūca, ae *f* (garment of) sheepskin.

mastrūcātus 3 clothed in sheepskins.

masturbor 1 to masturbate; *hence* **masturbātor, ōris** *m.*

matara, ae *f and* **-ris, is** *f* Gallic javelin.

matella, ae *f* (chamber-)pot.

matelliō, ōnis *m* small pot, vessel.

māter, tris *f* mother; parent, producer, origin, source.

mātercula, ae *f* little mother.

māteria, ae *and* **-iēs, ēī** *f* matter, stuff; **a**) materials, wood, timber; **b**) provisions, store, resource; **c**) subject, subject-matter, topic, ground, theme; **d**) occasion, opportunity, cause; **e**) natural disposition, abilities.

māteriārius, ī *m* timber-merchant.

māteriātus 3 timbered.

māterior 1 to fetch timber.

māternus 3 a mother's, maternal, motherly.

mātertera, ae *f* mother's sister, maternal aunt.

mathēmatica, ae *f* mathematics; astrology.

mathēmaticus, ī *m* mathematician; astrologer.

mātri-cīda, ae *m* matricide, a mother's murderer.

mātricīdium, ī *n* matricide, the murder of a mother.

mātrimōnium, ī *n* wedlock, marriage; matrimony; *pl.* wives.

mātrīmus (*and* **-ĭmus**) 3 having a mother still living.

mātrīx, īcis *f* **a**) womb; **b**) parent stem of plants.

mātrōna, ae *f* wife, matron; woman of rank, lady.

mātrōnālis, e belonging to a matron *or* married woman.
mattea, ae *f* dainty bit.
matula, ae *f* vessel, (chamber-)pot; simpleton.
mātūrātē in good time.
mātūrēscō, ruī, — 3 to become ripe, ripen; to come to maturity.
mātūritās, ātis *f* ripeness; **a**) full time, perfection; **b**) proper time; **c**) promptness.
mātūrō 1 **1.** to make ripe; **P.** to become ripe; a) to do early, betimes; b) to hasten, accelerate, dispatch; to hurry, precipitate (*alqd; alci alqd*); **2.** *intr.* to make haste.
mātūrus 3 **a**) ripe, mature; developed, mellow; grown up, marriageable, of age, advanced in life; **b**) seasonable, timely, early, speedy; premature.
mātūtīnus 3 of the morning, early in the morning.
maxilla, ae *f* jaw.
maximē (-umē) *adv.* in the highest degree, most of all; **quam ~** as much as possible; **a**) particularly, especially; **b**) essentially, principally, just, precisely; **c**) certainly, very well.
maximitās, ātis *f* greatness.
maximus (-umus) 3, *superl. of* **magnus.**
māzo-nomus, ī *m* large dish.
meātus, ūs *m* **a**) a going, passing, course, flight; **b**) way, path, channel.
mē-castor *int.* by Castor!
mēchanicus, ī *m* engineer.
meddix, *see* **medix.**
medeor, — 2 to heal, cure (*with dat.*); to relieve, amend, correct, restore.
mediastīnus, ī *m* common servant, menial, drudge.
mēdica, ae *f* lucerne.
medicābilis, e curable.
(**medicāmen, inis** *and*) **medicāmentum, ī** *n* remedy; **a**) medicament, medicine, plaster; **b**) drug, poison; **c**) dye, paint; **d**) charm; artificial means; antidote.
medicātus, ūs *m* charm.
medicīna, ae *f* **a**) the healing art, medicine; **b**) surgery; **c**) remedy, medicine.
medicō 1 to add drugs *or* poison to; to dye; to produce by drugs *or* charms.
medicor 1 to heal, cure (*with dat.*).
medicus 3 healing; *subst.* **~, ī** *m* physician, surgeon.
medietās, ātis *f* the middle, mean.
medimnum, ī *n* (*and* **-us, ī** *m*) Greek bushel.
mediocris, e middling; **a**) moderate, inferior, inconsiderable; **b**) tolerable, ordinary.
mediocritās, ātis *f* the middle state; moderation; mean; mediocrity.
medioxumus 3 in the middle.
meditāmentum, ī *n* (*and* **-āmen, inis** *n*) preparation, practice.
meditātiō, ōnis *f* a thinking over, contemplation (*with gen.*); preparation, exercise.
medi-terrāneus 3 inland.
meditor 1 to think over, contemplate, reflect; to plan, design; to study, practise; **meditātus** 3 thought upon, considered, studied, devised, prepared.
medius 3 **1.** mid, mean, middle, in the middle, in the midst; (**in**) **mediō forō** in the midst of the Forum; **medium tempus** intervening time; **mediā nocte** at midnight; **2.** standing between two extremities; a) middling, tolerable, common, moderate; b) neutral, undecided; ambiguous; c) mediating; **3.** *subst.* **medium, ī** *n* the middle, the midst, the middle point, centre; a) the public, community, publicity, human society; b) common weal; **de medio tollere** to put out of the way; **de medio recedere** to go away; **in medio relinquere** to leave undecided; **in medio ponere** to place in the sight of all; **in medium proferre** to publish; **in medium procedere** to come forward, appear in public; **in medium vocare** to summon before the public; **in medium consulere** to care for the public good.
mēdius fidius, *see* **fidius.**
medix tuticus *m* the highest magistrate of the Oscans.
medulla, ae *f* marrow, the inmost part, kernel, heart.
medullitus *adv.* from the marrow, inwardly, heartily.

medullula, ae *f* soft marrow.
mefītis, *see* **mephitis.**
megistānēs, um *m/pl.* grandees, magnates.
meherclē (*and* **meherc(u)lēs**) *int.* by Hercules!
mēiō, —, — 3 to make water.
mel, mellis *n* honey; sweetness.
melan-cholicus 3 melancholy.
melandryum, ī *n* salted tunny-fish.
melculum, ī *n* little honey.
melichrūs (μελίχρους) honey-complexioned.
melicus 3 lyrical, melodious.
meli-lōtos, ī *m* sweet clover.
meli-mēlum, ī *n* sweet apple.
Mēlinum, ī *n* pipeclay.
melior, *comp. of* **bonus.**
melisphyllum, ī *n* balm.
melius, *see* **bonus.**
meliusculus 3 rather better.
mell(in)a, ae *f* mead; sweetness.
melli-fer 3 honey-bearing.
mellilla, ae *f* little honey.
mellīna, ae *f* bag of marten-skin.
mellītus 3 sweet with honey; lovely, darling.
melos (*pl.* **melē**) *n* tune, song.
membrāna, ae *f* skin, membrane; parchment.
membrānula, ae *f* (thin) parchment.
membrātim *adv.* by pieces.
membrum, ī *n* limb, member; part, portion, division.
mē-met, *see* **met.**
meminī —, isse to remember, recollect **a**) to think of (*with gen.* or *acc.; acc.c.inf.*); **b**) to make mention of, mention.
memor, oris 1. mindful, remembering (*gen.*); a) thankful; unrelenting, relentless; b) having a good memory; **2.** recalling, mentioning.
memorābilis, e memorable, remarkable, famous.
memorandus 3 = **memorabilis.**
memorātor, ōris *m*, **-trīx, īcis** *f* narrator.
memorātus, ūs *m* mention.
memoria, ae *f* memory; **a**) remembrance, recollection; **post hominum memoriam** since the memory of man; **b**) record, historical account; **c**) period of recollection, time; history.
memoriālis, e relating to memory.
memoriola, ae *f* memory.
memoriter *adv.* with a good memory.
memorō 1 to call to mind, mention, recount, relate (*alqd*).
menda, ae *f* = **mendum.**
mendāci-loquus 3 lying, mendacious.
mendācium, ī (*dimin.* **-iunculum**) *n* lie, untruth; fiction, falsehood.
mendāx, ācis given to lying, *m* a liar; **a**) false, deceptive; **b**) feigned, counterfeit.
mendīcābulum, ī *n* beggar (?).
mendīcātiō, ōnis *f* begging.
mendīcitās, ātis *f* beggary, pauperism.
mendīcō *and* **-or** 1 to beg, ask alms.
mendīculus 3 beggarly.
mendīcus 3 beggarly, needy; *subst.* ~ **ī** *m* beggar; poor, paltry, pitiful.
mendōsus 3 full of faults, faulty, incorrect; blundering.
mendum, ī *n* fault, error, blunder.
mēns, tis *f* mind, intellect, understanding; **a**) judgment, discernment; **b**) disposition, feeling, character, heart, soul; spirit, courage, boldness, passion, impulse; **c**) thought, idea, opinion; **d**) plan, purpose.
mēnsa, ae *f* table; **a**) meal, food, course; table; ~ **secunda** dessert; **b**) sacrificial table; **c**) counter of a money-changer.
mēnsārius, ī *m* banker; finance commissioner.
mēnsiō, ōnis *f* a measuring, measure.
mēnsis, is *m* month.
mēnsor, ōris *m* measurer, surveyor.
mēnstruālis, e monthly.
mēnstruus 3 monthly, lasting a month; *subst.* **-um, ī** *n* a month's provisions; monthly term of office.
mēnsula, ae *f* little table.
mēnsūra, ae *f* a measuring, measure, standard; extent, capacity, limit.
ment(h)a, ae *f* mint.
mentiō, ōnis *f* a calling to mind, mention; suggestion, hint.
mentior, ītus sum 4 **a**) to lie, be a liar, to invent; **b**) to assert falsely, feign; **c**) to fail in a promise, break one's word, deceive, cheat; **mentītus** 3 counterfeit, feigned.
mentula, ae *f* penis.
mentum, ī *n* chin.

meō 1 to go, pass.
mephītis, is *f* noxious vapour, malaria.
merāc(u)lus 3 unmixed, strong.
merācus 3 unmixed, pure.
mercābilis, e purchasable.
mercātor, ōris *m* **a)** trader, merchant; **b)** buyer.
mercātōrius 3 of a merchant.
mercātūra, ae *f* trade, commerce; goods.
mercātus, ūs *m* **a)** trade, traffic; **b)** market, fair.
mercēdula, ae *f* small wages; small rent.
mercēn(n)ārius 3 hired, serving for pay; paid, mercenary, bribed; *m* hireling, hired servant, mercenary.
mercēs, ēdis *f* reward, price, hire, pay; **a)** wages, fee, salary; **b)** punishment, injury; **c)** rent, revenue, income.
mercimōnium, ī *n* merchandise.
mercor 1 to trade, traffic, buy.
merda, ae *f* dung, excrement.
merenda, ae *f* afternoon meal.
mereō 2 *and* **mereor, ritus sum** 2 **a)** to deserve, merit; to earn, gain, acquire, obtain (*alqd*); **stipendia** to serve as a soldier; **equo** as a horse-soldier; **b)** to incur (*poenam, odium*); to deserve well *or* ill (*bene, male de alqo*); **merēns, tis** deserving, meriting; **meritus** 3 deserved, fit, just, right.
meretrīcium, ī *n* trade of a prostitute.
meretrīcius 3 relating to a harlot *or* prostitute.
meretrīcula, ae *f* prostitute, courtesan.
meretrīx, īcis *f* prostitute.
mergae, ārum *f/pl.* reaping-fork.
merges, itis *f* reaping-fork; forkful.
mergō, rsī, rsum 3 to dip in, immerse, plunge into water (*alqd in rem, in re*), sink, bury; **a)** to thrust *or* drive into; **b)** to cover, conceal, overwhelm.
mergus, ī *m* diver, gull.
merīdiānus 3 of midday, of noon; southerly.
merīdiātiō, ōnis *f* midday-rest, siesta.
merīdiēs, ēī *m* midday, noon; south.
merīdiō 1 to take a midday sleep.
meritō¹ 1 to earn, deserve.
meritō² *adv.* deservedly, justly.
meritōrius 3 earning money; hired, paid; *subst.* **-ia** *n/pl.* lodgings.
meritum, ī *n* desert; merit, worth; benefit, kindness, service; fault, offence.
mero-bibus 3 drinking unmixed wine.
merops, opis *m* bee-eater.
mersō 1, *intens. of* **mergo.**
merula, ae *f* **a)** blackbird; **b)** a fish.
meruleus 3 as black as a blackbird.
merus 3 unmixed, pure; **a)** nothing but, mere; **b)** genuine, unadulterated, true, real; *subst.* **merum, ī** *n* unmixed wine.
merx, cis (*nomin. also* **mers**) *f* goods, merchandise.
meso-chorus, ī *m* leader of a claque; hired applauder.
messis, is *f* harvest, gathering; **a)** harvest-time; **b)** crops.
messor, ōris *m* mower, reaper.
messōrius, 3 of a reaper.
met (*enclitic suffix*) self, own.
mēta, ae *f* **a)** turning post, goal; **b)** end, extremity; **c)** turning point, critical point.
metalli-fer 3 productive of *or* rich in metals.
metallum, ī *n* metal; mine.
meta-morphōsis, is *f* transformation.
mētātor, ōris *m* measurer.
mētior, mēnsus sum 4 to measure; **a)** to measure out, distribute (*alci alqd*); **b)** to pass over, traverse; **c)** to estimate, value (*alqd re*).
metō, (messuī,) messum 3 to reap, mow; **a)** to gather, collect, harvest; **b)** to cut down, destroy.
metōpo-scopus, ī *m* forehead-inspector, soothsayer.
mētor (*and* **mētō**) 1 to measure out, mark out, lay out.
metrēta, ae *f* a Greek measure (8—9 gallons).
metrum, ī *n* metre.
metūculōsus 3 **a)** afraid; **b)** frightening.
mētula, ae *f* little conical pillar.
metuō, uī, — 3 to fear (*alci, de re, alqd; ne, ne non, ut*).
metus, ūs *m* fear, apprehension, dread, anxiety.
meus 3 my, mine, my own, my dear; *pl.* **mei** my friends, relations, adherents, followers.

mīca, ae *f* grain, crumb, bit.
micō, cuī, — 1 **a**) to quiver, shake, tremble, beat, palpitate; **b**) to sparkle, shine, flicker, flash; **c**) (*digitis*) to hold up a number of the fingers for a moment and challenge someone to say how many fingers are raised (*a game, used also as a method of casting lots*).
micturiō 4 to want to make water.
migrātiō, ōnis *f* removal, migration; change of meaning.
migrō 1 **a**) to remove, depart, emigrate (*ab, ex, de re in* or *ad alqd*); **b**) *trans.* to transport; to transgress.
miles, itis *m* (*f*) soldier; **a**) foot-soldier, common soldier; **b**) soldiery, army; **c**) piece on a game board; **d**) follower.
mīlia, mīliārius, mīliēs, *see* **mill...**
mīlitāris, e of a soldier, of war, military; warlike, martial; **res mīlitāris** (art of) warfare.
mīlitārius 3 military.
mīlitia, ae *f* military service, warfare; **a**) war, expedition; **b**) soldiers, militia.
mīlitō 1 to perform military service, be a soldier.
milium, ī *n* millet.
mīlle *indecl.* (*pl.* **mīlia, ium**) *n* a thousand; innumerable; **mīlle (passuum)** a mile.
millēsimus 3 the thousandth.
milliārius 3 containing a thousand; *subst.* **milliārium, ī** *n* mile-stone, mile.
milliē(n)s *adv.* a thousand times.
mīluīnus (mīlvīnus) 3 resembling a kite; rapacious.
mīluus (mīlvus) ī *m* (*and f*) **a**) bird of prey, kite; **b**) a fish of prey.
mīma, ae *f* mime actress.
mīmiambī, ōrum *m/pl.* mimic verse in iambics.
mīmicus 3 farcical; *adv.* **-cē** like a mime-actor.
mīmula, ae *f dim. of* **mima.**
mīmus, ī *m* **a**) mime-actor; **b**) mime, farce.
mina, ae *f* a mina (*Greek money, 100 denarii*).
mināciae, ārum *f/pl.* threats.
minae, ārum *f/pl.* **a**) pinnacles; **b**) threats, menaces.
minanter *adv.* threateningly.
minātiō, ōnis *f* a threatening.
mināx, ācis a) overhanging; **b**) threatening.
mineō 2 to project.
mingō, nxī, (n)ctum 3 to make water.
miniāt(ul)us 3 coloured red.
minimus 3, *superl. of* **parvus**; **minimē** *superl.* of **parum.**
minister, trī *m* attendant, servant; helper, assistant, agent, accomplice.
ministerium, ī *n* **a**) attendance, service, employment, office; **b**) suite, train, helpers.
ministra, ae, *fem. of* **minister.**
ministrātor, ōris *m* attendant, helper.
ministrātōrius 3 for servants' use.
ministrātrīx, īcis *f* female attendant.
ministrō 1 to attend, wait upon, serve (*wine*); **a**) to furnish, supply, provide (*alci alqd*); **b**) to execute, carry out.
minitābundus 3 threatening.
minitor (*and* **-ō**) 1, *intens. of* **minor¹.**
minium, ī *n* red lead, vermilion.
minor¹ 1 **a**) to project, overhang; **b**) to threaten (*alci alqd, alqa re; acc.c.inf. fut.*).
minor², us, *comp. of* **parvus**; **minus** *comp.* of **parum.**
minuō, uī, ūtum 3 **a**) to make smaller, lessen, diminish; **P.** to grow less, decrease; **b**) to reduce, weaken, abate, break.
minusculus 3 rather little.
minūtal, ālis *n* minced food.
minūtātim *adv.* little by little, bit by bit, gradually.
minūtia, ae *f* fineness.
minūtulus 3, *dim. of* **minutus.**
minūtus 3 diminished; little, small, minute, trifling; **res minūtae** trifles.
mīrābilis, e a) wonderful, marvellous; admirable; **b**) extraordinary, strange, singular.
mīrābundus 3 astonished.
mīrācula, ae *f* monstrosity.
mīrāculum, ī *n* wonder, marvel, miracle; wonderful thing.
mīrandus 3 wonderful.
mīrātiō, ōnis *f* wonder, admiration.
mīrātor, ōris *m and* **-trīx, īcis** *f* admirer.
mīri-ficus 3 = **mirabilis.**
mīri-modīs wonderfully.

mirmillō, ōnis *m* gladiator with Gallic arms.
mīror (*and* **-ō**) 1 **a**) to wonder at; **b**) to admire, esteem.
mīrus 3 = **mirabilis.**
mis = **mei** (*gen.*).
miscellānea, ōrum *n/pl.* hashed food.
miscellus 3 mixed.
misceō, cuī, xtum (stum) 2 to mix, mingle, intermingle (*alqd re, cum re, alci rei*); **a**) to join, unite; **b**) to disturb, confound, throw into confusion.
misellus 3, *dim. of* **miser.**
miser, era, erum wretched, unfortunate, poor; **a**) pitiable, lamentable; **b**) worthless.
miserābilis, e pitiable, miserable, wretched; plaintive.
miserandus 3 = **miserabilis.**
miserātiō, ōnis *f* pity, compassion; pathetic speech.
misereor (rarely **-eō**), **ritus sum** 2 to feel pity *or* compassion, to commiserate (*gen.*).
miserēscō, —, — 3 = **misereor.**
miseret (*and* **-ētur,** rarely **-ēscit**), **-itum est** *me alcis* I feel pity for.
miseria, ae *f* wretchedness, misery, misfortune, distress.
misericordia, ae *f* compassion, sympathy, mercy.
miseri-cors, dis pitiful, compassionate, merciful.
miseror 1 to lament; to pity.
missīcius 3 discharged.
missiculō 1 to send often.
missilis, e that may be thrown, missile; *subst.* **missile, is** *n* missile, javelin.
missiō, ōnis *f* a sending away; **a**) release; **b**) discharge from service; **c**) quarter; **d**) cessation.
missitō 1 to send repeatedly.
missus, ūs *m* a sending, dispatching; throwing; bow-shot; round *or* heat (in a race).
mitella, ae *f, dim. of* **mitra.**
mitellītus 3 wearing a *mitella*; **-a cena** dinner at which *mitellae* were provided for guests.
mītēscō *and* **-īscō, —, —** 3 to grow mild, soft, gentle, ripe.
mīti-ficō 1 to make mild; to ripen; to digest.
mīti-ficus 3 gentle.
mītigātiō, ōnis *f* an assuaging, soothing, appeasing.
mītigō 1 to soften; **a**) to make mild, tender, soft; **b**) to soothe, assuage, appease.
mītis, e mild; **a**) mellow, ripe, soft; **b**) gentle, kind.
mitra, ae *f* head-band, turban.
mitrātus 3 wearing a *mitra*.
mitto, mīsī, missum 3 to send; **a**) to throw, hurl, cast; **b**) to send, cause to go; **sub iugum** under the yoke; *ad alqm* or *alci* to send word, send orders; **librum** *ad alqm* to dedicate; **c**) to yield, produce, furnish; to let out, put forth, emit, utter; **d**) to let go, drop, release, dismiss; to forgo, omit, pass over; to forget, put away.
mītulus, ī *m* mussel.
mixtim in combination.
mixtūra, ae *f* blending.
mnēmosynum, ī *n* keepsake.
mōbilis, e movable, quick; **a**) pliant, pliable, excitable; **b**) changeable, inconstant.
mōbilitās, ātis *f* movableness, mobility; **a**) agility, quickness; **b**) changeableness, fickleness.
mōbilitō 1 to impart motion to.
moderābilis, e moderate.
moderāmen, inis *n* **a**) rudder, helm; **b**) government.
moderanter with control.
moderātim gradually.
moderātiō, ōnis *f* guidance, government; moderation; self-control, temperance.
moderātor, ōris *m* manager, governor, ruler, controller.
moderātrīx, īcis *f* controller.
moderātus 3 **a**) moderate, temperate; **b**) within bounds, restrained.
moderor (*and* **-ō**) 1 **a**) to set bounds, restrain, to limit (*with dat.*); **b**) to govern, regulate, manage, direct.
modestia, ae *f* moderation; **a**) discretion, sobriety; **b**) unassuming behaviour, shyness, modesty; **c**) obedience, subordination; **d**) correctness of conduct, propriety.
modestus 3 moderate, keeping within bounds; **a**) calm, gentle; **b**) modest, forbearing; **c**) sober, discreet, orderly, virtuous.

modiālis, e containing a *modius.*
modicus 3 moderate; **a**) middling, small, mean, scanty; **b**) calm, temperate; **c**) unpretending.
modi-ficātiō, ōnis *f* measuring, scansion (*of verse*).
modi-ficō 1 to measure off.
modius, ī *m* (*a measure, about 2 gallons*).
modo (*and* **modō**) **1.** *adv.* only, but; **non modo ... sed etiam** not only ... but also; **non modo (non) ... sed ne ... quidem** not only not ... but not even; **2.** *with subj.* if only, provided that; **modo ne** provided that not; **3.** (*of time*) now, but now, just now, lately; presently; **modo ... modo** now ... now, sometimes ... sometimes.
modulātor, ōris *m* musician.
modulātus[1] 3 musical.
modulātus[2], **ūs** *m* playing, music.
modulor 1 to measure rhythmically, to modulate, sing, play.
modulus, ī *m* measure.
modus, ī *m* measure, standard measure; **a**) size, extent, quantity; **b**) time, rhythm, metre, melody; **c**) bound, limit; **d**) moderation, due measure; **e**) way, manner; **modo, in modum, ad modum** in the manner of; **nullo modo** by no means; **mirum in modum** wonderfully; **quodam modo** in a certain manner, somehow; **huius (eius) modi** of this *or* that kind.
moecha, ae *f* adulteress.
moechissō 1 to seduce.
moechor 1 to commit adultery.
moechus, ī *m* fornicator, adulterer.
moenerō = **munero.**
moenia[1], **ium** *n/pl.* defensive walls, city-walls, bulwarks, ramparts, fortifications; **a**) city enclosed by walls; **b**) the buildings of a city.
moenia[2], **ium** *n/pl.* = **munia.**
moenīmentum = **munimentum.**
mola, ae *f* **a**) millstone, grindstone; *pl.* mill; **b**) spelt coarsely ground and mixed with salt.
molāris, is *m* **a**) millstone; **b**) molar tooth.
mōlēs, is *f* huge, heavy mass, bulk; **a**) massive structure *or* apparatus, colossus, large building; **b**) dam, pier, mole, foundation; **c**) great quantity, multitude; weight, power; **d**) difficulty, labour, trouble.
molestia, ae *f* molestation, trouble; **a**) annoyance, vexation; **b**) affectation.
molestus 3 burdensome, troublesome, grieving, annoying; stiff, affected.
mōlīmen, inis *and* **mōlīmentum, ī** *n* a) exertion, effort; b) weight, importance.
mōlior 4 **1.** to set in motion, displace, remove (*alqd*); **a**) to hurl, weigh (*anchor*), wield; **b**) to set about, attempt (any thing difficult *or* laborious); to build, make, cause; c) to undertake, devise; **2.** to toil, exert oneself.
mōlītiō, ōnis *f* **a**) a removing, demolishing; **b**) a making (with labour).
mōlītor, ōris *m* builder, contriver, author.
mōlītrīx, īcis *f* she who contrives.
mollēscō, —, — 3 to become soft, effeminate.
molliculus 3 rather soft *or* voluptuous.
mollīmentum, ī *n* means of mitigation.
molliō 4 to soften, make pliant *or* supple; **a**) to mitigate, moderate; **b**) to render effeminate.
molli-pēs, pedis soft-footed.
mollis, e soft, impressionable; **a**) pliant, flexible, supple; **b**) mild, tender, delicate; **c**) quiet, calm, gentle; **d**) movable, fickle; **e**) effeminate, unmanly, weak; **f**) amatory, voluptuous.
mollitia, ae *f and* **mollitiēs, ēī** *f* softness; **a**) pliability, flexibility; **b**) tenderness, gentleness, mildness; **c**) weakness, effeminacy, voluptuousness.
mollitūdō, inis *f* = **mollitia.**
molō, uī, itum 3 to grind.
molocinārius, ī *m* dyer of mauve-coloured garments.
mōly, yos *n* a magic herb.
mōmen, inis *n* **a**) momentum; **b**) moving mass.
mōmentum, ī *n* **1.** moving power; a) weight; b) that which turns the scales; influence, impulse; cause, circumstance, importance, turning point; **2.** motion; a) alteration; b) moment, minute, instant; c) period.
mon-aulos, ī *m* single flute.

monēdula, ae *f* daw, jackdaw.
moneō, uī, itum 2 to remind, admonish (*alqm de re* or *gen.*); **a**) to warn; exhort, advise; **b**) to teach, instruct, punish; **c**) to announce, predict, foretell.
monēris, is *f* galley with one bank of oars.
monērula = **monēdula.**
monēta, ae *f* **a**) mint; **b**) coined money, coin; **c**) stamp, die.
monētālis, e of *or* relating to the mint; *subst. m* mint-master.
monetrīx, īcis *f* instructress.
monīle, is *n* necklace.
monimentum, ī *n* = **monumentum.**
monitiō, ōnis *f* a warning, admonition, advice.
monitor, ōris *m* admonisher, reminder; prompter; teacher.
monitum, ī *n* admonition, advice; prophecy.
monitus, ūs *m* = **monitum.**
mono-grammus 3 outlined, sketched.
mono-podium, ī *n* table with one foot.
mono-pōlium, ī *n* monopoly.
mono-tropus, ī *m* all alone.
mōns, tis *m* mountain, mount, range of mountains; rock.
mōnstrābilis, e remarkable.
mōnstrātiō, ōnis *f* a showing.
mōnstrātor, ōris *m* shower, pointer out, introducer, inventor.
mōnstrātus 3 distinguished, conspicuous.
mōnstri-fer 3 producing monsters.
mōnstri-ficus 3 working wonders, magic.
mōnstrō 1 to show, point out (*alci alqd*); **a**) to ordain, appoint, indicate; **b**) to inform against.
mōnstrōsus 3 = **monstruosus.**
mōnstrum, ī *n* omen; **a**) monster, monstrosity; **b**) miracle.
mōnstruōsus 3 wonderful, monstrous.
montānus 3 belonging to a mountain, of a mountain, mountainous; *subst.* ~, **ī** *m* mountain dweller.
monti-cola, ae *m* mountain dweller.
monti-fer 3 bearing (*i. e.* buried under) mountains.
monti-vagus 3 wandering over the mountains.
mont(u)ōsus 3 mountainous.
monumentum, ī *n* remembrance, **a**) memorial, monument; statue; memorial offering, sepulchre, tomb; **b**) tradition, chronicle, record.
mora[1], ae *f* division of Spartan infantry, battalion.
mora[2], ae *f* delay, procrastination; **a**) pause on a march; **b**) space of time; **c**) obstruction, hindrance.
mōrālis, e of morals, moral.
morātor, ōris *m* delayer, loiterer.
mōrātus 3 **a**) mannered, constituted; **b**) characteristic, expressive of character.
morbidus 3 unhealthy.
morbōsus 3 diseased, morbid.
morbus, ī *m* sickness, disease; distress.
mordāx, ācis biting; stinging, sharp, piercing.
mordeō, momordī, morsum 2 to bite, chew; **a**) to gnaw at; **b**) to clasp, take hold of; **c**) to indent, wash away; **d**) to bite, pain, hurt.
mordicibus *abl.* with bites (?).
mordicus *adv.* **a**) by biting, with the teeth; **b**) tenaciously.
mōrē *adv.* foolishly.
morētum, ī *n* a rustic dish, salad.
moribundus 3 dying; mortal.
mōri-geror (*or* **-ō**) 1 to comply with, humour (*alci*).
mōri-gerus 3 complying.
mōriō, ōnis *m* fool, jester.
morior, mortuus sum 3 to die; **mortuus** 3 dead, dead person; to die away, die out, decay, pass away.
mōro-logus 3 foolish.
moror[1] 1 **a**) to stay, delay, (*trans.* and *intr.*), to linger, loiter; **b**) to hold the attention of; to hinder; **nihil moror** I have nothing to say to, I do not heed, I do not care for.
mōror[2] 1 to be a fool.
mōrōsitās, ātis *f* peevishness, fretfulness, morosity.
mōrōsus 3 peevish, fretful, fastidious, morose, stubborn.
mors, tis *f* death; **a**) mode of death; **b**) dead body, corpse.
morsa, ōrum *n/pl.* small pieces.
morsiuncula, ae *f* a biting of the lips.
morsus, ūs *m* a biting, bite; **a**) an eating, corrosion; **b**) a seizing, holding; **c**) malicious attack; **d**) sting, pain, vexation.

mortālis, e mortal; *subst. m* man, mortal, human being; **a**) temporary, transient; **b**) earthly, human; **mortālia, ium** *n/pl.* human affairs.
mortālitās, ātis *f* mortality; **a**) mortal destiny; **b**) mortals.
mortārium, ī *n* mortar.
morticīnus 3 dead (*body*).
morti-fer 3 death-bringing, deadly.
mortuālia, ium *n/pl.* funeral songs.
mortuus 3, *see* **morior.**
mōrum, ī *n* **a**) mulberry; **b**) blackberry.
mōrus[1], **ī** *f* mulberry-tree.
mōrus[2] 3 foolish, silly.
mōs, mōris *m* habit, manner, custom, fashion; **a**) will, humour, precept, law; **mōrem gerere alci** = **morigerari; b**) quality, nature, mode, fashion; *pl.* conduct, behaviour, manners, morals, character.
mōtiō, ōnis *f* = **motus.**
mōtiuncula, ae *f* slight attack of fever.
mōtō 1 to move about.
mōtor, ōris *m* one who moves *or* rocks.
mōtus, ūs *m* a moving, motion; **terrae** earth-quake; **a**) movement, change; **b**) gesticulation, dancing; **c**) evolution; **d**) impulse, gesture, passion, agitation, emotion; **e**) thought, inspiration; **f**) political movement, tumult, commotion.
moveō, mōvī, mōtum 2 to move, set in motion; **1.** to stir, shake, disturb, remove; **arma** to take up arms; **se movēre** *and* **P.** to move *or* bestir oneself, to dance; a) to ponder; b) to change; c) to move, excite, affect, inspire, influence; d) to shake, cause to waver, to disturb, concern, trouble, torment; e) to occasion, cause, produce, begin; **2.** to remove, put out of its place (*alqd loco; re, de, ex, ab re in* or *ad alqd*); **castra movēre** to break up camp, march away; *intr.*, **se movēre** *or* **P.** to move from a place, betake oneself; to drive away, dislodge, expel.
mox *adv.* soon, directly, presently; then, thereupon.
mūcidus 3 **a**) running at the nose; **b**) mouldy.
mūcrō, ōnis *m* sharp point, edge; sword; sharpness.
mūcus, ī *m* nasal mucus.
mūgil(is), is *m* mullet.
mūgīnor 1 to dally, hesitate.
mūgiō 4 to low, bellow; to sound, roar.
mūgītor, ōris *m* bellower.
mūgītus, ūs *m* a lowing, bellowing; roaring.
mūla, ae *f* she-mule.
mulceō, sī, sum 2 to stroke, touch lightly; **a**) to soothe, appease, soften; **b**) to charm, delight, caress.
Mulciber, eris *and* **erī** *m* Vulcan; fire.
mulcō 1 to beat, cudgel, maltreat.
mulctra, ae *f and* **-trum, ī** *n and* **mulctrārium, ī** *n* milk-pail.
mulgeō, lsī, — 2 to milk.
muliebris, e a) of a woman, womanly, feminine; **b**) womanish, effeminate.
mulier, eris *f* woman, female, wife.
mulierārius 3 of a woman.
muliercula, ae *f* (weak) woman.
mulierōsitās, ātis *f* passionate love of women.
mulierōsus 3 fond of women.
mūlīnus 3 mulish.
mūliō, ōnis *m* muleteer.
mūliōnius 3 of a muleteer.
mullus, ī *m* red mullet.
mulsus 3 honey-sweet; *subst.* **mulsum, ī** *n* honey-wine.
multa, ae *f* penalty, fine, loss.
mult-angulus 3 having many angles.
multātīcius 3 accruing from fines.
multātiō, ōnis *f* penalty, fine.
multēsimus 3 very small, trifling.
multi-bibus 3 fond of drinking.
multi-cavus 3 many-holed, porous.
multīcia, -ōrum *n/pl.* fine-spun garments.
multifāriam *adv.* in many places.
multi-fidus 3 (much) split.
multi-fōrmis, e multiform, manifold.
multi-forus 3 pierced with many holes.
multi-generis, e *and* **multi-genus** 3 of many kinds.
multi-iugus 3 *and* **-gis, e** (yoked) many together.
multi-loquium, ī *n* much talk.
multi-loquos 3 talkative.
multi-modīs *adv.* in many ways, variously.
multi-plex, icis having many folds *or* windings; **a**) manifold; **b**) nume-

rous, various; **c**) many times as large; **d**) many-sided; versatile, changeable.
multiplicābilis, e manifold.
multiplicātiō, ōnis *f* a multiplying.
multiplicō 1 to multiply, increase.
multi-potēns, tis very mighty.
multi-sonus 3 loud sounding.
multitūdō, inis *f* large number, multitude; crowd, mob.
multi-vagus 3 wandering much.
multi-volus 3 desiring much.
multō 1 to punish.
multum 1. *as subst. n* a great part, much; *abl.* **multō** by much, by far, a great deal; **2.** *adv.* much, very much, greatly, often, frequently, far; **3.** *comp.* **plūs, plūris** *n* more, a greater part; a) **plūris** of more value, at a higher price; b) *adv.* **plūs** more, in a higher degree; **4.** *superl.* **plūrimum, ī** *n* very much, a great deal, most; a) *gen.* **plūrimī** of the greatest value *or* importance; at a very high price; b) *adv.* **plūrimum** very much, for the most part.
multus 3 **1.** much, many, numerous; **multī, ōrum** *m/pl.* many, the multitude, common people; **multa, ōrum** *n/pl.* many things; a) considerable, abundant, extensive, vigorous, zealous; b) far advanced (*multa nocte*); c) copious; **2.** *comp.* **plūrēs, a** more, in greater number; **3.** *superl.* **plūrimus** 3 very much, very many, most.
mūlus, ī *m* mule.
mundānus, ī *m* citizen of the world, cosmopolitan.
munditia, ae (*and* **-tiēs, ēī**) *f* **a**) cleanliness, cleanness; **b**) neatness, elegance.
mundulus 3 neat, elegant.
mundus[1] 3 **a**) clean, cleanly; **b**) nice, neat, elegant, fine, genteel; *adv.* **-ē** *and* **-iter; in mundō** prepared, in readiness.
mundus[2], **ī** *m* **a**) toilet-outfit; **b**) the universe, the world; **c**) mankind.
mūnerārius, ī *m* arranger of public games.
mūneri-gerulus 3 carrying presents.
(**mūnerō** *and*) **mūneror** 1 to reward, bestow, present.
mūnia *n/pl.* duties, functions.
mūni-ceps, cipis *m* (*and f*) citizen of a *municipium or* free town; fellow-citizen.
mūnicipālis, e belonging to a *municipium*, provincial.
mūnicipātim by *municipia*.
mūnicipium, ī *n* self-governing town (*esp.* in Italy).
mūnificentia, ae *f* liberality, bountifulness.
mūni-ficō 1 to present.
mūni-ficus 3 liberal, bountiful.
(**mūnīmen, inis** *and*) **mūnīmentum, ī** *n* **a**) defence; **b**) fortification.
mūniō 4 to wall, wall round; **a**) to build with walls; **b**) to fortify, defend, secure; **c**) (*viam*) to build *or* pave.
mūnis, e ready to serve.
mūnītiō, ōnis *f* a fortifying, entrenching; **a**) paving of roads; **b**) fortification, rampart.
mūnītō 1 to pave, make passable (*viam*).
mūnītor, ōris *m* fortifier, engineer, sapper.
mūnītus 3 fortified, protected.
mūnus, eris *n* **a**) duty, office, function; **b**) service, favour; the last service (*burial*); **c**) present, gift; public show.
mūnusculum, ī *n* small gift.
mūraena, ae, *f* = **murena.**
mūrālis, e of a wall, mural.
mūrēna, ae *f* (*a sea-fish*) muræna.
mūrex, icis *m* **a**) purple-fish; **b**) purple dye; **c**) projecting rock; **d**) spiked trap.
muria, ae *f* brine, pickle.
muriāticum, ī *n* pickled fish.
mūri-cīdus, ī *m* mouse-killer, coward.
murmillō, ōnis *m* = **mirmillo.**
murmur, uris *n* murmur, a murmuring, humming, buzzing, roaring, crashing, sounding.
murmurātiō, ōnis *f* murmuring.
murmurillum, ī *n* = **murmur.**
murmurō 1 to murmur, mutter, roar.
murra, ae *f* **1.** myrrh-tree, myrrh; **2.** fluor-spar.
murreus 3 **1.** myrrh-coloured (pale yellow); perfumed with myrrh; **2.** of fluor-spar.
murrinus 3 = **murreus; murrina, ae** *f* wine flavoured with myrrh.
murtētum, ī *n* grove of myrtles.
murteus 3 of myrtle; adorned with myrtle (*or* as dark as myrtle).

murtum, ī *n* myrtle-berry.
murtus, ī (*and* **ūs**) *f* myrtle; spear of myrtle-wood.
mūrus, ī *m* wall, rim; protection, defence.
mūs, mūris *m* mouse, rat.
Mūsa, ae *f* a muse; song, poem, poetry, sciences.
musca, ae *f* a fly; intruder.
muscārium, ī *n* fly-brush (also used as a clothes-brush).
mūs-cipula, ae *f and* **-um, ī** *n* mouse-trap.
mūscōsus 3 mossy.
mūsculus, ī *m* a little mouse; **a**) muscle; **b**) shed; **c**) mussel.
mūscus, ī *m* moss.
mūsica, ae *f* (*or* **-cē, ēs** *f*) *and* **mūsica, ōrum** *n/pl.* music; poetry; fine art.
mūsicus 3 belonging to the muses, to music, musical; *subst.* **~, ī** *m* musician; **mūsicē** elegantly.
mussitō 1 = **musso a**), **b**).
mussō 1 **a**) to murmur, mutter, buzz; **b**) to bear in silence; **c**) to wonder *or* brood in silence.
mustāceum, ī *n* wedding-cake.
mustēla, ae *f* weasel.
mustēlīnus 3 of a weasel.
musteus 3 must-like, quite new.
mustum, ī *n* must; vintage.
mūtābilis, e mutable, changeable.
mūtābilitās, ātis *f* mutability.
mūtātiō, ōnis *f* change, alteration; interchange.
mūtātor, ōris *m* one who changes *or* barters.
mutilō 1 to maim, mutilate.
mutilus 3 maimed, mutilated.
mūtiō 4, *see* **muttio.**
mūtō[1] 1 **1.** to move, remove, to move from its place; **2.** to change, alter; **vestem mūtāre** to put on mourning; a) to exchange; b) to take in exchange (*alqd alqa re*).
mūtō[2], **ōnis** *m* penis; *hence* **mūtūniātus** 3.
muttiō 4 to mutter, mumble.
muttītiō, -ōnis *f* muttering.
mūtuātiō, ōnis *f* a borrowing.
mūtuitō 1 to seek to borrow.
mūtuō, *adv. of* **mutuus.**
mūtuor 1 to borrow; to obtain, get (*alqd ab alqo*).
mūtus 3 dumb, mute, speechless; silent, still.
mūtuus 3 borrowed; lent; **a**) mutual, reciprocal, on both sides; *subst.* **mūtuum, ī** *n* **a**) a return of like for like; **b**) loan.
myo-parō, ōnis *m* a pirate's vessel.
myrīca, ae *f* tamarisk.
myrmillō, ōnis *m, see* **mirmillo.**
myrobalanum, ī *n* balsam.
myro-pōla, ae *m* perfume-dealer.
myro-pōlium, ī *n* perfumer's shop.
myro-thēcium, ī *n* unguent-box.
myrrha, ae *f* = **murra** (1).
myrtum, myrtus etc., *see* **murt...**
myst-agōgus, ī *m* a guide to mysteries *or* temples, cicerone.
mystērium, ī *n* secret, mystery; *pl.* **-ia, iōrum** secret rites *or* worship.
mystēs, ae *m* priest at the mysteries.
mysticus 3 mystic, secret.
myxa, ae *f* curved spout of a lamp; lamp-wick.

N

nablium, ī *n* lute, mandolin.
nae *int.* = **nē**[1].
naenia, ae *f*, *see* **nenia.**
naevus, ī *m* birth-mark, mole.
Nāias, adis *and* **Nāis, idis** *f* water-nymph, Naiad.
nam *cj.* for, for instance; *as enclitic with an interrogative:* **quisnam** who?; **ubinam** where?
nam-que *cj.* = **nam.**
nancīscor, nactus *and* **nanctus sum** 3 to light (up)on, meet with, find, get, obtain, incur.
nānus, ī *m* dwarf.
Napaeae, -ārum *f/pl.* nymphs of woodland valleys.
nāpus, ī *m* swede.
narcissus, ī *m* narcissus, daffodil.
nardinum, ī *n* nard-wine.
nardum, ī *n and* **nardus, ī** *f* nard, nard-oil.
nāris, is *f* nostril, *pl.* the nose; perception, sagacity.
nārrābilis, e that can be told *or* related.
nārrātiō, ōnis *f* a telling, narrating, relating.
narrātiuncula, ae *f* anecdote.
nārrātor, ōris *m* relater, narrator.
nārrātus, ūs *m* narration, narrative.
nārrō 1 **a**) to tell, narrate, relate; **b**) to say, mention.
narthēcium, ī *n* ointment-box.
nārus 3 = **gnarus.**
nāscor, nātus sum 3 to be born, be produced, (*abl.; ex alqo*); **a**) to spring from, proceed, rise (*ab, ex re*); **ex hoc nāscitur, ut** hence it follows that; **b**) to grow, be found; — **nātus** 3 born (*abl.; ex alqo*); **a**) destined, designed, intended (*dat.; ad* or *in alqd*); **b**) constituted by nature, fitted; **c**) (*with an expression of time*) old; *subst. m* son, *f* daughter, *pl. m* children, young ones.
nassa, ae *f* trap, net, snare.
nassiterna, ae *f* watering-pot.
nāsturtium *or* **-cium, ī** *n* cress.
nāsus, ī *m* (*and* **-um** *n*) nose; sense of smell, perception.
nāsūtus 3 large-nosed; sarcastic.
nāta, ae *f* daughter.
nātālicius 3 relating to a birthday; *subst.* **-ia, ae** *f* birthday entertainment.
nātālis, e pertaining to birth, of birth; **dies** *or subst. m* birthday; *pl.* origin, family.
natātiō, ōnis *f*, **natātus, ūs** *m* swimming.
natātor, ōris *m* swimmer.
nātiō, ōnis *f* **1.** birth; **2.** a) nation, people; b) race, species, class, set, kind, breed.
natis, is *f* (*usu. pl.*) buttocks.
nātīvus 3 born; inborn, innate, natural.
natō 1 to swim, float; **a**) to be flooded, be full of; **b**) to fluctuate, waver.
natrix, icis *f* (and *m*) water-snake.
nātūra, ae *f* **1.** birth; **2.** nature; a) natural quality, constitution; disposition, character, inclination, bent, temper; b) human nature; c) the order of the world, course of things, laws of nature; d) the world, universe; e) element, substance, essence; f) organ of generation.
nātūrālis, e natural, by birth; **a**) produced by nature, according to nature; **b**) relating to nature.
(**nātus, ūs** *m* birth, age); **magnus** *or* **grandis nātū** old, aged; **minimus nātū** the youngest.
nau-archus, ī *m* captain of a vessel.
nauclēricus 3 belonging to a skipper.
nau-clērus, ī *m* skipper.
naucula = **navicula.**
nauculor 1 to sail.
(**naucum** *n*); **non nauci esse** to be of no value.
nau-fragium, ī *n* shipwreck; **a**) storm; **b**) ruin, loss; **c**) remnants, remains.
nau-fragus 3 **a**) shipwrecked, wrecked; ruined; **b**) causing shipwreck.
naulum, ī *n* passage-money.
nau-machia, ae *f* mock sea-fight; place in which such fights were held.

naumachiārii, ōrum *m/pl.* fighters in a mock naval battle.
nausea, ae *f* sea-sickness, vomiting, nausea.
nauseō 1 **a**) to be sea-sick, to vomit **b**) to cause disgust.
nauseola, ae *f* squeamishness.
nausia, ae *f* = **nausea.**
nausiābundus 3 sea-sick, bilious.
nausiātor, ōris *m* one subject to sea-sickness.
nauta, ae *m* **a**) sailor, seaman, mariner; **b**) trader, merchant, ship-owner; **c**) passenger.
nautea, ae *f* a stinking liquid.
nauticus 3 nautical, naval; *subst. m* = **nauta.**
nāvālis, e relating to ships, nautical, naval; **socii nāvālēs** seamen, marines; *subst.* **nāvāle, is** *n* **a**) station for ships, harbour; **b**) *pl.* dockyard, tackling, rigging.
nāvicula, ae *f* little ship, boat.
nāviculāria, ae *f* business of shipping.
nāviculārius, ī *m* ship-owner.
nāvi-fragus 3 causing shipwreck.
nāvigābilis, e navigable.
nāvigātiō, ōnis *f* a sailing, navigation, voyage.
nāvi-ger 3 bearing ships.
nāvigiolum, ī *n* = **navicula.**
nāvigium, ī *n* vessel, ship.
nāvigō 1 **a**) to sail, voyage, cruise; **b**) to sail over *or* through (*alqd*), to navigate; **c**) to earn by navigation.
nāvis, is *f* vessel, ship; boat; ~ **longa** man-of-war, ~ **onerāria** transport-ship.
nāvita, ae *m* = **nauta.**
nāvitās, ātis *f* assiduity, zeal.
nāviter, *adv. of* **navus.**
nāvō 1 to do zealously, assiduously, diligently; **operam nāvāre alci** to render assistance; to accomplish, effect (*alqd in alqm*).
nāvus 3 active, busy, diligent, assiduous.
nē[1] *int.* verily, truly.
-ne[2] *interrog. particle:* **1.** *in simple direct or indirect questions* (*sometimes* = **nonne**), **videsne, videmusne** do you (we) see?; do you not see?; **2.** *in compound questions* (*direct* or *indirect*): **-ne ... an** = **utrum ... an; nec-ne** or not.
nē[3] *particle of negation and cj.;* **1. nē ... quidem** noteven; **2.** *with subj.* (*or imperat.*) *to express a negative desire, purpose, command, etc.:* not, that not, lest, so that not.
nebris, idis *f* fawn-skin worn by worshippers of Bacchus.
nebula, ae *f* mist, cloud; smoke.
nebulō, ōnis *m* paltry, worthless fellow; idler.
nebulōsus 3 misty, foggy, cloudy.
nec *and* **neque 1.** = **non; 2.** and not, nor, neither; **neque quisquam** and no one, **neque umquam** and never; **neque vero** and indeed not; **neque enim** for not; **neque tamen** and yet not; **nec-nōn** and besides; **neque aut ... aut** and neither ... nor; **nec ... nec, neque ... neque** neither ... nor; **nec-ne** or not.
nec-dum *adv.* and not yet.
necessāriō *and* **-ē** *adv.* necessarily.
necessārius 3 necessary; **a**) indispensable; **b**) unavoidable, inevitable; **c**) pressing, compulsory, essential; **d**) connected, related; *subst.* ~**, ī** *m* relation, kinsman, friend.
necesse (*and* **-sum**) **esse** to be necessary, indispensable, inevitable (*with inf., acc. c. inf., dat. c. inf., subj.; ut*); ~ **habēre** to consider necessary.
necessitās, ātis *f* necessity; **a**) inevitableness; **b**) compulsion, force, exigency; **c**) fate, destiny; **d**) need, poverty, want; *pl.* necessaries, necessary expenses; **e**) connection, relationship, friendship.
necessitūdō, inis *f* **1.** necessity, compulsion, want, need, distress; **2.** close connection, relationship, friendship; relations, friends.
necessum (*obsolete*) = **necesse.**
nec-ne or not.
nec-nōn (*see* **nec**).
necō 1 to kill, slay.
nec-opīnāns, tis not expecting, unaware.
nec-opīnātus 3 unexpected; *adv.* **-ō.**
nec-opīnus 3 not expecting; unexpected.
nectar, aris *n* nectar, drink of the gods.
nectareus 3 of nectar; delicious.
nectō, nex(u)ī, nexum 3 to tie, bind, fasten, connect (*alqd re*), weave together; **a**) to fetter, confine; **b**) to attach (*alqd ex re*); **c**) to

devise; *subst.* **nexus, ī** *m* prisoner for debt; **nexum, ī** *n* personal obligation, voluntary assignment of the person for debt.

nē-cubi *cj.* with *subj.* lest anywhere.

nē-cunde *cj.* with *subj.* lest from anywhere.

nē-dum 1. *cj.* with *subj.* much less, still less, not to speak of; **2.** *adv.* not to say, much more.

ne-fandus 3 = **nefarius.**

ne-fārius 3 abominable, impious, execrable; *subst.* **-ium, ī** *n* = **nefas.**

ne-fās *n* (*indecl.*, only *nom.* and *acc. sg.*) unlawful, criminal, sinful thing; abominable wretch.

ne-fāstus 3 **1.** forbidden, unholy; **2.** a) unlucky, inauspicious; b) sinful, profane, wicked.

negantia, ae *f* negation.

negātiō, ōnis *f* a denying, negation.

negitō 1 to persist in denying.

neglēctiō, ōnis *f*, **neglēctus, ūs** *m* a neglecting, neglect.

neglēctus 3 *and* **neglegēns, tis,** *see* **neglego.**

neglegentia, ae *f* **a**) carelessness, negligence; **b**) coldness, disrespect.

neg-legō, lēxī, lēctum 3 to neglect, disregard, slight, take no heed of; **a**) to despise, contemn; **b**) to overlook, pass over; **neglegēns, tis** negligent, careless, indifferent; prodigal, extravagant; **neglēctus** 3 neglected, disregarded.

negō 1 **a**) to say no; **b**) to deny, to maintain *or* assert that a thing is not; **c**) to refuse.

negōtiālis, e relating to business.

negōtiātiō, ōnis *f* wholesale business, banking business.

negōtiātor, ōris *m* wholesale dealer, merchant, banker.

negōtiolum, ī *n* little business.

negōtior 1 to carry on (a wholesale) business, to trade, traffic; **negōtiāns, tis** *m* trader, merchant, banker.

negōtiōsus 3 full of business, busy, occupied.

neg-ōtium, ī *n* business, employment, occupation; **a**) affair, undertaking; **b**) difficult affair, difficulty, pains, trouble, labour; **~ alci facessere** *or* **exhibēre** to cause trouble to; **nullo negōtio** easily; **c**) public business, affairs of state; **d**) trade, banking business; **e**) domestic affairs, management of a household; **f**) matter, thing.

nēmō (**nūllīus, nēminī, nēminem, nūllō** no man, no one, nobody; **non nēmō** some one, **nēmō non** every one.

nemorālis (*and* **-ēnsis**), **e** of a grove *or* wood, sylvan.

nemori-cultrīx, īcis *f* inhabitant of the woods.

nemori-vagus 3 wandering in the woods.

nemorōsus 3 full of woods *or* trees.

nem-pe *adv.* truly, certainly, of course, indeed; namely.

nemus, oris *n* wood, grove, forest; plantation.

nēnia, ae *f* **a**) funeral song, dirge; mournful song; **b**) magic song, incantation; **c**) song, nursery song, lullaby.

neō, nēvī, nētum 2 to spin, weave.

nepa, ae *f* scorpion; crab.

nepōs, ōtis *m* **a**) grandson; **b**) descendant, nephew; **c**) spendthrift.

nepōtātus, ūs *m* prodigality.

nepōtor 1 to squander.

nepōtulus, ī *m* little grandson.

neptis, is *f* granddaughter.

nē-quam (*indecl.*, *comp.* **nēquior,** *superl.* **nēquissimus**) good-for-nothing, worthless, useless, bad, wicked.

nē-quāquam *adv.* by no means.

ne-que, *see* **nec.**

neque-dum, *see* **necdum.**

ne-queō, īvī *and* **iī, itum, īre** to be unable (*with inf.*).

nē-quīquam *adv.* in vain, to no purpose, without good reason; for nothing.

nēquiter, *adv. of* **nequam.**

nēquitia, ae (*and* **nēquitiēs, ēī**) *f* worthlessness, badness, wickedness, profligacy.

nervōsus 3 sinewy, wiry, energetic.

nervulus, ī *m* vigour, strength.

nervus, ī *m* sinew, tendon; **a**) cord, string, *pl.* stringed instrument; **b**) bowstring; **c**) leather cover of a shield; **d**) thong, fetter, prison; **e**) vigour, force, strength, energy; **f**) penis.

ne-sciō 4 **a**) not to know, to be ignorant; **nesciō an** I know not whether, perhaps, probably; **nescio (-)quis** I know not who, some one; **nescio-quōius** 3 someone's; **b**) to be unacquainted with.

ne-scius 3 **a**) unknowing, ignorant, unaware; **b**) unable, incapable; **c**) unknown.

neu = **neve.**

neuter, tra, trum neither of the two; of neither sex *or* gender.

ne-uti-quam *adv.* by no means.

neutrō *adv.* to neither side.

neutr-ubi *adv.* in neither place.

nē-ve *and* **neu** *cj.* **a**) and not, nor, or not, and that not, and lest; **neu ... neu** neither ... nor.

ne-vult etc. = **nōn vult** etc.

nex, necis *f* murder, violent death; the blood of the slain.

nexilis, e tied *or* bound together.

nexum, ī *n, see* **necto.**

nexus, ūs *m* a binding together, interlacing, entwining; **a**) a bond; **b**) personal obligation of a debtor, assignment of the person for debt.

nī *cj.* **1.** unless, if not; **2.** = **nē**[3] not, that not.

nīcātor, ōris *m* victor.

nīcētērium, ī *n* prize of victory.

nictō 1 to wink; to flicker.

nīdāmentum, ī *n* materials of a nest.

nīdi-ficus 3: *-um ver* the season of nesting.

nīdor, ōris *m* vapour, steam, smell.

nīdulus, ī *m* little nest.

nīdus, ī *m* nest; nestling; dwelling, home; book-case.

niger, gra, grum black, dark, dusky; **a**) gloomy; **b**) unlucky, unpropitious; **c**) wicked, bad.

nigrēscō, gruī, — 3 to become black.

nigrō 1 **a**) to be black; **b**) to blacken.

nigror, ōris *m* blackness.

nihil (*indecl.*, only *nom.* and *acc.*; *gen.* **nūllīus reī,** *dat.* **nūllī reī,** *abl.* **nūllā rē**) nothing, a nothing, of no value; **non nihil** something, **nihil non** everything, **nihil aliud nisi** *or* **quam** nothing else but; **nihil** *adv.* in nothing, in no respect, not at all.

nihil-dum *adv.* nothing as yet.

nihilum, ī *n* nothing; **nihilī** for nothing, of no account; **ad nihilum recidere, in nihilum occidere** come to nothing; **nihilō** (*abl.*) by nothing, not at all; **pro nihilo** for nothing; **de nihilo** without cause; **nihilō(-)minus** *adv.* nevertheless.

nīl = **nihil; nīlum** = **nihilum.**

nimbātus 3 (shrouded in rain-clouds); humbugging (?).

nimbi-fer 3 storm-bringing.

nimbōsus 3 cloudy, stormy.

nimbus, ī *m* cloud, rain-cloud; **a**) stormy rain, rain-storm, heavy shower; **b**) cloud, mass, multitude.

nī-mīrum *adv.* without doubt, certainly, surely, to be sure, forsooth.

nimis *adv.* **a**) too much, overmuch, excessively; **non nimis** not very much, not particularly; **b**) greatly, very much.

nimius 3 too great, too much, excessive, beyond measure; *adv.* (**nimiō** *and*) **nimium a**) = **nimis; b**) by far; **nimium quantum** very much indeed, as much as can be.

ningues *f/pl.* snow.

ning(u)it, ninxit, — 3 it snows.

ni-si *cj.* if not, unless; **a**) (*after negatives*) except, but, only; **nihil (aliud) nisi** nothing but; **non ... nisi** *or* **nisi ... non** only; **b**) **nisi si, nisi quod** except, unless, save only; **nisi forte, nisi vero** unless perhaps.

nīsus, ūs *m* a pressing *or* resting upon *or* against; **a**) a striving, exertion; **b**) step, flight, push, ascent; **c**) a giving birth.

nītēdula *and* **nītēl(l)a, ae** *f* small mouse, dormouse.

niteō, uī, — 2 to shine, glitter, be bright; **a**) to be well-fed, in good condition, to thrive; **b**) to flourish, abound; **c**) to be illustrious.

nitēscō, tuī, — 3 to begin to shine, become sleek.

nitidiusculus 3 a little more shiny.

nitidus 3 shining, glittering, bright; **a**) sleek, fat, healthy-looking; **b**) handsome, neat, elegant; **c**) flourishing, blooming; **d**) cultivated, refined.

nitor[1], **ōris** *m* brightness, splendour, lustre, sheen; **a**) beauty, elegance, charm, grace; **b**) dignity, excellence.

nītor[2], **nīxus** *or* **nīsus sum** 3 to rest, lean *or* support oneself upon (*alqa re, in alqd*); **a**) to tread, press forward; to climb, ascend, push up towards a height; **b**) to strive, exert oneself, endeavour; **c**) to rest, rely, depend upon.

nitrātus 3 containing soda.
nitrum, ī *n* natural carbonate of soda.
nivālis, e snowy; snow-white, covered with snow; cold.
nivārius 3 filled with snow.
nivātus 3 cooled with snow.
nī-ve *cj.* or if not; or lest.
niveus 3 = **nivalis.**
nivōsus 3 full of snow, snowy.
nix, nivis *f* snow; white hair.
nīxor 1 = **nītor**[2].
nīxus, ūs *m* = **nisus.**
nō 1 to swim, sail, flow, fly.
nōbilis, e knowable; **a)** well-known, noticeable, celebrated, renowned, famous, notorious; **b)** of noble birth, noble, highborn; **c)** excellent, superior.
nōbilitās, ātis *f* fame, renown, celebrity; **a)** noble birth, nobility; **b)** the nobility, the nobles; **c)** excellence, superiority.
nōbilitō 1 to make known, famous, notorious.
nocēns, tis a) hurtful, injurious; **b)** culpable, criminal.
noceō, uī, itum 2 to harm, hurt, injure (*alci*).
nocīvus 3 hurtful, injurious.
nocti-fer ī *m* evening-star.
nocti-lūca, ae *f* the moon.
nocti-vagus 3 night-wandering.
noctū *adv.* at night, by night.
noctua, ae *f* night-owl, owl.
noctuābundus 3 (travelling) in the night-time.
noctuīnus 3 of an owl.
nocturnus 3 by night, nocturnal.
noctu-vigilus 3 awake at night.
nocuus 3 injurious.
nōdō 1 to tie in a knot, to knot, fetter.
nōdōsus 3 knotty; intricate.
nōdus, ī *m* knot; **a)** knot *or* knob on the joint of an animal, knot in the wood of plants; **b)** bud; **c)** band, grip, girdle, bond, obligation; **d)** entanglement, difficulty, impediment.
noenu(m) (*obsolete*) = **non.**
nōlō, luī, —, nōlle not to wish, to be unwilling (*with inf., acc.c.inf.*); to wish ill, be adverse (*alci*).
nōmen, inis *n* name, appellation; **nōmen mihi est Gaio** *or* **Gaius** I am called G.; **nōmen dare alci** to give a name, to call; **nōmen dare, edere, profiteri** to give in one's name, to enlist; **nōmen alcis deferre** to give information against, to accuse judicially; **a)** title; **b)** gentile name, race, family, nation; person; **c)** fame, repute, renown; **d)** the mere name, pretext, pretence; **e)** name of a debtor in an account-book, bond, obligation, security for a debt; **nōmen solvere** to pay a debt; **nōmina exigere** to collect one's debts; **nōmine** by name, under the name, in the name of, on the ground, on account *or* behalf of; **meo nōmine** in my name, on my behalf.
nomen-clātiō, ōnis *f* a calling by name.
nōmen-c(u)lātor, ōris *m* name--caller.
nōminātim *adv.* by name, expressly.
nōminātiō, ōnis *f* a naming, nomination.
nōminitō 1 to name.
nōminō 1 to name, call by name; **P.** to be called; **a)** to name, mention, make famous; **b)** to nominate for office; **c)** to accuse, arraign.
nomisma, atis *n* coin.
nomos, ī *m* song.
nōn *aov.* **a)** not; **b)** (*in answers*) no.
Nōnae, ārum *f/pl.* the nones (*the fifth* or *seventh day of a month*).
nōnāgēsimus 3 the ninetieth.
nōnāgiē(n)s *adv.* ninety times.
nōnāgintā ninety.
nōnānus 3 belonging to the ninth legion.
nōnāria, ae *f* prostitute.
nōn-dum *adv.* not yet.
nōngentī 3 nine hundred.
nōn-ne *adv. interr.* not?
nōn-nēmō someone, many a one.
nōn-nihil something; somewhat.
nōn-nūllus 3 some, several; considerable.
nōn-numquam *adv.* sometimes.
nōnus 3 the ninth; *subst.* **nōna, ae** *f* the ninth hour.
norma, ae *f* carpenter's square, measure, standard, rule; precept.
nōs we; I.
nōscitō 1 to observe, perceive; to recognize.

nōscō, nōvī, nōtum 3 to become acquainted with, to learn to know; *perf.* to know; **a**) to recognize; **b**) to acknowledge, allow, admit; **c**) to investigate a case.

noster, tra, trum our, ours; **nostrī, ōrum** *m/pl.* our friends, troops, countrymen; **a**) favourable to us; **b**) = **meus.**

nostrās, ātis of our country, native.

nota, ae *f* mark, token, sign; **a**) written character, cipher; note, criticism; mark of punctuation; **b**) mark on a cask of wine; **c**) branded mark, brand; mark of ignominy; **d**) reproach, disgrace, official censure; **e**) nod, sign.

notābilis, e remarkable, noteworthy, extraordinary.

notārius, ī *m* shorthand-writer; secretary.

notātiō, ōnis *f* a marking, noting; **a**) degradation by a censor; **b**) a noticing, observing; **c**) analysis of meaning.

notātus 3 **a**) marked, recognizable; **b**) perceptible (*alci*).

nōtēscō, tuī, — 3 to become known.

nothus 3 bastard; counterfeit.

nōtiō, ōnis *f* a becoming acquainted with; **a**) examination, investigation, inquiry; **b**) idea, conception, notion.

nōtitia, ae (*and* **-iēs, ēī**) *f* acquaintance; **a**) a being known; fame; **b**) knowledge; **c**) conception, idea.

notō 1 to mark, designate with a mark; **a**) to note down, write; **b**) to denote, indicate, signify; **c**) to observe; **d**) to blame, censure, reprimand.

nōtor, ōris *m* witness to identity

notus[1], **ī** *m* the south wind.

nōtus[2] 3 known; *subst. m* an acquaintance; **a**) familiar, friendly; **b**) common, customary; **c**) notorious, of ill repute.

novācula, ae *f* razor.

novālis, is *f and* **novāle, is** *n* fallow land; cultivated land; crop.

novātrīx, īcis *f* she that renews.

novellō 1 to plant young vines.

novellus 3 new, young, fresh.

novem (*indecl.*) nine.

November, bris, bre belonging to November; (*mensis m*) November.

noven-diālis, e a) of nine days, lasting nine days; **b**) on the ninth day.

novēnī 3 nine each.

noverca, ae *f* step-mother.

novercālis, e of a step-mother.

novīcius 3 new, fresh; new comer, novice.

noviē(n)s *adv.* nine times.

novitās, ātis *f* newness, novelty; rareness, strangeness; **a**) new acquaintance; **b**) newness of rank, upstart condition.

novō 1 to make new, renew, renovate; **a**) to invent; **b**) to change, alter, fashion anew; **res novāre** to effect a revolution, overthrow the government.

novus 3 new, fresh, recent; **novae res** political innovations, revolution; **homo novus** upstart, the first of a family to hold a curule office, newly ennobled; **a**) new, novel, strange, singular, unusual, unheard of; **b**) inexperienced, unaccustomed, unused, unacquainted with; *superl.* **novissimus** 3 the latest, last, extreme; **agmen novissimum** the rear; *adv.* **novē**, in a new fashion; **novissimē** lately, recently, a short time ago; lastly, finally.

nox, noctis *f* night; darkness; **a**) death; **b**) sleep, dream; **c**) the lower world; **d**) confusion, gloom, blindness.

noxa, ae *f* harm, injury, damage; **a**) crime, fault, offence; **b**) punishment.

noxia, ae *f* **a**) guilt, crime; **b**) hurt, damage, injury.

noxiōsus 3 injurious.

noxius 3 **a**) hurtful, noxious; **b**) criminal, guilty; *m* a criminal.

nūbēcula, ae *f* little cloud.

nūbēs, is *f* cloud; **a**) multitude; **b**) darkness, obscurity, concealment, veil; **c**) sad condition, gloom, misfortune; **d**) phantom.

nūbi-fer 3 cloud-bringing; cloud--capped.

nūbi-gena, ae *m, f* cloud-born.

nūbilis, e marriageable.

nūbilus 3 cloudy, overcast; *subst.* **-um, ī** *n* cloudy weather, *pl.* clouds; **a**) dark, gloomy; **b**) unfavourable; unhappy.

nūbi-vagus 3 wandering in the clouds.

nūbō, nūpsī, ptum 3 to veil; (*of a bride*) to be married, to marry (*alci*); **nupta, -ae** *f* wife, spouse, bride.

nucētum, ī *n* plantation of nut trees.

nuci-frangibulum, ī *n* nutcracker, tooth.

nuc(u)leus, ī *m* kernel, nut.

nu-diūs it is now the ... day; ~ **tertius** the day before yesterday.

nūdō 1 to bare, uncover, strip, (*alqd re*); **a**) to leave undefended; **b**) to rob, spoil, plunder; **c**) to expose, disclose.

nūdus 3 naked, bare, unclothed; **a**) in light attire; **b**) unarmed, unprotected; **c**) deprived of, destitute; **d**) needy, poor; **e**) bare, mere, alone, only; **f**) simple, unadorned.

nūgae, ārum *f/pl.* jests, trifles, nonsense, silly things, trumpery; foolish, trifling fellow.

nūgātor, ōris *m* babbler, trifler.

nūgātōrius 3 trifling, silly, worthless, frivolous.

nūgāx, ācis jesting, trifling.

nūgi-gerulus, ī *m* dealer in trumpery.

nūgi-vendus, ī *m* seller of trumpery.

nūgor 1 to trifle, be frivolous; to lie.

nūllus 3 none, no, not any, nobody; **nūllo ordine** without (any) order; **nūllus non** every one; **non nūllus** some; **a**) non-existent; **b**) insignificant, of no account, worthless.

nūllus-dum none as yet.

num *interrog. particle* **a**) *introducing a direct question, gen. suggesting a negative answer*; really? surely not?; **numne** = **num; b**) *in indirect questions:* whether.

numella, ae *f* fetter (*for slaves*).

nūmen, inis *n* nod, command; **a**) divine will, divine command, divine authority, divinity, divine majesty, god, goddess; **b**) oracle.

numerābilis, e that can be counted; easily counted.

numerātiō, ōnis *f* payment.

numerō 1 to count, reckon, number; **a**) to count out, pay down; **numerātus** 3 in ready money; *subst.* **-um, ī** *n* ready money, cash; **b**) to reckon under (*alqd in re, inter alqos*), class under, consider, hold; **c**) to recount, relate.

numerōsus 3 **a**) numerous, manifold, populous; **b**) measured, rhythmical.

numerus, ī *m* **1.** measure, rhythm, melody, harmony, numbers, verse, metre; **2.** number, certain number; calculation; a) class, category, estimation; **in hostium numero ducere** to count as enemies; b) rank, place, condition, position; c) mass, heap; quantity, body, party, collection; d) a mere number, nothing; *abl. as adv.* **numerō** at the proper time; too soon.

nummārius 3 belonging to money; bribed.

nummātus 3 provided with money.

nummulāri(ol)us, ī *m* money-changer.

nummulus, ī *m* paltry money.

nummus, ī *m* coin, piece of money; *pl.* money; **a**) sesterce; **b**) penny, trifle.

num-ne, *see* **num.**

numquam *adv.* never; **non** ~ sometimes; ~ **non** always.

num-quī *interrog. adv.* in any way? at all?

num-quid 1. *in direct questions:* a) anything? b) *simply as an interrog. particle*; **2.** *in indirect questions*: whether.

nunc *adv.* **a**) now, at present; **nunc ipsum** at this very moment; **nunc ... nunc** now ... now, at one time ... at another; **b**) under these circumstances, as matters are; **nunc autem,** ~ **vero** but now, now however.

nuncĭam = **nunc.**

nuncupātiō, ōnis *f* public proclamation.

nuncupō 1 to call by name, name; to pronounce publicly, utter, vow, nominate as heir.

nūndinae, ārum *f/pl.* (ninth day) market-day, market, trade, traffic, business.

nūndinālis cocus a nine-day cook (once-a-week cook).

nūndinātiō, ōnis *f* a trafficking, trade, buying and selling.

nūndinor 1 **a**) to go to market, trade, traffic; **b**) to purchase.

(**nūndinus** of nine days) **a**) *see* **nundinae; b**) **trīnum nūndinum** period of three market-days (*about 20 days*).

nunquam, *see* **numquam.**
nūntia, ae *f* she that announces, female messenger.
nūntiātiō, ōnis *f* augur's right of announcing his observations.
nūntiō 1 to announce, report, make known, give orders.
nūntius, 3 announcing, bringing news; *subst.* **~, ī** *m* **a**) messenger, announcer; **b**) (*also* **-ium** *n*) message, news, tidings; command, order.
nū-per *adv.* (*superl.* **nūperrimē**) newly, lately, not long ago.
nūperus 3 newly arrived.
nuptiae, ārum *f/pl.* (*and* **nuptus, ūs** *m*) nuptials, marriage, wedding.
nuptiālis, e relating to a marriage, nuptial.
nurus, ūs *f* daughter-in-law; young married woman.
nusquam *adv.* **a**) nowhere; **b**) to no place; **c**) on no occasion, in nothing; **d**) for nothing.
nūtāmen, inis *n* a waving.
nūtātiō, ōnis *f* a tottering, going to ruin.
nūtō 1 to nod, move up and down, totter, waver.
nūtrīcātus, ūs *m* a suckling, bringing up.
nūtrīcium, ī *n* nursing.
nūtrīcius, ī *m* foster-father.
(**nūtrīcō** *and*) **nūtrīcor** 1 to nourish; to sustain.
nūtrīcula, ae *f* nurse.
(**nūtrīmen, inis** *and*) **nūtrīmentum, ī** *n* **a**) nourishment; **b**) fuel; training.
nūtriō (*and* **-or**) 4 **a**) to suckle, nourish, feed, bring up; **b**) to tend, take care of, cherish, cultivate.
nūtrītor, ōris *m* breeder, rearer.
nūtrīx, īcis *f* nurse, foster-mother; breast.
nūtus, ūs *m* a nodding, inclination; **a**) downward tendency, gravity; **b**) command, will, hint.
nux, nucis *f* nut; nut-tree; almond-tree.
nympha, ae *and* **nymphē, ēs** *f* **a**) bride, young woman; **b**) nymph; water.

O

ō *int.* o! oh!
ob *prep.* with *acc.* **a)** towards, to; **b)** at, before, in front of, over against, **ob oculos versari; c)** on account of, for, because of, for the sake of.
ob-aerātus 3 involved in debt.
ob-agitō 1 to disturb.
ob-ambulō 1 to walk before *or* near; to walk up and down.
ob-ārdēscō, ārsī, — 3 to blaze up.
ob-armō 1 to arm against.
ob-arō 1 to plough up.
obba, ae *f* a vessel for holding wine.
ob-brūtēscō 3 to become stupid.
ob-dō, didī, ditum 3 **a)** to set, put, place before *or* against (*alqd* with *dat.*); **b)** to expose; **c)** to shut, close.
(ob-dormiō 4 *and*) **ob-dormīscō, [mīvī,** — 3 to fall asleep.]
ob-dūcō 3 **1.** to lead against, bring forward; **2.** a) to draw over (*alqd* with *dat.*), draw in front; b) to cover over, overspread; c) to swallow; to pass (time); **obductus** 3 overspread, clouded, scarred over, wrinkled.
ob-ductiō, ōnis *f* a covering.
ob-ductō 1 to bring in as a rival.
ōb-dūrēscō, ruī, — 3 to become hard *or* insensitive.
ob-dūrō 1 to hold out, persist.
obeliscus, ī *m* obelisk.
ob-eō, iī (īvī), itum, īre 1. *intr.* to go to (*in alqd*); a) to go to meet, go against; b) to go down, set, to die, perish; **2.** *trans.* to reach, betake oneself to, to visit, travel over, wander through (*alqd*); a) to run over, survey, review; b) to surround; c) to engage in, apply oneself to, perform, execute, accomplish; **mortem** *or* **diem (supremum)** to die.
ob-equitō 1 to ride up to (*dat.*).
ob-errō 1 to wander about; blunder.
ob-ēsitās, ātis *f* fatness, stoutness.
ob-ēsus 3 fat, plump; coarse.
ōbex, icis *m and f* bolt, bar; barrier, barricade, obstacle.
ob-f..., ob-g..., *see* **off..., ogg...**
ob-fuī, *see* **obsum.**
ob-haereō 2, **ob-haerēscō** 3 to stick fast, cleave to.
ob-iaceō 2 to lie against, in the way (*dat.*).
ōb-iciō (*and* **ŏb-**)**, iēcī, iectum** 3 **1.** to throw against *or* in the way of, to oppose (*alci alqd*); **2.** to throw before, throw to, cast, offer, present (*alci alqd*); a) to expose; b) to hold before as a defence *or* protection; c) to cast up at (as an accusation *or* reproach).
obiectātiō, ōnis *f* reproach.
ob-iectō 1 to set against, throw at (*alqd alci rei*); a) to abandon, expose; **b)** to cast up at (as a reproach).
ob-iectus, ūs *m* **a)** a placing *or* putting before *or* against; **b)** a lying against *or* opposite.
ob-iiciō, *see* **obicio.**
ob-īrāscor 3 to grow angry at.
ob-iter *adv.* on the way; by the way, incidentally.
ob-itus, ūs *m* **a)** meeting; **b)** ruin, destruction, death.
ob-iūrgātiō, ōnis *f* a chiding, reproof, scolding.
ob-iūrgātor, ōris *m* chider, blamer.
ob-iūrgātōrius 3 reproachful.
ob-iūrgitō 1 to chide, rebuke.
ob-iūr(i)gō 1 to chide, scold, reprove; to deter by reproof; to chastise.
(ob-languēscō), guī, — 3 to become languid.
ob-lātrātrīx, īcis *f* she who barks at.
ob-lātrō 1 to bark at *or* against.
(oblectāmen, inis *and*) **oblectāmentum, ī** *n* delight, amusement, pleasure.
oblectātiō, ōnis *f* a delighting, pleasing, delight.
ob-lectō 1 to delight, please, amuse.
ob-lēniō 4 to soothe.
ob-līdō, sī, sum 3 to squeeze together, compress.
ob-ligātiō, ōnis *f* a pledging, obligation.

ob-ligō 1 **a**) to bind *or* fasten; **b**) to bind up, bandage; **c**) to put under obligation, make liable; to involve in (*alqm alqa re*); **d**) to pledge, mortgage; **obligātus** 3 bound, under an obligation, indebted, devoted, mortgaged.
ob-līmō 1 to cover with slime *or* mud; to lavish, squander.
ob-linō 3 to daub, smear over, besmear, bedaub; **a**) to cover over, load; **b**) to stain, pollute, defile.
oblīquō 1 to turn sideways *or* aside, turn awry.
ob-līquus 3 **a**) slanting, sideways, oblique; **b**) indirect, covert; envious.
ob-litēscō, tuī, — 3 to hide oneself.
ob-litterō 1 to erase; to blot out of memory; to cancel.
oblitus *part. pass. of* **oblino; oblītus** *of* **obliviscor.**
oblīviō, ōnis *f* **a**) forgetfulness, oblivion; **b**) amnesty.
oblīviōsus 3 **a**) forgetful; **b**) causing forgetfulness.
ob-līvīscor, oblītus sum 3 to forget (*with gen.* or *acc.*).
oblīvium, ī *n* = **oblivio.**
ob-locūtor, ōris *m* contradictor.
ob-longus 3 oblong.
ob-loquor 3 to speak against, reproach; to accompany in song, to sound in accompaniment.
ob-luctor 1 to struggle *or* strive against.
ob-lūdiō (?) 1 to jest.
ob-mōlior 4 to build *or* pile against (as a defence *or* obstruction).
ob-murmurō 1 to murmur at *or* against.
ob-mūtēscō, tuī, — 3 to become dumb; to cease.
ob-nātus 3 growing on.
ob-nītor 3 to press against, resist; **obnīxus** 3 steadfast, firm, resolute.
ob-noxiōsus 3 slavish.
ob-noxius 3 **a**) liable to, addicted to (*dat.*), guilty of (with *dat.* or *gen.*); **b**) subject, exposed to (*dat.*); submissive, servile; **c**) obliged, indebted, responsible (*dat.*).
ob-nūbilus 3 clouded over.
ob-nūbō 3 to cover, veil.
ob-nūntiātiō, ōnis *f* announcement of evil omens.
ob-nūntiō 1 to announce bad omens *or* news.
oboediēns, tis obedient, compliant (*dat.*).
oboedientia, ae *f* obedience.
ob-oediō, īvī, ītum 4 to give ear, hearken, listen; to obey (*dat.*).
ob-oleō 2 to emit a smell, smell of (*acc.*); to attract by smell (*dat.*).
ob-orior 4 to arise, appear, spring up (before someone).
ob-p..., *see* **opp...**
ob-rēpō, rēpsī, rēptum 3 to creep up; to approach stealthily, come up suddenly.
ob-rēptō 1 = **obrepo.**
ob-rētiō 4 to entangle.
ob-rigēscō, guī, — 3 to become stiff *or* hard.
ob-rōdō 3 to gnaw at.
ob-rogō 1 to repeal a law by another.
ob-ruō 3 to cover over (*alqd re*); **a**) to hide, bury, sink; **b**) to overwhelm, conceal, eclipse, obscure; **c**) to overload, weigh down, oppress.
obrussa, ae *f* the testing of gold by fire.
ob-saepiō 4 to hedge in, fence in, enclose.
ob-saturor 1 to have more than enough of.
obscaenus 3, *see* **obscenus.**
ob-scaevō 1 to give bad omens.
obs-cēnitās, ātis *f* impurity, unchastity, lewdness.
obs-cēnus 3 filthy, repulsive, offensive; **a**) impure, indecent, lewd, obscene; **b**) ill-omened, inauspicious.
obscūrātiō, ōnis *f* a darkening.
obscūritās, ātis *f* darkness, obscurity; **a**) indistinctness, unintelligibility; **b**) low birth.
obscūrō 1 to darken, obscure; **a**) to hide, conceal; **b**) to make indistinct, unintelligible; **c**) to make unknown, forgotten, to eclipse.
ob-scūrus 3 dark, obscure; **a**) hidden, concealed, secret; **b**) indistinct, unintelligible; **c**) reserved; **d**) unknown, not celebrated, ignoble, mean.
ob-secrātiō, ōnis *f* earnest entreaty; **a**) public prayer *or* supplication; **b**) appeal.
ob-secrō 1 to entreat earnestly (*alqm; ut*), to implore, supplicate, conjure.

ob-secundō 1 to be compliant, subservient, to yield (*dat.*).
ob-sēpiō 4, *see* **obsaepio.**
obsequēl(l)a, ae *f* = **obsequium.**
ob-sequēns, tis compliant, obedient, yielding (*dat.*).
obsequentia, ae *f* = **obsequium.**
obsequiōsus 3 compliant, obsequious.
obsequium, ī *n* compliance, complaisance, obedience, indulgence, submission.
ob-sequor 3 to comply with, obey, submit, indulge in (*with dat.*).
ob-serō[1] 1 to bolt, bar, fasten, shut up.
ob-serō[2], **sēvī, situm** 3 to sow, plant, cover over, fill (*alqd re*).
ob-servābilis, e remarkable.
ob-servāns, tis attentive, respectful.
observantia, ae *f* respect, esteem.
observātiō, ōnis *f* **a**) an observing, watching; **b**) accuracy, circumspection.
ob-servātor, ōris *m* watcher, observer.
observitō 1 to watch, observe diligently.
ob-servō 1 to observe, watch; **a**) to attend to, guard, keep, regard; **b**) to respect, esteem, honour.
ob-ses, idis *m*, *f* hostage; surety, pledge, security.
ob-sessiō, ōnis *f* = **obsidio.**
ob-sessor, ōris *m* besieger, blockader, haunter.
ob-sideō, sēdī, sessum 2 to sit at (*acc.*); **a**) to sit *or* stay by; **b**) to beset, besiege, invest, blockade; to occupy, fill, haunt; **c**) to look out for, watch for.
obsidiālis, e relating to a siege *or* blockade.
obsidiō, ōnis *f* siege, blockade; pressing danger.
obsidium[1], **ī** *n* condition of a hostage.
obsidium[2], **ī** siege, blockade; danger.
ob-sidō, sēdī, sessum 3 to beset, to occupy.
ob-signātor, ōris *m* sealer, witness.
ob-signō 1 **a**) to seal; **b**) to attest under seal; **c**) to impress.
ob-sipō 1 to sprinkle over.
ob-sistō, stitī, — 3 to stand in the way; to withstand, resist (*dat.*); *subst.* **obstita, ōrum** *n/pl.* things struck by lightning.
obsole-fīō, factus sum, fierī 3 = **obsolesco.**
obsolēscō, lēvī, (lētum) 3 to decay, wear out, fall into disuse, grow old *or* shabby; **obsolētus** 3 worn out; decayed, shabby; **a**) common, mean; **b**) obsolete.
obsōnātor, ōris *m* buyer of victuals.
obsōnātus, ūs *m* purchase of provisions.
obsōnium, ī *n* relish, victuals; fish.
ob-sonō[1], 1 to interrupt in speech.
obsōnō[2] *and* **-or** 1 to buy provisions.
ob-sorbeō 2 to swallow, gulp down.
ob-stetrīx, īcis *f* midwife.
obstinātiō, ōnis *f* firmness, steadfastness, persistence, obstinacy.
obstinātus 3 firmly resolved, persistent, stubborn, obstinate.
ob-stinō 1 to resolve, determine firmly, persist (*alqd;* with *inf.*).
ob-stipēscō = **obstupesco.**
ob-stīpus 3 inclined, bent, turned aside.
obstita, ōrum *n/pl.*, *see* **obsisto.**
ob-stō, stitī, (stātūrus) 1 to stand against, to be in the way; to resist; hinder, obstruct (*alci; ne, quominus*).
ob-strepō 3 to make a noise at *or* against (*dat.*); to interrupt with a noise, drown with clamour, shout down.
ob-strigillō 1 to be a hindrance.
ob-stringō 3 **a**) to bind,fasten, tie to; **b**) to bind, fetter, put under an obligation; **c**) to entangle, involve, make guilty of (*alqm re*).
ob-structiō, ōnis *f* hindrance, obstruction.
obs-trūdō = **obtrudo.**
ob-struō 3 to build before *or* against; **lūminibus alcis** to block up the light, build before the windows; to block up, close, hinder.
ob-stupefaciō 3 to astonish, astound, amaze, stupefy.
ob-stupēscō, puī, — 3 to become senseless, astounded, amazed.
ob-stupidus 3 amazed, stupefied.
ob-sum, fuī, esse to be in the way, hinder, injure.
ob-suō 3 to sew on *or* up.
ob-surdēscō, duī, — 3 to become deaf.
ob-taedēscit it starts to weary.
ob-tegō 3 to cover; **a**) to protect; **b**) to conceal, veil, hide.
ob-temperātiō, ōnis *f* compliance, obedience.

ob-temperō 1 to comply, obey, submit (*dat.*).
ob-tendō, ndī, ntum 3 to stretch *or* spread before; **a**) to plead as an excuse; **b**) to hide, conceal; **P.** to lie opposite (*dat.*).
ob-tentus, ūs *m* **a**) a stretching *or* spreading before; **b**) pretext, pretence, excuse.
ob-terō 3 to trample, crush, to bruise; **a**) to destroy; **b**) to put down, degrade.
ob-testātiō, ōnis *f* adjuration, earnest entreaty.
ob-testor 1 to call to witness; **a**) to assert solemnly (*alqd; acc. c. inf.*); **b**) to conjure, implore, entreat (*alqm; ut*).
ob-texō 3 to overspread.
ob-ticeō 2 to be silent.
ob-ticēscō, cuī, — 3 to become silent.
ob-tineō, tinuī, tentum 2 to hold fast; **a**) to occupy, possess, keep; **b**) to assert, maintain; **c**) to obtain; *intr.* to stand, continue.
ob-tingō, tigī, — 3 to fall to the lot of, happen (*alci; ut*).
ob-torpēscō, puī, — 3 to grow stiff, torpid, insensible.
ob-torqueō 2 to twist *or* turn round; to wrench.
ob-trectātiō, ōnis *f* detraction, disparagement.
ob-trectātor, ōris *m* detractor, disparager, rival.
ob-trectō 1 to disparage.
ob-trūdō 3 to thrust upon; to gulp down.
ob-truncō 1 to kill, slaughter.
ob-tueor 2 to gaze on, see clearly.
ob-tundō, tudī, tū(n)sum 3 to beat upon (*alqd*); **a**) to make blunt *or* dull, to stun, deafen; **b**) to annoy, tire; **obtū(n)sus** 3 blunt, dulled, stupid, weak.
ob-turbō 1 to disturb, disorder, confuse; **a**) to trouble; **b**) to interrupt, distract.
ob-turgēscō 3 to swell.
ob-tūrō 1 to stop up, close.
ob-tūtus, ūs *m* a looking at, beholding, gaze.
ob-umbrō 1 to overshadow; **a**) to darken; **b**) to conceal, cover; **c**) to cast into the shade.
ob-uncus 3 hooked.
ob-ustus 3 burnt into, hardened by fire.
ob-vāgiō 4 to whimper at.
ob-vallō 1 to wall round.
ob-veniō 4 **a**) to come up to, come to meet; **b**) to occur; **c**) to fall to the lot of.
ob-versor 1 to move up and down before; to hover before; to appear (*dat.; ante alqm*).
ob-versus 3 **a**) turned towards; **b**) inclined to; *subst.* opponent.
ob-vertō 3 to turn towards *or* against (*alqd in* or *ad alqd*); **P.** to face, turn oneself to.
ob-viam *adv.* in the way, towards, against, meeting (*dat.*); **obviam ire** to come to meet; to oppose, resist, contend against, prevent.
ob-vigilō 1 to be watchful.
obvius 3 in the way, meeting, to meet (*dat.*); **a**) exposed to, open to, subject to; **b**) ready, at hand; **c**) affable, courteous.
ob-volvō 3 to wrap round *or* up, envelop.
ob-vors-, -vort- = **ob-vers-, -vert-.**
oc-caecō 1 to make blind; **a**) to darken, obscure, overcloud; **c**) to hide from sight.
oc-callātus 3 indurated.
oc-callēscō, luī, — 3 to become thick-skinned, callous.
oc-canō, nuī, — 3 to sound for action.
occāsiō, ōnis *f* opportunity, favourable moment; surprise attack.
occāsiuncula, ae *f* opportunity.
oc-cāsus, ūs *m* setting; the west; downfall.
occātiō, ōnis *f* a harrowing.
occātor, ōris *m* harrower.
oc-cēdō 3 to go up to.
oc-centō 1 to sing a (satirical) song to *or* at.
oc-ceptō 1 to begin.
occidēns, tis *m* the west.
occīdiō, ōnis *f* massacre, complete slaughter, extermination.
oc-cidō[1], cidī, (cāsūrus) 3 to fall down; **a**) to go down, set; **b**) to fall, perish, die, be ruined, be lost.
oc-cīdō[2], cīdī, cīsum 3 to strike down; **a**) to cut down, kill; **b**) to plague to death, to undo; **occīsissumus** most completely ruined.
occiduus 3 sinking; setting, western.
occillō 1 to batter, smash.
oc-cinō, cinuī (cecinī), — 3 to sing inauspiciously, to croak.

oc-cip iō, cēpī, ceptum 3 to begin
oc-cipitium, ī (*and* **occiput, itis**) *n* back of the head.
oc-cīsiō, ōnis *f* massacre, slaughter.
oc-cīsor, ōris *m* killer.
oc-clāmitō 1 to cry aloud.
oc-clūdō, sī, sum 3 to shut up, close.
ocō 1 to harrow, till.
cc-cubō, —, — 1 to lie down, lie dead.
oc-culcō 1 to trample down.
oc-culō, culuī, cultum 3 to hide, conceal, keep secret.
occultātiō, ōnis *f* concealing.
occultātor, ōris *m* concealer.
occultō 1, *intens. of* **occulo.**
occultus 3 hidden, concealed, secret, imperceptible; reserved, close; *subst.* **occultum, ī** *n* secret; hiding-place.
oc-cumbō, cubuī, cubitum 3 to fall down, fall in death, die.
occupātiō, ōnis *f* **a**) a seizing, taking possession of; **b**) business, employment, affairs.
occupātus 3 busy, engaged.
occupō 1 to take possession of, seize; **a**) to fill, occupy with (*alqd re*); **b**) to fall upon, attack (before an enemy); **c**) to anticipate, do anything first (*inf.*); **d**) to put out *or* invest money.
oc-currō, (cu)currī, cursum 3 to run to meet, hasten to meet (*alci*); **a**) to attack; **b**) to come to, be present at; **c**) to come in the way of, present itself, meet the eye, come into the thoughts, appear, occur, happen; **d**) to resist, oppose, counteract; to come to the help of, assist, prevent; **e**) to reply, answer (*dat.*).
occursātiō, ōnis *f* a running to meet; greeting, attention.
occursiō, ōnis *f* assault.
oc-cursō 1 to go to meet (*dat.*); **a**) to attack; **b**) to approach; **c**) to forestall; **d**) to occur to (the mind).
oc-cursus, ūs *m* a meeting, falling in with; movement.
ocellātus 3 marked with eyes, spotted (dice *or* marbles).
ocellus, ī *m* little eye.
ōcimum, ī *n* basil (*a plant*).
ōcior, us (*comp.*) swifter; *comp. adv.* **ōcius** (more) swiftly; *superl.* **ōcissimē.**
ocliferius 3 striking the eye.
ocrea, ae *f* metal greave.
ocreātus 3 wearing greaves.
octāvus 3 the eighth.
octiē(n)s *adv.* eight times.
octingentēsimus 3 eight hundredth.
octingentī 3 eight hundred.
octi-pēs, edis eight-footed.
octō (*indecl.*) eight.
Octōber, bris, bre belonging to October; (*mensis*) *m* October.
octō-decim (*indecl.*) eighteen.
octōgēnārius 3 containing eighty; eighty years old.
octōgēnī 3 eighty each.
octōgēsimus 3 the eightieth.
octōgiē(n)s *adv.* eighty times.
octōgintā (*indecl.*) eighty.
octō-iugis, e eight together.
octōnī 3 eight each.
octō-phoros, on carried by eight bearers; *subst.* **-on, ī** *n* litter carried by eight bearers.
octuplicātus 3 multiplied by eight.
octuplus 3 eightfold; *subst.* **octuplum, ī** *n* eightfold payment.
octussis, is *m* eight asses.
oculātus 3 having eyes, seeing; conspicuous.
oculeus 3 having many eyes.
oculissumus 3 dearest (apple of my eye).
oculus, ī *m* eye; **a**) bud; **b**) pearl (*metaph.*).
ōdēum (*and* **ōdīum**), **ī** *n* concert-hall.
ōdī, ōdisse (**ōsūrus**) to hate, dislike, be displeased with.
odiōs(s)icus 3 = **odiōsus.**
odiōsus 3 hateful, odious, annoying.
odium, ī *n* hatred, enmity; **a**) aversion; **b**) object of hatred.
odor (*and* **odōs**), **ōris** *m* smell, odour; **a**) perfume, spice; **b**) scent, suspicion.
odōrātiō, ōnis *f* a smelling smell.
odōrātus[1], **ūs** *m* sense of smell.
odōrātus[2] 3 fragrant.
odōri-fer 3 fragrant; producing perfumes.
odōrō 1 to make fragrant.
odōror 1 **a**) to smell at *or* out, scent; **b**) to aspire to; **c**) to get a smattering of (*acc.*).
odōrus 3 **a**) sweet-smelling; **b**) keen-scented.
odōs, ōris *m* (*obsolete*) = **odor.**
oeno-phorum, ī *n* wine-basket.
oeno-pōlium, ī *n* wine-shop.
oenus 3 (*obsolete*) = **unus.**

oestrus, ī *m* gadfly; frenzy.
oesus, ūs *m* (*obsolete*) = **usus.**
oesypum, ī *n* cosmetic made from wool-grease.
ofella, ae *f* bit, mouthful.
offa, ae *f* **a**) ball of meal; **b**) cutlet; **c**) tumour; **d**) abortion, shapeless mass.
offātim by bits.
offendiculum, ī *n* stumbling-block, obstacle.
of-fendō, endī, ēnsum 3 to hit, strike, knock, dash against; **1.** a) to come upon, meet with (*in re*); b) to suffer disaster, receive an injury; c) to offend, make a mistake, blunder; **2.** to offend, shock, displease; **offēnsus** 3 a) offended, displeased; b) offensive, odious.
offēnsa, ae *f* a striking against; **a**) offence, affront, enmity; **b**) disfavour, displeasure.
of-fēnsātiō, ōnis *f* blunder.
offēnsiō, ōnis *f* a striking against; **a**) indisposition, illness, complaint; **b**) a stumbling; offence, injury; **c**) hatred, enmity, aversion, disgust, dislike, disfavour; **d**) accident, misfortune, failure, defeat.
offēnsiuncula, ae *f* **a**) slight offence; **b**) slight failure.
offēnsō 1 to strike against.
offēnsus 3, *see* **offendo.**
of-fēnsus, ūs *m* shock; disfavour.
of-ferō, obtulī, oblātum, offerre to bring to, place before, present, show, exhibit (*alci alqd*); **a**) to offer, bring forward; **b**) to expose; **c**) to cause, occasion, bestow, inflict; — **P.** *or* **se offerre** to present oneself, oppose oneself.
offerumentae, ārum *f/pl.* presents (= blows).
officīna, ae *f* workshop, manufactory.
of-ficiō, fēcī, fectum 3 to be in the way of, hinder, oppose, obstruct, thwart (*dat.*).
officiōsus 3 obliging, courteous, serviceable; dutiful.
officium, ī *n* **1.** service, kindness; a) attention, complaisance, friendly service; b) respect, courtesy, deference; c) office, service, employment, work; **2.** duty, obligation, business, function; a) sense of duty, dutifulness, conscience; b) obedience, allegiance.
of-fīgō, —, — 3 to fix, fasten.
of-firmō 1 to hold fast to; **offirmātus** 3 firm; obstinate.
of-flectō 3 to turn round.
of-fōcō 1 to choke.
of-frēnātus 3 bound, fettered.
of-fūcia, ae *f* paint; deceit.
offula, ae *f* bit, morsel.
of-fulgeō, -lsī, — 2 to shine upon, appear.
of-fundō 3 to pour before *or* round; to spread over, cover.
og-ganniō 4 to growl at.
og-gerō 3 to bring to, press upon.
oh! *int.* oh! ah!
ōhē (*and* **ŏ, ĕ**) *int.* hi there! stop!
oi, oiei alas!
olea, ae *f* = **oliva.**
oleāginus 3 of the olive-tree.
oleārius 3 of oil; *subst.* oil-dealer.
oleaster, trī *m* wild olive-tree.
olēns, tis smelling; **a**) fragrant; **b**) stinking.
oleō, oluī, — 2 (*and* **olō** 3) to emit a smell, smell; to smell of (*alqd*), indicate, betray.
olētum, ī *n* faeces, excrement.
oleum, ī *n* oil; wrestling-school; rhetorical exercise.
ol-faciō 3 to smell, to scent out [*alqd*).
ol-factō 1 to smell.
olidus 3 smelling; stinking.
ōlim *adv.* **a**) formerly, some time ago, of old; **b**) one day, hereafter, at a future time; **c**) at times, often, for some time past.
olitor, ōris *m* kitchen-gardener.
olitōrius 3 relating to vegetables.
olīva, ae *f* **a**) olive; **b**) olive-tree; olive-branch; staff of olive-wood.
olīvētum, ī *n* olive-garden.
olīvi-fer 3 olive-bearing.
olīvum, ī *n* olive-oil; unguent; wrestling-school.
ōlla, ae *f* pot, jar.
ōllāris, e preserved in a jar.
olle *and* **ollus** (*obsolete*) = **ille.**
olor, ōris *m* swan.
olōrīnus 3 relating to a swan.
olus, eris *n* kitchen-herbs, vegetables, cabbage.
olusculum, ī *n* = **olus.**
omāsum, ī *n* bullock's tripe; paunch.
ōmen, inis *n* omen, sign, augury, token, foreboding; solemn usage, ceremony.
ōmentum, ī *n* **a**) fat; **b**) bowels.
ōminātor, ōris *m* prophet.

ōminor 1 to forebode, presage, predict, prophesy.
ōminōsus 3 ominous.
o-mittō 3 to let go, let alone, let loose, let fall; **a**) to give up, leave off; **b**) to leave unmentioned, to omit, overlook.
omni-genus 3 of all sorts.
omni-modīs in every way.
omnīnō *adv.* **a**) altogether, wholly, entirely, totally; **b**) in general, in all; **c**) to be sure; **omnīnō non** not at all.
omni-parēns, tis all-producing.
omni-potēns, tis all-powerful.
omnis, e all, each, every; **a**) all, whole, complete; **b**) of all kinds.
omni-tuēns, ntis all-seeing.
omni-vagus 3 wandering everywhere.
omni-volus 3 all-wishing.
onager *and* **onagrus, ī** *m* wild ass.
onāgos, ī *m* ass-driver.
onerārius 3 of burden; *subst.* **-a, ae** *f* merchant-vessel, transport.
onerō 1 to load, burden; **a**) to weigh down, oppress, overload; **b**) to pile up, aggravate; **c**) to stow away.
onerōsus 3 heavy, burdensome.
onocrotalus, ī *m* pelican.
onus, eris *n* load, burden, freight, cargo; weight; **a**) trouble, charge, difficulty; **b**) public burden, tax, expense, debt.
onustus 3 loaded, burdened (*re*), freighted; filled; weighed down.
onyx, ychis *m* and *f* onyx; onyx box, perfume-box.
opācitās, ātis *f* shadiness.
opācō 1 to shade, overshadow.
opācus 3 shaded, shady; dark, obscure.
opella, ae *f* a little work.
opera, ae *f* pains, effort, exertion, work; **operam dare** to see to, attend to, deal with (*alci rei* or *ut*); **operae pretium est** it is worth while; **a**) service, help; **b**) leisure, spare time; **c**) a day's work; workman, hired assistant; *plur.* hired mob, gang.
operārius 3 working; *subst.* **~, ī** *m* day-labourer, workman.
operculum, ī *n* lid, cover.
operīmentum, ī *n* a covering, cover.
operiō, eruī, ertum 4 to cover, cover over; **a**) to bury; **b**) to cover, shut, overwhelm; **c**) to hide, conceal, dissemble; **opertus** 3 hidden, covered; *subst.* **-um, ī** *n* secret; secret place.
operor 1 to work, labour, be busied (*alci rei*); to be engaged in worship *or* sacrifice.
operōsus 3 **a**) painstaking, active, busy; efficacious; **b**) troublesome, toilsome, difficult; **c**) elaborate, artfully constructed.
opertōrium, ī *n* covering.
opēs, um *f/pl., see* **ops.**
ophītēs, ae *m* serpentine.
opicus 3 uncivilized.
opi-fer 3 helpful, helping.
opi-fex, icis *m, f* **a**) worker, framer; **b**) mechanic, artisan.
opi-ficīna, ae *f* workshop.
ōpiliō, ōnis *m* shepherd. [dance.]
opīmitās, ātis *f* richness, abun-
opīmus 3 fat, well-fed; **a**) fruitful, fertile; **b**) rich, copious; **c**) sumptuous, splendid; overloaded (*speech*).
opīnābilis, e conjectural.
opīnātiō, ōnis *f* conjecture, opinion.
opīnātor, ōris *m* one who holds an opinion.
opīnātus 3 supposed, fancied.
opīnātus, ūs *m* supposition.
opīniō, ōnis *f* opinion, conjecture, supposition, belief; **a**) impression; **b**) expectation; **c**) reputation; **d**) fame, report.
opīnor (*and* **-ō**) 1 to be of opinion, believe, think, suppose.
opi-parus 3 splendid, sumptuous.
opistho-graphus 3 covered with writing on the back.
opitulor 1 to help, aid.
opo-balsamum, ī *n* balsam.
oportet, uit, — 2 it is necessary, proper, becoming.
op-pangō, pēgī, — 3 to impress.
op-pectō 3 to pick (food).
op-pēdō, —, — 3 to insult (*alci*).
op-perior, pertus (*rarely* **perītus**) **sum** 4 to wait (for).
op-petō 3 to go to meet; to encounter, suffer (*alqd*).
oppidānus 3 belonging to a (small) town; *subst.* **~, ī** *m* inhabitant of a (small) town.
oppidātim in each town.
oppidō *adv.* quite, exceedingly, exactly (*also* **oppidō quam**).
oppidulum, ī *n* little town.
oppidum, ī *n* fortification; **a**) town, provincial town; **b**) fortified place.

op-pignerō 1 to pledge, pawn.
op-pīlō 1 to shut up, block up.
op-pingō, pēgī, — 3 to impress.
op-pleō, ēvī, ētum 2 to fill, fill up (*alqd re*).
op-pōnō 3 to set against, put *or* place opposite *or* before (*alqd alci rei, ad alqd*); **a**) to oppose, interpose, expose, **b**) to bring forward, present, adduce, allege; **c**) to place in comparison; **d**) to pledge, mortgage.
opportūnitās, ātis *f* fitness, convenience, appropriateness, suitability; **a**) right time, opportunity; **b**) advantage.
op-portūnus 3 fit, suitable, appropriate; **a**) opportune, favourable, serviceable, advantageous, useful (*dat.; ad alqd*); **b**) exposed to, liable to.
op-positus, ūs *m* a setting *or* placing against *or* opposite, opposition.
op-pressiō, ōnis *f* force; violent seizure; overthrow.
oppressiuncula, ae *f* a slight touching *or* feeling.
oppressor, ōris *m* suppressor.
op-pressus, ūs *m* pressure.
op-primō, pressī, pressum 3 **1.** to press down *or* together, to sink; a) to crush, stifle, extinguish, close; b) to weigh down; c) to suppress, conceal, hide; d) to overpower, overthrow, prostrate, subdue; **2.** to fall upon, surprise, seize, catch.
opprobrāmentum, ī *n* reproach.
op-probrium, ī *n* reproach, abuse; disgrace, scandal, dishonour.
op-probrō 1 to reproach, taunt (*alci alqd*).
op-pugnātiō, ōnis *f* a storming; attack, assault.
op-pugnātor, ōris *m* attacker.
op-pugnō 1 to strike with the fist; to storm; to attack, assault, fight against.
ops ..., opt ..., *see* **obs ..., obt ...**
ops, opis *f* **a**) might, power, strength; **b**) assistance, help, aid, succour; *pl.* **opēs, um a**) means, property, wealth, riches, resources; **b**) forces, troops; **c**) influence, power.
optābilis, e to be wished for, desirable.
optātiō, ōnis *f* wish.
opthalmiās, ae *m* a fish.
optimās, ātis one of the best; *subst.* (*gen.* **optimātēs, ium** *pl.*) *m* aristocrat(s).
optimus 3 *and* **optimē,** *superl. of* **bonus** *and* **bene.**
optiō[1]**, ōnis** *f* free choice, option.
optiō[2]**, ōnis** *m* adjutant, assistant.
optīvus 3 chosen.
optō 1 **a**) to choose, select; **b**) to wish for, desire (*alqd; ut*); **optandus** 3 desirable; **optātus** 3 wished for, desired, dear, welcome; **optātum, ī** *n* wish; **optātō** as desired.
optumus 3 (*obsolete*) = **optimus.**
opulēns, tis = **opulentus.**
opulentia, ae (*and* **-titās, ātis**) *f* riches, wealth; power, greatness.
opulentō 1 to enrich.
opulentus 3 rich, wealthy (with *abl.* or *gen.*); **a**) splendid, sumptuous; **b**) powerful, mighty.
opus, eris *n* work; **1.** labour; a) action, deed, achievement, performance, business, undertaking; b) artistic work, workmanship, art; **2.** product of labour; a) work, book, composition; b) building, structure; c) military work, fortification, entrenchment; siege-apparatus; **3. opus est** there is need, it is required, useful (*alci res* or *re; inf.* or *acc. c. inf.*).
opusculum, ī *n* a little work.
ōra[1]**, ae** *f* ship's cable.
ōra[2]**, ae** *f* edge, border, margin, end; **a**) sea-coast; **b**) region, country, clime, zone.
ōrāc(u)lum, ī *n* **a**) oracle, divine announcement, prophecy, wise speech; **b**) place where oracles are given.
ōrāmentum, ī *n* (?) coaxing.
ōrārius 3 belonging to the sea-coast.
ōrātiō, ōnis *f* **1.** a speaking; a) speech, use of language, faculty of speech, language; b) manner of speech, style, expression; c) a language; prose; d) subject, theme; **2.** set speech; a) harangue, oration; b) eloquence; c) imperial message, rescript.
ōrātiuncula, ae *f* short speech.
ōrātor, ōris *m* **a**) speaker, orator; **b**) negotiator, spokesman.
ōrātōrius 3 oratorical.
ōrātrīx, īcis *f* female suppliant.
ōrātus, ūs *m* request, entreaty.
orbātiō, ōnis *f* deprivation.
orbātor, ōris *m* one who deprives of children.
orbiculātus 3 circular, round.

orbis, is *m* circle, ring, orbit; circuit; **a**) a winding, circular motion; **b**) routine; **c**) rotation; **d**) rounded period of speech; **e**) circular surface, shield, wheel, table, eye, quoit; disk of the sun *or* moon, the heavens; **f**) (*terrae, terrarum*) the earth, the universe; region, territory; mankind.
orbita, ae *f* (wheel-)rut, track.
orbitās, ātis *f* bereavement, childlessness; want.
orbitōsus 3 full of cart-ruts.
orbō 1 to bereave of children *or* parents, to deprive (*alqm re*).
orbus 3 deprived; **a**) bereft, destitute (*re, a re*); **b**) bereaved of parents *or* children, widowed; **~, ī** *m and* **orba, ae** *f* orphan, widow.
orca, ae *f* jar, barrel; dice-box.
orchas, adis *f* a kind of olive.
orchēstra, ae *f* place where the senate sat in the theatre.
orcīnus (*or* **-īvus**) 3 of the underworld.
Orcus, ī *m* (the god of) the underworld; death.
ōrdia prīma *n/pl.* = **primordia.**
ōrdinārius 3 ordinary, regular.
ōrdinātim *adv.* in succession, in good order.
ōrdinātiō, ōnis *f* a regulating, arranging, appointment.
ōrdinātor, ōris *m* one who sets in order (*a law-suit*).
ōrdinō 1 to set in order, arrange; **a**) to settle, regulate; **b**) to appoint; — **ōrdinātus** 3 arranged, orderly.
ōrdior, ōrsus sum 4 to begin, to commence; *subst.* **ōrsa, ōrum** *n/pl.* **a**) a beginning, undertaking; **b**) speech.
ōrdō, inis *m* series; **a**) line, row, order, rank; **b**) array, file; **c**) band, troop, company, centuria; **d**) centurionship, command, centurion; **e**) order, rank, class, degree; **f**) order, succession; **g**) regularity, rule, usage, custom.
orēas, adis *f* mountain-nymph, oread.
orexis, is *f* appetite.
organicus, ī *m* musician.
organum, ī *n* instrument.
orgia, ōrum *n/pl.* orgies, secret festival, nocturnal festival of Bacchus.
ori-chalcum, ī *n* yellow copper, brass.
ōricilla, ae *f* = **auricilla.**
ōricula, ae *f* = **auricula.**
oriēns, tis *m* the rising sun; the east, orient; the sun-god.
orīgō, inis *f* origin, source, descent, lineage, birth; record of early history.
orior, ortus sum (**oritūrus**) 4 **a**) to rise, arise, become visible; **b**) to spring from, come forth, take origin (*ab, ex re*); to be born from (*ab, ex alqo, alqo*), descend, originate; to grow; **c**) to begin.
oriundus 3 descended, springing from (*ab alqo; ab, ex re*).
ōrnāmentum, ī *n* equipment, accoutrement; **a**) furniture; **b**) ornament, decoration; **c**) honour, ornament, distinction.
ōrnātrīx, īcis *f* lady's maid.
ōrnātus, ūs *m* equipment, outfit, accoutrements, furniture; **a**) dress, attire; **b**) ornament, decoration, embellishment.
ōrnō 1 to equip, fit out, provide, supply (*alqd re*); **a**) to adorn, embellish, decorate, set off; **b**) to honour, distinguish, praise, extol; — **ōrnātus** 3 fitted out, provided; **a**) adorned, decorated, embellished, handsome, beautiful; **b**) honoured, distinguished; **c**) admirable, excellent, eminent, illustrious.
ornus, ī *f* mountain-ash.
ōrō 1 to speak (*alqd*); **a**) to speak as an orator, treat, plead, argue; **b**) to beg, pray, entreat (*alqm alqd; ut, ne*).
ōrsa, ōrum *n/pl., see* **ordior.**
ōrsus, ūs *m* a beginning, undertaking.
ortho-graphia, ae *f* orthography.
ortho-pȳgium, ī *n* the raised tail of a bird.
ortus, ūs *m* a rising, sunrise; **a**) east; **b**) birth, origin, source.
oryx, ygis *m* wild goat.
oryza, ae *f* rice.
ōs[1]**, ōris** *n* the mouth, jaws, (bird's *or* ship's) beak; **a**) tongue, lips, speech, talk; **b**) opening, mouth; **c**) face, look, expression, presence; mask; impudence, boldness.
os[2]**, ossis** *n* bone; marrow; inmost part, heart.
os-cen, inis *m* (*f*) bird of augury.
ōscillum, ī *n* little mask (*of Bacchus*).

ōscitanter *adv.* drowsily; negligently.
ōscitātiō, ōnis *f* yawning.
ōs-citō (*and* **ōs-citor**) 1 to open the mouth, gape, yawn; to be sleepy, listless, negligent.
ōsculābundus 3 kissing repeatedly.
ōsculātiō, ōnis (*and* **-lentia[?], ae**) *f* a kissing.
ōsculor 1 to kiss; to caress.
ōsculum, ī *n* little mouth; kiss.
ōsor, ōris *m* hater.
osseus 3 of bone, bony.
ossi-fraga, ae *f* (bone-breaker) sea-eagle, osprey; *or* the bearded vulture.
os-tendō, ndī, ntum (*and* **nsum**) 3 to stretch out (*alci alqd*); **a**) to show, expose to view, exhibit, display, lay open, disclose, betray, make known, promise; **b**) to express, indicate, declare; **se ostendere** *and* **P.** to become visible.
ostentātiō, ōnis *f* a showing, displaying, revealing; **a**) boasting, ostentation; **b**) pomp, false show, pretence, simulation.
ostentātor, ōris *m* displayer, boaster, vaunter.
os-tentō 1 to hold out, present to view, show, point out, indicate; **a**) to display, exhibit; **b**) to boast of (*alqd*); **c**) to promise, offer, threaten; **d**) to declare, make known, disclose (*alqd; acc.c.inf.*).
ostentuī (*dat.*) for a show, sign *or* pretence.
ostentum, ī *n* prodigy, portent.
ōstiārium, ī *n* door-tax.
ōstiārius, ī *m* doorkeeper, porter.
ōstiātim *adv.* from door to door.
ōstium, ī *n* door; entrance, mouth.
ostrea, ae *f and* **-um, ī** *n* mussel, oyster.
ostreātus 3 (covered with oyster--shells) covered with weals.
ostri-fer 3 producing oysters.
ostrīnus 3 purple.
ostrum, ī purple(-dye); purple dress *or* covering.
ōtiolum, ī *n* a little leisure.
ōtior 1 to be idle, at leisure.
ōtiōsus 3 idle, at leisure, disengaged, unoccupied; **a**) free from public affairs and duties; **b**) quiet, calm, undisturbed; **c**) passionless, indifferent, neutral, unconcerned.
ōtium, ī *n* leisure, idleness, ease; **a**) literary work, study, fruit of leisure; **b**) rest, repose, quiet; **c**) peace.
ovātus, ūs *m* rejoicing, triumph.
ovīle, is *n* sheepfold, fold for goats; enclosure for voting in the Campus Martius.
ovillus 3 of sheep.
ovis, is *f* sheep; wool; simpleton.
ovō 1 **a**) to rejoice, exult; **b**) to celebrate a lesser triumph.
ōvum, ī *n* egg; egg-shaped ball.
oxy-garum, ī *n* mixture of vinegar and fish-sauce.

P

P. *abbr.* = **Publius.**
pābulātiō, ōnis *f* a foraging.
pābulātor, ōris *m* forager.
pābulor 1 to forage.
pābulum, ī *n* fodder; food, nourishment.
pācālis, e relating to peace, peaceful.
pācātor, ōris *m* pacifier, conqueror.
pācātus 3 pacified, quieted, peaceful; *subst.* **pācātum, ī** *n* friendly country.
pāci-fer 3 peace-bringing.
pāci-ficātiō, ōnis *f* a peacemaking, pacification.
pāci-ficātor, ōris *m* peace-maker.
pācificātōrius 3 peace-making.
(**pāci-ficō** *and*) **pāci-ficor** 1 to make peace, reconcile, appease.
pāci-ficus 3 peace-making.
paciscor, pactus sum 3 **a**) to make a contract *or* agreement, to agree (*cum alqo; ut; inf.*); **b**) to stipulate, bargain for (*alqd*); **c**) to barter, exchange; **pactus** 3 agreed upon, stipulated, settled; betrothed; **pacta, ae** *f* betrothed woman.
pācō 1 to reduce to peace, to pacify, subdue.
pacta, ae *f, see* **paciscor.**
pactiō, ōnis *f* **a**) agreement, contract, covenant, treaty; underhand agreement; **b**) (*verborum*) form of words.
pactor, ōris *m* negotiator.
pactum, ī *n* **1.** = **pactio; 2.** (*abl. only*) way, means; **nullo, aliquo, alio, hoc pacto.**
paeān, ānis *m* **a**) hymn (to Apollo); **b**) = **paeon.**
paedagōgium, ī *n* training school for page-boys; page-boys.
paed-agōgus, ī *m* slave in charge of children; guardian, leader.
paedīcō 1 to practise unnatural vice.
paedīcō, ōnis (*and* **paedīcātor, ōris**) *m* practiser of unnatural vice.
paedor, ōris *m* dirt, filth.
paegniārius 3 belonging to sport.
paelex, icis *f* concubine, mistress.
paelicātus, ūs *m* concubinage.
paene *adv.* nearly, almost.
paen-īnsula, ae *f* peninsula.
paenitentia, ae *f* repentance.
paeniteō, uī, — 2 **a**) to repent, regret; to displease; **paenitendus** regrettable, to be ashamed of; **b**) **me paenitet** (*alcis rei* or with *inf.* or *quod*) it repents me, grieves, makes sorry, I am displeased *or* vexed; it offends, dissatisfies; **non paenitet** I am content, satisfied.
paenula, ae *f* travelling-cloak, mantle.
paenulātus 3 clothed in the *paenula.*
paeōn, ōnis *m a metrical foot.*
paetus (*and* **-tulus**) 3 having a slight squint *or* cast in the eye.
pāgānicus 3 = **paganus;** *subst.* **-a** (*sc.* **pila**), **ae** *f* ball stuffed with feathers.
pāgānus 3 belonging to a village, rustic; *subst.* **~, ī** *m* villager, peasant, countryman; civilian.
pāgātim *adv.* by villages.
pāgella, ae *f* = **pagina.**
pāgina, ae *f* page, leaf of paper; sheet; tablet, poem.
pāginula, ae *f* (little) page.
pāgus, ī *m* **a**) district, canton, region; **b**) village; villagers, country people.
pāla, ae *f* spade; socket *or* bezel of a ring.
palaestra, ae *f* wrestling-school, wrestling-place, gymnasium; **a**) wrestling; **b**) rhetorical exercise; **c**) brothel.
palaestricus 3 of the *palaestra.*
palaestrīta, ae *m* director of a *palaestra.*
palam 1. *adv.* openly, publicly, plainly, without concealment; **2.** *prep.* with *abl.* in the presence of, before.
Palātīnus 3 of the Palatine hill; of the imperial house.
Palātium, ī *n* the Palatine hill; palace.

palātum, ī *n and* **palātus, ī** *m* the palate; **a**) taste, judgment; **b**) vault.
palē, ēs *f* wrestling.
palea, ae *f* chaff.
palear, āris *n* dew-lap (*of an ox*).
palim-psēstus, ī *m* palimpsest, parchment rewritten after erasure.
pālitor (?) 1 to wander.
paliūrus, ī *m* Christ's thorn.
palla, ae *f* long robe, outer garment, mantle; curtain.
pallaca, ae *f* concubine.
Palladium, ī *n* image of Pallas.
pallēns, tis a)pale, wan; pale-yellow, pale-green; **b**) causing paleness; **c**) sickly.
palleō, uī, — 2 to be pale, be faded; to be anxious, fearful (of).
pallēscō, luī, — 2 to turn pale, grow yellow; to become afraid.
palliātus 3 dressed in a long Greek robe; Greek.
pallidulus 3 pale.
pallidus 3 = **pallens.**
palliolātus 3 covered with a *pallium; adv.* **palliolātim.**
palliolum, ī *n* little Greek mantle; hood.
pallium, ī *n* Greek cloak; coverlet.
pallor, ōris *m* paleness; fear, alarm.
pallula, ae *f, dim. of* **palla.**
palma[1], **ae** *f* palm, flat hand, hand; oar-blade.
palma[2], **ae** *f* palm-tree; **a**) date; **b**) palm-branch; **c**) palm-wreath, token of victory, prize, reward, victory; **d**) broom of palm-twigs; **e**) branch, twig.
palmāris, e deserving the palm, excellent.
palmārium, ī *n* masterpiece.
palmātus 3 embroidered with palm--twigs.
palmes, itis *m* vine-shoot; vine; branch.
palmētum, ī *n* palm-grove.
palmi-fer 3 palm-bearing.
palmōsus 3 full of palm-trees.
palmula, ae *f* oar(-blade); date.
pālor 1 to wander about, to roam, be dispersed, straggle.
palpātiō, ōnis *f* caress.
palpātor, ōris *m* flatterer.
palpebra, ae *f* (*usu. pl.*) eyelid.
palpitō 1 to quiver, throb.
(**palpō** *and*) **palpor** 1 to stroke, touch gently; to flatter
palpō, ōnis *m* flatterer.
palpum (*or* **-us**?), **ī** *n* a stroking, flattering.
palūdāmentum, ī *n* military cloak.
palūdātus 3 clothed in a military cloak.
palūdōsus 3 marshy, boggy.
palumbēs, is *m, f* (*and* **-us, ī** *m*) woodpigeon, ring-dove.
pālus[1], **ī** *m* stake.
palūs[2], **ūdis** *f* swamp, marsh, bog, pond, pool.
palūx, ūcis *f* = **balux.**
palūster, tris, tre marshy, swampy.
pampineus 3 of vine (shoots).
pampinus, ī *m* (*f*) shoot, tendril (of vines, &c.).
panaca, ae *f* wine-glass.
pan-acēa, ae *f* a plant said to heal all diseases; panacea.
pānāri(ol)um, ī *n* bread-basket.
pan-chrēstus 3 useful for everything.
pan-craticē like an athlete.
pan-cration *and* **-cratium, ī** *n* gymnastic contest (*wrestling and boxing*).
pandiculor 1 to stretch oneself.
pandō, pandī, passum 3 to extend, spread out; to open, throw open, disclose.
pandus 3 bent, curved.
pāne *n* = **panis.**
pan-ēgyricus, ī *m* eulogy.
pangō, pepigī (panxī), pāctum 3 to fasten, fix, drive in; **a**) to make, compose, write; **b**) to settle, agree upon, contract.
pāniceus 3 of bread.
pāniculus, ī *m* thatch.
pānicum, ī *n* wild millet.
pāni-ficium, ī *n* (the making of) bread, cakes.
pānis, is *m* bread, loaf.
pannāria, ōrum *n/pl.* presents of cloth.
panniculus, ī *m* small garment.
pannōsus 3 ragged; shrivelled.
pannūceus (*and* **-ius**) 3 tattered; shrivelled.
pannus, ī *m* piece of cloth, garment; rag, patch.
pānsa, ae *adj.* broad-footed.
pantex, icis *m* belly, bowels.
panthēra, ae *f* panther.
panthērīnus 3 like a panther; mottled(?).
panto-mīmicus 3 of a pantomimus.
panto-mīmus, ī *m*, **-mīma, ae** *f* dumb-show actor, actress.

panto-pōlium, ī *n* general store.
papae *int.* indeed! strange!
pāpās *m* father; tutor.
papāver, eris *n* (*and m*) poppy (seed).
papāvereus 3 of poppies.
pāpiliō, ōnis *m* butterfly, moth.
papilla, ae *f* nipple, teat, breast.
pappō 1 to eat.
pappus, ī *m* old man; (thistle) down.
papula, ae *f* pimple, pustule.
papȳri-fer 3 producing papyrus.
papȳrus, ī *f and* **-um, ī** *n* papyrus, paper-reed, paper.
pār, paris 1. equal, like, equally strong, a match; adequate, suitable, proper; **2.** *subst. m and f* comrade, mate; *n* a pair.
parābilis, e procurable.
para-bolē, ēs *f* comparison.
parārius, ī *m* agent, broker.
parasīta, ae *f* (female) parasite.
parasītaster, tri *m* mean parasite.
parasītātiō, ōnis *f* parasitism.
parasīticus 3 parasitic.
parasītor 1 to play the parasite.
para-sītus, ī *m* guest, parasite.
parātiō, ōnis *f* a procuring, striving after (*gen.*).
para-tragoedō 1 to speak in tragic style *or* pompously.
parātus[1] 3 **a**) prepared, ready, provided, furnished, fitted, equipped, skilled; easy; **b**) bought.
parātus[2], **ūs** *m* preparation, provision; outfit; clothing.
parce-prōmus 3 niggardly.
parcitās, ātis *f* sparingness.
parcō, peperci, (**parsūrus**) 3 **a**) to spare, be sparing, use moderately (*alci rei*); **b**) to preserve by sparing (*with dat.*); to abstain, forbear, leave off, desist, cease (*dat.*).
parcus 3 **a**) sparing, frugal, thrifty; moderate; scanty, small, little, slight; **b**) narrow-minded, niggardly.
pardus, ī *m* panther.
pārēns[1], **tis** obedient; *subst.* **pārentēs, ium** *m/pl.* subjects.
parēns[2], **tis** *m and f* parent, father, mother, *pl.* parents; **a**) ancestor, progenitor, *pl.* relations, kindred; **b**) father, founder, inventor, author.
parentālis, e a) of parents, parental; **b**) belonging to the festival in honour of dead parents; *subst.* **parentālia, ium** *n/pl.* festival in honour of dead parents.
parenti-cīda, ae *m* parricide.
parentō 1 to offer a sacrifice in honour of parents *or* relatives (*alci*); to revenge, appease, satisfy (*alci*).
pāreō, uī, (**pāritūrus**) 2 **1.** to appear, be visible; **pāret** it is clear, evident, manifest; **2.** to obey, be obedient; to submit to, comply with, gratify, yield (*alci*).
pāri-cīda, ae *m, see* **parricida.**
pariēs, etis *m* wall of a building.
parietinae, ārum *f/pl.* fallen walls, ruins.
parilis, e similar, like, equal.
pariō, peperī, partum (**paritūrus**) 3 **a**) to bring forth, bear, beget; **b**) to produce; **c**) to get, win, acquire, procure (*alqd; sibi alqd ab alqo*); to occasion; *subst.* **parta, ōrum** *n/pl.*acquisitions,possessions.
pariter *adv.* **a**) equally, in like manner, as well, alike; **b**) at the same time, together (~ *cum re*).
paritō 1 to prepare; to be about to (*inf.*).
parma, ae *f* small round shield, target.
parmātus 3 armed with a round shield.
parmula, ae *f* little round shield.
parmulārius, ī *m* partisan of gladiators armed with the *parmula.*
parō 1 to prepare, furnish, provide, contrive, design, dispose (*alqd; alci alqd*); **a**) to intend, be on the point of, be about, prepare oneself, make arrangements (*inf.*); **b**) to procure, acquire, get, obtain, buy.
par-ochus, ī *m* purveyor; host, entertainer.
par-opsis, idis *f* (dessert) dish.
parra, ae *f* owl.
parri-cīda, ae *m and f* **a**) parricide, murderer of a parent *or* near relative; **b**) traitor, rebel.
parricīdium, ī *n* **a**) murder of a parent *or* relation, of a citizen; **b**) high treason, rebellion.
pars, tis *f* part; **magnam, maximam partem** for the most part, in great part = **magnā, maximā ex parte; (ex) aliquā parte** to some extent; **omnī (ex) parte** entirely, in every respect; **a**) portion, share; **prō virīlī parte** to the best of one's abilities; **b**) part, place, region, district; **c**) direction,

relation, respect; **in utramque partem disputāre** for and against; **in omnēs partēs** in every respect; altogether; **d**) division, section, species, branch; **e**) party, faction, side; **f**) *pl.* part, character (*on the stage*); office, duty, function.

parsimōnia, ae *f* thriftiness, parsimony.

parthenicē, ēs *f* an unknown plant.

parti-ceps, cipis sharing, partaking (*with gen.*); *subst. m* sharer, partaker, partner.

participō 1 to give a share to (*alqm alcis rei*), to impart; to share with (*alqd cum alqo*); to partake of (*alqd*).

particula, ae *f* small part, little bit, particle.

particulātim piecemeal.

partim a) = **partem; b**) *adv.* partly; **c**) **partim ... partim** one part ... another part.

partiō, ōnis *f* a giving birth.

partior (*and* **partiō**) 4 **a**) to divide (*alqd in partes*); **b**) to distribute, apportion, share, part.

partītē *adv.* with proper divisions.

partītiō, ōnis *f* **a**) a sharing, partition; **b**) division; **c**) distribution.

partitūdō, inis *f* = **partio.**

parturiō 4 to be in travail *or* labour; **a**) to teem with; **b**) to be pregnant with, brood over, meditate (*alqd*); **c**) to be anxious *or* concerned.

partus, ūs *m* a bringing forth, bearing, birth; **a**) time of delivery; **b**) beginning; **c**) offspring, child, young one.

parum *adv.* too little, not enough, not sufficiently; *as subst.* a little, too little, not enough; *comp.* **minus** less; not at all, not; **non minus** no less, just as much; *superl.* **minimē** least of all, in the smallest degree; by no means, not at all.

parum-loquium, ī *n* talking too little.

parum-per *adv.* for a little while.

parvitās, ātis *f* smallness.

parvulus 3 very little *or* small, slight; very young; **a parvulo** *or* **-is** from childhood.

parvus 3 *adj.* little, small (*comp.* **minor, us,** *superl.* **minimus** 3); **a**) young; (**natu**) **minor** younger; **minimus** youngest; **b**) short, brief; **c**) insignificant, trifling, petty, unimportant; **d**) low, mean, poor; *subst.* **a**) **parvus, ī** *m* boy, child; **a parvo** *or* **-is** from childhood; **b**) **minōrēs, um** *m/pl.* descendants, posterity; **c**) **parvum, ī** *n* a little, trifle; *adv.* **minimum** very little.

pasceolus, ī *m* little money-bag.

pāscō, pāvī, pāstum 3 to feed, supply with food; **a**) to feed cattle, lead to pasture; **b**) to feed, nourish, maintain, support; to let grow, cultivate; to feast, satisfy, gratify; **c**) to use (land) as pasture; (of animals) to graze (on); **P. pāscor, pāstus sum** 3 **a**) to feed, eat, graze on, browse, to feed on; **b**) to feast oneself.

pāscuus 3 fit for pasture, for grazing; *subst.* **pāscua, ōrum** *n/pl.* pastures.

passer, eris *m* **a**) sparrow; **b**) a flat fish; **c**) ~ **marīnus** ostrich.

passerculus, ī *m* little sparrow.

passim *adv.* scattered about, here and there, far and wide, in every direction, confusedly, at random, promiscuously.

passum, ī *n* raisin-wine.

passus 3 (*pf. part. P.* of **pandō**) spread out; dried; curdled.

passus, ūs *m* step, stride, pace; footstep.

pāstillus, ī *m* lozenge, pastille.

pāstiō, ōnis *f* a pasturing, pasture.

pāstor, ōris *m* herdsman, shepherd.

pāstōrālis, e *and* **pāstōricius** 3 (*also* **pāstōrius** 3) relating to a shepherd, pastoral.

pāstus, ūs *m* food, pasture.

patagiārius, ī *m* maker of fringes.

patagiātus 3 furnished with fringes.

pate-faciō 3 to open, throw open; to make visible, disclose, expose, display, reveal, detect.

patefactiō, ōnis *f* a throwing open.

patella, ae *f* pan, dish, platter; sacrificial dish.

patellāriī dī platter-gods, Lares.

patēns, tis open, unobstructed, accessible, passable; evident.

pateō, uī, — 2 to be open, stand open, lie open to (*alci*); **a**) to be accessible *or* passable; **b**) to stretch out, extend; **c**) to be exposed to; **d**) to be visible, manifest.

pater, tris *m* father, *pl.* fathers, parents, forefathers; **a**) *pl.* senators; **b**) creator, author, chief, head.

patera, ae *f* sacrificial dish.
paternus 3 fatherly, paternal; native, ancestral.
patēscō, tuī, — 3 to be opened, lie open; **a**) to extend; **b**) to become visible *or* manifest.
pathicus 3 submitting to unnatural lust; licentious.
patibilis, e a) endurable, tolerable; **b**) sensitive.
patibulātus 3 fastened on a gallows, crucified.
patibulum, ī *n* gibbet, gallows, cross.
patiēns, tis bearing, enduring, suffering (*with gen.*); **a**) patient; **b**) firm, hard, unyielding.
patientia, ae *f* endurance, patience; **a**) perseverance; **b**) want; of spirit; **c**) forbearance, indulgence; **d**) submission to lust; humility, subjection.
patina, ae *f* dish, pan.
patinārius 3 pertaining to a dish.
patiō (*archaic*) = **patior.**
patior, passus sum 3 to suffer, bear, endure, undergo; to allow, permit, let (*alqd; with acc.c.inf.; ut*); to submit to lust.
qatrātor, ōris *m* accomplisher, achiever.
patrātus, ī *m, see* **patro.**
patria, ae *f* fatherland, native land, native town, home.
patricē *adv.* in a fatherly manner.
patriciātus, ūs *m* the status of patrician.
patricius 3 patrician, noble; *subst.* **~, ī** *m* a patrician, nobleman.
patrimōnium, ī *n* inherited property, inheritance, patrimony, estate.
patrīmus (*and* **īmus**) 3 whose father still lives.
patrissō 1 to be like one's father.
patrītus 3 paternal.
patrius 3 of a father, paternal; inherited, ancestral; relating to one's country.
patrō 1 to accomplish, achieve, perform, execute; **pater patrātus** *m* the chief of the fetiales.
patrōcinium, ī *n* **a**) protection, defence, patronage; **b**) defence in a court of law.
patrōcinor 1 to protect, defend.
patrōna, ae *f* protectress, patroness.
patrōnus, ī *m* **a**) protector, defender, patron; **b**) advocate before a court of justice.
patruēlis, e of a father's brother; of a cousin; *m* cousin.
patruus, ī *m* a father's brother, paternal uncle; severe censor; *adj.* 3 of an uncle.
patulus 3 standing open; spreading; extended.
pauci-loquium, ī *n* talking little.
paucitās, ātis *f* small number, fewness.
pauculī 3 very few.
paucus 3 **a**) small; **b**) *pl.* few, a few; a select few; **c**) **pauca** *n/pl.* a few things, little, a few words.
paul(l)ātim *adv.* gradually, little by little.
paul(l)īs-per *adv.* a little while.
paul(l)ulus 3, *dim. of* **paul(l)us.**
paul(l)us 3 small, little; *subst.* **paulum, ī** *n* a little, trifle, a little while; **paulō post** a little later.
pauper, eris poor, not wealthy; scanty, meagre; *subst. m* a poor man.
pauperculus 3 poor.
pauperiēs, ēī *f* = **paupertas.**
pauperō 1 to impoverish.
paupertās, ātis *f* poverty.
pausa, ae *f* pause, cessation, end.
pausārius, ī *m* time-keeper for rowers.
pausea *and* **-ia, ae** *f* a kind of olive.
pauxillātim *adv.* gradually.
pauxillīs-per *adv.* in a very little time.
pauxill(ul)us 3 very small.
pave-factus 3 frightened, alarmed.
paveō, —, — 2 to tremble, quake with fear, be afraid, terrified.
pavēscō, —, — 3 = **paveo.**
pavidus 3 **a**) quaking, frightened, excited; **b**) causing fear, making timorous.
pavīmentātus 3 furnished with a pavement.
pavīmentum, ī *n* pavement.
paviō 4 to beat, strike.
pavitō 1 to tremble with fear (at).
pāvō, ōnis (*and* **pāvus, ī**) *m* peacock.
pāvōnīnus 3 made of, *or* coloured like, a peacock's tail.
pavor, ōris *m* a trembling, quaking, terror, fear, dread; excitement.
pāx, pācis *f* peace; treaty of peace, time of peace; **pāce tuā** with your good leave; **a**) goddess of peace; **b**) peace of mind, tranquillity; assistance *or* favour (*of the gods*).

P.C. = **patres conscripti.**
peccātum, ī *n* (*and* **-us, ūs** *m*) fault, error, sin, transgression, crime.
peccō 1 to commit a fault, to sin, transgress, offend (*alqd; in re; in alqm*); to go wrong, *or* astray.
pecorōsus 3 abounding in cattle.
pecten, inis *m* comb; **a**) reed (i.e. toothed bar) of a loom; loom; weaver's shuttle (?); comb for carding wool, &c.; **b**) a kind of shell-fish; **c**) quill for striking the strings of a lyre; **d**) rake; **e**) a kind of dance.
pectō, pexī, pexum 3 to comb (hair, wool, flax, .&c.).
pectus, oris *n* breast; **a**) heart, soul, courage, feelings; **b**) mind, understanding, character.
pecū *plur.* **pecua** *n* **a**) flocks, herds; **b**) money.
pecuārius 3 of cattle *or* sheep; *subst.* **a**) **~, ī** *m* cattle-breeder, grazier; **b**) **-ia, ae** *f* cattle-breeding; **c**) **-ia, ōrum** *n/pl.* herds of cattle *or* sheep.
pecūlātor, ōris *m* embezzler of public money.
pecūlātus, ūs *m* embezzlement of public money.
pecūliāris, e as private property, one's own; special.
pecūliātus 3 provided with money.
pecūliō 1 to give a present to.
pecūliōsus 3 possessing savings.
pecūlium, ī *n* savings, personal property (of slaves, *or* other members of a household;) small sum of money.
pecūnia, ae *f* **a**) property (*in cattle*), riches, wealth; **b**) money.
pecūniārius 3 relating to money, pecuniary.
pecūniōsus 3 rich, wealthy.
pecus[1], **oris** *n* cattle, swine, sheep; flock.
pecus[2], **udis** *f* domestic animal (head of cattle, sheep &c.); wild animal; brute (as term of abuse).
pedālis, e of the length *or* breadth of a foot.
pedārius (**senator**) senator of inferior rank.
pedātus[1], **ūs** *m* an advance, attack.
pedātus[2] 3 provided with feet.
pedes, itis *m* walker; (*as adj.*) on foot; foot-soldier, infantry.
pedester, tris, tre on foot, pedestrian; **a**) of infantry, on land; **b**) simple, plain; in prose, prosaic.
pede-temptim *adv.* step by step; slowly; cautiously.
pedica, ae *f* fetter, snare.
pēdis, is *m and f* louse.
pedi-sequus, ī *m and* **-a, ae** *f* servant, attendant, lackey, footman, waiting-woman.
peditāstellus, ī *m* poor little infantryman.
peditātus, ūs *m* infantry.
pēdō, pepēdī, pēditum 3 to break wind.
pēdor, ōris *m* = **paedor.**
pedum, ī *n* a shepherd's crook.
pēgma, atis *n* **a**) book-case, shelf; **b**) stage machine, movable platform.
peii..., *see* **peri...**
pē-i(i)erō 1 to swear falsely, forswear oneself; **iūs pēierātum** false oath.
pēior, pēius, *see* **malus.**
pelagius 3 relating to the sea, of the sea.
pelagus, ī *n* (*plur.* **-gē**) the open sea, ocean.
pēlamys, ydis *f* young tunny-fish.
pēlex, icis *f* = **paelex.**
pell-, *see also* **perl-.**
pellācia, ae *f* enticement.
pellāx, ācis deceitful.
pellecebrae, ārum *f/pl.* inducements.
pel-lēctiō, ōnis *f* a reading through, perusal.
pel-legō = **perlego.**
pel-liciō, lexī, lectum 3 to allure, entice, seduce, decoy; to win over.
pellicula, ae *f* small skin *or* hide.
pelliō, ōnis *m* furrier, skinner.
pellis, is *f* hide, skin, felt, pelt; leather, leather cover, leather tent.
pellītus 3 clothed in hides.
pellō, pepulī, pulsum 3 to set in motion, strike, push; **a**) to beat, knock (*alqd*); **b**) to move, touch, make an impression on; **c**) to drive out *or* away, expel; to put to flight, drive back; to banish.
pelōris, idis *f* giant mussel.
pelta, ae *f* light crescent-shaped shield.
peltastēs, ae *m* soldier armed with the *pelta.*
peltātus (*and* **pelti-fer**) 3 armed with the *pelta.*

pelvis, is *f* basin.
penārius 3 relating to provisions.
penātēs, ium *m/pl.* the Penates (*guardian gods of the household store-cupboard and the state stores*); a dwelling, home.
penāti-ger 3 carrying the Penates.
pendeō, pependī, — 2 **a**) to hang, hang down (*in, ex, ab, de re*); **b**) to be flabby, weak; **c**) to hover, be suspended *or* poised; **d**) to depend upon (*re, ex re*); **e**) to be in suspense, undecided, unfinished; to be ready to fall.
pendō, pependī, pēnsum 3 to suspend; **a**) to weigh, weigh out; to pay (out); **b**) to ponder, consider; **c**) to value, esteem (*alqd magni, parvi,* &c.); **d**) to have a certain weight; — **pēnsus** 3 weighed, valued; **nihil pēnsī habēre** to attach no value to, care nothing about; **pēnsum, ī** *n* portion (*of wool*) weighed out, day's work, task.
pendulus 3 hanging down; in suspense.
penes *prep.* with *acc.* **a**) in the possession *or* power of; **b**) belonging to, with.
penetrābilis, e penetrable; piercing.
penetrālis, e a) inward, inner, internal; **penetrāle, is** *n* (*mostly pl.* **-ālia, ium**) inner part, inner room, secret place, sanctuary; **b**) piercing.
penetrō 1 **a**) to set *or* place in; to enter, penetrate, betake (oneself) (*in, ad alqd*); **b**) *trans.* to pierce, to penetrate.
pēnicillus, ī *m* (*and* **-um, ī** *n*) painter's brush.
pēniculus, ī *m* **a**) brush; **b**) sponge; **c**) thatch (?).
pēnis, is *m* tail; the penis; lust.
penitus[1] 3 inner, inmost.
penitus[2] (*also* **-tē**) *adv.* inwardly, internally, deeply; **a**) far within; **b**) accurately, thoroughly; **c**) wholly, entirely.
penna, ae *f* feather; **a**) wing; plumage; **b**) flight; **c**) (feather on an) arrow.
pennātus 3 winged.
penni-ger 3 feathered, winged.
penni-pēs, edis wing-footed.
penni-potēns, entis winged.
pēnsilis, e hanging, suspended.
pēnsiō, ōnis *f* a paying, payment; instalment; rent.
pēnsitō 1 to weigh out; **a**) to weigh, consider, think over; **b**) to pay (*alci alqd*).
pēnsō 1 to weigh, weigh out; **a**) to compare; **b**) to counterbalance, compensate, repay, requite, atone for (*alqd re*); **c**) to ponder, consider, examine, judge (*alqd ex re*).
pēnsum *and* **pēnsus,** *see* **pendo.**
pentēris, idis *f* = **quinqueremis.**
penuārius, see **penarius.**
pēnūria, ae *f* want, scarcity.
penus, oris *n and* **penus, ūs** *f and* **ī** *m or* **penum, ī** *n* provisions, victuals, store of food.
peplum, ī *n and* **-us, ī** *m* robe of state of Athene at Athens.
per *prep.* with *acc.* **1.** (*of space*) through, through the midst of, throughout, along, over (*per medios hostes, per Alpes proficisci, vigiles disponere per urbem, per oram, per muros, per municipia; per manus tradere* from hand to hand; *cives per domus invitati* from house to house); **2.** (*of time*) through, during, in the course of, within (*per idem tempus, multos per annos, per noctem*); **3.** (*of agency*) a) through, by, by means of, by the hands of, by the agency of (*per speculatores cognoscere, per servum nuntiare; per se* in person, alone, for oneself); b) under pretence of, by the pretext of, in the name of (*per fidem fallere, decipere aliquem per indutias*); c) (*in entreaties, oaths*) *per deos immortales* by the immortal gods; d) for, for the sake of, on account of, by, as far as concerns (*per metum, per ambitionem; per leges non licet, per me licet*); e) (*of manner*) by, through, with, in (*per vim* violently, *per iocum* in sport, *per iniuriam, per dolum, per speciem*).
pēra, ae *f* bag, wallet.
per-absurdus 3 very absurd.
per-accommodātus 3 very convenient.
per-ācer, cris, cre very sharp.
per-acerbus 3 very harsh.
per-acēscō, acuī, — 3 to become much vexed.
per-āctiō, ōnis *f* a finishing, completion.
per-acūtus 3 very sharp, clear.
per-adulēscēns, tis *and* **peradulēscentulus, ī** *m* very young (man).

per-aequē *adv.* equally.
per-agitō 1 to harass; to excite.
per-agō 3 **1.** to pierce through; **2.** to drive about, harass; a) to stir up, cultivate; b) to bring to an end, complete, finish, accomplish; to pass through, traverse; to live through, pass (*a time*); to play (*a part*) through; to prosecute till a conviction is obtained; c) to set forth, go through, go over.
per-agrātiō, ōnis *f* travelling.
per-agrō 1 to go over, travel through, traverse.
per-amāns, tis very loving.
per-ambulō 1 to travel through.
per-amoenus 3 very pleasant.
per-amplus 3 very large.
per-angustus 3 very narrow.
per-annō 1 to live through a year.
per-antīquus 3 very old.
per-appositus 3 very fit *or* suitable.
per-arduus 3 very difficult.
per-argūtus 3 very acute *or* clever.
per-armātus 3 well-armed.
per-arō 1 to furrow; to write down; to write on.
pērātus 3 in a wallet.
per-attentus 3 very attentive.
per-audiendus 3 that must be heard to the end.
per-bacchor 1 to revel through.
per-beātus 3 very happy.
per-bellē *adv.* very prettily.
per-bene *adv.* very well.
per-benevolus 3 very friendly.
per-benignē *adv.* very kindly.
per-bibō 3 to drink up, swallow.
per-bītō 3 to perish.
per-blandus 3 very charming.
per-bonus 3 very good.
per-brevis, e very short.
perca, ae *f* perch (the fish).
per-calefactus thoroughly warmed.
(**per-calēscō** 3) **-caluī** to become heated through.
(**per-callēscō** 3) **-calluī** a) to become quite hardened; **b**) to get to know thoroughly.
per-cārus 3 very dear.
per-cautus 3 very cautious.
per-celebrō 1 to speak of frequently.
per-celer, is, e very swift, sudden.
per-cellō, culī, culsum 3 to strike, hit, beat; **a**) to throw down, strike down, overthrow, shatter; **b**) to ruin, destroy; to scare, unnerve; **c**) to thrill.
per-cēnseō 2 **a**) to count through *or* over, to enumerate; **b**) to survey, review, examine; **c**) to judge, criticize; **d**) to travel through.
perceptiō, ōnis *f* gathering, harvesting; comprehension; concept.
per-cīdō 3 to strike, beat; to cut to pieces.
per-cieō 2 (*and* **-ciō** 4) to stir, excite; **percitus** 3 **a**) aroused, excited; **b**) excitable, irritable.
per-cipiō, cēpī, ceptum 3 to seize, lay hold of, catch; **a**) to take to oneself, assume; **b**) to get, receive, gather, harvest; **c**) to perceive, be sensible of, hear, feel; **d**) to learn, know, comprehend, understand; — *subst.* **perceptum, ī** *n* principle, rule.
per-cīvīlis, e very polite, courteous.
per-cognōscō 3 to become acquainted with thoroughly.
per-cōlō 1 to allow to pass through.
per-colō 3 to adorn, honour exceedingly, crown.
per-cōmis, e very friendly.
per-commodus 3 very convenient *or* suitable.
per-cōnor 1 to persist in effort.
percontātiō, ōnis *f* inquiry.
percontātor, ōris *m* inquirer.
per-contor 1 to ask, inquire, question (*alqd ab, ex alqo; alqm de re; alqm alqd*).
per-contumāx, ācis very obstinate.
per-cōpiōsus 3 full of invention.
per-coquō 3 to cook *or* heat thoroughly; to ripen; to scorch.
per-crēb(r)ēscō, b(r)uī, — 3 to become very frequent, spread abroad.
per-crepō 1 to resound, ring with.
per-crucior 1 to be in great auxiety.
per-cunctor 1 = **percontor.**
per-cupidus 3 very fond of.
per-cupiō 3 to desire greatly.
per-cūriōsus 3 very inquisitive.
per-cūrō 1 to heal thoroughly.
per-currō, (cu)currī, cursum 3 **a**) to run along *or* over, to traverse; to run *or* hasten through, run over.
per-cursātiō, ōnis *f* a running *or* travelling through.
per-cursiō, ōnis *f* a running through, rapid survey.

per-cursō 1 to wander about.
percussiō, ōnis *f* a) a striking against, beating; **b**) measure of time, a beating time.
percussor, ōris *m* murderer.
percussus, ūs *m* = **percussio.**
per-cutiō, cussī, cussum 3 **a**) to strike through, pierce, cut (*alqd re*); **b**) to strike, beat, hit; **c**) to wound, kill, slay; to execute, behead; **d**) to affect, move, shock, astound.
per-decōrus 3 very seemly *or* becoming.
per-dēlīrus 3 very foolish.
per-depsō 3 to knead well.
per-difficilis, e very difficult.
per-dīgnus 3 very worthy.
per-dīligēns, tis very careful.
per-discō 3 to learn thoroughly.
per-disertē *adv.* very eloquently.
perditor, ōris *m* ruiner, destroyer.
perditus, ūs *m* ruin.
per-diū *adv.* a very long time.
per-diuturnus 3 lasting very long.
per-dīves, itis very rich.
perdīx, īcis *f* partridge.
per-dō, didī, ditum 3 to destroy, ruin, undo; **a**) to waste, squander; **b**) to throw away, lose; — **perditus** 3 lost, ruined, wretched, miserable, desperate, hopeless; immoderate; abandoned, profligate, incorrigible.
per-doceō 1 to teach *or* instruct thoroughly.
per-doctus 3 very learned.
per-dolēscō, luī, — 3 to feel great pain *or* grief.
per-domō 1 to tame thoroughly; to subdue thoroughly.
per-dormīscō 3 to sleep through.
per-dūcō 3 **1.** to lead *or* bring to (*alqd ad* or *in alqd*); a) to seduce (*a woman*); b) to carry on, continue, prolong; c) to persuade, induce, win over; **2.** to spread over, smear over (*alqd re*).
per-ductō 1 to lead to *or* round.
per-ductor, ōris *m* a) guide; **b**) pander.
per-dūdum *adv.* very long ago.
per-duelliō, ōnis *f* high-treason.
per-duellis, is *m* enemy.
perduim, perduint, *subj. of* **perdo.**
per-dūrō 1 to last, endure.
per-edō 3 to eat up, consume, devour.
per-egrē *and* **-ī** *adv.* **a**) away from home, abroad, in a foreign country; from abroad; **b**) to foreign parts.
peregrīnābundus 3 travelling about.
peregrīnātiō, ōnis *f* sojourn abroad, travelling.
peregrīnātor, ōris *m* habitual traveller.
peregrīnitās, ātis *f* foreign manners and customs; the status of a foreigner.
peregrīnor 1 to be *or* live abroad, to travel about; to be a stranger, alien, foreigner.
peregrīnus 3 **a**) foreign, strange, *subst.* **~, ī** *m* foreigner, stranger, alien; **b**) unversed, inexperienced in.
per-ēlegāns, tis very pretty, neat, elegant.
per-ēloquēns, tis very eloquent.
per-emnia, ium *n/pl.* auspices taken on crossing a river *or* spring.
per-ēmptor, ōris *m* killer.
perendiē *adv.* on the day after to-morrow.
perendinus 3 after to-morrow.
per-ennis, e lasting throughout the year; lasting, everlasting, ever-flowing; unceasing, perpetual.
perenni-servus, ī *m* slave for life-time.
perennitās, ātis *f* duration, continuance.
perennō 1 to last, endure.
per-eō, iī, itum, īre to pass away, be lost, perish, die; **a**) to be desperately in love (with *acc.* or *abl.*); **b**) to be wasted, spent in vain.
per-equitō 1 to ride through, ride about.
per-errō 1 to wander through, roam over, look over.
per-ērudītus 3 very learned.
per-excelsus 3 very high.
per-exiguus 3 very small, very little, very short.
per-expedītus 3 very easy.
per-fabricō 1 to deceive, cheat.
per-facētus 3 very witty.
per-facilis, e very easy; very willing.
per-familiāris, e very intimate, familiar; *m* intimate friend.
perfectiō, ōnis *f* perfection, completion.
perfector, ōris *m* one who perfects.
perfectus 3 perfect, complete, finished.
per-ferō 3 to carry through, bear *or* bring to a certain place (*alqd ad* or *in alqd*); **a**) to bring, convey;

b) to bring news, announce; c) to bring to an end, carry out, complete, accomplish, to carry through (*legem*); d) to bear, suffer, endure.

per-fica, ae *f adj.* perfecting.

per-ficiō, fēcī, fectum 3 to complete; a) to make perfect, bring about, effect, execute, carry out, accomplish, achieve; b) to finish, bring to an end; c) to carry through, cause.

per-fidēlis e very faithful.

perfidia ae *f* faithlessness, perfidy, treachery.

perfidiōsus 3 = **perfidus.**

per-fidus 3 faithless, perfidious, treacherous.

per-fīgō 3 to pierce.

per-flābilis, e that can be blown through.

per-flāgitiōsus 3 very shameful.

per-flō 1 to blow through, blow over.

per-fluctuō 1 to surge through.

per-fluō 3 to flow to waste, leak out.

per-fodiō 3 to dig through, pierce through, perforate.

per-forō 1 to bore *or* pierce through.

per-fortiter very bravely.

per-fossor, ōris *m* housebreaker.

per-fremō 3 to roar *or* snort along.

per-frequēns, tis much visited, frequented.

per-fricō 1 to rub over, scratch; **ōs** to lay aside shame.

per-frīgefaciō 3 to make very cold, to terrify.

per-frīgēscō, frīxī 3 to catch cold.

per-frīgidus 3 very cold.

per-fringō, frēgī, frāctum 3 to break through; a) to break to pieces, shiver, shatter; b) to violate; c) to overpower.

per-fruor 3 to enjoy fully (*abl.*).

per-fuga, ae *m* deserter, fugitive.

per-fugiō 3 to flee away, to flee for refuge; to go over, desert.

perfugium, ī *n* place of refuge, asylum, shelter.

per-fūnctiō, ōnis *f* a performing, discharging.

per-fundō 3 a) to soak, wet, flood, dye (*alqd re*); b) to besprinkle, bathe, anoint; c) to bestrew, scatter over; d) to inspire, fill, imbue

per-fungor 3 to perform, discharge, accomplish, execute (*abl.*); a) to undergo, endure; b) to come to the end of.

per-furō 3 to rage on furiously (through, *acc.*).

per-fūsōrius 3 a) superficial; b) trumped-up, vexatious.

per-gaudeō 2 to be very glad.

pergō, perrēxī, perrēctum 3 to continue, proceed with, go on (*alqd; inf.*); a) to (continue to) speak; b) to proceed, go, march.

per-graecor 1 to revel in Greek fashion.

per-grandis, e very large, very great, very old.

per-graphicus 3 very artful.

per-grātus 3 very pleasant, very agreeable.

per-gravis, e very heavy; very important.

pergula, ae *f* shed, loggia; observatory, school; brothel.

per-hauriō 4 to devour greedily.

per-hibeō 2 to bring forward, adduce; to say, assert (*alqd; acc.c.inf.*).

perhīlum *adv.* very little.

per-honōrificus 3 very honourable; very respectful.

per-horrēscō 3 to shudder, shake with terror; to shudder at (*alqd*).

per-horridus 3 very dreadful.

per-hūmānus 3 very kind; *adv.* **-niter.**

perīclitātiō, ōnis *f* experiment.

perīclitor 1 to try, test; a) to risk, hazard, endanger; b) to be in danger, run risk.

perīculōsus 3 dangerous, perilous, hazardous, threatening.

perīculum (*and* **perīclum**), **ī** *n* **1.** trial, experiment, test; **perīculum facere alcis rei** to make a trial of, experience; attempt in authorship, essay; **2.** a) danger, peril, risk, hazard, dangerous deed; b) trial, action, suit; c) judicial record, register.

per-idōneus 3 very suitable.

perierātiuncula, ae *f* a little false swearing.

per-ierō 1, *see* **peiero.**

per-illūstris, e very evident; very distinguished.

per-imbēcillus 3 very weak.

per-imō, ēmī, ēmptum 3 a) to destroy, annihilate, to kill; b) to prevent, frustrate.

per-impedītus 3 very much obstructed.

per-incommodus 3 very inconvenient, very troublesome.

per-inde *adv.* in the same manner; **perinde ac** *or* **ut** *or* **quam** just as.
per-indīgnē *adv.* very indignantly.
per-indulgēns, tis very indulgent.
per-īnfāmis, e very infamous.
per-īnfirmus 3 very weak.
per-ingeniōsus 3 very clever.
per-ingrātus 3 very ungrateful.
per-iniquus 3 **a**) very unfair; **b**) very much upset, displeased.
per-īnsignis, e very conspicuous *or* remarkable.
per-invalidus 3 very weak.
per-invīsus 3 much hated.
per-invītus 3 very unwilling.
peri-odus, ī *f* (rhetorical) period.
peri-patēticus 3 Peripatetic, Aristotelian.
peri-petasma, atis *n* = **peri-stroma.**
peri-phrasis, is *f* circumlocution.
per-īrātus 3 very angry.
peri-scelis, idis *f* knee-band, garter.
peri-strōma, atis *n* coverlet curtain, carpet.
peri-stȳl(i)um, ī *n* court surrounded by a colonnade, peristyle.
perītia, ae *f* experience, knowledge, skill.
perītus 3 experienced, skilled, practised, expert, trained (with *gen.* or *abl., ad alqd, de re*).
per-iūcundus 3 very agreeable.
per-iūriōsus 3 full of perjury.
per-iūrium, ī *n* perjury.
per-iūrō = **peiero.**
per-iūrus 3 perjured, lying.
perl..., *see also* **pell...**
per-labor 3 to glide over *or* through; to travel, make one's way.
per-laetus 3 very joyful.
per-lātē *adv.* very widely.
per-lateō 2 to remain hidden.
per-lātus 3, *part. of* **perfero.**
per-lēctiō, ōnis *f* perusal.
per-legō 3 to survey thoroughly, examine all over; to read through, peruse.
per-lepidē very nicely.
per-levis, e very (s)light.
per-libēns, tis very willing.
per-līberālis, e well-bred; *adv.* **-iter** very liberally, graciously.
per-lībrō 1 **a**) to weigh; **b**) to whirl, hurl.
per-liciō 3 = **pellicio.**
per-litō 1 to sacrifice with favourable omens.
per-longinquus 3 very lengthy.
per-longus 3 very long, tedious; *adv.* **-gē** very far.
per-lubēns, tis = **perlibens.**
per-lubet it pleases much.
per-lūceō 2 to shine through; to be transparent, clear.
per-lūcidulus 3 transparent.
per-lūcidus 3 translucent; very bright.
per-lūctuōsus 3 very mournful.
per-luō 3 to wash off, bathe.
per-lūstrō 1 to wander through; to examine, survey.
per-madefaciō 3 to drench.
per-madēscō, maduī 3 to become wet *or* soft.
per-magnus 3 very great.
per-male *adv.* very badly.
per-mānanter *adv.* by flowing through.
per-mānāscō 3 to flow through.
per-maneō 2 to remain, stay, abide (*in re*); **a**) to endure, continue; **b**) to persist.
per-mānō 1 to flow through *or* to (*in* or *ad alqd*); to penetrate.
per-mānsiō, ōnis *f* a remaining.
per-marīnus 3 accompanying through the sea.
per-mātūrēscō, ruī, — 3 to become quite ripe.
per-mediocris, e very moderate.
per-meditātus 3 well prepared *or* trained.
per-meō 1 to go through, pass through *or* over; to penetrate.
per-mereō 2 to perform military service (in a country, *acc.*).
per-mētior 4 to measure out; to traverse.
per-mingō, minxī, — 3 to make water upon, defile.
per-mīrus 3 very wonderful.
per-misceō 2 to mix together, intermingle; **a**) to throw into confusion; **b**) to unite.
per-missiō, ōnis *f* leave, permission; surrender.
per-missū *m, only abl.* by permission (of ...).
permitiālis, e destructive.
permitiēs, *f* ruin.
per-mittō 3 to let go, let loose; **equum, se permittere** to gallop, rush; **a**) to give up, yield, leave, surrender, intrust, commit (*alci alqd*); to use without restraint; **b**)

to sacrifice; **c**) to permit, allow, grant (*ut; inf.*); **permissum, ī** *n* permission.
permixtē *and* **-tim** *adv.* confusedly.
per-mixtiō, ōnis *f* a mixing together, mixture; confusion.
per-modestus 3 very modest, very moderate.
per-modicus 3 very small.
per-molestus 3 very troublesome; *adv.* **-tē** with much vexation.
per-molō 3 to grind; to debauch.
per-mōtiō, ōnis *f* movement, agitation; emotion.
per-moveō 2 to move thoroughly, excite, rouse; **a**) to induce, influence, prevail on; **b**) to agitate, disturb.
per-mulceō 2 **a**) to stroke, touch gently; **b**) to flatter, please, charm; **c**) to soothe, appease, soften.
per-multus 3 very much, very many.
per-mūniō 4 to fortify completely; to finish fortifying.
per-mūtātiō, ōnis *f* change, alteration; exchange.
per-mūtō 1 to change, alter; to exchange.
perna, ae *f* leg of pork, ham.
per-necessārius 3 **a**) very necessary; **b**) very intimate.
per-necesse est it is very necessary.
per-negō 1 to deny obstinately.
per-neō 2 to spin to an end.
perniciābilis, e = **perniciosus.**
per-niciēs, ēī *f* destruction, ruin, death.
perniciōsus 3 destructive, ruinous, pernicious, dangerous.
pernīcitās, ātis *f* swiftness, briskness.
per-niger 3 quite black.
per-nimium *adv.* too much, very much.
pernīx, īcis swift, brisk, nimble.
per-nōbilis, e very famous.
per-noctō 1 to pass the night.
pernōnidēs, ae *m* son of a ham.
per-nōscō 3 to learn throughly, become thoroughly acquainted with.
per-nōtēscō, tuī, — 3 to become generally known.
per-nōtus 3 well known.
per-nox, ctis through the night.
pernula, ae *f* = **perna.**
per-numerō 1 to count out.
pērō, ōnis *m* rustic boot.
per-obscūrus 3 very obscure.
per-odiōsus 3 very annoying.
per-officiōsē *adv.* very courteously.
per-oleō 2 to emit a penetrating odour.
pērōnātus 3 wearing the *pero.*
per-opportūnus 3 very seasonable, convenient.
per-optātō *adv.* very much to one's wish.
per-opus *indecl.* very necessary.
per-ōrātiō, ōnis *f* conclusion of a speech, peroration.
per-ōrnō 1 to adorn much.
per-ōrō 1 to speak to the end, plead throughout; to end, conclude, finish.
per-ōsculor 1 to kiss repeatedly.
per-ōsus 3 hating (*acc.*).
per-pācō 1 to pacify completely.
per-parcē *adv.* very sparingly.
per-parvulus 3 very small.
per-parvus 3 very little.
per-pāstus 3 well fed.
per-paucī 3 very few.
per-pauculī 3 very few.
per-paul(l)um, ī *n* a very little.
per-pauper, eris very poor.
per-pauxillum, ī *n* a very little.
per-pavefaciō 3 to terrify.
per-pellō 3 to drive on, urge, compel, prevail upon (*alqm; ut, ne*).
perpendiculum, ī *n* plumb-line.
per-pendō, pendī, pēnsum 3 to weigh carefully.
perperam *adv.* wrongly, falsely, untruly.
perpes, petis uninterrupted.
perpessīcius 3 patient.
perpessiō, ōnis *f* a suffering.
per-petior, pessus sum 3 to bear *or* suffer steadfastly.
per-petrō 1 to complete, achieve, effect, execute, perform.
perpetuārius 3 continually at work.
perpetuitās, ātis *f* uninterrupted duration, continuity, succession.
perpetuō[1] 1 to cause to continue, perpetuate.
perpetuō[2] *adv.* uninterruptedly, for ever.
perpetuus 3 **a**) uninterrupted, continuous, whole, entire; **b**) constant, perpetual, lasting, permanent; **in perpetuum** for ever; **c**) universal, general.

per-placeō 2 to please greatly.
perplexābilis, e obscure.
per-plexor 1 to cause confusion.
per-plexus 3 entangled, intricate, involved, confused; ambiguous, obscure; *adv.* **-xē** *and* **-xim.**
per-plicātus 3 entangled.
per-pluō 3 to let the rain through; to pour itself into.
per-poliō 4 to polish thoroughly, to make perfect; **perpolītus** 3 accomplished, refined.
per-populor 1 to ravage *or* devastate completely.
per-pōtātiō, ōnis *f* drinking-bout.
per-pōtō 1 to continue drinking; to drink off (*alqd*).
per-primō, pressī, pressum 3 to press hard *or* continually.
per-propinquus 3 very nearly related.
per-prūrīscō 3 to itch all over.
per-pugnāx, ācis very pugnacious.
per-pulcher 3 very beautiful.
per-pūr(i)gō 1 to cleanse thoroughly; **a**) to clear up, explain; **b**) to confute, refute.
per-pusillus 3 very small, very little.
per-putō 1 to explain.
per-quam *adv.* exceedingly.
per-quīrō, quīsīvī, quīsītum 3 to search for eagerly, inquire diligently, examine.
per-quīsītius *comp. adv.* more critically.
per-quīsītor, ōris *m* seeker out.
per-rārus 3 very rare.
per-reconditus 3 very hidden.
per-rēpō 3 to creep along.
per-rēptō 1 to crawl (over).
per-rīdiculus 3 very ridiculous.
per-rogātiō, ōnis *f* enactment of a law.
per-rogō 1 to ask in succession (*alqd*).
per-rumpō 3 to break through, force a way through; to shatter; to overcome.
per-saepe *adv.* very often.
per-salsus 3 very witty.
per-salūtātiō, ōnis *f* general salutation.
per-salūtō 1 to greet in succession.
per-sānctē 3 very solemnly.
per-sapiēns, tis very wise.
per-scienter *adv.* very knowingly.
per-scindō 3 to tear to pieces.
per-scītus 3 very clever.
per-scrībō 3 to write down explicitly, at length; **a**) to note down, enter in a register, to record; **b**) to enter in an account-book; **c**) to assign money by writing, pay by draft; **d**) to announce, recount, detail.
per-scrīptiō, ōnis *f* a writing down, entry; draft (of money).
per-scrīptor, ōris *m* book-keeper.
per-scrūtātiō, ōnis *f* a searching.
per-scrūtor (*and* **-ō**) 1 to search through, examine.
per-secō 1 **a**) to dissect, lay bare; **b**) to cut out.
per-sector 1 **a**) to pursue; **b**) to investigate.
per-sedeō 2 to sit continuously.
per-sēgnis, e very sluggish *or* inactive.
per-sentiō 4 to feel deeply; to perceive distinctly.
per-sentīscō 3 = **persentiō.**
per-sequor 3 to follow constantly, follow after, pursue (*acc.*); to press upon, chase; **a**) to pursue hostilely, punish; **b**) to prosecute judicially; **c**) to note down, record, register; **d**) to pursue eagerly; to busy oneself with; **e**) to imitate, copy, be a follower of; **f**) to search over *or* through; **g**) to continue, carry on, carry out, perform, execute, accomplish; **h**) catch up, overtake; **i**) to set forth, relate, expound, describe, explain.
persevērāns, tis, persistent, persevering.
persevērantia, ae *f* perseverance, persistence.
per-sevērō 1 to remain steadfast, persevere in, persist, proceed with, continue (*in re; inf.*).
per-sevērus 3 very severe, strict.
per-sīdō, sēdī, sessum 3 to settle down; to penetrate through.
per-signō 1 to note down carefully.
per-similis, e very like.
per-simplex, icis very simple.
per-sistō 3 to persist.
persōlla, ae *f* (a little mask) an ugly fright.
per-sōlus 3 quite alone.
per-solvō 3 **a**) to pay, pay off, pay out (*alci alqd*); **b**) to render, fulfil, discharge an obligation; **c**) to suffer *or* to inflict (punishment); **d**) to explain.

persōna, ae *f* mask (*worn by actors*); **a**) character, part (*in a play or in life*), person; **b**) station, rank, condition.
persōnātus 3 in a mask, masked; in an assumed character.
per-sonō 1 **a**) to resound, re-echo; to make a loud noise; **b**) to fill with sound (*alqd*); to cry aloud, shout.
per-sonus 3 resounding.
per-spectē intelligently.
per-spectō 1 to inspect; to see to the end.
perspectus 3 clearly perceived, well known.
per-speculor 1 to explore thoroughly.
per-spergō 3 to besprinkle.
perspicāx, ācis sharp-sighted, acute.
perspicientia, ae *f* clear perception, full knowledge.
per-spiciō, spexī, spectum 3 to look through; to see clearly; **a**) to look at, examine, view, inspect; **b**) to read through; **c**) to mark, observe, perceive.
perspicuitās, ātis *f* clearness, perspicuity.
perspicuus 3 transparent; clear, evident, manifest, conspicuous.
per-spissō *adv.* very slowly.
per-sternō 3 to pave throughout.
per-stimulō 1 to stimulate incessantly.
per-stō, stitī (stātūrus) 1 to remain standing, stand firm; **a**) to remain unchanged, last; **b**) to persist in, persevere (*in re*).
per-strepō 3 to make a great noise.
per-stringō 3 to touch lightly, graze; **a**) to affect deeply, strike, move; to dazzle; to deafen; **b**) to scold, blame, reproach; **c**) to touch on in speaking.
per-studiōsus 3 very eager, *or* fond.
per-suādeō 2 (*with dat.*) **a**) to persuade, induce, prevail upon (with *ut* or *ne*); **mihi persuādētur** I am persuaded, prevailed upon; **b**) to convince (of a fact) (*alci de re* or with *acc.* and *inf.*); **mihi persuāsum est** I am convinced.
persuāsiō, ōnis *f* persuasion; conviction, belief, opinion.
per-suāstrīx, īcis *f* she who persuades.
persuāsus, ūs *m* = **persuasio.**
per-subtīlis, e very subtle; very fine.
per-sultō 1 to leap about; to range through (*alqd*).
per-tābēscō, buī, — 3 to waste away.
per-taedet, taesum est 2 it wearies, disgusts.
pertaesus 3 disgusted at (*acc.*).
per-tegō 3 to cover all over.
per-temptō 1 **a**) to prove thoroughly, try, put to the test; **b**) to penetrate, affect deeply, try severely.
per-tendō, tendī, (tēnsum *or*) **tentum** 3 to push on, proceed; to carry through.
per-tentō 1 = **pertempto.**
per-tenuis, e very weak, very slight.
per-terebrō 1 to bore through.
per-tergeō 2 to wipe; to touch *or* brush lightly.
per-terreō 2 to terrify.
perterri-crepus 3 sounding terribly.
per-texō 3 to weave throughout, to complete.
pertica, ae *f* pole, (measuring) rod, staff.
per-timefactus 3 greatly frightened.
per-timēscō, muī, — 3 to be very much afraid, fear exceedingly.
pertinācia, ae *f* stubbornness; perseverance.
per-tināx, ācis tenacious; **a**) persevering, firm; **b**) obstinate, stubborn; stingy.
per-tineō, tinuī, — 2 to reach *or* extend to, stretch to; **a**) to belong, relate, pertain, concern, refer to; **b**) to be applicable *or* suitable, tend, lead, conduce to (*ad alqd*).
per-tingō, —, — 3 to reach, extend.
per-tolerō 1 to endure to the end.
per-torqueō 2 to distort.
per-tractātē in a hackneyed style.
per-tractātiō, ōnis *f* a being busy with (*gen.*).
per-tractō 1 to touch, handle; to busy oneself with, treat, study.
per-trahō 3 to draw along, drag; to entice *or* allure to a place
per-trectō 1 = **pertracto.**
per-tribuō 3 to give.
pertrīcōsus 3 hard to understand (*or* trifling?).
per-trīstis, e very sad *or* gloomy.
per-trītus 3 trite.

per-tumultuōsē *adv.* with much agitation.
per-tundō, tudī, tūsum 3 to thrust *or* bore through.
per-turbātiō, ōnis *f* confusion, disorder; **a**) disturbance, revolution; **b**) passion, emotion.
per-turbātrīx, īcis *f* disturber.
per-turbō 1 **a**) to confuse, disturb, throw into disorder; **b**) to disquiet, discompose, embarrass;— **perturbātus** 3 confused, troubled, disturbed; agitated; discomposed.
per-turpis, e very disgraceful.
pērula, ae *f* little wallet.
per-ungō 3 to besmear, anoint.
per-urbānus 3 very polite, refined, witty.
per-urgeō 2 to urge strongly.
per-ūrō 3 to burn up; **a**) to inflame, rub sore; **b**) to consume; to nip (with cold).
per-ūtilis, e very useful.
per-vādō 3 to go, come, pass through, to extend; to reach, arrive at.
per-vagor 1 **a**) to rove *or* wander over *or* about (*alqd*); **b**) to spread out, extend (*in re*); **pervagātus** 3 wide-spread, well known.
per-vagus 3 wandering about.
per-variē *adv.* very variously.
per-vāstō 1 to devastate.
per-vehō 3 **a**) to carry *or* convey through; **b**) to lead, conduct, bring, convey to; **P.** to pass through, to travel, sail to.
per-vellō 3 to pull, pluck; to pinch, hurt; to excite; to revile, disparage.
per-veniō 4 to come, arrive; to reach, attain (*ad, in alqd*).
per-vēnor 1 to hunt through.
per-versāriō *adv.* crazily.
perversitās, ātis *f* perversity.
per-versus 3 turned the wrong way, awry; perverse; wrong.
per-vertō 3 to turn upside down, overthrow, throw down; to destroy, ruin, undo.
per-vesperī *adv.* very late in the evening.
per-vestīgātiō, ōnis *f* investigation.
per-vestīgō 1 to track out; to investigate, search into.
per-vetus, eris *and* **per-vetustus** 3 very old.
per-vicācia, ae *f* persistence; stubbornness.
per-vicāx, ācis unyielding, persevering; obstinate, headstrong, wilful.
per-videō 2 **a**) to behold, survey, review; **b**) to look through, perceive, discern.
per-vigeō, uī, — 2 to flourish continually; to remain strong.
per-vigil, is ever watchful.
per-vigilātiō, ōnis *f* vigil.
per-vigilium, ī *n* **a**) a remaining awake throughout the night; **b**) vigil.
per-vigilō 1 to remain awake throughout the night.
per-vīlis, e very cheap.
per-vincō 3 to conquer completely; **a**) to prevail upon; **b**) to carry one's point, to effect (*ut*), to outbid; to prove.
per-vius 3 passable, accessible, unobstructed; *subst.* **pervium, ī** *n* thoroughfare, passage.
per-vīvō 3 to live on.
per-volitō 1 to fly through.
per-volō[1] 1 **a**) to fly through *or* about (*alqd*); **b**) to fly *or* hasten to (*in alqd*).
per-volō[2]**, voluī, velle** to wish greatly, be very desirous.
per-volūtō 1 to roll over and over; to unroll, read.
per-volvō 3 **a**) to roll over; **b**) to unroll, read through; **c**) **P.** to make oneself familiar with (*in re*).
per-vors-, -vort- = **per-vers-, -vert-**.
per-vulgō 1 to make common *or* public, to publish, make known; to prostitute oneself; to visit often, haunt; **pervulgātus** 3 well known, common.
pēs, pedis *m* foot; **pedibus** on foot; by land; **pedem ferre** to go *or* come; **conferre** to come to close quarters; **referre** to return, go back; **in sententiam pedibus ire** to vote for a motion in the senate;— **a**) foot (*of animals*), talon, hoof; **b**) step, gait, course; **c**) sheet, sail-rope; **d**) foot (*as a measure*); **e**) metrical foot, kind of verse.
pessimus 3, *superl. of* **malus.**
pessulus, ī *m* bolt (*of a door*).
pessum *adv.* to the ground, to the bottom, downwards; **~ īre** to be ruined, to perish; **~ dare** to destroy, ruin.

pesti-fer 3 destructive, fatal, injurious.
pestilēns, tis unhealthy, pestilential; deadly, fatal.
pestilentia, ae (*and* **pestilitās, ātis**) *f* unhealthy air *or* weather; plague, pestilence.
pestis, is *f* **a**) plague, pestilence; **b**) destruction, ruin, death; **c**) injurious person, curse, bane.
petasātus 3 wearing a *petasus or* travelling cap.
petasō, ōnis (*dimin.* **-sunculus, ī**) *m* shoulder of pork.
petasus, ī *m* traveller's hat.
petaurum, ī *n* acrobat's apparatus (? = spring-board, see-saw, wheel).
petessō, —, — 3 to long for, strive after.
petītiō, ōnis *f* **a**) attack, blow; **b**) a soliciting, requesting; **c**) application for office, candidature; **d**) claim, suit.
petītor, ōris *m* **a**) seeker; candidate; **b**) plaintiff.
petīturiō 4 to desire to be a candidate.
petītus, ūs *m* a falling towards.
petō, tīvī (*or* **tiī**), **tītum** 3 to seek, aim at; a) to make for, go to (*acc.*); b) to fall upon, attack, assail; c) to go to seek, fetch; d) to pursue, aim at; to demand, exact, desire; e) to ask, request (*ut*); to solicit, be a candidate for; f) to demand at law, sue for, claim.
petorritum, ī *n* open four-wheeled carriage.
petra, ae *f* rock, stone.
petrō, ōnis *m* old ram.
petulāns, tis forward, pert, petulant; wanton, impudent.
petulantia, ae *f* impudence, forwardness; heedlessness.
petulcus 3 butting.
pexātus 3 dressed in a garment of new wool.
pexus 3 of new wool.
phaecasium, ī *n* white shoe worn by priests; *hence* **phaecasiātus** 3.
phalanga, ae *f* wooden roller.
phalangītēs, ae *m* heavy-armed soldier (*of the phalanx*).
phalanx, angis *f* band of soldiers; Macedonian phalanx, heavy-armed men in close array.
phalārica, ae *f* = **falarica.**
phalerae, ārum *f/pl.* metal ornament worn on the breast.
phalerātus 3 wearing the *phalerae*; fine-sounding.
phantasma, atis *n* ghost, spectre.
pharetra, ae *f* quiver.
pharetrātus 3 and **pharetriger** 3 wearing a quiver.
pharmaco-pōla, ae *m* seller of drugs, quack.
phasēlus, ī *m* and *f* kidney-bean; swift-sailing yacht.
phengītēs, ae *m* transparent crystal.
phiala, ae *f* shallow cup.
philēma, atis *n* kiss.
Philipp(ē)us (**nummus**) *m* gold coin worth 20 drachmae.
philitia, ōrum *n/pl.* public meals of the Lacedemonians.
philo-logia, ae *f* (love of) learning; literary exposition.
philo-logus, ī *m* learned man.
philo-sophia, ae *f* philosophy; phi osophical question, sect.
philosophor 1 to study philosophy.
philo-sophus, ī *m* philosopher; *adj.* 3 philosophical.
philtrum, ī *n* love-potion.
philyra, ae *f* inner bark of a linden--tree.
phīmus, ī *m* dice-box.
phōca, ae (*and* **-ē, ēs**) *f* sea-calf, seal.
phoenīco-pterus, ī *m* flamingo.
phoenīx, īcis *m* phœnix.
phōn-ascus, ī *m* voice-teacher.
phrenēsis, is *f* madness.
phrenēticus 3 mad, frantic.
phrygiō, ōnis *m* gold-embroiderer.
phthisis, is *f* tuberculosis.
phylaca, ae *f* prison.
phȳl-archus, ī *m* chief of a tribe, prince, sheik.
phyrgiō = **phrygiō.**
phȳsētēr, ēris *m* a kind of whale.
physicus 3 relating to nature, natural, physical; *subst.* ~, **ī** *m* natural philosopher; **-a, ae** *f and* **-a, ōrum** *n/pl.* natural philosophy, physics.
physio-gnōmōn, onis *m* physiognomist.
physio-logia, ae *f* natural philosophy.
piābilis, e expiable.
piāculāris, e atoning, expiating.
piāculum, ī *n* means of expiating, expiatory sacrifice; **a**) expiation, expiatory victim; **b**) sin, guilt, guilty person.
piāmen, inis *n* = **piaculum.**

pīca, ae *f* magpie.
picāria, ae *f* pitch-works.
picea, ae *f* pitch-pine.
piceus 3 pitchy, pitch-black.
picō 1 to pitch; **picātus** 3 with a pitchy taste.
pictor, ōris *m* painter.
pictūra, ae *f* art of painting, painting; **a**) a painting, picture; **b**) a painting in words.
pictūrātus 3 painted; embroidered.
pīcus, ī *m* wood-pecker; griffin.
pietās, ātis *f* dutifulness, sense of duty; **a**) piety, religiousness, devotion; **b**) filial love, affection, patriotism; **c**) justice; **d**) kindness, tenderness.
piger, gra, grum slow, dull, lazy (*ad alqd*), indolent, inactive; sluggish; unfruitful.
piget, uit (*and* **itum est**) 2 **a**) it grieves, troubles, displeases (*alqm alcis rei; inf.*); **b**) = **paenitet.**
pigmentārius, ī *m* dealer in paints *or* unguents.
pigmentum, ī *n* paint, colour, pigment; decoration, ornament.
pignerātor, ōris *m* one who takes a pledge.
pignerō 1 to pledge, pawn, mortgage; **-or** 1 to take as a pledge; to appropriate, make one's own.
pignus, oris (*or* **eris**) *n* pledge, pawn, security; **a**) mortgage; **b**) hostage; **c**) wager, stake; **d**) assurance, proof; **e**) *pl.* pledges of love (*children*).
pigritia, ae (*and* **-iēs, ēī**) *f* sloth, laziness, indolence.
pigror (*and* **-ō**) 1 to be slow, sluggish.
pīla[1], **ae** *f* mortar.
pīla[2], **ae** *f* pillar; pier.
pila[3], **ae** *f* (game of) ball.
pīlānus, ī *m* soldier of the third line (= **triarius**).
pīlātus 3 closely packed (*or* armed with the *pilum*).
pīleātus 3 = **pilleatus.**
pīlentum, ī *n* carriage, coach.
pīleus, *see* **pilleus.**
pili-crepus, ī *m* ball-player.
pilleātus 3 wearing a felt cap.
pilleolus, ī *m* small felt cap.
pilleus, ī *m and* **-um, ī** *n* felt cap (a token of freedom).
pilō 1 to depilate.
pilōsus 3 hairy, shaggy.
pīlum, ī *n* **a**) heavy javelin of the legionaries; **b**) **primum pīlum** the first maniple of the *triarii.*
pilus[1], **ī** *m* hair; trifle.
pīlus[2], **ī** *m* = **pilum b**).
pin(n)a, ae *f* a shell-fish.
pīnētum, ī *n* pine-wood.
pīneus 3 of pine.
pingo, pinxī, pictum 3 to paint; to stain, dye, colour; **a**) to represent, depict, portray; **b**) to embroider; **c**) to tattoo; **d**) to decorate, variegate; to colour, embellish; — **pictus** 3 **a**) painted, coloured; **b**) variegated, tattooed; **c**) adorned; unreal.
pinguēscō, —, — 3 to grow fat *or* fertile.
pinguiārius, ī *m* a lover of fat.
pinguis, e fat, plump, thick, well fed; oily, greasy; *subst.* **pingue, is** *n* fat, grease; **a**) rich, fertile; **b**) dull, heavy, awkward, stupid; **c**) bombastic; **d**) calm, quiet, comfortable.
pīni-fer 3 pine-bearing.
pīni-ger 3 pine-bearing.
pinna[1], **ae** *f* = **penna.**
pinna[2], **ae** *f* fin; pinnacle, battlement.
pinnātus 3 feathered, winged.
pinni-ger 3 **a**) = **pinnatus; b**) provided with fins.
pinni-pēs, edis = **pennipes.**
pinni-rapus, ī *m* crest-seizer, a kind of gladiator.
pinnula, ae *f* little wing.
pīno-tērēs, ae *m* small crab.
pīnsātiō, ōnis *f* pounding.
pīnsitō 1 to grind.
pīnsō, (pīnsuī, pistum) 3 to pound.
pīnus, ūs *and* **ī** *f* **a**) pine, fir; **b**) ship; **c**) torch; **d**) wreath of pine-leaves; **e**) oar.
piō 1 to appease, propitiate; to atone for, expiate, purify.
piper, eris *n* pepper.
piperātus 3 peppered; thievish.
pīpilō 1 to chirp, twitter.
pīpulum, ī *n* outcry.
pīrāta, ae *m* sea-robber, pirate.
pīrāticus 3 of pirates, piratical; *subst.* **-ca, ae** *f* piracy.
pirum, ī *n* pear.
pirus, ī *f* pear-tree.
piscārius 3 belonging to fish.
piscātor, ōris *m* fisherman, fishmonger.

piscātōrius 3 of fishermen, fishing-...

piscātus, ūs *m* fishing, catch of fish.

pisciculus, ī *m* little fish.

piscīna, ae *f* fish-pond, swimming-pool.

piscīnārius, ī *m* owner of a fish-pond.

piscis, is *m* fish.

piscor 1 to fish.

piscōsus 3 abounding in fish.

pisculentus 3 full of fish.

pistillum, ī *n* pestle.

pistor, ōris *m* miller, baker.

pistōrius 3 pertaining to a baker.

pistrilla, ae *f* little pounding-mill.

pistrīnēnsis, e belonging to a pounding-mill.

pistrīnum, ī *n* (*and* **-na, ae** *f*) corn-mill; bakery.

pistrīx, īcis *f* sea-monster (*also* **pristis** *and* **pistris, is**).

pithēcium, ī *n* little ape.

pītuīta, ae *f* phlegm, catarrh, cold.

pītuītōsus, 3 full of phlegm.

pius 3 dutiful; **a)** pious, religious; *pl.* the blessed, departed; **b)** affectionate, filial, loving, devoted; patriotic; **c)** holy, sacred, just, right.

pix, picis *f* pitch.

plācābilis, e 1. easily appeased, placable; **2.** effective in appeasing.

plācābilitās, ātis *f* placability.

plācāmen, inis *and* **plācāmentum, ī** *n* means of appeasing.

plācātiō, ōnis *f* an appeasing.

plācātus 3, *see* **placo.**

placenta, ae *f* cake.

placeō, uī *and* **placitus sum, itum** 2 to please, be pleasing, agreeable, acceptable (*alci*); **sibi placēre** to flatter oneself, be satisfied with oneself; **a)** to find favour; **b) placet** (*perf.* **placuit** *or* **placitum est**) it seems good, is settled, resolved; **si placet** if you please.

placidus 3 gentle, quiet, calm, peaceful, placid; kind, mild.

placitō 1 to please.

placitus 3 **a)** pleasing, agreeable; **b)** agreed on; *subst.* **placitum, ī** *n* that which is agreeable; opinion, doctrine.

plācō 1 **a)** to quiet, soothe, calm, appease; **b)** to reconcile; **plācātus** 3 soothed, calmed, reconciled; quiet, gentle, still.

plāga[1]**, ae** *f* blow, stroke; **a)** cut, thrust, wound; **b)** loss, injury, misfortune, disaster.

plaga[2]**, ae** *f* (mesh of a) net, snare, trap.

plaga[3]**, ae** *f* tract, region, district, zone.

plagiārius, ī *m* kidnapper; plagiarist.

plāgi-ger 3, **-gerulus** 3, **plāgi-patida, ae** *m* one who is flogged.

plāgōsus 3 fond of flogging.

plagula, ae *f* curtain.

plagūsia, ae *f* a kind of fish.

planctus, ūs *m* = **plangor.**

plango, anxī, anctum 3 to strike, beat; to make a noise by beating; to lament aloud, bewail; **-or** to beat one's breast.

plangor, ōris *m* a striking, beating, loud lamentation, wailing.

plāni-loquus 3 plain-speaking.

plāni-pēs, pedis *m* bare-footed mime-actor.

plānitās, ātis *f* distinctness.

plānitia, ae *and* **plānitiēs, ēī** *f* level ground, plain.

planta[1]**, ae** *f* shoot for propagation, cutting.

planta[2]**, ae** *f* sole of the foot.

plantāria, ium *n/pl.* **a)** young plants *or* trees; **b)** sandals; **c)** hair; **plantāris, e** on the soles of the feet.

planus[1]**, ī** *m* vagabond, impostor.

plānus[2] 3 **a)** level, flat, even; **b)** plain; distinct; *subst.* **plānum, ī** *n* plain; *adv.* **plānē** clearly, distinctly; entirely, quite; by all means, to be sure.

plasma, atis *n* affected modulation of the voice.

platalea, ae *f* spoonbill; pelican.

platanōn, ōnis *m* grove of plane-trees.

platanus, ī (*and* **ūs**) *f* plane-tree.

platēa (*and* **platĕa**) **ae** *f* street.

plaudō, sī, sum 3 **a)** to clap, slap, beat, to stamp; to strike together; **b)** to clap the hands, applaud, approve.

plausibilis, e worthy of applause.

plausor, ōris *m* applauder.

plaustrum, ī *n* wagon, cart.

plausus, ūs *m* a clapping, noise; a clapping of hands, applause.

plēbēcula, ae *f* rabble, mob.

plēbēius 3 of the common people, plebeian; common, vulgar.

plēbēs, (e)ī *f* = **plebs.**

plēbi-cola, ae *m* friend of the common people.

plēbs, is *f* a) the common people, commons; b) populace, lower class, mob.
plectilis, e plaited.
plector, — 3 to be beaten *or* punished.
plēctrum, ī *n* a) plectrum for striking the chords of a stringed instrument; b) lyre, lute; c) rudder.
plēnus 3 full, filled (*with gen.; abl.*); a) stout; b) strong, sonorous; c) pregnant; d) filled, satisfied, sated; e) abundant, copious, substantial; full, at full length; f) much frequented, numerous; g) entire, complete, whole, finished.
plērus 3 = **plerusque.**
plērus-que, plēraque, plērumque a very great part, most; a) **plērumque** *subst. n* the greatest part, *adv.* for the most part, mostly, commonly; b) **plērīque** 3 the greater part, majority, very many; **in plērīsque** in the majority of cases.
plexus 3 plaited.
plicātrīx, īcis *f* one who folds clothes.
plicō, —, ātum 1 to fold together, coil up.
plōdō, sī, sum 3 = **plaudo.**
ploerēs = **plures.**
ploerus 3 = **plerus.**
plōrābilis, e lamentable.
plōrābundus 3 lamenting.
plōrātor, ōris *m* mourner.
plōrātus, ūs *m* lamentation.
plōrō 1 to cry aloud, wail, lament, weep; to bewail (*acc.*).
plōstellum, ī *n* small wagon.
plōstrum, ī *n* = **plaustrum.**
ploxenum (-inum), ī *n* the frame of a Gallic cart (?).
pluit, pluit (plūvit) 3 it rains.
plūma, ae *f* soft feather, down.
plūmātile, is *n* robe with feather-trimming.
plūmātus 3 covered with feathers; embroidered.
plumbeus 3 of lead; lead-coloured; a) dull; poor; b) heavy, oppressive.
plumbum, ī *n* lead, leaden ball; (leaden) pipe *or* pencil.
plūmeus 3 filled with feathers; like feathers.
plūmi-pēs, edis feather-footed.
plūmōsus 3 feathered.
plūrēs, plūrimus, plūs, *see* **multus.**
plūrifāriam *adv.* in many places.
plūsculus 3 a little more.
pluteus, ī *m* (*and* **pluteum, ī** *n*) a) penthouse, shed; b) parapet, breastwork; c) (the back of) a couch; d) desk; shelf; e) bier.
pluvia, ae *f* rain.
pluviālis, e = **pluvius.**
pluvius 3 rainy; causing *or* bringing rain.
P.M. *abbr.* = **pontifex maximus.**
pōcillum, ī *n* small cup.
pōc(u)lum, ī *n* drinking vessel, cup; drink, drinking-bout; draught.
podagra, ae *f* gout in the feet.
podagrōsus *and* **podagricus** 3 gouty.
pōdex, icis *m* fundament, anus.
podium, ī *n* balcony; terrace.
poēma, atis *n* poem.
poēmatium, ī *n* short poem.
poena, ae *f* indemnification, compensation, recompense, expiation; a) punishment, penalty (*poenas alcis rei dare* to be punished for); b) hardship, suffering, pain; c) the goddess of vengeance.
poeniceus = **pūniceus.**
poeniō *and* **-ior** = **punio(r).**
poenitentia, ae *f and* **poenitet,** *see* **paenitentia** *and* **paenitet.**
poenītiō, ōnis *f, see* **punitio.**
poēsis, is *f* poetry, poesy; poem.
poēta, ae *m* poet.
poēticus 3 poetic, poetical; *subst.* **-ca, ae** *and* **-cē, ēs** *f* the poetic art.
poētria, ae (*and* **-tris, idis**) *f* poetess.
pol *int.* by Pollux! indeed! truly!
polenta, ae *f* peeled barley, barley-groats.
polentārius 3 of barley-groats.
poliō 4 to smooth, polish; a) to whitewash; b) to embellish, adorn, decorate, refine; — **polītus** 3 polished; refined, accomplished, polite.
polīticus 3 of *or* belonging to the state *or* government.
polītūra, ae *f* polishing.
pollen, inis *n* (*and* **pollis, inis** *m, f*) fine flour.
pollēns, entis, *see* **polleo.**
pollentia, ae *f* might, power.
polleō, (ui), — 2 to be strong, mighty, powerful, able, efficacious; to prevail, avail; **pollēns, tis** strong, mighty.
pollex, icis *m* the thumb; the big toe.
pol-liceor, licitus sum 2 to offer, promise (*alci alqd; acc. c. inf.*); *subst.* **pollicitum, ī** *n* promise.

pollicitātiō, ōnis *f* promise.
pollicitor 1 to promise repeatedly.
pollinārius 3 for fine flour.
polli(n)ctor, ōris *m* washer and anointer of corpses.
pollingō, inxī, inctum 3 to wash and anoint a corpse.
pollūceō, xī, ctum 2 to present as a sacrifice; to serve up; to serve, entertain.
pollūcibiliter *adv.* sumptuously.
pollūctūra, ae *f* splendid dinner.
pol-luō, uī, ūtum 3 to defile, pollute, contaminate, dishonour, violate; **pollūtus** 3 defiled; vicious, unchaste.
polus, ī *m* pole of the earth; the sky, the heavens.
poly-phagus, ī *m* gormandizer.
pōlypōsus 3 with a polypus in the nose.
pōlypus, ī *m* polypus; greedy person; polypus in the nose.
pōmārium, ī *n* orchard.
pōmārius, ī *m* fruiterer.
pōm(o)ērium, ī *n* open space on each side of the walls of a city.
pōmi-fer 3 fruit-bearing.
pōmōsus 3 abounding in fruit.
pompa, ae *f* solemn procession; retinue; **a**) funeral procession; **b**) display, ostentation, pomp.
pōmum, ī *n* fruit; fruit-tree.
pōmus, ī *f* fruit-tree.
ponderō 1 to weigh; to ponder, consider (*alqd ex re, re*).
ponderōsus 3 weighty.
pondō a) (*abl. sg.*) in weight; **b**) (*with libra,* &c. *understood*) pound, pounds.
pondus, eris *n* weight, heaviness; **a**) balance, equilibrium; **b**) burden, load, heavy body; **c**) mass, quantity, sum; a pound weight; **d**) consequence, importance; stability.
pōne 1. *adv.* behind; **2.** *prep.* with *acc.* behind.
pōnō, posuī (*and* **posīvī**), **positum** (*and* **postum**) 3 to put, place, set, lay; **1.** a) to put *or* set down (*alqd in re*) **librum in mensa, sellam sub quercu;** to plant (*trees*); b) to set before (*to eat and drink*); c) to lay out; to bury; d) to invest, put out at interest; e) to propose as a prize; f) to wager, stake; g) to spend, employ (*time, trouble*); h) to dedicate (*a votive offering*); i) to station (*troops*); to put a person in some position *or* office, to appoint; to erect, set up (*statuam in foro*), build (*domum, castellum in monte*), **castra pōnere** to pitch a camp; j) to represent, picture; k) to lay down *or* aside, take off, remove, give up (*vestem, arma, librum de manu*); **2.** to put, place (*omnem spem in consule* or *in fuga*); a) **P. positus esse in re** to be based *or* founded upon, to rest upon, depend on; b) to apply (*omnem curam in salute*); c) to fix, give (*nomen alci*); to ordain (*laws*); d) to reckon, count, consider, regard; e) to lay down as true, assert, maintain, assume; f) to put away, dismiss, forgo, leave off, lay down, surrender.
pōns, tis *m* bridge; **a**) gangway; **b**) passage; **c**) drawbridge; **d**) deck of a ship.
ponticulus, ī *m* little bridge.
ponti-fex, icis *m* high priest.
pontificālis, e *and* **-ficius** 3 pontifical, relating to the high priest.
pontificātus, ūs *m* office of a high priest, pontificate.
pontō, ōnis *m* large flat boat; transport.
pontus, ī *m* the sea.
popa, ae *m* priest's attendant at sacrifices.
popanum, ī *n* sacrificial cake.
popellus, ī *m* the common people, rabble.
popīna, ae *f* cook-shop, eating-house, low tavern; food sold at a cook-shop.
popīnō, ōnis *m* frequenter of eating--houses, glutton.
poples, itis *m* hollow of the knee; knee.
poplus, ī *m* = **populus.**
poppysma, atis *n* a clicking with the tongue (sign of approval).
populābilis, e that can be devastated.
populābundus 3 laying waste, ravaging.
populāris, e relating to the people, popular, designed for the people; **a**) agreeable to the people; **b**) democratic, demagogic; **c**) of the same people *or* country, native; — *subst. m* fellow-countryman, associate, *pl.* the popular party, democrats; *n/pl.* the common people's seats in the theatre.

populāritās, ātis *f* a) fellow-citizenship; b) desire to please the people.
populātiō, ōnis *f* devastation.
populātor, ōris *m and* **-trīx, īcis** *f* devastator, plunderer.
populātus, ūs *m* devastation.
pōpuleus 3 of a poplar.
pōpuli-fer 3 poplar-bearing.
pōpulnus 3 of poplar wood.
populor *and* **-lō** 1 to lay waste, devastate, plunder, destroy.
populus[1], **ī** *m* a people, political community, the citizens; multitude, crowd, throng.
pōpulus[2], **ī** *f* poplar.
porca, ae *f* sow.
porcellus, ī *m* little pig.
porcīnārius, ī *m* dealer in pork.
porcīnus 3 of pigs; *subst.* **-īna, ae** *f* pork.
porclēna, ae *f* little sow.
porculus, ī *m* little pig.
porcus, ī *m* hog, pig.
porgō = **porrigo**[2].
porphyrēticus 3 purple-red.
por-rēctiō, ōnis *f* a stretching out, extension.
por(r)iciō, —, rēctum 3 to offer as a sacrifice; **inter caesa et porrēcta** between the killing of a victim and the laying of its entrails on the altar, i. e. at the last moment.
porrīgō[1], **inis** *f* scurf, scab.
por-rigō[2], **rēxī, rēctum** 3 to stretch out, reach out, extend; a) to stretch on the ground, lay at full length; b) to lengthen; c) to offer, present, hold out to (*alci alqd*).
porrō *adv.* forward; a) onward, to *or* at a distance; b) henceforward, furthermore; c) besides, moreover, again.
porrum, i *n and* **-us, ī** *m* leek.
porta, ae *f* gate; avenue, entrance, passage.
portātiō, ōnis *f* a carrying, conveying.
por-tendō, ndī, ntum 3 to point out, indicate, foretell, presage, portend (*alqd; acc. c. inf.*).
portenti-ficus 3 creating monsters (*or* wonder-working).
portentōsus 3 prodigious, portentous, monstrous.
portentum, ī *n* marvel, prodigy, portent; a) monster, monstrosity; b) strange tale, wonderful story, fiction.
porthmeus (*dissyllabic*) *m* ferryman.
porticula, ae *f* little gallery *or* portico.
porticus, ūs *f* colonnade, arcade, portico; a) entrance; b) gallery (*in a siege*); c) the Stoic school.
portiō, ōnis *f* share, portion; instalment; proportion.
portisculus, ī *m* coxswain's hammer (for beating time).
portitor, ōris *m* a) ferryman; waggoner (*constellation*); b) custom-house officer.
portō 1 to carry, convey.
portōrium, ī *n* tax, toll, duty.
portula, ae *f* small gate.
portuōsus 3 having many harbours.
portus, ūs *m* harbour, haven; refuge; river-mouth.
pōsca, ae *f* drink made of egg, vinegar, and water.
poscō, poposcī, — 3 to beg, demand, request, desire (*alqd ab alqo* or *alqm alqd*); a) to require, need; b) to inquire, ask (*alqd*); c) to challenge to fight; d) to offer a price, bid for; e) to call, call upon, invoke.
positiō, ōnis *f* placing, position, situation; affirmation.
positor, ōris *m* founder, builder.
positūra, ae *f* situation, structure.
positus, ūs *m* position, place, situation; arrangement.
possessiō, ōnis *f* a) a taking possession, possessing; b) possession, property, estate.
possessiuncula, ae *f* small property *or* estate.
possessor, ōris *m* possessor.
pos-sideō, sēdī, sessum 2 to possess, have, hold.
pos-sīdō, sēdī, sessum 3 to occupy, take possession of.
possum, potuī, posse a) to be able; I can (*with inf.*); b) to avail, have influence *or* efficacy (*multum*).
post 1. *adv.* behind; afterwards, after, subsequently; **2.** *prep.* with *acc.*; a) behind; b) after, since.
post-eā *adv.* after, after that, afterwards.
posteā-quam *cj.* = **postquam.**
posteritās, ātis *f* after-ages, posterity, future generations.
posterus 3 coming after, following, next, future; **in posterum** for the future, for the next day; *subst.* **posterī, ōrum** *m/pl.* descendants,

posterity; — *comp.* **posterior, ius** following after, later, posterior, inferior, worse; — *sup.* **postrēmus** 3 hindmost, last, lowest, meanest, worst; *adv.* **postrēmum** for the last time; **postrēmō** at last, finally; **postumus** 3 last born, posthumous.
post-ferō 3 = **postpono.**
post-genitī, ōrum *m/pl.* posterity, descendants.
post-habeō 2 = **postpono.**
post-hāc *adv.* henceforth, after this, in future.
post-ibi *adv.* after that, afterwards.
postīculum, ī *n* back-premises.
postīcus 3 hinder, back; *subst.* **postīcum, ī** *n* back-door.
postid(eā) *adv.* = **postea.**
postilēna, ae *f* crupper.
postiliō, ōnis *f* claim of a god for a forgotten sacrifice.
post-illā(c) afterwards.
postis, is *m* door-post; door, gate.
post-līminium, ī *n* right to return home with citizen-rights.
pos(t)-merīdiānus 3 in the afternoon.
post-modo *and* **-modum** *adv.* soon after, presently.
post-partor, ōris *m* subsequent acquirer, descendant.
post-pōnō 3 to put after, esteem less, disregard.
post-prīncipiō in the sequel.
post-putō 1 to esteem less.
post-quam *cj.* after, when.
postrēmus 3, *see* **posterus.**
postrī-diē (*and* **postrī-duō**) *adv.* on the following day.
post-scaenia, ōrum *n/pl.* that which is behind the scenes.
post-scrībō 3 to write after *or* under.
postulātīcius 3 demanded, requested.
postulātiō, ōnis *f* claim, demand; **a**) complaint, expostulation; **b**) application to the prætor to admit a complaint.
postulātor, ōris *m* claimant.
postulātum, ī *n* demand.
postulātus, ūs *m* complaint, (law-) suit.
postulō 1 to demand, claim; **a**) to request (*alqd ab alqo; alqm alqd, de re; ut, ne*); **b**) to summon, prosecute (*alqm de re*); **c**) to ask leave to prosecute.
postumus 3, *see* **posterus.**
pōtātiō, ōnis *f* drinking-bout.
pōtātor, ōris *m* drinker.
pote, *see* **potis.**
potēns, tis mighty, powerful, ruling over; able, capable, efficacious; possessed of, master of, in control of.
potentātus, ūs *m* power *or* command in a state, dominion.
potentia, ae *f* power, might, force; **a**)(unconstitutional)political power, rule, dominion, command; **b**) influence, efficacy.
potērium, ī *n* drinking-vessel.
potestās, ātis *f* ability, capacity, power to do something; **a**) legal power, control; **b**) political power, authority, dominion, rule, sovereignty; official authority, office, magistracy, magistrate; **c**) opportunity, ability, leave, permission; **potestātem sui facere alci** to give an opportunity of speaking to *or* fighting with one.
potīcius 3 childish (?).
potin? = **potes-ne?, potest-ne?**
pōtiō, ōnis *f* a drinking, drink; magic potion, love-potion, poisonous draught.
potiō 4 to put into the power of (*alqm alcis*).
pōtiōnātus 3 having been given a draught *or* potion.
potior[1]**, ius,** *comp.* of **potis.**
potior[2]**, tītus sum** 4 to become master of, take possession of, obtain, acquire (*with gen., abl., acc.*); to possess, hold, occupy, enjoy.
potis, pote able, capable, possible; **potis sum** = **possum; potis** *or* **pote est** = **potest** it may be, can be, is possible; — *comp.* **potior, us** better, preferable, more important; *adv.* **potius** rather, preferably, more; — *superl.* **potissimus** 3 chief, principal, most important; *adv.* **potissimum** especially, above all, of all people, of all things.
pōtitō 1 to drink often.
pōtiuncula, ae *f* small potion.
pōtō, āvi, pōtum *or* **pōtātum** 1 to drink, absorb; — **pōtus** 3 **a**) drunk, drunk up; **b**) drunken, intoxicated.
pōtor, ōris *m* drinker, drunkard.
pōtrīx, īcis *f* female tippler.
pōtulentus 3 **a**) drinkable; **-um, ī** *n* drink; **b**) drunken.
pōtus[1] 3, *see* **poto.**
pōtus[2]**, ūs** *m* a drinking, drink.
P. R. *abbr.* = **populus Romanus.**

prae 1. *adv.* before, in front; **praeut, praequam** *cj.* in comparison with (what); **2.** *prep.* with *acc.* a) before, in front of; **prae manu** at hand; **prae se ferre** to display, boast of; b) in comparison with; c) because of, on account of, for **prae lacrimis loqui non posse.**
prae-acūtus 3 sharp, pointed.
prae-altus 3 very high *or* deep.
prae-beō, uī, itum 2 to hold forth, reach out (*alci alqd*); **a**) to proffer, offer, present, furnish, afford; **b**) to give, occasion, cause; **c**) to show, exhibit, represent (*se virum, se misericordem praebere*).
prae-bibō, bibī, — 3 to drink to (*alci*).
praebitor, ōris *m* furnisher, purveyor.
prae-calidus 3 very warm *or* hot
prae-calvus 3 very bald.
prae-cantrīx, īcis *f* sorceress.
prae-cānus 3 quite white (*or* prematurely white?).
prae-caveō 2 **a**) to use precaution, take care, be on one's guard (*a re; ne*); **b**) to take care for (*with dat.*).
prae-cēdō 3 to go before, precede; to surpass, outdo.
prae-celer, eris, ere very swift.
prae-celerō 1 to hurry forward (*intrans. or trans.*).
prae-cellō, —, — 3 to surpass, excel (*alqm re*), distinguish oneself; **praecellēns, tis** excellent, eminent, distinguished.
prae-celsus 3 very high, very lofty.
prae-centiō, ōnis *f* prelude.
prae-centō 1 to utter incantations before (*alci*).
prae-ceps, cipitis head-foremost, headlong; **a**) steep, precipitous, abrupt; *subst.* steep place, precipice; danger, critical circumstances; **b**) hasty, rapid; rash, reckless; **c**) inclined, prone (*in alqd*); **praeceps** (*as adv.*) down headlong; into peril.
praeceptiō, ōnis *f* **a**) precept; **b**) preconception; **c**) legacy paid before the winding-up of an estate.
praeceptīvus 3 didactic.
praeceptor, ōris *m* teacher, instructor.
praeceptrīx, īcis *f* preceptress.
praeceptum, ī *n* precept, order, injunction; rule, maxim.
prae-cerpō, psī, ptum 3 to pluck *or* gather prematurely; to forestall, intercept.
prae-cīdō, cīdī, cīsum 3 **a**) to cut off; **b**) to refuse; **c**) to cut short, abridge; **d**) to cut in pieces; **e**) to break off suddenly.
prae-cingō 3 to gird about; to surround, encircle (*alqd re*).
prae-cinō, cinuī (*and* **cecinī**), **centum** 3 **a**) to recite *or* play before; **b**) to foretell, predict.
praecipes, ipis = **praeceps.**
prae-cipiō, cēpī, ceptum 3 **a**) to take *or* obtain in advance, to anticipate, to enjoy in anticipation; **b**) to conjecture; **c**) to advise (*alci alqd; ut, ne, inf.*), warn, instruct, prescribe, command, give rules.
praecipitātiō, ōnis *f* a headlong fall.
praecipitium, ī *n* precipice.
praecipitō 1 **1.** to cast down headlong; a) to destroy, ruin; b) to hurry, hasten (*alqd; inf.*); **2.** *intr.* to throw oneself down, to rush headlong, fall down, sink to ruin; — **praecipitanter** headlong.
praecipuē *adv.* chiefly, principally, especially.
praecipuus 3 **a**) received in advance; **b**) particular, peculiar, especial; principal, distinguished, eminent; — *subst.* **praecipuum, ī** *n* desirable *or* important thing.
prae-cīsus 3 broken off, steep, abrupt, precipitous; short; *adv.* concisely, positively.
prae-clārus 3 very clear, very bright; **a**) splendid, noble, excellent, admirable; **b**) famous, celebrated.
prae-clūdō, sī, sum 3 to shut off, shut, close.
praecō, ōnis *m* crier, herald; auctioneer; publisher, eulogist.
prae-cōgitō 1 to think *or* consider beforehand.
prae-cognōscō 3 to know *or* see beforehand.
prae-colō 3 to cultivate beforehand; to honour prematurely.
prae-compositus 3 arranged beforehand.
praecōnius 3 of a public crier; *subst.* **praecōnium, ī** *n* office of a public crier; proclamation, publication; laudation.
prae-cōnsūmō 3 to waste *or* spend beforehand.

prae-contrectō 1 to feel *or* handle beforehand.
prae-cordia, ōrum *n/pl.* **1.** midriff, diaphragm; **2.** internal organs; a) breast; b) heart, feeling, mind.
prae-corrumpō 3 to bribe beforehand.
prae-cox, -cocis *and* **-coquis, e** premature; precocious.
prae-cultus 3 highly ornamented.
prae-cupidus 3 very fond of.
prae-currō, (cu)currī, cursum 3 to run before, hasten on before; **a)** to precede, anticipate (*alqd*); **b)** to exceed, surpass, excel (*alqm re*).
prae-cursiō, ōnis *f* **a)** previous occurrence; **b)** preliminary skirmish.
prae-cursor, ōris *m* forerunner; advanced guard; scout.
prae-cursōrius 3 sent in advance.
prae-cutiō, cussī, cussum 3 to shake *or* brandish before.
praeda, ae *f* booty, spoil, plunder; **a)** prey, game; **b)** gain, profit, advantage.
praedābundus 3 ravaging, plundering.
prae-damnō 1 to condemn beforehand; to give up in advance.
praedātiō, ōnis *f* (*and* **-dātus, ūs** *m*) a pillaging.
praedātor, ōris *m and* **-trīx, īcis** *f* plunderer; hunter; greedy person.
praedātōrius 3 plundering, predatory.
prae-dēlassō 1 to weary out beforehand.
prae-dēstinō 1 to decree beforehand (*alci alqd*).
praediātor, ōris *m* dealer in estates.
praediātōrius 3 relating to the sale of estates.
praedicābilis, e praiseworthy.
praedicātiō, ōnis *f* proclamation, publication; **a)** praise, commendation; **b)** declaration.
praedicātor, ōris *m* commender.
prae-dicō[1] 1 to publish, proclaim; **a)** to declare publicly, assert, announce, boast of; **b)** to praise, commend.
prae-dīcō[2] 3 to say *or* mention before; **a)** to foretell, predict, prophesy; **b)** to prearrange; to order beforehand.
prae-dictiō, ōnis *f* prediction.
prae-dictum, ī *n* **a)** prediction; **b)** order, command; **c)** agreement, concert.
praediolum, ī *n* small farm *or* estate.
prae-discō 3 to learn beforehand.
prae-dispositus 3 arranged beforehand.
prae-ditus 3 endowed, gifted *or* provided with; possessed of (*abl.*).
praedium, ī *n* farm, estate.
prae-dīves, itis very rich.
prae-dīvīnō 1 to have a presentiment.
praedō, ōnis *m* plunderer, robber; pirate.
prae-doceō 2 to instruct beforehand.
prae-domō 1 to overcome beforehand.
praedor 1 **1.** to make booty, plunder; **2.** *trans.* to carry off as prey; to plunder, rob.
prae-dūcō 3 to draw *or* construct in front of (*dat.*).
prae-dulcis, e very sweet.
prae-dūrus 3 very hard, very tough.
prae-ēmineō, 2 = praemineo.
prae-eō to go before (*alci*), lead the way; to dictate (a formula); to order, dictate.
prae-fātiō, ōnis *f* religious form of words, formula; preface, introduction.
praefectūra, ae *f* office of a *praefectus*; **a)** command, administration; **b)** district, province; city governed by a prefect; prefecture.
praefectus, ī *m* overseer, superintendent; **a)** commander, governor; **b)** prefect.
prae-ferō 3 to bear *or* carry before, in front (*alci alqd*); **a)** to show, display; manifest, betray; **b)** to put before; **c)** to prefer, choose rather (*alci alqd*); **d)** to anticipate; **P.** to ride *or* march past.
prae-ferōx, ōcis very defiant *or* headstrong.
prae-ferrātus 3 in irons.
prae-fervidus 3 very hot, glowing.
prae-festīnō 1 **a)** to hasten too much; **b)** to hasten past.
prae-fica, ae *f* woman hired to lament at a funeral.
prae-ficiō, fēcī, fectum 3 to set *or* place over, place in authority over (*alqm alci rei*), appoint to command.
prae-fīdēns, tis over-confident.
prae-fīgō 3 **a)** to fix *or* fasten in front *or* on the end; **b)** to point with; **c)** to pierce.

prae-fīniō 4 to determine beforehand, prescribe; **praefīnītō** (*as adv.*) as prescribed.
prae-fiscinē (-**nī**) *adv.* may no evil befall us!; meaning no harm, without offence.
prae-flōrō 1 to rob of its bloom beforehand.
prae-fluō, —, — 3 to flow by *or* past (*alqd*).
prae-fōcō 1 to choke.
prae-fodiō 3 **a**) to dig in front of (*alqd*); **b**) to bury beforehand.
prae-for 1 to say beforehand, utter in advance; **a**) to utter a preliminary prayer; **b**) to preface; **c**) to invoke; **d**) to foretell, prophesy.
prae-frāctus 3 abrupt; stern, harsh.
prae-frīgidus 3 very cold.
prae-fringō, frēgī, frāctum 3 to break off at the end.
prae-fulciō 4 to prop up; to use as a prop; to fence round; to secure.
prae-fulgeō 2 to shine forth, beam, glitter; to be conspicuous; to outshine.
prae-fulgurō 1 to flash forth; to fill with brightness (*acc.*).
prae-furō 3 to rage violently.
prae-gaudeō 2 to rejoice greatly.
prae-gelidus 3 very cold.
prae-gestiō 4 to desire greatly.
prae-gnā(n)s, (n)tis pregnant, with child, big with, full of.
prae-gracilis, e very slender.
prae-grandis, e very large; very powerful *or* great.
prae-gravis, e very heavy; **a**) burdensome; **b**) wearisome.
prae-gravō 1 to oppress with, encumber, burden; to depress, weigh down.
prae-gredior, gressus sum 3 **a**) to go before *or* in advance; **b**) to pass by, go past (*acc.*).
praegressiō, ōnis *f* a preceding, precedence.
praegressus, ūs *m* previous development.
prae-gustātor, ōris *m* one who tastes first, taster.
prae-gustō 1 to taste beforehand.
prae-hibeō 2 = **praebeo.**
prae-iaceō, —, — 2 to lie before *or* in front of (*acc.*).
prae-iūdicium, ī *n* previous judgment, preliminary decision; **a**) precedent, example; **b**) premature decision; **c**) prejudice, disadvantage.
prae-iūdicō 1 to judge *or* decide beforehand (*de re*); **praeiūdicātus** 3 decided previously, prejudged; **opinio praeiūdicāta** prejudice.
prae-lābor 3 to glide *or* flow past *or* along (*acc.*).
prae-lambō, —, — 3 to lick *or* taste before.
prae-largus 3 very prodigal of.
prae-lautus 3 very sumptuous.
prae-legō 3 **a**) to sail past; **b**) to lecture on.
prae-lībō 1 to taste beforehand.
prae-ligō 1 to bind in front; to bind up; **praeligātus** 3 obdurate.
prae-longus 3 very long.
prae-loquor 3 to speak before someone else; to speak by way of preface.
prae-lūceō 2 to shine before; to outshine, surpass (*alci*).
prae-lūdō 3 to say by way of preface.
prae-lūsiō, ōnis *f* prelude.
prae-lūstris, e magnificent.
prae-mandō 1 to order beforehand; *subst.* **praemandātum, ī** *n* warrant of arrest.
prae-mātūrus 3 too early, untimely, premature.
prae-medicātus 3 protected by medicines *or* charms.
prae-meditātiō, ōnis *f* a considering beforehand.
prae-meditor 1 to consider *or* meditate beforehand.
prae-mercor 1 to buy before.
prae-metuō, —, — 3 to fear beforehand; **praemetuenter** anxiously.
prae-mineo, —, — 2 to surpass, excel (*acc.*).
praemior 1 to stipulate for a reward.
prae-mittō 3 to send in advance; to send out; to say first.
praemium, ī *n* **1.** profit, advantage, gain; prerogative, distinction; **2.** reward, recompense; prize; exploit; booty.
prae-molestia, ae *f* trouble beforehand, apprehension.
prae-mōlior 4 to prepare.
prae-moneō 2 **a**) to forewarn, admonish beforehand (*ut, ne*); **b**) to foretell, presage.
prae-monitus, ūs *m* a forewarning.
prae-mōnstrātor, ōris *m* guide.
prae-mōnstrō 1 to show, guide, warn; to predict, presage.
prae-mordeō 2 to bite off.

prae-morior 3 to die prematurely.
prae-mūniō 4 **a**) to fortify, protect, secure; **b**) to place before as a defence; **c**) to say beforehand to obviate objections.
prae-mūnītiō, ōnis *f* preparation.
prae-nārrō 1 to relate beforehand.
prae-natō 1 to swim before *or* past, to flow by.
prae-nāvigō 1 to sail past; to pass through.
prae-niteō 2 to outshine (*alci*).
prae-nōmen, inis *n* first *or* personal name; title.
prae-nōscō 3 to learn beforehand, foreknow.
prae-nōtiō, ōnis *f* preconception, innate idea.
prae-nūbilus 3 very cloudy, very dark.
prae-nūntiō 1 to announce, foretell.
prae-nūntius, ī *m and* **-nūntia, ae** *f* foreteller, foreboder; **-nūntium, ī** *n* sign, omen.
prae-occupātiō, ōnis *f* a seizing beforehand.
prae-occupō 1 to seize *or* take possession of before; **a**) to anticipate, prevent; **b**) to hasten to do sooner.
prae-olit mihi I smell in advance.
prae-optō 1 to prefer.
prae-pandō, —, — 3 to spread out before, extend; to open.
prae-parātiō, ōnis *f* preparation.
prae-parō 1 to prepare, make ready, provide (*alqd ad alqd*).
prae-pedīmentum, ī *n* hindrance, impediment.
prae-pediō 4 to tether, shackle, fetter; to hinder, obstruct.
prae-pendeō, pendī, — 2 to hang down in front.
prae-pes, petis quick in flight, fleet; auspicious; *subst. m* and *f* bird; bird of good omen.
prae-pilātus 3 tipped with a ball.
prae-pinguis, e very fat, rich.
prae-polleō 2 to be very powerful, exceed in power.
prae-ponderō 1 to preponderate; to outweigh, surpass.
prae-pōnō 3 to put *or* set before; **a**) to put over, set over, place at the head of (*alqm alci rei*); **b**) to prefer; *subst.* **praepositus, ī** *m* = **praefectus; praepositum, ī** *n* preferable, desirable thing.
prae-portō 1 to carry in front; to show.
prae-positiō, ōnis *f* **a**) preference; **b**) preposition.
prae-posterus 3 reversed, inverted, perverse, preposterous; unseasonable.
prae-potēns, tis very mighty *or* powerful.
prae-properus 3 too hasty, precipitate; *adv.* **-rē** *and* **-ranter.**
prae-pūtium, ī *n* foreskin.
praequam, *see* **prae.**
prae-queror 3 to complain beforehand.
prae-radiō 1 to outshine.
prae-rapidus 3 very rapid.
prae-rigēscō, 3 to become very stiff.
prae-ripiō, ripuī, reptum 3 **a**) to seize first *or* prematurely; to forestall; **b**) to frustrate.
prae-rōdō 3 to gnaw (off).
prae-rogātīvus 3 voting before others; *subst.* **praerogātīva, ae** *f* **a**) century that voted first (also *n/pl.* the votes of the first centuries); **b**) previous choice; **c**) sign, omen.
prae-rumpō 3 to break off short.
prae-ruptus 3 steep, precipitous; headstrong; harsh.
praes, praedis *m* surety, bondsman; property of a surety.
praesaepe, is *n* (*and* **-saepēs** *or* **-saepis, is** *f*) **a**) manger; **b**) stall, stable, fold; home; **c**) beehive.
prae-saepiō 4 to barricade.
prae-sāgiō (*and* **-ior**) 4 to have a presentiment; to forebode.
praesāgitiō, ōnis *f* presentiment, foreboding.
praesāgium, ī *n* presentiment, foreboding, presage, prediction.
prae-sāgus 3 foreboding; predicting.
prae-sciō 4 to know beforehand.
prae-scīscō, īvī, (iī), — 3 to learn *or* find out beforehand.
prae-scius 3 knowing beforehand.
prae-scrībō 3 to prefix in writing; **a**) to use as a pretext; **b**) to dictate; **c**) to order, direct, prescribe (*alci alqd; ut, ne*); **d**) to outline in advance.
prae-scrīptiō, ōnis *f* title; **a**) pretext, excuse; **b**) order, rule; **c**) captious objection.
prae-scrīptum, ī *n* prescribed limit; task; order, rule.
prae-secō 1 to cut off short.

prae-segmen, inis *n* clippings.
praesēns, tis 1. present, in person; **2.** at hand, immediate, instant; a) ready, prompt, efficacious, powerful; b) pressing, urgent; c) aiding; propitious; d) determined, resolute; — **in praesēns** (*tempus*) for the present, for the moment; **in praesentī** at present, now; *subst.* **praesentia, ium** *n/pl.* the present, present circumstances.
prae-sēnsiō, ōnis *f* presentiment; preconception.
praesentāneus 3 having a quick effect.
praesentārius 3 = **praesens.**
praesentia, ae *f* presence, a being present; effect, efficacy.
prae-sentiō 4 to feel *or* perceive beforehand.
praesēpe, is *n*, *see* **praesaepe.**
praesertim *adv.* especially, chiefly.
prae-serviō 4 to serve by preference.
prae-ses, sidis presiding, protecting, guarding; *subst. m* and *f* **a**) protector, guardian, defender; **b**) chief, ruler.
prae-sideō, sēdī, (**sessum**) 2 to sit before; to protect, guard; to preside over, govern.
praesidiārius 3 serving as a guard *or* garrison.
praesidium, ī *n* protection, defence; **a**) aid, assistance, support; **b**) escort, convoy; **c**) guard, garrison, patrol, post, picket, troops; **d**) station, camp, fortification.
prae-significō 1 to indicate beforehand.
prae-signis, e remarkable before others.
prae-solidō 1 to solidify.
prae-sonō 1 to sound first.
prae-spargō 3 to strew before.
praestābilis, e = **praestans.**
praestāns, tis distinguished, excellent, superior, pre-eminent.
praestantia, ae *f* excellence, superiority.
praestātiō, ōnis *f* guarantee.
prae-sternō 3 to strew before; to lay in front; to deck, make ready; to smooth the way.
prae-stes, itis protecting.
praest(r)īgiae, ārum *f/pl.* deceptions, illusions, trickery.
prae-st(r)īgiātor, ōris *m*, **-trīx, īcis** *f* conjurer, cheat.
praestinō 1 to buy.
prae-stituō, uī, ūtum 3 to determine beforehand (*alci alqd*).
prae-stō[1] *adv.* at hand, ready, present, here, at one's service (*alci, ad alqd*); present in a hostile manner.
prae-stō[2], **stitī, stitum** (**stātūrus**) 1 **1.** to stand out, stand before; a) to distinguish oneself, excel (*alci re; alqm re*), be superior; b) **praestat** it is preferable *or* better (*dat.; dat. c. inf.*); **2.** *trans.* to perform, to execute, fulfil; **fidem** to keep one's word; a) to give, offer, furnish (*alci alqd*); b) to show, exhibit, prove, evince, manifest; **se praestare** to show *or* prove oneself (*constantem, fortem*); c) to answer, be responsible for, warrant (*alqm* or *alqd, de re; alci alqd; acc. c. inf.*).
praestōlor 1 to wait for (*alqd*), stand ready for (*alci*).
prae-stringō 3 to draw together, fasten up, bind fast; to blunt, dazzle, weaken.
prae-struō 3 to build before, block up; **a**) to secure beforehand; **b**) to prepare.
prae-sūdō 1 to sweat *or* labour greatly.
prae-sul, ulis *and* **-sultātor, ōris** *m* leader in a dance *or* procession.
prae-sultō 1 to leap *or* dance before.
prae-sum, fuī, (**futūrus**), **esse** to be leader, be set over, preside, rule, command, superintend (*with dat.*).
prae-sūmō 3 to take beforehand; **a**) to enjoy beforehand, anticipate; **b**) to imagine beforehand, to suppose, take for granted, presume, presuppose.
prae-sūmptiō, ōnis *f* expectation, hope.
prae-suō, —, sūtum 3 to sew up; to cover (*alqd re*).
prae-tegō 3 to cover, shelter.
prae-temptō 1 to feel, try *or* test beforehand.
prae-tendō, ndī, ntum 3 to stretch forth *or* forward; **a**) to place, hold *or* spread before (*alqd alci rei*); **P.** to lie before *or* in front; **b**) to pretend, hold before as a pretext.
prae-tentō 1, *see* **praetempto.**
(prae-tepēscō), praetepuī, — 3 to grow warm before.
praeter 1. *adv.* (*used as cj.*) unless it be, except; **2.** *prep.* with *acc.* past, in front of, along; a) except; b) above, besides; **c**) beyond, contrary to.

praeter-agō 3 to drive past.
praeter-bītō 3 to go by.
praeter-dūcō 3 to lead by.
praeter-eā *adv.* besides, beyond this, further; **a**) moreover; **b**) henceforth, thereafter.
praeter-eō to go by, pass by (*alqd*); **a**) to pass, elapse; **b**) to flow past *or* along; **c**) to escape the notice of, be unknown to; **d**) to neglect, omit, not to mention, leave unnoticed *or* unpractised; **e**) to go beyond, surpass, excel; to pass in a race; **praeteritus** 3 gone by, past, departed.
praeter-equitō 1 to ride past.
praeter-feror to go past (*alqd*).
praeter-fluō 3 to flow by *or* past (*alqd*); to pass away.
praeter-gredior, gressus sum 3 to walk by; to surpass.
praeter-hāc *adv.* further.
praeter-itus 3, *see* **praetereo.**
praeter-lābor 3 to glide past (*alqd*).
praeter-meō 1 to go by.
praeter-missiō, ōnis *f* omission, neglect.
praeter-mittō 3 to let pass; **a**) to omit, neglect, leave undone; **b**) to overlook.
praeter-nāvigō 1 to sail past.
prae-terō 3 to rub off.
praeter-quam *cj.* more than; except, beyond, unless it be; ~ **quod** except that, apart from the fact that.
praeter-vectiō, ōnis *f* a place where people sail by.
praeter-vehor 3 to pass, drive, ride, sail by (*alqd*).
praeter-volō 1 to fly by *or* past; to slip by, escape; to pass over cursorily.
prae-texō 3 **a**) to fringe, border, edge; **b**) to adorn in front; **praetextus** 3 bordered with purple (*also* = **praetextātus**); **c**) to cover, conceal (*alqd re*); **d**) to pretend, allege as an excuse.
praetexta, ae *f* **a**) (*toga*) purple-bordered toga (worn by the higher magistrates and by free-born boys); **b**) (*fabula*) tragedy dealing with Roman life.
praetextātus 3 wearing a *toga praetexta*; under age; indecent.
praetextum, ī *n* pretence, pretext; ornament.
praetextus, ūs *m* outward appearance, show, adornment; pretence, pretext.
prae-timeō 2 to fear beforehand.
prae-tinctus 3 moistened beforehand.
praetor, ōris *m* leader, chief, president; **a**) commander, general; **b**) praetor, magistrate; **c**) governor.
praetōriānus 3 prætorian, belonging to the imperial bodyguard; *subst. m* one of the imperial body-guard.
praetōricius 3 of a prætor.
praetōrius 3 **a**) relating to a prætor, of a prætor; **b**) of a general; **cohors praetōria** a general's *or* emperor's body-guard; **porta, -ia** the gate near the general's tent; **c**) belonging to a proprætor; — *subst.* **a**) **-ius, ī** *m* a past prætor; **b**) **-ium, ī** *n* a general's tent; council of war; place before the general's tent; residence of a governor; palace, imposing residence; imperial body-guard.
prae-torqueō 2 to twist, wring.
prae-tractō 1 to discuss beforehand.
prae-trepidō 1 to be excited.
prae-trepidus 3 palpitating; disquieted.
prae-truncō 1 to cut off.
praetūra, ae *f* prætorship.
prae-umbrō 1 to overshadow, to obscure.
prae-ustus 3 burned at the end *or* point; frost-bitten.
praeut, *see* **prae.**
prae-vādō 3 to obtain a discharge from (*acc.*).
prae-valeō, uī, — 2 to be very strong *or* powerful, to be stronger, have greater power *or* worth, be superior, prevail.
prae-validus 3 very strong *or* powerful; too strong.
prae-vallō 1 to fortify in front.
praevāricātiō, ōnis *f* collusion.
praevāricātor, ōris *m* collusive advocate, sham accuser.
prae-vāricor 1 to play a double part, be a false advocate.
prae-vehor 3 to drive, ride, fly, forward *or* in front; to flow past.
prae-veniō 4 to come before, get the start of, to forestall.
prae-verrō 3 to sweep.
prae-vertō *and* **-vertor** 3 **a**) to do first *or* in preference, attend to first; to be wholly occupied with, intent on; **b**) to go before, precede, outrun;

c) to interfere with, anticipate, prevent; **d**) to possess first; **e**) to be of more importance, outweigh.
prae-vetitus 3 forbidden.
prae-videō 2 to see first; to foresee.
prae-vitiō 1 to corrupt beforehand.
prae-vius 3 going before.
prae-volō 1 to fly before, in advance.
prae-vortō, *see* **prae-vertō.**
prāgmaticus 3 skilled in state business.
prandeō, ndī, ānsum 2 to lunch (on); **prānsus** 3 having lunched.
prandium, ī *n* lunch.
prānsitō 1 to lunch on.
prānsor, ōris *m* guest at lunch.
prasinus 3 (leek-)green.
prātēnsis, e growing in meadows.
prātulum, ī *n* small meadow.
prātum, ī *n* meadow; meadow grass; flat surface.
prāvitās, ātis *f* crookedness, deformity; **a**) perversity; **b**) viciousness, wickedness.
prāvus 3 crooked, distorted, deformed; **a**) perverse; **b**) bad, wicked, vicious.
precārius 3 **a**) obtained by begging *or* entreaty; **b**) uncertain, precarious; *adv.* **precāriō** by entreaty; on sufferance.
precātiō, ōnis *f* a begging, entreating, prayer.
precātor, ōris *m* pleader, intercessor.
precātus, ūs *m* prayer.
precēs, um *f/pl.* (*sing. rare*) wish, entreaty; **a**) prayer; **b**) curse, execration.
preciae, ārum *f/pl.* a kind of vine.
precor 1 to beg, pray, beseech, entreat; to pray to, invoke (*alqm, alqd, alqd ab alqo; ut, ne*); to wish good *or* evil (*alci alqd*), curse.
prehendō, ndī, ēnsum 3 to grasp, seize, lay hold of; **a**) to catch, occupy; to reach; **b**) to arrest, detain.
prehēnsō 1 = **prenso.**
prēlum, ī *n* wine-press, olive-press; clothes-press.
premō, pressī, pressum 3 **1.** to press, compress; **a**) to press out, express, obtain by pressing; **b**) to press with the body, stand, sit *or* lie on (*torum, humum, currum*); **vestigia alcis** to follow in the footsteps of; **c**) to press down, burden, load, freight (*magno onere alqm*); **d**) to cover, conceal by covering; to bury; **e**) to press hard upon, keep close to; to pursue closely, follow up; to importune, vex; **f**) to depress, lower; **2.** to press into, force in; a) to plant; b) to impress, mark; c) to press down, weigh down, sink; to oppress, overwhelm; d) to degrade, humble, disparage, depreciate; e) to check, tighten, repress, restrain; f) to shorten, prune; g) to keep down, rule; h) to overshadow; to compress, close, shut; i) to abridge, condense.
prēndō = **prehendo.**
prēnsātiō, ōnis *f* a canvassing for office.
prēnsō 1 **a**) to grasp, seize, lay hold of; **b**) to canvass.
pressiō, ōnis *f* leverage; contrivance for raising a heavy mass.
pressō 1 to press.
pressus[1] 3 compressed; **a**) low (*voice*); moderate; **b**) concise; **c**)restrained, plain, without ornament; **pressē** *adv.* distinctly; concisely; simply; exactly.
pressus[2], **ūs** *m* pressure.
prēstēr, ēris *m* **a**) fiery whirlwind; **b**) serpent whose bite causes burning thirst.
pretiōsus 3 valuable, precious, costly; extravagant.
pretium, ī *n* worth, value, price; **pretio** by purchase; bribe; ransom; wages, reward; punishment; **operae pretium est** it is worth while.
precem, -ī, -e, *see* **preces.**
prīdem *adv.* long ago, long since.
prīdiānus of the day before, yesterday's.
prī-diē *adv.* on the day before; **a**) **prīdiē quam** a day earlier than; **b**) **prīdiē eius diei** the day before.
prīm-aevus 3 youthful.
prīmānus, ī *m* soldier of the first legion.
prīmārius 3 of the first rank, principal, excellent.
prīmi-genus 3 original, first.
prīmi-pīlāris, is *m and* **prīmi-pīlus, ī** *m* the first centurion of a legion.
prīm-itiae, ārum *f/pl.* firstlings, firstfruits; first attempt.
prīmitus *adv.* at first; for the first time.
prīm-ōrdium, ī *n* first beginning, origin, original element; beginning of a new reign.

prīmōris, e a) at the extreme edge *or* tip of; **b**) first, chief, principal (*also as subst.*).

prīmulus 3 first, early; *adv.* **-um** first.

prīmus 3 first; at the extremity of; **prīmum agmen** the van; **prīmā nocte** at the beginning of the night; **in prīmā prōvinciā** at the entrance of the province; the first, chief, principal, most excellent; — *subst.* **a**) **prīmae, ārum** *f/pl.* (*scil. partes*), the chief *or* leading part, first rank; **b**) **prīmum, ī** *n* the van, first part, beginning; — *adv.* **prīmum:** for the first time; firstly; **ubi prīmum** as soon as; **quam prīmum** as soon as possible; **prīmō** at first, at the beginning; firstly.

prīn-ceps, ipis 1. *adj.* = **prīmus; 2.** *subst. m* a) author, founder; mover; b) leader, head, chief, master, superior, director, ruler, prince, sovereign, emperor; **prīncipēs, um** *m/pl.* **a**) the first, most eminent, most noble; **b**) soldiers of the second line (*between the hastati and triarii*); *sing.* a company of the *principes*, centurion(ship) of the *principes*.

prīncipālis, e a) first, original, primitive; **b**) princely, imperial; **c**) chief, principal.

prīncipātus, ūs *m* the first place, pre-eminence; **a**) highest place, commandership; **b**) rule, reign, sovereignity, dominion, empire; **c**) principle; **d**) beginning.

prīncipiālis, e in the beginning, earliest.

prīncipium, ī *n* a beginning, commencement; (**in** *or* **a**) **prīncipiō** at the beginning, at first; **a**) foundation, element, principle; **b**) (*pl.*) the foremost rank, front line of soldiers; **c**) (*pl.*) head-quarters, principal place in a camp.

prior, us *comp.* **a**) former, previous, prior, first; **b**) better, superior; **c**) (in) front, fore; *subst.* **priōrēs, um** *m/pl.* ancestors; **prius** *adv.* earlier, previously.

prīscus 3 of former times, old, olden, ancient; **a**) antique, venerable; **b**) former, previous; **c**) old-fashioned, severe, strict.

prīstinus 3 **a**) former, early, primitive, original; **b**) just past, previous.

pristis, is *f* **a**) a sea-monster, whale; **b**) ship of war.

prius-quam *cj.* before; **non prius quam** not until.

prīvātim *adv.* apart from state affairs, as an individual, for oneself, privately, separately; at home.

prīvātiō, ōnis *f* a freeing from (*gen.*).

prīvātus 3 apart from the state, belonging to an individual, private, personal; **a**) common, out of office, not princely; **b**) *subst.* **~, ī** *m* private individual; **-um, ī** *n* private property, private use, privacy.

prīvīgna, ae *f* step-daughter.

prīvīgnus, ī *m* step-son.

prīvi-lēgium, ī *n* law relating to a single person only; privilege, prerogative.

prīvō 1 to bereave, deprive of (*alqm re*); to free, release.

prīvus 3 single, each, every, one each; private, peculiar, particular.

prō[1] *int.* oh! ah! alas! (with *voc.: pro sancte Juppiter;* with *acc.: pro deum hominumque fidem*).

prō[2] *prep.* with *abl.* **1.** (*of place*) a) before, in front of, in face of (*aciem pro castris instruere, pro templis praesidia collocare*); b) from, on (the front of) (*pro tectis* or *pro litore stare, orationem habere pro rostris*); **2.** (*of relation*) a) for, on behalf of, for the benefit of, in the service of (*pro patria pugnare, pro libertate mori, oratio pro Milone*); b) in the place of, instead of, for, as good as (*Cato unus mihi est pro centum milibus, pro vallo carros obiecerant, aliquem pro deo colere, se pro cive gerere, Volsci pro victis abierunt*); c) as a reward, in exchange *or* return for (*pro beneficiis gratiam referre*); d) in proportion to, according to, by virtue of (*proelium atrocius quam pro numero pugnantium, alqm pro dignitate laudare, pro viribus agere, consilium pro tempore et pro re capere, pro mea parte* for my part, *pro se quisque* each one according to his strength). **prō quam** = **proquam.**

pro-āgorus, ī *m* chief magistrate *of a place* (*in Sicily*).

pro-auctor, ōris *m* ancestor.

pro-avia, ae *f* great grandmother.

pro-avītus 3 ancestral.

pro-avus, ī *m* great grandfather; ancestor.

probābilis, e that may be believed *or* approved; pleasing, acceptable; probable, credible, likely.
probābilitās, ātis *f* probability, credibility.
probātiō, ōnis *f* proving, examination; **a**) approval, assent; **b**) proof, demonstration.
probātor, ōris *m* approver.
probātus 3 **a**) approved, tried and found good; **b**) pleasing, acceptable.
prōbet = **prohibet.**
probitās, ātis *f* honesty, uprightness.
probō 1 **1.** to try, test, prove, examine, inspect; a) to judge; b) to approve, esteem good; **2.** a) to represent *or* commend as good *or* serviceable; **P.** *or* **se probāre alci** to render oneself acceptable, to recommend oneself to; b) to show, prove, demonstrate (*alci alqd*).
pro-boscis, idis *f* trunk (*of an elephant*).
probriperlecebrae, ārum *f/pl.* enticements to vice.
probrōsus 3 shameful, ignominious, infamous, abusive.
probrum, ī *n* **a**) shameful *or* disgraceful deed; unchastity, lewdness; **b**) disgrace, infamy; reproach, abuse, insult.
probus 3 good, proper, excellent; **a**) upright, honest, virtuous, honourable; **b**) modest.
procācitās, ātis *f* impudence.
procāx, ācis importunate, bold, insolent, shameless, forward.
prō-cēdō 3 to go forth *or* before; **a**) to proceed, advance, go forward; **b**) to appear, show oneself, step forward; **c**) to advance, make progress; to run on, pass, elapse; to continue, remain; to go on; **eo prōcēdere** to go so far; **d**) to turn out, result, succeed well, prosper.
procella, ae *f* storm, tempest; onset, charge, stormy attack.
prō-cellō 3 to throw forward.
procellōsus 3 stormy.
procerēs, um *m/pl.* (*and sing.* **-rem**) chiefs, nobles, princes.
prōcēritās, ātis *f* tallness, height, length.
prō-cērus 3 tall, long, extended.
prōcessiō, ōnis *f* advance.
prōcessus, ūs *m* advance, progress.
prō-cidō, cidī, — 3 to fall down *or* forward.
prōciduus 3 fallen, prostrate.
(**prō-cinctus** *m*) **in prōcinctū** on the battle-field, ready for action.
prō-clāmātor, ōris *m* shouter, noisy advocate.
prō-clāmō 1 to call out, cry out.
prō-clīnō 1 to turn, incline; **-nātus** turned in someone's favour; going downhill.
prō-clīvis, e sloping down, steep; **a**) inclined, prone to (*ad alqd*); **b**) easy; *subst.* **-clīve, is** *n* descent; *adv.* **-clīve, -clīvī** downhill, easily, readily.
prō-clīvitās, ātis *f* slope; inclination, tendency.
prō-clīvus 3 = **proclivis; planus ex prōclīvō** flat instead of steep; easy instead of difficult, plain instead of obscure.
procoetōn, ōnis *m* anteroom.
prō-cōnsul, ulis *m* proconsul.
prōcōnsulāris, e proconsular.
prōcōnsulātus, ūs *m* proconsulship.
procor 1 to ask, demand.
prōcrāstinātiō, ōnis *f* a putting off from day to day.
prō-crāstinō 1 to put off till tomorrow.
prō-creātiō, ōnis *f* procreation.
prō-creātor, ōris *m* begetter (*pl.* parents); creator, producer.
prō-creātrīx, īcis *f* she who brings forth, mother.
prō-creō 1 to beget; produce, cause, make.
prō-crēscō 3 to spring; to grow.
prō-cubō 1 to lie stretched out.
prō-cūdō 3 to forge, hammer out, produce.
procul *adv.* far off, far away, at a distance; from afar; **procul dubio** without doubt.
prō-culcō 1 to tread down, trample upon; *hence* **prōculcātiō, ōnis** *f.*
proculēna, ae *f* little sow.
prō-cumbō, cubuī, cubitum 3 to lean, bend *or* fall forward; **a**) to fall *or* sink down, prostrate oneself; **b**) to fall to ruin.
prōcūrātiō, ōnis *f* a taking care of; **a**) administration, management, charge; **b**) office of a procurator; **c**) expiatory sacrifice, expiation.
prōcūrātiuncula, ae *f* a trifling post *or* duty.
prō-cūrātor, ōris *m* manager, administrator; **a**) agent, deputy; **b**) imperial finance-officer *or* governor.

prōcūrātrīx, īcis *f* governess, protectress.
prō-cūrō (*and* **prŏ-**) 1 **a**) to take care of, attend to, look after, administer (as an agent or procurator); **b**) to expiate.
prō-currō, (cu)currī, cursum 3 to run *or* rush forward; to project.
prō-cursātiō, ōnis *f* sally, skirmishing.
prōcursātor, ōris *m* skirmisher.
prō-cursō 1 to run forth, to skirmish.
prō-cursus, ūs *m* a running forward, sally, attack.
prō-curvō 1 to bend forwards.
prō-curvus 3 bent *or* curved forward.
procus, ī *m* wooer, suitor; canvasser.
prō-deambulō 1 to walk out.
prōd-eō to go *or* come forth (*ex re in alqd*); **a**) to appear, show oneself, to appear in public; **b**) to advance, go forward.
prō-dīcō 3 to put off, defer.
prō-dictātor, ōris *m* vice-dictator.
prōdigentia, ae *f* profusion, prodigality.
prōdigiālis, e a) averting unnatural portents; **b**) unnatural, monstrous.
prōdigiōsus 3 wonderful, strange, unnatural.
prōdigium, ī *n* **a**) prodigy, portent, omen, token, sign; **b**) monster.
prōd-igō, ēgī, — 3 to drive forth; to use up, squander.
prōdigus 3 wasteful, prodigal; **a**) rich, generous; **b**) not sparing.
prōditiō, ōnis *f* betrayal, treachery, treason.
prōditor, ōris *m* betrayer, traitor.
prō-dō, didī, ditum 3 to give *or* bring forth; **a**) to produce, bear; **b**) to put forth in writing, to hand down, transmit (*alci alqd*); **c**) to publish, proclaim relate, report; **d**) to appoint; **e**) to discover, reveal, betray; **f**) to betray perfidiously, surrender, abandon (*alci alqd*); **g**) to prolong.
prō-doceō 2 to teach, inculcate.
pro-dromus, ī *m* forerunner, messenger; wind blowing before the rising of the Dog-star.
prō-dūcō 3 **1.** to lead forth, to bring out (in front of), conduct; a) to produce, introduce; b) to cause to appear; c) to promote, advance; d) to induce; **2.** to draw *or* stretch out, lengthen; a) to beget; b) to protract, put off; c) to bring up, cultivate.
prō-ductiō, ōnis *f* a lengthening, prolonging, a putting off.
prō-ductō 1 to spin out.
prō-ductus 3 lengthened, prolonged, drawn out; **prōducta, ōrum** *n/pl.* = **proegmena.**
pro-ēgmena, ōrum *n/pl.* preferable things.
proeliāris, e pertaining to a battle.
proeliātor, ōris *m* warrior.
proelior 1 to fight (*cum alqo*).
proelium, ī *n* battle, fight, combat; *plur.* warriors.
pro-fānō 1 to desecrate, profane.
pro-fānus 3 not sacred, profane; common; impious; ill-boding.
pro-fātus, ūs *m* an uttering.
profectiō, ōnis *f* a setting out, departure; source, origin.
pro-fectō *adv.* truly, surely, really, indeed.
prōfectus, ūs *m* advance, progress, increase, profit.
prō-ferō 3 **1.** to carry forward *or* bring forth; a) to extend, stretch out; b) to make known, produce in public, discover, reveal, invent; c) to bring to light, perform, produce; d) to utter, quote, mention; **2.** a) to advance, move forward, extend, lengthen; b) to put off, postpone.
professiō, ōnis *f* **a**) public acknowledgment, declaration, return (of name, property, &c.); **b**) business, profession.
professor, ōris *m* public teacher.
professōrius 3 of a school-master.
pro-fēstus 3 not festival, common.
prō-ficiō, fēcī, fectum 3 to advance; **a**) to make progress, to effect *or* gain something (*alqd in re, ad alqd*); **b**) to be useful, serviceable (*ad alqd*).
pro-ficīscor (*and* **-cō;** *also* **prōficīscor**), **fectus sum** 3 **a**) to set out, march, depart, go, travel; **b**) to set out from, begin with, go on; **c**) to spring *or* arise from.
pro-fiteor (*and* **prō-**), **fessus sum** 2 to declare publicly, acknowledge, confess, avow; **a**) to profess an art *or* science (*philosophiam, ius*); **b**) **se profitērī** to profess to be something (*se philo-*

sophum) **c**) to offer, propose, promise; **d**) to give in one's name (for service), make a return (of property, &c.);— **professus** 3 acknowledged.

prō-flātus, ūs *m* breathing forth, snoring.

prōfligātor, ōris *m* spendthrift.

prōfligātus 3 **a**) degraded, abandoned; **b**) advanced (age).

prō-flīgō 1 to strike to the ground, overthrow, overcome; **a**) to ruin, destroy; **b**) to lower, debase; **c**) to bring nearly to an end.

prō-flō 1 to blow *or* breathe forth.

prō-fluēns, tis, *see* **profluo.**

prō-fluentia, ae *f* a flowing forth.

prō-fluō 3 to flow forth; to issue, proceed; **prōfluēns, tis** flowing along; *subst. f* running water, stream.

prō-fluvium, ī *n* a flowing forth.

pro-for 1 to say *or* speak out.

prō-fringō 3 to break up, to till.

pro-fugiō 3 to flee away, escape; to flee before *or* from (*acc.*).

pro-fugus 3 fleeing, fugitive; banished.

pro-fundō (*and* **prō-**) 3 to pour *out or* forth; **P.** *or* **se profundere** to gush forth, to burst forth; **a**) to utter; **b**) to bring forth, produce; **c**) to spend, sacrifice, lavish, squander; **d**) to stretch *or* lay out.

pro-fundus 3 deep, profound, bottomless, immoderate, inexhaustible; *subst.* **-um, ī** *n* depth, the deep, sea.

pro-fūsiō, ōnis *f* profusion, prodigality.

pro-fūsus 3 lavish, excessive; extravagant, profuse; **profūsē** *adv.* in disorder.

prō-gener, erī *m* granddaughter's husband.

prō-generō 1 to beget, generate.

prōgeniēs, ēī *f* descent, lineage, race; progeny, offspring.

prō-genitor, ōris *m* ancestor, progenitor.

prō-gignō 3 to beget, bear, produce.

prō-gnāriter *adv.* expertly, properly.

prō-gnātus 3 born, descended.

prō-gredior, gressus sum 3 **a**) to go forth *or* out (*ex re, in alqd*); to go forward, advance; **b**) to go on, proceed (*in speech*).

prōgressiō, ōnis *f, fig.* = **progressus.**

prō-gressus, ūs *m* **a**) advance, progression, progress; **b**) a beginning; **c**) growth, increase, advancement.

progymnastēs, ae *m* a slave who teaches gymnastics.

pro-hibeō, uī, itum 2 **1.** to hold back, keep in check, keep off, verta (*alqm* or *alqd re, a re*); **commeatu** to cut off from supplies; **senatu** to exclude from the senate; a) to prevent, hinder (*inf.; acc. c. inf.; ne, quominus, quin*); b) to forbid, prohibit; **2.** to preserve, defend, protect (*alqd a re*).

prohibitiō, ōnis *f* a forbidding.

prō-iciō, iēcī, iectum 3 **a**) to throw forth *or* before (*alci alqd*); **b**) to throw, thrust, drive *or* put out, to stretch out, extend (*bracchium, pedem, hastam*); **P.** to project; **c**) to cast out, expel, exile, banish; **d**) to throw down *or* away, let go, abandon; to give up, yield, resign, neglect.

prō-iectīcius 3 cast out, exposed.

prō-iectiō, ōnis *f* a stretching out.

prō-iectō 1 to blame.

prō-iectus[1] 3 stretched out, jutting out, projecting; **a**) prominent, conspicuous; **b**) inclined, prone (*in alqd*); **c**) abject, contemptible; downcast.

prō-iectus[2], **ūs** *m* stretching-out.

prō-iiciō, *see* **proicio.**

proin, proinde *adv.* **a**) therefore, so; **b**) just so; ~ **ac, ut** just as; ~ **quasi** just as if.

prō-lābor 3 **1.** to glide forward, to slide *or* slip along; a) to go on, proceed; b) to fall into (a feeling *or* state); **2.** to slip out, escape; a) to fall down; b) to fall into decay; c) to fail, err; d) to sink, decline, go to ruin.

prō-lāpsiō, ōnis *f* a slipping, falling.

prō-lātiō, ōnis *f* a bringing forward, mentioning, citing; **a**) extension, enlargement; **b**) a putting off, delay.

prō-lātō 1 **a**) to extend, enlarge; **b**) to put off, delay, postpone.

prō-lectō 1 to allure, entice.

prōlēs, is *f* offspring, progeny, race, stock; **a**) descendants; **b**) young men.

prōlētārius 3 common, vulgar; *subst. m* citizen of the lowest class.

prō-liciō, —, — 3 to allure forth, to excite.

prō-lixus 3 a) extended, wide, broad; b) willing, well-disposed; favourable, fortunate.
prō-logus, ī *m* preface, prologue; the deliverer of a prologue.
prō-loquor 3 to speak out, utter, declare.
prō-lubium, ī *n* desire, inclination.
prō-lūdō 3 to practise beforehand (*ad alqd*); to rehearse.
prō-luō, uī, ūtum 3 a) to wash, wet, moisten; b) to wash off *or* away.
prō-lūsiō, ōnis *f* preliminary exercise.
prō-luviēs, ēī *f* a) overflow, inundation; b) refuse, filth.
prō-mercālis, e on sale.
(**prō-mereō** *and*) **prō-mereor** 2 a) to deserve, merit, be worthy of (*alqd; ut*); b) to deserve well (*de alqo*); c) to earn (the good-will of).
prō-meritum, ī *n* desert, merit (*in alqm*); guilt.
prō-mineō, —, — 2 to stand out, jut, project, overhang; to reach out, extend; *subst.* **prōminēns, tis** *n* projection.
prō-miscuus (*and* **-cus**) 3 mixed, not distinct *or* separate, indiscriminate, in common; mean, ordinary; *adv.* **-c(u)ē, -cam.**
prō-missiō, ōnis *f* a promising.
prōmissor, ōris *m* promiser, boaster.
prōmissum, ī *n* promise.
prō-missus 3 hanging down, long.
prō-mittō 3 **1.** to let grow, let hang down; **2.** to promise, give hope of (*alci alqd, de re, acc. c. inf.*); a) to promise to come, engage oneself to dine (*ad alqm*); b) to foretell, predict.
prōmō, mpsī, mptum 3 a) to take out, bring forth (*alqd ex re*), produce, put *or* draw forth; b) to bring to light, disclose; c) to utter, tell, express (*alqd*).
prō-moneō, —, — 2 to remind.
prōmontorium, ī *n* = **promunturium.**
prōmōta, ōrum *n/pl.* = **proegmena** *or* **producta.**
prō-moveō 2 to move forward, push onward; a) to cause to advance; b) to extend; c) to bring to light; d) to promote; e) to postpone.
prōmptāria cella *f* store-chamber; prison.
prōmptō 1 to distribute; to have the disposal of.
prōmptus[1] 3 **1.** visible, apparent, manifest; **2.** at hand, ready; a) inclined, disposed; b) enterprising; resolute, courageous; c) easy, practicable.
prōmptus[2], **ūs** *m*; *only* **in prōmptū** a) public, open, visible, before the eyes; b) ready, at hand; c) easy.
prōmulgātiō, ōnis *f* public announcement.
prō-mulgō 1 to publish, promulgate.
prō-mulsis, idis *f* a relish taken before a meal, hors d'œuvre.
prōmunturium, ī *n* headland, promontory.
prōmus, ī *m* steward, butler; keeper.
prō-mūtuus 3 advanced, lent beforehand.
prō-nectō 3 to spin out.
pro-nepōs, ōtis *m* great grandson.
pro-neptis, is *f* great granddaughter.
pro-noea, ae *f* providence.
prō-nuba, ae *f* bride's attendant, brides-woman; patroness of marriage.
prō-nūntiātiō, ōnis *f* publication, proclamation; a) decision of a judge; b) proposition (*in logic*); c) utterance, delivery.
prō-nūntiātor, ōris *m* narrator, relater.
prōnūntiātum, ī *n* proposition, axiom.
prō-nūntiō 1 a) to publish, proclaim, announce, make known, disclose (*alci alqd*); b) to relate, report; c) to order; d) to recite, declaim, deliver; e) to decide, pronounce a judgment.
prō-nūper = **nūper.**
prō-nurus, ūs *f* a grandson's wife.
prōnus 3 inclined forward, hanging down, face downwards; a) stooping; flying headlong; setting, sinking; b) sloping, precipitous, steep; c) inclined, well disposed, favourable; d) easy; *subst.* **prōnum, ī** *n* slope.
pro-oemior 1 to make a preface *or* introduction.
pro-oemium, ī *n* introduction, preface.
propāgātiō, ōnis *f* a) an extending, enlarging, prolonging; b) propagation.

propāgātor, ōris *m* enlarger, extender.
pro-pāgō[1] (*and* **prō-**), **inis** *f* sucker, layer, shoot; **a**) offspring, child; **b**) progeny, posterity.
pro-pāgō[2] (*and* **prō-**) 1 to propagate; **a**) to enlarge, extend; **b**) to prolong.
prō-palam *adv.* publicly, openly.
prō-patulus 3 open *or* uncovered in front; **in prōpatulō** in the open air; publicly.
prope (*comp.* **propius,** *superl.* **proximē** *and* **-umē**) **1.** *adv.* near, nigh; a) not far distant; b) at hand; c) nearly, almost; **2.** *prep.* with *acc.* a) (*of place*) near, near by, hard by; b) (*of time* and *other relations*) close to, near to, about (*res prope secessionem venit*); **3.** a) *comp. adj.* **propior, ius** nearer, nigher; **propiora** *n/pl.* places lying nearer; later, more recent; more nearly related, more like, more intimate, concerning more nearly; b) *superl.* **proximus** (*and* **-umus**) 3 the nearest, next, very near; *subst.* **proximum, ī** *n* neighbourhood, nearest place *or* point; next preceding *or* following (**proximē** shortly before *or* after); the next in value *or* quality, most like *or* similar, most closely related; *subst.* **proximī, ōrum** *m/pl.* nearest relatives, those standing next.
prope-diem *adv.* very soon.
prō-pellō (*and* **prŏ-**), **pulī, pulsum** 3 to drive, push *or* urge forward (*alqd ex re in rem*); **a**) to drive out *or* away; **b**) to drive on, move, impel; **c**) to keep off (*alqd ab alqo*).
prope-modum *and* **-modo** *adv.* nearly, almost.
propempticon, ī *n* farewell address.
prō-pendeō, pendī, pēnsum 2 to hang down; **a**) to preponderate, weigh more; **b**) to be inclined *or* disposed.
prō-pēnsiō, ōnis *f* inclination, propensity.
prō-pēnsus 3 hanging down; **a**) heavy (*i.e.* rich); important; **b**) coming near, approaching; **c**) inclined, disposed, ready, willing (*in* or *ad alqd*).
properanter *adv.* hastily, speedily, quickly.
properantia, ae *and* **properātiō, ōnis** *f* haste, speed.
properātō *adv.* = **properanter.**
properi-pēs, pedis swift-footed.
properō 1 **a**) to do in haste, hasten; **b**) *intr.* to make haste, be quick.
properus 3 hastening, quick, speedy.
prō-pexus 3 combed forward, hanging down.
propīnātiō, ōnis *f* a drinking to someone's health, a toast.
prō-pīnō (*and* **prŏ-**) 1 to drink to one's health; to deliver, yield up.
propinquitās, ātis *f* **a**) nearness; **b**) relationship.
propinquō 1 **a**) to come near, draw near, approach; **b**) to hasten, accelerate.
propinquus 3 near, nigh, neighbouring; **a**) near in time, at hand; **b**) similar; **c**) kindred, related; *subst.* **propinquus, ī** *m and* **-a, ae** *f* relation, kinsman, kinswoman; **propinquē** *adv.* near.
propior, ius, *comp. of* **prope.**
propitiō 1 to appease, propitiate.
propitius 3 favourable, inclined, well disposed, gracious (*alci*).
pro-pnigēum, ī *n* fire-place (*of a bath*).
prō-pōla, ae *m* retailer of eatables.
prō-polluō 3 to defile *or* pollute.
prō-pōnō 3 to put *or* set forth, lay out, expose to view; **a**) to expose for sale, offer; **b**) to make known, publish; **c**) to bring forward, declare, state a proposition; **d**) to propose, promise, offer as a reward (*alci alqd*); **P.** to threaten, menace; to set before the mind, imagine, conceive (*sibi spem*); to propose, make a proposal; **e**) to purpose, intend, design, resolve.
prōporrō furthermore, moreover.
prō-portiō, ōnis *f* proportion, symmetry, analogy.
prō-positiō, ōnis *f* = **propositum.**
prō-positum, ī *n* **1.** a) design, purpose, intention; b) notion; conception; c) manner *or* course of life; **2.** main point, principal subject, theme; **3.** first proposition in a syllogism.
prō-praetor, ōris *m* proprætor.
propriē *adv.* personally, as one's own, individually; **a**) peculiarly, characteristically; **b**) especially; **c**) properly, accurately, in the proper sense.
proprietās, ātis *f* a property, peculiar quality; ownership.

proprius 3 lasting, permanent; **a**) one's own, peculiar, proper; *subst.* **proprium, ī** *n* property; **b**) characteristic, essential, especial; **c**) exclusive, personal, individual.
prōprōmptū, in ~ = in prōmptū.
propter 1. *adv.* near, hard by; **2.** *prep.* with *acc.* a) near, close to; b) on account of, because of, for.
propter-eā *adv.* therefore, on that account.
pro-pudiōsus 3 shameful, infamous.
pro-pudium, ī *n* **a**) shameful act; **b**) shameful person, villain, rascal.
prōpugnāculum, ī *n* bulwark, rampart, fort; **a**) defence, protection; **b**) grounds of defence.
prō-pugnātiō, ōnis *f* defence.
prō-pugnātor, ōris *m* defender, protector.
prō-pugnō 1 **a**) to fight in the front, go forth to fight; **b**) to fight in defence.
prō-pulsātiō, ōnis *f* a repelling.
prō-pulsō 1 to drive back, repel, ward off, avert (*alqd a re*).
prōquam in proportion as, according as.
prōra, ae *f* forepart of a ship, prow, bow; ship.
prō-rēpō 3 to creep forward, crawl out.
prōrēta, ae *m* watchman at the prow of a ship.
prō-ripiō, ripuī, reptum 3 to snatch, drag, tear forth; **se prōripere** to rush forward, hurry away.
prō-rītō 1 to attract.
prō-rogātiō, ōnis *f* prolongation; a deferring.
prō-rogō 1 to prolong, protract (*alci alqd*); to put off, defer.
prō(r)sus (*and* **prō(r)sum**) *adv.* straight forward; **a**) utterly, entirely, wholly, absolutely; **b**) in a word, in short.
prō-rumpō 3 **a**) *intrans.* (*and* **P.**) to break *or* burst forth; to break out; **b**) *trans.* to cause to break forth.
prō-ruō 3 **a**) to rush forth; **b**) to tumble down; **c**) *trans.* to throw down, pull down; **d**) **se ~** to rush.
prōsa (*sc. oratio*) *f* prose.
prō-sāpia, ae *f* family, race.
pro-scaenium, ī *n* the stage.
prō-scindō 3 **a**) to rend, to plough; **b**) to revile, censure.
prō-scrībō 3 to make public; **a**) to offer publicly for sale, advertise; **b**) to confiscate; **c**) to proscribe, outlaw.
prō-scrīptiō, ōnis *f* **a**) advertisement of sale; **b**) proscription.
prōscrīpturiō 4 to desire a proscription.
prō-secō 1 to cut off; to plough; *subst.* **prōsecta, ōrum** *n/pl.* parts cut off for sacrifice, entrails.
prō-seda, ae *f* prostitute.
prō-sēminō 1 to sow, to propagate.
prō-sentiō 4 to perceive beforehand.
prō-sequor 3 to follow, accompany, attend, escort (*acc.*); **a**) to pursue, attack; **b**) to go on *or* proceed with; **c**) to honour, present *or* treat with, wait upon; **d**) to go on, continue, follow up, describe at length.
prō-serō[1] 3 to extend, thrust out.
prō-serō[2] 3 to produce by sowing.
prō-serpō 3 to creep forward.
proseucha, ae *f* Jewish place of prayer.
prō-sicō = prō-secō.
prō-siliō, siluī (*and* **silīvī, siliī**), — 4 to spring *or* leap forth, burst forth, start out; to rush, hasten to a place.
prō-socer, erī *m* a wife's grandfather.
prō-spectō 1 to look forth, see afar off; **a**) to look at *or* out; **b**) to look for, await, expect.
prōspectus, ūs *m* (distant) view, prospect; **a**) (faculty of) sight; **b**) a sight.
prō-speculor 1 = **prospecto.**
prosperitās, ātis *f* good fortune, prosperity, success.
prosperō 1 to make successful, happy, prosperous (*alci alqd*).
prosperus 3 **a**) fortunate, according to one's wishes; **b**) favourable, lucky, prosperous, propitious.
prōspicientia, ae *f* foresight, precaution.
prō-spiciō, spexī, spectum 3 **1.** to look forward, into the distance, look out; to exercise foresight, take care of, provide for (*alci; ut, ne*); **2.** to see afar, command a view of; a) to have a wide prospect; b) to foresee; c) to provide, procure (*alci alqd*).
prō-sternō 3 to strew before, throw to the ground, cast down; to overthrow, destroy, ruin.
prō-stibilis, is *f*, **-stibulum, ī** *n* prostitute.
prō-stituō, uī, ūtum 3 to prostitute; **-ūta, ae** *f* prostitute.
prō-stō, stitī, — 1 to be on sale.

prō-subigō 3 to dig up.
prō-sum, prōfuī, (**prōfutūrus**), **prōdesse** to be useful, to be of use (*alci*).
prō-tegō 3 to cover in front; to protect, defend; to ward off.
prō-tēlō 1 to drive away.
prōtēlum, ī *n* line, succession.
prō-tendō, ndī, ntum 3 to stretch forth *or* out.
prō-tenus *adv.* = **protinus.**
prō-terō 3 to tread upon, trample down, crush, maltreat.
prō-terreō 2 to frighten away.
protervitās, ātis *f* boldness, impudence, wantonness.
protervus (*and* **prō-**) 3 vehement; **a**) bold, forward; **b**) impudent, wanton.
pro-thȳmē *adv.* willingly.
pro-thȳmia, ae *f* readiness, willingness.
prō-tinam = **prōtinus.**
prō-tinus *adv.* **a**) forward, further on; **b**) straightway, on the spot; immediately, at once; **c**) continuously, uninterruptedly.
prō-tollō 3 to stretch forth; to prolong; to defer.
prō-tonō 1 to thunder forth.
prōto-prāxia, ae *f* priority in a claim.
prōto-tomus 3 cut first; *subst. m* early greens.
prō-trahō 3 to draw *or* drag forth; **a**) to compel, force; **b**) to bring forth, produce, bring to light, reveal; to drag on, defer.
prō-trūdō 3 to thrust forth, push forward; to put off, defer.
prō-turbō 1 to drive on *or* away; to throw down.
pro-ut *cj.* according as, just as.
prō-vehō 3 to carry forward *or* away; **a**) to conduct, lead on, carry; **b**) to promote, advance, exalt, raise; **P.** to go on, ride, drive, *or* sail on; to advance, make progress; **prōvectus aetāte** advanced in life.
prō-veniō 4 to come forth, appear; **a**) to grow up, arise; to go on, advance; **b**) to thrive, prosper, flourish.
prōventus, ūs *m* growth, produce, harvest; issue, result, success.
prō-verbium, ī *n* old saying, proverb.
prō-vidēns, tis foreseeing, prudent.
prōvidentia, ae *f* foresight; **a**) precaution, forethought; **b**) providence.
prō-videō 2 to see from afar; **a**) to foresee; **b**) to look out, take care, care for (*dat.; de re; ut, ne*); **c**) to provide; **prōvīsō** with foresight.
prōvidus 3 foreseeing (*gen.*); **a**) cautious, provident, prudent; **b**) caring for (*gen.*).
prōvincia, ae *f* **1.** official duty, sphere of duty; business, office; **2.** province, administration of a province.
prōvinciālis, e of a province, provincial; *subst. m* provincial, inhabitant of a province.
prōvinciātim *adv.* province by province.
prō-vīsiō, ōnis *f* = **providentia.**
prō-vīsō 3 **a**) to go to see; **b**) to be on the look-out for.
prōvīsor, ōris *m* foreseer; provider.
prō-vīsus, ūs *m* = **providentia.**
prō-vīvō 3 to go on living.
prō-vocātiō, ōnis *f* appeal (in law).
prō-vocātor, ōris *m* challenger; a kind of gladiator.
prō-vocō 1 to call forth *or* out; **a**) to summon, invite, incite; **b**) to challenge; to emulate; **c**) to appeal (in law); to appeal to.
prō-volō 1 to fly forth; to rush forth.
prō-volvō 3 to roll forward *or* along; **P.** *and* **se prōvolvere a**) to throw oneself down, prostrate oneself; **b**) to be expelled.
prō-vomō 3 to vomit forth.
prō-vulgō 1 to make known publicly.
proxenēta, ae *m* agent, broker.
proximē *adv., see* **prope.**
proximitās, ātis *f* nearness, similarity; near relationship.
proximus 3, *superl. of* **prope.**
prūdēns, tis 1. knowing, with intention; foreseeing; **2.** a) skilled, experienced, practised (*gen.*); b) wise, discreet, prudent.
prūdentia, ae *f* **1.** a foreseeing; **2.** a) knowledge, skill; b) prudence, practical wisdom, discretion.
pruīna, ae *f* hoar-frost, rime; **a**) snow; **b**) winter.
pruīnōsus 3 covered with hoar-frost.
prūna, ae *f* burning *or* live coal.
prūniceus 3 of plum-tree wood.
prūnum, ī *n* plum.
prūnus, ī *f* plum-tree.
prūrīgō, inis *f* itch; itching desire.
prūriō 4 to itch; to long for.

prytanēum *and* **-īum, ī** *n* town hall, council-hall.
prytanis, is *m* prytanis (*Greek magistrate*).
psallō, lī, — 3 to play on *or* sing to the cithara.
psaltērium, ī *n* a stringed instrument.
psaltria, ae *f* female player on the cithara.
psecas, adis *f* hair-dresser.
psēphisma, atis *n* decree of a Greek popular assembly.
Pseudo-catō, ōnis *m* a sham Cato.
pseudomenos, ī *m* sophistical syllogism.
pseudo-thyrum, ī *n* secret door.
psīlo-citharistēs, ae *m* one who plays on the cithara without singing.
psīlōthrum, ī *n* a depilatory.
psithia (**vītis**) *f* a kind of vine.
psittacus, ī *m* parrot.
psȳcho-mantīum, ī *n* place where the souls of the dead were interrogated.
psythia = **psithia.**
-pte (*suffix*) self, own.
ptisanārium, ī *n* decoction of barley-groats.
pūbēns, tis mature, exuberant.
pūbertās, ātis *f* maturity, puberty; manhood; downy beard.
pūbēs[1], **is** *f* **a**) the genitals; **b**) young men; men, people.
pūbēs[2], **eris** adult, grown up; downy.
pūbēscō, buī, — 3 to arrive at the age of puberty; **a**) to grow up, arrive at maturity; **b**) to be covered *or* clothed (of plants).
pūblicānus, ī *m* farmer of state-revenues; **muliercula -a** wench of a tax-farmer.
pūblicātiō, ōnis *f* confiscation.
pūblicē *adv.* **a**) in the name, at the command of the state; **b**) in the interest of the state; **c**) at the cost of the state; **d**) all together, in a body.
pūblicitus *adv.* **a**) = **publice; b**) publicly, in public.
pūblicō 1 to make public; **a**) to appropriate to the public use; to confiscate; **b**) to give over to the public use; to prostitute; to publish.
pūblicus 3 belonging to the people, to the state, to the community; **a**) in the name, on account, at the cost of the state; **b**) public, common, general, universal; — *subst.* **a**) **rēs pūblica** public affair, state business, commonwealth, republic, state; public property, state treasury; the public interest; **b**) **pūblicum, ī** *n* state property; public revenue, treasury, money; public place, street; **in pūblicō** publicly, openly, in the street.
pudeō 2 **a**) to be ashamed; **b**) to make ashamed; mostly *impers.* **pudet** (*perf.* **puduit** *or* **puditum est**) **me alcis rei** I am ashamed of; **pudēns, tis** bashful, modest, chaste; **pudendus** 3 shameful, disgraceful, scandalous.
pudibundus 3 shamefaced, bashful.
pudīcitia, ae *f* bashfulness, modesty, chastity, virtue.
pudīcus 3 bashful, modest, chaste, virtuous.
pudor, ōris *m* sense of shame, shyness, bashfulness; **a**) honour; **b**) modesty, decency, sense of propriety; **c**) chastity; **d**) shame, disgrace.
puella, ae *f* girl, maiden; **a**) daughter; **b**) mistress, sweetheart; **c**) young woman.
puellāris, e girlish, maidenly.
puellula, ae *f*, *dim. of* **puella.**
puellus, ī *m* = **puerulus.**
puer, erī *m* **a**) child; boy; **b**) youth, young man; **c**) servant, slave; **d**) bachelor.
puera, ae *f* girl.
puerāscō 3 to grow up into boyhood.
puerculus, ī *m* little boy.
puerīlis, e boyish, childish, youthful.
puerīlitās, ātis *f* childishness.
pueritia, ae *f* boyhood, childhood.
puer-pera, ae *f* woman in childbirth.
puerperium, ī *n* childbirth.
puer-perus 3 aiding childbirth.
puertia, ae *f* = **pueritia.**
puerulus, ī *m* little boy.
pūga, ae *f* rump, buttocks.
pugil, ilis *m* boxer, pugilist.
pugilātōrius follis punching-ball.
pugilātus, ūs *m and* **-ātiō, ōnis** *f* boxing.
pugilicē like a boxer.
pugillārēs, ium *m/pl.*, **pugillāria, ium** *n/pl.* little writing-tablets.

pūgiō, ōnis *m* dagger, poniard.
pūgiunculus, ī *m* small dagger.
pugna, ae *f* **a**) fight, battle, combat; **b**) contention, quarrel; **c**) line of battle.
pugnācitās, ātis *f* desire of fighting.
pugnāculum, ī *n* fortified place, fort.
pugnātor, ōris *m* fighter, combatant.
pugnātōrius 3 of a fighter.
pugnāx, ācis fond of fighting, combative, warlike; obstinate.
pugneus 3 pertaining to the fist.
pugnō 1 to fight; **a**) to contradict; **b**) to struggle, contend.
pugnus, ī *m* the fist; boxing.
pulcer, cra, crum = **pulcher.**
pulchellus 3 pretty little.
pulcher, chra, chrum beautiful, fair, handsome; fine, excellent, glorious, noble; fortunate.
pulchritūdō, inis *f* beauty; **excellence.**
pūlēium, ī *n* an aromatic plant.
pūlex, icis *m* flea.
pullārius, ī *m* feeder of fowls.
pullātī, ōrum *m/pl.* persons in mourning dress; the common people.
pullēiāceus 3 = **pullus²**.
pullulō 1 to shoot up, sprout; to swarm with (*abl.*).
pullus¹, ī *m* young animal, chicken.
pullus² 3 dark grey, very dark, gloomy; *subst.* **pullum, ī** *n* dark *or* grey stuff.
pulmentārium, ī *n* = **pulpamentum.**
pulmentum, ī *n* portion of food.
pulmō, ōnis *m* the lung.
pulmōneus 3 of the lungs.
pulpa, ae *f* flesh.
(**pulpāmen, inis** *n and*) **pulpāmentum, ī** *n* flesh, meat; a relish, tasty food.
pulpitum, ī *n* platform, stage, tribune.
puls, tis *f* thick pap, porridge.
pulsātiō, ōnis *f* a striking.
pulsātor, ōris *m* striker, player (*of a lyre*).
pulsō 1 to beat, strike, knock; to move, agitate, alarm.
pulsus, ūs *m* a beating, striking; impulse, influence.
pultātiō, ōnis *f* knocking (at a door).
pulti-phagus 3 porridge-eating (*i.e.* Roman).
pultō 1 = **pulsō.**
pulvereus 3 full of dust, dusty; raising dust.
pulverulentus 3 dusty.
pulvīllus, ī *m* small cushion.
pulvīnar, āris *n* couch of the gods (*pl.* feast of the gods); cushioned seat.
pulvīnārium, ī *n* ship's berth.
pulvīnus, ī *m* cushion, pillow.
pulvis, eris *m* (*f*) dust, sand, ashes; **a**) dust of the circus, arena, field; toil; **b**) scene of action.
pulvisculus, ī *m* dust; **cum pulvisculo** dust and all, completely.
pūmex, icis *m* (*and f*) pumice-stone; porous stone, lava bed.
pūmiceus 3 of pumice; dry as a stone.
pūmicō 1 to smooth with pumice-stone.
pūmiliō, ōnis *m and f* (*and* **pūmilus, ī** *m*) dwarf.
punctim *adv.* by stabbing.
punctiuncula, ae *f* prick; pricking pain.
punctum, ī *n* puncture; **a**) point, voting-mark; **b**) small portion of time, moment; **c**) brief clause, short section.
pungō, pupugī, punctum 3 to prick, puncture; to sting, vex, grieve, disturb, afflict, annoy.
pūniceus 3 bright red.
pūniō *and* **pūnior** 4 to punish; to avenge (*alqm; alqd*).
pūnītor, ōris *m* punisher, avenger.
pūpa, ae *f* **a**) girl; **b**) doll.
pūpilla, ae *f* orphan-girl; pupil of the eye.
pūpillāris, e of an orphan.
pūpillus, ī *m* orphan-boy; ward.
puppis, is *f* stern *or* poop; ship, vessel; back.
pūpula, ae *f* (pupil of) the eye.
pūpulus, ī *m* (**pūpus, ī** *m*) little boy, child.
pūrgāmen, inis *and* **pūrgāmentum, ī** *n* **a**) filth, dirt, sweepings; **b**) means of purgation *or* expiation.
pūrgātiō, ōnis *f* a cleansing; **a**) a purging; **b**) justification.
pūrgitō 1 to make clean.
pūrgō (*and* **-rigō**) 1 to cleanse; **a**) to purge, free oneself from; **b**) to cleanse morally, purify, expiate; **c**) to excuse, justify, exculpate; to disprove; to clear up.
pūri-ficō 1 to cleanse, purify.
pūriter, *adv. of* **purus.**

purpura, ae *f* purple dye, purple; **a**) purple garment; **b**) purple robe of a king, high dignity.
purpurātus 3 clad in purple; *subst. m* high officer, courtier.
purpureus 3 **a**) violet, crimson, purple (of many shades); **b**) clad in purple; **c**) shining, bright, beautiful.
purpurissātus 3 dyed with purple.
purpurissum, ī *n* purple dye.
pūrulentus 3 discharging pus, festering.
pūrus 3 (*adv.* **-ē** *and* **-iter**) pure, clean; **a**) clear, bright, serene; **b**) purifying; **c**) purified, expiated; **d**) spotless, unspotted; undefiled; **e**) unadorned, simple, plain, unmixed, unadulterated; **f**) pure, honest; chaste; **g**) unconditional, absolute.
pūs, pūris *n* matter from a sore, pus; gall, bitter speech.
pusillus 3 tiny, petty.
pūsiō, ōnis *m* little boy.
pūs(s)ula *and* **pustula, ae** *f* pimple, pustule; refined silver (melted so as to form bubbles).
pustulātus 3 blistered; refined.
puta (imperative of *puto*) suppose, for instance.
putāmen, inis *n* husk, nut-shell.
putātiō, ōnis *f* a pruning.
putātor, ōris *m* pruner.
puteal, ālis *n* stone-enclosure of a well; stone-enclosure.
puteālis, e of a well.
puteārius, ī *m* well-digger.
pūtēfaciō 3 (?) to make rotten.
pūteō 2 to stink; to rot.
puter, tris, tre rotten, decaying, stinking, putrid; **a**) crumbling, soft, flabby; **b**) languishing.
pūtēscō, tuī, — 3 to rot, decay, putrefy.
puteus, ī *m* **a**) pit; dungeon; **b**) well, cistern; **c**) spring.
pūtidiusculus 3 rather disgusting *or* tedious.
pūtidus (*and* **pūtidulus**) 3 rotten, decaying, putrid; **a**) withered; **b**) disgusting, affected, unnatural.
putillus, ī *m* little boy.
putō 1 **1.** to prune; **2. a**) to estimate, reckon, value, consider; **b**) to think, reflect; **c**) to believe, suppose.
pūtor, ōris *m* stench.
putre-faciō 3 to make rotten, cause to putrefy; to soften.
putrēscō 3 to rot.
putridus 3 *and* **putris, e** = **puter.**
putus 3 pure, complete, out and out.
pyctēs *and* **-ta, ae** *m* boxer, pugilist.
pyelus, ī *m* bath-tub.
pȳga, ae *f* = **puga.**
pȳgargus, ī *m* antelope.
pyra, ae *f* funeral pile, pyre.
pȳramis, idis *f* pyramid.
pyrethrum, ī *n* a plant.
pyrōpus, ī *m* gold-bronze.
pyrrhicha, ae *f* war-dance.
pȳthaulēs, ae *m* one who accompanies an actor on a flute.
pȳtisma, atis *n* wine spit out after tasting.
pȳtissō 1 to spit out (wine, after tasting).
pyxis, idis *f* small box, casket.

Q

Q. *abbr.* = **Quintus** *or* **que.**
quā (*interrog. and relat.*) **a)** by what way, on which side, where; **b)** in so far as; **quā ... quā** partly ... partly, as well ... as; **c)** in what manner, in any manner.
quā-cumque by *or* in whatever way, wherever.
quādam ... tenus *adv.* to a certain point, so far.
quadra, ae *f* a quarter (of a circular loaf, cake, cheese, &c.).
quadrāgēnārius 3 forty years old.
quadrāgēnī 3 forty each.
quadrāgēsimus 3 the fortieth.
quadrāgiē(n)s *adv.* forty times.
quadrāgintā forty.
quadrāns, tis *m* fourth part, quarter; quarter of an as, *or* of a pint.
quadrantal, ālis *n* a liquid measure *of* 8 *congii* (= *amphora*).
quadrantārius 3 **a)** reduced to a fourth part; **b)** costing a quarter of an as.
quadrātus 3 squared, square; *subst.* **quadrātum, ī** *n* a square; quartile aspect (*in astrology*).
quadrī-duum, ī *n* space of four days.
quadri-ennium, ī *n* period of four years.
quadri-fāriam *adv.* into four parts.
quadri-fidus 3 split into four parts.
quadrīgae, ārum *f/pl.* (*sing. rare*) team of four; four-horse chariot.
quadrīgārius 3 (*and subst. m*) (of a) chariot-racer.
quadrīgātus 3 stamped with a quadriga.
quadrīgulae, ārum *f/pl.* small quadrigae.
quadri-iugus 3 (*and* **-iugis, e**) of a team of four; *subst.* **quadriiugī, ōrum** *m/pl.* four-horse chariot.
quadri-lībris, e weighing four pounds.
quadri-mēstris, e of four months.
quadrīm(ul)us 3 four years old.
quadringēnārius 3 consisting of four hundred each.
quadringēnī 3 four hundred each.
quadringentēsimus 3 the four hundredth.
quadringentī 3 four hundred.
quadringentiē(n)s *adv.* four hundred times.
quadri-partītus *or* **-pertītus** 3 divided into four parts.
quadri-pedāns, -pēs, -plex, *see* **quadru-.**
quadri-rēmis, e with oars worked by four rowers; *subst. f* quadrireme.
quadri-vium, ī *n* cross-roads.
quadrō 1 **a)** to make full *or* complete; **b)** to arrange properly; **c)** *intr.* to agree, fit, to accord, correspond with.
quadrum, ī *n* square.
quadru-pedāns, tis galloping; *subst.* horse, steed.
quadru-pedō at a trot.
quadru-pēs, pedis four-footed; *subst. m* and *f* quadruped, horse.
quadrup(u)lātor, ōris *m* **a)** informer; **b)** fraudulent arbitrator; **c)** exaggerator.
quadru-plex, icis = **quadruplus.**
quadru-plicō 1 to quadruple.
quadrup(u)lor 1 to be a public informer.
quadru-plus 3 fourfold; *subst.* **-um, ī** *n* four times as much.
quadru-vium, ī *n*, *see* **quadrivium.**
quaeritō 1 to seek eagerly.
quaerō, sīvī *and* **siī, sītum** 3 to seek, search for (*alqd*); **a)** to miss, want; **b)** to seek to obtain *or* procure; to get, earn, acquire (*alqd; alci alqd*); **c)** to wish to know, ask, inquire, demand (*alqd; de re: alqd ab, ex, de alqo*); **d)** to investigate, examine, make inquiry; **e)** to inquire into judicially, to examine under torture (*de alqo in alqm*).
quaesītiō, ōnis *f* inquisition.
quaesītor, ōris *m* president of a criminal investigation.
quaesītus 3 **a)** far-fetched, affected; **b)** sought out, uncommon, extraordinary; — *subst.* **quaesītum, ī** *n* question; gain.

quaesō, 3 **1.** = **quaero; 2.** to beg, beseech, entreat (*alqd ab alqo; ut, ne*); **quaeso** I pray, please; **quaesumus** we beg.

quaesticulus, ī *m* small profit.

quaestiō, ōnis *f* an asking, seeking; question, inquiry, examination; **a**) judicial inquiry, investigation with torture; subject of investigation, evidence; commission of inquisition, criminal court; **b**) scientific inquiry, subject of debate, matter, case, cause, dispute.

quaestiuncula, ae *f* little question.

quaestor, ōris *m* quæstor **a**); financial and administrative assistant to a magistrate *or* provincial governor; **b**) officer of the treasury; **c**) investigator of capital crimes.

quaestōrius 3 of a quæstor; *subst.* **a**) **quaestōrius, ī** *m* ex-quæstor; **b**) **quaestōrium, ī** *n* tent *or* dwelling of a quæstor.

quaestuāria, ae *f* prostitute.

quaestuōsus 3 **a**) gainful, profitable; **b**) greedy of gain, eager for profit; **c**) having much gain, rich.

quaestūra, ae *f* office of a quæstor, quæstorship.

quaestus, ūs *m* gain, profit, advantage; source of gain; business, trade.

quā-libet *and* **quā-lubet** *adv.* where you will; anyhow.

quālis, e 1. (*interr., exclam.*) of what sort, kind *or* nature; **2.** (*rel.*) of such a kind as, such as; **3.** (*indef.*) having some quality *or* other.

quālis-cumque 2 **a**) of whatever kind *or* sort; **b**) any whatever.

quālis-libet 2 of what sort you will.

quālis-nam 2 of what kind then?

quālitās, ātis *f* quality, property, condition.

quāliter *adv.* just as.

quālus, ī *m* (*and* **-um, ī** *n*) wicker-basket, wool-basket.

quam 1. (*interrog.* or *exclamatory*) how greatly, how much, how; **2.** (*rel.*) as; **tam ... quam** as (much) ... as; (with *superl. adj.* or *adv.*) **quam maximus** as great as possible, **quam celerrime** as quickly as possible; — (*after comp.*) than.

quam-diū how long? as long as.

quam-libet *adv.* however much.

quam-ob-rem a) on what account? why?; **b**) wherefore; **c**) therefore.

quam-prīmum *adv.* as soon as possible.

quam-quam *cj.* though, although; (*in transitions*) however, yet.

quam-vīs 1. *adv.* as you will, however (much), ever so much; **2.** *cj.* however (much), although.

quā-nam by what way.

quandō 1. *adv.* **a**) at what time?; when?; **b**) at any time, ever; **2.** *cj.* when (*v. rare*); since, as (*causal*).

quandō-cumque a) whenever, as often as; **b**) at some time *or* other.

quandō-que *cj.* whenever; since, as; *adv.* at some time.

quando-quidem *cj.* since, as.

quanquam = **quamquam.**

quantillus 3 = **quantulus.**

quantitās, ātis *f* greatness, quantity.

quantopere a) how greatly, how much; to what an extent; **b**) as much as.

quantulus 3 how little, how small.

quantulus-cumque 3 however small *or* little.

quantus 3 (*interr., exclam., relat.*) **a**) how great; how much; **b**) as great as, as much as; — **quantum** how much; as much as, as far as; — **quantī** of what value, at what price; **quantō** (*abl.*) by how much, by as much as; **quantō ... tantō** the more ... the more.

quantus-cumque 3 however great; however small; **quantumcumque** as much as ever; **quanticumque** at whatever price.

quantus-libet = **quantusvis.**

quantus-quantus 3 = **quantuscumque.**

quantus-vīs 3 as great as you will.

quantumvīs as much as you please.

quā-propter wherefore?; therefore.

quāquā by whatever way, wherever.

quāque, *see* **usque.**

quā-rē (*interr.* and *rel.*) **a**) whereby (?); **b**) wherefore (?) why (?); **c**) therefore.

quārtadecumānī, ōrum *m/pl.* soldiers of the fourteenth legion.

quārtānus 3 of the fourth day; *subst.* **quārtāna, ae** *f* quartan fever; **quārtānī, ōrum** *m/pl.* soldiers of the fourth legion.

quārtārius, ī *m* the fourth part; quarter of a sextarius.

quārtus 3 the fourth.

qua-si *cj.* as if, as though, as; *adv.* as it were, so to speak; nearly, almost.
quasillum, ī *n* (*and* **-us, ī** *m*) wool--basket (*for spinning*).
quassābilis, e that can be shaken.
quassātiō, ōnis *f* a shaking.
quassō 1 **a)** *intens.* of **quatio**; **b)** *intrans.*, to shake; to rattle.
quassus, ūs *m* a shaking.
quate-faciō 3 to shake, weaken.
quā-tenus a) how far?; up to what point?; **b)** as far as; **c)** in so far as, inasmuch as; **d)** since, as.
quater *adv.* four times.
quaternī 3 four each.
quatiō, —, quassum 3 to shake, wield, brandish; **a)** to beat, strike; **b)** to drive, chase; **c)** to crush, batter, shatter, beat to pieces; **d)** to agitate, touch, affect, trouble, vex, harass, plague.
quattuor (*indecl.*) four.
quattuor-decim fourteen.
quattuor-virātus, ūs *m* office of the *quattuorviri*.
quattuor-virī, ōrum *m/pl.* commission of four members.
-que *cj.* and; **que ... que** (*or* **et, ac**) as well ... as, both ... and.
quem-ad-modum a) in what manner, how; **b)** as, just as, as for instance.
queō, quīvī, (*or* **iī, itum), īre** to be able, I can.
quercētum, ī *n* an oak-wood.
querceus 3 of oak.
quercus, ūs *f* oak; garland of oak--leaves.
querēl(l)a, ae *f* complaint; **a)** wailing, cry; **b)** physical complaint.
queribundus 3 complaining, plaintive.
querimōnia, ae *f* = **querela.**
queritor 1 to complain vehemently.
quern(e)us 3 of oak.
queror, questus sum 3 to complain, lament, bewail (*alqd; de re*); **a)** to make complaint; **b)** to lament, sing plaintively.
querquētulānus 3 of an oak-wood.
querulus 3 **a)** complaining, querulous; **b)** plaintive.
questus, ūs *m* a complaining, complaint.
quī[1]**, quae, quod 1.** *interrog.* what?; what kind of a?; **2.** *relat.* a) who, which, what, that; b) he who, that which; c) such as; **quō ... eō** the more ... the more.
quī[2]**, qua** (*and* **quae**), **quod** *indef.* any, some, any one.
quī[3] **1.** (*abl.* = **quō**), **quīcum** = **cum quo; 2.** a) *interrog.* how?; why?; b) *relat.* by which, with which; c) somehow; d) oh that! (in wishes).
quia *cj.* because; **quianam?** why?; **quiane?** because?
quic-quam, *see* **quisquam.**
quic-quid, *see* **quisquis.**
quīcum, *see* **quī**[3]**.**
quī-cumque, quae-, quod- a) whoever, whatever, whichever, all that; **b)** any, every possible.
quī-dam, quae-dam, quiddam (*subst.*) *and* **quoddam** (*adj.*) a certain, a certain one; **a)** somebody, one, something; *pl.* some, certain ones; **b)** a kind of, so to speak.
quidem *adv.* assuredly, certainly, in fact, indeed, at least, in truth; for instance, for example; **ne ... quidem** not even; not ... either.
quid-nī *adv.* why not?
quiēs, ētis *f* rest, repose, quiet; **a)** sleep; **b)** sleep of death; **c)** dream; **d)** silence; peace, neutrality; **e)** resting-place.
quiēsco, ēvī, ētum 3 to rest, repose, keep quiet; **a)** to sleep, be asleep; **b)** to be silent, still, calm; **c)** to be at peace, be neutral; **d)** to do nothing, be inactive; to cease, refrain from; **e)** to come to rest, to be quiet, undisturbed, free from trouble.
quiētus 3 quiet; **a)** sleeping, resting; **b)** inactive; **c)** free from trouble *or* agitation, peaceful; **d)** retired, taking no part in politics; neutral; **e)** undisturbed, restful; **f)** calm, mild; indolent.
quī-libet, quae-libet, quid-libet (*subst.*) *and* **quod-libet** (*adj.*) any one, any thing you please; any without distinction, the first that comes.
quīn 1. *adv.* a) why not?; wherefore not?; how not?; b) rather, nay, indeed, verily, in fact; **2.** *cj.* a) that not, without; b) that, but that (*only after negatives*).
quī-nam 3 who, which, what?
quīnavīcēnārius 3, **-ia lēx** relating to minors under twenty-five.
Quīnctīlis, e, *see* **Quintilis.**
quīnctus 3 = **quintus.**

quinc-ūnx, ūncis *m* **a**) five twelfths of a whole, of an *as*; **b**) a quincunx (five objects arranged like the five pips on dice or playing-cards).
quin-deciē(n)s *adv.* fifteen times.
quin-decim (*indecl.*) fifteen.
quindecimvirālis, e of a commission of fifteen members.
quindecim-virī, ōrum *m/pl.* commission of fifteen members.
quingēnī 3 five hundred each.
quingentēsimus 3 the five hundredth.
quingentī 3 five hundred.
quingentiē(n)s *adv.* five hundred times.
quīnī 3 five each.
quinquāgēnī 3 fifty each.
quinquāgēsimus 3 the fiftieth; *subst.* **-a, ae** *f* the fiftieth part.
quinquāgintā (*indecl.*) fifty.
quinquātrūs, uum *f/pl.* (*and* **-tria, ium** *n/pl.*) festival in honour of Minerva.
quinque (*indecl.*) five.
quinquennālis, e occurring every five years; lasting five years.
quinqu-ennis, e five years old; *subst.* **-ia** *n/pl.* games held every fifth year.
quinqu-ennium, ī *n* period of five years.
quinque-partītus *and* **-pertītus** 3 divided into five parts.
quinque-rēmis, e with oars worked by five rowers; (**navis**) quinquereme.
quinque-vir, ī *m* one of a commission *or* college of five.
quinque-virātus, ūs *m* office of a *quinquevir*.
quinquiē(n)s *adv.* five times.
quinqui-plex, icis fivefold, with five leaves.
quinqui-plicō 1 to make fivefold.
quintadecimānī, ōrum *m/pl.* soldiers of the fifteenth legion.
quintāna, ae *f* (*sc.* **via**) road in a Roman camp; market.
quintānī, ōrum *m/pl.* soldiers of the fifth legion.
Quintīlis, e belonging to July, *subst.*, ~ (*sc. mensis.*) July.
quintus 3 the fifth.
quintus-decimus 3 the fifteenth.
quippe *adv.* **a**) of course, to be sure, obviously, naturally, indeed; **b**) **quippe quī** since he, inasmuch as he.
quippiam = **quidpiam,** *see* **quispiam.**
quippinī why not?; certainly, to be sure.
Quirīs, ītis *m* Roman citizen.
quirītātiō, ōnis *f and* **-tus, ūs** *m* shriek, scream, cry of distress.
quirītō 1 to shriek, wail; to cry aloud.
quis (*subst.* and *adj.*), **quid** (*subst.*) **1.** (*interr.*) who?; which one?; what?; a) **quid** for what purpose?; why?; b) what!; how!; why!; **quid ita** why so?; how so?; **quid quod** what of the fact that ...?; moreover; **2.** (*indef.*) anyone, anybody, anything; someone, something (mostly after *ne, num, si, nisi, cum*).
quis-nam, quid-nam who then?; what then?
quis-piam, quae-piam (*subst.* and *adj.*), **quid-piam** (*subst.*) *and* **quod-piam** (*adj.*) someone, something.
quis-quam, quid-quam *or* **quicquam** (*subst.* only) anyone, anything (*in negative sentences*); **nec quisquam** and no one.
quis-que, quae-que, quid-que (*subst.*) *and* **quod-que** (*adj.*) each, every, every one, every thing; **a**) **decimus quisque** every tenth; **quinto quōque anno** every fifth year, every four years; **primus quisque** the first possible, the very first; **b**) (*with superl.*) **optimus quisque** all the best, every good man; **optima quaeque** all the best things.
quisquiliae, ārum *f/pl.* rubbish, sweepings, refuse.
quisquis, quidquid *or* **quicquid** (*subst.*) whoever, whatever; also rarely = *quisque*; *adv.* **quidquid** however much *or* far.
quī-vīs, quae-vīs, quid-vīs (*subst.*) *and* **quod-vīs** (*adj.*) whoever you will, whatever you please, any (one), anything.
quivīscumque, quae-, quod- any whatsoever.
quō 1. *adv.* a) *interrog.* and *relat.* whither, to what place, where; to whom, into what family; to what purpose; by what *or* which means, whereby; b) *indef.* to any place, anywhere; **2.** *cj.* (in order) that, that thereby, that ... the more; **non quō** not because, not that; **quō ... eo** the more ..., the more.

quoad a) how long?; **b**) as long as, until, as far as.
quō-circā *adv.* therefore.
quō-cumque whithersoever.
quod (*relat. pron.* and *cj.*) (as to) the fact that, in so far as, because, on the ground that; **quod sī** and if, but if.
quōdam-modo *adv.* in a certain manner *or* measure.
quodsī, *see* **quod.**
quōiās, ātis (*also nomin.* **quōiātis**) = **cūiās.**
quōius; quoi (archaic) = **cūius; cui.**
quōius(nam) 3 = **cūius** 3.
quō-libet *adv.* to any place whatever.
quom (*archaic*) = **cum.**
quō-minus *cj.* with *subj.* used after verbs of preventing and refusing (by which ... not, so that ... not).
quō-modo a) how (*interrog.*, *exclam.*, *relat.*); **b**) just as.
quōmodo-cumque in whatever way.
quōmodo-nam *adv.* how then?
quō-nam *adv.* whither? how far? how long?
quondam *adv.* **a**) at one time, once, formerly; **b**) sometimes; **c**) at some future time.
quon-iam *cj.* now that, since, seeing that.
quō-piam *adv.* to some *or* any place.
quoppiam = **quodpiam,** *see* **quispiam.**
quō-quam *adv.* to any place.
quoque *adv.* also, too.
quōque-versus = **quoquoversus.**
quō-quō whithersoever.
quōquō-versus *and* **-versum** *adv.* in every direction.
quōr (archaic) = **cūr.**
quōrsum *and* **-us** *adv.* **a**) whither, to what place?; **b**) to what purpose?
quot (*indecl.*) **a**) how many? **b**) as many as.
quot-annīs *adv.* every year, yearly.
quot-cumque (*indecl.*) however many.
quotēnī 3 how many each.
quotīdiānus, quotīdiē, *see* **cot...**
quotiē(n)s *adv.* **a**) how often?, how many times?; **b**) (*rel.*) as often as.
quotiē(n)s-cumque *adv.* however often, as often as.
quot-quot (*indecl.*) however many.
quotumus 3 = **quotus.**
quotus 3 which? (in the series 1st, 2nd, 3rd, &c.); **quota hōra?** what hour?; **quota pars?** what fraction?; **quotus quisque est?** how few there are!; **quotacumque pars** what a small fraction!, the smallest possible part.
quo-usque *adv.* **a**) how far?; **b**) how long?; until when?
quō-vīs *adv.* to any place, anywhere.
quum an incorrect spelling of **cum** (*cj.*).
qūr = **cūr.**

R

R. *abbr.* = **Romanus** *or* **Rufus.**
rabidus 3 furious, raving, enraged, mad; inspired.
rabiēs, (ēī) *f* rage, madness, frenzy; **a**) anger, fury; **b**) fierceness; **c**) inspiration.
rabiō, —, — 3 to rave, be mad.
rabiōsulus 3 a little mad.
rabiōsus 3 = **rabidus.**
rabula, ae *m* ranter.
racēmi-fer 3 cluster-bearing.
racēmus, ī *m* cluster of grapes, bunch of berries; wine.
radiātus 3 shining, emitting rays; irradiated.
rādīcēscō 3 to strike root.
rādīcitus *adv.* with the root; radically, utterly.
rādīcula, ae *f* little root.
radiō *and* **radior** 1 to shine; *subst.* **radiāns, tis** *m* the sun.
radiōs(s)us 3 beaming.
radius, ī *m* staff, stake; **a**) spoke of a wheel; **b**) measuring-rod; **c**) radius of a circle; **d**) weaver's shuttle; **e**) a kind of long olive; **f**) beam, ray of light.
rādīx, īcis *f* root; **a**) radish; **b**) lower part, foot (*of a hill*) (*mostly plur.*); **c**) ground, basis, origin, source; **d**) foundation.
rādō, sī, sum 3 to scrape, scratch, shave; **a**) to rub, smooth; **b**) to lacerate; **c**) to shave off, erase; **d**) to touch in passing, graze.
raeda, ae *f* travelling-carriage.
raedārius, ī *m* coachman.
rallus 3 thin.
rāmālia, ium *n/pl.* (*sing.* **rāmāle** *rare*) branches, twigs, brushwood.
rāmentum, ī *n* (*and* **-ta, ae** *f*) chip, bit, morsel.
rāmes, itis *m* small tube of the lung.
rāmeus 3 of boughs *or* branches.
rāmex, icis *m* varicose veins, varicocele.
rāmōsus 3 full of boughs, branching.
rāmulus, ī *m* twig, sprig.
rāmus, ī *m* branch, bough; club; tree.
rāna, ae *f* **a**) frog; **b**) a sea-fish.
rancēns, tis = **rancidus.**
rancid(ul)us 3 stinking, tainted; disgusting.
rānunculus, ī *m* little frog.
rapācida, ae *m* 'son of a robber'.
rapācitās, ātis *f* greediness, rapacity.
rapāx, ācis grasping, rapacious; **a**) prone to grasp; **b**) greedy, insatiable; *m* robber.
raphanus, ī *m* radish.
rapiditās, ātis *f* rapidity.
rapidus 3 snatching, seizing, carrying off, hurrying away; consuming, rapacious; impetuous, whirling, rapid.
rapīna, ae *f* robbery, plundering; prey, booty.
rapiō, puī, ptum 3 **1.** to snatch to oneself, seize and carry off, seize hastily; a) to lead away with haste, hurry away *or* off; b) to tear, pluck, drag; **2.** to snatch away, carry off; a) to rob, ravish, plunder, ravage, carry off as plunder; b) to lay waste; c) to carry away, lead astray, transport, draw irresistibly; d) to seize by violence, steal; *subst.* **raptum, ī** *n* plunder, booty.
raptim *adv.* hastily, hurriedly.
raptiō, ōnis *f* seizing, abduction.
raptō 1 **a**) to carry away, hurry away, drag away *or* along; **b**) to rob, plunder.
raptor, ōris *m* robber, plunderer; abductor.
raptum, ī *n, see* **rapio.**
raptus, ūs *m* **a**) a carrying off, abduction, rape; **b**) a rending, tearing off; **c**) plunder.
rāpulum, ī *n* turnip.
rāpum, ī *n* turnip; knob of tree-roots.
rārē-faciō 3 to make thin, rarefy.
rārēscō, —, — 3 to grow thin, lose density; to widen out.
rāritās, ātis *f* want of density, looseness of texture; fewness, thinness.
rārus 3 (*adv.* **rārō**) loose in texture, thin, wide apart, with large meshes;

a) with large intervals, scattered, scanty, dispersed; **b**) few in number, rare, nor frequent; **c**) uncommon, extraordinary, remarkable, distinguished in its kind.
rāsilis, e polished, smoothed.
rāsitō 1 to shave.
rāstellus, ī *m* = **rastrum.**
rāstrum, ī *n and* **rāster, trī** *m* toothed hoe.
ratiō, ōnis *f* a reckoning; **1.** account, computation, calculation; **ratiō constat** the account is correct; **ratiōnem inire** *or* **habere** to make a computation; **conficere** *or* **(com)putare** to settle an account; **in ratiōnem inducere** to bring into one's account; **ratiōnem reddere alci** to give an account; **ratiōnem repetere ab alqo** to call to account; — a) roll, register, list; b) money-transaction, business, affair; connection, relation, reference; **ratiōnem habere cum alqo** to have to do with; **2.** respect, regard, consideration, concern; **ratiōnem habere** *or* **ducere alcis rei,** to consider, have regard for; **ratiōnem habere hominis** to accept a man as a candidate (at an election); interest, advantage (*alcis ratiōnibus consulere, ratiōnēs meas vestrae saluti antepono*); **3.** judgment, understanding; a) reason; b) way, manner, course, method (**ratiō belli gerendi; vitae ratiōnēs** plan of life; **ratiōne** methodically); procedure, plan; c) reason, motive, ground, principle; d) argument, reasoning; **4.** system; a) theory, doctrine, science, knowledge, philosophy; b) rule, order, principle; c) fashion, manner, way (**omni ratiōne** by all means).
ratiōcinātiō, ōnis *f* **a**) deliberate consideration, reasoning; **b**) syllogism.
ratiōcinātīvus 3 belonging to reasoning *or* syllogisms.
ratiōcinātor, ōris *m* reckoner, computer.
ratiōcinor 1 to reckon, compute, calculate; to deliberate; to argue, reason, conclude.
ratiōnābilis, e endowed with reason.
ratiōnālis, e a) endowed with reason; **b**) rational, logical.
ratiōnārium, ī *n* statistical survey.
ratis, is *f* raft, pontoon; float (for swimming on); boat, ship.
ratiuncula, ae *f* **a**) little reckoning *or* account; **b**) slight reason *or* ground; **c**) petty syllogism.
ratus 3 reckoned, calculated; **a**) fixed, defined, settled, established; **b**) confirmed, sure, certain; valid; **prō ratā (parte)** proportionately.
rauci-sonus 3 hoarse-sounding.
raucus 3 hoarse; hollow-sounding, deep-voiced; roaring, ringing, growling.
raudus, eris *n, see* **rudus 2.**
raudusculum, ī *n* small sum of money.
rāviō 4 to talk oneself hoarse.
răvis, is *f* hoarseness.
rāvus 3 yellowish-grey.
rea, ae *f, see* **reus.**
reāpse *adv.* indeed, really.
reātus, ūs *m* state of an accused person.
rebellātiō, ōnis *f* = **rebellio.**
reballātrīx, īcis *f* = **rebellis.**
rebelliō, ōnis *f* renewal of war; revolt, rebellion.
rebellis, e insurgent, rebellious; refractory.
re-bellō 1 to renew a war; to revolt, rebel.
re-bītō 3 to go back, return.
re-boō 1 to (make to) resound, echo.
re-calcitrō 1 to kick back; to reject advances.
re-caleō, —, — 2 to be warm again.
re-calēscō, luī, — 3 **a**) to grow warm again; **b**) to regain one's heat, to be rekindled.
re-calfaciō 3 to make warm again.
re-calvus 3 with a bald forehead.
re-candēscō, duī, — 3 **a**) to begin to glow; **b**) to grow white.
re-canō 3 to resound.
re-cantō 1 **a**) to recall, recant, revoke; **b**) to charm away; **c**) to re--echo.
re-cēdō 3 **a**) to go back, retire, withdraw, recede, retreat, be distant; **b**) to go away, depart, vanish, disappear (*ab, ex re in alqd*); **c**) to depart from, abandon (*a re*); to resign, yield, desist; **d**) to be removed, cut off.
re-cellō, —, — 3 to spring *or* fly back.
recēns, tis a) just come, lately arisen, modern; subsequent to, fresh from

(*a re, re*); **b**) fresh, vigorous, young, recent; — *adv*. (**recēns**) lately, recently, newly, just.
re-cēnseō, suī, sum (*or* **situm**) 2 to count, number, muster, survey, review, examine; **a**) to go over, reckon up; **b**) to consider; **c**) to recount (*in words*).
recēnsio, ōnis *f* a numbering, mustering.
recēnsus, ūs *m* a reviewing, mustering.
receptāculum, ī *n* **a**) reservoir, magazine, receptacle; **b**) place of refuge, retreat, shelter.
re-ceptiō, ōnis *f* receiving.
re-ceptō 1 **a**) to take back, draw back; **b**) to receive habitually, to harbour.
receptor, ōris *m* concealer.
receptrīx, īcis *f* concealer.
receptum, ī *n* obligation.
receptus, ūs *m* **a**) a taking back; **b**) a retiring, retreat; place of retreat, refuge; withdrawal.
re-cessim *adv*. backwards.
recessus, ūs *m* a going back, retiring; **a**) retreat, escape, withdrawal; **b**) nook, corner, recess, retired spot, inner room; solitude.
recidīvus 3 restored; constantly renewed.
re(c)cidō, re(c)cidī, recāsūrus 3 **a**) to fall back, return, recoil; to be thrown back, relapse; **b**) to sink, be subdued, be reduced, fall into (*ex re, in* or *ad alqd*); to fall into a certain time (*in tempus*).
re-cīdō, cīdī, cīsum 3 to cut away, down *or* off; to hew; **a**) to extirpate; **b**) to lop off, cut away, prune away.
re-cingō 3 to ungird; **P.** to ungird *or* divest oneself of (*alqd*).
re-cinō, —, — 3 a) to resound, echo; to keep on hooting (*or* to hoot in warning tones); **b**) to cause to resound; to celebrate, praise in song.
reciperō 1 = **recupero.**
re-cipiō, cēpī, ceptum 3 **1.** to take, draw, get, bring, fetch back (*alqd ab* or *ex re, in* or *ad alqd*); **se recipere** to withdraw, retire, retreat; a) to draw back (*troops*), cause to retreat; **signum recipiendi** signal for retreat; b) to save, deliver (*alqm ex re*); **2.** to get back, rescue, receive again, regain, recover, (re)conquer, take possession of, occupy; **se recipere** to recover *or* collect oneself, regain courage; **3.** to admit, accept; a) to take to oneself, take in, receive, welcome (*tecto* or *domum suam*); b) to admit (*to a class*) (*alqm in ordinem senatorium, in civitatem, in amicitiam, in fidem*); c) to receive *or* entertain a charge against one; d) to admit, allow; e) to take upon oneself, assume (*mandatum, officium*); f) to guarantee, to promise, be responsible for.
reciprocō 1 **a**) to move backwards and forwards, to turn back, move back, reverse; **b**) **P.** *and intr*. to ebb and flow, alternate.
reciprocus 3 returning, ebbing.
recitātiō, ōnis *f* a reading aloud.
recitātor, ōris *m* reader, reciter.
re-citō 1 to read aloud.
re-clāmātiō, ōnis *f* shout of disapproval.
re-clāmitō 1 to contradict loudly, oppose.
re-clāmō to cry out against; **a**) to contradict loudly; **b**) to resound.
re-clīnis, e leaning back.
re-clīnō 1 to bend back, cause to lean back; to relieve; to rest.
re-clūdō, sī, sum 3 to unclose, open; to disclose; (*rarely*) to close.
re-cōgitō 1 to think over again.
re-cognitiō, ōnis *f* inspection.
re-cognōscō 3 to know again; **a**) to recall to mind; to recognize; **b**) to inspect, review, examine, revise.
re-colligō 3 to collect again, to regain; **se recolligere** to collect oneself, take courage (again); to reconcile.
re-colō 3 to cultivate again; **a**) to practise again; **b**) to restore, renew; to revisit; to reinvest; **c**) to think over again.
re-commentor 1 to recall to mind.
re-comminīscor 3 to remember.
re-compōnō 3 to readjust; to appease.
re-conciliātiō, ōnis *f* a reconciling; restoration.
re-conciliātor, ōris *m* restorer.
re-conciliō 1 to restore, repair; **a**) to re-unite, reconcile; **b**) to win over again.
re-concinnō 1 to repair, set right again.
re-conditus 3 put out of the way; **a**) hidden, concealed, far removed, sequestered; **b**) profound, abstruse.

re-condō 3 to put back *or* away (*alqd in alqd*); **oculos** to shut again; **a**) to lay up, store away, hoard; **b**) to hide, conceal (*alqd in re, re*).
re-cōnflō 1 to rekindle.
re-coquō 3 to cook *or* boil again; to melt *or* forge again.
re-cordātiō, ōnis *f* recollection, remembrance.
re-cordor 1 to remember, recollect (*alqd; de re; acc. c. inf.*), to think over.
re-corrigō 3 to reform.
re-creō 1 to make *or* create anew; to revive, restore, refresh, invigorate.
re-crepō, —, — 1 to resound.
re-crēscō 3 to grow again.
re-crūdēscō, duī, — 3 to break open afresh (*vulnera*); to break out again.
rēctā (*sc.* **viā**) *adv.* straight, right on.
rēctiō, ōnis *f* a ruling, direction.
rēctor, ōris *m* (*and* **-trīx, īcis** *f*) controller, director, governor; steersman, tutor.
rēctus 3 straight; **a**) upright; erect; **b**) right, correct, proper, appropriate, suitable, due; **c**) plain, simple, natural; **d**) honest, upright, virtuous, good; — *subst.* **rēctum, ī** *n* the right, the good, virtue; *adv.* **rēctē** straight; rightly, duly, well; (*in answers*) all right.
re-cubō, —, — 1 to lie on the back, to recline.
rēcula, ae *f* small property.
re-cumbō, cubuī, — 3 to lie backwards, recline (*at table*), lie down; to fall, sink down.
recuperātiō, ōnis *f* a regaining, recovery.
recuperātor, ōris *m* **a**) regainer, recoverer; **b**) judicial umpire, arbitrator.
recuperātōrius 3 of umpires.
recuperō 1 to regain, recover.
re-cūrō 1 to cure, restore.
re-currō, currī, cursum 3 to run back, hasten back (*in* or *ad alqd*); **a**) to come back to, return; **b**) to have recourse to.
re-cursō 1 to run back, return.
re-cursus, ūs *m* a running back, return, retreat.
re-curvō 1 to bend *or* curve backward.
re-curvus 3 bent back.
re-cūsātiō, ōnis *f* a declining, refusal; counter-plea; objection.
re-cūsō 1 to decline, refuse, reject (*alqd; de re; inf.; ne, quominus, quin*); to object, protest.
re-cutiō, —, cussum 3 to shake, cause to rebound *or* reverberate.
recutītus 3 circumcised; chafed.
red-ambulō 1 to come back.
red-amō 1 to love in return.
red-ārdēscō 3 to blaze up again.
red-arguō, uī, — 3 to confute, refute, contradict (*acc.*).
red-auspicō 1 to take return-auspices, to go back.
red-dō, didī, ditum 3 **1.** to bring back; **P.** *and* **se reddere** to return; **2.** to give *or* put back, restore, return; a) to recite, rehearse; b) to render, make, cause to be (*mare tutum, servitutem lenem, alqm iratum*); **3.** a) to repay (*beneficium, gratiam*); b) to take vengeance for (*hostibus cladem*); c) to pay back (*debts*), suffer (*punishment*); d) to deliver, assign, bestow, grant, to render, give what is due; **rationem reddere** to render an account; **ius reddere** to administer justice; e) to give out *or* forth, to reply; f) to imitate, represent, express; to translate, render (*alqd Latine*).
red-dūcō = **reduco**
red-ēmptiō, ōnis *f* a buying back, ransoming; **a**) a bribing; **b**) farming.
red-ēmptō 1 to ransom, redeem.
red-ēmptor, ōris *m* contractor, farmer, purveyor.
redēmptūra, ae *f* a contracting, farming.
red-eō to go *or* come back, return; **ad se redire** to recover one's senses; to return to one's natural bent; **in gratiam cum alqo** to be reconciled with; **a**) to return, recur (*to a former topic*); **b**) to come in (*as revenue*); **c**) to come to, be brought to, betake oneself to, have recourse to.
red-hālō 1 to breathe out again.
red-hibeō 2 to give back.
red-igō, ēgī, āctum 3 to drive, bring *or* lead back; **a**) to collect, raise, call in (*money*); to confiscate; **b**) to bring *or* reduce to a state *or* condition, force (*Galliam in potestatem, in dicionem, sub imperium*),

to make, render; **in provinciam** to reduce to a province; **ad vanum et irritum** to make fruitless, to frustrate; **c**) to lessen, reduce.
redimīculum, ī *n* band, fillet, bond.
redimiō 4 to bind *or* wreathe round, to crown.
red-imō, ēmī, ēmptum 3 **a**) to buy back; to redeem, ransom, set free; **b**) to buy off, avert; **c**) to buy, procure by purchase; farm, hire, contract for, undertake.
red-integrō 1 to make whole again; **a**) to restore, renew; **b**) to refresh, revive.
red-ipīscor 3 to get back.
red-itiō, ōnis *f* return.
red-itus, ūs *m* a coming back, return; **a**) revolution, circuit; **b**) income, revenue.
redivia, ae *f* = **reduvia.**
redivīvus 3 used again; *subst.* **-um, ī** *n* old building materials used as new.
red-oleō, uī, — 2 to smell of (*alqd*); to be discernible (by smell).
re-domitus 3 subdued again.
re-dōnō 1 to give back; to resign.
re-dormiō 4 to sleep again.
re-dūcō 3 **a**) to bring, lead *or* draw back, to call back; **b**) to restore; to re-marry.
re-ductiō, ōnis *f* a bringing back.
re-ductor, ōris *m* one who leads back; restorer.
re-ductus 3 **a**) drawn back; **b**) retired, sequestered, remote.
red-uncus 3 bent *or* curved back.
redundantia, ae *f* superfluity, superabundance.
red-undō 1 to stream over, overflow; to be swimming with (*re*); **a**) to flow forth freely; **b**) to abound in, to be in excess.
reduvia, ae *f* hangnail.
re(d)-dux, ucis a) bringing back; **b**) brought back, returned.
re-fectiō, ōnis *f* a repairing, restoring.
re-fector, ōris *m* restorer.
re-fellō, fellī, — 3 to refute, confute, rebut.
re-ferciō, rsī, rtum 4 to stuff full, fill up; **refertus** 3 crammed, filled (with *abl.* or *gen.*).
re-feriō, —, — 4 to strike back.
re-ferō, rettulī, relātum, referre 3 **1.** to bear, carry, bring back (*alqd in* or *ad alqd*); a) to bring back as a trophy, booty, present; b) to bring back a message, to report, announce, relate; c) to move back, remove backwards (*castra*; *pedem* or *se referre* or **P.** to go back, retreat, withdraw, return); d) to call to mind, think over; to refer to, assign to, give credit for; to judge by, measure according to a certain standard; e) to pay back, repay, pay in return, give back; f) **gratiam** to make a return, to show one's gratitude; g) to reply, return, answer; to repeat; to echo, resound; h) to restore, renew, revive; i) to call back to memory; to represent, recall; **2.** to bring, deliver, transmit (*pecuniam in aerarium*); a) to note down, register, record; b) to tell, say, assert, relate; c) to bring before *or* refer to (*ad senatum*); d) to include (in a list), enter (*nomen in tabulas, alqm in proscriptos*).
rē-fert, rē-tulit, rē-ferre it matters, concerns, is of advantage *or* importance (*meā, tuā, suā;* with *gen.;* with *inf.* or *acc. c. inf.*).
refertus 3, *see* **refercio.**
re-ferveō, —, — 2 to boil up *or* over again.
re-fervēscō 3 to bubble up.
re-ficiō, fēcī, fectum 3 to make again; **a**) to choose again; **b**) to restore, repair, re-establish; **c**) to make up to full strength; **d**) to refresh, revive; **e**) to get back (*money*), get in return.
re-fīgō 3 to unfasten, unloose; to abolish, abrogate, repeal.
re-fingō 3 to form anew.
re-flāgitō 1 to demand back.
re-flātus, ūs *m* contrary wind.
re-flectō 3 to bend *or* turn backward; to turn about, to change, to bring back.
re-flō 1 to blow against *or* contrary; to breathe out again.
re-fluō 3 to flow back.
refluus 3 flowing back.
re-fodiō 3 to dig up.
re-fōrmātiō, ōnis *f* reformation.
re-fōrmātor, ōris *m* reformer.
re-formīdātiō, ōnis *f* dread.
re-formīdō 1 to dread, shun.
re-fōrmō 1 to form again, remould, transform.
re-foveō 2 to refresh, revive.

refrāctāri(ol)us 3 stubborn, over bearing.
re-frāgor 1 to oppose, withstand (*dat.*).
re-frēnātiō, ōnis *f* a restraining.
re-frēnō 1 to bridle, check.
re-fricō, cuī, cātum 1 to rub *or* scratch open again; to renew.
re-frīgerātiō, ōnis *f* a cooling.
re-frīgerō 1 to make cool; **P.** to cool oneself, grow cool.
re-frīgēscō, frīxī, — 3 to grow cool (again); to lose vigour *or* interest, to abate, fail.
re-fringō, frēgī, frāctum 3 to break up, off, *or* open; to break in pieces, check, destroy.
re-fugiō 3 to flee back; **a**) to flee away, escape, take to flight (*ex* or *a re*); **b**) to turn away from, avoid, shun (*alqd*).
refugium, ī *n* place of refuge.
re-fugus 3 receding; fugitive.
re-fulgeō, fulsī, — 2 to shine *or* gleam back.
re-fundō 3 to cause to flow back *or* overflow.
refūtātiō, ōnis *f* (**refūtātus, ūs** *m*) refutation.
re-fūtō 1 to drive back; **a**) to repel, resist; to contemn; **b**) to confute, refute.
rēgāliolus, ī *m* (*a little bird*) wren.
rēgālis, e kingly, princely.
re-gelō 1 to thaw.
re-gemō 3 to groan.
re-gerō 3 to bear, carry *or* bring back; to return.
rēgia, ae *f* royal palace, castle, residence; **a**) royal city *or* tent; **b**) court, courtiers; **c**) basilica, public hall.
rēgi-ficus = **regius a**).
re-gignō 3 to reproduce.
rēgillus 3 royal, splendid.
regimen, inis *n* a guiding, direction; **a**) government; **b**) rudder; **c**) ruler, governor.
rēgīna, ae *f* queen, princess, lady.
regiō, ōnis *f* **1.** direction, line, situation; **e regiōne** in a straight line, directly, opposite; **2.** boundary line, boundary; a) region of the heavens *or* of the earth; b) tract, territory, neighbourhood; c) district, province; sphere; d) quarter of a city.
regiōnātim *adv.* by districts.
rēgius 3 of a king, royal, regal; **a**) splendid, magnificent; **b**) despotic, tyrannical; **c**) = **regalis;** *subst.* **rēgiī, ōrum** *m/pl.* royal troops; courtiers, satraps.
re-glūtinō 1 to unglue, separate.
rēgnātor, ōris *m* = **rex.**
rēgnātrīx, īcis *f* ruling, imperial.
rēgnō 1 to be king, to rule, reign; **a**) to rule as a king; **b**) to be master, to domineer.
rēgnum, ī *n* royal power, monarchy; sovereignty, absolute power, despotism; kingdom, realm.
regō, rēxī, rēctum 3 to guide, conduct, direct (*acc.*); **a**) to rule, govern, control; **b**) to regulate.
re-gredior, gressus sum 3 to go back, retreat, march back, withdraw.
re-gressus, ūs *m* return; **a**) retreat; **b**) going back; **c**) recourse.
rēgula, ae *f* **a**) straight piece of wood, board; ruler, rule; **b**) model, pattern, example.
rēgulus, ī *m* petty king, chieftain; prince.
re-gustō 1 to taste repeatedly.
rē-iciō, iēcī, iectum 3 to throw back; **a**) to repel, drive back, cast back, cast up *or* away (*a ship*); **b**) to reject, refuse, scorn, disdain; **c**) to throw away, remove; **d**) to expel, relegate; **e**) to put off, defer (*in alqd*); **f**) to refer.
rēiculus 3 **a**) worthless; **b**) misspent, wasted.
rēiecta *and* **rēiectānea, ōrum** *n/pl.* rejectable things.
rēiectiō, ōnis *f* rejection.
rē-iectō 1 to throw back.
re-lābor 3 to slide, glide, sink back; to glide *or* flow down.
re-languēscō, guī, — 3 to grow languid *or* faint.
re-lātiō, ōnis *f* report, proposition, motion; throwing back; returning; repetition.
re-lātor, ōris *m* mover, proposer.
relātus, ūs *m* report; recital.
re-laxātiō, ōnis *f* relaxation, easing, alleviation.
re-laxō 1 to loosen, open; **a**) to relax, abate; **b**) to ease, relieve, mitigate; to release.
relēgātiō, ōnis *f* banishment.
re-lēgō[1] 1 to send away, dispatch; **a**) to banish; **b**) to put aside, reject; **c**) to refer.

re-legō[2] 3 to gather together, collect again; **a**) to travel over *or* traverse again; **b**) to read again; **c**) to consider again.
re-lentēscō, —, — 3 to slacken.
re-levō 1 to lift up, raise; to relieve, alleviate, mitigate; to free from (*abl.*); to lighten.
relictiō, ōnis *f* a forsaking, abandoning.
relicuos (-cuus) 3 = **reliquus.**
religātiō, ōnis *f* a binding *or* tying up.
religiō, ōnis *f* **1.** a) scrupulousness; superstitious awe, scrupulous fear; religious scruples, scruples of conscience; **religiōnī mihi est** it is a matter of conscience; b) anxiety, punctiliousness, conscientiousness; **2.** a) religious feeling, reverence of the gods, fear of god, religion, piety, devoutness; superstition; b) worship of the gods; religious observance, ceremony; c) religious system, mode of worship, faith, cult; **3.** sacredness, sanctity; a) sacred obligation; b) holy object, sacred place, consecrated things; c) religious liability, sin, curse.
religiōsus 3 **a**) careful, anxious, scrupulous; **b**) conscientious, pious, devout, religious; superstitious; **c**) holy, sacred; **d**) forbidden by religious scruples.
re-ligō 1 to bind back *or* fast.
re-linō, lēvī, — 3 to unseal, open; to take out.
re-linquō, līquī, lictum 3 **1.** to leave behind; a) to leave; to leave behind by death, bequeath; b) to let remain, suffer to be (*alqm insepultum, alqd in medio*); **2.** to leave remaining, leave over, leave to (*alci alqd*); *subst.* **relictum, ī** *n* remains, remnant; **3.** to go away from, abandon, forsake, desert, give up; a) to leave in the lurch; b) to neglect, slight; to leave unpunished; c) to pass over, not to mention.
reliquiae, ārum *f/pl.* remainder, remains, relics, rest, fragments; ashes.
reliquus 3 **a**) left behind *or* over, remaining; *subst.* **reliquum, ī** *n* rest, remainder; **b**) outstanding, in arrear; *subst.* **-um, ī** *n* residue, remaining debt; **c**) other, rest; **reliquī** *pl.* 3 the others, the rest; **d**) subsequent, future.
rellig-, relliqu-, *see* **relig-, reliqu-.**
re-lūceō, xī, — 2 to shine back.
re-lūcēscō, lūxī, — 3 to become bright again.
re-luctor 1 to strive *or* struggle against (*dat.*).
re-macrēscō, cruī, — 3 to grow lean again.
re-maledīcō 3 to revile back.
re-maneō 2 **a**) to stay behind; **b**) to be left, remain.
re-mānō 1 to flow back.
re-mānsiō, ōnis *f* a staying behind, remaining.
re-meābilis, e continually returning.
remediābilis, e curable.
re-medium, ī *n* remedy, medicine; means of healing *or* aid.
remeligō, inis *f* dawdler.
re-meō 1 to go *or* come back, return.
re-mētior 4 to go over again, to retrace, traverse again; to give back in equal quantity.
rēmex, igis *m* rower.
rēmigātiō, ōnis *f* a rowing.
rēmigium, ī *n* a rowing; oars; rowers.
rēmigō 1 to row.
re-migrō 1 to wander back, return.
re-minīscor, — 3 to call to mind, recollect, remember.
re-misceō 2 to mix up, mingle.
re-missiō, ōnis *f* **a**) a sending back; **b**) a letting down, lowering; **c**) a relaxing, slackening; remission; **d**) recreation; **e**) mildness, laxness.
re-missus 3 relaxed, languid; **a**) mild, gentle, indulgent, soft, yielding; **b**) gay, cheerful, merry; **c**) slack, careless.
re-mittō 3 **1.** to send back; to dismiss; a) to throw back; b) to give back, give out, yield, return (*beneficium*); c) to give back from oneself, give up, reject, resign; **2.** to loosen, relax, slacken; to melt; thaw; a) to leave off, abate, remit; **se remittere** to leave off work, refresh oneself; to become milder, to cease; b) to pardon, remit; c) to give up, allow, concede, grant; d) to cease, omit.
re-mōlior 4 to press *or* push back.
re-mollēscō, —, — 3 to become soft again; **a**) to be touched, moved, influenced; **b**) to be enervated.
re-molliō 4 to make weak *or* effeminate.
re-mora, ae *f* delay.

re-morāmen, inis *n* hindrance.
re-mordeō, mordī, morsum 2 to bite back; to torment, vex.
re-moror 1 a) to stay, tarry, linger; **b**) *trans.* to detain, delay, hinder.
re-mōtiō, ōnis *f* removal.
re-mōtus 3 removed; distant, far off; **a**) remote; free from, disconnected; **b**) rejectable.
re-moveō 2 to move back *or* away, withdraw, remove, lay aside, put away, abolish.
re-mūgiō 4 **a**) to bellow again; **b**) to bellow back; to resound.
re-mulceō 2 to stroke; to put (a tail) between the legs.
remulcum, ī *n* towing cable.
remūnerātiō, ōnis *f* recompense, reward.
re-mūneror 1 to repay, reward, recompense (*alqm re*).
re-murmurō 1 to murmur back.
rēmus, ī *m* oar.
re-nārrō 1 to relate again.
re-nāscor 3 to be born again, to rise *or* grow again.
re-nāvigō 1 to sail back.
re-neō 2 to unspin, unravel.
rēnēs, um *and* **ium** *m/pl.* the kidneys.
re-nīdeō, —, — 2 to shine *or* gleam back; to beam with joy, smile.
re-nīdēscō 3 to reflect light.
re-nītor 3 to withstand, resist.
re-nō[1] 1 to swim back.
rēnō[2], **ōnis** *m* reindeer skin, fur-cloak.
re-nōdō 1 **a**) to tie back; **b**) to untie.
re-novāmen, inis *n* renewal, new form.
re-novātiō, ōnis *f* a renewing.
re-novō 1 a) to renew, restore, repeat; **b**) to refresh, revive, recreate; **se renovāre** *or* **P.** to recover, be renewed in strength.
re-numerō 1 to pay back; to count up.
re-nūntiātiō, ōnis *f* proclamation, declaration, report.
re-nūntiō 1 to bring back a message (*alci alqd*); **a**) to report, announce; **b**) to proclaim, declare elected; **c**) to revoke, recall, renounce.
re-nūntius, ī *m* bringer-back of news.
re-nuō, uī, — 3 to deny (*by nodding*), to refuse.
re-nūtō 1 to refuse.
re-nūtus, ūs *m* refusal.
reor, ratus sum 2 to think, believe, suppose, judge (*alqd*; *acc. c. inf.*).
repāgula, ōrum *n/pl.* bars *or* bolts of a door; barrier.
re-pandus 3 bent upwards.
re-parābilis, e reparable, retrievable.
re-parcō 3 to spare; to abstain from.
re-parātor, ōris *m* restorer, renewer.
re-parō 1 **1.** to get back, a) to restore, repair, renew; b) to retrieve; c) to refresh, revive; **2.** to take in exchange.
re-pastinātiō, ōnis *f* a digging up again.
re-pectō, —, pexum 3 to comb again.
re-pellō, reppulī, repulsum 3 **a**) to drive *or* thrust back; **b**) to drive away; **c**) to keep off, remove; **d**) to reject, repulse, spurn, scorn; **e**) to refute.
re-pendō, pendī, pēnsum 3 to weigh back; **a**) to weigh in return, pay in equal weight; **b**) to repay, purchase, ransom, redeem; **c**) to requite, recompense.
repēns, tis a) sudden, unexpected (*adv.* **-te** and **repēns**); **b**) fresh, recent.
re-pēnsō 1, *intens. of* **rependo.**
repentīnus 3 unexpected, sudden, hasty; upstart.
re-percō 3 = **re-parcō.**
repercussus, ūs *m* a rebounding, reverberation.
re-percutiō 3 to strike, push *or* drive back; **P. a**) to rebound, echo; **b**) to be reflected.
re-periō, repperī, repertum 4 **a**) to find again; **b**) to find out, discover; **c**) to perceive, learn, ascertain; **d**) to acquire, obtain; **e**) to invent, devise.
repertor, ōris *m* discoverer, inventor, deviser, author.
repetentia, ae *f* recollection.
re-petītiō, ōnis *f* repetition.
repetītor, ōris *m* one who asks back.
re-petō 3 **1.** a) to attack *or* fall upon again; b) to seek again, go to again, return; **2.** a) to fetch back; to repeat, renew, begin again; **memoriam** (*rei*) to call to mind again; to repeat by words *or* writing; to think over again; to reckon again; b) to ask

back, to demand restitution *or* satisfaction (*res repetere*); (**pecuniae**) **repetundae, ārum** *f/pl.* (property which is being sought back) the crime of extortion; to claim, demand as one's right; **poenam** to punish; to derive, to trace from; to begin, to undertake.

re-pleō, plēvī, plētum 2 **a**) to fill again, fill up; to replenish, complete; **b**) to make full; satisfy, supply.

re-plicātiō, ōnis *f* a folding back.

re-plicō 1 to fold back, unroll, open.

rēpō, rēpsī, — 3 to crawl, creep.

re-pōnō 3 **a**) to put *or* place back; to lay up, store, preserve; **b**) to lay aside, store up, put away; to lay in the earth, bury; **c**) to give back, restore, requite, retaliate, make compensation (*alci alqd pro re*); **d**) to place back, replace; to restore to a former condition; **e**) to repeat, renew; to answer again; **f**) to place, lay, put (in the proper *or* natural place); to place, count, reckon, class; **g**) to cause to rest on (*alqd in re*).

re-portō 1 to bear, carry *or* bring back; **a**) to bring back information, to report (*alqd alci*); **b**) to carry home.

re-poscō, —, — 3 to demand back; to claim.

re-positōrium, ī *n* dinner-wagon, tray.

repostor, ōris *m* restorer.

repos(i)tus 3 remote, distant.

repōtia, ōrum *n/pl.* a revelling on the day after an entertainment.

re-praesentātiō, ōnis *f* payment in cash.

re-praesentō 1 to make present *or* manifest, to display, show; **a**) to pay in ready money; **b**) to perform immediately, realize, accomplish instantly, hasten.

re-prehendō 3 to hold fast, detain, check; to blame, censure; to refute; to restore.

reprehēnsiō, ōnis *f* blame, censure; check; refutation.

re-prehēnsō 1 to hold back, repeatedly.

reprehēnsor, ōris *m* blamer, censurer; reformer.

re-prēndō 3 = **reprehendo.**

re-pressor, ōris *m* restrainer.

re-primō, pressī, pressum 3 to press *or* hold back; **a**) to restrain, check; **se reprimere** to restrain oneself; **b**) to limit, confine.

re-prōmissiō, ōnis *f* counter-promise.

re-prōmittō 3 to promise in return.

rēptābundus 3 creeping.

rēptō 1 to crawl, walk slowly.

repudiātiō, ōnis *f* refusal.

re-pudiō 1 to reject, refuse, disdain, scorn, repudiate.

repudiōsus 3 shocking, offensive, objectionable.

repudium, ī *n* a casting off; putting away; divorce, separation.

re-puerāscō, —, — 3 to become a boy again.

re-pugnāns, tis contrary, opposed.

re-pugnantia, ae *f* contradiction.

re-pugnō 1 **a**) to resist, oppose, withstand (*dat.*); **b**) to be inconsistent, incompatible.

re-pullulō 1 to sprout again.

repulsa, ae *f* rejection, repulse; refusal, denial.

re-pulsō 1 **a**) to re-echo; **b**) to reject.

re-pulsus, ūs *m* reflection of light, echo.

re-pungō, —, — 3 to prick *or* goad again.

re-pūrgō 1 to cleanse again; to clear away.

reputātiō, ōnis *f* consideration, thinking over.

re-putō 1 to reckon, count; to think over, consider.

re-quiēs, ētis (*also* **requiem, requiē**) *f* rest, repose, recreation.

re-quiēscō, quiēvī, — 3 to rest, repose, to sleep; to be relieved; *rarely trans.* to lay to rest.

re-quiētus 3 rested, refreshed.

re-quīritō 1 to inquire after.

re-quīrō, sīvī *or* **siī, sītum** 3 **a**) to seek again, search for; **b**) to miss, want, require, demand, desire; **c**) to ask for, inquire after (*alqd; de re; alqd ab* or *ex alqo*); to investigate.

rēs, rēī (*and* **rĕī**) *f* **1.** thing, matter, affair; a) *pl.* the world, the universe, nature; b) condition, position, circumstances; respect, relation; **in omnibus rēbus** in every respect, from every point of view; **rem renuntiare** to relate the state of affairs; **rēs secundae** *or* **prosperae** (*adversae*) good (bad) fortune; fate, lot; ground, reason; c) business, affair, matter of business; **rēs mili-**

taris *or* **bellica** military affairs; **r. maritima** *or* **navalis** naval affairs; **frumentaria** corn-supply, **rustica** agriculture, *pl.* **rēs divinae** religion; **rem suscipere** to undertake a task; d) lawsuit, action; commonwealth, state, republic, public interest *or* power, government, = **rēs publica** (*see* **publicus**); e) benefit, profit, advantage, interest (*rebus suis consulere, in rem meam est* it is useful for me); **2.** property, possessions, estate, wealth; **rēs familiaris** private affairs *or* property; **3.** deed, action; a) exploit, battle, engagement, affair; b) event, occurrence, facts, history; **rērum scriptor** historian; c) actual thing, reality, truth; nature of a thing; d) contents, substance.

re-sacrō 1 to free from a curse.

re-saeviō 4 to rage again.

re-salūtātiō, ōnis *f* responsive greeting.

re-salūtō 1 to greet in return.

re-sānēscō, nuī, — 3 to become sound again.

re-sarciō 4 to patch up *or* mend again; to repair.

re-scindō 3 **a**) to tear open again; **b**) to break up, tear off *or* away, to force open; **c**) to annul, repeal.

re-scīscō 3 to find out, ascertain.

re-scrībō 3 **a**) to write back; to answer in writing; to rewrite; **b**) to re-enlist; **c**) to transfer; **d**) to place (money) to someone's credit, to pay back.

re-scrīptum, ī *n* imperial rescript.

re-secō 1 to cut a part off, cut back; to curtail, check.

re-secrō 1 to adjure repeatedly.

re-sēminō 1 to sow *or* produce again.

re-sequor 3 to answer, reply.

re-serō 1 to unlock, unclose; to open, reveal, begin.

re-servō 1 to keep back, reserve (*alqd ad* or *in alqd*); **a**) to save, preserve; **b**) to retain.

re-ses, idis inactive, lazy.

re-sideō, sēdī, sessum 2 to be seated; **a**) to rest, keep a festival *or* holiday; **b**) to reside, be left, remain.

re-sīdō, sēdī, sessum 3 to sit down, settle; **a**) to sink, fall; **b**) to abate, grow calm, subside.

residuus 3 remaining, left behind; *subst.* **-um, ī** *n* remainder, residue.

re-signō 1 **a**) to unseal, open; to reveal; **b**) to annul, destroy; **c**) to pay back, resign.

re-siliō, luī, — 4 to leap *or* spring back; to contract, shrink.

re-sīmus 3 turned up.

rēsīna, ae *f* resin.

rēsīnātus 3 smeared *or* flavoured with resin.

re-sipiō, —, — 3 to taste *or* smack of.

re-sipīscō, pīvī (**piī** *and* **puī**), — 3 to recover one's senses.

re-sistō, stitī, — 3 **a**) to stand back, to halt, stop; to remain behind; to pause, stay; to recover a footing; **b**) to resist, oppose, withstand (*alci, contra alqd; ne, quin*).

re-solvō 3 to untie, unbind, loosen; **a**) to open; **b**) to relax, unnerve; **c**) to annul, cancel, abolish; **d**) to free, dispel, dissolve, melt; **e**) to pay (back).

re-sonābilis, e resounding.

re-sonō 1 to resound, echo; **a**) to sound; **b**) to fill with sound, cause to resound.

re-sonus 3 resounding.

re-sorbeō, —, — 2 to suck back, swallow again.

re-spectō 1 to look back, round *or* about (*ad alqd*); **a**) to gaze at, look upon (*alqd*); **b**) to regard, care for; **c**) to look for, expect (*alqd ab alqo*).

respectus, ūs *m* a looking back *or* about; **a**) regard, respect, consideration; **b**) refuge, retreat.

re-spergō, rsī, rsum 3 to besprinkle, bestrew (*alqd re*).

respersiō, ōnis *f* a besprinkling.

re-spiciō, exī, ectum 3 **a**) to look back, behind *or* about (*ad alqd*); to have respect to; **b**) to look back at (*alqd*), to see behind; **c**) to reflect upon, think of, to consider, care for, regard, have a care for (*alqd*).

re-spīrāmen, inis *n* windpipe.

re-spīrātiō, ōnis *f* a breathing out, breathing; exhalation; a taking breath.

re-spīrō 1 a) to breathe out; **b**) to take *or* recover breath, to recover, revive, be refreshed; **c**) to abate, cease.

re-splendeō, uī, — 2 to shine back, glitter.

re-spondeō, ndī, ōnsum 2 to promise in return; **a**) to answer, reply, make answer (*alci alqd; de re; acc. c.*

inf.); **b**) to give decisions, to give advice (*ius*, *de iure*); **c**) to answer to one's name, to appear, be present; **d**) to answer, correspond, agree, be equal *or* a match for (*dat.*); to requite, return; to be punctual in paying.
re-spōnsiō, ōnis *f* answer, reply.
respōnsitō 1 to give advice professionally.
respōnsō 1 **a**) to answer, echo; **b**) to withstand, defy.
re-spōnsor, ōris *m* one who gives an expert's opinion.
respōnsum, ī *n* **a**) answer; **b**) answer of a lawyer, priest, *or* oracle.
rēs-pūblica, ae *f*, *see* **publicus.**
re-spuō 3 to spit back *or* out; to reject, refuse, spurn.
re-stāgnō 1 to overflow; to be inundated.
re-staurō 1 to restore, repair.
resticula, ae *f* cord, line.
restinctiō, ōnis *f* a quenching.
re-stinguō, inxī, inctum 3 to quench, extinguish; to mitigate, appease; to destroy.
restiō, ōnis *m* rope-maker; one who is whipped with ropes.
re-stipulātiō, ōnis *f* counter-obligation.
re-stipulor 1 to stipulate in return.
restis, is *f* rope, cord.
restitō 1 to tarry, hesitate.
restitrīx, īcis *f* she who remains behind.
re-stituō, uī, ūtum 3 **1.** to replace; a) to bring *or* call back; b) to give back, restore, deliver up (*alci alqd*); **2.** to reinstate, restore to the former state, bring back; a) to renew, rebuild, revive, repair; b) to make restitution of, make good again, compensate; c) to revoke, make void, reverse.
restitūtiō, ōnis *f* a replacing, reinstating; restoring; recalling.
restitūtor, ōris *m* restorer.
re-stō, stitī, — 1 **a**) to stay back *or* behind; **b**) to withstand, resist; **c**) to be left, remain alive; **restat ut** it remains that; to be in store for; **quod restat** for the future.
re-strictus 3 bound fast, tight, close; **a**) strict, stern; **b**) niggardly, stingy; **c**) moderate.
re-stringō 3 to bind back *or* fast; **a**) to tighten; **b**) to confine, restrict.
re-sūdō 1 to sweat out.
re-sultō 1 to rebound, spring back; **a**) to resound; **b**) to be repugnant.
re-sūmō 3 to take again *or* back; **a**) to renew, repeat; **b**) to obtain again.
re-supīnō 1 to throw down (on the back).
re-supīnus 3 lying on the back; arrogant ('with his nose in the air').
re-surgō 3 to rise up again, to reappear.
re-suscitō 1 to rouse again.
re-sūtus 3 unstitched, come apart.
re-tardātiō, ōnis *f* a retarding, delaying.
re-tardō 1 to retard, delay, detain, hinder.
re-taxō 1 to censure in return.
rēte, is *n* net.
re-tegō 3 to uncover, make bare; to open; to reveal.
re-temptō 1 to try again.
re-tendō, ndī, ntum *or* **ēnsum** 3 to unbend (*a bow*).
re-tentiō, ōnis *f* a keeping back.
re-tentō[1] 1 to hold back *or* fast; to preserve.
re-tentō[2] 1 = **retempto.**
re-texō 3 **a**) to unweave, unravel; to annul, cancel, reverse; **b**) to weave anew, to renew, repeat.
rētiārius, ī *m* fighter furnished with a net.
reticentia, ae *f* silence, a keeping silence; pause.
re-ticeō, cuī, — 2 **a**) to be silent; **b**) to keep secret.
rēticulum, ī *n* fishing-net; net-bag; hair-net.
retināculum, ī *n* band, halter, rope, cable.
re-tinēns, tis holding fast, tenacious (*gen.*).
re-tinentia, ae *f* a remembering.
re-tineō, tinuī, tentum 2 to hold back *or* fast, to detain (*alqm in re*); **a**) to hold in check, restrain; **b**) to fetter; **c**) to keep, preserve, retain, maintain.
re-tinniō 4 to resound.
re-tonō, —, — 1 to thunder back.
re-torqueō 2 to twist, bend *or* turn back; to change.
re-torridus 3 parched up, withered: old, cunning.
re-tractātiō, ōnis *f* **a**) recollection; **b**) drawing back, refusal.
retractātus 3 revised, corrected.

re-tractō 1 **a**) to draw back, take back, recall, retract; to refuse; **b**) to handle again, take in hand again, go over again, retouch, renew; to consider again, revise.
retractus 3 retired, remote.
re-trahō 3 **a**) to draw, drag, fetch back; to keep back, prevent, detain from (*alqm a re*); **se retrahere** to withdraw oneself; **b**) to draw *or* drag again; to draw forth again; **c**) to draw towards (*alqm in alqd*).
re-trectō 1 = **retracto.**
re-tribuō 3 to give again *or* back; to return, restore, repay.
re-trītus 3 rubbed down.
retrō *adv.* backwards, back, behind; in the past.
retro-agō 3 to turn back *or* aside.
retrōrsum (*and* **-us**) *adv.* = **retro.**
retrō-versus 3 turned backwards.
re-trūdō 3 to push back; to thrust into a corner; to hide.
re-tundō, rettudī, retū(n)sum 3 to beat back; **a**) to blunt, make dull; **b**)to check; **retū(n)sus** 3 blunt, dull.
reus, ī *m and* **rea, ae** *f* a party in a law-suit; accused person, defendant; one who is bound *or* answerable for something (*gen.*).
re-valēscō, luī, — 3 to become well again, to recover, be restored.
re-vehō 3 to carry back; **P.** to come, sail, ride back.
re-vellō 3 to tear, pull *or* pluck off *or* away; to do away with, abolish; to tear up, open.
re-vēlō 1 to unveil, uncover.
re-veniō 4 to come back, return.
rē-vērā *adv.* indeed, in truth, truly.
re-verberō 1 to beat back; to cause to rebound.
re-verēns, tis respectful, reverent.
reverentia, ae *f* reverence, awe, respect.
re-vereor 2 to feel awe *or* respect, to fear, be afraid of.
re-verrō 3 to sweep back again.
re-versiō, ōnis *f* a turning back; return, recurrence.
re-vertor (rarely **-ō**), *perf.* **revertī, reversum** 3 to turn back, return, come back; *part.* **reversus** having returned.
re-videō 2 to go back to see.
re-vīlēscō 3 to become cheap.
re-vinciō 4 **a**) to bind back; **b**) to bind fast, fasten; to bind around, fetter.
re-vincō 3 to conquer, subdue; to convict, refute.
re-virēscō, ruī, — 3 to become green again; to become young *or* vigorous again.
re-vīsō, sī, — 3 to revisit; to go back to see.
re-vīvīscō, vīxī, vīctum 3 to come to life again, revive.
re-vocābilis, e revocable.
re-vocāmen, inis *n* a calling back, warning.
re-vocātiō, ōnis *f* a calling back.
re-vocō 1 **1.** to call back, recall (*alqm de, ex, a re in* or *ad alqd*); a) to draw, turn, fetch back; b) to call off, withdraw, check; divert; c) to demand back; to recall; d) to renew, restore; e) to revoke, retract, cancel; f) to apply, reduce, refer; **2.** to call anew, ask again, invite in return; a) to recall (*players*), to encore; b) to summon again.
re-volō 1 to fly back.
re-volūbilis, e that may be rolled back.
re-volvō 3 to roll back; **a**) to unroll, open again, read over, repeat, think over; **b**) **P.** to return, recur; — **re-volūtus** 3 returning, elapsed.
re-vomō 3 to vomit up.
re-vorr-, -vors-, -vort- = **re-verr-, -vers-, -vert-.**
rēx, rēgis *m* king, monarch, prince; *adj.* ruling, supreme; — **a**) *pl.* royal family, princes; **b**) arbitrary ruler; despot, tyrant; **c**) high priest; **d**) leader, head, chief, master, lord; **e**) mighty person, great man, patron, protector.
rhadinē *f adj.* (ῥαδινή) delicate.
rhaps-ōdia, ae *f* lay, book (*of a poem*).
rhētor, oris *m* **a**) teacher of rhetoric; **b**) = **orator.**
rhētoricus 3 rhetorical, of an orator; *subst.* **-a, ae** *f and* **ōrum** *n/pl.* art of rhetoric.
rhīno-cerōs, ōtis *m* rhinoceros; vessel made of rhinoceros horn.
rhō *n* (*indecl.*) the Greek letter r.
rhombus, ī *m* **a**) a magician's circle; **b**) turbot.
rhonchus, ī *m* **a**) snore; **b**) grunt of contempt, sneer.
rhythmicus, ī *m* one who teaches the art of preserving rhythm in poetry.

rhythmus (-os), **ī** *m* rhythm.
rhytium, i *n* drinking-horn.
rīca, ae *f* veil.
rīcinium, ī *n* small veil, kerchief.
rictum, ī *n and* **rictus, ūs** *m* wide open mouth.
rīdeō, sī, sum 2 to laugh; to smile; **a**) to look cheerful, be favourable, to smile at (*alci; ad alqm*); **b**) to beam; **c**) to laugh at (*acc.*), deride, mock.
rīdibundus 3 laughing.
rīdiculāria, ōrum *n/pl.* fun, drollery.
rīdiculus 3 exciting laughter, funny, amusing, droll; *subst.* **-um, ī** *n* jest, joke.
rigēns, tis = **rigidus.**
rigeō, guī, — 2 **a**) to be stiff *or* numb; **b**) to stand on end, bristle up.
rigēscō, riguī, — 3 to become stiff.
rigidō 1 to stiffen, confirm.
rigidus 3 stiff, hard, inflexible; **a**) rigid; rocky; **b**) stern, rough, cruel.
rigō 1 to conduct (*water*); to wet, moisten, water.
rigor, ōris *m* stiffness; **a**) cold, chilliness; **b**) hardness, severity, sternness.
riguus 3 watering; watered.
rīma, ae *f* chink, fissure, cleft.
rīmor 1 to lay open, cleave; **a**) to turn over, pry into, search; **b**) to examine, investigate thoroughly.
rīmōsus 3 full of chinks *or* fissures.
ringor, — 3 to show the teeth; to snarl.
rīpa, ae *f* bank of a river (*rarely,* sea-coast).
rīpula, ae *f* small bank.
riscus, ī *m* trunk, chest.
rīsiō, ōnis *f* a laughing, laughter.
rīsor, ōris *m* mocker.
rīsus, ūs *m* laughter, laughing, laugh; **a**) object of laughter; **b**) mockery.
rīte *adv.* according to (*religious*) usage *or* ceremonies, according to rites; **a**) properly, fitly, justly, rightly, duly; **b**) fortunately, luckily.
rītus, ūs *m* religious usage, ceremony, rite; custom, usage, manner, mode; **rītū** (*with gen.*) in the manner *or* fashion of.
rīvālis, is *m* rival, competitor.
rīvālitās, ātis *f* rivalry.
rīvulus, ī *m* rivulet, streamlet.
rīvus, ī *m* brook, stream.
rixa, ae *f* quarrel, brawl, dispute.
rixor 1 to quarrel, brawl, dispute.
rōbīginōsus 3 rusty; corroding, envious.
rōbīgō, inis *f* rust; **a**) blight, mildew tartar (*or* decay?) on the teeth; rustiness (through lack of use).
rōboreus 3 oaken.
rōborō 1 to strengthen, invigorate.
rōbur, oris *n* hard-wood, oakwood, oak-tree; **a**) things made of hard wood, bench, club, lance; **b**) underground dungeon in the prison at Rome; **c**) hardness, firmness, strength; **d**) the best *or* strongest part, the pick; the flower of troops; stronghold.
rōbus 3 red.
rōbustus 3 oaken; hard, firm, solid, strong, vigorous, robust.
rōdō, sī, sum 3 to gnaw; to eat away, consume, corrode; to slander, disparage.
rogālis, e of a funeral pile.
rogātiō, ōnis *f* **a**) proposed law, bill; **b**) entreaty, request; question, interrogation.
rogātiuncula, ae *f* little question; little bill.
rogātor, ōris *m* **a**) proposer of a bill; **b**) collector of votes; beggar.
rogātus, ūs *m* request, entreaty.
rogitātiō, ōnis *f* proposed law.
rogitō 1 to ask (repeatedly).
rogō 1 **1.** to ask, question; **rogātum, ī** *n* question; a) **alqm sententiam** to ask an opinion, call upon to vote; b) **populum** *or* **lēgem** to propose a law; **magistrātum** to propose for election; **2.** to ask for, beg, entreat, request (*alqd ab alqo; alqm; ut, ne*); to invite.
rogus, ī *m* funeral pile; grave.
rōrārii. ōrum *m/pl.* skirmishers.
rōridus 3 = **roscidus.**
rōri-fer 3 dew-bringing.
rōrō 1 **a**) to drop dew; **rōrat** dew falls; to trickle, drip, be moist; **b**) to bedew, moisten.
rōs, rōris *m* dew, dewdrops; moisture, water; **rōs marīnus, ī** *m* rosemary.
rosa, ae *f* **a**) rose-bush; **b**) rose, wreath of roses.
rosārius 3 of roses; *subst.* **-ium, ī** *n* = **rosētum.**
rōscidus 3 **a**) full of dew, dewy, dripping; **b**) moistened, wet.

rosētum, ī *n* rose-garden.
roseus 3 of roses; rosy.
rōsidus 3 = **roscidus.**
rōstrātus 3 having a beak; **columna** (*or* **corōna**) **-a** adorned with beaks of vessels.
rōstrum, ī *n* bill, beak, snout; **a**) beak of a ship; **b**) *pl.* platform for speakers in the Forum (adorned with ships' beaks).
rota, ae *f* wheel; **a**) potter's wheel; **b**) wheel for torture; **c**) roller; **d**) wheel of a chariot, chariot; **e**) vicissitude, alternation, fickleness.
rotātus, ūs *m* whirling motion.
rotō 1 to turn, whirl *or* swing round; *intr.* to roll round.
rotula, ae *f* little wheel.
rotundō 1 to make round; to round off.
rotundus 3 round; **a**) rounded, circular, spherical; **b**) rounded, perfect, elegant.
rube-faciō 3 to make red.
rubellus 3 pale red.
rubeō, uī, — 2 to be red; to redden, blush.
ruber, bra, brum red, ruddy.
rubēscō, buī, — 3 to grow *or* turn red.
rubēta, ae *f* a species of venomous toad.
rubētum, ī *n* bramble-thicket.
rubeus 3 of a bramble-bush.
rubicund(**ul**)**us** 3 red.
rubidus 3 blackish red.
rubor, ōris *m* redness; **a**) flush, blush; **b**) bashfulness, modesty; **c**) shame, disgrace.
rubrīca, ae *f* red ochre; (title of) a law.
rubus, ī *m* bramble-bush; blackberry.
rūctābundus 3 belching frequently.
rūctō (*and* **-or**) 1 to belch.
rūctus, ūs *m* a belching.
rudēns (*and* **rū-**), **tis** *m* and *f* rope, cable.
rudiārius, ī *m* discharged gladiator.
rudīmentum, ī *n* first attempt, trial, essay, beginning, novitiate.
rudis[1], **is** *f* gladiator's practice-foil (presented to gladiators on retirement).
rudis[2], **e** unwrought, roughly made; untilled; unskilled, untrained, inexperienced (*gen.*; *in re*); uncultured.
rudō (*and* **rūdō**), **īvī,** — 3 to roar, bellow, bray.
rūdus, eris *n* **1.** rubbish, debris, broken stone, plaster; — **2.** formless piece of metal used as money.
rūf(**ul**)**us** 3 dull yellowish *or* brownish red; red-haired.
rūga, ae *f* wrinkle, frown, gloomy look.
rūgō 1 to be wrinkled.
rūgōsus 3 wrinkled.
ruīna, ae *f* a tumbling, falling down, fall; **a**) disaster, calamity, overthrow, ruin; **b**) slip; **c**) destruction, death; **d**) fallen building, ruins.
ruīnōsus 3 **a**) going to ruin; **b**) fallen, ruined.
rumex, icis *m* and *f* sorrel.
rūmi-ferō 1 to praise publicly.
rūminātiō, ōnis *f* a chewing the cud, rumination; reflection.
rūminō 1 to chew again.
rūmor, ōris *m* vague sound; **a**) cry of applause; **b**) common talk, report, hearsay; **c**) popular voice, common opinion, fame.
rumpia, ae *f* long sword.
rumpō, rūpī, ruptum 3 to break, burst, tear, rend, break asunder; **a**) to burst to pieces, break open, break through; **viam** to force a way (*also* **sē rumpere** *and* **P. rumpī**); **b**) to cause to break forth; **c**) to violate, destroy, annul, interrupt, cut short.
rūmusculus, ī *m* idle talk, gossip.
runcō 1 to depilate.
ruō, ruī, rutum (**ruitūrus**) 3 **1.** to hasten, hurry, run, rush; a) to fall with violence, tumble down, go to ruin; b) to rush, hasten, hurry, dash (*in alqd*); **c**) to fall, be ruined; **2.** *trans.* to cause to fall, cast down, to throw up in a heap.
rūpēs, is *f* rock, cliff, cavern.
ruptor, ōris *m* breaker, violator.
rūri-cola, ae *m* and *f* inhabiting the country, rural, rustic.
rūri-gena, ae *m* and *f* countryman, -woman.
rūrō 1 to be in the country.
rūrsus *and* **rūrsum** *adv.* turned back, back, backwards; **a**) again, anew; **b**) on the contrary, on the other hand, in return.
rūs, rūris *n* the country, fields; **a**) country-seat, farm; **b**) rusticity; **rūs** into the country; **rūrī** *and* **rūre** in the country; **rūre** from the country.
rūscum, ī *n* butcher's-broom.
russātus 3 dressed in red.
russus 3 red.

rūsticānus 3 of the country, rustic.
rūsticātiō, ōnis *f* rural life.
rūsticitās, ātis *f* rustic behaviour, boorishness; simplicity.
rūsticor 1 to live in the country.
rūsticulus 3 = **rūsticus;** *subst. m* countryman; *f* grouse.
rūsticus 3 of the country, rural, rustic; *m* countryman, peasant; **a**) simple, plain; **b**) boorish, awkward, rude; coarse.
rūsum *and* **-us** = **rūrsum, -us.**
rūta[1], **ae** *f* rue (*a herb*); bitterness.
rūta[2] **(et) caesa** *n/pl.* minerals and timber.
rutābulum, ī *n* poker, fire-rake.
rūtātus 3 garnished with rue.
rutilō 1 **a**) to colour reddish; **b**) to shine with a reddish gleam.
rutilus 3 reddish yellow, golden red.
rutrum, ī *n* shovel, spade.
rūtula, ae *f* a little piece of rue.

S

sabbata, ōrum *n/pl.* Sabbath; Jewish festival.
sabbatāriae, ārum *f/pl.* Sabbath-keepers, Jewesses.
sabulum, ī *n* coarse sand, gravel.
saburra, ae *f* sand; ballast.
saburrō 1 to fill (with ballast; with food).
sacci-pērium, ī *n* cover for a purse.
saccō[1], **ōnis** *m* 'bagman', i.e. usurer.
saccō[2] 1 to strain, filter.
sacculus, ī *m* small bag.
saccus, ī *m* sack, bag, purse.
sacellum, ī *n* little sanctuary, chapel.
sacer, cra, crum holy, sacred, consecrated (with *gen.* or *dat.*); accursed, execrable.
sacerdōs, ōtis *m* and *f* priest, priestess.
sacerdōtālis, e priestly.
sacerdōtium, ī *n* priesthood.
sacrāmentum, ī *n* **a**) money deposited by the parties in a suit, forfeit-money; **b**) civil suit; dispute; **c**) military oath of allegiance; **d**) oath, obligation.
sacrārium, ī *n* **a**) shrine, sacristy; **b**) chapel, sanctuary.
sacrēs = **sacrī (sacer).**
sacri-cola, ae *m* sacrificing priest.
sacri-fer 3 bearing sacred things.
sacrificālis, e belonging to sacrificing.
sacrificātiō, ōnis *f* a sacrificing.
sacrificium, ī *n* sacrifice.
sacrificō 1 to sacrifice, offer a sacrifice (*alci re* or *rem*).
sacrificulus, ī *m* sacrificing priest.
sacri-ficus 3 sacrificial.
sacrilegium, ī *n* temple-robbery, sacrilege.
sacri-legus 3 **a**) stealing sacred things; robbing a temple, sacrilegious; **b**) impious, godless, wicked.
sacrō 1 to consecrate, dedicate, devote; **a**) to render sacred *or* inviolable; **b**) to immortalize, render imperishable; **c**) to devote to the infernal gods.
sacrō-sānctus 3 most holy, inviolable.
sacruficō = **sacrificō.**
sacrum, ī *n* **a**) sacred *or* holy thing; sanctuary; **b**) sacrifice, holy rite; victim; worship, divine service; festival; mystery; poetry.
saeculāris, e: a) **-ēs (lūdī)** centennial games; **b**) **-e carmen** hymn composed for such games.
saec(u)lum, ī *n* **a**) generation, age, lifetime; **b**) a hundred years, century; long period; the times, spirit of the age.
saepe *adv.* often, frequently.
saepe-numerō *adv.* often.
saepēs, is *f* hedge, fence; enclosure.
saepiculē pretty often.
saepīmentum, ī *n* hedge, enclosure.
saepiō, psī, ptum 4 to hedge in, fence in, enclose; to protect.
saeptum, ī *n* (*usu. pl.*) fence, enclosure, fold; barrier.
saeta, ae *f* stiff hair, bristle; part of a fishing-line.
saeti-ger 3 bristle-bearing; *subst. m* boar.
saetōsus 3 bristly.
saevi-dicus 3 spoken angrily.
saeviō 4 to rage, rave, be furious *or* fierce.
saevitia, ae *f* (*and* **-tūdō** *f*) rage, fury, fierceness, savageness, severity.
saevus 3 raging, furious, mad; fierce, cruel, savage, ferocious; *adv.* **-vē, -viter.**
sāga, ae *f* female soothsayer.
sagācitās, ātis *f* keenness (*of perception*), sagacity, acuteness.
sagātus 3 clothed in a military cloak.
sagāx, ācis keen in the scent; keen, acute, sagacious, clever.
sagīna, ae *f* a feeding, fattening: food, nourishment.
sagīnō 1 to feed, fatten, cram.
sāgiō 4 to perceive keenly.
sagitta, ae *f* arrow, bolt.
sagittārius, ī *m* archer.
sagittātus barbed.
sagitti-fer 3 arrow-bearing.
sagitti-potēns, tis mighty with arrows.
sagittō 1 to shoot with arrows.

sagmina, um *n/pl.* tuft of sacred grass.
sagulātus 3 wearing a *sagulum.*
sagulum, ī *n* = **sagum.**
sagum, ī *n* (military) cloak.
sāgus 3 prophetic.
sāl, salis *m* (*n*) salt; **a**) salt-water, brine, sea; **b**) acuteness, cunning, wit, good sense, elegance, brilliance; sarcasm.
salacō, ōnis *m* braggart.
salamandra, ae *f* salamander.
salapūtium, ī *n* little man, manikin.
salārius 3 of salt; *subst.* **~, ī** *m* dealer in salted fish; **salārium, ī** *n* salt-money, pension, salary, stipend.
salāx, ācis lustful, lecherous; provoking lust.
salebra, ae *f* rough *or* uneven road; roughness.
salebrōsus 3 rough, rugged, uneven.
saliātus, ūs *m* appointment *or* dignity of the *Salii.*
salictum, ī *n* willow plantation.
salignus 3 of willows.
Saliī, (ōr)um *m/pl.* the priests of Mars.
salillum, ī *n* salt-cellar.
salīnae, ārum *f/pl.* salt-works, salt-pits.
salīnum, ī *n* salt-cellar.
saliō, luī *or* **liī,** — 4 to leap, spring, bound, jump; *subst.* **salientēs, ium** *m/pl.* springs, fountains.
saliunca, ae *f* wild nard.
salīva, ae *f* spittle, saliva; taste, appetite.
salix, icis *f* willow.
salsāmentārius, ī *m* salt-fish dealer.
salsāmentum, ī *n* salted fish; brine.
salsi-potēns, ntis ruling the salt sea.
salsūra, ae *f* a salting, pickling.
salsus 3 salted, salt; **a**) biting, sharp; **b**) witty, satirical.
saltātiō, ōnis *f* a dancing, dance.
saltātor, ōris *m* dancer.
saltātōrius 3 of dancing.
saltātrīx, īcis *f* dancing-girl.
saltātus, ūs *m* = **saltatio.**
saltem (*and* **saltim**) *adv.* at least.
saltō 1 to dance, to represent in dancing.
saltuōsus 3 well-wooded.
saltus[1], **ūs** *m* forest- *or* mountain-pasture, wooded upland; mountain-pass; tight corner.
saltus[2], **ūs** *m* a leaping, leap.
salūbris, e (*and* **salūber, bris, bre**) **a**) healthful, wholesome, salubrious, salutary, serviceable; **b**) sound, vigorous.
salūbritās, ātis *f* healthfulness, wholesomeness; healthiness, health; means of deliverance.
salum, ī *n* open sea, sea; tossing at sea; river current.
salūs, ūtis *f* health; **a**) welfare, well-being, weal, good fortune; **b**) security, safety, deliverance, life; **c**) salutation, greeting; **salūtem dicere** to greet, to bid farewell.
salūtāris, e healthful, wholesome, beneficial.
salūtātiō, ōnis *f* a greeting, saluting; a waiting upon, visit.
salutātor, ōris *m* one who salutes; caller.
salūtātrīx, īcis *f* (*as adj.*) (of) greeting; of callers.
salūti-fer 3 health-bringing.
salūti-gerulus 3 carrying greetings.
salūtō 1 to greet, salute; **a**) to greet as, to name; **b**) to wait upon, to call upon, visit.
salveō, —, — 2 to be well, be in good health; **salvē, salvēte** greeting!; hail!; good day!; farewell!
salvus 3 safe, unhurt, preserved, sound, still alive; *adv.* **-vē** in good health, well, all right.
sambūca, ae *f* harp(-player).
sambūcistria, ae *f* female harpist.
sānābilis, e curable, healable.
sānātiō, ōnis *f* a healing, curing.
sanciō, sanxī, sānctum 4 to make sacred *or* inviolable; **a**) to appoint, order, establish, decree (*alqd; ut, ne*); **b**) to confirm, ratify; **c**) to forbid under penalty *or* punishment.
sānctimōnia, ae *f* = **sanctitas.**
sānctiō, ōnis *f* ordinance; penal clause, declaration of a penalty.
sānctitās, ātis *f* sacredness, sanctity; **a**) inviolability; **b**) holiness, purity, virtue, integrity, chastity; piety.
sānctitūdō, inis *f* = **sanctitas.**
sānctor, ōris *m* ordainer.
sānctus 3 sacred, inviolable; **a**) venerable, august, divine; **b**) virtuous, holy, pious; innocent, pure: chaste, just.
sandali-gerula, ae *f* female slave who carried her mistress' sandals.
sandalium, ī *n* slipper, sandal.

sandapila, ae *f* bier for poor people.
sandȳx, ȳcis *f* vermilion.
sānē *adv.* **1.** soberly, sensibly, reasonably; **2.** a) indeed, truly, forsooth, well, by all means; b) to be sure, certainly: c) (*with imperative*) then, if you will; d) exceedingly, extremely; **sānē quam** very much indeed, uncommonly.
sanguen, inis *n* = **sanguis.**
sanguināns, antis blood-stained; blood-thirsty.
sanguinārius 3 blood-thirsty.
sanguineus 3 bloody, of blood; **a**) stained with blood; **b**) bloodred; **c**) blood-thirsty.
sanguinolentus *and* **sanguinulentus** 3 = **sanguineus.**
sanguīs (*and* **-ĭs**), **inis** *m* blood; **a**) bloodshed; **b**) vigour, strength, life; **c**) consanguinity, race, family, blood; **d**) descendant, offspring.
saniēs, ēī *f* corrupted blood, bloody matter, venom, poison.
sānitās, ātis *f* health; **a**) soundness of mind, good sense, reasonableness; **b**) solidity, propriety.
sanna, ae *f* grimace.
sanniō, ōnis *m* buffoon.
sānō 1 to heal, cure, make sound; to restore, repair.
sānus 3 sound, healthy, whole; sober, reasonable, discreet.
sapa, ae *f* must, new wine boiled thick.
sāperda, ae *m* a cheap kind of salt fish.
sapiēns, tis wise, knowing, sensible, judicious, discreet; *subst. m* a wise man, philosopher.
sapientia, ae *f* good sense, prudence, discretion, wisdom; philosophy.
sapienti-potēns, tis mighty in wisdom.
sapiō, iī, — 3 a) to taste of (*alqd*); **b**) to have taste; **c**) to be sensible *or* wise; **d**) to understand.
sāpō, ōnis *m* soap.
sapor, ōris *m* taste, flavour; **a**) delicacy, pleasant odour; **b**) good taste, elegance.
saprophagō 3 to eat putrid food.
sarcina, ae *f* bundle, soldier's pack; load, burden; burden of the womb.
sarcinārius 3 belonging to baggage.
sarcinātor, ōris *m* one who patches *or* mends clothes.
sarcinātus 3 burdened with baggage.
sarcinula, ae *f* bundle, small baggage.
sarciō, rsī, rtum 4 to patch, mend, repair; to make good, make amends for; **sartus** 3 in good condition, in good repair.
sarco-phagus, ī *m* coffin.
sarculum, ī *n* hoe.
sardonyx, ychis *m* and *f* sardonyx.
sargus, ī *m* a sea-fish.
sariō 4 to hoe, weed.
sarīs(s)a, ae *f* Macedonian lance.
sarīso-phorus, ī *m* Macedonian lancer.
sarmen, inis *n* = **sarmentum.**
sarmentum, ī *n* (*pl.*) twigs, brushwood, faggots.
sarrācum, ī *n* = **serracum.**
sartāgō, inis *f* frying-pan.
sartor, ōris *m* one who hoes.
sartūra, ae *f* patching, patch.
sartus 3, *see* **sarcio.**
sat *adv.* = **satis.**
sata, ōrum *n/pl.* standing corn, crops.
sat-agius 3 over-anxious.
sat-agō 3 (= *satis agō*) **a**) to pay debts; **b**) to have enough to do, be in trouble.
satelles, itis *m* and *f* attendant, escort, life-guard; **a**) *pl.* train, retinue; **b**) follower, partner, accomplice.
satiās, (ātis) *f* = **satietas.**
satietās, ātis *f* **a**) sufficiency, abundance; **b**) satiety, fulness; **c**) loathing, disgust.
satillum *n* a small trifle.
satin' *and* **satine** = **satisne.**
satiō[1] 1 to fill (*alqm re*); **a**) to satisfy, satiate, appease; **b**) to overfill, disgust.
satiō[2], **ōnis** *f* **a**) a sowing, planting; **b**) sown field.
satira, ae *f* = **satura.**
satis enough, sufficiently, sufficient; **satis superque** more than enough; **a**) tolerably, moderately, well enough, pretty well, somewhat; **b**) **satis esse** to suffice; **satis habēre** to think sufficient, be satisfied, content; **satis agere,** *see* **satago; satis dare,** *see* **satisdo;** *comp.* **satius** better, preferable, more advantageous.
satis-datiō, ōnis *f* a giving of bail *or* security.
satis-dō 1 to give bail *or* security.

satis-faciō 3 to satisfy, give satisfaction; **a**) to pay (*a creditor*); **b**) to apologize, make excuse (*alci de re*); **c**) to make amends; **d**) to prove sufficiently (*alci acc. c. inf.*).
satis-factiō, ōnis *f* reparation, amends; apology.
sator, ōris *m* sower, planter; begetter, father, creator.
satrapēa *and* **-ia, ae** *f* satrapy, province of Persia.
satrapēs, is *and* **-pa, ae** *m* satrap, governor.
satur, ra, rum full, sated, satiated (*abl.* or *gen.*); fat, rich, fertile, abundant.
satura[1], **ae** *f* **a**) dish of various fruits, mixture, medley; **per saturam** confusedly; **b**) discursive composition; satire.
satura[2] *f* female satyr.
saturēia, ōrum *n/pl.* a herb.
saturiō *m* a well-fed man.
saturitās, ātis *f* fulness, repleteness; abundance.
saturō 1 = **satiō**[1].
satus[1], **ūs** *m* a sowing, planting; **a**) seed; **b**) a begetting, producing, origin, race.
satus[2] 3, *see* **sero**[2].
satyriscus, ī *m* little Satyr.
satyrus, ī *m* Satyr; Satyric drama.
sauciātiō, ōnis *f* a wounding.
sauciō 1 to wound, hurt; to cut.
saucius 3 wounded, hurt, damaged, weakened.
sāv-, *see* **suāv-**.
saxātilis, e (found) among rocks.
saxētum, ī *n* rocky place.
saxeus 3 rocky, stony.
saxi-fer 3 bearing *or* casting stones.
saxi-ficus 3 turning into stone, petrifying.
saxi-fragus 3 stone-breaking.
saxōsus 3 stony, rocky.
saxulum, ī *n* (little) rock.
saxum, ī *n* large stone, fragment of rock; rock; stone-wall.
S.C. *abbr.* = **senatūs cōnsultum.**
scabellum, ī *n* percussion instrument used at dramatic performances.
scaber, bra, brum rough, scurfy, untidy, scabby, mangy.
scabiēs, ēī *f* roughness, scurf; **a**) scab, mange, leprosy; **b**) an itching, longing, pruriency.
scabillum, ī *n* = **scabellum.**
scabiōsus 3 scabby, scurfy; mildewy, spoilt (*grain*).
scabō, scābī, — 3 to scratch.
scaena, ae *f* stage, theatre; **a**) scene; **b**) publicity, public; **c**) parade, show; **d**) pretext, pretence.
scaenālis, e = **scaenicus.**
scaenicus 3 of the stage, scenic, dramatic, theatrical; *subst.* **~, ī** *m* actor, player.
scaeva, ae *f* omen (*on the left hand*), portent.
scaevus 3 left.
scālae, ārum *f/pl.* flight of steps, staircase; ladder.
scalmus, ī *m* peg to hold an oar, thole, rowlock.
scalpellum, ī *n* scalpel, lancet.
scalpō, psī, ptum 3 to scratch, cut, carve; to tickle.
scalprum, ī *n* chisel, knife.
scalptūra, ae *f* carving.
scalpurriō 4 to scratch.
scambus 3 bandy-legged.
scammōnia (*and* **-ea**), **ae** *f* scammony.
scamnum, ī *n* bench, stool; throne.
scandō, ndī, (**ānsum**) 3 to climb, mount, ascend, mount into.
scandula, ae *f* roofing-lath.
scapha, ae *f* boat, skiff.
scaphium, ī *n* drinking-vessel, basin; chamber-pot.
scapulae, ārum *f/pl.* the shoulder-blades, shoulders.
scāpus, ī *m* rod forming part of a loom.
scarus, ī *m* (*a savoury sea-fish*).
scatebra, ae *f* a bubbling, spring--water.
scateō 2 (*and* **scatō** 3) to bubble *or* gush up; to swarm, abound (*abl.*).
scatur(r)īgō, inis *f* bubbling water, spring-water.
scatur(r)iō 4 to bubble.
scaurus 3 club-footed.
scazōn, ontis *m* 'limping' iambic line.
scelerātus 3 polluted by crime, defiled, profaned; **a**) wicked, vicious; **b**) annoying, troublesome.
scelerō 1 to pollute, defile.
scelerōsus (*and* **scelerus?**) 3 wicked.
scelestus 3 wicked, villanous, accursed, infamous, knavish; *m* rogue, scoundrel.

scelus, eris *n* wicked deed, crime, offence; **a**) wickedness, impiety; **b**) villain, scoundrel, rascal; **c**) misfortune.
scēptri-fer *and* **-ger** 3 sceptre-bearing.
scēptrum, ī *n* sceptre; dominion, kingdom, rule.
scēptūchus, ī *m* sceptre-bearer.
scheda, ae *f* = **scida.**
schĕma, ae *f and* **schēma, atis** *n* figure, fashion, manner.
schoenicula *f* scented with rush-perfume.
schoeno-batēs, ae *m* rope-dancer.
schoenus, ī *m* aromatic reed, perfume.
schola, ae *f* learned lecture *or* dispute; school; sect.
scholasticus 3 of a school, rhetorical; *subst.* **~, ī** *m* teacher *or* student of rhetoric; grammarian.
scida, ae *f* strip of papyrus bark, leaf of paper.
sciēns, tis knowing; **a**) knowingly, purposely, intentionally; **b**) skilled, versed, expert.
scientia, ae *f* knowledge; science, skill.
sci-licet *adv.* of course, obviously, naturally, no doubt, certainly, to be sure; doubtless; namely.
scilla, ae *f* squill (a plant).
scīn' = **scīsne.**
scindō, idī, issum 3 to cut, tear, rend, split, cleave, divide, break asunder; to destroy.
scindula, ae *f* = **scandula.**
scintilla, ae *f* spark.
scintillō 1 to sparkle, flash.
scintillula, ae *f* little spark.
sciō, scīvī *and* **sciī, scītum** 4 **a**) to know, have knowledge, perceive; **b**) to understand, be skilled in.
scīpiō, ōnis *m* staff.
scirpea, ae *f* basket-work made of rushes to form the body of a wagon.
scirpeus 3 of rushes.
scirpiculus, ī *m* rush-basket.
scirpus, ī *m* rush, bulrush.
scīscitātor, ōris *m* inquirer.
scīscitor (*and* **-ō**) 1 to seek to know, to inquire, question, examine (*alqd ex alqo, alqm de re*).
scīscō, scīvī, scītum 3 to decree, ordain (*alqd; ut*); to assent to, vote for (*alqd*); to inquire, ascertain.
scissus 3 rent, split, cleft; furrowed; harsh.
scītāmentum, ī *n* dainty.
scītor 1 = **sciscitor.**
scītulus 3 = **scitus**[2] (b).
scītum, ī *n* decree, ordinance.
scītus[1], **ūs** *m* (*only abl.*) = **scitum.**
scītus[2] 3 **a**) knowing, clever, shrewd, skilful (*gen.*), experienced, adroit; **b**) pretty, fine, elegant.
sciūrus, ī *m* squirrel.
scobis, is *f* sawdust, filings.
scomber, brī *m* mackerel.
scōpae, ārum *f/pl.* twigs; broom, besom.
scopulōsus 3 rocky, craggy.
scopulus, ī *m* rock, crag, cliff; difficulty, danger.
scordalus, ī *m* brawler.
scorpiō, ōnis *and* **scorpius, ī** *m* scorpion; a military engine; a sea-fish.
scortātor, ōris *m* fornicator.
scorteus 3 leathern; *subst.* **-ea, ae** *f* coat of leather.
scortillum, ī *n dim. of* **scortum** (b).
scortor 1 to whore.
scortum, ī *n* **a**) skin, hide; **b**) whore, prostitute.
screō 1 to hawk, clear the throat noisily; *hence* **screātor, ōris** *m*; **screātus, ūs** *m.*
scrība, ae *m* clerk, secretary.
scrib(i)līta, ae *f* cheese tart.
scrībō, psī, ptum 3 **a**) to scratch, engrave, draw; **b**) to write (*alqd alci, ad alqm, de re*); to beg, entreat, command by letter; **c**) to compose, draw up; **d**) to write of, describe; **e**) to enroll (*soldiers*).
scrīnium, ī *n* chest, box, case.
scrīptiō, ōnis *f* a writing; written composition, text.
scrīptitō 1 to write often *or* continually, to compose.
scrīptor, ōris *m* **a**) writer, scribe, copyist; **b**) author, composer; historian, poet.
scrīptula, ōrum *n/pl.* lines on a board for playing *duodecim scripta.*
scrīptum, ī *n* something written; writing, composition, essay, treatise, book, work, letter; **duodecim scrīpta** a game resembling draughts.
scrīptūra, ae *f* **a**) = **scriptio**; **b**) tax paid on public pastures.
scrīptus, ūs *m* office of a scribe.
scrīpulum, ī *n* = **scrupulum.**
scrobis, is *m* and *f* ditch, trench.

scrōfa, ae *f* a sow.
scrōfi-pāscus, ī *m* breeder of pigs.
scrūpeus 3 stony, rugged.
scrūpōsus 3 rugged; hard.
scrūpulōsus 3 full of sharp stones, rough, rugged; careful, anxious, scrupulous.
scrūpulum, ī *n* the 24th part of an ounce.
scrūpulus, ī *m* uneasiness, anxiety, scruple.
scrūpus, ī *m* = **scrupulus.**
scrūta, ōrum *n/pl.* trash, trumpery.
scrūtātiō, ōnis *f* search.
scrūtātor, ōris *m* searcher, examiner.
scrūtor 1 to search carefully, examine thoroughly, explore, investigate, find out, search out.
sculpō, psī, ptum 3 to carve, cut, chisel; to form, fashion.
sculpōneae, ārum *f/pl.* wooden shoes.
sculptilis, e carved, sculptured.
sculptor, ōris *m* stone-cutter sculptor.
sculptūra, ae *f* sculpture.
scurra, ae *m* buffoon, jester; dandy, man about town.
scurrīlis, e buffoon-like, scurrilous.
scurrīlitās, ātis *f* buffoonery.
scurror 1 to play the buffoon, be a parasite.
scūtāle, is *n* thong of a sling.
scūtārius, ī *m* shield-maker.
scūtātus 3 armed with a shield.
scutella, ae *f* little flat dish.
scutica, ae *f* lash, wip.
scūti-gerulus 3 shield-bearer.
scutra, ae *f* flat dish.
scutula[1], **ae** *f* wooden roller, cylinder.
scutula[2], **ae** *f* lozenge-shaped dish; patch over the eye.
scutulāta, ōrum *n/pl.* check-patterned garments.
scūtulum, ī *n* small shield.
scūtum, ī *n* shield, oblong shield.
scymnus, ī *m* whelp.
scyphus, ī *m* cup, goblet.
scytalē, ēs *f* a kind of snake.
S.D. *abbr.* = **salutem dicit.**
sē *acc., abl.* himself, herself, itself.
sēbum, ī *n* suet; tallow.
sē-cēdō 3 to go away *or* apart, to separate, withdraw, retire.
sē-cernō 3 to sunder, sever, divide, put apart, separate, disjoin (*alqd a re*); to discern.
secespita, ae *f* sacrificial knife.
sē-cessiō, ōnis *f* **a**) a going aside, withdrawal, retirement; **b**) secession, schism.
sē-cessus, ūs *m* retirement, solitude; retreat, hiding-place.
sē-clūdō, sī, sum 3 to shut off; to shut up *or* apart, to seclude, separate, remove (*alqd a re*).
sēclum, ī *n, see* **saeculum.**
secō, cuī, ctum 1 to cut; to cut off, up, down; **a**) to tear, wound, hurt; **b**) to divide, cleave, separate; **c**) to cut *or* pass through, traverse; **d**) to decide.
sēcrētiō, ōnis *f* separation.
sē-crētus 3 severed, separated; **a**) retired, remote, lonely, solitary; **b**) secret, hidden, concealed; **c**) deprived of, lacking; — *subst.* **sēcrētum, ī** *n* retirement, solitude, secrecy; secret; *adv.* **sēcrētō** in secret, apart, secretly, without witnesses, in private.
secta, ae *f* path, way; mode, manner, method; **a**) party, side; **b**) school, sect, faction.
sectārius 3 leading (the flock).
sectātor, ōris *m* follower, attendant, adherent, *pl.* train, retinue.
sectilis, e (that can be) cut, divided.
sectiō, ōnis *f* buying of confiscated goods; confiscated property.
sector[1], **ōris** *m* cutter; purchaser at a sale of confiscated goods.
sector[2] 1 to follow continually, attend, accompany (*acc.*); to follow after, pursue, chase.
sectūra, ae *f* a digging, mine.
sē-cubitus, ūs *m* a lying *or* sleeping alone.
sē-cubō, buī, — 1 to sleep *or* live alone.
sēculāris, sēculum, ī *n* = **saec-.**
secundānī, ōrum *m/pl.* soldiers of the second legion.
secundārius 3 of second quality *or* importance.
secundō[1] 1 to favour, further.
secundō[2] *adv.* secondly.
secundum *adv.* behind; *prep.* with *acc.* behind; along; besides; after; next to; in accordance with; in favour of.
secundus 3 following, next, second; **secundae** (**partes**) second part, inferior part, second rank; **a**) secondary, subordinate, inferior; **b**) following, accompanying, downward; **secundo flumine** down

stream, with the current; c) favourable, propitious, fortunate; **secundo populo** with the consent of the people; **res secundae** good fortune.

secūricula, ae *f* little axe.

secūri-fer *and* **-ger** 3 axe- *or* hatchet-bearing.

secūris, is *f* a) axe, hatchet; b) blow, wound, injury; c) *pl.* authority, power, sovereignty.

sēcūritās, ātis *f* a) freedom from care, peace of mind; confidence; b) safety, security.

sē-cūrus 3 free from care, fearless, untroubled, composed, quiet; a) cheerful, bright, serene; b) careless, negligent; c) safe, free from danger; d) dispelling care.

secus[1] *n* (*indecl.*) sex.

secus[2] *adv.* otherwise, not so; **non secus** even so, just so (with *atque* or *quam*); not well, wrongly; *comp.* **sequius** otherwise than good, ill, discreditable (sometimes written **secius;** *see also* **sētius**).

secūtor, ōris *m* pursuer; a kind of gladiator.

sed *cj.* a) (*after a negative*) but, but on the contrary; b) but, yet, however; c) (*in resuming a discourse*) but.

sēdāmen, inis *n* alleviation.

sēdātiō, ōnis *f* an allaying, assuaging.

sēdātus 3 composed, quiet, calm.

sē-decim (*indecl.*) sixteen.

sēdēcula, ae *f* little seat, stool.

sedentārius 3 sitting.

sedeō, sēdī, sessum 2 to sit (*in loco*); a) to sit in council, in judgment; b) to remain in a place, stay; to sit still *or* idle, to be inactive; c) to sit down, remain encamped; d) to hold fast, be fixed *or* established; e) to sink, subside.

sēdēs, is *f* seat; a) dwelling-place, residence, home; resting-place; b) place, spot, seat; foundation; c) station, rank.

sedīle, is *n* seat, stool, chair.

sēd-itiō, ōnis *f* a going apart; separation, dissension, quarrel; insurrection, rebellion, mutiny, military revolt.

sēditiōsus 3 factious, seditious, mutinous, turbulent.

sēdō 1 to soothe, still, allay, assuage, appease, stop, check.

sē-dūcō 3 to lead aside, take apart; to turn aside, separate, sever; **sēductus** 3 remote, withdrawn.

sē-ductiō, ōnis *f* a leading aside.

sēdulitās, ātis *f* a) assiduity, zeal, application; b) officiousness, obtrusiveness.

sēdulus 3 a) busy, diligent, zealous, assiduous, earnest, unremitting; b) officious, obtrusive; *adv.* **sēdulō.**

seges, etis *f* a) cornfield, standing corn; crop; b) multitude.

segmentātus 3 adorned with *segmenta.*

segmentum, ī *n* strip of brocade, &c., used as a border *or* trimming.

sēgnipes, edis slow-footed.

sēgnis, e slow, sluggish, inactive, lazy, dilatory; lingering, languid.

sēgnitia, ae (*and* **sēgnitās, ātis** *and* **-tiēs, ēī**) *f* slowness, sluggishness, tardiness, inactivity.

sē-gregō 1 to separate from the flock; to set apart, separate, sever, remove, segregate.

sē-grex, gregis separate.

sei = **sī.**

sē-iugātus 3 separated.

sē-iugis, e drawn by six horses; *pl.* **sēiugēs** *m* chariot drawn by six horses.

sē-iūnctim *adv.* separately.

sē-iūnctiō, ōnis *f* a separating.

sē-iungō 3 to disjoin, sever, separate; to distinguish.

sē-lēctiō, ōnis *f* selection.

se-lībra (*and* **sē-**), **ae** *f* half a pound.

sē-ligō, lēgī, lēctum 3 to choose out, select, single out.

sella, ae *f* seat, chair; a) teacher's chair; b) official chair of a magistrate; c) sedan-chair.

sellāria *n/pl.* lounge.

sellāriolus 3 for lounging in.

sellārius, ī *m* voluptuary.

selli-sternium, ī *n* banquet in honour of goddesses.

sellula, ae *f* little sedan-chair.

sellulārius, ī *m* sedentary mechanic.

sēmanimis, -us, *see* **sēmi...**

semel *adv.* a) a single time, once; **non semel** more than once; **semel atque iterum** once and again, repeatedly; b) once for all; c) first, the first time.

sēmen, inis *n* seed; a) shoot, seedling; b) stock, race; c) descendant, offspring; d) origin, ground, cause, element.

sēmenti-fer 3 fruitful.
sēmentis, is *f* a sowing; young crops.
sēmentīvus 3 of seed *or* sowing.
sēmermis, e *and* **-mus** 3, *see* **semiermis.**
sē-mē(n)stris, e of six months, half-yearly.
sēm-ēsus 3 half-consumed.
sē-met = **se** (*strengthened*).
sēmi-adapertus 3 half-opened.
sēmi-ambustus 3 half-burned.
sēmianimis, e *and* **-mus** 3 half--alive; half-dead.
sēmi-apertus 3 half-open.
sēmi-barbarus 3 half-barbarian.
sēmi-bōs, bovis *m* half-ox (*the Minotaur*).
sēmi-caper, prī *m* half-goat (= *Pan, faun*).
sēmi-cremātus *and* **-cremus** 3 half-burned.
sēmi-crūdus 3 half-raw; half-digested.
sēmi-cubitālis, e half a cubit long.
sēmi-deus 3 half-divine; *m* demigod.
sēmi-doctus 3 half-taught.
sēmiermis, e (*and* **-mus** 3) half-armed.
sēmiēsus 3 = **semesus.**
sēmi-factus 3 half-finished.
sēmi-fer 3 half-man and half-beast; half-savage.
sēmi-fultus 3 half-supported.
sēmi-germānus 3 half-German.
sēmi-graecus 3 half-Greek.
sēmi-gravis, e half-drunken.
sē-migrō 1 to go away, remove.
sēmi-hiāns, tis half-open.
sēmi-homō, inis half-human; half--man and half-beast.
sēmi-hōra, ae *f* half-hour.
sēmi-lacer 3 half-mangled.
sēmi-lautus 3 half-washed.
sēmi-līber, era, erum half-free.
sēmi-lixa, ae *m* half-sutler.
sēmi-marīnus 3 half in the sea.
sēmi-mās, maris *m* half-male, hermaphrodite; castrated.
sēmi-mortuus 3 half-dead.
sēminārium, ī *n* nursery-garden, nursery.
sēminātor, ōris *m* sower, producer, author.
sēmi-nex, necis half-dead.
sēminium, ī *n* seed; race, breed.
sēminō 1 to sow, beget, produce.
sēmi-nūdus 3 half-naked.
sēmi-pāgānus 3 half a yokel.
sēmi-perfectus 3 half-finished.
sēmi-plēnus 3 half-manned.
sēmi-putātus 3 half-pruned.
sēmī-rāsus 3 half-shaven.
sēmi-reductus 3 half-bent back.
sēmi-refectus 3 half-repaired.
sēmi-rutus 3 half-ruined.
sēmis, issis *m* a half-unit, half an as; a half.
sēmi-senex, senis *m* elderly man.
sēmi-sepultus 3 half-buried.
sēmi-somnus 3 (*and* **-nis, e**) half--asleep.
sēmi-supīnus 3 half on one's back.
sēmita, ae *f* narrow way, footpath; way, lane.
sēmitālis, e of footpaths.
sēmitārius 3 found in lanes.
sēmi-tēctus 3 half-covered.
sēmi-ustulātus *or* **-ustilātus** 3 = **semustulatus.**
sēmi-ustus 3 = **semustus.**
sēmi-vir, ī *m* half-man (half-beast); **a**) half-male, hermaphrodite; castrated; **b**) womanish, effeminate.
sēmi-vīvus 3 half-alive; half-dead.
sē-modius, ī *m* half-modius.
sē-move ō2 to move apart *or* away, to sever; **sēmōtus** 3 remote, distant; confidential.
semper *adv.* always, ever.
sempiternus 3 everlasting, perpetual, eternal.
semul = **simul.**
sēm-uncia, ae *f* half an ounce; the 24th part (of an *as*); a trifle.
sēmunciārius 3 containing the 24th part.
sēm-ustulātus, -ustilātus, *and* **sēm-ustus** 3 half-burned.
senāculum, ī *n* meeting-place of the senate.
sēnāriolus, ī *m*, *dim. of* **senarius.**
sēnārius 3 consisting of six each; (**versus**) ~ *m* verse of six feet.
senātor, ōris *m* senator.
senātōrius 3 senatorial.
senātus, ūs *m* senate, council of state; **a**) body of senators; **b**) meeting of the senate; **senātūs consultum** decree of the senate; **senātūs auctoritas** resolution of the senate.
senecta, ae *f* = **senectus**[2].
senectus[1] 3 = **senilis.**
senectūs[2], **ūtis** *f* old age; **a**) old men; **b**) gray hair; **c**) moroseness; **d**) maturity.

seneō, —, — 2 to be old.
senēscō, nuī, — 3 to grow old, become aged; to grow old in strength, to decay, waste away.
senex, senis old, aged (*comp.* **senior, ius**); *subst.* **senex** *m* and *f* old man *or* woman; **seniōrēs, um** *m/pl.* elderly persons (*between 45 and 60 years*).
sēnī 3 six each.
senīlis, e of an old man, of old age, senile.
sēniō, ōnis *m* the number six.
senium, ī *n* weakness *or* decay of old age; **a**) trouble, affliction; **b**) gloom, moroseness.
senius, ī *m* old man.
sēnsibilis, e perceptible by the senses.
sēnsifer 3 producing sensation.
sēnsilis, e having sensation.
sēnsim *adv.* gradually, by degrees, gently, slowly.
sēnsus, ūs *m* perception; **1.** power of perceiving, sensation, sense (*sēnsus videndi* or *oculorum*); consciousness; **2.** understanding, mind; a) feeling, common-sense; b) opinion, thought, view, notion; c) meaning, signification; **3.** sentiment, emotion, inclination, disposition, habit of mind, mode of thinking.
sententia, ae *f* opinion, thought, meaning, purpose; **ex animi sententiā** to the best of one's belief; **a**) way of thinking, judgment; **b**) determination, decision, sentence, vote (*of senators*); **c**) meaning, signification (*of a word*), purport of a speech; **d**) maxim, aphorism, axiom, saying.
sententiola, ae *f* short sentence, maxim.
sententiōsus 3 full of meaning, sententious.
senticētum, ī *m* thorn-bush.
sentīna, ae *f* bilge-water; ship's hold; sewer; dregs, refuse, rabble.
sentiō, sēnsī, sēnsum 4 to feel, perceive, discern by sense (*alqd, de re; acc. c. inf.*), be sensible of; **a**) to feel the effects of, to experience, learn, suffer; **b**) to understand, observe, notice, remark; **c**) to think, judge, imagine, suppose, believe, mean; **d**) to give an opinion, to vote, declare; **sēnsa, ōrum** *n/pl.* thoughts, opinions.
sentis, is *m* (*f*) thorn-bush, briar.
sentīscō 3 to perceive, observe.
sentus 3 rough, overgrown with thorns, uncared for.
se-orsum *and* **-sus** *adv.* asunder, apart, separately.
sē-par, paris separate, different.
sēparābilis, e separable.
sēparātim, *adv. of* **separatus.**
sēparātiō, ōnis *f* a severing, separation.
sēparātus 3 separated, severed, apart, distinct, particular, different; far off, remote.
sē-parō 1 to separate, divide.
sepelībilis, e that may be hidden.
sepeliō, pelīvī, pultum 4 to bury, inter (*also* to cremate); **a**) to destroy, ruin, suppress; **b**) to immerse, sink.
sēpēs, sēpiō, *see* **saepes, saepio.**
sēpia, ae *f* cuttle-fish; ink.
sēpiola, ae *f* little cuttle-fish.
sē-pōnō 3 to put *or* lay aside, apart; **a**) to keep back, reserve; **b**) to separate, pick out; to distinguish; **c**) to keep far off, exclude; **sēpositus** 3 choice, select; reserved; distant.
sēps, sēpis *m* and *f* poisonous snake-like lizard.
sēpse = **se ipse.**
sēpta, ōrum *n/pl., see* **saepta.**
septem (*indecl.*) seven.
September, bris, bre belonging to September; (*mensis*) *m* September.
septem-decim = **septendecim.**
septem-fluus 3 with seven streams *or* mouths.
semptem-geminus 3 sevenfold (with seven mouths, with seven hills).
septem-pedālis, e seven feet long.
septem-plex, icis sevenfold.
septem-triō, *see* **septentrio.**
septem-vir, ī *m* one of a college of seven.
septemvirālis, e of the *septemviri.*
septem-virātus, ūs *m* office of a *septemvir.*
septēnārius 3 consisting of seven; *subst. m* line containing seven (and a half) feet, septenarius.
septen-decim (*indecl.*) seventeen.
septēnī 3 seven each; seven at once; *sing.* sevenfold.
septentriō, ōnis *m* (*usu. pl.*) the seven stars of the Great *or* Little Bear; the north; (*sg.*) north-wind.
septentriōnālis, e northern.
septiē(n)s *adv.* seven times.

septimānī, ōrum *m/pl.* soldiers of the seventh legion.
septi-montiālis, e relating to the festival of the seven hills.
septimus 3 the seventh.
septingentēsimus 3 the seven hundreth.
septingentī 3 seven hundred.
septuāgēsimus 3 seventieth.
septuāgintā (*indecl.*) seventy.
septu-ennis, e seven years old.
septumus 3 = **septimus.**
sept-unx, uncis *m* seven ounces, seven twelfths.
sepulcrālis, e funeral.
sepulcrētum, ī *n* burial place.
sepulcrum, ī *n* burial-place; grave, tomb, sepulchre; dead person.
sepultūra, ae *f* a burying, burial, interment, cremation.
sequāx, ācis following quickly, pursuing penetrating.
sequester, tris, tre, (*and* **tra, trum**) mediating; *subst. m* mediator, go-between; *n* deposit, security.
sequius *adv., comp. of* **secus**[2].
sequor, cūtus sum 3 to follow, come after; to accompany; **a**) to pursue; **b**) to come next, succeed, ensue; **c**) to go to, have for a destination; to aim at, seek to gain; **d**) to accede to, imitate, take as a guide; **e**) to follow naturally, come of itself; **f**) to follow logically; **g**) to fall to, fall to the share of.
Ser. *abbr.* = **Servius.**
sera, ae *f* bar, bolt.
serēnitās, ātis *f* clearness, fair weather; favourableness.
serēnō 1 to make clear *or* bright.
serēnus 3 clear, bright, serene; *subst.* **-um, ī** *n* clear sky, fair weather; cheerful, glad.
serēscō to dry (*intrans.*).
sēria, ae *f* earthen vessel, jar.
sēricātus 3 dressed in silk.
sēricus 3 of silk; *subst.* **-ca, ōrum** *n/pl.* silk garments.
seriēs, ēī *f* row, succession, chain, series; lineage.
sēriola, ae *f* small jar.
sērius[1] 3 serious, earnest; *subst.* **sēria, ōrum** *n/pl.* serious things, earnestness; *adv.* **sēriō** in earnest, earnestly.
sērius[2] *adv., comp. of* **serus.**
sermō, ōnis *m* talk, conversation; **a**) learned talk, discourse, discussion; **b**) subject of conversation; **c**) ordinary speech, conversational language; familiar style; **d**) manner of speaking, language, expression, diction; dialect; **e**) common talk, report, rumour.
sermōcinātiō, ōnis *f* discussion
sermōcinor 1 to talk, converse.
sermunculus, ī *m* report, rumour, gossip.
serō[1], **(ruī,) rtum** 3 to join together, interweave, entwine; **serta, ōrum** *n/pl.* (*and* **sertae, ārum** *f/pl.*) garlands, wreaths; to connect, combine, compose.
serō[2], **sēvī, satum** 3 **a**) to sow, plant; *subst.* **sata, ōrum** *n/pl.* cornfields, standing crops; **b**) to beget, engender, bring forth; **satus** begotten, sprung, born (*abl.*); **c**) to spread abroad, disseminate, cause, occasion.
sērō[3], *adv. of* **serus.**
serpēns, tis *f and m* snake, serpent.
serpenti-gena, ae *m* sprung from a serpent.
serpenti-pēs, edis serpent-footed.
serperastra, ōrum *n/pl.* bandages, knee-splints.
serpillum, ī *n* = **serpyllum.**
serpō, psī, — 3 to crawl, creep; to move slowly, proceed imperceptibly; to extend gradually, spread abroad.
serpyllum, ī (*and* **serpullum, ī**) *n* wild thyme.
serra, ae *f* saw.
serrācum, ī *n* two-wheeled wagon, cart.
serrātus 3 notched on the edge; indented.
serrula, ae *f* little saw.
serta, ōrum *n/pl., see* **sero**[1].
serum[1], **ī** *n* whey, watery part of curdled milk.
sērus 3 (*adv.* **sērō**) late, belated, too late; *subst.* **sērum**[2], **ī** *n* late time; **sērō diei** late in the day, at a late hour; *comp.* **sērius** later, too late.
serva, ae *f* female slave, servant-maid.
servābilis, e that can be saved.
servantissimus 3 most observant.
servātor, ōris *m* preserver, saviour.
servātrīx, īcis, *fem. of* **servator.**
servilicola, ae *f* low prostitute.
servīlis, e servile; of slaves.
serviō 4 to serve, be a slave *or* servant, be in service (*apud alqm, alci*);

a) (*of land*) to be subject to burdens *or* obligations; **b**) to comply with, gratify, subserve, assist, be governed, enslaved by (*alci*).
servitium, ī *n* = **servitus** (a), (c).
servitrīcius 3 of slaves.
servitūs, ūtis *f* condition of a slave; **a**) slavery, servitude, service, subjection; **b**) (*of land*) liability to obligations; **c**) servants, slaves, body of servants.
servō 1 to observe, pay heed to, watch (*alqd*); **a**) to keep, preserve, guard, maintain; **b**) to keep for the future, lay up, reserve, retain, store; **c**) to keep safe; to rescue; **d**) to keep to, stay in (a place).
servolus, ī *m* = **servulus.**
servula, ae *f* servant maid.
servulus, ī *m* young slave.
servus 3 servile, slavish, subject; (*of lands*) subject to obligations; *subst.* **servus, ī** *m*, **serva, ae** *f* slave, servant.
sēsamum, ī *n* sesame.
sescenāris *adj.* (meaning unknown).
ses-cēnārius 3 consisting of six hundred.
ses-cēnī (*and* **-centēnī**) six hundred each.
ses-centēsimus 3 the six hundredth.
ses-centī 3 six hundred; countless.
ses-centiē(n)s *adv.* six hundred times.
sēsē = **sē.**
seselis, is *f* (*a plant*).
sēsqui *adv.* one half more, half as much again.
sēsqui-alter 3 one and a half.
sēsqui-hōra, ae *f* one hour and a half.
sēsqui-modius, ī *m* a modius and a half.
sēsqui-octāvus 3 of nine eighths.
sēsqui-opus, eris *n* the work of a day and a half.
sēsqui-pedālis, e one foot and a half long.
sēsqui-pēs, edis *m* a foot and a half.
sēsqui-plāga, ae *f* a blow and a half.
sēsqui-plex, icis one and a half times.
sēsqui-tertius 3 of one and a third.
sessibulum, ī *n* seat.
sessilis, e fit for sitting upon; dwarf (of plants).
sessiō, ōnis *f* a sitting; seat; session.
sessitō 1 to sit much.
sessiuncula, ae *f* small circle for conversation.
sessor, ōris *m* one who sits; rider; inhabitant.
sēstertiolum, ī *n* = **sestertium.**
sēs-tertius, ī *m* (*genit. pl.* **-tium**) sesterce (*a small silver coin, originally worth two and a half* asses): **decies sēstertium** (= *decies centena milia sēstertium*) a million sesterces; **sēstertium, ī** *n* (*usu. pl.* **sēstertia**) a thousand sesterces.
sēsuma, ae *f* sesame.
set *cj.* = **sed.**
sēta, ae *f* = **saeta.**
sētiger 3 = **saetiger.**
sētius *adv.* (confused with *sequius, see* **secus**) otherwise; not well, ill; **nōn sētius** none the less.
sētōsus 3 = **saetosus.**
seu = **sīve.**
sevēritās, ātis *f* seriousness, severity, sternness, strictness.
sevēritūdō, inis *f* = **sevēritās.**
sevērus 3 serious, grave, strict, austere, stern; harsh, hard.
sē-vocō 1 to call aside *or* away; to call off, withdraw (*alqd a re*).
sēvum, ī *n* = **sebum.**
Sex. *abbr.* = **Sextus.**
sex (*indecl.*) six.
sexāgēnārius 3 sixty years old.
sexāgēnī 3 sixty each.
sexāgēsimus 3 the sixtieth.
sexāgiē(n)s *adv.* sixty times.
sexāgintā (*indecl.*) sixty.
sex-angulus 3 hexagonal.
sexc..., *see* **sesc...**
sex-decim = **sedecim.**
sex-ennis, e of six years.
sex-ennium, ī *n* period of six years.
sexiē(n)s *adv.* six times.
sex-prīmī, ōrum *m/pl.* a board of six magistrates in provincial towns.
sextā-decimānī, ōrum *m/pl.* soldiers of the sixteenth legion.
sextāns, tis *m* the sixth part (*of an* as, iugerum, sextarius, &c.).
sextārius, ī *m* (*a liquid measure*) pint.
Sextīlis, e belonging to August; (*mensis*) *m* August.
sextula, ae *f* the sixth part of an *uncia*.
sextus 3 the sixth.
sexus, ūs *m* sex.
sī *cj.* if, if only, if ever, even if; in case, in the hope that, on the chance that.

sībilō 1 to hiss, whistle; to hiss at (*acc.*).
sībilus[1] 3 hissing, whistling.
sībilus[2], **ī** *m* (*plur. also* **sībila** *n*) a hissing, whistling, rustling; contemptuous hissing.
Sibylla *and* **Sibulla, ae** *f* prophetess, female soothsayer.
Sibyllīnus 3 Sibylline.
sīc *adv.* so, thus, in this manner; in this case, on this condition; **a**) **ut ... sic** as ..., so ...; **b**) so much, to such a degree; **c**) just so, yes.
sīca, ae *f* dagger, poniard; assassination.
sīcārius, ī *m* assassin, murderer.
siccitās, ātis *f* dryness, drought; **a**) firm, healthy condition; **b**) jejuneness, simplicity.
siccō 1 to dry, dry up; to drain.
sicc-oculus 3 having dry eyes.
siccus 3 dry; *subst.* **-um, ī** *n* dry land; **a**) thirsty; sober; **b**) firm, healthy; **c**) plain, insipid, dull.
sīcīlicula, ae *f* small sickle.
sicilicissitō 1 to be in the Sicilian manner.
sīcine *adv.* (*sīc* + *ne*) thus? indeed?
sī-cubi *cj.* if anywhere.
sīcula, ae *f* (small dagger) penis.
sī-cunde *cj.* if from anywhere.
sīc-ut(ī) *adv.* so as, just as, as; **sicuti ... ita** just as ... so; as it were, just as if, as for instance.
sīdereus 3 starry, of stars; **a**) bright, glittering; **b**) heavenly, divine.
sīdō, sēdī *and* **sīdī, sessum** 3 to sit down, settle; **a**) to sink down; **b**) to become fixed.
sīdus, eris *n* constellation; **a**) star; heavenly body; **b**) sky, heavens; **c**) time of year, day; **d**) climate, region; **e**) weather, storm; **f**) pride, glory.
sigillātus 3 adorned with little figures.
sigillum, ī *n* **a**) small figure *or* image; **b**) seal.
sigma *n* the Greek letter *Σ*; semicircular dining-couch.
signātor, ōris *m* one who seals; witness to a will *or* contract.
signi-fer 3 bearing figures, starry; **orbis** zodiac; *subst. m* standard-bearer.
significanter *adv.* plainly, clearly.
significātiō, ōnis *f* a pointing out, indicating, showing, sign, token; **a**) sign of assent, approbation, applause; **b**) meaning, signification (*of a word*).
signi-ficō 1 to give a sign *or* indication; **a**) to indicate, point out, make known; **b**) to foreshow, indicate future things; **c**) to mean, signify.
signō 1 to mark, mark out, designate; **a**) to engrave; to seal, seal up; **b**) to stamp, coin, impress, imprint; **c**) to observe, notice; **d**) to adorn, decorate.
signum, ī *n* **1.** sign, mark, token; a) signal, order, command, watchword, pass-word; b) standard, flag, banner; **signa movēre** *or* **convellere** to march away, **inferre** to attack, **signa conferre** to fight, come to close quarters; c) a small division of troops, company, maniple; **2.** figure, image, statue, picture; a) seal, signet; b) group of of stars, constellation.
sīlānus, ī *m* fountain.
silentium, ī *n* silence, stillness; **a**) freedom from disturbance in taking the auspices; **b**) repose, tranquillity, leisure.
sileō, uī, — 2 **1.** *intr.* a) to be still, silent, noiseless; *subst.* **silentēs, um** *m/pl.* the silent, the dead; Pythagoreans; b) to be inactive, to rest, cease; **2.** *trans.* to be silent about (*acc.*); *subst.* **silenda, ōrum** *n/pl.* secrets, mysteries.
siler, eris *n* a pliant plant.
silēscō, luī, — 3 to become silent.
silex, icis *m* (and *f*) flint, pebble; rock, crag.
silicernium, ī *n* funeral feast; old man.
silīgineus 3 of fine wheaten flour.
silīgō, inis *f* white flour.
siliqua, ae *f* husk, pod, shell, *pl.* pulse.
sillybus, ī *m* = **sittybus.**
silua, ae *f* = **silva.**
silūrus, ī *m* a river-fish.
sīlus 3 snub-nosed, flat-nosed.
silva, ae *f* wood, forest; **a**) grove, shrubbery; **b**) tree, undergrowth; **c**) crowded mass, crop, growth; plentiful supply; materials.
silvēscō, —, — 3 to grow wild.
(**silvester, tris, tre** *and*) **silvestris, e** of a wood *or* forest, wooded; **a**) living in the woods; **b**) growing wild, wild; rural, pastoral.

silvi-cola, ae *m* inhabitant of the woods.
silvi-cultrīx, īcis *f* living in the woods.
silvifragus 3 breaking trees.
ilvōsus 3 wooded.
sīmia, ae *f* (*and* **-ius, ī** *m*) ape, monkey.
simila, ae *f* fine wheaten flour.
similis, e like, resembling, similar (with *gen.* or *dat.*); **veri similis** likely, probable; *subst.* **simile, is** *n* comparison, simile.
similitūdō, inis *f* likeness, resemblance; imitation; sameness; **a**) analogy; **b**) comparison, simile.
sīmiolus, ī *m* little ape.
simitū (archaic) = **simul.**
sīmius, ī *m*, *see* **simia.**
sim-plex, icis simple; **a**) uncompounded, unmixed; **b**) single, one; **c**) plain, simple, natural; **d**) open, frank, guileless, artless, sincere; *adv.* **simpliciter** plainly, directly, openly, artlessly, simply.
simplicitās, ātis *f* simplicity; candour.
simplum, ī *n* an original sum *or* number (*without multiplication*).
simpulum, ī *n* sacrificial ladle.
simpuvium, ī *n* sacrificial bowl.
simul 1. *adv.* at once, at the same time, together; **simul cum** together with; **simul ... simul** partly ... partly, as well ... as; **2.** *cj.* **simul ac, simul atque, simul ut, simul** as soon as.
simula, ae *f* = **simila.**
simulācrum, ī *n* likeness; **a**) image, figure, portrait, statue; **b**) vision in a dream; shadow, shade; **c**) portraiture, characterization; **d**) phantom, mere image, appearance; **e**) imitation, reflection.
simulāmen, inis *n* copy.
simulātiō, ōnis *f* false show, feigning, shamming; pretence, deceit, hypocrisy.
simulātor, ōris *m* imitator; feigner, pretender, hypocrite.
simulātrīx, īcis *f* one who transforms (*men into the image of beasts*).
simulō 1 to make like (*alqd alci rei*); **a**) to imitate, copy, represent; **b**) to pretend, feign, counterfeit, simulate, assume the appearance of; **simulātus** 3 feigned, counterfeit, pretended.
simultās, ātis *f* jealousy, rivalry, enmity, quarrel.
simulter = **similiter,** in a similar way.
sīmus (*and* **-ulus**) 3 flat-nosed.
sīn *cj.* if however, but if; **sīn minus** but if not.
sināpi, *indecl. n and* **-pis, is** *f* mustard.
sincēritās, ātis *f* soundness, purity, integrity, uprightness.
sincērus 3 unadulterated; **a**) pure, unmixed, uninjured, whole; **b**) sound, candid, sincere; real, genuine.
sincipitāmentum, ī *n* pig's cheek.
sinciput, itis *n* **a**) pig's cheek; **b**) brain.
sindōn, onis *f* fine linen, muslin.
sine *prep.* with *abl.* without.
singillātim *adv.* one by one, singly; severally.
singulāris, e one by one, alone, single; **a**) singular; *subst. m* picked horseman; **b**) single in its kind, matchless, unique, extraordinary, exceptional; *adv.* **sing(u)lāriter.**
singulārius 3 single.
singulī, ae, a one each; single, several, one alone.
singultim *adv.* sobbingly; stammeringly.
singultiō 4 to throb.
singultō 1 to sob, gasp (out).
singultus, ūs *m* a sobbing, panting, gasping.
singulus 3, *see* **singuli.**
sinister, tra, trum left, on the left hand; *subst.* **sinistra, ae** *f* left hand, left side; **a**) awkward, wrong, perverse; **b**) unfavourable, unlucky, inauspicious; **c**) favourable, lucky. auspicious.
sinisteritās, ātis *f* awkwardness.
sinistrōrsum *and* **-sus** *adv.* to the left.
sinō, sīvī, situm 3 **a**) to lay, place, *or* put down; **b**) to let, suffer, allow, permit (*inf.; acc. c. inf.*); *imperative* **sine** let, be it so.
sīnum, ī *n* (*and* **sīnus, ī** *m*) vessel, pot, bowl, basin.
sinuō 1 to bend, wind, curve, swell out in curves.
sinuōsus 3 full of bendings *or* curves, sinuous.
sinus, ūs *m* curve, fold, hollow, coil; **a**) bay, gulf; hollow, valley; **b**) shore of a bay; **c**) fold of the toga, of a

garment, bosom, lap; purse; **d**) wind-filled sail; **e**) love, affection, intimacy, protection; **f**) interior, inmost part, heart; **g**) place of refuge.
sīparium, ī *n* small theatre-curtain; comedy.
sīparum, ī *n* = **supparum.**
sīphō, ōnis *m* **a**) siphon; **b**) fire-engine.
sīphunculus, ī *m* little tube *or* pipe.
si-quidem *cj.* **a**) if indeed; **b**) since, inasmuch as.
siremps(e) exactly the same.
Sirius, ī *m* the Dog-star.
sirp... = **scirp...**
sirpe, is *n* a North African plant.
sīs = **si vis** if you will, please.
siser, eris *n* a salad plant.
sistō, stitī *and* **stetī, statum** 3 **1.** to cause to stand, to place, put (*alqm* or *alqd in loco* or *loco*); a) to set up, to convey, bring, lead to; b) to erect, build; c) to cause to appear before a court; **se sistere** to appear, present oneself; d) to make stand still, to stop, check, arrest, detain; **se sistere** to halt, make a stand; **status** 3 set, fixed, appointed; **2.** *intr.* to stand; a) to appear; b) to stand still; c) to stand firm, continue, endure, remain.
sīstrātus 3 provided with a *sīstrum.*
sīstrum, ī *n* metal rattle.
sisymbrium, ī *n* a fragrant herb.
sitella, ae *f* urn for lots, ballot-box.
sitīculōsus 3 thirsty, dry, parched.
sitienter *adv.* greedily, eagerly.
sitiō 4 to thirst, be thirsty; to be dry, parched, arid; **sitiēns, tis a**) thirsty, dry; **b**) eager, greedy.
sitis, is *f* thirst; **a**) dryness, drought; **b**) eager desire, greediness.
sitītor, ōris *m* one who thirsts.
sittybus, ī *m* book-label.
situla, ae *f* bucket; urn used for drawing lots.
situs[1], **ūs** *m* **a**) situation, position, site; construction; **b**) want of cultivation, neglect; mould, dirt, rust; inactivity, sloth.
situs[2] 3 **a**) placed, lying, situated; **b**) built, erected; **c**) buried; **situm esse in re** to rest *or* depend upon.
sī-ve *or* **seu** *cj.* or if; or; **sīve potius** or rather; **sīve ... sīve** if ..., or if ...; whether ..., or ...
smaragdus, ī *m* and *f* emerald (*and other jewels*).
smīlax, acis *f* (*a plant*) bindweed.
smyrna, ae *f* myrrh.
sōbrietās, ātis *f* sobriety.
sobrīnus, ī *m and* **-a, ae** *f* cousin (*on the mother's side*).
sōbrius 3 not intoxicated; **a**) sober; moderate, continent; **b**) sensible; cautious.
soccātus 3 wearing *socci.*
socculus, ī *m, dim. of* **soccus.**
soccus, ī *m* light shoe; comedy.
socer (*and* **-erus**), **erī** *m* father-in-law; *pl.* parents-in-law.
sociābilis, e sociable, easily united.
sociālis, e of allies *or* partners; **a**) conjugal; **b**) sociable, social.
sociālitās, ātis *f* fellowship.
sociātrīx, īcis *f* uniting.
sociennus, ī *m* = **socius.**
societās, ātis *f* union, society; fellowship, association; **a**) political league, alliance, confederacy; **b**) partnership, association in business.
sociō 1 to join, unite, associate (*alqd cum alqo*); to hold in common, share, take part in.
socio-fraudus 3 one who deceives his comrades.
socius 3 united, associated, allied; shared, joint; *subst.* **socius, ī** *m and* **-ia, ae** *f* companion, associate, fellow, partner; ally, confederate.
socordia, ae *f* dulness, stupidity, indolence.
so-cors, rdis weak-minded; stupid; indolent.
socrus, ūs *f* mother-in-law.
sodālicius 3 relating to fellowship *or* companionship; *subst.* **-ium, ī** *n* = **sodalitas.**
sodālis, e of companions, friendly; *subst. m* **a**) comrade, companion, mate; **b**) member of a club, of a college of priests; **c**) table companion, boon companion; accomplice.
sodālitās, ātis *f* companionship, fellowship, friendship; **a**) association; **b**) religious brotherhood; **c**) club for feasting; **d**) secret, illegal society, political club.
sōdēs = **si audes** if you please.
sōl, sōlis *m* the sun; **a**) the sun-god; **b**) sunlight, sunshine, heat of the sun, sunny day; **c**) day; **d**) publicity, appearance in public; **e**) sun, star = distinguished person.
sōlāciolum, ī *n* a little comfort.

sōlācium, ī *n* consolation, comfort, relief, solace; **a)** an assuaging, means of help, refuge; **b)** amends, compensation; **c)** consoler.
sōlāmen, inis *n* comfort, consolation.
sōlāris, e relating to the sun.
sōlārium, ī *n* **a)** sun-dial; clock; **b)** flat roof, balcony.
sōlātium, ī *m* = **solacium.**
sōlātor, ōris *m* consoler, comforter.
soldurii, ōrum *m/pl.* vassals, liegemen.
soldus 3 = **solidus.**
solea, ae *f* **a)** sole, sandal; fetter for the feet; **b)** (*kind of fish*) sole.
soleārius, ī *m* sandal-maker.
soleātus 3 wearing sandals.
solemnis *and* **solennis, e** = **sollemnis.**
soleō, solitus sum 2 **a)** to be accustomed *or* wont (*inf.*); **ut solet** as is his custom; **b)** to cohabit with; — **solitus** 3 usual, customary; *subst.* **solitum, ī** *n* what is usual, the customary, custom.
soliditās, ātis *f* solidity.
solidō 1 to make dense *or* solid, to make firm, strengthen.
solidus 3 dense; **a)** massive, compact, firm, solid, hard; *subst.* **solidum, ī** *n* something firm, solid body, firm ground, mass, solidity; **b)** whole, complete, entire; **solidum, ī** *n* the whole sum, the total; **c)** true, real, enduring, substantial, trustworthy.
sōli-fer 3 sun-bringing.
sōli-gena, ae *m* child of the sun-god.
sōlitārius 3 solitary, alone, lonely, unsocial.
sōlitūdō, inis *f* loneliness, solitude; **a)** desert, wilderness; **b)** destitution, deprivation; **c)** retirement; **d)** helplessness.
solitum, ī *n and* **solitus** 3, *see* **soleo.**
solium, ī *n* seat, chair; **a)** throne, royal seat, royal dignity *or* power; **b)** arm-chair; **c)** coffin; **d)** bathing-tub.
sōli-vagus 3 wandering alone; lonely, single.
soll-emnis *and* **-ennis, e** annual; periodic; **a)** established; ceremonial, religious, solemn; **b)** usual, customary; *subst.* **sollemne, is** *n* festival, solemnity, sacrifice; custom, rite, ceremony.
soll-ers, rtis clever, skilful, adroit, expert, ingenious.
soll-ertia, ae *f* skill, cleverness, adroitness, ingenuity, expertness, shrewdness; trick.
sollicitātiō, ōnis *f* an inciting to mutiny *or* rebellion.
sollicitō 1 to move violently, stir, agitate, shake; **a)** to plough; **b)** to disturb, trouble, harass, annoy; **c)** to stir up, incite, instigate to revolt.
sollicitūdō, inis *f* uneasiness, disquiet, anxiety, care, trouble.
solli-citus 3 tossed, stirred up, agitated; **a)** troubled, disturbed, anxious, uneasy (*de re, pro alqo*); **b)** causing trouble, disquieting, painful; **c)** careful, busy.
solli-ferreum, ī *n* javelin of iron.
sollistimus 3 most perfect *or* auspicious.
sollus whole, entire.
sōlō 1 to empty; to lay waste.
soloecismus, ī *m* solecism.
sōlor 1 to comfort, console; **a)** to soothe, assuage, lessen; **b)** to compensate.
sōlstitiālis, e relating to the summer solstice, of midsummer, of summer heat; solar.
sōl-stitium, ī *n* (summer) solstice, summer time, heat of summer.
solum[1]**, ī** *n* the lowest part, bottom, ground, foundation; **a)** floor, pavement; **b)** sole of a foot; **c)** earth, soil; land, country; **d)** basis.
sōlum[2] *adv.*, *see* **solus.**
sōlus 3 alone, only, single, sole; **a)** lonely, solitary, deserted, widowed; **b)** unfrequented, uninhabited; *adv.* **sōlum** only, merely, barely; **non sōlum ... sed etiam** not only ... but also, **non sōlum (non) ... sed ne ... quidem** not only not ... but not even.
solūtilis, e easily coming asunder.
solūtiō, ōnis *f* **a)** a loosening; (dis-)solution; **b)** payment.
solūtus 3, *see* **solvo.**
solvō, solvī, solūtum 3 to loosen, untie, unbind (*alqd a* or *de re*), unfetter, release, open; **navem** to weigh anchor, to sail; **a)** to pay *or* discharge a debt; **solvendō non esse** to be insolvent; to pay, fulfil, perform a duty *or* promise (*alqd; alci alqd*); **poenam** to suffer punishment; **b)** to set free, release, relieve, acquit, absolve (*alqm re*); **c)** to

detach, remove, disjoin, break up (*pontem*), separate; to relax, weaken; **d**) to dissolve, bring to an end; to solve, explain; — **solūtus** 3 loosened; **a**) unbound, free; unburdened, independent, free from debt, care, *or* punishment; **b**) unrestrained, unchecked, wanton, disorderly, lax, remiss, careless; **c**) without metre, prose, loose, irregular; **d**) fluent, ready (*in speaking*).
somnīculōsus 3 sleepy, drowsy.
somni-fer 3 sleep-bringing.
somniō 1 to dream (*de alqo, alqm, alqd*); to talk foolishly.
somnium, ī *n* dream; vain imagination, fancy, nonsense.
somnus, ī *m* sleep, slumber; **a**) sleep of death; night; **b**) drowsiness, laziness, inactivity.
sonābilis, e = **sonans.**
sonāns, tis sounding, resounding, sonorous.
soni-pēs, pedis *m* horse, steed.
sonitus, ūs *m* sound, noise, din; thunder.
sonīvius 3 = **sonans; tripudium sonīvium** noise of the corn dropped by the sacred chickens (in augury).
sonō, nuī, (**sonātūrus**) 1 (*and* 3) **1.** *intr.* to make a noise, sound, resound, roar; **2.** *trans.* to speak, sound; to sing, celebrate; to mean.
sonor, ōris *m* = **sonitus.**
sonōrus 3 = **sonans.**
sōns, sontis guilty; *subst. m* criminal, sinner.
sonticus 3 serious, weighty.
sonus, ī *m* sound, noise; voice; tone.
sophia, ae *f* wisdom.
sophisma, atis *n* false conclusion, fallacy.
sophistēs *and* **-a, ae** *m* sophist.
sophos *and* **-us, ī** *m* wise (man).
sophōs *int.* bravo!, well done!
sōpiō[1] 4 to lull asleep, put to sleep; **P.** to fall asleep; **a**) to stun, stupefy; **b**) to calm, assuage, still, quiet.
sōpiō[2], **ōnis** penis (?).
sopor, ōris *m* deep sleep; **a**) sleepiness, lethargy; **b**) sleeping-potion; **c**) the god of sleep; **d**) death; **e**) temple of the head.
sopōrātus 3 **a**) put to sleep, stilled; **b**) soporific, stupefying.
sopōri-fer 3 causing deep sleep.
sopōrus 3 sleep-bringing; drowsy.
sōracum, ī *n* hamper.
sorbeō, buī, — 2 to suck in, swallow.
sorbillō 1 to suck in, sip.
sorbilō *adv.* in little drops, on a low diet.
sorbitiō, ōnis *f* draught, drink; broth.
sorbum, ī *n* sorb, service-berry.
sordeō, (uī), — 2 to be dirty; to be mean *or* despised (*alci*).
sordēs, is *f* (*usu. pl.*) dirt, filth; **a**) dirty clothes, mourning; **b**) meanness, low condition, baseness, stinginess, niggardliness, covetousness; **c**) rabble, dregs of the people.
sordēscō, duī, — 3 to become dirty.
sordidātus 3 in mourning attire.
sordidulus 3 dirty, mean.
sordidus 3 dirty, foul, filthy; **a**) in mourning attire; **b**) mean, despicable, vile; poor; base, disgraceful; niggardly, stingy.
sorditūdō, inis *f* = **sordes.**
sōrex, icis *m* shrew-mouse.
sōricīnus 3 of a shrew-mouse.
sōrītēs, ae *m* (*in logic*) conclusion drawn from accumulated arguments.
soror, ōris *f* sister; cousin.
sororcula, ae *f* little sister.
sorōri-cīda, ae *m* murderer of a sister.
sorōrius 3 of, for a sister.
sors, rtis *f* lot; *pl.* oracle; **a**) a casting lots; **b**) oracular response, prophecy; **c**) lot, share, money, capital; fate, destiny, chance; **d**) official duty.
sorsum *and* **-us** *adv.* = **seorsum.**
sorticula, ae *f* small tablet.
sorti-fer *and* **-ger** 3 oracular.
sorti-legus 3 foretelling, prophetic; *subst.* ~, **ī** *m* soothsayer.
sortior (*and* **-ō**) 4 to cast *or* draw lots; **a**) to assign by lot; **b**) to cast lots for, get by lot; to gain by fate, get, receive, obtain; **c**) to choose, select; — **sortītus** 3 gained by lot, appointed by lot.
sortis, is *f* = **sors.**
sortītiō, ōnis *f* a casting lots.
sortītō by lot, by destiny.
sortītor, ōris *m* one who draws lots.
sortītus, ūs *m* = **sortitio.**
sospes, itis safe and sound, unhurt, fortunate, happy.
sospita, ae *f* she who saves.

sospitālis, e bringing deliverance.
sospitō 1 to save, protect.
sōtēr, ēris *m* saviour.
sōtēria, ōrum *n/pl.* presents given on recovery from illness.
spādīx, īcis reddish brown.
spadō, ōnis *m* eunuch.
spargō, rsī, rsum 3 to strew, scatter, sprinkle; **a**) to scatter seeds, to sow; **b**) to throw, hurl, cast; **c**) to spread abroad, disseminate, disperse; **d**) to dissipate, squander; **e**) to distribute, divide, tear in pieces; **f**) to besprinkle; **sparsus** 3 dispersed; speckled, freckled.
sparsiō, ōnis *f* scattering.
spartum, ī *n* esparto (grass).
sparulus, ī *m* sea-bream.
sparus, ī *m* hunting-spear.
spatha, ae *f* broadsword; weaver's batten (for tightening the threads).
spatior 1 to walk about, take a walk; to spread out.
spatiōsus 3 roomy, of great extent, wide, spacious; lasting long.
spatium, ī *n* room, extent; **a**) size, length, breadth; **b**) interval, distance; **c**) race-course; lap; walk, promenade; open space, public place; **d**) space of time, interval, period; time, respite, leisure, opportunity; length of time; metrical time, measure.
speciālis, e individual, particular.
speciēs, ēī *f* **1.** a seeing, sight, look, view; **2.** appearance, mien, exterior, outside; a) vision, dream; b) beautiful form, beauty, splendour, display, show; c) likeness, image, statue; d) semblance, seeming, resemblance; **speciē** in appearance; **ad speciem** for the sake of outward show; **3.** idea, notion, conception; a) ideal, model; b) species, kind, sort.
specillum, ī *n* probe.
specimen, inis *n* mark, token; **a**) pattern, model, specimen, example, proof; **b**) ideal.
speciō, xī, (ctum) 3 to see, behold.
speciōsus 3 showy, fair, fine, beautiful, handsome, splendid; **a**) respectable; **b**) imposing, for show; specious, plausible.
spectābilis, e a) visible; **b**) worth seeing, admirable.
spectāculum (*and* **spectāclum**), **ī** *n* **1.** spectator's seat in a theatre; theatre; **2.** show, sight, spectacle; stage-play.
spectāmen, inis *n* proof, sign.
spectātiō, ōnis *f* a looking at, beholding; testing of money.
spectātor, ōris *m* looker-on; **a**) beholder, observer, spectator; **b**) examiner, connoisseur.
spectātrīx, īcis *f* female beholder.
spectātus 3 well tried *or* tested; excellent.
spectiō, ōnis *f* the right of observing *or* determining the auspices.
spectō 1 to look; to behold, view, observe, gaze at, contemplate (*alqd*); **a**) to attend as a spectator; **b**) to examine, try, prove; to keep in view, bear in mind, aim at, look for (*alqd; ut*); **c**) to intend, tend towards; **res ad arma spectat** things look like war; **d**) to look *or* face towards (*ad* or *in alqd*).
spectrum, ī *n* image; phantom.
spēcula[1], **ae** *f* slight hope.
specula[2], **ae** *f* height, eminence, watch-tower; **esse in speculis** to be on the watch.
speculābilis, e visible.
speculābundus 3 watching, on the watch.
speculāria, *gen.* **-iōrum,** *abl.* **-ibus** *n/pl.* window panes.
speculātor, ōris *m* watcher, spy, scout; explorer, examiner.
speculātōrius 3 relating to spies, of scouts; **-ia (navis)** scouting-ship.
speculātrīx, īcis *f* female spy *or* watcher.
speculor 1 **a**) to look around, spy; **b**) to look out, spy out, watch, explore, wait for.
speculum, ī *n* **a**) mirror; **b**) image.
specus, ūs *m* (*n*) cave, cavern, grotto; **a**) ditch, pit, canal, excavation; **b**) hollow.
spēlaeum, ī *n* cave, hole, den.
spēlunca, ae *f* cave, grotto.
spērābilis, e that may be hoped for.
spernāx, ācis contemptuous.
spernō, sprēvī, sprētum 3 **a**) to separate, sever, remove; **b**) to reject, disdain, despise.
spērō 1 to expect; to hope (*alqd; acc. c. inf.*); to trust in.
spēs, ēī *f* expectation; **1.** hope (*alcis rei*); **a**) object of hope; **b**) goddess of hope; **2.** fear, apprehension; anticipation.

sphaera, ae *f* ball, sphere.
sphaeristērium, ī *n* place for playing ball.
sphaeromachia, ae *f* boxing with padded iron balls fastened to the hands.
Sphinx, ingis *f* Sphinx.
spīca, ae *f* ear of corn, point, spike.
spīceus 3 of ears of corn.
spīci-fer 3 bearing ears of corn.
spiciō 3 = **speciō.**
spīculum, ī *n* point, sting; arrow, dart, javelin.
spīcum, ī *n* = **spica.**
spīna, ae *f* thorn, prickle; **a**) thorn-bush; **b**) spine, backbone; **c**) subtlety, perplexity; **d**) difficulty, pain, anxiety.
spīnētum, ī *n* thorn-hedge.
spīneus 3 thorny.
spīni-ger 3 thorn-bearing.
spīnōsus 3 thorny, prickly; galling; crabbed, obscure.
spinter, eris *n* metal armlet.
spintria, ae *m* male prostitute.
spinturnīcium, ī *n* bird of (ill) omen.
spīnus, ī *f* blackthorn, sloe.
spīra, ae *f* coil, twist, fold.
spīrābilis, e that can be breathed; life-giving.
spīrāculum, ī *n* air-hole, vent.
spīrāmen, inis *n* **a**) air-hole; **b**) puff of air.
spīrāmentum, ī *n* air-hole, pore; pause, breathing-time.
spīritus, ūs *m* **a**) breath, air, breeze; **b**) breath of life, life; **c**) spirit, soul, mind, inspiration, courage; haughtiness, pride.
spīrō 1 **a**) to breathe, draw breath; to be alive; **b**) to blow, pant; **c**) to exhale, emit odour, to smell; breathe out; **d**) to be full of, inspired with, to intend, aim at; to express, imitate.
spissāmentum, ī *n* stopper, plug.
spissātiō, ōnis *f* a packing tight, ramming.
spissēscō 3 to grow thick, condense.
spissi-gradus 3 walking slowly.
spissō 1 to condense.
spissus 3 thick, crowded, dense, close; tardy, slow, tiresome.
splēn, ēnis *m* spleen.
splendeō, (uī), — 2 to shine, glitter, be bright; to be distinguished *or* glorious.
splendēscō, duī, — 3 to become bright, begin to shine.
splendidus 3 bright, shining, brilliant; **a**) splendid, magnificent, noble, fine; **b**) sumptuous, showy; **c**) distinguished, illustrious, renowned; **d**) clear.
splendor, ōris *m* brightness, clearness; **a**) splendour, magnificence, honour; **b**) ornament.
splēniātus 3 having a face-patch on.
splēnium, ī *n* face-patch.
spoliārium, i *n* stripping-room in the amphitheatre; den of plunder.
spoliātiō, ōnis *f* a plundering, robbing, deprivation, robbery.
spoliātor, ōris *m* plunderer.
spoliātrīx, īcis, *fem. of* **spoliator.**
spoliō 1 to rob one of his clothes, to strip (*acc.*); to plunder, rob, despoil, deprive (*alqm re*).
spolium, ī *n* skin, hide; **a**) (*pl.*) plunder, booty, arms taken from an enemy, spoil; **b**) victory.
sponda, ae *f* **a**) frame of a couch, bedstead; **b**) bed, sofa; **c**) bier.
spondālia (*or* **-aulia**), **ōrum** *n/pl.* sacrificial song accompanied by the flute.
spondeō, spopondī, spōnsum 2 to promise solemnly, engage, pledge oneself (*alqd; alci alqd*); **a**) to warrant, be a security (*pro alqo, alqd pro alqo*); **b**) to betroth, promise in marriage; **c**) to vow; **d**) to forebode, to promise; *subst.* **spōnsus, ī** *m* bridegroom; **spōnsa, ae** *f* bride.
spondēus *and* **-īus, ī** *m* spondee (- -).
spondylus, ī *m* a shell-fish (?mussel).
spongia (*and* **-ea**), **ae** *f* sponge; open-worked coat of mail.
spōnsa, ae *f, see* **spondeo.**
spōnsālia, *gen.* **-iōrum,** *abl.* **-ibus** *n/pl.* betrothal.
spōnsiō, ōnis *f* solemn promise, engagement, pledge, surety, formal stipulation *or* treaty; legal wager.
spōnsor, ōris *m* surety.
spōnsum, ī *n* solemn promise *or* engagement.
spōnsus[1], ī *m, see* **spondeo.**
spōnsus[2], ūs *m* engagement, contract.
sponte *f* (*abl. sing.*) **a**) of one's own accord, voluntarily, willingly, freely; **b**) without aid, alone; **c**) of itself, for its own sake.
sporta, ae *f* a hamper, basket.

sportella, ae *f* = **sportula.**
sportula, ae *f* little basket; **a**) provision-basket; **b**) gift, present (*gen.* to clients).
S.P.Q.R. *abbr.* = **senatus populusque Romanus** the Senate and Roman people.
sprētiō, ōnis *f* a despising, contempt.
sprētor, ōris *m* despiser.
spūma, ae *f* foam, froth, scum; pomade for dyeing hair.
spūmātus, ūs *m* serpent's slaver.
spūmēscō, —, — 3 to begin to foam.
spūmeus 3 foaming.
spūmi-fer *and* **-ger** 3 foaming.
spūmō 1 to foam, froth; **spūmātus** 3 covered with foam.
spūmōsus 3 foaming, frothy.
spuō, uī, ūtum 3 to spit (out).
spurci-dicus 3 obscene.
spurci-ficus 3 polluting.
spurcitiēs, ēī *and* **-tia, ae** *f* filth.
spurcō 1 to defile, pollute; **spurcātus** 3 = **spurcus.**
spurcus 3 filthy, dirty, foul, obscene, impure.
spūtātilicus 3 despicable, detestable.
spūtātor, ōris *m* spitter.
spūtō 1 to spit out.
spūtum, ī *n* spittle.
squāleō, —, — 2 to be rough, scaly, stiff, *or* bristly (*alqa re*); **a**) to be dirty, neglected, foul, waste; **b**) to mourn in squalid garments.
squālidus 3 rough, stiff, scaly; **a**) unadorned, unpolished; **b**) dirty, filthy, squalid, neglected; **c**) in mourning attire.
squālor, ōris *m* roughness; **a**) filthiness, foulness; **b**) mourning attire.
squālus 3 stiff with dirt.
squāma, ae *f* scale; *pl.* scale-armour.
squāmeus 3, **squāmi-fer** 3, **squāmi-ger** 3, **squāmōsus** 3 scaly; *subst.* **-gerī** (*genit.* **-gerum**) *m/pl.* fishes.
squatus, ī *m* angel-fish.
squilla, ae *f* a shell-fish (? prawn).
st! *int.* hush!; 'sh!
stabilīmen, inis *n* stay, support.
stabilīmentum, ī *n* = **stabilimen.**
stabiliō 4 to make firm, to prop, support, establish.
stabilis, e standing; **a**) stable, firm; **b**) steadfast, constant, lasting, durable, immutable.
stabilitās, ātis *f* stability, steadfastness, durability, firmness.
stabilītor, ōris *m* establisher.
stabulārius, ī *m* tavern-keeper.
stabulor *and* **-lō** 1 to stand in a stable; to abide, dwell.
stabulum, ī *n* standing-place, abode; **a**) stable, stall, fold; **b**) tavern, brothel.
stacta, ae *f* juice of myrrh.
stadium, ī *n* **a**) race-course; **b**) stade (about 600 feet).
stāgnō 1 **a**) to form a pool of water; **b**) to overflow, inundate (*alqd*); **c**) to be inundated.
stāgnōsus 3 full of pools.
stāgnum[1], **ī** *n* standing water; **a**) lake, pond, pool; **b**) water (in general); sea.
stagnum[2], **ī** *n* alloy of silver and lead.
stalagmium, ī *n* ear-pendant.
stāmen, inis *n* **a**) warp of a web; thread; **b**) cloth; fillet; **c**) string of a lyre.
stāmineus 3 provided with threads.
stannum = **stagnum**[2].
statārius 3 standing firm; quiet; **~ia, ae** *f* (*sc.* **cōmoedia**) standing--still comedy (with little action); **~ius, ī** *m* actor in *statāria.*
statēra, ae *f* balance; yoke-pole.
staticulus, ī *m* a slow dance.
statim *adv.* **a**) firmly, steadily; **b**) on the spot, at once, immediately.
statiō, ōnis *f* **a**) a standing; **b**) station, position, abode, quarters; **c**) post, outpost, watch, picket, guard, sentinels; **d**) roadstead, anchorage.
statīvus 3 fixed, standing still; *subst.* **statīva, ōrum** *n/pl.* permanent camp.
stator, ōris *m* **a**) attendant of a magistrate; **b**) **Stator** (title of Jupiter) stayer of flight, supporter.
statua, ae *f* statue, image.
statuārius, ī *m* statuary, sculptor.
statūmen, inis *n* prop, support; rib of a ship.
statuō, uī, ūtum 3 to set up, cause to stand; to stop; **a**) to erect, build, raise, found; **b**) to fix, appoint, determine, decide, ordain (*alqd; ut*); to resolve, purpose (*inf.; ut*); **c**) to believe, be convinced, judge, consider.
statūra, ae *f* height, size, stature.
status[1] 3, *see* **sisto.**

status[2], **ūs** *m* a standing; **a**) position, posture, attitude; **b**) condition, state, circumstances, arrangement; **c**) standing, position in life; **d**) system *or* line of defence (in oratory).
statūtus 3 big, sturdy.
stega, ae *f* deck of a ship.
stēliō, ōnis *m* = **stellio.**
stēlla, ae *f* star; constellation; the sun.
stēllāns, tis a) starry; **b**) shining.
stēllātus 3 **a**) starry; **b**) placed in the heavens as a constellation; **c**) shining, bright.
stēlli-fer *and* **-ger** 3 star-bearing.
stēlliō, ōnis *m* lizard with spots.
stemma, atis *n* **a**) wreath hung on an ancestor's image; **b**) pedigree; **c**) antiquity.
stercoreus 3 dirty, filthy.
stercorō 1 to dung, manure.
sterculīnum, ī *n* dung-pit.
stercus, oris *n* dung, manure.
sterilis, e barren; **a**) empty, vain; **b**) making unfruitful.
sterilitās, ātis *f* unfruitfulness, barrenness.
sternāx, ācis throwing off the rider.
sternō, strāvī, strātum 3 **a**) to stretch out, spread out, extend, strew, scatter; **b**) to throw down, stretch on the ground; **c**) to level, pave (*a road*); **d**) to bestrew, cover; to cover with carpets, to saddle; to smooth over.
sternū(tā)mentum, ī *n* a sneezing.
sternuō, uī, — 3 to sneeze; to crackle.
sterquilīnum, ī *n* dung-pit.
stertō, —, — 3 to snore, snort.
stibadium, ī *n* semicircular couch.
stigma, atis *n* brand; mark of disgrace; cut.
stigmatiās, ae *m* branded slave.
stigmōsus 3 branded.
stilla, ae *f* drop.
stillārium, ī *n* a drop; gratuity, tip.
stilli-cidium, ī *n* dripping water (*esp.* from eaves of buildings).
stillō 1 **a**) to fall in drops, drip; **b**) to let drop, to distil.
stilus, ī *m* pointed instrument for writing, style; **a**) writing, composition; **b**) manner of writing, style; **c**) pointed stake.
stimulātiō, ōnis *f* incitement.
stimulātrīx, īcis *f* she who goads.
stimuleus 3 relating to the goad, of goads.
stimulō 1 to goad, prick; **a**) to torment, vex, trouble; **b**) to incite, spur, stimulate.
stimulus, ī *m* prick, goad; **a**) pointed stake; **b**) sting, torment, pain; spur, incentive, incitement.
stinguō, —, — 3 to extinguish.
stīpātiō, ōnis *f* throng, retinue.
stīpātor, ōris *m* attendant, satellite.
stipendiārius (stī-?) 3 **a**) serving for pay; **b**) liable to tribute, tributary.
stīpendium, ī *n* **a**) pay of a soldier; military service, campaign, a year's service; **b**) tax, tribute, contribution; penalty.
stīpes, itis *m* log, stump, trunk of a tree; **a**) tree; branch; **b**) blockhead, dunce.
stīpō 1 **a**) to press *or* crowd together, compress; **b**) to cram, stuff, fill full; **c**) to surround, attend, accompany.
stips, ipis *f* contribution in money; **a**) gift, alms; **b**) fee.
stipula, ae *f* stalk, stem, straw, stubble; reed-pipe.
stipulātiō, ōnis *f* agreement, covenant, stipulation.
stipulātiuncula, ae *f* a little stipulation.
stipulātor, ōris *m* bargainer.
stipulor 1 to stipulate, make a bargain *or* contract (*alqd*).
stīria, ae *f* icicle.
stirpēs *and* **stirpis, is** *f* = **stirps.**
stirpitus *adv.* by the roots, utterly.
stirps (**stirpēs, stirpis**), **is** *f* (*m*) lowest part of a tree, the trunk with the root; **a**) plant, shrub, tree; **b**) root, stem; shoot; **c**) family, origin, lineage; **d**) root, source, beginning; **e**) descendant, offspring.
stīva, ae *f* plough-handle.
stlāt(t)ārius 3 carried in ships, imported (?).
stlīs, ītis *f* (*archaic*) = **lis.**
stloppus, ī *m* the noise of a slap on the cheek.
stō, stetī (**stātūrus**) 1 **1.** to stand, be upright, remain standing; a) to be stationed (*troops*); to be at anchor; b) to stand on end, bristle up (*abl.*); c) to stand out with, to be full of, loaded with; d) to cost; e) to stand by, at the side of, adhere to (*cum* or *ab alqo*, *pro re* or *adversus alqm*); to rest upon, depend on; **per**

me stat it stands to my account, is my fault (*quominus, ne*); **2.** to stand firm, to endure, persist, remain; a) to be fixed, determined; b) to keep the stage (*of plays*).

stola, ae *f* gown, long robe of a woman; noble matron.

stolātus 3 in a woman's dress; befitting a matron.

stolidus 3 stupid, foolish, dull, rude.

stomachicus 3 suffering from disease of the stomach.

stomachor 1 to be angry, irritated, indignant.

stomachōsus 3 angry, irritable.

stomachus, ī *m* **a**) gullet; **b**) stomach; **c**) taste, liking; **d**) anger, irritation; **e**) **bonus** ~ good humour.

storea *and* **-ia, ae** *f* straw-mat, rush-mat.

strabō, ōnis *m* a squinting one, squinter.

strāgēs, is *f* a throwing down, overthrow, ruin; **a**) defeat, slaughter, massacre; **b**) fallen mass, confused heap.

strāgulus 3 fit for spreading out; **strāgula vestis** *and* **strāgulum, ī** *n* blanket, carpet.

strāmen, inis *n* straw, litter.

strāmentīcius 3 of straw.

strāmentum, ī *n* **a**) straw, litter; **b**) pack-saddle.

strāmineus 3 made of *or* covered with straw.

strangulō 1 to throttle, choke, strangle; to torment, torture.

strang-ūria, ae *f* difficulty in passing urine.

stratēgēma, atis *n* military artifice, stratagem.

stratēgus, ī *m* commander; president of a banquet.

stratiōticus 3 soldierly.

strātum, ī *n* covering, blanket; **a**) bed, couch; **b**) horsecloth, saddle; **c**) pavement.

strātūra, ae *f* a paving.

strēna, ae *f* omen, portent; new year's gift.

strēnuitās, ātis *f* quickness, activity, promptness.

strēnuus 3 **a**) active, quick, ready, prompt, brave; **b**) turbulent, restless.

strepitō 1 to make a loud noise.

strepitus, ūs *m* noise, din, rustling; sound.

strepō, puī, (pitum) 3 to make a noise, to rustle, rattle, roar; to sound, ring, resound.

striātus 3 ribbed, fluted.

strictim *adv.* closely; briefly, superficially.

strictūra, ae *f* mass of hot metal.

strictus 3 drawn together, narrow, close, tight; concise.

strīdeō, —, — 2 *and* **strīdō, dī, —** 3 to creak, hiss, hum, rustle, whistle.

strīdor, ōris *m* a creaking, hissing, humming, whistling, grunting, braying, whispering.

strīdulus 3 rustling, hissing, creaking, whistling, crackling.

strigilis, is *f* skin-scraper.

strigō 1 to stop; to jib.

strigor, ōris, *a word of doubtful sense; perhaps* = **strigosus.**

strigōsus 3 lean, thin, meagre.

stringō, strinxī, strictum 3 **a**) to touch lightly, graze upon; to wound; to touch, move; **b**) to draw *or* strip off, pluck; to draw, unsheath; **c**) to draw tight together, tie together.

stringor, ōris *m* shock, twinge.

strix, igis *f* screech-owl.

stropha, ae *f* trick.

strophiārius, ī *m* maker of breast-bands.

strophium, ī *n* breast-band; garland.

structilis, e of, for building.

strūctor, ōris *m* builder, mason; head-waiter.

structūra, ae *f* structure, building, construction; arrangement.

struēs, is *f* heap; heap of offering-cakes; phalanx of soldiers.

struīx, īcis *f* pile.

strūma, ae *f* tuberculous tumour.

strūmōsus 3 suffering from a tuberculous tumour.

struō, -uxī, -uctum 3 to heap up, pile, join together; **a**) to erect, build, construct, fabricate; **b**) to prepare, get ready; **c**) to arrange, put in order; **d**) to contrive, design, cause, occasion.

strūthea, ōrum *n/pl.* a kind of quinces.

studeō, uī, — 2 to give attention to, take pains with, apply oneself to, be busy with, strive after, pursue, desire (*alci rei; inf.; acc. c. inf.*); **a**) to be favourable *or* attached to, to side with; **b**) to study (*with dat.*).

studiōsus 3 zealous, eager, diligent, careful; **a**) devoted to, studious, fond of (*gen.*); **b**) partial, friendly, favourable, inclined to.
studium, ī *n* zeal, eagerness, application, enthusiasm, exertion, desire, study (*alcis rei*); **a**) favour, inclination, attachment, devotion, interest; **b**) partiality, partisanship, prejudice; **c**) employment, pursuit; propensity, favourite study; literary occupation, research.
stulti-loquentia, ae *f*, **-loquium, ī** *n* silly talk.
stulti-loquus 3 speaking foolishly.
stultitia, ae *f* folly, foolishness; silliness, stupidity.
stulti-vidus 3 seeing mistakenly.
stultus 3 foolish, stupid, silly, infatuated; *subst.* **∸, ī** *m* fool.
stupe-faciō 3 to stun, stupefy, astonish.
stupeō, uī, — 2 **a**) to be insensible, to be stunned, benumbed; **b**) to be amazed, surprised; **c**) to gaze at with wonder (*alqd*).
stupēscō, —, — 3 to be struck with wonder *or* awe.
stupiditās, ātis *f* insensibility; dulness, stupidity.
stupidus 3 senseless; amazed; stupid, foolish.
stupor, ōris *m* senselessness, dulness; **a**) astonishment, amazement; **b**) stupidity, foolishness.
stuppa, ae *f* coarse flax, tow.
stuppeus 3 of tow, flaxen.
stuprātor, ōris *m* ravisher.
stuprō 1 to defile, deflower, ravish.
stuprum, ī *n* a debauching; unchastity.
sturnus, ī *m* starling.
Stygius 3 of the river Styx; of the nether world; infernal.
Styx, ygis *f* a river in Hades (the abode of the dead).
suādēla, ae *f* a persuading.
suādeō, sī, sum 2 to advise, counsel, exhort, suggest, recommend (*alci alqd, ut, ne*); **a**) to impel, induce; **b**) to promote, support; **c**) to persuade.
suādus 3 persuasive.
suāsiō, ōnis *f* a recommending; advocacy, persuasive eloquence.
suāsor, ōris *m* adviser, exhorter; promoter (*gen.*).
suāsōria, ae *f* speech of advice.
suāsum, ī *n* dark dye.
suāsus, ūs *m* a persuading, exhorting.
suāve-olēns, tis sweet-smelling.
suāviātiō, ōnis *f* a kissing.
suāvi-dicus 3 speaking sweetly.
suāvi-loquēns, tis speaking sweetly.
suāvi-loquentia, ae *f* agreeable speech.
suāviolum, ī *n* little kiss.
suāvior 1 to kiss.
suāvis, e sweet, agreeable, pleasant, delightful, attractive.
suāvi-sāviātiō, ōnis *f* sweet kissing.
suāvitās, ātis *f* sweetness, pleasantness, agreeableness.
suāvitūdō, inis *f* = **suavitas.**
suāvium, ī *n* kiss.
sub 1. *prep.* with *acc.* a) (*of place, to express motion*) under; up towards; close up to, **sub iugum mittere, sub montem succedere, sub imperium** *or* **potestatem redigere;** b) (*of time*) about, close upon, just before, **sub noctem, sub idem tempus; 2.** *prep.* with *abl.* a) (*of place, to express position*) under, beneath, at the bottom of, at the foot of, **sub terra habitare, sub monte considere;** just behind; b) (*of condition*) under, beneath, **sub imperio, sub regno, sub dicione alcis esse, sub conditionibus;** c) (*of time*) at, at the same time as, **sub ipsa profectione, sub decessu suo.**
sub-absurdus 3 rather absurd *or* foolish.
sub-accūsō 1 to blame a little.
sub-āctiō, ōnis *f* training.
sub-aerātus 3 with bronze underneath.
sub-agrestis, e rather rustic.
sub-ālāris, e under the armpits.
sub-amārus 3 somewhat bitter.
sub-aquilus 3 dull black.
sub-arroganter somewhat arrogantly.
sub-auscultō 1 to listen secretly.
sub-basilicānus, ī *m* loafer, idler.
sub-bibō 3 to drink a little.
sub-blandior 4 to flatter *or* caress a little.
sub-c..., *see also* **succ...**
sub-cavus 3 hollow underneath.
sub-contumēliōsē somewhat insultingly.
sub-crispus 3 somewhat curled.

subcustōs, ōdis *m* under-guard.
sub-dēbilis, e somewhat crippled.
sub-difficilis, e rather difficult.
sub-diffīdō 3 to distrust a little.
subditīvus 3 substituted, not genuine, false, spurious.
sub-dō, didī, ditum 3 to put,place, *or* set under; to apply (*alqd alci rei*); **P.** to lie under *or* near; **a**) to subdue; **b**) to substitute, forge, suborn.
sub-doceō 2 to give supplementary lessons to.
sub-dolus 3 cunning, crafty, deceitful.
sub-domō 1 to tame, break in.
sub-dubitō 1 to doubt a little.
sub-dūcō 3 **1.** to draw up; to draw *or* take away; a) to draw away, remove, lead away, steal; **se subducere** *or* **P.** to withdraw secretly, steal away; b) to balance, calculate, compute; **2.** to draw up on high, lift up, draw ashore.
sub-ductiō, ōnis *f* a drawing a ship ashore; reckoning.
sub-dūrus 3 somewhat hard.
sub-edō 3 to eat away underneath.
sub-eō 1. to go under, come under (*alqd*); a) to enter, take cover in; b) to take upon oneself, to undergo, submit to, to sustain, undertake, encounter, endure; **2.** a) to go *or* come up, ascend, climb (*in, ad alqd*); b) to go to, approach, advance; to approach secretly *or* gradually (*alqd, ad alqd*); to steal into; to assail; c) to come into one's mind; d) to come immediately after, take the place of, follow (*alci* or *in locum alcis*).
sūber, eris *n* cork-oak; cork.
sub-f..., *see* **suff...**
sub-g..., *see* **sugg...**
sub-horridus 3 somewhat rough.
sub-iaceō 2 to lie below.
sūb-iciō (*and* **sŭb-**), **iēcī, iectum** 3 **1.** to throw, put, lay under (*alqd alci rei, sub alqd*); a) to subject, subdue; **P.** to be subject; to expose, make liable; b) to substitute, forge; to suborn; **2.** to place near *or* by, advance near (*alqd alci rei*); a) to present; b) to suggest, bring to mind, prompt, propose, whisper to (*alci alqd*); c) to put after; d) to connect, append, subjoin; to range *or* reckon under, subordinate, comprise in; e) to answer, reply; **3.** to throw from under, throw up on high, raise, lift up (*alqd in alqd*); **se sūbicere** to rise; — **subiectus** 3 lying under *or* near; a) adjacent; b) subjected, subject; c) exposed to; *subst.* **subiectī, ōrum** *m/pl.* subjects.
sub-iectiō, ōnis *f* a placing under; substitution, forgery.
sub-iectō 1 to throw up; to place underneath; to apply.
sub-iector, ōris *m* forger.
sub-iectus 3, *see* **subicio.**
subigitātiō, ōnis *f* touching, love-making.
subigitātrīx, īcis *f* woman who makes love.
sub-igitō 1 to touch, make love.
sub-igō, ēgī, āctum 3 **1.** to drive *or* bring up; **2.** to bring under; a) to force, compel, impel, oblige, constrain (*alqm ad* or *in alqd; inf.*); b) to overcome, conquer, subdue; c) to 'work up' in any way (to plough *or* dig soil, to plough through water, to propel a boat, to sharpen a tool); d) to discipline, train.
sub-iiciō, *see* **subicio.**
sub-impudēns, tis somewhat shameless.
sub-inānis, e rather vain.
sub-inde *adv.* **a**) immediately after, just after; **b**) from time to time, repeatedly.
sub-īnsulsus 3 somewhat insipid.
sub-invideō 2 to envy a little (*dat.*).
sub-invīsus 3 somewhat hated.
sub-invītō 1 to give a hint.
sub-īrāscor, — 3 to be a little angry (*dat.*).
sub-īrātus 3 somewhat angry.
subitārius 3 collected *or* built hastily, done in haste.
subitus 3 (*adv.* **subitō**) **a**) sudden, unexpected; *subst.* **subitum, ī** *n* sudden occurrence, surprise; **b**) = **subitarius.**
sub-iungō 3 to add, join, subjoin; to yoke, harness (*curru*); to subdue, subject (*alqd alci, sub alqd*).
sub-lābor 3 **a**) to glide imperceptibly; **b**) to fall down, sink.
sub-lātiō, ōnis *f* exaltation.
sub-lātus 3 elated, proud, haughty.
sub-lectō 1 to allure, decoy.
sub-legō 3 **a**) to gather, pick up; **b**) to take away secretly; to listen to secretly; **c**) to choose instead.
sublestus 3 weak, slight.
sub-levātiō, ōnis *f* alleviation.

sub-levō 1 to lift up, raise up, hold up; **a**) to support, assist, encourage; **b**) to lessen, to diminish, mitigate.
sublica, ae *f* stake, pile.
sublicius 3 resting upon piles.
sub-ligāculum, ī *and* **-ligar, āris** *n* loin-cloth, under-pants.
sub-ligō 1 to bind below.
sublīmis, e high, lofty; in the air, aloft; *adv.* **sublīme** (*and* **sublīmen** [?]) aloft, on high, upwards; **a**) elevated, exalted, sublime; **b**) distinguished.
sublīmitās, ātis *f* loftiness, sublimity.
sub-lingulō, ōnis *m* under-licker, cook's boy.
sub-linō 3 to besmear; ~ **ōs** (*alci*) to cheat.
sub-lūceō, —, — 2 to shine forth from below, glimmer.
sub-luō 3 to wash underneath.
sub-lūstris, e glimmering.
sub-m..., *see also* **summ...**
sub-merus 3 almost unmixed.
sub-molestus 3 somewhat vexatious; **-tē** *adv.* with some annoyance.
sub-mōrōsus 3 somewhat peevish *or* fretful.
sub-nāscor 3 to grow up under.
sub-natō 1 to swim underneath.
sub-nectō 3 to tie *or* bind on (under); to fasten.
sub-negō 1 to deny partly.
sub-niger, gra, grum dull black.
sub-nimium *a pun on subparum* (= *supparum*).
sub-nīsus *and* **-nīxus** 3 resting *or* leaning on (*abl.*); propped up; relying on.
sub-notō 1 to note (down); to annotate.
sub-nuba, ae *f* rival.
sub-nūbilus 3 somewhat cloudy.
subō 1 to be in heat *or* lustful.
sub-obscēnus 3 somewhat obscene.
sub-obscūrus 3 somewhat dark.
sub-odiōsus 3 somewhat odious.
sub-offendō 3 to give some offence.
sub-olēs, is *f* offspring, descendant.
sub-olēscō, —, — 3 to grow up.
sub-olet mihi I smell, have an inkling.
sub-orior 4 to spring up (as a replacement); *hence* **subortus, ūs** *m* replenishment.
sub-ōrnō 1 to furnish, provide, supply (secretly) (*alqm re*); to instruct privately, suborn.
sub-p..., *see* **supp...**
sub-rancidus 3 slightly tainted.
sub-raucus 3 somewhat hoarse.
sub-rēmigō 1 to paddle (under water).
sub-rēpō 3 to creep *or* crawl up (to), steal upon.
sub-rīdeō 2 to smile.
sub-rīdiculē *adv.* rather laughably.
sub-rigō 3 to raise up.
sub-ringor, —, — 3 to grin with annoyance.
sub-ripiō 3, *see* **surripio.**
sub-rogō 1, *see* **surrogo.**
sub-rōstrānī, ōrum *m/pl.* loungers (round the *rostra*).
sub-rubeō 2 to be reddish, to blush.
sub-rubicundus 3 somewhat red.
sub-rūfus 3 reddish.
sub-ruō 3 to dig under, undermine, overthrow, demolish; to subvert, destroy.
sub-rūsticus 3 somewhat clownish.
sub-rutilus 3 reddish.
sub-scrībō 3 to write beneath (*alqd alci rei*); **a**) to sign a charge; **b**) to subscribe, sign, support, assent to (*dat.*).
sub-scrīptiō, ōnis *f* a writing beneath; **a**) a noting down; **b**) register; **c**) a joining in an accusation.
sub-scrīptor, ōris *m* joint accuser.
subscūs, ūdis *f* the tenon of a dovetail.
sub-secīvus 3 = **subsicivus.**
sub-secō 1 to cut off, clip.
sub-sellium, ī *n* bench, seat; *pl.* court, tribunal.
sub-sentiō 4 to feel, notice, discover secretly.
sub-sequor 3 to follow, come after (*acc.*); **a**) to attend, accompany; **b**) to follow up, support.
sub-serviō 4 to serve, to accommodate oneself to (*alci*).
sub-sicīvus 3 left over, remaining; (of time) odd, spare; (of work) done in odd moments.
subsidiārius 3 belonging to a reserve; *pl. m* reserve-troops.
subsidior 1 to act as a reserve.
sub-sidium, ī *n* **a**) reserve line, reserve forces; **b**) aid, help, relief; **c**) place of refuge.
sub-sīdō, sēdī, sessum 3 to sit down, crouch down; **a**) to settle, sink, subside; **b**) to settle down, stop (in a place); **c**) to lie in wait for.

sub-signānī, ōrum *m/pl.* reserve-troops.
sub-signō 1 to enter in a register; to undertake, guarantee.
sub-siliō, siluī, — 4 to leap up.
sub-sistō, stitī, — 3 to stand still, remain standing, to stop, halt (*in loco*); **a**) to cease; **b**) to remain, stay; **c**) to resist, withstand (*alci*).
sub-sortior 4 to substitute by lot.
sub-sortītiō, ōnis *f* a choosing of substitutes by lot.
sub-stantia, ae *f* substance, essence; support, backing.
sub-sternō 3 **a**) to spread under *or* in front; to place under oneself *or* someone else; to place at someone's disposal, yield.
sub-stituō, uī, ūtum 3 **a**) to put under, next, *or* in front of; to present; **b**) to put instead, substitute.
sub-stō 1 to stand firm, hold out.
sub-strāmen, inis *n* something put underneath; rollers for transporting ships.
sub-stringō 3 to bind *or* draw up, **aurem** to prick the ear, listen attentively; to hold in.
sub-structiō, ōnis *f* foundation, substructure.
sub-struō 3 to build beneath; **a**) to lay the foundation of; **b**) to pave.
sub-sultim *adv.* by leaps and bounds.
sub-sultō 1, *intens. of* **subsilio.**
sub-sum,—,sub-esse to be under *or* behind (*dat.*); **a**) to be concealed in; **b**) to be subject to; **c**) to lie at the bottom, be underneath, near, at hand.
sub-sūtus 3 trimmed at the bottom.
sub-tēmen, inis *n* woof, weft; thread, yarn.
subter 1. *adv.* below, beneath; **2.** *prep.* with *acc.* and *abl.* below, beneath, under.
subter-dūcō 3 to withdraw secretly.
subter-fugiō, fūgī, — 3 to flee in secret, escape, evade, shun.
subter-lābor 3 to glide *or* flow under; to escape (*acc.*).
sub-terō 3 to wear away underneath.
sub-terrāneus 3 underground.
subter-volō 1 to fly beneath.
sub-texō 3 to draw in front; to cover, veil; to weave into, connect, join together, add.
subtīlis, e fine, thin; **a**) precise, exact, accurate; **b**) keen, delicate, acute, refined; **c**) plain, simple, unadorned.
subtīlitās, ātis *f* fineness, thinness; **a**) accuracy, exactness; **b**) discernment, subtlety; **c**) plainness, simplicity.
sub-timeō 2 to be a little afraid.
sub-trahō 3 **1.** to draw away from under (*dat.*); **2.** to take away secretly, remove, withdraw (*alci alqd*); **se subtrahere** *or* **P.** to withdraw, retire.
sub-trīstis, e somewhat sad.
sub-turpiculus 3 *and* **sub-turpis, e** somewhat disgraceful.
subtus *adv.* under, beneath.
sub-tūsus 3 somewhat bruised.
sub-ūcula, ae *f* under-tunic.
sūbula, ae *f* awl; small spear.
subulcus, ī *m* swineherd.
sub-urbānitās, ātis *f* nearness to the city.
sub-urbānus 3 near the city, suburban; *subst.* **-um, ī** *n* estate near Rome; **-ī, ōrum** *m/pl.* inhabitants of towns near Rome.
sub-urbium, ī *n* suburb.
sub-urgeō 2 to press to, drive close to.
sub-ūrō 3 to burn a little, to singe.
sub-vectiō, ōnis *f* a carrying, conveying.
sub-vectō 1 to carry, convey, bring to.
sub-vectus, ūs *m* a conveying.
sub-vehō 3 to carry *or* bring up; to convey, transport.
sub-veniō 4 **a**) to come to help, to assist, aid; **b**) to relieve, remedy, cure (*dat.*).
sub-ventō 1, *intens. of* **subvenio.**
sub-vereor 2 to fear a little.
sub-versor, ōris *m* overthrower, subverter.
sub-vertō 3 to overturn, upset, overthrow, to ruin, destroy.
sub-vexus 3 sloping upward.
sub-volō 1 to fly up.
sub-volturius 3 coloured like a vulture.
sub-volvō 3 to roll up.
sub-vortō 3 = **subverto.**
succēdāneus 3 substituted, taking the place of.
suc-cēdō 3 **1.** to go up under; a) to pass under, submit oneself to; b) to go to, approach, advance, march on

or up; to go into, enter; c) to turn out well, be successful, prosper, succeed; **2.** to go up, ascend (*ad alqd*; *dat.*); **3.** to come after, follow after *or* close upon, come into the place of, succeed; to supply the place of, relieve (*alci*).
suc-cendō, ndī, ēnsum 3 to set on fire, kindle; to inflame.
succēnseō 2 = **suscenseo.**
suc-centuriō[1]**,ōnis** *m* subcenturion.
suc-centuriō[2] 1 to enlist as a replacement; **-iātus,** placed in reserve.
suc-cernō 3 to sift.
suc-cessiō, ōnis *f* a succeeding, succession.
successor, ōris *m* successor, heir.
successus, ūs *m* **a**) advance; **b**) good progress, success.
succīdāneus 3 = **succedaneus.**
suc-cīdia, ae *f* flitch of bacon.
suc-cīdō[1]**, cīdī, cīsum** 3 to cut off below *or* from below; to cut down *or* through.
suc-cidō[2]**, cidī,** — 3 to sink down.
succiduus 3 sinking down.
suc-cinctus 3 concise.
suc-cingō 3 **a**) to tuck up the clothes; **b**) to gird round, surround (*alqd re*); to furnish, provide, equip.
suc-cingulum, ī *n* girdle.
suc-cinō, —, — 3 to sing with, chime in with.
suc-cipiō 3 = **suscipio.**
suc-clāmātiō, ōnis *f* a shouting, acclamation.
suc-clāmō 1 to shout to (*alci*).
suc-collō 1 to take upon the shoulders.
suc-contumēliōsē = **sub-c...**
suc-crēscō 3 to grow from below, grow up; to succeed to (*dat.*).
suc-crispus 3 = **sub-c...**
suc-cumbō, cubuī, cubitum 3 to sink down, to be overcome, to succumb, yield.
suc-currō, currī, cursum 3 to run under; **a**) to run to help, hasten to the aid of, to assist (*dat.*); **b**) to come into one's mind, suggest itself.
succussus, ūs *m* a shaking, jolting.
suc-custōs, ōdis *m* assistant watchman.
suc-cutiō, cussi, cussum 3 to shake up.
sūcidus 3 juicy, fresh.
sūcinum, ī *n* amber.
sūcinus 3 of amber.
sucula, ae *f* **a**) windlass; **b**) little sow; **c**) the constellation *Hyades.*
sūcus, ī *m* juice, sap, moisture; **a**) medicinal drink; **b**) taste, flavour; **c**) vigour, force.
sūdārium, ī *n* handkerchief.
sūdātiō, ōnis *f* sweating.
sūdātōrius 3 of *or* for sweating; *subst.* **-ium** *n* sweating-room.
sūdātrīx, īcis causing perspiration.
sudis, is *f* stake; bristle, fin(?).
sūdō 1 to sweat; to drip, be wet; to toil hard.
sūdor, ōris *m* sweat; moisture; exertion.
suduculum, ī *n* stick (*dimin. of* sudis).
sūdus 3 clear, serene; *subst.* **sūdum, ī** *n* bright sky, fair weather.
suēscō, ēvī, ētum 3 **a**) to become accustomed, *perf.* to be wont; **suētus** 3 accustomed, wont (*dat.*), customary, usual; **b**) to accustom to (*alqm re*).
sūfes, etis *m* judge, chief magistrate (*in Carthage*).
suf-farcinō 1 to stuff full, cram.
suf-ferō, sufferre to bear, support, endure, suffer.
suf-ficiō, fēcī, fectum 3 **1.** a) to afford, supply, furnish; b) to put in the place of another, substitute, choose as a substitute; **2.** to be sufficient, suffice, be adequate, avail; to stain.
suf-fīgō 3 to fix beneath, to fasten up(on).
(**suffīmen, inis** *and*) **suffīmentum, ī** *n* fumigation, incense.
suf-fiō 4 to perfume, fumigate.
sufflāmen, inis *n* drag, brake.
sufflāminō 1 to brake, check.
suf-flāvus 3 greyish yellow.
suf-flō 1 to blow (up), inflate.
suffōcātiō, ōnis *f* suffocation.
suf-fōcō 1 to throttle, choke, strangle.
suf-fodiō 3 to dig under, undermine; to pierce from below.
suffossiō, ōnis *f* undermining, mine.
suffrāgātiō, ōnis *f* **a**) a voting; **b**) favourable vote, support.
suffrāgātor, ōris *m* **a**) voter; **b**) favourer, supporter.
suffrāgātōrius 3 belonging to the support of a candidate.

suffrāgium, ī *n* voting-tablet; vote, suffrage; **suffrāgium ferre** to vote; **a**) right of voting; **b**) judgment, opinion; **c**) approbation, assent.

suf-frāgor 1 to vote for, support, favour, recommend, promote (*alci*).

suf-fringō, frēgī, frāctum 3 to break below.

su-fugiō, fūgī, — 3 to flee.

suf-fugium, ī *n* place of refuge.

suf-fulciō 4 to support beneath.

suf-fundō 3 to pour under, out, into, *or* upon, to overspread, suffuse, infuse; **suffūsus** 3 **a**) flowing; **b**) intermingled, bedewed, coloured, stained.

suf-fūror 1 to pilfer, filch.

suf-fuscus 3 brownish.

suffūsus 3, *see* **suffundo.**

sug-gerō 3 **a**) to put under; **b**) to pile up, erect; **c**) to put immediately after; **d**) to furnish, afford, supply, add, subjoin; **e**) to suggest, prompt.

suggestum, ī *n and* **-us, ūs** *m* elevated place; platform, stage.

suggillātiō, suggillō, *see* **sugi...**

sug-grandis, e pretty large *or* spacious.

sug-gredior, gressus sum 3 to come up, approach.

sūgillātiō, ōnis *f* affront, insult.

sūgillō 1 to beat black and blue; to taunt, insult, revile.

sūgō, xī, ctum 3 to suck, suck in.

suillus 3 of swine.

sulcātor, ōris *m* one who ploughs *or* cuts through.

sulcō 1 to furrow, plough, to sail over.

sulcus, ī *m* furrow; **a**) a ploughing; **b**) a cutting, trench, ditch; **c**) track, trail; **d**) wrinkle; **e**) vulva.

sulfur, uris *n* = **sulpur.**

sullāturiō 4 to want to play the part of Sulla.

sulphur, uris *n* = **sulpur.**

sulpur, uris *n* brimstone, sulphur.

sulpurātus 3 impregnated with sulphur; **-ta** *n/pl.* sulphur matches.

sulpureus 3 sulphurous, sulphur-yellow.

sultis = si vultis (*compare* **sīs**).

sum, fuī, esse 1. a) to be, exist, live; b) to happen, befall, occur, take place; c) to be present, be found, stay, abide; d) to be possible, to be the case that ... (*ut*); **2.** (*perf. tense*) to be a thing of the past, to be no more; **3.** *as a copula:* to be; a) *with gen. poss.* to belong *or* pertain to, be of, be peculiar to, characteristic of, be the duty of; b) *with gen. or abl. qualit.* to be of, be possessed of, belong to, have; c) *with numbers:* to be of, consist of; d) *with gen. or abl. of value:* to be valued at, cost; e) *with dat.* to have, possess (*patri est ampla domus*).

sumbolus, -um = **symbolus, -um.**

sūmen, inis *n* breast, teat, udder (*of a sow*); sow.

summa, ae *f* **1.** the sum, amount, contents, substance, quantity, number; a) sum of money; b) the whole, the chief point, chief thing, principal matter; **ad summam** on the whole, generally, in short; **summa imperii** chief command; **summa rerum** supreme power, the most vital issues *or* interests; **2.** pre-eminence, first place, first rank.

sum-mānō 1 to trickle over, wet.

summārium, ī *n* epitome of chief points, summary.

summās, ātis *m* and *f* of high birth, noble.

summātim *adv.* generally, summarily.

summātus, ūs *m* supremacy.

summē *adv.* exceedingly, very much.

sum-mergō 3 to dip *or* plunge under water, overwhelm, drown, submerge.

sumministrātor, ōris *m* supplier, abettor.

sum-ministrō 1 to furnish, supply (*alci alqd*).

summissim softly.

sum-missiō, ōnis *f* a) a letting down, lowering; lessening, diminishing; **b**) depression.

sum-missus 3 lowered; **a**) low, soft, gentle, calm, composed; **b**) mean, abject, crouching; humble, submissive.

sum-mittō 3 **1.** to let *or* put down, to lower, sink, drop; a) to relax, moderate, lessen, abate; b) to place under, submit, bring down, humble; **2.** to send privately, dispatch secretly (*alci alqd*), to send as aid *or* reinforcement, to send as a substitute; **3.** to let grow long; to rear, put forth, produce.

sum-moneō 2 to remind secretly.

sum-moveō 2 to move up *or* away, remove out of the way (*alqm a re*); **a**) to clear away, dislodge; **b**) to banish; **c**) to keep away from, withdraw, withhold, force from, induce to abandon (*alqm re, a re*).
summula, ae *f* trifling sum.
summus 3, *superl. of* **superus.**
sum-mūtō 1 to exchange, substitute.
sūmō, mpsī, mptum 3 to take, take up *or* in hand (*alqd ab alqo*); **a**) to take for use, put on; to wear, eat, consume, (**supplicium de alqo** to exact punishment); **b**) to take for granted, suppose, assert, affirm, maintain, cite, mention, adduce; **c**) to take, assume, choose, select, purchase, hire; **d**) to undertake, begin, enter upon; **e**) to claim, arrogate, appropriate; **f**) to wear out, harass.
sūmptiō, ōnis *f* premise of a syllogism.
sūmptuārius 3 pertaining to expense.
sūmptuōsus 3 **a**) expensive, costly; **b**) extravagant, prodigal.
sūmptus, ūs *m* charge, expense, cost; extravagance.
suō, suī, sūtum 3 to sew, stitch, to fasten together; *subst.* **sūtum, ī** *n* joint.
su-ove-taurīlia, ium *n/pl.* sacrifice of a pig, a sheep and a bull.
supellex, ectilis *f* household goods, movables, chattels, furniture.
super 1. *adv.* over; a) above, on the top, from above; b) besides, moreover; c) over and above; **2.** *prep.* a) *with abl.* over, above; (*of time*) during; about, concerning; b) *with acc.* over, above; beyond; during; more than (*super modum, super decem milia, super omnia* above all).
superā = **suprā.**
superābilis, e that may be surmounted *or* overcome.
super-addō 3 to add over and above.
superāns, antis prevailing, in the ascendant.
superātor, ōris *m* conqueror.
superbia, ae *f* pride, haughtiness, insolence, lofty spirit, noble pride.
superbi-ficus 3 acting proudly.
superbi-loquentia, ae *f* arrogant speech.
superbiō, —, — 4 to be proud, haughty; to boast (*abl.*); to look magnificent.
superbus 3 **a**) haughty, proud, arrogant, tyrannical; **b**) fastidious, nice; **c**) excellent, distinguished, splendid, magnificent.
superciliōsus 3 disdainful, censorious.
super-cilium, ī *n* eyebrow; **a**) severity, sternness, austerity; **b**) pride, haughtiness; **c**) ridge, summit of a hill.
super-currō 3 to exceed (in value).
super-ēmineō 2 to overtop, surmount.
super-ēvolō 1 to fly away over.
superficiārius 3 one who builds on another man's land.
super-ficiēs, ēī *f* surface; building with its ground.
super-fīō 3 to be left over, remain.
super-fīxus 3 fixed on the top.
super-fluō, —, — 3 to run over, overflow, to be in superfluity.
superfluus 3 **a**) overflowing; **b**) superfluous.
super-fugiō 3 to flee over.
super-fulgeō 2 to shine forth over.
super-fundō 3 **a**) to pour upon *or* over; **se superfundere** *and* **P.** to overflow, spread itself; **b**) to cover.
super-gredior, gressus sum 3 to go over, overstep; to surpass.
super-iaciō, iēcī, iectum (**iactum**) 3 **a**) to cast *or* throw over *or* upon; **b**) to surmount; to exceed, outdo (*acc.*).
super-immineō 2 to hang over.
super-impendeō 2 to overhang.
super-impōnō 3 to place *or* put upon.
super-incendō 3 to inflame still more.
super-incidō 3 to fall upon from above.
super-incubō 1 to lie upon.
super-incumbō, cubuī, — 3 to lay oneself down upon.
super-induō 3 to put on over.
super-ingerō 3 to pile on top.
super-īniciō 3 to throw *or* cast over.
super-īnsternō 3 to spread over.
super-īnstrepō 3 to sound over.
super-iūmentārius, ī *m* inspector of the drivers of beasts of burden.
super-lābor 3 to glide over.
super-lātiō, ōnis *f* exaggeration.

super-lātus 3 exaggerated, hyperbolical.
superne *adv.* **a**) from above; **b**) above.
supernus lying above, on high, upper; celestial.
superō 1 **1.** to be above, to project; a) to be superior, prevail, to have the upper hand, be conqueror, surpass; b) to abound, be in abundance; c) to remain, be left, be still alive, survive; **2.** *trans.* to surmount, pass over, mount, ascend; a) to overtop, surpass, excel, exceed; b) to sail past, go by; c) to conquer, overcome, vanquish, subdue.
super-obruō 3 to cover over, overwhelm.
super-occupō 1 to take by surprise.
super-pendeō 2 to overhang.
super-pōnō 3 to lay, place, put over *or* upon.
super-scandō 3 to climb over.
super-scrībō 3 to write over.
super-sedeō 2 **a**) to sit on; **b**) to forbear, desist, leave off, refrain (*abl.; inf.*).
super-stāgnō 1 to overflow.
super-sternō 3 to strew *or* spread over.
super-stes, stitis a) standing by (of a witness actually present); **b**) surviving, outliving, remaining.
super-stitiō, ōnis *f* superstition, superstitious rite; excessive religious awe; object of dread.
superstitiōsus 3 **a**) superstitious; anxious; **b**) prophetic.
superstitō 1 to be over and above; to preserve.
super-stō, —, — 1 to stand over *or* upon.
super-struō 3 to build upon *or* over.
super-sum, -fuī, -esse to remain, be left; **a**) to exist still; **b**) to survive, outlive; **c**) to be over and above, abound, be superfluous, be equal to (*dat.*); **d**) to protrude.
super-tegō 3 to cover over.
super-urgeō 2 to press from above.
superus 3 what is above, upper, higher; **a**) **superī, ōrum** *m/pl.* the celestial gods, men upon earth; **b**) **supera, ōrum** *n/pl.* the upper world; *comp.* **superior, us a**) higher, upper; **b**) past, gone by, former, last, first, older; **c**) superior, nobler, more important, conqueror; — *superl.* **suprēmus** 3 **a**) highest, uppermost, supreme; **b**) extreme, last; **suprēmus dies** the day of death; *subst.* **suprēma, ōrum** *n/pl.* death, funeral rites, last will; — *superl.* **summus** 3 highest, topmost, highest part, top of, surface of; **summum, ī** *n* top, surface (also as *adv.* at the utmost, at most); **a**) extreme, last; **summa aestas** midsummer, height of summer; **b**) greatest, most important, most excellent *or* distinguished, most valuable, best, chief; **summa res** the chief thing *or* point; **summum ius** strictest right, rigour of the law; **summa res** crisis, decisive point; **summo tempore** at a critical juncture, in an emergency; **summo opere** with all one's might (*adv.* **summē** in the highest degree, extremely); **c**) most perfect, whole, complete, entire; **summa res publica** the general welfare, the general cause.
super-vacāneus 3 over and above, superfluous, needless, useless, unnecessary.
super-vacuus 3 = **supervacāneus.**
super-vādō 3 to climb *or* pass over.
super-vehor 3 to ride, sail, pass beyond.
super-veniō 4 to follow up, overtake; **a**) to appear unexpectedly, come on by surprise, come on the scene; **b**) to be added; **c**) to surpass.
super-ventus, ūs *m* a coming up, arrival.
super-vīvō 3 to survive.
super-volitō 1 to fly over.
super-volō 1 to fly over.
supīnō 1 to turn up *or* over.
supīnus 3 **a**) lying on the back, face upwards; indolent; **b**) sloping *or* flowing up; **c**) (of verses) readable backwards.
sup-paenitet 2 it causes a little regret.
sup-palpor 1 to stroke a little, to flatter.
sup-pār, paris almost equal *or* contemporary.
sup-parasītor 1 to flatter a little like a parasite.
supparum, ī *n* **a**) woman's garment of linen; **b**) small sail.
suppeditātiō, ōnis *f* abundance.

sup-peditō 1 **a**) to furnish, afford, supply, procure (*alci alqd*); **b**) *intr.* to be available, be at hand, abound, be sufficient, suffice (*alci*).
sup-pēdō 3 to break wind a little.
sup-pernātus 3 hewn down.
suppetiae, ārum *f/pl.* aid, assistance.
suppetior 1 to aid, help, succour (*alci*).
sup-petō 3 *intr.* = **suppedito b**).
sup-pīlō 1 to steal; to rob.
sup-pingō 3 to fasten beneath.
sup-plantō 1 to trip up.
sup-plaudō 3 = **supplodo.**
sup-plēmentum, ī *n* a filling up; **a**) supply, supplement; **b**) recruiting, reinforcement.
sup-pleō, ēvī, ētum 2 to fill up, supply, complete, make full, repair, recruit.
sup-plex, icis bending the knee, kneeling; **a**) supplicating, suppliant. entreating (*alci; ut*); **b**) humble, submissive; *subst. m* humble petitioner.
sup-plicātiō, ōnis *f* public thanksgiving.
supplicium, ī *n* a kneeling down; **a**) humble entreaty, petition, supplication, prayer; **b**) = **supplicatio; c**) (capital) punishment, execution; penalty, torture, pain, distress.
sup-plicō 1 to kneel down to, pray *or* beseech humbly (*alci*); to pray, worship (*diis*).
sup-plōdō, sī, sum 3 to stamp (*pedem*).
supplōsiō, ōnis *f* a stamping.
sup-pōnō 3 to put, place *or* lay under (*alqd alci rei*); **a**) to make subject, submit; **b**) to put under something, annex, subjoin (*alci rei alqd*); **c**) to substitute (*alqd in locum, pro alqo*), forge.
sup-portō 1 to carry, bring up, convey.
suppositīcius 3 substituted, spurious.
sup-positiō, ōnis *f* substitution of a child.
sup-postrīx, īcis *f* she who substitutes.
sup-pressiō, ōnis *f* a keeping back, embezzlement.
sup-primō, pressī, pressum 3 to press down, press under; **a**) to hold back, check, restrain; to stop, sink (*a ship*); **b**) to suppress, conceal, hide, keep secret; to embezzle; — **suppressus** 3 subdued, low.
sup-prōmus, ī *m* under-butler.
sup-pudet 2 **me** I am somewhat ashamed (*alcis rei*).
suppūrātiō, ōnis *f* suppuration, abscess.
sup-pūrō 1 to suppurate, fester (*lit.* or *metaph.*).
suppus 3 upside down.
sup-putō 1 to count up, reckon, calculate.
suprā 1. *adv.* above, on the upper side, over, on the top; a) before, previously; b) more, further, beyond; **2.** *prep.* with *acc.* above, over; a) beyond; b) before; c) more than, above.
suprālātiō, suprālātus, *see* **superlatio, superlatus.**
suprā-scandō 3 to climb over.
suprēmus 3, *superl. of* **superus.**
supter, suptus = **subter, -tus.**
sūra, ae *f* calf of the leg.
surculus, ī *m* shoot, sprout, spring, sucker.
surdaster, tra, trum somewhat deaf.
surditās, ātis *f* deafness.
surdus 3 deaf (*ad alqd*); **a**) unheeding, regardless; **b**) not understanding (*in re*); **c**) silent, noiseless; **d**) faint, weak.
surgō, surrēxī, surrēctum 3 **a**) to rise, arise, get up; **b**) to grow up, appear, rise, spring up; **c**) to mount up, ascend; to increase.
surpiculus = **scirpiculus.**
surpite, surpuit, = **surripite, surripuit.**
sur-rēpō 3, *see* **subrepo.**
sur-repticius = **sur-rupticius.**
surrēxe, surrigō = **surrexisse, subrigo.**
sur-ripiō, ripuī, reptum 3 to snatch *or* take away secretly, to steal, filch, pilfer (*alqd alci* or *ab alqo*); **se surripere** to steal away, withdraw privily.
sur-rogō 1 to cause to be chosen as substitute.
sur-rupticius 3 stolen.
sūrsum (*and* **sūrsus**) *adv.* **a**) upwards; **b**) above, on high.
sūs[1]**, suis** *f* and *m* **a**) sow, swine, pig, hog; **b**) a fish.

sus[2] *adv.*, *see* **susque.**
sus-cēnseō, uī, — 2 to be angry, enraged (*alci; quod, acc. c. inf.*).
susceptiō, ōnis *f* an undertaking.
sus-cipiō, cēpī, ceptum 3 **1.** to catch (something as it falls), to support; a) to take up a new-born child, acknowledge; b) to have *or* beget a child from one (*ex alqa*); **2.** to take, accept, receive; a) to undertake, begin, take up (*alqd*); to submit to; b) to assume; c) to enter upon; d) to answer, take up a discourse.
sus-citō 1 to raise *or* stir up, raise on high, lift up; **a**) to cause to stand up, awake, excite, incite; **b**) to rekindle; **c**) to cause.
su-spectō 1 **a**) to look up at (*alqd*); **b**) to suspect, mistrust.
su-spectus[1], **ūs** *m* a looking up *or* upwards; height; admiration, esteem, respect.
su-spectus[2] 3 suspected, causing suspicion, mistrust *or* fear.
sus-pendium, ī *n* a hanging, hanging oneself.
sus-pendō, ndī, ēnsum 3 to hang up, hang (*alqd re, ex, de* or *a re*); **a**) to raise, lift up, to prop up; **b**) to keep in suspense, make doubtful *or* uncertain, leave undecided.
sus-pēnsūra, ae *f* vault; floor supported on pillars.
sus-pēnsus 3 suspended, hanging; poised, touching lightly, light; **a**) resting *or* depending upon (*ex re*); **b**) uncertain, doubtful, wavering, floating; **c**) fearful, anxious, timid.
suspicāx, ācis distrustful.
su-spiciō[1], **exī, ectum** 3 to look up (at, *acc.*); **a**) to look up to; **b**) to esteem, honour, admire; **c**) to suspect (v. rare; see *suspectus*).
su-spīciō[2], **ōnis** *f* **a**) suspicion, mistrust; **in suspīciōne esse alci** to be suspected by; **alqm in suspīciōnem adducere** to make one suspected; **b**) opinion, notion, conception, idea.
suspīciōsus 3 **a**) full of suspicion, mistrustful; **b**) causing suspicion, suspected.
suspicor (*and* **-ō**) 1 to suspect, conjecture, suppose (*alqd; acc. c. inf.*).
suspīrātus, ūs *m* a sighing, deep breath.
su-spīritus, ūs *m* deep breath, sigh, groan.
suspīrium, ī *n* **a**) deep breath, sigh; **b**) shortness of breath, panting; **c**) breath, respiration.
su-spīrō 1 to breathe deeply, heave a sigh, to long for (*alqd*); to exhale.
susque dēque *adv.* (up and down); of no importance; ~ **habeō** I don't care.
sustentāculum, ī *n* prop, stay.
sustentātiō, ōnis *f* a deferring, delay.
sus-tentō 1 to hold up, keep upright, sustain; **a**) to maintain, preserve, sustain with food; **b**) to hold out, bear, suffer, endure; **c**) to hold up, resist, check, put off, delay.
sus-tineō, nuī, — 2 to hold up, keep up, support, sustain; **a**) to bear, endure; to withstand, hold out against; to tolerate; **b**) to undertake, be equal to; **c**) to maintain, feed, nourish, sustain; **d**) to hold back, check, restrain, defer, delay, prolong.
sus-tollō, —, — 3 to raise *or* lift up; to take away, carry off.
sūsum = **sūrsum.**
susurrātor, ōris *m* whisperer.
susurrō 1 to whisper, murmur.
susurrus[1], **ī** *m* a whispering, murmuring, humming.
susurrus[2] 3 whispering.
sūtēla, ae *f* cunning trick.
sūtilis, e sewed together, fastened together.
sūtor, ōris *m* shoemaker.
sūtōrius 3 of a shoemaker.
sūtrīnus 3 = **sutorius**; *subst.* **sūtrīnum, ī** *n* shoemaking.
sūtūra, ae *f* a sewing, seam.
suus 3 *poss. adj.* his, her, its, their (own); *subst.* **a**) **suī, ōrum** *m/pl.* one's own troops, friends, dependents, countrymen; **b**) **suum, ī** *n* one's own property; proper, peculiar, suitable; appointed; favourable, propitious; independent, one's own master, free.
sȳcophanta, ae *m* false accuser, slanderer; cheat; flatterer, sycophant.
sȳcophantia, ae *f* cheating, deceit.
sȳcophantiōsē deceitfully.
sȳcophantor 1 to trick, deceive.
syllaba, ae *f* syllable; *pl.* verses.
syllabātim *adv.* syllable by syllable.
syllogismus, ī *m* syllogism.

sym-bola, ae *f* contribution, share of the cost of a meal; *pl.* 'feast' (*i.e.* a beating).
symbolus, ī *m and* **-um, ī** *n* token, sign.
sym-phōnia, ae *f* concerted music (vocal *or* instrumental).
symphōniacus 3 musical.
symplegma, atis *n* embrace.
syn-edrus, ī *m* councillor.
syn-grapha, ae *f* written agreement to pay, bond.
syn-graphus, ī *m* **a**) contract; **b**) passport.
syn-odūs, ontis *m* a sea-fish.
synthesina, ae *f* dressing-gown.
synthesis, is *f* **a**) dinner-service; **b**) suit of clothes; **c**) dressing-gown, house-coat.
syrma, atis *n* (tragic actor's) robe with a train; tragedy.
syrtis, is *and* **idos** *f* sandbank in the sea; *esp.* two dangerous shoals off the coast of North Africa.

T

T. = **Titus; Ti.** = **Tiberius.**

tabella, ae *f* small board, panel; **a**) gaming-board; **b**) little painting; **c**) fan; **d**) writing-tablet; letter; document, contract, deed, record; **e**) votive tablet; **f**) voting-tablet.

tabellārius 3 relating to voting; mail-carrying; *subst.* ~, **ī** *m* letter-carrier.

tābeō, —, — 2 **a**) to melt, waste away, fall away, be consumed; **b**) to drip.

taberna, ae *f* hut, shed; **a**) tavern, shop, stall, workshop; **b**) arcade (?) in the circus.

tabernāc(u)lum, ī *n* tent; place for observing the auspices.

tabernārius, ī *m* shopkeeper.

tabernula, ae *f* little shop *or* tavern.

tābēs, is *f* a melting away, putrefaction, decay; **a**) moisture of decay *or* melting; noxious fluid; **b**) wasting disease, pestilence, plague; **c**) decline.

tābēscō, buī, — 3 **a**) to melt gradually, waste away, be dissolved, decay; **b**) to pine away.

tābidulus 3 consuming.

tābidus 3 melting, wasting, decaying; corrupting, destructive.

tābi-ficus 3 dissolving, consuming.

tabula, ae *f* board, plank; **a**) gaming-board; **b**) picture, painting; **c**) writing-tablet; table of the law; **d**) auction; **e**) writing, document, record, note; register, list; contract; will; account-book.

tabulārium, ī *n* archives.

tabulārius, ī *m* revenue official.

tabulātiō, ōnis *f* a flooring, story.

tabulātus 3 boarded, floored; *subst.* **-um, ī** *n* a flooring, floor, story.

tābum, ī *n* **a**) corrupt moisture, matter, putrid gore; **b**) plague, pestilence.

taceō, uī, itum 2 **a**) to be silent, still; **b**) to pass over in silence (*alqd*).

taciturnitās, ātis *f* silence, taciturnity.

taciturnus 3 silent, taciturn; still, quiet.

tacitus 3 **a**) silent, not speaking, quiet; mute, noiseless; **b**) kept secret, passed over in silence, unmentioned; **c**) secret, concealed, hidden, silently assumed.

tāctilis, e tangible.

tāctiō, ōnis *f* a touching; sense of touch.

tāctus, ūs *m* **a**) a touching, touch; operation, influence; **b**) sense of touch, feeling.

taeda, ae *f* pine-tree; **a**) chip *or* plank of pine-wood; **b**) torch; nuptial torch; wedding.

taedet, uit *or* **taesum est** 2 to cause weariness *or* disgust; **taedet me** I am disgusted, weary (*alqm alcis rei; inf.*).

taedi-fer 3 torch-bearing.

taedium, ī *n* disgust, loathing, weariness.

taenia, ae *f* band, fillet, ribbon.

taeter, tra, trum nasty, foul, hideous, shocking, abominable.

tagāx, ācis thievish.

tālāris, e reaching *or* belonging to the ankles; *subst.* **tālāria, ium** *n/pl.* ankles; winged sandals *or* shoes; long garment reaching to the ankles; an instrument of torture.

tālārius 3 relating to dice.

tālea, ae *f* stake, bar.

talentum, ī *n* talent (*as a weight* = ½ cwt, *and as a sum money* = some hundreds of pounds).

tāliō, ōnis *f* punishment in kind ('an eye for an eye').

tālis, e such, of such a kind; **a**) of such a distinguished, remarkable kind; **b**) so bad *or* blamable; **c**) the following.

tālitrum, ī *n* rap with the knuckles.

talpa, ae *f* (*m*) mole.

tālus, ī *m* **a**) ankle, ankle-bone; heel; **b**) kind of dice.

tam *adv.* so, so very, to such a degree; **quam ... tam** as ... so; **tam ... quam** as much ... as, as well ... as; **non tam ... quam** not so much ... as.

tamarīx, īcis *f* tamarisk.

tam-diū *adv.* so long.
tamen *adv.* nevertheless, notwithstanding; yet at least, still.
tamendem (?) = **tamen.**
tamen-etsī *cj.* = **tametsi.**
tam-etsī *cj.* though, although.
tam-quam *adv.* as, just as; *cj.* with *subj.* as if, as though (= *tamquam si*); to the effect that, on the ground that.
tandem *adv.* at last, finally; *in interrogations:* pray, then, now.
tangō, tetigī, tāctum 3 to touch; **a**) to come to, arrive at, reach, enter; **b**) to border on, be connected with; **c**) to taste, eat, drink; **d**) to besprinkle, moisten, dye; **e**) to strike, hit; **f**) to move, touch, affect, impress; **g**) to touch upon, mention; **h**) to catch, cheat.
tan-quam = **tamquam.**
tantillus 3 = **tantulus.**
tantīs-per *adv.* just so long.
tant-opere *adv.* so much, so earnestly, to such a degree.
tantulus 3 so little, so small; *subst.* **-um, ī** *n* such a trifle.
tantus 3 so great, so much, so important; **a**) (*rarely*) so small, so slight; **b**) (*rarely*) *pl.* **tantī** so many; **c**) *subst.* **tantum, ī** *n* so much, such a quantity *or* number, so high a degree; **alterum tantum** as much again, twice as much; so little, such a trifle; **tantī** (*gen. of value*) of such value, worth so much, for so much; **tanti est** it is worth while; **tanto** by so much, so much the; **quanto ... tanto** the ... the; **d**) *adv.* **tantum** so much, so greatly, so far; only so much, so little; only, merely; **non tantum ... sed etiam** not only ... but also; **tantummodo** only, merely; **tantum non** nearly, almost; **tantum quod** only, only just, hardly.
tantus-dem 3 just so great *or* large; *subst.* **tantundem** *n* just as much; *adv.* just as far.
(**tapēs**), **ētis** *m and* **tap**(**p**)**ēte, is** *n* (*abl. pl. also* **tapētīs**) carpet, coverlet, tapestry.
tardēscō 3 to grow sluggish.
tardi-gradus 3 slowly stepping.
tardi-loquus 3 slow-speaking.
tardi-pēs, edis slow-footed.
tarditās, ātis *f* slowness, tardiness; dulness, stupidity.
tarditūdō, inis *f* slowness.
tardiusculus 3 rather slow.
tardō 1 **a**) to retard, stop, hinder; **b**) *intr.* to delay.
tardus 3 slow, tardy, sluggish; **a**) long, lasting; **b**) slow of approach, late; **c**) making slow; **d**) dull, heavy, stupid.
tarmes, itis *m* wood-worm.
tarpezīta, ae *m* money-changer, banker.
tata, ae *m* daddy.
tat(**ae**) *excl.*
taureus 3 of a bull *or* bull's hide; *subst.* **-ea, ae** *f* a whip of hide.
tauri-fer 3 producing bulls.
tauri-fōrmis, e bull-shaped.
taurīnus 3 of bulls *or* oxen.
taurus, ī *m* bull, ox.
taxātiō, ōnis *f* estimation.
taxeus 3 of yew-trees.
taxillus, ī *m* small dice.
taxō 1 **a**) to reproach; **b**) to appraise, estimate.
taxus, ī *f* yew-tree; javelin of yew-wood.
tech(**i**)**na, ae** *f* trick, artifice.
tēctor, ōris *m* plasterer.
tēctōriolum, ī *n* little plaster *or* stucco-work.
tēctōrium, ī *n* plaster, stucco, fresco-painting; paste for use on the face; hypocritical speech.
tēctōrius 3 for covering a roof.
tēctum, ī *n* roof; **a**) ceiling of a room; **b**) room, dwelling, house, temple, den, grotto.
tēctus 3 covered; **a**) roofed, decked; **b**) concealed, secret; **c**) close, reserved, cautious.
teges, etis *f* mat.
tegetīcula, ae *f* small mat.
tegillum, ī *n* little cover, hood.
tegimen, inis *n* cover; protection.
tegimentum, tegmentum, ī *n* cover, covering; protection.
tegmen, inis *n* = **tegimen.**
tegō, tēxī, tēctum 3 to cover (*alqd re*); **a**) to hide, conceal; to keep secret, cloak, dissemble; **b**) to protect, defend.
tēgula, ae *f* tile; tiled roof.
tegumen, tegumentum = **tegimen**(**tum**).
tegus, oris *n* = **tergus.**
tēla, ae *f* web; **a**) warp; **b**) loom; **c**) design, plan.
tēlinum, ī *n* a costly perfume

tellūs, ūris *f* the earth, globe; **a**) soil, ground; land, country, district, territory; **b**) estate; **c**) goddess of the Earth.
tēlum, ī *n* missile weapon; spear, javelin; weapon; sword, dagger; shaft of light.
temerārius 3 **a**) accidental; **b**) rash, inconsiderate, thoughtless, foolhardy.
temerātor, ōris *m* seducer, ravisher.
temere *adv.* by chance, accidentally, casually, without purpose; **a**) without reason, inconsiderately, rashly; **b**) **non temere** not easily, hardly.
temeritās, ātis *f* **a**) chance, accident; **b**) rashness, haste, thoughtlessness, indiscretion, foolhardiness.
temerō 1 to violate, defile, dishonour, disgrace.
tēmētum, ī *n* wine, intoxicating drink.
temnō, —, — 3 to contemn, despise (= **contemno**).
tēmō, ōnis *m* pole *or* beam of a wagon; wagon; *the constellation* Charles's Wain.
temperāmentum, ī *n* right proportion, measure, moderation; middle way.
temperāns, tis moderate, continent, sober, temperate.
temperantia, ae *f* moderation, temperance, continence.
temperātiō, ōnis *f* due admixture, just proportion, composition; proper regulation, order.
temperātor, ōris *m* one who regulates *or* moderates; tempering (metal).
temperātūra, ae *f* proper balance; temperature; constitution (*of the body*).
temperātus 3 **a**) properly arranged *or* prepared; **b**) moderate, temperate, mild, quiet, calm.
temperī *adv.* in due time.
temperiēs, ēī *f* = **temperatio;** moderate temperature.
temperō 1 **a**) to mingle in due proportion, to observe proper limits *or* measure; **b**) to compound properly (*vinum*); to arrange, order, regulate, govern, manage; **c**) to use with moderation, act temperately, to soften, qualify, temper; **d**) to keep back, restrain (*sibi, irae*); **e**) to be moderate, restrain oneself, forbear, abstain, spare.
tempestās, ātis *f* weather; **a**) bad weather, storm, tempest; **b**) storm, attack, fury; calamity, misfortune, danger; **c**) space *or* period of time, season.
tempestīvitās, ātis *f* fit time, seasonableness.
tempestīvus 3 happening *or* done at the proper time; **a**) seasonable, opportune, appropriate, timely, fitting, ripe; **b**) early.
templum, ī *n* space cut off, sacred space; **a**) space in the sky *or* on the earth marked out by the augur for observing the birds; open space; **b**) sanctuary, temple, chapel, shrine.
temporārius 3 proper for the time; temporary, changeable.
temporī *adv.* = **temperi.**
temptābundus 3 attempting.
temptāmen, inis *and* **temptāmentum, ī** *n* = **temptatio a**).
temptātiō, ōnis *f* **a**) trial, essay, proof; **b**) attack (*of disease*).
temptātor, ōris *m* tempter, assailant.
temptō 1 to touch, handle, feel; **a**) to attack, assail; **b**) to try, prove, test; to try, attempt, essay; **c**) to tempt, incite, disturb, sound, tamper with, work upon; **d**) to intend, purpose, undertake.
tempus[1], oris *n* time, division of time, section of time, period of time, space of time, distinct point of time; **anni tempus** season; **ex tempore** without preparation; **a**) right, proper, fit time, right occasion, opportunity; **tempus est** it is high time, it is the right time; **tempore** at the proper time; **b**) circumstances of time, the times, state *or* condition of things; **ex tempore** according to circumstances; dangerous *or* unfortunate circumstances, crisis, misfortune, calamity; emergency, extremity; **c**) time of life, years; **d**) measure (*of syllables*), quantity.
tempus[2], oris *n*, *mostly pl.*, temple on the forehead; head.
tēmulentus 3 drunken, intoxicated.
tenācitās, ātis *f* a holding fast, tenacity; avarice, niggardliness.

tenāx, ācis holding fast, gripping; **a**) tenacious, fast, firm, tough, sticky; **b**) constant, steadfast, persevering, persisting (*with gen.*); obstinate; **c**) stingy, niggardly, sordid.

tendicula, ae *f* **a**) snare, trap; **b**) clothes-stretcher.

tendō, tetendī, tentum (*and* **tēnsum**) 3 **1.** to stretch, stretch out, make tense (*alqd*); a) to distend, extend, **manūs alci** *or* **ad alqd;** to pitch (*a tent*); b) to hold out, offer, present, reach, extend (*alci alqd*); **insidias** to lay snares; c) to direct, turn; **2.** *intr.* a) to be encamped, be in tents, to encamp; b) to travel, run, sail, hold a course, direct oneself, move, march (*in* or *ad alqd*); c) to aim at, attack; d) to extend, stretch, reach to; e) to be inclined to, to tend; f) to strive, endeavour, struggle, contend, fight; to resist, withstand (*contra* or *adversus*).

tenebrae, ārum *f/pl.* darkness; **a**) night; blindness, swoon, darkness of death; dark place, lurking place, haunts; **b**) obscurity, low station *or* condition.

tenebricōsus 3 full of darkness, dark, gloomy, obscure.

tenebricus *and* **tenebrōsus** 3 dark, gloomy, obscure.

tenellulus 3 (*and* **tenellus** 3) very tender *or* delicate.

teneō, tenuī, (tentum) 2 to hold, keep, grasp, hold fast. **1.** to have in the hand, mouth etc., keep, seize, comprehend; a) to hold in mind, understand, conceive, comprehend, know; b) to hold one's way *or* course; to follow up, sail, steer, reach a place, land on, arrive at; c) to gain, acquire, obtain, attain; d) to convict, catch, detect; **2.** to hold in one's possession, have, possess, be master of; a) to inhabit, occupy, garrison; b) to comprise, comprehend; to include; c) to possess, master; to hold fast, keep in, hold back, bind, fetter, control; d) to preserve, maintain, retain, guard; to remember; **3.** a) to keep to, not to swerve from, remain true to; b) to last, endure, keep on; c) to charm, amuse, inspire; d) to bind, oblige; to maintain one's right; **4.** a) to hold back, repress, check, restrain, suppress; b) to detain, delay; c) to keep a thing away from (*alqd ab alqo*).

tener, era, erum soft, delicate, tender, smooth; **a**) young, youthful; **b**) tender, effeminate, sensitive; voluptuous; **c**) amorous; yielding.

tenerāscō 3 to grow soft.

teneritās, ātis *f* softness, tenderness.

teneritūdō, inis *f* = **teneritas.**

tēnesmos, ī *m* constipation.

tennō = **tendo.**

tenor, ōris *m* uninterrupted course, continuance, a keeping on, duration, career; **uno tenōre** uninterruptedly.

tēnsa, ae *f* chariot bearing the images of the gods.

tentābundus 3, *see* **temptabundus.**

tentāmen, inis *n*, *see* **temptamen.**

tentīgō, inis *f* passion, lust.

tentō 1, *see* **tempto.**

tentōrium, ī *n* tent.

tenuiculus 3 very thin, mean, *or* poor.

tenuis, e thin; **a**) slender, fine, slight; **b**) small, narrow; **c**) shallow; **d**) fine, subtle, exact, nice, ingenious; **e**) insignificant, unimportant, trifling, weak; **f**) miserable, poor, mean, bad; **g**) plain, simple, without ornament.

tenuitās, ātis *f* thinness, fineness; **a**) slenderness, leanness; **b**) poverty, indigence; **c**) simplicity, plainness.

tenuō 1 to make thin, fine, weak; to lessen, diminish, enfeeble.

tenus[1]**, oris** *n* snare.

tenus[2] *prep.* with *abl.* and *gen.* up to, as far as, unto; **verbō tenus** in words, nominally.

tenvis, e = **tenuis.**

tepe-faciō (*and* **tepē-**) 3 to make warm *or* tepid.

tepeō, uī, — 2 to be warm, tepid; to be in love (*alqo* with one); to be lukewarm (in love).

tepēscō, puī, — 3 **a**) to grow warm *or* tepid; **b**) to cool off.

tepidus 3 **a**) tepid, warm; **b**) cooling, cool; **c**) faint, languid.

tepor, ōris *m* **a**) lukewarmness, moderate heat; **b**) want of fire, languor.

ter *adv.* thrice, three times.

ter-deciē(n)s *adv.* thirteen times.

terebinthus, ī *f* turpentine-tree.

terebrō 1 to bore, pierce, perforate; to scrape out; to worm one's way in.
terēdō, inis *f* wood-worm.
teres, etis rounded off, polished; smooth; **a**) well-turned; **b**) finely shaped, graceful, refined, elegant.
ter-geminus 3, *see* **trigeminus.**
tergeō, sī, sum 2 to wipe off, dry, *or* clean; to tickle; to scrape, grate on; to polish.
tergīnum, ī *n* whip, leather scourge.
tergiversātiō, ōnis *f* evasion, subterfuge.
tergiversor 1 to make excuses, to practise evasion.
tergō 3 = **tergeo.**
tergum, ī *n* back, rear; **a**) ridge; **b**) surface; **c**) hide, leather; shield, bag, *or* other thing made of leather.
tergus, oris *n* = **tergum.**
termentum, ī *n* hurt, injury (?).
termes, itis *m* cut branch.
Terminālia, ium *and* **iōrum** *n/pl.* festival of the god Terminus.
terminātiō, ōnis *f* a fixing of limits; ending, clausula; sense of rhythm.
terminō 1 to bound, limit; **a**) to circumscribe, confine; **b**) to determine, define (*alqd re*); **c**) to end, terminate.
terminus, ī *m* boundary-mark, boundary-stone; **a**) boundary, limit; **b**) the god of boundaries; **c**) limit, end, term.
ternī 3 three each; threefold, triple.
terō, trīvī, trītum 3 to rub; **a**) to rub off; to polish, burnish, to turn at a lathe; **b**) to rub away, wear away; **c**) to thrash out, to grind, pound; **d**) to consume, waste, wear out, overdo with labour; **e**) to use often, tread often, frequent; **f**) to spend, pass (*tempus*).
terra, ae *f* the earth; **a**) land; **terrā marīque** by land and sea; ground, soil; **b**) land, country, region, district; *pl.* the world; **orbis terrārum** the earth, the world.
terrāneola, ae *f* crested lark.
terrēnus 3 **a**) of earth, earthen, earthy; *subst.* **terrēnum, ī** *n* earth, soil, ground; **b**) of the earth, terrestrial.
terreō, uī, itum 2 to frighten, terrify, alarm (*alqm; ne*) **a**) to chase with terror, frighten *or* scare away; **b**) to deter (*alqm a re; quominus*).
terrestris, e belonging to the earth, terrestrial, earthly, of the land.
terreus 3 of the earth.
terrebilis, e terrible, frightful, dreadful.
terriculum, ī *n* something that causes fright, bugbear, phantom.
terri-ficō 1 = **terreo.**
terri-ficus 3 = **terribilis.**
terri-gena, ae *m and f* earthborn.
terri-loquus 3 terror-speaking.
territō 1 to frighten, terrify, alarm greatly.
territōrium, ī *n* territory, district.
terror, ōris *m* terror, fright, fear, dread; object of fear, cause of alarm.
terruncius, ī *m* = **teruncius.**
tersus 3 wiped; clean, neat; elegant.
tertia-decumānī, ōrum *m/pl.* soldiers of the thirteenth legion.
tertiānus 3 recurring every other day; *subst.* ~, **ī** *m* soldier of the third legion.
tertius 3 the third; *adv.* **tertiō** *and* **-um** for the third time, thirdly.
tertius-decimus 3 the thirteenth.
ter-uncius, ī *m* (three ounces) a quarter of an *as* (= $^1/_{40}$ of a *dēnārius*); **hērēs ex teruncīō** heir to $^1/_{40}$ of an estate; **nullus** ~ not a farthing.
ter-venēficus, ī *m* arch-poisoner, arch-villain.
tesqua (*or* **tesca**), **ōrum** *n/pl.* deserts, wastes.
tessella, ae *f* small stone cube.
tessellātus 3 set with small square stones, tessellated.
tessera, ae *f* **a**) cube of stone *or* wood, dice; **b**) tablet containing watchword *or* orders; **c**) token, tally (for identification).
tesserārius, ī *m* officer who carried the watchword from the general through the camp.
tesserula, ae *f* = **tessera.**
testa, ae *f* **a**) tile, brick; **b**) earthen vessel, pot, urn, lamp; **c**) potsherd; **d**) shell of shell-fish, shell-fish; **e**) covering.
testāceus 3 of tiles *or* brick.
testāmentārius 3 belonging to a testament *or* will; *subst.* ~, **ī** *m* forger of a will.
testāmentum, ī *n* testament, last will.
testātiō, ōnis *f* a calling to witness.

testātor, ōris *m* testator.
testātus 3 attested; notorious, manifest, evident.
testiculus, ī *m* testicle, virility.
testificātiō, ōnis *f* a bearing witness; proof, evidence.
testi-ficor 1 **a**) to call to witness; **b**) to bear witness, testify, attest; **c**) to show, prove, demonstrate, declare.
testimōnium, ī *n* **a**) testimony, evidence; **b**) proof.
testis[1], **is** *m and f* witness; spectator.
testis[2], **is** *m* (*mostly pl.* **testēs, ium**) testicle.
testor 1 **a**) = **testificor; b**) *intr.* to make a will *or* testament.
testū (*indecl.*), **testum, ī** *n* earthenware cover *or* covered pot (for cooking).
testūdineus 3 like a tortoise; made of tortoise-shell.
testūdō, inis *f* tortoise; **a**) shell of the tortoise; **b**) arched room, arch, vault; **c**) ⚔ shed, shelter; covering of shields; **d**) stringed instrument, lyre; **e**) comb; **f**) a hedgehog's spines.
testula, ae *f* potsherd used as a voting-tablet.
tēter 3 = **taeter.**
tetrachmum, ī *n* four-drachma piece.
tetraō, ōnis *m* grouse, heath-cock.
tetrarchēs, ae *m* tetrarch.
tetrarchia, ae *f* tetrarchy.
tetrastichon, ī *n* poem of four lines.
tetricus 3 gloomy, harsh, grim, morose, severe.
texō, xuī, xtum 3 **a**) to weave, plait; **b**) to frame, construct, fabricate, make, compose.
textilis, e woven; *subst.* **textile, is** *n* web, stuff, cloth.
textor, ōris *m*, **textrīx, īcis** *f* weaver.
textōrius 3 woven; *(metaph.)* fine-spun, far-fetched.
textrīnum, ī *n* a weaver's shop; the art of weaving; ship-yard.
textum, ī *n* web, stuff, cloth; texture, construction.
textūra, ae *f* web, texture.
textus, ūs *m* web, texture; structure, connexion.
thalamēgus, ī *f* (barge) fitted with a cabin.
thalamus, ī *m* **a**) bedchamber; **b**) women's apartment, bridal bed, marriage; **c**) dwelling, habitation, abode.
thalassicus 3 of the sea.
thalassinus 3 purple (?).
thallus, ī *m* green twig.
theātrālis, e theatrical.
theātrum, ī *n* theatre, playhouse; **a**) the spectators, audience; **b**) place of exhibition, stage, sphere for any action.
thēca, ae *f* case, envelope, sheath, covering.
thema, atis *n* horoscope.
thensaurārius 3 of treasure.
thēnsaurus, ī *m* = **thesaurus.**
theo-logus, ī *m* theologian.
thermae, ārum *f/pl.* warm springs; warm baths.
thermo-pōlium (*and* **thermi-**), **ī** *n* shop where warm drinks are sold.
thermo-pōtō 1 to refresh with warm drinks.
thermulae, ārum *f/pl.* = **thermae.**
thēsaurus, ī *m* treasure, hoard, store; treasury, storehouse; repository, magazine.
thiasus, ī *m* Bacchic dance *or* troop of dancers.
tholus, ī *m* (round building with a) dome.
thōrāx, ācis *m* breastplate, cuirass.
thronus, ī *m* elevated seat, throne.
thunnus, ī *m* = **thynnus.**
thūs, ūris *n* = **tus.**
thȳias, adis *f* Bacchant.
thyius 3 (?) of citrus wood.
thȳlacistae *m/pl.* bag in hand, i.e. asking for money (?).
thymbra, ae *f* savory(*a kitchen herb*).
thymum, ī *n* thyme.
thynnus, ī *m* tunny(-fish).
thyrsi-ger 3 bearing the thyrsus.
thyrsus, ī *m* stalk, stem; staff of Bacchus twined with ivy and vine; goad, incitement.
Ti. *abbr.* = **Tiberius.**
tiāra, ae *f and* **tiārās, ae** *m* turban, tiara, diadem.
tībia, ae *f* shin-bone; flute, pipe.
tībiāle, is *n* legging.
tībī-cen, inis *m* **a**) piper, flute-player; **b**) pillar, prop.
tībīcina, ae *f* female fluteplayer.
tībīcinium, ī *n* a playing on the flute.
tigillum, ī *n* little beam of wood.

tignārius 3 relating to timber; **faber ~** carpenter.
tignum, ī *n* beam, log of timber.
tigris, idis *or* **is** *m and f* tiger, tigress; tiger skin.
tilia, ae *f* linden- *or* lime-tree.
time-facio 3 to terrify.
timeō, uī, — 2 to fear, be afraid of, dread, apprehend, be anxious (*alqd, alqm, de re; alci* for one; *with ne; ne non, ut; inf.*).
timiditās, ātis *f* fearfulness, timidity.
timidus 3 full of fear, timid, faint-hearted, cowardly.
timor, ōris *m* fear, dread, apprehension (*alcis rei*), alarm; cause *or* object of fear, terror.
tinctilis, e used for dipping.
tinea, ae *f* larva, grub, worm.
ting(u)ō, tinxī, tinctum 3 to moisten, wet, imbue (*alqd re*); **a**) to dip in, plunge; **b**) to stain, dye.
tinnīmentum, ī *n* a tinkling.
tinniō 4 to ring, tinkle, jingle.
tinnītus, ūs *m* a ringing, tinkling, jingling; jingle of words.
tinnulus 3 ringing, tinkling.
tintinnābulum, ī *n* bell.
tintinnāculus 3 tinkling, jingling.
tintinō 1 to ring, jingle.
tīnus, ī *f* laurustinus (?).
tippula, ae *f* water-spider; very light thing.
tīrō, ōnis *m* young soldier, recruit; beginner, novice, learner.
tīrōcinium, ī *n* first service of a soldier; **a**) young troops, recruits; **b**) inexperience; **c**) first trial *or* effort, first attempt.
tīrunculus, ī *m* young recruit, novice.
tis = **tui** (*gen.*).
tītillātiō, ōnis *f* a tickling.
tītillō 1 to tickle.
tittibilīcium, ī *n* trifle.
titubāns, tis wavering, faltering.
(**titubantia, ae** *f*), **titubātiō, ōnis** *f* a staggering, wavering.
titubō 1 to totter, stagger, reel; **a**) to stammer, falter; **b**) to hesitate, be perplexed; **c**) to blunder.
titulus, ī *m* inscription, superscription; **a**) title of a book; **b**) bill, placard; **c**) title of honour, rank *or* dignity; **d**) pretext, pretence.
tocullīō, ōnis *m* usurer.
tōfīnus 3 of tufa.
tōfus, ī *m* tufa, volcanic stone.
toga, ae *f* the toga (*upper garment of a Roman citizen in time of peace*); **a**) garment of peace; peace; **b**) political life; **c**) prostitute.
togātārius, ī *m* actor in a national Roman play.
togātulus, ī *m* humble citizen, client.
togātus 3 wearing the toga, clothed in a toga; **a**) in Roman dress, national; *subst.* **~, ī** *m* Roman citizen; **b**) in the garb of peace; **c**) **togāta, ae** *f* prostitute.
togula, ae *f* little toga.
tolerābilis, e bearable, tolerable, passable; enduring.
tolerāns, tis bearing, enduring, patient (*alcis rei*).
tolerantia, ae *f* a bearing, enduring.
tolerātiō, ōnis *f* = **tolerantia.**
tolerō 1 **a**) to bear, endure, sustain; **b**) to maintain, support, nourish.
tollēnō, ōnis *m* see-saw, swingbeam.
tollō, sustulī, sublātum 3 **1.** to lift *or* take up, raise; a) **signa tollere** to take up the standards, break up camp; **ancoras** to weigh anchor; **puerum, puellam** to accept, acknowledge, bring up; **sortes** to draw lots; b) to raise, exalt, elevate, extol; **animum** to cheer, encourage, animate, excite, make proud; **clamōrem** to raise a cry; **2.** a) to take away, remove, take *or* carry off, make away with, kill, destroy, ruin; b) to annul, cancel, abolish.
tolūtārius 3 trotting.
tolūtim *adv.* at a trot.
tomāc(u)lum, ī sausage.
tōmentum, ī *n* a stuffing, filling (*of cushions, matresses*).
tomus, ī *m* piece cut off; piece of writing-material.
tondeō, totondī, tōnsum 2 to shear, clip, shave; **a**) to mow, cut; **b**) to reap, pluck off, crop, graze, browse upon.
tonitrālis, e thundering.
tonitruālis, e pertaining to thunder.
tonitrus, ūs *m and* **tonitruum, ī** *n* thunder.
tonō, uī, — 1 to thunder; **a**) to sound, resound, roar; **b**) to thunder out.
tōnsa, ae *f* oar.
tōnsilis, e clipped.

tōnsillae, ārum *f/pl.* tonsils.
tōnsitō 1 to shear regularly.
tōnsor, ōris *m* hair-cutter, barber.
tōnsōrius 3 pertaining to shearing *or* shaving, of a barber.
tōnstrīcula, ae *f* hairdresser.
tōnstrīna, ae *f* barber's shop.
tōnstrīx, īcis *f* hairdresser.
tōnsūra, ae *f* a clipping, shearing, shaving.
tōnsus, ūs *m* style of hair-cutting.
tōphus, ī *m* = **tofus.**
topiārius 3 relating to landscape-gardening; *subst.* **~, ī** *m* landscape-gardener; **topiāria, ae** *f* landscape-gardening.
topper (*archaic adv.*) **a**) quickly; **b**) perhaps.
toral, ālis *n* couch-covering, sofa-cloth.
torculum, ī *n* wine-press; oil-press.
toreuma, atis *n* embossed work, work in relief.
tormentum, ī *n* windlass, pulley; **a**) engine for hurling, missile, shot; **b**) inducement, compulsion; **c**) torment, torture, rack, anguish, pain.
tormina, um *n/pl.* colic, gripes.
torminōsus 3 suffering from colic.
tornō 1 to turn in a lathe, to round off.
tornus, ī *m* lathe; chisel.
torōsus 3 muscular, brawny.
torpēdō, inis *f* **a**) = **torpor; b**) torpedo fish, electric ray.
torpeō, —, — 2 to be stiff, inert, immovable; to be benumbed, stupefied, dull, languid.
torpēscō, puī, — 3 to become stiff, inert, dull.
torpidus 3 stiff, benumbed, torpid.
torpor, ōris *m* numbness, stiffness, torpor; languor, indolence, dulness.
torquātus 3 adorned with a necklace.
torqueō, torsī, tortum 2 to wind, twist, turn round; **a**) to curl (*hair*); **b**) to throw with force, hurl, fling, whirl; **c**) to twist awry, wrest, distort, sprain, to put to the rack, torture; **d**) to turn, wrench, pervert; **e**) to put to the test, examine; **f**) to plague, harass, distress.
(**torquēs** *and*) **torquis, is** *m* (and *f*) twisted neck-chain, necklace, collar; **a**) coupling-collar for oxen; **b**) wreath, garland.
torrēns, tis a) burning, hot, heated; rushing, boiling, roaring; **b**) *subst. m* mountain stream, torrent.
torreō, torruī, tostum 2 to dry, parch; **a**) to burn, roast, singe; **b**) to inflame, fire.
torrēscō 3 to be burnt.
torridus 3 dried up, parched, dry, arid; frost-bitten.
torris, is *m* firebrand, piece of dry wood.
tortilis, e twisted.
tortō 1 to torture.
tortor, ōris *m* torturer; one who whirls.
tortuōsus 3 full of turns and windings, tortuous; intricate, perplexed, involved.
tortus[1]**, ūs** *m* a winding; whirling.
tortus[2] 3 crooked, twisted.
torulus, ī *m* tuft of hair.
torus, ī *m* a swelling, protuberance; **a**) muscle; **b**) pillow, cushion, couch, sofa, bed; **c**) bridal-bed, marriage, amour; **d**) bier; **e**) knot on a garland; **f**) bank, mound.
torvitās, ātis *f* sternness, fierceness.
torvus 3 stern, grim, fierce, wild, frightful.
tōsillae, ārum *f/pl.* = **tonsillae.**
tot (*indecl.*) so many.
toti-dem (*indecl.*) just so many.
totiē(n)s *adv.* so often, so many times.
tōtus (*gen.* **-īus** *and* **-ĭus,** *dat.* **-ī**) 3 whole, entire, all; *subst.* **tōtum, ī** *n* the whole, all.
tŏtus 3 **tŏta pars** as large a fraction.
toxicum, ī *n* poison (*for arrows*).
trabālis, e relating to beams of wood, of beams; beam-like.
trabea, ae *f* robe of state, robe of kings; the equestrian order.
trabeātus 3 in a robe of state.
trabs, abis *f* beam of wood; **a**) (trunk of) a tree; **b**) ship; **c**) battering-ram; spear-shaft; club; table.
tractābilis, e that can be handled, manageable, tractable; pliant, yielding, gentle.
tractātiō, ōnis *f* a handling, feeling; **a**) management, treatment; **b**) a using, use, usage.
tractātor, ōris *m* masseur.
tractātrīx, īcis *f* masseuse.
tractātus, ūs *m* = **tractatio.**
tractim *adv.* with a gentle stroke; gradually, continuously.

tractō 1 **1.** to drag along *or* about, to pull; **2.** to touch, handle, stroke, take in hand; a) to manage, work, exercise, practise (*alqd*); b) to treat, use; c) to handle, examine; to discuss; to negotiate.

tractum, ī *n* flock of wool drawn out for spinning.

tractus[1] 3 **a**) derived; **b**) flowing (*speech*).

tractus[2], **ūs** *m* a drawing, dragging, draught; track, course; **a**) extent, district, tract; **b**) a protracting; delay; slow movement; **c**) drawling.

trāditiō, ōnis *f* **a**) a giving up, delivering up, surrender; **b**) narrative.

trāditor, ōris *m* traitor.

trā-dō, didī, ditum 3 to give up, hand over (*alci alqd*); **per manūs** from hand to hand; **a**) to deliver, commit, intrust; **b**) to surrender, deliver up, betray; **c**) **se tradere** to devote oneself to (*alci rei, in alqd*); **d**) to leave behind, bequeath; **e**) to hand down to posterity, record, relate, transmit, recount; **f**) to teach.

trā-dūcō 3 to bring, carry, lead over (*alqm in alqd, ad alqm*); to lead *or* conduct across (*trans flumen*), **exercitum flumen** to transport over a river; **a**) to transfer, promote, advance, to win over, draw over, convert; **b**) to lead by (*alqm praeter, per, in alqd*); **c**) to spend, pass; **d**) to expose to ridicule.

trā-ductiō, ōnis *f* **a**) a carrying over, transferring, removal; **b**) course *or* lapse of time; **c**) exposure to disgrace.

trā-ductor, ōris *m* transferrer (*ad plebem*).

trā-dux, ucis *m* vine-branch, vine--layer.

tragi-cōmoedia, ae *f* drama composed of tragedy & comedy.

tragicus 3 of tragedy, tragic; **a**) in tragic style, lofty, sublime, grand; **b**) horrible; *subst. m* tragic dramatist *or* actor.

tragoedia, ae *f* tragedy; **a**) tragic scene, great tumult, disturbance, spectacle; **b**) tragic pathos, lofty diction.

tragoedus, ī *m* tragic actor, tragedian.

trāgula, ae *f* javelin (*of the Gauls and Iberians*).

tragus, ī *m* **a**) a fish; **b**) body-odour.

trahāx, ācis acquisitive.

trahea, ae *f* drag, sledge (for threshing).

trahō, traxī, tractum 3 to draw (*alqm* or *alqd ad, in, per alqd*) **1.** to drag, haul, trail, pull forth, drag away; to drag about; a) to dissipate, squander; b) to take into consideration, to consider, weigh; **2.** to draw to oneself; a) to allure, attract, influence; b) to draw *or* bring on, induce, cause; c) to appropriate, ascribe, refer; d) to interpret, explain, construe; **3.** a) to drag away violently, carry off, plunder; b) to draw along, lead on, be followed by; c) to draw apart, distract (*a re*); d) to draw in, take in, quaff, inhale; to take on, assume, acquire, get (*alqd ex, a re; nomen ex* or *a facinore*); to take to oneself, appropriate; e) to draw out, draw from, to deduce, derive (*ex, a re*); f) to draw together, contract; **4.** to draw out in length; a) to lengthen, protract, prolong, delay; b) to wear away, spend, pass.

trā-iciō, iēcī, iectum 3 **1.** to throw, cast, shoot over (*alqd ex loco in locum*); a) to bring *or* carry across *or* over; to transfer; **copias flumen** to transport across; b) *intr. or* **se trāicere** *or* **P.** to cross, pass over; **2.** to pass through, go over (*fluvium, mare*); **3.** to thrust through, shoot through, transfix, pierce (*alqd re, alci alqd*).

trā-iectiō, ōnis *f* transposition; passage; **stellae** shooting-star; exaggeration.

trā-iectus, ūs *m* = **traiectio.**

trā-l..., *see* **trans-l...**

trā-lātus 3, *see* **transfero.**

trā-loquor 3 to relate.

trā-m..., *see* **trans-m...**

trāma, ae *f* warp-thread, when raised by the *līcium*; bit of thread, trifle.

trāmes, itis *m* by-way, by-path; way, path, road, course.

trā-natō *and* **trā-nō** 1 to swim over, across, through; to fly through; to pass through; penetrate, permeate.

tranquillitās, ātis *f* quietness, stillness; **a**) calmness of the sea, still weather; **b**) rest, peace; **c**) mental calmness.

tranquillō 1 to calm, still, allay.

tranquillus 3 quiet, calm, still; *subst.* **tranquillum, ī** *n* = **tranquillitas.**

trāns *prep.* with *acc.* **a**) across, over; **b**) beyond, to *or* on the other side.
trāns-abeō to pass by; to pierce.
trāns-āctor, ōris *m* manager.
trāns-adigō 3 to thrust, drive *or* pierce through.
trāns-alpīnus 3 beyond the Alps, Transalpine.
trāns-bītō 3 to go *or* come across.
trānscendō, ndī, ēnsum 3 to climb *or* pass over, cross, overstep, surmount; *trans.* to overstep, transcend; to transgress, violate.
trāns-cīdō, cīdī, cīsum 3 to cut through.
trānscrībō 3 **a**) to transcribe, copy; **b**) to transfer in writing; to make over, assign, give over (*alqd in alqm*); to transfer (*alci alqd*), remove.
trāns-currō, (cu)currī, cursum 3 **a**) to run over *or* across; to pass over (*ad alqd*); **b**) to run *or* hasten through, traverse; to sail *or* travel past.
trāns-cursus, ūs *m* a running past *or* through.
trāns-dō 3, **trāns-dūcō** 3, *see* **trado, traduco.**
trānsenna, ae *f* fowler's net, snare; grille, lattice.
trāns-eō 1. to go *or* pass over; a) to go over to the enemy, desert; b) to be transformed *or* turned; c) to pass over (*in reading or writing*) (*ad alqd*); d) to pass by, elapse; e) to pass, go, sail through; **2.** to go through, pervade, penetrate (*alqd*); a) to pass beyond, transgress, violate; b) to outstrip, surpass; c) to go through briefly, to touch lightly on (*in speaking*); to go *or* pass by; to omit, leave unnoticed.
trānserō, — ertum 3 (*compound of* sero) to graft.
trāns-ferō 3 **1.** to carry, bring, convey over *or* across (*alqd ad alqm, in alqd*); a) to transfer, transport; to transform; b) to copy, transcribe; to translate; c) to turn, direct, apply to (*alqd in alqd, ad alqm*); to use figuratively; d) to put off, defer, delay; **2.** to carry along *or* in procession.
trāns-fīgō 3 to pierce *or* thrust through, transfix.
trāns-figūrō 1 to transform.
trāns-fodiō 3 = **transfigo.**
trāns-fōrmis, e transformed.
trāns-fōrmō 1 to transform.
trāns-forō 1 to pierce.
trāns-fretō 1 to cross the sea.
trāns-fuga, ae *m* deserter.
trāns-fugiō, fūgī, — 3 to flee over, desert.
trāns-fugium, ī *n* desertion.
trāns-fūmō 1 to penetrate like smoke.
trāns-fundō 3 to pour from one vessel into another; to transfer (*alqd ad* or *in alqm*).
trāns-fūsiō, ōnis *f* an intermingling.
trāns-gredior, gressus sum 3 **a**) to step *or* pass over *or* across; to proceed, go over to; **b**) to go beyond, surpass (*alqd*).
trāns-gressiō, ōnis *f* a going over, passage; transposition.
trāns-gressus, ūs *m* crossing.
trāns-iectiō, -iectus, *see* **trā- i...**
trāns-igō, ēgī, āctum 3 to drive through; **a**) to thrust *or* run through, pierce, transfix; **b**) to carry through, bring to an end, perform, finish, accomplish, transact; to settle a difference, adjust, agree; **c**) to pass, spend (*time*).
trāns-iciō 3, *see* **tra-icio.**
trānsiliō, siluī (*and* **silīvī** *or* **siliī**), — 4 **a**) to leap *or* spring over, leap across; **b**) to spring over something (*alqd*); to exceed, transgress, go beyond; to pass by, neglect.
trāns-itiō, ōnis *f* a passing over, passage; desertion; infection.
trānsitō 1 to pass through (?).
trānsitōrius 3 provided with a passage.
trāns-itus, ūs *m* **a**) a passing over, passage; **b**) desertion; **c**) gradual transition of shaded colours; **d**) a passing through; place to pass through, ford, pass; **e**) a passing by; change, transition.
trāns-lātīcius 3 traditional, customary, usual, common.
trāns-lātiō, ōnis *f* a transferring; transporting; **a**) metaphor, trope, **b**) a shifting, diversion, exchange.
trānslātīvus 3 that may be transferred.
trāns-lātor, ōris *m* transferrer.
trāns-lātus, ūs *m* a carrying past, procession.
trāns-legō 3 to read through.
trāns-lūceō 2 to shine *or* glimmer through; to be reflected.

trāns-marīnus 3 beyond sea, transmarine.
trāns-meō 1 to go over *or* across.
trāns-migrō 1 to migrate.
trāns-mineō 2 to pierce right through.
trāns-missiō, ōnis *f and* **-missus, ūs** *m* a passing over, passage.
trāns-mittō 3 to send over *or* across; **a**) to convey across, transmit, transfer; **b**) to let pass; **c**) to give over, entrust; resign, yield (*alci alqd*); **d**) to go, travel, pass over (*alqd*); to leave unnoticed, neglect; to pass (*time*); to endure.
trāns-montānus 3 beyond the mountains.
trāns-moveō 2 to remove, transfer.
trāns-mūtō 1 to change, shift, transpose.
trāns-natō, trāns-nō 1, *see* **tranato.**
trāns-nōminō 1 to change the name of.
trāns-padānus 3 beyond the Po.
trānspectus, ūs *m* seeing through.
trānspiciō 3 to see through.
trāns-pōnō 3 to remove, transfer (*alqd in locum*).
trāns-portātiō, ōnis *f* removal.
trāns-portō 1 to carry, convey *or* bring over, transport (*copias flumen*).
trāns-rhēnānus 3 beyond the Rhine.
trāns-scendō, -scrībō, -siliō, *see* **tran-...**
trāns-tiberīnus 3 beyond the Tiber.
trāns-tineō 2 to pass through.
trānstrum, ī *n* **a**) cross-beam; **b**) bench for rowers.
trānsultō 1 to leap over *or* across.
trānsūmō 3 to take up, assume.
trānsuō 3 to stitch through, pierce.
trāns-vectiō, ōnis *f* a carrying over *or* across; riding past.
trāns-vehō 3 **a**) to carry *or* convey over *or* to the other side, to transport; **b**) to carry by *or* along; **P.** to travel *or* sail over, go *or* pass by, pass away.
trāns-verberō 1 to strike through, pierce, wound.
trāns-versārius 3 lying across.
trāns-versus 3 lying across, transverse, athwart, crosswise; astray, in a wrong direction; *subst.* **trānsversum, ī** *n* cross direction *or* situation, **ex** *or* **de -ō** transversely; unexpectedly.
trāns-volitō 1 to fly through.
trāns-volō 1 **a**) to fly over, across, beyond; **b**) to fly past *or* by (*alqd*).
trāns-vorsus 3 (*archaic*) = **trans-versus.**
trapētus, ī *m* oil-press.
trapezīta, ae *m* money-changer, banker.
trapezo-phorum, ī *n* foot of a table.
trāsenna = **trānsenna.**
traulizī (τραυλίζει) she lisps.
trā-v..., *see* **trans-v...**
tre-cēnī ? three hundred each.
tre-centēsimus 3 three hundredth.
tre-centī 3 three hundred.
trecentiē(n)s *adv.* three hundred times.
trechedīpnum, ī *n* light garment worn when hastening to a dinner-party.
tre-decim (*indecl.*) thirteen.
tremebundus 3 trembling, shaking.
treme-faciō 3 to cause to tremble *or* quake.
tremendus 3 terrible, frightful.
tremēscō *and* **-īscō,** —, — 3 to tremble, quake for fear (at).
tremibundus 3 = **tremebundus.**
tremō, uī, — 3 to tremble (at), quake, quiver.
tremor, ōris *m* a trembling, quaking; earthquake; terror.
tremulus 3 trembling, quaking, quivering, tremulous.
trepidanter *adv.* in agitation.
trepidātiō, ōnis *f* confused hurry, agitation, anxiety, alarm.
trepidō 1 to hurry with alarm, hasten about, be agitated, be in alarm, in confusion; **a**) to be busy; **b**) to tremble at; **c**) to waver, hesitate.
trepidus 3 agitated, alarmed, restless, disturbed, anxious; **a**) boiling, bubbling (*of things*); **b**) perilous, critical, alarming; **in re trepida, in rebus trepidis** at a critical juncture.
trēs, tria, ium three; a few.
tressis, is *m* three *asses.*
trēs-virī, triumvir(ōr)um *m/pl.* board of three men.
tri-angulum, ī *n* triangle.
tri-angulus 3 triangular.
triāriī, ōrum *m/pl.* soldiers of the third rank in battle-order, the reserve.
tribas, adis *f* woman who practises homosexualism.
tribolus, ī *m* = **tribulus.**

tribuārius 3 relating to a tribe.
tribūlis, is *m* fellow tribesman; (at Athens) member of the same deme; proletarian.
trībulum, ī *n* threshing-sledge.
tribulus, ī *m* a kind of thistle.
tribūnal, ālis *n* raised platform for magistrates, judgment seat, tribunal; monumental mound.
tribūnātus, ūs *m* office of a tribune, tribuneship.
tribūnicius 3 of a tribune, tribunicial; *subst.* ~, **ī** *m* one that has been a tribune.
tribūnus, ī *m* tribune, the title of various Roman magistrates and officers, *esp.* **a**) tribune of the people; **b**) military tribune.
tribuō, uī, ūtum 3 **a**) to divide (*alqd in partes*); **b**) to distribute, assign, bestow, confer (*alci alqd*); to give, present, impart; **c**) to concede, grant, yield, allow; **d**) to ascribe, attribute, impute; **e**) to bestow, spend, devote.
tribus, ūs *f* tribe; third part of the Roman people; **a**) local division of the people, district (*31 rusticae* and *4 urbanae*); **b**) votes of a tribe.
tribūtārius 3 subject to tribute; **-ae tabellae** a note promising payment of money.
tribūtim *adv.* by tribes.
tribūtiō, ōnis *f* distribution.
tribūtum, ī *n* (*and* **-us, ī** *m*) tribute, tax, contribution.
tribūtus 3 arranged in tribes.
trīcae, ārum *f/pl.* nonsense; tricks.
trīcēnī 3 thirty each.
tri-ceps, cipitis three-headed.
trīcēsimus (*or* **-cēns-**) 3 thirtieth.
trichila, ae *f* arbour, bower.
trichōrum, ī *n* room divided into three parts.
trīciē(n)s *adv.* thirty times.
tri-clīnium, ī *n* **a**) table-couch, table-sofa; **b**) dining-room.
trīcor 1 to make difficulties, to shuffle, play tricks.
tri-corpor, oris having three bodies.
tri-cuspis, idis three-pointed.
tri-dēns, entis three-pronged; *subst. m* trident.
tridenti-fer 3 *and* **-ger** 3 trident-bearing.
tridenti-potēns, ntis ruling with the trident.
trī-duum, ī *n* space of three days.
triennia, ium *n/pl.* triennial festival.
tri-ennium, ī *n* space of three years.
triēns, tis *m* third part (esp. of an *as* or a *sextarius*).
trientābulum, ī *n* equivalent in land for the third part of a debt.
triēr-archus, ī *m* commander of a trireme.
triēris, is (**nāvis**) *f* trireme, ship propelled by groups of three oars.
trietēricus 3 happening every third year.
trietēris, idis *f* **a**) space of three years; **b**) triennial festival.
trifāriam *adv.* in three places, on three sides.
tri-faux, cis having three throats.
tri-fidus 3 split into three parts, three-forked.
tri-fīlis, e with three hairs.
tri-fōrmis, e having three shapes.
tri-fūr, ıs *m* arch-thief.
tri-furcifer, erī *m* arch-villain.
tri-geminus 3 **a**) threefold; **fratres trigemini** three brothers born together; **b**) triform.
trīgēsimus 3 = **tricesimus.**
trīgintā (*indecl.*) thirty.
trigōn, ōnis *m* playing-ball.
tri-lībris, e weighing three pounds.
tri-linguis, e three-tongued.
tri-līx, īcis woven with three threads.
tri-mē(n)stris, e three months old.
tri-metrus (*and* **-os**) 3 of three measures; *subst.* ~, **ī** *m* trimeter.
tri-modium, ī *n* vessel containing three modii.
trīmulus 3 = **trimus.**
trīmus 3 three years old.
trīnī 3 **a**) three each; **b**) triple, threefold.
tri-noctiālis, e of three nights.
tri-nōdis, e having three knots.
trīnum nūndinum *n*, *see* **nundinum.**
triō, ōnis *m* threshing ox; *pl.* the constellations of the two Bears.
triōbolus, ī *m* coin worth three obols (= half-drachma).
tri-parcus 3 very niggardly.
tri-partītus 3 divided into three parts, threefold; *adv.* **tripartītō** in three parts.
tri-pectorus 3 triple-breasted.
tri-pedālis, e three feet long.
tri-pertītus 3 = **tripartitus.**
tri-pēs, pedis three-footed.

tri-plex, icis threefold, triple; **a)** *subst.* **triplex** *n* threefold portion; **b)** *subst.* **triplicēs** *m/pl.* writing-tablet with three leaves.
triplus 3 threefold, triple.
tripudiō 1 to beat the ground with the feet; to dance.
tri-pudium, ī *n* **a)** a dancing in three measures; solemn dance; **b) tripudium sollistimum** favourable omen in augury.
tripūs, odis *m* three-footed vessel *or* seat, tripod; (the Delphic) oracle.
tri-quetrus 3 triangular; Sicilian.
tri-rēmis, e propelled by groups of three oars; *subst. f* trireme.
trīs *acc.* = **tres.**
tri-scurria, orum *n/pl.* gross buffooneries.
trīsticulus 3 somewhat sorrowful, rather sad.
trīsti-ficus 3 making sad, saddening.
trīstimōnia, ae *f* sadness.
trīstis, e a) sad, sorrowful, mournful, melancholy; **b)** bringing sorrow, saddening, doleful, dismal; **c)** gloomy, sullen, morose, severe, stern, harsh; **d)** distasteful, disagreeable.
trīstitia, ae (*and* **-tiēs, ēī**) *f* **a)** sadness, sorrow, melancholy; grief; **b)** moroseness, sternness, severity, harshness.
tri-sulcus 3 with three furrows, threefold, three-pronged.
trit-avus, ī *m* the father of an *atavus*, ancestor.
trīticeus (*and* **-cēius**) 3 of wheat, wheaten.
trīticum, ī *n* wheat.
trītor, ōris *m* one who rubs.
trītūra, ae *f* a threshing.
trītus[1] 3 rubbed; **a)** trodden, beaten, worn, frequented; **b)** much used, usual, commonplace; **c)** practised, expert.
trītus[2], **ūs** *m* a rubbing.
triumphālis, e of a triumph, triumphal; having had a triumph; **-ālia, -ium** *n/pl.* triumphal insignia.
triumphō 1 to celebrate a triumph, to triumph over (*ex* or *de alqo*); **a)** to exult, rejoice; **b)** to conquer completely (*alqm*); to obtain as booty.
triumphus, ī *m* triumph, triumphal procession; **triumphum agere ex** *or* **de alqo** to celebrate a triumph over; victory.
trium-vir, ī *m* triumvir, one of three associates in office, member of a board of three; *pl.* three joint commissioners.
triumvirālis, e of the triumvirs, triumviral.
triumvirātus, ūs *m* triumvirate, office of a triumvir.
tri-venēfica, ae *f* a thorough witch.
tri-viālis, e ordinary, commonplace.
trivium, ī *n* place where three roads meet, street-corner.
tri-vius 3 of the cross-roads; **Trivia, ae** *f* Diana *or* Hecate.
trochaeus, ī *m* trochee (*metrical foot consisting of one long and one short syllable*).
trochus, ī *m* boy's hoop.
troclea, ae *f* pulley.
Trōg(l)o-dytae, ārum *m/pl.* cave-dwellers.
tropa *adv.* at a game played with dice.
tropaeum, ī *n* trophy, memorial of victory; **a)** victory; **b)** monument, sign.
tropis (*acc.* **-in**) the sediment of wine.
trucīdātiō, ōnis *f* a slaughtering, massacre.
trucīdō 1 to cut down, slaughter, massacre, to ruin cruelly; to extinguish (*fire*).
truculentia, ae *f* fierceness, roughness, inclemency.
truculentus 3 grim, rough, harsh; savage, fierce, cruel.
trudis, is *f* pole, pike.
trūdō, sī, sum 3 to thrust, push, press on, drive forward; to put forth (*buds*); to force, impel (*alqm ad* or *in alqd*).
trulla, ae *f* **a)** ladle; **b)** fire-pan.
truncō 1 to cut off, maim, mutilate.
truncus[1], **ī** *m* **a)** trunk, stem of a tree; **b)** trunk of a body; side of meat; **c)** blockhead.
truncus[2] 3 maimed, mutilated, mangled, cut short; imperfect.
trūsō 1 to push violently.
trutina, ae *f* balance, pair of scales.
trutinor 1 to weigh.
trux, ucis fierce, ferocious, grim rough, savage, wild, furious.
tryblium, ī *n* dish.
trȳgōnus, ī *m* sting-ray.
tū thou, you.

tuātim *adv.* in your manner.
tuba, ae *f* trumpet.
tūber, eris *n* swelling, bump, hump, tumour; truffle (?).
tubi-cen, inis *m* trumpeter.
tubi-lūstrium, ī *n* festival for the purification of trumpets.
tubula, ae *f dimin. of* **tuba.**
tubulātus 3 provided with tubes.
tubur, uris *or* **eris** *m* a tree-fruit.
tuburcinor 1 to devour greedily.
tubus, ī *m* pipe.
tuccētum, ī *n* spiced meat-roll.
tuditāns, antis striking, beating.
tueor (*and* **tueō**), **tuitus sum** 2 to look at, view, behold, gaze upon (*alqd*); **a**) to care for, watch over, protect, defend; **b**) to maintain, uphold, preserve, keep up; **c**) to keep in mind; **d**) to keep in repair; **e**) to support, maintain, feed.
tugurium, ī *n* hut, cottage.
tuitiō, ōnis *f* protection.
tum *adv.* **a**) then, at that time; **b**) thereupon; then, afterwards; **c**) in the next place, next (*primum ... deinde ... tum ... postremo*); **d**) **tum ... tum** now ... now, as well ... as; **e**) **cum ... tum** in general ... and in particular, both ... and.
tume-faciō 3 to cause to swell; to puff up.
tumeō, —, — 2 to be swollen, blown *or* puffed up; **a**) to be puffed up with pride; **b**) to swell with anger, be excited; **c**) to be bombastic.
tumēscō, muī, — 3 to begin to swell; to swell with anger *or* pride; to begin to break out.
tumidus 3 swelling, swollen; **a**) puffed up, inflated, proud; **b**) pompous, bombastic; **c**) ambitious, arrogant, ready to break out; **d**) causing to swell.
tumor, ōris *m* a swelling, tumour; **a**) elevation; **b**) commotion, excitement, anger, wrath; **c**) pride, arrogance.
tumulō 1 to bury, inter.
tumulōsus 3 hilly.
tumultuārius 3 done *or* made in haste, confused, disorderly; brought together hastily, levied suddenly.
tumultuātiō, ōnis *f* confusion, bustle, tumult.
tumultuor (*and* **-ō**) 1 to be in confusion, in an uproar, to revolt; **tumultuātur** there is disorder.
tumultuōsus 3 confused, noisy, tumultuous; causing disturbance.
tumultus, ūs *m* noise, uproar, bustle, tumult, confusion; **a**) sedition, insurrection, revolt, mutiny; **b**) alarm, approaching war, civil war; **c**) disturbance, storm.
tumulus, ī *m* mound of earth, hill; sepulchral mound, grave.
tunc *adv.* **a**) then, at that time; **b**) thereupon, afterwards.
tundō, tutudī, tū(n)sum 3 to beat, strike; **a**) to thresh; **b**) to pound, bruise; **c**) to importune.
tunica, ae *f* under garment, shirt; coating, skin, peel.
tunicātus 3 clothed in a tunic; covered with skin.
tunicula, ae *f* little tunic.
tuor 3 = **tueor.**
turba, ae *f* tumult, noise, disturbance, confusion; **a**) crowd, throng, press, swarm; **b**) great number, multitude, band, mob.
turbāmentum, ī *n* means of disturbance.
turbātiō, ōnis *f* confusion, disorder, disturbance.
turbātor, ōris *m* disturber, stirrer--up.
turbātrīx, īcis *f* disturbing.
turbātus 3 troubled, disturbed, angered; confused, disorderly.
turbellae, ārum *f/pl.* disturbance, row.
turben, inis *m* (*and n ?*) top.
turbidus 3 confused, disturbed, stormy; muddy, turbid; dishevelled; **a**) impetuous, excited, enraged; **b**) troubled, surprised, astonished, perplexed; **c**) mutinous, turbulent.
turbineus 3 cone-shaped.
turbō¹, inis *m* whirling *or* spinning motion, revolution; **a**) whirlwind, storm; **b**) eddy; whirl; coil; **c**) spinning-top; wheel; reel; whorl; spindle.
turbō² 1 to throw into disorder *or* confusion, to disturb, disorder, trouble; **a**) to agitate, make turbid; **b**) to stir up, derange, put to the rout; **c**) to amaze, confound, trouble.
turbulentus 3 (*adv.* **-tē** *and* **-ter**) restless, full of commotion, stormy; turbid; **a**) disturbed, confused; **b**) causing disturbance, seditious.

turdus, ī *m* (*and* **turda, ae** *f*) thrush.
tūreus 3 of frankincense.
turgeō, (rsī), — 2 to be swollen; to be turgid *or* bombastic.
turgēscō, —, — 3 to begin to swell; to swell with passion.
turgidulus 3, *dim. of* **turgidus.**
turgidus 3 swollen, inflated; bombastic.
tūribulum, ī *n* censer, incense-pan.
tūri-cremus 3 incense-burning.
tūri-fer 3 incense-bearing.
tūri-legus 3 incense-gathering.
turma, ae *f* division of cavalry; squadron, troop, band, body.
turmālis, e of the same squadron; equestrian.
turmātim *adv.* by squadrons.
turpiculus 3 ugly; shameful.
turpi-ficātus 3 made foul, corrupted.
turpi-lucri-cupidus 3 greedy of dishonest gain.
turpis, e ugly, deformed; **a**) filthy, foul, nasty; **b**) disgraceful, shameful; infamous, base, indecent, obscene, scandalous.
turpitūdō, inis *f* ugliness, deformity; **a**) baseness; **b**) disgrace, dishonour, infamy.
turpō 1 to make ugly, to deform, pollute, defile.
turricula, ae *f* dice-box shaped like a tower.
turri-ger 3 tower-bearing, turreted.
turris, is *f* tower; **a**) castle, palace; **b**) siege-tower; **c**) dovecote; **d**) howdah.
turrītus 3 **a**) furnished *or* fortified with towers; **b**) adorned with a tower-crown; **c**) towering, lofty.
turtur, uris *m* turtle-dove.
turturilla, ae *f* (little turtle-dove); weakling.
tūs, tūris *n* incense, frankincense.
tūsculum, ī *n* a bit of incense.
tussicula, ae *f* fit of coughing.
tussiō 4 to cough.
tussis, is *f* cough.
tūtāmen, inis *n and* **tūtāmentum, ī** *n* means of protection.
tū-te (*emphatic*) = **tu.**
tūtē, *adv. of* **tutus.**
tūtēla, ae *f* care, charge, protection, defence, patronage; **a**) wardship, guardianship; **b**) thing protected, charge; **c**) guardian, tutor, protector; ward; **d**) property of a ward.
tuticus, *see* **medix.**
tūtō, *adv.* **tutus.**
tūtor[1]**, ōris** *m* protector, defender; guardian, tutor.
tūtor[2] (*and* **tūtō**) 1 to guard, protect, defend (*alqd a re; contra, adversus, ad alqm*); **a**) to keep, keep safe, preserve, watch; **b**) to ward off, avert (*alqd*).
tūtus 3 (*adv.* **tūtō** *and* **tūtē**) **a**) safe, secure, protected, guarded (*a re; adversus* or *ad alqd*); *subst.* **tūtum, ī** *n* safety, security, safe place, shelter; **b**) watchful, cautious, prudent; **c**) protecting.
tuus 3 thy, thine, your, yours; *subst.* **tuī** *m/pl.* your friends, people, *or* party; **tua** *n/pl.* your property.
tuxtax (imitation of the sound of blows).
tympanizō 1 to beat the tambourine.
tympano-triba, ae *m* one who plays on a tambourine; weakling.
ty(m)panum, ī *n* **a**) drum, tambourine; **b**) wheel without spokes, drum.
typus, ī *m* figure, image.
tyranni-cīda, ae *m* tyrant-slayer.
tyrannicus 3 of a tyrant, tyrannical, despotic.
tyrannis, idis *f* tyranny, arbitrary *or* despotic power.
tyranno-ctonus, ī *m* tyrant-killer, regicide.
tyrannus, ī *m* monarch, absolute ruler, king, prince; tyrant, arbitrary ruler, despot.
tyrianthina, ōrum *n/pl.* purple-violet robes.
tyro-tarīchum, ī *n* ragout of cheese and salt-fish.

U

ūber[1], **eris** *n* teat, udder, breast; **a**) fruitfulness, fertility, richness; **b**) fruitful field.
ūber[2], **eris** fertile, fruitful, productive (*with abl.*); rich, abounding, plentiful, copious.
ūbertās, ātis *f* fruitfulness, fertility; copiousness, fulness, plenty, richness.
ūbertim *adv.* copiously.
ūbertō 1 to make fruitful.
ubī (*and* **ubĭ**) **1.** *interr. adv.* where?; **2.** *rel. cj.* a) where; b) when, as soon as; c) whenever, as often as; **ubiubi** wherever.
ubi-cumque (*or* **-cunque**) **a**) wherever, wheresoever; **b**) anywhere, everywhere.
ubi-libet *adv.* anywhere.
ubi-nam *interr.* where?
ubi-quāque *adv.* anywhere; whenever(?).
ubī-que *adv.* everywhere, anywhere.
ubi-quomque = **ubicumque.**
ubi-vīs *adv.* where you will, everywhere.
ūdō, ōnis *m* shoe of felt *or* skin.
ūdus 3 moist, wet; sappy; drunk.
ulcerātiō, ōnis *f* sore, ulcer.
ulcerō 1 to cause to ulcerate, to make sore; to wound.
ulcerōsus 3 full of sores; wounded.
ulcīscor, ultus sum 3 to avenge (*acc.*); to avenge oneself; to take vengeance on, to punish, requite (*acc.*).
ulcus, eris *n* ulcer, sore; painful spot, sore place; *dimin.* **ulcusculum, ī** *n.*
ūlīgō, inis *f* moisture of the soil, dampness.
ūllus 3 any, any one.
ulmeus 3 of elm.
ulmi-triba, ae *m* elm-rubber, flogged slave.
ulmus, ī *f* elm, elm-tree.
ulna, ae *f* **a**) elbow; arm; **b**) ell.
ulpicum, ī *n* leek.
(**ulter, tra, trum**) (*not used*); **1.** *comp.* **ulterior, ius** farther, on the further side; a) at a greater distance, more remote *or* distant; b) beyond, farther on, farther; **2.** *superl.* **ultimus** 3 farthest; a) most distant, most remote, last, extreme; b) earliest, oldest, first; last, latest, final; c) utmost, greatest, highest, worst; d) lowest, meanest.
ultiō, ōnis *f* an avenging, revenge.
ultor, ōris *m* avenger, punisher.
ultrā 1. *adv.* farther on; a) beyond; b) further, moreover, besides, longer (*comp.* **ulterius**); **2.** *prep.* with *acc.* a) on the farther side of, beyond, past, over, across; b) more than, above.
ultrīx, īcis *f* avenging.
ultrō *adv.* **1.** a) to the farther side; beyond, on the other side; **ultrō et citrō** up and down, to and fro; b) even, moreover, actually; **2.** of one's own accord, of oneself, voluntarily, spontaneously.
ulula, ae *f* screech-owl.
ululātus, ūs *m* a howling, shrieking, wailing.
ululō 1 to howl, shriek, yell, wail; to call upon with howling (*acc.*); to ring with cries.
ulva, ae *f* sedge.
umbella, ae *f* sunshade.
umbilicus, ī *m* navel; **a**) middle, centre; **b**) (end of a) stick on which a manuscript was rolled; **c**) a shell-fish.
umbō, ōnis *m* knob, boss of a shield; shield; elbow; fullness (of a garment).
umbra, ae *f* shade, shadow; **1.** darkness; a) shadow in painting; b) shaded place; c) uninvited guest; **2.** shade, departed spirit, ghost; *pl.* the infernal regions, lower world; **3.** a) shelter, cover, protection; b) rest, leisure, retired *or* private life; c) shadow, phantom, semblance, show, pretext; d) a fish.
umbrāculum, ī *n* **a**) shady place; bower, arbour; school-room; **b**) parasol.
umbrāticulus = **umbrāticus.**

umbrāticus 3 (living, spent, *or* done) in the shade.
umbrātilis, e in the shade; **a**) private, retired, contemplative; **b**) scholastic, of the rhetorical schools.
umbri-fer 3 shady; shade-bearing.
umbrō 1 to shade, overshadow, cover.
umbrōsus 3 shady, giving shade.
ūmectō 1 to moisten, wet.
ūmectus 3 moist.
ūmeō, —, — 2 to be moist, wet, damp.
umerus, ī *m* shoulder, upper arm.
ūmēscō 3 to become moist.
ūmiditās, ātis *f* dampness.
ūmid(ul)us 3 moist, wet.
ūmi-fer 3 moist.
ūmor, ōris *m* moisture, liquid, fluid, dew, rain, tears, ocean.
umquam *adv.* ever, at any time; **nec umquam** and never.
ūna *adv., see* **unus.**
ūn-animāns, tis = **unanimus.**
ūnanimitās, ātis *f* unanimity, concord.
ūn-animus 3 of one mind, unanimous, concordant.
uncia, ae *f* twelfth part of a whole; ounce.
unciārius 3 containing a twelfth.
unciātim *adv.* by ounces.
uncīnātus 3 furnished with hooks, barbed.
unciola, ae *f* a paltry twelfth.
unctiō, ōnis *f* a besmearing, anointing.
unctitō 1 to anoint frequently.
unctiusculus 3 a little more oily.
unctor, ōris *m* anointer.
unctōrium, ī *n* anointing-room.
unctūra, ae *f* an anointing (*of the dead*).
unctus 3 **a**) anointed; **b**) oiled, greasy; **c**) rich; **d**) luxurious, sumptuous, voluptuous.
uncus[1], **ī** *m* hook, barb.
uncus[2] 3 hooked, crooked, curved.
unda, ae *f* wave; **a**) stream, water, fluid; **b**) moving air *or* smoke; **c**) agitation, surge; throng.
unde (*interr.* and *rel.*) from which place, whence; from whom; **unde unde** from somewhere or other.
ūn-deciē(n)s *adv.* eleven times.
ūn-decim (*indecl.*) eleven.
ūn-decimus 3 the eleventh.
unde-cumque from whatever point.
ūn-dēnī 3 eleven each.
ūn-dē-vīcēsimānī, ōrum *m/pl.* soldiers of the nineteenth legion.
ūn-dē-vīcēsimus 3 the nineteenth.
ūn-dē-vīgintī (*indecl.*) nineteen.
undique *adv.* from all parts *or* sides; on all sides, everywhere; in all respects.
undi-sonus 3 wave-sounding.
undi-vagus 3 wandering on waves.
undō 1 to rise in waves, to surge, swell; to wave, undulate; to overflow with (*alqo*); *trans.* to inundate.
undōsus 3 full of waves.
ūn-et-vīcēsimānī, ōrum *m/pl.* soldiers of the twenty-first legion.
ungō, unxī, unctum 3 to anoint.
unguen, inis *n* = **unguentum.**
unguentārius 3 of unguents; *m* dealer in ointments, *n* money to buy unguent.
unguentātus 3 anointed.
unguentum, ī *n* ointment, unguent, perfume.
unguiculus, ī *m* finger-nail, toe-nail.
unguis, is *m* finger-nail, toe-nail; claw, hoof, talon; **ad** *or* **in unguem** to a nicety, exactly; **unguis transversus** a finger's breadth.
ungula, ae *f* hoof; **a**) claw, talon; **b**) horse.
unguō 3 = **ungo.**
ūni-color, ōris of one colour.
ūnicus 3 one only, single; alone in its kind, singular, unique, unparalleled.
ūni-fōrmis, e uniform.
ūni-gena, ae only-begotten; born of the same parentage.
ūni-manus 3 one-handed.
ūniō, ōnis *m* single great pearl.
ūnitās, ātis *f* oneness, unity.
ūniter in(to) one.
ūni-versālis, e general, universal.
ūniversitās, ātis *f* the whole; the whole world, universe.
ūni-versus (*and* **-vorsus**) 3 **a**) combined into one, whole, entire, all together, collective; **b**) *subst.* **ūniversum, ī** *n* = **universitas**; **c**) *adv.* **ūniversē** *or* **in ūniversum** as a whole, in general.
ūn-oculus 3 one-eyed.
ūnorsum = **ūniversum.**
unquam *adv., see* **umquam.**
ūnus 3 one, a single, only one; **ad ūnum omnes** all to a man,

without exception; **in ūnum** into one place; **ūnus quisque** each single, every one; **a**) one and the same, the same, common; **b**) *adv.* **ūnā** at the same place, at the same time, together, at once.

ūpiliō, ōnis *m* = **opilio.**

upupa, ae *f* hoopoe; pick-axe.

urbānitās, ātis *f* life in Rome; **a**) city manners, city fashion, refinement, elegance, politeness, urbanity; **b**) wit, humour, pleasantry.

urbānus 3 belonging to the city (*Rome*), of the city, urban; *subst.* **~, ī** *m* city man, *pl.* townsfolk, citizens; **a**) Roman; **b**) in city fashion, refined, elegant, cultivated, polished; **c**) witty, pleasant; **d**) bold, forward.

urbi-capus, ī *m* taker of cities.

urbicus 3 belonging to the city, to Rome.

urbs, urbis *f* city, walled town, capital; city of Rome; the citizens.

urce(ol)us, ī *m* pitcher, water-pot.

ūrēdō, inis *f* blight (*upon plants*).

urgeō, ursī, — 2 to push, press, drive, urge (*acc.*); **a**) to press upon, bear hard upon, oppress, weigh down, burden, to press hard, beset; **b**) to crowd, hem in, confine; **c**) to insist upon, lay stress upon; **d**) to stick to, apply oneself to diligently, to push on with.

ūrīna, ae *f* urine; semen.

ūrīnātor, ōris *m* diver.

ūrīnor 1 to dive.

ūrios 3 giver of favourable wind.

urna, ae *f* pitcher, water-pot, jug, jar, urn; voting-urn, urn for lots; urn for the ashes of the dead; a liquid measure.

urnula, ae *f*, *dim. of* **urna.**

ūrō, ussī, ustum 3 to burn, destroy by fire; **a**) to burn in (*of encaustic painting*); **b**) to waste by burning, destroy, harass, distress, plague, vex, disquiet; **c**) to dry up, parch, scorch; **d**) to pinch with cold, chafe, gall, rub sore; **e**) to burn with passion; inflame.

ursa, ae *f* she-bear; (*constellation*) [the Bear.]

ursus, ī *m* bear.

urtīca, ae *f* (stinging-)nettle; sea-nettle; itching desire.

ūrus, ī *m* a kind of wild ox.

ūsitātus 3 usual, customary, wonted, common, familiar.

uspiam *adv.* anywhere.

usquam *adv.* **a**) anywhere, at any place; in any thing, in any way; **b**) to any place.

usque *adv.* all the way, right (up), continuously, without interruption, all the while; **a**) *with prep.* **ab, ex, ad;** **b**) *rarely as prep. with acc.* right up to, as far as; **c**) *with adv.* (**usque eō** to such a point; **usque quāque** everywhere, on all occasions); **d**) *with cj.* (**usque dum, dōnec**).

ustor, ōris *m* burner of dead bodies.

ustulō 1 to burn.

ūsū-capiō[1] 3 to acquire by use *or* prescription.

ūsū-capiō[2]**, ōnis** *f* acquisition by use.

ūsūra, ae *f* a using, use, enjoyment; **a**) use of money lent; **b**) interest, usury.

ūsūrārius 3 **a**) borrowed; **b**) lent.

ūsūrpātiō, ōnis *f* a making use of; employment.

ūsūrpō 1 to take into use, employ, apply, practise, enjoy (*alqd*); **a**) to seize, usurp, assume; **b**) to take possession of, acquire; **c**) to name, call; **d**) to have experience of; to perceive.

ūsus, ūs *m* a using, making use of, use, application, practice, exercise; **a**) use and enjoyment, usufruct; **b**) frequent use, acquired skill, experience, expertness; **ūsū venit** it happens, occurs; **c**) usage, custom; **d**) intercourse, familiarity, intimacy; **e**) usefulness, advantage, profit; **ex ūsū alcis esse** = **alci ūsuī esse** to be useful *or* advantageous; **f**) occasion, want, need, necessity.

ūsus-frūctus (*acc.* **ūsum-frūctum**) *m* use and enjoyment, usufruct.

ut 1. a) (*interr.*) how? b) (*exclam.*) how! c) *in indirect questions and exclamations, with subj. and indic.* (*vides ut ...?* do you see how ...?); d) *in indignant or repudiating questions, with subj.* (*te ut ulla res frangat?* can anything prevail upon you?); e) *rarely in wishes* = *utinam*; f) (*relat.*) as, just as (*perge, ut instituisti; ut potui, tuli*); α) (*in parenthesis*) **ut aiunt, ut supra demonstravimus, ut dixi, ut fit;**

β) (*in comparisons*) *with correlative* **sic, ita, eodem modo: ut initium, sic finis est; ut quisque ... sic (ita)** the more ... the more (*ut quisque est vir optimus, ita difficillime alios improbos esse suspicatur*); **ut ... ita** indeed ... but, although ... yet, **ut nihil boni est in morte, ita certe nihil mali**; γ) (*in attestations*) as it is true that: **ita vivam, ut maximos sumptus facio**; δ) (*to introduce an explanation or reason or limitation*) as, as being, inasmuch as, **quod non decet, poeta fugit ut maximum vitium; Diogenes liberius ut Cynicus locutus est; eloquens erat ut homo Thebanus** (for a Theban); ε) **ut si** *with subj.* as if; ζ) **ut qui** *with subj.* seeing that, since, **multa de me questus est Caesar, ut qui a Crasso in me esset incensus**; η) (*to introduce examples*) as, as for example, **multi gloriose mortui sunt, ut Leonidas; 2.** *cj.* a) *with ind.* (*of time*) when, as soon as, **repente, ut Roman venit, praetor factus est;** since, **ut Brundisio profectus es, nullas postea litteras a te accepi**; b) *with subj.* α) (*in final clauses*) that, in order that, for the purpose of (*neg.* **ne**); *with verbs of fearing* = **ne non** that not; β) (*to express a consequence*) that, so that (*neg.* **ut non**); γ) (*in concessive clauses*) although, granting that, **ut desint vires, tamen est laudanda voluntas**; δ) (*in indirect commands*) that; ε) (**eā condiciōne**) **ut** on condition that.

ut-cumque in whatever way, however; somehow; whenever.

ūtēns, tis using; *comp.* **ūtentior** better able to spend (?).

ūtēnsilia, ium *n/pl.* necessaries, materials, utensils.

uter¹, tris *m* leather bag *or* bottle.

uter², utra, utrum which of two, which; either.

uter-cumque 3 whichever of the two.

uter-libet 3 which of the two you please, either of the two.

uter-que 3 each of two, both.

uterus, ī *m* (*and* **uterum, ī** *n*) belly, paunch; womb; unborn child; inside.

uter-vīs 3 which of the two you will, either of the two.

utī = **ut.**

ūtibilis, e useful, serviceable.

ūtilis, e useful, serviceable, suitable, fit, proper, profitable (*alci, alci rei, ad alqd*).

ūtilitās, ātis *f* usefulness, serviceableness, use, profit, advantage.

uti-nam (*with subj.*) would that! oh that! **utinam ne** would that not!

utiquam, ne ~ = **neutiquam.**

uti-que *adv.* in any case, at any rate, by all means, certainly; at least; especially.

ūtor, ūsus sum 3 to use, make use of, employ (*with abl.*); **a**) to enjoy, partake of; to have, possess, avail oneself of, take advantage of; **b**) to practise, exercise, perform; **c**) to be intimate with, associate with.

ut-pote *adv.* seeing that, inasmuch as, as being, as.

utrārius, ī *m* water-carrier.

utriculārius, ī *m* bagpiper.

utrim-que *adv.* from both sides; on both sides.

utrō *adv.* to which of the two sides?

utrobīque *adv.* = **utrubīque.**

utrō-que *adv.* to both sides; in both directions.

utrubī (*and* **-ĭ**) on which side?

utrubīque *adv.* on each of the two sides, on both sides.

utrum (*in disjunctive questions*) whether; **utrum ... an** whether ... or.

ut-ut = **utcumque.**

ūva, ae *f* grape; cluster of grapes (*or* other fruits, *or* bees); vine.

ūvēns, ntis wet.

ūvēscō, —, — 3 to become moist *or* wet; to refresh oneself.

ūvid(ul)us 3 moist, wet; **a**) well-watered; **b**) drunken.

ūvi-fer 3 producing grapes.

uxor, ōris *f* wife, mate.

uxorcula, ae *f* little wife.

uxōrius 3 of a wife; devoted **to** one's wife, uxorious.

V

vacātiō, ōnis *f* freedom from, immunity, exemption; **a**) exemption from military service; **b**) price paid for exemption from military service.
vacca, ae *f* cow.
vaccīnium, ī *n* a purple flower (perhaps = *hyacinthus*).
vaccula, ae *f* little cow, heifer.
vacerrōsus 3 mad, crazy.
vacillātiō, ōnis *f* a reeling, wavering.
vac(c)illō 1 to waver, totter, reel, stagger, hesitate.
vacē-fīō to be made empty.
vacīvitās, ātis *f* emptiness.
vacīvus 3 empty, void.
vacō 1 to be empty *or* void; **a**) to be vacant, unoccupied; **b**) to be uncultivated, uninhabited; **c**) to have no master, be without a possessor; **d**) to be free from, to be without (*re, a re*); to be free from duties, be disengaged; to be at leisure for (*dat.*) have time for, be devoted to; *impers.* **vacat** there is time, leisure for (*inf., dat. and inf.*).
vacuē-faciō 3 to make empty *or* free; **vacuē-factus** 3 empty, unoccupied.
vacuitās, ātis *f* **a**) freedom (from), exemption; **b**) vacancy.
vacuō 1 to empty.
vacuus 3 **a**) void, empty, free from, without, exempt (*re, a re, ab alqo;* with *gen.*); *subst.* **vacuum, ī** *n* empty space, void, vacuum; **b**) free from care; heart-whole; **c**) single, unmarried, widowed; **d**) vacant, without an owner, unoccupied; **e**) free from duty, disengaged, at leisure, idle; quiet, calm; **f**) worthless, useless, vain.
vadimōnium, ī *n* bail, security, recognizance; (day of) appearance in court.
vādō 3 to go, walk.
vador 1 to bind over to appear in court; **vadātus** (as *pass.*) bound.
vadōsus 3 full of shallows.
vadum, ī *n* shallow water, shoal; ford; **a**) dangerous water (to ships); **b**) safe water (to swimmers); **c**) mass of water, sea, stream.
vae *int.* woe!, ah!, oh!; **vae tibi** (or **te,** *acc.*) alas for thee!
vae-cors, vae-grandis, vaesānus, *see* **ve-...**
vafer, fra, frum cunning, crafty, sly, artful, subtle.
vagātiō, ōnis *f* a wandering about.
vāgīna, ae *f* scabbard, sheath; husk; vagina.
vāgiō 4 to cry, scream, whimper.
vāgītus, ūs (*and* **vāgor, ōris**) *m* a crying, screaming.
vagor (*and* **vagō**) 1 to rove, ramble, roam, wander about.
vagus 3 wandering, strolling, rambling, roving; **a**) unsteady, inconstant, unsettled; **b**) aimless, indefinite, vague.
vāh *int.* ah! oh!
valdē *adv.* vehemently, strongly, very much.
valē-dīcō 3 to say good-bye, bid farewell.
valēns, tis strong, powerful; in good health, robust, vigorous, effective.
valentulus 3, *dim. of* **valens.**
valeō, uī, itūrus 2 to be strong; **a**) to be well *or* in health; **valē** (*as a farewell greeting*) farewell, good-bye; **b**) to be powerful, mighty, have weight *or* influence (*re, apud alqm; multum, plus, plurimum*) to prevail, have efficacy, avail, be effectual, succeed; **c**) to be able *or* capable; **d**) to be worth, valued at; to mean, signify.
valēscō, luī, — 3 to grow strong, gain strength.
valētūdinārius 3 invalid; **~ium** *n* hospital.
valētūdō, inis *f* state of health, bodily condition; **a**) good health; **b**) ill health, sickness, weakness.
valgus 3 bandy-legged.
validus 3 strong, vigorous; **a**) healthy, sound, robust; **b**) firm, fortified; **c**) powerful, mighty, influential, efficacious.

valitūdō, inis *f, see* **valetudo.**
vallāris, e of a rampart; ~ **corōna** wreath awarded for valour at an enemy's rampart.
(**vallēs** *and*) **vallis, is** *f* valley, vale.
vallō 1 to fortify with a rampart, entrench; to protect, defend (*alqd*).
vallum, ī *n* palisade; palisaded rampart, fortification; protection.
vallus, ī *m* stake, pole; **a**) palisade; **b**) rampart with palisades, stockade; **c**) tooth (*of a comb*).
valvae, ārum *f/pl.* leaves of a folding door.
vānēscō, —, — 3 to fade away, vanish, disappear.
vāni-dicus 3 bragging, lying.
vāni-loquentia, ae *f* a prating, vaunting.
vāni-loquidōrus, ī *m* liar.
vāni-loquus 3 lying; boasting.
vānitās, ātis *f* emptiness, unreality, mere show, vanity, untruth, deception; **a**) uselessness, failure; **b**) a boasting, vaunting, vainglory, lying, quackery.
vānitūdō, inis *f* lying talk.
vannus, ī *f* winnowing-fan.
vānus 3 empty, void, hollow; **a**) containing nothing, vain, unreal; without effect, fruitless, to no purpose; **b**) false, lying, untrue, deceitful, boastful, ostentatious, braggart; groundless, unreal; *subst.* **vānum, ī** *n* emptiness, groundlessness, mere show.
vapidus 3 mouldy, flat; spoilt, bad.
vapor (*and* **-ōs**), **ōris** *m* vapour, steam, smoke; **a**) exhalation; **b**) heat, warmth.
vapōrārium, ī *n* hot-air pipe.
vapōri-fer 3 giving out steam *or* heat.
vapōrō 1 to heat with steam, vapour, *or* smoke; to warm; to be hot, burn.
vappa, ae *f* spoiled *or* flat wine; a good-for-nothing.
vāpulāris, e of flogging.
vāpulō 1 to be flogged *or* whipped.
vāra, ae *f* forked pole (*for stretching nets*).
variātiō, ōnis (*and* **variantia, ae**) *f* diversity, difference.
varicōsus 3 with varicose veins.
vāricus 3 with legs wide apart.
varietās, ātis *f* **a**) variety, difference, diversity; **b**) vicissitude, change; difference in opinion; **c**) fickleness, inconstancy.
variō 1 **a**) to diversify, variegate, make particoloured, spot (*alqd*); to change, alter, interchange, make different, diverse, manifold; **b**) *intr.* to be particoloured; to be different, manifold, diverse; to differ in opinion; to waver, to differ, change, vary.
varius 3 variegated, particoloured; **a**) spotted, mottled; **b**) different, diverse, varying, manifold, changing, changeable; **c**) many-sided, versatile; fickle, inconstant, changeable.
varix, icis *f* and *m* dilated vein.
vārus 3 bent, crooked; **a**) with legs bent inward, knock-kneed; **b**) different, contrary.
vas[1], **vadis** *m* surety, bail.
vās[2], **vāsis** (*and* **vāsum**) *n* vessel, tool, utensil; **vāsa, ōrum** *n/pl.* luggage, baggage, military equipment.
vāsārium, ī *n* furniture-money, outfit.
vāsculārius, ī *m* worker in precious metals.
vāsculum, ī *n* small vessel.
vāstātiō, ōnis *f* a laying waste.
vāstātor, ōris *m* (*and* **-trīx, īcis** *f*) ravager, devastator.
vāsti-ficus 3 ravaging, devastating.
vāstitās, ātis (*and* **vāstitiēs, ēī**) *f* desolation, devastation, ruin, waste, desert.
vāstō 1 to make empty *or* void; **a**) to lay waste, desolate, ravage; **b**) to harass.
vāstus[1] 3 **a**) waste, desert, desolate, uncultivated, empty; **b**) devastated; **c**) rough, rude, uncouth, uncivilized.
vastus[2] 3 **a**) vast, huge, enormous; **b**) shapeless; monstrous.
vātēs (*and* **vātis**), **is** *m* and *f* soothsayer, diviner, seer, prophet; singer, bard, poet.
vāticinātiō, ōnis *f* prediction, prophecy.
vāticinātor, ōris *m* soothsayer, prophet.
vāticinor 1 to foretell, prophesy, divine; to utter teaching *or* warning; to rave, talk idly.
vāti-cinus 3 prophetic.
vatillum, ī *n* fire-pan.
ve *cj. enclitic* or, or perhaps; **ve ... ve** either ... or.

vēcordia, ae *f* madness, foolishness.
vē-cors, rdis mad, foolish, frantic.
vectātiō, ōnis *f* a riding, driving.
vectīgal, ālis *n* tax, impost, duty; **a**) contribution paid to a magistrate; **b**) private income, rents.
vectīgālis, e a) paid in taxes; **b**) liable to taxes, tributary; **c**) bringing in profit.
vectiō, ōnis *f* a carrying, conveyance.
vectis, is *m* lever; **a**) crowbar; **b**) bar, bolt.
vectō 1 to carry, convey.
vector, ōris *m* **a**) bearer, carrier; **b**) one who is carried, passenger, rider.
vectōrius 3 relating to conveying *or* transporting.
vectūra, ae *f* a carrying, conveying; conveyance, transport; passage-money, freight.
vegeō 2 to rouse, set in motion.
vegetus 3 vigorous, quick, active.
vē-grandis, e a) small, tiny; **b**) very great.
vehemēns, tis a) violent, vehement, furious, impetuous; **b**) strong, forcible, powerful, vigorous; *adv.* **vehementer** vehemently, violently, strongly, exceedingly, extremely, very much.
vehiculum, ī *n* vehicle, conveyance; litter, ship, wagon.
vehō, vēxī, vectum 3 to carry, bear, convey; to drive, draw; **P.** to be carried *or* conveyed; to ride, drive, sail, travel.
vel (*particle*) **a**) or, or rather; **vel ... vel** either ... or; **b**) even, actually; for example.
vēlāmen, inis *n* veil, covering, garment, clothing.
vēlāmentum, ī *n* **a**) = **velamen; b**) olive-branch wound round with wool.
vēlārium, ī *n* awning.
vēles, itis *m* skirmisher.
vēli-fer 3 sail-bearing.
vēlificātiō, ōnis *f* a sailing.
vēli-ficor (*and* **-ficō**) 1 to sail (through); to be zealous for (*with dat.*).
vēlitāris, e pertaining to skirmishers.
vēlitātiō, ōnis *f* a skirmishing.
vēlitor 1 to skirmish.
vēli-volāns, tis *and* **-volus** 3 flying *or* winged with sails.
vellicātiō, ōnis *f* taunting, fault-finding.
vellicō 1 to pluck, twitch; to criticize, rail at, taunt.
vellō, vellī (*and* **vulsī, volsī**), **vulsum** *and* **volsum** 3 to pluck, pull, twitch; to pluck out *or* off, to tear down.
vellus, eris *n* wool; **a**) fleece, sheepskin; **b**) skin of an animal; **c**) woollen band; **d**) silk; cloud; snow.
vēlō 1 to veil, cover; **a**) to wind about, encircle, surround; **b**) to hide, conceal, cloak.
vēlōcitās, ātis *f* quickness, swiftness, rapidity.
vēlōx, ōcis quick, swift, rapid.
vēlum[1], **ī** *n* sail; **vēla dare** to set sail.
vēlum[2], **ī** *n* drapery, curtain, awning, veil.
vel-ut(**ī**) **a**) as, even as, just as; **b**) for instance; **c**) **velut**(**sī**) (*with subj.*) just as if.
vēmēns, tis = **vehemens.**
vēna, ae *f* vein, blood-vessel; penis; **a**) water-course; **b**) vein in wood *or* stone; **c**) metallic vein; **d**) inmost nature, inmost *or* vital part, interior; **e**) vein of talent, disposition, natural bent, poetic genius.
vēnābulum, ī *n* hunting-spear.
vēnālīcius 3 for sale; *subst.* **~, ī** *m* slave-dealer.
vēnālis, e on sale; to be sold; *subst. m* slave; venal, that may be bribed.
vēnāticus 3 of the chase, for hunting.
vēnātiō, ōnis *f* a hunting, chase; hunting spectacle; wild beast fight; game.
vēnātor, ōris *m* hunter; explorer, searcher.
vēnātōrius 3 = **venaticus.**
vēnātrīx, īcis *f* huntress.
vēnātūra, ae *f* = **vēnātus.**
vēnātus, ūs *m* a hunting, chase; fishing.
vendibilis, e on sale, salable; popular, acceptable.
venditātiō, ōnis *f* a boasting, vaunting.
venditātor, ōris *m* boaster, vaunter.
venditiō, ōnis *f* a selling, sale, sale by auction; goods sold.
venditō 1 to offer for sale; **a**) to barter away, give for a bribe; **b**) to make traffic of; **c**) to praise, recommend.

venditor, ōris *m* seller.
vendō, didī, ditum 3 to sell; to have on sale; a) to sell by auction, to let out, farm out; **b**) to betray for money, give for a bribe; **c**) to cry up, praise, recommend.
venē-fica, ae *f* poisoner, sorceress, witch.
venēficium, ī *n* a poisoning, a preparing of poison; poisoned drink; magic, sorcery.
venē-ficus 3 mixing poison, magical; *subst.* **~, ī** *m* poisoner, sorcerer.
venēnārius, ī *m* poisoner.
venēnātus 3 **a**) poisoned, poisonous; **b**) bewitched, enchanted.
venēni-fer 3 poisonous.
venēnō 1 to poison.
venēnum, ī *n* **a**) dye, drug; **b**) poison, poisoned drink; **c**) ruin, destruction, bane; **d**) magic potion, charm, philtre, sorcery.
vēn-eō, iī, —, īre to be on sale, be sold.
venerābilis, e reverend, venerable.
venerābundus 3 respectful, reverent.
venerātiō, ōnis *f* reverence, respect, worship.
venerātor, ōris *m* reverer, adorer.
venereus *and* **-ius** 3, *see* **venus.**
veneror (*and* **venerō**) 1 to revere, worship, adore; to implore, pray reverently to *or* for; to beseech humbly.
venetus 3 (Venetian); blue.
venia, ae *f* favour, grace, indulgence, permission; **bonā tuā veniā** by your indulgence, by your leave; **a**) pardon; **b**) forgiveness, indulgence to faults.
veniō, vēnī, ventum 4 to come, come to, arrive; **a**) to advance, approach; **ventūrus** 3 coming, future; **b**) to come into, fall into a state *or* condition (*in periculum, in calamitatem, in potestatem alcis*); **c**) to come forth, appear; to grow; — **vēnit mihi in mentem** (*alcis*) I thought of.
vennū(n)cula, ae *f* = **vēnūcula.**
vēnō, *see* **vēnum.**
vēnor 1 to hunt; to chase, pursue, strive after (*acc.*).
vēnōsus 3 full of veins; over-exuberant, turgid (?).
venter, tris *m* belly, paunch; **a**) stomach; **b**) womb, fœtus; **c**) a swelling, protuberance; **d**) appetite, gluttony.
ventilō 1 to wave in the air; **a**) to winnow (*grain*), fan; **b**) to incite.
ventiō, ōnis *f* a coming.
ventitō 1 to come often.
ventōsus 3 full of wind, windy; of the wind; **a**) swift *or* light as the wind; **b**) vain, empty; conceited; **c**) unsteady, fickle, inconstant, changeable.
ventriculus, ī *m* belly; **cordis** ventricle of the heart.
ventriōsus 3 big-bellied.
ventulus, ī *m* breeze.
ventus, ī *m* wind; **a**) fortune, circumstances; **b**) favour of the people, vain applause; **c**) storm, disturbance; **d**) rumour.
vēnūcula, ae *f* a kind of grape.
vēnum (*acc.*), **vēnō** (*dat.*) sale; **vēnum dō = vendō; vēnum eō = vēneō; vēnō pōnō** to expose for sale.
venus, eris *f* **a**) love, pleasures of love; beloved person; **b**) loveliness, beauty, charm, attractiveness; **c**) **Venus** the goddess of love; the planet Venus; the highest throw in dice-play; *adj.* **venereus** *and* **venerius** 3 dedicated to Venus; relating to sexual love; *subst. m, n* the highest throw in dice-play.
venustās, ātis *f* loveliness, charm, beauty; **a**) attractiveness, gracefulness, sweetness; **b**) elegance, politeness.
venustulus 3, *dim. of* **venustus.**
venustus 3 charming, lovely, beautiful; attractive, fine.
vē-pallidus 3 very pale.
veprēcula, ae *f* little thorn-bush.
veprēs, is *m* (and *f*) thorn-bush, brier, bramble.
vēr, vēris *n* spring-time.
vērātrum, ī *n* hellebore.
vērāx, ācis truthful.
verbēna, ae *f* vervain; *pl.* sacred herbs *or* branches.
verbēnātus 3 decked with sacred twigs.
verber, eris *n* blow, lash; **a**) blows with a whip, a thrashing, flogging; **b**) cudgel, whip, scourge; **c**) thong of a sling.
verberābilis, e *and* **verbereus** 3 deserving to be flogged.
verberābundus 3 dealing blows.

verberātiō, ōnis *f* a beating, punishment.
verberō[1], **ōnis** *m* scoundrel.
verberō[2] 1 to beat, strike; **a**) to whip, scourge; **b**) to chastise, assail, harass, plague.
verbi-vēlitātiō, ōnis *f* skirmishing with words.
verbōsus 3 wordy, verbose.
verbum, ī *n* word, expression, *pl.* words, talk, discourse, speech; **verba facere** to speak, make a speech; **a**) utterance, saying, maxim, proverb; **b**) mere word, mere talk, stuff; **alci verba dare** to deceive, cheat; **c**) formula, incantation; — **verbō** in name, in theory; **ad verbum** word for word; **verbī causā** *or* **gratiā** for instance; **verbīs alcis** in the name of, in behalf of.
vērculum, ī *n* little spring.
vērē, *adv. of* **verus**.
verēcundia, ae *f* respect, awe, shyness, modesty; **a**) reverence, veneration; **b**) shame.
verēcundor 1 to be bashful, ashamed, shy.
verēcundus 3 bashful. modest; **a**) respectful; **b**) moderate.
verēdus, ī *m* swift horse.
vereor, veritus sum 2 **a**) to fear (*alqd, ne, ut*); **b**) to shrink from; hesitate (*inf.*), feel shame; **c**) to reverence, respect, stand in awe of; **verendus** 3 inspiring awe; *n/pl.* genital organs.
veretrum, ī *n* genital organs.
vergiliae, ārum *f/pl.* the seven stars (= Pleiades).
vergō, (rsī), —3 a) to incline *or* turn oneself to (*ad* or *in alqd*); to lie towards, be situated towards; **b**) to decline; **c**) *trans.* to pour in (*alqd in rem*); to incline, turn.
vēri-dicus 3 = **verax**.
vēri-loquium, ī *n* etymology.
vēri-similis, e probable, likely.
vēri-similitūdō, inis *f* probability.
vēritas, ātis *f* truth; **a**) reality, actual nature, real life; **b**) sincerity, candour, truthfulness; **c**) honesty, integrity.
vēri-verbium, ī *n* a speaking the truth.
vermiculātus 3 made in worm-pattern (mosaic).
vermiculus, ī *m* small worm, grub.
vermina, um *n/pl.* abdominal pains.
verminātiō, ōnis *f* pricking *or* itching pain.
verminō (*and* **-or**) 1 to itch; to have pricking *or* shooting pains.
vermis, is *m* worm.
verna, ae *m* (and *f*) home-born slave.
vernāculus 3 born in the house, domestic; *subst. m* house-jester, wit; **a**) native, indigenous, Roman; **b**) invented by an accuser (*crimen*).
vernīlis, e a) slavish, servile; **b**) abject, crouching; **c**) forward, saucy.
vernīlitās, ātis *f* **a**) fawning; **b**) pertness, sauciness.
vernō 1 to become spring-like, be renewed, grow green; to be youthful.
vernula, ae *m* (and *f*) *dimin. of* **verna**: *adj.* native.
vernus 3 relating to spring, spring-like.
vērō, *adv. of* **verus**.
verpa, ae *f* penis.
verpus, ī *m* a circumcised man.
verrēs, is *m* boar, male swine.
verrīnus 3 of a boar.
verrō,—versum 3 to sweep, brush; **a**) to sweep clean, to clean, to sweep out *or* together; **b**) to drag *or* sweep along, take away; **c**) to trail on the ground.
verrūca, ae *f* wart; small fault.
verrūcōsus 3 full of warts.
verruncō 1 to turn, **bene** to turn out well.
verrūtum, ī *n* = **verutum**.
versābilis, e movable, changeable.
versābundus 3 revolving.
versātilis, e turning round, revolving; versatile, adroit.
versātiō, ōnis *f* change.
versi-capillus 3 with greying hair.
versi-color, ōris changing in colour; particoloured.
versiculus, ī *m* little verse.
versi-pellis, e a) changed in appearance; **b**) subtle, crafty.
versō 1 **1.** to turn about often, to turn hither and thither, to turn round, roll; a) to turn, bend. shift, agitate, move about, drive round; b) to disturb, discompose, harass. vex; c) to handle, deal with; d) to revolve, consider, meditate; —**2. P. versor** 1 to turn oneself round; a) to stay, dwell, live; b) to be in a certain condition; c) to be occupied, busied, engaged in (*in re*), pay attention to, practise.

versum *adv.* = **versus**[2].
versūra, ae *f* **a**) the borrowing of money to pay a debt; **b**) a borrowing, loan.
versus[1] 3, *part. of* **verto** *and* **verro.**
versus[2] *adv.* towards, in the direction of, **in Italiam versus, ad mare versus.**
versus[3], **ūs** *m* a turning; **a**) furrow; **b**) row, line; **c**) verse, poetry; **d**) turn *or* step in a dance.
versūtia, ae *f* cunning, craftiness.
versūti-loquus 3 craftily-speaking.
versūtus 3 cunning, crafty, dexterous.
vertebra, ae *f* joint.
vertex, icis *m* whirl, whirlpool, eddy; **a**) whirlwind; **b**) coil of flame, pillar of fire; **c**) top *or* crown of the head, top, summit, head; **d**) the pole of the heavens; **e**) height, hill, elevation; **a vertice** from above.
verticōsus 3 full of whirlpools.
vertīgō, inis *f* a turning *or* whirling round; **a**) revolution; **b**) giddiness, dizziness.
vertō, rtī, rsum 3 (*archaic* **vortō**) **1.** to turn, turn round, up, back (*acc.*); a) to turn, direct, convert; **ad se** to appropriate (*pecuniam*); b) to ascribe, refer, construe as, impute; c) to change to, cause to pass to; d) to turn away (*lumina, vultum*); e) to turn round *or* back (*pedem, gradum*), to put to flight (*alqm in fugam*); **terga vertere** to flee; f) to turn up, dig up, plough (*terram aratro*); to overthrow, overturn, subvert, destroy, ruin; g) to alter, change, exchange, transform, metamorphose; to translate; **2.** *intr. and* **P.** to turn *or* direct oneself; a) to turn out, result; b) to move about, roll round, revolve; c) to be in a certain condition *or* state, lie in a certain direction; d) (*of time*) revolve, come round; e) to depend, rest upon, belong to; f) to be changed, change to, become.
vertragus, ī *m* greyhound.
verū, ūs (*and* **verum**) *n* spit; javelin.
veruīna, ae *f* small spit.
vērum, *see* **verus.**
vērum enim-vērō but truly.
vērum-tamen but yet, however, nevertheless.
vērus 3 true, real, actual, genuine, well-grounded, *subst.* **vērum, ī** *n* truth, reality, fact; **a**) truthful, true, veracious, upright; **b**) fitting, reasonable, just, proper; *subst.* **vērum, ī** *n* duty; **c**) *adv.* **vērē** truly, truthfully, rightly, in fact, really, actually; **d**) *adv.* **vērō** in truth, really. indeed, (*in answers*) certainly, to be sure; (*as adversative particle*) but in fact, but indeed; (*in climax*) even, indeed; **e**) **vērum** (as *adv.*) yes, certainly; (as *cj.*) but, but in truth, but still.
verūtum, ī *m* javelin.
verūtus 3 armed with a javelin.
vervēx, ēcis *m* wether; dolt.
vēsānia, ae *f* madness, insanity.
vēsāniēns, tis furious, raging.
vē-sānus 3 mad, insane, frantic, raging.
vescor, —, — 3 to feed on, eat (*alqa re*; rarely *alqd*); to use, enjoy.
vēscus 3 **a**) consuming, corroding; **b**) thin, slender, feeble, wretched.
vēsīca, ae *f* bladder; **a**) vulva; **b**) cap; **c**) lantern; **d**) bombast.
vēsīcula, ae *f* little bladder.
vespa, ae *f* wasp.
vesper, erī (*and* **-eris**) *m* **a**) the evening-star; **b**) evening, evening meal; **c**) the west; **vesperī** *and* **-e** in the evening.
vespera, ae *f* the evening.
vesperāscō, rāvī, — 3 to become evening, grow dark.
vespertīliō, ōnis *m* bat.
vespertīnus 3 of the evening; western.
vesperūgō, inis *f* evening-star.
vespillō, ōnis *m* corpse-bearer for the poor.
Vesta, ae *f* the goddess Vesta; **a**) hearth, fire on the hearth; **b**) temple of Vesta; *adj.* **Vestālis** belonging to Vesta; *subst. f* priestess of Vesta, Vestal virgin.
vester, tra, trum your, yours.
vestiārium, ī *n* clothing.
vestibulum, ī *n* **a**) entrance court, court-yard; porch, vestibule; **b**) entrance.
vestīgātor, ōris *m* spy.
vestīgium, ī *n* **a**) foot-print, foot-step, track; trace, mark, sign, *pl.* ruins; step, pace; **b**) sole of the foot; **c**) station, position, post; **d**) moment, instant; **e** *or* **in vestīgiō** on the spot, instantly.

vestīgō 1 **a**) to track, follow the trail of; **b**) to investigate, search out.
vestīmentum, ī *n* garment, article of clothing, *pl.* clothes.
vestiō 4 **a**) to clothe, dress; **b**) to cover, deck, adorn.
vesti-p(l)ica, ae *f* wardrobe-woman.
vestis, is *f* clothes, clothing, dress; **a**) carpet, tapestry; **b**) veil; **c**) spider's web; **d**) snake-skin.
vestītus, ūs *m* clothing; **a**) clothes, dress, attire; **b**) covering.
veterāmentārius 3, ~ **sūtor** mender of old shoes.
veterānus 3 (*and subst. m*) veteran.
veterārium, ī *n* (*sc. vinum*) old vintage wine.
veterāscō, āvi, — 3 to become old.
veterātor, ōris *m* old hand, old fox.
veterātōrius 3 cunning, crafty.
veterīnus 3 of a draught-horse.
veternōsus 3 sleepy, dreamy.
veternus, ī *m* **a**) old age; **b**) lethargy, drowsiness, laziness.
vetō, uī, itum 1 to forbid, prohibit (*alqm*; *acc.c.inf.*); **a**) to interpose a veto; **b**) to check, prevent.
vetulus 3 old.
vetus, eris (*comp.* **vetustior,** *superl.* **veterrimus**) old, aged, advanced in years; of long standing, ancient; *subst.* **veterēs, um** *m/pl.* the ancients, forefathers, men of old; *f* the old booths of money-changers in the Forum.
vetustās, ātis *f* old age, long existence, length of time; **a**) friendship of long standing; **b**) antiquity; **c**) late posterity.
vetustus 3 old, aged, ancient, old-fashioned, antique.
vexāmen, inis *n* shaking.
vexātiō, ōnis *f* a shaking; **a**) hardship, trouble; **b**) ill-treatment, vexation.
vexātor, ōris *m* harasser, disturber.
vexillārius, ī *m* **a**) standardbearer, ensign; **b**) *pl.* reserve of veterans; detachment of soldiers.
vexillātiō, ōnis *f* detachment of soldiers.
vexillum, ī *n* standard, flag; **a**) signal-flag; **b**) company of soldiers, troop; detachment.
vexō 1 to move violently, shake; **a**) to harass, trouble, plague; disturb, molest; **b**) to damage, maltreat, attack, abuse, annoy, injure, ruin.
via, ae *f* way, road; **a**) highroad; **b**) street in a town, lane; way, path, course; **c**) the right way, straight road; **d**) way, march, journey; way, manner, means, method.
viālis, e of the roads.
viārius 3 relating to highways.
viāticātus provided with travelling-money.
viāticus 3 relating to a journey; *subst.* **-cum, ī** *n* money for a journey; soldier's savings.
viātor, ōris *m* **a**) traveller, wayfarer; **b**) messenger of a magistrate.
vībīx, īcis *f* weal.
vibrō 1 to shake, brandish; **a**) to cause to vibrate, move to and fro; **P.** to tremble; to hurl; **b**) *intr.* to tremble, quiver; to flash, glitter, gleam.
vīburnum, ī *n* a kind of tree, wayfaring-tree.
vīcānus 3 of a village; *subst.* **~, ī** *m* villager.
vicārius 3 substituted, vicarious; *subst.* **~, ī** *m* substitute, deputy; under-slave.
vīcātim *adv.* **a**) from street to street; **b**) in villages.
vice *and* **vicem,** *see* **vicis.**
vīcēnī 3 twenty each.
vīcēnsimus 3 = **vicesimus.**
vicēs, *see* **vicis.**
vīcēsimānus, ī *m* soldier of the twentieth legion.
vīcēsimārius 3 derived from a five per cent tax.
vīcēsimus 3 the twentieth; *subst.* **-a, ae** *f* five per cent tax.
vicia, ae *f* vetch.
vīciē(n)s *adv.* twenty times.
vīcīnālis, e neighbouring.
(**vīcīnia, ae** *f and*) **vīcīnitās, ātis** *f* neighbourhood; the neighbours.
vīcīnus 3 **1.** neighbouring, near; a) *subst.* **~, ī** *m*, **-a, ae** *f* neighbour; b) **-um, ī** *n* neighbourhood, vicinity; **2.** a) near, approaching; b) similar, like.
vicis (*gen.*), *acc.* **em,** *abl.* **e,** *pl.* **vicēs,** *abl.* **vicibus** *f* change, interchange, alternation, turn; **a**) reply, answer, requital, compensation, equivalent, retaliation; **b**) lot, fate, fortune, destiny; **c**) position, place, office,

post, duty, part; **d**) *adv.* **vicem** *and* **vice** for the sake of, on account of, as, like; (**in**) **vicem** by turns; mutually; instead of.
vicissātim *adv.* = **vicissim.**
vicissim *adv.* **a**) in turn, again; **b**) on the other hand.
vicissitūdō, inis *f* change, interchange, alternation, vicissitude.
victima, ae *f* beast for sacrifice, victim; sacrifice.
victimārius, ī *m* assistant at sacrifices.
vīctitō 1 to live *or* feed upon (*alqa re*).
victor, ōris *m* conqueror, victor; victorious.
victōria, ae *f* victory, conquest; the goddess of victory.
victōriātus, ī *m* silver coin with the figure of Victory.
Victōriola, ae *f* small statue of Victory.
victrīx, īcis *f* (*and n*) victorious.
vīctus, ūs *m* **a**) means of living, nourishment, food, victuals; **b**) manner of life, mode of living.
vīculus, ī *m* hamlet.
vīcus, ī *m* **a**) village, hamlet; estate, farm; **b**) district of a town, street.
vidē-licet *adv.* **a**) clearly, plainly, obviously, manifestly; **b**) of course, to be sure; **c**) namely.
videō, vīdī, vīsum 2 **1.** to see; a) to have the power of seeing; b) to see, perceive, discern, to see again; to live to see, to experience; c) to look at, observe, behold; to go to see, visit; d) to see patiently, let pass, permit; e) to perceive mentally, observe, think, know, understand, comprehend; consider, reflect upon; f) to see to, take care, provide for, look after with care; **2. P. videor, vīsus sum** 2 a) to be seen, be looked upon, become visible, appear, to be evident *or* manifest; b) to seem, be regarded; **alci vidētur** it seems proper, right, good, it pleases; **si vidētur** if you please.
vidua, ae *f* widow; unmarried woman.
viduitās, ātis *f* widowhood; lack.
vidulus, ī *m* wicker trunk.
viduō 1 to deprive *or* bereave of, deprive of a husband.
viduus 3 widowed; unmarried, single, *see* **vidua**; **a**) deprived, bereft, destitute, without (*with abl.* or *gen.*); **b**) mateless, solitary.
viētus 3 shrivelled, withered.
vigeō, uī, — 2 to be lively, vigorous, strong, active; to flourish, bloom, be in repute, be esteemed; to prevail, be in vogue.
vigēscō, —, — 3 to become vigorous.
vīgēsimus 3 = **vicesimus.**
vīgessis, is *m* twenty *asses.*
vigil, ilis *m* watchman, sentinel; *adj.* watching, watchful, awake.
vigilāns, tis watchful, careful.
vigilantia, ae *f* wakefulness; watchfulness.
vigilāx, ācis watchful, wakeful.
vigilia, ae *f* a being awake, sleeplessness; **a**) a watching, keeping watch, watch, guard; **b**) watchmen, sentinels; **c**) a watch (a fourth part of the night); **d**) watchfulness, vigilance, attention.
vigil(i)ārium, ī *n* watch-tower.
vigilō 1 **a**) to keep awake, be wakeful; to watch, be vigilant *or* attentive; **b**) to watch through, to perform watching, execute by night.
vīgintī (*indecl.*) twenty.
vīgintī-virātus, ūs *m* office of *vīgintīvirī.*
vīgintī-virī, ōrum *m/pl.* commission *or* board of twenty men.
vigor, ōris *m* life, vigour, energy, liveliness.
vīlica, ae *f* female overseer; steward's wife.
vīlicō 1 to superintend, act as overseer.
vīlicus, ī *m* overseer, steward.
vīlis, e cheap, of little value, low, paltry, worthless, mean.
vīlitās, ātis *f* cheapness, low price; **a**) trifling value, worthlessness; **b**) disregard, contempt.
vīlla, ae *f* country-house, farm.
vīllica, -cō, -cus, *see* **vīlica, -co, -cus.**
villōsus 3 hairy, shaggy, rough.
vīllula, ae *f* small country house *or* villa.
vīllum, ī *n* a little wine, tipsiness.
villus, ī *m* shaggy hair, tuft of hair; nap of cloth.
vīmen, inis *n* pliant twig; **a**) withe, osier; **b**) wickerwork.
vīmentum, ī *n* osier, twig.

vīmineus 3 made of osiers, of wicker-work.
vīn' (= **visne**) wilt thou? will you?
vīnāceus, ī *m* grape-stone.
vīnālia, ium *n/pl.* wine festival.
vīnārius 3 of wine, for wine; *subst.* **~, ī** *m* wine-merchant; **-um, ī** *n* wine-pot, wine-flask.
vincibilis, e easily won.
vinciō, vinxī, vinctum 4 to bind, tie, fetter; **a**) to surround, encircle (*alqd alqa re*); **b**) to wind round; **c**) to bind, pledge, oblige; **d**) to restrain, confine.
vinclum, ī *n* = **vinculum.**
vincō, vīcī, victum 3 to conquer, overcome; **a**) to be victorious (*re*); **Olympia** (*acc.*) in the Olympian games; to prevail, get the mastery over, succeed, win; **b**) to overcome, overwhelm, subdue (*acc.*); **c**) to win over, cause to yield *or* give way; **d**) to outdo, surpass, exceed, excel; **e**) to show conclusively, carry a point.
vinculum, ī *n* band, tie; **a**) cord, rope, fetter; *pl.* fetters, bonds, prison; **b**) tie, band, restraint.
vīn-dēmia, ae *f* vintage; grapes, wine.
vīndēmiātor, ōris *m* grape-gatherer.
vīndēmiolae, ārum *f/pl.* little vintage; small income.
vīndēmitor, ōris *m* the vintager (the name of a star).
vindex, icis *m* **a**) protector, champion, deliverer; **b**) avenger, punisher.
vindicātiō, ōnis *f* claim; protection; punishment.
vindiciae, ārum *f/pl.* thing *or* person claimed at law; legal claim; protection; **vindicias decernere** *or* **dare** to pronounce judgment concerning a claim.
vindicō 1 **a**) to assert a claim, demand formally, ask judgment for; to claim, arrogate, demand as one's own, assume; **b**) to champion, rescue, deliver (*alqm* or *alqd in libertatem, ab alqo*); to defend, protect, save; **c**) to avenge, punish, inflict punishment, take vengeance on.
vindicta, ae *f* **a**) the freeing of a slave, deliverance, rescue; liberating-rod; **b**) vengeance, revenge, punishment.
vīnea, ae *f* **a**) vine; **b**) vineyard; **c**) roof, shed for shelter, penthouse.
vīnētum, ī *n* vineyard.
vīneus 3 of vine-wood.
vīnitor, ōris *m* vine-dresser.
vinnulus 3 charming, pleasant.
vīnolentia, ae *f* wine-drinking, intoxication.
vīnolentus 3 **a**) drunken with wine, given to wine; **b**) mixed with wine.
vīnōsus 3 full of wine; **a**) drunken; **b**) given to wine; **c**) like wine.
vīnulentia, vīnulentus, *see* **vino...**
vīnum, ī *n* wine; **a**) grape; **b**) vine.
viola, ae *f* **a**) violet; violet-colour; **b**) gillyflower, stock.
violābilis, e easily injured, **nōn ~** inviolable.
violārium, ī *n* bed of violets.
violārius, ī *m* one who dyes violet.
violātiō, ōnis *f* a violating, profaning.
violātor, ōris *m* violator, profaner.
violēns, tis = **violentus.**
violentia, ae *f* violence, vehemence; impetuosity, ferocity, fury.
violentus 3 violent, impetuous, boisterous, harsh.
violō 1 to treat with violence, maltreat, injure, hurt, outrage, dishonour, violate (*acc.*); **a**) to defile, profane; **b**) to transgress, break; **c**) to offend.
vīpera, ae *f* viper, adder, snake.
vīpereus 3 of a viper *or* snake; **a**) snaky-haired; **b**) poisonous.
vīperīnus 3 = **vipereus.**
vir, virī *m* a man, male person, adult male; **a**) husband; **b**) man of character *or* courage, worthy man, hero; **c**) soldier, warrior; **d**) a single man, individual; *pl.* = **homines** human beings, men, mortals.
virāgō, inis *f* a manlike woman, female warrior.
virectum, ī *n* green place, turf.
vireō, uī, — 2 to be green; to be blooming, fresh, vigorous.
virēscō, ruī, — 3 to grow green.
virētum, ī *n* = **virectum.**
virga, ae *f* twig, rod, wand, staff; **a**) graft, scion; **b**) *pl.* = *fascēs*; **c**) magic wand; **d**) branch of a pedigree; **e**) coloured stripe.
virgātor, ōris *m* flogger.
virgātus 3 **a**) made of twigs; **b**) striped.

virgētum, ī *n* osier-thicket.
virgeus 3 of rods *or* twigs.
virgi-dēmia, ae *f* rod-harvest, sound cudgelling.
virginālis, e (*and* **virginārius** 3) maidenly, of a maiden; *subst.* **-āle, is** *n* the vulva.
virginēs-vendōnidēs, ae *m* seller of maidens.
virgineus 3 of a maiden, of a virgin, maidenly.
virginitās, ātis *f* maidenhood, virginity, chastity.
virgō, inis *f* maiden, virgin; young woman; the constellation Virgo; a Roman aqueduct.
virgula, ae *f*, *dim. of* **virga.**
virgultum, ī *n* thicket, shrubbery, shrub; slip for planting.
virguncula, ae *f* young girl.
virid(i)ārium, ī *n* pleasure-garden.
viridis, e green; fresh, youthful.
viriditās ātis *f* greenness, verdure; freshness.
viridō 1 **a**) to be green; **b**) to make green.
virīlis, e of a man, like a man, manly, male; **a**) courageous, vigorous; **b**) adult; **c**) **prō virīlī parte** to the best of one's power.
virīlitās, ātis *f* manly age, manhood; virility.
vīripotēns, ntis all-powerful.
virītim *adv.* man for man, singly, separately.
vīrōsus 3 stinking, fetid.
virtūs, ūtis *f* manhood, manliness, virility; **a**) firmness, strength; **b**) courage, bravery, valour; constancy, resolution; gallant deeds; **c**) excellence, worth; **d**) virtue, goodness, moral perfection, good quality; *pl.* accomplishments.
vīrus, ī *n* slime: poison; strong smell; saltiness.
vīs (*acc.* **vim,** *abl.* **vī.;** *pl.* **vīrēs, ium**) *f* **1.** *sg.* force, power, strength; a) energy; b) hostile strength, violence, force, attack, impetuosity, fury, compulsion; c) power, might, influence, potency; force, meaning, nature, essence, sense, import; d) quantity, number, abundance; **2.** *pl.* **vīrēs, ium** powers, bodily strength; a) military forces, troops; b) means, resources; c) mental power, vigour.
viscātus 3 smeared with bird-lime; deceptive, ensnaring; laying under an obligation.
vīscerātiō, ōnis *f* public distribution of meat.
viscō 1 to smear, plaster, glue together.
viscum, ī *n* (*and* **viscus, ī** *m*) mistletoe; bird-lime.
vīscus, eris *n* (*usually pl.*) **a**) flesh, meat; **b**) internal organs; **c**) womb; one's own flesh, children; **d**) the inmost part, heart, centre, life **e**) bosom-friend, favourite.
vīsiō, ōnis *f* apparition, appearance; idea, conception.
vīsitō 1 to see often; to visit.
vīsō, sī, — 3 **a**) to look at carefully *or* attentively, to view; **b**) to go to see, visit; **vīsendus** 3 worth seeing.
vispillō, ōnis *m* = **vespillo.**
vīsum, ī *n* sight, appearance, vision; perception, image.
vīsus, ūs *m* **a**) a seeing, look, sight; **b**) appearance, thing seen.
vīta, ae *f* life, lifetime; **a**) soul, shade; **b**) way *or* manner of life, conduct of life, manners; **c**) life, biography; **d**) men living, the world.
vītābilis, e to be shunned.
vītābundus 3 avoiding, shunning, evading (*alqd*).
vītālis, e of life, vital; living, long-lived; life-sustaining; *subst.* **-lia** *n/pl.* **a**) vital parts; **b**) grave-clothes.
vītātiō, ōnis *f* an avoiding.
vitellus, ī *m* **a**) little calf; **b**) yolk of an egg.
vīteus 3 of the vine.
vīti-cola, ae *m* cultivator of vines.
vīticula, ae *f* little vine.
vītifer 3 vine-bearing.
vītigenus 3 produced from vines.
vitiō 1 to spoil, mar, corrupt, injure, damage, vitiate; **a**) to defile, debauch, ravish; **b**) to falsify, forge; **c**) to declare (*a day*) unfit for public business (on account of bad omens).
vitiōsitās, ātis *f* viciousness.
vitiōsus 3 full of faults, faulty, defective, bad, corrupt; **a**) vicious, wicked, depraved; **b**) contrary to the auspices.
vītis, is *f* vine, vine-branch: **a**) wine; **b**) centurion's staff; **c**) **alba** (*a plant*) bryony.

vīti-sator, ōris *m* planter of vines.
vitium, ī *n* fault, defect, blemish, imperfection; **a**) a failing, error, offence, crime; **b**) moral fault, vice.
vītō 1 to shun, avoid.
vītor, ōris *m* basket-maker.
vitreārius, ī *m* glass-blower.
vitreus 3 of glass; *subst. n/pl.* glass-ware; **a**) glassy, transparent, brilliant; **b**) brittle, precarious; **c**) blue-green.
vitricus, ī *m* stepfather.
vitrum[1], **ī** *n* glass.
vitrum[2], **ī** *n* (*a vegetable dye*) woad.
vitta, ae *f* ribbon, band, fillet.
vittātus 3 adorned with a fillet.
vitula, ae *f* calf, heifer.
vitulīnus 3 of a calf; *subst.* **-a, ae** *f* veal.
vītulor 1 to rejoice; to offer thanks.
vitulus, ī *m* **a**) calf; **b**) foal; **c**) ~ **marīnus** seal.
vituperābilis, e blamable.
vituperātiō, ōnis *f* a blaming, blame; blamable conduct.
vituperātor, ōris *m* blamer, censurer.
vituperō 1 **a**) to spoil (*an omen*); **b**) to blame, scold, censure.
vīvācitās, ātis *f* vital strength, longevity.
vīvārium, ī *n* park, preserve, aviary, fishpond.
vīvātus 3 lively, animated.
vīvāx, ācis long-lived; lively, vigorous; lasting.
vīvēscō 3 to grow lively *or* strong.
vīvidus 3 full of life, lively, animated, vigorous; life-like.
vīvi-rādīx, īcis *f* cutting with root.
vīvō, vīxī, vīctūrus 3 to live, be alive; **a**) to have *or* enjoy life; **b**) to live on, last, continue; **c**) to live upon (*abl.*), support life; **d**) to live in a certain manner, to live at a certain place.
vīvus 3 living, alive, having life; **mē vīvō** in my lifetime; **a**) fresh, active, lasting; **b**) natural, unwrought; *subst.* **vīvum, ī** *n* that which is alive, living flesh; capital of money, principal.
vix *adv.* with difficulty, hardly, scarcely, barely; (*of time*) scarcely, just.
vix-dum *adv.* scarcely yet.
vocābulum, ī *n* name, appellation.
vōcālis, e uttering sounds, sounding, sonorous, singing; *subst. f* vowel; conferring the power of speech.
vocāmen, inis *n* name.
vocātiō, ōnis *f* an inviting.
vocātor, ōris *m* inviter.
vocātus, ūs *m* a calling to *or* upon, invoking; invitation.
vōciferātiō, ōnis *f* an exclaiming, outcry, clamour.
vōciferor (*and* **-rō**) 1 to cry aloud, exclaim, shout; scream (*acc.c.inf.*; *ut*).
vocitō 1 to (be wont to) call; to shout loudly.
vocō 1 to call, summon (*acc.*); **a**) to cite; **b**) to invite; **c**) to challenge, defy, entice, urge, stimulate (*alqm ad alqd*); **d**) to call by name, to name; **e**) to bring into a certain condition (*alqm in odium, in periculum; alqd in dubium* to call in question).
vōcula, ae *f* weak voice; *pl.* soft notes, tones; spiteful remarks.
volaemum, ī *n* a kind of large pear.
volāticus 3 flying, volatile, fickle.
volātilis, e flying, winged; swift, transitory.
volātus, ūs *m* a flying, flight.
volēmum, ī *n* = **volaemum.**
volēns, tis willing; **a**) with purpose; **b**) of one's own accord, ready; **c**) well-disposed, kind, favourable, propitious, gracious; **d**) acceptable, pleasing.
volgus, volgāris (*archaic*) = **vulgus, vulgaris.**
volitō 1 to fly about *or* to and fro; to flit, hover.
volnerō, volnus (*archaic*) = **vulnero, vulnus.**
volō[1] 1 to fly, *subst.* **volantēs, ium** *f/pl.* birds; to fly, hasten.
volō[2], **luī, velle** to be willing, to wish, to choose, purpose, intend, desire; **a**) **velim, vellem** I should like, should be glad; **b**) **aliquem alqd velle** to want something of someone; **c**) **bene** (**male**) **alci velle** to wish well; **d**) **quid tibi vīs?** what are you driving at? what is your aim?; **e**) to command, ordain, appoint, determine; **f**) to believe, pretend, contend, maintain, say; **g**) to prefer, choose rather; **h**) to mean, signify, intend to say.
volō[3], **ōnis** *m* volunteer.

volpēcula, volpēs (*archaic*) = **vulpecula, vulpes.**
volsella, ae *f* pair of tweezers.
voltur-, voltus (*archaic*) = **vultur-, vultus.**
volūbilis, e that may be turned; **a**) turning, rolling, revolving; **b**) changeable, fickle, unstable; **c**) fluent, rapid (*of speech*).
volūbilitās, ātis *f* the power of being turned round easily; **a**) a rapid turning, whirling; **b**) mutability, inconstancy; **c**) fluency, volubility.
volucer (*and* **-cris**), **cris, cre** flying, winged; *subst.* **volucris** *f* (*and m*) bird, winged insect; **a**) rapid, quick, fleet; **b**) transient, changeable.
volūmen, inis *n* **a**) coil, whirl, fold; **b**) revolution; **c**) book, roll, volume.
voluntārius 3 willing, of freewill, voluntary; *subst.* volunteer.
voluntās, ātis *f* will, free-will; **a**) wish, desire, purpose, aim, resolution; **b**) good-will, favour, affection, readiness; **voluntāte** willingly; **c**) last will, testament; **d**) inclination, disposition.
volup *adv.* pleasantly, agreeably.
voluptābilis, e pleasing, pleasant.
voluptārius 3 relating to pleasure; **a**) giving enjoyment, pleasurable; **b**) devoted to pleasure, voluptuous; *subst.* **~, ī** *m* voluptuary, Epicure.
voluptās, ātis *f* pleasure, enjoyment, delight; **a**) desire, passion, sensual pleasures; **b**) *pl.* public shows, sports, spectacles, games; **c**) **mea voluptas** my darling.
voluptuōsus 3 agreeable, delightful.
volūtābrum, ī *n* hog-pool.
volūtābundus 3 wallowing about.
volūtātiō, ōnis *f* a rolling, wallowing; restlessness.
volūtō 1 to roll, turn; **a**) to roll about; **P.** to wallow, luxuriate; **b**) to turn over in the mind, consider, weigh.
volva, ae *f* womb (*esp. of a sow*).
volvō, lvī, lūtum 3 to roll, turn round *or* about, whirl round; **a**) to unroll (*books*), to read; **b**) to roll along, bring on, roll forth *or* down; **c**) **orbem** to form a circle; **d**) to pour forth (*words*), utter fluently; **e**) to revolve in the mind, to cherish, to consider, weigh, ponder, meditate; **f**) to roll on (*time*), bring on *or* round; **P.** to turn round, revolve, roll oneself round *or* about.
vōmer, eris *m* ploughshare.
vomica, ae *f* abscess, ulcer.
vōmis, eris *m* = **vomer.**
vomitiō, ōnis *f and* **-tus, ūs** *m* a vomiting.
vomitō 1 to vomit.
vomitor, ōris *m* one who vomits.
vomō, uī, itum 3 to vomit; to vomit up, throw up (*alqd*).
vorāginōsus 3 full of chasms *or* pits.
vorāgō, inis *f* **a**) chasm, abyss; **b**) whirlpool.
vorāx, ācis greedy, voracious, gluttonous.
vorō 1 to devour, swallow; to read eagerly.
vorrō 3 = **verrō.**
vors-, *see* **vers-.**
vorsōria, ae *f* sail-rope; **-am capiō** to tack.
vortex, vortō (*archaic*) = **vertex, verto.**
vōs you (*pl.*).
voster (*archaic*) = **vester.**
vōti-fer 3 bearing a votive offering.
vōtīvus 3 vowed, votive, promised by a vow, devoted.
votō 1 = **vetō.**
vōtum, ī *n* **a**) that which is vowed *or* promised by a vow, offering, gift; **b**) vow, promise to a god; **vōtī damnātus** *or* **reus** having attained one's prayer; **c**) wish, desire, longing, prayer.
voveō, vōvī, vōtum 2 **a**) to vow, promise solemnly, pledge (*alqd; acc.c.inf.*); **b**) to wish, desire.
vōx, vōcis *f* voice; **a**) sound, tone, utterance, cry, call; **b**) word, saying, speech, remark, proverb, maxim; language; formula; **c**) tone, accent.
vulgāris, e common, usual, vulgar, extending to all.
vulgātor, ōris *m* publisher, divulger.
vulgātus 3 common, public, known to all, notorious.
vulgi-vagus 3 roving, inconstant.
vulgō[1], *see* **vulgus.**
vulgō[2] 1 **a**) to spread among the multitude, make common, communicate; **b**) to prostitute; **c**) to publish, divulge.

vulgus, ī *n* (*acc.* also **vulgum** *m*) the people, the great multitude, the public, mob, rabble; **a**) the common soldiers; **b**) mass, crowd, throng, multitude; **c**) **vulgō** before all the world, openly, everywhere, generally, indiscriminately.
vulnerātiō, ōnis *f* a wounding, wound, injury.
vulnerō 1 to wound; to hurt, injure, grieve.
vulni-ficus 3 inflicting wounds.
vulnus, eris *n* wound; **a**) hurt, cut, blow, stroke; **b**) injury, misfortune, calamity, defeat, disaster; **c**) grief, pain, anguish, wound of love.
vulpēcula, ae *f* little fox.
vulpēs, is *f* fox.
vulpīnus 3 of a fox.
vulsus 3 with the hair plucked out, bald; effeminate.
vulticulus, ī *m* a mere look.
vultuōsus 3 making faces, full of grimaces; affected.
vultur, uris *m* vulture; avaricious man.
vulturīnus 3 of a vulture.
vulturius, ī *m* vulture; avaricious man; an unlucky throw at dice.
vultus, ūs *m* face, visage, countenance, features, looks, air, mien; **a**) bold, stern *or* angry look; **b**) look, appearance.
vulva, ae *f* = **volva.**

X

xenium, ī *n* present (given to a guest).
xērampelinae, ārum *f/pl.* dark red clothes.
xiphiās, ae *m* sword-fish.
xysticus, ī *m* athlete.
xystus, ī *m* (*and* **-um, ī** *n*) walk in a garden, promenade.

Z

zāmia, ae *f* damage, injury.
zēlotypus 3 jealous.
zephyrus, ī *m* west-wind.
zmaragdus, ī *m, f* = **smaragdus.**
zōdiacus, ī *m* the zodiac.
zōna, ae *f* girdle, belt (*of women*); **a**) money-belt; **b**) zone of the earth, climatic region.
zōnārius 3 of a belt; *subst. m* maker of girdles.
zōnula, ae *f* little girdle.
zō-thēca, ae *f*, **zō-thēcula, ae** *f* rest-room.

English-Latin Dictionary

A

a: twice a day bis in die.
abandon (*a person*) relinquo 3, desero 3; (*a task*) omitto 3; **~ed** perditus.
abase summitto 3.
abash ruborem inicio 3 (*alci*).
abate *v/t.* imminuo 3; *v/i.* remitto 3; **~ment** remissio *f.*
abbey abbatia *f.*
abbreviat|e imminuo 3; **~ion** contractio *f.*
abdicat|e abdico 1 (*me magistratu*); **~ion** abdicatio *f.*
abduct rapio 3.
aberration error *m.*
abet adiuvo 1; **~tor** minister *m.*
abeyance: be in ~ iaceo 2 (*leges*).
abhor abhorreo 2 (ab); **~rence** odium *n*; **~rent (to)** alienus (ab).
abide habito 1, maneo 2; **~ by** sto 1 (*abl.*, *in re*).
ability facultas *f*, ingenium *n.*
abject humilis.
abjure eiuro 1.
able potens, potis, pote; ingeniosus; **~-bodied** validus; **be ~** possum.
aboard in nave; **go ~** navem conscendo 3.
abode domicilium *n.*
abolish tollo 3, aboleo 2.
abomin|able infandus, detestabilis; **~ate** abominor 1; **~ation** nefas *n.*
aboriginal indigena *m and f.*
abortion abortus, us *m.*
abortive irritus.
abound abundo 1, circumfluo 3 (*abl.*); **~ing in** abundans (*abl.*).
about *prep.* circa, circum (*acc.*); de (*abl.*); *adv.* circa, fere.
above *prep.* super, supra (*acc.*); **~ all** ante omnia; *adv.* supra.
abreast a latere (*alcis*).
abridge contraho 3; **~ment** epitoma *f and* -e *f.*
abroad foris, peregre; **be ~** peregrinor 1.
abrogat|e abrogo 1, rescindo 3; **~ion** abrogatio *f.*
abrupt repentinus, subitus; **~ly** subito.
abscess vomica *f.*
abscond lateo 2, latito 1.
absence absentia *f*; **leave of ~** commeatus, us *m.*
absent absens; **~-minded** obliviosus; **be ~** absum.
absolute purus, absolutus; **~ power** infinita potestas *f*; **~ly** plane, prorsus.
absolve absolvo 3.
absorb bibo 3; **~ent** bibulus; **~ed** occupatus.
abstain abstineo 2 (*abl.*).
abstemious abstemius.
abstinen|ce abstinentia *f*; **~t** abstinens.
abstract separo 1; *adj.* cogitatione perceptus.
abstruse reconditus, abstrusus.
absurd absurdus, ineptus; **~ity** ineptia *f.*
abundan|ce affluentia *f*, abundantia *f*; **~t** amplus, largus.
abus|e abutor 3 (*abl.*); maledico 3 (*alci*); contumelia *f*; **~ive** contumeliosus.
abut adiaceo 2 (*ad alqd*, *dat.*); **~ting** finitimus.
abyss vorago *f*, barathrum *n.*
accede assentior 4 (*alci*).
accelerate accelero 1.
accent sonus *m* (vocis); **~uate** syllabam acuo 3.
accept accipio 3; **~able** gratus, acceptus; **~ance** approbatio *f.*
access aditus, us *m*; **~ible** pervius (*dat.*); facilis (*homo*).
accessory adiunctus; conscius *m.*
accident casus, us *m*; **by ~** casu; **~al** fortuitus.
acclamation clamor *m.*
accommodat|e accommodo 1 (*alqd alci*, *ad alqd*); **~ing** comis; **~ion** deversorium *n*; accommodatio *f.*
accompaniment: to the ~ of ad (*acc.*).
accompany comitor 1, prosequor 3.
accomplice conscius *m.*
accomplish conficio 3, efficio 3; **~ed** politus; **~ments** artes *f/pl.*
accord *v/t.* concedo 3; *v/i.* consentio 4; *subst.* consensus, us *m*; **of**

one's own ~ sua sponte, ultro; **in ~ance with** ex (*abl.*); **~ing to** pro (*abl.*); **~ingly** itaque.
accost appello 1.
account numero 1, duco 3; **~ for** causam affero 3; ratio *f*; narratio *f*; **on ~ of** ob, propter (*acc.*); **on no ~** nullo modo; **~ant** ratiocinator *m*; **~-book** tabulae *f/pl.*
accoutrements arma *n/pl.*
accrue cedo 3 (*alci, in alqm*).
accumulat|e cumulo 1; **~ion** congestus, us *m*.
accura|cy subtilitas *f*; **~te** subtilis; **~tely** accurate.
accursed sacer, exsecratus.
accus|ation accusatio *f*; **~e** accuso 1 (*alqm rei*); **~ed** reus *m*; **~er** accusator *m*.
accustom assuefacio 3 (*alqm re*); **be ~ed** soleo 2.
acerbity acerbitas *f*.
ache doleo 2; dolor *m*.
achieve perficio 3; **~ment** res *f* gesta.
acid acidus.
acknowledge fateor 2 (*acc. c. inf.*); agnosco 3 (*acc.*); **~ment** confessio *f*.
acme culmen *n*.
acorn glans *f*.
acquaint certiorem facio 3 (*alqm*); **~ance** consuetudo *f*, cognitio *f*.
acquiesce acquiesco 3 (*abl.*), contentus sum.
acqui|re acquiro 3; **~sition** comparatio *f*.
acquit absolvo 3 (*de re*); **~tal** absolutio *f*.
acre iugerum *n* (= $^2/_3$ *acre*).
acrimonious acerbus.
across trans (*acc.*).
act ago 3, me gero 3; *thea.* ago (*play* or *part*); factum *n*; *thea.* actus, us *m*; **~ of Parliament** lex *f*; **~ion** actio *f* (*also jur.*).
activ|e impiger, industrius; **~ity** industria *f*.
actor histrio *m*; **actress** mima *f*.
actual verus; **~ly** re vera.
acumen ingenii acies *f*.
acute acer.
adage proverbium *n*.
adapt accommodo 1.
add addo 3.
adder vipera *f*.
addicted to deditus (*dat.*).
addition accessio *f*.
address alloquor 3; alloquium *n*.
adduce profero 3.
adept peritus.
adequate par, satis magnus.
adhere haereo 2 (*in, ad*); sto 1 (*ab*); **~nt** assectator *m*.
adhesive tenax.
adieu vale(te).
adjacent finitimus.
adjoin adiaceo 2 (*dat., ad*).
adjourn *v/t.* differo 3 (**till** *in* + *acc.*)
adjudge adiudico 1 (*alci alqd*).
adjure obsecro 1.
adjust accommodo 1, compono 3.
adjutant optio *m*.
administer administro 1; **~ an oath** (*alqm*) iure iurando adigo 3.
administrat|ion procuratio *f*; **~or** procurator *m*.
admir|able admirabilis; **~ation** admiratio *f*; **~e** admiror 1.
admiral praefectus *m* classis.
admit (of) recipio 3; **~tance** aditus, us *m*.
admonish admoneo 2; **~ment** monita *n/pl.*
ado negotium *n*.
adolescent adulescens *m*.
adopt adopto 1; **~ion** adoptio *f*; **~ive** adoptivus.
adore veneror 1.
adorn decoro 1.
adrift: be ~ fluctuo 1.
adroit callidus; **~ness** sollertia *f*.
adulation assentatio *f*.
adult adultus.
adulterate corrumpo 3.
adulter|er adulter *m*; **~ess** adultera *f*; **~y** adulterium *n*; **commit ~y** adultero 1.
advance *v/t.* promoveo 2; *v/i.* progredior 3; **~ed** (*time*) provectus; **~ment** honor *m*.
advantage bonum *n*, commodum *n*; **~ous** utilis; **be ~ous** prosum.
adventure casus, us *m*.
advers|ary adversarius *m*; **~e** adversus; **~ity** res *f/pl.* adversae.
advert to attingo 3 (*acc.*).
advertise proscribo 3; **~ment** proscriptio *f*.
advice consilium *n*.
advise suadeo 2, moneo 2; **~dly** consulto; **~r** consiliarius *m*.
advoca|cy suasio *f*; *jur.* patrocinium *n*; **~te** suadeo 2; *jur.* patronus *m*.
aedile aedilis *m*; **~ship** aedilitas *f*.
aegis aegis *f*.

aerial aerius, aetherius.
afar procul.
affab|ility comitas *f*; **~le** comis.
affair res *f*, negotium *n*; **love ~** amor *m*.
affect afficio 3, moveo 2; simulo 1; **~ation** simulatio *f*; **~ed** molestus.
affection affectus, us *m*, amor *m*; **~ate** amans.
affiance spondeo 2.
affinity cognatio *f*.
affirm affirmo 1.
affix affigo 3.
afflict afflicto 1; **~ed with** affectus (*abl.*); **~ion** miseria *f*.
affluen|ce divitiae *f/pl.*; **~t** dives.
afford praebeo 2.
affront offendo 3; contumelia *f*.
afloat: be ~ navigo 1.
afoot pedibus; **set ~** moveo 2.
aforesaid supra commemoratus.
afraid timidus, pavidus; **be ~ (of)** timeo 2; metuo 3.
afresh de integro.
after *prep.* post, secundum (*acc.*); *cj.* postquam; **~noon** post meridiem; *adj.* postmeridianus; **~wards** post, postea.
again iterum, rursus, rursum; **~ and ~** etiam atque etiam.
against contra, adversus, in (*acc.*).
agape hians.
age aetas *f*, saeculum *n*; (*of things*) vetustas *f*; **old ~** senectus, utis *f*; **4 years of ~** quattuor annos natus.
aged senex, provectae aetatis.
agen|cy opera *f* (*chiefly in abl.*); **~t** actor *m*; minister *m*.
aggrandize augeo 2.
aggravate aggravo 1.
aggregate summa *f*.
aggress|ion incursio *f*; **~ive** infestus; **be the ~or** ultro arma infero 3.
aggrieve laedo 3.
aghast attonitus.
agil|e pernix; **~ity** pernicitas *f*.
agitat|e agito 1, perturbo 1; **~ed** sollicitus; **~ion** agitatio *f*, perturbatio *f*.
ago abhinc (*acc.*); **long ~** iam pridem, iam dudum; **some time ~** dudum.
agony cruciatus, us *m*, acerbissimus dolor *m*.
agrarian agrarius.
agree consentio 4 (*cum alqo, de re*); congruo 3, assentior 4; **~ upon** compono 3; **~able** gratus, commodus, suavis; **be ~d** constat; **be ~d upon** convenit; **~ment** consensus, us *m*, conventum *n*; pactio *f*.
agricultur|al rusticus, agrestis; **~e** agri cultura *f*, res *f/pl.* rusticae.
aground: run ~ sido 3.
ague febris *f*.
ah *int.* ah, a, heu.
ahead: go ~ antecedo 3 (*dat., acc.*); anteeo (*dat., acc.*).
aid adiuvo 1 (*acc.*), succurro 3 (*dat.*); auxilium *n*.
aide-de-camp optio *m*.
ail doleo 2, aegroto 1; **~ing** aegrotus, aeger; **~ment** morbus *m*.
aim intendo 3 (*alqd, in alqd, alci*), peto 3 (*alqm*); *fig.* affecto 1, peto 3; finis *m*, consilium *n*.
air aer *m*, aether *m*, aura *f*; species *f*, modus *m*; **in the open ~** sub divo; **take the ~** deambulo 1; **put on ~s** me iacto 1; **~ing** ambulatio *f*; **~y** aerius.
aisle ala *f*.
akin finitimus (*dat.*).
alacrity alacritas *f*.
alarm terreo 2; **be ~ed** perturbor 1; trepidatio *f*, tumultus, us *m*, terror *m*.
alas heu, eheu, hei.
albeit etsi.
alcove angulus *m*; recessus, us *m*.
alder alnus, i *f*.
ale fermentum *n*.
alert alacer, vigil.
alien externus, alienus; peregrinus *m*; **~ate** (ab)alieno 1; **~ation** alienatio *f*.
alight descendo 3 (ad pedes); desilio 4; **set ~** incendo 3.
alike par, similis; *adv.* pariter.
aliment alimentum *n*.
alive vivus; **be ~** vivo 3.
all omnis, cunctus, totus; **~ together** universus; **~ the better** tanto melius; **nothing at ~** nihil omnino; **in ~** omnino.
allay levo 1, sedo 1.
alleg|ation affirmatio *f*; **~e** praetendo 3 (*acc.*); refero 3 (*acc. c. inf.*).
allegiance fides *f*; **take oath of ~** in verba alicuius iuro 1.
allegory translationes *f/pl.*
alleviat|e levo 1; **~ion** levatio *f*.
alley angiportus, us *m*.
alli|ance societas *f*, foedus *n*, coniunctio *f*; **~ed** socius, foederatus.

allot distribuo 3, assigno 1, do 1; **~ment** assignatio *f.*
allow confiteor 2; patior 3 (*acc. c. inf.*; *ut*), sino 3 (*inf.*; *acc. c. inf.*), permitto 3 (*ut*, *inf.*); **~able** permissus; **~ance** diarium *n*; **make ~ances for** ignosco 3 (*dat.*); **it is ~ed** licet 2.
alloy corrumpo 3, misceo 2.
allude to tango 3, designo 1.
allur|e allicio 3; **~ement** blanditia *f*; **~ing** blandus.
ally socio 1; socius *m.*
almanac fasti *m/pl.*
almighty omnipotens.
almond amygdala *f.*
almost paene, fere, ferme.
alms stips *f.*
aloft sublime, in sublime, alte.
alone solus, unus; **let ~** abstineo 2 (*ab*).
along praeter (*acc.*), secundum (*acc.*), per (*acc.*).
aloof procul; **keep ~** removeo 2 me (*ab alqo*).
aloud clare.
alphabet litterae *f/pl.*
alpine alpinus.
already iam.
also etiam, quoque.
altar ara *f*, altaria *n/pl.*
alter *v/t.* muto 1; *v/i.* mutor 1; **~ation** mutatio *f.*
altercation iurgium *n.*
alternat|e vario 1; alternus; **~ely** alternis, invicem; **~ion** vicissitudo *f*; **have an ~ive** optio est (*alci*).
although quamquam, quamvis, (tam)etsi.
altogether omnino.
always semper.
amalgamate misceo 2.
amanuensis librarius *m.*
amass coacervo 1.
amatory amatorius.
amaz|e obstupefacio 3; **be ~ed** stupeo 2; **~ement** stupor *m*; **~ing** mirus.
ambassador legatus *m.*
amber sucinum *n.*
ambigu|ity ambiguitas *f*; **~ous** ambiguus.
ambitio|n ambitio *f*; **~us** cupidus gloriae.
ambrosia ambrosia *f.*
ambuscade, ambush insidior 1 (*dat.*); insidiae *f/pl.*
amenable oboediens (*dat.*).
amend corrigo 3, emendo 1; **make ~s** satisfacio 3 (*alci de re*).
amiab|ility suavitas *f*; **~le** suavis.
amicable amicus.
amid(st) inter (*acc.*).
amiss perperam; **take ~** moleste fero 3.
amity amicitia *f.*
ammunition apparatus, us *m*; arma *n/pl.*
amnesty venia *f.*
among inter (*acc.*); apud (*acc.*).
amorous amatorius.
amount summa *f*; **~ to** efficio 3, summa est.
amphitheatre amphitheatrum *n.*
ampl|e amplus; **~ify** dilato 1; **~y** abunde.
amputate seco 1.
amuse oblecto 1, delecto 1; **~ oneself** ludo 3; **~ment** delectatio *f.*
analogy similitudo, inis *f*, comparatio *f.*
analyse subtiliter dissero 3.
anarch|ical turbulentus; **~y** licentia *f.*
ancest|or avus *m*, proavus *m*; *pl.* maiores *m/pl.*; **~ral** avitus.
anchor ancora *f*; **weigh ~** ancoram tollo 3; **~age** statio *f.*
ancient antiquus, vetus, priscus.
and et, ac, atque, ...que.
anecdote fabula *f.*
anew denuo, de integro.
angel angelus *m.*
anger irrito 1; ira *f.*
angle piscor 1; angulus *m*; **~r** piscator *m.*
angr|ily iracunde; **~y** iratus; **be ~y** irascor 3.
anguish angor *m.*
angular angulatus.
animadver|sion animadversio *f*; **~t** animadverto 3.
animal animal *n*; pecus, udis *f*; fera *f.*
animat|e animo 1, excito 1; **~ed** alacer; **~ion** animatio *f*, vis *f.*
animosity odium *n.*
ankle talus *m.*
annals annales *m/pl.*
annex addo 3, subicio 3.
annihilat|e deleo 2; **~ion** internecio *f.*
anniversary dies *m* anniversarius.
annotate commentarium scribo 3 (*in alqd*).
announce (pro)nuntio 1; **~ment** pronuntiatio *f.*

annoy offendo 3, vexo 1; **~ance** molestia *f*, vexatio *f*; **be ~ed** moleste fero 3; **~ing** molestus.
annual anniversarius, annuus; **~ly** quotannis.
annuity annua *n/pl.*
annul tollo 3; **~ment** abrogatio *f.*
anoint ungo 3; **~ing** unctio *f.*
anon statim, mox.
anonymous sine auctoris nomine.
another alius; **one after ~** alius ex alio; **at ~ time** alias; **one ~** inter se; **~'s** alienus.
answer respondeo 2 (*alci alqd*; *de re*), rescribo 3; **~ for** praesto 1 (*alqm*; *alqd alci*); responsum *n.*
ant formica *f.*
antagonis|m odium *n*; **~t** adversarius *m.*
antechamber atriolum *n.*
anthem carmen *n.*
anticipate antevenio 4 (*dat.*; *acc.*); anteverto 3 (*dat.*); praecipio 3.
antics ineptiae *f/pl.*
antidote remedium *n.*
antipathy odium *n.*
antiquarian antiquarius.
antiqu|e antiquus, priscus; **~ity** antiquitas *f.*
antithesis *rhet.* contentio *f.*
antler cornu, us *n.*
anvil incus, udis *f.*
anxi|ety sollicitudo *f*, cura *f*; **~ous** anxius, sollicitus; **be ~ous to** laboro 1 (*ut*, *inf.*).
any ullus; qui, qua *or* quae, quod; aliqui, aliqua, aliquod; **~how** saltem, certe; **~one** aliquis; quis; quisquam; **~onesoever** quilibet, quivis; **~thing** aliquid; quid; quidquam.
apart separatim, seorsum; **~ from** praeter (*acc.*), extra (*acc.*); **~ment** conclave *n.*
apath|etic languidus; **~y** stupor *m.*
ape simia *f.*
aperture foramen *n*, hiatus, us *m.*
aphorism sententia *f.*
apiary alvus, i *f.*
apolog|ist defensor *m*; **~ise** excuso 1 (*me*, *aldq*); veniam peto 3 (*gen.*, *quod*); **~y** excusatio *f.*
appal exterreo 2.
apparatus apparatus, us *m.*
apparel vestio 4; vestis *f.*
apparent apertus, manifestus; simulatus, fictus; **be ~** appareo 2; **~ly** specie.
apparition simulacrum *n.*
appeal appello 1, provoco 1 (*also jur.*); obsecro 1, testor 1; obsecratio *f*; *jur.* appellatio *f*, provocatio *f.*
appear appareo 2, me ostendo 3; *jur.* adsum, me sisto 3; videor 2; **~ance** species *f*, aspectus, us *m.*
appease placo 1, sedo 1.
appellant appellator *m.*
append addo 3; **~age** appendix *f.*
appertain pertineo 2 (*ad alqd*).
appetite appetitus, us *m*; cupiditas *f*, fames *f.*
applau|d (ap)plaudo 3, faveo 2; **~se** plausus, us *m*; clamor *m.*
apple malum *n.*
applica|ble commodus (*dat.*); **~nt** petitor *m*; **~tion** petitio *f*; studium *n.*
apply *v/t.* adhibeo 2, admoveo 2; me confero 3 (*ad alqd*); *v/i.* pertineo 2 (*ad*); aggredior 3 (*alqm*).
appoint creo 1, facio 3, praeficio 3 (**to** *dat.*), constituo 3; **~ment** creatio *f*, constitutum *n.*
apportion divido 3.
apposite aptus.
appraise aestimo 1.
appreciate aestimo 1.
apprehen|d comprehendo 3, percipio 3; metuo 3; **~sive** timidus.
apprentice discipulus *m.*
apprize certiorem facio 3.
approach accedo 3 (*ad*, *acc.*, *dat.*); appropinquo 1 (*ad alqd*, *dat.*); accessus, us *m*; aditus, us *m.*
approbation approbatio *f.*
appropriate mihi arrogo 1, mihi ascisco 3, sumo 3; proprius, congruens (*dat.*).
approv|al approbatio *f*; **~e** laudo 3, approbo 1.
approximate accedo 3 (*ad*, *dat.*); proximus.
April Aprilis (mensis) *m.*
apt aptus, idoneus, pronus (*ad*); **~itude** ingenium *n.*
aquatic aquatilis.
aqueduct aquae ductus, us *m.*
aquiline aduncus.
arable land arvum *n.*
arbiter arbiter *m.*
arbitrar|ily ad libidinem (*alcs*); **~y** libidinosus.
arbitrat|e discepto 1; **~or** arbiter *m.*
arbour umbraculum *n.*
arc arcus, us *m.*
arcade porticus, us *f.*

arch fornix *m*, arcus, us *m*; lascivus; **~ed** fornicatus.
archer sagittarius *m*.
architect architectus *m*; **~ure** architectura *f*.
archives tabulae *f/pl*.
archon archon *m*.
arctic septentriones *m/pl*.; septentrionalis.
ard|ent ardens, vehemens; **~our** ardor *m*.
arduous arduus.
area area *f*; regio *f*.
arena arena *f*.
argu|e disputo 1, dissero 3; **~ment** argumentum *n*, ratio *f*, disputatio *f*.
aria canticum *n*.
arid aridus; **~ity** ariditas *f*.
aright recte.
arise (con)surgo 3; exorior 4 (*ex*); nascor 3.
aristocra|cy optimates *m/pl*.; **~tic** nobilis.
arithmetic arithmetica *n/pl*.
ark arca *f*.
arm *v/t*. armo 1; *v/i*. arma capio 3; bracchium *n*, lacertus *m*; **~s** arma *n/pl*., tela *n/pl*.; **be under ~s** sum in armis; **lay down ~s** arma pono 3.
armature copiae *f/pl*.
armistice indutiae *f/pl*.
armour arma *n/pl*.; **~-bearer** armiger *m*; **~er** faber *m*; **~y** armamentarium *n*.
armpit ala *f*, axilla *f*.
army exercitus, us *m*; agmen *n*; acies *f*.
aroma odor *m*; **~tic** odoratus.
around *prep*. circum, circa (*acc*.); *adv*. circa.
arouse suscito 1, excito 1.
arraign accuso 1.
arrange instruo 3, dispono 3, compono 3, ordino 1; **~ment** collocatio *f*, institutio *f*.
array instruo 3; **battle-~** acies *f*.
arrears reliqua *n/pl*.
arrest comprehendo 3; comprehensio *f*.
arriv|al adventus, us *m*; **~e** advenio 4, pervenio 4 (*in, ad*).
arrogan|ce arrogantia *f*, superbia *f*; **~t** arrogans.
arrogate sumo 3 (*mihi*).
arrow sagitta *f*; **~-head** cuspis, idis *f*.
arsenal armamentarium *n*.
arson incendium *n*.
art ars *f*; artificium *n*; opus *n*.
artery vena *f*.
artful callidus, vafer; **~ness** calliditas *f*.
artic|le res *f*, merx *f*, articulus *m*; **~ulate** distinctus; articulo 1; **~ulation** explanatio *f*.
artifice dolus *m*; **~r** artifex *m and f*.
artificial artificiosus, manu factus.
artillery tormenta *n/pl*.
artisan opifex *m and f*.
artist artifex *m and f*; pictor *m*; **~ic** artificiosus.
artless simplex.
as (*in comparisons*) atque, et, quam, ut; **~ ... ~** tam ... quam; **just ~** velut, tamquam, sicut; (*temporal*) dum; (*causal*) cum, quoniam; **~ regards** de (*abl*.), quod.
ascen|d ascendo 3 (*in, ad*); **~dency** potentia *f*; **~t** ascensus, us *m*.
ascertain comperio 4, cognosco 3.
ascetic austerus; **~ism** austeritas *f*.
ascribe ascribo 3, assigno 1.
ash(-tree) fraxinus, i *f*; **mountain ash** ornus, i *f*.
ashamed: be ~ pudet 2 (*alqm, alcis rei*).
ashes cinis, eris *m*.
ashore in terram, in terra.
ask rogo 1 (*alqd ab alqo; ut*); peto 3 (*ut*); quaero 3 (*alqd; de re*).
askance limus, obliquus.
aslant obliquus.
asleep: be ~ dormio 4; **fall ~** obdormio 4.
aspect facies *f*, aspectus, us *m*, vultus, us *m*.
aspen populus, i *f*.
asperity acerbitas *f*.
aspersions: cast ~ on calumnior 1.
aspir|ation studium *n*; **~e** aspiro 1 (*in, ad alqd*), peto 3; **~ing** appetens (*alcis rei*).
ass asinus *m*.
assail oppugno 1; invehor 3; **~ant** oppugnator *m*.
assassin percussor *m*, sicarius *m*; **~ate** caedo 3; **~ation** caedes *f*.
assault adorior 4; oppugnatio *f*, vis *f*.
assembl|e *v/t*. cogo 3, convoco 1; *v/i*. convenio 4; **~y** coetus, us *m*.
assent assentior 4; assensus, us *m*.
assert affirmo 1, vindico 1; **~ion** affirmatio *f*.
assess aestimo 1; **~ for taxes** censeo 2; **~ment** aestimatio *f*, census, us *m*; **~or** *jur*. assessor *m*.

assets bona *n/pl.*
asseverate assevero 1.
assidu|ity diligentia *f*; **~ous** sedulus.
assign (at)tribuo 3; *jur.* delego 1; **~ation** constitutum *n*; **~ment** assignatio *f.*
assist (ad)iuvo 1; **~ance** auxilium *n*, (ops,) opis *f*; **~ant** adiutor *m*, minister *m.*
assizes conventus, us *m.*
associate *v/t.* consocio 1; *v/i.* **~ with** utor 3 (*abl.*); socius *m.*
association societas *f.*
assort *v/i.* congruo 3; **~ment** varietas *f.*
assuage levo 1.
assum|e suscipio 3, induo 3, sumo 3 (*mihi*; *acc. c. inf.*); **~ption** arrogantia *f*; opinio *f.*
assur|ance fides *f*, fiducia *f*; **~e** confirmo 1, promitto 3; **be ~ed** confido 3; **~edly** profecto.
astern in puppi.
asthma anhelitus, us *m.*
astonish obstupefacio 3; **be ~ed** admiror 1, obstupesco 3; **~ment** admiratio *f*, stupor *m.*
astound obstupefacio 3; **be ~ed** obstupesco 3.
astray: go ~ erro 1; **lead ~** in errorem induco 3.
astringent asper.
astrolog|er astrologus *m*; **~y** astrologia *f.*
astronomer astrologus *m.*
astute callidus.
asunder: burst ~ dissilio 4.
asylum perfugium *n.*
at ad; apud; in (*abl.*); **~ the house of** apud (*alqm*); **~ home** domi; **~ Rome** Romae; **~ daybreak** prima luce; **~ the age of five** quinque annos natus; **~ a high price** magno pretio.
atheist impius.
athlet|e athleta *m*; **~ic** robustus.
atmosphere aer *m*, caelum *n.*
atom atomus, i *f*; corpora individua *n/pl.*
atone expio 1 (*alqd*); luo 3 (*alqd*); **~ment** piaculum *n.*
atroci|ous immanis; **~ty** atrocitas *f.*
attach adiungo 3, applico 1 (*ad alqd*, *alci rei*); **~ importance to** mea interest; **~ed to** devinctus (*alci*); **~ed by** alligatus (*abl.*); **~ment** caritas *f.*
attack adorior 4, oppugno 1, aggredior 3; *fig.* invehor 3 (*in alqm*); *med.* tempto 1; impetus, us *m.*
attain consequor 3, pervenio 4 (*ad*, *in alqd*); adipiscor 3.
attempt conor 1, molior 4; conatum *n.*
attend prosequor 3 (*acc.*); intersum (*in re*, *dat.*); **~ to** animadverto 3, curo 1; **~ance** assectatio *f*; **~ant** assectator *m.*
attent|ion attentus animus *m*; observantia *f*; **pay ~ to** operam do 1, studeo 2 (*dat.*); **~ive** attentus, observans.
attenuate extenuo 1.
attest testificor 1.
attic cenaculum *n.*
attire vestio 4; vestitus, us *m.*
attitude status, us *m*; **adopt an ~** me gero 3.
attorney cognitor *m.*
attract (at)traho 3; **~ion** illecebrae *f/pl.*; **~ive** blandus.
attribute (at)tribuo 3; **be an ~ of** insum (*in re*; *dat.*); proprium est (*gen.*).
auburn fulvus.
auction auctio *f*; **sell by ~** sub hasta vendo 3; **~eer** praeco *m.*
audac|ious audax, confidens; **~ity** audacia *f*, confidentia *f.*
audible clarus.
audience audientes *m/pl.*, auditores *m/pl.*; **grant ~ to** admitto 3.
audit dispungo 3.
auditor auditor *m.*
augment augeo 2; **~ation** incrementum *n.*
augur auguror 1, vaticinor 1; augur *m*; **~y** augurium *n*; **take the ~ies** auguror 1.
august augustus.
August (mensis) Sextilis *m*, Augustus *m.*
aunt (*paternal*) amita *f*; (*maternal*) matertera *f.*
auspices auspicium *n*; **take the ~** auspicor 1.
auspicious faustus.
auster|e severus, austerus; **~ity** severitas *f.*
authentic verus; **well ~ated** quod constat.
author auctor *m*, scriptor *m*; **~ity** auctoritas *f*, potestas *f*; **~ities** magistratus *m/pl.*; **~ize** potestatem do 1 (*alci*).
autograph chirographum *n.*
autonomy libertas *f.*

autumn autumnus *m*; **~al** autumnus.
auxiliar|y auxiliaris; **~ies** auxilia *n/pl.*
avail| o.s. of utor 3 (*abl.*); **it ~s** prodest; **be of no ~** nihil valeo 2; **~able** expeditus, in expedito.
avaric|e avaritia *f*; **~ious** avarus.
aveng|e ulciscor 3 (*acc.*); **~er** ultor *m*; **~ing** ultrix.
avenue aditus, us *m*; xystus *m*.
average: on the ~ circa.
averse aversus (*dat.*); **be ~ to** abhorreo 2 (*a re*).
aver|sion odium *n*; **~t** averto 3; **~t from** prohibeo 2 (*abl.*).
avidity aviditas *f*.
avocation officium *n*.
avoid vito 1, (de)fugio 3; **~ance** fuga *f*.
avow confiteor 2; **~al** confessio *f*.
await exspecto 1, maneo 2 (*acc.*).
awake *v/t.* excito 1, exsuscito 1; *v/i.* expergiscor 3; **be ~** vigilo 1.
award adiudico 1; addictio *f*.
aware gnarus; **be ~ of** sentio 4; **become ~ of** cognosco 3.
away: be ~ absum; **~ with you!** abi!
awe reverentia *f*; **stand in ~ of** vereor 2; **~-struck** pavidus.
awful verendus; terribilis.
awhile paulisper.
awkward laevus, rusticus; **~ness** inscitia *f*.
awning velum *n*.
awry perversus.
axe securis *f*.
axiom sententia *f*, pronuntiatum *n*.
axis, axle axis *f*.
aye ita, semper.
azure caeruleus.

B

baa balo 1.
babbl|e garrio 4; **~ing** garrulus.
baboon simia *f.*
baby infans *m*, parvulus *m*; **~hood** infantia *f*; **~ish** infans.
bacchan|al Bacchanalia *n/pl.*; **~te** Baccha *f.*
bachelor caelebs.
back *v/t.* adsum, adiuvo 1; *v/i.* pedem refero 3; **~ water** inhibeo 2 (*navem*); tergum *n*, dorsum *n*; **behind one's ~** clam (*alqm*); *adv.* retro, retrorsum; **~bite** rodo 3; **~bone** spina *f*; **~-door** posticum *n*; **~slide** deficio 3; **~ward** piger; **~wardness** pigritia *f*; **~wards** retro, retrorsum.
bacon laridum *n.*
bad malus, improbus, pravus.
badge insigne *n.*
badger maeles *f.*
badness malitia *f*, nequitia *f.*
baffle eludo 3.
bag saccus *m*, culleus *m*; **~gage** sarcinae *f/pl.*
bail spondeo 2 (*pro alqo*); vadimonium *n.*
bailiff vilicus *m.*
bait esca *f.*
bake coquo 3, torreo 2; **~r** pistor *m.*
balance libro 1; compenso 1; **~ accounts** rationes dispungo 3; libra *f*, trutina *f.*
balcony maenianum *n.*
bald calvus; *fig.* aridus; **~ness** calvitium *n.*
baldric balteus *m.*
bale egero 3; fascis *m*; **~ful** funestus.
balk frustror 1.
ball globus *m*, pila *f.*
ballad nenia *f.*
ballast saburra *f.*
ballot suffragium *n*, tabella *f*; **~-box** cista *f.*
balm balsamum *n*, solatium *n*; **~y** suavis.
balustrade cancelli *m/pl.*
ban interdico 3; interdictio *f.*
band vinculum *m*; manus, us *f*, caterva *f*; **~ together** coniuro 1.
bandage alligo 1; fascia *f.*
bandit latro *m.*
bandy-legged valgus.
bane venenum *n*, pernicies *f*; **~ful** perniciosus.
bang percutio 3, verbero 1; sonitus, us *m.*
banish aqua et igni interdico 3, eicio 3, pello 3; **~ment** eiectio *f*; exsilium *n.*
banister cancelli *m/pl.*
bank ripa *f*, tumulus *m*; argentaria *f*; **~ money** pecunias depono 3; **~er** argentarius *m*; **~rupt** decoctor *m*; **be ~rupt** conturbo 1, decoquo 3.
banner vexillum *n.*
banquet epulor 1; convivium *n*, epulae *f/pl.*
banter cavillor 1, iocor 1; iocus *m.*
bar obsero 1, intercludo 3, obsto 1; claustra *n/pl.*; vectis *m*; *fig.* impedimentum *n*; *jur.* cancelli *m/pl.*; **at the ~** forensis (*adj.*).
barb uncus *m*, hamus *m*; **~ed** hamatus.
barbar|ian barbarus *m*; **~ic** barbarus; **~ous** immanis, ferus.
barber tonsor *m.*
bard vates *m and f.*
bare nudus; *v/t.* aperio 4, nudo 1; **~faced** impudens; **~foot** nudo pede; **~ly** vix.
bargain paciscor 3; pactio *f*, pactum *n.*
barge linter, tris *f.*
bark latro 1; latratus, us *m*; cortex *m and f*, liber *m.*
barley hordeum *n.*
barm fermentum *n.*
barn horreum *n*, granaria *n/pl.*
baron princeps *m.*
barque ratis *f.*
barracks castra *n/pl.*
barrel dolium *n*, cupa *f.*
barren sterilis; **~ness** sterilitas *f.*
barricade obstruo 3; munimentum *n.*
barrier saepta *n/pl.*; claustra *n/pl.*
barrister advocatus *m*; patronus *m.*
barrow ferculum *n*; tumulus *m.*
barter muto 1 (*alqd alqa re*); paciscor 3; permutatio *f.*

base humilis, turpis; ~ **money** nummus *m* adulterinus; basis *f*; fundamentum *n*; **be ~d on** nitor 3; **~less** vanus; **~ness** turpitudo *f*.
bashful verecundus, pudens; **~ness** pudor *m*.
basilica basilica *f*.
basin crater *m*.
bask apricor 1.
basket canistrum *n*, fiscina *f*.
bas-relief toreuma *n*.
bass *mus.* gravis.
bastard nothus.
baste verbero 1.
bastion castellum *n*.
bat vespertilio *m*.
bath balneum *n*, lavatio *f*; **~-keeper** balneator *m*; **~-tub** alveus *m*.
bathe *v/t.* lavo 1; *v/i.* lavor 1.
battalion cohors *f*.
batter percutio 3; **~ing-ram** aries *m*.
battle pugna *f*, proelium *n*, acies *f*; **join ~** proelium committere; **~-cry** clamor *m*; **~-field** acies *f*; **~ment** pinna *f*.
bawd lena *f*.
bawl clamito 1.
bay badius; latro 1; sinus, us *m*; laurus, i *f*.
be sum; exsisto 3, me habeo 2.
beach litus *n*.
beacon ignis *m*.
bead lapillus *m*.
beak rostrum *n*; **~ed** rostratus; **~er** poculum *n*.
beam refulgeo 2; iubar *n*, radius *m*; tignum *n*, trabs *f*; **~ing** lucidus.
bean faba *f*.
bear fero 3; patior 3; pario 3; **~ with** morem gero 3 (*alci*); ursus *m*.
beard barba *f*; **~ed** barbatus; **~less** imberbis.
bear|er baiulus *m*; **~ing** gestus, us *m*; **have ~ing on** pertineo 2 ad.
beast belua *f*, bestia *f*, fera *f*; **~ly** immundus.
beat *v/t.* caedo 3, verbero 1; supero 1; *v/i.* palpito 1; **~ against** incutio 3; **~ing** ictus, us *m*; verbera *n/pl.*
beauti|ful pulcher, formosus; **~fy** orno 1.
beauty pulchritudo *f*.
beaver castor *m*.
because quia, quod; **~ of** propter (*acc.*).
beck nutus, us *m*; **~on** innuo 3 (*alci*).
becom|e fio 3; *impers.* decet 2 (*alqm*); convenit 4; **~ing** decorus, decens.
bed cubile *n*, lectus *m*; **go to ~** cubitum eo 4; **~-chamber** cubiculum *n*; **~-clothes** stragulum *n*; **~-post** fulcrum *n*.
bedeck orno 1.
bedew perfundo 3.
bee apis *f*; **~-hive** alvearium *n*.
beech fagus, i *f*.
beef bubula *f*.
beer fermentum *n*.
beet beta *f*.
beetle scarabaeus *m*.
befall contingo 3 (*alci*); evenio 4 (*alci*; *ut*).
befit deceo 2.
befool ludificor 1.
before *prep.* ante, ob (*acc.*); prae (*acc.*), pro (*abl.*); apud (*acc.*); coram (*abl.*); *adv.* ante, antea, antehac.
befoul inquino 1.
befriend adiuvo 1.
beg oro 1 (*alqm alqd*; *ut*); rogo 1 (*alqd ab alqo*; *ut*); peto 3 (*ut*); mendico 1.
beget gigno 3; procreo 1.
beggar mendicus *m*; egens; **~ly** mendicus.
begin coepi 3; incipio 3; exorior 4; **~ner** tiro *m*; **~ning** initium *n*; principium *n*.
begone abi!
begrudge invideo 2 (*alci*, *alci rei*).
beguile fallo 3.
behalf: on ~ of pro (*abl.*).
behave me gero 3; **~ towards** utor 3 (*abl.*).
behaviour mores *m/pl.*
behead securi ferio 4, percutio 3.
behind *prep.* post (*acc.*); *adv.* post, a tergo.
behold conspicio 3, tueor 2; *exclam.* ecce, en.
behove oportet 2 (*acc. c. inf.*).
being homo *m*.
belabour mulco 1.
belch (e)ructo 1.
beleaguer obsideo 2.
belie dissimulo 1.
belie|f opinio *f*; fides *f*; **~ve** credo 3 (*alci*, *acc. c. inf.*); puto 1; fidem habeo 2 (*dat.*).
bell tintinnabulum *n*.
belligerent bellicosus.
bellow mugio 4; **~ing** mugitus, us *m*.

bellows follis *m.*
belly venter, tris *m*, alvus, i *f*; **~ out** tumeo 2.
belong|to esse (*alcs, alci*); **~ings** bona *n/pl.*
beloved dilectus.
below infra (*acc.*); subter (*acc.*).
belt cinctus, us *m*; cingulum *n.*
bemoan gemo 3.
bench subsellium *n*; transtrum *n*; *jur.* subsellia *n/pl.*
bend *v/t.* flecto 3, curvo 1; *v/i.* flector 3; flexus, us *m*, flexio *f.*
beneath sub (*abl.*); infra, subter (*acc.*).
benefaction donum *n.*
benefi|cence beneficentia *f*; **~cent** beneficus; **~cial** salutaris; **~t** prosum (*dat.*); beneficium *n*; **for the ~t of** gratia (*gen.*).
benevolen|ce benevolentia *f*; **~t** benevolus.
benign benignus.
bent curvus; **~ on** attentus (*dat.*).
benumb stupefacio 3; **be ~ed** torpeo 2.
bequ|eath lego 1; **~est** legatum *n.*
ber|eave orbo 1; **~eft** orbus (*abl.*).
berry baca *f.*
berth statio *f.*
beseech oro 1, obsecro 1.
beset obsideo 2, circumvenio 4.
beside ad, prope, iuxta (*acc.*); **~s** *prep.* praeter (*acc.*); *adv.* praeterea.
besieg|e obsideo 2, circumsedeo 2; **~er** obsessor *m.*
besom scopae *f/pl.*
besotted demens.
bespatter aspergo 3.
besprinkle aspergo 3, irroro 1.
best optimus.
bestir oneself expergiscor 3.
bestow dono 1, largior 4; confero 3 (*in alqm*), impertio 4.
bet pignus do 1; pono 3; pignus *n*; sponsio *f.*
betake oneself me confero 3.
bethink oneself respicio 3.
betimes mature.
betoken denuntio 1.
betray prodo 3; **~al** proditio *f*; **~er** proditor *m.*
betroth (de)spondeo 2 (*alci alqm*); **~al** sponsalia *n/pl.*; **~ed** sponsa *f*; pactus.
better melior; **it is ~** praestat; satius est; **get the ~ of** vinco 3.
between inter (*acc.*).
beverage potio *f.*
bevy grex *m.*
bewail deploro 1.
beware caveo 2 (*acc.*; *ab re*; *ut, ne*).
bewildered perturbatus.
bewitch fascino 1.
beyond *prep.* ultra (*acc.*), extra (*acc.*), supra (*acc.*), praeter (*acc.*); *adv.* ultra, supra.
bias inclino 1; inclinatio *f.*
bicker rixor 1; **~ing** altercatio *f.*
bid iubeo 2; **~ a price** liceor 2; voco 1; **~ farewell** valedico 3; **~ding** licitatio *f*; **at the ~ding of** iussu.
bier ferculum *n.*
big ingens, magnus.
bilberry vaccinium *n.*
bile bilis *f.*
bilge-water sentina *f.*
bilk fraudo 1.
bill rostrum *n*; libellus *m*; syngrapha *f*; rogatio *f*; lex *f*; titulus *m.*
billet hospitium *n.*
bill-hook falx *f.*
billow fluctus, us *m*; **~y** undosus.
bin arca *f.*
bind vincio 4, necto 3; *fig.* obligo 1, obstringo 3; **~ over** vador 1; **~ing** fascia *f.*
birch betula *f.*
bird avis *f*; ales *m and f*; volucris *f*; **~-cage** cavea *f*; **~-catcher** auceps *m*; **~-lime** viscum *n*; **~'s nest** nidus *m.*
bireme biremis *f.*
birth ortus, us *m*; genus *n*; partus, us *m*; **give ~ to** pario 3; **~day** dies *m* natalis.
bit frenum *n*; frustum *n*; offa *f.*
bit|e mordeo 2; morsus, us *m*; **~ing** asper.
bitter amarus, acerbus; **~ness** amaritudo *f*; acerbitas *f.*
blab vulgo 1.
black niger, ater; **~ and blue** lividus; **~-berry** rubus *m*; morum *n*; **~bird** merula *f*; **~en** maledico 3 (*alci*); **~ing** atramentum *n*; **~smith** faber *m* (ferrarius).
bladder vesica *f.*
blade herba *f*; lamina *f.*
blame reprehendo 3; accuso 1; culpa *f*; reprehensio *f*; **~less** innocens, integer; **~worthy** noxius.
bland mitis.
blandishment blanditia *f*; lenocinium *n.*
blank purus; vacuus.

blanket stragula *f*, vestis *f*.
blaspheme maledico 3 (*alci*).
blast uro 3; perdo 3; flatus, us *m*.
blaze ardeo 2, flagro 1; ignis *m*.
bleach candidum facio 3.
bleak tristis, frigidus.
blear-eyed lippus.
bleat balo 1.
bleed *v/t*. sanguinem mitto 3; *v/i*. sanguis fluit.
blemish macula *f*; vitium *n*.
blend commisceo 2.
bless benedico 3; fortuno 1; **~ed** beatus; **~ing** bonum *n*.
blight lues *f*; uredo *f*.
blind caecus; caeco 1; velum *n*; **~-fold** oculos obligo 1; **~ly** temere; **~ness** caecitas *f*.
blink nicto 1.
bliss beatitudo *f*; **~ful** beatus.
blister pustula *f*.
blithe hilarus.
bloat tumefacio 3; **~ed** tumidus.
block moles *f*; massa *f*; **~ up** obstruo 3; **~ade** obsideo 2; obsessio *f*; **~head** stipes *m*.
blood sanguis *m*; cruor *m*; **~less** exsanguis, incruentus; **~-red** sanguineus; **~shed** caedes *f*; **~-stained** cruentus; **~-thirsty** cruentus; **~-vessel** vena *f*.
bloom floreo 2; flos *m*; **~ing** florens.
blot litura *f*; labes *f*, macula *f*; **~ out** deleo 2, exstinguo 3.
blow flo 1; spiro 1; inflo 1; **~ one's nose** emungo 3; **~ up** inflo 1; **~ upon** afflo 1; plaga *f*, ictus, us *m*.
bludgeon fustis *m*.
blue caeruleus.
bluff impolitus; abruptum *n*.
bluish lividus.
blunder erro 1; error *m*; **~ing** mendosus.
blunt hebes; inurbanus; *v/t*. hebeto 1; retundo 3.
blush erubesco 3; **~ at** pudet (*alqm*, *alcs rei*); rubor *m*.
bluster declamito 1; declamatio *f*.
boar verres *m*; aper, apri *m*.
board tabula *f*; mensa *f*, victus, us *m*; consilium *n*, collegium *n*; **go on ~** navem conscendo 3; **~ over** contabulo 1.
boast glorior 1 (*de re*, *re*); me iacto 1; iactatio *f*; **~ful** gloriosus.
boat scapha *f*; navicula *f*; **~man** nauta *m*.
bode vaticinor 1.
bodily corporeus.
body corpus *n*; globus *m*; manus, us *f*; collegium *n*; **~-guard** stipatores *m/pl*., satellites *m/pl*.
bog palus, udis *f*; **~gy** paluster.
boil *v/t*. (aqua ferventi) coquo 3; *v/i*. ferveo 2; aestuo 1; vomica *f*; **~ed** elixus.
boisterous turbidus.
bold audax, ferox; **~ness** audacia *f*.
bolster pulvinus *m*; **~ up** fulcio 4.
bolt obsero 1; fulmen *n*; telum *n*; repagula *n/pl*.; claustra *n/pl*.; clavus *m*.
bombastic tumidus.
bond vinculum *n*; nodus *m*; syngrapha *f*; **~age** servitus, utis *f*.
bone os *n*.
bonnet mitra *f*.
bony osseus.
book liber, bri *m*; libellus *m*; volumen *n*; codex *m*; **~-binder** glutinator *m*; **~case** foruli *m/pl*.; **~seller** librarius *m*.
boom mugio 4.
boon beneficium *n*; **~-companion** sodalis *m*.
boorish agrestis.
boot calceus *m*; caliga *f*.
booth taberna *f*.
booty praeda *f*.
booze poto 1.
border ora *f*; margo *m and f*; finis *m*; **~ on** attingo 3, contingo 3; **~ed with** praetextus; **~ing** finitimus.
bor|e perforo 1; obtundo 3; foramen *n*; **~ing** importunus, odiosus.
born natus; **be ~** nascor 3, orior 4.
borough municipium *n*.
borrow mutuor 1; **~ed** mutuus; alienus; **~ing** mutuatio *f*.
bosom sinus, us *m*; gremium *n*; pectus *n*.
boss bulla *f*; umbo *m*.
both ambo; uterque; **in ~ directions** utroque.
both ... and et ... et; cum ... tum.
bother vexo 1.
bottle ampulla *f*, amphora *f*.
bottom fundus *m*; imus, infimus.
bough ramus *m*; frons *f*.
boulder saxum *n*.
bounce salio 4.
bound *v/i*. exsilio 4; *v/t*. finio 4, termino 1; finis *m*; modus *m*; terminus *m*; **be ~ to** debeo 2; **be ~ for** tendo 3 (*in*, *ad*); **~ary** finis *m*; **~less** infinitus.

bount|iful benignus, liberalis; **~y** liberalitas *f*; praemium *n*.
bout certamen *n*.
bow flecto 3, inclino 1; demitto 3; saluto 1; arcus, us *m*; **~ed** curvus; **~-legged** valgus; **~man** sagittarius *m*.
bowels alvus, i *f*; viscera *n/pl*.
bower umbraculum *n*.
bowl crater *m*; patera *f*; **~ along** volvo 3.
bows prora *f*.
box arca *f*; cista *f*; colaphus *m*; pugnis certo 1; **~er** pugil *m*; **~ing glove** caestus, us *m*; **~-tree** buxus, i *f*.
boy puer, eri *m*; **~-hood** pueritia *f*.
brace firmo 1; fibula *f*; fascia *f*.
bracelet armilla *f*.
brag glorior 1; **~gart** gloriosus.
braid necto 3; intexo 3; limbus *m*.
brain cerebrum *n*; **~less** socors.
brake dumetum *n*.
bramble dumus *m*; sentis *m*.
bran furfur *m*.
branch ramus *m*; frons *f*; **~ into** dividor 3; **~ing** ramosus.
brand inuro 3; noto 1; torris *m*; stigma *n*.
brandish vibro 1; iacto 1.
brass aes *n*; orichalcum *n*.
brav|e fortis, acer; experior 4; **~ery** fortitudo *f*, virtus, utis *f*.
brawl rixor 1; rixa *f*.
brawn lacertus *m*; **~y** lacertosus.
bray rudo 3.
brazen aeneus, aeratus; impudens.
breach discutio 3; frango 3; violo 1; violatio *f*.
bread panis *m*; victus, us *m*.
breadth latitudo *f*.
break frango 3; rumpo 3; violo 1; **~ down** *v/i*. haereo 2; *v/t*. frango 3; **~ in** domo 1; **~ into** irrumpo 3; **~ off** dirumpo 3; **~ up** dissolvo 3; **~fast** prandium *n*; **~-water** moles *f*.
breast mamma *f*; pectus *n*; **~plate** lorica *f*.
breath spiritus, us *m*, anima *f*; **out of ~** exanimatus; **~e** spiro 1; anhelo 1; **~ing** respiratio *f*; **~ing-space** respirandi spatium *n*.
breeches bracae *f/pl*.
breed pario 3; genero 1; alo 3; genus *n*.
breeze aura *f*.
brevity brevitas *f*.
brew coquo 3.
brib|e (pecunia) corrumpo 3; largior 4; **~ery** largitio *f*; praemium *n*, donum *n*.
brick later *m*; **~-layer** structor *m*; **~work** latericium *n*.
bridal nuptialis; nuptiae *f/pl*.
bride nupta *f*; sponsa *f*; **~groom** sponsus *m*.
bridge pons *m*; pontem facio 3 (*in flumine*).
bridle infreno 1; frenum *n*.
brief brevis; *jur*. causa *f*; **in ~** ne multa.
brier vepres *m*.
brigade legio *f*.
brigand latro *m*; **~age** latrocinium *n*.
bright clarus, lucidus, nitidus; **~en** splendesco 3; **~ness** fulgor *m*, candor *m*.
brillian|cy splendor *m*, nitor *m*; **~t** splendidus, luculentus.
brim ora *f*; labrum *n*.
brimstone sulpur *n*.
brine muria *f*.
bring affero 3; adveho 3; **~ about** efficio 3; **~ forth** prodo 3; **~ forward (a law)** fero 3; **~ out** effero 3; **~ up the rear** agmen claudo 3.
brink margo *m*.
brisk alacer.
bristl|e horreo 2; seta *f*; **~y** setiger, hirsutus.
brittle fragilis.
broad latus, amplus.
broil torreo 2.
broken confectus.
broker interpres *m*.
bronze aes *n*; aeneus, aeratus.
brooch fibula *f*.
brood|(over) incubo 1 (*alci rei*); agito 1 (*rem*); fetus, us *m*.
brook rivus *m*; patior 3.
broom scopae *f/pl*.
broth ius *n*.
brothel lustrum *n*.
brother frater *m*; **~hood** sodalitas *f*; **~ly** fraternus.
brow supercilium *n*; frons *f*.
brown fuscus.
browse upon pascor 3; tondeo 2.
bruise contundo 3; contusum *n*.
bruit abroad vulgo 1.
brush detergeo 2; verro 3; scopae *f/pl*.; peniculus *m*; **~wood** virgulta *n/pl*.
brut|al saevus, inhumanus; **~ality** inhumanitas *f*; **~e** fera *f*.
bubble bulla *f*; **~ up** scateo 2.

buck cervus *m.*
bucket hama *f.*
buckle fibula *f.*
bucolic rusticus.
bud gemma *f*; gemmo 1.
budge me moveo 2.
buffet colaphus *m*; tundo 3.
buffoon scurra *m.*
bug cimex *m*; **~bear** terricula *n/pl.*
bugle tuba *f*; bucina *f.*
build aedifico 1; construo 3; condo 3; **~ upon** confido 3 (*alci*); **~er** aedificator *m*; **~ing** aedificium *n.*
bulb bulbus *m.*
bulge tumeo 2; tumor *m.*
bulk magnitudo *f*, moles *f*; maior pars *f*; **~y** magnus.
bull taurus *m*; **~ock** iuvencus *m.*
bulrush iuncus *m.*
bulwark munimentum *n*, propugnaculum *n.*
bump offendo 3; tuber *m.*
bumpkin rusticus *m.*
bunch racemus *m.*
bundle fascis *m*; sarcina *f.*
bung obturamentum *n.*
buoy fulcio 4; **~ancy** levitas *f*; **~ant** levis.
bur lappa *f.*
burden onero 1, opprimo 3; onus *n*; **beast of ~** iumentum *n*; **~some** gravis, molestus.
burgher municeps *m.*
burglar fur *m.*
burial funus *n*; sepultura *f*; **~-place** sepulcrum *n.*
burn *v/t.* uro 3, incendo 3; *v/i.* flagro 1, ardeo 2; **~ing** ardens.
burnish polio 4.
burnt-offering hostia *f.*
burrow cuniculus *m*; **~ under** suffodio 4.
burst *v/t.* (di)rumpo 3; *v/i.* dissilio 4; **~ into** *fig.* effundo 3 in (*alqd*).
bury sepelio 4, humo 1; condo 3.
bush dumus *m*; frutex *m.*
bushel medimnum *n.*
bushy fruticosus.
business negotium *n*; res *f*; occupatio *f*; quaestus, us *m*; ars *f.*
buskin cothurnus *m.*
bust imago *f.*
bustle trepido 1; tumultus, us *m.*
busy occupatus, negotiosus.
but sed, at, verum, autem; **all ~** tantum non.
butcher lanius *m*; obtrunco 1; **~y** caedes *f.*
butler promus *m.*
butt *fig.* ludibrium *n.*
butter butyrum *n.*
butterfly papilio *m.*
buy emo 3, paro 1; **~ back, off** redimo 3; **~er** emptor *m.*
buzz bombus *m.*
by ad (*acc.*), secundum (*acc.*), praeter (*acc.*); ab (*abl.*); per (*acc.*); **day ~ day** in dies; **~ night** de nocte; **~ the gods** per deos; **~ your leave** bona tua venia; **~gone** praeteritus, priscus; **~-road** deverticulum *n*; **~standers** circumstantes *m/pl.*

C

cab cisium *n.*
cabal coniurati *m/pl.*
cabbage brassica *f*; caulis *m.*
cabin casa *f*; cella *f.*
cabinet conclave *n*; armarium *n*; consilium *n.*
cable ancorale *n*; funis *m*; rudens *m and f.*
cackle strideo 2; strepitus, us *m.*
cadaverous cadaverosus.
cage cavea *f*; claustra *n/pl.*; includo 3 (*in*).
cajole blandior 4; **~ry** blanditia *f.*
cake libum *n*; placenta *f*; *v/i.* concresco 3.
calamit|ous funestus, exitiosus; **~y** calamitas *f*, clades *f*; malum *n.*
calculat|e computo 1; subduco (rationem) 3; **~ion** ratio *f*; calculus *m.*
calendar fasti *m/pl.*
calends Calendae *f/pl.*
calf vitulus *m*; sura *f.*
call appello 1, nomino 1; (ad)voco 1; **be ~ed** audio 4; **~ in** advoco 1; vox *f*; salutatio *f*; **pay a ~** saluto 1; **~ing** quaestus, us *m*; artificium *n.*
callo|sity callum *n*; **be ~us** obduresco 3, occalesco 3.
callow rudis.
calm placidus, tranquillus; sedo 1; tranquillitas *f*; malacia *f.*
calumn|iate criminor 1, calumnior 1; **~y** criminatio *f.*
camel camelus *m.*
camp castra *n/pl.*; **break up ~** castra moveo 2; **pitch ~** castra pono 3.
campaign expeditio *f*; stipendium *n.*
can possum; queo 4; scio 4; hama *f.*
canal fossa *f.*
cancel induco 3; tollo 3.
cancer cancer, cri *m.*
candid apertus, sincerus.
candidat|e candidatus *m*; **be a ~e for** peto 3; **~ure** petitio *f.*
candle candela *f*; cereus *m*; **~stick** candelabrum *n.*
candour candor *m.*
cane harundo *f*; virga *f*; verbero 1.
canine caninus.
canister pyxis *f.*
canker robigo *f.*
cannon tormentum *n.*
cannot non possum, nequeo 4; nescio 4.
canoe scapha *f.*
canon norma *f.*
canopy aulaea *n/pl.*
canton pagus *m.*
canvas linteum *n.*
canvass ambio 4; ambitio *f.*
cap pilleus *m.*
capab|ility facultas *f*; **~le** capax.
capaci|ous amplus, capax; **~ty** captus, us *m.*
cape promontorium *n*; sagum *n.*
caper exsulto 1; capparis *f.*
capital princeps; capitalis; caput *n*; sors *f.*
capitol capitolium *n.*
capitulat|e me dedo 3; **~ion** deditio *f.*
capon capo *m.*
capric|e libido *f*; **~ious** inconstans.
capsize evertor 3.
captain centurio *m*; praefectus *m*; nauarchus *m*; magister, tri *m.*
captious captiosus.
captivate delenio 4.
captiv|e captivus; **~ity** captivitas *f.*
capture capio 3.
car currus, us *m.*
caravan commeatus, us *m.*
carcass cadaver, eris *n*, corpus *n.*
card pecto 3; pecten *m.*
care cura *f*, sollicitudo *f*; curatio *f*; **take ~ (of)** caveo 2 (*alqd*); **take ~ (lest)** caveo 2 (*ne*); **~ for** curo 1; **I don't ~ for (about)** nihili facio 3 (*alqd*).
career cursus, us *m.*
care|ful diligens, attentus, curiosus; **~less** securus; neglegens; **~lessness** incuria *f*, neglegentia *f.*
caress blandior 4; mulceo 2; blanditia *f.*
cargo onus *n.*
carnage strages *f.*
carol carmen *n.*
carouse poto 1; comissor 1; **~r** comissator *m.*
carp at carpo 3, vellico 1.

carpenter faber *m* tignarius.
carpet stragulum *n*.
carriage raeda *f*, vehiculum *n*.
carry fero 3, gero 3, veho 3; porto 1; ~ **away** aufero 3; ~ **on** gero 3; ~ **out** exsequor 3; ~ **through** perfero 3.
cart plaustrum *n*.
carve caelo 1, sculpo 3; seco 1; ~**r** carptor *m*.
carving caelatura *f*; ~**-knife** culter, tri *m*.
cascade deiectus, us *m* aquae.
case res *f*, causa *f*; tempus *n*; involucrum *n*; **it is the ~ that** accidit ut.
casement fenestra *f*.
cash nummi *m/pl.*; pecunia *f*; numeratum *n*.
cashier exauctoro 1.
cask cupa *f*; ~**et** arcula *f*.
cast iacio 3, conicio 3; fundo 3; ~ **off** exuo 3; ~ **upon** confero 3; iactus, us *m*.
castanet crotalum *n*.
castaway naufragus.
caste ordo *m*.
castigate castigo 1.
castle castellum *n*; arx *f*.
casual fortuitus; ~**ty** casus, us *m*.
cat felis *f*.
cataract cataracta *f*.
catarrh gravedo *f*.
catastrophe ruina *f*.
catch capio 3; deprehendo 3; excipio 3; ~ **fire** ignem concipio 3; ~ **a disease** morbum contraho 3; praeda *f*.
cater obsono 1; ~**er** obsonator *m*.
cattle boves *m and f*; pecus *n*; pecudes *f/pl*.
cauldron lebes *m*; cortina *f*.
cause facio 3, efficio 3 (*alqd*, *ut*, *ne*); curo 1; creo 1; pario 3; causa *f*, materia *f*, effectio *f*; **with good ~** iure; **be the ~ of** per (*alqm*) fit ut, stat quominus; ~**less** vanus; ~**way** agger, eris *m*.
caustic acerbus.
cauterize aduro 3.
cauti|on cautio *f*; cura *f*; moneo 2; ~**ous** cautus, consideratus.
cavalry equitatus, us *m*; equites *m/pl.*; equestris; ~**-squadron** turma *f*; ~**man** eques *m*.
cave specus, us *m*; spelunca *f*; antrum *n*.
cavil at vellico 1.
cavity caverna *f*.
caw crocio 4.
cease desino 3 (*alcis rei*, *inf.*); desisto 3 (*re*, *inf.*); omitto 3 (*alqd*, *inf.*); consisto 3; ~**less** perpetuus.
cedar cedrus, i *f*.
ceiling lacunar *n*, tectum *n*.
celebrat|e celebro 1; ~**ed** celeber; ~**ion** celebratio *f*.
celery apium *n*.
celestial caelestis.
celiba|cy caelibatus, us *m*; ~**te** caelebs.
cell cella *f*.
cellar cella *f*.
cement ferrumen *n*; ~ **together** conglutino 1.
cemetery sepulcra *n/pl*.
censor censor *m*; noto 1; ~**ship** censura *f*.
censure vitupero 1; vituperatio *f*.
census census, us *m*; **hold the ~** censum habeo 2.
centaur centaurus *m*.
centr|al medius; ~**e** medium *n*; ~**e upon** situm esse (*in re*).
centurion centurio *m*; ~**ship** centuriatus, us *m*; ordo *m*.
century centuria *f*; ordo *m*; saeculum *n*.
ceremon|ial sollemnis; ~**y** caerimonia *f*; ritus, us *m*.
certain certus, exploratus; **a ~** quidam; **consider as ~** pro certo habeo 2; **be ~** certo scio 4; ~**ly** sane, profecto.
certify recognosco 3; certiorem facio 3.
cessation intermissio *f*.
chafe *v/t.* attero 3; *v/i.* stomachor 1.
chaff palea *f*; acus *n*; *fig.* quisquiliae *f/pl*.
chagrin dolor *m*.
chain catena *f*; vinculum *n*; *fig.* series *f*; **throw into ~s** catenas inicio 3 (*alci*).
chair sella *f*; cathedra *f*; ~**man** magister, tri *m*.
chalk creta *f*.
challenge provoco 1.
chamber conclave *n*; cubiculum *n*; cella *f*; ~**-servant** cubicularius *m*; ancilla *f*.
champion propugnator *m*.
chance fors *f*; casus, us *m*; spes *f*; **by ~** forte, casu; **it ~d** accidit (*ut*).
chandelier candelabrum *n*.
change *v/t.* (com)muto 1; verto 3;

v/i. mutor 1; me verto 3; (com-) mutatio *f*; vicis (*gen.*) *f*; vicissitudo *f*; **~able** mutabilis; **~ling** subditus.
channel canalis *m*; fretum *n*.
chant canto 1; cantus, us *m*.
chapel aedicula *f*; sacellum *n*.
chaplet sertum *n*.
chapter caput *n*.
char amburo 3.
character littera *f*; mores *m/pl.*; habitus, us *m*; *thea.* persona *f*; partes *f/pl.*; **of good ~** honestus; **~istic** proprius (*gen.*).
charcoal carbo *m*.
charge incurro 3; signa infero 3 (*in*); mando 1, committo 3 (*alci ut*); arguo 3 (*alqm alcis rei*; *acc. c. inf.*); impetus, us *m*; mandatum *n*; cura *f* (*gen.*); crimen *n*; sumptus, us *m*; **be in ~ of** praesum.
chariot currus, us *m*; **~eer** auriga *m*; quadrigarius *m*.
charit|able benignus, mitis; **~y** benignitas *f*; stips *f*.
charm fascino 1; delenio 4; cantio *f*; dulcedo *f*; **~ing** suavis, lepidus.
chart tabula *f*.
chase caelo 1; sector 1; agito 1; venatio *f*; venatus, us *m*.
chasm hiatus, us *m*.
chaste castus, pudicus, purus.
chastise castigo 1.
chastity castitas *f*.
chat garrio 4; **~ter** effutio 4; clamor *m*; crepitus, us *m*.
cheap vilis; **~ly** bene; **~ness** vilitas *f*.
cheat fraudo 1; circumvenio 4; fraudator *m*.
check cohibeo 2, contineo 2, retineo 2; comprimo 3; incommodum *n*.
cheek gena *f*, mala *f*, bucca *f*.
cheer *v/t.* erigo 3, hilaro 1; *v/i.* plaudo 3; clamorem tollo 3; clamor *m*; **be of good ~** bono animo sum; **~ful** alacer, hilaris.
cheese caseus *m*.
chequer vario 1; **~ed** varius.
cherish foveo 2; colo 3.
cherry cerasus, i *f*.
chess-board latruncularia tabula *f*.
chess-man latrunculus *m*.
chest arca *f*; armarium *n*; pectus *n*.
chestnut castanea *f*.
chew mando 3.
chicanery calumnia *f*.
chicken pullus *m*.
chick-pea cicer *n*.
chide obiurgo 1.
chief princeps, praecipuus, summus; princeps *m*; procer *m*; dux *m*.
child puer, eri *m*; infans *m*; **~birth** partus, us *m*; **~hood** pueritia *f*; **~ish** puerilis; **~ren** liberi *m/pl.*
chill refrigero 1; frigidus; frigus *n*.
chime sono 1.
chimera commentum *n*.
chimney caminus *m*.
chin mentum *n*.
china fictilia *n/pl.* tenuia.
chine tergum *n*.
chink rima *f*.
chip assula *f*.
chirp pipilo 1.
chisel scalprum *n*.
choice delectus, us *m*; conquisitus.
choir chorus *m*.
choke strangulo 1; suffoco 1.
choleric iracundus.
choose deligo 3, eligo 3; **~ rather** malo.
chop dolo 1; caedo 3; **~ off** detrunco 1; **~per** securis *f*.
chord chorda *f*; nervus *m*.
chorus chorus *m*.
Christian christianus; **~ name** praenomen *n*.
chronic diuturnus.
chronicles annales *m/pl.*
chuckle rideo 2.
church ecclesia *f*; aedes *f*.
churlish inhumanus, agrestis.
cinder cinis, eris *m*.
cipher numerus *m*; nota *f*.
circle orbis *m*; circulus *m*; corona *f*.
circuit ambitus, us *m*; **make a ~** circumeo 4.
circula|r rotundus; **~te** diffundo 3; percrebresco 3.
circumcise circumcido 3.
circum|ference ambitus, us *m*; **~locution** ambages *f/pl.*; **~navigate** circumvehor 3; **~scribe** circumscribo 3; **~spect** cautus; **~stance** res *f*; tempus *n*; **~vent** circumscribo 3.
circus circus *m*.
cistern cisterna *f*.
citadel arx *f*.
cite profero 3.
cithern cithara *f*.
citizen civis *m and f*; **~ship** civitas *f*.
city urbs *f*; urbanus.
civil civilis; comis; **~ian** civis, is *m and f*; civilis; **~ization** cultus, us *m*; **~ized** humanus.

clad vestitus (*abl.*).
claim postulo 1; exigo 3; vindico 1; postulatio *f*; **~ant** petitor *m*.
clamber scando 3.
clammy umidus.
clamour clamor *m*; **~ for** flagito 1.
clamp confibula *f*.
clan gens *f*.
clandestine clandestinus.
clang strepo 3; clangor *m*.
clansman gentilis *m*.
clap plaudo 3; **~ping** plausus, us *m*.
clarify explano 1.
clash concrepo 1; confligo 3; crepitus, us *m*.
clasp complector 3; necto 3; fibula *f*; amplexus, us *m*.
class genus *n*; ordo *m*; **~ification** discriptio *f*; **~ify** discribo 3.
clause articulus *m*; incisum *n*; caput *n*.
claw unguis *m*.
clay lutum *n*; argilla *f*.
clean mundus, purus; (per)purgo 1; detergeo 2; **~liness** munditia *f*.
clear liquidus, serenus; clarus; purus; apertus; expedio 4, purgo 1; **~ oneself** me purgo 1; **it is ~** apparet; **~ up** explano 1; **~ness** claritas *f*.
cleave findo 3, scindo 3; **~ to** adhaereo 2.
cleft hiatus, us *m*; rima *f*.
clemency clementia *f*.
clench comprimo 3.
clerk scriba *m*.
clever sollers, callidus, ingeniosus; vafer; **~ness** calliditas *f*.
click crepo 1.
client cliens *m and f*; consultor *m*.
cliff cautes *f*; scopulus *m*.
climate caelum *n*.
climax gradatio *f*.
climb scando 3, ascendo 3.
cling adhaereo 2 (*dat.*).
clip tondeo 2.
clique factio *f*; globus *m*.
cloak pallium *n*; lacerna *f*; dissimulo 1.
clock horologium *n*; clepsydra *f*.
clod glaeba *f*.
clog impedio 4; sculponeae *f/pl*.
cloister porticus, us *f*.
close claudo 3; comprimo 3; coeo 4; confertus, densus, creber; *adv.* prope, iuxta; finis *m*; exitus, us *m*; **~ to** iuxta (*acc.*), prope (*acc.*).
closet cella *f*.
clot concresco 3.
cloth textile *n*; **~e** vestio 4; induo 3; **~ed in** amictus; **~es** vestis *f*; vestitus, us *m*; vestimenta *n/pl*.
cloud nubes *f*; nubila *n/pl.*; **storm-~** nimbus *m*; **~ over** nubem induco 3; **~y** nubilus.
cloven bisulcus.
clown scurra *m*.
club fustis *m*; clava *f*; sodalitas *f*; collegium *n*.
clue *fig.* indicium *n*.
clums|iness inscitia *f*; **~y** inscitus; rusticus.
cluster racemus *m*.
clutch arripio 3; **~es** manus, us *f*.
coach currus, us *m*; raeda *f*; **~man** raedarius *m*.
coagulate concresco 3.
coal carbo *m*.
coalition societas *f*; coitio *f*.
coarse crassus, rudis; incultus.
coast ora *f*; litus *n*; **~ along** lego 3; praetervehor 3.
coat lacerna *f*; tegmentum *n*; illino 3.
coax palpo 1; blandior 4; **~ing** blandimentum *n*.
cobble sarcio 4; **~r** sutor *m*.
cobweb aranea *f*.
cock gallus *m*; **game ~** gallus *m* rixosus; mas; erigo 3; **~roach** blatta *f*; **~scomb** crista *f*.
code leges *f/pl*.
coerce cogo 3.
coeval aequalis (*dat.*).
coffer arca *f*.
coffin sarcophagus *m*.
cog dens *m*.
cogent gravis.
cognizance cognitio *f*.
cognomen cognomen *n*.
cohere cohaereo 2; **~nce** contextus, us *m*.
cohort cohors *f*.
coil spira *f*; **~ up** glomero 1.
coin nummus *m*; signo 1; novo 1; **~age** moneta *f*.
coincide concurro 3; congruo 3; **by ~nce** forte.
colander colum *n*.
cold frigidus; frigus *n*; gravedo *f*; **be ~** frigeo 2.
collapse concido 3.
collar collare *n*; monile *n*; comprehendo 3.
colleague collega *m*.
collect colligo 3, congero 3; **~ion**

congeries *f*; collatio *f*; **~ive** universus; **~or** exactor *m*.
college collegium *n*.
colli|de confligo 3, concurro 3; **~sion** concursus, us *m*.
colloquial familiaris, vulgaris.
collu|de colludo 3; **~sion** collusio *f*; praevaricatio *f*.
colonel praefectus *m*; tribunus *m*.
colon|ial colonicus; **~ist** colonus *m*; **~izing** deductio *f*.
colonnade porticus, us *f*.
colony colonia *f*; **found a ~** coloniam deduco 3.
colossal vastus.
colour color *m*; pigmentum *n*; *fig.* species *f*; **~s** signum *n*; coloro 1; inficio 3; rubesco 3; **~ed** coloratus.
colt eculeus *m*.
column columna *f*; *mil.* agmen *n*.
comb pecto 3; pecten *m*.
combat repugno 1; pugna *f*; proelium *n*; certamen *n*.
combin|ation coniunctio *f*; conspiratio *f*; **~e** (con)iungo 3; confero 3 (in unum); conspiro 1.
come (per)venio 4; advehor 3; **~!** age, agite; **~ about** fieri; **~ down** descendo 3; **~ forth** prodeo 4; **~ in** incedo 3; **~ up with** consequor 3.
comed|ian comoedus *m*; **~y** comoedia *f*.
comely pulcher.
comet cometes, ae *m*.
comfort consolor 1; solatium *n*; consolatio *f*; **~able** commodus; **~er** consolator *m*.
comic comicus; ridiculus.
command impero 1 (*dat.*); iubeo 2 (*acc.*); praesum (*dat.*); imperium *n*, mandatum *n*, iussum *n*; **put in ~** praeficio 3; **~er** imperator *m*, dux *m*.
commemorate celebro 1.
commence incipio 3; exordior 4; **~ment** initium *n*.
commend commendo 1 (*alci alqd*); laudo 1 (*acc.*); **~able** laudabilis.
commensurate dignus (*abl.*).
comment sententia *f*; dictum *n*; **~ary** commentarii *m/pl.*
commerce mercatura *f*, mercatus, us *m*; commercium *n*.
commission mandatum *n*; mando 1 (*alci*).
commit mando 1, committo 3 (*alci alqd*); **~ (a crime)** committo 3; **be ~ted to** obligor 1 (*dat.*).
commodity merx *f*.
common communis; publicus; vulgaris; **in ~** in commune; communiter; **~s** plebs *f*; populus *m*; **~wealth** res *f* publica; civitas *f*.
commotion motus, us *m*; tumultus, us *m*; turba *f*.
commune colloquor 3.
communica|te impertio 4; communico 1; **~tion** communicatio *f*; commercium *n*.
commun|ion communio *f*; societas *f*; **~ity** commune *n*; civitas *f*.
compact solidus, compactus; pactum *n*, foedus *n*.
companion socius *m*; comes *m and f*; **~ship** sodalitas *f*.
company coetus, us *m*; convivae *m/pl.*; *mil.* manipulus *m*; societas *f*.
compar|e comparo 1, confero 3 (*alqd cum re*; *dat.*); **~ison** comparatio *f*; **in ~ison with** ad, adversus (*acc.*).
compartment pars *f*.
compass spatium *n*; **~es** circinus *m*.
compassion misericordia *f*; **~ate** misericors.
compatible conveniens.
compatriot civis *m and f*, popularis *m and f*.
compel cogo 3, subigo 3.
compendium summarium *n*.
compensat|e compenso 1 (*aldq re*); **~ion** compensatio *f*.
compete certo 1; contendo 3; **~ for** peto 3; **~nt** capax; locuples.
competit|ion certamen *n*; **~or** competitor *m*.
compile compono 3.
complain (con)queror 3 (*alqd, de re*); **~t** querela *f*, querimonia *f*.
complaisan|ce obsequium *n*; **~t** commodus.
complement supplementum *n*.
complete plenus, integer; perfectus; compleo 2, expleo 2; **~ly** omnino, prorsus.
complex multiplex; **~ion** color *m*.
complian|ce obtemperatio *f*; **~t** facilis.
complicat|ed involutus; **~ion** implicatio *f*.
complicity conscientia *f*.
compliment laudo 1; officium *n*; **pay one's ~s to** saluto 1.
comply with pareo 2, obtempero 1 (*dat.*).
component pars *f*; elementum *n*.

compos|e compono 3; sedo 1; **be ~ed of** consto 1 (*ex, in; abl.*); **~ed** placidus; **~er** auctor *m*; **~ition** compositio *f*; scriptio *f*; scriptum *n*; **~ure** aequus animus *m*.
compound misceo 2; **~ interest** anatocismus *m*.
comprehen|d percipio 3, intellego 3, comprehendo 3; **~sion** intellectus, us *m*.
compress concludo 3, coarto 1.
comprise comprehendo 3; contineo 2.
compromise implico 1; transigo 3 (*rem*).
compulsion vis *f*, necessitas *f*.
compunction paenitentia *f*.
compute computo 1.
comrade sodalis *m*, contubernalis *m*.
concave (con)cavus.
conceal celo 1 (*alqd, alqm*); abdo 3; occulto 1; **~ment** occultatio *f*; latebra *f*.
concede permitto 3, concedo 3.
conceit superbia *f*; **~ed** superbus.
conceive concipio 3; comprehendo 3.
concentrate cogo 3, contraho 3; operam do 1; intendo 3 animum.
concept, conception imago *f*, notio *f*.
concern attinet, pertinet (*ad*); interest, refert; **~ oneself about** curo 1 (*alqd*); **be ~ed in** versor 1; **be ~ed about** sollicitus sum; negotium *n*; cura *f*; sollicitudo *f*; **~ing** de (*abl.*).
concert concentus, us *m*.
concession concessio *f*.
conciliate concilio 1.
concise brevis, concisus; **~ness** brevitas *f*.
conclu|de concludo 3; perficio 3; **~sion** conclusio *f*; finis *m*; **~sive** certus.
concord concordia *f*.
concourse concursus, us *m*; frequentia *f*.
concubine concubina *f*, paelex *f*.
concur concurro 3; assentior 4.
condemn damno 1, condemno 1 (*alcis rei, de re*); improbo 1; **~ation** damnatio *f*.
condense spisso 1; premo 3; **~d** densus.
condescend descendo 3; me demitto 3.
condition status, us *m*; sors *f*, fortuna *f*; condicio *f*; lex *f*; **on ~ that** ea condicione ut.
condole consolor 1; **~nces** consolatio *f*.
condone condono 1.
conduc|e to conducit (*dat.*); proficit (*ad*); **~ive** utilis (*ad*).
conduct adduco 3, perduco 3; **~ oneself** me gero 3; mores *m/pl.*; vita *f*; administratio *f*; **~or** dux *m*.
conduit aquaeductus, us *m*; canalis *m*.
cone conus *m*.
confectioner pistor *m*; libarius *m*; **~y** crustum *n*.
confedera|cy foedus *n*; foederatae civitates *f/pl.*; **~te** foederatus; socius *m*.
confer *v/t.* confero 3, tribuo 3 (*alci alqd*); *v/i.* colloquor 3; **~ence** colloquium *n*; congressus, us *m*.
confess confiteor 2, fateor 2; **~ion** confessio *f*.
confid|ant conscius *m*; familiaris; **~e** *v/i.* confido 3 (*dat., abl.*); *v/t.* committo 3; **~ence** fides *f*; fiducia *f*; confidentia *f*; **~ent** confidens; **~ential** secretus.
confine includo 3, coerceo 2, contineo 2; **~d** artus; **~ment** vincula *n/pl.*; partus, us *m*.
confirm confirmo 1; comprobo 1.
confiscat|e proscribo 3; publico 1; **~ion** proscriptio *f*.
conflagration incendium *n*.
conflict certamen *n*; pugna *f*; **~ with** repugno 1.
confluence confluens *m*.
conform|(to) accommodo 1 (*me ad, dat.*); **~ity** convenientia *f*; **in ~ity with** ex (*abl.*), secundum (*acc.*).
confound confundo 3, misceo 2; obstupefacio 3.
confront compono 3; me oppono 3.
confus|e confundo 3; **~ion** perturbatio *f*; stupor *m*.
confute confuto 1.
congeal concresco 3.
congenial commodus.
congratulat|e gratulor 1; **~ion** gratulatio *f*.
congregat|e (me) congrego 1; **~ion** coetus, us *m*.
congress conventus, us *m*.
conjectur|al opinabilis; **~e** conicio 3; coniectura *f*.
conjugal coniugalis; maritus.
conjuncture discrimen *n*.

conjur|ation carmen *n*; obsecratio *f*; **~e** obtestor 1; **~er** praestigiator *m*.
connect conecto 3, coniungo 3 (*cum re, dat.*); **be ~ed with** contingo 3 (*alqm*); **~ion** colligatio *f*; necessitudo *f*.
connive coniveo 2 (*in alqa re*).
connoisseur intellegens *m and f*.
conquer vinco 3, supero 1; **~or** victor *m*, victrix *f*.
conquest victoria *f*.
conscien|ce conscientia *f*; religio *f*; **~tious** religiosus; diligens.
conscious conscius (*alcis rei, alci rei*); **~ness** conscientia *f*.
conscript tiro *m*; **~ion** dilectus, us *m*.
consecrate consecro 1, dedico 1.
consecutive continuus.
consent annuo 3; **~ to** accipio 3; **~ that** permitto 3 (*ut*); consensus, us *m*.
consequence eventus, us *m*; **it is of no ~** nihil refert; **be the ~ of** consequor 3.
consequently ergo, igitur.
consider cogito 1 (*de*); considero 1 (*alqd, de*); delibero 1 (*alqd, de*); rationem habeo 2 (*alcis rei*); **~able** aliquantus; **~ate** humanus; **~ation** respectus, us *m*; deliberatio *f*.
consign committo 3.
consist consto 1 (*ex, in re*); *abl.*); consisto 3 (*in*); **~ency** constantia *f*; **~ent** consentaneus (*dat.*); **be ~ent with** consentio 4.
consol|ation solatium *n*; **~e** consolor 1.
consolidate stabilio 4.
consort coniunx *m and f*; **~ with** utor 3 (*abl.*).
conspicuous insignis, conspectus.
conspir|acy coniuratio *f*; **~ator** coniuratus *m*; **~e** coniuro 1.
constable vigil *m*.
constan|cy constantia *f*; fides *f*; **~t** constans; fidelis; perpetuus.
constellation sidus *n*.
consternation pavor *m*; perturbatio *f*.
constitut|e constituo 3; statuo 3; compono 3; **~ion** habitus, us *m*; natura *f*; res *f* publica; civitas *f*; **~ional** legitimus, innatus.
constrain cogo 3; **~t** necessitas *f*.
construct (con)struo 3; facio 3; **~ion** constructio *f*; structura *f*.
construe interpretor 1.
consul consul *m*; **~ar** consularis; **~ate** consulatus, us *m*.
consult *v/t.* consulo 3 (*alqm de re*); *v/i.* consulto 1; **~ation** deliberatio *f*.
consum|e consumo 3; abutor 3; conficio 3; edo 3; **~er** emptor *m*.
consummate perficio 3; perfectus.
consumption tabes *f*.
contact, contagion contagio *f*.
contain capio 3; contineo 2.
contaminate contamino 1.
contemplat|e intueor 2; considero 1; **~ion** contemplatio *f*.
contemporary aequalis.
contempt contemptio *f*; **~ible** abiectus, contemptus; **~uous** fastidiosus.
contend contendo 3; certo 1; **~ against** adversor 1.
content contentus (*abl.*); **be ~** satis habeo 2 (*inf., si*).
content|ion discordia *f*; controversia *f*; **~ious** pugnax.
contentment aequus animus *m*.
contest contendo 3 (*cum alqo de re*); certamen *n*; contentio *f*; **be ~ed** in controversiam venio 4.
contiguous confinis (*dat.*).
continen|ce continentia *f*; **~t** continens; continens *f*.
contingen|cy casus, us *m*; **~t** fortuitus.
continu|al perpetuus; assiduus; **~ance** perpetuitas *f*; **~ation** continuatio *f*; **~e** *v/i.* persevero 1 (*inf., in re*); permaneo 2 (*in*); pergo 3; *v/t.* continuo 1; prorogo 1; **~ous** continens, perpetuus; **~ously** continenter.
contort contorqueo 2.
contour forma *f*.
contraband illicitus.
contract contraho 3; astringo 3; **~ a debt** aes alienum contraho 3; **~ for** loco 1; conduco 3; locatio *f*; pactio *f*; **~or** conductor *m*; redemptor *m*.
contradict adversor 1 (*dat.*); repugno 1; **~ion** repugnantia *f*; **~ory** repugnans.
contrary contrarius, diversus, adversus; **~ to** contra (*acc.*); contrarium *n* (*gen.*); **on the ~** contra; immo.
contrast confero 3; discrepo 1 (*cum, a re*); discrepantia *f*.
contravene violo 1.

contribut|e confero 3; affero 3 (*ad*); **~ion** collatio *f*; collecta *f*; stips *f*.
contriv|ance excogitatio *f*; ars *f*; machina *f*; **~e** struo 3; machinor 1; invenio 4; **~er** machinator *m*.
control moderor 1 (*dat.*); coerceo 2; moderatio *f*; potestas *f*.
controversy concertatio *f*, controversia *f*.
contumacious contumax.
contumel|ious contumeliosus; **~y** contumelia *f*.
convalesce convalesco 3; **~nt** convalescens.
convene (con)voco 1.
convenien|ce commoditas *f*; opportunitas *f*; utilitas *f*; **at your, his ~ce** commodo tuo, suo; **~t** commodus; opportunus.
convention conventus, us *m*; pactio *f*; mos *m*; **~al** usitatus.
converge in unum tendo 3.
convers|ant peritus (*gen.*); **~ation** colloquium *n*; sermo *m*; **~e** colloquor 3 (*cum*); congressus, us *m*; contrarium *n*.
convert (com)muto 1.
convex convexus.
convey (ad)veho 3; conveho 3; deporto 1; significo 1; **~ance** vehiculum *n*.
convict convinco 3 (*alqm alcs rei*); condemno 1; **~ion** damnatio *f*; opinio *f*.
convince persuadeo 2 (*alci*); **be ~d** persuasum habeo 2.
conviviality convivia *n/pl.*
convoy commeatus, us *m*.
convuls|e concutio 3; **~ion** perturbatio *f*.
coo queror 3.
cook coquo 3; coquus *m*; coqua *f*.
cool frigidus; impavidus; *v/t.* refrigero 1; *v/i.* refrigesco 3; **~ness** frigus *n*; impudentia *f*.
coop cavea *f*; **~ up** includo 3.
cooperat|e adiuvo 1; operam confero 3; **~ion** auxilium *n*; opera *f*.
coot fulica *f*.
cope (with) contendo 3 (*cum*).
copious largus, uber, abundans.
copper aes *n*; aenum *n*; aeneus.
copse fruticetum *n*, dumetum *n*.
copulate coeo 4.
copy describo 3, exscribo 3; imitor 1; exemplar *n*; similitudo *f*; **~ist** librarius *m*.
coral corallium *n*.
cord funis *m*; constringo 3; **~age** rudentes *m/pl.*
cordial benignus.
cordon corona *f*.
core medulla *f*.
cork suber, eris *n*; cortex *m*.
corn frumentum *n*; frumentarius; **standing ~** seges *f*; **~-merchant** frumentarius *m*; **~ supply, price of ~** annona *f*.
corner angulus *m*; recessus, us *m*.
cornet bucina *f*.
coronet diadema *n*.
corpor|ation collegium *n*; municipium *n*; **~eal** corporeus.
corpse cadaver, eris *n*, corpus *n*.
corpulen|ce opimus habitus, us *m*; **~t** pinguis.
correct rectus, accuratus; corrigo 3; emendo 1; **~ion** correctio *f*; castigatio *f*.
correspond congruo 3 (*cum, inter se, dat.*); respondeo 2 (*dat.*); litteras scribo 3; **~ence** convenientia *f*; litterae *f/pl.*; **~ing** par (*dat.*).
corroborate confirmo 1.
corrode erodo 3.
corrugate corrugo 1.
corrupt corrumpo 3; depravo 1; putridus; corruptus; **~er** corruptor *m*; **~ible** venalis; **~ion** corruptio *f*; corruptela *f*; largitio *f*.
corselet lorica *f*; thorax *m*.
cosmetics medicamina *n/pl.*; fucus *m*.
cosmopolitan mundanus *m*.
cost (con)sto 1; pretium *n*; impensa *f*; damnum *n*; **at what ~?** quanti?; **~ly** pretiosus; carus.
costume vestitus, us *m*.
cot lectulus *m*.
cottage casa *f*.
couch lectus *m*; cubile *n*; subsido 3; (*in language*) dico 3.
cough tussis *f*; tussio 4.
council concilium *n*, consilium *n*; **~ of war** praetorium *n*; **town-~lor** decurio *m*.
counsel moneo 2; consilium *n*; patronus *m*; **~lor** consiliarius *m*.
count numero 1; duco 3; **~ upon** fidem habeo 2 (*alci*).
countenance vultus, us *m*; facies *f*; indulgeo 2.
counter calculus *m*; mensa *f*; **run ~ to** repugno 1; **~act** occurro 3; **~-balance** compenso 1 (*alqd cum*);

~feit simulo 1; adulterinus; fictus; **~pane** stragulum *n*.
countless innumerabilis.
countrified agrestis.
country rus *n*; agri *m/pl.*; terra *f*; fines *m/pl.*; **native ~** patria *f*; **in the ~** ruri; **~-house, ~ seat** villa *f*; **~man** rusticus *m*; homo *m* agrestis.
coup d'état res *f/pl.* novae.
couple copulo 1; par *n*; iugum *n*; bini, ae, a (*adj.*).
courage virtus, utis *f*; animus *m*; **~ous** fortis, animosus.
courier nuntius *m*.
course venor 1; curro 3; cursus, us *m*; iter, ineris *n*; curriculum *n*; ratio *f*, consilium *n*; **race-~** circus *m*; **in the ~ of** in (*abl.*), inter (*acc.*); **of ~** sane; scilicet; videlicet.
court peto 3; ambio 4; capto 1; aula *f*; atrium *n*; regia *f*; **law-~** basilica *f*; subsellia *n/pl.*; iudicium *n*; **~eous** comis; **~esy** comitas *f*; **~esan** meretrix *f*; **~ier** comes *m*; **~ing** ambitio *f*.
cousin consobrinus *m*; consobrina *f*.
cove sinus, us *m*.
covenant stipulor 1; pactum *n*.
cover (in)tego 3; operio 4; obduco 3; velo 1; operculum *n*; praesidium *n*; **~ing** tegmen *n*, tegimentum *n*; **~let** stragulum *n*; **~t** occultus; obliquus; dumetum *n*.
covet concupisco 3; **~ous** avarus; **~ousness** avaritia *f*.
cow vacca *f*, bos *f*; terreo 2; **~-herd** pastor *m*, armentarius *m*.
coward|ice ignavia *f*; **~ly** ignavus, timidus.
cower tremo 3.
coxcomb crista *f* (galli); nugator *m*.
coy verecundus.
crab cancer, cri *m*; **~bed** morosus.
crack findo 3; dissilio 4; concrepo 1; rima *f*; crepitus, us *m*.
cradle cunae *f/pl.*; incunabula *n/pl.*; foveo 2.
craft ars *f*; artificium *n*; dolus *m*; scapha *f*; **~sman** artifex *m*, opifex *m*; **~y** callidus.
crag scopulus *m*; **~gy** asper.
cram refercio 4; stipo 1; sagino 1.
cramp comprimo 3.
crane grus, gruis *f*; tolleno *m*.
crash fragor *m*; **~ down** ruo 3.
crate corbis *f*.
crater crater, eris *m*.
crav|e oro 1, obsecro 1 (*alqm alqd*); **~en** ignavus; **~ing** desiderium *n*.
crawl repo 3; serpo 3.
craz|iness furor *m*; **~y** imbecillus.
creak strideo 2; concrepo 1.
cream flos *m* lactis.
crease corrugo 1; ruga *f*.
creat|e creo 1; pario 3; fingo 3; **~ion** mundus *m*; opus *n*; **~or** genitor *m*; (pro)creator *m*; auctor *m*; **~ure** animal *n*; animans *m and f*.
creden|ce fides *f*; **~tials** auctoritates *f/pl.*
credible credibilis.
credit fides *f*; existimatio *f*; gratia *f*; **be to one's ~** honori esse alci; fidem habeo 2 (*alci*); **~able** honestus; **~or** creditor *m*.
credul|ity credulitas *f*; **~ous** credulus.
creek aestuarium *n*.
creep serpo 3, repo 3; **~ up on** obrepo 3 (*dat.*, *ad*, *in*).
cremate cremo 1.
crescent luna *f*; lunatus.
crest crista *f*; iuba *f*; vertex *m*; **~ed** cristatus; **~fallen** demissus.
crevice rima *f*.
crew nautae *m/pl.*; remiges *m/pl.*; remigium *n*.
crib praesaepe *n*; lectulus *m*.
cricket cicada *f*.
crier praeco *m*.
crim|e facinus *n*; scelus *n*; **~inal** nefarius; sons *m*.
crimson coccineus; coccum *n*.
cring|e adulor 1 (*alqm*, *alci*); **~ing** proiectus.
cripple *fig.* accido 3; **~d** claudus; mancus.
crisis discrimen *n*; tempus *n*.
criterion obrussa *f*.
criti|c iudex *m*, criticus *m*; **~cal** intellegens; dubius; **~cism** iudicium *n*; **~cise** iudico 1 (*de*); reprehendo 3.
croak cano 3; crocio 4; occino 3; **~ing** clamor *m*.
crock olla *f*; **~ery** fictilia *n/pl.*
crocodile crocodilus *m*.
crone anus, us *f*.
crook pedum *n*; **~ed** pravus.
crop seges *f*; fruges *f*; carpo 3; tondeo 2.
cross transeo 4; me traicio 3; obsto 1 (*alci*); **~ the mind** occurro 3 (animo); crux *f*; quincunx *m*; transversus; difficilis; **~-examination** interrogatio *f*; **~ing** transitus, us *m*; trivium *n*.

crouch subsido 3.
crow cornix *f*; cano 3.
crowd turba *f*; vulgus, i *n*; frequentia *f*; stipo 1; compleo 2; **~ around** circumfundor 3 (*alci*); **~ together** conglobo 1 (me); **~ed** celeber; frequens.
crown corona *f*; diadema *n*; *fig.* cumulus *m*; diadema impono 3 (*capiti*); cingo 3.
crucify cruce afficio 3.
crude rudis.
cruel crudelis, atrox; **~ty** crudelitas *f*.
cruise (per)vagor 1.
crumb frustum *n*; **~le** frio 1; contero 3; corruo 3.
crumpled rugosus.
crush opprimo 3; frango 3.
crust crusta *f*; **~ of bread** frustum *n*.
crutch baculum *n*.
cry clamo 1; fleo 2; vagio 4; **~ out at** acclamo 1; clamor *m*; vox *f*.
crystal crystallum *n*.
cub catulus *m*.
cuckoo cuculus *m*.
cucumber cucumis *m*.
cudgel fustis *m*; baculum *n*; fuste verbero 1.
cue signum *n*; **give a ~** innuo 3.
cuff colaphus *m*.
cuirass lorica *f*.
cull lego 3.
culmination fastigium *n*; summum *n*.
culp|able nocens; **~rit** noxius *m*.
cultivat|e colo 3; **~ed** cultus; **~ion** cultura *f*; cultus, us *m*; **~or** cultor *m*.
culture cultura *f* (animi).
cumbersome inhabilis.
cumin cuminum *n*.
cunning callidus, dolosus; astutia *f*.
cup poculum *n*, calix *m*; **~board** armarium *n*.
cupidity cupiditas *f*.
cur canis *m*.
curable sanabilis.
curator curator *m*.
curb (re)freno 1; coerceo 2; frenum *n*; crepido *f*.
curdle *v/t*. coagulo 1; *v/i*. concreso 3.
cure medeor 2 (*dat.*); sano 1; sanatio *f*; remedium *n*.
curio|sity curiositas *f*; cura *f*; **~us** curiosus; elaboratus; rarus.
curl torqueo 2; cincinnus *m*; cirrus *m*; **~y** crispus, cincinnatus; **~ing iron** calamister *m*.
currant acinus *m*.
curren|cy moneta *f*; **~t** vulgaris, usitatus; **be ~t** vigeo 2; percrebresco 3; flumen *n*; aestus, us *m*; **~t of air** aura *f*.
curse exsecror 1; exsecratio *f*; preces *f/pl*.
curtail coarto 1.
curtain aulaeum *n*.
curve sinus, us *m*; flexus, us *m*; flecto 3; curvo 1; **~d** curvatus; sinuosus.
cushion pulvinus *m*.
custod|ian curator *m*; **~y** custodia *f*.
custom mos *m*; consuetudo *f*; institutum *n*; commercium *n*; **~ary** translaticius; usitatus; **~er** emptor *m*.
cut caedo 3; seco 1; **~ down** excido 3; **~ off** praecido, intercludo 3; vulnus *n*; **a short ~** via *f* compendiaria.
cutter celox *f*.
cutting acerbus.
cuttle-fish sepia *f*.
cycle orbis *m*.
cylinder cylindrus *m*.
cymbal cymbalum *n*.
cynical mordax.
cypress cupressus, i *f*.

D

dabble tingo 3.
dagger pugio *m*, sica *f*.
daily cotidianus, diurnus; *adv.* cotidie; in dies.
daint|iness fastidium *n*; **~ies** cuppedia *n/pl.*; **~y** fastidiosus; delicatus.
dall|iance lusus, us *m*; **~y** ludo 3; moror 1.
dam moles *f*; mater *f*; **~ up** obstruo 3.
damage laedo 3; affligo 3; damnum *n*; incommodum *n*; **~s** *jur.* damnum *n*.
dame matrona *f*.
damp umidus; umor *m*; restinguo 3.
damsel virgo *f*.
dance salto 1; saltatus, us *m*; **~r** saltator *m*; saltatrix *f*.
dandruff porrigo *f*.
dandy (homo) delicatus *m*.
danger periculum *n*; discrimen *n*; **~ous** periculosus; gravis.
dangle pendeo 2 (*ab, de re*).
dank umidus.
dappled varius; maculosus.
dare *v/i.* audeo 2; *v/t.* provoco 1 (*alqm in pugnam*).
daring audax; audacia *f*.
dark obscurus; ater; **it grows ~** advesperascit 3; **after ~** de nocte; **keep in the ~** celo 1 (*alqm alqd*); **~en** obscuro 1, occaeco 1; **~ness** tenebrae *f/pl.*; caligo *f*.
darling deliciae *f/pl.*
darn sarcio 4.
dart iaculor 1; provolo 1; emico 1; telum *n*, iaculum *n*.
dash ruo 3; **~ against** affligo 3 (*ad*); **~ to pieces** elido 3; **have one's hopes ~ed** spe depellor 3; impetus, us *m*; **~ing** animosus.
dastardly ignavus.
date dies *m and f*; tempus *n*; (*fruit*) palmula *f*; diem ascribo 3; **~ from** incipio 3 (*abl.*).
daub illino 3 (*alqd re*).
daughter filia *f*; **~-in-law** nurus, us *f*.
daunt percello 3; **~less** ferox, impavidus.
dawdle cesso 1.
dawn (prima) lux *f*; aurora *f*; dilucesco 3.
day dies *m and f*; lux *f*; **~ after ~** diem ex die; **every ~** in dies; **every other ~** alternis diebus; **the ~ before** pridie; **the ~ after** postridie; **~light** dies *m and f*, lux *f*.
dazz|le perstringo 3; **~ling** splendidus.
dead mortuus; **the ~** manes *m/pl.*; inferi *m/pl.*; **~ of night** nox *f* intempesta; **~en** obtundo 3; **~ly** funestus; capitalis.
deaf surdus; **~en** obtundo 3; **~ness** surditas *f*.
deal infligo 3 (*alci*); **~ out** dispertio 4; **~ with** tracto 1 (*alqm*); **~er** negotiator *m*, mercator *m*; **~ings** commercium *n*.
dear carus; pretiosus; **~ness** caritas *f*.
dearth inopia *f*.
death mors *f*; letum *n*; obitus, us *m*.
debar prohibeo 2.
debase adultero 1.
debate disputo 1 (*alqd, de re*); controversia *f*.
debauch stupro 1; perdo 3; **~ery** stuprum *n*.
debilitate debilito 1.
debit expensum fero 3 (*alci*).
debt aes *n* alienum; debitum *n*; **be in ~** in aere alieno sum; **~or** debitor *m*.
decant diffundo 3.
decapitate securi ferio 4; detrunco 1.
decay tabesco 3; putesco 3; minuor 3; tabes *f*; senium *n*.
decease obitus, us *m*; **~d** demortuus.
deceit fraus *f*; dolus *m*; **~ful** fallax, dolosus.
deceive decipio 3; fallo 3.
December (mensis) December, bris *m*.
decemvir decemvir *m*; **~ate** decemviratus, us *m*.
decen|cy pudor *m*; honestas *f*; **~t** honestus; decens.
deception fraus *f*; dolus *m*.
decide *v/t.* decerno 3; diiudico 1; *v/i.* constituo 3.
decimate decimo 1.
decisi|on decretum *n*, arbitrium *n*,

iudicium *n*; **~ve** supremus (*proelium*); certus.
deck orno 1; pons *m*.
declaim declamo 1; **~ against** invehor 3 (*in*); **~er** declamator *m*.
declar|ation professio *f*; **~e** *v/t*. declaro 1; renuntio 1; *v/i*. affirmo 1; **~e war** bellum indico 3.
decline *v/i*. senesco 3, deficio 3; *v/t*. recuso 1 (*alqd*; *inf*.); deminutio *f*.
decompose putesco 3.
decorat|e (ex)orno 1; **~ion** decus *n*; ornamentum *n*; insigne *n*.
decorous decorus.
decoy illicio 3.
decrease (de)minuor 3; imminutio *f*.
decree decerno 3; censeo 2; decretum *n*; **~ of the senate** senatus consultum *n*.
decrepit decrepitus.
decry obtrecto 1.
dedicat|e dedico 1 (*dat*.); **~ion** dedicatio *f*.
deduce concludo 3.
deduct deduco 3; **~ion** deductio *f*; conclusio *f*.
deed factum *n*; res *f*; facinus *n*; tabula *f*.
deem existimo 1.
deep altus, profundus; altum *n*; **~en** altiorem facio 3; **~ly** penitus.
deer cervus *m*.
deface deformo 1.
defam|ation obtrectatio *f*; **~e** maledico 3 (*dat*.).
defeat vinco 3; supero 1; frustror 1; clades *f*; repulsa *f*.
defect vitium *n*; **~ion** defectio *f*; **~ive** vitiosus.
defence defensio *f*; tutela *f*; *jur*. patrocinium *n*; praesidium *n*; **~less** inermis.
defend defendo 3; tueor 2; **~ant** reus *m*; rea *f*; **~er** propugnator *m*.
defer differo 3 (*alqd in*); **~ to** obtempero 1; **~ence** observantia *f*.
defian|ce: in ~ce of contra (*acc*.); **~t** ferox.
deficien|cy inopia *f*; **be ~t** desum; deficio 3.
defile contamino 1; angustiae *f/pl*.
defin|e circumscribo 3; definio 4; **~ite** definitus, certus; **~ition** definitio *f*.
deflect deflecto 3.
deform deformo 1; **~ed** pravus; **~ity** pravitas *f*.
defraud fraudo 1 (*alqm, alqa re*).
defray suppedito 1.
deft scitus.
defy provoco 1; contemno 3.
degenerate degenero 1 (*ab*); perditus.
degrad|ation ignominia *f*; **~e** moveo 2 (*abl*.); abicio 3; **~ing** indignus.
degree gradus, us *m*; **in some ~** aliquantum; **by ~s** gradatim.
deign dignor 1 (*inf*.).
deity deus *m*; dea *f*; numen *n*.
dejected demissus.
delay moror 1; cunctor 1; mora *f*.
delegat|e defero 3 (*ad*); legatus *m*; **~ion** legatio *f*.
delete deleo 2.
deliberat|e consulo 3, delibero 1 (*de*); cogitatus; **~ely** consulto; **~ion** deliberatio *f*.
delica|cy humanitas *f*; cuppedia *n/pl*.; **~te** subtilis, tener, suavis.
delicious suavis.
delight *v/t*. delecto 1; *v/i*. gaudeo 2 (*abl*., *inf*., *quod*); delectatio *f*; voluptas *f*; **~ful** iucundus.
delineate describo 3.
delinquent noxius *m*.
deliver libero 1; eripio 3; reddo 3, trado 3; **~ a speech** orationem habeo 3; **~ance** salus, utis *f*; **~y** *rhet*. actio *f*; *med*. partus, us *m*.
dell vallis *f*.
delude decipio 3.
deluge inundatio *f*; inundo 1.
delusi|on error *m*; **~ve** fallax.
demagogue contionator *m*.
demand postulo 1, flagito 1; postulatio *f*.
demean me demitto 3; **~our** habitus, us *m*.
demented demens.
demesne ager, gri *m*.
demigod semideus *m*.
demise obitus, us *m*.
democra|cy civitas *f* popularis; **~tic** popularis.
demolish demolior 4.
demonstrat|e demonstro 1; **~ion** indicium *n*.
demur dubito 1; haesito 1; dubitatio *f*.
demure verecundus.
den latibulum *n*.
denial negatio *f*.
denizen incola *m*.
denote indico 1, significo 1.
denounce defero 3 (*nomen alcis*).
dense densus, confertus.

dent vulnus *n*.
denude (de)nudo 1.
denunciation delatio *f*; accusatio *f*.
deny nego 1; infitior 1; abnuo 3.
depart abeo 4, discedo 3 (*ab, ex, de*); *fig*. descisco 3 (*ab*); **~ment** provincia *f*; munus *n*; **~ure** discessus, us *m*.
depend pendeo 2 (*abl., ex*); nitor 3 (*abl.*); consisto 3 (*in re*); **~ant** cliens *m*; **~ent (on)** obnoxius (*dat.*).
depict (de)pingo 3; describo 3.
deplor|able miserabilis; **~e** deploro.
deploy explico 1.
depopulat|e vasto 1; depopulor 1; **~ion** vastatio *f*.
deport relego 1; **~ation** relegatio *f*; exsilium *n*; **~ment** habitus, us *m*.
depose abrogo 1 (*magistratum alci*); moveo 2; testificor 1.
deposit depono 3 (*apud alqm*); depositum *n*; pignus *n*.
depot horreum *n*.
deprav|ed corruptus; **~ity** pravitas *f*.
deprecate deprecor 1 (*alqd ab alqo*).
depreciate detraho 3 (*de*).
depredation direptio *f*.
depress deprimo 3; **~ed** fractus; **~ion** tristitia *f*.
deprive privo 1 (*abl.*); adimo 3 (*alqd alci*); **~d of** orbus (*abl.*).
depth altitudo *f*; **~s** altum *n*; **in ~** in agrum.
deput|ation legatio *f*; **~e** mando 1 (*dat.*); **~y** procurator *m*; legatus *m*.
derange perturbo 1; **~d** insanus.
deri|de derideo 2; **~sion** irrisus, us *m*.
deriv|ation declinatio *f*; **~e** duco 3, traho 3 (*originem ab, ex*).
derogatory indignus.
descend descendo 3 (*de, ex, in, ad*); degredior 3; pervenio 4; **~ant** progenies *f*; **~ants** posteri *m/pl.*; **~ed** ortus (*abl.*).
descent descensus, us *m*; genus *n*.
describe describo 3; exprimo 3; expono 3.
descry conspicio 3.
desecrate violo 1.
desert desero 3, relinquo 3; desertus, vastus; deserta *n/pl.*; **~s** meritum *n*; **~er** desertor *m*, perfuga *m*.
deserve mereor 2; dignus sum; **~dly** merito, iure.
design describo 3; formo 1; cogito 1; descriptio *f*; consilium *n*; **~ate** designo 1; **~edly** consulto; **~er** architectus *m*; auctor *m*.
desir|able optabilis; **~e** cupio 3; (ex)opto 1; gestio 4; cupiditas *f*; studium *n*; libido *f*; **~ous** cupidus (*gen.*).
desist desisto 3 (*re, inf.*).
desk scrinium *n*.
desolat|e vastus, desertus; orbus; vasto 1; **~ion** vastatio *f*; solitudo *f*.
despair despero 1 (*de*; *alqd*; *acc. c. inf.*); desperatio *f*.
despatch mitto 3; perficio 3, conficio 3; litterae *f/pl.*
desperate desperatus, periculosus.
despise contemno 3, sperno 3.
despite *prep*. etiamsi; *cj*. quamvis.
despoil spolio 1.
despond despero 1, animum demitto 3.
despot tyrannus *m*; **~ic** tyrannicus.
dessert bellaria *n/pl.*
destin|e destino 1; **~ed** fatalis (*ad*); **~y** fatum *n*.
destitut|e inops, egens, expers; **~ion** egestas *f*, inopia *f*.
destroy deleo 2, everto 3, perdo 3; **~er** perditor *m*.
destruct|ion pernicies *f*; exitium *n*; **~ive** exitialis.
desultory inconstans.
detach eximo 3, abripio 3; disiungo 3; removeo 2; **~ment** manus, us *f*.
detail enarro 1; **~s** singula *n/pl.*; **in ~** singillatim.
detain teneo 2; retineo 2.
detect deprehendo 3; comperio 4.
deter deterreo 2 (*a re, ne*).
deteriorate corrumpo(r) 3.
determin|ate certus; **~ation** sententia *f*; constantia *f*; **~e** statuo 3, constituo 3 (*inf., ut*); decerno 3 (*alqd*; *acc. c. inf.*; *ut*); **~ed** firmus, constans.
detest odi; abominor 1; **~able** foedus, detestabilis.
dethrone regno expello 3.
detonation fragor *m*.
detour circuitus, us *m*.
detract detraho 3, derogo 1 (*de*); **~or** obtrectator *m*.
detriment damnum *n*, detrimentum *n*.
devastat|e vasto 1, populor 1; **~ion** vastatio *f*.
develop *v/t*. dilato 1, explico 1; amplifico 1; alo 3; *v/i*. cresco 3; **~ment** incrementum *n*.

deviat|e declino 1 (*de*); **~ion** declinatio *f.*
device insigne *n*; artificium *n.*
devil diabolus *m.*
devise excogito 1; fingo 3.
devoid expers (*gen.*); vacuus (*abl.*).
devolve *v/t.* defero 3 (*alci*); *v/i.* pervenio 4 (*ad*); obvenio 4 (*dat.*).
devot|e devoveo 2 (*dat.*); confero 3 (*dat.*); **~e oneself to** incumbo 3 (*in, ad*); **~ed** sacer; studiosus (*gen.*); **~ion** studium *n*; **~ions** preces *f/pl.*
devour devoro 1.
devout pius.
dew ros *m*; **dew-lap** palearia *n/pl.*; **~y** roscidus.
dexter|ity calliditas *f*; **~ous** callidus.
diadem diadema *n.*
diagram descriptio *f.*
dial solarium *n.*
dialect lingua *f*; **~ical** dialecticus; **~ics** dialectica *f.*
dialogue sermo *m*; dialogus *m.*
diamond adamas *m.*
diaphragm praecordia *n/pl.*
diary ephemeris *f.*
dice tali *m/pl.*; tesserae *f/pl.*; **game of ~** alea *f*; **~-board** alveus *m*; **~-box** fritillus *m.*
dictat|e impero 1; praescribo 3; dicto 1; praeceptum *n*; **~ion** arbitrium *n*; **~or** dictator *m*; **~orial** arrogans; **~orship** dictatura *f.*
diction dictio *f.*
die talus *m*; tessera *f*; morior 3; obeo 4; pereo 4; **~ out** obsolesco 3.
diet cibus *m*; victus, us *m*; diaeta *f.*
differ differo 3, discrepo 1, disto 1 (*ab, inter se*); **~ence** differentia *f*, distantia *f*; **it makes a ~ence** interest (*utrum ... an*); **~ent** diversus, varius, alius, dispar.
difficult difficilis, arduus; **~y** difficultas *f*; angustiae *f/pl.*; **with ~y** aegre, vix.
diffident verecundus.
diffuse diffundo 3; diffusus, verbosus.
dig fodio 3.
digest concoquo 3.
dignif|ied gravis; **~y** honesto 1.
dignity dignitas *f*, maiestas *f.*
digress digredior 3, declino 1; **~ion** digressio *f.*
dike fossa *f*; agger, eris *n.*
dilapidated ruinosus.
dilate (upon) dilato 1.
dilatory tardus.
dilemma complexio *f*; angustiae *f/pl.*
diligen|ce diligentia *f*, industria *f*; **~t** diligens, industrius.
dilute diluo 3.
dim obscurus, hebes; obscuro 1; **grow ~** hebesco 3.
dimension modus *m*; amplitudo *f.*
dimin|ish minuo 3; levo 1; **~utive** parvus, exiguus.
dimness obscuritas *f.*
dimple gelasinus *m.*
din sonitus, us *m*; strepitus, us *m.*
dine ceno 1.
dingy squalidus.
dining|-couch, ~-room triclinium *n.*
dinner cena *f.*
dint ictus, us *m*; **by ~ of** per (*acc.*).
dip *v/t.* tingo 3; mergo 3 (*abl.*); *v/i.* me inclino 1; **~ into** perstringo 3.
diplomatist legatus *m.*
dire dirus.
direct rectus; dirigo 3; intendo 3 (*in, ad*); doceo 2; rego 3; iubeo 2; **~ion** cursus, us *m*; iter, ineris *n*; administratio *f*; praeceptum *n*; inscriptio *f*; **in all ~ions** passim; **in the ~ion of** in, ad, ... versus; **~ly** recta; statim; **~or** magister, tri *m*; curator *m.*
dirge nenia *f.*
dirt sordes *f*; caenum *n*, lutum *n*; **~y** sordidus, squalidus; foedo 1.
disable debilito 1; **~d** mancus, debilis.
disabuse errorem tollo 3.
disadvantage incommodum *n*; **~ous** incommodus, iniquus.
disaffect alieno 1; **~ion** alienatio *f*; seditio *f.*
disagree dissentio 4, dissideo 2 (*ab, cum, inter se*); **~able** molestus, difficilis; **~ment** dissensio *f*; discordia *f.*
disappear evanesco 3; dilabor 3.
disappoint fallo 3; **~ing** fallax.
disapprov|al reprehensio *f*; **~e** improbo 1.
disarm exuo 3 armis.
disarrange turbo 1.
disast|er clades *f*; calamitas *f*; **~rous** calamitosus.
disavow infitior 1 (*alqd*).
disband dimitto 3.
disbelieve fidem non habeo 2.
disburse expendo 3; **~ment** erogatio *f.*

discard excutio 3.
discern discerno 3 (*alqd a re*); dispicio 3; **~ing** acutus; **~ment** iudicium *n*.
discharge evomo 3; (im)mitto 3; *mil.* dimitto 3, exauctoro 1; (per-) fungor 3 (*abl.*); coniectus, us *m*, missio *f*; *jur.* absolutio *f*.
disciple discipulus *m*.
discipline disciplina *f*; **good ~** modestia *f*; coerceo 2.
disclaim infitior 1.
disclos|e patefacio 3; ostendo 3; **~ure** indicium *n*.
dis|colour infusco 1; **~comfit** perturbo 1; **~comfort** vexatio *f*; **~composed** commotus; **~concert** perturbo 1; **~consolate** maerens.
discontent molestia *f*; **~ed** iniquus (*animus*).
discontinue desisto 3 (*abl.*, *inf.*).
discord discordia *f*; **~ant** discors.
discount deduco 3; decessio *f*.
discountenance perturbo 1.
discourage animum frango 3; deterreo 2 (*alqm a re, ne*); **be ~d** animum demitto 3.
discourse sermo *m*; oratio *f*; **~ upon** dissero 3 (*de*).
discourteous inhumanus.
discover invenio 4; reperio 4; deprehendo 3; **~er** inventor *m*; **~y** inventum *n*.
discredit invidia *f*; fidem non habeo 2 (*alci*); **~able** inhonestus.
discreet prudens.
discrepancy discrepantia *f*.
discretion prudentia *f*; arbitratus, us *m*; arbitrium *n*; **at his ~** arbitratu, arbitrio suo.
discriminat|e diiudico 1 (*acc.*, *inter*); **~ing** acutus; **~ion** discrimen *n*.
discuss disputo 1, dissero 3 (*de*); **~ion** disceptatio *f*.
disdain despicio 3; contemno 3; fastidium *n*; **~ful** fastidiosus.
disease morbus *m*; **~d** aeger, morbo affectus.
disembark *v/t.* expono 3; *v/i.* egredior 3 (ex navi).
disengage expedio 4.
disentangle explico 1.
disfavour offensio *f*.
disfigure deformo 1.
disfranchise civitatem adimo 3 (*alci*).
disgorge evomo 3.
disgrace dedecoro 1; ignominia *f*, turpitudo *f*; dedecus *n*; **be ~d** infamiam habeo 2, capio 3; **~ful** turpis, foedus.
disguise dissimulo 1; persona *f*; simulatio *f*.
disgust fastidium *n*, taedium *n*; fastidium pario 3, affero 3; taedet (*me alcis rei*); **~ing** foedus.
dish patina *f*, lanx *f*.
dishearten exanimo 1.
dishevelled passus.
dishonest fraudulentus, mendax; **~y** fraus *f*, improbitas *f*.
dishonour dedecoro 1; stupro 1; ignominia *f*; stuprum *n*; **~able** inhonestus.
disinclined: be ~ abhorreo 2 (*a re*).
disinherit exheredo 1.
disinterested integer.
disjointed disiunctus.
dislike odi; abhorreo 2 (*ab*).
dislocate extorqueo 2.
dislodge (sum)moveo 2; deicio 3.
disloyal perfidus.
dismal tristis, maestus.
dismay percello 3; perturbo 1; perturbatio *f*; pavor *m*.
dismember discerpo 3.
dismiss (di)mitto 3; moveo 2; **~al** missio *f*.
dismount descendo 3 (*ex equo*); desilio 4.
disobey non pareo 2.
disobliging inhumanus.
disorder perturbo 1; perturbatio *f*, turba *f*; **~ly** inordinatus, turbulentus.
disown infitior 1.
disparage detraho 3 (*de*).
dispel dispello 3.
dispens|ation immunitas *f*; **~e** tribuo 3; **~e with** remitto 3.
disperse *v/t.* dissipo 1; *v/i.* dilabor 3.
displace summoveo 2.
display praebeo 2; ostendo 3; ostentatio *f*.
displeas|e displiceo 2; **be ~ed** aegre fero 3; **~ure** offensio *f*.
dispos|al dispositio *f*; dicio *f*; **~e** ordino 1; **~ed** propensus (*in*, *ad*); inclinatus (*ad*); **~ition** natura *f*; indoles *f*.
dispossess expello 3.
disproportionate inaequalis.
dispute discepto 1 (*de*); altercor 1 (*cum alqo*); controversia *f*.
disqualif|ication impedimentum *n*; **~y** impedio 4; impedimento est (*alci*).

disquiet sollicito 1; sollicitudo *f*.
dis|regard neglego 3; **~reputable** infamis; **~repute** infamia *f*; **~respectful** contumeliosus; **~robe** vestem detraho 3.
dissatisf|action molestia *f*; **be ~ied** me paenitet (*alcis rei*).
dissemble dissimulo 1; obtego 3.
disseminate dissemino 1.
dissen|sion dissensio *f*; **~t** dissentio 4 (*ab alqo*).
dissertation schola *f*.
dissimilar dissimilis (*gen*., *dat*.).
dissipat|e dissipo 1; **~ed** dissolutus; **~ion** libidines *f*/*pl*.
dissociate separo 1.
dissol|ute dissolutus; **~ve** (dis)solve 3.
dissuade dissuadeo 2 (*ne*).
distan|ce spatium *n*; **at a ~ce** longe, procul; **~t** disiunctus; longinquus; **be ~t** absum; disto 1 (*ab*).
distaste fastidium *n*; **~ful** odiosus.
distend distendo 3.
distil stillo 1.
distinct clarus; distinctus; alius (*ac*, *atque*); **~ion** discrimen *n*; distinctio *f*; honor *m*; **~ive** proprius; **~ly** clare; diserte.
distinguish discerno 3; distinguo 3 (*alqd ab alqo*); **~ oneself** emineo 2; **~ed** insignis, egregius.
distort detorqueo 2.
distract distraho 3; **~ed** amens; **~ion** perturbatio *f*.
distress affligo 3; ango 3; dolor *m*, angor *m*; **~ing** miser.
distribut|e distribuo 3; dispertio 4; **~ion** partitio *f*.
district regio *f*; tractus, us *m*; ager, gri *m*.
distrust diffido 3 (*dat*.); diffidentia *f*.
disturb perturbo 1; sollicito 1; **~ance** turba *f*; tumultus, us *m*; perturbatio *f*.
disunite dissocio 1.
disuse desuetudo *f*; **fall into ~** obsolesco 3.
ditch fossa *f*.
ditty nenia *f*.
dive mergo(r) 3 (*in rem*, *in re*); **~r** urinator *m*.
diverg|e decedo 3 (*de via*); deflecto 3 (*a*, *de*); **~ing** diversus.
divers|e varius, diversus; **~ion** derivatio *f*; oblectamentum *n*.
divert derivo 1; averto 3; oblecto 1; *mil*. distringo 3; **~ing** festivus, facetus.
divest exuo 3, depono 3; **~ oneself of** exuo 3 (*alqd*).
divide seco 1; divido 3; dispertio 4.
divin|ation divinatio *f*; **~e** divino 1 (*alqd*, *acc. c. inf*.); conicio 3; divinus; sacer; **~ely** divinitus; **~ity** numen *n*, deus *m*.
division partitio *f*; discidium *n*; pars *f*; (*for voting*) discessio *f*.
divorce divortium *n*; divortium facio 3 (*cum*).
divulge divulgo 1.
dizziness vertigo *f*.
do facio 3; ago 3; **have to ~ with** rationem habeo 2 (*cum*); **how ~ you ~?** quid agis?; **~ without** careo 2.
docile tractabilis.
dock navalia *n*/*pl*.; cancelli *m*/*pl*.; subduco 3 navem; praecido 3.
doctor medicus *m*.
doctrine ratio *f*; disciplina *f*.
document tabula *f*.
dodge elabor 3 (*ex*); declino 1 (*alqd*).
doe cerva *f*.
dog canis *m and f*; investigo 1; **~ged** pertinax; **~matic** arrogans; **~star** Sirius *m*.
doing factum *n*.
dole diurnum *n*; diurnus cibus *m*; stips *f*; **~ out** divido 3; **~ful** maestus.
doll pupa *f*.
dolphin delphinus *m*.
dolt baro *m*.
domain regnum *n*; dicio *f*.
dome tholus *m*.
domestic domesticus, familiaris; famulus *m*; famula *f*.
domicile domus, us *f*; domicilium *n*.
dominat|e regno 1, dominor 1 (*in*); **~ion** dominatio *f*.
domineering imperiosus.
dominion imperium *n*; potestas *f*.
donation stips *f*.
done: well ~! euge!
donkey asinus *m*.
doom fatum *n*; exitium *n*; condemno 1; **~ed** fatalis.
door ianua *f*; fores *f*/*pl*.; ostium *n*; **in~s** domi; **out of ~s** foris; **back-~** posticum *n*; **~keeper** ianitor *m*; **~way** limen *n*.
dose medicamentum do 1.
dot punctum *n*.
dot|age deliratio *f*; **~ard** senex *m* delirus; **~e upon** depereo 4.
double duplex, geminus; duplum *n*;

duplico 1; flecto 3; **~-dealing** fraus *f*; versutus.
doubt dubito 1 (*de re*; *quin*); dubitatio *f*; **without ~** sine dubio; **~ful** dubius, incertus; anceps; **~less** nimirum; scilicet.
dove columba *f*.
down[1] lanugo *f*; plumae *f/pl.*
down[2] *prep.* de (*abl.*); **~ stream** secundum flumen; *adv.* deorsum; **~cast** demissus; **~fall** ruina *f*; **~-hill** declivis; **~right** merus; plane, prorsus.
dowry dos *f*; **having a ~** dotata.
doze dormito 1.
drag traho 3; **~on** draco *m*.
drain sicco 1; (ex)haurio 4; cloaca *f*.
drama fabula *f*; **~tic** scaenicus; **~tist** poeta *m*.
drapery amictus, us *m*.
draught potio *f*; **game of ~s** latrunculi *m/pl.*
draw traho 3; educo 3 (*gladium*); haurio 4 (*aquam*); duco 3 (*spiritum*); **~ back** pedem refero 3; **~ near** appropinquo 1; **~ up (in words)** concipio 3; *mil.* instruo 3; **~ing** tabula *f*; descriptio *f*.
dread formido 1; formido *f*; **~ful** terribilis, atrox.
dream somnio 1; somnium *n*.
dreary vastus; tristis.
dregs faex *f*; sentina *f*.
drench perfundo 3.
dress induo 3 (*sibi*, *alci*, *alqd*); vestio 4 (*alqm veste*); como 3 (*capillos*); obligo 1 (*vulnera*); vestis *f*; vestitus, us *m*; habitus, us *m*; **~ing** fomentum *n*.
drift deferor 3 vento.
drill perforo 1; exerceo 2; terebra *f*; exercitium *n*.
drink bibo 3; **~ to** propino 1 (*alci*); potio *f*; potus, us *m*; **~er** potor *m*; **~ing-bout** potatio *f*.
drip stillo 1; mano 1 (*alqa re*); **~ping (with)** madidus (*abl.*).
drive *v/t.* ago 3; *v/i.* vehor 3; **~ away** abigo 3; **~ back** repello 3; **~ from, out** exigo 3; pello 3; **~r** agitator *m*, auriga *m*.
droll ridiculus.
drone fucus *m*; bombus *m*.
droop *v/i.* pendeo 2; langueo 2; *v/t.* demitto 3; **~ing** languidus, fractus.
drop *v/t.* demitto 3; *v/i.* stillo 1; delabor 3; decido 3; **~ in on** venio 4 (*ad*); gutta *f*.
dropsy hydrops *m*.
drought siccitas *f*.
drove grex *m*; **~r** pastor *m*; armentarius *m*.
drown summergo 3; *fig.* mergo 3.
drows|iness somnus *m*; **~y** somniculosus.
drudge mediastinus *m*; **~ry** labor *m*.
drug medicamentum *n*, venenum *n*; medico 1 (*alqd*).
druids Druides *m/pl.*
drum tympanum *n*.
drunk ebrius; **~ard** ebriosus *m*; **~enness** ebrietas *f*.
dry siccus, aridus; **~ land** aridum *n*; *v/t.* sicco 1; abstergeo 2; *v/i.* aresco 3; **~ness** siccitas *f*.
dubious dubius.
duck anas *f*; summergor 3.
due debitum *n*; vectigal *n*, portorium *n*; debitus, meritus; **in ~ time** tempore, tempori.
duel certamen *n*.
dug uber, eris *n*.
dull hebes; tardus; obtusus; subnubilus; frigidus; obtundo 3; hebeto 1; **~ness** tarditas *f*.
dumb mutus; **~founded** obstupefactus.
dun fuscus.
dung stercus *n*.
dungeon carcer, eris *n*.
dunghill sterquilinum *n*.
dupe ludifico 1; credulus homo *m*.
duplicate exemplar *n*.
duplicity fraus *f*.
dura|ble firmus, stabilis; **~tion** spatium *n*; tempus *n*; **of long, short ~tion** diuturnus, brevis.
during per (*acc.*), inter (*acc.*); in (*abl.*); *cj.* dum.
dusk crepusculum *n*; **~y** fuscus, obscurus.
dust pulvis *m*; tergeo 2; verro 3; **~y** pulverulentus.
dutiful pius; officiosus; **~ness** pietas *f*.
duty officium *n*; munus *n*; *mil.* **on ~** in statione (*esse*); **pay ~** vectigal pendo 3; **it is my ~** debeo 2.
dwarf pumilio *m and f*.
dwell habito 1 (*in*); incolo 3; **~ upon** commoror 1; **~ing** domicilium *n*; habitatio *f*.
dwindle decresco 3, minuor 3.
dye tingo 3; inficio 3; color *m*; **~r** infector *m*.
dynasty domus, us *f*.

E

each quisque; **~ and every** unus quisque; **~ of two** uterque; **~ other** inter se; **one ~** singuli.
eager avidus, cupidus (**for** *gen.*); acer; **~ness** aviditas *f*; studium *n.*
eagle aquila *f*; **~-bearer** aquilifer *m.*
ear auris *f*; **give ~ to** aures do 1, praebeo 2 (*alci*); **~ of corn** spica *f.*
earliness maturitas *f.*
early matutinus, maturus; antiquus; *adv.* mane, mature.
earn mereo(r) 2; consequor 3.
earnest acer; serius; arrhabo *m*; **~ly** magnopere, vehementer.
earnings merces *f.*
earth terra *f*, tellus *f*; **~en** fictilis; **~enware** fictilia *n/pl.*; **~ly** terrestris; humanus; **~quake** terrae motus, us *m*; **~work** agger, eris *m.*
ease remitto 3; relaxo 1; levo 1; otium *n*; quies *f*; facilitas *f*; **at ~** otiose.
east oriens *m*; solis ortus, us *m*; **~er** pascha *f*; **~ern** Eous; **~ wind** eurus *m.*
easy facilis; expeditus; commodus.
eat edo 3; vescor 3 (*abl.*); **~ up** comedo 3; consumo 3; **~ables** cibaria *n/pl.*; **~ing-house** popina *f.*
eaves-drop subausculto 1.
ebb recedo 3; *fig.* decresco 3; (aestus) recessus, us *m*; **be at a low ~** iaceo 2.
ebony ebenum *n.*
echo imago *f*; refero 3; resono 1; itero 1.
eclipse defectio *f*; obscuro 1; **be ~d** deficio 3.
eclogue ecloga *f.*
econom|ical parcus; **~y** parsimonia *f.*
ecsta|sy insania *f*; laetitia *f*; **~tic** insanus.
eddy vertex *m.*
edge ora *f*; margo *m*; **cutting ~** acies *f*; praetexo 3.
edible esculentus.
edict edictum *n.*
edifice aedificium *n.*
edify excolo 3.
edit edo 3.
educat|e educo 1; instituo 3; **~ion** educatio *f*; disciplina *f.*
eel anguilla *f.*
efface deleo 2; oblittero 1.
effect efficio 3; effectus, us *m*; eventus, us *m*; vis *f*; **in ~** reapse, re vera; **have ~ on** valeo 2 (*apud*); **~ive** efficax; **~s** bona *n/pl.*
effeminate effeminatus, mollis, muliebris.
effervesce effervesco 3; **~nce** fervor *m.*
efficac|ious efficax; **~y** vis *f.*
efficient idoneus.
effigy imago *f.*
effort conatus, us *m*; labor *m.*
effrontery impudentia *f*; os *n.*
egg ovum *n*; **~ on** incito 1; **~-shell** ovi putamen *n.*
egregious insignis.
eight octo; **~een** duodeviginti; **~eenth** duodevicesimus; **~-fold** octuplus; **~h** octavus; **~ hundred** octingenti; **~y** octoginta.
either alteruter; utervis, uterlibet; **on ~ side** utrimque; **~ ... or** aut ... aut; vel ... vel.
ejaculate exclamo 1.
eject deicio 3.
eke out parco 3.
elaborate expolio 4; elaboratus, accuratus.
elapse praetereo 4.
elated elatus (gaudio, superbia).
elbow cubitum *n.*
elder maior natu; **~ly** aetate provectus; **the ~ly** seniores *m/pl.*
elect creo 1; deligo 3; designatus; **~ion** suffragium *n*; comitia *n/pl.*; **~ioneering** petitio *f*, ambitio *f*; **~or** suffragator *m.*
elegan|ce munditia *f*; urbanitas *f*; **~t** elegans, urbanus.
eleg|iacs elegi *m/pl.*; **~y** elegia *f.*
element elementum *n*; **~s** principia *n/pl.*; elementa *n/pl.*; **~ary** simplex.
elephant elephantus *m.*
elevat|e effero 3; excolo 3; **~ed** celsus, elatus; **~ion** elatio *f.*
eleven undecim; **~th** undecimus.

elicit elicio 3.
eligible optabilis.
eliminate tollo 3.
ell ulna *f*.
elm ulmus, i *f*.
elocution pronuntiatio *f*.
elope (ef)fugio 3.
eloquen|ce eloquentia *f*, facundia *f*; **~t** eloquens, disertus, copiosus.
else alioqui(n); aliter; **some one ~** alius; **~where** alibi.
elucidate illustro 1.
elu|de effugio 3; elabor 3 (*abl.*); eludo 3; **~sive** fallax.
emaciat|e macero 1; **~ion** macies *f*.
emanate emano 1.
emancipat|e manumitto 3; libero 1; **~ion** manumissio *f*.
emasculate enervo 1.
embalm condio 4.
embankment agger, eris *m*; moles *f*.
embargo prohibitio *f*.
embark *v/t.* impono 3 (*in navem*); *v/i.* navem conscendo 3; **~ upon** ineo 4 (*alqd*).
embarrass impedio 4; implico 1; **be ~ed** haereo 2; perturbor 1; **~ment** scrupulus *m*; angustiae *f/pl.*
embassy legatio *f*.
embellish orno 1; **~ment** ornamentum *n*.
embers cinis, eris *m*.
embezzle averto 3; **~ment** peculatus, us *m*; **~r** peculator *m*.
embitter exacerbo 1.
emblem indicium *n*.
embolden confirmo 1.
embrace amplector 3, complector 3; complexus, us *m*.
embroider pingo 3.
embroil implico 1.
emerald smaragdus, i *m and f*.
emerge emergo 3, exsisto 3 (*ex*); **~ncy** tempus *n*, discrimen *n*.
emigrat|e (e)migro 1; **~ion** migratio *f*.
eminen|ce tumulus *m*; praestantia *f*; **~t** praeclarus; nobilis.
emissary legatus *m*.
emit emitto 3; iacio 3.
emotion motus, us *m*; commotio *f*.
emperor imperator *m*, princeps *m*.
empha|sis vis *f*; **~size** vehementer dico 3.
empire imperium *n*; regnum *n*.
employ utor 3; adhibeo 2; **~ment** quaestus, us *m*.
empower potestatem do 1 (*alci*).
empt|iness inanitas *f*; **~y** vacuus; inanis; vanus; exinanio 4; exhaurio 4.
emulat|e aemulor 1 (*acc.*); **~ion** aemulatio *f*.
enable facultatem do 1 (*alci*).
enact sancio 4 (*legem, lege alqd, ut*); scisco 3 (*alqd, ut*); constituo 3; **get ~ed** perfero 3; **~ment** lex *f*; scitum *n*.
enamoured: be ~ depereo 2 (*alqm*).
encamp castra pono 3; consido 3.
enchant fascino 1; capio 3; **~ing** venustus; **~ment** carmen *n*; **~ress** venefica *f*.
encircle cingo 3; circumdo 1 (*alqd re*).
enclos|e includo 3; **~ure** saepta *n/pl.*
encore revoco 1.
encounter offendo 3; congredior 3; oppeto 3 (*mortem*); experior 4 (*periculum*); congressus, us *m*.
encourage confirmo 1; hortor 1; **~ment** cohortatio *f*.
encroach upon occupo 1; imminuo 3 (*ius etc.*).
encumb|er impedio 4; **~rance** impedimentum *n*.
end finis *m*; **make an ~** finem facio 3 (*gen.*); **put an ~ to** finem affero 3 (*dat.*); dirimo 3; **in the ~** postremo; **to no ~** frustra; **to this ~** ideo; extremus; *v/t.* finio 4; *v/i.* desino 3.
endanger periclitor 1.
endeavour conor 1; conatum *n*.
end|ing exitus, us *m*; **~less** infinitus.
endow dono 1 (*alqm re*); instruo 3; **~ed** praeditus.
endur|ance patientia *f*; fortitudo *f*; **~e** patior 3; (per)fero 3; duro 1; **~ing** patiens (*gen.*); perennis.
enemy hostis *m and f*, inimicus *m*.
energ|etic acer; strenuus; **~y** vis *f*; impetus, us *m*.
enervate enervo 1.
enfeeble debilito 1.
enforce exerceo 2.
enfranchise civitatem do 1 (*alci*).
engage *v/t.* conduco 3; *v/i.* congredior 3 (*cum hostibus*); (*in me*) recipio 3; promitto 3 (*acc. c. inf.*); **~ in** suscipio 3; **~d** occupatus (*in re*); sponsus; **~ment** sponsio *f*; negotium *n*; proelium *n*.
engender gigno 3.
engin|e machina *f*; tormentum *n*; **~eer** machinator *m*.

engrave incido 3; caelo 1; **~r** sculptor *m*, sculptor *m*.
engross occupo 1.
engulf devoro 1.
enhance amplifico 1; augeo 2; **~ment** amplificatio *f*.
enigma aenigma *n*.
enjoin praecipio 3 (*alci alqd*).
enjoy fruor 3, utor 3 (*abl.*); delector 1 (*abl.*); **~ment** gaudium *n*; voluptas *f*.
enlarge augeo 2; dilato 1; **~ upon** uberius loquor 3, dico 3.
enlighten erudio 4; certiorem facio 3.
enlist *v/t.* conscribo 3; *v/i.* nomen do 1, edo 3, sacramentum dico 3.
enliven exhilaro 1.
enmity inimicitia *f*; simultas *f*.
enorm|ity immanitas *f*; scelus *n*; **~ous** ingens; immanis.
enough satis; **~ and to spare** satis superque; **not ~** parum.
enrage exaspero 1.
en|rapture delecto 1; **~rich** locupleto 1; **~rol** ascribo 3 (*in*, *dat.*); **~sconce oneself** consido 3.
ensign signum *n*; vexillum *n*.
enslave in servitutem abduco 3, abstraho 3; **~ment** servitus, utis *f*.
ensnare irretio 4.
ensue sequor 3.
ensure curo 1; provideo 2 (*ut*, *ne*).
entail affero 3.
entangle implico 1.
enter ingredior 3 (*intra*, *in*); venio 4 (*in*); intro 1 (*alqd*, *in*, *ad*); refero 3 (*alqd in libellum*); **~ upon** ineo 4 (*alqd*); **~prise** inceptum *n*, consilium *n*; audacia *f*; **~prising** promptus, audax.
entertain excipio 3; invito 1; oblecto 1; **~ment** hospitium *n*; epulae *f/pl.*
enthusias|m studium *n*; ardor *m*; **~tic** studiosus (*gen.*); **be ~tic** ardeo 2 (*studio*).
entic|e allicio 3, illicio 3; **~ement** illecebra *f*; **~ing** blandus.
entire totus; integer; universi; **~ly** omnino; plane.
entitle inscribo 3; **be ~d to** ius habeo 2 (*gen.*); dignus sum (*abl.*, *qui*).
entrails viscera *n/pl.*
entrance introitus, us *m*; aditus, us *m*; capio 3.
entreat oro 1, obsecro 1; flagito 1; **~y** preces *f/pl.*; obsecratio *f*.
entrust credo 3 (*alqd alci*).
entry introitus, us *m*; aditus, us *m*; **make an ~** refero 3 (*in*).
entwine implico 1 (*alqd alqa re*).
enumerate enumero 1.
envelop involvo 3; **~e** involucrum *n*.
env|iable fortunatus; **~ious** invidus; **~oy** legatus *m*; **~y** invidia *f*; invideo 2 (*dat.*).
ephemeral caducus, brevis.
epic epos *n*; epicus.
epigram epigramma *n*.
epistle epistula *f*.
epitaph elogium *n*.
epoch tempus *n*; saeculum *n*.
equable aequus.
equal aequus; aequalis; par; (ad-) aequo 1; aequipero 1; **~ity** aequabilitas *f*; **~ize** aequo 1.
equanimity aequus animus *m*.
equestrian equester; eques *m*.
equinox aequinoctium *n*.
equip orno 1; instruo 3; **~ment** arma *n/pl.*; apparatus, us *m*; instrumentum *n*.
equit|able aequus; **~y** aequitas *f*.
equivocal ambiguus.
equivocate tergiversor 1.
era tempus *n*.
eradicate exstirpo 1.
eras|e deleo 2; induco 3; **~ure** litura *f*.
ere prius, ante quam.
erect exstruo 3; statuo 3; erectus; **~ion** aedificatio *f*; aedificium *n*.
erotic amatorius.
err erro 1; pecco 1.
errand mandatum *n*; **~-boy** nuntius *m*.
err|atic vagus; **~oneous** falsus; **~or** error *m*; erratum *n*; peccatum *n*.
erudit|e doctus, eruditus; **~ion** eruditio *f*.
eruption eruptio *f*.
escape effugio 3; elabor 3 (*ex*); **it ~s one's notice** fallit; praeterit; effugium *n*.
escort prosequor 3; deduco 3; praesidium *n*; comitatus, us *m*.
especial praecipuus; **~ly** praecipue; praesertim.
espy conspicor 1.
essay tento 1; periculum *n*.
essen|ce substantia *f*; **~tial** necessarius.
establish instituo 3, statuo 3; stabilio 4; **~ that** vinco 3 (*acc. c. inf.*); **~ment** constitutio *f*; familia *f*.

estate status, us *m*; ager *m*; fundus *m*.
esteem diligo 3; magni facio 3; existimatio *f*.
estimat|e aestimo 1; iudicium *n*; aestimatio *f*; **~ion** existimatio *f*; opinio *f*.
estrange alieno 1; **~ment** alienatio *f*.
estuary aestuarium *n*.
etern|al aeternus; sempiternus; **~ity** aeternitas *f*.
ether aether, eris *m*; **~eal** aetherius.
ethic|al moralis; **~s** philosophia *f* moralis.
etiquette mos *n*.
eulog|ize laudo 1; **~y** laudatio *f*; laus *f*.
eunuch eunuchus *m*.
evacuate vacuefacio 3; *mil.* deduco 3 praesidium; excedo 3 (*abl.*).
evade subterfugio 3; fraudem facio 3 (*legi*).
evaporate exhalo 1.
evasion ambages *f/pl.*; **practise ~** tergiversor 1.
eve: on the ~ of pridie (*gen.*).
even aequus, planus; *adv.* etiam; vel; **not ... ~** ne ... quidem; **~ if** etiamsi.
evening vesper *m*; **good ~!** salve; **in the ~** vesperi; vespertinus; **~ star** Hesperus *m*.
evenness aequitas *f* (animi).
event res *f*; eventus, us *m*; **at all ~s** certe; **~ful** memorabilis; **~ually** postremo; ad postremum.
ever semper; **if ~** si quando; **nor ... ~** nec ... umquam; **~ since** ex eo tempore quo; **~lasting** sempiternus.
every quisque; omnis; **any and ~** quivis; **~ day** cotidie; **~ year** quotannis; **~body** quisque; omnes; nemo ... non; **~thing** quidque; omnia *n/pl.*; **~where** ubique; passim.
evidence testimonium *n*; indicium *n*; argumentum *n*; **give ~** testificor 1.
evident manifestus; apertus; evidens; **it is ~** apparet 2; **~ly** aperte; scilicet.
evil malus; improbus; pravus; malum *n*; incommodum *n*.
evince praesto 1.
evoke evoco 1.
ewe ovis *f*.
ewer urceus *m*.
exact exigo 3; impero 1; sumo 3 (*poenas*); subtilis; accuratus; diligens; **~itude** diligentia *f*.
exaggerate augeo 2; exaggero 1; in maius (vero) fero 3, extollo 3.
exalt effero 3; augeo 2; **~ed** celsus.
examin|ation investigatio *f*; interrogatio *f*; probatio *f*; **~e** investigo 1; interrogo 1; quaero 3; probo 1.
example exemplum *n*; exemplar *n*; documentum *n*; **for ~** verbi causa.
exasperate irrito 1.
excavat|e (ex)cavo 1; **~ion** cavum *n*.
exceed egredior 3 (*extra, acc.*); **~ingly** valde.
excel praesto 1 (*dat.*); excello 3 (*dat.*); **~lence** virtus, utis *f*; excellentia *f*; **~lent** optimus; praestans.
except excipio 3; nisi quod; nisi ut; praeter (*acc.*); **~ing you two** exceptis vobis duobus; **~ion** exceptio *f*; **without ~ion** omnes; **~ional** rarus; eximius.
excess nimium *n*; luxuria *f*; **~ive** nimius; immoderatus.
exchange muto 1 (*alqd alqa re*); inter se dare; permutatio *f*; **~ of money** collybus *m*.
exchequer aerarium *n*; fiscus *m*.
excise vectigalia *n/pl.*
excit|able fervidus; **~e** commoveo 2; excito 1, concito 1 (*ad*); **~ement** commotio *f*; perturbatio *f*.
exclaim exclamo 1; conclamo 1; **~ against** acclamo 1 (*dat.*).
exclamation vox *f*; exclamatio *f*.
exclu|de prohibeo 2; excludo 3; **~sion** interdictio *f*; **~sive** proprius.
excrement stercus *n*.
excruciating acerbissimus.
exculpate purgo 1.
excus|able venia dignus; **~e** me purgo 1, excuso 1 (*alci*); veniam do 1; ignosco 3; excusatio *f*; venia *f*.
execrate exsecror 1.
execut|e exsequor 3; perficio 3; supplicium sumo 3 (*de*); supplicio afficio 3; **~ion** supplicium *n*; mors *f*; **~ioner** carnifex *m*.
exempl|ary egregius; **~ify** exemplum do 1, prodo 1.
exempt libero 1; solvo 3 (*alqm alqa re*); immunitatem tribuo 3; immunis (*abl.*); **~ion** immunitas *f*; vacatio *f*.
exercise exerceo 2; exercitatio *f*; **take ~** ambulo 1.
exert exerceo 2; utor 3; **~ oneself** nitor 3; laboro 1; **~ion** contentio *f*.

exhal|ation exhalatio *f*; **~e** exhalo 1.
exhaust exhaurio 4; defatigo 1; debilito 1; **be ~ed** deficio 3; **~ed** confectus; defessus; effetus; **~ion** lassitudo *f*.
exhibit propono 3; expono 3; exhibeo 2; praesto 1; ostento 1; **~ion** spectaculum *n*; munus *n*.
exhilarate exhilaro 1.
exhort (ad-, co-)hortor 1; **~ation** hortatio *f*.
exigency necessitas *f*.
exile eicio 3; aqua et igni interdico 3; pello 3; exsilium *n*; exsul *m and f*; extorris; **be an ~, live in ~** exsulo 1; **go into ~** solum verto 3.
exist sum; exsisto 3; exsto 1; **~ence** vita *f*.
exit exitus, us *m*.
exonerate libero 1 (*culpa*).
exorbitant immodicus.
exordium exordium *n*.
expan|d pando 3; extendo 3; **~se** spatium *n*.
expect exspecto 1 (*alqd*); spero 1 (*alqd, acc. c. inf.*); credo 3 (*acc. c. inf.*); **~ation** exspectatio *f*; spes *f*; **contrary to ~ation** praeter spem.
expedien|cy utilitas *f*; **~t** utilis; **be ~t** expedit.
expedit|e maturo 1; **~ion** expeditio *f*.
expel (ex)pello 3; eicio 3.
expen|d impendo 3; **~se** impensa *f*; sumptus, us *m*; **~sive** sumptuosus; carus.
experience experior 4; patior 3; usus, us *m*; peritia *f*; **~d** peritus (*gen.*).
experiment periculum *n*; experimentum *n* (facio 3).
expert peritus (*gen.*), sciens (*gen.*); **~ness** peritia *f*.
expiat|e expio 1 (*alqd alqa re*); **~ion** expiatio *f*.
expire exspiro 1; animam, vitam edo 3; exeo 2.
expl|ain explico 1; explano 1; expono 3; **~anation** explanatio *f*; ratio *f*; **~icit** apertus.
explode dirumpor 3; explodo 3 (*sententiam*).
exploit res *f* gesta; facinus *n*.
explore exploro 1; speculor 1.
explosion fragor *m*.
export exporto 1.
expos|e expono 3; profero 3 (*rem*); nudo 1; **~e to** obicio 3; **~ed** apertus; obnoxius (*dat.*); **~ition** explicatio *f*; **~tulate** expostulo 1 (*cum alqo de, acc. c. inf.*); **~ure** frigus *n*.
expound expono 3.
express effero 3; dico 3; significo 1; **~ion** verba *n/pl.*; oratio *f*; vultus, us *m*; significatio *f*; **~ive** significans; **~ly** diserte.
exquisite conquisitus, exquisitus.
extant: be ~ exsto 1.
extempor|ary subitus; **~e** subito.
extend extendo 3, distendo 3; porrigo 3; propago 1.
extens|ion propagatio *f*; **~ive** amplus, latus.
extent spatium *n*; **to this ~, that** hactenus ... ut; **to what ~** quatenus.
extenuate levo 1.
exterior exterior; species *f*.
exterminate ad internecionem deleo 2, redigo 3; deleo 2.
external externus; **~ things** quae extra sunt.
extinct mortuus; **~ion** interitus, us *m*.
extinguish exstinguo 3.
extirpate exstirpo 1.
extol laudo 1; laudibus effero 3.
extort extorqueo 2; exprimo 3; **crime of ~ion** (pecuniae) repetundae *f/pl.*; **~ionate** rapax.
extra praecipuus; *adv.* praeterea.
extract extraho 3; exprimo 3; **make an ~** excerpo 3; **~ion** evulsio *f*; genus *n*.
extraneous alienus.
extraordinar|ily extra ordinem *or* modum; **~y** extraordinarius; insolitus.
extravagan|ce luxuria *f*; sumptus *m/pl.*; **~t** immodicus; prodigus, profusus.
extreme extremus; summus; ultimus; **~s** extrema *n/pl.*
extricate (me) expedio 4, extraho 3.
exuberan|ce hilaritas *f*; **~t** laetus; luxuriosus.
exude sudo 1.
exult gestio 4; exsulto 1; gaudeo 2 (*abl.*); **~ant** laetus; **~ation** laetitia *f*.
eye oculus *m*; lumen *n*; **before one's ~s** ante oculos, in oculis, in conspectu; aspicio 3; **~ball** pupula *f*; **~brow** supercilium *n*; **~lid** palpebra *f*; **~sight** acies *f*; **~-witness** arbiter, tri *m*.

F

fable fabula *f*; **~d** fabulosus.
fabric textile *n*; textum *n*; fabrica *f*; **~ate** *fig.* comminiscor 3; **~ation** commentum *n*.
fabulous commenticius, fabulosus.
face os *n*; facies *f*; vultus, us *m*; frons *f*; **~ to ~** coram (*abl.*); **in the ~ of** in (*abl.*); obviam eo 4 (*dat.*); me oppono 3, offero 3 (*dat.*); **~ (towards)** aspecto 1 (*acc.*); vergo 3 (*in, ad*); **~ about** signa converto 3.
facetious facetus.
facil|itate facilius reddo 3; **~ity** facilitas *f*; facultas *f*.
facing adversus (*acc.*).
fact res *f*; factum *n*; **in ~** re vera.
facti|on factio *f*; pars *f*; **~ous** factiosus.
factor procurator *m*; **~y** officina *f*.
faculty facultas *f*; ingenium *n*.
fade palleo 2; pallesco 3; cado 3.
faggot fascis *m*; sarmenta *n/pl.*
fail *v/i.* deficio 3; desum (*dat.*); cado 3; male evenit; *v/t.* destituo 3; **without ~** certe; **~ure** defectio *f*.
fain: I would ~ velim, vellem.
faint hebes; languidus; confectus; intermorior 3; animus relinquit (*alqm*); **~hearted** ignavus; **~ness** languor *m*.
fair candidus; pulcher; sudus, serenus (*tempestas*); mediocris; secundus (*ventus*); aequus; nundinae *f/pl.*; **~ly** satis; **~ness** aequum *n*; candor *m*; **~ weather** sudum *n*.
faith fides *f*; **put ~ in** fidem habeo 2 (*dat.*); **keep good ~** fidem servo 1; **break ~** fidem violo 1; **in good ~** ex bona fide; **~ful** fidelis; fidus; **~less** perfidus.
fall cado 3; labor 3; praecipito 1; ruo 3; **~ away** descisco 3 (*ab*); **~ in with** incido 3 (*in c. acc.*); **~ out** dissideo 2 (*inter se*); **~ short of** desum (*dat.*); **~ to** obtingit (*sors, etc., alci*); accidit (*alci*); **~ upon** invado 3 (*in c. acc.*); casus, us *m*; lapsus, us *m*; ruina *f*; deminutio *f*.
fallac|ious fallax; **~y** captio *f*.
fallow novalis, inaratus; **~ land** novalis *f*; novale *n*; **lie ~** cesso 1.
fals|e falsus; fictus; mendax; perfidus; **~ehood** mendacium *n*; commentum *n*; **~ify** corrumpo 3; vitio 1.
falter titubo 1; haereo 2.
fame gloria *f*; fama *f*; nomen *n*.
familiar familiaris (**with** *dat.*); notus; **be on ~ terms with** familiariter utor 3 (*alqo*); **~ity** familiaritas *f*; usus, us *m*; **~ize** assuefacio 3 (*alqm alqa re*).
family domus, us *f*; mei, tui, sui; familia *f* (*of common descent*); domesticus; gentilis.
famine fames *f*.
famished fame confectus.
famous clarus, praeclarus, celeber, nobilis.
fan flabellum *n*; ventilo 1.
fancy fingo 3 (cogitatione, animo); puto 1; cogitatio *f*; somnium *n*; species *f*; libido *f*; **as I ~** ut libet (*mihi*).
fang dens *m*.
fantastic commenticius; vanus.
far procul; longe; **by ~** longe, multo; **be ~ (removed) from** longe absum (ab); **as ~ as** tenus (*abl.*); *adv.* quatenus, quoad; **thus ~** hactenus; **~-fetched** arcessitus; **~-off** longinquus.
farce mimus *m*.
fare me habeo 2 (*bene, male*); mihi evenit; cibus *m*; vectura *f*; **~well** vale.
farm fundus *m*; praedium *n*; ager, gri *m*; colo 3; conduco 3 (*vectigalia*); **~ out** loco 1; **~er** agricola *m*; colonus *m*; **~house** villa *f*; **~ing** agri cultura *f*.
farthing: not a ~ nullus teruncius *m*; **I don't care a ~** non flocci facio 3.
fasces fasces *m/pl.*
fascinat|e capio 3; delenio 4; **~ion** blanditiae *f/pl.*
fashion fabricor 1; effingo 3; forma *f*; mos *m*; **after the ~ of** more (*gen.*); **~able** elegans; **it is ~able** moris est.
fast firmus; stabilis; celer; velox;

ieiunus sum; ieiunium *n*; **make ~** deligo 1; **be ~ asleep** arte dormio 4.
fasten figo 3 (*alqd in re*); annecto 3 (*ad alqd;dat.*); deligo 1 (*ad*); **~ing** claustra *n/pl.*; vinculum *n*.
fastidious fastidiosus.
fat pinguis; opimus; obesus; pingue *n*; adeps *m and f*.
fatal fatalis; funestus; perniciosus; **~ity** fatum *n*.
fate fatum *n*; **~d** fatalis (*ad*).
father pater *m*; parens; **~-in-law** socer *m*; **~less** orbus; **~ly** paternus.
fathom *fig.* mente comprehendo 3; **~less** profundus.
fatigue fatigo 1; (de)fatigatio *f*.
fatness pinguitudo *f*, obesitas *f*.
fatt|en sagino 1; farcio 4; **~y** pinguis.
fatuous fatuus.
fault culpa *f*; delictum *n*; peccatum *n*; vitium *n*; **find ~ with** accuso 1; **commit a ~** pecco 1; **it is my ~** per me stat (*quominus, ne*); **~less** emendatus; perfectus; **~y** mendosus, vitiosus.
favour faveo 2, foveo 2, studeo 2 (*dat.*); gratia *f*; studium *n*; beneficium *n*; **confer a ~** beneficium confero 3; **win the ~ of** gratiam ineo 4 (*ab, apud*); **in ~ of** pro (*abl.*); **~able** prosperus; secundus; **~ite** gratus; carus; dilectus; deliciae *f/pl.*; **~itism** studium *n*.
fawn hinnuleus *m*; **~ upon** adulor 1 (*alqm*).
fear timeo 2, metuo 3; vereor 2; **~ for** diffido 3 (*dat.*); metus, us *m*, timor *m*; **~ful** timidus; atrox; **~less** fidens.
feast convivium *n*; epulae *f/pl.*; dies *m* festus; epulor 1; convivor 1.
feat factum *n*; res *f*.
feather penna *f*, pluma *f*.
feature proprium *n*; **~s** vultus, us *m*; lineamenta *n/pl.*
February Februarius (mensis) *m*.
fecundity fecunditas *f*.
federation civitates *f/pl.* foederatae.
fee merces *f*.
feeble infirmus; imbecillus; **~ness** infirmitas *f*, imbecillitas *f*.
feed *v/t.* alo 3; nutrio 4; pasco 1; *v/i.* vescor 3 (*abl.*); pascor 1.
feel tento 1; tango 3; contrecto 1; sentio 4; percipio 3; **~ing** tactus, us *m*; sensus, us *m*; **~ings** animus *m*.
feign fingo 3; simulo 1.
felicitate gratulor 1 (*alci de re, quod*).
fell dirus; caedo 3.
fellow socius *m*; homo *m*; **~-citizen** civis *m and f*; **~-countryman** popularis *m*; **~-slave** conservus *m*; **~ship** societas *f*; sodalitas *f*; **~-soldier** commilito *m*.
felt coactum *n*.
female femineus; femina *f*.
feminine muliebris; femineus.
fen palus, udis *f*.
fence saepes *f*; saepta *n/pl.*; rudibus certare; **~ in** saepio 4.
ferment fermentum *n*; *fig.* aestus, us *m*; **be in a ~** ferveó 2; fermentor 1.
fern filix *f*.
feroci|ous trux; **~ty** atrocitas *f*.
ferret out eruo 3.
ferry transveho 3; **~man** portitor *m*.
fertil|e fertilis; fecundus; **~ity** fecunditas *f*; **~ize** laetifico 1.
ferv|ent ardens; **~our** ardor *m*.
fester suppuro 1.
festiv|al dies *m* festus; sollemne *n*; feriae *f/pl.*; **~e** festus; festivus; **~ity** sollemnia *n/pl.*
festoon serta *n/pl.*
fetch fero 3; arcesso 3.
fetid fetidus.
fetter compes *m*; vinculum *n*; catena *f*; catenas inicio 3 (*alci*).
feud simultas *f*.
fever febris *f*; **~ish** *fig.* furiosus.
few pauci; aliquot; rarus.
fibre fibra *f*.
fickle levis; mobilis; **~ness** levitas *f*.
ficti|on commentum *n*; fabula *f*; **~tious** fictus.
fidelity fidelitas *f*.
field ager, gri *m*; arvum *n*; *fig.* campus *m*; locus *m*; **~ of battle** acies *f*; **in the ~** militiae.
fiendish inhumanus.
fierce atrox; saevus; acer; **~ness** atrocitas *f*.
fiery igneus, ardens; ferox.
fif|teen quindecim; **~teenth** quintus decimus; **~th** quintus; **~tieth** quinquagesimus; **~ty** quinquaginta.
fig ficus, i *and* us *f*.
fight pugno 1, dimico 1; (con)certo 1; **~ a battle** proelium committo 3; pugna *f*; certamen *n*; **~er** pugnator *m*.

figur|ative translatus; **~e** figura *f*; forma *f*; signum *n*; **~e of speech** translatio *f*.
filament filum *n*.
filch surripio 3.
file lima *f*; *mil.* ordo *m*; **rank and ~** gregarii milites *m/pl.*; limo 1.
filial pius.
fill impleo 2, compleo 2 (*alqd alqa re*); celebro 1 (*locum, aures etc.*); inicio 3 (*spem, etc. alci*).
fillet vitta *f*; fascia *f*.
film membrana *f*.
filter liquo 1; colum *n*.
filth sordes *f/pl.*; caenum *n*; illuvies *f*; **~iness** squalor *m*; **~y** sordidus; spurcus; foedus.
final ultimus, extremus; **~ly** ad extremum; postremo; denique.
finance pecuniam solvo 3 (*pro re*); **(public) ~s** aerarium *n*.
find invenio 4; reperio 4; nanciscor 3; **~ guilty** damno 1; **~ out** comperio 4; **~ing** inventum *n*.
fine praeclarus; pulcher; bellus; tenuis; subtilis; multo 1 (*alqm pecunia*); multa *f*; **~ness** tenuitas *f*; **~sse** argutiae *f/pl.*
finger digitus *m*; attrecto 1; **~-tips** extremi digiti *m/pl.*
finish conficio 3, perficio 3; perago 3; finio 4; **~ off** absolvo 3; absolutio *f*; **~ed** perfectus.
fir abies *m*; pinus, us *f*; **of ~-wood** abiegnus.
fire ignis *m*; incendium *n*; ardor *m*; **set on ~** incendo 3; **be on ~** ardeo 2; **catch ~** exardesco 3; **~-brand** fax *f*; **~-place** focus *m*; **~wood** ligna *n/pl.*
firm firmus, stabilis; constans; societas *f*; **make ~** firmo 1; **stand ~** sto 1; **~ament** caelum *n*; **~ness** firmitas *f*; constantia *f*.
first primus; princeps; **at ~** primo; **~ly, in the ~ place** primo, primum; **for the ~ time** primum; **~-fruits** primitiae *f/pl.*
fish piscis *m*; piscor 1; **~ for** capto 1; **~erman** piscator *m*; **~ing boat** piscatoria navis *f*; **~ing rod** harundo *f*; **~monger** cetarius *m*; **~pond** piscina *f*.
fist pugnus *m*.
fit aptus (*alci*; *ad alqd*); idoneus; accommodatus; *v/t.* accommodo 1 (*alci ad alqd*); *v/i.* convenio 4 (*ad*); **~ out** instruo 3; impetus, us *m*; **~ful** incertus; **~ting** decens; **it is ~ting** oportet.
five quinque; **~ hundred** quingenti, **~ times** quinquies.
fix figo 3; constituo 3; destino 1; defigo 3 (*oculos in alqd*); **~ed** certus; constans.
flabby, flaccid mollis; enervatus.
flag languesco 3; refrigesco 3; vexillum *n*, signum *n*.
flagon lagoena *f*.
flame flamma *f*; flagro 1; **~-coloured** flammeus.
flamen flamen *m*.
flank latus *n*; ilia *n/pl.*; *mil.* **on the ~s** a lateribus.
flap *v/t.* plaudo 3 (*pennis etc.*); *v/i.* fluito 1; lacinia *f*.
flare flagro 1.
flash fulgeo 2; corusco 1; mico 1; fulgor *m*; **lightning ~** fulgur *n*.
flask ampulla *f*.
flat aequus; planus; campester; pronus; *fig.* frigidus; campus *m*; **~ness** planities *f*; **~ten** complano 1.
flatter adulor 1 (*acc.*); blandior 4, assentor 1 (*dat.*); **~er** assentator *m*; **~ing** blandus; **~y** adulatio *f*.
flatulent inflatus.
flaunt ostento 1.
flavour sapor *m*; **have a ~** sapio 3 (*acc.*).
flaw vitium *n*, mendum *n*; **~less** emendatus.
flax linum *n*; carbasus, i *f*; **~en** flavus.
flay pellem deripio 3.
flea pulex *m*.
flee fugio 3; in fugam me do 1, confero 3.
fleec|e vellus *n*; expilo 1; **~y** laniger.
fleet celer; classis *f*; **~ing** fugax; **~ness** velocitas *f*.
flesh caro *f*; corpus *n*.
flexib|ility mollitia *f*; **~le** flexibilis; lentus.
flicker mico 1; corusco 1.
flight volatus, us *m*; lapsus, us *m*; fuga *f*; **put to ~** in fugam do 1, conicio 3 (*alqm*); **~ of stairs** scalae *f/pl.*; **~y** levis.
flimsy subtilis; pertenuis.
flinch abhorreo 2 (*ab*).
fling iacio 3; **~ away** pro-, ab-icio 3.
flint silex *m*; **~y** *fig.* ferreus.
flippant nugax.
flit volito 1.
float fluito 1; inno 1; fluo 3; ratis *f*.

flock grex *m*; pecus *n*; floccus *m*; ~ **to, towards, together** confluo 3; congregor 1.
flog verbero 1; **~ging** verberatio *f*; verbera *n/pl.*
flood diluvies *f*, diluvium *n*; unda *f*; *fig.* flumen *n*; inundo 1.
floor solum *n*; pavimentum *n*; contignatio *f*.
florid rubicundus; floridus.
flounce instita *f*.
flounder mergor 3; haereo 2.
flour farina *f*.
flourish floreo 2; vigeo 2; iacto 1; flos *m*; clangor *m* (*tubarum*).
flout contemno 3.
flow fluo 3; mano 1; ~ **down, into, past** de-, in-, praeter-fluo 3; flumen *n*; lapsus, us *m*; accessus, us *m* (*aestus*).
flower flos *m*; flosculus *m*; floreo 2; **~y** floreus; floridus.
fluctuate me iacto 1; nato 1.
fluen|cy copia *f*, facultas *f* dicendi; **~t** volubilis, copiosus.
fluid liquidus; liquor *m*.
flurry trepidatio *f*; trepido 1.
flush rubeo 2; rubor *m*; flos *m*; planus.
flute tibia *f*; **~-player** tibicen *m*.
flutter volito 1; trepidatio *f*.
fly volo 1; fugio 3; ~ **at** involo 1; ~ **open** dissilio 4; musca *f*; **~ing** volucer.
foal eculeus *m*.
foam spumo 1; spuma *f*; **~ing** spumeus, spumosus.
fodder pabulum *n*.
foe hostis *m*; inimicus *m*.
fog caligo *f*, nebula *f*; **~gy** caliginosus.
foil eludo 3; rudis *f*; lamina *f*.
fold complico 1; ruga *f*, sinus, us *m* (*vestis*); saepta *n/pl.*; ovile *n*; **~ing-doors** valvae *f/pl.*
foliage frondes *f/pl.*
folk vulgus, i *n*.
follow (con-, in-)sequor 3; insisto 3 (*rationem, etc.*); utor 3 (consiliis); **as ~s** in hunc modum; **it ~s that** sequitur ut; **~er** assectator *m*; **the ~ing** proximus; **~ing** comitatus, us *m*.
folly stultitia *f*.
foment *fig.* concito 1.
fond amans, studiosus (*gen.*); indulgens (*in alqm*; *dat.*); **be ~ of** amo 1 (*acc., inf.*); **~le** mulceo 2; blandior 4.
food cibus *m*; alimentum *n*; pabulum *n*; victus, us *m*.
fool stultus *m*; ludificor 1 (*alqm*), ludo 3 (*alqm*); **~ery** ineptiae *f/pl.*; **~-hardy** temerarius; **~ish** stultus, ineptus.
foot pes *m*; *mil.* pedes *m/pl.*; pedites *m/pl.*; imum *n* (*adj.* imus); **at the ~ of** sub (*abl.*); **on ~** pedibus; pedestris; pedes; **~ing** status, us *m*; **~man** pedisequus *m*; **~path** semita *f*; **~print** vestigium *n*; **~stool** scamnum *n*.
foppish delicatus.
for *prep.* pro (*abl.*); ob, propter (*causam*); in, ad (*acc.*); ~ **my part** pro mea parte; **leave ~ dead** pro occiso relinquo 3; *cj.* nam; enim; quippe.
forage pabulor 1; frumentor 1; pabulum *n*.
forbear mitto 3, desino 3 (*inf.*); **~ance** patientia *f*.
forbid veto 1 (*acc. c. inf.*); impero 1 (*ne*).
force vis *f*; **be in ~** valeo 2; *v/t.* cogo 3 (*ut, inf.*); ~ **a way through, out of** perrumpo 3 per, erumpo 3 ex; ~ **out of** extorqueo 2; **~d** arcessitus; **~s** copiae *f/pl.*
forcible vehemens; gravis.
ford vadum *n*; vado transeo 4.
fore|bode portendo 3; praesentio 4; **~cast** praevideo 2; **~fathers** maiores *m/pl.*; **~finger** digitus *m* index; **~go** dimitto 3; **~head** frons *f*.
foreign externus; peregrinus; ~ **to** abhorrens ab; **~er** advena *m*; peregrinus *m*.
fore|knowledge providentia *f*; **~man** procurator *m*; **~most** princeps, primus; **~see** provideo 2; **~sight** providentia *f*.
forest silva *f*.
fore|stall anteverto 3 (*dat.*); **~tell** praedico 3.
forfeit multor 1 (*abl.*); multa *f*; commissus.
forge fabricor 1 (*gladium*); subicio 3; fornax *f*.
forget obliviscor 3 (*gen., acc.*); **~ful** immemor (*gen.*); obliviosus.
forgive ignosco 3 (*alci alqd*); **~ness** venia *f*.
fork furca *f*; **~ed** bifurcus.
forlorn destitutus; miser.
form forma *f*, figura *f*, species *f*; genus *n*; ritus, us *m*; scamnum *n*;

for ~'s sake dicis causa; (con-) formo 1; fingo 3; instruo 3 (*aciem*); ineo 4 (*consilium*).
formal|ities ritus *m/pl.*; iusta *n/pl.*; **~ly** rite.
former prior; superior; pristinus; **the ~** ille; **~ly** olim, quondam.
formidable gravis.
formula formula *f*; carmen *n*; praefatio *f*.
forsake desero 3.
forsooth scilicet, nempe.
forswear eiuro 1 (*alqd*); **~ oneself** periuro 1.
fort castellum *n*.
forth foras; **from that time ~** inde; **~with** protinus.
fortieth quadragesimus.
fortif|ication munitio *f*; munimentum *n*; moenia *n/pl.*; **~y** munio 4.
fortress castellum *n*; arx *f*.
fortuitous fortuitus; **~ly** fortuito, forte.
fortun|ate felix; fortunatus; **~e** fortuna *f* (*secunda, adversa*); fors *f*; **good ~e** felicitas *f*; res *f/pl.* secundae; divitiae *f/pl.*, fortunae *f/pl.*; res *f* (*familiaris*); **~e-teller** hariolus *m*.
forty quadraginta.
forum forum *n*.
forward porro, ante; **thence-~** iam inde; protervus; promptus; adiuvo 1; perfero 3 (*litteras*); **~ness** protervitas *f*.
foster foveo 2; nutrio 4; **~-child** alumnus *m*; **~-mother** nutrix *f*.
foul foedus; taeter; inquino 1; **~ness** foeditas *f*.
found condo 3, constituo 3; deduco (*coloniam*); **~ation** fundamentum *n*; sedes *f*; **~er** conditor *m*; auctor *m*; summergor 3.
foundry fornax *f*.
fountain fons *f*.
four quattuor; **~ each** quaterni; **~ times** quater; **~ hundred** quadringenti; **~fold** quadruplus; quadruplum *n*; **~footed** quadrupes; **~teen** quattuordecim; **~teenth** quartus decimus; **~th** quartus; **~thly** quarto.
fowl volucris *f*; gallina *f*; **~er** auceps *m*; **~ing** aucupium *n*.
fox vulpes *f*; **old ~** veterator *m*; vulpinus.
fract|ion pars *f*; **~ure** frango 3.
fragile fragilis.
fragment fragmentum *n*.
fragran|ce suavis odor *m*; **~t** odorus, suavis.
frail infirmus, fragilis.
frame compages *m*; forma *f*; **~ of mind** affectio *f*; animus *m*; compono 3; fabricor 1; formo 1; concipio 3 (*ius iurandum*); forma includo 3 (*tabulam*).
franchise civitas *f*; suffragium *n*.
frank liber; simplex; sincerus; **~ness** libertas *f*.
frantic fanaticus; insanus.
fratern|al fraternus; **~ity** sodalitas *f*.
fraud fraus *f*; dolus *m*; **~ulent** fraudulentus.
fray rixa *f*; detero 3.
freak monstrum *n*; **~ish** inconstans.
freckle macula *f*.
free liber (*re, a re*); vacuus (*a re*); expers (*gen.*); **be ~ from** careo 2 (*abl.*); **~ from blame** extra culpam; **~ from care** securus; **of one's own ~ will** sua sponte; libero 1 (*alqm re, a re*); manumitto 3 (*servum*); vindico 1 (*ab*); **~booter** latro *m*; **~born** ingenuus; **~dman** libertus *m*; **~dom** libertas *f*; vacuitas *f*.
freeze congelo 1; concresco 3; conglacio 1.
freight onus *n*; navem onero 1.
frenz|ied furiosus, insanus; **~y** furor *m*.
frequen|cy crebritas *f*; frequentia *f*; **~t** creber; frequens; celebro 1; **~ted** celeber; **~tly** crebro.
fresh recens; integer; **a~** de integro; **~en** increbresco 3 (*ventus*); **~ness** viriditas *f*.
fret sollicito 1; doleo 2; **~ful** morosus.
friction tritus, us *m*.
friend amicus *m*; familiaris *m*; **~ly** comes; benevolus, amicus (*erga, dat.*); **~ship** amicitia *f*; familiaritas *f*.
fright terror *m*; **~en** (per)terreo 2; **~ful** terribilis; atrox.
frigid frigidus.
frill segmenta *n/pl*.
fringe fimbriae *f/pl.*; limbus *m*.
fritter away dissipo 1.
frivol|ity levitas *f*; **~ous** levis; nugax.
fro: to and ~ ultro citroque.
frock stola *f*.
frog rana *f*.
frolic ludo 3; lascivio 4; lascivia *f*.

from a, ab (*abl.*); de (*abl.*); e, ex (*abl.*); ~ **all sides** undique; ~ **day to day** in dies; ~ **that time** inde; ~ **this, that place** hinc, illinc.
front frons *f*; ~ **of a column** primum agmen *n*; **in** ~ a fronte; **in** ~ **of** pro (*abl.*); ante (*acc.*); **in** ~ (*adj.*) adversus; obviam eo 4 (*alci*); aspecto 3 (*alqd*); **~ier** finis *m*; **~ing** adversus (*acc.*).
frost gelu *n*; pruina *f*; **~bitten** praeustus; **~y** gelidus.
froth spuma *f*; spumo 1.
frown frontem contraho 3; contractio *f* frontis.
frozen glacie, frigore concretus.
frugal frugi; parcus; **~ity** parsimonia *f*.
fruit fructus, us *m*; pomum *n*; fruges *f/pl.*; baca *f*; **~erer** pomarius *m*; **~ful** fructuosus; frugifer; fecundus; **~less** irritus; **~tree** pomum *n*.
frustrate dirimo 3; disturbo 1.
fry frigo 3; **~ing-pan** sartago *f*.
fuel ligna *n/pl.*; **gather** ~ lignor 1; *fig.* **add** ~ **to** faces subicio 3 (*dat.*).
fugitive caducus; fugax; profugus *m*; fugitivus *m*.
fulfil expleo 2; perfungor 3; exsequor 3.
full plenus (*abl.*); refertus (*abl.*, *gen.*); frequens; satur (*cibo*); **~y** copiose.
fulminate intono 1.
fume fumus *m*; stomachor 1.
fumigate fumigo 1; vaporo 1.
fun iocus *m*; ludus *m*.
function officium *n*, munus *n*; **~ary** magistratus, us *m*.
fund copia *f* (pecuniae); **~amental** ultimus.
funeral funus *n*; exsequiae *f/pl.*; funebris.
funnel infundibulum *n*.
funny ridiculus.
fur pellis *f*; villi *m/pl.*, pili *m/pl.*
furbish interpolo 1.
furious iratus; furibundus.
furlong stadium *n*.
furlough commeatus, us *m*.
furnace fornax *f*.
furnish praebeo 2; suppedito 1; orno 1 (*alqd re*).
furniture supellex *f*.
furrow sulcus *m*; sulco 1.
furry villosus.
further ulterior; consulo 3 (*dat.*); *adv.* longius; praeterea; amplius; **~more** porro.
furtive furtivus.
fury furor *m*; rabies *f*; furia *f*.
fuse fundo 3; *fig.* confundo 3.
fuss perturbatio *f*.
fustian *fig.* tumor *m*; tumidus.
futile futilis; vanus.
future futurus; **in, for the** ~ in futurum, in posterum; futura *n/pl.*

G

gable fastigium *n*.
gad-fly asilus *m*.
gag praeligo 1; obturamentum *n*.
gage pignus *n*.
gaiety hilaritas *f*.
gain lucror 1; consequor 3, pario 3; paro 1; lucrum *n*; quaestus, us *m*; **~ful** lucrosus.
gainsay nego 1; contra dico 3.
gait incessus, us *m*.
gale ventus *m*.
gall fel *n*; bilis *m*; mordeo 2.
gallant fortis; amator *m*; **~ry** virtus, utis *f*.
gallery porticus, us *f*; pinacotheca *f*.
galley navis *f* longa.
galling mordax.
gallop: at a ~ citato equo.
gallows crux *f*; patibulum *n*.
gambl|e alea ludo 3; **~er** aleator *m*; **~ing** alea *f*.
gambol lascivio 4.
game ludus *m*; lusus, us *m*; venatio *f*.
gaming alea *f*.
gammon perna *f*.
gander anser, eris *m*.
gang caterva *f*; operae *f/pl*.
gaol carcer, eris *m*; **~er** custos *m*.
gap lacuna *f*; **~e** dehisco 3; hio 1; stupeo 2 (**at** *alqd*).
garb vestitus, us *m*.
garbage quisquiliae *f/pl*.
garden hortus *m*; **~er** hortulanus *m*.
garland corona *f*; sertum *n*.
garlic allium *n*.
garment vestimentum *n*.
garnish decoro 1.
garret cenaculum *n*.
garrison praesidium *n*; praesidio confirmo 1.
garrulous loquax.
garter periscelis, idis *f*.
gash plaga *f*; vulnus *n*; seco 1.
gasp anhelo 1; anhelitus, us *m*.
gate porta *f*; **~post** postis *m*; **~way** limen *n*.
gather colligo 3; confero 3; cogo 3; lego 3; *fig*. conicio 3 (*ex re*); **~ in** meto 3; **~ing** coetus, us *m*.
gaudy versicolor.
gauge metior 4; modulus *m*.
gauntlet caestus, us *m*.
gay hilaris, hilarus; festus.
gaze intueor 2; contemplo 1; obtutus, us *m*.
gazette acta *n/pl*. diurna.
gear instrumentum *n*.
gelding canterius *m*.
gem gemma *f*.
gender genus *n*.
general generalis; communis; universus; **become ~** increbresco 3; **in ~** ad summam; dux *m*, imperator *m*; **~ities** loci *m/pl*. communes; **~ize** universe loquor 3; **~ly** plerumque; vulgo.
generat|e pario 3; genero 1; **~ion** saeculum *n*; aetas *f*.
gener|osity liberalitas *f*; **~ous** liberalis, generosus.
genial benignus, comis.
genius ingenium *n*.
genteel politus.
gentile gentilis.
gentle lenis, mitis; nobilis; **~man** generosus *m* (homo); **~manly** honestus; **~ness** lenitas *f*; mansuetudo *f*.
genuine sincerus, verus, merus.
geography geographia *f*.
geomet|er geometres, ae *m*; **~ry** geometria *f*.
germ germen *n*; semen *n*; **~ane** affinis; **~inate** germino 1.
gest|iculate gestum ago 3; **~iculation** gestus, us *m*; iactatio *f*; **~ure** gestus, us *m*; motus, us *m*.
get adipiscor 3; nanciscor 3; pario 3; percipio 3 (*fructus*); impetro 1 (*quod postulo*); **~ something done** curo 1 alqd faciendum; *v/impers*. fit; **~ abroad** percrebresco 3; **~ along, on** procedo 3; **~ back** recupero 1; **~ out** descendo 3 (*e curru*); **~ to** pervenio 4 (*ad*); **~ up** surgo 3.
ghastly pallidus; foedus.
ghost umbra *f*; Manes *m/pl*.; larva *f*.
giant vir *m* eximia corporis magnitudine; gigas, ntis *m*; praegrandis.
gibbet furca *f*; patibulum *n*.
gidd|iness vertigo *f*; **~y** levis.

gift donum *n*; munus *n*; facultas *f*; **~ed** praeditus (*alqa re*); ingeniosus.
gig cisium *n*.
gigantic immanis.
giggle cacchinno 1.
gild inauro 1.
gill quartarius *m*.
gilt aureus, inauratus.
gimlet terebra *f*.
gin pedica *f*, plaga *f*.
gingerly pedetemptim.
gird cingor 3 (*alqa re*); **~le** cingulum *n*.
girl puella *f*; virgo *f*; **~ish** virginalis.
girth cingula *f*.
gist summa *f*.
give do 1; dono 1; tribuo 3; **~ one's word** fidem interpono 3; **~ place, way to** (de)cedo 3 (*alci*); **~ away** largior 4; **~ back** reddo 3; **~ in** me dedo 4 (*alci*); **~ out** me fero 3; **~ up** trado 3; dimitto 3; **~ way to** indulgeo 2 (*dat.*).
glad laetus; **be ~** gaudeo 2; **~den** hilaro 1.
glade saltus, us *m*; nemus *n*.
gladiator gladiator *m*; **of a ~** gladiatorius.
gladly libenter.
glance oculos adicio 3 (*dat.*); aspectus, us *m*.
gland glandula *f*.
glar|e torvis oculis aspicio 3; fulgor *m*; **~ing** fulgens; *fig*. manifestus.
glass vitrum *n*; **drinking ~** poculum *n* (vitreum); **looking ~** speculum *n*; **~ware** vitrea *n/pl.*; **of ~** vitreus.
gleam fulgeo 2; fulgor *m*, nitor *m*; **~ing** nitidus.
glean spicas lego 3; colligo 3.
glee hilaritas *f*.
glen convallis *f*.
glib blandus; volubilis.
glide labor 3.
glimmer subluceo 2.
glimpse conspicio 3; aspectus, us *m*.
glitter fulgeo 2; corusco 1; fulgor *m*.
gloat pascor 3 (*alqa re*).
globe globus *m*; orbis *m* (terrarum).
gloom tenebrae *f/pl.*; caligo *f*; **~y** tenebricosus, tenebrosus; tristis; ater.
glori|fy celebro 1; augeo 2; **~ous** praeclarus, amplus.
glory gloria *f*; decus *n*; **~ in** glorior 1 (*in re*).
gloss nitor *m*; interpretatio *f*; **~y** nitidus.
gloves manicae *f/pl.*
glow candeo 2, caleo 2; *fig*. ardeo 2; calor *m*; ardor *m*; **~worm** cicindela *f*.
glue gluten *n*; **~ together** coagmento 1.
glut satio 1; satietas *f*; **~ton** helluo *m*; lurco *m*; **~tony** edacitas *f*; gula *f*.
gnarled nodosus.
gnash frendeo 2.
gnat culex *m*.
gnaw rodo 3.
go eo 4; vado 3; **~ well** bene procedit 3 (*alci*); **let ~** dimitto 3, omitto 3; **~ astray** erro 1; **~ away** discedo 3; **~ before** anteeo 4 (*dat.*, *acc.*); **~ by** praetereo 4; sequor 3; **~ on** fio 3; **~ over** transeo 4; **~ up to** subeo 4.
goad stimulus *m*; **~ on** stimulo 1 (*ad*, *in*, *ut*).
goal meta *f*; calx *f*.
goat caper, pri *m*; capra *f*.
go-between internuntius *m*.
gobble devoro 1.
goblet poculum *n*; scyphus *m*.
god deus *m*; numen *n*; **~dess** dea *f*; **~less** impius; **~like** divinus.
gold aurum *n*; aureus; **~-leaf** brattea *f*; **~smith** aurifex *m*.
good bonus; probus; utilis (*ad*); bonum *n*, commodum *n*; **~s** bona *n/pl.*; merx *f*; **a ~ deal** aliquantum (*gen.*); **a ~ many** complures; **do ~ to** prosum (*dat.*); **make ~** sarcio 4; **~-bye** vale; **~ day** salve; **~-for-nothing** nequam; **~-natured** comis; **~-will** benevolentia *f*.
goose anser, eris *m*.
gore cruor *m*.
gorge fauces *f/pl.*; ingurgito 1 (*me re*).
gorgeous magnificus.
gormandise helluor 1.
gory cruentus.
gossip rumor *m*; sermo *m*; sermonem confero 3 (*cum alqo*); garrio 4; **~ing** garrulus.
gourd cucurbita *f*.
gout podagra *f*; **~y** arthriticus.
govern impero 1 (*dat.*); rego 3, guberno 1, moderor 1 (*acc.*); **~ment** administratio *f*; imperium *n*; res *f* publica; qui rei publicae praesunt; **~or** gubernator *m*; proconsul *m or* pro consule; praetor *m*; legatus *m*; praefectus *m*; **be ~or** praesum (*dat.*).

gown stola *f*; palla *f*.
grace gratia *f*; venia *f*; elegantia *f*; decoro 1 (*alqd alqa re*); **get into the good ~s of** gratiam concilio 1 (*alcs*); **~ful** decorus, venustus.
gracious propritius, benignus.
grade gradus, us *m*; locus *m*.
gradually gradatim; paulatim; sensim.
graft insero 3; surculus *m*.
grain frumentum *n*; granum *n*, mica *f*.
grammar grammatica *f*; **~ian** grammaticus *m*.
granary horreum *n*.
grand grandis; magnificus; sublimis; **~daughter** neptis *f*; **~eur** maiestas *f*; **~father** avus *m*; **~iloquent** grandiloquus; **~mother** avia *f*; **~son** nepos *m*.
grange villa *f*.
grant concedo 3; permitto 3; tribuo 3.
grape uva *f*; acinus *m and* -um *n*; **~vine** vitis *f*.
graphic vividus.
grappl|e luctor 1 (*cum*); **~ing-iron** manus *f* ferrea.
grasp comprehendo 3, complector 3 (*also fig.*); complexus, us *m*; manus, us *f*; **~ at** appeto 3; **~ing** avarus.
grass gramen *n*; herba *f*; **~y** herbidus, herbosus.
grate (con)tero 3; strideo 2; focus *m*.
grateful gratus; **be ~** gratiam habeo 2 (*alci*).
grati|fication expletio *f*; voluptas *f*; **~fy** gratificor 1 (*alci*); morem gero 3 (*alci*); expleo 2; **~fying** gratus; **~tude** gratia *f*.
gratuit|ous gratuitus; **~y** corollarium *n*.
grave gravis, serius; austerus; sepulcrum *n*; **from the ~** ab inferis.
gravel glarea *f*.
grave|stone monumentum *n*; **~-yard** sepulcra *n/pl*.
gravity gravitas *f*; severitas *f*; momentum *n*.
gravy ius *n*.
graze *v/t.* pasco 3; perstringo 3 (*alqd alqa re*); *v/i.* pascor 3.
grease adeps *m and f*; pingue *n*; ungo 3.
great magnus; ingens; grandis; **as, how ~** quantus; **so ~** tantus; **~-grandfather** proavus *m*; **~ly** magnopere; valde; **~ness** magnitudo *f*, amplitudo *f*.
greed avaritia *f*; edacitas *f*; **~y** avarus, avidus; cupidus (*gen.*).
green viridus; prasinus; crudus; **~s** olus *n*; **be ~** vireo 2; **~horn** tiro *m*; **~ness** viriditas *f*; cruditas *f*; **~sward** herba *f*; caespes *m*.
greet saluto 1; **~ing** salutatio *f*.
grey canus, albus; glaucus; **~ hair** cani capilli *m/pl.*; canities *f*.
grief dolor *m*; luctus, us *m*; maeror *m*.
griev|ance querel(l)a *f*; iniuria *f*; **~e** *v/t.* dolore afficio 3 (*alqm*); ango 3; *v/i.* doleo 2 (*acc., abl., quod*); piget 2 (*me alcs rei*); **~ous** acerbus, gravis.
grill torreo 2.
grim torvus, atrox.
grimace os torqueo 2.
grimy squalidus.
grin rideo 2.
grind (con)tero 3; molo 3; frendeo 2 (*dentibus*); **~ down** opprimo 3; **~stone** cos *f*.
grip comprehendo 3; manus, us *f*.
grisly horridus.
grizzled canus.
groan (in)gemo 3 (*alqd*); gemitus, us *m*.
groin inguen *n*.
groom agaso *m*.
groove canalis *m*.
grope praetento 1 (*iter*).
gross crassus; indecorus; **~ness** magnitudo *f*; turpitudo *f*.
grotto antrum *n*.
ground terra *f*; solum *n*; humus, i *f*; locus *m* (*aequus etc.*); **~s** causa *f*, ratio *f*; **on, to the ~** humi; **gain ~** percrebresco 3 (*rumor*); proficio 3; **~less** vanus, inanis; **~work** fundamentum *n*.
group circulus *m*; globus *m*; dispono 3.
grove lucus *m*; nemus *n*.
grovel me abicio 3 (*ad pedes*); **~ling** humilis.
grow *v/i.* cresco 3; adolesco 3; nascor 3; *fig.* fio 3; *v/t.* colo 3, sero 3; **~ long** promitto 3 (*capillos etc.*).
growl fremo 3; fremitus, us *m*.
grow|n up adultus; **~th** incrementum *n*; auctus, us *m*.
grub vermiculus *m*; **~ up** eruo 3.
grudge invideo 2 (*dat.*); simultas *f*;

bear a ~ against succenseo 2 (*alci*).
gruel puls *f*.
gruff asper.
grumble murmuro 1.
guarantee fides *f*; pignus *n*; fidem do 1 (*alci*); satisdo 1.
guard custodio 4; tueor 2; praesideo 2 (*dat.*); custodia *f*; praesidium *n*; custos *m*; vigiliae *f*/*pl.* (*by night*); **mount ~** custodiam ago 3; **be on one's ~** caveo 2 (*alqd*); **off one's ~** incautus; **~ed** cautus; **~ian** praeses *m and f*; tutor *m*.
guess conicio 3; divino 1; coniectura *f*.
guest hospes *m*; hospita *f*; conviva *m*.
guidance consilium *n*.
guide duco 3; rego 3; dux *m*.
guild sodalitas *f*, societas *f*; collegium *n*.
guile dolus *m*; **~ful** dolosus.
guilt noxa *f*; scelus *n*; culpa *f*; **~less** innocens; **~y** noxius, sons, nocens.
guise species *f*.
gulf sinus, us *m*, gurges *m*.
gull mergus *m*; ludificor 1.
gullet gula *f*.
gullible credulus.
gully fauces *f*/*pl.*
gulp singultus, us *m*; **~ down** absorbeo 2.
gum gingiva *f*; gummi *n*; lacrima *f*.
gurgle murmuro 1.
gush me profundo 3; emico 1.
gust aura *f*; flatus, us *m*; **~y** ventosus.
gut exintero 1.
guts intestina *n*/*pl.*, viscera *n*/*pl.*
gutter fossa *f*; cloaca *f*; imbrex *f*.
gymnas|ium palaestra *f*, gymnasium *n*; **~tic** gymnicus; **~tics** palaestra *f*.

H

habit mos *m*; consuetudo *f*; habitus, us *m*; **be in the ~ of** soleo 2; **~ation** domicilium *n*; **~ual** usitatus.
hack concido 3; caballus *m*; **~neyed** tritus.
haft manubrium *n*.
hag anus, us *f*; **~gard** macie confectus.
hail saluto 1; salvere iubeo 2 (*alqm*); *int.* salve; grando *f*; **it ~s** grandinat.
hair capillus *m*; crinis *m*; pilus *m*; **~dresser** tonsor *m*; cinerarius *m*; **~less** glaber, calvus; **~y** pilosus, villosus.
hale validus.
half dimidius; dimidia pars *f*; dimidium *n*; **~-breed** hibrida *m and f*; **~ hour** semihora *f*; **~-moon** luna *f* dimidia; **~-pound** selibra *f*; **~-witted** stultus; **~yearly** semestris.
hall atrium *n*.
hallow sacro 1; **~ed** sanctus.
hallucination error *m* (mentis); somnium *n*.
halo corona *f*.
halt *v/t.* constituo 3; *v/i.* consisto 3; haesito 1; claudico 1; claudus; **~er** capistrum *n*.
ham perna *f*; poples *m*.
hamlet viculus *m*.
hammer malleus *m*; tundo 3 (malleo).
hamper qualus *m*; impedio 4.
hamstring poplites succido 3 (*alci*).
hand manus, us *f*; palma *f*; **right, left ~** dext(e)ra, laeva; **at ~** praesto, ad manum; **be at ~** adsum (*dat.*); **by ~** manu; **in ~** in manibus; **on the one ~, on the other ~** quidem ... sed, at ... contra; **~ to ~** comminus (*pugnare*); **come to ~** venire ad manum; **have a ~ in** intersum (*dat.*); **~ down, over** trado 3; **~ in** profiteor 2 (*nomen etc.*); **~ round** circumfero 3; **~book** libellus *m*; **~cuffs** manicae *f/pl.*; **~ful** manipulus *m*.
handi|craft artificium *n*; **~work** opus *n*.
handkerchief sudarium *n*.
handle tracto 1; ansa *f*; manubrium *n*.
hand|maid ancilla *f*; **~some** pulcher, decorus, speciosus; liberalis; **~writing** chirographum *n*; manus, us *f*; **~y** habilis, dexter.
hang *v/t.* suspendo 3 (*alqm, alqd, re, ex, de, in re*); affigo 3 (*ad, dat.*); *v/i.* pendeo 2; **~ back** dubito 1; **~ over** immineo 2 (*dat.*); **let ~** demitto 3; **~er-on** assecla *m*; **~ing** suspendium *n*; **~ings** aulaea *n/pl.*; **~man** carnifex *m*.
hanker after cupio 3.
hap|hazardly temere; **~less** infelix; **~ly** fortasse.
happen accido 3 (**that** *ut*); contingo 3 (*dat.*); evenio 4; fio.
happ|iness felicitas *f*; **~y** felix, beatus, fortunatus.
harangue contionor 1 (*apud*); contio *f*.
harass sollicito 1; vexo 1; fatigo 1.
harbinger (prae)nuntius *m*.
harbour portus, us *m*; *fig.* refugium *n*; excipio 3.
hard durus; asper; difficilis, arduus; *adv.* valde, sedulo; **~ by** prope, iuxta; **be ~ pressed** premor 3; **~en** duro 1; **become ~ened** obduresco 3; **~hearted** ferreus; **~ly** vix, aegre; **~ness** duritia *f*; **~ship** iniuria *f*; labor *m*; **~ware** ferramenta *n/pl.*; **~y** robustus.
hare lepus, oris *m*.
harlot meretrix *f*.
harm laedo 3; noceo 2 (*dat.*); iniuria *f*; incommodum *n*; **~ful** nocens; **~less** innocens.
harmon|ious concors; **~ise** concino 3; consentio 4; **~y** concentus, us *m*; concordia *f*.
harness freni *m/pl.*; frenos impono 3.
harp cithara *f*; **~ upon** canto 1.
harrow rastrum *n*; occo 1.
harsh asper, austerus, durus.
hart cervus *m*.
harvest messis *f*; demeto 3, percipio 3; **~er** messor *m*.
hast|e propero 1, festino 1; festina-

tio *f*; celeritas *f*; **~en** accelero 1, maturo 1; **~ily** propere, raptim; **~y** properus, praeceps; iracundus.
hat petasus *m*.
hatch excludo 3; coquo 3 (*consilium*).
hatchet securis *f*.
hate odi; **~ful** invisus, odiosus; **be ~ful to** odio sum (*alci*).
hatred odium *n*.
haught|iness superbia *f*, arrogantia *f*; **~y** superbus, arrogans.
haul traho 3, rapio 3; **~ down, up** de-, sub-duco 3 (*naves*); praeda *f*.
haunch clunis *f or m*.
haunt celebro 1, frequento 1; inquieto 1; latebra *f*.
have habeo 2; teneo 2; est mihi; utor 3; **I ~ to do this** hoc mihi faciendum est.
haven refugium *n*.
havoc caedes *f*, clades *f*.
hawk accipiter *m*; *v/i*. exscreo 1; *v/t*. vendito 1; **~er** institor *m*.
hay faenum *n*; **~-loft** faenilia *n/pl*.
hazard in discrimen committo 3, voco 1; in aleam do 1; periculum *n*; alea *f*; **~ous** periculosus.
haze nebula *f*.
hazel corylus, i *f*.
he ille; **~ who** is qui; **~ himself** ipse.
head caput *n*; vertex *m*; princeps *m*; **be ~ of** praesum (*dat*.); *mil*. **~ of a column** primum agmen *n*; **~ foremost** pronus; **be brought to a ~** in discrimen adducor 3; **hang over one's ~** supra caput est; **lay ~s together** capita conferre; **make ~way** proficio 3; **~ache** capitis dolor *m*; **~band** vitta *f*; **~land** promontorium *n*; **~long** praeceps; **~quarters** principia *n/pl*.; **~strong** pervicax.
heal sano 1; medeor 2 (*dat*.); coeo 4 (*vulnera*); **~er** medicus *m*; **~ing** sanatio *f*; salutaris.
health sanitas *f*, valetudo *f*; **good, bad ~** bona, infirma valetudo *f*; **drink one's ~** propino 1 (*salutem alci*); **~ful** salubris, salutaris; **~y** sanus, validus.
heap acervus *m*; cumulus *m*; **~ up** coacervo 1; **~ upon** congero 3 (*in alqm*).
hear audio 4 (*acc., acc. c. inf*.); percipio 3; *fig*. cognosco 3; **~ing** auditus, us *m*; audientia *f*; **give a ~ing** aures praebeo 2 (*alci*).
hearken ausculto 1 (*alci*).
hearsay auditio *f*; rumor *m*.
heart cor *n*; *fig*. pectus *n*; animus *m*; viscera *n/pl*.; **know by ~** memoria teneo 2; **~-breaking** miserabilis; **~felt** sincerus; **~en** confirmo 1.
hearth focus *m*.
heart|ily summo studio; vehementer; **~iness** studium *n*; **~less** ferreus; **~y** sincerus, comis.
heat calor *m*, ardor *m*; aestus, us *m*; calefacio 3.
heath planum *n*; loca *n/pl*. virgultis obsita.
heathen paganus; barbarus.
heave *v/i*. tumeo 2; tumesco 3; *v/t*. tollo 3; **~ a groan, sigh** gemitum, suspirium do 1, duco 3.
heaven caelum *n*; *fig*. superi *m/pl*.; di *m/pl*. immortales; **~ly** caelestis, divinus.
heav|iness gravitas *f*; **~y** gravis; crassus; aeger (animi); magnus (*imber etc*.).
hecatomb hecatombe *f*.
hectic febriculosus; *fig*. incitatus.
hedge saepes *f*; saepio 4; **~hog** erinaceus *m*.
heed oboedio 4 (*dat*.); **take ~** curo 1; caveo 2; **~ful** memor, cautus; **~less** immemor (*gen*.); incautus.
heel calx *f*; **take to one's ~s** me in pedes conicio 3.
heifer iuvenca *f*.
height altitudo *f*; proceritas *f*; locus *m* editus, superior; *fig*. fastigium *n*; summus; **~en** amplifico 1; augeo 2.
heinous atrox, nefarius.
heir heres *m and f*.
hell inferi *m/pl*.; **~ish** infernus; nefandus.
helm gubernaculum *n*; clavus *m*.
helmet galea *f*, cassis *f*; **~ed** galeatus.
helmsman gubernator *m*.
help adiuvo 1; subvenio 4 (*dat*.); opem fero 3; porrigo 3 (*cibus*); **I can't ~** facere non possum quin; auxilium *n*, ops *f*; **~er** adiutor *m*; **~ful** utilis; **~less** inops.
hem ora *f*, instita *f*; **~ in** circumsedeo 2; claudo 3.
hemlock cicuta *f*.
hemp cannabis *f*.
hen gallina *f*.
hence hinc; ita, ex quo; **~forth** dehinc, posthac.
her suus; eius.

herald praeco *m*; praenuntio 1.
herb herba *f*.
herd grex *m*; pecus *n*; **~sman** pastor *m*.
here hic; **~ and there** passim; **be ~** adsum; **~abouts** hic alicubi; **~after** posthac, aliquando.
hereditary hereditarius; paternus.
here|sy prava opinio *f*; **~tical** pravus.
hereupon hic.
heritage hereditas *f*.
hermit homo *m* solitarius.
hero heros *m*; vir *m* fortissimus; **~ic** heroicus; **~ine** heroina *f*, herois *f*; **~ism** virtus, utis *f*, fortitudo *f*.
heron ardea *f*.
herself ipsa.
hesita|ncy haesitatio *f*; **~te** dubito 1; haesito 1, cunctor 1; **~tion** haesitatio *f*.
hew caedo 3; dolo 1.
hiccup singulto 1; singultus, us *m*.
hide *v/t.* celo 1; abdo 3, condo 3; dissimulo 1; *v/i.* lateo 2; corium *n*; pellis *f*.
hideous foedus, taeter, informis.
hiding verbera *n/pl.*; **~place** latebrae *f/pl.*
high altus; (ex)celsus; sublimis; *fig.* summus, amplus; magnus (*price, etc.*); **~-born** generosus; **~lands** loca *n/pl.* montuosa; **~ly** magni (*aestimo*); **~-priest** pontifex *m*; **~-spirited** ferox; **~way** via *f*; **~wayman** latro *m*.
hilarity hilaritas *f*.
hill collis *m*; clivus *m*; tumulus *m*; **~y** clivosus.
hilt manubrium *n*.
himself ipse; se(met); **by ~** solitarius, solus.
hind cerva *f*; posterior.
hind|er impedio 4 (*alqm a re*; *ne, quin, quominus*); obsto 1 (*alci*; *ne, quominus*); **~rance** impedimentum *n*, mora *f*.
hinge cardo *m*; **~ on** vertor 3 (*in re*).
hint significo 1; significatio *f*; signum *n*.
hip coxendix *f*.
hire conduco 3; merces *f*; **~ling** mercenarius *m*.
his suus; eius.
hiss sibilo 1; **~ off** explodo 3; **~ing** sibilus, us *m*.
histor|ian rerum scriptor *m*; **~ical** historicus; **~y** historia *f*; res *f/pl.* (gestae).
hit ferio 4; percutio 3; **~ upon** invenio 4; plaga *f*.
hitch impedimentum *n*; **~ up** succingo 3.
hither huc; **~to** adhuc; antehac.
hive alvearium *n*.
hoard recondo 3; thesaurus *m*.
hoar|frost pruina *f*; **~iness** canities *f*.
hoarse raucus.
hoary canus; priscus.
hoax fallo 3; fallaciae *f/pl.*
hobble claudico 1.
hobby studium *n*.
hoe sarculum *n*.
hog porcus *m*.
hoist tollo 3; **~ sail** vela do 1.
hold teneo 2; gesto 1; capio 3; habeo 2, possideo 2; gero 3 (*magistratum*); **~ the belief that** existimo 1, censeo 2; **~ good** convenit 4 (*ad*); **~ one's tongue** conticesco 3; **~ out** sustineo 2; **~ with** consentio 4; caverna *f*; manus, us *f*; **catch ~ of** comprehendo 3; arripio 3.
hole cavum *n*; foramen *n*.
holiday feriae *f/pl.*; dies *m* festus; **keep ~** ferior 1; ferias ago 3.
holiness sanctitas *f*; numen *n*.
hollow cavus; *fig.* vanus; fucatus; caverna *f*, cavum *n*; **~ out** (ex-) cavo 1.
holy sanctus, divinus.
homage observantia *f*, veneratio *f*.
home domus, us *f*; domicilium *n*; **at ~** domi; **~(wards)** domum; **from ~** domo; **drive, strike ~** adigo 3; domesticus; **~ly** rusticus; **~sickness** suorum desiderium *n*.
honest probus, sincerus; **~y** probitas *f*.
honey mel *n*; **~comb** favus *m*; **~ed** mellitus.
honorary honorarius.
honour honor *m*; dignitas *f*; honestas *f*; **word of ~** fides *f*; **~s** iusta *n/pl.*; honoro 1; honesto 1; in honore habeo 2; orno 1, colo 3; **~able** honestus.
hood cucullus *m*; **~wink** ludificor 1.
hoof ungula *f*.
hook hamus *m*; uncus *m*; hamo capio 3; **~ed** aduncus.
hoop circulus *m*.
hoot cano 3; *fig.* obstrepo 3 (*alci*).
hop salio 4.

hope spero 1 (*alqd, acc. c. inf.*); exspecto 1 (*alqd*); spes *f*; **lose, give up ~** despero 1.
horizon prospectus, us *m*; **~tal** aequus.
horn cornu *n*; bucina *f*; corneus; **~ed** cornutus.
horri|ble horribilis, atrox, foedus; **~fy** terreo 2; percello 3.
horror horror *m*, pavor *m*.
horse equus *m*; **on ~back** (in) equo; **~man** eques *m*; **~-race** certamen *n* equorum; **~shoe** solea *f*; **~-whip** flagellum *n*.
hose tibiale *n*.
hospit|able hospitalis; **~al** valetudinarium *n*; **~ality** hospitium *n*; liberalitas *f*.
host hospes *m*; multitudo *f*; **~age** obses *m*; **~elry** caupona *f*; **~ess** hospita *f*.
hostil|e hostilis; inimicus, infestus, infensus; **~ity** inimicitiae *f/pl.*; **~ities** bellum *n*.
hot calidus; aestuosus; **be ~** caleo 2; aestuo 1; **~-headed** fervidus, calidus.
hound canis *m or f* (venaticus); **~ on** stimulo 1, agito 1.
hour hora *f*; **half an ~** semihora *f*; **from ~ to ~** in horas; **~-glass** horologium *n*.
house domus, us *f*; domicilium *n*; aedes *f*; tectum *n*; **at my ~** apud me; domo excipio 3; condo 3; **~-breaker** fur *m*; **~hold** familia *f*; **~hold gods** Lares *m/pl.*, Penates *m/pl.*; **~keeper** dispensator *m*; **~-maid** ancilla *f*; **~wife** materfamilias *f*.
hovel gurgustium *n*.
hover (circum)volito 1; *fig.* obversor 1 (*alci*; *ante alqm*).
how quomodo, quemadmodum; *int.* quam, ut; **~ much** quantus; **~ many** quot; **~ever** utcumque; tamen.
howl ululo 1; ululatus, us *m*.
hubbub clamor *m*.
huckster institor *m*.
huddled together confertus.
hue color *m*.
huff: be in a ~ stomachor 1.
hug amplector 3; complexus, us *m*.
huge ingens, vastus, immanis.
hull alveus *m* (navis).
hum murmuro 1; musso 1; bombus *m*; fremitus, us *m*.
human humanus; **~ beings** homines *m/pl.*; **~e** humanus; **~ity** humanitas *f*; genus *n* humanum.
humble humilis; demissus; deprimo 3.
humbug tricae *f/pl.*
humid umidus.
humili|ate deprimo 3; **~ation** dedecus *n*; **~ating** indignus; **~ty** modestia *f*.
humorous facetus, festivus.
humour ingenium *n*; facetiae *f/pl.*; **be in the ~ to** libet 2 (*alci c. inf.*); morem gero 3 (*alci*); gratificor 1.
hump gibba *f*.
hunchbacked gibber.
hundred centum; **a ~ times** centies; **~th** centesimus.
hunger fames *f*; inedia *f*; esurio 4.
hungry ieiunus.
hunt venor 1; venatus, us *m*, venatio *f*; **~er** venator *m*; **~ing spear** venabulum *n*; **~ress** venatrix *f*.
hurdle crates f.
hurl conicio 3 (*in*); iaculor 1.
hurricane procella *f*.
hurr|ied praeceps; praeproperus; **~iedly** raptim; **~y** *v/i.* festino 1, propero 1, curro 3; *v/t.* rapio 3; festinatio *f*.
hurt noceo 2; laedo 3; doleo 2; **be ~** acerbe fero 3 (*alqd*); **~ful** noxius.
husband maritus *m*; vir *m*; **~man** agricola *m*; **~ry** agri cultura *f*; parsimonia *f*.
hush st!, tace, tacete; sedo 1; **~ up** celo 1.
husk folliculus *m*; vagina *f*.
husky raucus.
hustle trudo 3.
hut tugurium *n*; casa *f*.
hutch cavea *f*.
hyena hyaena *f*.
hymeneal nuptialis.
hymn carmen *n*; cano 3.
hyperbole superlatio *f*.
hypocri|sy (dis)simulatio *f*; **~te** (dis)simulator *m*; **~tical** simulatus, fictus.
hypothesis sumptio *f*; **on this ~** hoc posito.

I

I ego.
ic|e glacies *f*; **~icle** stiria *f*; **~y** glacialis, gelidus.
idea notio *f*; notitia *f*; imago *f*; **~l** perfectus; exemplum *n*.
identi|cal idem; **~fy** agnosco 3.
ides idus, uum *f/pl.*
idiocy fatuitas *f*.
idiom proprietas *f* (linguae); **~atic** proprius.
idiot imbecillus, fatuus (homo *m*).
idle otiosus, vacuus; deses, ignavus; (*of things*) vanus, irritus; **be ~** cesso 1, vaco 1; **~ness** pigritia *f*, desidia *f*.
idol simulacrum *n*; *fig.* deliciae *f/pl.*; **~ise** veneror 1.
if si; **~ not** sin, si minus; **~ ... not** nisi; **~ only** dummodo; **but, even ~** quod si, etiamsi; **I ask ~** rogo 1 num.
ignite *v/t.* accendo 3; *v/i.* exardesco 3.
ignoble ignobilis; turpis.
ignominious turpis.
ignor|ance ignoratio *f*, ignorantia *f*; inscitia *f*; **~ant** ignarus, imprudens (*gen.*); rudis; **be ~ant** ignoro 1; nescio 4; **~e** praetereo 4; neglego 3.
ill aeger, aegrotus; malus; malum *n*; **be ~** aegroto 1; laboro 1; morbo afficior 3; **speak ~ of** maledico 3 (*alci*); **~-advised** temerarius; **~-bred** inhumanus, agrestis.
illegal contra leges.
illegitimate spurius, haud legitimus.
ill-|fated infelix; **~ health** valetudo *f*.
illiterate illiteratus, indoctus.
ill|natured malevolus; **~ness** morbus *m*; valetudo *f*; **~omened** dirus, infaustus; **~ temper** stomachus *m*; **~-tempered** iracundus, difficilis.
illuminate illustro 1.
illus|ion error *m*; species *f*; **~ory** vanus.
illustrat|e illustro 1; **~ion** exemplum *n*.
illustrious praeclarus, illustris.
image imago *f*; simulacrum *n*; effigies *f*; species *f*.
imagin|ary commenticius; **~ation** cogitatio *f*; **~e** animo fingo 3; puto 1.
imbue imbuo 3, inficio 3 (*alqd alqa re*).
imitat|e imitor 1; effingo 3; **~ion** imitatio *f*; imago *f*; **~or** imitator *m*.
immaculate integer.
immature crudus.
immeasurable immensus.
immediate praesens; proximus; **~ly** statim, protinus, continuo.
immense ingens, immanis.
immerse mergo 3.
immigrant advena *m*.
imminent praesens; **be ~** immineo 2.
immoderate immoderatus, nimius.
immodest impudicus.
immoral pravus, turpis; **~ity** pravitas *f*; luxus, us *m*.
immortal immortalis; aeternus; **~ity** immortalitas *f*.
immovable immobilis.
immun|e immunis; **~ity** immunitas *f*.
immure includo 3.
impair infringo 3; imminuo 3; elevo 1.
impart impertio 4 (*alci alqd*); communico 1 (*cum alqo*).
impartial aequus, integer; **~ity** aequitas *f*.
impassable invius.
impatien|ce ardor *m*; **~t** impatiens (*gen.*); avidus (**for** *gen.*); **be ~t for** gestio 4 (*inf.*).
impeach accuso 1; postulo 1.
impediment impedimentum *n*; **~ of speech** haesitantia *f* (linguae).
impel impello 3 (*ad alqd*, *ut*).
impend impendeo 2; **~ing** praesens, futurus.
impenetrable invius, inaccessus.
imperative necessarius.
imperceptibly sensim.
imperfect imperfectus; mancus, mendosus; **~ion** vitium *n*.
imperial imperatorius; augustus.
imperious imperiosus.
imperishable immortalis.
impersonate partes sustineo 2 (*alcs*).

impertinen|ce contumelia *f*; os *n*; **~t** contumeliosus.
imperturbable tranquillus.
impervious (to) surdus (ad).
impetuous acer, fervidus.
impetus vis *f*.
impious nefarius, impius.
implacable implacabilis; atrox.
implant insero 3.
implement instrumentum *n*.
implicate implico 1; **be ~d** affinis, conscius sum.
implicit tacitus.
implore oro 1, obsecro 1.
impl|y: be ~ied in inest (in).
impolite inhumanus.
import importo 1 (*in*); significatio *f*; **~s** merces *f/pl.* (importaticiae).
importan|ce momentum *n*, pondus *n*; **be of ~ce** interest (**to me** mea); **~t** gravis, magnus; amplus.
importun|ate improbus; **~e** flagito 1.
impos|e impono 3 (*alqd alci*); **~e upon** impono 3 (*alci*); **~ition** fraus *f*.
impossible: it is ~ fieri non potest (*quin*).
impostor planus *m*.
imprecation preces *f/pl.*
impregna|ble inexpugnabilis; **~te** inicio 3.
impress (per)moveo 2; inculco 1; imprimo 3; **~ion** impressio *f*; opinio *f*; **~ive** gravis.
imprison in vincula, carcerem conicio 3; includo 3; **~ment** vincula *n/pl.*
improbable haud veri similis.
improper indecorus.
improve *v/t.* corrigo 3; meliorem facio 3, reddo 3; *v/i.* melior fio; proficio 3.
improvident improvidus.
imprudence temeritas *f*, imprudentia *f*.
impuden|ce impudentia *f*; os *n*; **~t** impudens.
impugn impugno 1.
impulse impulsus, us *m*; impetus, us *m*.
impunity: with ~ impune.
impure impurus.
impute do 1, attribuo 3, imputo 1 (*alci qlqd*).
in in (*abl.*); **~ Rome** Romae; **~ summer** aestate; **~ the writings of** apud (*alqm*); **~ that** quod.
in|accessible invius; difficilis; **~accurate** parum diligens; **~action** otium *n*; **~active** iners; **~activity** inertia *f*.
in|adequate impar (*dat.*); **~advertently** per imprudentiam; **~animate** inanimus; **~appropriate** parum aptus.
inasmuch as quoniam; **~ he** quippe qui.
in|attentive parum attentus; **~augural** aditialis; **~augurate** inauguro 1; **~auspicious** dirus; **~cantation** carmen *n*.
incapa|ble: be ~ble of non possum; alienus sum (ab); **~city** inscitia *f*.
in|cautious incautus; **~cense** tus *n*; incendo 3 (*ira*); **~centive** incitamentum *n*; **~cessant** continuus, assiduus; **~cest** incestum *n*.
inch uncia *f*.
incident casus, us *m*; res *f*; **~ally** casu.
incite incito 1; **~ment** stimulus *m*.
in|civility inhumanitas *f*; **~clement** asper.
inclin|ation voluntas *f*; animus *m*; studium *n*; **~e** inclino 1; induco 3; clivus *m*; **be favourably ~ed to** inclinor 1 ad; **I am ~ed to think** haud scio 4 an, nescio 4 an.
include includo 3; ascribo 3.
incom|e vectigal *n*; **~parable** singularis; **~patible** repugnans; **~petence** inscitia *f*; **~plete** imperfectus.
incon|clusive infirmus; **be ~gruous** discrepo 1; **~siderate** inconsideratus; **~sistent** inconstans; absonus, alienus (*ab*); **~stant** inconstans, levis; **~venience** incommodum *n*; incommodo 1 (*alci*); **~venient** incommodus.
in|corporate contribuo 3; ascribo 3; **~correct** falsus, mendosus; **~correctly** perperam, prave; **~corrigible** perditus; **~corruptible** integer.
increase *v/t.* augeo 2; amplifico 1; *v/i.* cresco 3; incrementum *n*.
incred|ible incredibilis; **~ulous** incredulus.
in|criminate culpam (*in alqm*) transfero 3; **~culcate** inculco 1.
incur suscipio 3; incurro 3 (*alqd*).
in|curable insanabilis; **~cursion** incursio *f*.

indebted obnoxius; **be ~** pecuniam debeo 2 (*alci*); *fig.* acceptum refero 3 (*alqd alci*).

indecen|cy turpitudo *f*; **~t** turpis.

indeci|sion dubitatio *f*; **~sive** dubius, anceps.

indeed quidem; vero; ain' (vero)?

inde|fatigable impiger; **~finable** nescio quis; **~finite** infinitus.

indelicate putidus.

indemnify damnum sarcio 4; remuneror 1.

independen|ce libertas *f*; **~t** liber, solutus; sui iuris (*homo*).

inde|structible perennis; **~terminate** anceps, dubius.

index index *m*.

indicat|e indico 1, significo 1; **~ion** indicium *n*; signum *n*.

indict accuso 1; reum facio 3; **~ment** accusatio *f*; crimen *n*.

indifferen|ce aequus animus *m*; neglegentia *f*; **~t** neglegens; (*of things*) indifferens; **be ~t to** parvi facio 3 (*alqd*).

indi|genous indigena; **~gent** inops; **~gestible** gravis; **~gestion** cruditas *f*.

indign|ant: be ~ indignor 1 (*alqd*); stomachor 1 (*alqa re*); **~ation** indignatio *f*; ira *f*; **~ity** contumelia *f*, indignitas *f*.

indirect obliquus.

indis|creet imprudens; **~criminate** promiscuus; *adv.* passim.

indispos|ed aegrotus; **~ition** valetudo *f*.

indis|putable certus; **~tinct** obscurus, obtusus.

individual proprius; singuli.

indolen|ce inertia *f*; **~t** iners.

indomitable invictus.

indoor domesticus; **~s** domi.

induce adduco 3, induco 3 (*alqm ut*); persuadeo 2 (*alci ut*); **~ment** praemium *n*; illecebra *f*.

indulge indulgeo 2 (*dat.*); morem gero 3 (*alci*); expleo 2 (*alqd*); **~nce** indulgentia *f*; venia *f*; **~nt** indulgens, remissus.

industr|ious industrius, sedulus, navus; **~y** industria *f*.

inebriated ebrius.

in|effectual irritus; **~efficient** invalidus; **~ept** ineptus; **~ert** segnis, immobilis; **~ertness** segnitia *f*; **~evitable** necessarius; **~exhaustible** infinitus; **~exorable** inexorabilis, durus; **~expensive** vilis.

inexper|ience imperitia *f*; **~ienced** imperitus, rudis (*gen.*); **~t** inscitus.

in|explicable inexplicabilis; **~expressible** infandus; **~fallible** certus.

infam|ous infamis; flagitiosus; **~y** flagitium *n*.

infan|cy (prima) pueritia *f*, infantia *f*; **~t** infans *m and f*; **~tile** infans; **~try** pedes *m/sg. and pl.*, pedites *m/sg. and pl.*; peditatus, us *m*; pedester.

infatuat|ed demens; **~ion** dementia *f*.

infect inficio 3; **~ion** contagio *f*.

infer colligo 3; **~ence** coniectura *f*.

inferior inferior, deterior; impar (*dat.*).

infernal infernus; **~ regions** inferi *m/pl.*

infinit|e infinitus, immensus; **~y** infinitas *f*.

infirm infirmus, imbecillus; **~ity** infirmitas *f*.

inflam|e in-, ac-cendo 3; **be ~ed** flagro 1; **~matory** turbulentus.

inflat|e inflo 1; **be ~ed** turgeo 2; **~ion** tumor *m*.

inflexib|ility pertinacia *f*; **~le** obstinatus, rigidus.

inflict infero 3; impono 3 (*alqd alci*); **~ punishment** poenam sumo 3 (*de alqo*).

influen|ce momentum *n*; auctoritas *f*; **have ~ce with** possum apud; moveo 2; **~tial** gravis, amplus.

inform certiorem facio 3 (*alqm*); doceo 2; **be ~ed** cognosco 3; **~ against** nomen defero 3 (*alcs*); **~ation** nuntius *m*; **~er** delator *m*, index *m*.

infringe violo 1, imminuo 3; **~ment** imminutio *f*.

infuse infundo 3.

ingen|ious sollers; **~uity** sollertia *f*; **~uous** ingenuus.

inglorious inglorius, turpis.

ingrained insitus.

ingrati|ate gratiam ineo 4 (*apud alqm*); **~tude** ingratus animus *m*.

inhabit teneo 2, incolo 3; habito 1; **~able** habitabilis; **~ant** incola *m and f*.

inhere inhaereo 2 (*re, in re*); insum.

inherit hereditatem adeo 4, capio 3; **~ance** hereditas *f*; **~ed** hereditarius.

inhospitable inhospitalis; inhumanus.

inhuman immanis, crudelis.
iniquit|ous improbus; **~y** scelus *n*.
initia|l primus; **~te** initio 1 (*alqm alci rei*).
injudicious inconsultus.
injunction mandatum *n*.
injur|e noceo 2, obsum (*dat*.); laedo 3; **~ious** noxius, gravis; **~y** damnum *n*, incommodum *n*; vulnus *n*; iniuria *f*.
injustice iniustitia *f*; iniuria *f*.
ink atramentum *n*.
inland mediterraneus, interior.
inlet aestuarium *n*.
inmate inquilinus *m*.
inmost intimus.
inn caupona *f*; deversorium *n*.
innate insitus, innatus.
inner interior.
innkeeper caupo *m*.
innocen|ce innocentia *f*; **~t** innocens; insons; castus.
innovat|e novo 1; **~ion** res *f/pl*. novae.
innumerable innumerabilis.
inoffensive innocens.
inopportune inopportunus.
inordinate immoderatus.
inquir|e quaero 3 (*alqd ab, de, alqo*); percontor 1 (*alqd ab alqo*; *alqm de re*); interrogo 1 (*alqm*); **~e into** inquiro 3 (*in alqd*); **~y** percontatio *f*, interrogatio *f*; quaestio *f*.
inquisitive percontator *m*.
inroad incursio *f*; **make an ~** incurro 3 (*in*).
insan|e insanus, vecors; **~ity** insania *f*.
insatiable insatiabilis.
inscri|be inscribo 3 (*alqd in re*); **~ption** inscriptio *f*; titulus *m*.
insect insectum *n*.
insecure instabilis.
insensib|ility lentitudo *f*; **~le** lentus.
insert insero 3 (*alqd in alqd, dat*.); includo 3 (*in re, in rem*).
inside intra (*acc*.); *adv*. intus; interiora *n/pl*.
insight cognitio *f*.
insignia insignia *n/pl*.
in|significant exiguus; nullius momenti; **~sincere** fictus, simulatus.
insinuate me insinuo 1 (*alci*); significo 1.
insipid insulsus, frigidus.
insist flagito 1; urgeo 2; insto 1.
insolen|ce insolentia *f*, contumacia *f*; **~** superbus.
insolvent: be ~ decoquo 3.
insomuch adeo (*ut*).
inspect inspicio 3; recenseo 2 (*exercitum*); **~ion** recensio *f*, recognitio *f*; **~or** curator *m*.
inspir|ation afflatus, us *m*; instinctus, us *m*; **~e** *fig*. inicio 3, incutio 3 (*alci alqd*); **~ed** instinctus (*re*).
instal|l inauguro 1; **~ment** pensio *f*.
instance *n* exemplum; **for ~** verbi gratia.
instant praesens; momentum *n* (temporis); **~ly** continuo, statim.
instead of pro (*abl*.); loco (*gen*.).
instigat|e instigo 1; **at your ~ion** instigante, auctore te.
instil instillo 1.
instinct impetus, us *m*; natura *f*; **~ive** naturalis.
institut|e in-, con-stituo 3; **~ion** institutum *n*.
instruct instituo 3; doceo 2; praecipio 3; mando 1 (*alci ut*); **~ion** institutio *f*; mandatum *n*; **~ive** utilis; **~or** magister *m*.
instrument instrumentum *n*; organum *n*; machina *f*; **~ality: by your ~** tua opera.
insubordinate seditiosus.
insufferable intolerabilis.
insufficien|cy inopia *f*; **~t** non satis (magnus).
insulate segrego 1.
insult probrum *n*; contumelia *f*; contumeliam impono 3 (*alci*), iacio 3 (*in alqm*); **~ing** contumeliosus.
insupportable intolerabilis.
insure caveo 2 (*ut*).
insur|gent turbulentus, seditiosus; **~rection** tumultus, us *m*; defectio *f*.
intact integer, incolumis.
integr|al necessarius; **~ity** integritas *f*, innocentia *f*.
intell|ect mens *f*; ingenium *n*; **~igence** mens *f*; intellegentia *f*; ingenium *n*; sollertia *f*; **~igent** intellegens; ingeniosus.
intempera|nce intemperantia *f*; **~te** intemperans, immoderatus.
intend in animo habeo 2, in animo est (mihi) (*inf*.); destino 1 (*alqd*).
intense magnus, acer.
intens|ify incendo 3; **~ity** vis *f*; ardor *m*.
intent intentus (*re, in re*); totus (*in re*); **be ~ on** animum intendo 3 in (*re*); **~ion** consilium *n*; **~ionally**

consulto; de industria; **~ness** intentio *f.*
inter sepelio 4.
intercalary intercalarius.
intercede deprecor 1 (**for** alqm; *ut, ne*).
intercept intercipio 3; excipio 3.
intercession deprecatio *f.*
interchange commuto 1 (*inter se*); vices *f/pl.*; vicissitudo *f.*
intercourse usus, us *m*; consuetudo *f*; commercium *n.*
interdict interdico 3 (*alci alqa re, alci alqd*).
interest delecto 1; capio 3; **~ oneself** incumbo 3 (*dat.*); utilitas *f*; commodum *n*; **it is of ~** interest (*alcs, ad alqd*); studium *n*; faenus *n* (*on money*); **gain the ~ of** gratiam concilio 1 (*alcs*); **~ing** iucundus.
interfere me interpono 3 (*dat., in alqd*); intercedo 3, intervenio 4 (*dat.*); **~nce** intercessio *f.*
interim: in the ~ interim.
interior interior; pars *f* interior; interiora *n/pl.*
interlude *thea.* embolium *n.*
intermedia|ry internuntius *m*; **~te** medius.
interment sepultura *f.*
intermingle misceo 2.
intermission intermissio *f*; **without ~** assidue.
internal intestinus, domesticus; interior.
interpose interpono 3; intercedo 3.
interpret interpretor 1; explano 1; **~ation** interpretatio *f*; **~er** interpres *m.*
interrogat|e interrogo 1; **~ion** interrogatio *f*; quaestio *f.*
interrupt interrumpo 3 (*orationem, etc.*); interpello 1 (*alqm*); **~ion** interpellatio *f.*
intersperse misceo 2.
interval spatium *n* (*inter*); intervallum *n*; **after an ~ of a year** anno interiecto; **in the ~** interim.
interven|e intercedo 3, intersum; interpello 1; intervenio 4; **~ing** medius; **~tion** intercessio *f.*
interview admitto 3; colloquor 3 (*cum alqo, inter se*); colloquium *n.*
intestate intestatus.
intestines intestina *n/pl.*
intima|cy familiaritas *f*, necessitudo *f*; **~te** familiaris; intimus *m*; significo 1; **~tion** denuntiatio *f.*
intimidat|e terreo 2; **~ion** minae *f/pl.*
into in (*acc.*).
intolera|ble intolerabilis; **~nt** intolerans.
intoxicat|ed ebrius; **~ion** ebrietas *f.*
intrench vallo et fossa munio 4; **~ment** vallum *n*, munimentum *n.*
intrepid intrepidus, fortis; **~ity** fortitudo *f.*
intricate implicatus.
intrigue dolus *m*; fallaciae *f/pl.*
introduc|e intro-, in-duco 3; inveho 3; **~tion** inductio *f*; *liter.* prooemium *n*, exordium *n*; praefatio *f*; **give an ~ion** commendo 1 (*alqm alci*); **letter of ~ion** litterae *f/pl.* commendaticiae.
intrude inculco 1 (*me alci*).
inundat|e inundo 1; **~ion** diluvies *f*, diluvium *n.*
inure duro 1.
invade invado 3 (*in*); bellum infero 3 (*dat.*).
invalid aegrotus (*homo*); irritus; **~ate** infirmo 1; labefacto 1.
invaluable inaestimabilis.
invariable constans.
invasion irruptio *f.*
invective convicium *n.*
inveigh against invenor 3 (*in*); insector 1, incesso 3.
inveigle pellicio 3.
invent reperio 4; excogito 1; **~ion** inventum *n*; commentum *n*; **~or** inventor *m*, auctor *m.*
invert inverto 3.
invest inauguro 1 (*alqm magistratum*); addo 3 (*alqd alci rei*); circumsedeo 2 (*urbem, etc.*); colloco 1 (*pecuniam in re*).
investigat|e investigo 1; quaero 3; **~ion** investigatio *f*; quaestio *f.*
inveterate inveteratus.
invidious invidiosus, invisus.
invigorate corroboro 1; confirmo 1.
in|vincible invictus; **~violate** inviolatus, sacrosanctus; **~visible** obscurus, caecus.
invit|ation invitatio *f*; **~e** invito 1, voco 1 (*alqm in, ad*); arcesso 3; **~ing** gratus, blandus.
invoke invoco 1, imploro 1.
involuntar|y coactus; **~ily** imprudenter; haud sponte.
involve contineo 2; affero 3; admisceo 2; **be ~d in** versor 1, implicor 1 (*abl.*).

inward interior; **~ly** penitus.
irascible iracundus.
ire ira *f.*
irk piget 2 (*me alcs rei*); **~some** molestus.
iron ferrum *n*; ferreus; **~s** vincula *n/pl.*; **~mongery** ferramenta *n/pl.*
irony ironia *f*; dissimulatio *f.*
irrational fatuus; brutus.
irreconcilable repugnans.
ir|recoverable irreparabilis; **~refutable** certissimus.
irregular inaequabilis, incompositus, tumultuarius (*milites*).
irrelevant: be ~ nihil attinet.
ir|religious impius; **~reparable** irreparabilis; **~reproachable** integer; **~resistible** invictus; **~resolute** dubius; **~revocable** irrevocabilis.
irrigat|e irrigo 1; **~ion** irrigatio *f.*
irrita|ble stomachosus; **~te** stomachum moveo 2 (*alci*); irrito 1; **~tion** stomachus *m.*
island insula *f*; **~er** insulanus *m.*
isolate intercludo 3; secerno 3.
issue *v/i.* evenio 4; *v/t.* edo 3; metior 4 (*frumentum*); **~ forth** egredior 3; eventus, us *m*; exitus, us *m*; egressus, us *m*; res *f*; liberi *m/pl.*; **the main ~** summa *f.*
it id.
itch prurio 4; *fig.* gestio 4; prurigo *f.*
iterat|e itero 1; **~ion** iteratio *f.*
itinerant vagus.
ivory ebur *n*; eburneus.
ivy hedera *f.*

J

jackdaw monedula *f.*
Jack-of-all-trades omnis Minervae homo *m.*
jaded defessus.
jagged scopulosus.
jail carcer, eris *n*; **~er** custos *m.*
jam conditae baccae *f/pl.*
jamb postis *m.*
January Ianuarius (mensis) *m.*
jar discrepo 1; olla *f*; cadus *m* (*wine*); **a~** semiapertus; **~ring** discors, dissonus.
jaunty hilaris.
javelin pilum *n*, iaculum *n.*
jaw malae *f/pl.*; maxilla *f*; *fig.* fauces *f/pl.*
jealous invidus, aemulus; **be ~ of** invideo 2 (*alci*); **~y** invidia *f*, aemulatio *f.*
jeer cavillor 1, derideo 2; irrisio *f.*
jeopard|ise periclitor 1; **~y** periculum *n.*
jest iocor 1; cavillor 1; iocus *m*; **in ~** per iocum; **~er** cavillator *m*, sannio *m*, scurra *m.*
jet: ~ of water aqua *f* saliens; **~-black** niger; **~ty** moles *f*, crepido *f.*
Jew Iudaeus *m.*
jewel gemma *f*; **~led** gemmeus; **~ler** aurifex *m.*
Jewish Iudaicus.
jibe convicium *n.*
jilt repudio 1.
jingle tinnio 4.
job opus *n*; negotium *n.*
jockey eques *m.*
joc|ose iocosus; **~und** hilaris.
join (con)iungo 3; connecto 3; me adiungo 3 (*alci*, *ad*); **~ in** intersum (*dat.*); **~ together** coeo 4; **~er** faber, bri *m.*
joint commissura *f*; articulus *m*; nodus *m*; communis.
joist tignum *n.*
joke iocus *m*; iocatio *f*; iocor 1 (*de*); cavillor 1.
jolly hilaris, festivus.
jolt quasso 1, iacto 1; iactatio *f.*
jostle trudo 3.
jot: not a ~ ne pilus quidem; **I don't care a ~** non pili facio 3 (*alqd*).
journal ephemeris *f*; commentarii *m/pl.*
journey iter, ineris *n*; iter facio 3; proficiscor 3.
jovial hilaris.
joy gaudium *n*; laetitia *f*; gaudeo 2; **~ful** laetus.
jubilant exsultans.
judge iudico 1; reor 2, existimo 1, aestimo 1; iudex *m*, quaesitor *m*; existimator *m*; **~ment** iudicium *n*; arbitrium *n*; **pronounce ~ment** ius dico 3; **good ~ment** consilium *n.*
judic|ial iudicialis, iudiciarius, forensis; **~ious** prudens.
juic|e sucus *m*; **~y** sucosus.
jug urceus *m.*
juggl|er praestigiator *m*; **~ing** praestigiae *f/pl.*
July Quintilis (mensis) *m*; Iulius (mensis) *m.*
jumble confundo 3.
jump salio 4; saltus, us *m.*
juncture tempus *n.*
June (mensis) Iunius *m.*
jungle loca *n/pl.* obsita (*virgultis etc.*).
junior minor natu.
juniper iuniperus, i *f.*
juris|consult iuris consultus *m*; **~diction** iurisdictio *f*; **~t** iuris consultus *m.*
jur|or iudex *m*; **~y** iudices *m/pl.*
just iustus, aequus; meritus; *adv.* vix; modo; **~ as** perinde ac; **~ when** cum maxime; commodum ... cum.
just|ice iustitia *f*; **~ifiably** iure; **~ification** purgatio *f*; **~ify** purgo 1, excuso 1.
jut| out exsto 1; promineo 2; **~ting** proiectus.
juvenile iuvenilis.

K

keel carina *f.*
keen acer, sagax; studiosus; **~ness** sagacitas *f*, acies *f.*
keep teneo 2, retineo 2; servo 1 (*fidem etc.*); habeo 2; custodio 4; condo 3 (*frumentum etc.*); **~ accounts** tabulas conficio 3; **~ away** abstineo 2 (*me, alqm*); **~ company** congregor 1 (*cum*); **~ holiday** festum diem celebro 1; **~ in the dark** celo 1 (*alqd alqm*); **~ off** arceo 2; **~ up** tueor 2; **~up with** subsequor 3; arx *f*; **~er** custos *m*; **~ing** custodia *f*; **in ~ing with** conveniens (*dat.*); **~sake** pignus *n.*
keg cadus *m.*
kennel cubile *n.*
kerchief sudarium *n.*
kernel nucleus *m.*
kettle olla *f.*
key clavis *f*; **~hole** foramen *n.*
kick calce ferio 4, peto 3; calx *f.*
kid haedus *m.*
kidnap surripio 3.
kidneys renes *m/pl.*
kill interficio 3, occido 3, caedo 3; neco 1; **~ing** caedes *f.*
kiln fornax *f.*
kin propinqui *m/pl.*, necessarii *m/pl.*
kind benignus, comis; genus *n*; **of this ~** huiusmodi; **of such a ~** talis ... (qualis).
kindle *v/t.* ac-, in-cendo 3; inflammo 1; *v/i.* exardesco 3.
kindness benignitas *f*, comitas *f*; beneficium *n*; officium *n.*
kindred propinqui *m/pl.*, necessarii *m/pl.*; cognatus, consanguineus; *fig.* finitimus.
king rex *m*; **be ~** regno 1; **~dom** regnum *n*; **~ly** regius.
kinsman necessarius *m.*
kiss suavior 1, osculor 1; suavium *n*, osculum *n.*
kitchen culina *f.*
kite milvus *m.*
knack sollertia *f.*
knapsack sarcina *f.*
knav|e nebulo *m*, furcifer *m*, scelestus *m*; **~ery** nequitia *f*; **~ish** nequam, improbus.
knead subigo 3.
knee genu *n*; **~l** nitor 3 genibus.
knife culter *m.*
knight eques *m*; **~ly** equester.
knit: ~ the brows supercilium contraho 3.
knob bulla *f*; umbilicus *m*; nodus *m.*
knock pulso 1; ferio 4; **~ at the door** fores pulso 1; **~ down** sterno 3; (*at an auction*) addico 3 (*alqd alci*); pulsatio *f*; **~-kneed** varus.
knot nodus *m*; *fig.* vinculum *n*; (*of people*) circulus *m*; nodo 1; **~ty** nodosus.
know scio 4; (cog)nosco 3; **not to ~** nescio 4, ignoro 1; **be ~n** constat 1; **make ~n** declaro 1; **~ledge** scientia *f*; cognitio *f*; doctrina *f*; **without the ~ledge of** clam (*abl.*); **to my ~ledge** quod sciam; **well-~n** notus, celeber.

L

label titulus *m.*
laborious operosus.
labor laboro 1; contendo 3 (*inf.*); labor *m*; opera *f*; partus, us *m*; **~er** operarius *m*, mercenarius *m*.
lace necto 3; alligo 1.
lacerate lacero 1.
lack egeo 2, careo 2; mihi deest; inopia *f*; defectio *f*.
lackey pedisequus *m*.
lacking: be ~ deficio 3, desum.
lad puer *m*.
ladder scalae *f/pl*.
lade onero 1; **~n** onustus, gravis.
ladle trulla *f*.
lady matrona *f*, mulier *f*; **~ship** domina *f*, era *f*.
lag cesso 1; **~gard** cessator *m*.
lake lacus, us *m*; stagnum *n*.
lamb agnus *m*; (*meal*) agnina *f*.
lame claudus; **be ~** claudico 1; **~ness** claudicatio *f*.
lament lugeo 2; miseror 1; lamentor 1; **~able** miserandus; **~ation** lamentatio *f*; plangor *m*.
lamp lucerna *f*.
lampoon versus *m/pl*. probrosi, famosi.
lamprey murena *f*.
lampstand lychnuchus *m*.
lance hasta *f*, lancea *f*; telum *n*; incido 3.
land terra *f*, tellus, uris *f*; solum *n*; ager, gri *m*; terrestris; *v/t*. expono 3; *v/i*. egredior 3 (e nave).
land|ing egressus, us *m*; **~lady** caupona *f*; **~lord** caupo *m*; **~mark** lapis *m*; **~owner** (agri) possessor *m*; **~slide** lapsus, us *m* terrae; **~-tax** vectigal *n*.
lane angiportus, us *m*.
language lingua *f*; oratio *f*, verba *n/pl.*, sermo *m*.
langu|id languidus; **be ~id** langueo 2; **~ish** tabesco 3; **~or** lassitudo *f*.
lank strigosus.
lantern lanterna *f*.
lap gremium *n*; sinus, us *m*; lambo 3.
lapse labor 3; error *m*; **~ of time** spatium *n*.
larceny furtum *n*.
lard adeps *m*; laridum *n*; **~er** carnarium *n*.
large magnus, grandis, amplus, ingens; **~ss** donativum *n*; largitio *f*.
lark alauda *f*.
lascivious libidinosus.
lash flagello 1; flagellum *n*; verbera *n/pl*.
lass puella *f*.
lassitude lassitudo *f*.
last ultimus, postremus; extremus; **~ night** proxima nocte; **in the ~ three days** his tribus diebus; **~ but one** proximus a postremo; forma *f*; **at ~** postremo, ad extremum, demum, denique; duro 1; maneo 2; **~ing** diuturnus; **~ly** denique.
late serus; **~ at night** sera, multa nocte; **~ in life** provecta iam aetate; **the ~** (de)mortuus (*alqs*), recens (*alqd*); *adv*. sero; **~ly** nuper, modo, recens.
lath tignum *n*.
lathe tornus *m*.
lather spuma *f*.
Latin Latinus; **speak ~** Latine loquor 3.
latitude libertas *f*.
latter posterior; **the ~** hic; **~ly** nuper.
lattice cancelli *m/pl*.
laudable laudabilis.
laugh rideo 2; cachinno 1; **~ at** irrideo 2 (*acc.*); risus, us *m*; **~able** ridiculus; **~ing-stock** ludibrium *n*.
launch deduco 3 (*naves*); **~ at** iaculor 1 (*in*); inmitto 3 (*in*).
laurel laurus, i *f* (*tree and wreath*); laureus.
lavish pro-, ef-fusus; profundo 3; largior 4 (*alqd alci*).
law lex *f*; **the ~** ius *n*; **go to ~** litem intendo 3 (*alci*); **propose, enact a ~** fero 3, scisco 3 legem; **~ful** legitimus; **~less** seditiosus; **~lessness** licentia *f*.
lawn pratum *n*.
lawsuit lis *f*.
lawyer iuris consultus *m*.
lax dissolutus, remissior, neglegens; **~ness** neglegentia *f*.

lay pono 3; loco 1; edo 3 (*ova*); ~ **aside** repono 3; ~ **before** defero 3, propono 3; ~ **down arms** ab armis discedo 3; ~ **hold of** prehendo 3; ~ **plans** consilium capio 3, ineo 4; ~ **siege to** obsideo 2; ~ **upon** impono 3; ~ **waste** vasto 1; cantus, us *m*.
layer tabulatum *n*.
laz|iness pigritia *f*; ~**y** ignavus, piger.
lead[1] plumbum *n*; plumbeus.
lead[2] duco 3; ~ **back, out, round** re-, e-, circum-duco 3; ~ **a life** vitam ago 3; ~**er** dux *m*; **be** ~**er** praesum (*dat.*).
leading primus, princeps; ~ **men** principes *m/pl.*
leaf folium *n*; (*of book*) scheda *f*, pagina *f*; (*of door*) foris *f*; **be in** ~ frondesco 3; ~**y** frondosus.
league societas *f*; **be in** ~ conspiro 1, coniuro 1.
leak perfluo 3; rima *f*; ~**y** rimosus.
lean macer; (in)nitor 3 (*abl.*); incumbo 3 (*in alqd*); ~**ness** macies *f*.
leap salio 4; saltus, us *m*.
learn disco 3; cognosco 3, certior fio; ~**ed** doctus, eruditus; ~**ing** doctrina *f*, eruditio *f*.
lease conduco 3; loco 1; locatio *f*.
least minimus; **at** ~ saltem, certe.
leather corium *n*; scorteus.
leave relinquo 3, destituo 3 (*acc.*); discedo 3 (*ab*, *ex*); excedo 3 (*ex loco*); (*at death*) lego 1; ~ **off** desino 3; ~ **out** omitto 3; potestas *f*; ~ **of absence** commeatus, us *m*; **by your** ~ bona tua venia.
lecherous salax.
lecture schola *f*, acroasis *f*; scholas habeo 2; ~**-room** schola *f*.
ledge tabula *f*; pluteus *m*; ~**r** codex *m*.
leech hirudo *f*.
leek porrum *n*.
lees faex *f*.
left laevus, sinister; ~ **over** reliquus; **be** ~ **over** resto 1.
leg crus, uris *n*.
legacy legatum *n*; ~**-hunter** captator *m*.
legal legitimus; ex lege.
legate legatus *m*; legatio *f*.
legend fabula *f*; ~**ary** commenticius.
legion legio *f*; ~**ary** legionarius *m*.
legislate leges scribo 3.
legitimate legitimus; germanus.
leisure otium *n*; **at** ~ otiosus, vacuus; **be at** ~ vaco 1; ~**ly** lentus.
lend mutuum (*alqd*) do 1 (*alci*); commodo 1 (*alqd alci*).
length longitudo *f*; diurnitas *f* (temporis); **at** ~ tandem; demum; late, fuse (*loqui*); ~**en** produco 3; ~**wise** in longitudinem.
lenient mitis, lenis.
lentil lens *f*.
less minor; *adv.* minus; **much, still** ~ nedum (*subj.*); ~**ee** conductor *m*; ~**en** minuo 3.
lesson *fig.* documentum *n*; **take** ~**s** disco 3; audio 4 (*alqm*).
lessor locator *m*.
lest ne.
let permitto 3; sino 3; loco 1 (*agrum etc.*); ~ **alone** abstineo 2 (*me re*); ~ **down** demitto 3; ~ **loose, go** emitto 3.
lethargy veternus *m*.
letter littera *f*; epistola *f*, litterae *f/pl.*; ~**-carrier** tabellarius *m*.
lettuce lactuca *f*.
level planus, aequus; ~ **place** planities *f*; *fig.* gradus, us *m*; **make** ~ **with** exaequo 1 (*alqd alci rei*); sterno 3 (*muros*).
lever vectis *m*.
levity iocatio *f*.
levy delectus, us *m*; delectum habeo 2, scribo 3; impero 1 (*alqd alci*).
lewd incestus.
liable obnoxius (*dat.*).
liar (homo *m*) mendax.
libation libamentum *n*; **make** ~ libo 1.
libel diffamo 1; libellus *m* (famosus).
liberal liberalis, benignus; ~**ity** liberalitas *f*.
liberat|e solvo 3; libero 1; ~**ion** liberatio *f*.
liberty libertas *f*; **be at** ~ **to** licet 2 (*dat. c. inf.*).
library bibliotheca *f*.
licen|ce potestas *f*; venia *f*; licentia *f*; ~**se** potestatem do 1 (*alci*); ~**tious** libidinosus.
lick lambo 3, lingo 3.
lictor lictor *m*.
lid operculum *n*; **eye**~ palpebra *f*.
lie mentior 4 (*in alqa re*); iaceo 2; cubo 1, recumbo 3; (*of places*) situm esse; **as far as in me** ~**s** quantum in me est; ~ **in wait** insidior 1 (*dat.*); mendacium *n*.

lieu: in ~ of loco (*gen.*).
lieutenant legatus *m.*
life vita *f*; anima *f*; vigor *m*, viriditas *f*; **~(time)** aetas *f*; **in his ~time** vivus (*adj.*); **~less** exanimis; frigidus.
lift tollo 3; levo 1; sublevo 1; effero 3.
ligature ligamentum *n.*
light lux *f*; lumen *n*; **see in a good, unfavourable ~** in mitiorem, deteriorem partem accipio 3 (*alqd*); **set ~ to** accendo 3; illustris; levis; **grow ~** lucesco 3; **make ~** illustro 1; **make ~ of** contemno 3; **~ upon** offendo 3 (*acc.*); **~-armed troops** levis armatura *f*; velites *m/pl.*
lighten *v/t.* levo 1; *v/i.* fulguro 1, fulgeo 2.
light|house pharus, i *f*; **~ness** levitas *f*; **~ning** fulmen *n.*
like similis (*gen.*); par (*dat.*); *adv.* similiter (*ac*); modo, ritu (*gen.*); velut(i); me iuvat 1; amo 1 (*inf.*); mihi libet 2, placet 2; **~ly** veri similis; **it is ~ly** fieri potest (*ut*); **~n** comparo 1; **~ness** similitudo *f*; effigies *f*; **~wise** item.
liking animus *m.*
lily lilium *n.*
limb membrum *n*; articulus *m.*
lime calx *f*; **bird-~** viscum *n*; **~ tree** tilia *f.*
limit finis *m*; modus *m*; terminus *m*; finio 4; circumscribo 3; **~ed** circumscriptus, certus; **~less** infinitus.
limp claudico 1; languidus; **~et** lepas *f.*
limpid liquidus.
line linea *f*; (*battle*) acies *f*; (*of march*) agmen *n*; (*poetry*) versus, us *m*; **~s** ordines *m/pl.*; **~ up** in ordinem instruo 3, dispono 3.
line|age genus *n*; **~ament** lineamentum *n.*
linen linteum *n*; linteus, lineus.
linger moror 1, cunctor 1; **~ing** tardus.
link connecto 3; iungo 3; vinculum *n.*
lion leo *m*; **~ess** leaena *f.*
lip labrum *n*; *fig.* os *n.*
liqu|efy liquefacio 3; **~id** liquidus; liquidum *n*; liquor *m.*
lisping blaesus.
list tabula *f*; index *m.*
listen ausculto 1; audio 4; **~er** auditor *m.*
listless languidus.
litera|lly ad litteram; **~ture** litterae *f/pl.*
litigate litigo 1.
litter lectica *f*; fetus, us *m.*
little parvus, exiguus; (*time*) brevis; **for a ~ time** paulisper; **a ~** paulum; **too ~** parum.
live vivo 3, spiro 1; vitam ago 3; **~ in** habito 1 (*acc.*); **~ on, off** vescor 3 (*abl.*); vivus.
livel|ihood victus, us *m*; **~iness** alacritas *f*; **~y** alacer, laetus.
liver iecur *n.*
livid lividus.
living vivus; victus, us *m.*
lizard lacerta *f.*
lo ecce, en.
load onero 1 (*abl.*); *fig.* congero 3 (*alqd in alqm*); onus *n*; **~ed** onustus.
loaf panis *m.*
loam lutum *n.*
loan: make a ~ mutuum do 1 (*alqd*); **obtain a ~** mutuor 1 (*alqd*).
loath invitus.
loath|e odi; fastidio 4; **~ing** fastidium *n*; **~some** foedus, taeter.
lobby vestibulum *n.*
lobster locusta *f.*
locality locus *m.*
lock obsero 1; sera *f*; floccus *m*; **~ out** excludo 3; **~ up** concludo 3; **~s** crines *m/pl.*
locust locusta *f.*
lodge deversor 1, deverto 3 (*in, apud*); maneo 2; **~r** inquilinus *m*; deversor *m.*
lodging deversorium *n*, hospitium *n.*
loft cenaculum *n*; **~iness** excelsitas *f*; **~y** excelsus, altus, sublimis.
log tignum *n*; stipes *m.*
loggerheads: be at ~ discordo 1 (*ab, inter se*).
logic dialectica *f*; **~al** dialecticus; **~ian** dialecticus *m.*
loin lumbus *m.*
loiter cunctor 1, cesso 1.
lonel|iness solitudo *f*; **~y** solus, solitarius.
long longus; procerus; (*time*) diuturnus; promissus (*capillus*); *adv.* diu; **~ ago** iam pridem; **~ after, before** multo ante, post; **how ~** quamdiu; **~ to** aveo 2, gestio 4 (*inf.*); **~ for** desidero 1; **~ed-for** exspectatus; **~ing** desiderium *n.*
look speciem habeo 2, praebeo 2 (*honesti, ridentis, etc.*); **~ (at)**

aspicio 3; intueor 2 (*alqd*); ~ **after** colo 3; ~ **down (on)** despicio 3 (*acc.*); ~ **for** quaero 3; ~ **forward** exspecto 1; ~ **out!** cave; ~ **round** circumspicio 3; ~ **towards** specto 1; ~ **up (to)** suspicio 3; aspectus, us *m*; obtutus, us *m*; vultus, us *m*; **~er-on** spectator *m*; **~ing-glass** speculum *n*.
loom tela *f*.
loop retinaculum *n*; **~hole** fenestra *f*; locus *m*.
loose laxus, solutus; mobilis; *fig.* dissolutus; **let** ~ emitto 3; **~n** laxo 1; remitto 3; solvo 3; **~ness** pravitas *f*.
lop amputo 1; **~-sided** inaequalis.
loquacious loquax.
lord dominus *m*; ~ **it over** dominor 1 (*in*); **~ly** regius, superbus.
lore doctrina *f*.
lose amitto 3; perdo 3; ~ **heart** animo deficio 3; ~ **an opportunity** tempori desum; ~ **the day** vincor 3.
loss damnum *n*, detrimentum *n*; **be at a** ~ haereo 2.
lot sors *f*; *fig.* fortuna *f*; **by** ~ sorte, sortito; **cast ~s (for)** sortibus utor 3; sortior 4 (*acc.*); **it falls to my** ~ mihi contingit 3.
loud magnus, clarus.
lounge otior 1; desideo 2.
louse pediculus *m*; pedis *m*.
love amo 1, diligo 3; me iuvat 1, cordi est mihi (*alqd*, *inf.*); amor *m*; studium *n*; caritas *f*; **fall in** ~ **with** adamo 1; **~-affair** amor *m*; **~liness** venustas *f*; **~ly** venustus, amabilis; **~r** amator *m*; amans *m*.
loving amans.
low humilis, demissus; gravis; summissus; obscurus; sordidus, abiectus; mugio 4; **~-born** ignobilis; **~er** inferior; demitto 3; abicio 3; **~ering** minax; **~est** infimus, imus; **~ing** mugitus, us *m*; **~lands** loca *n*/*pl.* campestria; **~-spirited** demissus.
loyal fidelis, fidus; **~ty** fides *f*.
lozenge pastillus *m*.
lubricate ungo 3.
lucid lucidus, clarus.
luck fors *f*, fortuna *f*; **good** ~ felicitas *f*; **~less** infelix; **~y** felix, fortunatus; faustus.
lucrative fructuosus.
ludicrous ridiculus.
luggage impedimenta *n*/*pl.*; sarcinae *f*/*pl.*
lukewarm tepidus; frigidus.
lull sedo 1; sopio 4; **~aby** nenia *f*.
lumber scruta *n*/*pl.*
lumin|ary lumen *n*; **~ous** lucidus.
lump massa *f*; glaeba *f*; **~ish** crassus.
lun|acy insania *f*; **~ar** lunaris; **~atic** insanus.
lunch prandium *n*; ~ **(on)** prandeo 2.
lung pulmo *m*.
lurch: leave in the ~ derelinquo 3.
lure pellicio 3; esca *f*; illecebrae *f*/*pl.*
lurk lateo 2; latito 1.
luscious praedulcis.
lust libido *f*; **~ful** libidinosus.
lustra|l lustralis; **~tion** lustratio *f*.
lustre nitor *m*, splendor *m*.
lusty validus.
luxuri|ant luxuriosus; **~ous** lautus, delicatus.
luxury luxuria *f*, lautitia *f*; luxus, us *m*.
lying mendax; **~-in** puerperium *n*.
lynx lynx *m and f*; **~-eyed** lynceus.
lyre lyra *f*, cithara *f*; fides *f*/*pl.*; **~-player** citharoedus *m*.
lyric lyricus; carmen *n* lyricum.

M

machin|ations fallaciae *f/pl.*, artes *f/pl.*; **~e** machina *f*; **~ery** machinatio *f*.
mackerel scomber, bri *m*.
mad insanus; **be ~** furo 3.
madam domina *f*.
mad|den mentem alieno 1 (*alci*); irrito 1; **~man** homo *m* furiosus; **~ness** insania *f*; furor *m*.
magazine armamentarium *n*.
maggot vermiculus *m*.
magic magicus; magica ars *f*; **~ian** magus *m*.
magist|erial imperiosus; **~racy** magistratus, us *m*; **~rate** magistratus, us *m*.
magnanim|ity magnanimitas *f*; **~ous** magnanimus.
magnet lapis *m* magnes.
magnificen|ce magnificentia *f*; **~t** splendidus, lautus.
magni|fy amplifico 1; **~tude** magnitudo *f*.
magpie pica *f*.
maid virgo *f*, puella *f*; **~enly** virginalis, puellaris; **~servant** ancilla *f*.
mail squamae *f/pl.*; spongia *f*; litterae *f/pl.*; tabellarius.
maim mutilo 1; **~ed** mancus, truncus.
main praecipuus, primus; **~ point** summa *f*; **~ road** via *f*; pontus *m*; **~land** continens *f*; **~ly** plerumque, praecipue.
maintain conservo 1; sustineo 2; contendo 3, affirmo 1 (*alqd, acc. c. inf.*).
majest|ic augustus, regius; **~y** [maiestas *f*.]
major|-domo dispensator *m*; **~ity** plerique *m/pl.*; maior pars *f*.
make facio 3; fingo 3; reddo 3 (*mare tutum, alqm iratum*); cogo 3 (*alqm alqd facere*); **~ as if** simulo 1 (*acc. c. inf.*); **~ away with** tollo 3; **~ for** peto 3; **~ good** sarcio 4; **~ light of** contemno 3; **~ much of** magni facio 3; **~ up** expleo 2 (*numerum*); **~ up one's mind** certum est (*inf.*); **~ war** bellum infero 3; **~ way** decedo 3 (*alci*); **~r** fabricator *m*, creator *m*.
malady morbus *m*.
male mas, virilis.
malediction dirae *f/pl*.
malevolen|ce malevolentia *f*; **~t** malevolus.
malice malitia *f*.
malign obtrecto 1.
malleable ductilis, lentus.
mallet malleus *m*.
maltreat vexo 1.
man homo *m*; genus *n* humanum, mortales *m/pl.*; vir *m*; **our men** nostri *m/pl.*; compleo 2 (*naves*); **~servant** servus *m*.
manacle manica *f*.
manage curo 1; administro 1; gero 3; tracto 1; **~able** tractabilis; **~ment** cura *f*, administratio *f*; **~r** (pro)curator *m*; magister, tri *m*.
mane iuba *f*.
manful fortis.
manger praesaepe *n*.
mangle lanio 1.
manhood: reach ~ togam virilem sumo 3; **in ~** iuvenis, vir.
mania insania *f*.
manifest manifestus, apertus; declaro 1, ostendo 3.
manifold multiplex, varius.
maniple manipulus *m*.
manipulate tracto 1.
man|kind genus *n* humanum; **~liness** fortitudo *f*; **~ly** fortis.
manner modus *m*; ratio *f*; mos *m*; **~s** mores *m/pl.*; **~ed** affectatus.
manœuvre decursio *f*.
manor praedium *n*.
mansion domus, us *f*.
manslaughter caedes *f*.
mantle palla *f*.
manual libellus *m*.
manufacture fabrica *f*; fabricor 1.
manumi|ssion manumissio *f*; **~t** manumitto 3.
manure stercus *n*.
many multi, plerique; **a good ~** complures; **how ~** quot.
map tabula *f*; **~ out** describo 3.
maple acer, eris *n*.
mar deformo 1, corrumpo 3.
marauding praedatorius.

marble marmor *n*; marmoreus.
March (mensis) Martius *m*.
march iter facio 3; progredior 3; incedo 3; iter, ineris *n*; agmen *n*; **on the ~** in itinere.
mare equa *f*.
margin margo *f*.
marigold caltha *f*.
mari|ne marinus; (miles *m*) classicus; **~ner** nauta *m*; **~time** maritimus.
mark noto 1, operam do 1 (*dat.*); nota *f*; signum *n*, indicium *n*; **~ out** denoto 1; **~ed** gravis.
market forum *n*, macellum *n*; mercatus, us *m*; **~ (day)** nundinae *f/pl.*; nundinor 1; obsono 1.
marriage coniugium *n*; matrimonium *n*; nuptiae *f/pl.*; **~able** nubilis; **~-contract** pactio *f* nuptialis.
marrow medulla *f*.
marry (in matrimonium) duco 3 (*alqm uxorem*); nubo 3 (*alci viro*); colloco 1 (in matrimonium)(*filiam*); matrimonio iungor 3.
marsh palus, udis *f*; **~y** paluster.
marshal instruo 3.
martial bellicosus, bellicus.
marvel miror 1 (**at** *alqd*); **~lous** mirus.
masculine virilis, masculinus.
mash farrago *f*; contundo 3.
mask persona *f*; *fig.* integumentum *n*; dissimulo 1.
mason structor *m*.
mass moles *f*; multitudo *f*; vulgus, i *n*; congrego(r) 1.
massacre trucido 1; caedes *f*.
massive solidus.
mast malus *m*; glans *f*.
master dominus *m*, erus *m*; magister, tri *m* (*societatis, ludi, navis*); potens (*gen.*); peritus (*in re*); **be ~ of** potior 4 (*abl.*); domo 1; **~ful** imperiosus; **~ly** artificiosus; **~y** potestas *f*, victoria *f*.
masticate mando 3.
mat teges *f*; storea *f*.
match (ex)aequo 1, comparo 1; par sum; certamen *n*; **~less** singularis.
mate socius *m*; coeo 4.
material corporeus; materia *f*; textile *n*.
maternal maternus.
mathematic|al mathematicus; **~ian** mathematicus *m*.
matrimony matrimonium *n*.
matron matrona *f*; **~ly** matronalis.
matter corpus *n*; res *f*; materia *f*; **what is the ~?** quid est?; **it ~s** refert 3 (*parvi, magni, etc.*).
mattress culcita *f*.
matur|e adultus; maturus; maturo 1; **~ity** maturitas *f*.
maxim sententia *f*; praeceptum *n*.
May (mensis) Maius *m*.
may licet 2 (*alci*); possum (*inf.*); **~be** forsitan, fortasse.
mayor praefectus *m* urbi(s).
maze labyrinthus *m*.
me me; **to ~** mihi.
meadow pratum *n*.
meagre exilis, exiguus.
meal prandium *n*; farina *f*; **chief ~** cena *f*.
mean humilis; illiberalis; medius; in animo est (*mihi inf.*); significo 1, volo (mihi) (*verba etc.*); dico 3; medium *n*; mediocritas *f*; **~s** modus *m*; **by all ~s** omnino; **by no ~s** haudquaquam, nullo modo; **by ~s of per** (*acc.*); **~ing** significatio *f*; sententia *f*; **~ness** sordes *f*; humilitas *f*; **~while** interea, interim.
measure metior 4; mensura *f*; modus *m*; consilium *n*; **in some ~** aliqua ex parte; **take ~s** provideo 2 (*ut, ne*); **~d** moderatus; **~ment** mensura *f*.
meat caro, carnis *f*.
mechani|c faber, bri *m*; **~sm** machina *f*.
meddle me immisceo 2 (*alci rei*).
mediat|e me interpono 3; **~or** deprecator *m*; intercessor *m*.
medic|al medicinus; **~ate** medico 1; **~ine** medicina *f*; medicamentum *n*, medicamen *n*.
mediocr|e mediocris; **~ity** mediocritas *f*.
meditat|e volvo 3; cogito 1 (*de*); in animo est mihi (*inf.*); **~ion** cogitatio *f*.
medium medius, mediocris; modus *m*.
medley farrago *f*.
meed praemium *n*.
meek mitis, demissus; **~ness** animus *m* demissus.
meet aptus, accommodatus (*ad*); obviam fio (*alci*); convenio 4 (*alqm*); incido 3 (*alci*); oppeto 3 (*mortem etc.*); **go to ~** obviam eo 4 (*alci*); **~ together** convenio 4; **~ing** coetus, us *m*; conventus, us *m*; contio *f*.
melancholy tristis; tristitia *f*.

mellow mitis, maturus, lenis; maturesco 3.
melod|ious canorus; **~y** modus *m*; cantus, us *m*.
melon melopepo *m*.
melt *v/t.* liquefacio 3; *v/i.* liquefio, liquesco 3; **~ away** dilabor 3.
member membrum *n*; socius *m*.
memor|able memorabilis; insignis; **~ial** monumentum *n*; **~y** memoria *f*; recordatio *f*.
menac|e minor 1 (*alci alqd*); minae *f/pl.*; **~ing** minax.
mend *v/t.* sarcio 4; emendo 1; corrigo 3; *v/i.* melior fio.
mendacious mendax.
mendicant mendicus.
menial sordidus; mediastinus *m*.
mention (com)memoro 1; mentionem facio 3 (*gen.*, *de*); **not to ~** ne dicam; mentio *f*.
mercenary mercenarius, conductus (miles *m*).
merchan|dise merx *f*; res *f/pl.* venales; **~t** mercator *m*; **~t-ship** navis *f* oneraria.
merc|iful clemens, misericors; **~iless** durus; **~y** misericordia *f*, venia *f*; **show ~y** ignosco 3.
mere merus, unus; lacus, us *m*.
merge confundo 3.
merit mereo(r) 2; meritum *n*; virtus utis *f*; **~ed** meritus.
merry hilarus, festivus.
mesh macula *f*; plaga *f*.
mess squalor *m*.
mess|age nuntius *m*; **~enger** nuntius *m*; tabellarius *m*.
metal metallum *n*.
metamorphose transformo 1; verto 3.
metaphor translatio *f*; **~ical** translatus.
meteor fax *f*.
methinks ut mihi videtur.
method ratio *f*; modus *m*; **~ically** disposite.
metonymy immutatio *f*.
metr|e numerus *m*; **~ical** metricus.
metropolis caput *n*; urbs *f*.
mettle ferocitas *f*; **~some** ferox, animosus.
mews stabula *n/pl.*
mid medius; **~day** meridies *m*; meridianus.
middle medius; medium *n*; **~-aged** senior.
middling mediocris.
midge culex *m*.
mid|land mediterraneus; **~night** media nox *f*; **~riff** praecordia *n/pl.*
midst medius.
mid|summer media aestas *f*; **~wife** obstetrix *f*; **~winter** bruma *f*.
might vis *f*, potestas *f*; **~y** validus, (prae)potens.
migrate migro 1.
mild mitis, clemens, facilis; tepidus.
mildew robigo *f*; situs, us *m*.
mildness lenitas *f*, mansuetudo *f*.
mile mille passuum; **~stone** milliarium *n*.
military militaris, bellicus; militares copiae *f*; **~ service** militia *f*.
militate against contra facio 3 (*alqm*).
milk mulgeo 2; lac *n*; **~y** lacteus.
mill tero 3; mola *f*; pistrinum *n*; **~er** pistor *m*; **~stone** mola *f*.
millet milium *n*.
million decies centena milia.
mime imitor 1; mimus *m*.
mince conseco 1; **not to ~ matters** ut plane aperteque dicam; **~d meat** minutal *n*.
mind curo 1; **~ one's own business** meum negotium ago 3; mens *f*; animus *m*; ingenium *n*; sensus, us *m*; sententia *f*; **be out of one's ~** insanio 4; **bear in ~** memini; **call to ~** recordor 1; **change one's ~** sententiam muto 1; **have a ~ to** mihi libet; mihi in animo est; **to my ~** ex mea sententia; **~ful** memor (*gen.*).
mine meus; (ef)fodio 4; *mil.* cuniculos ago 3; metallum *n*; cuniculus *m*; **~r** metallicus *m*; **~ral** metallum *n*.
mingle (im)misceo 2 (*alqd alci rei*); confundo 3 (*alqd in alqd*).
miniature minutus.
minimum minimus.
minion minister, tri *m*; satelles *m*.
minister praefectus *m*; **~ to** servio 4 (*dat.*); prosum (*dat.*).
ministry ministerium *n*.
minor minor; filius *m* familias; **~ity** minor pars *f*; aetas *f* nondum adulta.
minstrel vates *m*.
mint cudo 3; moneta *f*; mentha *f*.
minus sine (*abl.*).
minute minutus, pusillus; subtilis; momentum *n* (temporis); commentarius *m*.

mirac|le miraculum *n*, prodigium *n*; **~ulous** mirus.
mire lutum *n*.
mirror speculum *n*; imaginem reddo 3.
mirth hilaritas *f*, laetitia *f*; **~ful** hilarus.
misadventure casus, us *m*.
misanthropic inhumanus.
misapply abutor 3.
mis|apprehension error *m*; **~behave** indecore me gero 3.
miscalculat|e erro 1; **~ion** error *m*.
miscarriage abortus, us *m*.
miscellan|eous promiscuus, varius; **~y** farrago *f*.
mischance incommodum *n*.
mischie|f incommodum *n*; maleficium *n*; pestis *f*; **~vous** improbus, noxius.
miscon|duct peccatum *n*; **~strue** male interpretor 1.
misdeed delictum *n*.
miser homo *m* avarus; **~able** miser; **~y** miseria *f*, angor *m*.
misfortune adversa *n/pl.*; incommodum *n*; calamitas *f*.
misgivings: have ~ diffido 3.
mis|govern male administro 1; **~guided** demens; **~hap** incommodum *n*; **~interpret** male interpretor 1; male iudico 1; **~lay** amitto 3; **~lead** decipio 3; **~represent** in deteriorem partem interpretor 1; **~rule** male administro 1.
miss aberro 1 (*abl.*); frustra mittor 3 (*telum etc.*); amitto 3 (*occasionem etc.*); desidero 1 (*alqm*); requiro 3 (*alqd*); puella *f*; domina *f*.
misshapen deformis, pravus.
missile telum *n*, missile *n*.
missing: be ~ desideror 1; desum.
mission legatio *f*; officium *n*.
mist nebula *f*; caligo *f*.
mistake error *m*; erratum *n*; mendum *n*; **by ~ for** pro (*abl.*); **be ~n** erro 1, fallor 3 (*in re*).
mistletoe viscum *n*.
mistress era *f*, domina *f*, mater *f*-familias; puella *f*, amica *f*.
mistrust diffido 3; diffidentia *f*.
misty nebulosus.
misunderstand haud recte intellego 3; **~ing** error *m*.
misuse iniuriose tracto 1.
mite teruncius *m*.
mitigat|e mitigo 1; levo 1; **~ion** levamentum *n*.
mix (ad)misceo 2 (*alqd re*); commisceo 3 (*alqd cum re*); **~ed** promiscuus, varius; **~ture** mixtura *f*.
moan gemo 3; gemitus, us *m*.
moat fossa *f*.
mob turba *f*; multitudo *f*; vulgus, i *n*; circumfundor 3 (*dat.*).
mobile mobilis.
mock irrideo 2, derideo 2 (*acc.*); illudo 3 (*dat.*); fictus; **~er** derisor *m*; **~ery** irrisio *f*; irrisus, us *m*; ludificatio *f*.
mode modus *m*; ratio *f*.
model exemplum *n*, exemplar *n*; fingo 3.
moderat|e modicus, moderatus, modestus; tempero 1, mitigo 1; moderor 1 (*dat.*); **~ion** modus *m*; moderatio *f*, mediocritas *f*.
modern recens, novus.
modest modicus; verecundus, demissus; **~y** verecundia *f*; pudor *m*.
modify tempero 1; immuto 1; accommodo 1 (*alqd*; **to suit** *ad alqd*).
modulat|e flecto 3; **~ion** flexio *f*.
moist umidus; **~en** madefacio 3; rigo 1; **~ure** umor *m*.
molar molaris *m*.
mole talpa *f*; moles *f*; naevus *m*.
molest vexo 1, sollicito 1; **~ation** vexatio *f*.
mollify mitigo 1.
moment punctum *n*, momentum *n* (temporis); **in a ~** statim; **at the ~ when** cum maxime; **of great ~** magni momenti; **~ary** brevis; **~ous** maximi momenti; **~um** impetus, us *m*.
monarch rex *m*, princeps *m*; **~ical** regius; **~y** regnum *n*.
monastery monasterium *n*.
money pecunia *f*; nummi *m/pl.*; nummarius; **~-bag** fiscus *m*; **~-changer** nummularius *m*; **~-lender** faenerator *m*; **~ed** pecuniosus.
mongrel hibrida *m and f*.
monkey simia *f*.
monograph libellus *m*.
monoton|ous similis; **~y** similitudo *f*.
monster, monstrosity belua *f*; monstrum *n*.
monstrous monstruosus, portentosus; nefarius.
month mensis *m*; **~ly** menstruus.
monument monumentum *n*.

mood animus *m*; mens *f*; affectus, us *m* (*mentis etc.*); **~y** morosus.
moon luna *f*; **~light** lunae lumen *n*.
moor religo 1, deligo 1; loca *n/pl.* patentia; **~ings** retinacula *n/pl.*; statio *f*.
mop detergeo 2.
moral moralis; probus; **~s** mores *m/pl.*; officia *n/pl.*; **the ~ is** significat; **~ity** honestas *f*.
morbid morbosus, insanus.
more plus, magis; ultra (*acc.*, *quam*); amplius; **no ~** non iam, non diutius; **~over** praeterea.
morning matutinum tempus *n*; **in the ~** mane; matutinus; **good morning!** salve.
morose tristis, difficilis.
morrow posterus dies *m*; crastinus dies *m*.
morsel offa *f*; frustum *n*.
mortal mortalis; mortifer, funestus; **~ity** mortalitas *f*; mortes *f/pl.*
mortar mortarium *n*; calx *f*.
mortgage pignus *n*; pignero 1.
mortif|ication offensio *f*; indignitas *f*; **~y** *v/t.* offendo 3 (*alqm*); *v/i.* putresco 3.
mosaic tessellatus (*opus*, *pavimentum*, *etc.*).
mosquito culex *m*.
moss muscus *m*; **~y** muscosus.
most plurimus; plerique; *adv.* maxime, plurimum; **at the ~** summum; **for the ~ part** plerumque, fere, maximam partem.
moth blatta *f*.
mother mater *f*; **of a ~** maternus; **~-in-law** socrus, us *f*; **~ tongue** patrius sermo *m*.
motion motus, us *m*; agitatio *f*; rogatio *f*; sententia *f*; **adopt a ~** in sententiam (*alcs*) discedo 3; innuo 3 (*dat.*); **~less** immotus.
motive causa *f*, ratio *f*.
motley, mottled versicolor; varius, maculosus.
motto sententia *f*.
mould fingo 3; formo 1; forma *f*; robigo *f*; situs, us *m*; **~er** putresco 3; **~ering, ~y** puter, mucidus.
moult pennas exuo 3.
mound tumulus *m*; agger, eris *m*.
mount scando 3, conscendo 3 (*alqd*); ascendo 3 (*alqd*, *in alqd*); equum conscendo 3; **~ guard** in statione sum.
mountain mons *m*; **~eer** montanus (homo) *m*; **~ous** montuosus; **~ range** iugum *n*.
mourn lugeo 2, maereo 2, doleo 2 (*acc.*); **~ful** tristis, luctuosus; lugubris; **~ing** luctus, us *m*; squalor *m*; sordes *f/pl.*; **be in ~ing** squaleo 2; **go into ~ing** vestitum muto 1.
mouse mus *m*; **~-trap** muscipula *f*.
moustache labri superioris capilli *m/pl.*
mouth os *n*; rostrum *n*; ostium *n*; **~ful** bucca *f*.
move *v/t.* moveo 2; commoveo 2 (*alqm ad*); (re)fero 3 (*legem*, *rogationem*, *etc.*); *v/i.* moveor 2, me moveo 2; migro 1; **~ables** bona *n/pl.* (mobilia); **~ment** motus, us *m*.
moving miserabilis, flebilis.
mow seco 1, meto 3.
much multus; multum *n*; *adv.* multum; multo (*with comparatives*); **as ~ as** tantus ... quantus; **how ~** quantus; **too ~** nimius; nimium *n*; **~ less** nedum.
mud lutum *n*, caenum *n*; limus *m*; **~dle** confundo 3; perturbo 1; **~dy** lutulentus, limosus; turbidus.
muffle involvo 3, obvolvo 3.
mug poculum *n*; **~gy** umidus.
mulberry morum *n*; **~-tree** morus, i *f*.
mule mulus *m*; **~teer** mulio *m*.
mulish pervicax.
mullet mullus *m*.
multi|ply *v/t.* multiplico 1, augeo 2; *v/i.* cresco 3; **~tude** multitudo *f*; vis *f*; vulgus, i *n*.
mumble murmuro 1; musso 1.
munch mando 3.
municipal municipalis; **~ity** municipium *n*.
munificen|ce liberalitas *f*; **~t** liberalis.
murder neco 1; interficio 3; obtrunco 1; caedes *f*, nex *f*; **~er** homicida *m*; sicarius *m*; percussor *m*; **~ous** cruentus.
murky caliginosus, obscurus.
murmur murmuro 1; fremo 3 (*acc. c. inf.*); murmur *n*; fremitus, us *m*.
musc|le lacertus *m*; nervus *m*; **~ular** lacertosus.
muse meditor 1, cogito 1; Musa *f*.
mushroom fungus *m*; boletus *m*.
music musica *f and n/pl.*; cantus, us *m*; modi *m/pl.*; **~al** musicus, cano-

rus; musicorum studiosus; **~ian** musicus *m.*
muslin sindon *f.*
must debeo 2 (*inf.*); oportet me (*inf.*); necesse est mihi (*inf.*, *ut*); **I ~ go** eundum est mihi; mustum *n.*
mustard sinapi *indecl. n*, sinapis *f.*
muster *v/t.* cogo 3; lustro 1; *v/i.* congregor 1; recensio *f.*
musty mucidus.
mutability inconstantia *f.*
mute mutus, tacitus.
mutilate mutilo 1, (de)trunco 1.
mutin|ous seditiosus, turbulentus; **~y** seditio *f*; seditionem facio 3.
mutter murmuro 1, musso 1; murmur *n.*
mutton ovilla (caro) *f.*
mutual mutuus.
muzzle os *n*; fiscella *f.*
my meus.
myriad sescenti.
myrrh murra *f.*
myrtle myrtus, i *f*; myrteus.
myself (me) ipse.
myster|ious occultus, arcanus; **~y** arcanum *n*; res *f* occulta.
mystic mysticus.
mystification ambages *f/pl.*
myth fabula *f*; **~ical** fabulosus.

N

nag caballus *m.*
nail unguis *m*; clavus *m*; clavis (con)figo 3 (*dat.*).
naive simplex.
naked nudus; apertus.
name nomen *n*, vocabulum *n*; **family ~, sur~** cognomen *n*; **first ~** praenomen *n*; **good ~** fama *f*, existimatio *f*; **in ~** nomine; **in my ~** meis verbis; **in the ~ of** per (*deos*); nomino 1, appello 1, nuncupo 1; dico 3; **~ly** dico, inquam.
nap villus *m*; brevis somnus *m.*
nape cervix *f.*
napkin mappa *f.*
narcotic somnifer.
nard nardum *n.*
narrat|e (e)narro 1; **~ion, ~ive** narratio *f*; historia *f*; **~or** narrator *m.*
narrow angustus, artus; angustior fio; **~ly** diligenter; haud multum abest quin ...; **~ness, ~s** angustiae *f/pl.*
nasty foedus, taeter.
natal natalis.
nation gens *f*, natio *f*; populus *m*; cives *m/pl.*; res *f* publica; **~al** communis; **~al assembly** concilium *n* populi.
native indigena *m and f*; **be a ~ of** natus sum; **~ land** patria *f*; **~ language** patrius sermo *m.*
natural naturalis; nativus; proprius (*gen.*); **~ parts** ingenium *n*; **~ize** civitatem do 1 (*alci*); **~ly** natura, naturaliter.
nature natura *f* (rerum); ingenium *n*; indoles *f*; vis *f.*
naught nihil; **set at ~** parvi facio 3, contemno 3; **~y** improbus.
nause|a nausea *f*; fastidium *n*; **~ate** fastidium facio 3; **~ating** taeter, foedus.
nautical nauticus.
naval navalis, maritimus.
navel umbilicus *m.*
naviga|ble navigabilis; **~te** navigo 1; **~tor** nauta *m*, gubernator *m.*
navy classis *f.*
nay immo; minime (vero).
near prope, ad, iuxta (*acc.*); propinquus, vicinus; *adv.* prope, iuxta; appropinquo 1 (*ad*; *dat.*); **be ~ at hand** adsum; advento 1 (*tempus*).
nearer propior; *adv.* propius.
nearest proximus; *adv.* proxime.
near|ly prope, paene; fere, ferme; haud multum afuit quin ...; **~ness** propinquitas *f.*
neat mundus, nitidus; **~ness** munditia *f.*
necess|ary necessarius; **it is ~ary** necesse est (*inf.*); opus est (*nom.*; *abl.*); **~aries** necessaria *n/pl.*; **~itate** cogo 3 (*inf.*); **~ity** necessitas *f*; egestas *f*; res *f* necessaria; tempus *n.*
neck cervix *f*; collum *n*; angustiae *f/pl.*; **~lace** monile *n.*
nectar nectar *n.*
need egeo 2 (*abl.*); requiro 3 (*alqd*); egestas *f*, inopia *f*; **there is ~ of** (mihi) opus est (*nom.*; *abl.*); **there is no ~** nihil attinet 2 (*inf.*); **~ful** opus; necessarius.
needle acus, us *f.*
need|less sine causa; **~y** egens.
nefarious nefarius.
negat|ion negatio *f*; **~ive** negans; **give a ~ive answer** nego 1; intercedo 3 (*dat.*).
neglect neglego 3, praetermitto 3; desum (*dat.*); incuria *f*, neglegentia *f*; **~ful of** neglegens (*gen.*).
negligen|ce neglegentia *f*; **~t** remissus.
negotiat|e ago 3 (*de re*); **~ion** pactio *f.*
negro Aethiops *m.*
neigh hinnio 4; hinnitus, us *m.*
neighbour vicinus *m*; *fig.* alter *m*; **~hood** vicinitas *f*; **~ing** vicinus, finitimus, propinquus.
neither neuter, neutri; **~ ... nor** neque ... neque, nec ... nec; neve ... neve.
nephew fratris *or* sororis filius *m.*
nerv|e nervus *m*; **~ous** anxius, trepidus; **~ousness** metus, us *m*; anxietas *f.*
nest nidus *m*; nidum facio 3.
net rete *n*; plaga *f*; plagis capio 3.

nether infernus; **~most** infimus, imus.
nettle urtica *f.*
neuter neuter.
neutral medius; neutrius partis; **remain ~** quiesco 3.
never numquam; **and ~** nec umquam; **nevermore** numquam posthac; **~theless** nihilominus, (at)tamen, verumtamen.
new novus, recens; **~comer** advena *m*; **~ly** nuper, modo, recens; **~ness** novitas *f.*
news nuntius *m*; **what ~?** quid novi?; **~ was brought** nuntiatum est (*acc. c. inf.*); **~paper** acta *n/pl.* diurna.
newt lacertus *m.*
next proximus (*dat.*); insequens; posterus; **on the ~ day** postridie; *adv.* deinceps, proxime; **~ before** proximus ante; **~ after, to** secundum (*acc.*); iuxta (*acc.*); deinde, postea.
nib acumen *n.*
nibble rodo 3; **~ at** arrodo 3.
nice subtilis, exquisitus; elegans; suavis, dulcis; **to a ~ty** ad unguem.
niche angulus *m.*
nick incido 3; **in the ~ of time** in ipso articulo temporis.
nickname cognomen *n.*
niece fratris *or* sororis filia *f.*
niggardly sordidus, parcus.
night nox *f*; **all ~** pernox; **at ~fall** sub noctem; **by ~** noctu, de nocte; nocturnus; **~ingale** luscinia *f*; **~-watch** vigiliae *f/pl.*, excubiae *f/pl.*
nimble pernix.
nine novem; **~ hundred** nongenti; **~ times** novies; **~teen** undeviginti; **~teenth** undevicesimus; **~tieth** nonagesimus; **~ty** nonaginta; **ninth** nonus.
nip mordeo 2; vellico 1; uro 3; **~pers** forceps *f.*
nipple papilla *f.*
nitre nitrum *n.*
no nullus; immo; minime (vero); **~ one** nemo; **and ~ one** nec quisquam; **~ more than** nihilo magis quam; **~ news** nihil novi; **~ sooner ... than** ubi primum.
nob|ility nobilitas *f*; nobiles *m/pl.*; generosus animus *m*; **~le** nobilis, generosus, excelsus; praeclarus; **~leman** vir *m* nobilis.
nobody nemo.
nocturnal nocturnus.
nod nuto 1; nutus, us *m*; **~ (assent) to** annuo 3 (*alci*; *alqd alci*); **~ding** nutans.
nois|e sonitus, us *m*; strepitus, us *m*; crepitus, us *m*; **~e abroad** effero 3; **~eless** tacitus, silens; **~ome** taeter, foedus; **~y** clamosus, tumultuosus, argutus.
nomadic vagus.
nominally nomine; verbo; specie (*gen.*).
nominat|e nomino 1, dico 3; **~ion** nominatio *f.*
none nemo; nullus; **~ the less** nihilominus.
nones nonae *f/pl.*
nonsens|e nugae *f/pl.*, ineptiae *f/pl.*; **~ical** absurdus, ineptus.
nook angulus *m.*
noon meridies *m*; **~day** meridianus.
noose laqueus *m.*
nor neque, nec; neu.
normal solitus.
north septentrio *m*; septentriones *m/pl.*; septentrionalis; **~-east** inter septentriones et orientem; **~-east wind** aquilo *m*; **~-west** inter septentriones et occasum solis; **~-west wind** caurus *m*; **~-wind** aquilo *m.*
nose nasus *m*; nares *f/pl.*; **~gay** fasciculus *m* (florum).
nostril naris *f.*
not non; haud; minus; **and ~** neque, nec; **~ even** ne ... quidem; **~ that ... but** non quod ... sed; **~ yet** nondum.
nota|ble memorabilis; **~ry** scriba *m*; **~tion** notatio *f.*
notch incisura *f.*
note nota *f*; codicilli *m/pl.*; vox *f*; **~s** commentarius *m*; noto 1; animadverto 3, intellego 3; **~book** pugillares *m/pl.*; **~d** insignis; **~worthy** memorabilis.
nothing nihil; nihilum *n.*
notice animadverto 3; proscriptio *f*; titulus *m*; **attract ~** conspicior 3; **escape ~** fallo 3 (*alqm*; *acc. c. inf.*); lateo 2; **give ~** denuntio 1, praenuntio 1; **~able** notabilis.
notif|ication denuntiatio *f*; **~y** denuntio 1.
notion notio *f*, suspicio *f.*
notor|iety infamia *f*; **~ious** notus, infamis, famosus.
notwithstanding nihilominus, attamen.

noun nomen *n*.
nourish nutrio 4; alo 3; **~ment** alimentum *n*; cibus *m*.
novel novus; **~ty** novitas *f*, insolentia *f*.
November (mensis) November, bris *m*.
novice tiro *m*.
now nunc, iam, hodie; **~ ... ~** modo ... modo; **~ (for a long time)** iam diu, iam pridem; *particle* quidem, nunc; **~adays** nunc; hodie; **~ and then** aliquando.
no|where nusquam; **~wise** haudquaquam.
noxious nocens.
nude nudus.
nudge fodico 1.
nuisance: be a ~ molestum est.
null irritus; **~ify** infirmo 1; irritum facio 3.
numb torpens; **be ~** torpeo 2.
number numerus *m*; **a ~** pars *f*; **a considerable ~** aliquot; **large ~s, a large ~** multi *m/pl.*, complures *m/pl.*; multitudo *f*, copia *f*; **what, such a ~** quot?, tot; (e)numero 1; **~less** innumerabilis.
numbness torpor *m*.
numerous multi, plurimi, plures.
nuptial nuptialis; **~s** nuptiae *f/pl.*
nurse nutrix *f*; *fig.* altrix *f*; nutrio 4, alo 3; assideo 2 (*aegrotanti*); **~ry** (*for plants*) seminarium *n*.
nurture educatio *f*.
nut nux *f*.
nutri|ment, ~tion alimentum *n*; cibus *m*; **~tious** alibilis.

O

O, oh! o.
oak quercus, us *f*; ilex *f*; aesculus, i *f*; quern(e)us; aesculeus; **~wood** robur *n*.
oar remus *m*; **~blade** palma *f*; **~sman** remex *m*.
oat avena *f*; avenaceus.
oath ius *n* iurandum; **military ~** sacramentum *n*; **swear an ~ to** iuro 1 in verba (*alcs*); **tender, take an ~** ius iurandum defero 3 (*alci*), accipio 3.
obdurate obstinatus, durus.
obedien|ce oboedientia *f*; **~t** oboediens (*dat.*); dicto audiens (*alci*).
obese obesus.
obey pareo 2, oboedio 4, obtempero 1 (*dat.*).
object| (to) improbo 1, gravor 1 (*acc.*); repugno 1 (*dat.*); recuso 1 (*alqd, ne; after neg.: quin, quominus*); res *f*; consilium *n*; finis *m*; **I have no ~ion** per me licet (*inf., subj.*); **~ionable** ingratus; **~ive** externus.
obligat|ion officium *n*; **be under an ~ion** obnoxius, obligatus sum (*alci*); **lay under an ~ion** obligo 1, obstringo 3; **~ory** necessarius.
oblig|e cogo 3; gratificor 1 (*alci*); beneficium confero 3 (*in alqm*); gratum facio 3 (*alci*); **~ing** comis, facilis.
oblique obliquus.
obliterate deleo 2; oblittero 1.
oblivi|on oblivio *f*; **~ous** immemor, ignarus (*gen.*).
obloquy vituperatio *f*.
obnoxious ingratus, invisus; noxius [cens.]
obscen|e obscenus, turpis; **~ity** obscenitas *f*.
obscur|e obscurus, reconditus; ignobilis; obscuro 1; **~ity** obscuritas *f*; tenebrae *f/pl*.
obsequies exsequiae *f/pl*.
obsequious obsequens, ambitiosus.
observ|ance conservatio *f*; mos *m*; **~ation** observatio *f*, contemplatio *f*; sententia *f*; **~e** observo 1, contemplor 1; dico 3; conservo 1.
obsolete obsoletus; **become ~** obsolesco 3.
obstacle impedimentum *n*.
obstina|cy pertinacia *f*, pervicacia *f*; **~te** pertinax, pervicax, obstinatus.
obstruct *v/t.* obstruo 3 (*dat.*); *v/i.* obsto 1 (*dat.*); **~ion** impedimentum *n*.
obtain adipiscor 3, consequor 3; nanciscor 3; obtineo 2; impetro 1.
obtru|de inculco 1 (*alqd, se, alci*); ingero 3 (*alqd alci*); **~sive** molestus.
obtuse hebes, obtusus.
obviate occurro 3 (*dat.*).
obvious apertus, manifestus.
occasion occasio *f*; tempus *n*; causa *f*; efficio 3; **~ally** per occasionem, aliquando.
occult arcanus.
occup|ation occupatio *f*, possessio *f*; negotium *n*; quaestus, us *m*; **~y** occupo 1; obsideo 2; obsido 3; teneo 2; **be ~ied with** versor 1 (*in re*); totum sum in (*re*).
occur accido 3, contingo 3; evenio 4; in mentem venio 4, occurro 3 (*dat.*); **~rence** res *f*.
ocean oceanus *m*.
October (mensis) October, bris *m*.
odd impar; insolitus, mirus; ridiculus; subsicivus (*tempus etc.*); **be at ~s with** dissideo 2 (*ab; inter se*).
ode carmen *n*.
odi|ous invisus, odiosus; **~um** invidia *f*.
odour odor *m*; **be in bad ~ with** invidiam suscipio 3 (*apud alqm*).
of de (*abl.*), ex (*abl.*); **each ~ you** uterque vestrum; **one ~ you** unus ex vobis.
off: (the coast of) prope, propter (*acc.*); **be well ~ for** abundo 1 (*abl.*); **far ~** longe (*ab*); **make ~** me conicio 3 (*in*); **some way ~** procul (*ab*).
offal quisquiliae *f/pl*.
offen|ce delictum *n*, peccatum *n*; offensio *f*; **~d** offendo 3 (*acc.*); laedo 3; pecco 1; **~d against** violo 1 (*ius etc.*); **~sive** odiosus, molestus; putidus; **take the ~sive** bellum, signa infero 3 (*in*).
offer offero 3, defero 3; porrigo 3;

adhibeo 2 (*preces etc.*); macto 1 (*hostia*); condicio *f*; **~ing** donum *n*.
office officium *n*, munus *n*; magistratus, us *m*; ministerium *n*; **hold ~** magistratum obtineo 2; **~r** praefectus *m*.
official publicus, civilis; minister, tri *m*; lictor *m*.
officious molestus.
offset compenso 1 (*alqd alqua re, cum alqua re*).
offspring progenies *f*; liberi *m/pl.*
often saepe, saepenumero; **as ~ as** quotiescumque; **how ~** quoties; **so ~** toties.
ogre larva *f*.
oil oleum *n*; **of ~** olearius.
ointment unguentum *n*; **eye ~** collyrium *n*.
old vetus, antiquus, vetustus; senex, senior; **four years ~** quattuor annos natus; **~ age** senectus, utis *f*; **~er** maior natu; **~-fashioned** priscus, pristinus; obsoletus; **~ man** senex *m*; **~ woman** anus, us *f*.
olive (tree) olea *f*, oliva *f*; **~-oil** oleum *n*.
omen omen *n*; auspicium *n*; **obtain good ~s** lito 1.
ominous infaustus, infelix.
omission praetermissio *f*.
omit praetermitto 3, omitto 3; praetereo 4; relinquo 3.
on in (*abl.*); super (*acc.*); **~ all sides** undique; **~ foot** pedibus; **~ the right** a dextra parte; **~ the subject of** de (*abl.*); *adv.* porro.
once semel; **at ~** simul, uno tempore; ilico, statim; **~ (upon a time)** olim, quondam.
one unus; **~ and all** cuncti; **~ and the same** idem; **~ another** inter se; **~ by ~** singuli; singillatim; **~ day** olim, aliquando; **~ of** unus ex, quidam ex (*abl.*); **~ or two** unus vel alter; **~ ... ~** alius ... alius; **~ who** is qui; **~-eyed** luscus; **~-sided** inaequalis, iniquus.
onerous gravis.
onion caepa *f*, caepe *n*.
only unus, solus, unicus; *adv.* solum, modo, tantum.
onset, onslaught impetus, us *m*; incursus, us *m*.
onward porro.
ooze mano 1.
opaque caecus.
open apertus, patens; manifestus; simplex; patefacio 3; aperio 4; pando 3; *fig.* exordior 4 (*orationem*); **be, lie ~** pateo 2; **in the ~ air** sub divo; **~ing** exordium *n* (*orationis*); foramen *n*; os *n*; *fig.* ansa *f*, opportunitas *f*; **~ly** palam, aperte.
operat|e ago 3, facio 3; *med.* seco 1; **~e upon** moveo 2; **~ion** res *f*; actio *f*; **~ive** efficax.
opin|e opinor 1; **~ion** opinio *f*, sententia *f*; **good ~ion** existimatio *f*; **give an ~ion on** censeo 2 (*de*).
opponent adversarius *m*.
opportun|e opportunus, idoneus, tempestivus; **~ity** occasio *f*, opportunitas *f*; tempus *n*.
oppose *v/t.* oppono 3 (*alqd alci, alci rei*); *v/i.* adversor 1, repugno 1, obsto 1 (*dat.*).
opposit|e adversus, contrarius, diversus; **~e to** contra (*acc.*); e regione (*gen.*); adversus (*acc.*); **~ion** repugnantia *f*; adversarii *m/pl.*
oppress premo 3; affligo 3; vexo 1; **~ion** vexatio *f*; iniuriae *f/pl.*; **~ive** iniquus, gravis, acerbus.
opprobrious turpis.
option optio *f* (eligendi).
opulen|ce divitiae *f/pl.*; **~t** locuples, dives.
or aut; **either ... ~** aut ... aut; vel ... vel; **whether ... ~** sive ... sive, seu ... seu; *interrog.* utrum ... an; **~ not** annon (*direct*); necne (*indirect*).
oracle oraculum *n*; responsum *n*.
orally voce, verbis.
orange(-coloured) luteus.
orat|ion oratio *f*; contio *f*; **~or** orator *m*; **~orical** oratorius; **~ory** rhetorica *f*; eloquentia *f*; facundia *f*.
orb orbis *m*; **~it** orbis *m*; ambitus, us *m*.
orchard pomarium *n*.
orchestra symphoniaci pueri *m/pl.*, servi *m/pl.*
ordain sancio 4; statuo 3; decerno 3.
ordeal discrimen *n*.
order dispono 3; iubeo 2 (*acc. c. inf.*); impero 1 (*alci ut*); edico 3 (*ut*); ordo *m*, descriptio *f*; iussum *n*, mandatum *n*; imperium *n*, imperatum *n*; **~ of battle** acies *f*; **the equestrian ~** equester ordo *m*; **the lower ~s** vulgus, i *n*; **by, without ~ of** iussu, iniussu (*gen.*);

money ~ perscriptio *f*; **in good ~** ordine, in ordinem, ex ordine; **~ly** compositus; modestus.
ordinance edictum *n*.
ordinary usitatus, cottidianus, vulgaris; mediocris.
ore metallum *n*.
organ pars *f*; membrum *n*; organum *n*; **~isation** descriptio *f*, temperatio *f*; **~ise** dispono 3, compono 3; tempero 1; **~ism** animal *n*; animans *n*.
orgies orgia *n/pl.*; *fig.* comissatio *f*.
orient oriens *m*.
orifice os *m*.
origin origo *f*; principium *n*; primordia *n/pl.*; genus *n*; **~al** pristinus; principalis; singularis; exemplar *n*, exemplum *n*; **~ate** *v/t.* instituo 3; *v/i.* orior 4 (*ex*, *ab*); principium, initium duco 3 (*ab*); nascor 3 (*ex*); **~ator** auctor *m*.
ornament ornamentum *n*; ornatus, us *m*; *fig.* decus *n*; lumen *n*.
ornate pictus.
orphan orbus.
oscillat|e agitor 1, iactor 1; **~ion** agitatio *f*.
osier vimen *n*; vimeneus.
ostensibly per speciem.
ostentat|ion ostentatio *f*; **~ious** gloriosus.
ostler agaso *m*.
ostrich struthiocamelus *m*.
other alius, (**than** *atque*); **the ~ (of two)** alter; **the ~s** ceteri *m/pl.*, reliqui *m/pl.*; **of ~s** alienus; **~wise** aliter, secus; alioquin, sin aliter.
otter lutra *f*.
ought debeo 2 (*inf.*); oportet (*acc. c. inf.*).
ounce uncia *f*.
our noster; **~selves** (nos) ipsi.
oust eicio 3.
out foris (*esse*, *cenare*, *etc.*); foras (*ire*); **~ of** e, ex (*abl.*); **(one) ~ of, (made) ~ of** de (*abl.*); **~ of fear** per, propter metum; **~break** impetus, us *m*; **~cast** extorris; **~cry** clamor *m*; acclamatio *f*; **~do** supero 1; vinco 3; **~doors** foris, foras.
outer exterior; **~most** extremus.
out|fit apparatus, us *m*; **~house** tugurium *n*; **~landish** barbarus; **~law** proscribo 3; proscriptus *m*; latro *m*; **~lay** impensa *f*; **~let** exitus, us *m*; emissarium *n*; **~line** lineamenta *n/pl.*; **~live** supersum; **~look** prospectus, us *m*; **~number** superiores esse (numero); **~post** statio *f*.
outrage vexo 1; violo 1; iniuria afficio 3; vexatio *f*; iniuria *f*; facinus *n*; **~ous** indignus, turpis.
out|right plane, prorsus; **~set** principium *n*; **~side** extra (*acc.*), *adv.* extrinsecus, foris; externus; species *f*; **~skirts** suburbanus; **be ~spoken** aperte loquor 3; **~standing** reliquus; praestans; **~strip** supero 1; **~ward** externus; **~wardly** specie; **~weigh** praepondero 1; antiquius sum (*alqd alci*); **~wit** decipio 3; **~work** munitio *f*.
oven furnus *m*; fornax *f*.
over super (*acc. and abl.*); supra (*acc.*); trans (*flumen, etc.*); plus (*numbers*); per (*Alpes, etc.*); **~ and above** praeter (*acc.*); **~ and ~ (again)** saepenumero, identidem; **be ~** praesum (*dat.*); **it is all ~ with** actum est de (*alqo*); **place, appoint ~** praeficio 3 (*alqm alci rei*).
over|awe deterreo 2; **~bearing** insolens; **~burden** praegravo 1; **~cast** obscuratus, obductus; **~coat (cloak)** lacerna *f*; **~come** vinco 3; supero 1; **~flow** me effundo 3; redundo 1; **~grow** obsitus (*abl.*); **~hang** immineo 2 (*dat.*); **~head** insuper; **~hear** excipio 3; **~lay** induco 3 (*alqd re*); **~look** prospicio 3; coniveo 2; ignosco 3 (*alci alqd*); **~much** nimis; nimium; **~power** opprimo 3; **~reach** circumvenio 4; **~run** percurro 3 (*alqd*); potior 4 (*abl.*); **~seer** curator *m*; **~shadow** obscuro 1, obumbro 1; **~take** consequor 3 (*alqm*); *fig.* deprehendo 3, opprimo 3; **~throw** everto 3, prosterno 3; ruina *f*.
overtly aperte.
overtures: make ~ of peace condicionem fero 3; **make ~ to** sollicito 1 (*alqm*).
over|turn everto 3; **~whelm** obruo 3, opprimo 3.
owe debeo 2 (*alqd alci*).
owing to propter (*acc.*); **be ~** stat 1 (*per alqm quominus*).
owl bubo *m*, noctua *f*.
own meus, tuus, suus, *etc.*; meus ipsius; (meus) proprius; possideo 2, teneo 2, habeo 2; **~ that** confiteor 2 (*acc. c. inf.*); **~er** dominus *m*.
ox bos *m*.
oyster ostrea *f*.

P

pace passus, us *m*; gradus, us *m*; spatior 1; incedo 3.
pacify paco 1, sedo 1.
pack colligo 3 (*sarcinas etc.*); stipo 1; sarcina *f*; grex *m*, turba *f*; **~et** fasciculus *m*; **~horse** iumentum *n*.
pact pactio *f*; pactum *n*.
pad farcio 4; **~ding** tomentum *n*.
paddle remus *m*; remigo 1.
paddock saeptum *n*.
page pagina *f*; puer, eri *m*.
pageant spectaculum *n*.
pail hama *f*.
pain dolor *m*; **mental ~** aegritudo *f*; **be in ~** doleo 2; *v/t.* dolore afficio 3 (*alqm*); **~ful** acerbus; **~s** opera *f*; **take ~s** operam do 1 (*ut, ne*); elaboro 1 (*in alqa re; ut*); **~staking** operosus, industrius.
paint pingo 3; fuco 1; pigmentum *n*; **~brush** penicillus *m*; **~er** pictor *m*; **~ing** tabula *f*; **art of ~ing** pictura *f*.
pair par *n*; bini, ae, a; iungo 3; compono 3 (*combatants etc.*).
palace regia *f*.
palat|able iucundus; **~e** palatum *n*.
pale pallidus, albus; palus *m*; obscuror 1; **grow, be ~** palleo 2.
palisade vallum *n*.
pall pallium *n*; satietatem pario 3.
pallet grabatus *m*.
palliate lenio 4; extenuo 1.
pallor pallor *m*.
palm palma *f*; **~ off upon** suppono 3 (*alqd alci*).
palpable manifestus.
palpitate salio 4; palpito 1.
palsy paralysis *f*.
paltry vilis, exiguus.
pamper indulgeo 2 (*dat.*); foveo 2 (*acc.*).
pamphlet libellus *m*.
pan patina *f*, patella *f*; **frying-~** sartago *f*.
pander leno *m*.
panegyric laudatio *f*.
panel tabula *f*; **~led** laqueatus; **~led ceiling** lacunar *n*.
pang dolor *m*.
panic pavor *m*; **~stricken** pavidus, exterritus.
pannier clitellae *f/pl.*
pansy viola *f*.
pant anhelo 1; **~ing** anhelitus, us *m*.
panther panthera *f*.
pantry cella *f* (penaria).
pap puls *f*.
paper charta *f*; papyrus, i *f*; libellus *m*.
papyrus papyrus, i *f*.
parade pompa *f*; *mil.* decursus, us *m*; ostento 1; *mil.* decurro 3.
paragon specimen *n*.
paralys|e debilito 1; *fig.* percello 3; **~is** paralysis *f*.
paramount summus; antiquissimus.
paramour adulter *m*; meretrix *f*.
parapet pluteus *m*.
paraphernalia apparatus, us *m*.
paraphrase interpretor 1.
parasite parasitus *m*.
parasol umbraculum *n*.
parcel fasciculus *m*; **~ out** partior 4.
parch torreo 2; uro 3; **~ed** torridus, aridus.
parchment membrana *f*.
pardon ignosco 3 (*alci alqd*); veniam do 1 (*alci*); venia *f*, excusatio *f*.
pare reseco 1; circumcido 3.
parent parens *m and f*; genitor *m*, genetrix *f*; **~age** genus *n*; stirps *f*; **~al** patrius.
park horti *m/pl.*; vivarium *n*.
parlance sermo *m*.
parley colloquor 3; colloquium *n*.
parliament concilium *n*; senatus, us *m*.
parlour conclave *n*.
parody per iocum imitor 1.
parole fides *f*.
parricide parricida *m*; parricidium *n*.
parrot psittacus *m*.
parry eludo 3; propulso 1.
parsimon|ious parcus; **~y** parsimonia *f*; sordes *f/pl.*
part pars *f*; *thea.* partes *f/pl.*; persona *f*; **~s** loca *n/pl.*; **in, to, foreign ~s** peregre; **for my ~** equidem;

for the most ~ plerumque; **in great ~** magna ex parte; **do one's ~** officium servo 1; **play a ~** partes ago 3; **take in good, bad, ~ in** bonam, malam, partem accipio 3 (*alqd*); **take ~ in** intersum (*dat.*); me immisceo 2 (*dat.*); attingo 3 (*alqd*); **have no ~ in** expertem sum (*gen.*); **it is my ~** meum est; **it is the ~ of a king** regis est; *v/t.* seiungo 3; separo 1; divido 3; *v/i.* **~ from** discedo 3, digredior 3 (*ab*).
partake particeps sum (*gen.*); intersum (*dat.*).
partial cupidus; iniquus; **~ity** studium *n*; **~ly** ex aliqua parte.
particip|ant particeps; **~ate** particeps sum.
particle particula *f.*
particular proprius; praecipuus; subtilis; **~ly** praecipue, praesertim.
parting digressus, us *m.*
partisan fautor *m*; **be a ~ of** studiosus sum (*gen.*).
partition partitio *f*; paries *m.*
partly partim; (aliqua) ex parte.
partner socius *m*; consors; **~ship** societas *f.*
partridge perdix *f.*
party pars *f*, factio *f*; convivium *n*; **~ to** affinis (*dat.*).
pass *v/t.* ago 3, dego 3 (*tempus*); trado 3 (*alci alqd*); perfero 3 (*legem*); *v/i.* intercedo 3; transeo 4 (*dies, etc.*); pervenio 4 (*hereditas, etc.*); **~ away** intereo 4; **~ by** praetereo 4, praetervehor 3 (*acc.*); **~ for** habeor 2 (*pro alqo*); **~ on** *v/t.* trado 3; *v/i.* pergo 3; **~ over** transeo 4 (*alqd; ad*); praetermitto 3; **come to ~** fio, evenio 4; angustiae *f/pl.*, fauces *f/pl.*; discrimen *n.*
passable tolerabilis.
passage transitus, us *m*; via *f*; iter, ineris *n*; transitio *f*; (*of book*) locus *m.*
passenger vector *m.*
passer-by qui praeterit.
passion (animi) motus *m/pl.*; cupiditas *f*; libido *f*; ira *f*; iracundia *f*; studium *n*; **~ate** ardens, vehemens; iracundus.
passive iners, lentus.
password tessera *f.*
past praeteritus; praeterita *n/pl.*; praeteritum tempus *n*; *prep.* praeter, ultra (*acc.*).
paste gluten *n.*
pastille pastillus *m.*
pastime ludus *m.*
pastoral pastoralis.
pastry crustum *n*; **~-cook** pistor *m*; crustularius *m.*
pastur|age pabulum *n*; pastus, us *m*; **~e** pascuum *n*; pasco 3.
pat permulceo 2; palpo 1.
patch sarcio 4; pannus *m*; **~work** cento *m.*
patent apertus, manifestus; diploma *n*, privilegium *n.*
paternal paternus, patrius.
path semita *f*; trames *m*; via *f*; iter, ineris *n.*
pathetic miser, miserabilis.
pathless invius.
patien|ce patientia *f*; **with ~ce** aequo animo; **~t** patiens; aeger *m*, aegrotus *m.*
patrician patricius.
patriot bonus, optimus civis *m*; **~ic** amans patriae.
patrol custodiae *f/pl.*, vigiliae *f/pl.*
patron patronus *m*; praeses *m*; **~age** patrocinium *n*; clientela *f*; **~ize** faveo 2 (*dat.*).
pattern exemplar *n*, exemplum *n* specimen *n*; signum *n.*
paucity paucitas *f.*
paunch venter, tris *m.*
pauper inops.
pause subsisto 3; intermitto 3; intermissio *f.*
pave munio 4; **~ment** pavimentum *n.*
pavilion tabernaculum *n.*
paw pes *m*; pulso 1.
pawn (op)pignero 1; pignus *n.*
pay solvo 3; pendo 3 (*pecuniam pro*); **~ down, out** numero 1; **~ off** exsolvo 3 (*aes alienum, etc.*); **~ penalty** poenas do 1; **~ respects** saluto 1 (*alqm*); merces *f*; **soldier's ~** stipendium *n*; **~master** tribunus *m* aerarius; **~ment** solutio *f.*
pea pisum *n.*
peace pax *f*; otium *n*; **~ of mind** securitas *f*; **~able** tranquillus; **~ful** pacatus, placidus.
peach Persicum *n.*
peacock pavo *m.*
peak cacumen *n*; vertex *m.*
peal sono 1; fragor *m.*
pear pirum *n*; **~-tree** pirus, i *f.*
pearl margarita *f.*
peasant rusticus, agrestis.
pebble calculus *m.*

peck vellico 1; modius *m.*
peculation peculatus, us *m.*
peculiar proprius; singularis; **~ity** proprium *n*; proprietas *f.*
pedant scholasticus *m*; **~ry** molestia *f.*
peddle vendito 1.
pedestal basis *f.*
pedestrian pedester.
pedigree stemma *n.*
pediment fastigium *n.*
peel cutis *f*; membrana *f*; reseco 1.
peep strictim aspicio 3 (**at** *alqd*).
peer rimor 1 (**at** *alqd*); par; **~less** unicus.
peevish stomachosus, morosus.
peg clavus *m.*
pell-mell passim.
pelt iacio 3 (*alqd in alqm*); peto 3 (*alqm telis, etc.*).
pen calamus *m*; (*for animals*) saepta *n/pl.*; scribo 3; includo 3.
penalty poena *f*; supplicium *n*, damnum *n*; **pay, exact the ~** poenas do 1, sumo 3.
pencil penicillus *m.*
pending dum.
penetrat|e pervado 3 (*ad, per*); penetro 1, pervenio 4 (*in, ad*); **~ion** sagacitas *f.*
peninsula paeninsula *f.*
penitent: be ~ paenitet (*me alcs rei, quod, inf.*).
pennant vexillum *n.*
penniless inops.
penny as *m* (*a copper coin*).
pension annua *n/pl.*
penthouse vinea *f.*
penur|ious inops; **~y** egestas *f.*
people homines *m/pl.*; populus *m*; **common ~** plebs *f*; vulgus, i *n*; incolo 3; frequento 1; **of the ~** publicus.
pepper piper *n.*
perceive percipio 3; sentio 4; intellego 3.
perch insido 3 (*dat.*); sedile *n* (avium).
perchance forte.
percussion ictus, us *m.*
perdition exitium *n.*
peremptorily praecise.
perfect perfectus; integer; merus; perficio 3; **~ion** perfectio *f*, absolutio *f*; **~ly** plane, prorsus.
perfid|ious perfidus; **~y** perfidia *f.*
perforate perforo 1.
perforce per vim; invitus.
perform persequor 3; exsequor 3; fungor 3 (*abl.*); praesto 1 (*munus, fidem, etc.*); *thea.* ago 3; **~ance** functio *f.*
perfume odor *m*; unguentum *n*; **~d** odoratus.
perhaps fortasse; forsan, forsitan; forte; nescio an; haud scio an.
peril periculum *n*, discrimen *n*; **~ous** periculosus.
period tempus *n*; aetas *f*; spatium *n* temporis.
perish pereo 4, intereo 4; **~able** caducus.
peristyle peristylum *n.*
perjur|ed periurus; **~y** periurium *n*; **commit ~y** peiero 1.
permanen|ce stabilitas *f*; **~t** diuturnus, mansurus; **~tly** perpetuo.
permeate permano 1 (*in*).
permission potestas *f*; **with your ~** bona tua venia; **without the ~ of** iniussu (*alcs*); invito (*alqo*); **give ~** potestatem facio 3 (*alci faciendi*); **have ~** licet (*per alqm*).
permit permitto 3 (*alci ut*); sino 3 (*inf.*; *acc. c. inf.*); **it is ~ted** licet (*alci inf.*; *acc. c. inf.*).
pernicious perniciosus.
peroration peroratio *f.*
perpendicular (di)rectus.
perpetrate committo 3; admitto 3 (*facinus*; *facinus in me*).
perpetua|l perennis, sempiternus, perpetuus; **~te** perpetuo 1.
perplex distraho 3; sollicito 1; **be ~ed** haereo 2; **~ity** dubitatio *f.*
persecut|e insector 1; **~ion** insectatio *f*; **~or** insectator *m.*
persever|ance perseverantia *f*; **~e** persevero 1, persto 1 (*in re*); **~ing** pertinax.
persist persto 1, persevero 1 (*in re*); permaneo 2; **~ent** pertinax.
person homo *m*; caput *n*; persona *f*; **in ~** ipse; **~age** persona *f*; **~al** privatus; proprius; **~al appearance** habitus, us *m*; **~ality** mores *m/pl.*
perspicaci|ous perspicax; **~ty** acumen *n.*
perspir|ation sudor *m*; **~e** sudo 1.
persuade persuadeo 2 (*alci ut, ne*); adduco 3 (*alqm in, ad, ut*).
pert procax.
pertain attineo 2, pertineo 2 (*ad*).
pertinacious pertinax.
pertinent aptus, appositus.
pertness procacitas *f.*

perturb (per)turbo 1; sollicito 1; **~ation** perturbatio *f.*
perus|al pellectio *f*; **~e** perlego 3.
pervade permano 1 (*in*, *ad*); pervado 3 (*acc.*, *in*, *per*).
perverse perversus, pravus; pertinax.
perver|sion depravatio *f*; **~t** depravo 1; corrumpo 3.
pest pestis *f*; **~er** vexo 1; **~ilence** pestilentia *f.*
pestle pilum *n.*
pet deliciae *f/pl.*; amores *m/pl.*
petition preces *f/pl.*; libellus *m*; libellum do 1 (*alci*); **~er** supplex *m.*
petrif|y in lapidem me verto 3; *fig.* **be ~ied** obstupesco 3.
petticoat tunica *f.*
pettish stomachosus.
petty minutus, angustus.
petulant stomachosus.
pew subsellium *n.*
phantom simulacrum *n.*
pheasant phasianus *m.*
phenomenon res *f* (mirabilis, nova).
phial laguncula *f.*
philanthrop|ic beneficus, humanus; **~y** humanitas *f.*
philolog|ical grammaticus; **~ist** grammaticus *m*; **~y** grammatica *f.*
philosoph|er philosophus *m*; sapiens *m*; **~ize** philosophor 1; **~y** philosophia *f.*
philtre amatorium *n.*
phlegm pituita *f*; **~atic** lentus.
phoenix phoenix *m.*
phrase verba *n/pl.*; dico 3, loquor 3.
physic medicamentum *n*; **~al** physicus; **~al strength** corporis vires *f/pl.*; **~ian** medicus *m*; **~s** physica *n/pl.*
physiognomy vultus, us *m*; oris lineamenta *n/pl.*
pick carpo 3, lego 3; **~ out** vello 3; eligo 3; **~ up** tollo 3, colligo 3; **the ~ of the troops** robus *m* militum; **~axe** dolabra *f*; **~ed** lectus, electus; **~et** statio *f*; stationem dispono 3.
pickle condo 3; condio 4; muria *f.*
pickpocket fur *m.*
picture tabula *f*; depingo 3; fingo 3 (animo).
pie crustum *n.*
piece frustum *n*; *thea.* fabula *f*; *mus.* carmen *n*; sarcio 4; **~ of money** nummus *m*; **break in ~s** comminuo 3; **fall to ~s** dissolvor 3; **tear in ~s** discerpo 3; lanio 1.
pied versicolor.
pier moles *f*; pila *f.*
pierc|e confodio 4, traicio 3; perforo 1, terebro 1; *fig.* ango 3; **~ing** acutus, acer.
piety pietas *f.*
pig porcus *m*; sus *f and m*; porcinus.
pigeon columba *f*; palumbes *m and f.*
pigmy pumilio *m and f.*
pigsty hara *f.*
pike hasta *f*; (*fish*) lupus *m.*
pile acervus *m*; cumulus *m*; strues *f*; palus *m*; sublica *f*; **funeral ~** rogus *m*; (*of cloth*) villus *m*; **~ up** congero 3, exstruo 3; coacervo 1.
pilfer surripio 3 (*alqd alci*); **~er** fur *m.*
pill pilula *f.*
pillage *v/t.* diripio 3; populor 1; *v/i.* praedor 1; rapina *f*, direptio *f.*
pillar columna *f*; *fig.* columen *n.*
pillow pulvinus *m*; cervical *n.*
pilot gubernator *m*; guberno 1.
pimp leno *m.*
pimple pusula *f*, pustula *f.*
pin acus, us *f*; fibula *f*; affigo 3 (*alqd ad alqd*, *dat.*).
pincers forceps *f.*
pinch vellico 1; uro 3 (*frigus*, *calcei*, *etc.*); urgeo 2 (*inopia*).
pine tabesco 3; consenesco 3; pinus, us *f.*
pinion vincio 4; pinna *f.*
pink roseus.
pinnacle fastigium *n.*
pint sextarius *m.*
pious pius, religiosus.
pip semen *n*; granum *n.*
pipe fistula *f*; tibia *f*; tubus *m*; tubulus *m*; **reed ~** calamus *m*; tibia cano 3; **~r** fistulator *m*; tibicen *m.*
piquant acer; salsus.
pique offensio *f.*
pira|cy latrocinium *n*; **~te** praedo *m*; pirata *m*; piraticus.
pit fovea *f*, fossa *f*; barathrum *n*; **arm~** ala *f*; excavo 1; **~ against** oppono 3 (*dat.*).
pitch pono 3 (*castra*); conicio 3; pix *f*; **to such a ~** eo (*gen.*); **highest ~** fastigium *n*; **musical ~** vox *f*; **~ed battle** universae rei dimicatio *f*; **~er** urceus *m*; **~fork** furca *f*; **~pipe** fistula *f*; **~y** piceus.
piteous miserabilis.

pitfall *fig.* laqueus *m*; plagna *f*.
pith medulla *f*; *fig.* summa *f*; **~y** sententiosus.
pit|iable, ~iful miserabilis, afflictus; **~iless** durus, ferreus.
pittance mercedula *f*.
pity misereor 2 (*gen.*); me miseret (*gen.*); misericordia *f*, miseratio *f*; **~ing** misericors.
pivot cardo *m*.
placard libellus *m*.
placate placo 1.
place locus *m*; sedes *f*; gradus, us *m*; officium *n*; **in this, that ~** hic, illic; **in the same ~** ibidem; **in the ~ of** loco (*gen.*); **take ~** fio; accido 3; **out of ~** ineptus; pono 3; (col)loco 1; statuo 3.
placid placidus, tranquillus.
plagiari|sm furtum *n*; **~ze** compilo 1 (*alqd*).
plague pestilentia *f*; pestis *f*; molestus sum, vexo 1.
plain planus, manifestus, apertus, clarus; inornatus, subtilis, purus, simplex; campus *m*; planities *f*; aequum *n*; **~ly** simpliciter (*loqui, etc.*); **~ness** simplicitas *f*.
plaint querela *f*.
plaintiff petitor *m*, actor *m*, accusator *m*.
plaintive querulus, miserabilis.
plait intexo 3, nodo 1.
plan consilium *n*; ratio *f*; descriptio *f*; consilium capio 3; excogito 1; describo 3.
plane tero 1; rado 3; lima *f*, runcina *f*; **~-tree** platanus, i *f*.
planet stella *f* errans.
plank tabula *f*.
plant sero 3, consero 3; pono 3; herba *f*; **~ation** arbustum *n*; **~er** sator *m*.
plaster induco 3 (*alqd alci rei*); tectorium *n*.
plate lamina *f*; lanx *f*, patella *f*; **silver ~** argentum *n*.
platform tribunal *n*; suggestus, us *m*; (*in Forum*) rostra *n/pl.*
plaudits plausus, us *m*.
plausible probabilis, speciosus.
play ludo 3; cano 3 (*abl.*); ago 3 (*fabulam*); ludus *m*; *thea.* fabula *f*; **~er** histrio *m*; **~ful** lascivus; iocosus; **~mate** collusor *m*.
plea excusatio *f*; *jur.* exceptio *f*; **~d** excuso 1, causor 1 (*alqd*); obsecro 1 (*ut*); defendo 3 (*acc. c. inf.*); **~d a case** causam dico 1, ago 3; **~der** orator *m*.
pleasant iucundus, amoenus; suavis; **~ry** facetiae *f/pl.*
please placeo 2 (*dat.*); delecto 1 (*acc.*); gratificor 1 (*alci*); **~!** amabo te; **as you ~** quod libet; **if you ~** si libet.
pleas|ing gratus; **be ~ing** cordi est (*alci*); **~ure** voluptas *f*; libido *f*; arbitratus, us *m*; **it is the ~ure of** placet 2, videtur 3 (*dat.*).
plebeian plebeius; **~ order** plebs *f*.
pledge spondeo 2 (*alqd alci*; *acc. c. inf.*); promitto 3; oppignero 1, obligo 1 (*alqd*); pignus *n*; fides *f*.
plent|iful largus, uber; **~y** copia *f*; **~y of** satis (*gen.*).
pliable lentus; flexibilis.
plight obligo 1; miseria *f*.
plot coniuro 1; molior 4; coniuratio *f*; consilium *n*; *thea.* argumentum *n*; **~ of land** agellus *m*.
plough aro 1; aratrum *n*; **~share** vomer, eris *n*.
pluck carpo, lego 3; vello 3; **~ up courage** bono animo sum, utor 3; **~y** fortis.
plug obturo 1; obturamentum *n*.
plum prunum *n*; **~-tree** prunus, i *f*.
plumage pinnae *f/pl.*, plumae *f/pl.*
plumb(-line) perpendiculum *n*.
plume penna *f*, pinna *f*; **~ oneself on** me iacto 1 (*de*).
plump pinguis, nitidus.
plunder praedor 1; diripio 3; praeda *f*; **~ing** rapina *f*; praedatorius.
plunge *v/t.* (im)mergo 3, summergo 3 (*in*); *v/i.* me mergo, *etc.* (*in*).
plural pluralis; **~ity** multitudo *f*.
ply exerceo 2, urgeo 2.
poach furor 1; **~er** fur *m*.
pocket sacculus *m*; intercipio 3; **~-book (tablets)** pugillares *m/pl.*; **~-money** peculium *n*.
pod siliqua *f*.
poem poema, atis *n*, carmen *n*.
poet poeta *m*; **~ess** poetria *f*; **~ical** poeticus; **~ry** carmen *n*; poesis *f*; versus *m/pl.*
poignant acerbus.
point acumen *n*; mucro *m*; punctum *n*; locus *m*; res *f*; **the main ~** summa *f*; caput *n*; **to this ~** huc; **to such a ~** eo; **on the ~ of speaking** locuturus; **be to the ~** attineo 2; **~ out** (de)monstro 1; designo 1;

significo 1; ostendo 3; **~ed** (prae-) acutus; salsus; **~er** index *m*; **~less** frigidus, insulsus, ineptus.
poise libro 1.
poison venenum *n*; venenum do 1 (*alci*); veneno 1 (*alqd*); **~er** veneficus *m*; **~ing** veneficium *n*; **~ous** venenatus.
poke fodio 3; fodico 1; **~r** rutabulum *n*.
polar septentrionalis.
pole contus *m*; axis *m*; **~cat** feles *f*.
polemics controversiae *f/pl.*
police vigiles *m/pl.*
policy consilia *n/pl.*; ratio *f*.
polish polio 4; *fig.* limo 1; nitor *m*; lima *f*; **~ed** (per)politus.
polite comis, humanus; urbanus; **~ness** comitas *f*; humanitas *f*.
politic prudens.
politic|al civilis, politicus; **~s** res *f* publica; **take part in ~s** in re publica versor 1.
poll suffragium *n*.
pollut|e inquino 1, contamino 1; polluo 3; **~ion** colluvio *f*.
pomp pompa *f*; apparatus, us *m*; **~osity** magnificentia *f*; **~ous** inflatus.
pond stagnum *n*.
ponder considero 1; animo voluto 1; **~ous** gravis.
poniard pugio *m*.
pony mannus *m*.
pool stagnum *n*; lacus, us *m*.
poop puppis *f*.
poor pauper, inops, egens; miser; exilis.
pop crepito 1; **~ out** exsilio 4; crepitus, us *m*.
pope pontifex *m*.
poplar populus, i *f*; populeus.
poppy papaver, eris *n*.
populace plebes *m/pl.*; vulgus, i *n*.
popular popularis; gratus, acceptus; vulgaris; **~ party** populares *m/pl.*; **~ity** favor *m* (populi); studium *n*; **~ly** populariter.
population populus *m*.
populous frequens, celeber.
porcelain fictilis.
porch vestibulum *n*; porticus, us *f*.
porcupine hystrix *f*.
pore foramen *n*; **~ over** animum, considerationem intendo 3 (*in alqd*).
pork porcina *f*.
porridge puls *f*.
port portus, us *m*.
portal porta *f*.
portcullis cataracta *f*.
portend portendo 3; significo 1.
portent prodigium *n*, portentum *n*, monstrum *n*; **~ous** prodigiosus.
porter ianitor *m*; ostiarius *m*; baiulus *m*.
portfolio scrinium *n*.
portico porticus, us *f*.
portion pars *f*; divido 3; partior 4; **marriage ~** dos *f*.
portly plenus.
portmanteau mantica *f*.
portrait imago *f*.
portray pingo 3; depingo 3, describo 3.
pose *v/t.* (pro)pono 3 (*quaestionem*); *v/i.* simulo 1 (*acc. c. inf.*); status, us *m*.
position locus *m*; situs, us *m*; *fig.* status, us *m*; gradus, us *m*.
positive certus, firmus; **be ~ that** pro certo habeo 2.
possess possideo 2, habeo 2, teneo 2; est mihi; **~ed** insanus; **~ion** possessio *f*; **take ~ion of** occupo 1, capio 3 (*locum, animum, etc.*); **~ions** bona *n/pl.*
possible: it is ~ fieri potest (*ut*); **as quickly as ~** quam celerrime.
possibly fortasse; fieri potest (*ut*).
post (col)loco 1; constituo 3 (*milites*); do 1 (*litteras*); **~ up** propono 3, figo 3 (*in publicum*); palus *m*; cippus *m*; statio *f*, locus *m*, praesidium *n*; officium *n*; **door~** postis *m*; tabellarius.
posteri|or posterior; **~ty** posteri *m/pl.*; posteritas *f*.
postman tabellarius *m*.
postpone differo 3, profero 3.
postulate pono 3.
posture status, us *m*.
pot olla *f*.
poten|cy vis *f*; **~t** efficax, potens; **~tate** princeps *m*, rex *m*.
potion potio *f*.
potsherd testa *f*.
potter figulus *m*; **~y** fictilia *n/pl.*
pouch pera *f*; sacculus *m*.
poultry altiles *m/pl.*
pounce upon insilio 4; involo 1 (*in alqm*).
pound tero 3, tundo 3; libra *f*.
pour fundo 3; **~ down** *v/i.* me deicio 3; *v/t.* praecipito 1; **~ forth, out** *v/t.* profundo 3; *v/i.* me eicio 3, effundor 3.

poverty paupertas *f*, egestas *f*.
powder pulvis *m*; tero 3 (*in pulverem*).
power vis *f*; ops *f*; potestas *f*, potentia *f*; imperium *n*, dicio *f*; **be in one's ~** in manu sum (*alcs*); **~ful** validus; potens, valens; efficax; **be very, most ~ful** multum, plurimum possum; **be ~less** nihil possum.
practical experience, practice usus, us *m*; tractatio *f*; exercitatio *f*.
practise exerceo 2; celebro 1; meditor 1; **~d** exercitatus, peritus.
praetor praetor *m*; **~ian guard** praetoriani *m/pl.*; praetorium *n*; **~ship** praetura *f*.
praise laudo 1; celebro 1 (*laudibus*); laus *f*; **~-worthy** laudabilis, laudandus.
prance exsulto 1.
prank iocus *m*.
prate, prattle garrio 4, blatero 1.
pray precor 1, obsecro 1; oro 1 (*alqm, alqd, ut*); quaeso 3 (*alqd ab alqo, ut*); **~ to the gods** adoro 1 (*acc.*); supplico 1 (*dat.*); **~er** preces *f/pl.*; precatio *f*.
preach doceo 2.
preamble praefatio *f*; exordium *n*.
precarious incertus.
precaution: take ~s praecaveo 2 (*ne*).
precede praeeo 4; antecedo 3 (*acc., dat.*); ante fio, sum (*quam*).
precedence: give ~ to cedo 3 (*alci*); praevertor 3 (*alqd, alci rei*).
preced|ent exemplum *n*; **~ing** proximus, superior.
precept praeceptum *n*.
precinct templum *n*.
precious pretiosus.
precipi|ce locus *m* praeceps, abruptus; **~tate** *v/i.* me praecipito 1, deicio 3; *v/t.* maturo 1 (*alqd*); praeceps, temerarius; **~tous** praeceps, praeruptus.
precis|e subtilis, exactus; **~ion** subtilitas *f*; cura *f*.
preclude prohibeo 2 (*inf., ne*).
precocious praecox.
precon|ceived praeiudicatus; **~ception** praeiudicata opinio *f*; **~certed** compositus.
pre|decessor proximus; **~determine** praefinio 4; **~dicament** angustiae *f/pl.*
predict praedico 3; **~ion** praedictum *n*; praedictio *f*.
pre|dilection studium *n*; **~dominate** plus, plurimum possum; superiores sunt; **~eminent** praecipuus.
preface praefatio *f*; praefor 1 (*pauca*).
prefect praefectus *m*; **~ure** praefectura *f*.
prefer malo (*alqd, inf.*); antepono 3, praepono 3 (*acc., dat.*); **~ a charge against** nomen defero 3 (*alcs de re*); **~able** potior, antiquior; **~ably** potius.
prefix praescribo 3, praepono 3.
pregnan|cy graviditas *f*; **~t** gravida, praegnans.
prejud|ge praeiudico 1; **~ice** praeiudicata opinio *f*; laedo 3.
preliminary: ~ exercise prolusio *f*; **make some ~ remarks** pauca praefor 1.
prelude proemium *n*; *fig.* prolusio *f*.
premature praematurus, immaturus.
premeditate praemeditor 1; **~dly** consulto, de industria.
premier princeps *m*.
premise propositio *f*, assumptio *f*; **~s** aedificia *n/pl.*
premium praemium *n*.
premonition augurium *n*.
preoccupied occupatus.
prepar|ation praeparatio *f*; **~e** (prae)paro 1; meditor 1; me comparo 1 (*ad alqd*).
preponderate plus, plurimum polleo 2.
preposterous praeposterus, absurdus.
presage portendo 3; significo 1.
prescribe praescribo 3.
presence praesentia *f*; conspectus, us *m*; **~ of mind** praesens animus *m*; praesentia *f* animi; **in the ~ of** coram (*abl.*); **in my ~ce** me praesente.
present praesens; **at the ~** in praesenti; **for the ~** in praesens; **at the ~ day** hodie; **be ~** adsum, intersum (*dat.*); introduco 3; offero 3, obicio 3; praebeo 2, dono 1 (*alqm dono*); **~ itself** occurro 3; obvenio 4; donum *n*, munus *n*; **~iment** augurium *n*; **~ly** mox, brevi.
preserv|ation conservatio *f*; **~e**

(con)servo 1; tueor 2; (*fruit*) condio 4; **~ed** conditivus; **~er** servator *m*.

preside praesideo 2 (*dat.*); **~nt** praefectus *m*.

press premo 3 (*alqd, alqm*); **~ hard** urgeo 2; insto 1 (*dat.*); **~ together** comprimo 3; prelum *n* (*for wine, olives, clothes, etc.*); turba *f*; **~ing** praesens; **~ingly** vehementer, impense; **~ure** pressus, us *m*.

prestige gloria *f*.

presum|e sumo 3 (*mihi ut*); audeo 2; **~ption** arrogantia *f*; coniectura *f*; **~ptuous** arrogans.

preten|ce simulatio *f*, species *f*; **~d** simulo 1; dictito 1; fingo 3; **~der** qui regnum affectat; **~sion** ostentatio *f*; **have ~sions to** affecto 1 (*alqd*).

preternatural monstruosus; **~ly** praeter modum.

pretext species *f*; **put forward as a ~** praetendo 3 (*alqd alci rei*).

pretty bellus, pulcher, lepidus.

prevail vinco 3; valeo 2; **~ upon** impetro 1 (*alqd ab alqo*; *ut*).

prevalent creber, vulgatus; **become ~** increb(r)esco 3.

prevaricate tergiversor 1.

prevent prohibeo 2 (*alqm*; *quominus*; *acc. c. inf.*); obsto 1 (*dat.*; *quominus*).

previous proximus, superior, prior; **~ to** prius quam; **~ly** antea, antehac.

prey praeda *f*; **~ upon** praedor 1; *fig.* sollicito 1.

price pretium *n*; **~ of corn, food** annona *f*; **sell at a high, low ~** magno, parvo vendo 3; *v/t.* pretium constituo 3; **~less** pretiosissimus.

prick pungo 3; *fig.* stimulo 1; **~ up one's ears** aures erigo 3; stimulus *m*; aculeus *m*; **~le** spina *f*; **~ly** spinosus.

pride superbia *f*; fastidium *n*; **~ oneself on** glorior 1 (*de, in re*).

priest sacerdos *m and f*; **~hood** sacerdotium *n*.

prima|cy principatus, us *m*; **~ry** primus.

prime optimus; erudio 4 (*alqm de*); **be in the ~** floreo 2, vigeo 2; **~val** priscus.

primitive priscus, pristinus, antiquus, principalis.

prince rex *m*, princeps *m*; regulus *m*; **~ly** regalis; **~ss** regina *f*; regis filia *f*.

principal praecipuus, primus; magister, tri *m*; (*money*) caput *n*; **~ity** regnum *n*.

principle principium *n*, elementum *n*; institutum *n*, decretum *n*; **man of ~** vir *m* probus, integer.

print imprimo 3 (*alqd in re*); nota *f* (*impressa*); tabula *f*.

prior potior; **~ to** ante (*acc.*).

prison carcer, eris *n*; vincula *n/pl.*; **~er** captivus *m*; *jur.* reus *m*; **take ~er** capio 3.

priva|cy solitudo *f*; secretum *n*; secessus, us *m*; **~te** privatus; proprius; secretus; domesticus; **in ~te** privatim; secreto; **~te soldier** miles *m* gregarius; **~tion** inopia *f*.

privet ligustrum *n*.

privilege ius *n*; commodum *n*.

privy secretus; **~ to** conscius (*dat.*).

prize praemium *n*; praeda *f*; magni facio 3.

probab|ility veri similitudo *f*; **~le** veri similis; probabilis; **~ly** nescio an.

probation rudimenta *n/pl.*; **~er** tiro *m*.

probe scrutinor 1; tento 1.

probity probitas *f*.

problem quaestio *f*.

procedure ratio *f*.

proceed pergo 3; procedo 3, progredior 3; **~ against** persequor 3 (*alqm iudicio*); *fig.* **~ from** proficiscor 3; **~ing** ratio *f*; **~ings** acta *n/pl.*; **~s** fructus, us *m*.

process *jur.* actio *f*; **~ion** pompa *f*.

procla|im pronuntio 1; renuntio 1, declaro 1 (*alqm consulem, etc.*); edico 3; **~mation** praedicatio *f*; edictum *n*.

proconsul proconsul *m*; pro consule.

procrastinat|e cunctor 1; **~ion** mora *f*; cunctatio *f*.

procur|ator procurator *m*; **~e** comparo 1, adipiscor 3; **~er** leno *m*.

prodigal prodigus.

prodig|ious immanis; **~y** portentum *n*, prodigium *n*; miraculum *n*.

produce profero 3, produco 3; pario 3; (ef)fero 3; efficio 3, moveo 2; fructus, us *m*; ferus, us *m*.

product fructus, us *m*; opus *n*; **~ive** ferax; fecundus.

profan|ation violatio *f*; **~e** profanus; impius; violo 1; polluo 3.

profess profiteor 2 (*alqd*; *acc. c. inf.*); **~ion** professio *f*; artificium *n*.
proffer polliceor 2.
proficient prudens, peritus (*gen.*).
profile obliqua imago *f*.
profit prosum (*dat.*); proficio 3 (*ad*); commodum *n*, bonum *n*; emolumentum *n*, lucrum *n*; quaestus, us *m*; **get ~ from** proficio 3 (*abl.*); **~able** fructuosus, quaestuosus; **~less** inutilis.
profliga|cy flagitia *n/pl.*; **~te** perditus.
profound altus, profundus; **~ly** penitus, valde.
profus|e prodigus, profusus; **~ion** copia *f*.
progeny progenies *f*.
programme consilium *n*.
progress progredior 3; iter, ineris *n*; progressus, us *m*; progressio *f*; **make ~** proficio 3 (*in alqa re*); progressus facio 3; **~ion** progressio *f*.
prohibit veto 1, prohibeo 2 (*acc. c. inf.*); interdico 3 (*alci alqd*; *ne*); **~ion** interdictum *n*.
project emineo 2 (*ex*, *in*, *super*); consilium *n*; **~ile** missile *n*; **~ing** eminens, projectus.
proletariat vulgus, i *n*.
prolific fecundus.
prolix verbosus.
prologue prologus *m*.
prolong produco 3; prorogo 1 (*imperium*); **~ation** propagatio *f*; **~ed** diuturnus.
prominent eminens; praestans.
promise promitto 3; polliceor 2, profiteor 2; promissum *n*; **keep, break a ~** fidem servo 1, fallo 3.
promontory promunturium *n*.
promot|e proveho 3, produco 3 (*alqm ad honorem*); servio 4, consulo 3 (*alci rei*); **~ion** amplior honoris gradus, us *m*.
prompt promptus, paratus (*ad*); impello 3 (*alqm in*, *ut*); subicio 3 (*verba etc.*); **~itude** celeritas *f*.
promulgate promulgo 1.
prone pronus; **~ to** pronus, propensus (*ad.*).
prong dens *m*.
pronounce pronuntio 1 (*sententiam etc.*); enuntio 1, loquor 3 (*litteras*).
pronunciation appellatio *f*.
proof documentum *n*, argumentum *n*, indicium *n*; **be a ~** documento sum; **make ~ of** experior 4; **~ against** invictus (*ab*, *adversus*).

prop adminiculum *n*, columen *n*; **~ up** fulcio 4, sustineo 2.
propagat|e propago 1; dissemino 1; **~ion** propagatio *f*.
propel impello 3.
propensity proclivitas *f*; **have a ~ to** propensus, pronus sum (*ad*).
proper proprius; decorus; **it is ~** decet (*acc. c. inf.*); **~ly** proprie; recte, commode; **~ty** proprium *n*; proprietas *f*; bona *n/pl.*; res *f*; fortunae *f/pl*.
prophe|cy praedictio *f*; praedictum *n*; oraculum *n*; **~sy** vaticinor 1, ominor 1, divino 1; praedico 3; **~t** vates *m and f*; **~tic** divinus.
propinquity propinquitas *f*.
propitiat|e placo 1; **~ion** placatio *f*; piaculum *n*.
propitious propitius, faustus, prosperus.
proportion ratio *f*; **in ~, ~ally** pro portione; **in ~ to** pro (*abl.*); **sense of ~** modus *m*.
propos|al condicio *f*; consilium *n*; **carry a ~al** (*for a law*) rogationem perfero 3; **~e** in animo est (*mihi*), cogito 1 (*inf.*); pono 3; fero 3, rogo 1 (*legem*); **~er** lator *m* (*legis*); auctor *m*; **~ition** condicio *f*; propositio *f*, propositum *n*.
propound expono 3, propono 3.
propriet|or dominus *m*; **~y** decorum *n*.
prorogue differo 3; prorogo 1.
proscri|be proscribo 3; **~ption** proscriptio *f*.
prose soluta oratio *f*; solutus.
prosecut|e nomen (*alcs*) defero 3; accuso 1 (*alqm rei*, *de re*); exsequor 3, persequor 3; **~ion** accusatio *f*, delatio *f*; **~or** accusator *m*, actor *m*.
prospect prospectus, us *m*; spes *f*.
prosper *v/t.* adiuvo 1; *v/i.* secunda, prospera fortuna utor 3; floreo 2; bene procedit (*mihi*); **~ity** res *f/pl.* secundae, prosperae; **~ous** secundus, prosperus, florens.
prostitute vulgo 1; meretrix *f*.
prostrate sterno 3; **~ oneself** procumbo 3, me proicio 3, prosterno 3 (*humi*, *ad pedes alcs*); **be ~d** iaceo 2, fractus sum.
protect defendo 3, tueor 2; protego 3; **~ion** tutela *f*; praesidium *n*; **~or** defensor *m*, praeses *m*.
protest obtestor 1 (*acc. c. inf.*); **~ against** recuso 1 (*ne*, *quominus*).

protract (pro)duco 3; **~ed** diuturnus.
protrude *v/t.* protrudo 3; *v/i.* emineo 2.
protuberan|ce tuber, eris *n*; **~t** eminens.
proud superbus, arrogans; **be ~ of** glorior 1 (*de, in re*).
prove *v/t.* probo 1, confirmo 1, efficio 3; experior 4; *v/i.* me praesto 1, praebeo 2; evado 3.
proverb proverbium *n*.
provide (com)paro 1; praebeo 2; **~ against** caveo 2, provideo 2 (*ne*); **~ for** provideo 2 (*dat.*); **~d with** instructus (*abl.*); **~d that** dum(modo), modo.
providen|ce providentia *f*; **~t** providus; **~tially** divinitus.
provinc|e regio *f*; provincia *f* (*also fig.*); **~ial** provincialis.
provision: make ~ for provideo 2; **make ~ that** caveo 2 (*ut, ne*); **~s** frumentum *n*; res *f* frumentaria; commeatus, us *m*; cibaria *n/pl.*; **~ally** ad tempus.
provocation contumelia *f*.
provok|e irrito 1, lacesso 3; moveo 2 (*alqd*); **~ing** molestus.
prow prora *f*.
prowess virtus, utis *f*.
prowl vagor 1.
proxim|ate proximus; **~ity** propinquitas *f*.
proxy procurator *m*; vicarius *m*.
prude|nce prudentia *f*; **~nt** cautus, prudens; **~ry** pudor *m*.
prun|e (am)puto 1 (*also fig.*); **~ing knife** falx *f*.
pry into rimor 1, exploro 1.
puberty pubes aetas *f*.
public publicus; **~ affairs, ~ life** res *f* publica; **appear in ~** prodeo 4 in publicum; **in ~** in publico; **at ~ expense** publice; **make ~** vulgo 1; **the ~** populus *m*; vulgus, i *n*; **~ house** caupona *f*; **~an** caupo *m*; **~ity** lux *f*.
publish effero 3; pervulgo 1; edo 3 (*librum etc.*).
pudding placenta *f*.
puddle lacuna *f*.
puerile puerilis, ineptus.
puff *v/t.* fio 1; *v/i.* anhelo 1; **~ out** infio 1; **be ~ed up** *fig.* me effero 3, tumeo 2.
pugilist pugil *m*.
pugnacious pugnax.
pull traho 3, vello 3, rapio 3; **~ down** demolior 4, destruo 3; **~ out** revello 3, evello 3, eripio 3; nisus, us *m*; **~ey** troclea *f*; **~ing** tractus, us *m*.
pulp caro *f*.
puls|ate agitor 1; **~e** pulsus, us *m* venarum.
pulverise tero 3.
pumice pumex *m*.
pump antlia *f*; **~ out** exhaurio 4 (*sentinam, aquam, etc.*); **~kin** pepo *m*.
pun iocus *m*; iocor 1.
punch pertundo 3, terebro 1 (*alqd alqa re*); pulso 1, ferio 4 (*alqm*); ictus, us *m*.
punctilious religiosus.
punctual diligens; **~ly** ad tempus, tempore.
punctuat|e interpungo 3; **~ion mark** interpunctum *n*.
puncture pungo 3; punctum *n*.
pungent acer.
punish punio 4; animadverto 3; poenas sumo 3, capio 3 (*de alqo*); **~ment** poena *f*; supplicium *n*; animadversio *f*.
puny pusillus.
pupil discipulus *m*; **~ of the eye** pupilla *f*, pupula *f*.
puppet pupa *f*.
puppy catellus *m*; catulus.
purchase emo 3; comparo 1; emptio *f*; merx *f*; **~r** emptor *m*.
pure purus, merus; castus, integer.
purge purgo 1 (*alvum, urbem, etc.*).
puri|fy purgo 1; lustro 1; **~ty** castitas *f*, integritas *f*.
purloin surripio 3.
purple purpureus, conchyliatus; purpura *f*; conchylium *n*.
purport volo (*esse etc.*); significatio *f*, sententia *f*; summa *f*; **what is the ~** quo spectat?
purpose propositum *n*, consilium *n*; animus *m*; finis *m*; voluntas *f*; **with this ~** eo, ideo (... *ut*); **on ~** consulto; de industria; **to no ~** frustra, nequicquam; **it is to the ~** multum refert (*si, utrum, etc.*); in animo habeo 2, est; consilium est (*inf.*); **~less** vanus, inutilis, irritus; **~ly** consulto.
purse crumena *f*; marsupium *n*; sacculus *m*; astringo 3.
pursu|ance: in ~ance of ex (*abl.*); secundum (*acc.*); **~e** (per)sequor 3,

insequor 3; insisto 3 (*acc.*, *dat.*); **~it** studium *n.*

purvey comparo 1; praebeo 2; **~ food** obsono 1.

push trudo 3, impello 3, expello 3; **~ on** contendo 3, pergo 3; iter facio 3; impulsus, us *m*; impetus, us *m.*

pusillanimous timidus, ignavus.

puss feles *f.*

put pono 3; colloco 1; **~ aside** *fig.* (de)pono 3; **~ away** condo 3; **~ back** repono 3; **~ down** depono 3; comprimo 3 (*seditionem*); **~ forth** summitto 3, effero 3; **~ in** impono 3, insero 3 (*alqd in rem*); **~ into shore** applico 1 (*navem ad terram*); **~ off** *v/t.* differo 3 (*alqd in posterum diem*); *v/i.* navem solvo 3; **~ on** impono 3 (*alqd alci*, *in alqd*); induo 3 (*vestem alci*, *mihi*); **~ out** eicio 3, exstinguo 3 (*ignem*); effodio 3 (*oculum*); *fig.* perturbo 1 (*alqm*); **~ out of the way** tollo 3; **~ to sea** navem solvo 3; **~ up at** deverto 3 (*ad*, *apud*); **~ up for** peto 3 (*consulatum*); **~ up for sale** propono 3 (*alqd venale*); **~ up with** tolero 1, devoro 1.

putr|ify putesco 3; **~id** puter, putridus.

puzz|le aenigma *n*; quaestio *f*; dubium facio 3; perturbo 1; **be ~ed** haereo 2, dubito 1; **~ing** obscurus, ambiguus, dubius.

pygmy pumilio *m.*

pyramid pyramis *f.*

pyre rogus *m.*

Q

quack pharmacopola *m*, circulator *m*.
quadrangle quadratum *n*.
quadruped quadrupes *m and f*.
quadruple: in ~ in quadruplum.
quaff haurio 4.
quail trepido 1; **~ before** pertimesco 3 (*alqd*); coturnix *f*.
quaint facetus, insolitus.
quak|e tremo 3; tremor *m*; **~ing** trepidus.
quali|fication potestas *f*; exceptio *f*; **~fied** idoneus, aptus (*ad*); dignus (*abl.*); **~fy** idoneum facio 3 (*alqm*); deminuo 3 (*alqd de voluptate, etc.*); **~ty** ingenium *n*; natura *f*; virtus, utis *f*.
quandary angustiae *f/pl*.
quantity magnitudo *f*; numerus *m*; vis *f*; **small ~** aliquantulum *n*.
quarrel rixor 1, altercor 1; iurgium *n*, altercatio *f*, rixa *f*; **~some** litigiosus, pugnax.
quarry lapicidinae *f/pl.*; praeda *f*; excido 3.
quart duo sextarii *m/pl*.
quarter in quattuor partes divido 3; in hospitia deduco 3 (*milites*); quarta pars *f*; quadrans *m*; locus *m*, regio *f*; (*of a town*) vicus *m*; **ask for ~** in deditionem venio 4; **fight without ~** sine missione pugno 1; **give ~** parco 3, veniam do 1; **~s** hospitium *n*; *mil.* castra *n/pl.*; **general's ~s** praetorium *n*; **come to close ~s** manum consero 3 (*cum alqo*); **at close ~s** comminus.
quash rescindo 3; irritum facio 3.
quavering vibrans, tremulus, tremens.
quay crepido *f*.
queen regina *f*.
queer insolitus; absurdus; mirificus.
quell comprimo 3; sedo 1.
quench exstinguo 3; expleo 2 (*sitim*).
querulous queribundus, querulus.
query quaestio *f*.
quest inquisitio *f*; **be in ~ of** quaero 3 (*acc.*).
question interrogo 1, percontor 1 (*alqm*); dubito 1 (*de re*); (inter)rogatum *n*; dubitatio *f*; quaestio *f*; res *f*; **the ~ is** quaestio est (*an*); **put someone to the ~** quaestionem habeo 2 (*de alqo*); **~able** anceps, incertus; **~ing** interrogatio *f*.
quibbl|e captio *f*; captiose dico 3; **~ing** captiosus.
quick celer, velox; alacer, impiger; promptus (*ad*); acutus, callidus; **be ~** propero 1; vivum *n*; **cut to the ~** mordeo 2; **~en** *v/t.* accelero 1; excito 1; *v/i.* vigeo 2; **~ness** celeritas *f*, alacritas *f*; acumen *n*; **~silver** argentum *n* vivum; **~-tempered** iracundus; **~witted** acutus, sagax.
quiet quietus, tranquillus; tacitus, taciturnus; placo 1, sedo 1; quies *f*, tranquillitas *f*; otium *n*; **be ~** sileo 2, taceo 2; **~ness** otium *n*.
quill penna *f*.
quince cydonium *n*.
quintessence medulla *f*.
quip dictum *n*.
quit excedo 3 (*abl.*, *ex*); relinquo 3 (*acc.*); **~ of** exemptus, solutus (*abl.*).
quite prorsus, plane, admodum; omnino; **not ~** parum.
quiver tremo 3, trepido 1; tremor *m*; (*for arrows*) pharetra *f*; **~ing** tremebundus, tremulus.
quoit discus *m*.
quot|ation dictum *n*; **~e** profero 3, laudo 1 (*auctores, testes*).
quoth ait, inquit.

R

rabbit cuniculus *m*.
rabble turba *f*; colluvio *f*.
rabid rabidus.
race certo 1; gens *f*; genus *n*; stirps *f*; certamen *n* (*equorum etc.*); **chariot-~** curriculum *n*; **~-course** stadium *n*, curriculum *n*.
rack torqueo 2; equuleus *m*; tormentum *n*; carnificina *f*; cratis *f*; **be ~ed** (ex)crucior 1; **~et** strepitus, us *m*.
racy salsus.
radia|nce fulgor *m*, splendor *m*; **~nt** nitidus, fulgens, splendidus; **~te** fulgeo 2.
radical totus; *pol.* popularis; **~ly** penitus, omnino.
radish radix *f*.
radius radius *m*.
raft ratis *f*.
rafter trabs *f*.
rag pannus *m*; **~s** panni *m/pl.*
rage ira *f*; furor *m*; rabies *f*; furo 3, saevio 4.
ragged pannuceus (*vestis*); pannosus (*homo*).
raid incursio *f*; incursionem facio 3 (*in*).
rail palus *m*; longurius *m*; **~ at** maledico 3 (*dat.*); convicium facio 3 (*alci*); **~ing** pali *m/pl.*, saepes *f*; convicium *n*; **~lery** iocatio *f*.
raiment vestis *f*.
rain pluvia *f*; imber *m*; **it ~s** pluit; **~bow** arcus, us *m* (pluvius); **~water** aquae *f/pl.* pluviae; **~y** pluvius, pluvialis.
raise tollo 3 (*alqd*; *clamorem*; *cachinnum*); (sub)levo 1; erigo 3 (*caput, oculos, animum*); effero 3 (*alqm ad dignitatem*); sero 3 (*fruges*); cogo 3 (*pecuniam*); conscribo 3 (*exercitum*).
raisin uva *f* passa.
rake rado 3; **~ up** excito 1; rastrum *n*; *fig.* ganeo *m*.
rally *v/t.* restituo 3 (*ordines, aciem*); irrideo 2 (*alqm*); *v/i.* me colligo 3; concurro 3 (*milites*).
ram aries *m*; arietinus; **~ down** fistuco 1.
rambl|e vagor 1, erro 1; **~ing** vagus.
rampart vallum *n*; agger, eris *m*; moenia *n/pl.*
ranco|rous infensus; **~ur** simultates *f/pl.*; invidia *f*.
random fortuitus; **at ~** temere.
range *v/t.* dispono 3; *v/i.* (per)vagor 1; ordo *m*; genus *n*; *fig.* campus *m*, area *f* (*orationis etc.*); **mountain ~** iugum *n*; **~ of a weapon** teli iactus, us *m*.
rank numero 1; habeo 2 (*alqm in numero*); ordo *m*; series *f*; gradus, us *m*; dignitas *f*; status, us *m*; luxuriosus; fetidus, rancidus; *fig.* merus.
ransack diripio 3; perscrutor 1.
ransom redimo 3; pretium *n*; redemptio *f*.
rant bacchor 1.
rap ferio 4; pulso 1; ictus, us *m*.
rapaci|ous rapax; **~ty** rapacitas *f*.
rape rapio 3; raptus, us *m*.
rapid celer, rapidus; **~ity** celeritas *f*, velocitas *f*.
rapier gladius *m*.
rapine rapina *f*.
rapt stupens; **~ure** laetitia *f*.
rar|e rarus; tenuis (*aer*); singularis; **~efy** extenuo 1; **~ely** raro; **~eness** raritas *f*, paucitas *f*.
rascal verbero *m*, furcifer *m*; **~ly** nequam, flagitiosus.
rasp *v/t.* rado 3; *v/i.* strideo 2; scobina *f*.
rat mus *m*.
rate aestimo 1 (*alqm, alqd, magni*); censeo 2; increpo 1; pretium *n*; vectigal *n*; **~ of interest** faenus *n*; **at a high ~** magno; **at any ~** utique, certe.
rather potius, prius, libentius; quin, immo; **I would ~** malo, mallem.
ratif|ication sanctio *f* (*foederis*); **~y** sancio 4; confirmo 1.
rating aestimatio *f*.
ration (diurnus) cibus *m*; **soldier's ~** cibaria *n/pl.*
rational rationis particeps (*homo*); consentaneus; **~ity** ratio *f*.

rattle crepitus, us *m*; crotalum *n*; crepo 1, crepito 1.
ravage vasto 1, populor 1; diripio 3.
rave furo 3, bacchor 1; saevio 4.
raven corvus *m*; **~ous** rapax, edax.
ravine fauces *f/pl.*; vallis *f* praerupta.
raving furens, insanus, rabidus.
ravish rapio 3; stupro 1; **~ing** suavissimus.
raw crudus; *fig.* rudis, imperitus; **~ soldier** tiro *m*.
ray radius *m*; iubar *n*.
raze to the ground solo aequo 1 (*alqd*); funditus everto 3, deleo 2.
razor novacula *f*.
reach *v/i.* pervenio 4 (*ad*); attingo 3, tango 3 (*alqd*); *v/i.* pertineo 2 (*ad*); **~ out** porrigo 3; spatium *n*; iactus, us *m* (*teli*); **beyond ~ of** extra (*acc.*).
react upon afficio 3 (*alqm, alqd, invicem*).
read lego 3 (*alqd, librum*); volvo 3 (*librum*); **~ aloud** recito 1; **~ through** perlego 3; **~er** lector *m*; **~ing** lectio *f*, recitatio *f*.
readily ultro, libenter.
ready paratus, promptus (*ad*); celer, facilis; **be ~** praesto sum; **get ~** (com)paro 1; **~ money** praesens pecunia *f*.
real verus, germanus, solidus; **~ property** fundus *m*; **~isation** effectus, us *m*; **~ise** *v/t.* perficio 3; redigo 3 (*pecuniam*); *v/i.* intellego 3; mente concipio 3; **~ity** veritas *f*; verum *n*; **in ~ity** re vera.
really re vera; vero, profecto.
realm regnum *n*; *fig.* regio *f*.
reanimate recreo 1.
reap meto 3; *fig.* percipio 3 (*fructum ex re, rei*); **~er** messor *m*.
reappear redeo 4.
rear *v/t.* educo 1 *and* 3; alo 3; *v/i.* me erigo 3; tergum *n*; **in the ~** a tergo; **~ of a column** novissimum agmen *n*; **bring up the ~** agmen claudo 3.
reason ratio *f*, mens *f*; causa *f*; **with ~** ratione; **without ~** temere; **the ~ for ... is** idcirco (*alqd facio*) ... quod; **ask the ~ for** quaero 3 cur, quamobrem; **by ~ of** propter (*acc.*); ratiocinor 1; disputo 1 (*de re*); dissero 3 (*de re, cum alqo*); **~able** prudens; probabilis (*coniectura*); aequus; mediocris, modicus; **~er** disputator *m*; **~ing** ratio *f*, ratiocinatio *f*.
reass|emble redeo 4; **~ure** confirmo 1 (*animos etc.*).
rebel descisco 3 (*ab*); seditionem, rebellionem facio 3, commoveo 2; hostis *m*; **~lion** seditio *f*, rebellio *f*; defectio *f*; tumultus, us *m*; **~lious** seditiosus, turbulentus.
rebound resilio 4.
rebuff sperno 3, repello 3; repulsa *f*.
rebuild restituo 3, reficio 3.
rebuke increpo 1; reprehendo 3; reprehensio *f*.
rebut refello 3.
recall revoco 1 (*ad; in animum*); reduco 3; revocatio *f*; receptus, us *m*.
recant revoco 1 (*alqd*).
recede recedo 3.
receive accipio 3, excipio 3, recipio 3, capio 3.
recent recens; **~ly** recens, nuper.
recep|tacle receptaculum *n*; **~tion** aditus, us *m*; admissio *f*; congressus, us *m*; **~tive** studiosus, capax.
recess recessus, us *m*; secessus, us *m*.
reciproc|al mutuus; **~ate** refero 3.
reci|tal narratio *f*, enumeratio *f*; **~e** recito 1, pronuntio 1.
reckless temerarius, incautus; incuriosus (*gen.*); **~ness** temeritas *f*.
reckon duco 3; refero 3 (*alqm, alqd, in numero*); ascribo 3 (*in numerum*); **~ up** (e)numero 1, computo 1, aestimo 1; **~ing** ratio *f*; enumeratio *f*; numerus *m*; **~ing on** fretus (*abl.*).
reclaim repeto 3, reposco 3; recupero 1.
recline recumbo 3, accumbo 3.
recogni|se cognosco 3, agnosco 3 (*alqm*); **~ that** intellego 3 (*acc. c. inf.*); **~tion** agnitio *f*.
recoil recido 3 (*in alqm*).
recollect memini; reminiscor 3; colligo 3 (*me, animum*); **~ion** memoria *f*.
recommence instauro 1, redintegro 1.
recommend commendo 1 (*alqm, alqd, alci*); suadeo 2 (*alci ut*); **~ation** commendatio *f*, laudatio *f*.
recompense remuneror 1 (*alqm re*); praemium *n*, munus *n*; remuneratio *f*; merces *f*.
reconcil|e reconcilio 1; in gratiam restituo 3; accommodo 1 (*alqd ad alqd*); **be ~ed** in gratiam redeo 4 (*cum*); **~iation** reconciliatio *f*.
recondite abditus, abstrusus.

reconnoitre exploro 1.
reconsider reputo 1, retracto 1 (*alqd*).
reconstruct restituo 3; *fig.* repeto 3 (*alqd memoria*).
record litteris mando 1; refero 3; historia *f*, narratio *f*; monumentum *n*; memoria *f*; tabula *f*; **~s** acta *n/pl.*; fasti *m/pl.*
recount enarro 1, commemoro 1.
recourse: have ~ to decurro 3 (*ad*); descendo 3 (*ad*).
recover *v/t.* recupero 1; recipio 3; **~ oneself** colligo 3 (*me, animum*); *v/i.* convalesco 3; emergo 3 (*ex*); **~y** recuperatio *f* (*rei*); refectio *f*; salus, utis *f*.
recreat|e recreo 1; **~ion** remissio *f*; relaxatio *f*; requies *f*; vacatio *f*.
recruit reficio 3; *mil.* (con)scribo 3; comparo 1; sacramento adigo 3; tiro *m*.
recti|fy corrigo 3; emendo 1; **~tude** probitas *f*.
recur redeo 4; **~rence** reditus, us *m*; assiduitas *f*.
red ruber, rubens, rubicundus, rufus, rutilus; **be ~** rubeo 2; **~den** (e)rubesco 3.
redeem redimo 3; **~er** liberator *m*.
red-handed: catch ~ manifesto deprehendo 3 (*alqm*).
red|-hot candens; **~ lead** minium *n*; **~ness** rubor *m*.
redolent redolens (*alqd*).
redouble ingemino 1.
redress corrigo 3; restituo 3.
reduc|e minuo 3; redigo 3 (*alqm in alqd*); subigo 3, vinco 3 (*alqm*); **be ~ed to** recido 3 (*in alqd*); redeo 4 (*ad*); **~tion** deminutio *f*.
redundant supervacaneus; **be ~** redundo 1.
re-echo refero 3.
reed harundo *f*; calamus *m*.
reef saxa *n/pl.*; scopuli *m/pl.*; contraho 3 (*vela*).
reek fumo 1.
reel vacillo 1, titubo 1; fusus *m*.
re|elect reficio 3; **~establish** restituo 3.
refer refero 3 (*rem ad alqm, ad alqd*); reicio 3 (*rem ad alqm; alqm ad rem*); **~ to** memoro 1; attingo 3 (*alqd*); **~ee** arbiter, tri *m*; **~ence** mentio *f*; locus *m*; **have ~ence to** attineo 2 (*ad*).
refill repleo 2.
refine defaeco 1 (*vinum etc.*); *fig.* expolio 4; excolo 3 (*alqd*); **~d** humanus, politus; **~ment** humanitas *f*, urbanitas *f*.
reflect reddo 3 (imaginem); **~ upon** reputo 1, considero 1, recordor 1 (*alqd*); **~ion** imago *f*; cogitatio *f*, deliberatio *f*; **cast a ~ion upon** reprehendo 3.
reform emendo 1; corrigo 3; restituo 3, reficio 3; correctio *f*; **~er** corrector *m*.
refractory contumax.
refrain (me) abstineo 2, tempero 1 (*re, a re, quin, quominus*); me contineo 2, contineor 2 (*re, a re*).
refresh recreo 1, renovo 1; reficio 3; **~ment** cibus *m*.
refuge perfugium *n*, refugium *n*, asylum *n*; **take ~ with** confugio 3 (*ad*); **~e** exsul *m*; profugus *m*.
refund reddo 3.
refus|al recusatio *f*, repudiatio *f*, repulsa *f*; **~e** recuso 1 (*acc., ne, quin, quominus*); abnuo 3 (*acc.*); nolo (*inf.*); nego 1 (*alqd alci, acc. c. inf.*); purgamentum *n*; *fig.* faex *f*; quisquiliae *f/pl.*
refut|ation reprehensio *f*, dissolutio *f*; **~e** refello 3, refuto 1, revinco 3 (*acc.*).
regain recipio 3.
regal regius; **~ia** insignia *n/pl.* regia.
regard specto 1, aspicio 3; intueor 2, respicio 3; habeo 2 (*alqm pro amico*); duco 3 (*alqm amicum etc.*); cura *f*, respectus, us *m*; honor *m*; **have ~ to** rationem habeo 2 (*gen.*); **~less** neglegens, incuriosus (*gen.*); **as ~s** quod.
regen|cy procuratio *f* regni; **~t** procurator *m* regni.
regimen victus, us *m*.
regiment legio *f*, cohors *f*.
region regio *f*; tractus, us *m*.
regist|er in tabulas refero 3; perscribo 3; tabulae *f/pl.*; album *n*; **~rar** actuarius *m*; **~ry** tabularium *n*.
regret piget 2, paenitet 2 (*me alcs rei, inf.*); doleo 2 (*acc., abl., acc. c. inf., quod*).
regular constans, certus; ordinarius; aequabilis; iustus (*bellum etc.*); status (*sacrificia, dies etc.*); **~ troops** legionarii milites *m/pl.*; **~ity** ordo *m*; constantia *f*.
regulat|e ordino 1, compono 3; moderor 1 (*dat.*); administro 1;

~ion administratio *f*; praeceptum *n*, institutum *n*.
rehearse meditor 1; narro 1.
reign regno 1; dominor 1 (*dat.*); regnum *n*, imperium *n*.
reimburse remuneror 1.
rein habena *f*; frenum *n*; **take, hold the ~s** habenas accipio 3, teneo 2; **~ in** coerceo 2, freno 1.
reinforce firmo 1; **~ments** subsidia *n/pl.*, auxilia *n/pl.*
reiterate itero 1.
reject reicio 3; repudio 1; sperno 3; **~ion** repudiatio *f*.
rejoic|e *v/i.* gaudeo 2 (*acc. c. inf.*; *quod*); laetor 1 (*abl.*, *acc. c. inf.*); *v/t.* delecto 1; **~ing** laetitia *f*.
rejoin redeo 4 (*ad, in alqm, alqd*); respondeo 2 (*acc. c. inf.*); **~der** responsum *n*.
rekindle suscito 1.
relapse recido 3 (*in graviorem morbum*).
relate (e)narro 1, expono 3, refero 3 (*alqd*); trado 3 (*acc. c inf.*); **~ to** attinet 2 (*ad*); spectat 1 (*ad*); **~d** propinquus, cognatus (*dat.*); finitimus.
relation propinquus *m*; cognatus *m*; narratio *f*; **~ship** cognatio *f*, coniunctio *f*; necessitudo *f*.
relative propinquus *m*; cognatus *m*; **~ly** mediocriter.
relax *v/t.* relaxo 1; remitto 3; *v/i.* relanguesco 3; **~ation** remissio *f*, relaxatio *f*; otium *n*.
release libero 1; (ex)solvo 3; liberatio *f*; missio *f* (*from service*).
relent iram mitigo 1, mollio 4; **~less** atrox, saevus.
relevant quod attinet 2 (*ad*).
relia|ble fidus, certus; locuples; **~nce** fiducia *f*; **place ~nce on** fidem habeo 2 (*alci*).
relic *fig.* monumentum *n*; **~s** reliquiae *f/pl.* (*alcs*).
relief levamen *n*, levamentum *n* (*gen.*); *mil.* subsidium *n*, auxilium *n*; **carve in ~** caelo 1.
relieve (sub)levo 1; mitigo 1, exonero 1; succurro 3, subvenio 4 (*alci*); (*on duty etc.*) succedo 3 (*dat.*); excipio 3 (*alqm*).
religi|on religio *f*; sacra *n/pl.*; **~ous** religiosus, sacer, sollemnis.
relinquish remitto 3, concedo 3, relinquo 3.
relish delector 1 (*re*); sapor *m*; condimentum *n*.
reluctant invitus; **be ~** nolo.
rely confido 3 (*dat.*, *abl.*); fidem habeo 2 (*alci*); **~ing on** fretus (*abl.*).
remain (per)maneo 2; moror 1; resto 1; supersum; **it ~s that** restat 1 ut; **~der** reliquum *n*; **the ~der of** ceteri *m/pl.*; **~ing** reliquus, residuus, superstes; **~s** reliquiae *f/pl.*
remark animadverto 3; dico 3; dictum *n*; **~able** singularis, insignis.
remedy remedium *n*, medicamentum *n*; medicamentum do 1; sano 1; medeor 2 (*dat.*); corrigo 3.
rememb|er memini; reminiscor 3 (*gen.*, *acc. c. inf.*); recordor 1 (*acc.*; *acc. c. inf.*); memor sum (*gen.*); **~er me to** saluta (*alqm*); **~rance** recordatio *f*, memoria *f*.
remind (ad)moneo 2, commoneo 2, commonefacio 3 (*alqm de re*, *gen.*).
reminiscence recordatio *f*.
remiss neglegens; **~ion** remissio *f*.
remit mitto 3 (*pecuniam*); remitto 3 (*poenam*); **~tance** pecunia *f*.
remnant reliquum *n*; reliquiae *f/pl.*; **the ~ of** reliquus, ceterus.
remonstrate reclamo 1; **~ with** obiurgo 1 (*alqm*, *quod*).
remorse conscientia *f* (**for** *gen.*); **feel ~ for** paenitet 2 (*me alcs rei*, *quod*); **~less** immisericors.
remote remotus, semotus (*abl.*); *fig.* alienus, disiunctus (*ab*); **~ness** longinquitas *f*.
remov|al amotio *f*; migratio *f*; **~e** *v/t.* removeo 2, amoveo 2; tollo 3; segrego 1; *v/i.* (e)migro 1, commigro 1.
remunerat|e remuneror 1 (*alqm*); **~ion** remuneratio *f*; praemium *n*.
rend scindo 3; lacero 1, lamio 1.
render reddo 3, trado 3, tribuo 3; ago 3 (*gratias*); (*with double acc.*) facio 3, efficio 3, reddo 3; **~ up** dedo 3, trado 3; **~ an account** rationes refero 3.
rendezvous constitutum *n*.
renew renovo 1, instauro 1, redintegro 1; **~al** renovatio *f*.
renounce renuntio 1, eiuro 1; abdico 1 (*me re*).
renovate renovo 1.
renown gloria *f*, fama *f*; **~ed** clarus.
rent conduco 3; **~ out** loco 1; merces *f*; vectigal *n*; **~er** conductor *m*.
renunciation abdicatio *f*.
reopen (iterum) recludo 3.

repair reficio 3, restituo 3; sarcio 4; **~ to** me recipio 3 (*ad*); restitutio *f*, refectio *f*; **in good ~** sartus; **in bad ~** ruinosus.
reparation: make ~ satisfacio 3 (*dat.*).
repast cena *f*; epulae *f/pl*.
repay refero 3 (*alqd alci*); remuneror 1 (*alqm*; *alqd*); **~ment** remuneratio *f*; solutio *f*.
repeal abrogo 1; rescindo 3.
repeat itero 1, renovo 1; **~ often** decanto 1; **~edly** identidem; saepius, persaepe.
repel repello 3; propulso 1.
repent paenitet 2 (*me alcs rei*, *inf.*, *quod*); **~ance** paenitentia *f*.
repetition iteratio *f*, repetitio *f*.
repine queror 3.
replace repono 3; **~ ... with** substituo 3 (*alqm pro alqo*, *alci*); suppono 3 (*alqm pro alqo*); subrogo 1 (*alqm in locum alcs*).
reple|nish repleo 2; **~te** repletus, plenus (*abl.*).
reply respondeo 2; responsum *n*.
report (re)nuntio 1, refero 3 (*alqd*; *acc. c. inf.*); rumor *m*, fama *f*; relatio *f*, renuntiatio *f*; **~er** nuntius *m*, notarius *m*.
repose pono 3; quies *f*; ótium *n*; **enjoy ~** otiosus sum.
reprehen|d reprehendo 3; **~sible** vituperabilis.
represent repraesento 1, exprimo 3, imitor 1; propono 3 (*acc. c. inf.*); sto 1 (*pro alqo*, *alqa re*); **~ation** imago *f*; **~ative** vicarius *m*; procurator *m*.
repress reprimo 3; coerceo 2.
reprieve supplicium differo 3; veniam do 1; parco 3 (*dat.*); dilatio *f* (supplicii); venia *f*.
reprimand reprehendo 3.
reprisals ultio *f*.
reproach exprobro 1 (*alci alqd*; *quod*); obicio 3 (*alci alqd*; *acc. c. inf.*; *quod*); increpito 1 (*alqm*); opprobrium *n*, probrum *n*; vituperatio *f*; **~ful** obiurgatorius.
reprobate perditus.
reproduce propago 1; *fig.* refero 3; imitor 1.
repro|of obiurgatio *f*, reprehensio *f*; **~ve** reprehendo 3, obiurgo 1.
reptile serpens *f*.
republic res *f* publica; civitas *f* (libera, popularis); **~an** popularis.
repudiate repudio 1.
repugnan|ce odium *n*; fastidium *n*; **~t** aversus (*ab*); **be ~t to** odio sum; repugno 1 (*dat.*).
repuls|e repello 3; offensio *f*, repulsa *f*; **~ive** odiosus, foedus.
reput|able honestus; **~ation, ~e** fama *f*; **good ~e** existimatio *f*, laus *f*; honor *m*; **bad ~e** infamia *f*.
request peto 3, posco 3 (*alqd ab alqo*; *ut*); rogo 1 (*alqm alqd*; *ut*); rogatum *n*, postulatum *n*; preces *f/pl*.
require requiro 3 (*alqd*; *alqd ex alqo*); quaero 3; posco 3; desidero 1.
requisite necessarius.
requit|al remuneratio *f*, vicis *f* (*beneficii*); ultio *f* (*sceleris*); **~e** vindico 1 (*scelus*); ulciscor 3 (*alqm pro scelere*; *scelus*); (com)penso 1 (*alqd alqa re*); remuneror 1 (*alqm alqa re*).
rescind rescindo 3; abrogo 1.
rescue libero 1, vindico 1, eripio 3 (*alqm ab*); **come to the ~** subvenio 4 (*alci*).
research investigatio *f*.
resembl|ance similitudo *f*; **~e** similis sum (*gen.*, *dat.*); accedo 3 (*ad*).
resent aegre, moleste fero 3 (*alqd*, *quod*); **~ful** iracundus; **~ment** ira *f*, invidia *f*; dolor *m*.
reserv|ation exceptio *f*; **~e** (re)servo 1 (*alqd*, *alqm*, *ad*, *dat.*); sepono 3; taciturnitas *f*; **~es** subsidia *n/pl.*; subsidiarii *m/pl.*; **~ed** tectus, taciturnus.
reservoir cisterna *f*; lacus, us *m*.
reside habito 1; *fig.* consto 1 (*in*, *ex re*); **~nce** mansio *f*, habitatio *f*; domicilium *n*; domus, us *f*; **~nt** habitator *m*.
resign (con)cedo 3 (*alqd alci*); permitto 3, remitto 3, depono 3; summitto 3 (*me*, *animum*, *ad*, *dat.*); **~ation** abdicatio *f*; aequus animus *m*; patientia *f*; **~ed** patiens.
resin resina *f*.
resist resisto 3, obsisto 3, repugno 1 (*dat.*).
resolut|e firmus, fortis, obstinatus; **~ion** constantia *f*, firmitas *f*; solutio *f*; sententia *f*; **pass a ~ion** (de-)cerno 3.
resolve (dis)solvo 3; dissipo 1; statuo 3 (*inf.*; *ut*); constituo 3, decerno 3 (*inf.*; *acc. c. inf.*); certum est, concilium est (*mihi*, *inf.*); consilium *n*, propositum *n*; sententia *f*.

resort locus *m* celeber; **~ to** decurro 3, descendo 3, confugio 3 (*ad*).
resound resono 1, persono 1 (*alqa re*).
resource auxilium *n*, subsidium *n*; **~s** opes *f/pl.*, copiae *f/pl.*
respect observo 1; suspicio 3, colo 3; vereor 2; observantia *f*, honor *m*; **pay one's ~s to** saluto 1 (*alqm*); **as ~s** quod attinet 2 (*ad*); **in both ~s** in utramque partem; **in every ~** omnino; **in other ~s** ceterum; **~ability** honestas *f*; **~able** honestus; **~ful** observans (*gen.*), verecundus; **~ing** de (*abl.*).
respiration spiritus, us *m*; respiratio *f*.
respite mora *f*, intermissio *f*.
resplendent splendidus.
respond respondeo 2 (*dat.*).
responsib|ility officium *n*; cura *f*; **be ~le for** praesto 1 (*alqd*); **hold, make ~le for** rationem reposco 3 (*ab alqo alcs rei*).
rest (re)quies *f*; otium *n*; adminiculum *n*; **the ~** (*adj.*) reliquus, ceterus; reliquum *n*; *v/t.* repono 3 (*alqd in re*); *v/i.* (re)quiesco 3; quietem capio 3; **~ upon** nitor 3 (*abl.*); **~ with** situm est (*in alqo; in re*).
restitution: make ~ satisfacio 3 (*alci*); restituo 3 (*alqd*).
rest|ive ferox; **~less** turbidus, inquietus.
restor|ation refectio *f*; restitutio *f* (*bonorum*); **~e** renovo 1, redintegro 1; restituo 3, refero 3; reddo 3; **be ~ed** redeo 4; **~er** restitutor *m*.
restrain coerceo 2, retineo 2; comprimo 3; **~t** moderatio *f*; repagula *n/pl.*
restrict (de)finio 4 (*alqd*); circumscribo 3, includo 3 (*alqm*); **~ed** angustus; **~ion** modus *m*; finis *n*.
result evenio 4 (*ex re, ut*); evado 3 (*ex re*); fio 3 (*ut*); nascor 3 (*ab, ex*); eventus, us *m*; exitus, us *m*; fructus, us *m*.
resume repeto 1, recolo 3.
retailer venditor *m*.
retain retineo 2, teneo 2; servo 1; **~er** satelles *m and f.*
retaliat|e ulciscor 3 (*alqm, alqd*); **~ion** vicis *f* (*gen.*); ultio *f*.
retard retardo 1.
reticent taciturnus.
retinue comitatus, us *m*; satellites *m/pl.*
retire recedo 3, decedo 3; abeo 4; me recipio 3; **~d** remotus, quietus; **~ment** solitudo *f*; otium *n*.
retouch retracto 1.
retrace repeto 3; pedem refero 3.
retract renuntio 1.
retreat me recipio 3; pedem refero 3; recedo 3; receptus, us *m*; recessus, us *m*; latebrae *f/pl.*
retribution poena *f*; merces *f*.
retrieve recupero 1; sarcio 4.
return *v/i.* redeo 4; revertor 3; *v/t.* reddo 3; refero 3 (*gratiam*); remitto 3; renuntio 1 (*alqm consulem*); reditus, us *m*; regressus, us *m*; remuneratio *f*; quaestus, us *m*; fructus *m/pl.*
reunite reconcilio 1.
reveal patefacio 3; aperio 4; enuntio 1.
revel comissor 1; *fig.* bacchor 1, exsulto 1; comissatio *f*, bacchatio *f*.
revelation patefactio *f*.
reveller comissator *m*.
revenge ultio *f*; poena *f*; vicis *f* (*gen.*); **take ~ on** ulciscor 3 (*alqm*); **take ~ for** vindico 1 (*scelus in alqm*); **~r** vindex *m*.
revenue vectigal *n*; fructus, us *m*.
revere (re)vereor 2; veneror 1; **~nce** reverentia *f*; honor *m*; **~nd** venerabilis; **~nt** pius, reverens.
rever|se inverto 3; *fig.* recindo 3 (*legem, iudicium etc.*); infirmo 1; conversio *f*, commutatio *f*; *mil.* clades *f*; aversus, contrarius; **~t to** redeo 4 (*ad*).
review recenseo 2, recognosco 3, lustro 1; recensio *f*, recognitio *f* (*civium etc.*); **~er** censor *m*.
revile maledico 3 (*alci*).
revis|e corrigo 3, emendo 1; retracto 1 (*leges*); **~ion** emendatio *f*; lima *f*.
revisit reviso 3.
reviv|al renovatio *f*; **~e** *v/t.* reficio 3, recreo 1 (*alqm ex vulnere, morbo*); *fig.* excito 1, redintegro 1; *v/i.* me, animum recipio 3; renascor 3.
revoke renuntio 1, rescindo 3.
revolt deficio 3, descisco 3 (*ab alqo*); defectio *f*; tumultus, us *m*; **~ing** foedus.
revolution conversio *f*; circuitus, us *m*; commutatio *f*; *pol.* res *f/pl.* novae; **~ary** novus (*res*); seditiosus (*homo*); **~ise** novo 1.

revolve volvor 3, convertor 3; voluto 1 (*alqd animo*).
revulsion fastidium *n*.
reward praemium *n*; merces *f*; fructus, us *m*; praemio afficio 3 (*alqm*); remuneror 1.
rhetoric rhetorica *f*; **~al** rhetoricus, oratorius; **~ian** rhetor *m*.
rheum pituita *f*; **~atism** dolor *m* artuum.
rhinoceros rhinoceros *m*.
rhyme versus *m/pl.*; carmen *n*.
rhythm numerus *m*; modus *m*; **~ical** numerosus.
rib costa *f*.
ribald obscenus.
ribbon vitta *f*, taenia *f*.
rice oryza *f*.
rich dives, locuples, opulentus (*in abl.*); pretiosus; uber, fertilis (*terra etc.*); **~es** divitiae *f/pl.*, opes *f/pl.*; **~ness** ubertas *f*, copia *f*.
rid libero 1; **get ~ of** exuo 3, depono 3, tollo 3.
riddle aenigma *n*; ambages *f/pl.*; **be ~d with** confodior 3.
ride vehor 3 (*equo, curru*); **~r** eques *m*.
ridge dorsum *n*, iugum *n*.
ridicul|e risus, us *m*; irrideo 2 (*acc.*); **~ous** ridiculus.
rife: be ~ increbresco 3.
rifle compilo 1.
rift rima *f*; hiatus, us *m*.
rig armo 1; **~ging** armamenta *n/pl.*
right dexter (*manus etc.*); rectus, iustus, aequus; restituo 3, corrigo 3; fas *n*, iustum *n*; ius *n*; **on, to the ~** dextra, dextrorsum; **all ~** bene habet; **be ~** recte sentio 4, facio 3; **~ hand** dextra (manus) *f*; **~ on** recta; **~eous** integer, probus; **~ful** iustus, legitimus; **~ly** recte, iuste, iure.
rigid rigidus; severus.
rigo|rous durus, severus; **~ur** duritia *f*, asperitas *f*.
rill rivulus *m*.
rim labrum *n*; crepido *f*.
rime pruina *f*.
rind crusta *f*, cutis *f*; corium *n*.
ring tinnio 4, resono 1; circulus *m*; orbis *m*; (*of people*) corona *f*; (*for finger*) anulus *m*; (*for horses*) gyrus *m*; **~ing** clarus (*vox etc.*); **~let** cincinnus *m*.
rinse eluo 3.
riot turbae *f/pl.*; tumultus, us *m*; turbas efficio 3; **run ~** luxurior 1; **~ous** turbulentus; dissolutus.
rip scindo 3; **~ up** rescindo 3.
ripe maturus, tempestivus, coctus; **~ for** paratus (*ad*); **~n** maturesco 3; **~ness** maturitas *f*.
ripple trepido 1.
ris|e (ex)surgo 3; (ex)orior 4; me erigo 3; cresco 3; increbresco 3 (*ventus*); rebello 1; incrementum *n*; ortus, us *m*; collis *m*; tumulus *m*; **give ~e to** pario 3; **~ing** ortus, us *m* (*solis*); tumultus, us *m*; seditio *f*, rebellio *f*.
risk periclitor 1 (**one's life** *caput or capite*); periculum *n*, discrimen *n*; **run a ~** periculum facio 3, adeo 4 (*capitis*); **~y** periculosus.
rite ritus, us *m*.
rival aemulor 1 (*alqm*); aemulus *m*, competitor *m*; **~ in love** rivalis *m*; **~ry** aemulatio *f*, rivalitas *f*.
river flumen *n*; amnis *m*; fluvius *m*; **~-bed** alveus *m*.
rivet clavus *m*.
rivulet rivus *m*.
road via *f*; iter, ineris *n*; **~stead** statio *f*.
roam vagor 1.
roar rudo 3; fremo 3; fremitus, us *m*; clamor *m*.
roast torreo 2; frigo 3; assus.
rob *v/t.* compilo 1 (*templum*); spolio 1 (*alqm re*); adimo 3 (*alqd alci*); *v/i.* latrocinor 1; **~ber** latro *m*, fur *m*; **~bery** latrocinium *n*.
robe vestis *f*, palla *f*; vestio 4.
robust validus, robustus.
rock *v/t.* agito 1; moveo 2; *v/i.* vacillo 1, nuto 1; rupes *f*, cautes *f*; scopulum *n*, saxum *n*; **~y** saxosus, scopulosus.
rod virga *f*; **fishing ~** harundo *f*.
roe cerva *f*; (*of fish*) ova *n/pl.*; **~buck** cervus *m*.
rogue veterator *m*, furcifer *m*.
roll *v/t.* volvo 3; *v/i.* volvor 3; volutor 1; globus *m*; (*of writing*) volumen *n*; (*of names*) album *n*; **~er** (*for ships*) scutula *f*, phalangae *f/pl.*; cylindrus *m*.
roman|ce fabula *f*; **~tic** commenticius.
romp lascivio 4; lascivia *f*.
roof tectum *n*, culmen *n*; tego 3.
room locus *m*; spatium *n*; conclave *n*; cella *f*; **~y** amplus.
roost stabulor 1.

root radix *f*; *fig.* fons *f*; **take ~** coalesco 3; **become ~ed** inveterasco 3; **~ up** radicitus evello 3; **~ed** inveteratus.
rope funis *m*; restis *f*; rudens *m*; **~-walker** funambulus *m*.
rose rosa *f*.
rostrum rostra *n/pl.*
rosy roseus.
rot *v/i.* putesco 3; *v/t.* putrefacio 3; tabes *f*.
rotat|e volvor 3; me converto 3; convertor 3; **~ion** conversio *f*.
rotten put(r)idus.
rotund rotundus.
rouge fucus *m*; fuco 1.
rough asper, horridus; incultus, incomptus; **~ness** asperitas *f*.
round globosus, rotundus; flecto 3 (*promontorium*); ambitus, us *m*; orbis *m*; anfractus, us *m*; circuitio *f* (*vigiliarum*); *adv. and prep.* circum, circa (*acc.*); **~ about** circiter (*eandem horam*; *septuaginta*); ad (*centum*); **all the year ~** toto anno; **~ off** torno 1; concludo 3.
round|about devius; **~about way** circuitio *f*; **~ly** libere, aperte.
rouse suscito 1, excito 1; **~ oneself** expergiscor 3.
rout turba *f*; fuga *f*; fundo 3, fugo 1.
route iter, ineris *n*.
routine usus, us *m*; consuetudo *f*.
rove vagor 1, erro 1.
row ordo *m*; versus, us *m*; turba *f*; tumultus, us *m*; **~ of seats** gradus, us *m*; remigo 1; **~er** remex *m*; **~ing** remigatio *f*.
royal regius, regalis; **~ty** regnum *n*.
rub (per)frico 1; tero 3; **~ off** detergeo 2; **~ out** deleo 2; induco 3.
rubbish quisquiliae *f/pl.*, nugae *f/pl.*
rubble rudus *n*.
ruby carbunculus *m*.
rude rudis, inconditus, rusticus; inhumanus, asper, insolens; **~ness** rusticitas *f*; inhumanitas *f*.
rudiment|s elementa *n/pl.*; **~ary** incohatus, rudis.
rue ruta *f*; paenitet 2 (*me alcs rei*); **~ful** maestus.
ruffian latro *m*; sicarius *m*.
ruffle agito 1.
rug stragulum *n*.
rugged asper, praeruptus.
ruin perdo 3; profligo 1; affligo 3; corrumpo 3; interitus, us *m*; exitium *n*; pernicies *f*; calamitas *f*, clades *f*; **~ed** ruinosus (*aedes*); afflictus; **~ous** exitiosus, funestus.
rule *v/t.* rego 3; impero 1 (*dat.*); moderor 1; *v/i.* praesum (*dat.*); regno 1; decerno 3, edico 3 (*ut*); (*for measuring*) regula *f*; *fig.* regula *f*, norma *f*; praescriptum *n*, praeceptum *n*, institutum *n*; lex *f*; dicio *f*, imperium *n*; **~r** moderator *m*, gubernator *m*, rector *m*; regula *f*.
rumble mugio 4; murmur *m*.
rumour rumor *m*; fama *f*.
rumple ruga *f*.
run curro 3; fluo 3 (*aqua*), labor 3, mano 1; **~ aground** eicior 3; **~ away** aufugio 3; **~ out** exeo 4; **~ over** *fig.* percurro 3; **~away** fugitivus *m*; **~ner** cursor *m*.
rupture rumpo 3; *fig.* dissidium *n*.
rural rusticus.
rush iuncus *m*; impetus, us *m*; incursio *f*; concursus, us *m*; ruo 3, curro 3; me praecipito 1; **~ at** me inicio 3 (*in*); occurso 1 (*dat.*); **~ out** evolo 1; me effundo 3; **~ing** praeceps; **~-basket** scirpiculus *m*; **~y** iunceus, scirpeus.
russet fulvus.
rust robigo *f*; *v/i.* robigine laedor 3; *v/t.* robigine laedo 3.
rustic agrestis; rusticus.
rustle crepo 1, crepito 1; crepitus, us *m*.
rusty robigine laesus.
rut orbita *f*.
ruthless immitis, saevus, crudelis.

S

Sabbath sabbata *n/pl.*
sable niger, ater.
sabre gladius *m.*
sack saccus *m*; direptio *f* (*urbis*); diripio 3, populor 1; **~cloth** vestis *f* cannabina; **~er** direptor *m.*
sacred sacer, sanctus.
sacri|fice *v/t.* immolo 1; *fig.* profundo 3 (*alqd pro*); condono 1 (*alqd dat.*); *v/i.* sacrifico 1; (sacrifium) facio 3 (*alci hostiis*); sacrificium *n*; res *f* divina; *fig.* iactura *f*; **~lege** sacrilegium *n*; **~sty** sacrarium *n.*
sad maestus, tristis; **be ~** maereo 2; **~den** contristo 1.
saddle ephippium *n*; sterno 3; *fig.* **~ with** impono 3 (*alqd alci*); **pack-~** clitellae *f/pl.*
sadness tristitia *f*, maestitia *f.*
safe tutus, salvus, incolumis; cella *f*; (*for money*) arca *f*; **~-conduct** fides *f*; **~guard** cautio *f*; **~ty** salus, utis *f.*
saffron crocum *n and* crocus *m*; croceus.
sagaci|ous prudens, sagax; **~ty** sagacitas *f.*
sage sapiens *m.*
sail navigo 1; **~ round** circumvehor 3; velum *n*; **set ~** vela do 1; navem solvo 3; **~ing** navigatio *f*; **~or** nauta *m.*
saintly sanctus, pius.
sake: for the ~ of (*alcs, rei*) causa, gratia; pro (*abl.*).
salamander salamandra *f.*
salary merces *f.*
sale venditio *f*; **for ~** venalis; **offer for ~** venum do 1; **public ~** hasta *f*; **~sman** venditor *m.*
salient praecipuus.
saline salsus.
saliva saliva *f.*
sallow pallidus, luridus.
sally eruptio *f*; **make a ~** eruptionem facio 3.
salmon salmo *m.*
salt sal *m*; **~-cellar** salinum *n*; **~-works** salinae *f/pl.*; **~y** salsus.
salubrious salubris.
salutary salutaris, utilis.
salut|ation salutatio *f*; salus, utis *f*; **~e** saluto 1.
salvation salus, utis *f.*
salve unguentum *n.*
salver scutella *f.*
same idem (**as** *qui, atque*).
sample exemplum *n.*
sanct|ify sacro 1, consecro 1; **~ion** ratum facio 3; sancio 4 (*legem etc.*); permitto 3 (*alci ut*); auctoritas *f*; confirmatio *f*; **~ity** sanctitas *f*; **~uary** asylum *n.*
sand arena *f*, saburra *f*; **~-pit** arenaria *f.*
sandal solea *f*, crepida *f.*
sandy arenosus.
sane sanus.
sanguine: be ~ spero 1 (*acc. c. inf.*); magnam spem habeo 2.
sanit|ary purus, saluber; **~y** sanitas *f.*
sap sucus *m*; subruo 3, labefacto 1; **~ling** arbor *f* novella.
sapper munitor *m.*
sapphire sapphirus, i *f.*
sarcas|m cavillatio *f*; **~tic** dicax, acerbus.
sardine sarda *f.*
sash cingulum *n.*
satchel loculus *m.*
sate, satiate satio 1, saturo 1; expleo 2.
satiety saturitas *f.*
satir|e satura *f*; **~ical** satiricus; dicax; **~ist** saturarum scriptor *m.*
satis|faction: give ~faction satisfacio 3 (*dat.*); placet 2 (*dat.*); **~factorily** ex sententia (mea); **~factory** idoneus, probabilis; **~fy** expleo 2 (*alqd*); satisfacio 3 (*alci*); **be ~fied** satis habeo 2; mihi persuasum est (*acc. c. inf.*).
satrap satrapes *m.*
saturate saturo 1.
satyr satyrus *m.*
sauce ius *n*; condimentum *n*; **~pan** cacabus *m*; **~r** patella *f.*
saucy petulans, protervus.
saunter spatior 1.
sausage botulus *m*; tomaculum *n.*
savage ferus; immanis, saevus;

homo *m* incultus, barbarus; **~ry** feritas *f*, immanitas *f*, atrocitas *f*; barbaria *f*.
sav|e servo 1; eripio 3; salutem affero 3 (*alci*); **~e up** reservo 1; *adv. and prep.* praeter (*acc.*); nisi (*quod*); **~ing** compendium *n* (*alcs rei*); **~iour** servator *m*.
savour sapor *m*; **~ of** (red)oleo 2 (*alqd*); **~y** conditus; **be ~y** sapio 3.
saw serra *f*; proverbium *n*; *v/t.* serra seco 1 (*alqd*); *v/i.* serram, duco 3; **~dust** scobis *f*.
say dico 3; loquor 3 (*alqd*); **~ yes** aio; **~ that ... not** nego 1; **said I** inquam, aio; **said he** inquit, ait; **as Homer ~s** ut ait Homerus; **they (men) ~ that** ferunt 3, traditum est (*acc. c. inf.*); **he is said to be** traditur 3, dicitur 3 (esse); **~ing** dictum *n*, proverbium *n*; **as the ~ing is** ut aiunt.
scab scabies *f*.
scabbard vagina *f*.
scaffold machina *f*; *fig.* securis *f*, supplicium *n*.
scal|e conscendo 3; lanx *f*; squama *f* (*piscis etc.*); *fig.* gradus, us *m*; modus *m*; **pair of ~es** trutina *f*; **~ing-ladder** scalae *f/pl.*
scalp cutis *f* capitis.
scalpel scalpellum *n*.
scaly squamosus.
scamp verbero *m*, furcifer *m*.
scan intueor 2; contemplor 1, considero 1.
scandal opprobrium *n*, dedecus *n*; **~ise** offendo 3 (*dat.*); **~ous** probrosus, infamis, turpis.
scant|iness exiguitas *f*; inopia *f*; **~y** exiguus, tenuis.
scapegoat piaculum *n*.
scar cicatrix *f*.
scarc|e rarus; **~ely** vix; **~ely yet** vixdum; **~ity** inopia *f*, paucitas *f*.
scare terreo 2; **~crow** formido *f*.
scarf velamen *n*; rica *f*.
scarlet coccum *n*; coccinus.
scarred cicatricosus.
scatter *v/t.* spargo 3; dissipo 1; disicio 3; *v/i.* dissipor 1, disicior 3; **~ing** dissipatio *f*.
scene locus *m*; spectaculum *n*; *thea.* scaena *f*; **come on the ~** intervenio 4; **~ry** scaena *f*; species *f* loci.
scent odoror 1 (*cibum etc.*); odor *m*; **get ~ of** olfacio 3, odoror 1 (*alqd*); **~ed** odoratus.
sceptical: be ~ dubito 1.
sceptre sceptrum *n*; scipio *m*.
schedule tabula *f*.
scheme consilium *n*; ars *f*; insidiae *f/pl.*; ratio *f*; molior 4.
scholar vir *m* doctus, eruditus; discipulus *m*; **~ly** doctus; **~ship** litterae *f/pl.*; doctrina *f*.
school schola *f* (philosophorum); (*for boys*) ludus *m*; *fig.* disciplina *f*, secta *f* (*Platonis etc.*); erudio 4; **~ed** expertus (*gen.*); **~fellow** condiscipulus *m*; **~master** magister *m*.
schooner actuaria *f*.
scien|ce scientia *f*, disciplina *f*, doctrina *f*; ars *f*, ratio *f*; **~ce of war** res *f* militaris; **~tific** physicus.
scion proles *f*, progenies *f*.
scissors forfex *f*.
scoff at irrideo 2, derideo 2 (*acc.*); **~ing** irrisio *f*; irrisus, us *m*.
scold increpo 1, obiurgo 1; **~ing** obiurgatio *f*.
scoop ligula *f*; **~ out** excavo 1 (*alqd*).
scope campus *m*; area *f*; locus *m*.
scorch amburo 3; torreo 2; **~ed, ~ing** torridus.
score noto 1; nota *f*; (*total*) summa *f*; viginti; **reckon the ~** rationem computo 1.
scorn contemno 3, sperno 3; **~er** contemptor *m*; **~ful** fastidiosus (*gen.*); arrogans, superbus.
scorpion scorpio *m*.
scot-free incolumis.
scoundrel nebulo *m*, furcifer *m*.
scour (de)tergeo 2; verro 3; *fig.* pervagor 1.
scourge virgis caedo 3; verbero 1; flagellum *n*.
scout explorator *m*, speculator *m*; exploro 1; repudio 1, sperno 3.
scowl frontem contraho 3; frontis contractio *f*; **~ing** trux.
scraggy strigosus.
scramble (up) conscendo 3, scando 3 (*arcem etc.*).
scrap frustum *n*.
scrape rado 3; angustiae *f/pl.*; **~r** strigilis *f*.
scratch rado 3; seco 1; nota *f*.
scream vociferor 1; clamo 1, clamito 1; ululo 1; clamor *m*; vociferatio *f*.
screech ululo 1; ululatus, us *m*.
screen tego 3; vela *n/pl.*; *fig.* species *f*.
screw clavus *m*.

scribe scriba *m*; librarius *m*.
script scriptio *f*, scriptura *f*.
scrofula struma *f*.
scroll volumen *n*.
scrub tergeo 2.
scrup|le scrupulus *m*; religio *f*; cunctor 1, dubito 1 (*inf.*); **~ulous** religiosus, diligens; **~ulousness** religio *f*, diligentia *f*.
scrutinise (per)scrutor 1.
scuffle rixa *f*.
scull palma *f*.
sculp|tor sculptor *m*; **~ture** sculptura *f*; sculpo 3.
scum spuma *f*; *fig.* sentina *f*; quisquiliae *f/pl.*
scurf porrigo *f*.
scurrilous scurrilis, probrosus.
scuttle summergo 3.
scythe falx *f*.
sea mare *n*; pelagus, i *n*; **by ~ and land** terra marique; **be at ~** fluctuo 1; marinus, maritimus; **~ board, coast** ora *f* (maritima); **~gull** mergus *m*.
seal (ob)signo 1 (*epistolam, testamenta*); signum *n*; phoca *f*; **~ed** obsignatus; **~ing-wax** cera *f*.
seam sutura *f*.
seaman nauta *m*.
sear uro 3.
search (per)scrutor 1; **~ for** quaero 3; indago 1; **~ into** investigo 1; **~ out** exploro 1; investigatio *f*; **~ing** diligens.
seasick nauseabundus; **be ~** nauseo 1; **~ness** nausea *f*.
seaside maritimus.
season tempus *n*; condio 4 (*cibum*); **~able** tempestivus; **~ably** ad tempus; **~ing** condimentum *n*; sal *m*.
seat sedes *f*, sella *f*; **(rows of) ~s** subsellia *n/pl.*; **~ oneself** consido 3; **be ~ed** sedeo 2.
seaweed alga *f*.
secede descisco 3 (*ab*).
seclu|ded secretus; **~sion** solitudo *f*.
second secundus (*ad, ab*); alter; **a ~ time** iterum; momentum *n* (temporis); adiuvo 1; **~ary** secundarius, posterior; **~er** suasor *m*; **~ly** deinde; **~-rate** inferior.
secre|cy secretum *n*; **~t** occultus, tectus, arcanus; clandestinus; occultum *n*; commissa *n/pl.*; **keep a ~t** occultum teneo 2 (*alqd*); **keep ~t from** celo 1 (*alqd alqm*); **~tary** scriba *m*.
secrete abdo 3.
secretly clam, occulte.
sect secta *f*, schola *f*.
section pars *f*.
secure tutus; confirmo 1; tueor 2; munio 4 (*me contra alqd*).
security salus, utis *f*; cautio *f*; pignus *n*, vas *m*; **give ~** caveo 2 (*alci de re*), cautionem praesto 1; **get ~ from** caveo 2 (*ab alqd*); **be ~ for** vas fio (*alci*).
sedan-chair lectica *f*.
sedate sedatus, gravis.
sedentary iners.
sedge ulva *f*.
sediment faex *f*.
sediti|on seditio *f*; tumultus, us *m*; **~ous** seditiosus, factiosus.
seduc|e tempto 1; corrumpo 3; **~er** corruptor *m*; **~tion** corruptela *f*; stuprum *n*; **~tive** blandus.
sedulous assiduus.
see video 2; cerno 3; conspicor 1; specto 1 (*fabulam, ludos*); (*mentally*) intellego 3; percipio 3; sentio 4; **~ to** consulo 3 (*dat.*); video 2 (*alqd*); **go to ~** viso 3.
seed semen *n*.
seeing that quoniam, siquidem.
seek quaero 3; (ex)peto 3.
seem videor 2 (*inf.*); **~ing** fictus; **~ingly** ut videtur; **~ly** decens, decorus; **it is ~ly** decet 2 (*acc. c. inf.*).
seer vates *m*.
seethe ferveo 2.
segregate secerno 3.
seiz|e rapio 3; comprehendo 3, deprehendo 3; *mil.* occupo 1; invado 3; **~ure** comprehensio *f*.
seldom raro.
select deligo 3, eligo 3; lectus, exquisitus; **~ion** delectus, us *m*.
self ipse; **~-confidence** sui fiducia *f*; **~-control** modestia *f*, moderatio *f*; **be ~ish** mea causa ago 3; mihi (soli) consulo 3.
sell *v/t.* vendo 3 (*alqd auro*); *v/i.* veneo, venum eo 4; **~er** venditor *m*; **~ing** venditio *f*.
semblance imago *f*, umbra *f*; simulacrum *n*.
semicircle hemicyclium *n*.
senat|e senatus, us *m*; patres *m/pl.*; **~e-house** curia *f*; **~or** senator *m*; **~ors** patres *m/pl.* conscripti; **~orial** senatorius.
send mitto 3; **~ away** dimitto 3; **~ back** remitto 3; **~ for** arcesso 3;

~ **word** nuntio 1; certiorem facio 3 (*alqm*); (re)scribo 3; **~ing** missio *f*.
senil|e senilis; **~ity** senium *n*.
senior maior natu (*quam alqs, alqo*); superior (*aetate, gradu*); **~ity** superior aetas *f*, gradus, us *m*.
sensation sensus, us *m*.
sense sensus, us *m*; mens *f*, prudentia *f*; sententia *f* (*legis*); **out of one's ~s** mente captus; **~less** stultus, fatuus.
sensible prudens; **be ~** sentio 4 (*alqd*); intellego 3.
sensitive tener, mollis.
sensual voluptarius; **~ity** voluptates *f/pl*.
sentence sententia *f*; *jur*. iudicium *n*; damno 1, condemno 1, multo 1 (*alqm morte, exsilio*); **pass ~** sententiam fero 3.
sentiment sensus, us *m*; opinio *f*, sententia *f*; **hold the same ~s** eadem sentio 4.
sentinel, sentry vigil *m*, excubitor *m*; **sentinels** vigilia *f*, statio *f*; **be on sentry duty** in statione sum.
separa|ble separabilis; **~te** separo 1, disiungo 3 (*a re*); divido 3 (*alqd in partes*); (*mentally*) discerno 3, secerno 3; separatus, disiunctus; **~tion** disiunctio *f*.
September (mensis) September, bris *m*.
sepulchre sepulcrum *n*.
sequence ordo *m*; series *f*.
sequestrate sequestro pono 3, do 1 (*alqd*).
serene tranquillus, serenus.
serf servus *m*; **~dom** servitium *n*; servitus, utis *f*.
series series *f*; **a ~ of** continuus.
serious gravis (*homo, res*); severus (*homo*); serius (*res*); **~ matters** seria *n/pl.*; **~ness** gravitas *f*.
sermon oratio *f*.
serpent serpens *f*, anguis *m and f*; coluber, bri *m*, draco *m*; **~ine** sinuosus, multiplex.
serrated serratus.
serried confertus, densus.
servant famulus *m*, servus *m*; minister, tri *m*.
serve servio 4 (*dat.*); prosum (*dat.*); proficio 3 (*ad, in alqd*); *mil*. stipendia mereo(r) 2, milito 1; **~ for** sum (*pro re*); **~ up** appono 3 (*cibum alci*).
service ministerium *n*; opera *f*; officium *n*; **military ~** militia *f*; stipendia *n/pl.*; **good ~s** merita *n/pl.*; **be of ~ to** prosum (*dat.*); **~able** utilis; aptus (*ad*).
servi|le servilis; abiectus, humilis; **~lity** humilitas *f*, adulatio *f*; **~tude** servitus, utis *f*; servitium *n*.
session sessio *f*; **~s** conventus *m/pl*.
sesterce sestertius *m*; **a thousand ~s** sestertium *n*.
set status, ratus; series *f*; circulus *m*, globus *m*; *v/t*. pono 3; (col)loco 1; statuo 3; *v/i*. occido 3 (*sol*); **~ about** incipio 3; **~ against** oppono 3 (*alqd alci rei*); **~ apart** sepono 3; **~ at naught** contemno 3, nihili facio 3; **~ on fire** incendo 3; **~ out** proficiscor 3; **~ up** statuo 3, constituo 3; **~tee** lectus *m*; **~ting** occasus, us *m*.
settle *v/t*. constituo 3 (*gentem, pretium*); compono 3 (*controversias*); solvo 3 (*nomen, aes alienum*); deduco 3 (*coloniam, colonos*); *v/i*. consido 3 (*in*); **~d** certus, ratus; **~ment** deductio *f* (*coloniae*); colonia *f*; compositio *f*; **~r** colonus *m*; advena *m*.
seven septem; **~fold** septemplex; **~ hundred** septingenti; **~teen** septendecim; **~th** septimus; **~tieth** septuagesimus; **~ty** septuaginta.
sever disiungo 3.
several aliquot; (com)plures; singuli.
sever|e durus, austerus, severus; gravis, acerbus (*poena, morbus etc.*); **~ity** severitas *f*, gravitas *f*.
sew suo 3.
sewer cloaca *f*.
sex sexus, us *m*.
shabby obsoletus; pannosus (*homo*); sordidus.
shackle vinculum *n*; compes *f*.
shade umbra *f*; simulacrum *n*; **~s** manes *m/pl.*, inferi *m/pl.*; opaco 1; **put in the ~** officio 3 (*alci*; *nomini*); **sun-~** umbraculum *n*.
shadow umbra *f*; **~y** inanis, vanus.
shady opacus, umbrosus, umbrifer.
shaft telum *n*; sagitta *f*; hastile *n*; temo *m*.
shaggy villosus, hirtus.
shak|e *v/t*. quatio 3, concutio 3; agito 1; labefacto 1, commoveo 2; *v/i*. quatior 3; *fig*. horreo 2, horresco 3; **~e one's head** abnuo 3; **~y** tremebundus, instabilis.
shallow brevis; *fig*. vanus, levis; vadum *n*.

sham simulatus, falsus; simulo 1.
shame pudor *m*, verecundia *f*; rubor *m*; dedecus *n*, probrum *n*; ruborem, pudorem incutio 3 (*alci*); dedecoro 1 (*acc.*); **feel ~** pudet 2 (*me alcs rei*); **~faced** verecundus; **~ful** turpis, probrosus, flagitiosus; **~less** impudens, improbus; **~lessness** impudentia *f*.
shank crus, uris *n*.
shape forma *f*, figura *f*, facies *f*; fingo 3; (con)formo 1; **~less** informis, deformis; **~ly** formosus.
shard testa *f*.
share pars *f*; partior 4, communico 1, consocio 1 (*alqd cum alqo*); **~ out** divido 3; **have a ~ of** in partem habeo 2; intersum (*dat.*); **~d** communis; **~r** particeps *m*, socius *m*.
shark pistrix *f*.
sharp acutus; acer (*sensus*); sagax, argutus; mordax; **~en** acuo 3; **~er** fraudator *m*; **~ness** asperitas *f*, acerbitas *f*; acumen *n*; subtilitas *f*.
shatter frango 3, elido 3; quasso 1.
shav|e rado 3, tondeo 2; **~ings** ramenta *n/pl*.
shawl palla *f*.
she ea, haec, illa.
sheaf manipulus *m*; fascis *m*.
shear tondeo 2; **~ing** tonsura *f*; **~s** forfices *f/pl*.
sheath vagina *f*; **~e** recondo 3 (*gladium in vaginam*).
shed profundo 3, effundo 3 (*lacrimas, sanguinem, etc.*); **be ~** decido 3 (*ex alqa re*); tectum *n*, tugurium *n*.
sheen fulgor *m*.
sheep ovis *f*; **~fold** saepta *n/pl*.
sheer abruptus, praeruptus; merus, germanus.
sheet (*linen*) linteum *n*; (*paper*) scida *f*; (*metal*) lamina *f*; *naut.* pes *m*.
shelf pluteus *m*; pegma *n*.
shell concha *f*, testa *f* (*ostreae etc.*); putamen *n*; crusta *f*; **~fish** concha *f*.
shelter tego 3, defendo 3; in tutelam recipio 3; perfugium *n*; hospitium *n*.
shepherd pastor *m*.
shield scutum *n*; clipeus *m*; *fig.* praesidium *n*; tego 3 (*alqd ab alqa re*).
shift *v/t.* moveo 2; (per)muto 1; *v/i.* moveor 2, mutor 1; consilium *n*; stropha *f*; tunica *f*; mutatio *f*; **make ~** provideo 2; **~y** versutus, subdolus.
shin crus, uris *n*; **~bone** tibia *f*.
shine luceo 2, fulgeo 2, niteo 2; nitor *m*.
shingle calculi *m/pl*.
shining lucidus, nitidus, fulgens.
ship navis *f*; **merchant ~** navis *f* oneraria; **war~** navis *f* longa; in navem impono 3; **~owner** navicularius *m*; **~ping** naves *f/pl.*; **~wreck** naufragium *n*; **~wrecked** naufragus.
shirt tunica *f*, subucula *f*.
shiver *v/t.* comminuo 3; *v/i.* horreo 2; tremo 3; fragmentum *n*; horror *m*, tremor *m*.
shoal examen *n* (piscium); vadum *n*; syrtis *f*.
shock conflictus, us *m*; concursus, us *m*; impetus, us *m*; *fig.* offensio *f*; offendo 3; **be ~ed** obstupesco 3; **~ing** foedus, atrox, nefarius.
shoe calceus *m*; **indoor ~, horse~** solea *f*; calceo 1; **~maker** sutor *m*; **~string** lingula *f*.
shoot planta *f*, virga *f*; *v/t.* (e)mitto 3, conicio 3 (*telum*); vulnero 1 (*alqm*); *v/i.* volo 1; **~ing star** fax *f*.
shop taberna *f*; obsono 1; **~keeper** tabernarius *m*; **~ping** obsonatus, us *m*.
shore litus *n*; ora *f*; **~ up** fulcio 4.
short brevis; **be ~ of** egeo 2 (*abl.*); **fall ~ of** non contingo 3 (*alqd*); **in ~** denique; **~age** inopia *f*; **~-coming** delictum *n*; **~cut** compendiaria via *f*; **~en** contraho 3; **~hand** notae *f/pl.*; **~hand writer** notarius *m*; **~ly** brevi, mox; breviter; **~ness** brevitas *f*; **~sighted** hebes (*oculus*); *fig.* improvidus.
shot ictus, us *m*; **within, out of, ~** intra, extra ictum (teli).
shoulder umerus *m*; in umeros tollo 3 (*onus*).
shout clamo 1, vociferor 1; clamor *m*.
shove trudo 3.
shovel rutrum *n*; pala *f*.
show monstro 1 (*viam etc.*); praebeo 3, exhibeo 2, praesto 1 (*virtutem; me fortem*); **~ that** demonstro 1, doceo 2 (*acc. c. inf.*); **~ off** ostento 1 (*alqd, me*); ostentatio *f*, species *f*; spectaculum *n*.
shower imber, bris *m*; ingero 3, fundo 3 (*tela in alqm*); **~y** pluvius.
showy magnificus, speciosus.
shred conseco 1; fragmentum *n*.

shrewd sagax, acutus; **~ness** calliditas *f.*
shrewish importunus.
shriek ululo 1; ululatus, us *m.*
shrill (per)acutus.
shrine delubrum *n*, sacrarium *n.*
shrink me contraho 3; **~ from** refugio 3, abhorreo 2 (*ab*); detrecto 1, reformido 1 (*alqd*).
shrivel torreo 2; **~led** rugosus, torridus.
shroud involvo 3 (*alqd alqa re*).
shrub frutex *m*; **~bery** arbustum *n.*
shudder horreo 2; **~ at** perhorresco 3 (*alqd*); horror *m*, tremor *m.*
shuffle *v/t.* (per)misceo 2; *v/i.* tergiversor 1.
shun fugio 3; vito 1.
shut claudo 3, occludo 3; obsero 1 (*fores*); operio 4; **~ in** includo 3; **~ out** excludo 3; **~ter** foricula *f.*
shuttle radius *m.*
shy timidus, verecundus; consternor 1; **~ness** verecundia *f.*
Sibyl Sibylla *f*; **~line** Sibyllinus.
sick aeger, aegrotus; **be ~** aegroto 1; morbo afficior 3; vomo 3; nauseo 1; **be ~ of** taedet 2 (*me alcs rei*); **~en** *v/t.* fastidium moveo 2; *v/i.* in morbum cado 3, incido 3.
sickle falx *f.*
sick|ly aeger, invalidus; **~ness** morbus *m*; aegrotatio *f.*
side latus *n* (*corporis, collis*); pars *f*; factio *f*; **on this, that ~** hinc, illinc; **on this, that ~ of** citra (*acc.*), trans (*acc.*); **on both, all ~s** utrimque, undique; **on, at the ~** a latere (*alcs, exercitus etc.*); **be on the ~ of** sto 1 (*ab alqo*); **be on neither ~** nullius partis sum; **~long** obliquus, limus; **~ways** in obliquum.
siege obsidio *f*, obsessio *f*; **lay ~ to** obsideo 2 (*urbem*); oppugno 1; **~-works** opera *n/pl.*
sieve cribrum *n.*
sift perscrutor 1.
sigh suspiro 1; gemo 3; suspirium duco 3, traho 3; suspirium *n*; **~ing** suspiratus, us *m.*
sight visus, us *m*; acies *f* (*oculorum*); conspectus, us *m*; aspectus, us *m*; species *f*; spectaculum *n*; **at first ~** primo aspectu; **in ~ of** in conspectu (*alcs*); **catch ~ of** conspicio 3, conspicor 1 (*alqd*).
sign signum *n*, indicium *n*; nota *f*; vestigium *n*; **heavenly ~** omen *n*, portentum *n*; subscribo 3 (*dat.*); **~ with a seal** signo 1.
signal signum *n*; insignis, egregius; **give a ~** signum do 1; annuo 3; *mil.* cano 3 (*receptui etc.*).
sign|ature nomen *n*; **~et** signum *n*; **~et-ring** anulus *m.*
significan|ce significatio *f*; **~t** significans (*verbum*).
signify significo 1; sibi vult.
silen|ce silentium *n*; refuto 1 (*alqm*); **keep ~ce** taceo 2, sileo 2; **~t** tacitus, silens; **~tly** tacite.
silk serica *n/pl.*; bombyx *m*; **~en** sericus.
sill limen *n.*
sill|iness stultitia *f*; **~y** stultus, ineptus, fatuus.
silver argenteus; argentum *n*; argento induco 3 (*alqd*).
similar similis, par (*gen., dat.*); **~ity** similitudo *f.*
simile similitudo *f.*
simple simplex, merus; **~-minded** ineptus, credulus; **~ton** stultus (homo) *m.*
simpl|icity simplicitas *f*; candor *m*; **~ify** dilucide, apertius narro 1; explano 1; **~y** solum, simpliciter.
simulat|e simulo 1; **~ion** simulatio *f.*
simultaneously eodem tempore; simul.
sin peccatum *n*, delictum *n*; pecco 1.
since ex (*abl.*), ab (*abl.*); post (*acc.*); *conj.* postquam (*perf. indic.*); **it is many years ~** abhinc multos annos; **long ~** iamdudum; (*causal*) cum (*subj.*), quoniam (*indic.*).
sincer|e simplex, candidus, sincerus; **~ity** probitas *f*, sinceritas *f.*
sinew nervus *m*; lacertus *m*; **~y** nervosus.
sinful impius, pravus.
sing cano 3, canto 1 (*alqd*).
singe aduro 3, amburo 3.
sing|er cantator *m*, cantatrix *f*; **~ing** cantus, us *m.*
single unus, solus; **~ out** eligo 3; **in ~ combat** comminus.
singular singularis, unicus, egregius; novus, mirabilis.
sinister dirus.
sink *v/t.* deprimo 3 (*navem*); *v/i.* consido 3, desido 3; mergor 3 (*in aquam*); ruo 3; collabor 3.
sinner peccator *m.*
sinuous sinuosus.

sip sorbillo 1, degusto 1.
sire pater, tris *m*, genitor *m*.
Siren Siren *f*.
sister soror *f*.
sit sedeo 2 (*in sede*); ~ **down** consido 3; ~ **up** vigilo 1 (*de nocte*).
site situs, us *m*; locus *m*.
sitting (con)sessio *f*.
situat|ed situs (*in*); **be ~ed** iaceo 2; **~ion** situs, us *m*; locus *m*.
six sex; ~ **hundred** sescenti; **~teen** sedecim; **~teenth** sextus decimus; **~tieth** sexagesimus; **~ty** sexaginta.
size magnitudo *f*, amplitudo *f*; **of what ~?** quantus?
skein spira *f*.
skeleton ossa *n/pl.*; *fig.* larva *f*.
sketch adumbro 1; describo 3; adumbratio *f*; lineamenta *n/pl.*
skewer veru *n*.
skiff scapha *f*, navicula *f*.
skil|ful sollers, habilis; **~l** sollertia *f*, peritia *f*; artificium *n*; **~led** peritus (*gen.*, *abl.*); doctus, sciens (*gen.*).
skim despumo 1; ~ **over** percurro 3, perstringo 3, rado 3 (*alqd*).
skin cutis *f*; pellis *f*, tergum *n* (*bovis etc.*); pellem detraho 3 (*alci*); **dressed in ~s** pellitus; **~ny** macer.
skip exsulto 1; salio 4; lascivio 4 (*agnus etc.*); *fig.* praetereo 4, transilio 4; **~per** navicularius *m*; nauarchus *m*.
skirmish proelium *n* (leve); concursatio *f*; velitor 1, concurso 1; **~er** veles *m*, concursator *m*.
skirt limbus *m*; praetereo 4; *fig.* perstringo 3.
skittish lascivus.
skulk lateo 2; delitesco 3 (*in re*).
skull caput *n*.
sky caelum *n*; **~-blue** caeruleus; **raise to the skies** in caelum fero 3.
slab lapis *m*; tabula *f*.
slack laxus, remissus; piger; **~en** remitto 3; relaxo 1; **~ness** pigritia *f*, remissio *f*.
slake exstinguo 3, restinguo 3.
slander maledico 3 (*dat.*); criminor 1, obtrecto 1 (*alqm*); maledictio *f*, criminatio *f*, obtrectatio *f*; crimen *n*; **~er** obtrectator *m*; **~ous** maledicus.
slanting obliquus.
slap alapa *f*; pulso 1.
slash incido 3; plaga *f*.
slate (*roof*) tegula *f*; **writing-~** tabula *f*.
slaughter caedo 3, concido 3; trucido 1; caedes *f*, internecio *f*.
slave servus *m*; famulus *m*; **home-born ~** verna *m and f*; **female ~** ancilla *f*, serva *f*; (de)sudo 1; laboro 1; **~-dealer** venalicius *m*; **~ry** servitium *n*; servitus, utis *f*.
slay interficio 3, caedo 3, occido 3; neco 1; interimo 3; **~er** interfector *m*, percussor *m*.
sledge trahea *f*; **~hammer** malleus *m*.
sleek nitidus, nitens.
sleep dormio 4; quiesco 3; dormito 1, somnum capio 3; ~ **off** edormio 4; somnus *m*; quies *f*; sopor *m*; **go to ~** obdormisco 3; **during ~** in somnis; **~iness** somni cupido *f*; **~ing-draught** sopor *m*; **~less** insomnis; **be ~less** vigilo 1; **~lessness** insomnia *f*; **~y** semisomnus, somniculosus.
sleet grando *f*.
sleeve manicae *f/pl.*
sleigh trahea *f*.
sleight-of-hand praestigiae *f/pl.*
slender gracilis, tenuis; exilis; **~ness** gracilitas *f*.
slice concido 3; segmentum *n*.
slide labor 3; lapsus, us *m*.
slight levis, exiguus, parvus; despicio 3, contemno 3, parvi facio 3; neglego 3; indignitas *f*, neglegentia *f*; **~ingly** contemptim.
slim gracilis, tenuis.
slim|e limus *m*; lutum *n*; **~y** limosus.
sling funda *f*; mitto 3, conicio 3; suspendo 3 (*alqd e re*); **~er** funditor *m*.
slink away me subduco 3.
slip labor 3; **let ~** amitto 3 (*opportunitatem*); ~ **away** me subduco 3; ~ **out of** elabor 3; lapsus, us *m*; *fig.* error *m*; **make a ~** erro 1; **~per** solea *f*, crepida *f*; **~pery** lubricus; **~shod** dissolutus.
slit incido 3, scindo 3.
sloop lembus *m*.
slop|e clivus *m*; fastigium *n*; vergo 3; **~ing** declivis, acclivis, proclivis.
sloth segnitia *f*, desidia *f*; **~ful** segnis, ignavus, piger.
slovenly neglegens.
slow tardus, lentus, segnis; **~ness** tarditas *f*, pigritia *f*.
slugg|ard homo *m* ignavus; **~ish** piger, ignavus.

sluice cataracta *f*.
slumber sopor *m*; dormio 4.
slur macula *f*; **cast a ~ upon** maculo 1 (*alqd*).
slush tabes *f*.
sly callidus, astutus, vafer.
smack alapa *f*; sonus *m*; **fishing-~** lenunculus *m*; ferio 4; verbero 1; **~ of** sapio 3 (*alqd*); (red)oleo 2 (*alqd*).
small parvus, tenuis, brevis, exiguus; **how ~?** quantulus?; **~ness** exiguitas *f*, brevitas *f*.
smart lautus; acer, acerbus; sagax; mordeor 2, doleo 2; poenam do 1; morsus, us *m*, dolor *m*.
smash comminuo 3, confringo 3.
smear lino 3 (*alqd alqa re*); illino 3 (*alqd alci rei*).
smell olfacio 3, odoror 1; **~ of** (red)oleo 2 (*alqd*); odor *m*; **sense of ~** odoratus, us *m*; **sweet-~ing** odoratus.
smelt (ex)coquo 3.
smile (sub)rideo 2, renideo 2; risus, us *m*.
smite ferio 4.
smith faber, bri *m*; ferrarius *m*; **~y** officina *f* (ferraria); fabrica *f*.
smok|e *v/i*. fumo 1; *v/t*. fumigo 1; fumus *m*; vapor *m*; **~y** fumosus, fumidus.
smooth levis, teres; glaber; placidus, tranquillus (*mare*); levo 1; polio 4; rado 3; **~ness** levitas *f*, lenitas *f*; **~-tongued** blandus.
smother opprimo 3; suffoco 1; *fig*. reprimo 3, comprimo 3.
smoulder fumo 1.
smudge litura *f*.
smug mihi placens.
smuggle furtim, contra leges importo 1 (*alqd*).
smut fuligo *f*; **~ty** *fig*. obscenus.
snack cenula *f*.
snaffle frenum *n*.
snail cochlea *f*.
snak|e anguis *m and f*; coluber, bri *m*; serpens *f*; **~y** anguineus, vipereus.
snap *v/t*. praefringo 3; *v/i*. frangor 3, rumpor 3; crepo 1; concrepo 1 (*digitis*); **~ up** corripio 3; crepitus, us *m*.
snare plaga *f*, pedica *f*; laqueus *m*; *fig*. insidiae *f/pl*.; irretio 4; laqueo capto 1.
snarl gannio 4; ringor 3.
snatch rapio 3, carpo 3; **~ at** capto 1; **~ away from** avello 3; **~ up** arripio 3; **in ~es** carptim.
sneak correpo 3 (*in intra*); arrepo 3 (*ad*).
sneer irrideo 2, derideo 2, naso suspendo 3 (*alqm, alqd*); irrisio *f*; irrisus, us *m*.
sneez|e sternuo 3; **~ing** sternumentum *n*.
sniff odoror 1.
snip praecido 3; segmentum *n*.
snore sterto 3.
snort fremo 3; fremitus, us *m*.
snout rostrum *n*.
snow nix *f*; **it ~s** ningit 3; **~-white** niveus, nivalis; **~y** nivosus.
snub contemno 3, sperno 3; **~-nosed** simus, silus.
snuff (out) exstinguo 3.
snug commodus.
so ita, tam, adeo (... ut); **just ~** sic; ita; **and ~** itaque, ergo, igitur; **and ~ on** et cetera.
soak *v/t*. madefacio 3; macero 1; *v/i*. mano 1; **~ed** madidus.
soap sapo *m*.
soar sublime feror 3; subvolo 1; me tollo 3.
sob singulto 1; singultus, us *m*.
sob|er sobrius, siccus; sanus; modestus, temperans; **~riety** sobrietas *f*; continentia *f*, temperantia *f*.
sociab|ility facilitas *f*; **~le** sociabilis; comis.
social communis, civilis.
society societas *f*, communitas *f*, commune *n*; civitas *f*; sodalitas *f*, collegium *n*.
socket cavum *n*; sedes *f*.
socle basis *f*.
sod caespes *m*.
soda nitrum *n*.
sodden madidus.
sofa lectulus *m*.
soft mollis, lenis, tener; mitis, mansuetus; **~en** *v/t*. (e)mollio 4; mitigo 1 (*cibum, severitatem*); lenio 4, placo 1; *v/i*. mitesco 3, mansuesco 3; **~ness** mollitia *f*, lenitas *f*.
soil terra *f*; solum *n*; humus, i *f*; inquino 1, foedo 1.
sojourn (com)moror 1; commoratio *f*, mansio *f*.
solace consolor 1; consolatio *f*; solatium *n*.
solder ferrumen *n*; ferrumino 1.
soldier miles *m*; **common ~** gre-

garius (miles) *m*; **~ly** militaris; **~y** miles *m*.
sole planta *f*; solum *n*; solus, unus, unicus; **~ly** solum, tantum.
solemn sollemnis, festus; augustus, religiosus; severus, gravis, serius; **~ity** sollemne *n*; gravitas *f*, severitas *f*; **~ize** celebro 1.
solicit peto 3 (*alqd ab alqo*); flagito 1, obsecro 1 (*alqm*; *ut*); **~ation** flagitatio *f*; **~or** cognitor *m*; iuris consultus *m*; **~ous** officiosus; **~ude** anxietas *f*.
solid solidus; firmus, robustus; solidum *n*; **~ify** concresco 3.
soliloquize mecum loquor 3.
solit|ary solitarius (*homo*); desertus, solus, secretus; **~ude** solitudo *f*.
solo solus.
solstice: summer ~ solstitium *n*; **winter ~** bruma *f*.
solution dilutum *n*; explicatio *f*.
solve (dis)solvo 3; enodo 1; **be ~nt** solvendo sum.
sombre tristis, tenebrosus.
some aliqui, nonnullus; aliquot (*pl.*); aliquid, aliquantum *n*; **~ ... others** alii ... alii; **~body, ~one** aliquis, quidam, nescio quis; **~how** aliqua; **~thing** aliquid, nescio quid; **~time** aliquando; **~times** aliquando, interdum, nonnunquam; modo ... modo; **~where** alicubi.
son filius *m*; **~-in-law** gener, eri *m*.
song cantus, us *m*; carmen *n*.
sonorous sonorus, clarus.
soon mox, brevi, iam; **~ after** post paulo; **as ~ as** simul atque, ac; statim ut; cum primum, ubi primum; **as ~ as possible** quamprimum; **~er** ante ... quam; libentius.
soot fuligo *f*.
soothe mitigo 1, sedo 1, placo 1.
soothsayer augur *m*, haruspex *m*, vates *m*.
sooty fuliginosus, fumosus.
sop *fig.* delenimentum *n*.
sophist sophistes *m*; cavillator *m*; **~ical** captiosus; **~ry** captiones *f/pl.*; **~icated** urbanus.
soporific soporifer, somnificus.
sorcer|er veneficus *m*; magus *m*; **~ess** maga *f*, saga *f*; **~y** veneficia *n/pl.*
sordid sordidus.
sore ulcus *n*; acerbus, gravis (*dolor etc.*); **be ~** doleo 2 (*caput etc.*); *fig.* aegre fero 3 (*alqd*; *quod*); **~ly** graviter; **~ness** dolor *m*.
sorrel lapathus *m*.
sorrow dolor *m*, maeror *m*; luctus, us *m*; doleo 2, lugeo 2; **~ful** maestus, maerens, tristis.
sorry miser, miserabilis; **be ~** paenitet 2, piget 2 (*me alcs rei*; *inf.*; *quod*).
sort genus; **a ~ of** quidam; **of this, that ~** huiusmodi, eiusmodi; **of such a ~** is, talis; **of all ~s** omnis; digero 3, dispono 3; **~ with** consentio 4 (*cum*).
sortie eruptio *f*, excursio *f*; **make a ~** erumpo 3.
sot potator *m*.
soul animus *m*; anima *f*; **with all my ~** ex animo, toto pectore; **not a ~** nemo (omnium); **~less** hebes.
sound sanus; salvus, incolumis; artus (*somnus*); sonus *m*; sonitus, us *m*; vox *f*; *v/t.* cano 3 (*classicum*; *signum*; *fidibus*); tento 1 (*vadum*); scrutor 1 (*animos*); **~ the praises of** celebro 1 (*laudem*; *alqm*); *v/i.* sono 1, cano 3; sonitum reddo 3; **~ness** sanitas *f*, gravitas *f*.
soup ius *n*.
sour acerbus; acidus; amarus; **turn ~** (co)acesco 3.
source fons *m*; caput *n*; origo *f*; **have its ~ in** orior 4 (*ab*).
south meridies *m*; australis, meridianus; **~ wind** auster, tri *m*; **~-east** inter meridiem et solis ortum; **~-east wind** eurus *m*; **~-pole** polus *m* australis; **~-west** inter meridiem et occasum solis; **~-west wind** Africus *m*.
sovereign rex *m*, princeps *m*; potentissimus; validus; **~ty** principatus, us *m*; regnum *n*; imperium *n*.
sow scrofa *f*, porca *f*; (con)sero 3; **~er** sator *m*; **~ing** sementis *f*, satio *f*.
spac|e locus *m*; spatium *n*, intervallum *n*; **~ious** amplus, latus, capax; **~iousness** amplitudo *f*.
spade pala *f*.
span palmus *m*; spatium *n* (*temporis*); iungo 3 (*flumen ponte*).
spangled distinctus (*stellis etc.*).
spar|e exilis; subsicivus (*tempus*, *opera*); parco 3 (*dat.*); parce utor 3 (*abl.*); **~ing** parcus (*in re*; *gen.*).
spark scintilla *f*; igniculus *m*; **~le** mico 1, corusco 1, scintillo 1; **~ling** micans, coruscus.
sparrow passer, eris *m*.
sparse rarus.
spasm convulsio *f*; **~odic** *fig.* rarus.

spatter aspergo 3.
speak dico 3, loquor 3 (*de re*); **~ out** eloquor 3; **~ to** alloquor 3, appello 1 (*alqm*); **~er** orator *m.*
spear hasta *f*; telum *n*; hasta transfigo 3 (*alqm*); **~man** hastatus *m*; iaculator *m.*
special proprius, peculiaris; praecipuus, extraordinarius; **~ity** proprium *n*; quod proprium est (*gen., dat.*); **~ly** praecipue.
species genus *n.*
specif|ic peculiaris; certus; **~ically** subtiliter; diserte.
specimen exemplum *n*, exemplar *m*; specimen *n.*
specious probabilis, speciosus.
speck macula *f*; **~led** maculosus, varius.
specta|cle spectaculum *n*; **~tor** spectator *m.*
spectre larva *f*; simulacrum *n*, imago *f.*
speculat|e cogito 1 (*de re*); inquiro 3 (*rem*); conicio 3; coniecturam facio 3; **~ion** coniectura *f.*
speech oratio *f*, lingua *f*; contio *f*; sermo *m*; verba *n/pl.*; **make a ~** orationem, contionem habeo 2; **~less** mutus.
speed celeritas *f*; accelero 1, maturo 1; fortuno 1; **~y** celer, citus.
spell carmen *n*; cantus, us *m*; litteras ordino 1.
spend impendo 3, insumo 3. (*alqd in alqd*); ago 3, dego 3, consumo 3 (*tempus*); **~thrift** nepos *m*; profusus (homo) *m.*
spent: be ~ defervesco 3 (*ira, cupido etc.*).
spew vomo 3.
sphere sphaera *f*; globus *m*; *fig.* campus *m*; provincia *f*, area *f.*
sphinx Sphinx *f.*
spice odor *m*; condimentum *n*; condio 4; **~d** odoratus.
spider's web aranea *f.*
spike clavus *m*; cuspis *f*; spica *f.*
spill effundo 3; assula *f.*
spin *v/t.* neo 2; deduco 3; verso 1; *v/i.* versor 1; **~ out** duco 3; **~dle** fusus *m.*
spine spina *f.*
spinster innupta *f.*
spiral spira *f*, coc(h)lea *f*; **in a ~ shape** in cocleam.
spirit animus *m*; anima *f*; mens *f*, ingenium *n*; vigor *m*; voluntas *f*, sententia *f* (*legis*); **high ~s** animi *m/pl.*, spiritus *m/pl.*; **~s of the dead** Manes *m/pl.*; **~ed** animosus, ferox, acer; **~less** ignavus; abiectus (animo).
spit spuo 3; veru (con)figo 3 (*carnem*); veru *n.*
spite malevolentia *f*, malignitas *f*, invidia *f*; laedo 3; malevolentia utor 3 (*in alqm*); **~ful** malevolus, infestus.
spittle sputum *n.*
splash aspergo 3 (*alqm alqa re*); sonitus, us *m.*
spleen lien *m*; bilis *f*; stomachus *m.*
splend|id splendidus, lautus, magnificus; praeclarus; **~our** splendor *m*; lautitia *f.*
splenetic stomachosus.
splinter assula *f*; fragmentum *n.*
split *v/t.* (dif)findo 3, scindo 3; *v/i.* dissilio 4; fissum *n*; fissura *f.*
splutter crepo 1, crepito 1; balbutio 4.
spoil spolio 1; corrumpo 3; vitio 1; (nimium) indulgeo 2 (*dat.*); praeda *f*; spolia *n/pl.*
spoke radius *m.*
spokesman interpres *m*, orator *m.*
spondee spondeus *m.*
sponge spongia *f*; spongia detergo 3.
spontaneous voluntarius; **~ly** sua sponte, ultro.
spoon cochlear *n.*
sporadic rarus.
sport ludo 3; ludus *m*; lusus, us *m*; ludibrium *n*; **make ~ of** ludifico 1 (*alqm*); **be the ~ of** ludibrio sum (*alcs*); **~ive** ludicer, iocosus; **~sman** venator *m.*
spot macula *f*, nota *f*; locus *m*; **on the ~** ibidem; conspicio 3; **~less** integer, purus; **~ted** maculosus, varius.
spouse coniunx *f and m.*
spout os *n*; prosilio 4; emico 1.
sprain intorqueo 2.
sprawl fundor 3 (*humo*).
spray aspergo 3; aspergo *f*; ramulus *m.*
spread extendo 3, pando 3; **~ abroad** *v/t.* sero 3, differo 3, divulgo 1; *v/i.* diffundor 3; serpo 3; evagor 1; increbresco 3, percrebresco 3, peragro 1 (*rumores etc.*); **~ing** patulus.
sprig ramulus *m.*
sprightly alacer, hilaris.

spring ver *n*; fons *m*; saltus, us *m*; vernus; salio 4, exsilio 4; ~ **down** desilio 4; ~ **from** nascor 3 (*ab, ex re; alqo*); ~ **up** coorior 4 (*tempestas etc.*); exorior 4 (*seditio etc.*); exsilio 4 (*de sella*); **~-time** vernum tempus *n*.
sprinkle aspergo 3, inspergo 3 (*alqd alqa re; alqd alci rei*).
sprout cresco 3, emergo 3 (*ex*); surculus *m*.
spruce nitidus, lautus.
spume spuma *f*.
spur calcar *n*; (*of mountains*) iugum *n*; calcaribus concito 1; calcaria subdo 1 (*equo*); *fig.* concito 1.
spurious falsus.
spurn aspernor 1; reicio 3.
spurt emico 1; nisus, us *m*; impetus, us *m*.
spy explorator *m*, speculator *m*; ~ **out** exploro 1.
squabble altercor 1, rixor 1; iurgium *n*.
squadron (of cavalry) turma *f*, ala *f*.
squal|id sordidus, squalidus; **~or** squalor *m*.
squall procella *f*; vagio 4.
squander effundo 3; dissipo 1; **~er** nepos *m*.
square quadratum *n*; quadratus; quadro 1; ~ **with** consentio 4 (*cum*); ~ **accounts** rationem subduco 3.
squash obtero 3.
squat subsido 3; consido 3; brevis, humilis.
squeak strideo 2; stridor *m*.
squeamish fastidiosus.
squeeze comprimo 3, premo 3.
squint strabonem sum; limis (oculis) intueor 2; **~ing** strabo, paetus.
squire armiger, eri *m*.
squirrel sciurus *m*.
stab (con)fodio 3, percutio 3; vulnus *n*.
stability stabilitas *f*.
stable stabilis, firmus, solidus; stabulum *n*.
stack coacervo 1; acervus *m*; strues *f*.
staff baculum *n*; scipio *m*; *fig.* columen *n*; **military** ~ legati *m/pl.*
stag cervus *m*.
stage pulpitum *n*, proscaenium *n*; scaena *f*; gradus, us *m*.
stagger titubo 1, vacillo 1.
stagnant iners; *fig.* frigidus; **be** ~ stagno 1; ~ **water** stagnum *n*.
stagnat|e refrigesco 3, torpesco 3; **~ion** cessatio *f*; torpor *m*.
staid severus.
stain tingo 3, inficio 3; maculo 1, foedo 1; macula *f*; *fig.* labes *f*, nota *f*; **~less** purus.
stair scala *f*; gradus, us *m*; **~case** scalae *f/pl.*
stake palus *m*; stipes *m*; sudes *f*; pignus *n*; **be at** ~ in discrimen venio 4; pono 3.
stale obsoletus, vulgaris; mucidus.
stalk stirps *f*, caulis *m*; *v/i.* incedo 3; *v/t.* (vestigiis) persequor 3.
stall stabulum *n*, tectum *n*; taberna *f*.
stallion (equus) admissarius *m*.
stamina robur *n*; vires *f/pl.*
stammer (lingua) haesito 1; balbutio 4; haesitatio *f*; **~ing** balbus.
stamp signo 1; imprimo 3; pedem supplodo 3; moneta *f*, forma *f*; nota *f*; (pedis) supplosio *f*.
stand *v/i.* sto 1; *v/t.* tolero 1; patior 3, perfero 3; statio *f*; **raised** ~ suggestus, us *m*; **be at, come to, a** ~ consisto 3; **bring to a** ~ constituo 3; **make a** ~ resisto 3; ~ **by** adsum (*dat.*); ~ **firm** consisto 3; ~ **for** peto 3 (*magistratum*); ~ **round** circumsto 1 (*acc.*); ~ **still** subsisto 3, consisto 3; ~ **thus** se habet 2 (*res*); **it ~s to reason** dubitari non potest (*quin*); ~ **up** (con)surgo 3; ~ **up for** adsum (*dat.*).
standard signum *n*, vexillum *n*; norma *f*, regula *f*; **~-bearer** aquilifer, eri *m*; signifer, eri *m*.
standing status, us *m*; locus *m*.
standstill: be at a ~ cesso 1; haereo 2.
star stella *f*; sidus *n*, astrum *n*; *fig.* lumen *n*.
starboard dextra *f*; **to** ~ ad dexteram; dextera.
starch amylum *n*.
stare stupeo 2; ~ **at** intueor 2 (*alqd; in alqd*); (oculorum) obtutus, us *m*.
stark naked plane nudus.
starling sturnus *m*.
starry sidereus, stellans.
start *v/i.* tremo 3; proficiscor 3; incipio 3 (*alqd; inf.*); coepi (*inf.*); *v/t.* instituo 3; aggredior 3 (*alqd, ad alqd*); **~ing-place** carcer, eris *n*.
startle terreo 2; timorem, metum inicio 3 (*alci*).
starv|ation fames *f*, inedia *f*; **~e**

fame conficior 3, consumor 3; *fig.* privo 1 (*alqm alqa re*).
state condicio *f*; status, us *m*; locus *m*; res *f* publica, civitas *f*; pompa *f*; publicus, civilis; profiteor 2; declaro 1, affirmo 1, explico 1; **~liness** lautitia *f*, gravitas *f*; **~ly** magnificus, gravis; **~ment** affirmatio *f*, professio *f*; testimonium *n*; **~sman** qui in re publica versatur; vir *m* rei publicae gubernandae peritus.
station locus *m*; condicio *f*; ordo *m*; statio *f*; (dis)pono 3; **~ary** fixus, immotus; **~ery** chartae *f/pl.*
statue statua *f*; signum *n*.
stature statura *f*.
statute lex *f*.
stave scipio *m*; **~ off** arceo 2, prohibeo 2.
stay *v/i.* maneo 2, commoror 1 (*apud*, *in*); *v/t.* moror 1; mora *f*; commoratio *f*; *fig.* columen *n*, praesidium *n*.
stead: in his ~ pro eo; **~fast** constans; firmus; **~fastness** constantia *f*; **~iness** stabilitas *f*; **~y** firmus, stabilis; frugi, honestus.
steak frustum *n* (*carnis*); offa *f*.
steal furor 1; surripio 3; **~ away** me subduco 3; dilabor 3; **~ over, upon** irrepo 3 (*in alqd*); **~ up to** arrepo 3 (*ad*); **~ing** furtum *n*.
stealth: by ~ clam; furtim; **~y** furtivus, clandestinus.
steam vapor *m*; *v/i.* fumo 1; *v/t.* vaporo 1.
steed equus *m* (bellator).
steel chalybs *m*; ferrum *n*; duro 1.
steep praeceps, arduus, praeruptus; madefacio 3; **~le** turris *f*.
steer guberno 1; rego 3; iuvencus *m*; **~ing** gubernatio *f*; **~sman** gubernator *m*.
stem stirps *f*; stipes *m*; obsisto 3, resisto 3 (*dat.*).
stench fetor *m*; foedus odor *m*.
stenograph|er notarius *m*; **~y** notae *f/pl.*
step gradus, us *m*; vestigium *n*; *fig.* **~s** consilium *n*; incedo 3, ingredior 3; **~ by ~** pedetemptim; **~-daughter** privigna *f*; **~-father** vitricus *m*; **~mother** noverca *f*; **~-son** privignus *m*.
steril|e sterilis, inutilis; **~ity** sterilitas *f*.
stern severus, durus, rigidus; puppis *f*; **~ness** severitas *f*.
stew coquo 3; caro *f* elixa.
steward vilicus *m*; procurator *m*.
stick *v/t.* (de)figo 3 (*alqd in re*); *v/i.* haereo 2 (*re*; *in re*); adhaereo 2 (*in re*); adhaeresco 3 (*ad*; *in re*); baculum *n*; clava *f*; **~y** tenax, lentus.
stiff rigidus; durus, severus; **~en** rigeo 2; rigesco 3; **~ness** rigor *m*; duritia *f*.
stifle strangulo 1, suffoco 1; *fig.* reprimo 3.
stigma nota *f*; stigma *n*; **~tize** noto 1.
still immotus, tranquillus, quietus; placo 1, sedo 1; *adv.* adhuc, etiam; etiamnunc, etiamtum; semper, usque; nihilominus, (at)tamen, verumtamen; **~ness** quies *f*; silentium *n*.
stilted inflatus.
stimul|ate excito 1, incendo 3, stimulo 1; **~us** stimulus *m*; incitamentum *n*.
sting pungo 3; *fig.* mordeo 2, uro 3; aculeus *m*; morsus, us *m*.
sting|iness sordes *f/pl.*; **~y** sordidus, parcus.
stink male oleo 2; fetor *m*.
stint parco 3 (*dat.*); pensum *n*.
stipend merces *f*; annuum *n*.
stipulat|e (de)paciscor 3 (*ut*); statuo 3 (*ut*); **~ion** condicio *f*.
stir (com)moveo 2; motus, us *m*; tumultus, us *m*; turba *f*; **~ up** excito 1; misceo 2.
stitch suo 3.
stock stirps *f*; genus *n*; copia *f*; instrumentum *n*, merces *f/pl.*; pecus *n*; instruo 3, repleo 2 (*alqd alqa re*); tritus, usitatus; **well-~ed** abundans, frequens (*abl.*).
stockade vallum *n*.
stocking tibiale *n*.
stocks compedes *f/pl.*
stoic Stoicus; durus; Stoicus *m*.
stole palla *f*.
stolid hebes, stolidus.
stomach stomachus *m*; concoquo 3.
stone lapis *m*; saxum *n*; nucleus *m* (*olivarum etc.*); lapideus; lapidibus cooperio 4 (*alqm*); **~-quarry** lapicidinae *f/pl.*
stony lapidosus, saxosus, saxeus; **~-hearted** ferreus.
stook manipulus *m*.
stool scamnum *n*.
stoop demitto 3, summitto 3; *fig.* descendo 3 (*ad alqd*).

stop *v/t.* teneo 2, retineo 2; sisto 3; *fig.* cohibeo 2; comprimo 3, reprimo 3; *v/i.* consisto 3, insisto 3, subsisto 3; maneo 2; commoror 1 (*apud alqm*); desino 3, omitto 3 (*inf.*); ~ **up** obturo 1, obsaepio 4; interpunctum *n*; **put a ~ to** dirimo 3, comprimo 3; moram facio 3 (*alci rei*); ~**per** obturamentum *n*.
store condo 3, repono 3; copia *f*; ~**s** commeatus, us *m*; ~**house** apotheca *f*, cella *f*; horreum *n*; ~**keeper** cellarius *m*.
storey tabulatum *n*.
stork ciconia *f*.
storm tempestas *f*; procella *f*; *v/t.* expugno 1; *v/i.* saevio 4; ~**ing** expugnatio *f*; ~**y** turbulentus, turbidus.
story fabula *f*; res *f*; **there is a ~** ferunt 3 (*acc. c. inf.*); ~**-teller** narrator *m*.
stout pinguis, opimus; validus; ~**-hearted** impavidus, fortis; ~**ness** habitus, us *m* opimus (corporis).
stove caminus *m*; focus *m*.
stow repono 3, condo 3; ~ **away** me condo 3, abdo 3.
straggle vagor 1, palor 1.
straight rectus, directus; *adv.* recta; ~**en** corrigo 3; ~**forward** directus, sincerus, simplex; ~**way** statim, continuo.
strain *v/t.* contendo 3; intendo 3 (*aciem*); intorqueo 2 (*talum*); liquo 1, colo 1 (*vinum*); *v/i.* nitor 3, me intendo 3 (*ut, ne*); contentio *f*; nixus, us *m*; labor *m*; cantus, us *m*; modus *m*; ~**ed** arcessitus (*dictum etc.*); ~**er** colum *n*.
strait fretum *n*; angustiae *f/pl.*; ~**-laced** rigidus.
strand litus *n*; **be ~ed** eicior 3 (in litore).
strange insolitus, inusitatus, mirus, novus; peregrinus, externus; alienus (*ab*; *dat.*); ~**ly** mirabiliter; nescio quo pacto; ~**ness** insolentia *f*; ~**r** peregrinus *m*; hospes *m*; homo *m* ignotus; *fig.* **a ~r to** ignarus, rudis, imperitus (*gen.*).
strangle strangulo 1.
strap lorum *n*; loris vincio 4; ~**ping** validus.
stratagem insidiae *f/pl.*; machina *f*; dolus *m*.
strategy consilium *n*; belli ratio *f*.
straw stramentum *n*; culmus *m*; *fig.* pilus *m*; stramenticius; ~**berry** fragum *n*.
stray (ab)erro 1, vagor 1, palor 1; errans.
streak linea *f*; ~**ed** virgatus.
stream rivus *m*; flumen *n*; **down ~** secundo flumine; **up ~** adverso flumine; labor 3; me effundo 3; ~**er** vexillum *n*.
street via *f*; vicus *m*; platea *f*.
strength vis *f*; vires *f/pl.*; robur *n*; firmitas *f*, firmitudo *f*, ~ **of mind** constantia *f*; **on the ~ of** fretus (*abl.*); ~**en** (con)firmo 1; stabilio 4.
strenuous acer, impiger.
stress vis *f*; impetus, us *m*; pondus *n*; **lay ~ on** (magni) momenti facio 3 (*alqd*).
stretch *v/t.* (in)tendo 3, contendo 3; *v/i.* pateo 2; patesco 3, pandor 3; ~ **forth, out** porrigo 3, extendo 3; contentio *f*, intentio *f*; tractus, us *m*; spatium *n*; ~**er** lectica *f*.
strew sterno 3, spargo 3.
stricken: ~ **in years** aetate confectus.
strict severus, durus; intentus, diligens.
stricture reprehensio *f*.
stride magnis gradibus incedo 3; magnus gradus, us *m*.
strife discordia *f*; iurgia *n/pl.*; lites *f/pl.*
strigil strigilis *f*.
strike *v/t.* ferio 4; percutio 3, caedo 3, ico 3; signo 1 (*nummos*); pello 3 (*lyram, nervos*); percello 3, percutio 3 (*animum, mentem*); incurro 3, incurso 1 (*in oculos, aures*); *v/i.* sono 1; ~ **against** infligo 3, offendo 3 (*alqd alci*); ~ **at, down** subverto 3, everto 3; ~ **camp** castra moveo 2; **it ~s me** mihi occurrit 3, venit 4 in mentem; ~ **out** induco 3.
striking insignis, gravis, mirus.
string linum *n*; nervus *m* (*lyrae, arcus*); chorda *f* (*lyrae*); **shoe~** corrigia *f*; ~ **together** conecto 3; ~**ed instrument** fides *f/pl.*
stringent severus.
strip *v/t.* spolio 1, nudo 1, exuo 3 (*alqm alqa re*); *v/i.* vestem depono 3; ~ **off** stringo 3, exuo 3, detraho 3 (*alqd*); ~ **of paper** (papyri) scida *f*; ~ **of cloth** fascia *f*.
stripe virga *f*; **purple ~** clavus *m* (latus, angustus); ~**s** verbera *n/pl.*, vulnera *n/pl.*; ~**d** virgatus.

striv|e (e)nitor 3 (*ut*; *ad*, *pro*); contendo 3 (*inf.*; *ut*; *ad alqd*; *contra alqm*); conor 1 (*inf.*); **~ing** contentio *f*, appetitio *f* (*gen.*).
stroke (per)mulceo 2; ictus, us *m*; plaga *f*; pulsus, us *m* (remorum); linea *f*.
stroll inambulo 1, spatior 1; ambulatio *f*.
strong validus, robustus, firmus, fortis; gravis, acer; potens; vehemens; **be ~** valeo 2; **~-box** arca *f*; **~hold** arx *f*; praesidium *n*.
structure compages *f*; aedificium *n*; *fig.* ratio *f*.
struggle luctor 1, pugno 1 (*cum*); nitor 3 (*ut*); contendo 3 (*inf.*); dimico 1 (*cum*; *de*); certamen *n*; dimicatio *f*.
strut magnifice incedo 3; magnifice me iacto 1.
stubble stipula *f*.
stubborn pertinax, pervicax, obstinatus; **~ness** pertinacia *f*.
stud equaria *f*; equi *m/pl.*
studded distinctus (*alqa re*).
stud|ent qui studet (*litteras*, *doctrinas etc.*); homo *m* litterarum studiosus; **~ent of rhetoric** scholasticus *m*; **~ied** meditatus, exquisitus; **~ious** studiosus (*litterarum*, *doctrinae*).
study studeo 2 (*dat.*); operam do 1, incumbo 3 (*dat.*); cognosco 3; meditor 1; meditatio *f*; studium *n*; opera *f*; litterarum studia *n/pl.*; ars *f*; bibliotheca *f*.
stuff materia *f*; textile *n*; farcio 4, refercio 4; sagino 1; **~ing** fartum *n*; (*of cushions*) tomentum *n*.
stumble offendo 3 (*pedem ad alqd*); labor 3; **~ upon** incido 3 (*dat.*).
stump stipes *m*.
stun (ob)stupefacio 3; consterno 1; **be ~ned** sopior 4.
stunted minutus.
stupe|faction stupor *m*; **~fy** (ob-)stupefacio 3; consterno 1; **~ndous** permirus.
stupid stultus, stupidus, stolidus; **~ity** stultitia *f*.
sturdy robustus, validus, firmus.
sturgeon acipenser, eris *m*.
stutter balbutio 4; haesito 1; **~ing** balbus.
sty hara *f*.
styl|e ratio *f*; modus *m*; **literary ~e** genus *n*; oratio *f*; stilus *m*; sermo *m*; apello 1, voco 1; dico 3; **~ish** lautus, magnificus.
subaltern optio *m*.
subdue subicio 3, subigo 3, redigo 3; domo 1.
subject subicio 3 (*alqm sub alqd*; *dat.*); oppono 3 (*alqm alci rei*); subiectus, dicto audiens; **~ to** obnoxius (*dat.*); civis *m*; privatus *m*; res *f*; argumentum *n*; materia *f*; quaestio *f*; **~ion** servitus, utis *f*.
sub|join subicio 3; **~jugate** subigo 3, redigo 3; domo 1.
sublim|e elatus, excelsus; **~ity** elatio *f*.
submarine marinus, summersus.
submerge summergo 3, demergo 3; inundo 1.
submi|ssive humilis, summissus, supplex; **~t** me summitto 3, subicio 3 (*dat.*); (con)cedo 3 (*dat.*); subeo 4; perfero 3 (*labores etc.*); refero 3 (*alqd ad alqm*).
subordinate subicio 3 (*alqd alci rei*); secundus, inferior; minister, tri *m*.
suborn suborno 1.
subpoena testimonium denuntio 1 (*alci*).
subscri|be subscribo 3; assentior 4 (*alci*, *sententiae*); confero 3 (*pecuniam*); **~ption** subscriptio *f*.
subsequent posterior, proximus; **~ly** postea, deinde.
subsid|e resido 3, remitto 3; cado 3; defervesco 3 (*ira etc.*); **~iary** secundus; subsidiarius (*cohortes etc.*); **~ise** pecunias praebeo 2; **~y** collatio *f*.
subsist sustineor 2; consto 1; sum; **~ence** victus, us *m*.
substan|ce res *f*; natura *f*; corpus *n*; summa *f*; **~tial** solidus; gravis, magnus; amplus; **~tiate** probo 1 (*crimen*); argumentis confirmo 1.
substitute vicarius *m*; **as a ~ for** pro (*alqo*); in vicem (*alcs*); substituo 3, suppono 3 (*alqm*, *alqd*, *in locum alcs*, *pro alqo*).
subterfuge tergiversatio *f*; dolus *m*.
subterranean subterraneus.
subtle subtilis, acutus, acer; callidus; **~ty** subtilitas *f*; acumen *n*; astutia *f*.
subtract deduco 3.
suburb suburbium *n*; **~an** suburbanus.
subver|sion eversio *f*; **~t** everto 3.

succeed *v/t.* succedo 3 (*alci*); excipio 3 (*annus annum*; *regnum*); *v/i.* succedit 3 (mihi); prospere evenit 4 (*mihi*); efficio 3 (*ut*); ~ **in** perficio 3 (*alqd*).
success res *f/pl.* secundae, prosperae; felicitas *f*; **~ful** felix, fortunatus; secundus, bonus; **~ion** continuatio *f*, series *f*; **in ~ion** ex ordine; **~ive** continuus; **~or** successor *m*.
succinct brevis.
succour subvenio 4, succurro 3 (*dat.*); auxilium *n*.
succulent sucosus.
succumb (con)cedo 3, succumbo 3 (*dat.*).
such talis, huiusmodi, eiusmodi; ~ **a man as to** is ... qui; ~ **a good man** tam bonus vir; **to ~ an extent** adeo; **in ~ a way** ita.
suck sugo 3; sorbeo 2; bibo 3; **~ing** lactens; **~le** mammam do 1, praebeo 2 (*dat.*).
sudden subitus, repentinus, repens; **~ly** repente, subito.
sue litem, actionem intendo 3 (*alci*); ~ **for** peto 3, rogo 1, precor 1 (*alqd ab alqo*).
suet sebum *n*.
suffer subeo 4, accipio 3, patior 3, perpetior 3, (per)fero 3 (*labores etc.*); permitto 3 (*alci inf.*; *ut*); sino 3 (*acc. c. inf.*; *inf.*; *subj.*); ~ **from** afficior 3 (*abl.*); laboro 1 (*abl.*); **~er** aeger, gri *m*; **~ing** miseria *f*; labor *m*; **~ing from** afflictus (*abl.*).
suffice sufficio 3 (*dat.*; *ad*; *ut*); suppeto 3 (*dat.*); satis sum.
sufficien|cy, ~t satis (*alcs rei*).
suffocate suffoco 1, strangulo 1.
suffrage suffragium *n*.
suffuse suffundo 3 (*alqd alqa re*).
sugar saccharon *n*; mel *n* (*lit. honey*).
suggest subicio 3, inicio 3 (*alqd alci*); admoneo 2 (*ut*); ~ **itself** animo occurrit 3; **~ion** admonitus, us *m*; consilium *n*; **at my ~ion** me auctore.
suicid|al funestus, fatalis; **~e** mors *f* voluntaria; **commit ~e** mihi mortem conscisco 3.
suit *v/t.* accommodo 1 (*alqd ad*); *v/i.* convenio 4 (*in*, *ad alqd*; *dat.*; *acc. c. inf.*); congruo 3 (*cum*; *dat.*); decet 2 (*alqm*); placet 2 (*alci*); **~able** idoneus, aptus (*ad*); commodus, opportunus; dignus.
suite comitatus, us *m*; satellites *m/pl.*, comites *m/pl.*
suitor procus *m*.
sulky morosus, difficilis.
sullen tristis, severus, tetricus.
sully contamino 1.
sulphur sulfur *n*.
sultr|iness aestus, us *m*; **~y** aestuosus.
sum summa *f*; pecunia *f*; caput *n*; ~ **up** subduco 3; **~marily** sine mora; **~mary** brevis, subitus; breviarium *n*; **give a ~mary** breviter describo 3.
summer aestas *f*; aestivus.
summit cacumen *n*, culmen *n*; vertex *m*; summus mons *m*.
summon voco 1 (*also jur.* in ius), arcesso 3; appello 1; **~s** arcessitus, us *m*.
sumptuous sumptuosus, lautissimus.
sun sol *m*; ~ **oneself** apricor 1; **~beam** solis radius *m*; **~burnt** adustus; **~dial** solarium *n*.
sunken depressus, humilis, cavus.
sun|ny apricus; **~rise** solis ortus, us *m*; **~set** solis occasus, us *m*; **~shine** sol *m*; lux *f*.
sup ceno 1.
superabundan|ce abundantia *f*; **~t** abundans.
superannuated qui annuum accipit 3; obsoletus.
superb magnificus, lautus.
super|cilious arrogans, superbus, fastidiosus; **~ficial** levis; **~fluous** supervacaneus; **~human** (paene) divinus.
superintend praesum (*dat.*); curo 1 (*alqd*); **~ence** cura *f*; administratio *f*; **~ent** (pro)curator *m*; praefectus *m*.
superior superior, melior; amplior; praestans; **be ~ to** supero 1.
super|lative praestans, singularis; **~natural** divinus; **~scription** titulus *m*; **~stition** superstitio *f*, religio *f*; **~stitious** superstitiosus, religiosus; **~vision** cura *f*, curatio *f*.
supine supinus, iners.
supper cena *f*.
supple flexibilis, lentus.
supplement accessio *f*, appendix *f*.
suppli|ant supplex *m and f*; **~cate** supplico 1 (*dat.*); oro 1, obsecro 1 (*alqm*); **~cation** preces *f/pl.*; **~catory** supplex.

suppl|y praebeo 2, suppedito 1, ministro 1 (*alqd alci*); suppleo 2, (re)sarcio 4 (*damna*); copia *f*, facultas *f*; **~ies** commeatus, us *m*; copiae *f/pl.*
support sustineo 2, sublevo 1; perfero 3, tolero 1 (*labores*); alo 3, sustento 1 (*familiam*); adiuvo 1 (*alqm*); adsum (*alci*); firmamentum *n*, adminiculum *n*; *fig.* columen *n*; praesidium *n*; alimentum *n*; **~er** fautor *m*, adiutor *m*.
suppos|e pono 3; fingo 3 (animo); puto 1, opinor 1; **~ition** opinio *f*; **~itious** subditus, subditivus.
suppress reprimo 3, opprimo 3; supprimo 3, celo 1 (*famam etc.*).
suprem|acy principatus, us *m*; imperium *n*; **~e** summus, supremus.
sure certus; compertus (*res*); fidus (*homo*); **be ~** pro certo habeo 2; certe scio 4; compertum habeo 2; **be ~ to** cura 1 (*ut*)!; **~ly** certe, certo, nimirum; **~ty** vas *m*, sponsor *m*; **be ~ty for** spondeo 2 (*pro alqo*).
surf fluctus *m/pl.*
surface aequor *n*; summum *n*; *adj.* summus.
surfeit satietas *f*; satio 1.
surge fluctus, us *m*; aestus, us *m*; aestuo 1, surgo 3.
surge|on chirurgus *m*; **~ry** chirurgia *f*.
surl|iness morositas *f*; **~y** morosus, difficilis.
surmise suspicor 1; coniectura *f*.
surmount transcendo 3 (*alqd*); *fig.* (ex)supero 1; vinco 3.
surname cognomen *n*.
surpass (ex)supero 1; vinco 3; praesto 1.
surplus residuum *m*, reliquum *n*.
surpris|e admiratio *f*; res *f* improvisa; opprimo 3, adorior 4 (*alqm*); occupo 1 (*urbem etc.*); **be ~ed** miror 1 (*acc.*; *acc. c. inf.*; *quod*; *si*); **~ing** mirus, mirabilis.
surrender *v/t.* cedo 3, trado 3; *v/i.* me dedo 3, arma trado 3; deditio *f*, traditio *f*.
surreptitious furtivus, clandestinus; **~ly** furtim, clam.
surround circumsto 1 (*acc.*); circumdo 1, cingo 3 (*alqd, alqm, alqa re*); circumsedeo 2 (*urbem*); **~ed by** circumfusus, cinctus (*abl.*).
survey contemplor 1, considero 1; contemplatio *f*; mensura *f* (*agri etc.*); **~or** finitor *m*, metator *m*.
surviv|e supersum, superstes sum (*dat.*); supero 1; **~ing** superstes.
susceptib|ility mollitia *f* (animi); **~le** obnoxius (*dat.*).
suspect suspicor 1 (*alqd*; *acc. c. inf.*); suspectum habeo 2 (*alqm*); **be ~ed** in suspicione sum (*alci alcs rei*); suspectus sum.
suspend suspendo 3 (*alqd re*; *e, de re*); intermitto 3 (*proelium etc.*); moveo 2 (*alqm magistratu*).
suspense dubitatio *f*; **in ~** suspensus, incertus, dubius.
suspension intermissio *f*.
suspici|on suspicio *f*; **~ous** suspiciosus (*in alqm*; *res*).
sust|ain sustineo 2; alo 3, sustento 1; patior 3; **~enance** victus, us *m*; alimentum *n*.
swaddling-clothes incunabula *n/pl.*
swagger magnifice incedo 3; magnifice me iacto 1.
swallow hirundo *f*; devoro 1; haurio 4.
swamp palus, udis *f*; inundo 1; deprimo 3 (*navem*); **~y** paludosus.
swan cygnus *m*.
sward caespes *m*.
swarm examen *n*; *fig.* turba *f*, multitudo *f*; congregor 1, glomeror 1; **~ out of** effundor 3 (*abl.*); **~ up** scando 3.
swarthy fuscus, adustus.
swathe fascia *f*.
sway *v/t.* agito 1; *v/i.* vacillo 1, fluito 1; *fig.* dirigo 3, rego 3; imperium *n*; dicio *f*.
swear iuro 1 (*per alqm*; *in alqd*; *acc. c. inf.*); iusiurandum accipio 3; **~ at** exsecror 1 (*alqm*); **~ in** iureiurando obstringo 3 (*alqm*); iusiurandum adigo 3 (*alqm*); **~ allegiance to** iuro 1 in nomen (*alcs*); **~ing** exsecrationes *f/pl.*
sweat sudor *m*; sudo 1.
sweep verro 3 (*vias, purgamenta, etc.*); (de)tergeo 2 (*vias*); percurro 3 (*alqd oculo*); **~ings** purgamenta *n/pl.*
sweet dulcis, suavis, iucundus; **~en** iucundum facio 3; **~heart** deliciae *f/pl.*; **~ness** dulcedo *f*, suavitas *f*.
swell *v/i.* tumeo 2; tumesco 3, turgesco 3; cresco 3; *v/t.* distendo 3; inflo 1; fluctus, us *m*; **~ing** tumor *m*.

swerve declino 1 (*ab, de*).
swift celer; velox, rapidus; **~ness** velocitas *f*.
swim nato 1; **~mer** natator *m*; **~ming** natatio *f*.
swindle fraudo 1 (*alqm pecunia*); decipio 3 (*alqm*); fraus *f*; **~r** fraudator *m*.
swine sus *f and m*; **~herd** subulcus *m*.
swing *v/t.* agito 1 (*huc illuc*); *v/i.* vacillo 1, fluito 1; *fig.* **~ round** me verto 3 (*in*).
swirl torqueor 2; vertex *m*.
swish strepitus, us *m*.
switch virga *f*; *v/t.* muto 1; *v/i.* mutor 1.
swollen tumidus, turgidus.
swoon collabor 3.
swoop lapsus, us *m*; impetus, us *m*; **~ down (on)** (de)labor 3 (*in*); **~ upon** involo 1, incurro 3 (*in*).
sword gladius *m*; ferrum *n*.
sycophant assentator *m*.
syllable syllaba *f*.
symbol signum *n*; imago *f*.
symmetr|ical aequalis, congruens; **~y** convenientia *f*.
sympath|etic misericors; **~ise** misereor 2 (*gen.*); **~y** misericordia *f*; concordia *f*.
symphony concentus, us *m*; symphonia *f*.
symptom indicium *n*, signum *n*.
syndicate societas *f*.
synonymous quod idem declarat 1 (*verbum*).
synopsis epitoma *f*.
syntax constructio *f* verborum.
synthesis coniunctio *f*.
syringe sipho *m*.
system ratio *f*, institutio *f*, descriptio *f*; disciplina *f* (*philosophiae*); **~atic** ordinatus; **~atise** ordino 1.

T

table mensa *f*; *fig.* cena *f*; index *m*.
tablet tabula *f*, tabella *f*, tessera *f*.
tacit tacitus; **~urn** taciturnus.
tack *v/t.* figo 3 (*alqd in re*); **~ together, up** (con)suo 3 (*alqd*); *v/i.* reciprocor 1; clavulus *m*.
tackle armamenta *n/pl.*, instrumenta *n/pl.*; obviam eo 4 (*dat.*).
tact prudentia *f*, humanitas *f*; **~ful** prudens.
tactics belli ratio *f*; consilium *n*.
tag pittacium *n*; **~ after** subsequor 3 (*alqm*).
tail cauda *f*.
tailor vestiarius (homo) *m*.
taint contamino 1, inquino 1; imbuo 3; contagio *f*; vitium *n*.
take capio 1, sumo 3; accipio 3; duco 3; **~ after** similis sum (*alcs*); **~ away** adimo 3, aufero 3, tollo 3 (*alqd*); **~ down** detraho 3; **~ fire** ignem accipio 3, concipio 3; **~ for** habeo 2 (*pro amico etc.*); **~ hold of** comprehendo 3; **~ in** recipio 3, accipio 3 (*hospitem*); comprehendo 3, percipio 3 (*mente*); decipio 3 (*alqm dolo*); **~ off** depono 3 (*vestem*); **~ out** eximo 3, eripio 3; **~ (oneself) to** me confero 3; **~ place** fio 3; **~ up** sumo 3 (*arma*); consumo 3 (*tempus*); suscipio 3 (*bellum, partem alcs*).
tale fabula *f*, narratio *f*, historia *f*.
talent ingenium *n*; indoles *f*; **~ed** ingeniosus.
talk (col)loquor 3 (*cum alqo*); sermo *m*; colloquium *n*; **~ative** loquax, garrulus; **~ativeness** loquacitas *f*.
tall procerus; grandis; longus; **~ness** proceritas *f*.
tallow sebum *n*.
tally convenio 4 (*cum re*); tessera *f*; ratio *f*.
talon unguis *m*.
tambourine tympanum *n*.
tame mansuetus, cicur, domitus; ignavus; mansuefacio 3; domo 1; **~ness** lentitudo *f*; **~r** domitor *m*.
tamper with *fig.* sollicito 1 (*alqm*).
tan pelles conficio 3; coloro 1 (*corpus*).
tangle implico 1; implicatio *f*; nodus *m*.
tank lacus, us *m*; cisterna *f*; **~ard** cantharus *m*.
tanner coriarius *m*.
tantamount idem (*ac*); par (*dat.*).
tap leviter pulso 1; ictus, us *m*.
tape taenia *f*.
taper cereus *m*; fastigor 1; **~ing** fastigatus (*in cacumen etc.*).
tapestry tapetia *n/pl.*
tar pix *f*.
tard|iness tarditas *f*; **~y** tardus, lentus.
tare lolium *n*.
target *fig.* meta *f*.
tarnish maculo 1, vitio 1.
tarry (com)moror 1.
tart scriblita *f*; acidus; mordax.
task opus *n*, negotium *n*, pensum *n*; onus impono 3 (*alci*); **~master** exactor *m* (operis).
tassels fimbriae *f/pl.*; cirri *m/pl.*
taste *v/t.* (de)gusto 1, (de)libo 1 (*alqd*); *v/i.* sapio 3 (*alqd; bene*); sapor *m*; gustatus, us *m*; *fig.* intellegentia *f*; iudicium *n*; elegantia *f*; **~ful** elegans, intellegens; **~less** insulsus.
tast|er praegustator *m*; **~y** sapidus, conditus.
tatter pannus *m*; **~ed** pannosus.
tattle garrio 4.
tattoo compungo 3.
taunt obicio 3 (*alqd alci*); opprobrium *n*, convicium *n*.
tavern caupona *f*.
tawdry fucosus.
tawny fulvus.
tax vectigal *n*; incuso 1 (*alqm alcs rei*); vectigal impono 3 (*alci*); censeo 2 (*alqm*); **~-collector** exactor *m*.
teach doceo 2 (*alqm alqd; inf.*); erudio 4, instruo 3 (*alqm alqa re*); **~er** magister, tri *m*; doctor *m*, praeceptor *m*; **~ing** doctrina *f*, institutio *f*; praecepta *n/pl.*
team iugum *n*.
tear[1] lacrima *f*; **shed ~s** lacrimas fundo 3; **~ful** lacrimans.
tear[2] scindo 3; **~ to pieces** lanio 1; discindo 3; convello 3; scissura *f*.

tease obtundo 3 (*alqm*); vexo 1.
teat mamma *f*.
tedious lentus, longus, molestus.
teem abundo 1, scateo 2 (*alqa re*).
tell (e)narro 1 (*rem alci*); dico 3 (*acc. c. inf.*); memoro 1 (*alqd*); iubeo 2 (*alqm alqd facere*); **~ing** gravis, validus.
temerity temeritas *f*.
temper tempero 1; lenio 4; animus *m*; **bad ~** iracundia *f*; **bad-~ed** morosus, difficilis; **~ament** habitus, us *m*; **~ance** temperantia *f*, modestia *f*; **~ate** temperatus, temperans.
temperature temperatura *f*; **high ~** calor *m*; **low ~** frigor *m*.
tempest tempestas *f*; **~uous** procellosus.
temple templum *n*; aedes *f*; tempus *n* (*capitis*); **~-keeper** aedituus *m*.
tempor|arily ad tempus; in tempus; **~ary** temporarius; **~ise** cunctor 1; tempori servio 4.
tempt tempto 1, sollicito 1; **~ation** sollicitatio *f*; illecebra *f*; **~er** temptator *m*; **~ing** illecebrosus.
ten decem; **~ times** decies.
tenac|ious pertinax, tenax; **~ity** tenacitas *f*, pertinacia *f*.
tenant conductor *m*; incola *m*.
tend *v/t.* colo 3; curo 1; *v/i.* tendo 3; pertineo 2; specto 1; **~ency** inclinatio *f*.
tender tener, delicatus, mollis; defero 3, offero 3; **~ness** teneritas *f*; indulgentia *f*.
tendon nervus *m*.
tendril pampinus *m*.
tenet institutum *n*, dogma *n*.
tenor cursus, us *m*; ratio *f*.
tens|e tentus; intentus; tempus *n*; **~ion** intentio *f*.
tent tabernaculum *n*; **general's ~** praetorium *n*.
tentacle bracchium *n*.
tenth decimus.
tenuous exiguus, rarus.
tepid tepidus.
term finis *m*; spatium *n*; tempus *n*; verbum *n*; nuncupo 1, appello 1; **~s** condicio *f*; **be on good (bad) ~s (with)** est mihi amicitia (inimicitia) (*cum alqo*).
termin|ate finio 4; concludo 3; **~ation** finis *m*; exitus, us *m*; **~ology** vocabula *n/pl.*, verba *n/pl.*
terrestrial terrestris, terrenus.
terrible, terrific terribilis, horribilis.
territory fines *m/pl.*; ager, gri *m*; terra *f*.
terror terror *m*, pavor *m*; **~ize** terreo 2.
terse pressus, astrictus; **~ness** brevitas *f*.
test experior 4; tento 1, specto 1, periclitor 1; periculum *n*, experimentum *n*; obrussa *f*.
testa|ment testamentum *n*; **~tor** testator *m*.
testicle testis *m*.
testify (to) testificor 1, testor 1, declaro 1 (*alqd*; *acc. c. inf.*).
testimony testimonium *n*.
testy stomachosus.
tether religo 1.
text verba *n/pl.*; oratio *f*.
textile textilis; textile *n*.
texture textus, us *m*; textum *n*.
than quam, atque.
thank gratias ago 3 (*alci*); **~ you** benigne; **~ful** gratus; **~less** ingratus; **~s** gratia *f*, gratiae *f/pl.*; **~sgiving** supplicatio *f*, gratulatio *f*.
that ille; is; iste; *relat.* qui, quae, quod; *cj.* ut; **~ not** ut non, ne; **oh ~!** utinam.
thatch stramentum *n*.
thaw *v/t.* (dis)solvo 3; *v/i.* tabesco 3, resolvor 3.
the ille; **~ more ... ~ more** quo magis ... eo magis.
theatr|e theatrum *n*; scaena *f*, cavea *f*; spectaculum *n*; **~ical** theatralis, scaenicus.
theft furtum *n*.
their suus, sua, suum.
theme propositum *n*, argumentum *n*; res *f*.
then tum, tunc; deinde, inde, post, postea; igitur, ergo; **~ and there** ilico.
thence inde, illinc; hinc; **~forth** ex eo tempore, inde.
theolog|ian theologus *m*; **~y** theologia *f*.
theor|etically scientia; **~y** ratio *f*; scientia *f*.
there ibi, illic; eo; **~abouts** circa; **~after** exinde; **~fore** igitur, ergo, itaque; **~upon** tum, subinde, inde.
thesis propositum *n*, argumentum *n*.
thick densus, crassus, artus; creber, confertus; **in the ~ of** in medio

(*proelio etc.*); **~en** denso 1; **~et** dumetum *n*; **~ness** crassitudo *f*.
thie|f fur *m and f*; **~ve** furor 1; **~vish** furax.
thigh femur *n*.
thin tenuis; rarus; gracilis; subtilis; exilis, macer; attenuo 1, extenuo 1.
thing res *f*; negotium *n*.
think cogito 1; arbitror 1, opinor 1, puto 1, existimo 1; credo 3; censeo 2; **~ about, over** cogito 1 (*alqd*; *de re*); reputo 1 (*alqd*); **~er** philosophus *m*; **~ing** cogitatio *f*.
third tertius; tertia pars *f*; **~ly** tertio.
thirst sitis *f*; sitio 4 (*alqd*); **~y** sitiens, siccus.
thirt|een tredecim; **~eenth** tertius decimus; **~ieth** trigesimus; **~y** triginta.
this hic, haec, hoc.
thistle carduus *m*.
thither illuc, eo.
thong lorum *n*.
thorn spina *f*; **~bush** sentis *m*; **~y** spinosus.
thorough germanus, perfectus; **~bred** generosus; **~fare** pervium *n*; **~ly** penitus, omnino, plane.
though quamquam, quamvis; etsi, etiamsi.
thought cogitatio *f*; cogitatum *n*; notio *f*; **~ful** providus; **~fulness** cura *f*; **~less** inconsultus, neglegens; **~lessness** temeritas *f*.
thousand mille, *pl.* milia; **a ~ times** miliens; **~th** millesimus.
thrall servus *m*.
thrash tero 3, tundo 3 (*frumentum*); verbero 1; **~ing** verbera *n/pl.*
thread filum *n*, linum *n*; cursus, us *m* (*verborum*); filum in acum conicio 3; **~ one's way** me insinuo 1; **~bare** obsoletus.
threat minae *f/pl.*; **~en** *v/t.* minor 1 (*alqd alci*; *acc. c. inf.*); intendo 3 (*alqd alci, in alqm*); denuntio 1 (*alqd alci*); *v/i.* impendeo 2; insto 1; **~ening** minax.
three tres, tria; **~ days** triduum *n*; **~ each** terni; **~ hundred** trecenti; **~ times** ter; **~ years** triennium *n*; **~fold** triplex; **~legged** tripes.
thresh tero 3, tundo 3; **~ing** tritura *f*; **~ing floor** area *f*.
threshold limen *n*.
thrice ter.
thrift frugalitas *f*; **~y** frugi; parcus.
thrill agito 1 (*alqm, mentem*); commoveo 2; stringor *m*, horror *m*; **~ed** attonitus.
thriv|e vigeo 2, floreo 2, vireo 2; **~ing** vegetus, vigens, laetus.
throat guttur *n*, iugulum *n*; fauces *f/pl.*; gula *f*; **cut the ~** iugulo 1.
throb palpito 1; salio 4; pulsus, us *m*.
throes dolor *m*.
throne solium *n*; *fig.* regnum *n*.
throng frequentia *f*, multitudo *f*, turba *f*; *v/t.* frequento 1, celebro 1 (*locum*); *v/i.* confluo 3.
throttle strangulo 1, suffoco 1.
through per (*acc.*); propter (*acc.*); **~out** per (*totam urbem, noctem etc.*); *adv.* penitus, semper.
throw iacio 3, conicio 3, mitto 3; iacto 1; excutio 3, deicio 3 (*equitem*); **~ across** traicio 3; **~ away** proicio 3, abicio 3; **~ oneself down** me proicio 3; iactus, us *m*; coniectus, us *m*.
thrush turdus *m*.
thrust trudo 3, pello 3; plaga *f*.
thud fragor *m*.
thumb pollex *m*.
thump tundo 3.
thunder tonitrus, us *m*; tono 1; **~bolt** fulmen *n*; **~ing** tonans; **~struck** attonitus, obstupefactus.
thus ita, sic.
thwart obsto 1 (*dat.*); disturbo 1 (*alqd*); transtrum *n*.
thyme thymum *n*.
thyrsus thyrsus *m*.
tiara tiara *f*.
tick crepito 1; pedis *m*.
ticket tessera *f*.
ticking crepitus, us *m*.
tick|le titillo 1; **~ling** titillatio *f*; **~lish** *fig.* lubricus.
tide aestus, us *m*.
tid|iness munditia *f*; **~y** mundus.
tidings nuntius *m*.
tie (al)ligo 1; vincio 4; vinculum *n*; necessitudo *f*, coniunctio *f* (*amicitiae etc.*).
tier ordo *m*.
tiger tigris *m*.
tight strictus, contentus, astrictus, artus; **~en** (a)stringo 3, contendo 3.
tile tegula *f*, imbrex *f*; later, eris *m*.
till colo 3; dum, donec, quoad; *prep.* (usque) ad (*acc.*); **~er** cultor *m*, arator *m*; gubernaculum *n*; clavus *m*.

tilt proclino 1, inclino 1.
timber materia *f*, materies *f*; ligna *n/pl*.
time tempus *n*; tempestas *f*, aetas *f*; spatium *n*; **at that ~** tum; ea tempestate; **at ~s** aliquando, interdum; **at the same ~** simul; **at a good ~, in ~** tempore, in tempore, ad tempus; **at another ~** alias; **for the first ~** primum; **what is the ~?** hora quota est?; **keep ~** servo 1 numerum, modum; **in ~** in numerum; **be in ~** (tempus) metior 4, **~ly** tempestivus, opportunus, maturus; **~piece** horologium *n*.
timid timidus, trepidus; **~ity** timiditas *f*.
timorous pavidus.
tin stannum *n*.
tincture color *m*; tingo 3.
tinder fomes *m*.
tinge tingo 3, imbuo 3.
tingle ferveo 2.
tinkle tinnio 4; crepito 1; crepitus, us *m*; tinnitus, us *m*.
tinsel brattea *f*; bratteatus.
tint color *m*; tingo 3.
tiny parvulus, pusillus, exiguus.
tip cacumen *n*; apex *m*; **finger~** extremus digitus *m*; praefigo 3 (*caput hastae*); **~ up** inclino 1.
tipple poto 1; **~r** potator *m*.
tipsy ebrius, temulentus.
tiptoe: stand on ~ in digitos me erigo 3.
tirade declamatio *f*.
tire (de)fatigo 1; **I am ~d of** taedet 2 me (*alcs rei*); **~d** (de)fessus, lassus; **~some** odiosus, molestus; laboriosus.
tiro tiro *m*.
tissue textus, us *m*.
titbit cuppedium *n*; mattea *f*.
tithe decima (pars) *f*.
title titulus *m*; inscriptio *f*; nomen *n*; **~d** nobilis.
to ad (*acc.*), in (*acc.*); *final cj.* ut; **~ and fro** huc illuc; **all ~ a man** omnes ad unum.
toad bufo *m*; **~stool** fungus *m*.
toady assentor 1 (*alci*); adulor 1 (*alqm, alci*); assentator *m*.
toast torreo 2; frigo 3; propino 1 (*poculum alci*; *salutem*); propinatio *f*.
today hodie; hodiernus dies *m*.
toe digitus *m*.
toga toga *f*.
together simul, una; **~ with** (una) cum (*abl.*).
toil labor *m*; laboro 1; **~s** plagae *f/pl*.
toilet ornatus, us *m*; cultus, us *m*.
toilsome laboriosus.
token signum *n*.
tolera|ble tolerabilis; mediocris; **~bly** satis; **~nce** indulgentia *f*; **~nt** patiens (*gen.*); indulgens; **~te** tolero 1; patior 3, fero 3; indulgeo 2 (*dat.*).
toll vectigal *n*.
tomb sepulcrum *n*, monumentum *n*; **~stone** lapis *m*.
tomorrow cras; crastinus dies *m*; **after ~** perendinus.
tone sonus *m*, vox *f*; color *m*.
tongs forceps *f*.
tongue lingua *f*.
tonight hac nocte.
tonsils tonsillae *f/pl*.
too et, etiam; quoque; nimis; **~ long** nimis longus; longior; **~ much** nimis, nimium; **~ little** parum.
tool instrumentum *n*, ferramentum *n*; *fig*. minister, tri *m*.
tooth dens *m*; **~less** edentulus; **~pick** dentiscalpium *n*.
top summus; summum cacumen *n*, fastigium *n*, caput *n*, culmen *n*; vertex *m*; turbo *m*; **on the ~ of the hill** in summo monte.
toper potator *m*.
topic res *f*; locus *m*; argumentum *n*.
topmost summus.
topography locorum descriptio *f*.
topsy-turvy sursum deorsum (*versare omnia*).
torch fax *f*; taeda *f*.
torment (ex)crucio 1; ango 3; vexo 1; cruciatus, us *m*.
tornado turbo *m*.
torp|id piger, iners; **~or** inertia *f*, pigritia *f*; torpor *m*.
torrent torrens *m*.
torrid torridus.
tortoise(-shell) testudo *f*.
torture (ex)crucio 1; (ex)torqueo 2; tormenta *n/pl.*; quaestio *f*, cruciatus, us *m*; **~r** carnifex *m*.
toss iacto 1; iactus, us *m*.
total totus, cunctus; summa *f*; **~ly** omnino.
totter titubo 1, vacillo 1, labo 1.
touch tango 3, attingo 3; *fig*. moveo 2; flecto 3, afficio 3; **~ in at** navem appello 3 (*ad*); **~ upon** tango 3, attingo 3, perstringo 3; tactus, us

m; contagio *f*; **~ing** quod ad; de (*abl.*); **~stone** index *m*; *fig.* obrussa *f*; **~y** difficilis, stomachosus.
tough lentus, durus; difficilis.
tour iter, ineris *n*; (*abroad*) peregrinatio *f*; circuitio *f*; iter facio 3, circumeo 4; **~ist** peregrinator *m*.
tow stuppa *f*; (remulco) traho 3; **~-line** remulcum *n*.
towards ad, adversus, in (*acc.*); sub (*noctem*); erga (*alqm*).
towel mantele *n*.
tower turris *f*; **~ up** emineo 2.
town urbs *f*; oppidum *n*; municipium *n*; urbanus; **~ councillors** decuriones *m/pl.*; **~ crier** praeco *m*; **~hall** curia *f*; **~sman** oppidanus *m*, municeps *m*.
toy crepundia *n/pl.*; *fig.* ludicrum *n*, ludibrium *n*; ludo 3.
trace vestigium *n*, indicium *n*; significatio *f*; habena *f*, lorum *n* (*equi*); sequor 3; indago 1.
track vestigium *n*; callis *f*; **~ out, down** odoror 1, indago 1, vestigo 1; **~less** avius, invius.
tract tractus, us *m*; regio *f*; libellus *m*.
tractable tractabilis, docilis.
trade commercium *n*; mercatura *f*; negotium *n*; artificium *n*; negotior 1; **~r** mercator *m*; **~sman** caupo *m*.
trading vessel navis *f* oneraria.
tradition mos *m* (maiorum); fama *f*, memoria *f*; **there is a ~** traditur; tradunt; memoria proditum est (*acc. c. inf.*); **~al** a maioribus traditus.
traduce maledico 3 (*dat.*); obtrecto 1 (*alqm*).
traffic commercium *n*; commercium habeo 2 (*cum alqo*); (merces) muto 1.
trag|edian tragoedus *m*; **~edy** tragoedia *f*; **~ic** tragicus; *fig.* tristis, miserabilis.
trail traho 3; vestigo 1, odoror 1; vestigia *n/pl.*
train instituo 3; doceo 2, exerceo 2; exercito 1; assuefacio 3 (*alqm alqa re*; *inf.*); pompa *f*; commeatus, us *m*; tractus, us *m*; ordo *m*; series *f*; **~er** exercitor *m*; **~ing** disciplina *f*, exercitatio *f*.
trait nota *f*.
traitor proditor *m*; **~ous** perfidus.
trample on calco 1, conculco 1; obtero 3.
tranquil tranquillus, placidus; **~lity** otium *n*.
transact transigo 3, conficio 3, ago 3; **~ion** res *f*, negotium *n*.
transcend supero 1.
transcri|be transcribo 3; **~pt** exemplar *n*.
transfer traduco 3, transfero 3; translatio *f*.
transfix traicio 3, transfigo 3; *fig.* **~ed** (ob)stupefactus.
transform muto 1; verto 3.
transgress violo 1; transcendo 3; **~ion** violatio *f*, delictum *n*.
transient fluxus, caducus, brevis.
transit transitus, us *m*.
translat|e converto 3, reddo 3; interpretor 1; **~or** interpres *m*.
trans|lucent pellucidus; **~marine** transmarinus; **~mit** transmitto 3; **~parent** pellucidus; **~plant** transfero 3.
transport transporto 1; traicio 3, transveho 3; *fig.* **be ~ed** exardesco 3, efferor 3 (*gaudio etc.*); vectura *f*; navis *f* oneraria.
transverse transversus.
trap pedica *f*, plaga *f*; insidiae *f/pl.*; **mouse~** muscipulum *n*; irretio 4.
trappings ornatus, us *m*; insignia *n/pl.*
trash scruta *n/pl.*; quisquiliae *f/pl.*; **~y** vilis.
travail dolor *m*, labor *m*.
travel iter facio 3; peregrinor 1; **~ over** perlustro 1 (*acc.*); peregrinatio *f*; **~ler** viator *m*, peregrinator *m*.
traverse obeo 4; perlustro 1.
tray ferculum *n*, repositorium *n*.
treacher|ous perfidus, perfidiosus; lubricus; **~y** perfidia *f*.
tread insisto 3 (*in re*; *dat.*); **~ upon** calco 1 (*alqd*); gradus, us *m*; vestigium *n*.
treason maiestas *f*; proditio *f*; **commit ~** maiestatem minuo 3, laedo 3.
treasur|e thesaurus *m*; gaza *f*; coacervo 1; plurimi facio 3, aestimo 1; **~er** aerarii praefectus *m*; **~y** aerarium *n*; fiscus *m*; thesaurus *m*.
treat tracto 1; accipio 3 (*alqm bene*); habeo 2 (*alqm pro amico, in honore*); utor 3 (*abl.*); curo 1 (*aegrotum*); dissero 3, disputo 1 (*de re*); **~ lightly** parvi facio 3 (*rem*); **~ with** ago 3, paciscor 3 (*cum alqo*); **~ise** liber, bri *m*; **~ment** tractatio *f*; curatio *f*; **~y** foedus, *n*, pactio *f*; pactum *n*.

treble acutus (*sonus*); triplex.
tree arbor *f.*
trellis cancelli *m/pl.*
trembl|e tremo 3, contremisco 3 (*alqd*); **~ing** tremor *m*; tremens, tremulus.
tremendous immanis, ingens.
trem|or tremor *m*; **~ulous** tremulus.
trench fossa *f*; sulcus *m.*
trepidation trepidatio *f.*
trespass pecco 1; **~ upon** *fig.* praesumo 3 (*alqd*); immineo 3.
tress crinis *m*; coma *f.*
trial experientia *f*; periculum *n*; probatio *f*; conatus, us *m*; *jur.* iudicium *n*; quaestio *f*; **make ~ of** periclitor 1; **put on ~** postulo 1 (*alqm de re*).
triang|le triangulum *n*; **~ular** triangulus, triquetrus.
tribe gens *f*, natio *f*; tribus, us *f.*
tribunal iudicium *n*; quaestio *f.*
tribun|ate tribunatus, us *m*; **~e** tribunus *m* (*plebis, militum*); **~icial** tribunicius.
tribut|ary stipendiarius, vectigalis; **~e** tributum *n*, vectigal *n*; *fig.* munus *n.*
trice momentum *n.*
trick dolus *m*; fallacia *f*; fallo 3; ludificor 1; **~ery** dolus *m*; artificium *n.*
trickle mano 1; stillo 1.
tricky difficilis.
trident tridens *m.*
tried spectatus, probatus.
trifl|e nugae *f/pl.*; nugor 1; ludo 3; **~e with** illudo 3 (*acc.*); **~ing** levissimus; inconstans; ineptiae *f/pl.*
trill vibro 1; **~ing** tremulus.
trim mundus, nitidus; tondeo 2; puto 1; como 3 (*capillos*); **~mer** qui temporibus servit.
trip offendo 3 (pedem); *fig.* erro 1; **~ up** supplanto 1 (*alqm*); iter, ineris *n.*
tripartite tripartitus.
tripe omasum *n.*
tri|ple triplex; **~pod** tripus, odis *m*; **~reme** triremis *f.*
trite tritus, pervulgatus.
triumph victoria *f*; **Roman general's ~** triumphus *m*; ovatio *f*; exsulto 1; triumpho 1; **~ over** supero 1; **~al** triumphalis; **~ant** victor.
triumvir triumvir *m*; **~ate** triumviratus, us *m.*
trivial levis.
troop caterva *f*, manus, us *f*; grex *m*; turma *f* (*equitum*); confluo 3; **~er** eques *m*; **~s** copiae *f/pl.*; milites *m/pl.*
trophy tropaeum *n.*
troth fides *f.*
trouble opera *f*; labor *m*; negotium *n*; molestia *f*; incommodum *n*; dolor *m*; res *f/pl.* adversae; sollicito 1, perturbo 1; molestiam exhibeo 2 (*alci*); **~ oneself** curo 1 (*alqd*; *ut*; *inf.*); **be ~d with, by** laboro 1 (*morbo etc.*); **~some** molestus, gravis.
trough alveus *m.*
trousers bracae *f/pl.*
truant vagus.
truce indutiae *f/pl.*
truck carrus *m.*
trudge pedibus eo 4.
true verus; germanus, sincerus; fidus; rectus; **be ~ of** cadit 3 (*in*); convenit 4 (*dat.*).
truffle tuber, eris *n.*
truly profecto.
trump up comminiscor 3.
trumpet bucina *f*; *mil.* tuba *f*; **~ abroad** celebro 1, vulgo 1; **~er** bucinator *m*, tubicen *m.*
truncheon scipio *m.*
trunk truncus *m*; stirps *f*; truncus *m* corporis; proboscis *f* (*elephanti*); arca *f*, cista *f.*
truss fascia *f*; fascis *m.*
trust confido 3 (*alci*; *alqa re*); fidem habeo 2 (*alci*); fides *f*; mandatum *n*, depositum *n*; **~ful** credulus; **~worthy** certus, fidus, gravis (*auctor, testis*); **~y** fidus, fidelis.
truth veritas *f*; vera *n/pl.*; fides *f*; **in ~** vero; **~ful** verax.
try conor 1, tento 1 (*inf.*); experior 4, periclitor 1 (*alqd*); *jur.* iudico 1; cognosco 3 (*causam*; *de re*); **~ing** incommodus, difficilis.
tub labrum *n*; cupa *f.*
tube fistula *f*; tubus *m.*
tuck up succingo 3.
tuft crista *f*; floccus *m*; **~ed** cristatus.
tug traho 3.
tuition institutio *f.*
tumble cado 3, concido 3; casus, us *m*; **~r** petaurista *m*; poculum *n.*
tumbrel plaustrum *n.*
tumour tumor *m.*
tumult tumultus, us *m*; turba *f*;

perturbatio *f*; **~uous** tumultuosus, turbulentus.
tun dolium *n*.
tune cantus, us *m*; carmen *n*; numeri *m/pl.*; **keep in ~** concentum servo 1; **be out of ~** discrepo 1; **out of ~** absonus; tendo 3; **~ful** canorus.
tunic tunica *f*.
tunnel cuniculus *m*.
turban mitra *f*.
turbid turbidus.
turbot rhombus *m*.
turbulent turbulentus, tumultuosus.
turf caespes *m*; herba *f*.
turgid tumidus, turgidus.
turmoil tumultus, us *m*; turba *f*.
turn *v/t.* (con)verto 3; verso 1; torqueo 2; flecto 3 (*oculos, equum, cursum, promontorium*); intendo 3 (*oculos, iter, animum*); *v/i.* (con)vertor 3; me (con)verto 3; fio; **~ against** descisco 3 (*ab*); **~ aside** declino 1 (*de via etc.*); **~ away** aversor 1 (*ab*); **~ bad** vitior 1; **~ in** devertor 3 (*apud*); **~ into** *v/t.* verto 3, muto 1 (*alqd in, ad*); *v/i.* muto 1, mutor 1; me converto 3; **~ off** averto 3; **~ out** eicio 3, exigo 3; moveo 2; *v/i.* cado 3, evenio 4, accido 3 (*bene, male, etc.*); evado 3 (*sapiens, orator*); **~ round** verso 1, contorqueo 2 (*rotam etc.*); **~ sour** (co)acesco 3 (*vinum*); **~ to use, one's advantage** utor 3 (*abl.*); ad utilitatem meam refero 3 (*alqd*); **~ upon** vertor 3; situm est (*in alqo, alqa re*); **~ upside down** everto 3; conversio *f*; flexus, us *m* (*viae*); commutatio *f*, vicissitudo *f*; ambulatio *f*; **a good, bad ~** beneficium *n*, iniuria *f*; **in ~** invicem; **by ~s** alternis; **~ing point** discrimen *n*.
turnip rapum *n*.
turnkey ianitor *m* (carceris).
turpentine terebinthus, i *f*.
turret turris *f*.
turtle-dove turtur *m*.
tusk dens *m*.
tutelary praeses.
tutor magister, tri *m*; praeceptor *m*; doceo 2; instituo 3.
twang sonitus, us *m*; sono 1.
twelfth duodecimus.
twelve duodecim; **~ each** duodeni; **~ times** duodecies; **~month** annus *m*.
twentieth vicesimus.
twenty viginti; **~ each** viceni; **~ times** vicies.
twice bis; **~ as much** bis tantum; **~ over** semel atque iterum.
twig surculus *m*; virga *f*.
twilight crepusculum *n*.
twin geminus.
twine linum *n*; *v/t.* circumplico 1, circumplector 3 (*alqd alqa re*); *v/i.* **~ around** complector 3 (*alqd*).
twinge morsus, us *m* (doloris).
twinkle mico 1, corusco 1.
twirl verso 1.
twist (con)torqueo 2; intorqueo 2; spira *f*.
twit vellico 1; irrideo 2 (*acc.*).
twitch vellico 1; vello 3; motus, us *m*.
twitter pipilo 1; garrio 4.
two duo, duae, duo; bini; **~ days** biduum *n*; **~ hundred** ducenti; **~ years** biennium *n*; **~fold** duplex.
typ|e exemplar *n*, exemplum *n*; forma *f*; lltterae *f/pl.*; **~ical** proprius; **~ify** exemplum sum.
tyrann|ical tyrannicus, superbus; **~ize** dominor 1 (*alqd*; *in alqm*); opprimo 3; **~y** tyrannis *f*; dominatus, us *m*, dominatio *f*.
tyrant tyrannus *m*; dominus *m*.

U

udder uber, eris *n*.
ugl|iness deformitas *f*; foeditas *f*; **~y** deformis, informis; pravus.
ulcer ulcus *n*; suppuro 1.
ulterior occultus.
ultimate ultimus, postremus; **~ly** ad postremum.
umbrage: take ~ offendor 3.
umbrella umbraculum *n*.
umpire arbiter, tri *m*.
unabashed intrepidus, impudens.
unable: be ~ nequeo 4; non possum (*inf*.).
un|acceptable ingratus, invisus; **~accountable** inexplicabilis.
unaccustomed insolitus (*ad*); insolens, insuetus (*gen*.).
un|acquainted ignarus, expers (*gen*.); **~affected** simplex, sincerus; **~alterable** immutabilis; **~ambitious** modestus.
unanim|ity consensio *f*; consensus, us *m*; **~ously** una voce; consensu omnium.
un|armed inermis; **~asked** sponte, ultro; **~assuming** modestus, humilis; **~authenticated** sine auctore; incertus; **~availing** irritus, vanus; **~avenged** inultus; **~avoidable** quod vitari non potest; necessarius.
unaware inscius, ignarus (*gen*.); **~s** (de) improviso; **take ~s** imprudentem, inopinantem capio 3 (*alqm*).
un|bar resero 1; aperio 4; **~bearable** intolerabilis; **~becoming** indecorus; alienus (*abl*.); **~bend** remitto 3; **~bending** rigidus; **~biassed** incorruptus; **~bidden** iniussus; invocatus; **~bind** (re)solvo 3; **~blemished** purus, integer; **~bolt** resero 1; **~born** nondum natus; **~bosom oneself** me patefacio 3; **~bounded** infinitus; **~bridled** effrenatus; **~broken** continuus, perpetuus; **~burden oneself** me patefacio 3; onus allevo 1; **~buried** inhumatus, insepultus; **~button** (re)solvo 3; **~ceasing** continuus, perpetuus.
uncertain dubius, incertus; anceps; **be ~** dubito 1; haereo 2; **it is ~** incertum est; **~ty** dubium *n*; dubitatio *f*.
unchange|able immutabilis; **be ~d** permaneo 2.
un|charitable malevolus, iniquus; **~chaste** impudicus; **~checked** liber; **~civil** inhumanus, rusticus; **~civilised** barbarus, incultus.
uncle patruus *m* (*paternal*); avunculus *m* (*maternal*).
un|clean impurus; **~clouded** serenus; **~coil** evolvo 3; **~comfortable** incommodus, gravis; **~common** rarus, insolens, insolitus; **~concerned** otiosus; **~connected** disiunctus; **~conquered** invictus.
unconscious inscius, ignarus (*gen*.); **~ness** oblivio *f*; defectio *f* (*animi*).
unconstitutional non legitimus; illicitus; **~ly** contra rem publicam.
un|controlled impotens, effrenatus; **~couple** disiungo 3; **~couth** incultus, rudis, inhumanus; **~cover** recludo 3; aperio 4; **~cultivated** incultus; **~damaged** integer; **~daunted** intrepidus, impavidus; **~deceive** errorem tollo 3 (*dat*.); **~decided** anceps; dubius; **~defended** nudus; **~deniably** certe.
under sub (*acc*.; *abl*.); subter, infra (*acc*.); per (*acc*.); **~ a pretence of** specie; **~ arms** armatus; **~ ten days** intra decem dies; **~garment** subucula *f*; **~go** subeo 4; perfero 3, patior 3; **~ground** sub terra; subterraneus; **~growth** virgulta *n/pl*.; **~hand** clandestinus, perfidus; **~line** noto 1; **~ling** assecla *m*; **~mine** labefacto 1; detraho 3 (*alqd de re*); **~neath** infra, subter (*acc*.).
understand intellego 3, comprehendo 3; teneo 2; accipio 3, percipio 3; certior fio; audio 4; **~ing** mens *f*; ingenium *n*.
undertak|e suscipio 3 (*alqd*); spondeo 2; recipio 3, promitto 3 (*alqd*; *acc. c. inf*.); **~er** libitinarius *m*; **~ing** inceptum *n*, facinus *n*.
un|deserved immeritus; **~developed** immaturus; crudus; **~digested** crudus; **~diminished** integer; **~-**

disputed certus; **~do** (dis)solvo 3, resolvo 3; pessum do 1; irritum facio 3; **be ~done** pereo 4; **leave ~done** omitto 3; **~doing** dissolutio *f*; **~doubted** certus, haud dubius; **~dress** vestem exuo 3, detraho 3; **~dressed** nudus.
undulate fluctuo 1.
un|duly nimis; **~earth** detego 3; **~earthly** mirus, monstruosus; **~easiness** perturbatio *f*, aegritudo *f*; **~educated** indoctus, illitteratus, ineruditus; **~employed** vacuus, otiosus.
unequal impar, dispar; **~led** singularis, unicus.
un|equivocally plane; **~erring** certus; **~even** inaequabilis, asper; **~exampled** inauditus, unicus; **~expected** inopinatus, inexpectatus; necopinatus; improvisus; **~failing** perennis; **~fair** iniquus, iniustus.
unfaithful perfidus, infidus; **be ~** fidem fallo 3.
un|familiar novus, insolitus; **~fasten** refigo 3; **~favourable** iniquus, alienus, adversus, inopportunus; **~feeling** durus; **~finished** imperfectus, rudis; **~fit** inutilis, inhabilis; indignus; **~fold** explico 1; evolvo 3; **~foreseen** improvisus; **~forgiving** implacabilis, atrox; **~formed** crudus, informis; **~fortunate** miser, infelix; **~founded** vanus; **~friendly** inimicus; **~fulfilled** inanis, vanus; **~furl** solvo 3, pando 3; **~gainly** imperitus, rusticus; **~gentlemanly** illiberalis; **~godly** impius; **~gracious** inhumanus; **~grateful** ingratus; immemor (beneficii); **~guarded** parum custoditus; incautus; **~happy** miser, infelix; **~harmed** incolumis; **~healthy** pestilens (*locus*); valetudine affectus; **~heard (of)** inauditus; **~hesitatingly** audacter; **~holy** impius, nefarius; **~hurt** incolumis.
uniform aequabilis; ornatus, us *m* militaris; **~ity** aequabilitas *f*.
un|impaired integer; **~important** nullius momenti; **~inhabitable** inhabitabilis; **~inhabited** desertus; **~injured** incolumis; **~intelligible** obscurus; **~intentional** haud meditatus, cogitatus.
union consociatio *f*; concilium *n*; societas *f*; coniunctio *f*.
unique unicus, singularis.
unison: in ~ una voce.
unit|e *v/t.* (con)iungo 3; consocio 1; *v/i.* coniuro 1; consocior 1; **~ed** consociatus; **~y** consensus, us *m*; concordia *f*.
univers|al communis; **~ally** in universum, universe; **~e** mundus *m*; **~ity** academia *f*.
un|just iniquus, iniustus; **~kempt** horridus, incomptus; **~kind** haud benignus; crudelis, inhumanus; **~known** ignotus, incognitus; **~lace** solvo 3.
unlawful illicitus, vetitus; **it is ~** nefas est; **~ly** contra legem; contra ius.
unless nisi, ni.
un|like dissimilis, dispar (*gen.*, *dat.*); **~limited** infinitus; **~load** expono 3; **~lock** resero 1; **~looked-for** necopinatus, inexspectatus; **~loose** solvo 3; **~lucky** infelix; **~manageable** intractabilis; **~manly** mollis; **~mannerly** agrestis, inhumanus; **~married** caelebs; **~mentionable** infandus; **~merciful** immitis; **~mindful** immemor (*gen.*); **~mistakeable** certissimus; **~mixed** merus; **~moved** immotus.
unnatural immanis, nefarius; arcessitus (*oratio*); **~ly** praeter naturam.
un|necessary haud necessarius; supervacaneus; **~nerve** frango 3.
unnoticed: pass ~ lateo 2.
un|occupied vacuus; **~palatable** *fig.* molestus; **~patriotic** improbus, malus; **~pleasant** iniucundus, molestus; **~polished** impolitus, rudis.
unpopular invidiosus, invisus, ingratus; **~ity** invidia *f*; offensio *f*.
un|practised inexpertus; **~precedented** inauditus, novus; **~prepossessing** iniucundus; **~principled** improbus; nequam; **~propitious** iniquus, infaustus; **~provoked** ultro (*adv.*); **~punished** impunitus; **~questionably** facile, certe; **~ravel** retexo 3; *fig.* enodo 1; **~reasonable** absurdus; contra rationem.
un|refined crudus; rudis; **~relenting** atrox; **~remitting** assiduus; **~restrained** effrenatus, liber; **~ripe** crudus; **~rivalled** unicus; praestantissimus; **~roll** evolvo 3; **~ruffled** aequus; **~ruly** impotens; **~saddle** stratum detraho 3; **~safe** infestus, lubricus, periculosus; **~-**

seal resigno 1; aperio 4; **~seasonable** immaturus, ineptus; **~seemly** indecorus; **~seen** invisus; **~serviceable** inutilis.

unsettled dubius; perturbatus; vagus; **leave ~** in medio relinquo 3.

un|sheath educo 3, eripio 3 (e vagina); **~sightly** turpis, foedus; **~skilled** imperitus (*gen.*); **~sociable** difficilis; **~sophisticated** simplex; **~sound** infirmus, morbosus; **~sparing** profusus, prodigus (*gen.*); **~speakable** infandus; **~stable, ~steady** instabilis, fluxus; **~successful** infelix; adversus, irritus; **~suitable** incommodus, ineptus; alienus (*ab*); **~suspecting** incautus; **~thinking** inconsideratus; **~tie** (dis)solvo 3; laxo 1.

until ad, in (*acc.*); *cj.* dum, quoad, donec; **not ~** non prius (ante) ... quam.

un|timely immaturus; **~tiring** assiduus; **~touched** intactus, integer; **~toward** adversus; **~tried** inexpertus; **~troubled** securus, tranquillus; **~true** falsus; **~truth** mendacium *n*; **~used** insuetus (*gen.*); insolitus (*ad*; *gen.*); integer; **~usual** insolitus, insolens, novus; **~varnished** haud fucatus; **~veil** detego 3; *fig.* patefacio 3, aperio 4; **~versed in** imperitus (*gen.*); **~warlike** imbellis; **~wary** imprudens, incautus; **~wearied** impiger; **~welcome** iniucundus, ingratus; **~well** aeger; **~wholesome** gravis (*cibus*); noxius; **~wieldy** inhabilis.

unwilling invitus; **be ~** nolo (*inf.*); **~ly** invitus.

un|wind revolvo 3; **~wise** insipiens; **~witting** imprudens; **~wonted** insuetus, insolitus; **~worthy** indignus (*abl.*; *qui*); alienus (*ab*); **~wrap** evolvo 3; explico 1; **~written** non scriptus; **~yielding** firmus, obstinatus.

up sursum; **~ and down** sursum deorsum; **~ in the air** sublime; **~ to** ad (*acc.*); in (*acc.*); **~ to this year** usque ad hunc annum.

up|braid obiurgo 1; **~-country** in interiora; **~hill** acclivis, arduus; **~hold** sustineo 2, sustento 1; **~land** editus.

upon in, super (*acc.*, *abl.*); **~ the right** a dextra.

upper superior, superus; **~most** supremus, summus.

upright rectus; integer, honestus, bonus; **~ness** probitas *f.*

uproar tumultus, us *m*; turba *f.*

uproot evello 3.

upset everto 3, subverto 3; sollicito 1 (*alqm*).

upshot exitus, us *m.*

upside: turn ~ down sursum deorsum verso 1.

up|start novus homo *m*; terrae filius *m*; **~stream** adverso flumine; in adversum flumen.

upwards sursum; sublime; **~ of** amplius, plus.

urge suadeo 2 (*alci ut*; *alqd alci*); hortor 1 (*alqm ut*; *alci alqd*); impello 3 (*alqm ad alqd*); **~ on** incito 1; impello 3; **~nt** gravis, praesens; **~ntly** vehementer.

urn urna *f.*

usage mos *m.*

use utor 3 (*abl.*); adhibeo 2 (*alqd ad alqd*; *in re*); tracto 1 (*alqm*); usus, us *m*; utilitas *f*; commodum *n*; **be of ~** prosum; usui sum; **make ~ of** utor 3 (*alqa re*); **in common ~** usitatus; **~ up** consumo 3; **~d to** assuetus, assuefactus; **~ful** utilis, commodus; **~less** inutilis, vanus, irritus; **it is ~less** nihil prodest; **~lessly** frustra.

usher in introduco 3; *fig.* infero 3.

usual solitus, usitatus, consuetus; **be ~** soleo 2; **~ly** plerumque; fere.

usufruct usus, us *m.*

usurer faenerator *m*; **be a ~** faeneror 1.

usurp invado 3 (*in alqd*; *alqd*); usurpo 1.

usury faeneratio *f*; faenus *n.*

utensils supellex *f*; instrumenta *n/pl.*

utility utilitas *f.*

utmost extremus, ultimus, summus; **to my ~** quantum in me est; omnibus viribus.

utter totus, merus, germanus; dico 3, emitto 3, loquor 3; **~ance** dictum *n*; **~ly** omnino, funditus; **~most** ultimus, extremus.

V

vacan|cy (vacuus) locus *m*; inane *n*; **~t** vacuus, inanis.
vacat|e vacuefacio 3; **~ion** feriae *f/pl.*
vacillat|e vacillo 1; **~ion** dubitatio *f.*
vacuum inane *n.*
vagabond vagus; erro *m.*
vagary libido *f.*
vagrant vagus; erro *m.*
vague incertus, dubius; vagus; **~ness** obscuritas *f.*
vain vanus, inanis, irritus, levis; gloriosus (*homo*); **in ~** frustra, nequiquam; **~glorious** gloriosus.
vale vallis *f.*
valet cubicularius *m.*
valiant fortis.
valid firmus, certus, ratus; **~ity** auctoritas *f*, gravitas *f.*
valley vallis *f.*
valour virtus, utis *f.*
valu|able pretiosus; magni (pretii); **~ation** aestimatio *f.*
value aestimo 1, habeo 2, facio 3, duco 3, pendo 3 (*alqd magni, pluris, parvi, etc.*); diligo 3; pretium *n*; aestimatio *f*; virtus, utis *f*; honor *m*; **be of ~** prosum (*alci*); **~less** minimi pretii.
vampire lamia *f.*
van *mil.* primum agmen *n.*
vanish evanesco 3, dilabor 3.
vanity vanitas *f*; iactatio *f*, gloria *f.*
vanquish vinco 3; supero 1.
vapour vapor *m*; halitus, us *m*; exhalatio *f.*
variable varius, mutabilis, mobilis.
variance discordia *f*; discrepantia *f*; **be at ~ with** pugno 1 cum; **at ~ with** discors.
variation varietas *f*, commutatio *f.*
varicose varicosus; **~ vein** varix *f.*
var|ied varius, diversus; **~iegate** vario 1; **~iety** varietas *f*, diversitas *f*; **~ious** varius, diversus, multiplex; **~ious opinions were expressed** alius aliud dixit.
varnish *fig.* fucus *m.*
vary vario 1, muto 1; distinguo 3.
vase amphora *f.*
vast ingens, maximus, immensus.
vat dolium *n.*
vault salio 4; fornix *f*; camera *f*; saltus, us *m*; **~ed** fornicatus.
vaunt iacto 1, ostento 1 (*alqd*); glorior 1 (*acc. c. inf.*); iactatio *f*, ostentatio *f.*
veal vitulina *f.*
veer (me) verto 3 (*in, ad*).
vegetable planta *f*; **~s** olus *n.*
vehemen|ce vis *f*; **~t** vehemens, ardens.
vehicle vehiculum *n.*
veil velum *n*, velamentum *n*; rica *f*; velo 1; tego 3.
vein vena *f.*
velocity velocitas *f*, celeritas *f.*
venal venalis.
vend vendo 3; **~or** venditor *m.*
venera|ble venerabilis, gravis, augustus; **~te** veneror 1; **~tion** veneratio *f.*
vengeance ultio *f.*
venison ferina *f.*
venom virus, i *n*, venenum *n*; **~ous** venenatus; mordax.
vent foramen *n*; **give ~ to** erumpo 3 (*abl.*; *alqd*); erumpo 3, effundo 3 (*alqd in alqm*).
ventilat|e *fig.* in medium profero 3; **~ion** perflatus, us *m.*
venture audeo 2 (*alqd*; *inf.*); conor 1 (*alqd*; *inf.*); periclitor 1 (*alqd*); in periculum infero 3 (*alqm, alqd*); in aleam do 1; periculum *n*, discrimen *n*; alea *f*; **at a ~** temere; **~some** audax, audens.
verac|ious verax, verus; **~ity** fides *f*, veritas *f.*
verb verbum *n*; **~ally** verbum pro verbo (*reddere etc.*); sermone (*iubere*); **~atim** totidem verbis; **~ose** verbosus.
verdict sententia *f*; iudicium *n*; **pronounce ~** pronuntio 1.
verdure viriditas *f.*
verg|e margo *m*; ora *f*; **~ing on** proximus (*dat.*).
verify probo 1, confirmo 1.
vermilion miniatus.
vernacular patrius sermo *m.*
vernal vernus.

versatile varius, multiplex.
vers|e versus, us *m*; carmen *n*; **~ed in** peritus (*gen.*), exercitatus (*in re*).
vertebra vertebra *f*.
vertical rectus, directus; **~ly** ad lineam.
very *adv.* valde, maxime, admodum (*bonus etc.*); **not ~** non ita; **~ much** magnopere, vehementer; *adj.* germanus; **this ~** hic ipse; **at that ~ moment** ea ipsa hora.
vessel vas *n*; navis *f*.
vest subucula *f*.
vestal vestalis (virgo) *f*.
vestibule vestibulum *n*.
vestige indicium *n*, signum *n*; nota *f*.
vetch vicia *f*.
veteran veteranus (miles) *m*; vetus.
veto intercessio *f*; intercedo 3 (*dat.*).
vex sollicito 1, vexo 1; **~ation** stomachus *m*; **~atious** molestus, odiosus.
vibrate tremo 3; vibro 1.
vice flagitium *n*, vitium *n*; pravitas *f*, turpitudo *f*; **~roy** praefectus *m*.
vicious flagitiosus, pravus, nequam.
vicinity vicinitas *f*; vicinum *n*.
vicissitudes vices *f/pl.*, vicissitudines *f/pl.*
victim victima *f*, hostia *f*.
victor victor *m*, victrix *f*; **~ious** victor; **be ~ious** vinco 3; **~y** victoria *f*; triumphus *m*; **gain ~y** victoriam consequor 3.
victuals victus, us *m*; cibaria *n/pl.*
vie with certo 1, contendo 3 (*cum*).
view conspectus, us *m*; acies *f*; *fig.* sententia *f*, opinio *f*; iudicium *n*; **~ down, over** despectus, us *m*; **be in ~** sum in prospectu; **come into ~** venio 4 in conspectum (*alcs*); **in ~** in conspectu; ante oculos; *fig.* **in my ~** meo iudicio; mihi videtur; **take the same ~** idem sentio 4 (*quod, atque*); **with a ~ to** ut; gratia, causa (*alcs rei*); intueor 2, contueor 2; specto 1, contemplor 1.
vigilan|ce vigilantia *f*; **~t** vigilans, providus.
vigo|rous acer, strenuus, ferox; **~ur** ferocitas *f*; vis *f*.
vile turpis, perditus, nequam.
vilify maledico 3 (*dat.*).
villa villa *f*.
village pagus *m*, vicus *m*; **~r** rusticus *m*, agrestis *m*.
villain verbero *m*, furcifer *m*; **~y** nequitia *f*; flagitium *n*.
vindicate purgo 1.
vine vitis *f*; **~ leaf** pampineus *m*.
vinegar acetum *n*.
vin|eyard vinea *f*; vinetum *n*; **~tage** vindemia *f*.
viol|ate violo 1; **~ater** violator *m*; **~ence** vis *f*, violentia *f*; impetus, us *m*; **~ent** violentus, vehemens.
violet viola *f*.
viper vipera *f*.
virgin virgo *f*; innupta *f*; virginalis; **~ity** virginitas *f*.
viril|e virilis; mas; **~ity** virilitas *f*.
virtue virtus, utis *f*; probitas *f*; **in ~ of** pro (*abl.*); per (*acc.*).
virtuous honestus, probus.
virulen|ce acerbitas *f*; vis *f*; **~t** acerbus, gravis.
visage os *n*.
viscous lentus.
visible conspicuus, manifestus; **be ~** appareo 2.
vision visus, us *m*; aspectus, us *m*; visum *n*; imago *f*.
visit (in)viso 1; saluto 1; salutatio *f*; **~or** hospes *m and f*.
vista prospectus, us *m*; despectus, us *m*.
vital vitalis; necessarius; **~ity** alacritas *f*.
vitiate vitio 1.
vivaci|ous alacer, acer; **~ty** alacritas *f*.
vivid vivus, acer.
vocal sonorus.
vociferously magno clamore.
vogue mos *m*.
voice vox *f*; *fig.* sententia *f*, opinio *f*.
void inanis, vacuus; liber (*abl.*); irritus (*lex*); inane *n*; lacuna *f*; erumpo 3, evomo 3.
volition voluntas *f*.
volley *fig.* nubes *f*.
voluble loquax.
volum|e volumen *n*; liber, bri *m*; **~inous** copiosus.
volunt|arily mea (sua) sponte, voluntate; ultro; **~ary** voluntarius.
volunteer sponte, ultro offero 3 (*alqd*); *mil.* nomen do 1; (miles) voluntarius *m*.
voluptuous voluptarius, libidinosus.

vomit (e)vomo 3.
voracious avidus, vorax.
votary cultor *m.*
vot|e suffragium *n* (*populi*); sententia *f* (*iudicis*); *v/t.* censeo 2; decerno 3; *v/i.* suffragium fero 3; **~e for** suffragor 1 (*alci*); **~ing-tablet** tabella *f*; **~ing urn, box** cista *f.*
votive votivus.
vouch for praesto 1, confirmo 1 (*alqd*).
vouch|er auctoritas *f*; **~safe** concedo 3 (*alqd*); permitto 3 (*ut*).
vow (de)voveo 2; promitto 3; votum *n.*
vowel vocalis *f.*
voyage navigatio *f*; **make a ~** navigo 1.
vulgar vulgaris, communis; agrestis, insulsus, ineptus; **~ity** ineptiae *f/pl.*; **~ly** vulgo.
vulture vultur *m.*

W

waddle vacillo 1.
waft fero 3.
wag quasso 1; moveo 2; ioculator *m*.
wage gero 3 (*bellum etc. cum alqo*).
wager spondeo 2; pono 3; sponsio *f*; pignus *n*.
wages merces *f/pl.*; praemium *n*.
waggon plaustrum *n*; carrus *m*; **~er** bubulcus *m*; auriga, ae *m*.
wail ploro 1; fleo 2; ploratus, us *m*; fletus, us *m*.
wain plaustrum *n*.
waist medium corpus *n*.
wait exspecto 1, maneo 2, opperior 4 (*alqd*; *dum*); **~ on** ministro 1 (*alci*); **~er** puer, eri *m*; minister, tri *m*.
waive remitto 3 (*alqd*).
wake *v/t*. excito 1, suscito 1; *v/i*. expergiscor 3; vigilia *f*; **~ful** vigilans.
walk pedibus eo 4; ambulo 1, spatior 1; **~ in** inambulo 1 (*abl.*); ambulatio *f*; **~er** pedes *m*; **~ing stick** baculum *n*.
wall murus *m*; **city ~** moenia *n/pl.*; **house~** paries *m*; munio 4; **~ed** munitus; **~et** pera *f*.
wallow volutor 1.
walnut (tree) iuglans *f*.
wan pallidus.
wand virga *f*; caduceus *m*.
wander erro 1, vagor 1, palor 1; **~ing** vagus; erratio *f*.
wane decresco 3; minuor 3.
wanness pallor *m*.
want volo; aveo 2; careo 2 (*abl.*); desidero 1; inopia *f*, egestas *f*; **there ~s** deest; opus est (*nom.*; *abl.*); **be ~ing** deficio 3, desum, absum.
wanton libidinosus, protervus, procax; **~ness** protervitas *f*.
war bellum *n*; militia *f*; **make ~ on** arma, bellum infero 3 (*alci*); **wage ~** bellum gero 3; bello 1; **declare ~** bellum indico 3 (*alci*); **in ~ and peace** pace belloque; **~-cry** clamor *m*.
warble cano 3.
ward custodia *f*; pupillus *m*, pupilla *f*; regio *f* (*urbis*); **~ off** arceo 2; defendo 3, averto 3; **~en, ~er** custos *m*, excubitor *m*; **~ship** tutela *f*.
wares merces *f/pl.*
war|fare militia *f*; res *f* bellica; **~like** bellicosus.
warm calidus, tepidus; *fig*. acer; tepefacio 3; foveo 2; **~th** calor *m*, tepor *m*.
warn (ad)moneo 2 (*alqm alqd*; *ut*); **~ing** monitus, us *m*; admonitum *n*.
warp stamen *n*; torqueo 2.
warrant auctoritas *f*; mandatum *n*; spondeo 2; praesto 1; promitto 3.
warrior bellator *m*.
wary cautus, providus.
wash *v/t*. lavo 1; *v/i*. lavor 1; **~ against** alluo 3 (*acc.*); **~ing** lavatio *f*.
wasp vespa *f*.
waste consumo 3; perdo 3, tero 3 (*tempus etc.*); dissipo 1, profundo 3 (*rem*); vastus, desertus; **lay ~** vasto 1, populor 1; effusio *f*; vastitas *f*, solitudo *f*; **~ful** prodigus, effusus; **~fulness** luxuria *f*.
watch *v/t*. observo 1; custodio 4; exspecto 1; *v/i*. vigilo 1, excubo 1; vigilia *f*; excubiae *f/pl.*; custodia *f*; **keep ~ over** custodio 4; **set a ~** vigilias dispono 3; **~ful** vigilans; **~man** vigil *m*; **~-tower** specula *f*; **~word** tessera *f*.
water (ir)rigo 1; aqua *f*; **sea~** aqua *f* marina; **by land and ~** terra marique; **~-carrier** aquarius *m*; **~-clock** clepsydra *f*; **well ~ed** irriguus; **~fall** desiliens aqua *f*; **~ing-place** aquatio *f*.
wattle crates *f*.
wave unda *f*; fluctus, us *m*; *v/t*. iacto 1, agito 1; *v/i*. fluctuo 1, fluito 1; **~r** fluctuo 1, vacillo 1, dubito 1; **~ring** dubius, incertus.
wax cera *f*; *v/t*. cero 1; *v/i*. cresco 3 (*luna*); **~en** cereus.
way via *f*; cursus, us *m*; *fig*. modus *m*; ratio *f*; **on the ~** ex itinere; **out of the ~** devius, remotus, abstrusus; **get under ~** ancoram solvo 3; **~farer** viator *m*; **~lay** insidior 1 (*dat.*); **~side** ad viam; **~ward** pertinax, levis.
we nos.

weak infirmus, debilis, imbecillus, fractus, tenuis; **~en** infirmo 1; frango 3, comminuo 3; **~ness** infirmitas *f.*
weal vibix *f*; **common ~** bonum *n* publicum.
wealth divitiae *f/pl.*, opes *f/pl.*; copia *f*; **~y** dives, opulentus, locuples.
wean lacte depello 3.
weapon telum *n*; iaculum *n*; **~s** arma *n/pl.*
wear *v/t.* gero 3 (*vestem*); *v/i.* duro 1; **~ away** (con)tero 3; **~ out** conficio 3; tritus, us *m*; habitus, us *m*; **~ied** defessus; **~iness** lassitudo *f*; **~ing** amictus (*alqa veste*); **~isome** operosus, laboriosus.
weary defessus, defatigatus; (de-) fatigo 1; **be ~ of** taedet 2 me (*alcs rei*).
weasel mustela *f.*
weather tempestas *f*; caelum *n*; **fine ~** serenitas *f*; **bad ~** foeda tempestas *f*; *fig.* perfero 3; **~beaten** adustus.
weave (con)texo 3; **~r** textor *m.*
web tela *f*; textum *n.*
wed duco 3 (*uxorem*); nubo 3 (*maritum*); **~ded** maritus, nupta; *fig.* **~ded to** deditus (*dat.*); **~ding** nuptiae *f/pl.*
wedge cuneus *m.*
wedlock matrimonium *n.*
weed lolium *n*; runco 1.
week septem dies *m/pl.*
weep fleo 2; lacrimor 1; **~ over** defleo 2 (*alqd*), illacrimo 1 (*dat.*); **~ing** fletus, us *m.*
weevil curculio *m.*
weigh (ex)pendo 3; penso 1; *fig.* pondero 1; **~ down** premo 3, opprimo 3; gravo 1; **~t** pondus *n*; momentum *n*; gravitas *f*; auctoritas *f*; **have great, no ~t** multum, nihil valeo 2 (*apud alqm*); **~ty** gravis.
welcome gratus, acceptus; salvere iubeo 2; (benigne) excipio 3, accipio 3; saluto 1; *int.* salve!; salutatio *f.*
weld ferrumino 1.
welfare salus, utis *f*; bonum *n*, commodum *n.*
well puteus *m*; fons *m*; *adj.* valens, salvus; *adv.* bene, probe; **be ~** valeo 2; **~-being** felicitas *f*; **~-born** nobilis; **~-bred** urbanus, comis; **~-disposed to** benevolus (*erga, in alqm*); **~earned** (bene) meritus; **~-known** celebratus; **~-versed** peritus, versatus; **~-wisher** amicus *m.*
west occidens *m*; occasus, us *m* (solis); **~ern** ad occidentem; occidentalis; **~wards** in occasum; **~ wind** zephyrus *m.*
wet madefacio 3; umidus, udus, madidus; **be ~** madeo 2; **~ness** umor *m.*
whale balaena *f*, cetus *m.*
wharf crepido *f.*
what quid?, quod?; **~ kind of a** quod?, *exclam.* qui, qualis; *relat.* quod; **~ever** quicumque; quisquis.
wheat triticum *n.*
wheedle blandior 4 (*dat.*).
wheel rota *f*; **~ round** *v/t.* circumago 3; *v/i.* circumagor 3.
whelp catulus *m.*
when quando?; *cj.* cum, ubi, postquam, ut; **~ce** unde?; **~ever** quandocumque, quotiescumque, cum.
where ubi?, quo?; *relat.* qua, ubi; **~ ... from** unde?; **~ on earth** ubi gentium?; **~as** quoniam; **~by** qua ratione; **~upon** quo facto; **~ver** ubicumque.
whet acuo 3.
whether *interrog.* num; utrum ... (*an*); -ne ... (*an*); *cj.* **~ ... or** sive ... sive; seu ... seu.
whetstone cos *f.*
which quis?; *relat.* qui; **~ (of two)** uter?; *relat.* quis; **~ever** quicumque.
while *cj.* dum; donec, cum; tempus *n*; **for a little ~** parumper; **~ away** dego 3.
whim arbitrium *n*; libido *f.*
whimper vagio 4.
whimsical ridiculus.
whine vagio 4.
whip flagellum *n*; lora *n/pl.*; verbero 1.
whirl turbo *m*; **~ round** torqueor 2; **~pool** vorago *f*, vertex *m*; **~wind** turbo *m.*
whiskers capilli *m/pl.*
whisper (in)susurro 1; susurrus *m.*
whistle sibilo 1; sibilus *m*; fistula *f.*
white albus, candidus; canus (*capilli*); album *n*; **~n** albesco 3, canesco 3; **~ness** candor *m*; **~wash** dealbo 1.
whither quo?
who quis?; *relat.* qui; **~ever** quicumque.

whole totus, cunctus, omnis; integer, solidus; totum *n*; **as a ~** in universum; **on the ~** ad summam; **~sale dealer** mercator *m*; **~some** salutaris.
wholly omnino; ex omni ratione; prorsus.
whoop ululo 1; ululatus, us *m*.
whose cuius.
why cur?, quare?, quam ob rem?; **~ not** quidni?
wick filum *n*.
wicked scelestus, improbus, nefarius; **~ness** scelus *n*, flagitium *n*; nequitia *f*.
wicker vimineus; **~work** vimen *n*.
wide latus, amplus; *adv.* late; **~-spread** (per)vulgatus; **~-spreading** patulus (*rami*); **~n** laxo 1, dilato 1.
widow vidua *f*; **~ed** viduus; **~er** viduus homo *m*.
width latitudo *f*, amplitudo *f*.
wield gero 3; utor 3.
wife uxor *f*, coniunx *f*.
wig capillamentum *n*.
wild ferus, incultus; vastus; insanus; **~erness** desertum *n*; vastitas *f*; **~ness** feritas *f*.
wiles dolus *m*; fallaciae *f/pl.*
wilful pertinax, pervicax.
will voluntas *f*; consilium *n*, arbitrium *n*; testamentum *n*; **against my ~** me invito; invitus (*adj.*); **as you ~** ut libet.
willing libens; promptus (*ad*); **~ly** libenter; **~ness** studium *n*.
willow salix *f*.
wily vafer, astutus, callidus.
win vinco 3 (*in pugna etc.*); consequor 3, pario 3 (*alqd*); concilio 1 (*gratiam etc.*).
wind ventus *m*; volvo 3; glomero 1; **~ one's way into** me insinuo 1 (*in*); **~ed** anhelans; **~ing** flexuosus; ambages *f/pl.*; sinus, us *m*.
window fenestra *f*.
wind|pipe aspera arteria *f*; **~y** ventosus.
wine vinum *n*; **~-cellar** cella *f*; **~-press** prelum *n*.
wing ala *f*, penna *f*; cornu *n* (*exercitus*); volo 1; **~ed** volucer, pinniger.
wink nictus, us *m*; nicto 1; **~ at** coniveo 2 (*dat.*).
win|ner victor *m*; **~ning** victor; blandus, suavis.
winnowing fan vannus, i *f*.
winter hiems *f*; hiemo 1, hiberno 1; **~ solstice** bruma *f*; **~-quarters** hiberna *n/pl.*
wintry hiemalis, hibernus.
wipe (de)tergeo 2; **~ out** deleo 2.
wisdom sapientia *f*; consilium *n*.
wise sapiens, prudens, peritus.
wish volo (*inf.*); cupio 3, opto 1 (*inf.*); **~ for** volo, opto 1 (*alqd*); votum *n*, optatum *n*, desiderium *n*; optatio *f*, **against my ~es** me invito.
wit sal *m*; facetiae *f/pl.*; ingenium *n*, acumen *n*; **to ~** scilicet.
witch saga *f*; venefica *f*; **~craft** veneficium *n*; magicae artes *f/pl.*
with cum (*abl.*); **~ me** mecum; apud me; **it rests, lies ~ me** penes me est; **~draw** *v/t.* removeo 2; abduco 3, deduco 3; *v/i.* (re)cedo 3, me recipio 3.
wither *v/t.* torreo 2; *v/i.* languesco 3, aresco 3; **~ed** marcidus, rugosus.
withhold retineo 2; supprimo 3, recuso 1.
within in (*abl.*); intra, inter (*acc.*); cis, citra (*acc.*); *adv.* intus.
without sine (*abl.*); *cj.* quin; *adv.* extra, extrinsecus.
withstand obsto 1, resisto 3, obsisto 3 (*dat.*).
witness testis *m*; arbiter *m*, spectator *m*; video 2; conspicio 3; **bear ~, call to ~** testor 1, testificor 1 (*alqd*; *alqm*; *acc. c. inf.*); **bear ~ against** testimonium dico 3 (*in alqm*).
witt|icism dictum *n*; **~y** facetus, salsus.
wizard magus *m*.
woad vitrum *n*.
woe dolor *m*; **~ful** miser, tristis.
wolf lupus *m*.
woman mulier *f*, femina *f*; **old ~** anus, us *f*; **young ~** puella *f*; **~ish** muliebris, effeminatus; **~ly, ~'s** muliebris, femineus.
womb uterus *m*.
wonder admiratio *f*; miraculum *n*; (ad)miror 1 (*alqd*; *acc. c. inf.*; *quod*); **~ful** mirus, mirabilis, mirificus.
wont mos *m*; **be ~** soleo 2.
woo peto 3; *fig.* ambio 4.
wood lignum *n*; silva *f*; nemus *n*; **~cutter** lignator *m*; **~ed** silvestris; **~en** ligneus; **~-pigeon** palumbes *m*; **~y** lignosus, silvosus.
wooer procus *m*.

wool lana *f*; **~len** laneus.

word verbum *n*, vocabulum *n*, nomen *n*; vox *f*; **~s** dicta *n/pl.*; **in a ~, few ~s** paucis, breviter; **have ~s with** altercor 1 (*cum alqo*); **send (back) ~** (re)nuntio 1; **keep, break one's ~** fidem servo 1, fallo 3; **~y** verbosus.

work opus *n*; labor *m*; opera *f*; pensum *n*; **~ of art** opus *n*; ars *f*; artificium *n*; **~s** machinatio *f*; *v/i.* (e)laboro 1; *v/t.* subigo 3, colo 3 (*terram*); **~ at** exerceo 2 (*rem*); versor 1 (*in re*); **~ upon** flecto 3 (*animum etc.*); **~er** opifex *m*, artifex *m*; **~-house** ergastulum *n*; **~ing** cultus, us *m* (*terrae*); **~man** opifex *m*; **~shop** officina *f*.

world mundus *m*; orbis *m* terrarum; **all the ~** omnes (ad unum); nemo est quin (*subj.*); **where in the ~** ubi gentium?; **in the whole ~** usquam.

worm vermis *m*; tinea *f*; **~ one's way into** me insinuo 1 (*in*).

worry sollicito 1; exerceo 2; agito 1.

worse peior, deterior; **for the ~** in deterius; **grow ~, ~n** ingravesco 3.

worship colo 3; veneror 1; cultus, us *m*; veneratio *f*; **~per** cultor *m*.

worst pessimus, deterrimus, ultimus; **get the ~ of it** vincor 3.

worth dignus (*abl.*); pretium *n*; dignitas *f*; **it is ~ (while)** operae pretium est (*inf.*); **~less** nequam (*homo*); inutilis, vilis; **~y** dignus (*abl.*; *qui*); bonus.

would that utinam.

wound vulnus *n*; plaga *f*; vulnero 1; saucio 4.

wrangle altercor 1.

wrap involvo 3, obvolvo 3 (*alqd re*); **~per** involucrum *n*; tegumentum *n*.

wrath ira *f*.

wreath sertum *n*; corona *f*; volumen *n*; vertex *m*; **~e** necto 3 (*caput sertis*).

wreck frango 3, illido 3; naufragium *n*; **~ed** naufragus.

wrench, wrest extorqueo 2 (*alqd alci*).

wrestl|e luctor 1; **~er** luctator *m*; **~ing** luctatio *f*.

wretch homo *m* nequam, perditus, miser; **~ed** infelix, miserabilis; **~edness** miseria *f*.

wriggle torqueo 2 me.

wring torqueo 2, crucio 1; **~ from** extorqueo 2 (*alqd alci*).

wrinkle ruga *f*; **~d** rugosus.

writ litterae *f/pl.*; mandatum *n*.

write scribo 3; **~ back** rescribo 3; **~ out** perscribo 3; **~r** scriptor *m*, auctor *m*.

writing scriptio *f*, scriptura *f*; **~s** scripta *n/pl.*; **~-case** scrinium *n*; **~-paper** charta *f*.

wrong falsus; pravus, iniustus, iniquus; iniuriam infero 3 (*alci*); **be ~** erro 1; **~doer** maleficus *m*; **~ful** iniustus; **~ly** male, perperam, falso.

wry distortus.

Y

yacht phaselus *m*; celox *f*.
yard area *f*, cohors *f*; antenna *f* (*navis*).
yarn linum *n*; fabula *f*.
yawn oscito 1; *fig.* hio 1, dehisco 3; oscitatio *f*.
yea ita, certe.
year annus *m*; **~ly** anniversarius; *adv.* quotannis.
yearn| for desidero 1; **~ing** desiderium *n*.
yeast fermentum *n*.
yell ululo 1; ululatus, us *m*.
yellow flavus, luteus, croceus.
yelp gannio 4.
yes ita (vero); sane, certe, etiam; **say ~** aio.
yesterday heri; hesternus dies *m*.
yet tamen, vero, nihilominus, at; (*of time*) etiam(-nunc), adhuc; **not ~** nondum.
yew taxus, i *f*.
yield *v/t.* effero 3; *fig.* pario 3, affero 3; do 1, concedo 3, dedo 3; *v/i.* cedo 3, obsequor 3 (*dat.*); fructus, us *m*; **~ing** mollis.
yoke iugum *n*; iungo 3.
yolk vitellus *m*.
yonder *adj.* ille; *adv.* ecce, illic.
yore olim, quondam.
you tu, vos.
young iuvenis, parvus, adolescens; partus, us *m*, fetus, us *m*; **~er** iunior, minor natu.
your tuus, vester.
youth iuventus, utis *f*, adolescentia *f*; iuvenis *m*, adolescens *m*; **~ful** iuvenilis, puerilis.

Z

zeal studium *n*; ardor *m*; **~ous** studiosus, acer.
zephyr zephyrus *m*.
zero nihil.
zest gustatus, us *m*; studium *n*.
zigzag anfractus, us *m* (*viae etc.*); tortuosus.
zone zona *f*; regio *f*.

In the later Republican period the Latin alphabet consisted of the following twenty-one letters:

a b c d e f g h i k l m n o p q r s t u x

In the time of Augustus two new letters were introduced for use in words borrowed from Greek or other languages; *y* (for the Greek υ) and *z* (for the Greek ζ).

Notes: (1) The letter *c*, derived from the Greek γ, was at first used both for the sound of English *g* in *go*[1], and for the sound of *k*. As it continued to be used for *k*, the letter *k* eventually went almost out of use[2]. For the *g*-sound, a new letter, *G*, was formed in the third century B.C. by the addition of a small stroke to *C*.

(2) The letter *i* represented not only a vowel sound, but also a semivowel sound like that of the English *y* in *yet*. When the letter is used for this *y*-sound, it is generally called 'consonantal *i*', and is sometimes written *i̯*. In medieval texts it was often written as *j* — a practice still sometimes followed, though it has now become rare.

(3) The letter *u* (capital *V*) represented a vowel sound, and also a semivowel sound like that of the English *w*. In the latter case it is generally called 'consonantal *u*', and is sometimes written *u̯*. The medieval practice of writing it as *v* still remains common, but modern editors are tending to revert to the Roman practice of using *u* (capital *V*).

III. **Pronunciation.** No system of writing can be, and remain, entirely phonetic; but Latin spelling in the classical period was very nearly phonetic — more so even than modern Italian is. The classical pronunciation is known with a fair degree of accuracy. The ancient writers themselves, especially the grammarians, tell us something about it. Something can be inferred from the development of Latin sounds in Romance languages; for instance, most of the pure vowel sounds represented by Latin *a e i o u* are similar to those represented by these letters in Italian and French (with a few exceptions: e.g. the *u* of the French *plume* is quite different from the *u* of the Latin *pluma*). Another kind

---

[1] A survival of the original use of Latin *c* for *g* is seen in the abbreviations *C.* for *Gāius* and *Cn.* for *Gnaeus*.

[2] It was retained only in a very few words, e. g. *Kalendae* (abbreviated *Kal.* or *K.*).

Some Remarks on the Latin Language

I. Latin is one of several Italic languages, the most important of the others being Oscan — spoken by the Samnites, Campanians, Apulians, Lucanians, and other peoples of central and southern Italy — and Umbrian, which was spoken in the district called Umbria, and at one time, probably, in other parts of north-central Italy. Italic is one branch of the great family of languages known as Indo-European, which includes nearly all European languages — Greek, Celtic, Germanic, and Balto-Slavonic — and some of the languages of India and Persia, the oldest of these being Sanskrit, the sacred language of the Indian Brahmins.

Of the non-Italic branches of Indo-European, Latin shows most affinity to Celtic, which, besides the languages of ancient Gaul and Britain, includes Welsh, Breton, Manx, Irish, and Gaelic. This may mean that people speaking languages from which Latin and some Celtic languages (especially Irish) are derived lived at one time in close contact. We have no means of knowing when the Italic group of languages was brought into Italy — presumably from some part of central Europe —, except that it was certainly before 1,000 B.C. The oldest Latin inscriptions in existence date from the sixth century B.C., but inscriptions earlier than about 200 B.C. are few and short. The earliest extant Latin literature is the comedies of Plautus, who began to write in the last decade of the third century B.C.

II. **The Alphabet.** The ultimate source of the Latin alphabet, and of those of the other Italic languages, is the 'western' Greek alphabet used in parts of the Greek mainland, in the island of Euboea, and in some of the Greek colonies in southern Italy and Sicily. The Latin alphabet has a particularly close resemblance to that in use at Cumae in Campania, a colony founded from Chalcis in Euboea. The Romans probably derived it, however, not from these Campanian Greeks, but from the Etruscans of north-central Italy, who used a variety of the western Greek alphabet, although their language was not Indo-European[1].

[1] Nevertheless, Etruscan had a considerable influence upon the vocabulary of Latin. Not only are many Latin proper names of Etruscan origin (including, most probably, the name of Rome itself), but also a number of words connected with religion, the state, and the theatre.

PREFACE

The Latin-English section of this dictionary is an entirely revised edition of Professor K. Feyerabend's well-known dictionary, which went through several editions.

Our special thanks are due to Mr. S. A. Handford for the present revision, which takes account of recent scholarship and increases the number of entries by 2200 words.

A special feature is the marking of 'hidden' quantities. There is an introductory account of the development of the Latin language, and just before the main text there is a list of the Roman authors whose vocabulary is included, and information on the arrangement of the dictionary.

The English-Latin section of the dictionary, compiled by Mrs. Mary Herberg, offers a Classical prose vocabulary. Equivalents have been drawn wherever possible from Cicero and Caesar, and where notes on a word's construction are given they are likewise based on the best prose usage.

In a dictionary of this size it is not possible to distinguish fully between the different meanings of one English word. Often the notes on construction will help to show which sense is being translated, but if there is any doubt the word must be checked in the Latin-English section, and this rule holds good wherever the Latin word is unfamiliar.

LANGENSCHEIDT'S POCKET LATIN DICTIONARY

LATIN-ENGLISH
ENGLISH-LATIN

By

S. A. HANDFORD
Reader in Classics at King's College
University of London

and

MARY HERBERG
Formerly Assistant Lecturer
in Classics at King's College
University of London

LANGENSCHEIDT